THE NATIONAL COURTS' MANDATE IN THE EUROPEAN CONSTITUTION

The reform of the European Constitution continues to dominate news headlines and has provoked a massive debate, unprecedented in the history of EU law. Against this backdrop Monica Claes' book offers a 'bottom up' view of how the Constitution might work, taking the viewpoint of the national courts as her starting point, and at the same time returning to fundamental principles in order to interrogate the myths of Community law. Adopting a broad, comparative approach, she analyses the basic doctrines of Community law from both national constitutional perspectives as well as the more usual European perspective. It is only by combining the perspectives of the EU and national constitutions, she argues, that a complete picture can be obtained, and a solid theoretical base (constitutional pluralism) developed. Her comparative analysis encompasses the law in France, Belgium, Denmark, the Netherlands, Germany, Ireland, Italy and the United Kingdom and in the course of her inquiry discusses a wide variety of prominent problems.

The book is structured around three main themes, coinciding with three periods in the development of the judicial dialogue between the ECJ and the national courts. The first focuses on the ordinary non-constitutional national courts and how they have successfully adapted to the mandates developed by the ECJ in *Simmenthal* and *Francovich*. The second examines the constitutional and other review courts and discusses the gradual transformation of the ECJ into a constitutional court, and its relationship to the national constitutional courts. The contrast is marked; these courts are not specifically empowered by the case law of the ECJ and have reacted quite differently to the message from Luxembourg, leaving them apparently on collision course with the ECJ in the areas of judicial *Kompetenz-Kompetenz* and fundamental rights. The third theme reprises the first two and places them in the context of the current debate on the Constitution for Europe and the Convention, taking the perspective of the national courts as the starting point for a wide-ranging examination of EU's constitutional fundamentals. In so doing it argues that the new Constitution must accommodate the national perspective if it is to prove effective.

Volume 5 in the series Modern Studies in European Law

Modern Studies in European Law

Soft Law in European Community Law *Linda Senden*
The Impact of European Rights on National Legal Cultures *Miriam Aziz*
Partnership Rights, Free Movement and EU Law *Helen Toner*
National Remedies Before the Court of Justice *Michael Dougan*

The National Courts' Mandate in the European Constitution *Monica Claes*

The National Courts' Mandate in the European Constitution

Monica Claes

·HART·
PUBLISHING

HART PUBLISHING
OXFORD AND PORTLAND, OREGON
2006

Published in North America (US and Canada) by
Hart Publishing
c/o International Specialized Book Services
5804 NE Hassalo Street
Portland, Oregon
97213-3644
USA

Hart Publishing is a specialist legal publisher based in Oxford,
England. To order further copies of this book or to request a list of other
publications please write to:

Hart Publishing, Salters Boatyard, Folly Bridge, Abingdon Rd,
Oxford, OX1 4LB
Telephone: +44 (0)1865 245533 Fax: +44 (0)1865 794882
email: mail@hartpub.co.uk
WEBSITE: http//:www.hartpub.co.uk

British Library Cataloguing in Publication Data
Data Available

ISBN 10: 1-84113-476-7 (hardback)
ISBN 13: 978-1-84113-476-5 (hardback)

Typeset by Datamatics Technologies Ltd, India
Printed and bound in Great Britain by
TJ International Ltd, Padstow, Cornwall.

Acknowledgements

This book was originally written as a PhD thesis, which I defended at the Law Faculty of the University of Maastricht in June 2004. The original topic of my research had been the impact of Community law on the constitutional position of national courts (this ultimately became Part I). As I went along, I became more interested in the multifaceted theme of the relationship between legal orders and constitutionalism in a multi-level Constitution, which I decided to include in the book, and analysed from the perspective of national courts (this ended up being Part II of my book). When I returned to my research after maternity leave, the constitutional debate had been redirected, and was now phrased in terms of the Convention and the Draft Treaty establishing a Constitution for Europe. I decided to add a third (and final!) Part to my book, examining the impact of the Constitutional Treaty on the national courts' European mandate.

Writing this book took time and patience, and would never have been possible without the encouragement and support of many people. Being grateful to many, I would like to mention a few.

I would like to express my sincere gratitude to my supervisors, Bruno de Witte and Aalt Willem Heringa. I thank Bruno for his astute comments and sharp remarks, for his kind encouragement and his wise and flexible approach. He was always ready to share his wide knowledge and clear insights, first in Maastricht, later from Florence by e-mail. Bruno truly was and is my mentor, my *Doktorvater*. I thank Aalt Willem for his help, guidance and support, both with respect to my work and in human matters. His belief in me and my work gave me confidence. I hope and trust that I will continue to learn from both of them.

I would like to thank the members of the PhD committee: Hildegard Schneider, Sacha Prechal and Luc Verhey, for their time and support. I thank Leonard Besselink, Ellen Vos and Pierre Larouche for their comments and for the stimulating debate at the defense ceremony.

I thank my seconds ('*paranimfen*') Janneke Gerards and Margreet Keus, both of whom I admire greatly, and whose strength and dedication inspire me. Margreet and Janneke have supported me during the final stages of writing and in the preparation of my PhD defence. They have shared the legendary nervous last minutes before the start of the ceremony in the 'zweetkamertje' of the University of Maastricht.

Nettie Litjens kindly agreed to put the files together and produce a camera-ready manuscript, and did so with remarkable patience and

Acknowledgements

equanimity. She, in fact, gently forced me to finally bring my research to an end. The University of Maastricht provided the opportunity and the warm environment to conduct my research and write the book.

I am grateful to my family, friends, and colleagues who helped me in ways unknown to them. Above all, I thank my parents and my parents-in-law. Writing this book simply would not have been possible without their support.

Finally, words cannot express my gratitude to Eric, for his unfailing love and support. He put up with me during the entire process of writing and not writing, enquiring as to progress at the right times, respecting my grudging silence at others, patiently encouraging me to persevere all along. During the process, we were joined by our sons Lucas and Michiel; and after the completion of the manuscript, by Olivier. The boys took away much of our time and sleep, but they gave me the energy to bring this project to an end. I dedicate this book to my boys, all four of them.

Maastricht, October 2005

Contents

Contents

Table of Cases

Court of Justice

International Court of Justice

ECHR

All decisions are available on www.echr.coe.int

France

All decisions of the Conseil constitutionnel are available on
www.conseil-constitutionnel.fr

Germany

Decisions from 1998 onwards are available on
www.bundesverfassungsgericht.de

Italy

Corte costituzionale

Recent decisions available on www.cortecostituzionale.it; decisions
from 1973 onwards available in full on www.giurcost.it (older
cases are added regularly)

Corte Suprema di cassazione

Decisions from 2002 onwards available on www.giustizia.it/cassazione

Luxembourg

The Netherlands

From 1999 onwards a selection of decisions is available on
www.rechtspraak.nl

Spain

United States

Introduction

The Judge, his Mandate,
the National Constitution
and European Union Law

I

Setting the Stage

1. PROLOGUE

1.1. The First Stage

FORTY YEARS AFTER *Van Gend en Loos* and *Costa v ENEL*, it has become a truism to say that 'every national court in the European Community is now a Community law court'.[1] *'Juges communautaires de droit commun, (..), ils sont les juges des litiges qui naissent de l'insertion de droit communautaire dans les ordres juridiques nationaux'.*[2] To put it in the words of the Court of First Instance, 'when applying [Community law], the national courts are acting as Community courts of general jurisdiction'.[3] The national courts are first in line to enforce and apply Community law within the Member States. There is no provision in the Treaty transforming the national courts into Community courts. Rather, it is the catch-all provision of Article 10 EC (Article 5 of the old Treaty) which has come to serve as the Treaty basis for the Community law obligations of the national courts: the judicial authorities of the Member States are under an obligation to ensure that Community law is applied and enforced in the national legal system and that no measures are taken which could jeopardise the attainment of the objectives of the Treaties. Accordingly, national judges at all levels are potentially judges of Community law.[4] As revolutionary as this may have been in the 1960s, when national courts were hardly ever confronted with the area of international law, which was

---

1   J Temple Lang, 'The Duties of National Courts under Community Constitutional Law', (1997) *ELR*, 3, at 3.

2   F Grévisse and J-Cl Bonichot, 'Les incidences du droit communautaire sur l'organisation et l'exercice de la fonction juridictionnelle dans les États membres', in *L'Europe et le droit, Mélanges Jean Boulouis* (Paris, Dalloz, 1991) 297, at 297.

3   And the Court of First Instance continued: 'They will merely be applying – as they are bound to do by virtue of the primacy and direct effect of the Community rules on competition – the principles of Community law governing the relationship between Article 85(3) and Article 86. Accordingly, where a national court applies Article 86 to conduct enjoying exemption under Article 85(3), the uniform application of Community law – in this case, Article 85(3), the provisions implementing it, and Article 86- is fully guaranteed by the procedure for reference of questions of interpretation for a preliminary ruling under Article 177 of the Treaty', Case T-51/89 *Tetra Pak Rausing SA v Commission* [1990] ECR II-309, at para 42.

4   Lord Slynn of Hadley, 'What is a European Community Law Judge?', (1993) *CLJ*, 234, at 240.

considered first and foremost the field of the executive branch, it has now become self-evident, both from the point of view of Community law and from national law. It has become common ground.

The involvement of the national courts as common courts of Community law is grafted upon the twin doctrines of direct effect and supremacy of Community law. These doctrines mean nothing more or less, with respect to the judicial function, than that the Court of Justice invites, or rather instructs, the national courts to apply and enforce Community law, with precedence over conflicting national law, and that national law cannot be invoked to prevent the application of Community law. Case by case and jot by jot the Court of Justice has elucidated the national courts' obligations when acting as Community law courts. Its case law has witnessed a development in the definition of the tasks and functions entrusted to the national courts. In doing so, the Court has from time to time even deviated from the 'natural' – *i.e.* what is accepted as natural in a particular national context - tasks of the national courts, in order to ensure that in the context of Community law a sufficient level of judicial protection is achieved, that effective compliance with Community law is attained and that Community law is applied and enforced with a sufficient level of uniformity throughout the Community. Yet, for the national courts the instructions from Luxembourg become problematic when they do not coincide with the national (constitutional) role. What should a national court do when the Court of Justice requests it to do what would constitute a radical departure from the national Constitution? How should it act when 'caught in the middle' between two claims, one coming from the Court of Justice and requiring it to disapply an Act of Parliament on the one hand, and the national constitutional duty to abide by the laws made by Parliament on the other? Should the courts do what the Court of Justice requests? If so, on what ground should they: would it be some Community mandate? Or could the national courts refuse to co-operate with the Court and continue to follow the national mandate?

The answer from Luxembourg is unequivocal: the Court of Justice 'frees' the national courts from internal constitutional rules when interpreting and applying Community law. Accordingly, they do not have to worry about national constitutional rules and principles on the relations between state organs, separation of powers and the like. A case in point is *Simmenthal*,[5] the culmination of the principles of direct effect and supremacy, in which the Court held that the Italian courts simply had to defy the Italian constitutional rules which ordered them to leave judicial review of legislative rules to the *Corte costituzionale*. As simple as the case may have been from the point of view of Community law, its impact in

---

[5] Case 106/77 *Amministrazione delle Finanze dello Stato v Simmenthal SpA* [1978] ECR 585.

constitutional law terms was enormous. One can imagine that the Italian courts, and courts in other Member States for that matter, would at least feel uneasy about defying their own Constitution. Indeed, what the Court asked them to do had a vital impact on many deeply rooted constitutional principles, including the limits of their own mandate. A full acceptance of the absolute principle of supremacy as proclaimed by the Court of Justice and all its consequences, implies a definitive limitation on national sovereignty. At the same time it entails significant incursions on legislative sovereignty, the national Parliaments being limited by Community law and the national courts patrolling those limits. This new role for the national courts would cause a readjustment of the constitutional equilibrium, between courts and Parliament, and between the constitutional court on the one hand and the ordinary courts on the other.

What should the national courts do in such circumstances? Should the judges bow to the Court of Justice and overstep the limits of their constitutional mandate? Or should they uphold the Constitution and maintain their position in the constitutional equilibrium? Should they choose the constitutional mandate or the Community mandate? Put in these terms, it may even seem astonishing that the courts *have* actually achieved acceptance of what the Court wants, if not its logic, at least the result intended. *Why* have they done so? What was their *reasoning*? Have they really decided to set aside their constitutional mandate? Have they really made a choice between their constitutional mandate and their Community mandate?

At first glance, the meddling of the Court in the national judicial function and the acquiescence by national courts has led to the emergence of a double set of duties, powers and competences of national courts: one which applies to the strictly national mandate, and another belonging to their function as common courts of Community law. When faced with Community law, the judge must apply different standards of interpretation and construction, he must review legislation and administrative action even in circumstances where the applicable national law would not allow him to do so. Sometimes he must even offer remedies which simply are not available under national law. In short, Community law brings on a transmutation of the functions of national courts acting as Community judges.[6] This also implies that when a case touches upon issues of Community law, the court's constitutional position *vis-à-vis* the other state organs changes.[7] In States where the primary legislature, for instance, is

---

[6] J Temple Lang, 'The Duties of National Courts under Community Constitutional Law', 22 *ELR*, 1997, 3.

[7] See *e.g.* A Barav, 'La plénitude de compétence du juge national en sa qualité de juge communautaire', in *L'Europe et le droit, Mélanges en hommage à Jean Boulouis*, (Paris, Dalloz, 1991) 1; A Barav, 'Omnipotent Courts', in *Institutional Dynamics of European Integration. Essays in Honour of H.G. Schermers*, Vol 2 (Dordrecht, Nijhoff, 1994) 265; see also S Prechal, *Directives in European Community Law. A Study of Directives and Their Enforcement in National Courts* (Oxford, Clarendon Press, 1995) for instance at 185, 193, 364-367.

still considered, in law, to be sovereign and immune from judicial review, this no longer holds true within the scope of Community law. Where Community law is at stake, primary legislation loses its immunity from judicial reveiw by ordinary courts. In addition, in the realm of Community law, courts have the competence to grant interim relief against the Crown, even if that was unheard of before. Likewise, the State is no longer immune from actions in damages even for legislative wrong and even in those Member States which are still immune outside the sphere of Community law.

In cases with a Community law element, the courts are under an obligation to apply and enforce directly effective Community law, with precedence over conflicting national law. They must seek to interpret national law in conformity with Community law. They must have jurisdiction to suspend the application of a parliamentary Act and refer a question for preliminary ruling to the Court of Justice. National courts must have jurisdiction to hold the State liable in damages for infringements of Community law, even if those have been committed by Parliament or by a judicial organ. This is all part of the Community mandate.[8]

Yet, this 'Community mandate' is not an entirely separate mandate that is taken off the shelf when a case contains Community law elements. The reality is much more complex, since the Community mandate is closely intertwined with national law, and must be applied in a national legal environment. Under the principle of national procedural autonomy, national law decides issues concerning the competent court, the definition of rights that individuals derive from Community law, and procedural and remedial questions. In turn, this autonomy is limited by the principles of equivalence and effectiveness. In some cases, therefore, the national procedural or remedial rules will also have to be set aside, or adjusted to the requirements of effectiveness and effective judicial protection of the individual.

Do the national judges have a double mandate, one deriving from the national legal order, and one from the Court of Justice? Does it mean that their competences, powers and duties in a specific case vary, depending on whether or not Community issues are involved? If this is indeed the case, their powers and competences, and the remedies which they may offer to the citizen seeking relief, will differ from those available in a typical – non-Community law related – case. The powers, duties and remedies available in the Community context will have an impact on the place of the national judiciary in the constitutional setting in those situations. The courts gain powers of judicial review over the executive and legislative powers even in cases where they do not have those powers as a matter of national law. They are required to create new remedies, or to offer remedies that may not have been available under national law in similar cases.

---

8 As defined further below.

Within this first stage, the story is fairly well-known: the national courts have heeded, they have accepted that in the context of Community law they may have to set aside an Act of Parliament, they may have to suspend it, they may have to hold the State liable in damages for legislative acts or omissions. As a result, national courts are involved in enforcing Community loyalty upon all State organs, and their powers and competences are extended in Community law cases: in short, they are empowered by Community law. In the first part of the book, this story will be analysed from the perspective of national constitutional law: *how* and *why* have the national courts heeded? What were the national constitutional obstacles that may have prevented them from becoming the common courts of Community law, and how were these overcome? It further identifies the consequences of the national courts involvement from a national constitutional perspective: does it alter their position *vis-à-vis* the other State organs? Finally, it aims to test the hypothesis that the national courts have duties and competences that they derive directly from Community law, irrespective of their national constitutional mandate, *i.e.* the question of direct empowerment. Are the national courts empowered by Community law directly to set aside an otherwise immune Act, or is the source of this power to be found elsewhere?

1.2. The Second Stage

The tale of empowerment of the national courts as common courts of Community law does not however cover the full story. There is a parallel, yet distinct, narrative in which the Court of Justice has been less successful in convincing its interlocutors, the national courts. This story line features the national constitutional courts and other courts having constitutional jurisdiction[9] in dialogue with the Court of Justice. For these courts, the case law of the European Court presents constitutional difficulties which have not all been overcome, at least not entirely. All of these courts accept the case law of the Court with respect to the judicial function of the ordinary courts, at least in practical effect and be it with some limitations. But when it comes to their own national mandate as guardians of the Constitution, of core constitutional principles or fundamental rights, they are far more reluctant to heed the Court of Justice. In terms of judicial mandate, the message from Luxembourg would entail

---

[9]   The notions will be defined further below. Suffice it to say here that 'constitutional courts' are those which have been set up with the aim of reviewing the constitutionality of primary legislation; 'courts having constitutional jurisdiction' are those (ordinary) courts which are competent, in cases before them, to review the constitutionality of statutes, but which have not been set up especially with this competence in view. Taken together, both sets of courts could be labelled 'judicial review courts'.

a limitation of the powers, competences and responsibilities of the national courts having constitutional jurisdiction. Accepting the Community mandate may lead to an empowerment of these courts in some areas, but more importantly, it requests them to suspend some of their powers, and to submit to Community law and to the Court of Justice. Again, the Community side of the story is grafted upon the principle of supremacy, and is straightforward and uncompromising. The whole of Community law, be it a Treaty provision or a Commission decision takes precedence over the bulk of domestic law, including even the most fundamental principles of national constitutional law. *'Therefore, the validity of a Community measure or its effects within a Member State cannot be affected by allegations that it runs counter to either fundamental rights as formulated by the constitution of that State or the principles of a national constitutional structure'.*[10] As a consequence, all national courts are precluded from controlling Community law, and from letting constitutional provisions, rules and principles prevail over Community law. They are, put bluntly, requested to suspend their function of guardians of the Constitution. The conflict between the national mandate to guard the Constitution, and the Community mandate to ensure that Community law is applied and enforced even as against the national Constitution, is manifest.

In practice it has not appeared possible for most national constitutional courts to accept the broader constitutional implications of the concept of supremacy. The full extent of the principle has not been agreed to. National constitutional courts, and courts having constitutional jurisdiction, do accept Community law, but only on their own terms, and with reservations. More and more constitutional courts voice their reservations about the Court's case law. The 'rebellion' of the German *Bundesverfassungsgericht* is probably the most notorious. Famous, or infamous depending on the position adopted, are its *Solange* judgments and its *Maastricht Urteil*. But most of its brethren in other Member States adopt similar positions. The Italian *Corte costituzionale* has designed constitutional *controlimiti* against Community law. The Danish *Højesteret* has announced that Community law may not be applicable in Denmark, in certain circumstances, and that it will be for the Danish courts, not for the Court of Justice to rule on these cases. The position of the Belgian *Arbitragehof* may be more co-operative than that of the other constitutional courts, but its final position on several issues in not entirely clear.

The areas of conflict that still remain are, first, the question as to which court has jurisdiction to decide conflicts of competence between the Community or Union on the one hand and the Member States on the other hand. Second, while it may be true that in the context of fundamental

---

[10] Case 11/70 *Internationale Handelsgesellschaft mbH v Einfuhr- und Vorratsstelle für Getreide und Futtermittel* [1970] ECR 1125, at para 3.

rights the *Bundesverfassungsgericht* has made a peace-offering in the 2000 *Bananas III* decision, it is submitted that it may have put in place only a very fragile settlement, and that it has had no direct bearing on the threats made by other courts having constitutional jurisdiction. Third, the Court of Justice's reluctance to take account of international treaties, most particularly WTO law, when assessing the validity of Community law, is not shared by all national courts. Fourth, it is not yet clear what will be the role of national courts in the context of Union law which is not part of hard core Community law, especially in the scope of Titles IV and VI TEU. These issues will be considered in the second part of the book.

2. A KALEIDOSCOPIC VIEW OF THE RESEARCH AREA

The central theme of the book, the Community mandate of the national courts, is only one aspect of a much larger issue which, in its broadest sense, concerns the relationship between national and Community law, and is an evergreen in European legal studies. The problem which is central in this book is not limited to courts and judges. Courts merely make up the perspective adopted in the book. But the underlying theme is much greater and encompasses many different issues. The following are some of the perspectives which may be adopted on the issue.

2.1. Legal Orders

From the most general and theoretical perspective, the central theme is that of the relationship between *legal orders*, viewed as monolithic entities.[11] The notion of 'legal order' is then used in its widest sense, including both institutional arrangements of who does what and substantive provisions of law. In the framework of Community law, the central research questions posed in this respect are: how is the Community legal order to be defined? And: how do Community law and national law interrelate? The answers to these questions will vary according to the position adopted. The questions can, first, be asked from a Community perspective. The answer, then, will be easy and straightforward: from the Community point of view, the Community constitutes a new legal order, based on the constituting Treaties, its constitutional charter. It is integrated in the national legal order of the Member States and takes precedence over national law, including the Constitution. The tone is integrationist, and driven by *une*

---

[11] The book by Diarmuid Rossa Phelan is based on the concept of legal orders, see DR Phelan, *Revolt or Revolution. The Constitutional Boundaries of the European Community* (Dublin, Round Hall, 1997).

certaine idée de l'Europe.[12] It may be described as finding the legal parallel to the more political concept of 'supra-nationalism'. But then there are fifteen national perspectives, in which, on the basis of the constraints of the domestic legal order and from within, the same questions are being asked. Even when starting from the same *idée de l'Europe* the issue is considerably more complex since the broader constitutional implications immediately spring to mind. While some national systems may go along with the paradigm offered by the Court of Justice and Community law, many will not step out of the national legal order and prevailing principles, but rather seek to adapt existing rules principles and concepts to go along with the Court of Justice, so far as possible. More creativity will be required, since the conception of the relationship between legal orders must be blended with existing internal legal order conceptions, on the basis of a limited set of tools available in the Constitution or in constitutional law. This has led to a variety of images, involving bridges, pyramids, legal orders retreating from certain areas and the like. A third possible view would be the neutral perspective, that of the outsider, identifying with neither the one or the other legal order and belonging to neither. Yet, it may well be that there is no answer based on logic, to the question which legal order must take precedence, when two claim priority.[13]

This wider issue of relationship between legal orders will from time to time be considered in the book. The national courts have used their (changing) perception of the relation between legal orders in order to build their case with respect to their own judicial mandate.

2.2. Effective Judicial Protection of the Individual

From another angle, the focus is on the *citizen* seeking relief. While this was a novel theme in the foundational period, the individual being a new-comer in international law, it is now one of the most frequently used perspectives. The individual is the *jeune premier* at the centre of attention, and the objective of the Court seems to be the enhancement of his judicial protection before the national courts. On the basis of the principles of effectiveness and the effective judicial protection of the individual, the Court of Justice has developed an entire case law, known as second and

---

[12] There is however also a second, more marginal approach, which seeks to explain Community law and its relations with national law entirely on the basis of 'classic' international law, implying that Community law may not be so 'new'.

[13] A concept which may prove useful in this context would be that of the 'rule of recognition'; the central question would then be which rule of recognition would have priority over the other on the basis of logic.

third generation jurisprudence.[14] In this line of cases, the Court of Justice has indicated what the courts must do when a provision of Community law is directly effective and is opposed by a contrary provision of national law. The result has been the creation of new remedies and exceptions to national procedural rules. From the individual's perspective, it may be important to find out whether or not his case falls within or outside the scope of Community law: if the case is covered by Community law, there may be additional remedies available. This may trigger a Euro-law game: trying to find arguments based on European law in order to win the case. The co-existence of legal systems and the limited reach of the case law of the Court of Justice have sometimes created situations of unequal protection of rights, depending on whether the case is purely national, or contains a Community law element.

This development has been criticised for various reasons. One may wonder why Community law rights should be better protected than national rights. Second, while the Court of Justice is seeking to attain an acceptable level of uniformity Community wide, a new disparity is created, not between Member States, but *within* one legal order. Even leaving aside these disparities, it has been argued that Community law disrupts or even spoils the structure of national law. On the other hand, it has been pointed out that the innovations introduced in the area of Community law are sometimes extended to cases that lack the Community component. Consequently, Community law contributes to enhancing judicial protection generally and to the development of common law in Europe, even beyond what is being done through legislative harmonisation. The 'school' studying a developing *ius commune europeum*, a common standard in the judicial protection of the individual in the European Union, and across national legal boundaries, follows from this line of reasoning.

While the citizen will appear frequently in the book, the focus will be on courts.

---

[14] The 'generation' typology is frequently used in literature; see J Mertens de Wilmars, 'L'efficacité des différentes techniques nationales de protection juridique contre les violations du droit communautaire par les autorités nationales et les particuliers', (1981) *CDE*, 379; D Curtin and K Mortelmans, 'Application and Enforcement of Community Law by the Member States: Actors in Search of a Third Generation Script', in D Curtin and T Heukels (eds), *Institutional Dynamics of European Integration. Essays in Honour of H.G. Schermers*, Vol. 2 (Dordrecht, Nijhoff, 1994) 423. Second generation cases are those relating to the procedural and remedial rules governing cases involving Community law before national courts. The ECJ's approach is based on the principle of national procedural autonomy – even though the ECJ has never given it this label – restricted by the principles of equivalence and effectiveness. Third generation cases are those in which the ECJ introduces a new remedy, or extends it to cases in which it would not be available in similar national cases.

2.3. European Union Law and Parliamentary Sovereignty

Not only courts, but also other State organs have undergone tremendous shifts in their powers and competences as a consequence of their State's membership of the European Union. Powers – sovereign powers, *Hoheitsrechte*, or parts of national sovereignty – have been transferred to the European Union in order to be exercised in common, in what is sometimes called a pooling of sovereignty. The implications in national constitutional law are tremendous.[15] Parliaments cannot legislate in all areas, and even within the areas that remain strictly national, they are limited by Community law. Also from a formal legal perspective, Community law changes the prevailing rules and principles. In the hierarchy of norms, parliamentary legislation may no longer be the highest norm, just below the Constitution; the principle of legality may need a new content. There may even be a need to re-think democracy and constitutional foundations *tout court*, not only from a European perspective, but also in the context of the national Constitutions. The need to take these fundamental constitutional principles – shared throughout Western Europe – seriously may well be the most important message sent out by the *Bundesverfassungsgericht* in the *Maastricht Urteil*, which continues to carry importance, even after more recent and more 'pro-European' case law.

It may even be argued that Parliaments are no longer sovereign, while that was and still is the paradigm prevailing in most of the Member States in one form or other. National parliaments act in different capacities. When implementing a Community directive, especially one that does not leave much discretion to the Member States, they can hardly be regarded as sovereign legislators. The trend in the evolution goes in the opposite direction than in the case of courts: while national courts often gain powers when acting in the context of Community law, national legislatures lose.

Interest in the role of national parliaments in the context of the European Union has recently re-emerged. In the context of this book, the focus will however be on courts, but also their relationship with national parliaments. Indeed, Community law and in particular the case law of the Court of Justice has altered the position of the national courts *vis-à-vis* the national primary legislature. In the context of Community law, no Act of Parliament is now immune from judicial review, even in those Member States where the Sovereignty of Parliament and the immunity of primary legislation still forms one of the most fundamental foundations of the constitutional order.

---

[15] See e.g. LFM Besselink et al., *De Nederlandse Grondwet en de Europese Unie* (Groningen, Europa Law Publishing, 2002) chapter 3, 'De positie van de Staten-Generaal'.

2.4. European Union Law and Administrative Authorities

The same goes for national *executive organs and administrative bodies*, which are involved in the functioning of the Community. All national authorities may find themselves involved with Community law and may be asked and even ordered to administer Community law, whereby their Community mandate may conflict with their national constitutional function. The most obvious and problematic example is the independent obligation imposed on administrative authorities, whatever their rank or place in the national constitutional setting, to give effect to Community law and apply it, any conflicting rule of national law notwithstanding. In fact, the same duties and obligations that are imposed on national courts equally apply to administrative bodies. The Community rationale for these obligations is the same as for the courts and derives from the principles of direct effect, supremacy and the principle of Community loyalty as laid down in Article 10 EC. Yet, the national side of the story may be even more problematic than for the courts. Indeed, in a State governed by the rule of law, or *Rechtsstaatlichkeit*, administrative authorities are subject to the law, and they must apply it. They cannot of their own motion disapply it, even when they consider it to be in conflict with the Constitution. Community law does require such independent action by the administrative bodies and organs of whatever nature, be it the Minister adopting secondary legislation, the municipality implementing a decree, a tax authority, or a public law body responsible for the payment of social security benefits. These authorities have independent duties under Community law to abide by the Treaties and the law made under it.

The independent Community duties of public law bodies find a Treaty basis in Article 10 EC, which provides that 'the Member States' – and accordingly all their organs – are under a duty of loyalty and must ensure the fulfilment of the obligations arising out of Community law, and abstain from any measure which could jeopardise the attainment of the objectives of the Treaty. In addition, in the case law of the Court of Justice, the independent duties of administrative authorities follow logically from the functions and duties of the national courts.[16] Yet, these Community duties raise questions of legal certainty and equality, and if duly applied, may give rise to chaos on the national plane.

2.5. Actors on the Scene

The general theme, it has been explained, may feature many different actors and players. These are some of the actors involved: on the European

---

[16] Case 103/88 *Fratelli Costanzo SpA v Comune di Milano* [1989] ECR 1839.

scene, there are the Member States as the High Contracting Parties, and the European Community and Union and their institutions. Within the latter category, the Court of Justice as the ultimate (constitutional) interpreter of the Treaties, will play a leading role, as it has a privileged relationship with the national courts through the preliminary rulings procedure. On the national level, it could be said that all national authorities are involved in the European project: at all levels, whether central or federal, decentralised, municipal or provincial, and regional or federated, national authorities are engaged in the application and administration of European law. The Union does not possess a complete institutional structure and set up, and is to a large extent dependent on the co-operation of national authorities. Within the context of the European Union, national organs and institutions may accordingly operate in different capacities: as national organs, or as (part of) the European structure.

3. FOCUS ON COURTS

Featuring as central actors in this book are courts, and then first and foremost national courts and judges. The story line is defined by the Court of Justice, since it is the European level which is common to all legal systems. However, the Court of Justice may say what it wants and the national courts must pay heed. The study of European Union law is far too one-sided if it is only looked at from the European perspective: the picture emerging from the case-law of the Court of Justice may well be misleading. In order to gain a better understanding of the functioning of Union law, it must be looked at from a double perspective: top-down from the Community perspective and bottom-up from the national angle. The European side of the story must be completed with the national story lines. If the national courts had not taken up their mission as Community law courts and if they had not assisted in enforcing compliance with Community law and protecting Community rights of individuals, Community law would probably have remained a sub-set of international law, where compliance depends on the co-operation of the legislative, executive and administrative organs of the Member States, and where international liability is established at the international level only. Instead, in the European Union the national courts operate as agents of the Union within the national legal order. They make sure, for instance, that public authorities do not impede the operation of the common market by introducing conflicting legislation and, they make sure that Union law is given effect and that it is properly implemented. And they perform that function to a large extent in accordance with the instructions of the Court of Justice.

Since the focus in the book is on courts, it is also on pathology: if the legislative and administrative public bodies complied with their Community obligations, the national courts would much less often be confronted with Union law. Direct effect, supremacy, uniform interpretation and governmental liability mostly relate to the enforcement of Community law against *defying* Member States. The national courts are first and foremost, but not exclusively, involved in the enforcement of Union law against the Member States (and to a far lesser extent against the Union institutions – a task which is to a large degree entrusted to the Court of Justice).

The Court of Justice in its case law addresses 'the' national courts. Like the Treaty in Article 234 EC, the Court does not differentiate between national courts. The only distinction made in the Treaty is that between courts and tribunals against whose decisions there is no judicial remedy under national law, and other courts and tribunals. Yet, to approach 'the' national courts as one class should not obscure the fact that there are immense differences in powers, competences, and indeed in influence of those making up the group. This may make it difficult to make general pronouncements about the group. Is an Italian *pretore* to be dealt with in the same manner as the German *Bundesverfassungsgericht*? Can the English House of Lords be compared to the French *Conseil d'État*? It is obvious that each of these courts and institutions are coloured by their national institutional environment, their traditions, competences and the legal culture of the system in which they perform their functions. Their identity and self-perception may matter a great deal in how they face the Court of Justice and how willing they are to assume the function of Community courts. On the other hand, they are, as a group, distinct from other organs and institutions, such as the national legislative and the executive branches. I will address the national courts as a group, but some classification will be made.

The first group, on which the first part of the book concentrates, consists of ordinary national courts, including administrative, civil, tax and labour courts. In short, this group contains all courts except the national constitutional courts. Within this group the highest courts in the judicial organisation will play the leading roles, for obvious reasons. These are the courts against whose decisions there is no appeal possible within the national legal system, except, where available, by way of constitutional review. As an example, the French *Conseil d'État* belongs to this sub-category, as do the German *Bundesfinanzhof*, the English *House of Lords*, the Dutch *Hoge Raad* and the Belgian *Cour de cassation*. The second category, on which the second part of the book will focus, is made up of the constitutional courts of the Member States (such as the German *Bundesverfassungsgericht*, the Italian *Corte costituzionale*, the Belgian *Cour d'arbitrage* or *Arbitragehof*), together with those courts belonging to the first category which also perform the function of guardian of the Constitution, as part of the ordinary court system. The Danish *Højesteret* and the Irish *Supreme Court* accordingly belong to both categories. Nevertheless, even though the first part concentrates on the ordinary, non-constitutional courts (first group), the constitutional courts may also have an important role to play. Indeed, Community law on the judicial function was only agreed to after several constitutional issues had been resolved, often following intervention by the constitutional courts. Conversely, the second part of the book will primarily feature the constitutional courts and courts having constitutional jurisdiction. But from time to time, also other (ordinary) courts may appear, where they have taken up the role of guardian of the national Constitution.

4. OBJECTIVES

The book is an attempt to gain a better understanding of the involvement of national courts in the European Union judicial system, and its impact on the national constitutional position of the national courts. The main thrust is to explore *what* constitutional questions the courts have been confronted with, in several selected areas, and *how* despite the constitutional difficulties, they have come to apply and enforce Union law. And what were the *consequences* for their national constitutional position, and their relations with the other State organs? Next, *why* have the courts accepted it even in those systems where it appeared almost impossible for fundamental constitutional reasons? These questions ultimately lead to the source of judicial authority and the limits of the judicial function. The dilemma, for the national courts, is that the invitation by the European Court of Justice to become its ally in the enforcement and application of Community law, entails several duties and competences, which, in some cases, force the courts to overstep the constitutional limits of their function. Judges derive their authority from the Constitution, the legal source of all State authority, which also indicates the limits of their authority. The invitation by the Luxembourg Court may be at odds with the traditional conception of the judicial function; it may even collide head-on with it. Can a national judge overstep the constitutional limits of his powers when discharging his role as a Community *juge de droit commun*? Is that what national courts have done? And if so, what have they based it on? Is it fair to say that the national courts have indeed become *'les juges communs de droit communautaire'*, and that they sometimes act not as national courts, but in a different capacity of decentralised Community courts? Can they be considered agents of the Union within the Member States? What are the remaining pockets of resistance? Are there any insurmountable constitutional obstacles? And finally, how and to what extent can a European Constitution play a part in these matters?

5. METHOD

The book intends to tell the story of the national courts' involvement in the application and enforcement of Community law, both from the European and the national constitutional perspective. Since this involvement was requested by the Court of Justice, the story will first be told from the perspective of the Court of Justice and European Union law. Within each section, the issue will first be explained from the angle of Community law, or where relevant, Union law.[17] Since the book intends to give a complete picture, it will also include the national constitutional perspectives, and hence a second narrative will be added analysing the same issues from the national constitutional perspective of the national courts. To gain a complete understanding of the issues involved from a national perspective would require an analysis of fifteen legal systems and constitutional settings. However, this cannot be achieved in a reasonable time-limit and by one author, if only for reasons of language. The analysis has been restricted to a more limited number of Member States, including, for most issues, the Netherlands, Belgium, France, Germany, Italy, the United Kingdom and Ireland, sometimes Luxembourg and Denmark. The choice of these countries is related to linguistic skills. But there are other reasons: Belgium and the Netherlands have been included for obvious reasons: I have been educated in Belgium and an a Belgian national; I live and work in the Netherlands, and this research project was completed in the Netherlands at the University of Maastricht. In addition, both are small States, were founding Members of the European Communities and Union and have, until recently, been regarded as forerunners in the process of European integration. While the Netherlands Constitution and constitutional system was and is considered to be particularly apt to comply with the demands of the European Court, the Belgian Constitution was silent at the time when the founding Treaties were signed, and still is. Both countries have a tradition of judicial deference of courts *vis-à-vis* the primary legislature. However, Belgium has since established a constitutional court on the occasion of the federalisation of the State, and it is therefore interesting to find out whether this changes the national constitutional perspective on the issue. Germany, France and Italy were the three largest founding Member States, and are interesting both because of differences and similarities: France as the monist State, characterised by deference of the courts *vis-à-vis* the primary legislature; Germany and Italy as dualist States, with assertive constitutional courts and a strong post-war tradition of judicial protection of fundamental rights. The United Kingdom combines fundamental principles from France on the one hand (absence of judicial review of parliamentary

---

[17] With respect to the terminology, see below.

legislation) and Germany and Italy on the other (a dualist system). But the United Kingdom is different from all the foregoing Member States because of the peculiarities of its constitutional system based on the common law principle of parliamentary sovereignty and lacking a single, codified constitutional document. Moreover, it has a very distinct legal and judicial style, which is unlike any of those prevailing on the continent. Finally, the United Kingdom acceded when the basic traits of the Community conception of the relationship between national and Community law were already in place: 'they knew what they were getting into'. Irish law is partly based on similar lines (common law, dualism, later accession), but differs fundamentally from the British system in the area of constitutional law. While the style of reasoning and of writing may be comparable, the Irish do have a fairly young constitutional document, which has been adapted to conform to the changing conditions of evolving European integration. In addition, Ireland does have a system of constitutional review, but in contrast to the States already mentioned, this review is not reserved to a separate court set up to that end. At the end of the day, Ireland may well be the Member State which takes European integration most seriously from the national constitutional perspective, or, *vice-versa*, takes its Constitution most seriously in the context of European integration. No other country has amended its Constitution so regularly and consistently to follow the steps of integration, in an attempt to comply with constitutional and European requirements. Luxembourg has been included in the first Part of the book on ordinary supremacy and ordinary courts, since it was the smallest of the founding Member States, had no express constitutional provisions solving the question and is extremely receptive to international law as a whole. Denmark will be taken on in the second Part on courts having constitutional jurisdiction, obviously because of the famous or infamous *Maastricht* judgment of the *Højesteret*. Denmark is another smaller Member State, but, in contrast to Belgium, the Netherlands and Luxembourg, it acceded at a later stage – together with Ireland, another small Member State – and, more importantly, is not a prominent pro-European country: it is rather known for its sceptical European stance. The order of the discussion will not always be the same, and will depend on the relevant topic. Sometimes, Member States are left out when they add nothing to the discussion.

The approach will be a lawyer's. The wider context, political and sociological, will obviously be taken into account, but the perspective will remain a lawyer's. No interviews, for instance with judges, have been conducted. The underlying rationale as to *why* courts have done what they did will mostly remain unexposed in judicial decisions. Only the 'legal' why will be analysed. What were the constitutional obstacles hindering the reception of the message from Luxembourg? What would be the impact of accepting the Community mandate in terms of national constitutional relationships? Would it affect the constitutional equilibrium? And *how* did the courts reason? What legal techniques, tools and methods have the courts used to achieve the aim required by the Court of Justice?

The book is based on empirical observation. The analysis comprises a lot of judicial material. It is assumed that not every reader will be familiar with the case law of all the national courts concerned, from, say, the Italian, to the Irish, Netherlands and Belgian courts. Accordingly, the cases have sometimes been explained in rather lengthy manner. The reader who is familiar with a specific national system can pass over these sections and move on to others quickly. Likewise, for the scholar of Community law, the sections on Union law may seem extensive. I have included them for those readers who are less familiar with the funda- mentals of Union law. On the other hand, I also found it useful to go back to the basics, to re-examine *Van Gend en Loos*, *Costa v ENEL*, *Simmenthal* and the like, to put them in a national constitutional perspective, in order to gain a better understanding of the issues, and to check some of the myths concerning the case law of the Court of Justice. *Reculer pour mieux sauter...* Since the book concentrates on constitutional issues, the analysis focuses on the constitutional cases. Accordingly, it does not give a com- plete picture of the actual day to day application of Community law in national courts.[18]

Finally, the story being told – or the hypothesis that is being tested – is that of a 'transformation' of the national courts into the common courts of Community law, and of the dialogue between the Court of Justice and the national courts. Accordingly, recent legal and judicial history will play a role. It will be explained what the prevailing rules and principles were in a specific domestic system *before* the Court of Justice made explicit its requests to the national courts, showing the constitutional intricacies that the courts were confronted with. This will most often be followed by an explanation of exactly what it is the Court of Justice expects the courts to do or not to do. Finally, the reaction of the national courts is analysed, and its impact in national constitutional law.

What the book intends to do, is test the hypothesis that 'the national courts are the common courts of Community law acting under a Community mandate'. It further signals the areas of contention between the Court of Justice and the national courts. And third, it places these issues in the context of the broader discussion on the transformation and

---

18 Such a study would have to include all national cases involving Community law, includ- ing also those cases where the Community law component has not been taken on where it could or should have; each year some 1200 cases come to the attention of the Research and Documentation Department. An example of a study of the practical application of Community law in the context of the internal market and with respect to three Member States, the Netherlands, France and the United Kingdom may be found in M. Jarvis, *The Application of EC law by National Courts: The Free Movement of Goods* (Oxford, Clarendon Press, 1998).

constitutionalisation of Europe and the recent debate on the drafting of a
European Constitution.

6. STRUCTURE

The book is divided into three main themes. The first theme, discussed in
part 1, relates to the functions and duties of the (ordinary) national courts
as Community courts. In the exercise of their Community mandate,
national courts may and must assume certain types of jurisdiction which
do not belong to their national mandate and which entail a modification
of their relations with the other organs of the State, for instance the primary legislature. This shift in powers will have an effect on some of the
most fundamental principles of constitutional law, such as the separation
of powers, the principles of legality, of judicial deference to primary legislation, and the principle of democracy. Even though Union law and the
Court of Justice demand quite an effort of the national courts, and often a
great deal of creativity entailing a shift of their national constitutional
position, this part of the story is one of success: the national courts have
become the Court of Justice's accomplices, its natural allies, in the enforcement of Community law and the protection of Community law rights
which individuals derive therefrom.

The second theme, central in part 2, appears much more problematic.
It relates to the constitutional courts and other courts having constitutional jurisdiction. This will be a less friendly narrative, in which the
most fundamental national constitutional concerns concerning European
integration surface, such as those relating to the final say on the division of competences between the Member States and the Union, questions of fundamental rights protection, of whether there are
untouchable core elements of national sovereignty which cannot be
transferred, and accordingly, questions of the limits of European integration. It may be asked therefore, whether there is, in this area, a *guerre
des juges*. Is there a power struggle going on between the Court of
Justice and the national constitutional courts over who has the right to
have the final say on the most fundamental issues? Is there any solution to these questions?

Finally, the third theme, in part 3, will draw together the lines of the
first two themes, and place them in the context of the debate on the
Constitution of Europe and Convention on the Future of Europe. Such
Constitution may constitute a unique and huge constitutional moment, a
moment to fundamentally reconsider the reasons for European integration, its aims and objectives, and the price we are willing to pay in constitutional terms. It will be analysed whether and how a Constitution may
help to answer some of the questions raised in parts 1 and 2.

The division into three parts, covering three different sub-themes within the central topic and featuring different leading actors, coincides roughly with three *periods* in time. During the *first* period, lasting from *Van Gend en Loos* and *Costa v ENEL* until about the late 1980's, the national courts by and large, one after the other, to a large extent accepted their 'Community mandate', as the Court of Justice asked them to. This period roughly ends in 1990 when the *House of Lords* accepted the power of the English courts to review Acts of the United Kingdom Parliament in the light of Community law and to set them aside in case of a conflict. Only a year before, the French *Conseil d'État* had, after a long period of resistance, accepted the same competence. Central themes in the case law and academic literature during this period are the concept of direct effect, the principle of supremacy, the success of the preliminary ruling procedure, and the fundamental question of the relationship between the national and the Community legal orders. At the Community judicial level, this period ends with *Opinion 1/91*, where the Court of Justice termed the Community Treaties as the 'constitutional charter'.

During the *second* period, roughly covering the nineties, the emphasis is no longer on acceptance by the national courts, but on the remaining pockets of resistance, on the areas of contention between the Court of Justice and some of the national courts. The focus is on *conflict* rather than on co-operation, on *limits* of integration rather than on integration. While the European literature during this phase focuses on the second and even third generation issues, which further develops the issues which were central during the first phase (how can Community law be made more effective in the national legal order; what are the national courts to do to make Community law more effective; direct effect of directives; *Francovich* liability), there is a new and different sound also. It is connected with the deficiencies in the system of judicial protection in Union law: the issue of fundamental rights, the question of judicial *Kompetenz Kompetenz* (as the pendant of absolute supremacy and the expansion of Qualified Majority Voting), the issue of limits on integration, of core principles of the national Constitutions, of the untouchable nucleus of national sovereignty. The highlight of this period of conflict from the national perspective is the *Maastricht* decision of the German *Bundesverfassungsgericht*. The decision made painfully clear the imperfections of the Community legal system, in terms of the most fundamental principles of national constitutional law: democracy, protection of fundamental rights, the division of competences between the Union and the Member States and the monitoring thereof, the nature of the Union and its relations with the Member States and, in legal terms, the relation between the Treaties and the national Constitutions. At first sight, this appeared to be a judicial dialogue between the Court of Justice and the national (constitutional) courts. Yet, while the German Court did indeed address some of its objections to the Court of Justice, its concerns were much more fundamental and concerned the much deeper political and legal issues. The real addressees of the decisions were the Member States as *Herren der Verträge*, as the Constitution-making Power at the European level, and their national counterparts, those responsible for the Constitution at the national level.

The end of the nineties and the turn of the millenium marked the beginning of a new era. While the conflict between the *Bundesverfassungsgericht* and the Court of Justice seemed to settle down, the failure of the Amsterdam and Nice IGC's demonstrated the need for a renewed constitutional debate on the future of Europe and the need for a European Constitution. Starting from the EU Charter of Fundamental Rights, but especially in the Convention on the Future of Europe, an entirely new debate has commenced and is now taking place. The topic of a Constitution for Europe has become mainstream rather than *avantgarde*: it is in the air, and is no longer limited to European federalists and idealists. It has become *bon ton*. Yet, what at times seems to be forgotten in this debate, are the lessons to be drawn from the previous judicial dialogue between some national courts and the Court of Justice, which, as said, was rather a complaint of these national courts addressed to the political elite about the lack of constitutional foundation of Europe, European and national. What is striking is the absence of courts in the current debate. While before the constitutional debate in Europe was qualified as a *judicial* debate, with leading roles for Courts both at the European and national level, the debate has been removed from the judicial organs and has been transferred to the political organs. And rightly so: the debate on these fundamental constitutional issues are first and foremost the responsibility of the political institutions. It should however be remembered that these courts will at the end of the day, again have to decide cases under the new Constitution. Due regard should be paid to their prior considerations and warnings, if new conflicts and the resurgence of old conflicts are to be avoided.

This division in periods obviously is not watertight. The issues central in the second period for instance were signalled already during the first period; the issue of direct effect still causes much debate today and so forth. Perhaps these three periods could be characterised more as different moods in the intercourt and academic debates.

7. MATERIALS

The leading national constitutional cases concerning Community law up to 1994 have been published in English in A. Oppenheimer, *The*

Relationship Between European Community Law and National Law: The Cases.[19] References to cases involving a Community law component can also be found in the annual report of the Commission[20] on the application of Community law in the Member States, which contains an annex relating to application by national courts.[21] Until 1999, the survey only included decisions by national courts of final instance; since 2000 lower court decisions may be incorporated. Typically, the survey is structured on the basis of a *questionnaire*, asking about 'cases where a question for a preliminary ruling should have been referred by a final instance court but was not, or other decisions regarding preliminary rulings that merit attention'; about 'cases where a court contrary to *Foto-Frost* declared an act of a Community institution to be invalid'; about 'decisions noteworthy as setting a good or bad example' and about 'decisions that applied the rulings given in *Francovich*, *Factortame* and *Brasserie du Pêcheur*'.[22] It is regrettable that the data gathered by the Research and Documentation Department of the Court of Justice is not freely accessible. This would not only facilitate the work of academics, it could also be a useful tool for national courts to easily gather information about decisions handed by their counterpart other Member States.

A lot has changed over the past years in terms of availability of national court cases concerning Community law. Constitutional courts now have their own web-sites and judgments are available there.[23] In addition, there are many sites containing court judgments also from ordinary courts, obviously in their original language version.[24] Several final instance courts also have their own web-site.[25] English language versions of landmark decisions may be published in the Common Market Law Reports or in other journals.

---

[19] A Oppenheimer, *The Relationship Between European Community Law and National Law: The Cases* (Cambridge, Cambridge University Press, 1994).

[20] The survey is drawn up by the Commission, on the basis of data gathered by the Research and Documentation Department of the Court of Justice. According to the introduction preceding the survey, the Commission does not undertake a systematic analysis of the many judgments delivered each year by the superior courts in the various courts. Each year, some 1200 judgments relating to Community law come to the attention of the ECJ's Research and Documentation Department.

[21] The most recent surveys are also available on the ECJ's website.

[22] Other questions have from time to time been added. In 1999 for instance, the survey also contained 'decisions of the European Court of Human Rights which were of interest for the purposes of the survey'.

[23] For instance www.bundesverfassungsgericht.de; www.conseil-constitutionnel.fr; www.arbitrage.be; www.cortecostituzionale.it.

[24] Examples are www.legifrance.gouv.fr (for French law and judicial decisions); www.bailii.org (for the UK and Ireland); www.irlii.org (for Ireland); www.cass.be (for Belgium); www. rechtspraak.nl (for The Netherlands) and www.giurcost.org (Italian constitutional cases).

[25] For instance www.bundesgerichtshof.de; www.conseil-etat.fr.

8. TERMINOLOGY AND TREATY ARTICLES

The original names of the courts discussed have been retained: *Hoge Raad*, *Højesteret*, *Conseil d'État*, *Arbeitsgericht*, *Supreme Court*. It is a difficult venture to translate these terms, without loosing the specificity of the court. The Netherlands *Hoge Raad* and the Danish *Højesteret* for instance – which would possibly have the same name in English – have different powers of judicial review; it would be very difficult to reflect those in translation. Should they be translated as 'Supreme Court' (which carries the risk of suggesting similarities with the United States Supreme Court), or 'Supreme Council', 'High Council' (suggesting that they are not really a court)? The original language term is therefore retained. With respect to Belgian courts, reference will be made to either the French or Dutch language version (*Arbitragehof* or *Cour d'arbitrage*; *Cour de cassation* or *Hof van Cassatie*), which reflects the characteristics of the system.[26]

A uniform method was chosen to refer to national court judgments in footnotes, thus deviating from the various differing national approaches. In footnotes, reference will be made to the original language name of the court or tribunal; sometimes, where usual in national law – as for instance in references to decisions handed by the Corte costituzionale or the Conseil constitutionnel – a number; date of the decision; name of the parties or another name or label the case goes by; and source. Reference is made to the publications that are usual in the relevant system,[27] for the more recent cases to electronic publications and where possible to other publications that may be more easily accessible; where available, reference may also be made to an English language version. This type of reference diverges from what is usual in national systems, but is preferred since it is more complete: it indicates the court that handed the decision (in contrast to for instance English references, where it may not be clear which court handed it); the number (because scholars familiar with the system that uses numbers instead of names will recognise a number rather than a name); the date (which is absent for instance in the usual German or English references, but may be important in the story); a name (which makes the case more 'real' than a number and easier to recognise) and a source.

With respect to Treaty articles, it will be indicated each time whether the old or new numbering applies. However, as a general rule, where reference is made to an article of a Treaty as it stands after 1 May 1999 – the entry into force of the Treaty of Amsterdam, the number of the article is immediately followed by two letters indicating the Treaty concerned: EU

---

[26] The German language, which is the third official language in Belgium, has been left out.

[27] So for instance to the BVerfGE (*Entscheidungen des Bundesverfassungsgerichts*); to the All ER etc.

for Treaty on European Union and EC for the EC Treaty. Article 234 EC thus refers to that article in the new numbering after Amsterdam. Where reference is made to the old numbering, the number is followed by the words 'of the EC Treaty' or 'of the EU Treaty'. The old version of Article 234 EC may then be referred to as Article 177 of the EC Treaty. Often, where useful for the reader – or the author – a double reference will be made to both the old and new numbering.

II

The Theoretical Framework

THE NATIONAL JUDGES are under a Community obligation to ensure the full effect of Community law and effective judicial protection of the rights which individuals derive from Community law, in accordance with the case law of the Court of Justice. While the formal source of their judicial power remains within the national legal order, the content of their function as Community law courts is defined by Community law. And in the execution of their function as Community judges, the national courts are freed from any constitutional restrictions *vis-à-vis* the legislature and the executive that may exist under national constitutional law. The national judges obviously remain organs of the State which has appointed them. Only few authors would take the view that, when exercising the role of Community law judge, the national judge would in fact be outside the State legal system insofar as he then applies Community law.[1] The better view seems to be that the court, as organ of the State, operates under a Community 'mandate'. The term *mandate* is borrowed from the work of Van Panhuys.

1. SCHIZOPHRENIA CONCEPTUALISED

1.1. Van Panhuys' Notion of 'Mandate'

Van Panhuys employed the concept of *'mandate'* in a set of articles published in the mid-sixties, on the interaction between international and national scenes of law.[2] Van Panhuys' aim was to present an alternative to

---

[1] But see P Mengozzi and P Del Duca, *European Community Law from Common Market to European Union*, (Dordrecht, Nijhoff, 1992) at 71; B Walsh, 'Reflections on the Effects of Membership of the European Communities in Irish Law', in F Capotorti et al., *Du droit international au droit de l'intégration. Liber Amicorum Pierre Pescatore*, (Baden-Baden, Nomos, 1987) 805, at 807: '(..) within this sphere [of transferred competences, MC] when the Irish judge is applying or interpreting Community law he has in effect ceased to be a national judge and has become a Community judge. While this view may not be acknowledged by every Member State in the Communities (..) it is, however, a view which I think most Irish judges would accept as correct'.

[2] HF van Panhuys, 'Relations and interaction between international and national scenes of law', *Recueil des Cours de l'Académie de Droit international* (1964)II, 7; HF van Panhuys, 'De verhouding tussen het volkenrecht, het Gemeenschapsrecht en het recht der lid-staten in het licht van het mandaat van rechters', in HF van Panhuys et al., *De rechtsorde der Europese Gemeenschappen tussen het internationale en nationale recht*, (Deventer, Kluwer) 13.

the traditional conceptions of the relation between legal orders, namely monism and dualism.[3] His critique of the conventional approach was that it was flawed in viewing law as a system, as a set of rules establishing standards by which to define in an abstract manner the legal quality that rules of an international nature should possess. Instead, he advocated an approach to the study of international law aimed primarily at the *functioning* of rules introduced and applied either domestically or internationally. By looking at the problem of the relation between legal orders from the perspective of the specific *mandate* of the authority involved, a more realistic and comprehensive picture would emerge. In his articles, he sketched the environment in which international and national judges act, as the 'scene' or 'sphere' on which they appear, representing them as a stage for a play, partitioned into a number of other scenes. The audience – the readers – were placed outside these spheres and are given an overall view of the ongoing play. By choosing the perspective – or rather, the scene and the actor – and being aware that it is a choice of only one possible perspective – the intricacies of the relations between legal orders and the actors acting in them emerged.

He attempted to illustrate the relationship between municipal and international law by reference to a play produced in the Netherlands at the occasion of the commemoration of the 400th birthday of William the Silent. For the play, a horizontal partition of the stage made it possible for the audience to look at two scenes at a time, so that it could simultaneously see what was going on in the Spanish headquarters as well as in the Beggars' League. This construction of the scene inspired Van Panhuys to illustrate the relation between the 'scenes' of international and national law, with the additional complication that within each scene a further subdivision would have to be made: while international law knows of regional and other subsections, the variety of municipal legal systems is proportionate to the number of States. The partition of the scenes was by no means watertight: there was a continuous intercommunication between them and actors playing a role on one stage also appeared on the other.

Van Panhuys then proposed to shed light on only certain aspects of the immense issue of the relationship between legal orders, by choosing a particular viewpoint: that of each of the *dramatis personae* on the different scenes. Each chapter would be devoted to a specific category of actors, among which international courts, domestic courts, legislators and

---

3 Van Panhuys stated that from a logical point of view, that is if law is to be an objective structure of legal norms from which inductions and deductions can be made by pure logic, there seems to be no *tertium* between the dualist and monist conceptions, and that those pretending that an intermediate position was possible only camouflaged a monist or dualist point of view, see HF van Panhuys, 'Relations and interaction between international and national scenes of law', *Recueil des Cours de l'Académie de Droit international (RCADI)*, 1964-II, 7, at 14.

individual as the *jeune premier*. Each of these actors was distributed a mandate by the master mind of some visible or invisible stage-manager.[4] A judge's mandate consists, in general terms, in *applying* the law. But the mandate of a court to apply the law should by no means be identified with the legal system to which these rules belong: the mandate given to the courts of State A may imply a duty to apply certain rules belonging to the legal system of State B; yet, it does not say that to that extent the courts of State A are in the possession of a mandate given by State B.

The term 'mandate', crucial in his *exposé*, denoted *'the contractual or quasi-contractual relationship between the person, who has accepted to exercise a specific public authority/function and he who has created the function'*, in the case of national courts the State. If a person enters into the service of a State, for example as a judge, he contracts, or quasi-contracts, a relationship between himself and that State. For international organs it would be the community of States which, mostly on the basis of a treaty, has created the international function. In a figurative sense, he went on to explain, the 'mandate-relation' implied certain duties on the part of the principal, such as the obligation to pay a salary and supply the necessary facilities on the one hand and the commitment for the person employed to duly exercise his function on the other. These duties, and the concomitant rights constitute only the *formal* aspects of the relation. In contrast, the *substance* encompassed the rules and principles by which the person concerned must be governed in the fulfilment of his task. *'This substantive part of the mandate-relation must be filled in either by reference to legal provisions, mostly scattered throughout the Constitution and subordinate legislation, or by reference to general principles to be derived from the legal system as such'*, while the mandate of international judges was determined, as far as its substance was concerned, by rules of international law, for the greater part contained in treaties.[5]

Now, within a given legal order, the functions of persons holding a public office within that order was defined by their 'mandates'. In appropriate cases, the mandate of a court may imply the duty for these authorities to apply legal rules pertaining to other scenes. In such cases, their 'function' may be said to be multiple, according to the origin of the rules to be applied. The source of the mandate, however, remains the same in all cases, and originates from the scene they belong to. But while there is only one mandate, acts performed under it may have effects on different scenes.

In Van Panhuys' view, the focus on mandates of the individual actors rather than on scenes of law, would offer a more realistic impression of the relation between legal orders and of courts therein. It is within the limits

---

4 This is where Van Panhuys' image diverges from the reality of the relations between national and European law in the hands of national organs: the 'neutral' mastermind or stage manager is missing.
5 HF Van Panhuys, *RCADI*, 1964-II, at 9.

of their mandate that the courts may or must individualise or create law. If the mandate imposes upon a municipal court the duty 'to apply international law', this means in fact that the court, in individualising or creating law, may base its decisions on international sources of law. The authorisation to apply international law extends the range of allowable sources.

Van Panhuys identified two problems with his approach: *first,* there was the problem of how to construe the substance of the 'mandates' in the absence of written and unequivocal rules. Though his initial aim had been to offer an alternative to the monism-dualism divide, he had to admit that the whole discussion would re-surface when defining the substance of the mandate: It would be of importance to know whether the mandate had adopted a dualist or monist conception. But the view did have the advantage of taking from the logically irreconcilable antithesis between monism and dualism its dogmatic flavour, and to reduce it to practical devices. If a legal order is said to be dualist, this simply means that the courts are only empowered to base their decisions on international sources if these have been re-enacted by the laws of that State. The notion of transformation – read into the credo of the dualist school – would no longer be indispensable. *Second,* there remained the issue of whether or not a conflict between two mandates was possible or, as was more likely, between a mandate on the one hand and what Van Panhuys referred to as an 'imperative directive' addressed to the mandatory in question emanating from outside the legal order to which the mandate belongs, on the other.[6]

In the application of his theory to Community law, Van Panhuys was not entirely explicit. Writing after *Van Gend en Loos* but before *Costa v ENEL,* Van Panhuys argued that the national mandates of the domestic courts were not dramatically pushed aside by a contrary *command* emanating from the law of the Community. He read *Van Gend en Loos* as implying that Article 12 of the Treaty (*old*) must be enforced by the national courts, unless its penetration into the legal systems of the Member States was thwarted by general constitutional rules or principles prevailing under these systems. '*This would mean e.g. that in Italy, where a statute may derogate from an earlier treaty to which Italy is a party, and assuming that this principle will be maintained under Italian constitutional law even in respect of the law of the Communities, the Italian courts remain bound to apply the later statute. For it is from the Italian State that the Italian courts hold their mandate,* and it would be hazardous to maintain that this mandate would allow a deviation from a clear intention of the Italian legislature acting within its constitutional boundaries'.[7] In an article written after *Costa v ENEL* he defended the view that the conception of Community law as expressed by the Court of Justice implied an obligation imposed on

---

6 Van Panhuys, *RCADI,* 1964-II, at 15.
7 Van Panhuys, *RCADI,* 1964-II, at 30 (my emphasis).

the Member States to adjust their constitutional system to the new conception. The choice for the Italian legal system, he said, was between a silent revision of the judicial mandate by virtue of Article 11 of the Constitution or a formal amendment of the Constitution, introducing the appropriate mandate *expressis verbis*.[8]

The concept of 'mandate' may be useful to describe the situation of the national courts in the context of European Union law. In the picture as described by Van Panhuys, judges are in a mandate-relation with their State, which also defines the rules and principles by which the mandate must be executed. The State may also mandate the courts to apply international law, either as such or upon re-enactment; and this mandate may be filled in either by reference to legal provisions or by reference to general principles to be derived from the legal system as such. However, in some cases the imperative peremptory directives impose themselves even irrespective of the national mandate. Examples would be certain peremptory norms of international law such as the Nuremberg principles, prohibition of and responsiblity for war crimes at the level of general international law, and, at the level of regional European law, human rights and 'the peremptory norms of Community law'.[9] In such cases, the national mandate would no longer be decisive. In this way, international law may penetrate into the scene of national law regardless of the national mandates concerned. This penetration could not be reasoned away by dualist arguments.[10]

'*Community law has thus created a mandate for Community judges, as well as a complementary one for national judges*'.[11] The '*Community mandate of national judges*' would then denote the concrete instructions and commands deriving from Community law and voiced by the Court of Justice: 'review national law and set it aside in case of incompatibility', 'interpret national law in conformity with Community law', 'to hold the State liable in damages for harm done as a consequence of a violation of Community law', without making a statement about the formal mandate-relationship. The '*national mandate*' would in this approach denote the duties and obligations imposed by national law, reflecting also the constitutional position of the courts within the national constitutional construct, *i.e.* their relationship with the other State organs.

Attractive in the image presented by Van Panhuys, is that it allows the spectator to gain a good view of reality, as he is allowed to retain his seat

---

8   Van Panhuys, 'De verhouding tussen het volkenrecht, het gemeenschapsrecht en het recht der lid-staten in het licht van het mandaat van rechters', in *De rechtsorde van de Europese gemeenschappen tussen het internationale en nationale recht* (Deventer, Kluwer, 1966) 13, at 26.
9   MJ van Emde Boas, *Jonkheer Haro Frederik van Panhuys (1916-1976), Bibliographical Essay*, (The Hague, T.M.C. Asser Institute, 1987) at 14.
10   *Ibid.*, at 14.
11   *Ibid.*, at 17.

in the audience. This was also the position chosen when the research for this book was conducted: that of a neutral observer, who does not choose a particular perspective, but is at liberty to alter perspectives and angles. This does not imply that no choices can be made at all. But the aim will ultimately be to understand and reconcile positions, and to find solutions to conflicts which may arise, not by awarding precedence to one position, body or organ over the other, but rather by seeking a system which, with mutual agreement and understanding, is aimed at conflict avoidance, at peaceful co-existence.

1.2. Scelle's *'dédoublement fonctionnel'*

In Scelle's work,[12] the notion of *'dédoublement fonctionnel'* equally alludes to the schizophrenia of the national institutions or organs, which due to the inadequacy and deficiency of the international institutional framework are obliged to execute functions which would normally have to be exercised by international organs, in addition to their normal national functions. National organs accordingly become agents, or mandatories, of their proper national legal order and of the international legal order. Scelle defined the phenomenon of *dédoublement fonctionnel* in the following manner: *'les agents dotés d'une compétence institutionnelle ou investis par un ordre juridique utilisent leur capacité 'fonctionnelle' telle qu'elle est organisée dans l'ordre juridique qui les a institués, mais pour assurer l'efficacité des normes d'un autre ordre juridique privé des organes nécessaires à cette réalisation, ou n'en possédent que d'insuffisants'.*[13] The notion is not limited to the relationship between Community law or international law and national law, but can also be used to explain relationships within a State. It is, however, in the context of international law in the municipal legal order that it finds application in the fullest sense.

Where organs of the internal legal order exercise functions pertaining to another legal order, Scelle stated, the content of the *'compétences dédoublées'* would rarely coincide. For instance, national executive organs would have a more extensive legislative power on the international plane than would be the case in the national constitutional setting, and accordingly, the

---

[12] G Scelle, *Précis de Droit des gens, principes et systématique* (Paris, Recueil Sirey, 1932-1934); G Scelle, 'Le phénomène juridique du dédoublement fonctionnel', in W. Schätzel and H-J Schlochauer (eds), *Rechtsfragen der internationalen Organisation, Festschrift für Hans Wehberg zu seinem 70. Geburtstag,* (Frankfurt am Main, 1956) 324; L Kopelmanas, 'La théorie du dédoublement fonctionnel et son utilisation pour la solution du problème dit des conflits des lois', in *La technique et les principes du droit public, Etudes en l'honneur de Georges Scelle* (Paris, 1950) 753.

[13] G Scelle, 'Le phénomène juridique du dédoublement fonctionnel', in W. Schätzel and H-J Schlochauer (eds), *Rechtsfragen der internationalen Organisation, Festschrift für Hans Wehberg zu seinem 70. Geburtstag,* (Frankfurt am Main, 1956) 324, at 331.

legislative powers of the national Parliament would be diminished. He termed this phenomenen *'le déséquilibre du dédoublement fonctionnel'*.

Scelle's model has been followed by several authors. Canivet has also made use of the language of *dédoublement fonctionnel* in his description of *l'office du juge national face au droit communautaire*.[14] *'C'est bien évidemment sur le titre qu'il tient de l'organisation constitutionnelle de l'Etat dont il relève que le juge assied sa juridiction, même lorsqu'il applique les traités. Mais tant par les obligations procédurales qui lui sont faites que par les pouvoirs dérogatoires qui lui sont reconnus, sous le contrîle, voire les sanctions de la Cour de Justice, le titre de compétence du juge étatiques est ambigu. De cette ambiguâté inhérente à sa fonction, au carrefour des systèmes juridiques nationaux et communautaire, certains auteurs déduisent un* dédoublement fonctionnel *dans le titre du juge selon qu'il exerce sa juridiction dans l'ordre interne ou dans le système des traités'.* Canivet then exposed the complexities of the hypothesis. If the national judiciary in the framework of Community law operates as part of a supra-statal judicial organisation, this would entail a transfer of sovereignty which, at least in the French constitutional context, would require a prior revision of the constitution. In any case, on the substance, the profound alteration and transformation of the judicial function modified the position of the judge in the constitutional setting, resulting in an expansion of the powers and duties of the national courts.

Grévisse spoke of a *'dualisme juridictionnel'*: a split has developed within every Member State in the person of the same judge, depending on whether he acts as on the basis of his national or his Community mandate.[15] And entirely in line with the English traditions, Lord Slynn of Hadley spoke of national judges *'wearing a Community law wig'*.[16]

2. THE NATIONAL MANDATE OF THE COURTS

The mandate of the courts, the rules and principles by which the recipient of the mandate must be governed in the fulfilment of his task, are to be filled in, either by reference to legal provisions, mostly scattered throughout the Constitution and subordinate legislation, or by reference to general principles to be derived from the legal system as such.[17] From these norms, principles and traditions, there emerges an understanding of the courts' role in the constitutional setting. The position of the courts is a

---

[14] G Canivet, 'Le droit communautaire et l'office du juge national', *Droit et Société* (1992) 133, at 138.

[15] F Grévisse and J-Cl Bonichot, 'Les incidences du droit communautaire sur l'organisation et l'exercice de la fonction juridictionnelle dans les Etats membres', in *L'Europe et le droit, Mélanges en hommage à Jean Boulouis* (Paris, Dalloz, 1991) 297.

[16] Lord Slynn of Hadley, 'What is a European Community Law Judge?', *CLJ* (1993) 52, 234.

[17] HF van Panhuys, 'Relations and Interactions between International and National Scenes of Law', *Recueil des Cours*, 1964-II, 7, at 9.

function of these rules and principles. But while these rules are decisive for the position of the courts and their *Kompetenzbild*, some of them are hard to detect, and difficult to change. They form part of the 'collective understanding' of what it is that courts can and cannot do.

Like all other State organs, courts derive their powers from the national Constitution, or through the Constitution from the Nation or the People. In many Constitution, this formal mandate relationship is expressed in the Constitution stating that *'All powers derive from the Nation'*[18] or 'All State authority shall emanate from the people. It shall be exercised by the people through elections and voting and by specific organs of the Legislature, the executive power and the judiciary'.[19] The position of the courts *vis-à-vis* the other State organs may be derived from constitutional provisions[20] or principles.[21] It is further developed in statutory legislation[22] and case law of the courts themselves.

3. THE HYPOTHESIS IN TERMS OF 'MANDATE'

The hypothesis which is tested in the book is that the national courts operate under a Community mandate as the common courts of Community law. It is a commonly accepted view that while the national courts may remain organs of the State, they in practical effect operate as Community courts. Accordingly, the Judicial Power in the Community/Union is exercised by the Court of Justice (including the Court of First Instance and soon also the judicial panels) assisted by the national courts; or the Judicial Branch consists of the European and the national courts. While the latter remain organs of their State, they perform functions as if they were, to a limited extent, Community institutions. In that capacity, they would be released from their national mandate and become Community courts, with all the powers, competences, and duties coming with the function. Acting as Community courts, their powers are increased dramatically, they become almost 'omnipotent courts'.[23]

---

[18] So for instance Art. 33 of the Belgian Constitution: *'Alle machten gaan uit van de Natie. Zij worden uitgeoefend op de wijze bij de Grondwet bepaald'*; and in the French version: *'Tous les pouvoirs émanent de la Nation. Ils sont exercés de la manière établie par la Constitution'*.
[19] Article 20(2) of the German *Grundgesetz*.
[20] Examples may be found in the Netherlands Constitution, which delimits the powers of the judiciary *vis-à-vis* Parliament in Articles 120 and 94 of the Constitution.
[21] An obvious example is the English rule that Parliament is Sovereign; or the French principle that the *loi* is the expression of the sovereign will of the People, granting it a status comparable to that of the English Act of Parliament.
[22] Such as the French revolutionary statutes on the courts.
[23] So A Barav, 'Omnipotent Courts', in *Institutional Dynamics of European Integration. Liber Amicorum in Honour of HG Schermers* (Dordrecht, Nijhoff, 1994) 265; see also his 'La plénitude de compétence du juge national en sa qualité de juge communautaire', in *L'Europe et le droit. Mélange en hommage à Jean Boulouis*, (Paris Dalloz, 1991) 1.

But is it really true that the national courts act *qua* Community courts? Is that really how the national courts perceive their function under Community law? The national courts have indeed by and large complied with the requirements accompanying the Community mandate, or making up the mandate. But does it mean that they act in a different capacity, wearing a different wig when acting under that mandate? Or is it simply their national mandate, adapted to the requirements of Community law?

While there may be some doubt with respect to the ordinary courts, it seems that the constitutional courts do not accept another mandate than their national constitutional mandate. These courts clearly act under their national mandate – they derive their powers from the national Constitution – and even reject some or many of the duties and competences accompanying the European mandate. As for the ordinary courts, the following statement of Laws LJ in the English *metric martyrs* case may lift a tip of the veil: '*the courts have found their way through the* impasse *seemingly created by two supremacies, the supremacy of European law and the supremacy of Parliament*'; but: '*there are no circumstances in which the jurisprudence of the Court of Justice can elevate Community law to a status within the corpus of English domestic law to which it could not aspire by any route of English law itself. (..) But the traditional doctrine has in my judgment been modified. It has been done by the common law, wholly consistently with constitutional principle*'.[24]

4. THE THEORETICAL GROUNDWORK: A MULTI-LEVEL EUROPEAN CONSTITUTION

The view underlying the research is that of the *multi-level or mixed Constitution*. 'The' European Constitution, in my view, is a multi-layered Constitution, made up of the constitutional documents and principles formulated and developed at the European level, completed with those at the national level. The Treaties on which the Union is founded – and which are in European law considered to constitute its constitutional charter – have to be considered together with the Constitutions of the Member States, with which they form a multi-level Constitution, a *Constitution composée*, or *Verfassungsverbund*.[25]

The underlying theoretical context is that of *constitutional pluralism*, which holds that '*States are no longer the sole locus of constitutional authority, but are now joined by other sites, or putative sites of constitutional authority, most*

---

24 High Court, Queen's Bench Division, Administrative Court, decision of 18 February 2002, *Thoburn v Sunderland City Council; Hunt v London Borough of Hackney; Harman and Dove v Cornwall County Council and Collins v London Borough of Sutton (metric martyrs)* [2002] EWHC 195; available on www.bailii.org.
25 The term was coined by I Pernice see *e.g.* his 'Multilevel Constitutionalism and the Treaty of Amsterdam: European Constitution-Making Revisited?', (1999) 36 *CMLRev.*, 703; I Pernice and F Mayer, 'De la Constitution composée de l'Europe', (2000) 36 *RTDeur.*, 623; I Pernice, 'Zur Verfassungsdiskussion in der Europäischen Union', WHI Paper 2/01.

prominently (..) those situated at the supra-state level, and that the relationship between state and non-state sites is better viewed as heterarchical rather than hierarchical'.[26] Member State Constitutions must be viewed in the context of membership of the Union, and conversely, the Union's Constitution does not consist only of the Treaties and the principles espoused as fundamental by the Court of Justice, but must be viewed together with the national Constitutions. Such view begs the question of the relationship between the component parts of the overall Constitution. In its purest form, the pluralist view does not accept a hierachical relationship between these component parts.[27] Rather, there is mutual recognition, respect and co-existence.[28] The European order has developed beyond the traditional confines of inter-national law,[29] and now makes its own independent constitutional claims, but these exist alongside the continuing claims of States. The relationship between these orders, and claims, is horizontal rather than vertical heterarchical rather than hierarchical.[30]

This is not to say that, for instance, I would reject the idea that Community law should take precedence over national law or that I would assume that in a concrete case of conflict, a directly effective provision of Community law would be merely equal in rank to a later national Act of Parliament. However, the claim of *absolute and unconditional* supremacy proclaimed by the Court of Justice exists alongside similar claims of supremacy of the national Constitutions, professed and guarded by the national (constitutional) courts. Which of those claims should prevail? In reality there is no *legal* or *logical* answer to the question. The claim of European law will not convince those who argue from the perspective of the national Constitution, since they consider the Constitution as the ultimate source of legitimacy; conversely, the claim of supremacy of the national constitutions will not convince those who argue from the European perspective. Acceptance of a radically pluralistic conception of legal systems entails acknowledging that not every legal problem can be

---

[26] Definition by N Walker, 'Late Sovereignty in the European Union', in N Walker (ed), *Sovereignty in Transition*, (Oxford, Hart Publishing, 2003) 5, at 7. See also his 'The Idea of Constitutional Pluralism', 65 *MLR*, 2002, 317.

[27] For an explanation of various versions of pluralism see N Walker, 'The Idea of Constitutional Pluralism', (2002) 65 *MLR*, 317; and his 'Late Sovereignty in the European Union', in N Walker (ed), *Sovereignty in Transition*, (Oxford, Hart Publishing, 2003) 5.

[28] This is not unrelated also to Weiler's 'Principle of Constitutional Tolerance', suggesting that in ultimate analysis, the federal constitutional discipline in the European construct is based on an autonomous voluntary act; it is not imposed top-down, but rather accepted bottom-up. See for instance JHH Weiler, 'Federalism and Constitutionalism: Europe's *Sonderweg*', Jean Monnet Working Paper 10/00, available on www.Jeanmonnetprogram.org/papers.

[29] Nevertheless, to a large extent Community law and its most fundamental principles can be explained on the basis of classic international law.

[30] So N Walker, 'The Idea of Constitutional Pluralism', (2002) 65 *MLR*, 317, at 337.

solved *legally*.[31] Radical pluralism suggests that there is no resolution to conflicts: neither European or national constitutional law can claim absolute supremacy over the other: in other words, at the end of the day, there is no overall decisive resolution.

How then, should conflicts be dealt with? The most important element of the solution is that the occurrence of conflict should be avoided: The Court of Justice should always take due account of national constitutional values and sensitivities; conversely, national (constitutional) courts should interpret their constitutions with due regard to the fact that their State is voluntarily a member of the European Union and Community. That should not be taken to mean that constitutional values and principles should be abandoned in the context of Union and Community law; it merely means that the courts have a responsibility of their own for the success of the European legal community: '*It is not just open skies that are above these courts of last instance, a system of balance of powers between the European and Member State courts is developing*'.[32]

Nevertheless, this should not be a matter for the courts alone. While the courts may ultimately have to decide when head-on collision is imminent, they should be well prepared, and the situation should be such that conflict is limited to exceptional cases. How should this be achieved, and under whose responsibility? It is first and foremost the responsibility of the Member States at the Union level and of those responsible for drafting the Constitution at the national level, *i.e.* the political institutions. They must ensure that there is a sufficient degree of harmony between the constitutional values at both levels. For the national Constitution-Making Power, this would assume opening up the national legal order for European law, where necessary by amending or adapting the Constitution, and by ensuring that European law can be effective. At the European level, this would imply that the Member States – which for the time being remain

---

[31] So N MacCormick, *Questioning Sovereignty. Law, State and Nation in the European Commonwealth*, (Oxford, OUP, 1999) at 119. MacCormick finally opts for a less radical version of pluralism: pluralism under international law, which holds that conflicts between Community and Member State legal systems occur not in a legal vacuum but in a space to which international law is relevant. Accordingly, conflicts would always have to be approached with due regard to the principles of international law, such as *pacta sunt servanda*; and at the end of the day, there would always be a possibility of recourse to international arbitration or adjudication. I do agree that principles of international law may be important to help solving cases of conflict, both before the Court of Justice and the national courts. However, I do not envisage conflicts between the national and Community legal order being submitted for international adjudication. While international law is relevant to such conflict given the international origins and the continuing character of the Union as an international organisation, such conflict is at the same time an internal constitutional conflict between constituent parts of a composite legal order; to that extent, it escapes classic international law.

[32] So P Kirchhof, 'The Balance of Powers Between National and European Institutions', (1999) 3 *ELJ*, 225, at 241.

the *Herren der Verträge* – should ensure that the constitutional principles and values which are considered as fundamental at the national level, are not discarded at the European level. Democracy, the protection of fundamental rights, the rule of law: these are not principles which are restricted to the national legal order, or which should come into play only after the decision has been adopted at the European level. Rather, the Member States are bound to ensure that these fundamental principles and values are realised at the European level also. That, it is submitted, is not the responsibility of the national or European Courts: it is the duty of the Member States as *Herren der Verträge*.

Part 1

The National Courts as Common Courts of European Law

1

Introduction

THE STORY OF how the national courts have become the common courts of Community law may be marked as a success story. The very fact that it is now so difficult to remember the days when it was a question for discussion whether and in what sense the national courts could be confronted with issues of Community law and whether they would or should award it precedence, is telling in itself. This transformation of the national courts into common courts of Community law was part of the larger transformation of Europe.[1] The Court of Justice has involved the national courts and made them allies in the enforcement of Community law, first on the basis of the principles of direct effect and supremacy of Community law and developing from there. The most intricate constitutional problem facing the national courts during the first wave was the issue of judicial review of domestic primary legislation in the light of Community law. The effect of direct effect and supremacy for the national courts was, in the view of the Court of Justice, that they must set aside any conflicting provision of national law, whatever its status under national law and including pieces of primary, parliamentary, legislation. While it may have taken some time in some of the Member States, by the end of the 1980s, all national courts were applying Community law and enforcing it even as against the national Parliament.

The conversion of national courts into common courts of Community law is not, however, complete: it is an on-going story. In fact, much of the recent case law on standing for individual applicants under Article 230 EC refers those applicants back to the national courts as the natural interlocutors of private applicants and seeks to deviate non-privileged applicants via the national courts. In *Unión de Pequeños Agricultores*,[2] the Court of Justice held that Community acts must be reviewable before the national courts, which are in turn under an obligation to refer questions for preliminary ruling concerning the validity of Community law. The

---

[1] In telling the story of the transformation of Europe, Joseph Weiler has been second to none, see especially JHH Weiler, 'The Transformation of Europe' (1991) 100 *Yale Law Journal* 2403.

[2] Case C–50/00 P *Unión de Pequeños Agricultores v Council* [2002] ECR I–6677.

route via the national courts is, in the system of judicial protection developed by the Court, the regular and often the only available procedure for private individuals and companies to challenge the validity of Community acts not addressed directly to them. In fact, it appears from the Court's judgment in *Unión de Pequeños Agricultores* that the national courts are under an obligation to allow this type of case even where they would not be admissible in similar national situations. This is an aspect of the national courts' role as the common courts of Community law which has not become routine, perhaps not because of any opposition on the part of the national courts, but rather because private applicants do not always find a way to access a national court, or do not realise that national courts are the correct forum under Community law. In two of the numerous *tobacco* cases, English courts did allow actions challenging a national act on their validity under national constitutional law, claiming that the underlying Community act was invalid as a matter of Community law.[3] If the underlying directive were to be found invalid in Community law, the Government would not, under British constitutional law and the EC Act 1972, be competent to adopt the proposed provisions by way of statutory instrument. In that case, the proposed legislation could only be introduced in the form of an Act of Parliament. Accordingly, there must be a cause of action before a national court, since there is no direct access before the European Courts because of the restrictive interpretation of the notion of 'direct and concern' in Article 230 EC. The type of case in which the national court allows an action in *national* law in order to make it possible to challenge the validity of *Community* law is exceptional, and was due, in fact, to coincidences of national constitutional law and factual circumstances. It is submitted that the system developed by the Court of Justice is, albeit understandable for reasons of procedural economy,[4]

---

3   Reference for a preliminary ruling from the High Court of Justice, Queen's Bench Division (Administrative Court), in Case C–491/01 *The Queen v Secretary of State for Health, ex parte British American Tobacco (Investments) Ltd and Others* [2002] ECR I–11453; *High Court of Justice, Queen's Bench Division (Administrative Court)*, decision of 6 December 2001, *The Queen v Secretary of State for Health and HM Attorney General, ex parte British American Tobacco (Investments) Ltd and Others*, [2001] EWHC Admin 1046. In an earlier case, the ECJ did not answer a question concerning the validity of another tobacco directive, which had arisen in the same type of national procedure, because the question was answered on the same day on an action for annulment brought by Germany on the basis of Article 230 EC resulting in the annulment of the directive, see Case C–376/98 *Germany v Parliament and Council (tobacco advertising)* [2000] ECR I–8419, and Case C–74/99 *The Queen v Secretary of State for Health and Others, ex parte Imperial Tobacco Ltd and Others* [2000] ECR I–8599.

4   However, one may wonder whether the system chosen by the ECJ does indeed limit the number of cases reaching the ECJ once the system is in place. It is submitted that when actors start finding their way to the national courts and the latter actually start allowing this type of cases on grounds of the principle of effective judicial protection and refer them to Luxembourg, this may well lead to more cases reaching the ECJ than would be the case if the ECJ and the CFI would allow these cases in direct actions. For reasons of procedural economy it may be more effective for the European Courts to allow these cases in direct actions, than to await reference being referred from the (many) national courts confronted with challenges of the validity of Community acts, and ensuing liability claims.

flawed. The appropriate forum to challenge the validity of Community law is Luxembourg, as the Court has itself held in cases like *Foto-Frost*[5] and *Atlanta*.[6] Conversely, cases arising before national courts and containing a Community law element typically concern situations where the State, its organs or bodies or authorities linked to it, have infringed Community law, denying individuals the benefit of their Community law rights, levying taxes where they are not allowed to, and so forth. Sometimes these cases will concern horizontal relationships, but even in those cases, there will typically have been an infringement of Community law on the part of national public authorities, for instance consisting in a failure to adopt the necessary implementing legislation so as to allow one individual to enjoy his Community law rights in his relations with another private party. Nevertheless, even for the other type of cases, against the Community institutions, the Court of Justice appears inclined to transform the national courts into the common courts of first instance, at least for cases brought by private applicants.

The national courts' Community law mandate was built and developed on the firm foundation offered by fundamental Community principles, most notably direct effect and supremacy. For the national courts, these principles denote an obligation to apply directly effective provisions of Community law, with precedence over conflicting provisions of national law, even where their national constitutional mandate would not allow them to do so. Accordingly, national courts must, under their mandate of common courts of Community law, review domestic legislation, including primary legislation deriving from Parliament itself and even the Constitution, and set it aside where necessary in order for the State as a whole to comply with its Treaty obligations. This mandate, which was most clearly stated in *Simmenthal*[7] and is therefore termed the '*Simmenthal* mandate' causes fundamental constitutional questions, concerning the effect of Community law in the domestic legal order, the nature and extent of the State's obligations under the Community Treaties and most importantly, about the role and function of the national courts in the enforcement of those obligations in the national legal order. The national courts' mandate is not limited to *Simmenthal*: The obligation 'to apply and set aside' has been clarified, refined, and circumscribed. For instance, the Court has made it clear that Community law must be applied with precedence, but within the legal environment offered by national law: in principle, procedural and remedial rules are defined by national law, under the conditions of efficiency and equivalence. These cases involving 'second generation issues' often relate to fairly technical or procedural questions, and do not

---

5   Case 314/85 *Foto-Frost v Hauptzollamt Lübeck-Ost* [1987] ECR 4199.
6   Case C–465/93 *Altanta Fruchthandelsgesellschaft mbH and Others v Bundesamt für Ernährung und Forstwirtschaft* [1995] ECR I–3761.
7   Case 106/77 *Amministrazione delle Finanze dello Stato v Simmenthal SpA* [1978] ECR 629.

pose constitutional dilemmas from a national perspective. In addition, there are other duties and competences making up the Community mandate: for instance, national law must be interpreted in so far as is possible under the national mandate of the courts, in conformity with national law;[8] courts must have jurisdiction to provide interim relief to protect Community law rights which individuals may derive from Community law[9] etc. Many of these duties do not fundamentally alter the 'ordinary' routine of the national courts, and do not pose any problems of a constitutional nature. However, in some instances the Community mandate does pose constitutional problems concerning the role of the courts in their relationship with the political State organs, in particular the legislature. This section of the book will concentrate on these two facets of the Community mandate of national courts: the duty to scrutinise national primary legislation (the *Simmenthal* mandate) and the duty to hold the State liable in damages for legislative wrong (the *Francovich* mandate).[10] Both facets of the Community mandate of the national courts clash, in many cases, with their national constitutional mandate and accordingly pose fundamental issues of a constitutional nature.

---

[8] Case C–106/89 *Marleasing SA v La Comercial Internacionale de Alimentacion SA* [1990] ECR I–4135 and its aftermath.

[9] Case C–213/89 *The Queen v Secretary of State for Transport, ex parte Factortame Ltd and Others* [1990] ECR I–2433 and its aftermath.

[10] After the famous decision in Joined Cases C–6/90 and 9/90 *Andrea Francovich and Danila Bonifaci and Others v Italian Republic* [1991] ECR I–5357.

2

Before the West was Won: A Touch of Legal Archaeology

2.1. THE GENERAL PICTURE

THE COMMUNITY MANDATE of the national courts has become so generally condoned, at least in theory,[1] that it is hard nowadays to imagine the legal context in which *Van Gend en Loos*[2] and *Costa v ENEL*[3] were rendered and the mandate was formulated.[4] This context was, under the prevailing rules of international law, defined by national law: the question of the domestic effect of treaties, the issue as to whether courts could interpret and apply them, whether individuals could derive rights from them, what the courts should do in case of a conflict between a treaty provision and a domestic provision: all these questions had to be answered by domestic law. Public international law does not impose any

---

[1]   One should not forget that even today and even in Member States whose legal systems are considered generally to be well adapted to the application of Community law, courts tend to prefer not to be confronted with Community law. This appears, for instance, from a survey conducted by the Dutch *Stichting Studiecentrum Rechtspleging* among Dutch judges. More than 40% of the respondents said that they had very little to do with Community law; that cases involving Community law were considered very difficult because of the judges' lack of experience with and knowledge of Community law, the complexity of the subject matter involved and the inaccessibility of the documents; see AWH Meij, 'Europese rechtspraak in de Nederlandse rechtspleging: impressies uit Den Haag en Luxemburg', Preadvies, in *Internationale rechtspraak in de Nederlandse rechtsorde*, *Handelingen van de NJV*, (Deventer, Tjeenk Willink, 1999) vol I, 133, at 138. 'To say the least', the author and member of the European Court of First Instance wrote, '*the application of Community law has not become common knowledge*' (my translation); see also M Jarvis, *Application of EC law by national courts: the free movement of goods*, (Oxford, Clarendon Press, 1997).

[2]   Case 26/62 *Van Gend en Loos* [1963] ECR 1.

[3]   Case 6/64 *Costa v ENEL* [1964] ECR 585.

[4]   This should not be understood as meaning that before *Van Gend en Loos*, no national court had ever had to deal with issues of Community law: In an editorial in the first issue of the *Common Market Law Review*, launched in 1963, reference is made to pre-*Van Gend en Loos* judgments applying Community law and enforcing it against national law (in all cases subordinate legislation and administrative decisions) in Italy (*Consiglio di Stato*), France, and Germany, see 1 *CMLRev* 4, at 5–6; see also references in P Pescatore, 'L'application directe des traités européens par les juridictions nationales: la jurisprudence nationale', (1969) *RTDeur* 697.

rules on the domestic effect of treaties:[5] it is concerned only with the result – does the State in question ultimately comply with its treaty obligations or not – and not with the means and methods. At the time, the Treaties establishing the European Communities seemed to constitute 'ordinary' treaties, albeit incorporating some novel provisions and procedures and establishing institutions that were unheard of before. Even if one may have recognised, at the time, the peculiarity and the uniqueness of the Community Treaties and Community law, the domestic effect of those treaties and the law deriving from them seemed to be governed by the ordinary principles, since no specific arrangement was made in the Treaties. And at least in form, the founding Treaties belong to public international law.[6] Consequently, the domestic effect of Community law would be different in each of the Member States. There was a clear chance that national authorities in the six founding Member States would react in different ways to Community law. The substantial difference with other international treaties was, however, the establishment of the Court of Justice which would ensure that the law was observed in the application and the interpretation of Community law, and which could be seized by national courts by way of preliminary rulings. Nevertheless, it seems that the founding fathers had not taken full account of the difficulties that could arise from the variety of approaches to international law and attitudes on the domestic effect of treaties. Pierre Pescatore, who acted as legal adviser to the Luxembourg and Belgian Governments during the negotiation of the Treaties, recalled this initial lack of awareness at a conference held at the College of Europe in 1965: *'Il faut bien dire qu'au moment de conclure les Traités européens, nous n'avons pas eu de conscience claire de ces différences de structure* [of the constitutional contexts of each of the Member States] *et de mentalité* [of lawyers and judges, and their attitudes towards the international and Community phenomenon]. *Nous nous sommes engagés dans l'ignorance et même dans l'équivoque. C'est peu à peu seulement, à propos de difficultés rencontrées dans tel ou tel état membre, à propos surtout de décisions rendues par telle ou telle juridiction nationale, qu'on a pu se rendre compte que les conceptions juridiques qui ont cours de part et d'autres s'écartent largement de l'impératif d'unité économique et juridique sur lequel repose la Communauté'.*[7] It is as if the issue of the domestic effect of the Treaties and of the law deriving from them, and the

---

5   See *e.g.* Th. Buergenthal, 'Self-Executing and Non-Self-Executing Treaties in National and International Law', *Recueil des Cours, Collected Courses of the Hague Academy of International Law,* Tome 235, 1992-IV, (Dordrecht, Martinus Nijhoff, 1993) 322.

6   See on the early discussion of the nature of Community law in relation to international law P Pescatore, 'International Law and Community Law – a Comparative Analysis' (1970) 7 *CMLRev* 167 with references at 168.

7   P Pescatore in *Droit communautaire et droit national.* Semaine de Bruges, (Bruges, De Tempel, 1965), at 87–88.

corollary position of the national courts, was overlooked at the time of the negotiations.

Nonetheless, there were tremendous differences of approach in the area of the domestic effect of treaties and the role of the courts in the enforcement and application of treaty law in the internal legal order. It must however also be noted that, while Pescatore seems to be saying that the issue of the domestic effect of the Treaties was not fully appreciated by those who negotiated the terms of the Treaties, the relevance of the question was perceived in several Member States which amended their Constitution in order to prepare for European integration and new forms of re-enforced international co-operation and their effects in the internal legal order. While some countries, such as Italy, restricted the constitutional efforts to providing for the transfer of sovereign powers to international organisations *in abstracto*, France and The Netherlands incorporated provisions intended to involve the national courts in the application of international law.

The national attitude concerning the functions and duties of the national courts *vis-à-vis* treaties, is, to again cite Pescatore *'conditionnées beaucoup plus, (...), par des conceptions philosophiques et même par des attitudes affectives, plutôt que par l'idée d'obéir à des impératifs juridiques positifs'*.[8] And even where arguments are moulded in legal shape, the fundamental motives, consciously or unconsciously, are of a different nature and hold policy choices, relating to the role of the courts in international relations, the role of private actors as main users of courts in foreign policy, the involvement of democratically elected bodies in international relations and so forth.[9] Especially before the 1960's, but even today, many of these factors work against the courts' involvement in the enforcement of international treaties.[10]

This section gives a short impression of the national law defining the judicial mandate in the context of international treaties before 1963 and 1964.[11] The survey is confined to the legal systems of the six founding Member States, since they establish the context in which the Court

---

[8] P Pescatore, 'L'application directe des traités européens par les juridictions nationales: la jurisprudence nationale', (1969) *RTDeur* 697, at 722.

[9] See in the context of direct effect in WTO law the illuminating article by T Cottier and K Nadakavukaren Schefer, 'The Relationship between World Trade Organization Law, National and Regional Law' (1998) *JIEL* 83.

[10] See E Benvenisti, 'Judicial Misgivings Regarding the Application of International Law: An Anaysis of Attitudes of National Courts', (1993) 4 *EJIL* 159.

[11] Case 26/62 *Van Gend en Loos* [1963] ECR, 1 and Case 6/64 *Costa v ENEL* [1964] *ECR* 585. For an account of the practice of the national courts written even before the establishment of the ECSC, F Morgenstern, 'Judicial Practice and the Supremacy of International law', (1950) 27 *BYBIL*, 42; for early and thorough surveys see also *Droit communautaire et droit national. Semaine de Bruges*, (Bruges, De Tempel, 1965); AM Donner *et al*, *Le juge national et le droit communautaire*, (Leyden Sijthoff, 1966); M Gaudet, *Conflits du Droit Communautaire avec les Droits Nationaux*, (Nancy, Centre européen universitaire, 1967); M Waelbroeck, *Traités internationaux et juridictions internes dans les pays du Marché commun*, (Paris, Pedone, 1969); G Bebr, 'How Supreme Is Community Law in the National Courts?' (1974) 11 *CMLRev* 3.

initially formulated the Community mandate of the national courts. The six Member States can, tentatively, be categorised in three couples. First, the *Netherlands* and *French* Constitutions contained a provision which could be interpreted as granting a mandate to the courts to ensure the enforcement of (some) treaty law in the domestic legal order and hence, to review the compatibility of national law with treaty provisions. Second, in *Belgium* and *Luxembourg*, the Constitution was silent on the relationship between international and national law and the role of the courts in that field. The courts had to define their role on the basis of constitutional theory, general principles and the prevailing paradigms. The third couple consists of *Italy* and *Germany*, two dualist systems, both of which also dispose of a constitutional court that has exclusive power to review the constitutionality of primary legislation, and whose Constitutions are similarly silent on the relations between treaties and national law and the role of national courts in the matter.

2.2. THE NETHERLANDS

The Netherlands Constitution was probably the most modern on the issue and was best adapted to the enforcement of Community law.[12] Since the constitutional revisions of 1953 and 1956 provoked by imminent European integration,[13] judicial review of all legislation applicable in the Kingdom including the Constitution itself is authorised in the light of treaty provisions which are *'binding on anyone'*.[14] The case law of the Court of Justice thus did not create a novelty in the Dutch constitutional

---

[12] M Claes and B de Witte, 'Report on The Netherlands', in A-M Slaughter, A Stone Sweet and JHH Weiler (eds), *The European Court and National Courts – Doctrine and Jurisprudence. Legal Change in Its Social Context* (Hart Publishing, Oxford, 1998) 171; on the openness of the Dutch Constitution to international law, see also LFM Besselink, 'An Open Constitution and European Integration: The Kingdom of The Netherlands', in *Le droit constitutionnel national et l'intégration européenne*, (17th FIDE Kongress, Berlin, 1996) 361 and recently CAJM Kortmann, 'European Union Law and National Constitutions: The Netherlands', 20th FIDE Congress (London, 2002); B De Witte, 'Do Not Mention The Word: Sovereignty in Two Europhile Countries, Belgium and The Netherlands', in N Walker (ed), *Sovereignty in Transition* (Hart Publishing, Oxford, 2003) 359.

[13] The provision introduced to allow for the transfer of competences to international organisations was reportedly announced in the Chicago Daily Tribune under the title 'Less than a Nation', see LJ Brinkhorst, 'Le juge néerlandais et le droit communautaire' in AM Donner *et al* (eds), *Le juge national et le droit communautaire* (Sijthoff, Alphen aan den Rijn, 1966) 101, 102.

[14] These are some of the older contributions on the issue: JFM Duynstee, *Grondwetsherziening 1953. de nieuwe bepalingen omtrent de buitenlandse betrekkingen in de grondwet* (Kluwer, Deventer, 1953); L Erades, 'Recht en rechter in Nederland en in de Europese Gemeenschappen', (1960) *NTIR* 334; AJ P Tammes, ''Een ieder verbindende' verdragsbepalingen', (1962) *NJB* 69 and 89; L Erades, 'Enkele vragen betreffende de artikelen 65 en 66 van de Grondwet', (1962) *NJB* 357 and 385; L Erades, 'Poging tot ontwarring van de self-executing' knoop', (1963) *NJB* 845.

legal order. Nevertheless, when these constitutional provisions were adopted, they did themselves constitute a revolution in the constitutional system of The Netherlands. Indeed, under Article 131 of the Constitution, which remained in force until 1983 – well after the introduction of judicial review powers in the light of international treaties – Acts of Parliament were 'inviolable' and the courts were precluded from reviewing primary legislation for whatever reason.[15] Yet, the revisions of 1953 and 1956 did introduce that other form of review, of the *'conventionnalité'* of statutes. The new Article 65 resolved the controversy about the rank of international treaties,[16] by stating unambiguously: *'Legal provisions in force within the Kingdom shall not apply if the application should be incompatible with agreements which have been published in accordance with article 66 either before or after the enactment of the provisions'*. This is all the more remarkable given the absence of judicial review of the constitutionality of such acts, and their continuing 'inviolability' following the coming into force of Article 131. Article 66 held that *'Agreements shall be binding on anyone insofar as they will have been published'*. The article was meant to conform the monist vision about the relationship between national and treaty law and sanctioned the idea that the domestic courts could apply such provisions. The newly introduced articles were again revised in 1956. One modification was that the order of the articles was reversed, so that they featured in a more logical order, dealing first with the domestic effect of treaties (new Article 65) and with supremacy and its effects after that. A second change was not merely technical and removed all doubts about the extent of the competences of the courts. The 1953 version of the texts may have given the impression that *all* agreements were enforceable by the Dutch courts, but that was not the opinion of the Dutch Government. Already in 1953, the Government had been of the opinion that both articles were restricted to those treaty provisions that were 'self-executing', which according to their nature can be applied directly by the courts or to provisions that are directly effective *vis-à-vis* the citizens, as opposed to norms of instruction addressed to the Government or the Legislature.[17] The question whether a particular provision was directly effective or not was 'in full confidence' left for the courts to decide, since it amounted to an interpretation of the

---

[15] Art. 131 of the Constitution was deleted in 1983 and replaced by Art. 120 which now states that *'De rechter treedt niet in de beoordeling van de grondwettigheid van wetten en verdragen'*, 'The courts shall not review the constitutionality of Acts of Parliament and treaties' (my translation). It is considered to constitute an exeption to the general rule that the courts review the compatibility of lower rules with higher ranking law and set it aside in case of a conflict. See briefly on judicial review in the Netherlands Th L Bennekom and others, *Koopmans' Staatsrecht*, 9th edn, (Deventer, Kluwer, 2002) 270 *et seq.*
[16] See the discussion between proponents of the monist school and defenders of dualism in *Handelingen van de NJV*, 1937.
[17] Discussed in JFM Duynstee, *Grondwetsherziening 1953. de nieuwe bepalingen omtrent de buitenlandse betrekkingen in de grondwet* (Deventer, 1953) 33 et seq.

relevant provision.[18] The new formulation of the constitutional articles removed all doubts about the issue. They now read: '*Provisions of agreements which, according to their terms, can be binding on anyone, shall have such binding force after having been published*' (Article 65) and '*Legislation in force within the Kingdom shall not apply if this application would be incompatible with provisions of agreements* which are binding on anyone *and which have been entered into either before or after the enactment of such legislation*' (Article 66). The qualification 'binding on anyone' stems from the text of 1953, and aimed to protect the citizen, who could only be bound by treaty provisions that he could know. But in 1956, the same qualification was used to restrict the effect of treaties in the domestic order and to limit the review competences of the national courts.

Nevertheless, despite the express authorisation in the Constitution, the courts tended to shy away from using their new powers to review national legislation on its compatibility with treaty provisions, either by relying on the rule of construction, and interpreting national legislation in conformity with the treaty provision, or by denying the self-executing nature thereof.[19] Perhaps, the courts were reluctant to actually set aside national legislation on grounds of the traditional perception of their constitutional position *vis-à-vis* the primary Legislature, and the idea that it was not for the courts to censure Parliament. Indeed, Article 131 of the Constitution declaring the inviolability of statutes was maintained in force until 1983, alongside the new articles on judicial review in the light of treaties. Despite these hesitations, the constitutional mandate of the Dutch courts did comprise the power to review national legislation, including parliamentary legislation of a later date, in the light of certain international treaties. It was generally accepted that that was indeed the intention of the new constitutional provisions. The texts allowed for judicial review of the compatibility with certain provisions of Community law; nevertheless, the minds of the judges may not have been so inclined.

2.3. FRANCE

At the time of the entry into force of the ECSC Treaty in 1952 and the EEC and Euratom Treaties in 1958, the 1946 Constitution was still in force. Article 26 of that Constitution provided that '*Les traités diplomatiques régulièrement ratifiés et publiés ont force de loi dans le cas même où il seraient contraires à des lois françaises, sans qu'il soit besoin pour en assurer l'application*

---

[18] *Memorie van Antwoord*, Handelingen Eerste Kamer, (1952–53), 2700, nr 63a, at 3.

[19] See the judgments mentioned in HJ van Panhuys, 'The Netherlands Constitution and International Law' (1964) *AJIL* 88, at 102, note 65; see also M Waelbroeck, *Traités internationaux et juridictions internes dans les pays du Marché commun*, 1969, at 250–251.

d'autres dispositions législatives que celles qui auraient été nécessaires pour assurer leur ratification'. Article 28 added that *'Les traités diplomatiques régulièrement ratifiés et publiés ayant une autorité supérieure à celle des lois internes, leurs dispositions ne peuvent être abrogées, modifiées ou suspendues qu'à la suite d'une dénonciation régulière, notifiée par voie diplomatique'*.

On the other hand, the French conception of the place of the courts strongly opposed any form of judicial review, including review of the *conventionnalité*, of primary legislation. Before the constitutional revision of 1946, the *Matter* doctrine was generally considered to reflect the French view on the relationship between treaties and domestic law and the role of the courts therein. In the words of *procureur général* Matter *'à supposer qu'il y ait conflit entre la loi et la Convention, quels seraient les devoirs du juge? Ici, aucune doute, vous ne connaissez et ne pouvez connaître d'autre volonté que celle de la loi. C'est le principe même sur lequel reposent nos institutions judiciaires'*.[20] The courts had to solve conflicts by recourse to the rule of construction, based on the presumption that the Act of Parliament did not intend to infringe the treaty. The doctrine established a compromise between the courts' desire to ensure the supremacy of treaties and their concern not to appear to be encroaching on parliamentary prerogatives.[21] They[22] sought to avoid the issue either by relying on the rule of construction or by saying that the treaty in question was not intended for the facts of the case.[23] The 1946 constitutional provisions did not alter that attitude.[24] In short, the situation was comparable to the Dutch: while the constitutional text seemed to allow for review the *conventionnalité* of primary legislation, the courts did not act upon it since it so vitally contradicted their traditional mandate to apply primary legislation without ever questioning its validity.

The 1958 Constitution was somewhat less internationally oriented, but Article 55 still declares: *'Les traités ou accords régulièrement ratifiés ou approuvés ont, dès leur publication, une autorité supérieure à celle des lois, sous réserve, pour chaque accord ou traité, de son application par l'autre partie'*. Nevertheless, the provisions on the judicial function were not amended accordingly, or at least, the terms of the Constitution did not make it abundantly clear that the judicial function was altered as a corollary.

[20] Opinion of *procureur général* Matter in *Cour de cassation*, decision of 22 December 1931, Clunet, RDIP, 1933, 475.
[21] Ph. Manin, 'The Nicolo Case of the Conseil d'Etat: French constitutional law and the Supreme Administrative Court's Acceptance of the Primacy of Community Law over Subsequent National Statute Law' (1991) *CMLRev* 499, at 502.
[22] Including the administrative courts: the *Conseil d'état* had adopted the position of the ordinary courts.
[23] For references see A Blondeau, 'L'application du droit conventionnel par les juridictions françaises de l'ordre judiciaire', in P Reuter et al, L'application du droit international par le juge français, (Paris, Librairie Armand Colin, 1972) 43, 59.
[24] For instance P Francescakis, 'Remarques critiques sur le rôle de la Constitution dans le conflit entre le traité et la loi interne devant les tribunaux judiciaires', (1969) *RCDIP* 425.

The constitutional affirmation of the supremacy of treaties over national legislation did not immediately lead the courts to abandon the *Matter* doctrine. The principle of supremacy of international law over national law in itself was not questioned. The controversy concentrated on the issue of its consequences for the judicial function. The constitutional provisions were mostly regarded as too weak to constitute a constitutional authorisation for the courts to enforce the supremacy of international law.[25] The reluctance of the courts to do so was instigated by the fear to interfere with the legislative function and by the limited conception of the judicial function prevailing in France.[26] The deeply rooted judicial self-restraint of French courts since the Revolution and their strict adherence to the doctrine of the separation of powers, led them to reject the review power, or at least to try and avoid it.

Accordingly, even though the Constitution contained an article that could be interpreted as empowering the courts to review national legislation in the light of international treaties, and to set it aside in case of a conflict, the traditional ideas on the constitutional position of the courts triumphed and Article 55 was not perceived as comprising a judicial mandate.

2.4. BELGIUM

The Belgian and Luxembourg Constitutions did not contain any provision regulating the relationship between international and national law, nor the position of the courts in the issue. An express mandate similar to the Dutch Article 66 (now 94) of the Constitution, or a more general provision such as Article 55 of the French Constitution did not exist in these constitutions. On the other hand, such mandate was not expressly excluded. Yet, as in France and in The Netherlands, there was a strong tradition of rejecting judicial review of primary legislation, based on fundamental principles such as the sovereignty of the Legislature, the separation of powers and the subjection of the courts to Acts of Parliament.

In Belgium, the same arguments against judicial control of the constitutionality of Acts of Parliament were also raised against judicial review of their compatibility with treaty provisions. While the Constitution did not expressly rule out the constitutional review of primary legislation, it was considered to contravene the basic principles underlying the Constitution, such as the principles of the separation of powers and of democracy. Technically, treaties were considered to take on the nature of

---

[25] See P Reuter, 'Le droit international et la place du juge français dans l'ordre constitutionnel national', in P Reuter *et al* (eds), *L'application du droit international par le juge français* (Paris, Librairie Armand Colin, 1972) 17, 22.

[26] R Kovar, 'La primauté du droit communautaire sur la loi française', (1975) *RTDeur* 636, at 643.

the act that made them effective in the national legal order, mostly an Act of Parliament. Consequently, when a conflict between a treaty provision and a subsequent statute occurred before the courts, the latter would give precedence to the statute.[27] In a 1925 case relating to the Treaty of Versailles and a subsequent Belgian statute, the *Cour de cassation* held: '*Attendu qu'il appartient au législateur belge, lorsqu'il édicte des dispositions en exécution d'une convention nationale, d'apprécier la conformité des règles qu'il adopte avec les obligations liant la Belgique par traité; que les tribunaux n'ont pas le pouvoir de refuser d'appliquer une loi pour le motif qu'elle ne serait pas conforme, prétendûment, à ses obligations*'.[28] Consequently, the judgment confirmed the application of the *lex posterior* rule. Some scholars did criticise this stance as being *passé*, but they too agreed that such mandate for the courts must be inserted in the Constitution, and that without such constitutional authorisation, the courts were precluded from guaranteeing respect for Belgium's treaty obligations.[29] A committee of four law professors, charged to advise the Government on constitutional issues concerning Belgian participation in the creation of a supra-national political organisation, even rejected the idea of a new constitutional provision providing for an express mandate for the courts, *à la hollandaise*. It was considered contrary to Belgian constitutional traditions for the courts to be empowered to oppose the primary Legislature.[30] Accordingly, under the traditional stance prevailing before 1963, the courts were not mandated by the Constitution to review the compatibility of statutes with treaty provisions.

2.5. LUXEMBOURG

In Luxembourg,[31] as in Belgium, the Constitution was silent on the issue. But from 1950 onwards, the courts changed their original stance that a review of the compatibility of statutes with treaties would amount to reviewing their constitutionality, which was excluded. Distinguishing both types of conflict on the basis of a new conception of the nature of the

---

27 References can be found in M Waelbroeck, 'Le juge belge et le droit communautaire', in AM Donner et al (eds), *Le juge national et le droit communautaire* (Sijthoff, Alphen aan den Rijn, 1966) 29, 33 et seq.

28 Hof van Cassatie *(B)*, decision of 26 November 1925, *Schieble*, Pas., 1926, I, 76 (my emphasis).

29 H Rolin, 'La force obligatoire des traités dans la jurisprudence belge', (1953) *JT*, 561.

30 'Avis donné au Gouvernement par MM G Dor, WJ Ganshof van der Meersch, P De Visscher and A Mast, au sujet des dispositions constitutionnelles qu'il y aurait lieu à réviser en vue de permettre l'adhésion de la Belgique à une communauté politique supranationale', *Documents parlementaires*, Chambre, 1952–53, no. 696, at 9 *et seq.*

31 M Waelbroeck, *Traités internationaux et juridictions internes dans les pays du Marché commun*, (Paris, Pedone, 1969) 253; P Pescatore, 'Application directe des traités européens par les juridictions nationales: la jurisprudence nationale', (1969) *RDTeur.*, 697, at 718.

treaty provision effective in the domestic legal order, the *Cour supérieure de justice* accepted jurisdiction to set aside laws in favour of treaty provisions. In case of a conflict between a rule of treaty law and a provision of national law, the latter must give way: '(..)*pareil traité est une loi d'une essence supérieure ayant une origine plus haute que la volonté d'un organe interne; qu'en conséquence, en cas de conflit entre les dispositions d'un traité international et celles d'une loi nationale postérieure, la loi internationale doit prévaloir sur la loi nationale(..)*'.[32] The internally effective treaty provision was not equated with an internal provision, but considered *qua* treaty provision, and it was given a higher rank than national norms. The judicial mandate to give precedence to such superior provision seemed to follow automatically from that understanding.

Even though the Constitution did not, as in The Netherlands, expressly provide for review powers in the hands of the courts, and did not even, as in France, proclaim the primacy of international law over the internal legal order in principle, the courts assumed that function as part of their natural mandate. Pescatore has explained the ease with which the Luxembourg courts have accepted this jurisdiction by the history of the Grand Duchy, whose very existence was founded on international treaties, and which has always economically been dependent on international agreements establishing forms of economic integration: the *Zollverein*, the Belgo-Luxembourg Economic Union and the Benelux.[33]

2.6. GERMANY

Both the German and the Italian legal systems are strongly influenced by the dualist doctrine of the relationship between the national and international legal order. Treaty provisions only become effective in the domestic legal order upon transformation into domestic law, and assume the nature of the national act that makes them effective, mostly an ordinary statute. In addition, both Germany and Italy have a constitutional court that has exclusive jurisdiction to review the constitutionality of primary legislation. Such review can result in the annulment of the act under scrutiny. The very establishment of a specialised constitutional court with the power to review and invalidate statutes for failure to conform to the constitution is a compromise with the conception of the separation of powers that would deny such powers to all judicial organs.[34] The ordinary courts are barred from judicial review of primary statutes.

Article 25 of the German Basic Law of 1949 provides that 'The general rules of public international law shall be an integral part of federal law.

---

[32] *Cour supérieure de justice (cass.)*, decision of 14 July 1954, *Pagani*, Pas.lux., XVI, 150.
[33] Pescatore, *art. cit.*, at 718–19.
[34] See M Cappelletti, *The Judicial Process in Comparative Perspective* (Oxford, OUP, 1989) at 146.

They shall take precedence over statutes and shall directly create rights and duties for the inhabitants of the federal territory'.[35] Under Article 100(2) of the Constitution the ordinary courts must obtain a decision from the *Bundesverfassungsgericht* where, in the course of litigation, doubts have arisen as to whether a rule of public international law is an integral part of federal law and whether such rule directly creates rights and duties for the individual. The *Bundesverfassungsgericht* has jurisdiction to declare unconstitutional statutes that violate such rules.[36] However, Article 25 which seems to give proof of great openness towards international law, was interpreted as being restricted to customary international law, [37] and was not extended to treaty law,[38] which must be introduced in the national legal order by a national act and is transformed into national law in the course of it.[39]

2.7. ITALY

Article 10(1) of the Italian Constitution proclaims that *'Italy's legal system conforms with the generally recognised principles of international law'*, which is interpreted as authorising the *Corte costituzionale* to declare statutes unconstitutional for breach of general principles of international law.[40] Nevertheless, as in Germany, this jurisdiction is restricted to reviewing statutes in the light of general principles of international law. Treaty provisions cannot in the same way be enforced against the primary Legislature.[41] The doctrine of dualism was, and is, firmly rooted in Italy and there is a strict separation between the international and national legal order.[42] Treaties assume the legal character of the norm that has made them effective in the Italian legal order, mostly an ordinary Act of Parliament, and are applied and enforced as such.

[35]   English translation taken from SE Finer et al, *Comparing Constitutions* (Oxford, Clarendon Press, 1995). In the German version: *'die allgemeine Regeln des Völkerrechts'*.

[36]   *Bundesverfassungsgericht*, decision of 26 March 1957, *Reichskonkordat*, BVerfGE 6, 309.

[37]   Also H Mosler, *Das Völkerrecht in der Praxis der deutsche Gerichte* (Karlsruhe, 1957) at 39; K Doehring, *Die allgemeinen Regeln des völkerrechtlichen Fremdenrechts und das deutsche Verfassungsrecht* (Köln, 1963) at 129.

[38]   This could have been done directly, by counting treaty law among the rules of general international law, or indirectly, by virtue of *pacta sunt servanda* which is in any case a general principle or a rule of customary law.

[39]   See M Waelbroeck, *Traités internationaux et juridictions dans les pays du Marché commun*, (Paris, Pedone, 1969) 240 with references; see also JA Frowein and K Oellers-Frahm, 'Allemagne', in PM Eisemann (ed), *L'intégration du droit international et communautaire dans l'Ordre Juridique National. Étude à la pratique en Europe* (Kluwer, Amsterdam, 1996) 69, 81.

[40]   *Corte costituzionale*, decision of 22 December 1961.

[41]   *Corte costituzionale*, decision of 11 March 1961, Riv.dir.int., 1961, 670.

[42]   S Neri, 'Le juge italien et le droit communautaire', in AM Donner *et al* (eds), *Le juge national et le droit Communautaire* (Sijthoff, Alphen aan den Rijn, 1966) 77, 77.

2.8. CONCLUSION

'*La situation (..) est préoccupante, mais elle n'est pas, pour autant, sans espoir*', Pescatore concluded his presentation of the position of courts *vis-à-vis* treaties in the six original Member States.[43] Of the six, which had signed the Treaties without the clear confirmation that it would comprise the obligation of their courts to enforce Community law against the State and to review national legislation in its light, only The Netherlands and Luxembourg already recognised such mandate for the courts. In The Netherlands, it was included in the Constitution; in Luxembourg, the courts assumed this competence without an express constitutional authorisation. Of these two, only the Luxembourg courts had actually used the mandate. In France, authorisation could be deduced from the Constitution. However, the courts preferred not to act upon it, as they did not consider it part of their mandate to enforce the supremacy of treaty law over national law. Conflicts between treaty provisions and rules of national law were avoided by recourse to rules of construction, by the presumption that the Legislature did not intend to violate treaty obligations or by limiting the field of application of the statute or the treaty provision. Also in the Member States that did not in principle recognise the supremacy of treaties over national law, courts did take account of treaty provisions to interpret national law.[44] In the practice of the courts, the different theoretical starting points did not lead to great differences in practical effect.[45] However, while there were tendencies in The Netherlands, Luxembourg, Belgium and possibly in France to accept an extended commitment of the national courts in the area of treaty law, especially Germany and Italy remained dualist.[46]

---

[43] P Pescatore, 'L'application directe des traités européens par les juridictions nationales: la jurisprudence nationale' (1969) *RTDeur* 697, at 722.

[44] M Waelbroeck, *Traités internationaux et juridictions internes dans les pays du Marché commun*, (Paris, Pedone, 1969) 279 et seq.

[45] This is still true today, see for instance R Higgins, 'Dualism in the Face of a Changing Legal Culture' in M Andenas and D Fairgrieve (eds), *Judicial review in International Perspective. Liber Amicorum in Honour of Lord Slynn of Hadley*, Vol II, (The Hague, Kluwer Law International, 2000) 9.

[46] During the discussions at the Semaine de Bruges organised in 1965 on the relationship between national and international law, it was reportedly stated by Munch that, while it must have been the assumption of the drafters of the Treaties that the national courts would become involved in the application and enforcement thereof, they must have accepted that no uniformity would be achieved in this respect. '*This may be regrettable*', he was reported saying, '*but that cannot justify the acceptance of the federalist tendency – absolute supremacy of Community law – in the absence of a clear legislative text*', MJ van Emde Boas and LP Suetens, 'Gemeenschapsrecht en nationaal recht (Week van Brugge 1965)', (1965) *SEW*, 267, at 274; the authors were of the opinion that equal application and enforcement of Community law in the national legal orders could only be achieved by adapting the constitutional arrangements to the requirements of Community law, above *SEW*, 267, at 272.

This short presentation is restricted to a general view of the constitutional provisions on the position of national courts *vis-à-vis* treaties and their power of judicial review in case of a conflict between a treaty provision and an Act of Parliament. It fits in a wider image of national courts showing great deference to international treaties, and more importantly, to their governments' policies in the light of international law.[47] The constitutional provisions importing treaty law into national law were applied with reluctance, so as to limit the courts' obligations to enforce treaty provisions against national law. Courts used a number of 'avoidance doctrines', such as limiting the notion of 'self-executingness',[48] the doctrines of act of state,[49] *acte de gouvernement*, political questions doctrines or a theory of non-justiciability so as not to interfere with foreign affairs, which were considered to be the province of the Executive, possibly under the supervision of Parliament, but preferably not of the courts. Courts were not eager to become involved in foreign affairs, stepping on their government's toes, embarrassing it or upsetting the State's relations with other States.[50] Some courts did not even interpret treaty provisions themselves.[51]

This was the context in which the Court of Justice decided to involve the national courts in the enforcement of Community law, and make them common courts of Community law.

---

[47] Drawing on E Benvenisti, 'Judicial Misgivings Regarding the Application of International Law: An Analysis of Attitudes of National Courts', (1993) 4 *EJIL* 159. Benvenisti was not writing about the same pre-*Van Gend en Loos* era and national courts in the Original Six. His article is written in the present tense, and claims to demonstrate the existence of a similar pattern of behaviour in most jurisdictions today.

[48] B Conforti speaks of a veritable abuse of the notion of non-self-executing international rules: *'When state officials [including courts] do not want to apply an international rule, they say that the rule is not self-executing; they say in particular that the rule, especially owing to its vague content or incompleteness, is only a simple, although binding directive addressed to the legislator and nobody else within the State'.* Conforti explains this by pointing to the fact that the rule may be contrary to national interests, it may be difficult to apply or to interpret or simply be too progressive, B Conforti, 'Notes on the Relationship between International and National Law', *International Law FORUM du droit international*, (2001) 18, at 21.

[49] On the act of State doctrine, see C Flinterman, *De Act of State doctrine*, (Antwerpen, 1981).

[50] JH Jackson, 'Status of Treaties in Domestic Legal Systems: a Policy Analysis' (1992) 86 *AJIL* 310, at 326 *et seq.*

[51] Until 1990, the *Conseil d'état* referred questions of interpretation of treaties to the Foreign Minister and considered itself bound to the interpretation offered. Since 1990 (*Conseil d'é-tat*, decision of 29 June 1990, *GISTI*, Rec., 171) the Minister may be consulted or asked to submit his views, but the last say will be for the court. The practice of executive interpretation is still followed in the United States; the suggested interpretation is not binding but will be followed in most cases, see G Guillaume, 'The Work of the Committee on International Law in International Courts of the International Law Association', *International Law FORUM du droit international*, (2001) 34, at 38.

3

The Creation of a Community Mandate for National Courts

3.1. INTRODUCTION: NATIONAL COURTS AS COMMUNITY COURTS

JOHN TEMPLE LANG wrote in 1997: *'Every national court in the European Community is now a Community law court. National judges have a duty, in common with the Court of Justice, to see that Community law is respected in the application and interpretation of the Treaties.' 'In fact'*, he said, *'national courts probably interpret and apply Community law more often than the two Community courts do. (..) Every national court, whatever its powers, is a Community court of general jurisdiction, with power to apply all rules of Community law. This duty is imposed by the constitutional law of the Community'.*[1] The national courts share the judicial function in the Community with the Community courts. The Court of Justice and the Court of First Instance have referred to the mandate of the national courts as Community courts on many occasions and in various contexts.[2] National courts are

[1] J Temple Lang, 'The Duties of National Courts under Community Constitutional Law', (1997) 22 *ELRev* 3; the topic is Temple Lang's personal evergreen: see also his *The duties of national courts under the constitutional law of the European Community*, Dominik Lasok Lecture, Exeter, 1987; also 'The duties of national authorities under Community constitutional law', (1998) 23 *ELRev* 109; and 'The duties of co-operation of national authorities and Courts under Article 10 EC: two more reflections', (2001) 26 *ELRev* 84; Temple Lang also wrote the general report for the XIX FIDE Congress in Helsinki, 2000: 'General Report: The Duties of Co-operation of the National Authorities and Courts and the Community Institutions under Article 10 EC Treaty, in *XIX FIDE Congress*, (Helsinki, 2000) Vol I, 373, www.bitline.fi/fide/ with summary of the discussion.

[2] *'The judicial authorities of the Member States (..) are responsible for ensuring that Community law is applied and respected in the national legal system'*: Case 2/88 Imm. *Zwartveld and Others* [1990] ECR I–3365 (in proceedings under national criminal law where the rechter-commissaris had asked assistance from Community officials); *'(..) When applying Article 86, in particular to conduct exempt under Article 85(3), the national courts are acting as Community courts of general jurisdiction'*: Case T–51/89 *Tetra Pak Rausing SA v Commission (Tetrapak)* [1990] ECR II–309, at para 42 (referring to cases to be brought against private individuals or firms before national courts); *'judicial protection of individuals is ensured, in the Community system of remedies, not only by the various rights of access (..) before the Community judicature (..) but also by [the preliminary rulings procedure] in the context of actions brought before the national courts, which are the ordinary courts of Community law'*: Case T–219/95 R *Marie-Therese Danielson et al v Commission (Mururoa nuclear tests case)* [1995] ECR II–3051 (enforcement of the Euratom Treaty in an action for annulment of a Commission act).

Community courts and are bound to enforce Community law, sometimes in relations between individuals, most notably in the context of competition law, but more often as against national authorities, and also in cases involving question on the validity of Community law.[3] The national courts have become first-in-line Community courts, in most cases involving private parties. It is only in cases brought by Member States or Community institutions amongst themselves that national courts are not involved. In almost every case involving private individuals, national courts are the 'natural forum' for the enforcement of Community law. The Court of Justice seeks to direct these cases to the national courts.

Now, where does this Community mandate of the national courts come from? It is not in so many words to be found in the Treaties. The Treaty only contains traces of the involvement of national courts in the supervision of the enforcement of Community law, in Article 81(2) EC (old Article 85(2) of the EC Treaty), in Article 234 EC (old Article 177), and Article 249 EC (old Article 189) and in Article 10 EC (old Article 5). The mandate is for the most part the product of the case law of the Court of Justice, but in a direct dialogue with the national courts. Indeed, '*The ECJ can* say *whatever it wants, the real question is why anyone should* heed *it*'.[4] Much of the case law developing the doctrines of direct effect and supremacy is a direct answer to the problems indicated by the national courts, and, in some instances, to the defiance of some national courts to go along with the European Court.[5] Of course, most questions concerning direct effect and supremacy arise in proceedings before national courts, which refer them to the Court of Justice. Starting from the doctrines of direct effect and supremacy, but gradually evolving beyond them on the basis of the principle of Community loyalty laid down in Article 10 EC and by virtue of the principles of *effet utile* and effectiveness of Community law and the principle of effective judicial protection, the Court has refined the Community mandate for the national courts. Yet, this *Community* mandate is necessarily blended in with their *national* mandate. Community law is part of the law of the land, it is, in the famous wording of Lord Denning, '(..) *like an incoming tide. It flows into the estuaries and up the rivers. It cannot be held back*'.[6] Or, to quote the Court of Justice,

---

3 Case C–50/00 P *Unión de Pequeños Agricultores v Council* [2002] ECR I–6677; Case C–70/97 P *Kruidvat BVBA v Commission* [1998] ECR I–7183; Case C–321/95 P *Stichting Greenpeace Council (Greenpeace International) and Others v Commission* [1998] ECR I–1651.
4 KJ Alter, 'The European Court's Political Power', (1996) *West European Politics*, 458, at 459.
5 For instance, the language of Case 6/64 *Costa v ENEL* [1964] ECR 585 and Case 106/77 *Simmenthal* [1978] *ECR* 629, was tailored to the Italian case, but paid attention also to the other systems ('transfer of sovereign powers' and 'limitation of sovereignty'); Case 148/78 *Criminal proceedings against Tullio Ratti* [1979] *ECR* 1629 providing an alternative rationale for allowing the direct effect of directives after initial rejection by some national courts.
6 In *Court of Appeal*, decision of 22 May 1974, *Bulmer v Bollinger* 2 All ER 1226, 1231; Oppenheimer, *The Cases*, 735.

'*the EEC Treaty has created its own legal system which, on the entry into force of the Treaty, became an integral part of the legal systems of the Member States*'.[7] Within the domestic legal order Community law does not form a separate entity: it is not just foreign law. Community law is intertwined with national law. More so, since Community law mostly contains substantive provisions, and does not provide for sanction mechanisms, procedures and remedies, it is utterly dependent on national law for its enforcement and effectiveness under the principle of procedural autonomy. It is national authorities and courts that are first responsible for ensuring the enforcement of Community law. And since there is no Community scenario as to *how* this should be done laid down in the legislative texts, the Court of Justice, in the formulation of the mandate, will mostly have to rely on national rules and procedures. Since the Court of Justice is not empowered or equipped to develop a complete mandate for the national courts, the Community mandate is only partial and must be supplemented with national law.

The creation and development of a Community mandate of the national courts, confronted with this new body of case law and requiring from them the fulfilment of a number of duties which are not necessarily in conformity with their national mandate, raises a number of constitutional questions, mostly related to their own jurisdiction.

3.2. HINTS OF A ROLE FOR NATIONAL COURTS IN THE TREATIES

3.2.1. Article 177 of the EC Treaty[8]

National courts are mentioned *expressis verbis* only in the provisions on references for preliminary rulings, *i.e.* Article 177 of the EC Treaty (*old*, now Article 234 EC) and more recently also in the new provisions on a more restrictive preliminary rulings procedure in Title VI of the TEU (Article 35 EU), and Article 68 EC (Title IV). The provision does not say in so many words that the national courts become Community courts, but it must have been assumed by the framers of the founding treaties that national courts would be confronted in cases before them with the Treaties and the law deriving from them. The application of Community law would not be the affair of the Court of Justice alone but to some extent also that of the national courts. The preliminary rulings procedure, a novel judicial 'gadget' in international organisations,[9] was probably

---

[7]   Case 6/64 *Costa v ENEL* [1964] ECR 585.
[8]   Since I want to go back to the foundational period when the ECJ had to 'start from scratch', I prefer to use the old numbering (with reference to the new numbers).
[9]   Article 41 of the ECSC Treaty already provided for a preliminary rulings procedure; yet, it was restricted to questions of validity and had, accordingly, remained largely unused.

introduced in the Treaty on instigation of Nicola Catalano, the Italian member of the legal Working Group assisting the drafting of the Treaties.[10] The Italian system of constitutional review comprises a similar model of preliminary references from ordinary courts to the *Corte costituzionale*. The German member of the Group, also familiar with the system of *konkrete Normenkontrolle* in the German context, immediately agreed. The other members, most of whom supposedly did not realise the magnitude of the innovation,[11] did not oppose it. The introduction of the preliminary rulings procedure would prove to be crucial in the development of the ever closer union among the Member States. Without it, the principles of direct effect and supremacy would not have been spread among all the national courts. If those two doctrines are the twin-pillars of the Community legal order, Article 234 EC is the corner stone.

Yet, the preliminary reference procedure of itself does not transform the national courts into Community courts.[12] Indeed, the article only provides for a procedure by which the national court, if and when confronted with a problem of interpretation or questions of validity of Community law, may or must refer questions to Luxembourg. It makes the Court of Justice a beacon for the national courts when applying and interpreting

---

[10] So P Pescatore, 'De werkzaamheden van de "juridische groep" bij de onderhandelingen over de verdragen van Rome', (1981) Studia Diplomatica, 167, at 181; see also H van den Heuvel, *Prejudiciële vragen en bevoegdheidsproblemen in het Europees recht* (Deventer, 1962) 33, who conducted a comparative study to similar procedures. Besides the German and Italian constitutional references for preliminary rulings, he also looked at the French system of *questions prèjudicielles* and made some (peculiar) observations on the US system under Section 2403 of the US Code which provided that where the constitutionality of an Act of Congress is drawn into question, the Attorney General is informed and permitted to intervene. (It is not clear how this should compare to the preliminary rulings procedure under Art. 177 of the Treaty.)

[11] P Pescatore, 'De werkzaamheden van de "juridische groep" bij de onderhandelingen over de verdragen van Rome', (1981) Studia Diplomatica, 167, at 182: '*I am inclined to believe that most likely not everyone realised the importance of this novel procedure*' (my translation).

[12] It did in the interpretation of the ECJ in *Van Gend en Loos* where it said that '*the task assigned to the Court under Art. 177, the object of which is to secure uniform interpretation of the Treaty by national courts and tribunals, confirms that the States have aknowledged that Community law has an authority which can be invoked by their nationals before their national courts or tribunals*', Case 26/62 *Van Gend en Loos* [1963] ECR 1. In fact, that is not entirely true: the uniform interpretation of a Treaty provision would also be important without direct effect: it would then concern the interpretation of the content of the provisions, independent of the question of their applicability *qua* treaty provision or in their national transformed quality. The possibility to invoke a provision directly and as treaty provision does not follow automatically. See e.g. F Münch, 'Compètence des juridictions nationales. Leur tâche dans l'application du droit communautaire', in N Catalano et al, *Droit communautaire et droit national*, Semaine de Bruges (Bruges, De Tempel, 1965) 173, at 176 *et seq.*, who explained that most would agree that the national courts would have to decide on the applicability of the Community provision as interpreted by the ECJ, and on its relation with conflicting national law, in accordance with national constitutional law. Consequently, no uniformity of application could be achieved, and probably the Dutch courts would be the most loyal to the Community, while the German and Italian courts would be inclined to raise questions concerning the constitutionality of Community law.

Community law – for whatever reason and to whatever effect – but it says nothing about when and how national courts should apply Community law in cases before them. Moreover, the guiding role of the Court of Justice is, according to the text of Article 234 EC, restricted to the *interpretation* and *validity* of Community law, and it was not evident that the issue of whether and how the national courts should apply it in the domestic legal order – its *applicability* – was one for the European Court to decide.[13] *Interpretation* of Community law is for the Court of Justice, with a view to preserving uniformity, while the *application to the concrete case* would be for the national courts. Is the question of direct effect (or direct applicability), for instance, which is so closely connected to the role of the national courts, one of *interpretation* or of *application*? On the other hand, it is clear that even in the most fervent dualist States, questions of the interpretation of the substance of Community law, while transformed into national law, could emerge before the domestic courts. Indeed, to a large extent, Community law is implemented and executed by national authorities, and cases were bound to come up before national courts, including those in dualist States, in which the interpretation of Community law would be of importance for the solution of the case. The involvement of the domestic courts in the Community judicial system follows from the intertwinement of Community law and domestic law: It came naturally. Yet, without the doctrines of direct effect and supremacy and their progeny, as developed by the Court of Justice,[14] the national courts would probably not have become Community courts. It is likely that they would have applied Community law exclusively from the perspective of 15 different national systems, in the same way as the domestic application of international law differs from state to state.[15] While the interpretation of specific provisions may have been uniform, their effect would not have been. 'The judge was Dutch and behaved as such'...[16]

---

[13] This was also the argument put forward by the Belgium and Netherlands governments which intervened in the *Van Gend en Loos* case. They argued that since the question of direct effect concerned the application of Community law and not its interpretation, the ECJ did not have jurisdiction and the question should be answered on the basis of domestic constitutional law. It was only by making the question of direct effect one of the interpretation of Community law that the Court could justify its jurisdiction; for an early analysis of the notions of interpretation and application, AM Donner, 'Uitlegging en toepassing', in *Miscellanea Ganshof van der Meersch, Studia ab discipulis amicisque in honorem egregii professoris edita* (Bruylant, Brussels, 1972) 103.

[14] See on this question R Lecourt, 'Quel eût ètè le droit des Communautès sans les arrêts de 1963 et 1964?', in *L'Europe et le droit, Mèlanges en hommage de Jean Boulouis* (Dalloz, Paris, 1991) 349.

[15] So for instance H van den Heuvel, *Prejudiciële vragen en bevoegdheidsproblemen in het Europees recht* (Deventer, 1962) 14.

[16] See EA Alkema, 'The Application of Internationally Guaranteed Human Rights in the Municipal Order', in F Kalshoven (ed), *Essays on the Development of the International Legal Order in Memory of Van Panhuys* (Sijthoff, 1980) 181, at 181.

The questions referred to the Court by the domestic courts, were used as a springboard by the Community Court to argue the direct effect and the supremacy of Community law, which have an immediate bearing on the national courts and make them responsible for the enforcement and application of Community law in accordance with the Court's case law. At least some of the national courts did refer questions as to the effect of Community law in the domestic legal order and the fate of conflicting national law.[17] For them too, these questions apparently related to the *interpretation* rather than to the *application* of Community law.

3.2.2. Article 85(2) of the EC Treaty

Under Article 85(2) of the EC Treaty (now Article 81(2) EC) agreements or decisions prohibited pursuant to the provision shall be automatically void. Accordingly, they cannot be enforced in proceedings before national courts. Articles 85 and 86 of the EC Treaty (new Articles 81 and 82 EC) were from the outset among the provisions, which were considered as being clearly intended to be incorporated in national law and to be enforced by the national courts.[18]

3.2.3. Article 189 of the EC Treaty

Article 189 of the EC Treaty (now Article 249 EC) states that regulations are binding in their entirety and are 'directly applicable' in all Member States. Again, the tale of the origins of the notion is told by Pescatore;[19] it was he who suggested that the normative system should be improved in comparison to the ECSC Treaty. He proposed to distinguish between normative acts which would apply directly in the entire Community, and those which required further national implementation, similar to decisions of international organisations. All agreed with the suggestion without objection, including the issue of directly applicable norms. Only the label to be put on them was an issue. The notion of 'laws or statutes'[20] was rejected, as it would stand no chance of being accepted; instead, it was decided to take one step down on the ladder of terminology, and to speak of 'regulations'.

---

[17] *Van Gend en Loos* has been labelled as a reference to the ECJ of a question of interpretation of the Netherlands Constitution: under the Constitution, Article 12 of the Treaty would be given precedence if it was 'binding on anyone': was it?

[18] See for instance AG Roemer in his Opinion in Case 26/62 *Van Gend en Loos* [1963] ECR 1, at 20.

[19] P Pescatore, 'De werkzaamheden van de "Juridische Groep"bij de onderhandelingen over de Verdragen van Rome', *Studia Diplomatica* (1981) 167, at 179.

[20] Pescatore spoke of '*communautaire wetten*' ('*lois communautaires*' or 'Community Acts').

Article 189 of the Treaty made regulations 'directly applicable'. The notion was not entirely clear from the beginning: it was not clear, for instance, whether it meant the same as the notions used more often, namely 'self-executing' or 'directly effective'. What it intended to say was that regulations were legally perfect and immersed in the domestic legal orders.[21]

3.2.4. Article 5 of the EC Treaty (Article 10 EC)

The Treaty provision which is nowadays most linked with the Community role for the national courts[22] is Article 10 EC (previously Article 5 of the EC Treaty) which states that *'The Member States shall take all appropriate measures, whether general or particular, to ensure fulfilment of the obligations arising out of this Treaty or resulting from action taken by the institutions of the Community. They shall facilitate the achievement of the Community's tasks'.* The provision does not mention the national courts, but addresses the Member States as such. It has been interpreted to cover all the organs of the State, including the courts. Nevertheless, in the initial cases establishing the role of the national courts as Community courts, no reference was made to Article 10 EC. The provision has been added to the case law in order to strengthen the compliance pull of the Court's case law by reference to a solid Treaty basis. It is, of course, a rather vague provision, akin to the international law principle of good faith. Yet, it has developed into a provision of constitutional principle, and is now more akin to the principle of federal loyalty that to its more loose pendant in international law.[23] The provision has been used in order to formulate duties of national courts in the absence of direct effect, for instance the duty of conform interpretation[24] or the duty to hold the State liable in damages

---

[21] Temple Lang, in his 1997 contribution, referred to Art. 189 of the Treaty as the main ground for the involvement of the national courts: *'Why are national courts involved with Community law at all? (..) The legal reasons are in the Treaties, which say that some rules of Community law are binding in their entirety and directly applicable in all Member States, that is, they are part of national law which national courts must apply, without any national implementing national measure. [Article 177]'*, J Temple Lang, 'The Duties of National Courts under Community Constitutional Law', (1997) 22 *ELRev* 3, at 4. However, the direct applicability of regulations cannot serve as a ground for the involvement of the national courts in the enforcement of the Treaties and of other acts of secondary Community law.

[22] J Temple Lang, 'The Duties of National Courts under Community Constitutional Law', (1997) 22 *EL Rev* 3; J Temple Lang, 'The duties of cooperation of national authorities and Courts under Article 10 EC: two more reflections', (2001) 26 *ELRev* 84, and his other publications on the issue referred to above.

[23] V Constantinesco, 'L'article 5 CEE, de la bonne foi à la loyautè communautaire', in *Du droit international au droit de l'intègration. Liber Amicorum Pierre Pescatore* (Nomos, Baden, 1987) 97; O Due, 'Artikel 5 van het EEG Verdrag. Een bepaling met een federaal karakter?', (1992) *SEW*, 355.

[24] See Case 14/83 *Sabine Von Colson and Elisabeth Kamann v Land Nordrhein-Westphalen* [1984] ECR 1891, at para 26: 'However, the Member States' obligation arising from a

for violation of Community law.[25] It has also been referred to in those cases where the national courts are ordered to find in national law the relevant tools, procedures and remedies to effectively protect the rights that individuals derive from the direct effect of Community law, in order to explain the exact duties imposed on the national courts by virtue of the direct effect of Community law: *'It follows from the judgments of 16 December 1976 in the Rewe and Comet cases that, applying the principle of co-operation laid down in Article 5 of the EEC Treaty, it is the courts of the Member States which are entrusted with ensuring the legal protection which subjects derive from the direct effect of the provisions of Community law.'*[26] It is for the domestic legal system of each Member State to designate the courts having jurisdiction and determine the procedural conditions governing actions at law intended to safeguard the rights which subjects derive from the direct effect of Community law, it being understood that such conditions cannot be less favourable than those relating to similar actions of a domestic nature and that under no circumstances may they be such as to make it impossible in practice to exercise the rights which the national courts have a duty to protect. And finally, the national courts must, in accordance with the principle of co-operation of Article 10 EC, so far as possible interpret and apply national procedural rules governing the exercise of rights of action in a way that enables natural or legal persons to challenge before the courts the legality of any decision or other national measure relative to the application to them of a Community act of general application, by pleading the invalidity of the act.[27]

Today, Article 10 EC can safely be named the single most important Treaty basis for the Community mandate of national courts. It has been used to fill the gaps in the doctrine of direct effects in order to increase the effectiveness of Community law and to define the associated duties of the national courts.[28]

Directive to achieve the result envisaged by the Directive and their duty under Article 5 of the Treaty to take all appropriate measures, whether general or particular, to ensure the fulfilment of that obligation, is binding on all the authorities of Member States including, for matters within their jurisdiction, the courts. It follows that, in applying the national law and in particular the provisions of a national law specifically introduced in order to implement Directive no 76/207, national courts are required to interpret their national law in the light of the wording and the purpose of the Directive in order to achieve the result referred to in the third paragraph of Article 189'; see also Case C–106/89 *Marleasing SA v La Comercial Internacional de Alimentacion SA* [1990] ECR I–4135.

25 Joined Cases C–6/90 and C–9/90 *Francovich and Bonifaci v Italy* [1991] ECR I–5406.

26 Case 811/79 *Amministrazione delle finanze dello Stato v Ariete SpA* [1980] 2545, at para 12, and the many other cases on the right to recovery of undue payments.

27 Case C–50/00 P *Uniòn de Pequeños Agricultores v Council* [2002] ECR I–6677, at para 42.

28 On the ECJ's methodology relying on Art. 10 EC (new) to fill gaps in the doctrine of direct effect to increase the effectiveness of Community law, EF Hinton, 'Strengthening the Effectiveness of Community Law: Direct Effect, Article 5 EC and the European Court of Justice', 31 *NYJILP*, 1999, 307.

3.2.5. Final Remarks

None of the Treaty provisions discussed reveals even the beginning of the Community mandate of the national courts, as it exists today. The mandate is first and foremost the result of the case law of the Court of Justice, which, on the basis of the Treaty provisions mentioned and of general rules and principles, has bit by bit and case by case developed the mandate for the national courts. The absence of the Community mandate of the national courts in the primary text is not exceptional in the logic of the drafters. Community law is applied and implemented by the national authorities.[29] National administrative authorities give effect to Community law on a daily basis, and they are not mentioned either. All national authorities are hidden behind the 'Member State', as is usual in international law, and accordingly, so are the national courts.

Even today, forty years after *Van Gend en Loos*, the Community mandate of the national courts is absent from the Treaties. There are traces, however. In disguise, Member States have given a Treaty basis to direct effect and supremacy and their progeny: in the Protocol on the application of the principles of subsidiarity and proportionality, the Member States agree that these principles shall not affect the 'principles developed by the Court of Justice regarding the relationship between national and Community law', which can only be interpreted as an approval of the Court's case law on direct effect, supremacy and presumably of the Community mandate of the national courts as developed until then. Under Title VI of the Treaty on European Union, however, direct effect of decisions and framework decisions is denied *expressis verbis*.[30] What this implies for the mandate of the national courts will be discussed further below.

The Community mandate of the national courts is fleshed out in the case law of the Court of Justice. That is where the tasks and duties of the national courts when acting as Community courts are to be discovered. In its case law, the Court of Justice has made the national courts its allies and has introduced and initiated them in the Community judicial system. But the participation of the national courts is not pick and choose: the national courts must follow the guidance of the Court of Justice, which commissions the national courts as Community courts. The ensuing mandate is grafted upon the principles of direct effect and supremacy and further developed on the basis of general principles such as the uniformity, effectiveness or

---

[29] Due has suggested that the placing of Art 5 of the Treaty (*old*) immediately after Art 4 introducing the institutions of the Community is an indication that the Member States (and one might add therefore their organs) are, as it were, organs of the Communities, see O Due, 'Artikel 5 van het EEG Verdrag: Een bepaling met een federaal karakter?', (1992) *SEW*, 355, at 355.

[30] Art. 34 TEU.

l'effet utile of Community law and the effective judicial protection of the individual under Community law.

3.3. THE COMMUNITY MANDATE OF THE NATIONAL COURTS

Temple Lang and others[31] have listed duties imposed on the national courts in their capacity as Community courts, mostly in connection with Article 10 EC, used in combination with some other rule or principle of Community law which provides content to the general duty of co-operation. These duties include:[32]

– The duty to apply Community law in its entirety and protect rights which it confers on individuals and to accordingly set aside any provision of national law which may conflict with it;[33]
– the duty not to allow state authorities to rely on national laws which are inconsistent with directives which should have been implemented;[34]
– the duty to interpret and apply national laws as far as possible so as to make them compatible with and to fulfil the requirements of Community law;[35]
– the duty to give effective remedies for breach of Community law, in the form of compensation;[36]
– the duty to ensure that reparation of loss or damage sustained as a result of a violation of Community law by a Member State is adequate;[37]
– the duty to apply Community law under conditions, both procedural and substantive, which are analogous to those applicable to infringements of national law of similar nature and importance;[38]
– the duty to ensure the legal protection which persons derive from the direct effect of the provisions of Community law;[39]

---

[31] For instance EF Hinton, 'Strengthening the Effectiveness of Community Law: Direct Effect, Article 5 EC and the European Court of Justice', (1999) 31 *NYJILP*, 307.
[32] These are drawn from the publications of J Temple Lang, referred to above: This list of duties imposed by the Court of Justice on the national courts is of course not complete, nor are the references to the case law.
[33] Case 106/77 *Amministrazione delle Finanze dello Stato v Simmenthal* [1978] ECR 629.
[34] Case 148/78 *Pubblico Ministero v Ratti* [1979] ECR 1629.
[35] Case C–106/89 *Marleasing SA v La Comercial Internacionale de Alimentacion SA* [1990] ECR I–4135.
[36] Joined Cases C–6/90 and 9/90 *Francovich and Bonifaci v Italy* [1991] ECR I–5357.
[37] Joined Cases C–94/95 and C–95/95 *Bonifaci and others v INPS* [1997] ECR I–3969.
[38] Case 179/84 *Bozzetti v Invernizzi* [1985] ECR 2301.
[39] Case C–72/95 *Aannemersbedrijf Kraaijeveld BV v Gedeputeerde Staten van Zuid-Holland* [1996] ECR.

- – the duty to grant interim relief in order to protect rights which individuals derive from Community law;[40]
- – the duty to protect Community fundamental rights in the sphere of Community law;[41]
- – the duty to respect the jurisdiction of the Community institutions and to avoid conflicting decisions;[42]
- – the duty to refer to the European Court of Justice questions as to the validity of Community law;[43]
- – the duty to raise questions of Community law of their own motion where national law provides the same duty or power.[44]

These duties imposed on the national courts may demand quite a lot of the courts' judicial creativity. Sometimes, the issues raised to comply with the requests from Luxembourg will cause veritable constitutional problems with respect to the national constitutional mandate. What the Court is asking the national courts to do would imply an alteration of the national courts' constitutional position *vis-à-vis* the other State organs. In the case of two main sub-mandates the constitutional implications for the national courts' position are most apparent: the mandate to review national law, especially primary legislation, in the light of Community law and set it aside in case of conflict (the *'Simmenthal mandate'*) and the mandate to hold the State liable to compensate damage caused to individuals by breach of Community law (the *'Francovich mandate'*).

In what follows, these Community mandates with important national constitutional implications will be analysed in some depth. The analysis will consist of two perspectives: the Community perspective looking through the eyes of the Court of Justice, and the national perspectives of some of the national courts: what national constitutional problems have they had to overcome in order to give effect to the Community mandate imposed upon them? The bottom line is testing the hypothesis: have the national courts really become common courts of Community law? How have they? Do they operate under a double mandate?

---

[40] Case C–213/89 *The Queen v Secretary of State for Transport, ex parte Factortame Ltd and Others* [1990] ECR I–2433.

[41] Case 5/88 *Hubert Wachauf v Bundesamt für Ernährung und Forstwirtschaft* [1989] ECR 2609; Case C–2/92 *The Queen v Ministry for Agriculture, Fisheries and Food, ex parte Dennis Clifford Bostock* [1994] ECR I–955; Case C–260/89 *Elleniki Radiophonia Tiléorassi AE v Dimotiki Etairia Pliroforissis (ERT)* [1991] ECR I–2925; Case C–60/00 *Mary Carpenter v Secretary of State for the Home Department* [2002] ECR I–6279.

[42] Case C–234/89 *Stergois Delimitis v Henniger Bräu AG* [1991] ECR I–935.

[43] Case 314/85 *Foto-Frost v Hauptzollamt Lübeck-Ost* [1987] ECR 4199; C–465/93 *Atlanta Fruchthandelsgesellschaft mbH v Bundesamt für Ernährung und Forstwirtschaft* [1995] ECR I–3761.

[44] C–72/95 *Aannemersbedrijf Kraaijeveld BV v Gedeputeerde Staten van Zuid-Holland* [1996] I–5403; Joined Cases C–430/93 and C–431/93 *Van Schijndel en Van Veen v Stichting Pensioenfonds voor Fysiotherapeuten* [1995] ECR I–4705.

4

The Duty to Review National Law: the 'Simmenthal Mandate'

THE COMMUNITY MANDATE of the national courts obliges them to review national law against Community law, and to set it aside in case of a conflict. The obligation incumbent on the national courts is unequivocal and uncompromising: they must control the compatibility of *all* national legislation, including primary legislation, even subsequent to the rule of Community law.[1] The Court of Justice does not differentiate, in the development of the mandate of the national courts, as to the nature of the national rule in question, or the constitutional position of the body or organ that designed it. Likewise, the Court of Justice does not allow any exceptions to the mandate with regard to the constitutional position of national courts. *All* national courts, whatever their constitutional position *vis-à-vis* the national political organs, are compelled to execute this review, even if national constitutional law requires them to abide by the rule in question. The review conducted by the national courts must result at least in the disapplication of the conflicting provision of national law. They are not obliged to quash the national provision or to declare it void. On the other hand, the courts may be under an obligation to substitute a directly effective provision of Community law for the national provision that has been disapplied.

Judicial review of national law constitutes a specific tool in the hands of the national courts to give effect to Community law. The duty is grafted upon the principles of *supremacy* and *direct effect*.[2] The combined effect of these two principles obliges the courts to review national legislation and to set it aside in case of a conflict between a provision of national law and a directly effective provision of Community law. Yet, the two principles have a separate meaning, and consequences other than the duty of judicial review of national legislation. It is useful therefore to look into both principles and to distil from them the consequences for the duties of the national courts.

---

[1]   The relation between Community law and national constitutional law will be central in Part 2.

[2]   Especially Case 106/77 *Simmenthal* [1978] ECR 629.

4.1.1. Introduction

The doctrine of direct effect does not need much of an introduction. The line of cases in which the Court has introduced,[3] developed, extended[4] and circumscribed[5] the notion in Community law is well known and needs no repetition here. Nevertheless it is important to realise that the doctrine of direct effect changed the face of the Community once and for all, and that until this day, direct effect is pivotal in the decentralised enforcement of Community law. This is not to say that without it Community law would be unenforceable today. Yet, it does make Community law so much better enforceable than it would have been. After all, *'practical operation for all concerned, which is nothing else than direct effect, must be considered as being the normal condition of any rule of law'.*[6] Direct effect adds another layer to the Community judicial system. Judges and lawyers mostly do not doubt the direct effect of norms of national law, at least not in those terms. Community law has become part of the law of the land, and direct effect has been extended so much that one could perhaps say that direct effect has become the rule rather than the exception. And yet, the question of direct effect continues to be referred to the Court of Justice, and the doctrine is still being refined. There remain, in mainstream Community law, several issues for debate, such as, of course the issue of the direct effect of directives; in addition, the direct effect of WTO law is still a matter for discussion and the debate on the direct effect of non-Community Union law is only just beginning.

4.1.2. The Notion of Direct Effect

The European Court did not invent the notion of direct effect out of the blue. The notion is related to others, which in domestic law play a role in

---

3   Case 26/62 *Van Gend en Loos* [1963] ECR 1.
4   Case 57/65 *Lütticke* [1966] ECR 205 (direct effect in case of positive obligations imposed on the Member States by a Treaty provision); Case 41/74 *Van Duyn* [1974] ECR 1337 (direct effect of directives); Case 43/75 *Defrenne* [1976] ECR 455 (limited horizontal direct effect of a Treaty provision); Case 8/81 *Becker* [1982] ECR 53 (direct effect of directives restated); Case 104/81 *Kupferberg* [1982] ECR 3659 (direct effect of international agreements concluded by the Community).
5   Case 152/84 *Marshall* [1986] ECR 723 (no horizontal direct effect of directives); Cases 21–24/72 *International Fruit Company* [1972] *ECR* 1219 no direct effect of (certain provisions of) GATT 1947; The question as to whether the WTO agreement and GATT 1994 do produce direct effect in the Community legal order continues to be referred to the ECJ on a regular basis, see below.
6   P Pescatore, 'The Doctrine of "Direct Effect": An Infant Disease of Community law', (1983) *ELRev* 155, at 155.

determining the effect of provisions of international law in the internal legal order, such as 'internal effect' or the 'self-executing' nature of treaty provisions. While this is probably the area with which the notion is most associated today, it is also relevant in other fields. There are certain positive legal norms which by their nature or the intention of the organs which drafted them, do not have direct legal effects for citizens, and merely have effect for certain public authorities, legislative or administrative, or are designed as guidelines for them.[7] Many national constitutions contain such non-directly effective norms.[8] The courts cannot enforce them for lack of precision; and before implementation by the Legislature individuals cannot derive rights from them. Arguably, the absence of direct effect is not the normal state of the law. Any legal rule is devised so as to operate effectively. Some would even argue that if it is not operative, it is not a rule of law.[9] In the field with which the notion is mostly associated, that of the status of international law in the internal legal order of a State, direct effect of a treaty provision concerns its effectiveness in the domestic legal order. A treaty provision is, upon its entry into force, operative as between the Contracting Parties on the international plane; the question of direct effect relates to the effectiveness of the norm in the internal legal order.

Direct effect, direct applicability and analogous concepts existed long before the Court received the questions of the *Tariefcommissie* in the *Van Gend en Loos* case. With respect to international law the phenomenon was, at the time, generally referred to as the *self-executing* character of a norm. The issue was known in American law ever since Chief Justice Marshall in 1829 explained that *'Our Constitution declares a treaty to be the law of the land. It is, consequently, to be regarded in courts of justice as equivalent to an act of the legislature, whenever it operates of itself without the aid of any legislative provision. But when the terms of the stipulation import a contract, when either of the parties engages to perform a particular act, the treaty addresses itself to the political, not the judicial department; and the legislature must execute the contract before it can become a rule for the court'.*[10] He thus construed the essence of the self-executing character of treaty provisions in terms of the *justiciability* of the norm: if a treaty provision needs no further execution by

---

[7]   See also LFM Besselink, 'Curing a "Childhood Sickness"? On Direct Effect, Internal Effect, Primacy and Derogation from Civil Rights. The Netherlands Council of State Judgment in the *Metten* Case', (1996) *MJ*, 165, at 169.

[8]   Examples would be constitutional provisions granting a right to protection of the environment, as in Article 23 of the Belgian Constitution; other examples are social and economic right included in many Constitutions. For a comparison between direct effect of Irish constitutional provisions and Community law, see A Sherlock, 'Self-executing Provisions in EC Law and under the Irish Constitution (1996) 2 *EPL*, 103.

[9]   See P Pescatore, 'The Doctrine of "Direct Effect": An Infant Disease of Community Law', (1983) *ELR*, 155, at 155.

[10]   Supreme Court (US), *Foster and Elam v Neilson*, US SC, 1829, 2 Peters (US) 253.

the political branches, it becomes a rule for the court. A self-executing norm is one that is legally perfect and thus lends itself to application by courts of law. The quote also demonstrates that there is a question that precedes direct effect, namely that of the insertion in the domestic legal order, or at least of the openness of the legal order to international law, whether with or without transformation.[11] One question is whether international law is at all relevant in the domestic legal order. The next question is whether a court can take cognisance of the rule, generally speaking, and then, whether it can apply a particular norm to a case brought before it. Under the US Constitution, treaties are considered to form part of the law of the land. The subsequent question then is whether treaty provisions can also be applied in court proceedings. There apparently is no reason why a court should not, generally speaking, apply international law, since it is considered to be part of the law of the land. The last question, of whether a particular norm can be applied in a particular case, depends on its 'self-executing' character; in other words, whether it is legally perfect and needs no further execution.

One hundred years later, the Permanent Court of International Justice in the *Jurisdiction of the Courts of Danzig* case[12] discussed the 'direct effect' of Treaty provisions on the rights and obligations of individuals: *'the very object of an international agreement, according to the intention of the contracting Parties, may be the adoption by the Parties of some definite rules creating individual rights and obligations and enforceable by the national courts.'* International treaties may not only operate between States at the international, inter-state level, they may also be intended to affect the rights and obligations of individuals.[13]

In fact, the reference to the notion in the *Danzig* decision of the Permanent Court was rather exceptional, since under classic interna-

---

[11] This resembles the difference between 'direct applicability' and 'direct effect', see J Winter, 'Direct Applicability and Direct Effect: Two Distinct and Different Concepts in Community Law', (1972) 9 *CML Rev* 425; and more recently P Elefteriadis, 'The Direct Effect of Community Law: Conceptual Issues', (1996) *YEL*, 205, who makes a different distinction between both notions than Winter did. The ECJ uses them interchangeably, lumping both issues together.

[12] *Permanent Court of International Justice*, Advisory Opinion of 3 March 1928, *Jurisdiction of the Courts of Danzig*, PCIJ Series B, no. 15, at 17.

[13] Spiermann claims that the ECJ's understanding of the position under international law on the direct effect of treaties was inadequate, and did not correspond to the reality of international courts and tribunals' mention of the possibility of direct effect. He mentions some other decisions; however, it is submitted that none of the examples mentioned by Spiermann which make reference to direct effect, use the notion in the way it was used by the ECJ In one case, the principle is used to grant a right of standing to an individual before the Arbitral Tribunal of Upper Silezia; while this is remarkable under international law, it is not the version of direct effect used in *Van Gend en Loos*; other examples which he brings forward concern the military tribunals concerning crimes committed by individuals against the international rules on warfare, which constitutes a very specific situation; O Spiermann, 'The Other Side of the Story: An Unpopular Essay on the Making of the European Community Legal Order', (1999) *EJIL*, 763, at 765–71.

tional law, the question of direct effect and the applicability of provisions of international law is a matter of national (constitutional) law. Indeed, the question of the relation between international law and national law, at least as far as the domestic effect of international law in the domestic legal orders is concerned, depends on national preferences concerning the version of monism or dualism towards international law. Each of the six original Community Member States, prior to 1963, had their own vision of the applicability of treaties by the domestic courts in general.[14]

The notion of direct effect existed: there was nothing novel about it. What, then, is so special about direct effect in the Community legal order, that it has been elevated to the level of constitutional principle?[15] What was unusual in *Van Gend en Loos* was that an international court decided the issue[16] on the basis of Community law and for all the national courts alike, whereas under international law the question is answered on the basis of domestic constitutional rules and principles.[17] In *Van Gend en Loos* the Court of Justice formulated the basic tenets of the relationship between Community law and national law for all the national legal systems and for all the national courts, irrespective of their constitutional principles and traditional attitudes towards international law. What was different and novel was that an international court ruled on the effect of the Treaty in the domestic legal order, implicitly declaring the constitutional provisions and traditions irrelevant. Whereas for classic international agreements the national courts had to solve issues of applicability, justiciability and the creation of rights and obligations for individuals by recourse to constitutional principles and attitudes, these principles and attitudes became redundant in the case of Community law, and the Court of Justice positioned itself as the judge of the direct effect of Community law in the national legal orders, by making it a question of the interpretation of the relevant provision.

---

[14] P Pescatore, 'De werkzaamheden van de "juridische groep" bij de onderhandelingen over de Verdragen van Rome', *Studia Diplomatica*, (1981) 167, at 179–80.

[15] On the constitutionalising effect of direct effect and supremacy: E Stein, 'Toward Supremacy of Treaty-Constitution by judicial fiat in the European Economic Community', *Riv.dir.int.*, 1965, 3; E Stein, 'Lawyers, Judges and the Making of a Transnational Constitution', (1981) 75 *Am J of Int Law*, 1; GF Mancini, 'The Making of a Constitution for Europe', (1989) 26 *CML Rev*, 595; JHH Weiler, 'The Transformation of Europe', 100 *Yale LJ*, 1991, 2403, also published in his *The Constitution of Europe* (Cambridge, CUP, 1999) 10.

[16] The issue is not the question as to whether a particular provisions has direct effect in a legal system where the possibility of treaty provisions in general has been accepted, but rather the question as to whether it is at all possible for a provision to be directly effective, irrespective of the domestic preferences as to monism or dualism.

[17] The fact that the ECJ assumed jurisdiction to answer the question was therefore crucial, see below.

4.1.3. *Van Gend en Loos*

Some words about the legal background of the *Van Gend en Loos* case are in order.[18] To begin with, it was hardly a coincidence that the question of direct effect of a Treaty provision was referred by a Dutch court. The (then) article 65 of the Netherlands Constitution held that *'provisions of agreements which, according to their terms, can be binding on anyone shall have such binding force after having been published'*. Article 66 added: *'Legislation in force within the Kingdom shall not apply if this application would be incompatible with provisions of agreements which are binding upon anyone and which have been entered into before or after the enactment of such legislation'*. While the first provision was perceived to open up the Dutch legal order for international law, the second decided on the fate of national law that conflicted with the international provisions effective in the domestic legal order. Yet, the courts' traditional deference to primary legislation and the express rejection of judicial review in the Constitution, prevented the courts from acting in line with the constitutional provision on treaties. The constitutional provisions had during the first ten years of their existence never led to a judicial review of an Act of Parliament in the light of treaty provisions.

The preliminary rulings procedure of Article 177 of the EEC Treaty introduced the Court of Justice as a *deus ex machina*. In a 1962 case,[19] the *Hoge Raad* ruled that the question whether provisions of a Treaty were 'binding on anyone' could, as a matter of Dutch law, only be answered on the basis of interpretation of the Treaty provisions. Since the question of the *effect* in the domestic legal order therefore became one of *interpretation*, it could in the case of Community law be referred to the Court of Justice. This way, the Court of Justice became involved in upholding the Dutch Constitution.[20] The Dutch and Belgian Governments intervened in *Van Gend en Loos* and denied jurisdiction of the Court of Justice. In their opinion, the question of direct effect related to the application of Community law and was one that, as for ordinary international law, was to be decided on the basis of national constitutional law.

The Court of Justice followed the cue of the *Tariefcommissie* and the *Hoge Raad* that the question of direct effect was one of interpretation of Community law. The Court therefore was automatically competent to answer the question referred to it, not only for the Dutch courts, but for all other courts throughout the Community. The Court then distinguished the

---

[18] See also M Claes and B De Witte, 'Report on The Netherlands', in *The European Court and National Courts – Doctrine and Jurisprudence. Legal Change in its Social Context* (Oxford, Hart Publishing, 1998) 171.

[19] *Hoge Raad*, decision of 18 May 1962, *De Geus en Uitenbogerd v Robert Bosch GmbH*, NJ, 1965, 115.

[20] So also B De Witte, 'Direct Effect, Supremacy and the Nature of the Legal Order', in P Craig and G de Búrca (eds), *The Evolution of EU Law* (Oxford, OUP, 1999) 177, at 180.

Community Treaties from other international treaties in its famous statement that *'The Treaty is more than an agreement which merely creates mutual obligations between the contracting states'*, and *'the Community constitutes a new legal order of international law (..)'*.

The fact that the particular Article 12 of the Treaty was given direct effect in the case at hand was not so shocking, given the text of the provision.[21] Yet, what was critical was that the question of direct effect was removed from national constitutional law and laid in the hands of the Court of Justice. From now on, constitutional and judicial traditions would no longer instruct judges as to the effect and applicability of Community law. The national courts were drawn into the Community judicial system with the Court of Justice instructing the courts on the effect of Community law in the domestic legal order. Accordingly a decentralised enforcement system was set up.

4.1.4. The Meaning of Direct Effect

4.1.4.1. *Creation of Rights for Individuals*

The notion of direct effect is difficult to define and contains several elements.[22] In the early days, the emphasis was on the *creation of rights for individuals*. As stated already in *Van Gend en Loos*, directly effective provisions of Community law create rights for individuals.[23] Conversely, individuals derive rights from directly effective provisions of Community law. Yet, the language of rights is confusing, not only due to the inherent intricacies of the concept in legal theory, but also since the concept is understood differently in different legal systems.[24] In

---

[21] It did give proof of a generous attitude *vis-à-vis* direct effect, since the provision is formulated in the form of obligations imposed on the Member States, rather than as rights for individuals; On the other hand, it is a clear and unconditional prohibition, which was legally perfect and apt for judicial application.

[22] The matter of the difference between direct effect and direct applicability will not be discussed, since the ECJ does not make the distinction. See on this issue J Winter, 'Direct Applicability and Direct Effect: Two Distinct and Different Concepts in Community law', (1972) 9 *CML Rev* 425; and more recently P Elefteriadis, 'The Direct Effect of Community Law: Conceptual Issues', (1996) *YEL*, 205.

[23] As Bruno De Witte has rightly pointed out, the ECJ did not, in Van Gend en Loos make direct effect coincide with the creation of rights: 'Article 12 of the Treaty (..) produces direct effects *and* creates individual rights which national courts must protect', Case 26/62 *Van Gend en Loos* [1963] ECR 1, at 16, emphasis added.

[24] See *eg* M Ruffert, 'Rights and Remedies in European Community Law; A Comparative View', (1997) 34 *CML Rev* 307; W Van Gerven, 'Of Rights, Remedies and Procedures', (2000) 37 *CML Rev* 501; S Prechal, *Directives in European Community Law* (Oxford, Clarendon Press, 1995) at 129 *et seq*; and her 'Does Direct Effect Still Matter', (2000) 37 *CML Rev* 2000, 1047, at 1053 *et seq.*; C. Hilson and T Downes, 'Making Sense of Rights: Community Rights in EC Law', (1999) 24 *ELR* 121.

Salgoil,[25] the Court of Justice made it clear that the meaning of the notion and the consequences thereof for the jurisdiction of the courts, for the procedures and remedies are to be decided by the national systems. The Court did use the language of rights in the context of direct effect, but as a non-dogmatic notion.[26] The translation into national rights categories, of the Community law concept into national legal concepts is for the national courts, as long as they ensure the effective protection of those 'rights', whatever their classification in national law. Consequently, the classification of the effects of the provision will vary from procedure to procedure[27] and from Member State to Member State.[28] Moreover, Community law may also create 'rights' without being directly effective, for instance a right to compensation where the Member State has infringed a non-directly effective provision which was intended to create rights for individuals.[29] The *'creation of rights'* and *'direct effect'* formula

---

[25]   Case 13/68 *Salgoil* [1968] ECR 661, where the Rome *Corte d'Appello* sought clarification on the nature of the legal protection granted to the subjective position of the individual as regards the State. The question concerned the distinction in Italian law between subjective rights and legitimate interests, which separates the jurisdiction of the civil and the administrative courts. The court was in fact asking about the classification under national law of the position which the individual derived from the direct effect of Community law. The ECJ held that the courts must award direct and immediate protection, but it was for national law to classify these rights and to designate the courts having jurisdiction; see also Case C–236/92 *Comitato di Coordinamento per la Difesa della Cava and others v Regione Lombardia and others* [1994] ECR I–483; the referring court inquired about the classification of the right which an individual may derive from the directive on waste which had not been correctly implemented. In fact the court referred a whole series of interesting questions as to what a court should do if disapplication of conflicting measures of national law did not suffice to solve the case before him, and could even lead to another infringement, giving rise to State liability. The ECJ denied the direct effect of the relevant provision of the directive holding that it did not create rights for individuals, which they may invoke against the State. The other questions therefore needed no answer. The ECJ denied direct effect in the sense of the creation of rights for individuals, and did not go into the other right, of judicial review – the application of the provision as a standard of review.

[26]   The Community law version of the notion of 'rights' is a-dogmatic; the concrete implications are left to national law and national legal theory. The ECJ is concerned only with the result, namely the immediate and adequate protection of the position of individuals under Community law. While this is probably the only option for the ECJ, it continues to cause confusion on the part of the national courts. Yet, the ECJ does not seem to care much about the theory of rights, see Case C–287/98 *Luxembourg v Berthe Linster and Others* [2000] ECR I–6917.

[27]   Depending, for instance, on whether the provision is applied, to use the French approach and terminology, in a *recours objectif* or a *recours subjectif*.

[28]   The classification of *'rights'*, as *'subjective rights'* (*diritti soggettivi*) or *'legitimate interests'* (*interesse legitimi*), is crucial, for instance, in the Italian legal system for the division of labour between the administrative and the civil courts. German law is notoriously sophisticated in the classification of rights. English law uses an entirely different distinction between private and public law rights, for the protection of which different causes of action and different remedies are available; an additional complication in the case of common law systems is the focus on remedies rather than rights.

[29]   For instance Joined Cases 6/90 and 9/90 *Francovich and Bonifaci v Italy* [1991] ECR I–5357.

cannot completely be equated. In some cases, especially in the area of directives, provisions may not of themselves create rights for individuals and yet
they may be used as a standard for review of the legality of Member State
action[30] or as a defence in criminal proceedings.[31] In short, to say that direct
effect exclusively means the creation of rights for individuals seems to be a
rather formalistic and limited way of presenting things.[32]

Nevertheless, it appears that the notion of direct effect is always linked
in some way or other to individuals as addressees. Direct effect assumes
effects towards citizens.[33] In contrast, non-directly effective provisions
may also concern citizens – though not directly: some other intervention
is required in order to achieve the effects intended by the provision – but
they have public authorities as their addressees. There are cases which do
not involve individuals, and where the question of direct effect was raised
nonetheless. In the *Grosskrotzenburg* case,[34] the Commission brought
infringement proceedings against Germany for failure to fulfil its obligations by not having achieved the result intended by the environmental
impact assessment directive. More in particular, the District Office
Darmstadt had granted consent for the construction of a new block at the
Grosskrotzenburg thermal power station without carrying out a preliminary environmental impact assessment required by the directive. The
alleged violation of Article 10 and 249 EC (then Article 5 and 189 of the
EC Treaty) thus consisted in an incorrect concrete implementation or
application rather than a mere failure to adopt the necessary implementing
legislation. The German Government alleged that the procedure should
be held inadmissible *inter alia* because the case law of the Court of Justice

---

[30] An early example is *Becker* where the ECJ separated direct effect from the creation of rights
holding that 'Wherever the provisions of a directive appear, as far as their subject matter
is concerned, to be unconditional and sufficiently precise, those provisions may, in the
absence of implementing measures adopted within the prescribed period, be relied upon
as against any national provision which is incompatible with the directive *or* insofar as the
provisions define rights which individuals are able to assert against the State', Case 8/81
Ursula Becker v Finanzamt Münster-Innenstadt [1982] ECR 53, at para 25, emphasis added.

[31] It is possible to also bring these effects under the umbrella of the creation for rights, by
extending the notion of 'rights' to 'procedural rights', besides the more common creation
of substantive rights; the individual derives a 'right to judicial review' and a right not to
have a conflicting measure applied against him. This is not the approach of the ECJ (see
the *Becker* case mentioned above) and it seems rather artificial.

[32] See *eg* Case C–431/92 *Commission v Germany (Grosskrotzenburg)* [1995] ECR I–2189, where
Germany had argued that the ECJ had only awarded direct effect to directives where
they confer specific rights to individuals; the ECJ rejected the argument: *'The question
which arises is thus whether the directive is to be construed as imposing* [the obligation flowing directly from the directive to conduct an environmental impact assessment, MC].
*That question is quite separate from the question whether individuals may rely as against the
State on* [directives]', at para 26.

[33] LFM Besselink, 'Curing a "Childhood Sickness"? On Direct Effect, Internal Effect,
Primacy and Derogations from Civil Rights. The Netherlands Council of State Judgment
in the *Metten* Case', (1996) 3 *MJ*, 165, at 169.

[34] Case C–431/92 *Commission v Germany (Grosskrotzenburg)* [1995] ECR I–2189.

recognized the direct effect of the provisions of a directive only where they confer specific rights on individuals, which the relevant provisions did not. Since the Commission itself had not argued that the contested decision granting development consent failed to take account of the legal position of individuals protected by the directive, the latter's provisions could not have direct effect irrespective of whether they were unconditional and sufficiently precise. The German authorities were not therefore required to apply them directly before implementing the directive. The Court dismissed the argument, stating that the case did not concern the question whether individuals may rely as against the State on provisions of an unimplemented directive which were unconditional and sufficiently clear and precise, a right which had been recognized by the Court of Justice. It was only concerned with the question whether the directive could be construed as imposing an obligation to assess the environmental impact of the project concerned. In other words, direct effect had nothing to do with the case, as it did not involve the question whether individuals could rely on the relevant provisions.

Other cases which at first sight have no relation to direct effect are those in which a Member State seeks to rely on the provisions of WTO law or GATT to challenge the validity of Community law. While these cases are of course relevant to individuals and companies, they are not involved in the proceedings at hand which are conducted between a Member State and the Community institutions. In *Germany v Council (bananas)*[35] the German Government submitted that compliance with GATT rules was a condition for the lawfulness of Community acts, *regardless of any question as to the direct effect of GATT*, and that the Regulation infringed certain basic provisions of GATT. The Court did not exactly answer in terms of direct effect, but it held that those features of GATT, from which the Court had in other cases concluded that an individual within the Community could not invoke it in a court to challenge the lawfulness of a Community act, also precluded the Court from taking provisions of GATT into consideration to assess the lawfulness of a regulation in an action brought by a Member State. The special features of the GATT rules demonstrated that these were not unconditional and that an obligation to recognize them as rules of international law which are directly applicable in the domestic legal systems of the contracting parties could not be based on the spirit, general scheme or terms of GATT. The Court may not have equated direct effect and the possibility of a Member State to rely on GATT in an annulment action, but it came very close, and the rationale appeared to be exactly the same. This has been confirmed with respect to the WTO Agreement and GATT 1994 in the *Portuguese Textiles* case and in *Parfums Christian Dior*.[36]

[35] Case C–280/93 *Germany v Council (bananas)* [1994] ECR I–4973.
[36] Case C–149/96 *Portugal v Council (Portuguese Textiles Case)* [1999] ECR I–8395; Joined Cases C–300/98 and C–392/98 *Parfums Christian Dior SA v TUK Consultancy BV and Assco Gerüste GmbH and Rob van Dijk v Wilhelm Layher GmbH & Co KG and Layher BV* [2000] ECR-11307.

Turning back then to the definition of direct effect as related to the creation of rights, Cottier and Nadakavukaren Schefer have in relation to WTO law suggested a definition reminiscent of remedies. Direct effect, for them, intends to signify *'that a private person in a State (or Union, respectively) may base a claim in, and be granted relief from, the domestic courts of that state against another private person or the state on the basis of the state's obligations under an international treaty. (..) Direct effect brings about the empowerment of three actors: the administration, private actors and the courts'.*[37] In the context of Community law, the definition would require some adjustments,[38] but it does have some attractive elements by focusing on the remedy rather than the right created.[39]

In the more recent case law on the direct effect of the Europe Agreements, the Court apparently limits the content of the right to a procedural right to invoke the directly effective provision. The Court held, after affirming that the relevant provisions established *'a precise and unconditional principle which is sufficiently operational to be applied by a national court and which is therefore capable of governing the legal position of individuals'*, that *'the direct effect which those provisions must therefore be recognised as having means that (..) nationals relying on them have the right to invoke them before the courts of the host Member State'.*[40]

4.1.4.2. Invokability

The concept of direct effect is also described in terms of invokability.[41] In many cases, when considering the direct effect of a provision, the Court says that the provision *'may be relied upon by individuals and must be applied by the national courts'.*[42] The creation of rights formula is omitted and put

---

[37] T Cottier and K Nadakavukaren Schefer, 'The Relationship Between World Trade Organization Law, National and Regional Law', (1998) *JIEL*, 83, at 89.

[38] The passage 'against another person' would have to be abandoned under Community law, because of the distinction between horizontal and vertical direct effect.

[39] On the rights-remedies issue see W van Gerven, 'Of Right, Remedies and Procedures', (2000) 37 *CML Rev* 501.

[40] Case C–63/99 *The Queen v Secretary of State for the Home Department, ex parte Gloszczuk and Gloszczuk* [2001] ECR I–6369; Case C–257/99 *The Queen v Secretary of State for the Home Department, ex parte Barkoci and Malik* [2001] ECR I–6557; Case C–235/99 99 *The Queen v Secretary of State for the Home Department, ex parte Kondova* [2001] ECR I–6427; Case C–268/ 99 *Jany and Others v Staatssecretaris van Justitie* [2001] ECR I–8615. The recognition of direct effect of the provisions did not save the case of the nationals involved, given the content given to them, see A Pedain, 'A hollow victory: The ECJ rules on direct effect of freedom of establishment provisions in Europe Agreements', (2002) *CLJ*, 284 and by the same author '"With or without me": The ECJ adopts a pose of studied neutrality towards EU enlargement', (2002) 51 *ICLQ*, 981.

[41] For a recent discussion PV Figueroa Regueiro, 'Invocability of Substitution and Invocability of Exclusion: Bringing Legal Realism to the Current Developments of the Case Law of "Horizontal" Direct Effects of Directives', Jean Monnet Working Paper, 7/02.

[42] Case 8/81 *Ursula Becker* [1982] ECR 53, at para 25, emphasis added.

in more objective terms, referring to the capacity of the norm to be invoked by individuals in national courts.[43] In *Becker*, and on numerous occasions since, the Court stated that '(..) *wherever the provisions of a directive appear, as far as their subject-matter is concerned, to be unconditional and sufficiently precise, those provisions may, in the absence of implementing measures adopted within the prescribed period, be relied upon as against any national provision which is incompatible with the directive* or *in so far as the provisions define rights which individuals must be able to assert against the State'*. It seems that the Court of Justice places both types of effects – creation of rights and invokability as standard for review – under the umbrella 'direct effect'. Direct effect is broader than the creation of rights, and also covers the situation of a (directly effective) provision being invoked as a *standard for review of national law*, besides the cases where rights as such are awarded.[44] The definition of invokability has further been distinguished according to the intended effects of the norm invoked, between *invocabilité de substitution* and *invocabilité d'exécution*.[45]

Also, provisions may be sufficiently clear and precise to be invoked in one case and not in another. For instance, in *Francovich* when discussing whether relevant provisions of the directive were sufficiently clear and unconditional to be invoked directly against the State, the Court held that they were indeed with respect to the amount due and the definition of the creditors, but not with respect to the debtor. Since the State had discretion with respect to the identity of the agency or fund obliged to pay the amounts due, the provisions could not be enforced directly against the State. Does this mean that it cannot be directly effective in other cases? It

---

[43] Among the many examples, note the following definitions: *'le droit de toute personne de demander à son juge de lui appliquer traités, règlements, directives ou décisions communautaires'*, R Lecourt, *L'Europe des juges* (Brussels, 1976) at 248; *'the possibility for an individual to invoke the Community law provisions concerned before his national court in order to protect his interests'*, J Mertens de Wilmars, 'De directe werking van het Europese recht', (1969) *SEW*, 66 (my translation).

[44] Michel Waelbroeck distinguished between *'effet direct positif'* or *'imméditateté'* on the one hand and *'effet direct simple ou négatif'* on the other, M Waelbroeck, 'L'immédiateté communautaire, caractéristique de la supranationalité: quelques conséquences pour la pratique', in *Le droit international de demain*, (Neuchâtel, 1974), 85-90; David Edward distinguishes between objective and subjective direct effect, D Edward, 'Direct Effect, the Separation of Powers and the Judicial Enforcement of Obligations', in *Scritti in onore di Giuseppe Federico Mancini, Vol II, Diritto dell' Unione Europea*, (Milano, Giuffrè, 1998) 423, at 442.

[45] Y Galmot and J-Cl Bonichot, 'Le Cour de justice des Communauté européennes et la transposition des directives en droit national', (1988) *RFDA*, 1; These authors seem to restrict the notion of direct effect to the alternative of *invocabilité de substitution*. Others add also the *invocabilité d'interprétation conforme* and the *invocabilité de réparation*, each of which would require different conditions of clarity and unconditionality: D Simon and A Rigaux, under Case C–334/92 *Wagner-Miret* [1993] ECR I–6911, Europe, February 1994, 9–10; Manin distinguishes between *'invocabilité dans le cadre de l'effet direct'* and *'invocabilité au-delà de l'effet direct'*, Ph Manin, 'L'invocabilité des directives: Quelques interrogations', (1990) *RTDeur*, 669.

may well be that in other cases, the directive could be invoked, for instance to set aside a national measure that was clearly not compatible with the provisions of the directive.

It has been argued that the *Becker*-type of direct effect is not really about direct effect,[46] but rather about a right to call for judicial review or a public law effect of a provision.[47] This resembles the French distinction between the *invocabilité d'exclusion* and the *invocabilité de substitution*. While these refinements may be helpful to understand the full extent of the notion of direct effect, and certainly have some appeal, introducing a distinction between direct effect and public law effect or similar classifications, adds to the confusion, rather than clarifying the notion of direct effect. Directly effective provisions must be enforced and applied in national courts in national procedures, giving rise, most often to national remedies. What would be the use of distinguishing between direct effect and public law effects? The practical effects of the difference between the two types of effects – both of which are in the case law of the Court brought under the expression direct effect – follow matter of factly from the type of procedure and the remedy sought. Crucial, in both cases, is the *possumus* and *non-possumus* of the courts.

Yet, the definition of direct effect with reference to the capacity of the directly effective provision to be invoked or relied on before the national courts is not entirely satisfactory either.[48] First, provisions of Community law may be invoked before national courts also in cases where direct effect is denied, for instance in State liability cases.[49] The Community norm is invoked in order to establish a breach of Community law committed by the State and causing harm to the individual, giving rise to a right to compensation. The notion of invokability does not therefore sufficiently differentiate between directly effective and non-directly effective provisions. Second, directly effective provisions of Community law may,

---

[46] For instance D Edward, 'Direct Effect, the Separation of Powers and the Judicial Enforcement of Obligations', in *Scritti in onore di Giuseppe Federico Mancini*, (Milano, Giuffrè, 1998) Vol II, 423, who stated that the case did not involve direct effect in the traditional sense and it would perhaps be as well to find another formula to avoid confusion, for instance the right to call for judicial review; J Scott has suggested that this type of cases should be referred to as instances not of direct effect but rather of 'public law effect', J Scott, *EC Environmental Law*, (London, Longman, 1998) at 123–124, 157–157; on the discussion see also C Hilson and T Downes, 'Making Sense of Rights: Community Rights in EC Law', (1999) 24 *ELR* 121; S Prechal, 'Does Direct Effect Still Matter?' (2000) 37 *CML Rev*, 1047, at 1051 *et seq*.

[47] A similar distinction was proposed by AG Saggio in his Opinion in Case C-149/96 *Portugal v Council (Portuguese Textiles Case)* [1999] ECR I-8395, at para 18.

[48] B de Witte, 'The Nature of the Legal Order', in P Craig and G de Burca (eds), *The Evolution of EU Law* (Oxford, OUP, 1999) 177, at 187.

[49] The obvious example is *Francovich* where the ECJ denied direct effect. The relevant provisions could not be relied upon to claim outstanding wages from the State; yet the applicants could claim compensation for the harm caused as a consequence of the violation of Community law on the part of the State.

and sometimes must, be applied by courts of their own motion, without having been invoked by an individual.[50]

4.1.4.3. *Justiciability*

Inherent both in *'the creation of rights'* and the *'invokability'* formulas is always the reference to the *duties of national courts* to apply directly effective Community law provisions. This is what direct effect is all about: a provision that has direct effect is one that is sufficiently legally perfect and that is suitable for judicial enforcement in a particular case: it all boils down to justiciability. A provision has direct effect when it is capable of judicial adjudication. This means, according to Pescatore, *'that "direct effect" of Community law rules in the last analysis depends less on the intrinsic qualities of the rules concerned than on the possumus or non possumus of the judges of the different Member States, on the assumption that they take these attitudes in a spirit of goodwill and with a constructive mind. To this extent, direct effect appears to be in a way 'l'art du possible', as from the point of view of Community law it is to be expected that national courts are willing to carry the operation of the rules of Community law up to the limits of what appears to be feasible, considering the nature of the judicial function. Within these bounds a rule has direct effect, whereas beyond them this effect must be denied'.*[51]

A hint of this definition of direct effect can be found for instance in *Fink-Frucht* where the Court held: *'The prohibition [of Article 95(2) of the EC Treaty] is therefore self-sufficient and legally complete and is thus capable of having direct effects on the legal relationships between the Member States and those subject to their jurisdiction. Although this provision involves the evaluation of economic factors, this does not exclude the right and duty of national courts to ensure that the rules of the Treaty are observed whenever they can ascertain (..) that the conditions necessary for the application of the articles are fulfilled'.*[52] More clearly, in several decisions concerning the Europe Agreements concluded with Central and Eastern European countries, the Court stated that the provisions in question established *'a precise and unconditional principle which is sufficiently operational to be applied by a national court and which is therefore capable of governing the legal position of individuals'.*[53] In the same vein, Advocate General van Gerven defined

---

[50] Joined Cases C–430/93 and 431/93 *Van Schijndel en van Veen v SPF* [1995] ECR I–4705; C–72/95 *Aannemersbedrijf Kraaijeveld BV v Provinciale Staten Zuid-Holland* [1996] ECR I–5403.

[51] P Pescatore, 'The Doctrine of "Direct Effect": An Infant Disease of Community Law', (1983) *ELR* 155, at 177.

[52] Case 27/67 *Firma Fink-Frucht GmbH v Hauptzollamt München-Landsbergerstrasse* [1968] ECR 227, at 232.

[53] Case C–63/99 *The Queen v Secretary of State for the Home Department, ex parte Gloszczuk and Gloszczuk* [2001] ECR I–6369; Case C–257/99 *The Queen v Secretary of State for the Home Department, ex parte Barkoci and Malik* [2001] ECR I–6557; Case C–235/99 *The Queen v Secretary of State for the Home Department, ex parte Kondova* [2001] ECR I–6427; Case C–268/99 *Jany and Others v Staatssecretaris van Justitie* [2001] ECR I–8615.

the directly effective provision as one that is *'sufficiently operational in itself to be applied by a court'*[54] in a given case. This is reminiscent of the long-standing definition of Chief Justice Marshall. The question of direct effect relates directly to the separation of powers and the definition and limits of the judicial function: the question is whether the provision is apt for judicial application, whether the courts can and should give effect to the provision. If, however, direct effect coincides with the question of *possumus* and *non-possumus, i.e.* with the question of what is feasible considering the 'nature of the judicial function', national and sub-national disparities re-surface, given the fact that 'the judicial function' is perceived differently in each system. *L'art du possible'* is not exactly a strict and uniform standard.[55] On the other hand, whether or not a provision has direct effect ultimately has to be decided by the Court of Justice, any national preconceptions about the judicial function notwithstanding.

The question of justiciability is a *technical* question (is the provision sufficiently clear, precise and unconditional), but it hides questions of *policy*: it concerns the appropriate role for a court to apply and enforce the provision. This is the essence of direct effect: it is the bottom line under general national constitutional law *concerning* international agreements, it was the crucial question in *Van Gend en Loos*, it is central in the discussion on the direct effect of directives, the question of direct effect under Title VI and concerning the direct effect of WTO law, namely whether it is *appropriate* for the courts to apply and enforce a particular provision, or whether, rather, intervention by other State organs is needed. At the same time, direct effect is not only about the relationship between courts and other State organs: it also refers to the relationship between the Union and the national levels. Acknowledging the direct effect of an EU rule in fact triggers the principle of primacy; it entails an obligation to set aside conflicting national rules without any prior intervention of national norm-giving authorities.[56] The

---

[54] Opinion of AG van Gerven in Case C–128/92 *Banks v British Coal* [1994] ECR I–1209, at para 27.

[55] AW Heringa has demonstrated that the courts may use the issue of direct effect (or rather, of *'één ieder verbindend'* under the Netherlands Constitution), which he considered to be a formal preliminary issue, in order to escape a decision on the merits, *ie* to check the compatibility of the content of a paritcular measure with a treaty provision. In order to avoid abuses and confusion on the notion, he suggested that it may have to be omitted. AW Heringa, 'Terug naar af: waarom het begrip een ieder verbindende bepalingen van verdragen slechts tot verwarring leidt', *Staatkundig Jaarboek*, (1985).

[56] So A Verhoeven, *The European Union in Search of a Democratic and Constitutional Theory* (Kluwer, 2002) at 312–313. It must however be stressed that supremacy has other effects, beyond direct effect; in other words, non-directly effective provisions of Community law are also supreme, but the obligations of national courts following from them will be different; this is further developed below.

discussion on the direct effect of WTO law may help clarifying these fundamental considerations.[57]

4.1.4.4. The Policy of Direct Effect

The Court of Justice has con sistently denied direct effect of GATT provisions: the latter could not be invoked and enforced before the national courts because of the spirit, general scheme and the terms of GATT, given the flexibility of its wording and the inadequacy of its dispute settlement system.[58] The Court also held that for the same reasons, the Court itself was precluded from taking into consideration the provisions of GATT when reviewing the lawfulness of Community acts in an action for annulment brought by a Member State.[59] The Court thus established a link between the possibility of invoking an international agreement for reviewing the validity of a Community and the fact that certain provisions of this agreement may be relied upon by individuals before national courts.[60] The absence of direct effect of an international agreement thus protects the validity of Community acts.[61] The denial of the direct effect of GATT and its unenforceability before the European Courts is particularly remarkable in the light of the case law of the Court of Justice relating to other international agreements agreed by the Community and its Member States, which can under certain circumstances have direct effect. When assessing the internal legal effects of international obligations of the EC, the Court applies a two-stage procedure. First, it examines the purpose and nature of the agreement itself, and secondly, if the agreements

---

[57] The issue is still hotly debated, see Joined cases C-364/95 and C-365/95, *T. Port GmbH* [1998] I-1023, in which the German referring court urged the ECJ to declare the direct effect of GATT 1994, since it could be invoked before a German court (at para 53). Since GATT did not apply to the facts of the case anyway, the ECJ did not go into the issue of direct effect. In Case C-149/96 *Portugal v Council (Portuguese Textiles Case)* [1999] ECR I-8395 the ECJ ruled out the direct effect of WTO law. On the direct effect of WTO and GATT see P Van den Bossche, 'The European Community and the Uruguay Round Agreements', in J Jackson and A Sykes (eds), *Implementing the Uruguay Round*, (Oxford, Clarendon Press, 1997) 23, at 92ff; P Eeckhout, 'The Domestic Legal Status of the WTO Agreement: Interconnecting Legal Systems', (1997) 34 *CML Rev*, 11; Th Cottier and K Nadakavukaren Schefer, 'The Relationship between World Trade Organization Law, National and Regional Law', (1998) *JIEL*, 83; J H J Bourgeois, 'The European Court of Justice and the WTO: Problems and Challenges', in J H H Weiler (ed), *The EU, the WTO and the NAFTA. Towards a Common Law of International Trade?*, (Oxford, OUP, 2000) 71; G de Búrca and J Scott (eds) *The EU and the WTO. Legal and Constitutional Issues*, (Oxford, Hart Publishing, 2001).

[58] Joined Cases 21-24/72 *International Fruit Company v Produktschap voor Groenten en Fruit* [1972] ECR 1219.

[59] Case C–280/93 *Germany v Council (Bananas)* [1994] ECR I–4973.

[60] GA Zonnekeyn, 'The Status of WTO Law in the EC Legal Order. The Final Curtain?', (2000) 34 *JWT*, 111, at 120.

[61] G Bebr, 'Agreements concluded by the Community and their possible direct effect: From International Fruit Company to Kupferberg', (1983) 20 *CML Rev* 35, at 46.

meets the required standards, it examines its wording.[62] With respect to GATT, the Court has never reached the second stage of scrutiny. For various other international agreements it has: the Court has awarded direct effect to provisions contained in Association Agreements intended to lead to membership,[63] Free Trade Agreements,[64] and to association agreements conferring non-reciprocal advantages on third States.[65] The stark distinction between GATT and other international agreements certainly is the weakest and least convincing aspect of its position on the direct effect of GATT.[66]

In the *Portuguese Textiles case,*[67] the Court had to give the long-awaited answer to the question whether the new GATT 1994 and the WTO Agreement would be awarded direct effect before national courts, and be enforceable before the European Courts, given the new dispute settlement procedure, and the more precise nature of its provisions. The Portuguese Government argued that the case was not about direct effect, but concerned the circumstances in which a Member State may rely on the WTO Agreements before the Court for the purpose of reviewing the legality of a Council regulation. Advocate General Saggio took up the distinction and stated that the provisions of international agreements may be held not to have direct effect and confer rights on individuals on which they may rely before national courts, but that did not exclude the possibility of the same provisions to be used as a criterion of legality to review the validity of Community acts. Saggio would allow the claim. The Court,

---

[62] *'It is settled case-law that a provision of an agreement entered into by the Community with non-member countries must be regarded as being directly applicable when, regard being had to the wording, purpose and nature of the agreement, it may be concluded that the provision contains a clear, precise and unconditional obligation which is not subject, in its implementation or effects, to the adoption of any subsequent measure'*, Joined Cases C–300/98 and C–392/98 *Parfums Christian Dior SA v TUK Consultancy BV and Assco Gerüste GmbH and Rob van Dijk v Wilhelm Layher GmbH & Co KG and Layher BV* [2000] ECR 11307, at para 42. See S Griller, 'Judicial Enforceability of WTO Law in the European Union. Annotation to Case C–146/96 *Portugal v Council'*, (2000) *JIEL*, 441, at 444–445.

[63] Case 17/81 *Pabst* [1982] ECR 1331 (Association agreement with Greece); see also Case C–63/99 *The Queen v Secretary of State for the Home Department, ex parte Gloszczuk and Gloszczuk* [2001] ECR I–6369; Case C–257/99 *The Queen v Secretary of State for the Home Department, ex parte Barkoci and Malik* [2001] ECR I–6557; Case C–235/99 99 *The Queen v Secretary of State for the Home Department, ex parte Kondova* [2001] ECR I–6427; Case C–268/99 *Jany and Others v Staatssecretaris van Justitie* [2001] ECR I–8615 (Europe agreements).

[64] For instance Case 104/81 *Kupferberg* [1982] ECR 3641 (Free trade agreement with Portugal).

[65] Case C–18/90 *Kziber* [1991] ECR I–199 (Maghreb agreements); Case 87/75 *Bresciani* [1976] ECR 129 (Yaoundé); Case C–469/93 *Chiquita Italia* [1995] ECR I–4533 (Lomé).

[66] See *e.g.* S Griller, 'Judicial Enforceability of WTO Law in the European Union. Annotation to Case C–146/96 *Portugal v Council'*, (2000) *JIEL*, 441; S Peers, 'Fundamental Right or Political Whim? WTO Law and the European Court of Justice', in G de Búrca and J Scott (eds), *The EU and the WTO Legal and Constitutional Issues* (Oxford, Hart Publishing, 2001) 111, at 119;

[67] Case C–149/96 *Portugal v Council (Portuguese Textiles Case)* [1999] ECR I–8395.

however, did not. It was implied in the judgment that the denial of WTO law as standard of legality of Community law in direct actions brought by Member States is understood in terms of direct effect.[68] The rationale for this denial was the question of justiciability and ultimately of the constitutional position of the courts: the Court of Justice considered it inappropriate for the 'domestic' courts (both European and national) to apply provisions of WTO law, since such may trepass on the province of legislative or executive organs of the Contracting Parties. Direct effect relates to the limits of the judicial function, and the appropriateness of the courts' involvement, as is clear from the following passages: '*to require the judicial organs to refrain from applying the rules of domestic law which are inconsistent with the WTO agreements would have the consequence of depriving the legislative or executive organs of the contracting parties of the possibility afforded by Article 22 of that memorandum of entering into negotiated arrangements even on a temporary basis*' and '*to accept that the role of ensuring that Community law complies with those rules devolves directly on the Community judicature would deprive the legislative or executive organs of the Community of the scope for manoeuvre enjoyed by their counterparts in the Community's trading partners*'.[69] The Court concluded by noting that its findings corresponded with the statements made by the Council in the preamble to the Decision approving the WTO Agreement and its Annexes on behalf of the Community.[70] It followed that, having regard to their nature and structure, the WTO agreements were not in principle among the rules in the light of which the Court was to review the legality of measures adopted by the Community institutions. In later cases the Court would state clearly that in the same vein, the provisions of WTO law lacked direct effect, and for the same reasons as those mentioned in the *Portuguese Textiles* case, were not '*such as to create rights upon which individuals may rely directly before the courts by virtue of Community law*'. However, in areas where the Community had already legislated, the judicial authorities of the Member States were required by virtue of Community law, when called upon to apply national rules with a view to ordering provisional measures for the protection of rights falling within such a field, to do so as far as possible in the light of the wording and purpose of Article 50 of TRIPs. And in a field in respect of which the Community had not yet legislated and which consequently fell within the competence of the Member States, the protection of intellectual property rights, and measures adopted for that purpose by the judicial authorities, did not fall within the scope of Community law. Accordingly, Community law neither required

---

[68] The notion of 'direct applicability' is used, para 44; as is the notion of the 'effect in the internal legal order', at para 34 and the notion of 'rules applicable by the judicial organs when reviewing the legality of their rules of domestic law', at para 43.

[69] Case C–149/96 *Portugal v Council* [1999] ECR I–8395, at paras 40 and 46.

[70] Decision 94/800 [1994] OJ L 336/1.

nor forbade that the legal order of a Member State should accord to individuals the right to rely directly on the rule laid down by Article 50(6) of TRIPs or that it should oblige the courts to apply that rule of their own motion. In other words, in those areas the question of direct effect was left to national law.[71] Clearly, these are all political decisions of a Court that does not want to become involved in trade wars.

Turning back to mainstream Community law: can it be said, with reference to Pescatore and Chief Justice Marshall, that the answer is in fact as simple as this: the judge should do with the norm exactly what he would do with it if it were 'an act of the national legislature', the direct effect of which is never questioned? That direct effect has become the normal state of Community law? Maybe, in the context of most of Community law, this is what the question of direct effect has become: it was a childhood sickness that has been cured, and direct effect has become the normal state of Community; the only question which the national court, if necessary upon a reference to Luxembourg, must answer is whether the provision is legally perfect and can be applied in a court of law, for various reasons: to be applied to the facts of the case, or as a standard of review.[72] The policy questions as to whether it is appropriate for the national courts to apply and enforce Community law have been answered: they have become the common courts of Community law, they are first in line in the application and enforcement of Community law. This is also the limit of the definition of direct effect in the sense of justiciability in the context of Community law: it only works in the context of the enforcement of *Community* law, and not in the context of WTO law for instance, when Community law is under attack: there, the question of direct effect is more than one of *technical* justiciability, since the underlying *policy* question – is it appropriate for the courts enforce the obligations imposed on the Community and the Member States against the Community? – has been answered differently. Nevertheless, also in mainstream Community law there are exceptions to the ground rule that direct effect coincides with the question of justiciability once the policy question of the appropriateness of judicial application is answered. In the case of directives, for instance, *horizontal* direct effect is still excluded, even if the provision is sufficiently clear and precise to be applied by a court. However, direct effect triggers supremacy, it does not only involve the national courts in a neutral manner: it transforms them into review courts. Even in the context of mainstream Community law, direct effect is more than a technical question of justiciability.

---

[71] For a critique of the decision see G Bontinck, 'The TRIPs Agreement and the ECJ: A New Dawn? Some comments About Joined Cases C–300/98 and C–392/98 *Parfums Dior and Assco Gerüste'*, Jean Monnet Working Paper 16/01.

[72] 'Community law can be applied be national courts if it meets the requirements for the specific judicial use sought', see G Isaac, *Droit communautaire général* (Paris, Masson, 1994) at 169.

4.1.4.5. *Justiciability and Corrections*

The notion of justiciability does not therefore cover the full extent of the notion of direct effect: it does not, for instance, include the obligation of other authorities than courts to give effect to directly effective provisions of Community law.[73] In *Costanzo*, the Court held that *'when the conditions under which the Court has held that individuals may rely on the provisions of a directive before the national courts are met, all organs of the administration, including decentralised authorities such as municipalities, are obliged to apply those provisions'*.[74] The definition of the content of the concept of direct effect given by Prechal is helpful: *'Direct effect is the obligation of a court or another authority to apply the relevant provision of Community law, either as a norm which governs the case or as a standard for judicial review'*.[75]

To sum up, what is direct effect? Probably the most complete answer would be: All of the above. Direct effect has to do with the creation of rights for individuals, with the possibility to be relied on before national courts and other tribunals, and it concerns the justiciability of the provision and its applicability by administrative organs.[76]

4.1.5. The Conditions for Direct Effect

The conditions for direct effect mirror the idea of justiciability: a provision is considered to produce direct effects where is it sufficiently clear, precise, and unconditional. What is required is that the provision is legally perfect. The concrete measure of precision and unconditionality varies according to the concrete case and procedure and the remedy requested. In cases restricted to judicial review of national legislation

---

[73] The definition of direct effect in terms of justiciability does not answer all questions. There are more technical questions: What does 'to apply' mean? *How* should it apply it? To what effect? What should the court do with it? These questions have been answered by the Court in its case law on second-generation issues, discussed below.

[74] Case 103/88 *Fratelli Costanzo SpA v Comune di Milano* [1989] ECR 1839.

[75] S Prechal, *Directives in European Community law'* (Oxford, Clarendon Press, 1995) at 276; In the context of classic international law, John Jackson has defined 'direct applicability' as expressing the notion that the international treaty instrument has a 'direct' statute-like role in the domestic legal system, but it is not meant to differentiate between different kinds of such direct roles, see JH Jackson, 'Status of Treaties in Domestic Legal Systems: A Policy Analysis', (1992) 86 *AJIL*, 310, at 310; he does make the proviso that his definition will not in all respects coincide with the notion of direct effect in Community law.

[76] In Case C–431/92 *Commission v Germany (Grosskrotzenburg)* [1995] ECR I–2189, the notion of direct effect *vis-à-vis* administrative authorities (the duty to implement them directly) was linked to the sufficiently clear and obligations imposed by the directive; the case is special because it was an infringement procedure and involved no private parties. Germany based its defense on a restrictive definition of direct effect. Also in the early cases allowing for direct (or rather similar) effect of directives was the right of individuals to rely on the directive intimately linked to the obligations imposed on the State, Case 41/74 *Van Duyn* [1974] ECR 1337.

aimed at setting it aside, the courts may take into consideration provisions which leave a certain discretion to the national authorities, and are accordingly not entirely unconditional as the original definition would have it. The fact that the Member States have discretion under the directive does not preclude judicial review of the question whether the national authorities have exceeded their powers.[77] If however the directly effective provision must be applied by way of substitution of the disapplied norm, or in the absence of such norm, the measure of clarity required will be greater, given that the courts must not take over the role of the authorities entitles to make the discretionary decisions left open in the Community provision. Direct effect is not only awarded on grounds of the clarity and precision of the relevant provisions. It has been demonstrated that in the context of international agreements and WTO, regard will also be had to the spirit, aim and purpose of the agreement. Provisions must be intended to have direct effect.

4.1.6. The Effects of Direct Effect

4.1.6.1. Empowerment

Direct effect brings about an *empowerment* at three levels: *Individuals* are granted rights by Community law directly – with all the caveats discussed above – without the need for intervention by national law. National *administrative authorities* must equally apply directly effective Community law, and must not await the intervention by the Legislature. Third, and most importantly in this context, the *national courts* are drawn into the application and enforcement of Community law. They must protect the rights which individuals derive directly from Community law, and use Community law as a standard of reference when ruling on the validity of national law. Conversely, the denial of direct effect means that individuals cannot rely on these provisions directly and that courts cannot as such apply and enforce them. The implementation of the provision is left to the competent administrative and legislative authorities. As for the courts, they may have other obligations in the presence of a non-directly effective

---

[77]   Case 51/76 *Verbond van Nederlandse Ondernemingen (VNO)* [1977] ECR 113; Case 38/77 *Enka BV v Inspecteur der Invoerrechten en Accijnzen* [1977] ECR 2203; Case 21/78 *Knud Oluf Delkvist v Anklagemyndigheden* [1978] ECR 2327; Case C–72/95 *Aannemersbedrijf Kraaijeveld BV v Gedeputeerde Staten van Zuid-Holland* [1996] ECR I–5403; Case C–435/97 *WWF and Others v Autonome Provinz Bozen and Others* [1999] ECR I–5613; Case 287/98 *Luxembourg v Berthe Linster and Others* [2000] ECR I–6917; for administrative authorities, a similar obligations is apparent from Case C–431/92 *Commission v German (Grosskrotzenburg)* [1995] ECR I2189, where the ECJ held that despite the fact that there was some discretion left to the national authorities, they were (at least) under an obligation to carry out an environmental impact assessment.

provision of Community law: they may have to interpret conflicting national law as far as possible in line with the non-directly effective provision. They may also have to hold a public body liable for violations of non-directly effective provisions of Community law. Direct effect may be the alpha of the judicial mandate under Community law; it is not its omega.

4.1.6.2. Decentralised Enforcement

Through the notion of direct effect, individuals and national courts have been involved in the judicial enforcement of Community law against the Member States.[78] The Treaties provide for only one form of enforcement of Community obligations against the Member States, which is mainly a traditional internationalist mechanism: the enforcement procedure of Articles 226 and 227 EC. This form of public enforcement[79] is deficient for several reasons.[80] The limitations of public enforcement have been alleviated by the Court of Justice by making the national courts its allies in *Van Gend en Loos*. The Court of Justice and the Commission are no longer solely responsible for ensuring the enforcement of Community obligations of the Member States; that task is now shared with the national courts. Likewise, the Commission is assisted by 'vigilant individuals'. Public enforcement through Article 226 EC and private enforcement before the national courts are essentially different in their effects at the remedial level. Whereas enforcement actions can only lead to a declaratory judgment by the Court of Justice establishing that a Member State has infringed its Treaty obligations, enforcement before the national courts intends to provide an adequate sanction and effective protection for those concerned. Decentralised enforcement also has the advantage that it brings the Member States before their own courts, which they cannot disobey.[81] Direct effect mostly concerns the protection of the individual who derives rights from Community law. The protection of the Community right of individuals often at the same time also leads to the enforcement of Community law against the Member State who is forced to comply with its obligations. In some cases will direct effect impose obligations on individuals.

---

[78] See Chr Boch, 'The Iroquois at the Kirchberg: Some Naïve Remarks on the Status and Relevance of Direct Effect', in JA Usher (ed), The State of the European Union: Structure *Enlargement and Economic Union* (London, Longman, 2000) 21.

[79] See PP Craig, 'Once upon a Time in the West: Direct Effect and the Federalization of EEC Law', (1992) *OJLS*, 453, at 454.

[80] See above.

[81] See JHH Weiler, 'The Transformation of Europe', (1991) *Yale LJ*, 2403, at 2421; and PP Craig, 'Once upon a Time in the West: Direct Effect and the Federalization of EEC Law', (1992) *OJLS*, 453, at 456.

4.1.6.3. Securing Compliance

Direct effect makes provisions of (Community) law real; it gives them teeth. The fate of provisions of WTO law in the case law of the Court of Justice proves the point: while WTO law may be enforced at the WTO level under the new dispute settlement system, it remains to some extent ineffective, since it lacks direct enforcement by national courts. This is probably the reason also why the Member States have chosen to expressly deny direct effect to decisions and framework decisions in the context of Title VI of the TEU. At the end of the day, direct effect, especially when coupled with supremacy, concerns the issue of how serious the obligations under the Treaty are considered to be.

4.1.7. The Usefulness of Direct Effect

Does direct effect still matter?[82] It has been argued that direct effect is merely a childhood sickness that can be overcome and make the patient stronger.[83] Some have suggested that the notion of direct effect may be abused by national courts to escape their obligations under Community law, and should therefore be omitted.[84] Others argue that it is too confusing and that it now restricts rather than extends the application of Community law by the national courts. Prechal has made the strongest case against the preservation of direct effect in the context of Community law. I would agree with many of her observations: the concept has become diluted and may lead to confusion rather than assist in addressing the relevant issues. 'Direct effect' has as many meanings as there are domestic legal systems in the Union, as the concept is understood differently in the various legal systems. The context in which the concept is operating nowadays has changed, with the national courts involved in reviewing the State's behaviour in the international context, and the national legislative, administrative and judicial institutions acting as 'agents' of the Community legal order.[85]

---

[82] Sacha Prechal has argued that 'the process of integration has reached a level at which the usefulness of the concept of direct effect must be questioned, to say the least', S Prechal, 'Does Direct Effect Still Matter?', (2000) 37 *CML Rev*, 1047, at 1067–1068; see also by the same author, 'Direct Effect Reconsidered, Redefined and Rejected', in JM Prinssen and A Schrauwen (eds), *Direct Effect. Rethinking a Classic of EC Legal Doctrine* (Groningen, Europa Law Publishing, 2002) 15.

[83] P Pescatore, 'The Doctrine of 'Direct Effect: An Infant Disease of Community Law', (1983) 8 *ELR* 155.

[84] See in the context of Netherlands constitutional law AW Heringa, 'Terug naar af: waarom het begrip een ieder verbindende bepaling van verdragen slechts tot verwarring leidt', *Staatkundig Jaarboek*, (1985).

[85] So S Prechal, 'Direct Effect Reconsidered, Redefined and Rejected', in JM Prinssen and A Schrauwen (eds), *Direct Effect. Rethinking a Classic of EC Legal Doctrine* (Groningen, Europa Law Publishing, 2002) 15, at 23.

I would argue, however, that the notion of direct effect still matters a great deal and that it should not be rejected in the context of Union law. First, it would seem irresponsible to remove the notion of direct effect, with, it is agreed, all its imperfections and difficulties, from the dialogue between national courts and the Court of Justice. It has become the language of Community law, and still matters a great deal in fine-tuning the involvement of national courts in the application and enforcement of Community law. What message would the Court be sending to the national courts if it answered a court asking whether a particular provision produced direct effect, that it did not really matter? Second, while it may be true that in the context of mainstream Community law direct effect has become so widespread and diluted that it has lost its explanatory value and says nothing about Community law which cannot also be said about national law, Community law *is* not national law. It *is* still 'foreign' law of a special kind, which takes precedence over national law, and which may impose special duties on the national courts and create new remedies for individuals. Third, the notion still plays an important role in the case of directives, where the exclusion of horizontal direct effect has to do only with the character of the parties, not with justiciability and the quality of the provision.[86] The other obvious area is that of WTO law where the policy question hidden in the notion of justiciability is answered differently. Furthermore, and this is a very important point, the notion may well begin a new life and gain relevance once questions concerning non-Community Union law start reaching the Court. Direct effect, and the role of the Court of Justice in deciding issues related to the notion, may well become an important element to distinguish between mainstream Community law and non-Community Union law, even if the formal distinction were to disappear should the pillars be merged. The very fact that direct effect may appear to have become superfluous in the context of first pillar law, does not mean that it can simply be rejected. Precisely because of its significance in distinguishing Community law from non-Community Union law, it retains its fundamental importance in the context of the European Union.[87] In addition, the number of international agreements concluded in and outside the framework of Community and Union law is rapidly increasing. In this area the notion is certainly still necessary in order to differentiate and define the duties of national courts. Finally, it may well be that the question of direct effect is just a label for a phenomenon inherent in all legal contexts in establishing

---

[86] Admittedly, Prechal does not make 'direct effect' coincide with justiciability; she seems to consider it as a preliminary condition, above, at 1067.

[87] Sacha Prechal agrees, in a footnote, that the question may be different in the context of non-Community Union law, but she does not elaborate the issue further. In my view, the difference between manistream Community law and the remainder of Union law proves the continuing importance of the notion.

in specific cases who is actually bound by a legal act or who is addressed by it.[88] In that sense, and given that the principle has not proved inadequate to answer this type of questions, there is no reason to omit it.[89]

4.1.8. Direct Effect of Non-Community Union Law?

Direct effect has expanded from Community Treaty provisions, over regulations, directives, decisions and certain international agreements. However, what is the internal effect of the law deriving from the second and third pillars, *i.e.* non-Community Union Law? Can it be invoked before the national courts? Can or must the national courts protect rights which individuals may derive from it? Do individuals derive any rights from it? There are two important elements which complicate the case for direct effect. First, Article 34 EU expressly excludes direct effect of framework decisions and decisions adopted under Title VI EU. Second, the Court of Justice has very reduced jurisdiction in the third pillar, and none in the second pillar.

Article 34 (2)(b) and (c) EU state that *framework decisions* and *decisions* adopted in the framework of Title VI EU '*shall not entail direct effect*'. It is for the first time that the text of the Treaties mentions the notion of '*direct effect*'. Until the Treaty of Amsterdam, the notion was absent from the text of the Treaties, and had remained entirely judge-made, even if it is considered one of the cornerstones of the European constitutional construct, one of its 'twin pillars'. At a time when the usefulness concept of direct effect is being questioned in the context of Community law,[90] it is excluded *expressis verbis* from part of European Union law. The policy question has now been answered by the Member States in the constitutional document: courts should not be involved (in a specified manner) in the enforcement of these decisions, and individuals are not considered to derive rights directly from them. Or with a touch of malice: are the decisions and framework decisions not to be considered excessively compulsory?

What exactly does it mean that framework decisions and decisions '*shall not entail direct effect*'? The exclusion may either be absolute in the sense that direct effect is excluded both as a matter of Union law and from the national perspective; or it may, alternatively, be restricted to an exclusion

---

88 LFM Besselink, 'Curing a 'Childhood Sickness'? On Direct Effect, Internal Effect, Primacy and Derogation from Civil Rights. The Netherlands Council of State Judgment in the *Metten* Case', (1996) 3 *MJ*, 165, at 170.

89 S Prechal suggests that direct effect could be omitted and be replaced with the 'usual' questions relating to the applicability of the rule to a particual legal relationship, etc., which play a role in the context of applying any norm. I fail to see how and why the exclusion of direct effect would make the answer to such questions any easier.

90 S Prechal, 'Does Direct Effect Still Matter?', (2000) 37 *CML Rev*, 1047, at 1067–68.

as a matter of Union law. The latter alternative would imply that it is a matter for national law whether or not the relevant provisions may entail direct effect. Direct effect is, then, denied only as a matter of European law, and the question may be answered differently from the point of view of national constitutional law. National courts, may, in cases coming before them, have to answer the issue on the basis of their own national constitutional rules, as was the case with Community law before *Van Gend en Loos*.[91] Consequently, the question of the direct effect of a provision of a framework decision or a decision may be answered differently in various Member States, and Title VI law will not be uniformly applied and enforced. Nevertheless, even if it is assumed that the issue of direct effect may be answered in accordance with national constitutional law, direct effect will most likely be rejected. In order to ascertain whether a norm produces direct effects or is self-executing, the judge will first look at the text of the Treaty. In this case the Treaty expressly denies direct effect and the national judge will probably accept the expressed intention of the Contracting Parties and deny direct effect.

Direct effect in Community law means that individuals and national courts become involved, as a matter of Community law and in each Member State alike, in the application and enforcement of Community law; individuals can derive rights from directly effective provisions of Community law and national courts are under an obligation, a 'mandate', to protect them. Direct effect adds, to public enforcement procedure of Article 226 EC,[92] a form of 'private enforcement', whereby the national courts become the common courts of Community law and, mostly on the instigation of individuals, enforce Community law, most often against defiant Member States. The tenor of the entire Title VI of the EU is the denial of the involvement of individuals,[93] and courts, both national[94]

---

[91] See the submissions of the Netherlands and Belgian Governments in Case 26/62 *Van Gend en Loos* [1963] ECR 1.

[92] There is virtually no parallel to Art. 226 EC (Art. 169 of the Treaty) infringement actions against the Member States. A partial substitute is to be found in Art. 35(7) EU granting jurisdiction to the Court to rule on any dispute between Member States regarding the interpretation or the application of acts adopted under Art. 34(2) EU whenever such dispute cannot be settled by the Council within six months; and jurisdiction to rule on any dispute between Member States and the Commission regarding the interpretation or application of conventions under Art. 34(2)(d) EU.

[93] In a Title on Police and Judicial Cooperation in Criminal Matters, which is so related to individuals and their (fundamental) rights! Art. 6 EU does proclaim the Union's respect for human rights and fundamental freedoms and states that the Union shall respect fundamental rights, as guaranteed by the ECHR and as they result from the common constitutional traditions of the Member States, as general principles of Community law. Yet, while under Art. 46 EU the Court's jurisdiction applies to Art. 6 EU, it does not grant additional jurisdiction where it did not already exist under the EC Treaty or the EU Treaty.

[94] Through the denial of direct effect.

and European.[95] The Court of Justice has acquired competences under this Title, but these are aimed mostly at controlling the Union institutions, not the Member States, who escape review, both from the Court of Justice[96] and their own courts.[97] The question will arise whether the Strasbourg Court of Human Rights may become involved instead.[98] On the other hand, given that there is a system of preliminary references under Article 35 EU, it must have been presumed that national courts could be confronted with cases under Title VI of the TEU, including decisions and framework decisions. In fact, the first references for preliminary ruling have been made, in the cases of *Hüseyn Gözütok and Klaus Brügge*. In these cases, one of the courts had asked about the effect of a provision of the Schengen Implementing Convention. The Advocate General stated that the Court did not have jurisdiction to answer the question and had to restrict itself to explaining the autonomous interpretation of the relevant provisions.[99] It may be recalled that in *Van Gend en Loos*, the mere existence of the preliminary rulings procedure was used by the Court as one of the grounds for accepting the direct effect doctrine: *'In addition, the task assigned to the Court of Justice under Article 177, the object of which is to secure uniform interpretation of the Treaty by national courts and tribunals, confirms that the states have acknowledged that Community law has an authority which can be invoked by their nationals before those courts and tribunals'*.[100] In the case of Title VI, the Court would have to refine this statement, and add that 'an authority which can be invoked by their nationals before those courts' would have to mean something other than 'direct effect' in the sense of first pillar law.

As to the merits, what exactly does it mean that a provision *'shall not entail direct effect'*? It seems logical simply to reverse what direct effects means. With respect to the initial meaning of 'direct effect' as creating rights for individuals, the exclusion of direct effect could be taken to mean that a framework decision 'does not create rights for individuals': individuals must await the implementation of the framework decision by the national authorities and until such time as the framework decision is of no avail to them. In the context of the more procedural notion of invokability – direct effect as the possibility to invoke a provision – exclusion of direct effect would then mean that individuals cannot rely on the relevant

---

95   This aspect is developed further below. as M Shapiro put it: *'To exclude the Court of Justice from the pillar of justice is a bit much'*, in M Shapiro, 'The European Court of Justice', in P Craig and G de Búrca (eds), *The Evolution of EU Law*, (Oxford, OUP, 1999), 321, at 344.
96   In the absence of a 'real' enforcement procedure.
97   Due to the absence of direct effect.
98   The question will be discussed further below.
99   Opinion of AG Ruíz-Jarabo-Colomer in Cases C–187/01 *Criminal proceedings against Hüseyn Gözütok* and C–385/01 *Criminal proceedings against Klaus Brügge* [2003] ECR I–1345.
100   Case 26/62 *Van Gend en Loos* [1963] ECR 1, at p 12.

provision before a national court. Where direct effect is meant to connote the justiciability of the norm or 'the obligation of a court or another authority to apply the relevant provision of Community law, either as a norm which governs the case, or as a standard for review',[101] the exclusion of direct effect would mean something like national courts and other authorities being precluded from applying the relevant provision either as a norm governing the case or as a standard for review.

Now, given that the express exclusion of direct effect amounts to an exception in Union law, it can be argued that it must be interpreted restrictively. The denial of direct effect could be limited to a denial of 'the creation of rights for individuals', while allowing the provision to be invoked as a criterion of legality for national acts.[102] In line with the French approach distinguishing between the *'invocabilité de substitution'* and the *'invocabilité d'exclusion'*, the refutation of direct effect could be taken to rule out the possibility for a national judge to apply a provision of a framework decision or a decision to a concrete case, but to permit him to merely set aside conflicting national law. Thus the courts would have an important part[103] in enforcing these measures against the Member States.

Guidance on the interpretation of the denial of direct effect in Article 34 EU may come from the Court of Justice: it may not grant direct effect to decisions and framework decisions, yet, it may interpret the provisions of Title VI themselves, and thus may be interrogated about the meaning of the phrase *'shall not entail direct effect'* in Article 34 (2)(b) and (c) EU. Nevertheless, the notion of *'interpretation'* is the same as under Article 234 EC, which, ever since *Van Gend en Loos*, includes the interpretation of the effects of particular measures of Community law in the domestic legal order including the issue of direct effect. For this type of Union law, however, the answer is given in the Treaty: these provisions are not to be awarded direct effect. It is not likely that the Court will derive from the text of Article 34 EU and decide to make it a question for the Court to answer. As the Court stated long time ago in *Kupferberg 'Only if* [the question concerning the internal effects] *has not been settled by the agreement does it*

---

[101] S Prechal, *Directives in European Community Law* (Oxford, Clarendon Press, 1995) 276; see also her 'Does Direct Effect Still Matter?', (2000) 37 *CML Rev* 1047, at 1048.

[102] Similar to the distinction proposed by AG Saggio in his Opinion in Case C–149/96 *Portugal v Council (Portuguese Textiles Case)* [1999] ECR I–8395, at para 18, concerning the issue whether, in an action for annulment brought by a privileged applicant, the provisions of GATT or the WTO Agreement could be recognized as binding on the Community institutions and therefore as a criterion of legality, even though such provision may be held not to produce direct effects in the sense that they conferring rights for individuals which they may invoke before national courts. The Court rejected the distinction in its judgment. See *eg* GA Zonnekeyn, 'The status of WTO law in the Community legal order: some comments in the light of the *Portuguese Textiles* case', (2000) 25 *ELR* 293.

[103] The role of the ECJ is extremely limited in this respect in the absence of a veritable enforcement procedure and the restricted preliminary rulings procedure.

fall for decision by the courts having jurisdiction in the matter, and in particular by the Court of Justice within the framework of its jurisdiction under the Treaty, in the same manner as any question of interpretation relating to the application of the agreement in the Community'.[104] In the case concerning the direct effect of WTO the Court referred to the exclusion of direct effect in the Decision of the Council adopting the WTO Agreement on the part of the Community.[105]

Finally, for the remainder of non-Community Union law, other than the decisions and framework decisions, with respect to which the Treaty is silent, the question of direct effect will have to be answered by the Court of Justice and the national courts. The only complicating factor is that given the restricted version of preliminary rulings in this context, not all national courts may be able to invoke the assistance of the Court of Justice. They will then have to address the question of direct effect themselves.

4.2.   THE DOCTRINE OF SUPREMACY

If direct effect, for the national courts, constitutes an instruction to apply Community law in a certain way,[106] supremacy explains its relation to national law and implies mostly an obligation for the national courts to disapply conflicting measures of Community law, resulting from the duty to apply Community law (with precedence). As in the case of direct effect, the Treaty is silent on the question of the relationship between national law and Community law. It was created or discovered by the Court of Justice. The question of the *domestic* relation of treaty provisions with conflicting provisions of national law is one, which, in traditional international law is for the national legal order to decide. International law prevails over national law before international courts, but there is no rule in international law, which imposes supremacy of the international norm *before national courts.* Evidently, the failure of the national courts to enforce the international obligations of the State may entail the international liability of the State if the failure to award supremacy to the treaty provision leads to a violation of the State's obligations thereunder. Nonetheless, there is no obligation under international law for domestic courts to grant precedence to treaties over national law. In contrast, the Court of Justice dictates

---

[104] Case 104/81 *Hauptzollamt Mainz v CA Kupferberg & Cie KG a.A* [1982] ECR 3641, at para 17.
[105] It did not however use it as one of its main arguments. It merely seemed to add it to its other argument, almost like an obiter. Yet, there is an important distinction with the case of the TEU where the exclusion is part of the body agreed upon by the Contracting Parties, while in the case of the WTO the denial of direct effect is contained in a unilateral document.
[106] As a rule governing the case or a standard for review: The duties of national courts reach beyond the limits of direct effect: conform interpretation, 'indirect effect' and the Francovich mandate are the main examples, see below.

supremacy as an inherent feature of Community law, and the domestic constitutional rules and principles relating to the status of Community law in the internal legal order cannot prevent acceptance of the principle.

4.2.1. The Meaning of Supremacy

The Community version of supremacy – or primacy – is unequivocal and uncompromising: within the scope of Community law, the bulk of Community law *including 'the most minor piece of technical Community legislation ranks above the most cherished constitutional norm'*.[107] The principle was first stated[108] in that other constitutional case, *Costa-ENEL*,[109] which immediately focused on *judicial* supremacy (or priority or precedence), rather than *normative* supremacy, which would imply that the Community norms is higher in rank than national law.[110] Judicial supremacy means that because of its very nature, Community law, deriving from an autonomous source and constituting an integral part of the national legal orders cannot be *judicially* overridden by domestic legal provisions, however framed.[111] Consequently, supremacy implies that national courts cannot allow national law to override Community law, and must accordingly set aside conflicting national law. This is the mature formula of precedence in the hands of the national courts: *'a national court which is called upon, within the limits of its jurisdiction, to apply provisions of Community law is under a duty to give full effect to those provisions, if necessary refusing of its own motion to apply any conflicting provision of national legislation, and it is not necessary for the court to request or await the prior setting aside of such provision by legislative or other constitutional means'.*[112]

But the principle of supremacy is much greater, and is addressed to *all* state authorities. For the *national legislatures*, supremacy means that they are under an obligation to bring national law in line with Community law[113] and that they are precluded from validly adopting new legislative

---

[107] S Weatherill, *Law and Integration in the European Union* (Oxford, OUP, 1995) 106.
[108] Though not in those words: the ECJ has never used the word 'supremacy'. It rather refers to the principle as 'precedence'; also the notion of 'primacy' is used, so C–118/00 *Gervais Larsy v Inasti* [2001] ECR I–5063; Case C–224/97 *Erich Ciola v Land Vorarlberg* [1999] ECR I–2517; Joined Cases C–397/98 and C–410/98 *Metalgesellschaft Ltd and Hoechst v Commissioners of Inland Revenu* [2001] ECR I–1727.
[109] Case 6/64 *Costa v ENEL* [1964] ECR 585.
[110] It is submitted that this is not the only way of viewing the relationship between the national and Community legal order, while allowing for the precedence of Community law. This point is discussed below.
[111] The English version of *Costa v ENEL* is not conclusive; the French version, however, clearly states that Community law *'ne pourrait se voir judiciairement opposer un texte interne quel qu'il soit'.*
[112] Case C–184/89 *Helga Nimz v City of Hamburg* [1991] ECR I–297, at para 19.
[113] Case 48/71 *Commission v Italy* [1972] ECR 527; Case 167/73 *Commission v France (French maritime labour code)* [1974] ECR 365; Case 104/86 *Commission v Italy* [1988] ECR 1799; Case C–197/96 *Commission v France (nightwork for women)* [1997] ECR I–1489.

measures to the extent to which these would be incompatible with Community provisions.[114] The latter statement in *Simmenthal* was clarified in *IN.CO.GE. '90* where the Court explained that it cannot be inferred from *Simmenthal* that the incompatibility with Community law of a subsequently adopted rule of national law has the effect of rendering that rule of national law non-existent: Faced with such a situation, the national court is, however, obliged to disapply that rule, provided always that this obligation does not restrict the power of the competent national courts to apply, from among the various procedures available under national law, those which are appropriate for protecting the individual rights conferred by Community law.[115]

Under *Costanzo*,[116] administrative authorities, including decentralised authorities such as municipalities, are equally obliged to give effect to Community law and to refrain from applying conflicting provisions of national law. The case is often discussed under the heading 'administrative direct effect', rather than as an aspect of supremacy. In fact, the case concerned both the direct effect and supremacy of Community law before administrative authorities; but it is the supremacy aspect of the principle which is most shocking from a national constitutional perspective. In *Ciola* the Court said: *'While the Court initially held that it is for the national court to refuse if necessary to apply any conflicting provision of national law* [Simmenthal], *it subsequently refined its case law in two respects. Thus it appears from the case law, first, that all administrative bodies, including decentralised authorities, are subject to that obligation as to primacy, and individuals may therefore rely on such a provision of Community law against them* [Fratelli Costanzo].[117] From a Community perspective, this position is unsurprising and the reasoning of the Court, based on Article 10 EC (Article 5 of the old Treaty) seems convincing.[118] The duty imposed on the administrative authorities to ensure that the rules, which they apply comply with

---

[114] Case 106/77 *Simmenthal* [1978] ECR 585, para 17; some concluded from this statement that conflicting subsequently adopted legislation would be non-existent, see for instance, A Barav, 'Les effets du droit communautaire directement applicable', (1978) *CDE*, 265, at 273 *et seq.*

[115] Joined Cases C–10/97 to C–22/97 *Ministero delle Finanze v INCOGE'90 Srl and others* [1998] ECR I–6307, at para 21.

[116] Case 103/88 *Fratelli Costanzo SpA v Comune di Milano* [1989] ECR 1839.

[117] Case C–224/97 *Erich Ciola v Land Vorarlberg* [1999] ECR I–2517, at paras 29–30. The Court continued: *'Second, provisions of national law which conflict with such a provision of Community law may be legislative or administrative [reference omitted]. It is consistent with that case law that those administrative decisions of national law should include not only general abstract rules but also specific individual administrative decisions'*, paras 31–32.

[118] 'It would, moreover, be contradictory to rule that an individual may rely upon the provisions of a directive (..) before the national courts seeking an order against the administrayive authorities and yet to hold that those authorities are under no obligation to apply the provisions of the directive and to refrain from applying provisions of national law which conflict with them', Case 103/88 *Fratelli Costanzo SpA v Comune di Milano* [1989] ECR 1839, at para 31.

Community law derives from the supremacy of Community law and the obligation imposed on the State as such, and therefore *all* state authorities including administrative organs, that Community law is duly enforced. Yet, from a national constitutional perspective, what the Court of Justice is requesting from the administrative authorities is tantamount to a constitutional enormity. In all Member States, the administrative authorities are subjected to the law: such is the essence of the rule of law. Nevertheless, the Court is asking these administrative organs to review and set aside national primary legislation in the light of Community law.[119]

Turning back now to the national courts, the general principle of supremacy may cover two types of cases: substantive supremacy on the one hand and structural or procedural supremacy on the other. *Substantive supremacy* concerns the primacy of a substantive provision of Community law over a norm of national law: '(..) *Every national court must, in a case within its jurisdiction, apply Community law in its entirety and protect rights which the latter confers on individuals and must accordingly set aside any provision of national law which may conflict with it, whether prior or subsequent to the Community rule.*'[120] This substantive supremacy is the essence of supremacy and covers the 'normal' use of the notion.[121] *Structural supremacy* concerns the duty of national courts to set aside procedural rules of national law which prevent them from giving effect to Community law: '*any provision of a national legal system and any legislative, administrative or judicial practice which might impair the effectiveness of Community law by withholding from the national court having jurisdiction to apply such law the power to do everything necessary at the moment of its application to set aside national legislative provisions which might prevent, even temporarily, Community law from having full force and effect are incompatible with those requirements, which are the very essence of Community law*'[122] While this paragraph seems to express a general principle, it will be argued further that this is not really the case. Within each category, of substantive and structural supremacy, another distinction can be made between ordinary supremacy and ultimate supremacy. *Ordinary* supremacy is the supremacy of Community law over infra-constitutional national law, so

---

[119] This point is developed further in Chapter 10.

[120] Case 106/77 *Simmenthal* [1978] ECR 585, at para 21.

[121] See also AG Jacobs in *Joined Cases C–430/93 and C–431/93 van Schijndel en van Veen v Stichting Pensioenfonds voor Fysiotherapeuten* [1995] ECR 4705, at para 24. As Sacha Prechal has correctly pointed out, these 'substantive' provisions of Community law may include 'procedural rules', where Community law provides for them, S Prechal, 'Community Law in National Courts: The Lessons from van Schijndel', (1998) 35 *CML Rev* 681, at 685.

[122] This was the technique applied in Case 106/77 *Simmenthal* [1978] ECR 585; and Case C–213/89 *R v Secretary of State for Transport, ex parte Factortame* [1990] ECR I–2433; see also Case C–118/00 *Gervais Larsy v Inasti* [2001] ECR 5063, which even applies the principle of structural supremacy to the duties of national administrative authorities, see *infra*.

anything below the Constitution and higher principles, but including Acts of Parliament, and provisions of administrative law, including specific administrative decisions.[123] *Ultimate* supremacy refers to the priority of Community law over the national Constitutions.[124] *Simmenthal* is a complex case since it covers several aspects of supremacy in order to be able to award precedence to a substantive provision of Community law over an Italian statute (substantive, ordinary, supremacy), the Italian court must set aside a procedural rule obliging it to refer the case to the *Corte costituzionale* (structural supremacy), even if that rule is constitutional in nature (ultimate, structural, supremacy).

From the perspective of Community law, and in a normative frame, there may seem to be no difference between ultimate and ordinary given the absolute nature of supremacy: *all* Community law takes precedence over *all* national law. Yet, the distinction has explanatory value from the perspective of national courts and their mandate. Ordinary supremacy[125] has important constitutional implications for the ordinary (non-constitutional) courts which must set aside conflicting national legislation, including Acts of Parliament and thus become review courts: ordinary courts are empowered. Ultimate supremacy carries consequences for all courts, but it will be most controversial in the case of national courts having constitutional jurisdiction that are precluded from upholding the Constitution *vis-à-vis* Community law: Community law implies a curb on their national constitutional mandate.[126]

4.2.2. The Effects of Supremacy on the National Courts

For most national courts, and in combination with direct effect, supremacy first and foremost implies that they must become judicial review courts: *'every national court must, in a case within its jurisdiction, apply Community law in its entirety and protect the rights which the latter confers on individuals and must accordingly set aside any provision of national law*

---

[123] Case C–224/97 *Erich Ciola v Land Vorarlberg* [1999] ECR I–2517, at 31–32: '(..) provisions of national law which conflict with such a provision of Community law may be legislative or administrative (..) those administrative provisions of national law should include not only general abstract rules but also specific individual administrative decisions'.

[124] Case 11/70 *International Handelsgesellschaft mbH v Einführ- und Vorratsstelle für Getreide und Futtermittel* [1970] ECR 1125; see also the question referred in Case C–446/98 *Fazenda Pública v Câmara Municipal do Porto* [2000] *ECR* 11435; since the directive in question could also be implemented in a manner consistent with the Constitution, there was no incompatibility between the directive and the Constitution.

[125] This would be the *Costa v ENEL* and *Simmenthal* type of cases, and indeed most cases where national courts are confronted with incompatibilities between national and Community law. This is the aspect of supremacy which is central in this chapter.

[126] This aspect of supremacy will be analysed in the next section on courts having constitutional jurisdiction.

which may conflict with it, whether prior or subsequent to the Community rule'.[127] All courts, including those which under their national mandate are precluded from reviewing primary legislation, are obliged to give precedence to Community law and consequently, to set aside or disapply conflicting measures of national law, including primary legislation. Constitutional obstacles which may restrain the courts from exercising this mandate must be set aside. Each and every national court must be in a position, in a case within its jurisdiction and properly brought, to award precedence to Community law. Courts having constitutional jurisdiction whose obligation it is under national law to ensure that the Constitution is observed, are restrained from exercising their constitutional functions if and in so far as this would hinder the full effect of Community law. This latter element of supremacy will be developed and analysed in the second part of this book.[128]

In combination with direct effect, the principle of supremacy transforms the courts into review courts. In some cases, Community law provisions will be applied to the facts of the case instead of the disapplied provision of national law. The principle of supremacy operates, in such cases, as a *rule of conflict*. These are the cases, which the French would discuss under the notion of *invocabilité de substitution*. In other cases, the directly effective provisions of Community law are invoked as a *standard for review*, against which the validity or applicability of the national norms is tested.[129] In case of a conflict, the national norm is simply set aside. Nevertheless, the doctrine of supremacy reaches beyond direct effect and entails additional functions and duties for the national courts. In case of a non-directly effective provision of Community law, the courts are still under an obligation to make sure that the useful effect, *effet utile*, of Community law is ensured, for instance by conform interpretation or by holding the State liable to compensate.

4.2.3. The Limits of Supremacy

Supremacy applies only to Community law that is validly adopted: *ultra vires* Community law is not supreme over conflicting national law. This limit of the supremacy of Community law is extremely important: it triggers the question of who has the authority to decide where the *vires* of Community law are. The question is easily answered from the point of view of Community law: only the Court of Justice is competent to rule on

---

[127] Case 106/77 *Simmenthal* [1978] ECR 585, at para 21.

[128] Also, this chapter is not concerned with the relationship between Community law and international law before the ECJ or the national courts.

[129] See also S Prechal, *Directives in European Community law* (Oxford, Clarendon Press, 1995) 276.

the validity of Community law, including the issue of whether a Community act has been lawfully adopted, or in other words, whether the Community institutions were acting *intra vires*. However, several national courts have claimed that they had a say in it. Indeed, the question of the limits of the competences of the Communities is about where Community competences stop and where national competence re-surface. The Community only has those competences which have been transferred to it by the Member States in a contract; and the interpretation of the contract is a matter not exclusively left to one of the parties. These national courts claim that they too have a say in the interpretation of the limits of the Community competences, and accordingly, on the limits of its applicability in the national legal order. If a Community act is *ultra vires* in their opinion, it will not be applicable in their domestic legal order, and will certainly not be supreme over conflicting national law. This issue of *Kompetenz Kompetenz* will be discussed in the second part of this book.

4.2.4. Supremacy of Non-Community Union law?

Is non-Community Union law, *i.e.* second and third pillar law, supreme over national law in the same sense as mainstream Community law? This highly important question has not been analysed by the Court of Justice as yet, and it may take a while until it is referred, given the restrictions on preliminary references under those pillars. Some remarks can be made. First, from an international perspective, there is no doubt that non-Community Union law is as supreme over national law as mainstream Community law, and before the Court of Justice, an international court, a Member State would not be allowed to invoke national law to escape its obligations under the second and third pillar. But more important is the question whether second and third pillar law should also be supreme over national law *before the national courts*.

Now, does non-Community Union law deriving from the second and third pillar take precedence over conflicting national law? In the context of the *third pillar*, the Treaty itself excludes direct effect of framework decisions and decisions. This issue has been discussed before. However, the Treaty is silent on the supremacy or primacy of these same acts, and of any of the other acts adopted under Title VI, or indeed on the supremacy of the relevant Treaty provisions themselves. The exclusion of direct effect does not of itself entail the absence of supremacy. As discussed below, also in mainstream Community law, non-directly effective provisions as such are supreme over conflicting measures of national law. The difference is that the courts cannot draw the same consequences from this primacy, as they cannot 'apply' the non-directly effective provisions. They can, on the other hand, and are under an obligation to, interpret conflicting measures of national law in conformity with Community law, including non-directly effective provisions; and they have jurisdiction to hold the State or other governmental bodies liable in damages for harm caused by its infringements of Community law, including (some) directly effective provisions. Direct effect and supremacy are accordingly separate and independent issues.

One way to answer the question is to go back to *Costa v ENEL* and to check whether the reasons adduced by the Court of Justice to proclaim the precedence of Community law as a general principle apply with the same force to second and third pillar law. In my opinion, they do not, at least not as forcefully. In *Costa v ENEL*, the Court of Justice derived the principle of precedence from *'the special and original nature of the law stemming from the Treaty, an independent source of law'. 'By creating a Community of unlimited duration, having its own institutions, its own personality, its own legal capacity and capacity of representation on the international plane, and more importantly, real powers stemming from a limitation of sovereignty or a transfer of powers from the States to the Community, the Member States have limited their sovereign rights, albeit within limited fields, and have thus created a body of law which binds both their nationals and themselves'*. Furthermore, the terms and general spirit of the Treaty made it impossible as a corollary to accord precedence to unilateral and subsequent measures. And the Court completed its argumentation with references to provisions of the Treaty: Article 5(2) of the EEC Treaty (now Article 10 EC), Article 7 of the EEC Treaty (prohibition of discrimination); the fact that several provisions provided for specific procedures if Member States wanted to derogate from the Treaty; and the fact that regulations are 'directly applicable' under Article 189 of the EC Treaty (now Article 249 EC).

In the context of non-Community Union law, it seems that these criteria apply to a much more limited extent.[130] The terms and spirit of the second and third pillar would rather argue against the acceptance of the principle of supremacy. It was precisely to escape the intervention by the Court of Justice, and in order not to open up co-operation in the areas of common foreign and security policy and justice and home affairs to the same characteristics of mainstream Community law, that they were put in separate 'pillars'. Likewise, some of the other criteria cannot support a claim of primacy with the same force, at least not formally speaking: the 'Union' does not have its own institutions,[131] it does not have legal

---

[130] See also Chr Timmermans, 'The Constitutionalisation of the European Union', (2002) *YEL*, 1, at 9.

[131] But see the unitary view defended for instance by B De Witte, 'The Pillar Structure and the Nature of the European Union: Greek Temple or French Gothis Cathedral?', in T Heukels et al (eds), *The European Union After Amsterdam* (London, Kluwer, 1998) 51; D Curtin and I Dekker, 'The EU as a 'Layered' International Organization: Institutional Unity in Disguise', in P Craig and G de Búrca (eds), *The Evolution of EU Law* (Oxford, OUP, 1999) 83. This is developed further below, in Part 2.

personality,[132] it does not have capacity of representation; more importantly, there is no sense of limitation of sovereignty or transfer of powers: in common parlance, the second and third pillars are intended not to be supra-national, but instead were kept separate because the Member States preferred to confine these areas to intergovernmental co-operation. In addition, Article 5 of the EC Treaty (now Article 10 EC), which is nowadays considered the main Treaty basis for the principle of precedence, has no equivalent under the Union Treaty.[133] And finally, the text argument of Article 189 of the EEC Treaty (now Article 249 EC), equally leads to the opposite result, given the express exclusion of direct effect of framework decisions and decisions. The argumentation of the Court of Justice in *Costa v ENEL* accordingly does not offer the same support in favour of a principle of supremacy of non-Community Union law.

On the other hand, it can be argued that the quality and characteristics of the Community legal order have some radiation effect (*Reflexwirkung*) on the Union's legal system.[134] The case law of the Court of Justice gives an example of such radiation effect in the context of the Brussels I Convention on the recognition and enforcement of judgments in civil and commercial matters.[135] It is argued that the characteristics of the Community legal order spread out and affect the second and third pillar law. The unity thesis gives additional force to the argument: in fact, it is argued, the Union is not separate from the Communities: both organisations use the same institutional structure, they are based on common principles and aim to achieve common objectives; they are in fact the same actors, acting in different capacities and with varying competences and under varying procedures. However, these elements cannot do away with the fact that the second and third pillars are just that: separate pillars,[136] which have not been brought under the Community system, precisely because the High Contracting Parties did not want the law deriving from these pillars to have the same characteristics, and to be governed by the same principles.

---

[132] That is to say, it has not expressly been awarded such personality in the *corpus* of the Treaty. One can argue, however, that the Union does have *de facto* legal personality, on the basis of the principles as laid down by the International Court of Justice in *the Reparation for Injuries Case*, see *International Court of Justice*, Advisory Opinion of 11 April 1949, *Reparation for Injuries Suffered in the Service of the United Nations*, available on www.icj-cij.org.

[133] But see for an argument in favour of the development of a similar principle of loyalty in Union law, D Curtin and I Dekker, 'The Constitutional Structure of the European Union: Some Reflections on Vertical Unity-in-Diversity', in P Beaumont, C Lyons and N Walker (eds), *Convergence and Divergence in European Public Law* (Oxford, Hart Publishing, 2002) 59.

[134] See Chr Timmermans, 'The Constitutionalisation of the European Union', (2002) *YEL*, 1, at 10.

[135] See Case 288/82 *Duijnstee* [1983] ECR 3663. The Convention has now been transformed into a regulation.

[136] Despite the fact that, I agree, the image of the Greek temple with three pillars overstates the differences rather than the commonality between the various forms of cooperation. In this context, however, these differences outweigh the commonality.

Let us now change the perspective, and try and argue the case starting not from the Community orthodoxy, but from a wider angle. What was unique and novel in *Costa v ENEL* was *not* the fact that the Court of Justice, an international court, accorded priority to a Treaty over conflicting national law: *Pacta sunt servanda*, and it is only natural for an international court to emphasize that. It may not even have been so special that the Court of Justice stated that Community law was also to have precedence *before a national court*: if asked, any international court would come to the same decision, because the State would (probably) infringe international obligations if the courts did otherwise. But what made the difference for Community law was that there was a court which could hold, for all the Member State courts alike, and *in the course of a procedure before a national court*, that Community law takes precedence, in the sense that Member States cannot deviate unilaterally from what they have agreed in common. Under classic international law, an international court will only have to decide whether the State as such (and including all its organs) has violated an obligation under international law, *ex post facto*. So while it has been maintained for a long time that international law does not oblige national courts to apply international law and award precedence to international obligations,[137] it is also clear that if a court does indeed deny precedence to these obligations, it most likely contributes to the State's violation of the Treaty and thus causes the international liability of the State to arise. The preliminary rulings procedure, however, makes it possible for 'the clock to be stopped':[138] in the context of Community law, it is not necessary to wait until the end and ask the question whether indeed the national court has contributed to causing the State's international liability to arise: the Court of Justice can interfere at an earlier stage, and prevent the national courts from contributing to the violation of the Treaty.

The same may happen in the context of Title VI, where the Court has limited jurisdiction to give preliminary rulings. However, there are important differences with the situation in mainstream Community law: the Court only has jurisdiction to answer preliminary rulings in so far as a Member State has accepted this jurisdiction. While most Member States have done so, it is by no means obligatory, and in addition, the Member States could chose between various options, as to whether lower and/or highest courts could or must make references. What would be the effect

---

[137] But see arguments to the contrary, for instance the *Danzig* case referred to above, and recently the *La Grand* case, discussed below. See for a discussion of more modern approaches in international law concerning the principle of direct effect, A Nollkaemper, 'The Direct Effect of Public International Law', in JM Prinssen and A Schrauwen (eds), *Direct Effect. Rethinking a Classic of EC Legal Doctrine* (Groningen, Europa Law Publishing, 2002) 157.

[138] See D Wyatt, 'New Legal Order, or Old?', (1982) *ELR* 147.

of a decision of the Court of Justice, awarding precedence to a particular provision of an act adopted under Title VI, if some national courts cannot make references on the issue? Are they to the same effect bound by that decision? Underlying the principle of supremacy of Community law is *pacta sunt servanda*, and the notion of uniformity of Community law:*The executive force of Community law cannot vary from one State or another in deference to subsequent domestic laws, without jeopardising the attainment of the objectives set out in Article 5(2) [now Article 10 EC] and giving rise to the discrimination prohibited by Article 7'.*[139] Hence, it should be binding on all courts.

Nevertheless, and irrespective of this procedural problem, it would seem anomalous for the Court of Justice not to accept the supremacy of non-Community Union law – to the extent that it has jurisdiction. With the same force as for Community law, it must be accepted that the Member States cannot unilaterally detract from legal rules accepted on the basis of reciprocity.[140] This is a simple application of the principle of *pacta sunt servanda*. Once the clock is stopped, an international court will naturally state that treaty obligations take precedence, otherwise the international liability of the State will arise. The difficulty is that the clock is not stopped in the same way in the various Member States, and that the decision of the Court may not have the same (uniform) effect for each and every national court.

More problematic is the case for an absolute and unconditional version of supremacy. Consider the objections raised by the national courts against the principle of supremacy of mainstream Community law. Some of these objections concerned the place of the courts in the constitutional structure, and these have been overcome in one way or another. But others were more principled, and were most powerful in the context of conflicting provisions of national constitutional law and Community law. In the case of *Internationale Handelsgesellschaft*, the *Bundesverfassungsgericht* argued against the primacy of Community law, that the Community legal order lacked a sufficient protection of fundamental rights; accordingly, this protection had to be offered at the national level. In the context of Community law, the Court of Justice has been able to counter this argument by the development of the theory of general principles of Community law which include fundamental rights: the protection offered at the national level was replaced by protection at the Community level and accordingly there was no need for the national courts to retain jurisdiction to review Community law. It is well-known that the Court of Justice has been able to convince the *Bundesverfassungsgericht* to a large extent. Now, the argument was powerful in the context of Community

[139] Case 6/64 *Costa v ENEL* [1964] ECR 585, at 594.
[140] See, once again, Case 6/64 *Costa v ENEL* [1964] ECR 585, at 594.

law, where the Court of Justice can indeed state that it is able to replace the national courts in the protection of fundamental rights. However, that is not the case in the context of Title VI where the Court of Justice has only very limited jurisdiction, and cases may not reach the Court, because the more limited version of the preliminary rulings procedure, and of actions for annulment, which are in any case precluded for private applicants. In addition, there are other deficiencies in the system of Title VI, which would seem to add force to objections of national courts against the supremacy of acts adopted under this Title. The very limited democratic legitimation of acts adopted under Title VI is probably one of the most important.[141]

Where does all this leave us? The question of supremacy can arise before the Court of Justice, and the natural tendency of the Court of Justice will go in favour of the acceptance of supremacy also in the area of Title VI. However, the context is so different from that of the first pillar, that there are good reasons to argue against applying the same absolute and unconditional version of supremacy.

4.3. DIRECT EFFECT AND SUPREMACY: THE 'SIMMENTHAL MANDATE'

Direct effect and supremacy constitute the groundwork of the Community mandate of the national courts. The essence of the Community mandate is contained in those two doctrines, the culmination of which for the mandate of the national courts is *Simmenthal*, where the Court held that every national court must in a case within its jurisdiction apply Community law in its entirety and protect rights which individuals derive from it, and must set aside any provision which may conflict with it, whether prior or subsequent to the Community rule.

4.3.1. 'Setting Aside or Disapply'

The first questions relating to the exact duties and obligations of the national courts acting as Community courts were put before the Court soon after *Van Gend en Loos* and *Costa-ENEL*. In *Lück*, the *Finanzgericht Düsseldorf* sought a clarification of the consequences of the principle of primacy with regard to provisions of national law incompatible with

---

[141] It may be be objected that when *Costa v ENEL* and *Simmenthal* were decided, the Community was not more democratic than is the case now in the second and third pillar. However, one may and must accept a higher level of democratization now, with progressing integration and maturing of the system. In addition, the decisions adopted in the third pillar probably touch upon individuals' lives more directly and more intrusively than was the case with economic decisions adopted in the early days.

Community law: what is their fate? Would they be 'void', 'non-existent', 'to be annulled'? The Court held that Article 95 of the then EEC Treaty merely had the effect of *'excluding the application of any national measure incompatible with it'*. Disapplying the conflicting measure is the most general remedy that individuals may claim from national courts.[142] The supremacy of Community law requires, in the case at hand, that the conflicting rule find no application,[143] is set aside, 'disapplied', or declared 'unenforceable'.[144] Community law does not automatically render the conflicting rule null and void. The national norm remains in existence and can be applied to cases in which they do not lead to an infringement of Community law. Community law only dictates the non-application of the conflicting measure, whether prior or subsequent, in cases where Community law would otherwise be infringed.[145] The precedence of Community law imposes an *obligation de résultat* rather than an *obligation de moyens* on the national courts.[146]

4.3.2. An Obligation to Annul Conflicting Law?

However, the Court continued to say in *Lück* that the duty to disapply did not *'restrict the powers of the competent national courts to apply, from among the various procedures available under national law, those which are appropriate for the purpose of protecting the individual rights conferred by Community law'.*[147] Disapplication is only a minimum requirement: it does not restrict the powers of the national courts to choose other procedures available under national law which are appropriate to protect the Community rights of individuals. Yet, is a court having *jurisdiction* to annul a measure under national law under a Community *obligation* to do

---

[142] W van Gerven, 'Of Rights, Remedies and Procedures', (2000) 37 *CML Rev* 501, at 507–8.

[143] It has already been explained that the duty to refuse to apply any conflicting provision of national law is imposed not only on the courts, but equally on all adminstrative authorities, including decentralised authorities, Case 103/88 *Fratelli Costanzo v Comune di Milano* [1989] ECR 1839; Case 224/97 *Erich Ciola v Land Vorarlberg* [1999] ECR I–2517; should they not set aside conflicting national legislation, the courts must disregard these administrative decisions.

[144] See also Case 84/71 *Marimex* [1972] ECR 89 (the direct applicability of a regulation precludes the application of legislative measures which are incompatible with its provisions) and Case 48/71 *Commission v Italy* [1972] *ECR* 527 (direct applicability entails a prohibiton having the full force of law against applying a national rule recognized as incompatible with a Community provision).

[145] Joined Cases C–10/97 to C–22/97 *Ministero delle Finanze v INCOGE '90 Srl and Others* [1998] ECR I–6307. In the case the Court also made it clear that questions as to jurisdiction and procedure are a matter for national law.

[146] D Simon, 'Les exigences de la primauté du droit communautaire: continuité ou métamorphoses?', in *L'Europe et le droit. Mélanges en hommage à Jean Boulouis* (Paris, Dalloz, 1991) 481, at 485.

[147] Case 34/67 *Firma Gebrüder Lück v Hauptzollamt Köln-Rheinau* [1968] ECR 245, at 251.

so for infringement of Community law? Such obligation does not follow from *Lück* where the Court considered it only a possibility. It does however follow from the principle of equivalence in *Rewe* and *Comet*[148] that *'in the absence of any relevant Community rules, it is for the national legal order of each Member State to (..) lay down the procedural conditions governing actions at law intended to ensure the protection of rights which citizens have from the direct effect of Community law, it being understood that such conditions cannot be less favourable than those relating to similar actions of a domestic nature'*.[149] If a national court has jurisdiction to annul administrative decisions or regulations for breach of a higher national norm under domestic law, it must also annul them if their invalidity derives from an infringement of Community law.[150] Any national measure that appears to infringe Community law, must be annulled where the court has jurisdiction to do so under national law, in comparable situations under national law.[151]

Accordingly, judicial review courts, which have jurisdiction to annul *primary* legislation – mostly for unconstitutionality – should also annul[152]

---

[148] Case 33/76 *Rewe-Zentralfinanz eG and Rewe-Zentral AG v Landwirtschaftskammer für das Saarland* [1976] ECR 1989; Case 45/76 *Comet BV v Produktschap voor Siergewassen* [1976] ECR 2043. In fact, the German referring court in the first case had asked whether the citizen had a right to the annulment or revocation of the administrative measure infringing Community law. The second limb of the question concerned time limits, and the judgment seems to focus especially on the latter issue (which was also the issue in *Comet*). While the issue of annulment or revocation seems to concern the type of remedy rather than a procedural rule, it seems to be implied in the case that where a court has jurisdiction to annul, it must annul for infringement of Community law; see also Case C–159/00 *Sapod Audic v Eco-Emballages SA* [2002] ECR I–5031.

[149] Case 33/76 *Rewe* [1976] ECR 1989, at 1997–98.

[150] A case in point is Case C–224/97 *Erich Ciola v Land Vorarlberg* [1999] ECR I–2517, where it was argued on behalf of the Austrian government that to hold that Community law took precedence over an individual administrative decision which had become final would be liable to call into question the principles of legal certainty, protection of legitimate expectations or the protection of lawfully required rights. The ECJ ducked the question and stated that the dispute at hand did not concern the fate of the administrative act itself, but the question whether such act must be disregarded when assessing the validity of a penalty imposed for failure to comply with an obligation hereunder, because of its incompatibility with Community law. To this question the answer seemed easy on the basis of the established case law and the ECJ ruled that a specific individual administrative decision that has become final (even before the Austrian accession) must be disregarded when assessing the validity of a fine imposed for failure to comply with that prohibition after the date of accession. What would, however, been the answer where the individual sought the annulment of the decision without awaiting a procedure being brought against him for violation of the decision (which appears to be impossible under Austrian law on grounds of the principles mentioned)? Questions of this type were referred in Case C–453/00 *Kühne & Heitz NV v Productschap voor Pluimvee en Eieren*, judgment of 13 January 2004, nyr.

[151] Implicit in Case C–72/95 *Aannemersbedrijf Kraaijeveld BV v Gedeputeerde Staten van Zuid-Holland* [1996] ECR I–5403, at para 60.

[152] Or 'nullify'; or 'declare void'. The objection that a court only pronounces the unconstitutionality of a law and not its legality or validity otherwise, seem rather formalistic and not compatible with the principle of equivalence (which does not require identity). This issue is further developed in the chapter on courts having constitutional jurisdiction.

such legislation for violation of Community law. The ultimate aim of the principle of supremacy imposed on all national authorities is to eliminate conflicting norms, measures and situations. The principle of primacy in itself does not grant the national courts jurisdiction to annul conflicting legislation. Yet, when this *jurisdiction* exists under national law, it *must* also be exercised in the context of Community law.[153]

4.3.3. Declaration of Incompatibility

What other measures could a national court take? In the *Equal Opportunities Commission (EOC)* case,[154] the House of Lords gave a *declaration* that certain provisions of the Employment Protection (Consolidation) Act 1978, a piece of primary legislation, were incompatible with European Community law. The Equal Opportunities Commission (EOC) is a semi-autonomous statutory agency funded by the Home Office and whose function it is to promote equal opportunities for women. The EOC has funded a large number of preliminary references brought to the Court of Justice and has pushed the Commission to bring enforcement actions against the United Kingdom in the area of equal treatment for women. In this particular case, the EOC challenged the compatibility of the Act with Community law before the English courts. In order to elicit a decision open to judicial review and accordingly have access to the courts,[155] the EOC invited the Minister to reconsider the allegedly discriminatory provisions of the Act in question. When the Minister, in a letter, denied incompatibility with the equal treatment provisions in Community law, the EOC sought judicial review. The case raised important issues, relating to standing of the EOC, to the issue whether there was indeed a decision susceptible to judicial review, and, whether the courts could give a declaration that primary legislation was incompatible with Community law. In the Divisional Court,[156] the application for judicial review was refused. The Court held that in any event, it had no jurisdiction to grant relief requiring the Secretary of State (either directly through mandamus or obliquely through a declaration) to obtain amendment of the 1978 Act.

---

[153] The consequence of the incompatibility of national measures and their inapplicability as regards the severity of the sanction such as nullity or unenforceability of a contract are, under the same conditions of equivalence and effectiveness, a matter of national law, Case C-159/00 *Sapod Audic v Eco-Emballage SA* [2002] ECR I–5031, at para 52.

[154] *House of Lords*, decision of 3 March 1994, *R v Secretary of State for Employment, ex parte Equal Opportunities Commission* [1994] 2 WLR 409; [1995] 1 AC 1.

[155] There is no possibility, in English law, to bring an action directly against an Act of Parliament.

[156] *High Court, Queen's Bench Division, Divisional Court*, decision of 10 October 1992, *R v Secretary of State for Employment, ex parte Equal Opportunities Commission* [1992] 1 All ER 545.

The House of Lords held that the Secretary of State had not reached a decision capable of judicial review, but that, nonetheless, the Divisional Court did have jurisdiction to issue a declaration that primary legislation was incompatible with Community law. The ruling widens the scope of available remedies for the enforcement of Community law in Britain and, in effect, the courts may and must now order the Government and Parliament to bring legislation in line with Community law. This can even be done outside the framework of a concrete case, therefore creating a type of abstract review of primary legislation, 'giving Britain its first taste of a constitutional court'.[157] The judgment is all the more remarkable since courts in other countries which do have jurisdiction to declare primary legislation unconstitutional or even annul it, do not always assume that jurisdiction to declare legislation incompatible with Community law. It demonstrates an increasing willingness and even boldness of the English courts to use their judicial review powers.[158]

The Human Rights Act 1998 attempts to combine positive legal protection and enforcement of human rights with the preservation of parliamentary sovereignty. The Act itself is not entrenched, but Section 3 of the Act obliges all courts to interpret statutes in conformity with the human rights norms contained in the Act. They remain unable, however, to invalidate a statute by reference to these norms.[159] The superior courts may however make a declaration of incompatibility with Convention rights. Such declaration does not affect the validity, continuing operation or enforcement of the provisions in respect of which it is given,[160] it merely triggers a special procedure for the relevant provisions to be reconsidered by Parliament. However, the provisions may in practical effect become inoperative, for every time they are applied to an individual that individual may have recourse to Strasbourg, in the same way as the person in whose case the provision was declared incompatible in the first place. In practical effect, the declaration of incompatibility comes very close to enabling judicial review of parliamentary legislation.[161] In any case, it cannot be said that Parliament remains sovereign in exactly the same way as before.

[157] In an editorial *The Times* wrote: '*Britain may now have, for the first time in history, a constitutional court ... The House of Lords ... has, in effect, struck down as 'unconstitutional' an Act of Parliament which is still believed – in some quarters more than in others – to be 'sovereign'... by its methods in the EOC case, the House of Lords has given Britain the first taste of a constitutional court.*' Editorial: 'Profound Judgment How the Law Lords tipped Britain's constitutional Balance', *The Times*, 5 March 1994.

[158] C Harlow and E Szyszczak, case commentary in (1995) 32 *CML Rev* 641, at 652.

[159] On the Human Rights Act and the courts, see for instance Lord Hope of Craighead, 'The Human Rights Act 1998 – The Task of the Judges', in *Judicial Review in International Perspective. Liber Amicorum in Honour of Lord Slynn of Hadley*, Vol II, (The Hague, Kluwer Law International, 2000) 415.

[160] Section 4(6)(a) of the Human Rights Act 1998.

[161] AW Bradley, 'The Sovereignty of Parliament – Form or Substance?', in J Jowell and D Oliver (eds), *The Changing Constitution*, 4th edn, (Oxford, OUP, 2000) 23, at 55.

4.3.4. Invocabilité de substitution and invocabilité d'exclusion

The distinction has been discussed already in the context of direct effect. The conditions for direct effect have been stretched so far that even where a provision of Community law is not unconditional – and can accordingly not be applied as such to the facts of the case – the courts have to take it into consideration as a reference standard when reviewing national law. There is some discussion as to whether this duty of the courts still comes under the heading 'direct effect' or rather creates another duty for the courts[162] and a right to have national law reviewed where no (substantive) rights are created for individuals. The discussion thus centres on the definition of direct effect and its limits. In *Linster*, the question was put before the Court in so many words: the *Tribunal d'arrondissement du Luxembourg* asked the Court essentially whether a national court may only conduct review whether the national legislature has kept within the limits of discretion set by the directive if it produces direct effect.[163] The question implied an uncoupling of direct effect and the possibility of relying on a directive. The Court did not answer the question with reference to the notion of direct effect.[164] Yet, it is implied in the judgment that these cases of judicial review of the limits of discretion on national authorities are covered by the notion 'direct effect', be it that the conditions are less restrictively applied and that some discretion on the part of the national authorities in the implementation of the directive does not preclude it being invoked as a standard of legality. The issue has to do with the conditions for direct effect, namely the measure of unconditionality and clarity required in a particular case, rather than with the limits of direct effect.

In some cases, non-application of the conflicting norm will suffice to decide the case. In other cases – this is where the conditions of direct effect are strict and sufficient clarity, precision and unconditionality is

---

[162] Or even 'the *right* of a national court, responsible for reviewing the legality of [national law] to take account of a directive which has not been fully transposed (..)', Case C–287/98 *Luxembourg v Berthe Linster and Others* [2000] ECR I–6917, at 31 (emphasis added).

[163] The Linsters had argued that taking account of an unimplemented directive did not necessarily involve an appraisal of its direct effect. Such direct effect was necessary only in order for the directive to have an effect by way of substitution for an existing legal norm. On the other hand, it is the principle of primacy, which required the national court to disapply national legislation contrary to Community law, even where the Community provision at issue lacked direct effect. They thus argued that 'direct effect' was limited to cases of *invocabilité de substitution*, and was not required in cases of *invocabilité d'exclusion*.

[164] AG Léger did discuss the issue in quite some detail; he arrived at the conclusion that there was no need for prior consideration of the direct effect of the provisions relied on, *'at least in the sense in which the term 'direct effect' is understood'* (that seems to be the point exactly); and: *'it must be possible to exercise rights contained in a directive that has not been transposed, irrespective of the terms in which they are couched, where they are invoked for the purposes of reviewing the legality of rules of domestic law'*; at paras 81–82.

required – the provision of Community law is applied instead of the dis-applied rule of national law. In between is a range of cases where some creativity is required of the national courts and authorities. In *Kraaijeveld*, for instance, the Court held that where the national court finds that discretion allowed by a directive has been exceeded and consequently the national provisions must be set aside, it was for the authorities of the State, according to their respective powers, to take all the general or particular measures necessary to ensure that the directive is given effect.[165]

4.4. SUPREMACY BEYOND DIRECT EFFECT?

4.4.1. The Case of Alman Metten

In the remarkable *Metten* case,[166] the Netherlands Judicial Division of the Council of State concluded from the case law of the Court of Justice that the principle of supremacy of Community law also held for provisions which were not directly effective. Alman Metten, a Member of the European Parliament, had asked to see the minutes of a number of meetings of the Ecofin Council. He requested access to those minutes from the Netherlands Minister for Finance, on the basis of the Dutch Act on Open Government *(Wet openbaarheid van bestuur)*. The Minister refused on grounds of what was then Article 18 of the Rules of Procedure of the Council, and in the alternative, on a provision in the Dutch Act stating that information could not be provided when outweighed by the interests of the conduct of international relations with foreign States and international organisations.[167] In final instance, the case came before the Council of State, which based its judgment on the case law of the Court of Justice, and held that the Rules of Procedure took precedence, even if they were not directly effective. The references made, however, could not bear the conclusion drawn by the Council of State: *Costa v ENEL*, *Walt Wilhelm* and *Simmenthal* all concerned the supremacy of directly effective provisions of Community law, and the statements of the Court of Justice, while sweeping, are restricted to that category of Community law provisions. In the *Hormones* case, the Court stated that the Rules of Procedure were binding on the Council, and that a failure to comply with them constituted an

---

[165] Case C-72/95 *Aannemersbedrijf Kraaijeveld BV v Gedeputeerde Staten van Zuid-Holland* [1996] ECR I-5403, at para 61.

[166] *Raad van State, Afdeling Bestuursrechtspraak*, decision of 7 July 1995, *Alman Metten v Minister for Finance*, AB 1997/117, commented by AAL Beers; English translation in (1996) 3 MJ, 179.

[167] Rules of Procedure, [1979] OJ L 268/1; since replaced by Rules of Procedure, [1993] OJ L 304/1.

infringement of an essential procedural requirement.[168] The case has however no bearing on the question of direct effect or supremacy, which concerns the relation with the national legal order and national law before national courts. In fact, the Court has never said that the obligation imposed on the national courts to set aside conflicting measures of national law also applies in the absence of direct effect.[169]

Does this imply that there *is* no supremacy beyond direct effect? *Au contraire*, the whole of Community law takes precedence over national law. The supremacy of Community law is absolute and unconditional: *all* Community law takes precedence over *all* national law. Nevertheless, this does not mean that national law must be set aside when it conflicts with Community law provisions which are not directly effective. *Simmenthal* is restricted to directly effective provisions: 'in accordance with the principle of the precedence of Community law, the relationship between provisions of the Treaty and *directly applicable measures of the institutions* on the one hand and the national law of the Member States on the other is such that those provisions and measures not only by their entry into force render automatically inapplicable any conflicting provision of current national law but – in so far as they are an integral part of, and take precedence in, the legal order applicable in the territory of each of the Member States – also preclude the valid adoption of new national legislative measures to the extent to which they would be incompatible with Community provisions'. And 'every national court must, in a case within its jurisdiction, apply Community law in its entirety and *protect rights which the latter confers on individuals* and must accordingly set aside any provision of national law which may conflict with it, whether prior or subsequent to the Community rule'.

4.4.2. Consistent Interpretation

What effect does supremacy have in the case of a provision that lacks direct effect? The courts are under an obligation to interpret national law in conformity with Community law, even where it is not directly effective. The duty of consistent interpretation is founded on the principle of loyalty contained in Article 10 EC, and on the principle of the precedence of Community law over all provisions of national law.[170] Consistent

---

[168] Case 68/86 *United Kingdom v Council (hormones)* [1988] ECR 855, at paras 40–49.

[169] See also LFM Besselink, 'Curing a 'Childhood Sickness'? On Direct Effect, Internal Effect, Primacy and Derogation from Civil Rights. The Netherlands Council of State Judgment in the Metten Case', (1996) 3 *MJ*, 165, at 171.

[170] See for instance AG van Gerven in Case C–106/89 *Marleasing SA v La Comercial Internacional de Alimentacion SA* [1990] I–4135, at marginal number 9.

interpretation is a technique that is not unique to Community law.[171] It is used in the context of national law, where lower norms must be interpreted so as to conform to higher norms, including the Constitution (for instance the doctrine of *Verfassungskonforme Auslegung* in Germany), and is quite common for national courts interpreting national law so as not to infringe international law obligations imposed on the State. This is true both in dualist and in monist systems. In the context of Community law, consistent interpretation was used as a technique to give effect to Community law in the domestic legal orders by national courts even before the Court of Justice made it part of their Community law mandate, and thus made it compulsory.[172]

Supremacy shows itself in a double guise in the context of conform interpretation. First, supremacy as a general principle is one of the foundations of the duty imposed on courts and administrative authorities to seek an interpretation of national law that is consistent with Community law obligations, whether directly effective or not. Supremacy is however not often mentioned as a rationale for the duty of consistent interpretation: it is chiefly regarded as an element of the duty of loyalty as laid down in Article 10 EC. Second, supremacy can also be used to denote the supremacy of Community-consistent interpretation over national techniques and canons of construction.[173]

The duty of conform interpretation may cause problems for national courts concerning their constitutional position. (For instance, are they under a Community law obligation to give national primary legislation a different meaning than intended by Parliament? Or, what are the constitutional limits of the judicial creativity which is required in the context of conform interpretation?) It may cause serious problems of legal certainty. In the context of directives, for instance, it is a much debated issue whether consistent interpretation can be used to achieve the result excluded by the absence of horizontal direct effect. Can obligations be imposed on individuals through consistent interpretation of national law, where this cannot be done by applying Community law directly? On the other hand, interpretation is the very essence of the judicial function and only in a limited number of cases will these constitutional issues arise. In addition, where consistent interpretation goes as far as changing the wording of the inconsistent texts, it in fact becomes a form of judicial review. The detailed analysis of the doctrine of conform

---

[171] See eg G Betlem, 'The Doctrine of Constistent Interpretation – Managing Legal Uncertainty', (2002) 22 *OJLS*, 397, at 398.

[172] See HM Wissink, *Richtlijnconforme interpretatie van burgerlijk recht* (Deventer, 2001) 30 and 121 *et seq.*

[173] So H M Wissink, *Richtlijnconforme interpretatie van burgerlijk recht* (Deventer, 2001) 121 *et seq.*

interpretation and its effects on the constitutional position of national courts has therefore been omitted.

4.4.3. Governmental Liability

The principle of supremacy also underlies the principle of the liability of the Member States for infringements of (higher ranking) Community law, even where it is not directly effective. When the Court formulated this State liability as a principle inherent in the Treaty, it did refer to *Costa v ENEL* and *Simmenthal*, the ground-breaking decisions stating supremacy as a principle and explaining its consequences for the national courts, although it did not mention the principle in so many words. Advocate General Mischo did. He pointed out that the Court had already held in *Humblet* that it followed from the principle of precedence that the Member States were obliged to make reparation for any unlawful consequences which may have ensued from any legislative or administrative measures adopted contrary to Community law.[174] He also alluded to the principle of supremacy in another sense, namely that the Member States could not take refuge behind the immunity of the legislature, even if this had the status of a constitutional principle, in order to escape the obligation to make good damage, under reference to *Costa v ENEL* and *Internationale Handelsgesellschaft*.[175]

4.4.4. The Principle of Supremacy and National Procedural Rules

Supremacy does however have its limits when applied in a concrete case. It will be demonstrated further that the principle of structural supremacy may not be absolute, that it may not even be a principle. Sometimes, the enforcement and application of Community law may have to yield, and it must be recognised that the national legal environment in which Community law is applied, poses limits to its application.

4.5. CONCLUSION

Direct effect and supremacy, as said, form the alpha of the Community mandate of the national courts. They involve the national courts in the

---

[174] Case 6/60 *Humblet v Belgian State* [1960] ECR 559, at 569.
[175] Opinion of AG Mischo in Joined Cases C–6/90 and C–9/90 *Andrea Francovich and Others v Italian Republic* [1991] ECR I–5357, at marginal number 65.

application and enforcement of Community law and transform them into Community law courts. Yet, they are not the omega. It is one thing to say that the national courts must 'apply' and 'enforce' Community law and 'protect the rights which individuals derive from Community law'; but what exactly does that mandate entail? How are the national courts required to act in cases involving Community law? How is the mandate to be put into effect? That is what the second generation cases are about, and this is analysed in the next chapter.

5

Refining the Mandate: Second Generation Issues

IT IS NO longer disputed that directly effective provisions of Community law take precedence over conflicting national provisions and that national courts are under an obligation to disapply conflicting national law. Yet, this rule of thumb does not solve all problems for the national courts. What procedures, remedies and causes of action must be applied in the enforcement of Community law? Should a national court when acting as Community court, apply the same procedural and jurisdictional rules as in the case of national law and should it offer the same remedies? What should the court do if it lacks jurisdiction to award a particular remedy? The answers to these questions form what is generally called the second generation[1] case law and clarify the duties and obligations of the national courts when acting under their Community mandate. The case law is difficult to understand, since it follows various paths, applying several principles and techniques,[2] and the Court varies the intensity of its review of national procedural rules, without explaining which technique applies in which case. The Court does not explain where the Community requirements concerning the national courts' mandate stop and where

---

[1]   The term 'second generation' was coined by J Mertens de Wilmars, 'L'efficacité des différentes techniques nationales de protection juridique contre les violations du droit communautaire par les autorités nationales', CDE, 1981, 379. And counting on: D Curtin and K Mortelmans, 'Application and Enforcement of Community Law by the Member States: Actors in Search of a Third Generation Script', in Essays in Honour of Henry G Schermers (Nijhoff, Dordrecht, 1994) 423.

[2]   See on the various strands in the Court's case law, among others, S Prechal, 'Community Law in National Courts: The Lessons from Van Schijndel', (1998) 35 CML Rev 681; and her Directives in European Community Law (Oxford, Clarendon Press, 1995) Ch 8; F G Jacobs, 'Enforcing Community Rights and Obligations in National Courts: Striking the Balance', in J Lonbay and A Biondi (eds), Remedies for Breach of EC Law (Chichester, Wiley, 1997) 25 and AG Jacobs' Opinion in Van Schijndel and Peterbroeck, Joined Cases C–430/93 and C–431/93, Van Schijndel [1995] ECR I–4705 and Case C–312/93, Peterbroeck [1995] ECR I–4599; M Hoskins, 'Tilting the Balance: Supremacy and National Procedural Rules'' (1996) 21 ELR 365; A Biondi, 'The European Court of Justice and Certain National Procedural Limitations: Not Such a Tough Relationship' (1999) 36 CML Rev 1271; W van Gerven, 'Of Rights, Remedies and Procedures' (2000) 37 CML Rev 501.

national law takes over. It is a tricky exercise even to delineate the different strands in the Court's case law[3] and to find out why a particular case was decided under a particular principle,[4] or why it left the matter to the national court in some cases, while going into the particulars of national procedural law in other cases. What follows is only an attempt to shed some light on and bring some order to the complex and difficult case law.[5]

5.1. THE PRINCIPLE OF PROCEDURAL AUTONOMY

The first path in the Court's case law relies on the principle of *national procedural autonomy*, introduced in the *Rewe* and *Comet* cases of 1976,[6] and has been repeated on numerous occasions since. In essence, the principle means that apart from the fundamentals of the Community doctrines of

---

[3]   Various attempts have been made to bring order in the ECJ's case law: the diversity in outcomes has been explained in terms of a chronology, showing different periods with varying intensity of intervention in national procedural law, so C Kilpatrick, 'The Future of Remedies in Europe', in *The Future of Remedies in Europe* (Oxford, Hart Publishing, 2000) 1–9; van Gerven has explained the case law by distinguishing between rights, remedies and procedures, each requiring a different treatment: W van Gerven, 'Of Rights, Remedies and Procedures' (2000) 37 *CML Rev* 501; Others have analyzed the ECJ's approach to national procedural law within one sector, which allows a more complete view of the relationship between the techniques, and the objectives sought, for instance in terms of decentralized enforcement and protection of individual in a particular area, see the contributions in Part II of J Lonbay and A Biondi, *Remedies for Breach of EC Law* (Oxford, Wiley, 1997); and C Kilpatrick, 'Turning Remedies Around: A Sectoral Analysis of the Court of Justice', in G de Búrca and JHH Weiler (eds), *The European Court of Justice* (Oxford, OUP, 2001) 143.

[4]   See, for instance, J Lonbay and A Biondi, *Remedies for Breach of EC Law* (Oxford, Wiley, 1997); R Craufurd Smith, 'Remedies for Breaches of EU Law in National Courts: Legal Variation and Selection', in *The Evolution of EU Law* (Oxford, OUP, 1999) 286; A Biondi, 'The European Court of Justice and Certain National Procedural Limitations: Not Such a Tough Relationship' (1999) 36 *CML Rev* 1271; C Kilpatrick, T Novitz and P Skidmore (eds), *The Future of Remedies in Europe* (Oxford, Hart Publishing, 2000); W van Gerven, 'Of Rights, Remedies and Procedures' (2000) 37 *CML Rev* 501.

[5]   The approach will be rather technical and the focus is on the courts and the development of their Community mandate. The downside of this choice is that it may not do justice to the case law in the sense that the underlying policy issues – good or bad – do not come to the fore and the ECJ may seem to be going astray and make random choices. Claire Kilpatrick, for instance, has attempted to explain the different strands in the ECJ's case law on effective remedies and procedural autonomy in the area of gender equality and/or labour law, showing that the case law is not a pick and choose on the part of the ECJ but a search for the appropriate doctrinal rules in the context of procedures, with a view to their effects and outcomes on cases and in a continuing dialogue with the national courts. It goes without saying that her approach gives a more realistic and complete view of the issue. See C Kilpatrick, 'Turning Remedies Around: A Sectoral Analysis of the Court of Justice', in G de Búrca and JHH Weiler (eds), *The European Court of Justice* (Oxford, OUP, 2001) 143.

[6]   Case 33/76 *Rewe-Zentralfinanz eG and Rewe-Zentral AG v Landwirtschaftskammer für das Saarland* [1976] ECR 1989; Case 45/76 *Comet BV v Productschap voor Siergewassen* [1976] ECR 2043.

direct effect and supremacy themselves, the remaining questions must be answered on the basis of national law. In the absence of Community rules on this subject, it is for the domestic legal system of each Member State to designate the courts having jurisdiction, to lay down the detailed procedural rules governing actions at law and to provide for the remedies intended to ensure the protection of the rights which citizens derive from the direct effect of Community law.[7] *'Applying the principle of co-operation laid down in Article 5 of the Treaty, it is the national courts which are entrusted with ensuring the legal protection which citizens derive from the direct effect of the provisions of Community law. Accordingly, in the absence of Community rules on this subject, it is for the domestic legal system of each Member State to designate the courts having jurisdiction and to determine the procedural conditions governing actions at law intended to ensure the protection of rights which citizens have from the direct effect of Community law...'.* As pointed out by Advocate General Warner in the case, the Court had little choice in the matter. *'Where Community law confines itself to forbidding this or that kind of act on the part of a Member State and to saying that private persons are entitled to rely on the prohibition in their national courts, without prescribing the remedies available to them for that purpose, there really is no alternative to the application of the remedies and procedures prescribed by national law... Community law and national law operate in combination, the latter taking over where the former leaves off and working out its consequences'.*

It must accordingly be accepted that Community law is not made effective in all cases and that Community law rights are not at all times protected. As in the case of national law, there are other considerations than the full application of the law and the protection of rights, such as principles of legal certainty, rights of the defence, need for finality in litigation, rules of evidence and the like, which regulate the exercise of rights. Community law is enforceable through the domestic judicial systems, and must accept that national law puts restrictions on the exercise and protection of Community law rights, subject to two conditions: the national legal environment in which the Community rules are applied, enforced and protected must not be less favourable than those governing similar domestic actions *(principle of equivalence)* or render virtually impossible or excessively difficult *(principle of effectiveness)* the exercise of rights conferred by Community law. Yet, within these two limits, national procedural law regulates the concrete application of Community law and the protection of Community law rights. This may imply that Community rights at the end of the day are not protected, and that Community law is not correctly applied.

---

[7]   The notion procedural law must be taken in its widest sense and includes not only procedural law *strictu senso*, ie time limits and the like, but extends to more fundamental questions of jurisdiction of courts, types and nature of remedies, access to court and so on.

While the principles of procedural autonomy, effectiveness and equivalence appear to be clear in themselves, and their rationale is evident, the difficulty is, of course, in its application. Which action at law is comparable to the one applicable for the protection of a particular Community law right, in order to assess the principle of equivalence?[8] Which time limits are reasonable and therefore pass the test of effectiveness? What rules of evidence make it excessively difficult to exercise particular Community law rights? Many national courts do not feel confident to answer the questions of equivalence and effectiveness themselves, and refer the matter to Luxembourg. The Court has spent much valuable time deciding whether Community and national actions at law were comparable, whether particular time limits could be applied and so on, and has at times been lured into an analysis of national procedural law, which clearly is not its function, and seems not worth the time spent on it. On the other hand, how should a national court assess whether a particular procedural rule would pass the test? The more individual cases the Court decides for the national courts, the more courts will continue to refer questions. In addition, the Court has made mistakes, such as *Emmott*, which gave the wrong impression that Community law in general, and directives in particular, were so special that national procedural law would always have to yield to it.[9] The same impression has been created by the use of language of precedence and the duty to set aside even the most fundamental procedural rules of a constitutional nature for the sake of the effectiveness of Community law in *Simmenthal* and *Factortame*. However, it was also clear from the beginning that Community law accepts the limitations of national procedural law: in *Rewe* the applicant had argued that time limits would have to yield to the supremacy of

---

8   The ECJ has not formulated a yardstick, but pointed out that domestic actions and actions to enforce a Community right are similar where they pursue the same objective and the essential characteristics are the same in Case C–261/95 *Rosalba Palmisani v INPS* [1997] ECR I–4025; AG Léger did try to formulate a number of general criteria in Case C–326/96 *BS Levez v TH Jennings (Harlow Pools) Ltd* [1998] ECR I–7835; the Court did not follow its AG, but it did indicate that an Act adopted to give effect to the relevant Community rule cannot provide an appropriate ground of comparison against which to measure compliance with the principle of equivalence.

9   Case C–208/90 *Teresa Emmott v Minister for Social Welfare and Attorney General* [1991] ECR I–4296, where the ECJ ruled that time limits would only start to run when the directive is correctly implemented in national law; the ECJ has had to take back that statement, first distinguishing the case (Case C–338/91 *Steenhorst-Neerings* [1993] ECR I–5475 and Case C–410/92 *Johnson* [1994] ECR I–5483) and later holding that it was restricted to the case at hand given its particularities, Case C–188/95 *Fantask* [1997] ECR I–6783; While *Emmott* seemed justified at the time in order to enforce compliance by Member States and force them to implement directives timely and correctly, and in terms of protecting 'poor Teresa Emmott', it may have underestimated the financial consequences for the Member States, and the judgment proved to be exaggerated after the ruling in *Francovich*. *Emmott* may have been a simple mistake, or an 'audition' for a principle abandoned later, but it continues to confuse many national courts, and questions related to Emmott continue to be referred.

Community law. This line of reasoning was rejected by the Court and replaced by the principle of procedural autonomy, corrected by the principles of effectiveness and equivalence.[10]

In *Van Schijndel* and *Peterbroeck*, the Court refined the condition of *effectiveness*, and introduced a *rule of reason*[11] stating that *'For the purposes of applying those principles, each case which raises the question whether a national procedural provision renders application of Community law impossible or excessively difficult must be analysed by reference to the role of that provision in the procedure, its progress and its special features, viewed as a whole, before the various national instances. In the light of that analysis, the basic principles of the domestic judicial system, such as the protection of the rights of the defence, the principle of legal certainty and the proper conduct of procedure, must, where appropriate, be taken into consideration'.* The message seems to be that the national court must verify whether the individual who derives a right from Community law, has sufficient opportunity to seek judicial protection of that right before a court of law which may or must refer the case to the Court of Justice. Being a rule of reason, the test requires a balancing of many aspects, interests and principles. The difficulty, again, is in its application, as is demonstrated in the very cases in which it was introduced. In *Van Schijndel*, the fact that the national court was precluded from applying Community law of its own motion was justified and passed the test, thus restricting the application of Community law and (possibly) denying the protection of Community rights of the applicants. In *Peterbroeck*, however, the Belgian procedural rules, which equally had the effect of denying the possibility for the court to apply Community law of its own motion, were considered not to be justified, and Community law precluded their application. Put simply, the difference in outcome can be explained by the fact that taken as a whole, it was too difficult for the individuals in *Peterbroeck* to have their Community law rights protected before the referring court and impossible for the latter or any other Belgian court for that matter to apply Community law of its own motion and accordingly, to refer questions for preliminary ruling; in *van Schijndel*, on the other hand, the individuals had plenty opportunity to invoke their rights under Community law and have them protected in earlier instances, which also had the possibility to apply Community law of their own motion, and refer questions for preliminary ruling. Nevertheless, it remains to some extent a matter of taste whether a particular procedural rule in a given context makes it 'excessively difficult' or 'virtually impossible' to

---

[10]   This point will be developed further in the next section.

[11]   So S Prechal, 'Community Law in National Courts: The Lessons from *van Schijndel'* (1998) 35 *CML Rev* 681, at 690 *et seq*, see also A Biondi, 'The European Court of Justice and Certain National Procedural Limitations: Not Such a Tough Relationship' (1999) 36 *CML Rev* 1271, at 1277.

protect Community law right and make it effective. Questions continue to be referred, and the *van Schijndel* rule of reason apparently has not made the task of balancing principles any easier.

The principle of *equivalence* was put in perspective in *Edis* where the Court stated that '*That principle cannot, however, be interpreted as obliging a Member State to extend its most favourable rules governing recovery under national law to all actions for repayment of charges or levies in breach of Community law*'.[12] The Court attempted to withdraw from having to rule on the principle of equivalence and to leave it for the national courts: '*In order to determine whether the principle of equivalence has been complied with in the present case, the national court, which alone has direct knowledge of the procedural rules governing actions in the field of employment law – must consider both the purpose and the essential characteristics of allegedly similar domestic actions*' and extended the *Van Schijndel* rule of reason to equivalence: '*Furthermore, whenever it falls to be determined whether a procedural rule of national law is less favourable than those governing similar domestic actions, the national court must take into account the role played by that provision in the procedure as a whole, as well as the operation and any special features of that procedure before the different national courts*'.[13] Yet, it remains a delicate exercise, and to some extent, a matter of taste.

5.2. FROM A 'PRINCIPLE' OF STRUCTURAL SUPREMACY TO THE PRINCIPLE OF FULL EFFECTIVENESS

In another line of cases, the Court takes a more radical approach, based apparently on a very strong version of supremacy.[14] In *Simmenthal* the duty to conduct judicial review of a statute allegedly infringing Community law was excluded by a constitutional rule restricting jurisdiction of the ordinary courts. Indeed, in *Società industrie chimiche Italia*

---

12 Case C–231/96 *Edilizia Industriale Siderurgica Srl (Edis) v Ministero delle Finanze* [1998] ECR I–4951, at para36; see also Case C–260/96 *Ministero delle Finanze v Spac SpA* [1998] ECR I–4997; Joined Cases C–10/97 to C–22/97 *Ministero delle Finanze v INCOGE'90 Srl and Others* [1998] ECR I–6307; Case C–228/96 *Aprile Srl, in liquidation v Ministero delle Finanze dello Stato* [1998] ECR I–7141; Case C–343/96 *Dilexport Srl v Amministratzione delle Finanze dello Stato* [1999] ECR I–579; and in the context of employment Case C–326/96 *BS Levez v TH Jennings (Harlow Pools) Ltd* [1998] ECR I–7835, at paras 41 and 42: 'The principle of equivalence requires that the rule at issue be applied without distinction, whether the infringement alleged is of Community law or national law, where the purpose and cause of action are similar. (…) However, that principle is not to be interpreted as requiring Member States to extend their most favourable rules to all actions brought, like the main action in the present case, in the field of employment law'.

13 Case C–326/96 *BS Levez v TH Jennings (Harlow Pools) Ltd* [1998] ECR I–7835, at paras 43 and 44.

14 Without, however, using the notion. As has been mentioned, the ECJ never uses the notion of supremacy; it rather refers to the principle as precedence or primacy.

Centrale (ICIC)[15] the *Corte costituzionale* had declared that under Italian constitutional law, the setting aside of provisions of Italian law for incompatibility with Community law would not be the task of the ordinary Italian courts, but of the *Corte costituzionale* itself, holding that any subsequent national provision adopted in a field already governed by a Community regulation was incompatible with the principles of Community law and consequently with Article 11 of the Italian Constitution. Since it was accordingly a constitutional issue, the court hearing the case was bound to refer the matter to the constitutional court, which may declare the act unconstitutional for violation of Article 11 of the Constitution, and then refer the case back to the lower court for decision. The *Corte costituzionale* accepted the precedence of Community law, albeit on different grounds than the Court of Justice and with certain limitations,[16] but it did not accept the consequences of the principle for the judicial function. To accept that an ordinary court would choose between two conflicting norms and disapply an Act of Parliament would be tantamount to allowing it to declare the legislature not competent, a power which was certainly not given to the ordinary courts in the Italian legal order. At the end of the day, the conception of the Italian constitutional court did achieve the final result required by Community law: conflicting provisions of national law would not be applied. Even more so, they would even be eliminated from the law books. However, by forcing the courts to follow the cumbersome and time-consuming route via the *Corte costituzionale*, an additional burden was placed on individual litigants seeking protection of his Community law rights and the immediate application of Community law was not ensured.

The disagreement between the *Corte costituzionale* and the Court of Justice, which had started in *Costa v ENEL*, was manifest. Although the *Corte* had to a large extent given in with respect to the core principle of precedence, it did not recognise its full and immediate effect. It was the *pretore di Susa* who offered the Court of Justice the opportunity to once and for all explain the effects of the principles of direct effect and supremacy on the judicial function of *all* national courts. He asked the Court of Justice whether Community law was to be interpreted to the effect that any conflicting subsequent national provisions must be forthwith disregarded without waiting until those provisions had been eliminated by intervention of the legislature concerned (repeal) or of other constitutional authorities (the *Corte costituzionale*). The judgment of the Court was

---

[15]   *Corte costituzionale*, decision n. 232/1975 of 30 October 1975, *Società industrie chimiche Italia Centrale (ICIC)*, 45 Rac.uff. 395, 1975 Giur.cost. 2211; RTDE, 1976, 396; see also L Plouvier, 'L'arrêt de la cour constitutionnelle d'Italie du 22 octobre 1975 dans l'affaire ICIC', (1976) *RTDeur* 271.

[16]   See below.

straightforward and unequivocal, and elucidated the consequences of the principles of direct effect and supremacy for all national courts, irrespective of the position under the national constitution: *'(..) every national court must, in a case within its jurisdiction, apply Community law in its entirety and protect rights which the latter confers on individuals and must accordingly set aside any provision of national law which may conflict with it, whether prior or subsequent to the Community rule.* Accordingly any provision of a national legal system and any legislative, administrative or judicial practice which might impair the effectiveness of Community law by withholding from the national court having jurisdiction the power to do everything necessary at the moment of its application to set aside national legislative provisions which might prevent Community rules from having full force and effect are incompatible with those requirements which are the very essence of Community law. *This would be the case in the event of a conflict between a provision of Community law and a subsequent national law if the solution of the conflict were to be reserved for an authority with a discretion of its own, other than the court called upon to apply Community law, even if such an impediment to the full effectiveness of Community law were only temporary.'*[17]

No mention was made of the principle of national procedural autonomy, proclaimed only a few years back in *Rewe* and *Comet*. Crucial in *Simmenthal* is the principle of the *effectiveness* of Community law, or even its *full* effectiveness, and the duty of all courts to give full effect to Community law, with precedence over conflicting national law. At the end of the day, the judgment intended to create jurisdiction to conduct judicial review for the Italian courts where the constitutional mandate excludes it. The technique of structural supremacy was again applied in *Factortame*.[18]

The facts of the case are well known and need no repetition.[19] It will be remembered that the English courts claimed that they did not have jurisdiction under British law to offer interim relief to the Spanish fishermen by issuing an injunction against the Crown ordering the Minister to suspend the application of the Merchant Shipping Act which allegedly

---

[17] Case 106/77 *Simmenthal* [1978] ECR 585, at paras 21–23.

[18] Case C–213/89 *R v Secretary of State for Transport, ex parte Factortame Ltd and Others* [1990] ECR 2433. It was in this case, when referred back to the House of Lords, that the implications of the principle of supremacy for the English courts were finally accepted, see *infra*.

[19] In short, the effect of the newly adopted 1988 Merchant Shipping Act was that several UK fishing companies whose shareholders and directors were predominantly Spanish could no longer be registered, and could accordingly no longer benefit from the British fishing quota under the common fisheries regulations. They alleged before the English courts that the Act infringed Community law. That question was referred to the Court of Justice (Case C–221/89 *R v Secretary of State for Transport, ex parte Factortame Ltd and Others* [1991] ECR I–3905). Pending the case, and given that it was not likely that the ECJ would decide the case in less than two years, the issue of interim measures arose: would the Spanish fishermen be authorized to continue fishing in British waters in the meantime? If not, the financial consequences would be disastrous. On the aspect of interim relief in *Factortame*,

infringed Community law, for two reasons.[20] First, they could not issue an injunction against the Crown making an order for specific performance: such was explicitly excluded by S. 321 of the 1947 Crown Proceedings Act.[21] Second, under the presumption of validity of an Act of Parliament, it must be considered valid unless and until it has been declared otherwise by a competent authority.[22] When the case concerning the grant of interim relief reached the House of Lords, the question was whether in the absence of a right to interim relief under English law, the English courts would be so empowered *as a matter of Community law*, and if so, what the conditions for granting this remedy would be.

The case did show some similarities with *Simmenthal*: the English courts dealing with the case had pointed out that they lacked jurisdiction to award precedence to Community law in the case at hand. As in *Simmenthal*, they had to await a ruling of another Court – this time the Court of Justice – before giving full force and effect to Community law. In its judgment, the Court of Justice focussed exclusively on the similarity with *Simmenthal*.

The Court of Justice first reiterated the 'structural supremacy principle' as espoused in paragraph 22 of *Simmenthal* and continued that *'the full*

---

see A Barav, 'Enforcement of Community Rights in the National Courts: the case for jurisdiction to grant interim relief, (1989) 26 *CML Rev* 369; NP Gravells, 'Disapplying an Act of Parliament pending a Preliminary Ruling: Constitutional Enormity or Community law Right?', (1989) *PL* 568 (both written before the ECJ handed its judgment); L Papadias, 'Interim Protection under Community Law Before the National Courts: The Right to a Judge with Jurisdiction to grant Interim Relief' [1994] *LIEI* 153; J-Cl Bonichot, 'Les pouvoirs d'injonction du juge national pour la protection des droits conférés par l'ordre juridique communautaire', [1990] *RFDA* 912; J Bell, 'Sur le pouvoir du juge britannique d'addresser des injonction à la Couronne', [1990] *RFDA*, 920.

[20] See the questions referred by the House of Lords in para 15 of the judgment. The latter problem included two aspects: English courts lacked jurisdiction (1) to grant interim relief against the Crown and (2) to suspend the application of an Act of Parliament. The constitutional issues become even more apparent when the case is contrasted with its Irish pendant *Pesca Valentia*, where the Irish Supreme Court readily accepted that the Irish courts can temporarily suspend the application an Act alleged to infringe Community law, despite the presumption of constitutionality, *Supreme Court*, decision of 21 May 1985, *Pesca Valentia Ltd v Minister for Fisheries and Forestry, Ireland and the Attorney General* [1985] IR 193; [1986] IRLM 68; www.irlii.org.

[21] See on the state of English law on interim relief against the Crown at the time, MH Matthews, 'Injunctions, Interim Relief and Proceedings against Crown Servants', 8 *Oxford Journal of Legal Studies*, 1988, 154.

[22] The High Court *did* offer the interim relief sought on the basis of *Simmenthal*, and a *'qui peut le plus, peut le moins'* type reasoning: if a national court has jurisdiction to set aside conflicting legislation, it must also be competent to suspend the effects of an Act provisionally, *High Court, Queen's Bench Division*, decision of 10 March 1989, *R v Secretary of State for Transport, ex parte Factortame Ltd and Others* [1989] 2 CMLR 353. For a critique see A Barav, 'Enforcement of Community Rights in the National Courts: the case for jurisdiction to grant interim relief', 26 *CML Rev*, 1989, 369. The interim injunction was quashed by the Court of Appeal, on grounds mainly of the presumption of validity of an Act of Parliament, *Court of Appeal*, decision of 22 March 1989, *R v Secretary of State for Transport, ex parte Factortame Ltd and Others* [1989] 2 CMLR 353, at 392 *et seq*.

effectiveness of Community law would be just as much impaired if a rule of national law could prevent a court seized of a dispute governed by Community law from granting interim relief in order to ensure the full effectiveness of the judgment to be given on the existence of the rights claimed under Community law. It follows that a court which in those circumstances would grant interim relief, if it were not for a rule of national law, is obliged to set aside that rule.' The obligation of the English court to grant interim relief seems based primarily on the 'principle of structural precedence' (with the aim of ensuring substantive precedence of Community law and disapplication of the Merchant Shipping Act). In support of its judgment the Court repeated the principle of direct effect requiring that Community law is fully and uniformly applied, the principle of (substantive) precedence rendering automatically inapplicable conflicting national law; and also adduced additional arguments: the duty of co-operation under Article 5 of the EC Treaty (now Article 10 EC) obliging the courts to ensure legal protection of rights derived from direct effect, and the effectiveness of Article 177 of the EC Treaty (now Article 234 EC). As in *Simmenthal*, both aspects of supremacy, substantive and structural, were at stake: substantive supremacy of the Treaty over the Merchant Shipping Act (which was, strictly speaking, not part of the question referred; the English courts had said that they would at the end of the day be prepared to give priority to Community law rights over an Act of Parliament; the issue of whether there was actually an infringement of Community law was subject of prior reference of the High Court) and the structural supremacy: a procedural rule – the denial of jurisdiction to grant interim relief – must be set aside in order to be able to give full force and effect to Community law. In *Factortame*, as in *Simmenthal*, the effectiveness of Community law was constrained by a constitutional limit on the jurisdiction of the courts.

By implication, the English courts *did* have jurisdiction to offer the remedy of interim relief *as a matter of Community law*. When the case returned to the House of Lords, Lord Bridge accepted the jurisdiction of the English courts to grant interim relief against the Crown and consisting of the temporary setting aside of an Act of Parliament as a consequence of the supremacy of Community law.[23] Lord Donaldson, writing extra-judicially, did comment on the fact that the real problem of English law had not been that there was a barrier to the grant of interim relief in a particular case, which could simply be removed, but rather, and more fundamentally, that the English courts simply lacked jurisdiction to issue interim relief in the form sought in this case, namely an injunction against the Minister ordering him to suspend the application of an Act of

---

[23] *House of Lords*, decision of 11 October 1990, *Regina v Secretary of State for Transport, ex parte Factortame Ltd and Others* [1990] 3 CMLR 375, 380.

Parliament, which is claimed to conflict with Community law.[24] Advocate General Tesauro did discuss the issue, but he argued that the concept of interim protection was long anchored in the legal systems of the Member States, and pointed out that also the English courts were empowered to suspend the application of *subordinate* measures.

The Court of Justice did not, however, answer the subsequent question concerning the criteria to be applied in deciding whether or not to grant interim protection in a particular case. The Court presumably, left it for national law to decide.[25] It probably did not want to encroach upon the legislator's prerogatives.[26] In addition, the Court may not have considered it opportune to introduce a new principle fully worked out from the outset and preferred a one step at a time approach, introducing the principle in one decision, and leaving the elaboration of the conditions for future cases.[27]

Nevertheless, it remains remarkable that the Court did not even re-iterate the *Rewe* and *Comet* mantra of procedural autonomy. The difficulty is, of course, that *Rewe* and *Comet* start from the presumption that there *is* a national remedy available in the case. In *Factortame*, that was precisely the issue. On the other hand, the remedy of interim relief is not totally absent from English law. When the case returned to the House of Lords, Lord Goff stated that the jurisdiction of the courts to grant interim injunctions was to be found in Section 37 of the Supreme Court Act 1981, under which the courts have power to grant an injunction in all cases in which it appears to it to be just or convenient to do so, and have power to do so on such terms and conditions as it may think fit.[28] Guidelines for the exercise

---

[24] Lord Donaldson, who was Master of the Rolls at the time when Factortame was decided and who had sat on the Bench in the judgment of the Court of Appeal overruling the interim injunction granted by the High Court: *'The ruling of the European Court is based on a misunderstanding of English law and to that extent may be mistaken (…) The ruling appears to be based upon an assumption that the English law has a general power to grant interim injunctive relief which is subject to a special rule that this jurisdiction may not be exercised against the Crown. (…) [T]he appropriate ruling of the European Court would have been that Community law conferred a new jurisdiction on the English courts enabling them to issue interim injunctions against the Crown'*, Lord Donaldson, 'Can the Judiciary control Acts of Parliament?', (1991) *The Law Teacher*, 4, at 7–8.

[25] The failure of the Court to answer the question of the conditions for awarding interim relief has been criticised by several commentators, see JC Bonichot, 'Les pouvoirs d'injonction du juge national pour la protection des droits conférés par l'ordre juridique communautaire', *RFDA*, 1990, 912, at 918–19; D Simon and A Barav, 'Le droit communautaire et la suspension provisoire des mesures nationales. Les enjeux de l'affaire Factortame', (1990) *RMC*, 591, at 597.

[26] This is the explanation offered by Judge Kakouris, see L Papadias, 'Interim Protection under Community Law before the National Courts. The Right to a Judge with Jurisdiction to Grant Interim Relief', (1994) *LIEI*, 153, at 175.

[27] This is part of the explanation given by Judge Joliet, above at 176.

[28] *House of Lords*, decision of 11 October 1990, *Regina v Secretary of State for Transport, ex parte Factortame Ltd and Others* [1990] 3 CMLR 375, at 393, per Lord Goff.

of this jurisdiction were found in *American Cyanamid*, the 'normal' principles applying to interim injunctions cases.[29] The Court of Justice would later develop a Community test in *Zuckerfabrik Süderdithmarschen*,[30] concerning interim relief comprising the suspension of a *Community* measure alleged to be invalid. Before identifying the applicable criteria the Court held that the interim protection guaranteed to individuals before national courts cannot vary according to whether they contest the compatibility of national legal provisions with Community law or the validity of Community measures by way of secondary law, if the dispute in both cases is based on Community law itself. Accordingly, the criteria formulated in *Zuckerfabrik Süderdithmaschen* and developed later in *Atlanta*[31] equally apply to *Factortame* type situations, where a *national* measure is claimed to infringe Community law.

Structural supremacy has its limits. In fact, it is not a general rule and may not even exist as a principle; paragraph 22 of *Simmenthal*, which states that any measure of the national legal order preventing the court from giving full force and effect to Community law in a particular case must be set aside, is probably exaggerated, and certainly does not reflect a general principle: otherwise all time limits under national law would have to be set aside, and that is clearly not the case. Why then, did the Court decide *Simmenthal* and *Factortame* by reference to supremacy, presenting structural supremacy as a rule? Both in *Simmenthal* and in *Factortame*, the very principle of supremacy and the ensuing Community mandate of the national courts was at stake: '*the Court's intervention was necessary in order to enable national courts, before which claims based on Community law had been properly brought, to perform effectively the task conferred upon them under the system established by the Treaty*'.[32] Both *Simmenthal* and *Factortame* were cases in which the acceptance of Community law, its (substantive) supremacy and the ensuing mandate of all national courts still had to be consolidated.[33] The acceptance of their Community mandate was hindered not by some time limit, but by fundamental constitutional rules limiting their jurisdiction and making it impossible for them to give effect to Community law of their own motion. It is likely that the Court insisted

---

[29] See *eg* D Wyatt, 'Injunctions and Damages against the State for Breach of Community Law – a Legitimate Judicial Development', in *European Community Law in the English Courts* (Oxford, Clarendon Press, 1998) 87.

[30] Joined Cases C–1423/88 and C–92/89 *Zuckerfabrik Süderdithmarschen AG v Hauptzollamt Itzehoe and Zuckerfabrik Soest AG v Hauptzollamt Paderborn* [1991] ECR I–415.

[31] Case C–465/93 *Atlanta Fruchthandelsgesellschaft mbH v Bundesamt für Ernährung und Forstwirtschaft* [1995] ECR I–3761.

[32] Opinion of AG Jacobs in Joined Cases C–430/93 and C–431/93 *Van Schijndel and Van Veen v Stichting Pensioenfonds voor Fysiotherapeuten* [1995] ECR I–4705, at para 22.

[33] See also S Prechal, 'Community Law in National Courts: The Lessons from van Schijndel', (1998) 35 *CML Rev*, 681, at 686.

on the principle of substantive supremacy since English courts had never before *Factortame* actually given priority to Community law by setting aside an Act of Parliament and had, instead, found alternative routes mostly by virtue of rules of construction. The *Rewe* and *Comet* approach does not seem strong enough to confront such fundamental constitutional issues as the ones involved in *Factortame*, and cannot result in the creation of new jurisdiction; *Simmenthal* can. Once the fundamental principle is accepted, namely that all national courts must have jurisdiction in a case properly brought before them to award precedence to Community law, the principle of national procedural autonomy (and its corrections) takes over.

The limits of structural supremacy as a general rule became evident in *Van Schijndel*, concerning the rule under Netherlands law that an appeal in cassation is in principle confined to challenging an error of law made by the court whose decision is subject to the appeal. The question therefore arose whether, since the parties had not raised the issues of Community law before the lower courts, the latter should have done so *ex proprio motu* – otherwise there could not have been an error of law. The Spanish and Greek Governments argued before the Court of Justice that on grounds of the principle of primacy of Community law, and of effectiveness of Community law and the need for uniform application, national courts were required to consider, if necessary of their own motion, points of Community law notwithstanding any national procedural rules to the contrary. The position of the Spanish and Greek Governments was that as a matter of general principle, where national procedural rules constituted an obstacle to the application of Community law in a particular case, they must be set aside: structural supremacy.[34] Advocate General Jacobs rejected the assumption that it follows from the principle of primacy of Community law that national procedural rules must at all times yield to Community law.[35] Quite to the contrary: in the absence of Community procedural rules, the legal environment in which Community law is given effect, applied and enforced, is defined by national law, and Community law will only correct it where provisions of national law prevent Community law from being given full effect or interferes with the effective or adequate protection of Community law rights

---

[34] As Mark Hoskins formulated it: 'the supremacy is all argument', M Hoskins, 'Tilting the Balance: Supremacy and National Procedural Rules', (1996) 21 *ELR*, 265, at 375.

[35] 'What the principle of Community requires in the first place is a general rule that, when a national court is confronted with a conflict between a substantive provision of national law and a substantive provision of Community law, the Community principle should prevail', Opinion of AG Jacobs in *Joined Cases C–430/93 and C–341/93 Van Schijndel and Van Veen v Stichting Pensioenfonds voor Fysiotherapeuten* [1995] ECR 4705, at para 24. As Sacha Prechal has correctly pointed out, these 'substantive' provisions may include 'procedural rules', where Community law provides for them, S Prechal, 'Community Law in National Courts: The Lessons from van Schijndel', (1998) 35 *CML Rev*, 681, at 685.

of individuals. The 'setting aside' language of *Simmenthal* and *Factortame* may not be the consequence of the principle of supremacy, and rather be the result of the finding that, even though the legal environment is in principle defined by national law, it must nevertheless not render excessively difficult or virtually impossible the exercise of rights conferred by Community law; or in order for Community law rights to be effectively protected, courts hearing the case must have jurisdiction to apply Community law and set aside conflicting national law, even temporarily.

The *Simmenthal/Factortame* tandem has appeared again in other important cases. In *Francovich*, the Court referred to *Simmenthal* and *Factortame*[36] and in a wording reminiscent of both cases held that *'the full effectiveness of Community rules would be impaired and the protection of the rights which they grant would be weakened if individuals were unable to obtain redress when their rights are infringed by a breach of Community law for which a Member State can be held responsible'*. Only, the 'structural supremacy principle' that any measure of the national legal order preventing etc. must be set aside is not mentioned and there follows no 'accordingly, the rule preventing the court to…must be set aside', as in *Simmenthal* and *Factortame*, while it could easily be filled in: 'any rule of national law preventing the courts from holding the State liable where the breach of Community law is imputed to the national legislature must be set aside'.[37] The reasoning is no longer founded on a principle of 'structural supremacy'. Instead, the focus is on the principle of full effectiveness, taken on its own, supported by references to *Van Gend en Loos*, *Costa v ENEL* and Article 10 EC. In *Francovich*, the Court no longer seeks to hide that it is in fact creating a new remedy, the right to obtain damages when individual rights are infringed by breach of Community law for which a Member State can be held responsible. Connected with the right of individuals to obtain a remedy in damages, is the jurisdiction of the courts to offer that particular remedy, even for legislative wrong attributed to the primary legislature for which the State is immune under national constitutional law. The Court does not explain how this jurisdiction is created nor does it try to 'cover up' the fact that it is actually creating a new remedy by reference to an obstacle of national law. The Court merely states that Community law commands the existence of a particular remedy and, accordingly, a jurisdiction of the courts to provide that remedy. Structural supremacy was not the technique chosen by

---

[36] No reference was made to paragraph 22 stating the 'structural supremacy' of Community law; instead, the ECJ re-iterated the more general statement that it was the role of the national courts to ensure that Community law takes full effect and that the rights, which they confer on individuals are protected.

[37] Even in *Brasserie du Pêcheur* where the issue of the national rule of a constitutional nature denying the courts' jurisdiction to hold the State liable in damages for legislative wrong was in so many words put before the ECJ was the ruling not worded in the strongest version of paragraph 22 of *Simmenthal*.

the Court to decide the case.[38] *Simmenthal* and *Francovich* now stand for the proposition that the courts are under an obligation to give full effect to Community law and to provide protection for the rights which individuals derive from Community law, not for some 'principle of structural supremacy', which, it is submitted, does not exist as a general principle at all. It is a technique, applied in exceptional cases, not a general rule. The general rule is a more nuanced one, namely of national procedural autonomy, corrected by the principles of effectiveness and equivalence.

The structural supremacy formula returned in *Larsy*, not in the context of obligations under Community law of national courts, but rather of the duties of national administrative authorities, in a case concerning overlapping benefits in the determination of retirement pensions.[39] *Larsy*, a

---

[38]   There is a softer version of it in *Brasserie*, where the Court held that the *Francovich* principle applies irrespective of whether the breach was attributable to the legislature, the judiciary or the executive, and '*the fact that, according to national rules, the breach complained of is attributable to the legislature cannot affect the requirements inherent in the protection of the rights of individuals who rely on Community law and, in this instance, the right to obtain redress in the national courts for damages caused by that breach*', Joined Cases C–46/93 and C–48/93 *Brasserie du Pêcheur and Factortame III* [1996] ECR I–1029, at para 35.

[39]   Case C–118/00 *Gervais Larsy v Institut national d'assurances sociales pour travailleurs indépendants (Inasti)* [2001] ECR 5063. The applicant in this case, Gervais Larsy, had brought proceedings in the Belgian courts against the decision of Inasti, the competent Belgian authority, to reduce his pension in proportion to the retirement pension awarded by the competent French authorities. The Belgian court, the *Tribunal du travail de Tournai*, dismissed the action as unfounded. Since notice of the judgment had not been served, it did not become final. When the applicant's brother, Marius Larsy, who was in a similar legal and factual situation, also brought proceedings, the *Tribunal du travail de Tournai* decided to refer a question for preliminary ruling the Court of Justice. The Court held that the rule against overlapping could not apply where a person had worked in two Member States during one and the same period and had been obliged to pay contributions in both States during that time (Case C–31/92 *Marius Larsy v Inasti* [1993] ECR I–4543). Marius' action was upheld. Gervais Larsy requested that his situation be resolved in the same terms and upon a new application, he was awarded a full retirement pension, as of the date of the new application. Gervais Larsy then appealed against the seven year old judgment of the *Tribunal du travail de Tournai*, before the *Cour du Travail de Mons*, which upheld the appeal with regard to the full retirement pension with retroactive effect. The case then turned on the question of damages for breach of Community law: had Inasti committed a serious breach of Community law by not adopting of its own motion new decisions so as to comply with the judgment of the Court of Justice in *Marius Larsy*. The *Cour du Travail* decided to refer questions for preliminary ruling to the Court of Justice. The judgment of the Court turns on the issue of state liability, and the existence of a serious breach of Community law. Of interest here is the passage about the arguments invoked by Inasti explaining why it had not awarded retroactive effect to its decision to award full pension rights. According to Inasti, it did not have jurisdiction under Belgian law to review of its own motion an administrative decision that probably infringed Community law, given the fact that the decision had been upheld by a court judgment. In other words, Inasti claimed that it did not have the competence to review its decision because, under Belgian law, it was bound by a court judgment. Therefore, Gervais Larsy had to make a new application, and even then, under Belgian procedural law there was no procedural rule allowing the administrative authority to award a full pension with retroactive effect. The Court did not appreciate this basic rule that in a state governed by the rule of law, administrative authorities are bound by court judgments.

governmental liability case, turned on the extent of the Community mandate of administrative authorities and their competence to enforce Community law against conflicting national legislation. The question was whether administrative authorities are under a Community law obligation to set aside national law including a court decision having the force of *res judicata* in order to give effect to Community law.

The Court held:

> '*Suffice it to observe in that regard that the Court has held that any provision of a national legal system and any legislative, administrative or judicial practice which might impair the effectiveness of Community law by withholding from the national court having jurisdiction to apply such law the power to do everything necessary at the moment of its application to set aside national legislative provisions which might prevent, even temporarily, Community rules from having full force and effect are incompatible with those requirements, which are the very essence of Community law* [reference to paragraph 22 of *Simmenthal* and 20 of *Factortame*, the 'structural supremacy' paragraphs]'. And then it went on to say: '*Ce principe de primauté de droit communautaire impose non seulement aux juridictions, mais á toutes les instances de l'État membre de donner plein effet á la norme communautaire*[40] [reference omitted]'.[41] And it concluded: '*So, to the extent that national procedural rules precluded effective protection of Mr Larsy's rights derived under the direct effect of Community law, Inasti should have disapplied those provisions.*'[42]

Advocate General Léger had approached the issue rather differently, following the *Rewe* and *Comet* line of reasoning, leaving it to the national court to find out whether the lacuna in procedural law infringed the conditions of effectiveness and equivalence. He then added a remarkable statement, that should the procedural rules indeed have made it excessively difficult or virtually impossible to have Community rights protected, this may raise the question of the liability of the authority competent to draw up the procedural rules! However, no mention was made of the rule of reason in *Van Schijndel* and other cases, that other principles may also be taken into consideration: legal certainty, and presumably, the need for finality, *res judicata* and the principle of the rule of law.

---

[40] Case C–118/00 *Gervais Larsy v Inasti* [2001] ECR 5063, at para 52. The language of the case was French; the English version of the judgment is different, and rather bizarre: '*That principle of the primacy of Community law means that not only the lower courts but all the courts of the Member State are under a duty to give full effect to Community law (..)*'; the Dutch version coincides with the French version: '*(..) niet enkel de rechterlijke instanties, maar alle instanties van de lidstaat (..)*', at para 52.

[41] The references were to Case 48/71 *Commission v Italy* [1972] ECR 527 and Case C–101/91 *Commission v Italy* [1993] ECR I–191, which were concerned with a different issue, namely a declaration that the Member State has infringed Community law can be the consequence of an infringement on the part of the administrative authorities. This is the normal approach even under classic international law.

[42] Above 40, at para 53.

Gervais Larsy is a revolutionary case:[43] it draws extreme conclusions from the basic principles of Community law. It is implied in the judgment that national authorities must at all costs comply with Community law and with judgments of the Court of Justice, and add to *Costanzo* – which had already stated the principle that administrative authorities must set aside conflicting national legislation (substantive supremacy) – the obligation to set aside any provision of the legal system and any legislative, judicial or administrative practice which might impair the effectiveness of Community law (structural supremacy), for instance, the rule that administrative authorities are bound by court judgments. And with one stroke, the liability in damages is added. *Gervais Larsy* is *Simmenthal* (structural supremacy) and *Francovich* applied to the *Costanzo* mandate of the national administrative authorities. If that is indeed the meaning of the decision,[44] this explains the reference to structural supremacy. Once it is commonly accepted that administrative authorities are under the same Community mandate as courts in principle, the *Rewe* and *Comet* rule of procedural autonomy may be introduced.

To sum up, there does not seem to be a general principle of structural supremacy, implying that indeed any legislative, administrative or judicial practice which prevents the application of Community law in a given case must always be set aside. Community law must be applied with precedence over national law, but it is to be applied in the national legal environment, which, as a starting point, defines the procedural and remedial rules. Only in controversial cases, where the opposition from the national courts and authorities based on constitutional arguments is strongest, does the Court come up with the strongest weapon ruling out any contradiction: Community law must be applied, any national rule or practice notwithstanding.

5.3. THE PRINCIPLE OF EFFECTIVE JUDICIAL PROTECTION

The *Rewe/Comet* approach and the *Simmenthal/Factortame* approaches seem to be completely opposite: while the first technique starts from national law (with corrections), the second one starts from Community

---

[43]   On the other hand, it is a decision handed by a chamber of three judges, hardly the composition for such a principled judgment. The facts of the case may have influenced the outcome: if his brother Marius was awarded a full pension with retroactive effect, why not Gervais? The answer could have been: for reasons of procedure. It is normal, also under national law, that individuals in the same situation do not achieve the same outcome, depending on whether they have instituted court proceedings in time, have invoked certain arguments etc. The technique used – the reference to the strong versions of structural supremacy in *Simmenthal* and *Factortame* – may be a slip of the tongue.

[44]   Which is debatable as it was not handed by a full court.

law and rules out any national law restricting its *effet utile*. What both have in common is the concern for the effectiveness of Community law, both its effective enforcement and the effective judicial protection of individuals under Community law. In a third line of cases the emphasis is entirely on the principle of effectiveness, without reference to either the principle of national procedural autonomy or of structural supremacy. Effective judicial protection is elevated to a general principle of Community law, which can create jurisdiction for national courts, and new causes of action and remedies for individuals.

5.3.1. The Right to an Effective Remedy

The principle of effective judicial protection was introduced first to control whether a particular national remedy or sanction was appropriate to provide adequate protection of Community law rights as prescribed by a directive. The right in question was the right to equal treatment as laid down in Council Directive 76/207, Article 6 of which requires the Member States to introduce into their national legal systems such measures as are necessary to enable all persons who consider themselves wronged by discrimination to pursue their claim by judicial process.[45] In *Von Colson and Kamann*, the Court held that where compensation was chosen in national law as the remedy,[46] it must be adequate in relation to the damage sustained, based on the need for effective judicial protection required by the directive.[47] Since the remedy chosen in the German implementation law, compensation of the costs made – the bus-fare in the case at hand – did not comply with those conditions, the courts must instead seek another remedy available under national law and interpret their national law so as to comply with the conditions of effective judicial protection as required by the directive. In later cases, the requirement of an adequate remedy and of effective judicial protection would be elevated to a general principle, independent of any legislative prescriptions.

---

[45] Council Directive 76/207 of 9 February 1976 on the implementation of the principle of equal treatment of men and women as regards access to employment, vocational training and promotion and working conditions, OJ 1976, L 39, p40.

[46] Which operates as a sanction for the other party, and must accordingly have real deterrent effect.

[47] Case 14/83 *Sabine von Colson and Elisabeth Kamann v Land Nordrhein-Westfalen* [1984] ECR 1891; see also Case C–271/91 *Helen Marshall v Southhampton West Hampshire Area Health Authority* [1993] *ECR* 4367; Case C–185/97 *Belinda Jane Coote v Granada Hospitality Ltd* [1998] I–5199 (all concerning the interpretation of a remedy prescribed by a directive); Joined Cases C–46/93 and C–48/93 *Brasserie du Pêcheur SA v Germany and The Queen v Secretary of State for Transport, ex parte Factortame Ltd and Others* [1996] ECR 1029 (the reparation of loss caused by violation of Community law on the part of the Member State must be commensurate with the damage sustained).

5.3.2. The Right to Judicial Review

In *Johnston*,[48] the Court introduced the right to effective judicial review, and accordingly of access to a competent court, as an aspect of the *principle of effective judicial protection*. The Sex Discrimination (Northern Ireland) Order 1976 rendered judicially unreviewable the decision of the Chief Constable of the Royal Ulster Constabulary[49] and thus deprived Mrs Johnston of any judicial remedy.[50] Article 6 of Directive 76/207 required the Member States to introduce into their internal systems such measures as are needed to enable all persons who considered themselves to be wronged by discrimination to pursue their claims by judicial process. The Court held that the provision reflected a general principle of law, underlying the constitutional traditions common to the Member States and laid down also in Articles 6 and 13 of the ECHR. From Article 6 of the Directive, interpreted in the light of the general principle, the Court derived the right to obtain an effective remedy in a competent court. The provision in the Sex Discrimination Order was found contrary to the principle of effective judicial control laid down in the Directive.[51]

Although the principle of effective judicial protection[52] was linked to Article 6 of Directive 76/207, the judgment was formulated in general

---

[48] Case 222/84 *Johnston v Chief Constable of the Royal Ulster Constabulary* [1986] ECR 1651.

[49] Under Article 53(2) of the Act 'a certificate signed by or on behalf of the Secretary of State and certifying that an act specified in the certificate was done for [the purpose of safeguarding national security or of protecting public safety or public order] shall be conclusive evidence that it was done for that purpose'.

[50] Marguerite Johnston had performed the functions of a uniformed police officers, when, due to a newly introduced policy that male officers should carry fire-arms in the regular course of their duties, but that women would not be equipped with them, the chief constable refused to renew her contract. Mrs. Johnston lodged an application challenging the decision before the Industrial Tribunal claiming that she had suffered unlawful discrimination prohibited by the sex discrimination Order. In the proceedings before the Tribunal, the chief constable produced a certificate issued by the Secretary of State certifying that the refusal of the chief constabulary was done for the purpose of safeguarding national security and protecting public safety and public order, and was accordingly not open for judicial review.

[51] *Johnston* may therefore be considered as one of the instances where the principle of substantive supremacy would have lead to the setting aside of a national procedural rule, since the relevant provision of Community law was procedural in nature. Interestingly, Advocate General Darmon had suggested the approach based on structural supremacy, while the easier principle of substantive supremacy does the same, given that the requirement of judicial control was included in the directive, and there was a clear conflict between a provision in a national statute and a provision in the directive – as interpreted in the light of a general principle of effective judicial protection.

[52] While the case is built on the right of all persons to obtain an effective remedy in a competent court, the Court also gave away its other concern, and the pendant of the right to effective judicial protection of individuals by putting the question first in terms of whether Community law requires the Member States to ensure that their national courts and tribunals exercise effective control over compliance with the provisions of the directives and with the national legislation intended to put it into effect, Case 222/84 *Johnston v Chief Constable of the Royal Ulster Constabulary* [1986] ECR 1651, at para 13.

terms, and the principle was later extended to cases where there was no link with the principle of judicial protection in codified form.[53] In *Heylens*, a case decided on the basis of Article 48 of the Treaty, the right to a remedy of a judicial nature or effective judicial review against a decision refusing free access to employment in another Member State was derived from the fundamental character of both the right to free access to employment under the Treaty and the general principle of effective judicial protection in the form of judicial review. Accordingly, the authorities are under a duty to state reasons, which are open for review by the courts. No express mention was made of the *Rewe* and *Comet* principle of national autonomy and its limits,[54] nor of the principle of supremacy; these duties derived directly from the principle of effective judicial protection of fundamental Community law rights of individuals, a general principle of Community law deriving from the common constitutional traditions of the Member States and Articles 6 and 13 of the ECHR. The right to effective judicial protection of individual rights has become a source for new powers for national courts.[55] The principle of effective judicial protection and the principle of the effectiveness of Community law will often coincide: the effective remedy offered to the individual for the protection of his Community law rights, contributes to enforcing the correct application and the enforcement of Community law.

5.3.3. A 'Right' to Effective Judicial Protection before the European Courts?

The Court of Justice has not been so generous when it comes to its own jurisdiction. The fundamental right to effective judicial protection and access to a competent court has been invoked in order to convince the

---

[53] Case 222/86 *UNECTEF v Georges Heylens* [1987] ECR 4097, at para 14: 'the existence of a remedy of a judicial nature against any decision of a national authority refusing the benefit of that right is essential in order to secure for the individual effective protection of his right'.

[54] For an explanation: C Kilpatrick, 'Turning Remedies Around: A Sectoral Analysis of the Court of Justice', in G de Búrca and JHH Weiler (eds), *The European Court of Justice* (Oxford, OUP, 2001) 143, who argues that gender equality cases provide a perfect launching pad for more ambitious moves in the direction of procedural and remedial effectiveness, given the combination of 'vulnerable individuals', fundamental rights and State non-compliance with Community law.

[55] So for instance Case C–97/91 *Oleificio Borelli v Commission* [1992] I–6313 (action for judicial review of a preparatory administrative decision must be held admissible even if it would not be under national procedural law, where the national act is binding on the Commission taking the final decision); Joined Cases C–87/90, C–88/90 and C–89/90 *Verholen and Others v Sociale Verzekeringsbank* [1991] ECR I–3756 (on the extension of the rules of standing and individual interest to bring a case); Case C–226/99 *Siples Srl v Ministero delle Finanze* [2001] ECR I–277 (the power of judicial authorities to suspend the application of a decision derives from the principle of effective judicial protection).

Court to relax the conditions for standing for individuals in direct actions for annulment brought under Article 230(4) EC. In *Greenpeace*,[56] for instance, the applicants argued that if they were not awarded standing under Article 230(4) EC, they would not be able to obtain effective judicial protection, since they did not have standing under national law, and there was, accordingly, a gap in the 'complete system for judicial review of Community acts' which the Court claims to exist. Accordingly, Article 230(4) must be interpreted in such way as to safeguard fundamental environmental interests and protect individual environmental rights effectively. The Court dismissed the case as inadmissible, referring the applicants to the national courts.[57] The Court has systematically pretended that the indirect route via the national courts and the action for non-contractual liability pursuant to Article 235 EC and the second paragraph of Article 288 EC in all cases provide the relevant framework to achieve effective judicial protection of private individuals.

In *Jégo-Quéré*,[58] the Court of First Instance considered whether in a case where provisions of general application directly affect the legal situation of an individual, the latter's right would be effectively protected if he could not bring a direct action for annulment, and instead, had to follow the route via the national court,[59] or the route of an action for damages based on the non-contractual liability of the Community.[60] The Court of First Instance held that the right to an effective remedy before a court of competent jurisdiction was founded on the common constitutional traditions of the Member States and on Articles 6 and 13 of the ECHR and was reaffirmed by Article 47 of the EU Charter of Fundamental Rights, and arrived at the conclusion that the current restrictive interpretation of Article 230 (4) EC could no longer be considered compatible with the right to an effective remedy. Instead, the Court suggested that *'in order to ensure effective judicial protection for individuals, a natural or legal person is to be regarded as individually concerned by a Community measure of general application that concerns him directly if the measure in question affects his legal position, in a manner which is both definite and immediate, by restricting his rights by imposing obligations on him. The number and position of other persons*

---

[56] Case C–321/95 P *Stiching Greenpeace Council (Greenpeace International) and Others v Commission* [1998] ECR I–1651.

[57] See also Case C–70/97 P *Kruidvat BVBA v Commission* [1998] ECR I–7183.

[58] Case T–177/01 *Jégo-Quéré Cie SA v Commission* [2002] ECR II-2365.

[59] However, in the situation under analysis, where the general act directly affects the individual's legal position, *i.e.* without intervention by the national authorities, access to the national courts can only be obtained by knowingly infringing the act and awaiting judicial proceedings brought against him.

[60] Which cannot lead to the removal of the measure held to be illegal; there is no comprehensive judicial review, but is limited, in the type of cases under scrutiny, to the censuring of sufficiently serious infringements of rules of law intended to confer rights on individuals.

who are likewise affected by the measure, or who may be so, are of no relevance in that regard'.[61]

The Court of Justice, however, implicitly reversed *Jégo-Quéré* in *Unión de Pequeños Agricultores*. The Court did make a note of the principle of effective judicial protection of Community rights of individuals, a principle stemming from the common constitutional traditions of the Member States and Articles 6 and 13 of the ECHR.[62] However, in the complete system of legal remedies and procedures designed to review judicial protection of the legality of acts of the Community institutions, it was for the Member States to establish a system of legal remedies and procedures to ensure respect for the right to effective judicial protection... Accordingly the *national* courts are under an obligation to interpret *national* procedural law so as to enable natural and legal persons to challenge before the courts the legality of any decision or other *national* measure relative to the application to them of a *Community* act of general application, by pleading the invalidity of such an act. Yet, this was the point exactly, namely, that in some cases there *is* no national act operating as an interface between the Community act of general application and the legal position of the individual. The Court maintained its case law on direct and individual concern, *'although this last condition must be interpreted in the light of the principle of effective judicial protection by taking account of the various circumstances that may distinguish an applicant individually* [reference omitted], *such an interpretation cannot have the effect of setting aside the condition in question, expressly laid down in the Treaty, without going beyond the jurisdiction conferred by the Treaty on the Community Courts'.* It is striking that in this context the Court no longer speaks of a *right* to effective judicial protection, but only of a *principle* of effective judicial protection in the light of which Article 230 EC must be interpreted. It does not by and of itself create a right to judicial review or right to access to a Court having jurisdiction to conduct such review, as seemed to be the case for the national courts in *Johnston, Heylens* or *Borelli*.

5.4. THE REQUIREMENT OF UNIFORM APPLICATION OF COMMUNITY LAW

The need for a degree[63] of uniformity in the application[64] of Community law is another consideration in the case law of the Court. The need for

---

[61] Case T–177/01 *Jégo-Quéré et Cie SA v Commission* [2002] ECR II-2365, at para 51.
[62] Note that the reference to Art. 47 of the EU Charter is omitted.
[63] The vagueness is intentional; the question is of course what level of uniformity is required and feasible.
[64] The uniformity in the interpretation of Community law is ensured by the Court of Justice and the preliminary rulings procedure. Uniform *interpretation* does not however necessarily ensure uniform *application* due the procedural autonomy of the Member States.

uniformity was one of the arguments in favour of the precedence of Community law in *Costa v ENEL*.[65] However, given the fact that Community law depends on national law for its application and enforcement and given the principle of national procedural autonomy, this uniformity will be not be complete. There is not and cannot be a principle of full uniformity.[66] On the other hand, the Court has stated that the *'uniform application of [Community law] is a fundamental requirement of the Community legal order'*.[67]

The requirement of the uniformity of Community law is especially important in cases where the validity of a Community act is in question, in cases like *Foto-Frost*, *Zuckerfabrik Süderdithmarschen*, and in cases where a national rule threatens the application – any application – of Community law as in *Pafitis*.[68]

5.5. INTERMEDIATE CONCLUDING REMARKS

5.5.1. A Balancing Act

The formulation of the exact duties of the national courts and the Community approach to jurisdiction, procedural rules, remedies, and so on, is the result of a balancing exercise weighing various principles and fundamental requirements. In the absence of Community legislation providing remedies and prescribing the procedural rules to be applied to actions at law before national courts, Community law remains dependent on the national legal environment, and the courts will have to find a way to ensure effective protection of individuals, adequate remedies and effectiveness of Community law, while also having regard to principles of legal certainty, uniformity and so on.

5.5.2. Whose Balancing?

This balancing act is a joint exercise of the Court of Justice and the national courts. There is, however, no clear dividing line as to who does

---

[65] Case 6/64 *Costa v ENEL* [1964] ECR 585, at 594; see also Case 14/68 *Walt Wilhelm v Bundeskartellamt* [1969] *ECR* 1, at para 4.

[66] Or as van Gerven puts it: the ECJ does not regard the requirement of uniform application as an all-embracing principle which does not allow for national differences, W van Gerven, 'Of Rights, Remedies and Procedures', (2000) 37 *CML Rev*, 501, at 505.

[67] Joined Cases C–143/88 and C–92/89 *Zuckerfabrik Süderdithmarschen AG v Hauptzollamt Itzehoe and Zückerfabrik Soest AG v Hautzollamt Paderborn* [1991] ECR I–415, at 26.

[68] Case 441/93 *Paganis Pafitis and others v Traeza Kentrikis Ellados AE and others* [1996] ECR I–1347, at 68: 'It is for the Court of Justice, in relation to rights relied on by individuals on the basis of Community provisions, to verify whether the judicial protection available under national law is appropriate'.

what. Cases like *Van Schijndel* and *Levez* seem to encourage the national courts to take the responsibility to carry out the balancing function, by explaining the factors to be taken into account. On the other hand, there are other cases where the Court states that it is *its* role to control the appropriateness of national procedural rules for the judicial protection of Community law rights.[69] In some cases the Court simply refers back to the main rule of national procedural autonomy, effectiveness and equivalence and leaves the decision on a particular rule entirely to the national court;[70] in other cases, it dives into national procedural law to arrive at the conclusion that the relevant rule passes the test; or, in the alternative to hold that it does not. There is a problem of predictability: it is impossible to predict whether in a specific case the Court will scrutinise a particular procedural rule or not; if it does, it is difficult to predict whether a particular rule will pass the test or not. The difficulty for the Court's audience is, that it is never clear in advance which technique will apply, whether the Court will at all analyse the particular procedural rule or national legal problem put before it by the national court, and what level of intensity of scrutiny it will apply.

In theory, of course, the Court of Justice only interprets Community law and does not have jurisdiction to assess the compatibility of concrete measures of national law with the standards of Community law. Yet, in practice, the Court may solve the concrete case for the national court. The Court should however attempt not to be lured into such adventure. The Court of Justice is not an expert on national law, and does not know the intricacies of national procedural law in concrete cases.

5.5.3. The Key Word: Effectiveness

At the end of the day, the keyword is effectiveness. The main techniques all have the requirement of effectiveness in common: in the *Rewe* and *Comet* line of cases, the condition that national procedural law cannot make it excessively difficult or virtually impossible to protect rights under Community law, has been labelled 'the principle of effectiveness'. Of structural supremacy, which may have given the impression of existing as a principle in *Simmenthal* and *Factortame*, it is full effectiveness and the concomitant duty of the national courts to give full effect to Community law, which have survived as a general principle. And the fundamental right of effective judicial protection exists mainly as the duty in the hands of the

---

[69] So for instance Case C–441/93 *Panagis Pafitis and others v Trapeza Kentrikis Ellados AE and others* [1996] ECR I–1347, at 69, even though the Greek court had not submitted the question.
[70] For instance Case C–92/00 *Hospital Ingenieure Krankenhaustechnik Planungs-GmbH (HI) v Stadt Wien* [2002] ECR I–5553.

courts to provide effective protection of the rights which individuals derive from Community law. But at the end of the day, the principle of effectiveness is to be applied with reason in the national legal environment, under the supervision of the Court of Justice.

5.6. CHANGING THE PERSPECTIVE: THE CREATION OF NEW REMEDIES[71]

In the previous pages, an attempt was made to bring some order to the case law of the Court of Justice by reference to the techniques used by the Court and with the focus on the duties of national courts. When the perspective changes from the courts to the individual, the focus may be on remedies offered with a view to protecting Community rights. As is well-known, the Court of Justice in the *butter-buying cruises case* held that Community law does not intend to create new remedies in the national courts other than those already laid down by national law, while on the other hand, every type of action available under national law must also be available for the purpose of ensuring the observance of Community provisions having direct effect.[72] As has been described in the previous chapters, the Court has left it to national law to elaborate the specifics of the Community mandate of the national courts under the principle of national procedural autonomy, and to apply domestic remedies as long as the principle of effectiveness and equivalence are complied with. Procedural

---

[71] This is an evergreen in the literature on Community law in national courts. Few authors will however seek to define 'remedy' and 'new'. As for the latter notion, there are only so many remedies a court can offer in order to protect rights. Mostly, the 'new' remedy will not be so novel that it does not exist at all in the legal order of a Member State; the novelty will normally consist in the fact that a particular remedy is applied in new cases where it was not previously. The newness may have more to do with the fact that a particular remedy is prescribed as a matter of Community law and that Community law requires jurisdiction of the national courts to provide that remedy. The main difficulty, however, lies in the definition of the notion of 'remedy', see on this, M Ruffert, 'Rights and Remedies in European Community Law: Comparative View', (1997) 34 *CML Rev*, 307; W van Gerven, 'Of Rights, Remedies and Procedures', (2000) 37 *CML Rev*, 501.

[72] Case 158/80 *Rewe-Handelsgesellschaft Nord mbH and Rewe-Markt Steffen v Hauptzollamt Kiel (butter-buying cruises)* [1981] ECR 1805, at para 44. This was an unusual case: the plaintiffs in the main proceedings were traders who requested the courts to require national authorities to compel a third party to comply with obligations arising from Community law in a legal situation in which that trader was not involved but was indirectly economically adversely affected by the failure to observe Community law, because of the competitive advantage enjoyed by the plaintiffs competitors as a result of the failure of the authorities to enforce Community law. The Commission pointed out that the recognition of a personal right to have the prescribed customs duties applied would mean that individuals could request a national court to order the proper application of Community law in cases which did not directly concern them. According to the Commission, the legal system laid down by the Treaty prescribes that only the Court of Justice had jurisdiction in connection with an infringement of the Treaty by a Member State and then only on the application of the Commission or of another Member State.

autonomy also comprises remedial autonomy: it is first and foremost for the national legal order to provide the appropriate remedies. There are sufficient reasons why this should have been the starting point for the Court, and indeed why it was the only solution available. First, the Treaty and Community law did not (yet)[73] provide for a separate set of remedies.[74] On the contrary, the Treaty lacks a system of sanctions for breaches of Community law and of remedies for the individual whose rights have been violated by a Member State[75] or by an individual.[76] While the Treaty does provide for some, albeit limited, causes of action against the institutions and some protection of their rights in case of violations committed by them,[77] there is hardly anything to protect the individual from violations by national authorities. In the absence of sanctions and remedies provided in the Treaties, the Court had to mould them in its case law. Second, the Court did not wish to legislate detailed rules on remedies itself, leaving that for the Community legislature. Working out the details of available remedies does not seem part of the judicial function. In the absence of Community remedies, the only way forward was to rely on existing national remedies. Third, and irrespective of whether Community remedies would be created in legislation, there is much to be said for national procedures and remedies: in many areas of law, Community law and national law are so intertwined, that a separate set of Community procedures and remedies may complicate matters, rather than making them easier. In addition, national remedies are what national courts and the legal community in a given Member State are familiar with.

However, the Community rights/national remedies system would soon prove insufficient to secure the full and effective enforcement of Community law in the Member States and to ensure the effective protection of the Community rights of individuals. The Court would soon start to interfere with national remedies. The deficiencies of the system result from the limits of direct effect on the one hand and the unsuitability at times of national remedies on the other. The main problem with direct

---

[73] The Court did predict that there would be harmonization of remedies at some stage and in its national procedural and remedial autonomy mantra, the Court often refers to 'the present state of Community law'.

[74] There is a tendency now to prescribe remedies in Community legislation.

[75] As for infringements of Community law by the Members States, the Treaty only provides for the public enforcement mechanism of Article 226 EC, which does not formally involve the individual – in practice, most enforcement procedures are instigated upon complaints from individuals. The penalty payments or lump sums which since the Treaty of Maastricht may be imposed on the defying Member State under Article 228(2) EC do not benefit the individual.

[76] The exception is Article 81(2) EC that provides that agreements concluded in violation of Article 81 (1) are automatically void. This sanction is however not concerned with remedying damage suffered by other individuals.

[77] In Articles 230(4) and 288(2) read in conjunction with Article 235 EC.

effect as the basis for the judicial protection of individual Community law rights was, most strikingly, the lack of direct effect of directives in horizontal relations, which left a serious gap in the protection of individual rights. Non-implementation is a common violation, and it often causes damage to individuals, as many directives are intended, directly or indirectly, to benefit individuals, as entrepreneurs, consumers, tourists and so on. Direct effect, either on its own or in combination with supremacy could not secure a remedy for the individual in horizontal relationships. The Court attempted to fill the gap by having recourse to the old and familiar technique of conform interpretation, which would allow the courts to offer an adequate remedy.[78] Yet, there are limits to what a court can achieve by way of conform interpretation, mostly because of the limits of the judicial function: the courts may interpret or construe the law made by the legislature, but not re-write it to say the opposite of what was meant, in the absence of a sufficient reason to do so.[79] Conform interpretation cannot in all cases achieve effective judicial protection of Community law rights.

The second deficit of the system of Community rights/national remedies lies, at times, in the inaptness of those national judicial remedies. National remedies may not be adequate to protect Community law rights. They may even be completely absent in a particular case, leaving the individual entirely unprotected. In other cases, there may be substantial differences in national remedies available in the different Member States, creating an uneven level of protection. While Community citizens in all Member States may presumably enjoy the same rights, the remedies available to them in case of infringement may vary to such an extent that a sufficient level of uniformity is no longer attained.

Sometimes, the inaptness of the national system of remedies can equally be overcome by recourse to the technique of consistent interpretation. In *Von Colson and Kamann* for instance, the Court required the German courts to offer real and effective judicial protection and to interpret and apply German law in conformity with the requirements of the directive in question in so far as they were given discretion under German law. The duty of conform interpretation may allow the courts to offer suitable national remedies for Community law rights.[80] Yet, in other cases,

---

[78]   Cases in point are *Von Colson and Kamann*, *Marleasing* and *Faccini Dori*, where the technique of conform interpretation is presented explicitly as an alternative for direct effect.

[79]   Where there is direct effect, the courts may not only interpret the law so as to conform to the requirements of Community law, but even completely re-construe it and even set it aside.

[80]   See Ph Tash, 'Remedies for European Community Law Claims in Member State Courts: Toward a European Standard', (1993) 31 *Columbia Journal of Transnational Law*, 377, at 389 *et seq.*

consistent interpretation will not do to fill the gap. In some of those cases, the Court started to interfere more actively with the national system of remedies.

An example is offered by the case law on *access to national remedies*. In *Johnston*, for instance, there was no right to appeal against a particular type of decision; the Court held that this infringed the principle of effective judicial protection. In *Heylens*, the absence of a duty to state reasons was held to infringe the right to effective judicial review and the right to effective judicial protection. In *Borelli*, the Court rejected the rule under Italian administrative law that preparatory acts are not open to judicial review. In these cases, the Court extended the jurisdiction of the national courts and required them, by recourse to the principle of effective judicial protection, to provide a remedy, or at least, the possibility for an individual to seek a remedy. The area of restitution of unduly paid sums has formed a miniature laboratory for the Court to test the aptness of national procedural and remedial rules, and of setting standards of effectiveness of Community law, effective judicial protection, and of uniformity. Yet, these cases were still concerned with conditions on, and interferences with, *national* remedies.

The shortcomings of national procedures and remedies and the willingness of the Court to interfere was most striking in the *Factortame* case, relating to the remedy of interim relief. In contrast to the previous cases, the Court in *Factortame* did not interfere with a *national* remedy available in a particular case, nor did it clarify a remedy prescribed by a directive, but it created a *Community* law remedy which must in all Member States be available before the courts *as a matter of Community law*. This is at least the practical result of *Factortame*, and it certainly is the common manner of presenting the case. If this is indeed what happened in *Factortame*, the Court of Justice certainly attempted to conceal it. The decision is phrased not in terms of creating a new remedy, or, for that matter, of the court's jurisdiction to offer a particular remedy, but in terms of the 'principle' of structural supremacy and the duty of the national courts to set aside national rules preventing them from giving full effect to Community law and from granting effective judicial protection to individuals under Community law.[81]

---

[81] Peter Oliver has argued that there is very little difference between setting aside an obstacle to interim relief and creating interim relief as a fresh remedy, P Oliver, 'Interim Measures: Some Recent Developments', (1992) *CML Rev*, 7, at 16. While this may be true in practical terms and looking with the benefit of hindsight, it does matter a great deal as a matter of principle: the creation of a new remedy raises questions as to the the limits of the ECJ's judicial function, its likely interference with the legislative function and therefore as to its legitimacy, as was reflected in some reactions to *Francovich* in literature as well as in the submissions of several Governments in *Brasserie/Factortame*. More practically, it raises questions of the actual source of the jurisdiction of the national courts: can it really derive from Community itself, and if so, how must this be theorized?

The effect or result of *Factortame* was the creation of jurisdiction for the English courts to grant interim relief by suspending the application of a Statute, which would not be possible under English law. The wording of the judgment hides this effect: the Court pretends that the only reason why the courts did not award interim relief was a rule of national law preventing them doing so in a particular case.[82] Yet the case was more complicated: the English courts lacked jurisdiction, and in that sense it is remarkable that the case was solved under the *Simmenthal* reasoning:[83] it is difficult to maintain that by setting aside a lack of jurisdiction... jurisdiction is created: two negatives do not necessarily make a positive.

Factortame is often treated as the beginning of a line of cases, which in practical effect imply the creation of new remedies. Yet, one could go back even further in time, and characterise the setting aside of national law for violation of Community law as a remedy. *'Disapplying national measures which are found to be incompatible with Community law in themselves (..) is the most general remedy which individuals whose rights have been infringed may institute before a national court of law'.*[84] Where an individual derives a directly effective right from Community law, the national court must offer him the remedy of disapplication of conflicting national law. This remedy is imposed by Community law. In *Simmenthal*, the focus is on the jurisdiction of the *courts*, and the case is not often interpreted in terms of remedies. Few will remember who *Simmenthal* was and what was claimed before the Italian courts. But we do all know the Spanish fishermen whose Community law rights needed protection and who, given the inappropriateness of the English system of remedies, depended on the remedies available as a matter of Community law. However, also in *Simmenthal*, the Italian court was seized by an individual claiming that his rights had been infringed. In many cases, as in *Simmenthal*, the disapplying of conflicting national legislation will suffice to remedy the infringement causing harm to an individual.

The case which is most identified with the 'creation of Community remedies' is, of course, *Francovich*, the case that introduced the principle of the liability of the Member States for harm done as a consequence of

---

[82]   See *eg* J Temple Lang, 'The Principle of Effective Judicial Protection of Community Law Rights', in *Judicial Review in European Union Law. Liber Amicorum in Honour of Lord Slynn of Hadley*, Vol I, (The Hague, Kluwer Law International 2000) 235, at 240 *et seq.*

[83]   Perhaps the *Johnston/Heylens* approach *(see infra)* and *'the right to a judge having jurisdiction to (...)'* would have been more appropriate in this respect. However, it would have been difficult to convince the English courts that this would imply that they should assume jurisdiction of their own motion, without awaiting a legislative intervention creating it.

[84]   W van Gerven, 'Of rights, remedies and procedures', (2000) 37 *CML Rev*, 501, at 506.

violations of Community law. Becuase of the magnitude of the case, and because in terms of national constitutional law it poses a number of interesting questions, the *Francovich* mandate will be analysed in a separate chapter. But before turning to *Francovich*, the story of the development of the Community mandate of the national courts is interrupted, and the perspective is shifted from Community law to national law, in order to analyse the national reactions to the *Simmenthal* mandate.

6

The 'Simmenthal Mandate' Embraced

6.1. INTRODUCTION

THE DUTY INCUMBENT on the national courts to review national legislation, including primary legislation of a later date, has by and large been accepted in all the Member States. There are still some minor areas of resistance, but on the whole, the national courts have accepted the message from Luxembourg, and now assume a function which, for some courts, was unheard of before. The obstacles which had to be overcome by the various courts were not always the same. In some countries, the duty to review legislation in the light of Community law did not in principle alter the constitutional position of the courts. In The Netherlands, for instance, the competence of the courts to review primary legislation in light of certain treaties was provided for in the Constitution. The message from Luxembourg coincided with the constitutional mandate of the courts. In other States, however, there was great reluctance, in the beginning, to accept the new duty. The commands of the European Court conflicted with the national constitutional mandate of the courts. What the Court of Justice asked the courts to do was something that was unheard of in the constitutional framework. They were actually required by the Court to scrutinise the norms they had always adhered to. This reluctance, or hesitancy, was caused by a number of factors, such as a certain vision of the relationship between national and international law and of the organs which carried the responsibility to ensure respect for international treaties in the internal legal order; the prevailing under-standing of the constitutional position of the courts *vis-à-vis* the political organs; the existence of a constitutional court which has a constitutionally enshrined monopoly to scrutinise primary legislation; or a misperception of what the duty to review under Community law was really about. These obstacles have now largely been overcome, but this required, in some Member States, a dramatic change of view on all or some of the issues just mentioned. As will be demonstrated later on, in most of the Member States, and indeed, in all of the Member States which did not yet provide for judicial review in the light of treaties, the message from Luxembourg was finally accepted by way of judicial re-interpretation of the constitutional foundations, without any formal constitutional amendments having taken place. The constitutional building blocks remained identical; the edifice made out of them was different, and the national constitutional setting in which the courts operate was re-interpreted so as to accomodate the new mandate. The whole story is, in fact, one of adapting the existing constitutional framework to the requirements of the Court of Justice, which, with regard to judicial review, culminated in *Simmenthal*.

Before looking into the different obstacles which may have hindered the acceptance of the duty to review national legislation, it may be helpful to take a brief look at the evolution of the case law in the different Member States, so that the more detailed analysis of the different obstacles taken on their own, can be conducted against the general background of the whole story. The following pages are accordingly intended only as an introduction for those readers who are not familiar with the national case law.

6.2. GRADUAL ACCEPTANCE OF THE DUTY OF JUDICIAL REVIEW BY THE DOMESTIC COURTS: A BIRD'S EYE VIEW

6.2.1. The Netherlands

The constitutional doctrines concerning the relationship between international and national law and the judicial enforcement of the State's treaty obligations prevailing in The Netherlands were particularly apt for the courts to accept the commands of the European Court of Justice. In fact, the constitutional system materially coincided with what was expected from the courts by the Court of Justice. Yet even this seemingly uncomplicated narrative is interesting. It is in the context of Community law and with the assistance and support of the Court of Justice that the Netherlands courts have started to review national law in the light of international law. But for a long time and until very recently, the handling of the issue by the Netherlands, both by the courts and in legal writing, was surprisingly unprincipled. Even though the constitutional provisions were particularly apt to comply with the case law of the Court of Justice and the courts could therefore comply with both their national constitutional and Community mandate, the constitutional provisions were and still are generally considered irrelevant in the area of Community law: Community law takes precedence by and of itself, and the courts have the power of judicial review of national law, including Acts of Parliament, irrespective of the constitutional authorisation. The review powers are considered usually to follow from the case law of the Court of Justice, not from Article 94 of the Constitution. Now, forty years after *Van Gend en Loos* and *Costa v ENEL*, the question has been raised whether it would be appropriate to introduce new provisions in the Constitution to deal with the specific case of Community law.[1] Furthermore, the alternative view that Article 94 provides the proper basis for the courts' review powers in the context of Community law also is gaining ground.

6.2.2. Belgium

In Belgium, where the Constitution was silent on the question of the relation of international treaties and national law and the role of the courts, direct effect and supremacy of Community law were accepted by the *Cour de cassation* in its famous *Le Ski* judgment of 1971.[2] The acceptance of the pillar doctrines was not limited to Community law, but was part of a broader 'silent revision of the Constitution'[3] in respect of the relation between national law and treaty law in general, on grounds of 'the very nature of international law'. The essential principles have not been seriously challenged since then. However, the establishment of a constitutional court, the *Cour d'arbitrage*, has renewed the debate on the relation between international law and the Constitution, and even on whether Belgium is to be considered a monist or a dualist country. The *Cour d'arbitrage* has assumed competence to control the constitutionality of parliamentary acts of assent, and indirectly, of the content of the treaties they approve. The precedence of treaties in the domestic legal order may now be limited to treaties which are not unconstitutional. It is not clear as yet whether this restriction also applies to Community law. On the whole, however, the review powers of the ordinary courts have been accepted since *Le Ski* and the case law of the *Cour d'arbitrage* does not affect the acceptance of the *Simmenthal* mandate by the Belgian courts.

6.2.3. Luxembourg

The Luxembourg framework was particularly apt since the courts already accepted a *Simmenthal*-like mandate for the whole of international treaty law even in the absence of any constitutional provision to that effect. *Simmenthal* accordingly did not require any adaptations.[4]

---

[1]   LFM Besselink et al, *De Nederlandse Grondwet en de Europese Unie* (Groningen, Europa Law Publishing, 2002).

[2]   *Hof van Cassatie (B)*, decision of 27 May 1971, *SA Fromagerie franco-suisse Le Ski*, Pas., 1971, I, 886; Arr.Cass., 1971, 959; JT, 1971, 460; RW, 1971–1972, 424; CMLR, 1972, 330; RTDeur., 1971, 495; Oppenheimer, *The Cases*, at 245.

[3]   WJ Ganshof van der Meersch, 'Community Law and the Belgian Constitution', in St John Bates *et al* (ed), *In Memoriam JDB Mitchell* (London, 1983) 74, at 82.

[4]   Recently: G Wivines, 'Rapport Luxembourgeois', for *European Union Law and National Constitutions, XXth FIDE Conrgress*, (London, 2002) at 24–25.

6.2.4. Germany

Contrary to what may be expected, competence for the ordinary courts to review statutes in the light of Community law was fairly easily accepted in the 1971 *Lütticke* judgment, where the *Bundesverfassungsgericht*[5] held that as a result of the ratification of the EEC Treaty, an independent legal order had been created, and inserted in the German legal order. Article 24 of the Basic Law implied not only that the transfer of sovereign rights to inter-state institutions was permissible, but also that the sovereign acts of these institutions, including the decisions of the Court of Justice, were to be recognised as deriving from an original and sovereign authority. The German courts must apply those legal provisions having direct effect which superimpose themselves upon and displace conflicting national law. The *Bundesverfassungsgericht* did not itself have jurisdiction to review the compatibility of national law with Community law invested with priority, but the settlement of such a conflict of norms was a matter to be left to the trial courts.

The *Bundesverfassungsgericht* thus accepted both the principle of substantive supremacy and the review powers of the ordinary German courts. The jurisdictional issue of whether the review powers were restricted to the *Bundesverfassungsgericht* which also has exclusive power to review the constitutionality of statutes (*Verwerfungsmonopol*) or should extend to all courts was resolved without much ado. However, as will be demonstrated later on, the endorsement of the supremacy doctrine was not unconditional. Its limits were announced already in the decision relating to the constitutionality of EEC regulations,[6] specified in *Solange I*,[7] restricted in *Solange II*,[8] expanded in the *Maastricht Urteil*,[9] and clarified in the *Bananas III* judgment of June 2000.[10] In 1992, at the occasion of the Treaty of Maastricht, a new Euro-Article, Article 23, was introduced in the Basic Law.

6.2.5. Italy

The Italian acceptance of the *Simmenthal* mandate was much more complicated. There were many obstacles in constitutional theory: the dualist

---

[5] *Bundesverfassungsgericht*, decision of 9 June 1971, *Alphons Lütticke GmbH*, BverfGE 31, 145, Oppenheimer, *The Cases*, 415.

[6] *Bundesverfassungsgericht*, decision of 18 October 1967, *EEC regulations constitutionality case*, BverfGE 22, 293, Oppenheimer, *The Cases*, 410.

[7] *Bundesverfassungsgericht*, decision of 29 May 1974, *Internationale Handelsgesellschaft (Solange I)*, BverfGE 37, 271; [1974] 2 CMLR 540, Oppenheimer, *The Cases*, 419.

[8] *Bundesverfassungsgericht*, decision of 22 October 1986, *Wünsche Handelsgesellschaft (Solange II)*, BVerfGE 73, 339; [1987] 3 CMLR 225; Oppenheimer, *The Cases*, 461.

[9] *Bundesverfassungsgericht*, decision of 12 October 1993, *Treaty of Maastricht*, BverfGE 89, 155; [1994] 1 CMLR 57; Oppenheimer, *The Cases*, 520.

[10] *Bundesverfassungsgericht*, decision of 7 June 2000, *Bananas III*, BverfGE 102, 147.

tradition with regard to the relation between the national and international legal order, the conception of the separation of powers and the
monopoly of constitutional review in the hands of the *Corte costituzionale*
would prove to be true constitutional stumbling blocks. Contrary to the
hopes or expectations expressed by Advocate General Lagrange[11] in his
Opinion in the *Costa v ENEL* decision of the Court of Justice, that for a
country such as Italy which had always been in the forefront amongst the
promoters of the European idea, and for whom it should not be excessively difficult to find a constitutional means of allowing the Community
to live in full accordance with the rules created under its common charter,
the road to the Italian acceptance of the twin pillars of direct effect and
supremacy has been long and rocky. A leading role in the evolution is
played by the *Corte costituzionale*, but it was the ordinary courts that
forced the acceptance of the mandate by side-stepping the *Corte costituzionale* and making use of the direct link with the Court of Justice in the
preliminary rulings procedure. In its *Costa v ENEL* decision of 1964,[12] the
Corte costituzionale rejected precedence of Community law over national law,
since the Treaties had been approved by an ordinary statute and were thus
considered to be equal in force to subsequent statutes. The latter were
accorded precedence on the basis of *lex posterior*. In *Frontini*[13] the *Corte*
adapted its position, enunciating the doctrine of separate legal orders and
endorsing the principles of direct effect and supremacy, on the basis of
Article 11 of the Constitution, albeit with restrictions relating to constitutionally protected fundamental rights and core constitutional values.
However, the *Corte costituzionale* did not outline what an Italian court should
do when faced with a clash between Community law and subsequent provisions of domestic law. It was spelled out in *ICIC*,[14] where the *Corte costituzionale* opted for centralised judicial review. The choice of Article 11 of the
Constitution as the basis of supremacy of Community law implied that an
infringement of Community law would for that matter and at the same time
constitute a breach of Article 11 of the Italian Constitution. As a consequence, whenever a court finds itself confronted with a possible infringement of Community law, it must refer the matter to the *Corte costituzionale*,
which alone had jurisdiction to solve conflicts between statutes and the
Constitution. This supremacy *'all'italiana'*[15] was forcefully rejected by the
Court of Justice in *Simmenthal*, emphasising that direct applicability and

---

[11] Case 6/64, *Costa v ENEL* [1964] 585, at 606.
[12] *Corte costituzionale*, decision n. 14/64 of 7 March 1964, *Costa v ENEL*, Foro it., 1964, I, 465.
[13] *Corte costituzionale*, decision n. 183/73 of 27 December 1973, *Frontini*, 39 Rac.Uff. 395
     (1973); [1974] 2 CMLR 372; RTDeur., 1974, 148; Oppenheimer, *The Cases*, 629.
[14] *Corte costituzionale*, decision n. 232/75 of 30 October 1975, *ICIC v Ministerio Commercio
     Estero*, Foro it., 1976, I, 542; English summary in (1975) *CML Rev*, 439–41.
[15] So FP Ruggeri Laderchi, 'Report on Italy', in A-M Slaughter *at el* (eds), *The European Court
     and National Courts – Doctrine and Jurisprudence. Legal Change in Its Social Context* (Oxford,
     Hart Publishing, 1998) 147, at 164.

supremacy imposed the jurisdiction for all courts to enforce Community law, any contrary provision of national law notwithstanding. Consequently, *Simmenthal* required a radical move from *ICIC*. For the second time the *Corte costituzionale* found itself in a direct conflict with the Court of Justice. The conflict was solved in the *Granital* judgment of 1984,[16] when the *Corte costituzionale* in effect condoned decentralised review and accepted that the ordinary courts could of their own motion accord precedence to Community regulations, without the need for resort to constitutional review. In the version of supremacy of the *Corte costituzionale*, the Italian courts do not 'disapply' the conflicting national legislation; *they* do not set it aside, it simply is 'not applicable' in the case. The version of supremacy of the *Corte costituzionale* is one of 'direct applicability without supremacy'. Community law and national law are entirely separate and autonomous legal orders. Consequently, primacy of EC regulations means that municipal law does not operate in the domain covered by such regulations: it is covered by Community law exclusively. The *Corte* did not however give up all its review powers with regard to Community law: Community law does not, in the version of the *Corte costituzionale*, take precedence over the most fundamental principles of the constitutional order and the inalienable rights of man. The Italian Act giving effect to the Treaty could itself be the subject of review by the constitutional court with regard to the basic principles of the municipal legal order and the inalienable fundamental rights enshrined in the Constitution. *Granital* concerned the case of regulations, but the same principles were later extended to other acts, including the case law of the Court of Justice.[17]

6.2.6. France

The Community review powers of the French courts were only fully accepted in 1989, when the *Conseil d'Etat* handed its famous decision in the case of *Nicolo*.[18] The *Cour de cassation* had already accepted the

---

[16] *Corte costituzionale*, decision n. 170/84 of 8 June 1984, *Granital SpA v Amministrazione delle Finanze dello Stato*, Foro it., 1984, I, 2026; (1984) *CML Rev*, 757; CDE, 1986, 185; Oppenheimer, *The Cases*, at 643.

[17] *Corte costituzionale*, decision n. 113/85 of 19 April 1985, *Sp.a. BECA v Amministrazione delle Finanze dello Stato*, Riv.dir.int., 1985, 388; *Corte costituzionale*, decision n. 389/89 of 11 July 1989, *Provincia di Bolzano v Presidente Consiglio Ministri*, Riv.dir.int., 1989, 404 (both relating to the case law of the ECJ); *Corte costituzionale*, decision n. 64/90 of 18 January 1990, *Pesticides Referendum Case*, Foro Italiano, 1990, I, 747; RTDeur., 1991, 294; Oppenheimer, *The Cases*, 662; *Corte costituzionale*, decision n. 168/91 of 18 April 1991, *Spa Giampaoli v Ufficio del registro di Ancona*, 18 April 1991, Riv.dir.int., 1991, 108 (relating to directives).

[18] *Conseil d'État*, decision of 20 October 1989, *Nicolo*, RFDA, 1989, 824; [1990] 1 CMLR 173; Oppenheimer, *The Cases*, 335.

supremacy of Community law and the *Simmenthal* mandate much earlier in 1975 in a case *Jacques Vabre*.[19] The supreme civil court ruled that in the case of a conflict between an internal statute and a properly ratified international act, Article 55 of the Constitution accorded priority to the latter, and authorised the courts to accord precedence to treaty provisions and accordingly to set aside conflicting provisions of national law, even those contained in a *loi*. The *Conseil d'Etat* had adopted another view in the *Semoules* case of 1968,[20] when it accorded priority to a subsequent Act of Parliament. Judicial review of primary legislation was considered to be the exclusive competence of the *Conseil constitutionnel*, and to fall outside the province of the administrative courts. The *Conseil constitutionnel*, however, held that it did *not* have jurisdiction to review the conformity of statutes with treaty provisions: it had jurisdiction only to review the *constitutionnalité* of statutes, not their *conventionnalité*.[21] Articles 55 and 61 established two different kinds of judicial review of a different nature. Contrary to what the *Conseil d'Etat* presumed, judicial review of the compatibility of statutes with treaty provisions did not amount to a review of their constitutionality. Judicial review of the compatibility of French law including primary legislation was the business of the ordinary courts.[22]

The *Conseil d'Etat* was thus left in 'splendid isolation': the *Cour de cassation* and the *Conseil constitutionnel* had accepted that Article 55 of the Constitution empowered the ordinary courts to conduct review in the light of specified treaty provisions. The courts in the other Member States had by that time accepted the *Simmenthal* mandate. And clearly, the position of the *Conseil d'Etat* was in complete contradiction with the case law of the Court of Justice. Finally, in 1989, the *Conseil d'Etat* in *Nicolo* assumed competence to review the compatibility with Community law. Nevertheless, some limitations continue to exist.

For the other Member States the situation was different: they knew, when joining the Communities, that Community law was to be considered part of the law of the land, that it was to be supreme over national law and that the national courts were required to set aside conflicting national law.

---

[19]   *Cour de cassation*, decision of 24 May 1975, *Administration des Douanes v SociétéCafés Jacques Vabre*, D, 1975, 497; [1975] 2 CMLR 336; Oppenheimer, *The Cases*, at 287.

[20]   *Conseil d'État*, decision of 1 March 1968, *Syndicat Général de Fabricants de Semoules de France*, Rec., 149; [1970] CMLR 395.

[21]   *Conseil constitutionnel*, decision n. 74–54 DC of 15 January 1975, *Interruption volontaire de grossesse*, Rec., 1, www.conseil-constitutionnel.fr.

[22]   *Conseil constitutionnel*, decision n. 86–216 DC of 3 September 1986, *Loi relative aux conditions d'entrée et de séjour des étrangers en France*, Rec., 35; RFDA, 1987, 120; www.conseil-constitutionnel.fr.; In 1988, acting as an electoral court, the *Conseil constitutionnel* examined whether the Act of Parliament which it had to apply, was conform to the Protocol to the ECHR, *Conseil constitutionnel*, decision n. 88–1082 AN of 21 October 1988, *Val d'Oise, 5e circ.*, Rec., 183.

6.2.7. The United Kingdom

Before accession, the principle of supremacy and the ensuing obligations of judicial review were considered in the UK to be irreconcilable with the principle of parliamentary sovereignty. The principle of parliamentary sovereignty, in essence, means that Parliament can do anything and that no authority can asses the validity of Acts of Parliament. In addition, according to the orthodox view, no Parliament can bind its successors, and it would be impossible for Parliament to amend the rule of parliamentary sovereignty and provide for the precedence of Community law and for review powers of the British courts. Parliament could not prevent itself or any future Parliament from legislating contrary with Community law. In any case, such intention not to legislate contrary to Community law could not be monitored by the courts: Parliament would be considered simply to have 'changed its mind'. Nevertheless, when Britain did join the EC, the European Communities Act 1972 was adopted to make Community law effective in the domestic legal order. The Act contained several provisions which, without using the exact terms, were intended to allow for the direct effect and supremacy of Community law.

Nonetheless, during the first years of British membership, the English courts had recourse mainly to interpretation and construction techniques, so as not to be confronted with head on conflicts between Acts of Parliament and Community law. Yet, in 1989 the House of Lords in the famous *Factortame* case openly acknowledged the supremacy of Community law and the concomitant obligation of the courts to review national law, including Acts of Parliament and set them aside in case of a conflict. Lord Bridge, in his speech, disguised the novelty of this decision, and 'put the blame' on Parliament which had itself, in the 1972 EC Act, provided for such review.

Since *Factortame*, the review powers of the English courts in the context of Community law have been accepted, and, after initial hesitation, it is now by and large considered to constitute an exception to the principle of parliamentary sovereignty.

6.2.8. Ireland

Ireland was the first applicant State to make the necessary constitutional arrangements at the time of the accession in order to avoid constitutional quandaries later. Several provisions in the Constitution were at odds with membership. The 1937 Irish Constitution, Búnreacht Na héireann, states that all powers of government are to be exercised exclusively by or on the authority of the organs of State established by the Constitution, whereas membership implies a transfer of those powers to the European institutions.

In addition, Irish constitutional law adopts a dualist approach to the incorporation of treaties into domestic law. In order to make Irish membership constitutionally viable the Third Amendment to the Constitution was passed by referendum. This amendment *expressis verbis* authorised the accession to the Communities and went on to provide that *'no provision of this Constitution invalidates laws enacted, acts done or measures adopted by the State necessitated by the obligations of membership of the Communities or prevents laws enacted, acts done, or measures adopted by the Communities, or institutions thereof, from having force of law in the State'*. The precedence of Community law over the Constitution and the *Simmenthal* mandate of the courts are accordingly provided for. The amendment was complemented with the enactment of the European Communities Act 1972, which granted the necessary legislative authority for the incorporation of the Community treaties and the law deriving from them into Irish law.

With respect to the constitutional position of courts, the state of mind of Irish lawyers was very favourable to the acceptance of judicial review powers. In fact, the existing constitutional jurisprudence relating to constitutional review had already accustomed Irish courts to upholding the primacy of a higher law over inconsistent primary legislation and to asserting that rights created by a fundamental law must be enforced by the courts.[23] Ordinary supremacy of Community law over primary legislation has accordingly been embraced without much ado.[24] On the other hand, the debate is still ongoing on the relationship between Community law and the Irish Constitution.

6.2.9. Denmark

Denmark adheres to the dualist conception of the relation between international and national law. For treaty provisions to become directly applicable in Denmark, they must be transformed into Danish law, and rules thus transformed have no higher rank within the hierarchy of norms than the act transforming them. Under Section 20 of the Danish Constitution, inserted in 1953, powers vested in the Danish authorities may *'to such extent as shall be provided by statute'*, adopted by a majority of five-sixths in parliament or a simple majority followed by the direct approval of the electorate in a referendum, be delegated or transferred to international organisations as set up by mutual agreement with other States for the promotion of international rules of law and co-operation.

---

[23] B Walsh, 'Reflections of the Effects of Membership of the European Communities in Irish Law', in *Du droit international au droit de l'intégration. Liber Amicorum P Pescatore*, F Capotorti *et al* (eds) (Baden, Baden, 1987) 805, at 806.

[24] McMahon and Murphy, *European Community Law in Ireland* (Round Hall, Dublin, 1989) paras 14–15.

The 1972 Act on the accession to the European Communities was adopted under this provision. European law instruments that are directly effective seem to be so applied in the Danish courts. However, as has been noted by Ole Due, questions referred to the Court of Justice by Danish courts do not usually inquire about the direct effect of the provisions concerned. Danish courts prefer to find the solution in conform interpretation. A few judgments reportedly point to the supremacy of Community law, but the principle does not seem to have created any problems for the courts when it comes to the supremacy of Community law over administrative or legislative acts (ordinary supremacy).[25] According to Zahle, ever since the beginning of Danish membership in January 1973, more than 30 years ago, a real and open conflict between Community law and a Danish Act of Parliament has never even occurred![26]

6.2.10. Greece

In Greece, the ordinary supremacy of Community law and the resulting review powers of the courts have been accepted on the basis of Article 28 of the Constitution, providing for the direct effect and the primacy of international treaties in general.[27] The Greek constitutional system thus provides an apt environment for the acceptance of the *Simmenthal* mandate of the courts.[28] While there may have been some hesitations in the beginning, the Greek courts have accepted jurisdiction to set aside conflicting legislation.[29]

6.2.11. Spain

Article 96 of the Spanish Constitution provides that international treaties validly concluded, and officially published in Spain, will be part of

---

[25] O Due, 'Danish Preliminary References', in *Judicial Review in European Union Law. Liber Amicorum in Honour of Lord Slynn of Hadley*, Vol I, (The Hague, Kluwer Law International 2000) 363, at 373.

[26] H Zahle, 'National Constitutional Law and the European Integration', in *National Constitutional Law vis-à-vis European Integration. 17 FIDE Kongress* (FIDE, Berlin, 1996) 60, at 67.

[27] Article 28 (1) provides: '(1) The generally accepted rules of international law, as well as international treaties from the date of their ratification and entry into force, according to their own terms and conditions, constitute an inseparable part of the Greek legal order and supersede every contrary provision of law (..)', translation taken from A Oppenheimer, *The Cases*, at 577.

[28] So D Evrigenis, 'Legal and Constitutional Implications of Greek Accession to the European Communities', (1980) *CML Rev*, 157.

[29] J Iliopoulos-Strangas, 'Le droit constitutionnel national et l'intégration européenne', in *Le droit constitutionnel national et l'intégration européenne. 17. FIDE Kongress* (FIDE, Berlin, 1996) 120, at 122–123.

the domestic legal order. There is no express provision governing the rank or status of international law, but many commentators agree that Article 96(1) of the Constitution, providing that international rules can only be abolished, modified or suspended in the way provided for by the Treaty itself or by the general rules of international law, implicitly sanctions the primacy of treaty law in the internal legal order by granting them a higher rank.[30] Others however argue that Article 96(1) does not imply a hierarchy, but rather the existence of different legal spheres in which different competences apply. A case of a conflict implies that one norm has been adopted *ultra vires*. The consequence of this approach is that it would not be for the ordinary courts but rather for the constitutional court to resolve alleged conflicts with Community law. Under a third view, Article 96(1) of the Constitution was not relevant in the case of Community law: the priority of Community law was rather founded on Article 93 of the Constitution allowing for the transfer of powers to international organisations.[31]

The road to full recognition of the Community mandate of the Spanish courts has been rather bumpy.[32] The lower courts seem to have accepted their new role rather early and fairly easily,[33] but the higher courts have proved more reluctant. The *Tribunal Supremo* did, in a 1987 case, declare that Community law was directly applicable and was supreme over national law by virtue of the transfer of powers authorised in Article 93 of the Constitution, but in the *cigarette smuggling case*,[34] a criminal law case, the same court denied the direct effect of Articles 9(1) and 12 of the EC Treaty. The relevant provisions of the Treaty could not, according to the *Tribunal*, produce such effects, since they constituted mere guidelines for the Member States, and could not be interpreted as a source of rights and be invoked so as to allow the applicants to justify a crime under Spanish law. These are the provisions which were given direct effect in *Van Gend en Loos*! The judgment can only be explained by a lack of knowledge of Community law and its basic principles, and has been described as an *'affront honteux'* and an *'erreur gravissime'*.[35] However,

---

[30] References can be found in F Santaolalla Gadea and S Matrinez Lage, 'Spanish Accession to the European Communities: Legal and Constitutional Implications', (1986) 23 *CML Rev*, 11, at 21.

[31] So F Santaolalla Gadea and S Matrinez Lage, 'Spanish Accession to the European Communities: Legal and Constitutional Implications', (1986) 23 *CML Rev*, 11, at 22–23.

[32] See *e.g.* DJ Liñán Nogueras and J Roldán Barbero, 'The Judicial Application of Community Law in Spain', (1993) 30 *CML Rev*, 1135.

[33] L Bourgorgue Larsen, 'Espagne', in J Rideau (ed), *Les États membres de l'Union européenne. Adaptations, mutations résistances* (Paris, LGDJ, 1997) 135, at 182.

[34] *Tribunal Supremo (criminal chamber)*, decision of 21 December 1988, *cigarette smuggling case*, Aranzadi, 1988, n. 9680; English translation in Oppenheimer, *The Cases*, 690.

[35] A Mangas Martín, 'Le droit constitutionnel espagnol et l'intégration européenne', in *Le droit constitutionnel national et l'intégration européenne, 17. FIDE Kongress* (FIDE, Berlin, 1996) 206, at 218.

this seems to be an isolated case. Only one year later the administrative section of the *Tribunal Supremo* held,[36] under reference to a 1987 decision, that Community law has direct effect and takes precedence by virtue of the partial cession of sovereignty inherent in the accession of Spain to the Community, which was properly authorised by an Organic Act,[37] read in conjunction with Article 93 of the Constitution. The *Tribunal* further attributed to the Treaties establishing the Communities a supranational and para-constitutional nature.

Yet, the theoretical conception of the nature and status of Community law and of conflicting national law is even today not entirely clear. The debate centres around the issue as to whether a national provision infringing Community law is for that reason unconstitutional. In a 1990 decision, the *Tribunal Supremo* held: '*Le droit communautaire abroge les normes antérieures contraires, les normes postérieures contraires devant être réputées inconstitutionnelles pour incompétence – articles 93 et 96(1) de la Constitution –, sans qu'il y ait obligation pour le juge ordinaire de poser la question d'inconstitutionnalité (article 163 de la Constitution) afin de laisser inappliquée la norme étatique, ce dernier étant lié par la jurisprudence de la Cour de justice qui a établi le principe 'pro comunitate'.*'[38] The *Tribunal Supremo* thus seemed to combine different theories: the primacy of Community law over national law derives from Articles 96(1) and 93 of the Constitution,[39] and conflicting provisions are accordingly unconstitutional, but the jurisdiction of the ordinary courts to review Spanish law conflicting with Community law is imposed by the Court of Justice.

The *Tribunal constitucional*, for its part, accepted the *Simmenthal* mandate of the ordinary courts in a 1991 decision on the constitutionality of the Organic Law regulating the General Electoral System.[40] The applicant, the Basque Parliament, argued that the Organic Law infringed the EEC Council Decision concerning the Elections for the European Parliament. The action was declared inadmissible. From the date of its accession, Spain had been bound by Community law, which constituted, in the

---

[36] *Tribunal Supremo (administrative chamber)*, decision of 17 April 1989, *Canary Islands Customs Regulation*, Aranzadi, 1989, n. 4524; Oppenheimer, *The Cases*, 694.

[37] Organic Law No 10/1985 of 2 August 1985.

[38] *Tribunal Supremo*, decision of 24 April 1990, Aranzadi, 1990, n. 2747; translation taken from C Gimeno Verdejo, 'L'Espagne', in *La condition du droit communautaire dans le droit des Etats membres. Primauté et mise en oeuvre*, cliché, (CJCE, Division recherche et documentation, Luxembourg, 1994) 59, at 63; see also A Mangas Martín, 'Le droit constitutionnel espagnol et l'intégration européenne', in *Le droit constitutionnel national et l'intégration européenne, 17. FIDE Kongress* (FIDE, Berlin, 1996) 206, at 219.

[39] It had been argued in literature, however, that both provisions are mutually exclusive.

[40] *Tribunal constitucional*, decision n. 28/91 of 14 February 1991, *Electoral Law Constitutionality Case*, BOE of 15 March 1991; Oppenheimer, *The Cases*, 702; confirmed in *Tribunal constitucional*, decision n. 64/91 of 22 March 1991, *Aspesco*, BOE of 24 April 1991; Oppenheimer, *The Cases*, 705.

words of the Court of Justice, an independent legal order, integrated into
the legal systems of the Member States and which their courts are bound
to apply. However, this binding nature did not signify that by virtue of
Article 93 of the Constitution the norms of Community law were
endowed with constitutional rank and force. Nor did it imply that an
occasional violation of Community norms by Spanish legislative provisions necessarily entailed, at the same time, the contravention of Article
93. In addition, neither the Treaty of Accession to the Communities, nor
secondary Community law constituted a yardstick by which pursuant to
Article 96(1) of the Constitution the constitutionality of Spanish laws
must be examined. Article 96(1) merely had the effect of making treaty
provisions effective. Consequently, a conflict between a treaty provision
and national law was not a matter affecting the constitutionality of these
provisions of national law, but rather purely a problem of the selection of
the norm applicable to a particular case, which must be settled by the
ordinary courts. It was considered to be a conflict of 'infra-constitutional
norms',[41] to be resolved by the ordinary courts. No intervention was
called for on the part of the Constitutional Court.

6.2.12. Portugal

Article 8(2) of the 1976 Portuguese Constitution provides that *'Rules
provided for in international conventions that have been duly ratified or
approved, shall apply in national law following their official publication so long
as they remain internationally binding with respect to the Portuguese State'*.[42]
The provision sanctions the direct effect of treaties, but is silent on their
rank and relation with conflicting national law. Whether international
treaties have precedence over conflicting national law is still under
debate. In order to prepare for the Portuguese accession to the European
Communities, a third paragraph was added to the provision, stating that
*'Rules made by the competent organs of international organisations to which
Portugal belongs, apply directly in national law to the extent that the constitutive treaty provides'*. This provision also does not say whether these rules
take precedence over national law. Yet, Portuguese scholars generally
accept that the provision guarantees the supremacy of European law over
infra-constitutional norms, but it is also seen as conditioning that
supremacy and as holding to itself the ultimate power of authority.[43] In

---

[41] In a later case the *Tribunal Constitucional* altered this qualification and spoke of 'non-
constitutional norms', decision n. 180/93 of 31 May 1993, *Fogasa*, BOE of 5 July 1993.
[42] Translation taken from the official website of the Portuguese President: www.
presidencia republica.pt/en/republica/constituciao.
[43] M Poiares Maduro, 'EU Law and National Constitutions. Portuguese Report', report for
the XXth FIDE Congress (London, 2002) at 2, available on www.fide2002.org.

spite of these constitutional challenges there is reportedly an overall optimism in Portuguese scholarship on the prevention of conflicts between national constitutional law and EU law. There have not yet been any problematic decisions of Portuguese courts, including the constitutional court. In fact, there is no landmark decision of the latter court explaining the Portuguese constitutional perception of the relationship between EU law and national law at all.[44]

6.2.13. Sweden

As early as 1965 the Swedish Instrument of Government,[45] *Regeringsformen*, was amended in order to allow for the Swedish participation in the project of European integration. However, transfer of decision-making powers was made possible only 'to a limited extent'. When Swedish accession was actually envisaged, the provision was considered insufficient to provide the constitutional basis for accession to an ever closer Union with so many competences as the European Union and new constitutional provisions were introduced. These provisions are extensive and concentrate on pointing out the constitutional limits to the transfer of decision-making power. The proposed provisions in the government Bill offering an express constitutional basis for the supremacy of Community law were not passed. However, the Swedish courts have not encountered many difficulties in applying Community law, with precedence over conflicting provisions of Swedish law. Usually, the Swedish courts, like most other national courts, will seek to attain conform interpretation of Swedish law so as to avoid an open conflict. Nevertheless, they are prepared to set aside conflicting national law.

The leading case on the supremacy of Community law is *LassagÅrd*,[46] decided by the Supreme Administrative Court. *LassegÅrd* had been refused an aid on the basis of an EC regulation as the relevant time limit had expired. Under Swedish law, the decision was immune from judicial review. When the case did reach the Supreme Administrative Court, the provision excluding judicial review was found to infringe the general principle of Community law on judicial protection. The court referred to *Borelli* and stated that under the case law of the Court of Justice, there

---

[44] Ibidem.

[45] Sweden does not have a single document containing the Constitution: there are four constitutional documents: the Instrument of Government, the Act of Succession, the Freedom of the Press Act and the Fundamental Law on Freedom of Expression. The central rules are however contained in the Instrument of Government, *Regeringsformen*.

[46] *Regeringsrätten*, decision n. 219–1997 of 25 November 1997, *Lassagård*, Regeringsrättens Årsbok 1997, n. 65, see U Bernitz, 'Sweden and the European Union: On Sweden's Implementation and Application of European Law', (2001) 38 *CML Rev*, 903, at 925 *et seq*.

was a general right to judicial review in cases under Community law. Community law was held to take precedence over national law and the provision which denied judicial review of the decision was set aside. The Court permitted *LassagÅrd* a right to appeal the decision before a court of law and designated the competent court. Shortly after the decision, Swedish law was amended to provide for a general right of judicial review of administrative decision. There have been other cases since then of Swedish courts awarding precedence to Community law over conflicting national legislation. The courts do at times explicitly refer to *Simmenthal*.

6.2.14. Austria

Austria's accession to the European Union was considered to modify some of the basic principles of the Constitution (as laid down in so-called *Baugesetze*), and accordingly required a special procedure to amend the Constitution. These constitutional amendments did not however concern issues relating to the effect or rank of Community law in the Austrian legal order. The reception of Community and Union law into the Austrian legal order is perceived as causing a reception also of the consequences following from membership: direct applicability, direct effect and supremacy, and the ensuing duty of disapplication imposed on courts and administrative authorities.[47] Austrian courts have found no difficulty in accepting the *Simmenthal* mandate.[48] Any norm of Community law, whether contained in the constitutional treaties or in a legislative act, has primacy over any norm of national law, whether contained in the Constitution, or in 'simple' law. This applies even to the fundamental or basic principles of the Constitution (the so-called *Baugesetze*). Whether there are exceptions to this rule with respect to the most fundamental principles, democracy, rule of law, human rights, is not entirely clear.[49]

6.2.15. Finland

Direct effect and supremacy of Community law did not pose any difficulties at the time of accession. It was pre-supposed, as part of the *acquis communautaire*, but not explicitly mentioned. The primacy of Community

---

[47] See HF Köck, 'EU Law and National Constitutions – the Austrian Case', report for the XXth FIDE Congress (London, 2002) available on www.fide2002.org.
[48] P Fischer and A Lengauer, 'The Adaptation of the Austrian Legal System Following EU Membership', (2000) 37 *CML Rev*, 763, at 772 *et seq.*
[49] HF Köck, 'EU Law and National Constitutions – the Austrian Case', report for the XXth FIDE Congress (London, 2002) available on www.fide2002.org, at 26.

law over Finnish law is determined by the rules of Community law itself.[50] However, the environment was not particularly apt for the acceptance of the *Simmenthal* mandate. There is no tradition of judicial review of primary legislation, on grounds of an *a contrario* interpretation of a provision in the Constitution Act that lower legislation must be set aside if it conflicts with the Constitution or a Parliamentary Act. In addition, Finland has a dualist tradition of the relationship between international and national law.[51]

The new 2000 Constitution preserves the existing system's emphasis on the importance of anticipatory supervision of the constitutionality of legislation and the leading role of the Constitutional Law Committee in this area. However, anticipatory supervision was no longer thought sufficient to ensure the constitutionality of every single piece of legislation. The establishment of a special constitutional court for the retroactive supervision of constitutionality was not considered necessary, since it would mark a major departure from the foundations of the Finnish system of government. Instead, the current system was supplemented in the new Constitution by the introduction of a special provision on the legal precedence of the Constitution. This provision requires all courts to accord precedence to the provisions of the Constitution if in the individual case before the court the strict application of the relevant law would clearly be in conflict with these. Thus, the courts cannot make a general assessment in principle as to whether a particular legal provision is in conflict with the terms of the Constitution; the judgment must be tied to the application of the law in a specific concrete case. Section 106 of the Constitution is considered to emphasise the supremacy of Parliament, whose legislative decisions cannot be subjected to general retroactive challenge in the courts. While the new Finnish Constitution contains some provisions concerning Europe, and especially the involvement of the Finnish Parliament in the preparation of European legislation, it does not mention to obligations and responsibilities of the courts in this context.

6.3 FINAL REMARKS

And so the national courts became the common courts of Community law. By and large the national courts have embraced the *Simmenthal* mandate, and within the scope of Community law, they have become review courts. Their embrace of the Community mandate results in a shift

---

[50] K Pohjolainen, 'National Constitutional law and European Integration', in *Le droit constitutionnel national et l'intégration européenne. 17. FIDE Kongress* (Berlin, 1996) 399, at 416.
[51] K Kulovesi, 'International Relations in the New "Constitution of Finland"', (2000) 69 *Nordic Journal of International Law*, 513, at 520.

in the constitutional institutional balance. All courts now control the legislature and check whether Community law is complied with. This did not however happen overnight, and not without hesitation, in some countries more than in others. As appears from the foregoing pages, and will be developed in the rest of this chapter, many national courts had to overcome fundamental constitutional obstacles, which curbed their functioning as Community review courts. In some cases the embrace of the *Simmenthal* mandate required the courts to cast off some of the most fundamental principles relating to the conception of legal orders and of judicial function. Two clusters of constitutional difficulties can be detected on the basis of the overview. The first problem of a constitutional nature was a specific conception of the relationship between legal orders and of the effect and especially of the rank and status of international law in the internal legal order. The dilemma was particularly conspicuous in one of the most dualist countries among the six original Member States, Italy, and to a lesser extent in Belgium. Before judges in these countries could embrace their new mandate, they had to cast off a particular attitude and reconsider their fundamental beliefs. As the doctrines of direct effect and supremacy and the ensuing Community mandate had already been formulated at the time of the accession, the issue was less critical in other dualist Member States joining later, since the necessary constitutional arrangements could be made before accession.

The second cluster of constitutional obstacles relates to the place of the courts in the national constitutional landscape and the inherent limits of the judicial function. In every constitutional system there is a balance of powers and responsibilities between the organs of State. In many of the Member States this balance or separation of powers precludes judicial review of primary legislation by the ordinary courts. The role of guardian of the Constitution is most often attributed to a constitutional court (Germany, Italy, Belgium, and, though somewhat differently, France) or left to Parliament itself (The Netherlands, The United Kingdom). A traditionally limited conception of the judicial function, the principles of democracy and separation of powers and the pre-eminent role of Parliament in the constitutional arena are as many arguments to exclude judicial review of primary legislation in the light of higher law.

In the following chapters, each of these two clusters will be analysed in turn. Chapter 7 deals with the problems of the conceptual approach towards the relationship between national and Community law. Chapter 8 discusses the jurisdictional issue as an obstacle to the acceptance of *Simmenthal*. The constitutional limits to the supremacy of Community law, especially in the areas of fundamental rights and *Kompetenz Kompetenz* will be discussed in the second Theme on the courts having constitutional jurisdiction.

7

About Legal Orders

7.1. INTRODUCTION

THE CLASSIC CONSTITUTIONAL mandate of the courts is, in general terms, to apply and enforce 'the law'. Yet, the Constitution is hardly ever explicit on the exact category of norms which the courts are to enforce. The question whether the mandate also includes norms deriving from a foreign source, and in particular international legal provisions,[1] belonging to the body of law to be applied by the courts, and whether or not they must apply with precedence, is traditionally dealt with on the basis of a general theory about the relationship between legal orders.

In the absence of an explicit national constitutional mandate commanding the courts to grant international law precedence and to review national law and set it aside in case of a conflict, the domestic courts have to have recourse to the prevailing principles and rules dealing with conflicts of norms deriving from different polities. Several questions arise. First, are norms deriving from another polity at all relevant to a judge? This question is mostly phrased in terms of the domestic effect of the norm deriving from another polity or other legal order. Second, if the first question is answered in the positive,[2] what should a court do when confronted with a conflict between two norms, one deriving from another polity, the other from the domestic legal order? This question is typically phrased in terms of hierarchy. In some Member States, the traditional doctrine on these issues obstructed the acceptance of the Community mandate. In what follows these traditional doctrines will first be set out. Next, the orthodox Community law position will be defined, and the question will be analysed whether the Court of Justice imposes a particular vision of the relationship between the Community and national legal orders. Finally, the reaction of the national courts will be looked into. It will be demonstrated how some courts have construed a tailor-made theory for

---

[1]   A related question is that of the judicial application of foreign law under the rules of private international law.

[2]   Whether the treaty provision applies as such or as transformed into a national legal rule.

Community law, while maintaining the traditional views for the remainder of international law, while others have changed the traditional view altogether, also with respect to 'classic' treaties and international law.

7.2.   THE CLASSIC DICHOTOMY: MONISM AND DUALISM

7.2.1.   International Law

Under classic international law,[3] the effect of a treaty in the internal legal order of the Contracting Parties is determined by the domestic constitutional law of each participating State. There is no rule of international law requiring treaty law to be effective as such in the national legal order and with precedence over national law. The notions of 'direct effect', 'direct application' or 'self-executingness'[4] and of 'priority', 'precedence' or 'supremacy' of treaty provisions belong not to international law, but rather to the area of national constitutional law referred to in French literature as 'international constitutional law', *i.e.* the part of national (constitutional) law concerning the question whether and how international law takes effect in the national legal order. Obviously, *pacta sunt servanda*: contracting States must comply with the treaty provisions entered into between themselves. If the aim of an international agreement is to grant rights to individuals, and it is not given effect in the domestic legal order and the rights are not in effect granted (directly or indirectly), this constitutes an infringement of the treaty, and the international liability of the State in question may arise on the international plane. However, under

---

[3]   Recent contributions on this old topic include A Cassese, 'Modern Constitutions and International Law', 192 *Hague Recueil des cours*, 1985-III, 331; FG Jacobs and S Roberts (eds), *The Effect of Treaties in Domestic Law*, (London, Sweet & Maxwell, 1987); T Buergenthal, 'Self-Executing and Non-Self-Executing Treaties in National and International Law', 235 *Hague Recueil des cours*, 1992-IV, 303; JH Jackson, 'Status of Treaties in Domestic Legal Systems: A Policy Analysis', (1992) 86 *AJIL*, 310; M Fitzmaurice and C Flinterman (eds), *L Erades, Interactions Between International and Municipal Law: A Comparative Case Study*, (The Hague, TMC Asser Institute, 1993); PM Eisemann, *Intégration du droit international et communautaire dans l'ordre juridique national. A Study of the practice in Europe*, (The Hague, Kluwer, 1996); A Wasilkowski, 'Monism and Dualism at present', in *Theory of International law et the Threshold of the 21st Century. Essays in honour of Krzystof Skubiszewski*, (The Hague, Kluwer Law International, 1996) 323; Classics are H Kelsen, 'Les rapports de système entre droit interne et le droit international public', 14 *Hague Recueil des cours*, 1926-IV, 227; CH Triepel, 'Les rapports entre le droit interne et le droit international', 1 *Hague Recueil des cours*, 1923, 73.

[4]   In this section, the focus is not on whether a particular provision of an international treaty is apt to be invoked before a national court (*ie* the question of direct effect in the sense mostly used in the context of Community law), but rather on the preceding question of whether, as a general rule, treaty provisions are at all considered to be part of the national legal order. This is the issue often referred to as 'direct applicability' as opposed to 'direct effect'. Since the ECJ uses both notions interchangeably, the distinction has been played down in the previous section on the Community perspective.

classic international law it is considered to be a matter of national law *how* treaty provisions are given effect in the domestic legal order, whether as such, *i.e. qua* international norms, or transformed into national norms; there is not even a duty to bring national law in line with obligations under international law.[5] Traditional international law is concerned with the final result: fulfilment or non-fulfilment of an obligation.[6]

Under classic international law provisions contained in treaties always take precedence over conflicting national law, as does any other norm of international law. Before an international tribunal, national law will be considered as a mere fact, and in case of conflict between international law and national law, precedence will always be awarded to the former. Yet this merely means that a State cannot invoke its national law as an excuse for a failure to comply with its treaty obligations.[7] It does not, according to general opinion, imply that international law dictates the principles of direct effect and supremacy *before national courts in the internal legal order*. States are free to make their own rules on the domestic effect and rank of treaties in the municipal legal order. Nevertheless, the national arrangements so chosen may carry an effect on the international plane: whatever the method of applying international provisions in the domestic legal order, if the treaty provision is not applied – for instance because there is conflicting legislation and the courts do not award precedence to the treaty provision – they will have contributed to the violation of the international agreement by the State. The international liability of the State will only be established *ex post facto*, because there are no procedures available under international law to order the national courts to apply treaty provisions – whatever their legal nature under national law – with precedence over conflicting national legislation, so as to prevent the international liability of the State to arise. Nevertheless, as long as the result is achieved and the treaty obligations are complied with by the State – and its organs – international law does not concern itself with the specific arrangements in the Contracting States as to the method of making treaties effective and the theoretical approach as to the nature and rank of treaties. This is lucidly described by Derrick Wyatt who explained the 'new legal order' of Community law in terms of classic international law. In his opinion, the 'new legal order' is not really new. *Any* international tribunal would have decided *Van Gend en Loos* and *Costa v ENEL* the way the European Court did: '*direct effect is not rare in international law: it is*

---

5   A Cassese, *International Law* (Oxford, OUP, 2001) at 167.
6   Above. Cassese does however also indicate two recent developments: first, a number of treaties explicitly impose the duty to enact legislation for implementing certain provisions of the treaty; second, some norms of *jus cogens* require the State to adopt the necessary implementing legislation.
7   Article 27 of the Vienna Convention on the Law of Treaties states that 'A party may not invoke the provisions of its internal law as justification for its failure to perform a treaty (..)'.

simply a phenomenon invariably side-stepped by international adjudicatory machinery calculated to establish State responsibility' [ex post facto]. It is the preliminary rulings procedure which makes the difference: *'[W]hat the Article 177 procedure does allow is for "the clock to be stopped", and for question which would have traditionally been framed ex post facto in terms of responsibility, to be framed in terms of the duty of Member States, a duty in the case of treaty obligations apt for national judicial implementation, incumbent upon the courts of the Member States.'*[8]

7.2.2. Domestic Law

Turning now to domestic law, there are two[9] distinct abstract theories about the relation between international and national law, monism and dualism, which only reflect two extremes, while there is a wide variety of versions of both.[10] The monist view has a unitary perception of the 'law' and understands international and municipal law as forming part of one and the same legal order.[11] The monist State's legal system is considered to include international treaties to which the State is signatory.[12] In the most radical monist version, defended by Kelsen, the ultimate source of validity of all law derives from a basic rule (the *Grundnorm*) of international law. Consequently, all rules of international law are supreme over national law, which is null and void to the extent it conflicts with the

---

[8]   D Wyatt, 'New Legal Order, or Old?' (1982) *ELR* 147, at 153–54.

[9]   The monism–dualism partition is the most common way of categorising national legal attitudes towards international law. Other classifications are possible. Cassese starts from three principalle theories: first, the monistic view advocating the supremacy of national law ('nationalist' monism); second, dualism; and third, monism maintaining the unity of the various legal systems and the primacy of international law ('internationalist' monism, A Cassese, *International Law* (Oxford, OUP, 2001) at 162.

[10]   The classification in monist and dualist systems is made in different ways. Buergenthal focusses on the role of the legislature in making the treaty effective in the domestic legal order. If the treaty becomes effective directly upon ratification and approval, the system is categorized as monist. If the legislature does not take part in the formative process of the treaty and up to ratification, the system is considered dualist. Indeed in such a syustem the treaty will become effective only if the legislature adopts a separate legislative act, after ratification. In Buergenthal's theory, Italy and Germany are considered monist,. Ireland and the United Kingdom as dualist. This is not the most commonly adopted view in Europe. Generally, a system is considered monist if the treaty provision takes effect *as such*, as treaty provision. There may be several conditions, such as parliamentary approval, but the essence lays in the fact that the treaty provision retains its nature once effective in the domestic legal order. That is not the case in a dualist system, where the treaty provision is considered to become national upon entry in the domestic legal order. Its nature of international norm is transformed. The provision takes on the same nature and rank as the norm which allowed it to enter in the domestic legal order.

[11]   P Malanczuk, *Akehurst's Modern Introduction to International Law*, 7th revised edn, (London, Routledge, 1997) at 63.

[12]   So JH Jackson, 'Status of Treaties in Domestic Legal Systems: A Policy Analysis', (1992) 86 *AJIL*, 310, at 314.

higher ranking international norms; international law is of course directly applicable in the national legal orders (which are part of the same legal order). The more commonly accepted moderate monist position accepts international law as part of the law of the land, but also recognises that national law may impose conditions, for instance as to publication of the treaty, the participation of Parliament in the process or as to the nature of the treaty provision, for instance its self-executingness.

Dualism considers the international and the national legal orders to be separate and distinct; both systems exist independently of each other. In practical terms, monism and dualism take a different stance on the nature of the international norm once it has become effective. Under the monist view, treaty provisions takes effect *qua* international norm, while under the dualist view the international provision is transformed into a national norm when entering in the domestic legal order. Both systems will pose conditions to the entry of an international norm in the domestic legal order, relating to the involvement of the Parliament, publication in the domestic forum and entry into force at the international level. But in the dualist view, the international norm does not become effective as such: something more is needed.

It is not sufficient to know whether a system is monist or dualist. The notions only give an indication of the attitude taken in a specific system, since there is a wide variety of views within each of the two categories. The distinction is not conclusive on the rank of the international provision in the domestic legal order. Nor does it decide the issue of whether the courts have a mandate to apply these provisions and enforce them against conflicting national measures.

The choice between a monist or dualist position is not a choice about the beauty or logic of a theory: it is a choice about a nationalist or internationalist legal perspective.[13] States with a nationalist tendency incline to require transformation to make treaties effective; they put international treaties made effective on the same footing as national law of domestic origin. In contrast, States taking an international outlook tend to opt for automatic incorporation and often accord treaty provisions a higher rank than national legislation. Nevertheless, there are other policy issues involved, relating mainly to the principles of democracy and the involvement of the national Parliament in the making of the law applicable to individuals. Foreign affairs and the conclusion of treaties are typically the area of the Executive, and Parliament is often not involved until a late stage. As Jackson put it: '*there are sound policy reasons for a national legal system with typical democratic institutions to avoid the combination of direct domestic law application of treaties and higher status for those treaty norms than later-enacted statutory law. This conclusion depends greatly on the relative*

---

[13] A Cassese, *International Law* (Oxford, OUP, 2001) at 171.

degree to which constitution drafters trust international institutions and treaty-making processes compared with national institutions and legislative processes.'[14] The example of the United Kingdom demonstrates the issues involved: under the fundamental constitutional principle of parliamentary sovereignty, all legislative power is vested in the United Kingdom Parliament and all legislation is made by or under the authority of Parliament. Since the treaty making power is part of the royal prerogative and is vested in the Crown, treaties cannot of their own force be effective in the domestic legal order without putting the legislative monopoly of Parliament at risk.[15] The Crown does not have the authority to alter the rights and obligations of individuals within the United Kingdom. Hence, in order to become operative in the domestic legal order and to affect the rights and obligations of individuals, treaty provisions must be incorporated and transformed into British law. Until such act has been adopted, the treaty provisions do not carry effects in the internal legal order.[16]

It is important to note that international law is not necessarily better applied and enforced in monist systems. Courts may feel less inclined to apply norms of a foreign origin in a monist system, while in a dualist system the norms once transformed take on the guise of national provisions, and are accordingly applied in that way. In The Netherlands and France, for instance, which adopted the monist attitude towards international treaties even before 1963 and 1964, the courts were hesitant to actually apply international treaty provisions.[17] It is also possible that in a dualist

---

14   JH Jackson, 'Status of Treaties in Domestic Legal System: A Policy Analysis', (1992) 86 *AJIL*, 310, at 313.

15   JDB Mitchell, 'The Sovereignty of Parliament and Community Law: The Stumbling Block that isn't there', (1979) *International Affairs*, 33, at 38; G Anav, 'Parliamentary Sovereignty: An Anachronism?', (1989) 27 *Columbia J Transnational L*, 631, at 643.

16   '[I]t is elementary that these courts take no notice of treaties as such. We take notice of treaties until they are embodied in laws enacted by Parliament, and then only to the extent that Parliament tells us', per Lord Denning MR in Court of Appeal, decision of 10 May 1971, Blackburn v Attorney General [1971] 1 WLR 1037; [1971] 2 All ER 1380; Oppenheimer, The Cases, 731, at 732.

17   The new Netherlands constitutional provisions had been in place since 1953, but until *Van Gend en Loos*, no Dutch court had awarded precedence to an international treaty provision over an Act of Parliament. The issue had always been side-stepped by denying the conflict, by the technique of conform interpretation or by denying direct effect to the provision at issue, see *eg* L Erades, 'International Law and the Netherlands Legal Order', in HF Van Panhuys *et al*, (eds), *International Law in The Netherlands*, Vol III, (Alphen aan den Rijn, Sijthoff, 1980) 375; In the French case, Art. 55 of the 1958 Constitution, and before that Art. 26 of the 1946 Constitution were not considered to be addressed to the courts. So while the system was considered to adopt a monist stance as to the relation between international and national law, with priority over national law, it was not so applied in practice; see *eg* J Rideau, *Droit international et droit interne français*, (Paris, Librairie Armand Colin, 1971) 12 *et seq*; P Reuter, 'Le droit international et la place du juge français dans l'ordre constitutionnel national', in *L'application du droit international par le juge français*, (Paris, Librairie Armand Colin, 1972) 17; *'Nul ne doute que le traité soit supérieur à la loi ou même aux règles de fond de la Constitution: mais pour sanctionner cette supériorité il faut avoir reçu compétence à cet effet; il faut dans l'ordre des institutions avoir reçu un pouvoir'*, at 23.

system treaty provisions are granted a higher rank than an Act of Parliament.[18] In practice, however, it seems that in most dualist systems, the treaty provisions assume the nature and rank of the act which inserted them in the national legal order, which is at the most an Act of Parliament. Conflicts between norms of international origin and norms of national origin, both having the same rank in the domestic legal order, will have to be resolved by recourse to the normal general rules concerning conflicts of norms: *lex posterior derogat priori* and *lex specialis derogat generali*.

Whether a system is monist or dualist is hardly ever to be found in the text of the Constitution. It must be discovered in jurisprudence and in *la doctrine*. Most often, the self-perception of a system leads to a consensus as to which category the system belongs to. An exception is Belgium, which until the *le Ski* judgment of 1971 was considered both monist and dualist. The difficulty is in the definition. In the Belgian approach, a treaty provision which was duly published and ratified would have to give way to a later Act of Parliament.[19] Such treaty provisions were declared to be *équipollent à la loi*, yet what this meant exactly was not clear. Treaty provisions could be invoked before the *Cour de cassation* to found a claim that the law had been breached;[20] administrative decisions conflicting with treaty provisions could be set aside or annulled depending on the case. Yet, what was the exact nature of the treaty provision which was *équipollent à la loi*? Was it only equal in force and rank to an Act of Parliament, was it equivalent to it; or did it become an Act of Parliament? The precise meaning of the notion was debated in legal writing, and consequently so was the position of the Belgian approach as monist or dualist. The re-interpretation in *Le Ski* of the nature of the act of approval to treaties and of the nature of the treaty provisions themselves would lead to a revolution in its world view, and would finally make Belgium a truly monist State. Yet, when the *Cour d'arbitrage*, the constitutional court established

---

[18] Under Austrian constitutional law, for instance, the ECHR has been granted constitutional rank. The Austrian Constitution consists of the basic instrument, *ie* the Federal Constitution (the *Bundes-Verfassungsgesetz*) and many federal constitutional laws (*Bundesverfassungsgesetze* – note that the hyphen is missing when the notion is used in this context) which complement the Constitution properly called. The ECHR is one of the numerous constitutional laws outside the Constitution proper, see HF Köck, 'EU Law and National Constitutions – The Austrian Case', Report for the XXth FIDE Congress, (London 2002) available on the internet, www.fide2002.org/reports.htm; the Human Rights Act 1998 incorporating the ECHR into British law intends to produce a similar effect – the main difference with the Austrian situation lies in the judicial review powers of the English courts under the Act, which remain very limited with respect to Acts of Parliament and allow only for a declaration of incompatibility; moreover, the Human Rights Act is not entrenched and can be amended or repealed by a subsequent Act of Parliament. See among many other contributions A O'Neill, 'Fundamental Rights and the Constitutional Supremacy of Community law in the United Kingdom after Devolution and the Human Rights Act', (2002) *PL*, 724.

[19] The general reference is a 1925 judgment of the *Cour de cassation*, decision of 26 November 1925, *Schieble*, Pas., 1926, I, 76.

[20] In a 'recours en cassation pour violation de la loi'.

more than a decade after the adoption of the monist world view, set off to review the constitutionality of treaties – at least of the Acts approving them – the debate re-opened as to whether Belgium was to be considered monist or dualist. This discussion continues to date.[21]

Of the other founding Member States, Italy and Germany adopted an outspoken dualist perception and both still do. Treaties are considered to belong to a separate and distinct legal order, and in order to produce effects in the domestic legal order, an Act must be adopted to that end. In contrast to for instance the Irish and the English dualist conception, the treaty must not in its entirety be transcribed in a national document. Rather than being truly transcribed, the treaty is made effective by an order which makes it operative, the *ordine di esecuzione* or the *Vollzugsgesetz*.[22] At the same time, the provisions assume the nature and rank of the order, as if they were given new clothes. Consequently, they take precedence over existing provisions of the same rank, but they must give way to subsequent acts of the same nature and rank.

7.3.   WHAT RELATIONSHIP BETWEEN NATIONAL AND COMMUNITY LAW: IN SEARCH OF A DOCTRINAL BASIS[23]

Under the *Simmenthal* mandate national courts are under an obligation to set aside conflicting national law in order to give effect to Community

---

[21]   J Velu has argued that the Belgian position was monist and considered international and national law as belonging to one and the same legal order, with absolute priority of treaties over national law including the Constitution. He considered the decisions of the *Cour d'arbitrage* as reflecting an incorrect dualist position, J Velu, 'Toetsing van de grondwettigheid en toetsing van de verenigbaarheid met de verdragen', (1992–93) *RW*, 481, esp. 511 *et seq.*; see on this case law also C Naômé, 'Les relations entre le droit international et le droit interne belge après l'arrêt de la Cour d'arbitrage du 16 octobre 1991', (1994) *RDIC*, 24; Y Lejeune and Ph Brouwers, 'La Cour d'arbitrage face au controle de la constitutionnalité des traités', (1992) *JT*, 672; J Van Nieuwenhove, 'Over internationale verdragen, samenwerkingsakkoorden en "établissement". Enkele kanttekeningen bij de arresten 12/94, 17/94 en 33/94 van het Arbitragehof', (1995–96) *RW*, 449; J-V Louis, 'La primauté, une valeuuer relative', (1995) CDE, 22; P Popelier argued that the decisions of the *Cour d'arbitrage* could still be fitted into a monist appraoch, P Popelier, 'Ongrondwettige verdragen: de rechtspraak van het Arbitragehof geplaatst in een monistisch tijdsperspectief', (1994–1995) *RW*, 1076; Hervé Bribosia did not make the choice: he situated the Belgian position 'quelque part entre les deux', H Bribosia, 'Applicabilité directe et primauté des traités internationaux et du droit communautaire. Réflexions sur le point de vue de l'ordre juridique belge', (1996) *RBDI*, 33, at 55. Michel Melchior, president of the *Cour d'arbitrage* appears to tend more towards dualsim, and has declared that monism constitutes only a *'conception philosophique'* which is not imposed by international law and is not reflected in positive law. International practice and State behaviour prove the existence of a pluralism of legal orders, M Melchior and P Vandernoot, 'Controle de constitutionnalité et droit communautaire dérivé', (1998) *RBDC*, at 10.

[22]   An *ordine di esecuzione* in the Italian case; in Germany that result is achieved by the *Vollzugsgesetz*.

[23]   This will not be an in-depth analysis of the thinking about the relationship between legal orders on the basis of the theories of Kelsen, Hart or Dworkin, or on the basis of a systems theory; for a contribution using Hans Kelsen's theory of legal system to explain the

law, which takes precedence over national law. Now, why does Community law take precedence? From a normative perspective – why should Community law take precedence – the reasons are simple: without primacy, Community law could easily be overridden by national law and the national authorities would be in a position to depart from it. Such behaviour may lead to a declaratory judgment by the Court of Justice, but conflicting national legislation could not be struck down or set aside. In addition, the uniform application of Community law would be endangered and a veritable common market would become almost impossible to achieve. The direct effect and supremacy of Community law has been instrumental in enforcing Community law and achieving the internal market, something which the Court could not have done on its own: it simply lacks the means to effectively force the member States to live up to their treaty obligations.[24] Community law must take precedence: 'Nier sa supérioté, c'est nier son existence'. However, the fact that Community law should take precedence over national law is not sufficient in itself to say that it does indeed have precedence.

7.3.1. The Traditional Internationalist Doctrine: Constitutional Mandate[25]

Under the internationalist doctrine, the Community Treaties and the law deriving from them preserve all characteristics of the sphere they originated from, namely international law, and Community law takes precedence if and in so far as national law provides it. The courts will enforce the pre-eminence of Community law if and in so far as they have

Community legal order and its relation with the national legal orders, presenting alternative theories, see C Richmond, 'Preserving the Identity Crisis: Autonomy, System and Sovereignty in European law', in Constructing Legal Systems: 'European Union' in N MacCormick (ed), *Legal Theory*, (Dordrecht, Kluwer Academic Publishers, 1997) 47; a systems analysis may be found in I Maher, 'Community Law in the National Legal Order: A Systems Analysis', *JCMS*, 1998, 238; a Hartian view is presented in Jones, 'The Legal Nature of the European Community: A Jurisprudential Model Using HLA Hart's Model of Law and Legal System', 17 *Cornell International Law Journal*, 1984, 1; an orders approach is presented by DR Phelan, *Revolt or Revolution. The Constitutional Boundaries of the European Community*, (Dublin, Round Hall, 1997).

24 The focus on the intervention of courts – on pathology – presumes that there are instances where Member States intentionally or by oversight violate the Treaties. If they would not, there would not be any need for theories like direct effect and supremacy.

25 The notion may be somewhat confusing in that the internationalist doctrine often leads to national or even nationalist solutions. It merely refers to the school of thought which applies the classic principles of international law, under which it is national (constitutional) law which decides on the effect and rank of treaty law in the domestic legal order. The result can be very nationalist, if no precedence of treaties is provided for; it does not have to be.

been granted a constitutional mandate to that effect. Most of the Constitutions of the six original Member States were not adjusted in order to comply with the case law of the Court of Justice on the nature of Community law and its supremacy, especially in the dualist countries Germany and Italy, and in Belgium. One solution could have been to adopt a provision in the Treaty requiring the Member States to adjust their Constitutions so as to provide for the direct effect and supremacy of Community law and/or to empower the courts to enforce Community law with precedence. This solution was not adopted; on the contrary, appears not to have during the negotiations the subject come up. The issue did take an important place in the national constitutional debates. There were more general debates in several Member States about modernising their attitude towards international law and adjust it to the requirements of modern international society. The Dutch Constitution was modernised and an explicit judicial review mandate was included in 1953 following the French example of the 1946 Constitution. The Dutch participation in the ECSC was an important factor in the debate. In turn, the drafters of the 1958 Constitution of the Fifth Republic pointed to the Dutch Constitution as an example of a modern Constitution well adjusted to modern international relations. In Belgium, there was a strong doctrinal movement prompting a change of mind in the direction of monism and a constitutional mandate for the courts to enforce the pre-eminence of international law.[26] A constitutional revision was envisaged several times.[27] In Luxembourg, an international movement[28] manifested itself in

---

[26] Henri Rolin spoke of the *'caractère exceptionnellement rétrograde des conceptions prévalent dans la jurisprudence'* in the beginning of the nineteen fifties *i.e.* the dualist conception leading to the pre-eminence of the subsequent statute over a conflicting treaty provision, H Rolin, 'La force obligatoire des traités dans la jurisprudence belge', (1953) *JT*, 561; He urged those working on a revision to adjust the Constitution to the modern international society, after the example of the French and the Netherlands Constitutions; Rolin's plea for a change of attitude was also voiced by Hayoit de Termicourt and Ganshof van der Meersch, 'La Constitution belge et l'évolution de l'ordre juridique international', (1952) *ADSP*, T XII, 332, at 350ff and lead, in the absence of express constitutional reform, to a silent revision of the Constitution in the case law, see infra.

[27] Déclaration de révision of 1954, Moniteur belge/Belgisch Staatsblad 14 March 1954, 1892; Déclaration de révision of 1958, MB 30 April 1958, 3284; Déclaration de révision of 1965, MB 17 April 1965, 4143; Déclaration de révision 1968, MB 2 March 1968, 2051; see on this last proposed revision of the Constitution WJ Ganshof van der Meersch, 'Réflexions sur le droit international et la révision de la Constitution', mercuriale prononcée à l'audience solennelle de rentrée de la Cour de cassation le 2 septembre 1968, (1968) JT, 485; The express constitutional embracement of monism and the supremacy of the international legal order, along with the judicial review mandate to sanction it were originally thought indispensable in order to achieve a change of attitude. Later, such express constitutional mandate was considered superfluous; it was never adopted.

[28] The Luxembourg Chamber in 1965 however rejected a proposal tabled by the Government to insert a provision in the Constitution declaring the supremacy of international treaties over national Acts of Parliament and all other provisions of national law.

the case law of the courts, including the *Cour supérieure de justice*.[29] In Italy and Germany, traditionally truly dualist States, the post war Constitutions did provide for the pre-eminence of general or customary international law. Yet, the internal effect and the supremacy of international *treaty* law was not expressly provided for in the Constitution, despite their internationalist disposition. Consequently, conflicts between treaty law and internal law were addressed along the existing lines.

There was accordingly a mood of change in all the Member States,[30] and it may seem surprising, that no provision was made in the Community Treaties, at the time of their negotiation or ratification, obliging the Member States to amend their Constitutions so as to ensure the uniform application and the *effet utile* of Community law.

Other Member States, which acceded to the European Communities or the European Union after *Van Gend en Loos* and *Costa ENEL*, had the advantage that they 'knew what they were getting in to'. Some of them did arrange their constitutional provisions in order to provide for supremacy and what it entailed for the national courts, such as Ireland.

Now, as is clear from the overview of the national positions prevailing in the 1950's and 1960's in the Member States, it was clear that applying the rules of traditional international law to the Community treaties would lead to disparities in judicial protection and in the enforcement of Community law. Community law could be more binding on some States than on others. It was therefore important to convince the national courts that Community law was to be treated differently than 'ordinary' international treaty law. If the national rules on the relationship between international law on the one hand and international law are removed from the equation, arguments must be adduced to support the supremacy of Community law, irrespective of the national Constitutions.[31]

The Chamber took note of an internationalist tendency in the courts to the same effect, but deemed it immature to fix it in constitutional text, see WJ Ganshof van der Meersch, 'Le droit communautaire et ses rapports avec les droits des états membres', in WJ Ganshof van der Meersch (ed), *Droit des Communautés européennes, Les Novelles,* (Bruxelles, Larcier, 1969) 41, 67.

[29] *Cour supérieure de justice (cass.),* 14 July 1954, *Pagani,* Pas. lux., XVI, 150; case note by P Pescatore, JT, 1954, 697. The *Cour supérieure* held that a treaty has a higher rank than an Act of Parliament since it derives from a higher source than the will of an internal body. Conflicts must therefore not be solved on the basis of the *lex posterior* rule, but rather in accordance with the *lex superior derogat inferiori* rule.

[30] Eric Stein spoke of a trend towards the acceptance of supremacy of treaties, E Stein, 'Toward Supremacy of Treaty – Constitution by Judicial Fiat in the European Economic Community', *Riv.Dir.int.,* 1965, 3, at 20.

[31] See WJ Ganshof van der Meersch, 'Le droit communautaire et ses rapports avec le droit des états membres', in WJ Ganshof van der Meersch (ed), *Les Novelles, Droit des Communautés européennes,* (Bruxelles, Larcier, 1969) 41, at 53 *et seq*; other early contributions concerning the theoretical foundations of supremacy include M Gaudet, *Conflits du Droit Communautaire avec les Droits Nationaux* (Nancy, Publications du Centre européen Universitaire, 1967); R Lecourt, *Le juge devant le Marché commun,* (Genève, Institut

7.3.2. The Specificity of the Community Treaties

It was clear from the onset that the Community Treaties were different from 'ordinary' treaties. While in *form* there may not have been anything special about them, they were special as to the *aims and objectives* to be achieved even beyond the actual Treaties themselves,[32] and also as to the *methods* used: the creation of institutions with powers and competences of their own, including the power to adopt measures directly applicable in the domestic legal order of the Member States, the creation of a Court of Justice which has a direct link of communication with the national courts etc. However, the difficulty is to explain conclusively in what way these special aims and special procedures command the precedence of Community law over national law before the national courts. The explanation may be found in the *effet utile*, derived from the specificity of the Community legal order and the intention of the Contracting Parties: *'le système institué implique nécessairement la priorité du droit communauatire, faute de quoi il ne fonctionne plus et les Communautés ne peuvent pas réaliser leur objectif'*.[33] It was stated that the treaty itself embodies the principle that 'Community law supersedes national law'. *'This unwritten rule is necessarily implied by the treaties and by the very nature of the Community because it is functionally indispensable for the very existence of the Community and for the achievement of the objectives laid down by the member States in the treaty. The need for such a rule springs from the necessity to ensure uniform effect and application of Community law and thus to avoid divergencies and discrimination that might arise from the differing national constitutional practices (..)'*.[34] Nevertheless, even if the specificity is accepted to rule out the general constitutional rules, the question remains: why should Community law take precedence?

7.3.3. Hierarchical Subordination between Legal Orders?

The most straightforward and easiest way to pull off the absolute precedence of Community law is to argue that there is as a matter of

---

Universitaire de Hautes études Internationales, 1970); G Bebr, 'How Supreme is Community Law in the National Courts?' *CML Rev* 1974, 3.

[32] The treaties were adopted with a view to establishing a common market; they were also considered to be a first step on the road to closer integration of the Member States.

[33] WJ Ganshof van der Meersch, 'Le droit communautaire et ses rapports avec les droits des états membres', in WJ Ganshof van der Meersch (ed), *Les Novelles, Droit des Communautés européennes*, (Bruxelles, Larcier, 1969) 41, at 58; compare Constaninesco who stated that under this theory *'Sein'* followed automatically from *'Sollen'*, LJ Constantinesco, 'La spécificité du droit communautaire', *RTDeur* 1966, 3.

[34] E Stein, 'Toward Supremacy of Treaty – Constitution by Judicial Fiat in the European Economic Community', *RivDir.int.*, 1965, 3, at 22.

principle a hierarchical supra-ordination and subordination between both legal orders. Community law takes precedence because it is supreme, superior over national law: the Community legal order is higher in rank than the national legal order in the hierarchy of norms ('the pyramid'). This version of supremacy is absolute and unconditional: even the highest norm of national law including the Constitution and primary legislation must give way to the lowest provision of Community law.[35] The difficulty then is to prove *why* Community law should be higher in rank: how did Community law get to the apex of the pyramid?

7.3.4. The Federalist Doctrine

The so-called federalist doctrine,[36] or transfer of powers doctrine, denies any hierarchical relationship between Community and national norms, and proceeds on the basis of the separation of powers between the Community and the Member States. Under the federalist doctrine, the Member States have by ratifying the Treaties signed away some of their competences and attributed these to the Community institutions. Through an irreversible transfer of powers, the Member States have put in place a federal structure. In the field of these transferred powers, the national authorities are no longer competent to legislate; should they do so, the act is necessarily *ultra vires*. Conflicts do not arise in this approach: if two norms conflict, one of the law-making institutions at the national or the Community level has necessarily transgressed the boundaries of its powers and its act was not validly adopted. There is no hierarchical relationship between two legal orders: There are simply two spheres of law, existing side by side, each sovereign in their own realm. The courts simply have to decide which realm or sphere they are acting under. Advocate General Lagrange, who wrote the Opinion in *Costa v ENEL*, was an advocate of this view. He argued that Community law constituted an autonomous legal order created by a transfer of competences resulting from the Treaties, and in case of a conflict between Community law and national law, Community law took precedence: *'Il ne s'agit pas d'une primauté dans le sens*

---

[35] P Pescatore, in *Droit communautaire et droit national*. Semaine de Bruges, (Bruges, De Tempel, 1965) at 105; Pescatore claimed to be a fervent advocate of this approach, but he realised that it would not be acceptable to many lawyers with firm beliefs in the superiority of the Constitution and the inviolability of statutes.

[36] For instance WJ Ganshof van der Meersch, 'Le droit communautaire et ses rapports avec les droits des états membres', in *Droit des Communautés européennes, Les Novelles*, (Bruxelles, Larcier, 1969) 41, at 54 *et seq.*; J Rideau, *Droit international et droit interne français* (Paris, Librairie Armand Colin, 1971) at 22; the label 'federal' is not convincing, however. The line of reasoning based on a transfer of competences is not followed in most federal systems, see B De Witte, 'The Primacy of Community Law: A Not-So-Federal Principle?', unpublished paper, on file with the author.

d'une "hiérarchie" entre le droit communautaire prééminent et des droit nationaux subordonnés, mais d'une substitution *du droit propre de la Communauté au droit national dans les domaines où les transferts de compétence ont été opérés: dans ces domaines, c'est désormais la règle de droit communautaire qui s'applique. (..) l'analogie avec le système fédéral est ici difficilement contestable.'*[37]

It is understandable under this doctrine that secondary Community law takes precedence. Yet, why should the Treaties themselves, which establish the Community institutions and transfer powers to them, take precedence? The precedence of the Treaties themselves is difficult to explain by means of the federalist thesis.

7.4. THE RELATIONSHIP BETWEEN THE COMMUNITY AND NATIONAL LEGAL ORDER
        IN THE CASE LAW OF THE COURT OF JUSTICE

7.4.1. The Basic Rules

While the European Court's concept of supremacy is unequivocal – all Community law takes precedence over all national law – its reasoning and theoretical grounding is much less apparent. The Court is not dogmatic and does not seem to have chosen one doctrine or theory[38] of the relation between legal orders to base its version of supremacy, and the case law contains several elements which taken together must almost naturally lead to the acceptance of the supremacy of Community law.[39] The Court's task was a very difficult one. In order to achieve uniformity of Community law and to ensure the enforcement of Community law, the Court had to for-mulate a theoretical framework suitable for six very different national sys-tems, taking account of the legal conceptual ideology prevailing in all of these legal systems, apt to achieve an acceptable level of uniformity and to guarantee the enforcement of Community law in the national legal orders. The Court was well aware of the difficulties encountered by the national courts, and in order to achieve the outcome, it offered several

---

[37] M Lagrange, 'La primauté du droit communautaire sur le droit national', in *Droit com-munautaire et droit national, Semaine de Bruges*, (Bruges, 1965) 22, at 23–24; see also N Catalano, 'La position du droit communautaire dans le droit des états membres', in *Droit communautaire et droit national. Semaine de Bruges* (Bruges, Tempe, 1965) 56, at 66–86.

[38] See also G Bebr, 'How Supreme is Community Law in the National Courts?' *CML Rev* 1974, 3, at 3–7.

[39] A comprehensive analysis of the nature of the Community legal order as perceived from the Community perspective is offered by R Kovar, 'La contribution de la Cour de justice à l'édification de l'ordre juridique communautaire', *Collected Courses of the Academy of European Law*, (1993) Vol. IV Book 1, 15; see also J Wouters, 'National Constitutions and the European Union', (2000) *LIEI*, 25, at 64 *et seq.*; for a more neutral appraisal, B de Witte, 'Direct Effect, Supremacy and the Nature of the Legal Order', in P Craig and G de Búrca (eds), *The Evolution of EU Law* (Oxford, OUP, 1999) 177.

elements, from which the national legal systems could pick and choose to construe their own theory, as long as the result of direct effect and supremacy was achieved.[40] Hans Kutscher, judge at the European Court of Justice put it this way: *'[I]t may appear presumptuous for a judge of the Community to try to explain the effects of the Community law from the point of view of the national judge (..) [I]t is true that from the objective point of view the content of Community law and its legal relationship with national law remain unchanged; they can nevertheless be looked at from different perspectives (..) the Community judges are aware of this fact. (..) The Court (..) has endeavoured to make its view of Community law understandable to the national judge and to convince him. The complete and effective realisation of Community law is, however, a common task of the national judge and the Community judge.'* The Court hence had to argue the direct effect and especially the supremacy of Community law cogently without recourse to a specific provision in the Treaties imposing these principles *expressis verbis*. The second best argument, then, to convince the national courts, was to prove that even though the Member States had not stated it expressly, they had *intended* it. The Court presented several elements of a theory as to how the Community legal order and its relationship with the national legal orders may be viewed. Even though the main elements of the Court's view on the Community legal order are now proverbial, the following are, once again, the most significant paragraphs of the Court's case law describing the Community legal order and its relations with that of the Member States: '[T]his treaty is more than an agreement which merely creates mutual obligations between the contracting States' (..) '[T]he Community constitutes a new legal order of international law for the benefit of which the States have limited their sovereign rights, albeit within limited fields, and the subjects of which comprise not only Member States but also their nationals'.[41]

'By contrast with ordinary international treaties, the EEC Treaty has created its own legal system which, on the entry into force of the Treaty, became an integral part of the legal systems of the Member States and which their courts are bound to apply. By creating a Community of unlimited duration, having its own institutions, its own personality, its own legal capacity of representation on the international plane and, more particularly, real powers stemming from a limitation of sovereignty or a transfer of powers from the States to the Community, the member States have limited their sovereign rights, albeit within limited fields, and have thus created a body of law which binds both their nationals and themselves. (..)[T]he law stemming from the Treaty, an independent source of law,

---

[40] Hans Kutscher 'Community Law and the National Judge', (1973) *LQR*, 487, at 487; Kutscher was a member of the ECJ when he wrote the article.
[41] Case 26/62 *Van Gend en Loos* [1963] ECR 1, at 12.

could not, because of its special and original nature, be overridden by domestic legal provisions, however framed, without being deprived of its character as Community law and without the legal basis of the Community itself being called into question'.[42]

'In contrast, the EEC Treaty, albeit concluded in the form of an international agreement, none the less constitutes the constitutional charter of a Community based on the rule of law. As the Court of Justice has consistently held, the Community treaties established a new legal order for the benefit of which the States have limited their sovereign rights, in ever wider fields, and the subject of which comprise not only Member States but also their nationals [Van Gend en Loos] The essential characteristics of the Community legal order which has thus been established are in particular its primacy over the law of the Member States and the direct effect of a whole series of provisions which are applicable to their nationals and to the Member States themselves'.[43]

The Court uses elements of several doctrines, piling them together into a forceful narrative aimed at convincing the referring court and the rest of the audience. The result is not necessarily cohesive: as one commentator put it: *'Perhaps it is the Achilles heel of* Costa v ENEL *that the judgment puts forward too many, rather than too few, arguments to underpin the principle of primacy'.*[44] In the qualification of the Community legal order its specificity and its autonomy stand out.

7.4.2. The Specificity of the Community Legal Order

Ever since *Van Gend en Loos* and *Costa v ENEL* the Court has emphasised the *specificity* of the Community legal order, distinguishing Community law from international law.[45] The Treaties are more than an agreement creating obligations between Contracting States, but also include the citizens of the Member States. The Community legal order is a new legal order of international law, as a result of the limitation of sovereign rights on the part of the Member States. In *Costa v ENEL*, the Community legal order became a new legal order *simpliciter*, the reference to international law being omitted. What distinguishes the Community treaties from ordinary treaties in the Court's perception, are their *objectives*, the ever closer unity, and the *context* in which these are pursued: a new legal order was established for the benefit of which the Member States have limited their

---

[42] Case 6/64 *Costa v ENEL* [1964] ECR 585, at 593–4.
[43] Opinion 1/91 *EEA Agreement* [1991] I–6079, at para 21.
[44] J Wouters, 'National Constitutions and the European Union', (2000) *LIEI*, 25, at 68.
[45] The difference between the new legal order and public international law are diminishing, as described by E Denza, 'Two legal orders: divergent or convergent?', (1999) 48 *ICLQ*, 257.

sovereign rights or transferred sovereign powers for the benefit of the Community institutions, which now have powers of their own. The *subjects* of the new legal order comprised not only the Member States but also their nationals. All these qualities taken together make the Community legal order a new legal order, in the view of this Court which had *une certaine idée de l'Europe* in which the precedence of Community law follows naturally.[46]

In *Van Gend en Loos*, the new legal order was said to also include individuals, who could derive rights which national courts must protect, and operated as the foundation of direct effect. In *Costa v ENEL*, the special nature of the law stemming from the Treaty was presented as a foundation of the precedence of Community law: '..[T]he law stemming from the Treaty, (..) could not, because of its special and original nature, be overridden by domestic legal provisions..'.[47] While in the foundational judgment *Costa* the specificity is put forward as the basis for the supremacy of Community law, this is reversed in *Opinion 1/91* where the supremacy of Community law is presented as an argument for the specificity of the Community Treaties. The supremacy of Community law has acquired an axiomatic quality, which needs no further substantiation.[48]

The specificity of the Community legal order has been questioned, most notably by Derrick Wyatt and Bruno De Witte,[49] who have argued convincingly that the new legal order with precedence over national law could be explained entirely on the basis of prevailing international law, and was accordingly not so new after all. Yet, even if the direct effect and supremacy of Community law can be explained on the basis of the 'ordinary' rules of international law, this does not make the Community legal order less special: indeed, for Community law, direct effect and supremacy in the domestic legal order have been stated by an international court and imposed on the national courts who have accepted it. This had not (yet) happened in the context of classic international law. Furthermore, whether the Community legal order is new or old, the most important point is that the Court itself rejects public international law as an explanation of Community law.[50]

---

46 P Pescatore, 'The Doctrine of "Direct Effect": An Infant Disease of Community Law', (1983) *ELR* 155, at 157; see also M Sørensen, 'Autonomous Legal Orders: Some Considerations relating to a Systems Analysis of International organisations in the World legal Order', (1983) 32 *ICLQ*, 559, at 574.

47 Case 6/64 *Costa v ENEL* [1964] ECR 585, at 594.

48 Opinion 1/91 *EEA Agreement* [1991] 6079. In *Opinion 1/91* the Court puts very strong emphasis on the contrast between the Community Treaties and the EEA Agreement.

49 D Wyatt, 'New Legal Order, or Old?' (1982) *ELR* 147; B De Witte, 'Retour à "Costa". La primauté du droit communautaire à la lumière du droit international', (1984) *RTDeur*, 425; see the critique of the 'revisionist' view R Kovar, 'Ordre juridique communautaire', in *Juris-Classeur Europe*, fasc. 431.

50 DR Phelan, *Revolt or Revolution. The Constitutional Boundaries of the European Community* (Dublin, Round Hall, 1997) at 22–3.

For the national courts, the most important element of the specificity of Community law is that they must not treat it as any other treaty. The normal rules on the domestic effect of treaty provisions do not apply: different rules apply for Community law. The specificity argument allows them to discard the traditional beliefs in the context of Community law, without the need to re-phrase them for classic international law.[51] In addition, the specific characteristics of the Community legal order make direct effect and supremacy follow naturally: 'the judges had *"une certaine idée de l'Europe"* of their own, and it is this idea which has been received and not arguments based on the legal technicalities of the matter'.[52]

There have been a few important new developments in the context of 'classic' international law.[53] In the case of *Karl and Walter LaGrand*,[54] the International Court of Justice has stated that *'the clarity of [Article 36 (1) (b) and (c) of the Vienna Convention on Consular Relations] viewed in their context, admits of no doubt (..) Based on the text of these provisions, the Court concludes that Article 26, paragraph 1, creates individual rights, which by virtue of Article I of the Optional Protocol, may be invoked in this Court by the national State of the detained person'.[55]* And it further determined that *'Article 36, paragraph 1 creates individual rights for the detained person in addition to the rights accorded by the sending State, and that consequently the reference to "rights" in paragraph 2 must be read as applying not only to the rights of the sending State, but also to the rights of the detained individual'.[56]* The failure on the part of the American authorities to give full effect to the purposes for which the

---

[51] Different: DR Phelan, *Revolt or Revolution: The Constitutional Boundaries of the European Community* (Dublin, Round Hall, 1997) at 101.

[52] P Pescatore, 'The Doctrine of "Direct Effect": An Infant Disease of Community Law?' (1983) *ELR* 155, at 157.

[53] See for a modern view of the principle of direct effect in international law A Nollkaemper, 'The Direct Effect of Public International Law', in JM Prinssen and A Schrauwen (eds), *Direct Effect. Rethinking a Classic of EC Legal Doctrine* (Groningen, Europa Law Publishing, 2002) 155. He takes issue with the common view that 'direct effect' is a matter of domestic law exclusively. He argues that while public international law does not control direct effect in the same way as in EC law, the concept of direct effect straddles the boundaries of international and national law.

[54] *International Court of Justice*, decision of 27 June 2001, *LaGrand*, available on www.icj-cij.org. Karl and Walter LaGrand, two German nationals, arrested in 1982 on suspicion of capital offences in Arizona, had not been informed of their right to consular access. The LaGrands were tried and sentenced to death. Karl LaGrand was executed by way of lethal injection; Walter LaGrand died in the gas chamber of the State of Arizona. In the case of Walter, Germany had brought claims before the execution, and the Order of the Court called upon the United States to take all measures at its disposal to ensure his execution be stayed pending the Court's final decision in the matter. The case turned on the right to due process and the right to consular protection, and ultimately of course the right to life. Comments in M Feria Tinta, 'Due Process and the Right to Life in the Context of the Vienna Convention on Consular Relations: Arguing the *LaGrand* Case', (2001) 12 EJIL, 363. A full version of the article is available on www.ejil.org.

[55] At para 77.

[56] At para 89.

rights accorded under this article were intended constituted a violation of Article 36, paragraph 2.

In addition, the systems of international administration of Kosovo and East-Timor constitute a novelty in public international law.[57] The Constitutional Framework for Provisional Self-Government in Kosovo, for instance, forms a provisional constitutional framework for an internationalised territory, and enjoys supremacy over the laws in force in Kosovo and the legislation adopted by the provisional institutions of self-government. The Kosovo institutions have to exercise their powers in accordance with the Framework. Chapter 3 of the Constitutional Framework contains a list of international human rights documents, which 'shall be directly applicable in Kosovo as part of this Constitutional Framework'; they serve as a source for subjective rights for individuals, and as limitation of powers imposed on the acts of the provisional institutions. They take precedence over laws adopted by the Kosovo Assembly.[58]

These developments may go to show that Community law may no longer be as unique as it used to be.

7.4.3. The Autonomy of the Community Legal Order

The Community legal order is separate not only from international law but also from the national legal orders. The Community legal order derives from the Treaties and has been set up by the Member States who have transferred powers to it. The Court spoke both of a 'limitation of sovereignty' and a 'transfer of sovereign rights', which accommodates to both approaches detectable in national constitutional law.[59] Once these sovereign powers have been transferred, the Member States can no longer[60] exercise them

---

[57] See M Ruffert, 'The Administration of Kosovo and East-Timor by the International Community', (2001) 50 *ICLQ*, 613, at 613.

[58] This is explained further in C Stahn, 'Constitution Without a State? Kosovo Under the United Nations Constitutional Framework for Self-Government', (2001) 14 *LJIL*, 531.

[59] The 'limitation of sovereignty' language corresponds to the French or Italian approach, while the 'transfer of sovereign rights' corresponds more with the German formula allowing for transfers of sovereign rights see B De Witte, 'Sovereignty and European Integration: The Weight of Legal Tradition', (1995) 2 *MJ*, 145

[60] This leaves unaffected the possibility of a reversal of the initial transfer through a revision of the Treaties in accordance with the relevant Treaty provisions. In *Costa*, the Court speaks of a 'Community of unlimited duration' but this does not exclude the withdrawal of powers transferred. Also the reference to the 'permanent limitation of sovereign rights' (emphasis added) does not, in my view, exclude a reversal. Indeed, the Court qualifies this permanent limitation as one 'against which a subsequent unilateral act incompatible with the concept of the Community cannot prevail' (emphasis added). If the Member States, acting together as Masters of the Treaties, would choose to take back those rights, the limitation is no longer 'permanent'. Under ordinary international law, there are no restrictions to Treaty revision, with the only exception of *ius cogens*.

individually and unilaterally.[61] The new legal order is autonomous from the national legal orders: it derives from an autonomous, independent, source: the Treaties. The umbilical cord with the Member States is cut.

The autonomy of the Community legal order is much more difficult to argue than its specificity. The image conveyed in the cases is a difficult one: Community law derives from treaties concluded between States, which transfer powers to common institutions. The umbilical cord is cut and the Treaties become an independent source of law. Yet, the law deriving from this autonomous source does not remain separate: it becomes an integral part of the legal systems of the Member States. It becomes part of the national legal order *qua* Community law: it must be applied by the national courts, but it does not become national law; it must take precedence and cannot be over-ridden by conflicting national law. The most telling analogies are with Frankenstein's monster – '*Thus the Court affirms* [in Costa v ENEL] *that Community law is like Frankenstein's monster: independent from its creator, imbued with a life of its own, supreme throughout the States' territories, and immune from attack by their laws and Constitutions*'[62] – and with Baron von Munchhausen, lifting himself from the quicksands by pulling on his bootstraps.[63]

The principle of the autonomy of the Community legal order is most important in the context of its validity – once ratified in accordance with the constitutional requirements of the Member States, Community law does not depend on national law for its validity; it cannot be challenged on grounds that it infringes national (constitutional) law – and in the context of *Kompetenz Kompetenz*.[64] The message for the national courts is that Community law must be seen independent from the national Constitution, which is not the source, nor the limit of Community law deriving from an autonomous source and cannot therefore be affected by national law, however framed.

7.4.4. Constitutional Foundation or the Very Nature of Community Law?

It is widely accepted that under the Community orthodoxy that the direct effect and precedence of Community law must be based on Community law and its special nature alone, to the exclusion of constitutional foundations. More so, by basing the supremacy on the national Constitution, the national

---

[61] A commonly used phraseology is that there is a pooling of sovereignty in which the Member States can only exercise their sovereign rights commonly through the Community institutions and in accordance with the procedures and rules laid down in the treaties.

[62] B Rudden, *Basic Community Cases* (Oxford, Clarendon Press, 1987) at 52.

[63] B De Witte, 'Direct Effect, Supremacy and the Nature of the Legal Order', in P Craig and G de Búrca (eds), *The Evolution of EU Law* (Oxford, OUP, 1999) 177, at 199.

[64] See JHH Weiler and U Haltern, 'The Autonomy of the Community Legal Order: Through the Looking Glass', (1996) 37 *Harvard International Law Journal*, 411.

court would violate Community law.[65] Now, does it actually matter whether the direct applicability and precedence of Community law are founded on the Community theory, or are accepted on the basis of the national constitutional provisions? It is submitted that there is no reason why, from the Community perspective, the precedence of Community law and the more general question of the relation between legal orders could not be resolved on the basis of the Constitution or constitutional principles, *as long as* these comply with the basic requirements of Community law: direct effect, supremacy, *effet utile*.[66] Advocate General Lagrange in his Opinion in *Costa v ENEL* pointed out that the question of precedence was a constitutional issue. He trusted that Italy would find the constitutional means of allowing Community law to be effective.[67] The Court has in view a Community in which Community law is effectively applied and enforced with precedence over conflicting national law. That is what is essential and vital for the Community: *'Nier sa supériorité, c'est nier son existence'*. The special nature of the Treaties as instruments to European integration demands their precedence over national law. Yet, the very nature of the treaties and the law stemming from them may be a *reason why* Community law should take precedence, it is not necessarily the *theoretical foundation* for that supremacy. And even if it is the main argument in the Court's own perception and suggested to the national courts as an alternative explanation instead of the usual national view, that does not constrain the national courts to stick to that reasoning and renounce the national Constitution. As long as the aim is achieved, the ultimate foundation of precedence, either the very nature of Community law or a constitutional provision, is not important.[68] A constitutional foundation is not required – Community law takes precedence by its very nature – but it is not prohibited either.

---

[65] See *eg* R Kovar, 'The Relationship between Community law and national law', in *Thirty Years of Community Law*, 109, at 113.

[66] This is why it is not acceptable that Community law is transformed into domestic law: it must be effective *qua* Community law, it must remain visible as Community law, See Case 93/71 *Orsolina Leonesio v Ministry for Agriculture and Forstry of the Italian Republic* [1972] ECR 291; Case 39/72 *Commission v Italy (Premiums for slaugthering cows case)* [1973] ECR 101.

[67] Opinion of AG Lagrange in Case 6/64 *Costa v ENEL* [1964] ECR 585, at 604–606.

[68] In national constitutional theory, the constitutional foundation of the precedence of Community law often leads to the acceptance of constitutional limits to the principle of supremacy. In other words, since supremacy is based on a constitutional provision which must be interpreted and applied in the context of the entire Constitution, it does not apply to all constitutional articles. Some of those articles are considered to take precedence over Community law. In this version, the precedence of Community law is not absolute, as required by the Court of Justice. Such limitation on the absolute supremacy of Community law would obviously conflict with the requirements of Community law. This issue will be further elaborated in Part 2.

The Treaty of Maastricht dealt a serious blow to the new legal order and chose to design new forms of co-operation in new areas, which were, at the time, presented as separate pillars. Amsterdam confirmed the division of the Union. While the Court was allowed some jurisdiction in Title VI of the EU Treaty, the so-called third pillar, for instance, the Member States clearly stated in the Treaty that decisions and framework decision adopted under Title VI were not to be directly effective. Apparently, Title VI decisions are not to be part of the new legal order, at least not in the same way as mainstream Community law. It is as yet unclear what the relationship is of the law adopted under the second and the third pillar with first pillar law on the one hand, and national law on the other.

7.6. DEFINING THE COMMUNITY LEGAL ORDER
FROM THE NATIONAL PERSPECTIVE

7.6.1. Introduction

Quite a few national courts, in particular the constitutional courts, attempt to catch the European Treaties and the law stemming from it in a doctrinal matrix in order to explain their effects on national law. By defining the Community in suitable terms, the law deriving from it can be given a place in or with reference to the national legal system, often in contrast to 'ordinary' international treaties. These theoretical appraisals require a basic re-thinking of fundamental principles, and sometimes a good deal of creativity. The aim is to achieve the result required by the European Court of Justice, namely that Community law is applied and given precedence in all national courts, without however having to set aside the prevailing beliefs about the relation between the national and international legal order. The barriers on the road to acceptance were made up of constitutional principles and dogmas, related *inter alia* to the relation between legal orders. Today, it is difficult to argue that the European Treaties are like any other international treaty with no special internal relevance. National courts have given the Treaties and its law a place in the domestic legal order, either by re-defining the overall ideology on the relation between treaties and domestic law, as was the case in Belgium, or by reference to special nature of the Community, as in Italy and Germany. The need to define the Communities and the law deriving from them was especially strong in Italy and Germany which struggled with the peculiarities of the dualist doctrine. By distinguishing Community law from ordinary treaties and accepting its special nature, it could be given precedence in the internal legal order, while the traditional dualist tenets could be maintained for the remainder, and without the need for constitutional amendment.

7.6.2. Italy

In Italy, a rethinking of the relationship between the Community and the national legal order was essential for the Community mandate of the courts to be condoned.[69] Indeed, international agreements were still considered as foreign to the Italian legal order. The latter could be opened up to provisions contained in a treaty, but these would never be effective *qua* treaty provisions. In order to produce effects domestically, they would have to be brought to life by an *ordine di esecuzione*, mostly in the form of an Act of Parliament. The latter would also attach its nature and rank to the relevant treaty provisions. A transmutation would thus take place, the treaty provisions being disguised as national norms, casting off their quality of international treaty law and assuming the features and rank of a domestic norm. They would, in short, become the legal equivalents of Acts of the Italian Parliament.[70] If this view were equally applied to the EC Treaties and the law stemming from them, Community law would have the same rank and status as any other ordinary Act of Parliament and could thus be overridden by a later piece of primary legislation.

Nicola Catalano,[71] the first Italian member of the Court of Justice, presented an alternative view, based on Article 11 of the Italian Constitution, which authorised limitations of sovereignty in favour of certain international organisations. In his view, the ordinary Act of Parliament by which the European Treaties were consented to was of a different nature

---

[69] Surveys of the often contradictory case law of the *Corte costituzionale* and the difficult road towards acceptance of the Community mandate in the hands of all Italian courts can be found in A La Pergola and P Del Duca, 'Community law, International law and the Italian Constitution', (1985) *AJIL*, 598; M Cartabia, 'The Italian Constitutional Court and the Relationship between the Italian Legal System and the European Community', (1990) *Michigan J Int L*, 173; P Mengozzi, *European Community law from Common Market to European Union*, 1992, at 57ff; G Amoroso, 'La giurisprudenza costituzionale nell'anno 1995 in tema di rapporto tra ordinamento comunitario e ordinamento nazionale: verso un 'quarta' fase?', (1996) *Foro Italiano*, V–4; the Italian Report by L Daniele and S Bartole, in *Le droit constitutionnel national et l'intégration européenne*, 17th FIDE Congress (Berlin, 1996) 330; M Cartabia, 'The Italian Constitutional Court and the Relationship Between the Italian Legal System and the European Union', in *The European Court and National Courts – Doctrine and Jurisprudence. Legal Change in Its Social Context* (Oxford, Hart Publishing, 1998) 133 and FP Ruggieri Laderchi, 'Report on Italy', Above, 147.

[70] M Cartabia, 'The Italian Constitutional Court and the Relationship Between the Italian Legal System and the European Community', (1990) *Michigan J Int L*, 173, at 173·

[71] N Catalano, 'Portata dell'art. 11 della Costituzione in relazione ai trattati istitutive delle Comunità Europee', (1964) *Foro Italiano*, I, 465; N Catalano, 'La position du droit communautaire dans le droit des Etats membres', in *Droit communautaire et droit national*, *Semaine de Bruges*, (Bruges, De Tempel, 1965) 55, at 75ff.

to other such Acts. Indeed, the Community Treaties envisaged the transfer of normative, administrative and judicial powers and thus were of the kind referred to in Article 11 of the Constitution. The limitation of sovereignty referred to in the article implied derogations from certain constitutional provisions and brought about restrictions of the powers of the constitutional organs, and in particular of the legislative organs. An Article 11 limitation of sovereignty could be achieved by an ordinary Act of Parliament. Yet, even if such Act had the outward appearance of an ordinary Act of Parliament, its content and effect differed a great deal: it could to a limited extent modify the Constitution and restrict the powers of the Legislature. The ordinary Act of Parliament approving the Community Treaties had the effect of altering the Constitution and restricting the powers of the constitutional organs in the scope of the transferred powers. If Parliament were to pass contrary legislation in a domain that had been restricted by the Treaties it would abuse powers which it no longer possessed. The elements of the theory are the following. First, the Community Treaties are not ordinary treaties, but treaties as referred to in Article 11 of the Constitution, bringing about a limitation of sovereignty. Second, the Act of approval of these Treaties is of a different nature to ordinary Acts of Parliament and other Acts of approval, resulting in a modification of the Constitution and a restriction of the powers of the constitutional organs. Consequently, Parliament is restricted from legislating contrary to the treaties and the law stemming from it since it no longer has any legislative power in those areas: the powers conferred by the treaties are *ipso facto* removed from the regular constitutional organs of the Member States, which previously enjoyed them. Accordingly, conflicts of norms can always be reduced to conflicts of competences. There is no hierarchical relationship between the Community Treaties and Community law on the one hand and Italian law on the other. Both pertain to a different legal order. Parliament has simply withdrawn from domains specified in the Treaty and the Act of approval. In those areas, the Community institutions take over.

Catalano's theory presented a convenient and ingenious solution: the Italian legal community could preserve its dualist precepts, while at the same time Community law was granted a distinct character which allowed it to be given precedence. In addition, the precedence of Community law would not have to be formulated on the basis of lofty and abstract theories, but could be founded on the Constitution itself. The argument was advanced before the *Corte costituzionale* in the *Costa v ENEL* case,[72] but

---

[72] This is indeed the same case as the one that came before the ECJ. Mr Costa brought an action against his electricity bill to be paid to ENEL He argued before the giudice conciliatore of Milan that the law establishing ENEL was inconsistent with certain articles of the EEC Treaty and therefore with article 11 of the Constitution. The giudice conciliatore

rejected.[73] The *Corte costituzionale* recognised that the rule laid down by Article 11 did imply that it was possible to conclude treaties by which limitations of sovereignty were agreed to and that these may be brought into force by means of an ordinary law.[74] Yet it did not accept that Article 11 of the Constitution conferred a special status or rank to the parliamentary Act of approval, or altered the usual rules about the internal effects of treaties. Consequently, a conflict between a Community treaty provision – approved by an ordinary Act of Parliament – and a later parliamentary Act would have to be resolved by recourse to the *lex posterior* rule. In addition, a conflict would not amount to an indirect breach of Article 11 of the Constitution. The international responsibility of the State could be caused, but that did not deprive the later Act of Parliament of its full effects in the domestic legal order. Since no constitutional issue was involved, a clash between the Community Treaties and a later Act of Parliament fell into the province of the ordinary courts. The *Corte costituzionale* did not endorse the view that the Community Treaties were different from other Treaties and did not consider it essential to ascertain the exact nature of the Community.[75]

In view of the possible harmful effects this judgment for the application and enforcement of the Treaties and the entire project of European integration,[76] the Court of Justice was forced to forcefully denounce the view adopted by the *Corte costituzionale*. The judgment of the Court of Justice in *Costa v ENEL* is a constructive critique of the judgment from Rome. It contains a radical renunciation of the result obtained by the *Corte costituzionale*: It is '(..) impossible for the States (..) to accord precedence to a

was therefore confronted with a possible conflict and with the problem of precedence. To obtain certainty as to the interpretation of the EEC Treaty, he referred several questions to the ECJ In addition, he made a reference to the Corte costituzionale in order to find out whether he was entitled, under the principles of Italian constitutional law, to disregard the Statute in it were found to be contrary to the Treaty. The Italian Constitutional Court gave judgment on February 24, 1964; the ECJ decided its case a few months later on July 15, 1964; Both judgments were commented on in 2 *CML Rev* 1964–65, at 213 (by Sk.) and 226 (by N Catalano); see also E Stein, 'Toward Supremacy of Treaty—Constitution by Judicial Fiat in the European Economic Community', *Riv.dir.int.* 1965, 3.

[73] *Corte Costituzionale*, decision n 14/1964 of 24 February 1964, *Costa v ENEL*, Foro Italiano, 1964, I–30; English version in 1 *CML Rev* 1963–1964, 463, 465·

[74] The Constitution does not clearly say that an ordinary Act of Parliament, as opposed to constitutional amendment, suffices for the purpose of limiting sovereignty; neither does the Constitution clearly indicate the legal consequences of such limitation. In contrast, Art. 24 of the German Constitution expressly allows for the transfer of sovereign rights by ordinary law.

[75] The *Corte costituzionale* did not appear to show a great interest in and understanding of the Treaties and their essential features: it referred to the Commission as an 'ad hoc Commission' and a 'consultative commission' and to the Court of Justice as a 'High Court of Justice'.

[76] See eg the Opinion of AG Lagrange in Case 6/64 *Costa v ENEL* [1964] ECR 585. The warning that integration would fail if direct effect and supremacy were rejected was widespread in those days.

unilateral and subsequent measure over a legal system accepted by them on the basis of reciprocity' and *'the law stemming from the Treaty (..) could not (..) be overridden by domestic legal provisions, however framed (..)'.*[77] Yet it equally provides the *Corte costituzionale* with a number of ingredients for a new approach: the EEC Treaty is different from an ordinary international treaty; the EEC Treaty has created its own legal system which has become an integral part of the legal systems of the Member States and which the courts are bound to apply; the limitation of sovereignty on the part of the Member States have created a Community with real powers and a body of law which binds their nationals and themselves; the spirit of the Treaty and the special and original nature of the law stemming from them. All of these elements call for the precedence of Community law.

In *Frontini*[78] the *Corte costituzionale* re-defined its position.[79] Based on the limitation of sovereignty clause contained in Article 11 of the Constitution, the *Corte* described the Communities as a new inter-State organisation of a supra-national type to which the Member States have conferred certain sovereign powers and which is characterised by *'its own autonomous and separate legal order'*. Community law and the national law of the Member States had to be regarded as autonomous and distinct legal systems, albeit co-ordinated in accordance with the division of powers laid down and guaranteed in the Treaties. Community law was to be given effect in the Italian legal order as such without being reproduced by national rules. The *Corte costituzionale* thus recognised the constitutionality of the delegation of normative powers. The constitutional articles on the legislative function govern solely the legislative activity of the Italian State organs, and not of the Community organs.

The judgment, hailed as the acceptance of the precedence of Community law,[80] was not explicit as to the Community mandate of the

---

[77]   Case 6/64 *Costa v ENEL* [1964] ECR 585, at 594.

[78]   *Corte Costituzionale*, Decision n 183/1973 of 27 December 1973, *Frontini, 39 Rac.uff. 503 (1973)* [1974] 2 CMLR 372; French version in CDE, 1975, 114, with note by P de Caterini; RDI, 1989, 64; Oppenheimer, *The Cases, 629*.

[79]   The issue was whether the direct applicability of Community regulations violated the constitutional protection concerning the enactment of Statutes, and the principle of the *riserva di legge* (monopoly of Statute in certain areas). If the constitutional limitations on the enactment of laws were violated, it was argued, then the Italian Act of Parliament authorizing ratification of the Treaty was unconstitutional insofar as it authorized acceptance of such regulations.

[80]   There is, however, another element in the case which is much less Community friendly: Art. 11, according to the *Corte costituzionale*, also has its limits. It allows for a limitation of sovereignty effected by an ordinary law and without recourse to the normal procedures for constitutional amendment. Such limitation may bring about some modifications to the Constitution, but it cannot infringe upon the core principles of the Constitution and the inviolable rights of man as set out in the Constitution. The core principles of the Constitution cannot be affected by Community law. They constitute the limits of the supremacy of Community law. This aspect of Frontini is still good law. It will be discussed below.

Italian courts. The supremacy of Community law underpinned various parts of the judgment,[81] but what was an Italian court to do when confronted with two contrary provisions, deriving from different legal orders? The implications of the *Frontini* doctrine for the judicial function were set out in a subsequent judgment *ICIC*,[82] where the Court rejected the competence of the ordinary courts to declare conflicting national measures *void*,[83] or *inapplicable*.[84] An incompatibility between a Community provision and a measure of national law did raise the question of the latter's constitutionality and thus, had to be referred to the *Corte costituzionale*, which could declare it *unconstitutional*.[85] The reasoning builds on *Frontini* and goes as follows: Article 11 of the Constitution allows for a limitation of sovereignty in designated areas. The national authorities, including the Legislature, withdraw from those areas set out in the Treaties. Under Article 11 of the Constitution, the national authorities are bound to respect these new restrictions of their powers. Should they fail to do so, it is not for the ordinary courts to check the Legislature: Since the Legislature, by infringing a measure of Community law, at the

---

[81] According to Maestipieri, in 12 *CML Rev* 1975, at 435, who draws attention to the fact that the Corte costituzionale recognized exclusive normative powers in designated areas, and that the Corte acknowledged the vital importance of a uniform application of Community law throughout the Community; see also P de Caterini, 'La Cour constitutionnelle italienne et le droit communautaire', (1975) *CDE*, 122; L Plouvier, 'L'arrêt de la Cour constitutionnelle d'Italie du 22 octobre 1975 dans l'affaire ICIC', (1976) *RTDeur*, 271·

[82] *Corte costituzionale*, decision n. 232/75 of 30 October 1975, *ICIC*, *Foro Italiana*, 1975, I–2661; summary in English in 12 *CML Rev* 1975, 439–441 and above, 1976, 525–526 and 530–533; The case was referred to the *Corte costituzionale* by the *Corte di cassazione* and concerned the issue of the fate of a conflicting national provision (void or inapplicable?), and of which court had jurisdiction (*Corte costituzionale* or ordinary courts?).

[83] The Court reasoned that the effect of the transfer of normative powers to the Community institutions was not to emasculate entirely the sovereignty of the legislative bodies of the Member States; such a transfer raises the different problem of the constitutionality of the relevant legislative instruments.

[84] On this assumption, the courts would have to be regarded not as being empowered to choose between several applicable rules, but as being empowered to choose the only rule validly adopted, which would amount to admitting that the courts had the power to declare that the legislator was totally lacking in competence, a power which was certainly not attributed to them under the legal system in force. The ECJ's perspective on the question of the fate of the conflicting national measure was firmly established in Case 34/67 *Lück* [1968] ECR 245, where it held that Community law only commands the inapplicability of the conflicting measure, but that it does not preclude the courts from choosing other solutions available under national law. One can imagine other solutions such as a declaration of invalidity, declaring the norm null and void ab initio and erga omnes, etc. Yet, whichever solution is chosen under national law, all courts must be empowered to set aside the conflicting measure, see Case 106/77 *Simmenthal* [1978] ECR 629.

[85] Does a declaration of unconstitutionality of the norm meet the requirements of Case 34/67 *Lück* [1968] ECR 245, which imposes the minimum requirement of inapplicability but also allows for other solutions available under national law? The declaration of unconstitutionality, also available in Germany, was not raised in the *Lück* case, where the German referring court only spoke of inapplicability and annulment (null and void); the issue was discussed in Chapter 4 above.

same time violates Article 11 of the Constitution, a reference must be made to the *Corte costituzionale* which can remove the conflicting measure from the law books so that Community law is given precedence.

At the end of the day, Community law *is* accorded precedence and all legal effects of the national measure are eliminated. To that extent, it could even be argued that the Italian solution was even more Community friendly, as conflicting legislation would disappear from the law books. Yet, the solution did not conform with requirements of *immediate* applicability and precedence. Only a few years later, the *Pretore di Susa* asked the Court of Justice whether the Constitutional Court's insistence on centralised review was consistent with the requirements of Community law. The European Court in *Simmenthal* flatly rejected the Italian position as being contrary to the requirements of direct applicability and precedence. *All* national courts, and not only the constitutional court, must have jurisdiction to accord precedence to Community law and set aside conflicting national law.[86]

Finally, the *Granital* decision of 1984 marked the acceptance of the Community mandate in the hands of all Italian courts, without a dramatic revision of the existing principles.[87] The Community and Italian legal order are still regarded as autonomous and separate legal orders, co-ordinated on the basis of the division of powers established and guaranteed in the Treaty. In accordance with Article 11 of the Italian Constitution, Italy has limited its sovereignty and transferred competences to the Community institutions. Community law forms a separate legal system which is given direct applicability in the Italian legal order whilst at the same time remaining external to the municipal legal order. The national legal order opens itself up to those rules by allowing these provisions to be applied on Italian territory in the form in which they were enacted by the Community institutions. This is the same perception of the relation between Community law and Italian law as in *Frontini* and *ICIC*. What is new, however, are the consequences drawn from this theory for the judicial function and for the fate of the conflicting national measure. Where a Community regulation governs the case before a court, it must be applied, and no conflicting measure of national law can constitute an obstacle to the recognition of the force of law of that regulation. National law would not be abrogated or invalidated by the Community regulation: both norms belong to different legal orders; there cannot, therefore, be a hierarchical

---

[86]   Case 106/77 *Simmenthal* [1978] ECR 629.
[87]   *Corte costituzionale*, decision 170/1984 of 8 June 1984, Foro Italiano, 1984, 2062, with note A Tizzano; English translation in 21 *CML Rev* 1984, 756, with annotation by G Gaja; extract in French in *CDE*, 1986, 185, with note J-V Louis; other analyses include A Barav, 'Cour constitutionnelle italienne et droit communautaire: le fantôme de Simmenthal', (1985) *RTD Eur*, 313; RM Petriccione, 'Supremacy of Community law over national law', (1986) *ELR*, 320.

relationship between them. Municipal law simply does not operate in the domain covered by such regulation. Italian courts do not have to refer an incompatibility to the *Corte costituzionale*: the issue is not one of the constitutionality of the national measure. The measure simply is not relevant to the case and ordinary courts do not have to apply it. That does not mean that they pronounce themselves on the validity or even the applicability of the national rule. The conflicting norm must not even be 'disapplied': it simply is 'not applicable'. In this way the *Corte costituzionale* achieved the result required by the Court of Justice.[88]

This enigmatic and extremely abstract Italian version of the relation between legal orders, the precedence of Community law and the ensuing review powers of the Italian courts follows two paths. One emphasised the *separateness* of the two legal orders, an idea which is typical for a dualist attitude. In order to make Community law operative in the Italian legal order *qua* Community law and with precedence over national law, recourse is taken to the second element of the theory: Article 11 of the Constitution which has the effect of making the Italian authorities withdraw from certain areas of the Italian legal order to make room for Community law. Within those areas, and because of its separateness and lack of hierarchical or other relationship with Italian law, Community law takes precedence. All courts have jurisdiction to give full effect to Community law.[89] The highly dogmatic approach of the *Corte costituzionale* certainly is not the easiest one. The *Corte* grapples with concepts and terms in order to comply with the requirements of *Simmenthal* but on its own terms, and with certain exceptions. The Court is walking a tightrope and goes out of its way to avoid admitting the power of ordinary courts to 'disapply' conflicting legislation. The power of the Italian courts to not apply national law is not constitutive: conflicting law is not applicable even before the judge's intervention. It is simply a consequence of the relation between

---

[88] The *Corte costituzionale* admitted that its dualist views were based on different premises than those of the Court of Justice (monism), but insisted that at the end of the day corresponded to the latter's position. On the other hand. the qualifications as made in *Frontini*, that there are core principles of the Constitution over which Community law cannot be awarded precedence, do not comply with the Community orthodoxy. This is discussed in Theme 2.

[89] *Granital* concerned the precedence of Community regulations; In *Corte costituzionale*, decision 113/1985 of 19 April 1985, *Spa BECA*, 68 *Riv.dir.int.*, 1985, 388 and decision 389/1989, *Provincia di Bolzano*, 72 *Riv.dir.int.*, 1989, 404 the principle of precedence and judicial review was extended to the judgments of the ECJ and Treaty provisions; for a comment, see G Gaja, 'New Developments in a Continuing Story: The Relationship between EEC Law and Italian Law', (1990) 27 *CML Rev* 83, who claims that the Court has in these cases yet again changed its view on the relationship between orders, and replaced Granital implicitly with a simpler concept of supremacy, EEC law being higher in rank than national law, see also L Daniele, 'Après l'arrêt Granital: droit communautaire et droit national dans la jurisprudence récente de la Cour constitutionnelle italienne', (1992) *CDE*, 1.

the two legal systems. The Italian judges are thus situated at a cross-roads: they are on the State legal system's frontier, and monitor the boundaries between domestic law and Community law. As one author put it, 'The judge is outside the state legal system insofar as the judge then applies Community law'.[90] The fiction is thus brought to the extreme.[91]

7.6.3. Germany

At the outset, the German legal conceptions in this area of constitutional law were similar to those prevailing in Italy. Like Italy, Germany is a dualist State, where treaties are made effective in the domestic legal order by a domestic legal act which passes on its nature, status and rank to the treaty provisions thus executed. Another common feature is the existence of a constitutional court, with a monopoly of judicial scrutiny of primary legislation. Finally, both constitutional texts contain a provision on the effect and primacy of 'general international law', and provide for a 'transfer of powers' rule.[92]

And yet, the German constitutional court has not struggled for very long to arrive at a theory which allows for both the principle of supremacy of Community law and the *Simmenthal*-mandate. Certainly, the *Bundesverfassungsgericht* has clashed with the Court of Justice, and it certainly is one of its most ardent adversaries. And yet, in this particular area of the involvement of the ordinary courts in the enforcement of Community law even against the Legislature, the *Bundesverfassungsgericht* has shown itself lenient and co-operative.

Only a few years after *Van Gend en Loos* and *Costa v ENEL*, the *Bundesver fassungsgericht* handed down a very integration-friendly decision[93] in which it described Community regulations as acts of a special 'supranational' public authority, distinct and independent from the public authorities of the Member States, to which Germany, in accordance with Article 24 (1) of the Basic Law, had transferred *Hoheitsrechte*,

---

90   P Mengozzi, *European Community Law from Common Market to European Union*, (1992) at 71.
91   There may be advantages in this way of presenting matters: the judge would not be constrained by any national procedural rules, and would be free to accept all elements of his Community mandate without any restrictions. Yet, this is an impossible position to maintain: any judge needs rules on procedure, time limits, remedies, and Community law simply does not offer a complete system in this area. Further, hardly any case can be solved on the basis of Community law alone. The schizophrenic position of the judge is then complete!
92   The latter notion is here used in the abstract, without being fine-tuned for each of the systems individually.
93   *Bundesverfassungsgericht*, decision of 18 October 1967, *EEC Regulations Constitutionality Case*, 22 BVerfGE 293; Oppenheimer, *The Cases*, 410.

and which exercises sovereign rights of its own. Community law was autonomous both from international and from national law and could not be reviewed by the *Bundesverfassungsgericht* in constitutional complaint procedures.[94] The decision did not directly concern the supremacy of Community law over national law and the corresponding powers of the courts, but it did sanction the *de facto* supremacy of Community law.

The full acceptance of the Community judicial review mandate of the ordinary German courts came in the *Lütticke* decision.[95] In a wording that reflects the 1963 and 1964 decisions of the European Court, the *Bundesverfassungsgericht* held that as a result of the ratification of the EEC Treaty, an independent legal order had been created, which was inserted into the municipal legal order and which was to be applied by the German courts. Article 24(1) of the Basic Law not only permitted the transfer of *Hoheitsrechte*, but also implied that the sovereign acts of the Community organs were to be recognised as deriving from an original and exclusive sovereign authority. From that legal position it followed that German courts were obliged to apply those legal provisions which superimpose themselves upon and displace conflicting national law (*über-lagern und verdrängen entgegenstehendes nationales Recht*). The Constitutional Court was not competent to deal with the question whether a norm of ordinary municipal law was incompatible with a Community law provision invested with priority: the settlement of such a conflict of norms was a matter to be left to the ordinary courts. Without much constitutional difficulty the German constitutional court thus found a way out of the restrictions of the traditional German attitude towards international treaties and their lack of supremacy. Article 24(1) of the Grundgesetz was used as the constitutional foundation to open up the German legal order for Community law, and award it precedence.[96]

Since *Lütticke*, the description of Community law as supra-national and the recognition of the autonomy of Community law has gradually eroded.[97] More and more the emphasis is put on the *limits* on the transfers of *Hoheitsrechte* under Article 24(1). The provision opens up the national legal order to make room for direct effect and applicability of law from another source, and even its priority, but it does not allow for a transfer which would undermine essential structural parts of the Constitution and

---

[94] The procedure of Verfassungsbeschwerde can, after exhaustion of other legal remedies, be brought by anyone who claims that his rights have been violated by public authority: Art. 93(4a) GG.

[95] *Bundesverfassungsgericht*, decision of 9 June 1971, *Alfons Lütticke GmbH*, BVerfGE 31, 145; English translation in A Oppenheimer, *The Cases*, at 415.

[96] Ipsen spoke of an '*Integrationshebel*' contained in Article 24(1) of the Basic Law, HP Ipsen, note under *Lütticke*, BVerfGE 31, 145, Europarecht, 1972, 57.

[97] As pointed out by J Kokott, 'German Constitutional Jurisprudence and European Integration', (1996) *EPL*, 237, and 413, at 241.

in particular, the legal principles underlying the constitutional provisions on fundamental rights.[98] Nevertheless, the Constitutional Court has always been concerned to ensure that lower courts apply Community law, with precedence over conflicting legislation, and even in *Solange I* the *Bundesverfassungsgericht* stated: '*This Court – in this respect in agreement with the law developed by the Court of Justice – adheres to its settled view that Community law is neither a component part of the national legal system nor international law, but forms an independent system of law flowing from an autonomous legal source; for the Community is not a State, in particular not a federal State, but a 'sui generis community in the process of progressive integration', an 'inter-State institution' within the meaning of Article 24(1) of the Constitution. (..) the two legal spheres stand independent of and side by side one another in their validity, (..)'.*[99]

The nature of the Community and the Union and the effect and status of the law stemming from them are still under debate, in another, closely related area, of the constitutional limits to European law. As said, Article 24(1) of the Constitution is used as the device to open up the German legal order to Community law, and even to grant it priority.[100] The notorious and absolute low point in the description of the Communities and their relation with the German legal order was the *Maastricht Urteil* where the *Bundesverfassungsgericht* emphasised what the Union and the Community are *not*: they are not a State based on a European People; they do not constitute a '*Staatenbund*' or a '*Bundesstaat*' (but rather a '*Staatenverbund*'); there is no intention to establish a United States of Europe; co-operation exists only in limited areas, and the Member States remain the Masters of the Treaties, and at the end of the day, Germany remains a sovereign State in

---

[98] This *Solange* case law will be analysed more in the context of the review powers of the constitutional courts.

[99] *Bundesverfassungsgericht*, decision of 29 May 1974, *Internationale Handelsgesellschaft (Solange I)*, BVerfGE 37, 271; [1974] 2 CMLR 540; Oppenheimer, *The Cases*, 419, at 445–6.

[100] Even if the text of Article 24(1) does not mention such priority, see *Bundesverfassungsgericht*, decision of 22 October 1986, *Wünsche Handelsgesellschaft (Solange II)*, BverfGE 73, 339, Oppenheimer, *The Cases*, 461, at 484–85: '*It is true that article 24(1) of the Constitution does not itself (..) regulate the (..) question of priority (..)*'. Nor did such priority follow from general international law. '*Internal priority of validity or application only arises by virtue of an application-of-law instruction* [in German: '*Anwendungsbefehl*'] *to that effect under the internal law, and that applies too in the case of treaties the content of which obliges the parties to provide for internal priority of validity or application. Article 24(1) however makes it possible constitutionally for treaties which transfer sovereign rights to international institutions and the law established by such institutions to be accorded priority of validity or application as against the internal law of the Federal Republic by the appropriate internal application-of-law instruction. That is what took place in the case of the EC Treaties (..) From the application-of-law instruction of the Act of Accession to the EEC Treaty, which extends to Article 189(2) EEC, arises the immediate validity of the regulations (..) and the precedence of their application over internal law.*' The reasoning does not convince: what of the priority of the Treaties themselves? Or of other acts of the Community institutions other than regulations? Besides, Article 189 of the EEC Treaty (old) does not mention the priority of regulations either!

its own right; withdrawal remains possible at all times. Many of these statements are true, certainly under public international law and even from a Community law perspective. It is the tone that reveals the truth: the judgment bursts with distrust of the Communities and its Court, and with suspicion of constitutional limitations and restrictions. With respect to the effectiveness of Community law, the Court insists that the Community authority derives from the Member States and can have binding effect on German sovereign territory only by virtue of the German implementing order. The insistence is no longer on the *autonomy* of the Community legal order but on the *ancillary* character of the Community legal order. Ultimately, it derives from the States, the *Herren der Verträge*. The emphasis is on German restrictions, contained in the Constitution and in the Act of approval. The image of the relationship between the Community and the national legal order is that propagated by Kirchhof, the former member of the *Bundesverfassungsgericht* who is said to be responsible for writing the *Maastricht Urteil:* the Community and German legal order remain separate, and in order to be effective in Germany, Community law must pass over the bridge constituted by the Act of approval built on the constitutional authorisation of Article 23.[101] In order to be allowed to pass, Community law must fulfil certain conditions, and at the German side of the bridge, there is a *Brückenhäuschen* accommodating a guard, *i.e.* the *Bundesverfassungsgericht*. While the sharp edges of the *Maastricht Urteil* have been trimmed in subsequent cases, especially the *Bananas II* decision of June 2000,[102] the basic view is still that of separate legal orders linked by a bridge. The difference is that, as before, the *Brückenhäuschen* is not permanently staffed. [103]

7.6.4. Germany and Italy: an Appraisal

The positions of the German and Italian constitutional courts today still resemble one another, and are very often treated jointly where Community law is concerned. Both courts organise the internal effect and status of Community law on the basis of a transfer of powers or limitation of sovereignty article in the Constitution; both retain a dualist view of the relationship between Community law and national law; both also set constitutional limits to the effectiveness of Community law, sometimes even under reference to each other's case law. Yet, with respect to the

---

[101] Article 23 was introduced at the occasion of the Treaty of Maastricht, as Article 24 was no longer considered sufficient in the current state of integration.
[102] *Bundesverfassungsgericht*, decision of 7 June 2000, *Bananas III*, BVerfGE 102, 147; French version in 37 *RTDeur*, 2001, 155.
[103] This will be further developed below.

review powers of the ordinary courts, the German constitutional court has been much more lenient than its Italian counterpart. Its view of the relation between the Community and the national legal orders seems less principled, even if it is based on a similar reasoning of a similar provision in the Constitution. The mandate of the ordinary courts has never really been an issue before the *Bundesverfassungsgericht*, while it was crucial in the Italian case law, and the main issue in its polemic with the Court of Justice.

What is striking is that the tone of both the German and the Italian approaches to Community law is still *dualist*, in the sense that the emphasis is on the separateness of two distinct and autonomous legal orders. In that respect, no distinction is made with ordinary treaties. Yet, due to the special features of the Community and its goals of co-operation and integration, Community law is given a privileged position, with reference to a constitutional provision authorising a transfer of powers. On the basis of Article 11 of the Italian Constitution, the Italian authorities withdraw from specified areas to make room for Community law. As a consequence, there are two legal orders which produce effects on Italian territory: Italian law and, in some areas, Community law each being sovereign in its own realm. Article 24 of the German Basic Law, and now Article 23, operates as an *Integrationshebel* and has made it possible for the German Parliament to construe a bridge between the German and the Community legal order, over which Community law passes in order to enter the German legal system. In its effects, Community law thus wins over the constraints of dualism: in the areas vacated by the Italian legislature and once it has passed the German bridge, Community law operates *as such*, that is *qua* Community law, with precedence over conflicting legislation even deriving from the primary legislature.

7.6.5. Belgium

The third founding Member State to struggle with a separate legal orders vision and to seek a way of giving effect and priority to international treaty law was Belgium.[104] In contrast to Italy and Germany, which designed tailor-made theories exclusively for Community law, the Belgian strategy has been to re-define the entire attitude towards international law in general. Certainly, the Italo-German route was not available in Belgium, since the Constitution at the time lacked a transfer of powers

---

[104] For a recent survey of the direct effect and supremacy of Community and international law in Belgium, see H Bribosia, 'Applicabilité directe et primauté des traités internationaux et du droit communautaire. Réflexions générales sur le point de vue de l'ordre juridique belge', (1996) *RBDI*, 33; and M Melchior and P Vandernoot, 'Controle de constitutionnalité et droit communautaire dérivé', (1998) *RBDC*, 3.

provision. More importantly, the entire mood at the end of the fifties and throughout the sixties was different. Eminent Belgian lawyers had advocated a complete change of view in the direction of monism as espoused in France, The Netherlands and Luxembourg. The prevaling attitude, to view treaties as foreign to the Belgian legal order, which were given *force de loi* but nothing more in the internal legal order, was rejected as old-fashioned, and inappropriate in the new international environment.

The traditional stance was based on a 1925 *Schieble* judgment of the *Hof van Cassatie*, in which it held that in case of a contradiction, a treaty provision would have to give way to a later Act of Parliament.[105] The courts were refrained from disapplying Acts of Parliament in favour of treaty provisions, because that fell outside the limits of the judicial function. The issue was mainly jurisdictional: Parliament was considered sovereign in the sense that its action was not reviewable by the courts, in the light of the Constitution or any other law. Nevertheless, underlying that was also the other issue of the status of treaty law in the internal legal order and since treaty provisions were not considered to have any higher rank or overriding force, conflicts would have to be solved on the basis of the *lex posterior* rule.[106] Treaties which had been duly ratified and approved by Act of Parliament were considered to have *force de loi*, force of law. The expression had the advantage that treaty provisions became effective in the legal order, that they could serve as a standard for revision of any act inferior to Acts of Parliament, and that a breach of such treaty provision could constitute a basis for *cassation*, a ground to quash a judicial decision. On the other hand, they became *équipollent à la loi*, a phrase which denoted their equivalence and equal rank with Acts of Parliament.

The doctrinal debate running up to the *Franco-suisse Le Ski* judgment of 1971 which ultimately sanctioned the review mandate of courts in the light of international treaties, concentrated on the legal order dilemma and the rank and status of treaties in the domestic legal order. Once that hurdle was taken and treaty provisions were given a higher status, the review powers of the courts followed almost routinely. This is all the more remarkable since for a long time even the most ardent supporters of the

---

[105] '[I]l appartient au législateur belge, lorsqu'il édicte des dispositions en exécution d'une convention intrenationale, d'apprécier la conformité des règles qu'il adopte avec les obligations liant la Belgique par traités; (..) les tribunaux n'ont pas le pouvoir d erefuser d'appliquer une loi pour le motif qu'elle ne serait pas conforme, prétendument, à ces obligations', *Cour de cassation* (B), decision of 26 November 1925, *Schieble*, Pas., 1926, I, 76.

[106] Under Art. 159 (Art. 107 old) of the Belgian Constitution, courts must observe the rule of law and apply lower law in conformity with higher law. It is a written expression of the *lex superior* rule. The only exception are Acts of Parliament: Belgian courts do not have jurisdiction to control the constitutionality of Acts of Parliament. Since 1983, Belgium has a constitutional court, the *Cour d'arbitrage* or *Arbitragehof*, which has the competence to review the constitutionality of Acts of Parliament and of Decrees, ie their equivalents deriving from the parliaments of the federated entities.

supremacy of treaty law considered an express constitutional mandate indispensable to allow for judicial review of statutes on the conformity with treaty law.[107] Constitutional amendments were envisaged at several points, but never adopted.[108] In the end, the *lex posterior* adage was replaced by the *lex superior* rule for treaty-statute conflicts.

To begin with, the precedent in *Schieble* was drastically limited to non-directly effective treaty provisions, so as to deny that the *Cour de cassation* had ever pronounced itself on the status of directly effective treaty provisions.[109] A few years later Ganshof van der Meersch in two successive *mercuriales*[110] started a crusade against the prevailing views and proposed a radically different world view, which in his opinion did not require a constitutional revision. He repudiated the equivalence between treaty provisions and internal Acts of Parliament by a re-interpretation of the Act of Approval. Such Act, he said, is not a statute in its traditional sense, not as to its content nor as to its effect and the procedure. The treaty-making power lies with the Government; an Act of Approval is only *'un acte de haute tutelle'*, and not *'un acte de législation'*. It does not affect the nature of the treaty provisions, which therefore become effective as such, *qua* treaty provisions.

Once the equivalence between treaties and internal statutes had been done away with, Ganshof could construe a novel theory on the relation between legal orders. In his opinion, the international and national legal orders were not separated, but had to be considered as spheres of a general legal order, and the Belgian constitutional system was monist. The precedence of the treaty provision imposed itself for reasons of logic and social

---

[107] H Rolin, 'La force obligatoire des traités dans la jurisprudence belge', (1953) *JT*, 561, also published in Dutch in (1963) *RW*, 73.

[108] A proposal for constitutional amendment and introduction of an Art. 107bis was made at several instances. The text proposed read: 'Courts and tribunals will apply the law only in so far as they conform to the rules of international law and in particular to duly published treaties in force' (translation taken from WJ Ganshof van der Meersch, 'Community Law and the Belgian Constitution', in *In Memoriam JDB Mitchell*, St.John Bates (ed) (London, Sweet & Maxwell, 1983) 74, at 80), and was to be inserted as Art. 107*bis*, that is after the article sanctioning the rule of law principle for the courts, in the form of the lex superior rule of conflict. The underlying philosophy of the text and its place in the Constitution were thus based on the constitutional principles with regard to the hierarchy of norms and judicial control thereof. The draft was never adopted.

[109] R Hayoit de Termicourt, 'Le conflit traité-loi interne', mercuriale 1963, (1963) *JT*, 481 (French version); *RW*, 1963, 73 (Dutch version); a *mercuriale* is a lecture given by the *procureur-général* at the opening of new session of the supreme court (*Cour de cassation*) early September, every year. It treats a specific current legal problem in depth; the *Cour de cassation* seemed to follow the proposed line of reasoning in *Cour de cassation*, decision of 13 April 1964, *Ananou*, Pas., 1964, I, 849; the court did give precedence to a later Act of Parliament under reference to *Schieble*, but with the qualification that the relevant treaty provisions were not directly effective.

[110] WJ Ganshof van der Meersch, 'Réflexions sur le droit international et la révision de la Constitution', mercuriale 1968, (1968) *JT*, 485; id., 'Le juge belge à l'heure du droit international et du droit communautaire', mercuriale 1969, (1969) *JT*, 537.

morality, and because the pre-eminence of international law was embraced in the Constitutions of the Member States of the Communities, with the only exception of Belgium and Luxembourg. In addition, it was the duty of States to see that a rule of domestic law could not validly be set up against an international rule. The corollary of such obligation must be the superiority of the treaty rule over the domestic rule. The ultimate basis for the primacy of international law was its very nature: *'Le juge trouve dans la nature même de la règle de droit international (..) la justification de sa primauté'*: The judge finds a justification for the primacy of international law in its very nature'. Once that view is adopted, a constitutional article explicitly providing for the primacy of treaty law could only be declaratory.

The judicial mandate to enforce the primacy of treaties over primary legislation seems to follow automatically from the monist view, and the higher status of international law. This is surprising, since the limits of the judicial function and the prohibition imposed on the courts to review parliamentary acts had been a fundamental reason for the exclusion of the review mandate in the light of international law in *Schieble*. The jurisdictional argument seems to vanish in front of the new world view.

In the celebrated *Franco-suisse Le Ski*[111] judgment the *Cour de cassation* followed the lines set out by its *procureur général* and admitted to the precedence of directly effective treaty provisions over an Act of Parliament, based on their very nature. The case concerned Article 12 of the EEC Treaty, the *Van Gend en Loos* article. Yet, the judgment proceeds on the basis of a re-appraisal of the effect and status of international treaties in general and is not limited to Community law, as in Italy and Germany. The precedence of Community law is founded on the same principles but imposes itself with even greater force, *'a fortiori'*. 111 The reasoning of the *Cour de cassation* is short and simple: *'[9] In the event of a conflict between a norm of domestic law and a norm of international law which produces direct effects in the internal legal order, the rule established by the treaty shall prevail. The primacy of the treaty results from the very nature of international treaty law.*

---

[111] *Cour de cassation*, decision of 27 May 1971, *SA Fromagerie franco-suisse Le Ski*, JT, 1971, 460, with note JAA Salmon; *CDE*, 1971, 559, with note P Pescatore; [1972] CMLR 330; SEW, 1972, with note J Mertens de Wilmars; Oppenheimer, *The Cases*, 245; among the numerous comments see E Stein, 'Conflicts between Treaties and subsequently enacted statutes in Belgium. *Etat belge v Fromagerie franco-suisse Le Ski*', *Michigan Law Review*, 1972, 118; G Vandersanden, 'Primauté du droit communautaire sur le droit national', *RDIC*, 1972, 847; J-V Louis, 'La primauté du droit international et du droit communautaire après l'arrêt 'Le Ski'', in *Mélanges F Dehousse*, (Bruxelles, 1979), 237; for a recent analysis of the judgment and the subsequent practice and doctrine, J Velu, 'Contrôle de constitutionnalité et contrôle de compatibilité avec les traités', mercuriale 1992, *JT*, 1992, 729 and 749, published also in Dutch: J Velu, 'Toetsing van de grondwettigheid en toetsing van de verenigbaarheid met de verdragen', *RW*, 1992–1993, 481; and H Bribosia, 'Applicabilité directe et primauté des traités internationaux et du droit communautaire', *RBDI*, 1996, 33.

[10] This is a fortiori the case when a conflict exists, as in the present case, between a norm of internal law and a norm of Community law. The reason is that the treaties which have created Community law have instituted a new legal system in whose favour the Member States have restricted the exercise of their sovereign powers in the areas determined by those treaties. [11] Article 12 of the Treaty establishing the EEC is immediately effective and confers on individual persons rights which the national courts are bound to uphold. [12] It follows from all these considerations that it was the duty of the judge to set aside the application of provisions of domestic law that are contrary to this Treaty provision.'[112]

Accordingly, the supremacy of Community law and the powers of the courts to sanction that supremacy, are embedded in a much broader theory of international treaties and their effects in the internal legal order. The passage on the specificity of Community law does reflect the *Van Gend en Loos* and *Costa v ENEL* decisions of the Court of Justice,[113] but its direct impact on the supremacy of Community law is not entirely clear. In his Opinion in *Le Ski*, Ganshof van der Meersch did seem to make a distinction between both situations, of the effect and status of international treaties on the one hand and Community law on the other. The difference lay in the ultimate foundation of supremacy and its relation with the Constitutions. While at the end of the day the supremacy of international treaties was founded on international law itself,[114] Ganshof van der Meersch still linked it to the Constitution: the Belgian Constitution does not preclude the priority of treaties, on the contrary, it is *'d'inspiration moniste'*.[115] Yet that could be otherwise: a Constitution could limit the effects of a treaty in the domestic legal order,[116] but that was not so for Community

---

[112] *Cour de cassation*, decision of 27 May 1971, *Franco-suisse le Ski*, Oppenheimer, *The Cases*, at 266.

[113] Which, however, in the view of Ganshof van der Meersch did not as such bind the *Cour de cassation*.

[114] 'The subjection of the State – and therefore its laws – to international law in its international relations has its basis in the international legal system. This subjection implies the primacy of the rule of international law over that of domestic law', and 'if the international treaty obligation prevails over the rule of domestic law, this is because of its very nature, and the national authorities should respect this primacy, under pain of involving the international liability of the State. It is not for an organ of that State, not the judiciary or even the legislature to shirk the obligation incumbent on it to respect this primacy', Opinion of Ganshof van der Meersch in *Le Ski*, Oppenheimer, *The Cases*, at 252 and 264 respectively.

[115] Opinion of Ganshof van der Meersch, in *Le Ski*, Oppenheimer, *The Cases*, at 254: '(..) There is nothing, not only in the text of the Constitution but also in the constitutional system itself, which rules out the primacy of international law. It is above all in the very nature of international law (..) that the judiciary may find justification for this primacy.'

[116] WJ Ganshof van der Meersch, 'Réflexions sur le droit international et la revision de la Constitution', mercuriale 1968, JT, 1968, 485, at 496: *'La primauté du droit international demeure donc, dans une certaine mesure, affectée d'une condition suspensive: cette condition est la reconnaissance expresse ou tacite de la primauté du droit international, dans le système constitutionnel, ou, à tout le moins, l'absence d'incompatibilité du système avec cette primauté'*; on the other hand, in his Opinion in *Le Ski*, he stated that a constitutional provision providing for the supremacy of treaty law could only be declaratory.

law, where the supremacy based on the very nature of the Community legal order imposed itself independent of the constitutional provisions of the Member States.[117] Constitutional anchorage of the supremacy and direct effect of Community law is allowed, it is submitted, but it should not restrict or in any way hinder the full effect of Community law.

The issue of the relationship between international treaty law and Belgian law and the specificity of Community law has become interesting once again since the *Arbitragehof* has assumed competence to review the constitutionality of treaties through the acts approving them. In the vision of the *Arbitragehof*, the Constitution ranks higher, in the Belgian legal order, than treaties. Treaties take precedence over ordinary statutes, but only in so far as they are themselves compatible with the Constitution. The position reflects a dualist attitude.

The Belgian stance accordingly seems to have developed from a rather dualist perspective (pre-*Le Ski*), over a truly monist attitude (*Le Ski*) on the relationship of international treaties and Community law on the one hand and national law on the other, to the current position, which is not entirely clear yet. The position of the *Cour d'arbitrage* reflects a position of dualism without transformation, with an infra-constitutional but supra-legal status of treaty provisions. Melchior, president of the *Cour d'arbitrage* has proposed a way out of the dilemma, appreciating both the constraints of the Belgian Constitution and of Community law. Should the *Cour d'arbitrage* be asked to review the constitutionality of primary or secondary Community law, Article 34 of the Constitution could come into play,[118] as a constitutional sanction of the specificity of Community law.[119] The *Cour d'arbitrage* could then deny jurisdiction to review the constitutionality of Community law, whether primary or secondary, on grounds that the Framers of the Constitution have allowed the powers transferred to escape from the control of the constitutional court.

---

[117] Opinion of Ganshof van der Meersch in *Le Ski*, Oppenheimer, *The Cases*, 245, at 261, 'Community law is a specific and autonomous law which is binding on the courts of the Member States and makes it impossible to set against it any domestic law whatsoever. The very nature of the legal system instituted by the Treaties of Rome confers on that primacy its foundation, independently of the constitutional provisions in States.'

[118] Article 34 of the Constitution is the transfer powers provision of the Belgian Constitution. It is placed after the provision stating that all powers emanate from the people and are exercised in the manner provided for in the Constitution (Art. 33). Art. 34 then states that '*L'exercice de pouvoirs déterminés peut être attribué par un traité ou par une loi à des institutions de droit international public*'. The provision also served as the constitutional basis for the supra-constitutional effect of the case law of the ECJ in *Conseil d'état*, decision of 5 November 1996, *Orfinger v Belgian State*, (1997) JT, 254, note R Ergec; see *below*.

[119] See M Melchior and P Vandernoot, 'Controle de constitutionnalité et droit communautaire dérivé', (1998) *RBDC*, 3, at 12 *et seq*.

7.6.6. The Netherlands, France and Luxembourg

The three monist countries of the Original Six did not need to adapt their conceptions of the relationship between national and international law: the requirements of direct effect and supremacy could be fitted into the prevailing theories on the relationship between national and international law. Accordingly, there was no need to recognise the specificity of Community law, or to adapt the prevailing view on relations between the international and national legal orders. This is what predictably happened in France and Luxembourg: Community law is treated no differently from classic international treaty law. The French courts did struggle with the jurisdictional issue fully recognising the consequences of the principles of supremacy for their review powers, but the normative supremacy of Community law, as of any other international treaty law, was condoned. In the case of France, the failure on the part of the courts to recognise the specificity of Community law and the recourse to Article 55 of the Constitution has been the subject of much criticism. But since in the French narrative it was the jurisdictional issue that was most problematic, the development of the French case law is discussed in Chapter 8.

The situation in The Netherlands is remarkable. The constitutional system and the common understanding of the relationship between international treaty law and national law were in line with what the Court of Justice required in practical effect. Dutch courts have the unique luxury, unknown to most of their counterparts in other Member States, of avoiding any conflict of loyalty: their Community mandate as formulated by the Court of Justice coincides with the constitutional mandate. And yet, in the common academic view, the constitutional provisions were, until very recently, thought redundant in the context of Community law.[120] The direct effect and supremacy of Community law were recognised on the basis of the autonomous legal order theory of the Court of Justice. This position is both awkward and understandable: it is awkward, because the courts can fully comply with the case law of the Court of

---

[120] See on the discussion AW Hins and JL de Reede, 'Grondrechten, Europese integratie en nationale soevereiniteit', in *Europese Unie en nationale soevereiniteit*, LFM Besselink *et al*, Staatsrechtconferentie 1997, (Deventer, WEJ Tjeenk Willink, 1997), 1, at 22 *et seq*. references to the relevant literature can be found in M Claes and B De Witte, 'Report on The Netherlands', in A-M Slaughter *et al*, (eds), *The European Court and National Courts—Doctrine and Jurisprudence. Legal Change in Its Social Context* (Oxford, Hart Publishing, 1998) 171, at 183. Only a few authors took a different view. LFM Besselink has always claimed that the foundation for the direct effect and supremacy of Community law should remain the Constitutional provisions of Arts. 90–95; see e.g. his *Staatsrecht en buitenlands beleid*, (Nijmegen, Ars Aequi Cahiers, 1991), at 34–35; his 'Curing a 'Childhood Sickness'? On Direct Effect, Internal Effect, Primacy and Derogations from Civil Rights. The Netherlands Council of State Judgment in the *Metten* case', (1996) *MJ*, 165; and 'De zaak Metten: de Grondwet voorbij', (1996) *NJB*, 165.

Justice while acting under the constitutional provisions, which is exactly what courts in other countries attempt to achieve by the use of sometimes rather peculiar theories. Moreover, the constitutional legislature has made it clear on the occasion of the revision of the relevant articles that these provisions, interpreted in line with the case law of the Court of Justice, also served to provide for the direct effect and supremacy of Community law. It is at the same time understandable: if both positions coincide anyway, one might as well go all the way and take on also the Community source of the mandate, which, it is widely understood, is what the Court expects the national courts to do.[121]

Legal scholars hardly refer to judicial statements supporting their view. This is not surprising, since the courts generally exercise their review powers without indicating the legal basis for their action. In the 1960s the courts did refer to the constitutional articles as the origin of their competence to disapply national law conflicting with Community law. But this practice faded away without any revolutionary overruling or explicit pronouncements on the issue. The reference to the constitutional articles was simply left out without being replaced by another basis. The *Afdeling Geschillen van Bestuur van de Raad van State*, which ceased to exist in 1994, did make reference to Article 94 of the Constitution,[122] but these references were considered incorrect by legal writers.[123]

In recent years there seems to be a tendency to return to the constitutional provisions as the foundation of the *Simmenthal*-mandate of the Netherlands courts, with special reference to *Van Gend en Loos* and *Costa v ENEL*. At the conference of constitutional lawyers in 1997, for instance, it was argued that it is too simple and straightforward to establish these principles exclusively on the basis of the case law of the Court of Justice.[124] Where previously it was often stated that even if Articles 92–94 of the Constitution were abolished, Community law would still remain directly effective and supreme, it is now stressed that given these provisions, Community law would still be directly applicable in the Netherlands even if the European Court of Justice had not based the same principle on the spirit, substance and wording of the EEC Treaty.[125]

---

[121] While this may be a widely accepted view, I do not agree, see above, Chapter 7.4.4.

[122] *Raad van State, Afdeling Geschillen van Bestuur*, decision of 6 September 1990, AB, 1990/12; decision of 11 November 1991, AB, 1992/50; decision of 17 February 1993, (1993) *Milieu en Recht*, 305, comments by GH Addink.

[123] See GH Addink, comments on *Raad van State, Afdeling Geschillen van Bestuur*, decision of 17 February 1993, (1993) *Milieu en Recht*, 305, at 407.

[124] AW Hins and JL de Reede, 'Grondrechten, Europese integratie en nationale soevereiniteit', in *Europese Unie en nationale soevereiniteit*, LFM Besselink *et al*, Staatsrechtconferentie 1997 (Tjeenk Willink, 1997) 1, at 24.

[125] See AS Hartkamp, 'On European Freedoms and National Mandatory Rules: The Dutch Judiciary and the European Convention on Human Rights', (2000) 1 *ERPL*, 111, at 114.

7.6.7. Concluding Remarks on the Original Six

The new legal order dogma propagated by the Court of Justice, which was considered irreconcilable with the dualist attitude, did not transform the dualist into monist countries, not even in the context of Community law. Germany and Italy have remained dualist, also in the context of Community law which is not considered to apply and take precedence by and of itself. Community law is considered special, and is granted a special status, not on grounds of some monist view, but on grounds of the transfer of powers provision in the Constitution allowing for a 'special' theory designed to comply with the requirements of Community law. It is not the very nature of Community law which makes it effective and supreme, but a new interpretation of the Constitution.

France *and* Luxembourg make no distinction between Community law and international treaty law. Both are effective and take precedence on the same basis: their very nature in Luxembourg; Article 55 of the Constitution in France. The Netherlands position is peculiar in that, while like in France and Luxembourg, there is no need to give a special status to Community law, this has been done in the past. In Belgium, the central argument of the Court of Justice, 'the very nature of Community law', was extended to international treaty law in general and Community law a fortiori. The specificity of Community law did re-emerge with the creation of the constitutional court and in the context of the constitutionality of Community law.

7.6.8. The 'New' Member States: Ireland and the United Kingdom[126]

For the Member States joining the Communities and Union after the rulings in *Van Gend en Loos* and *Costa v ENEL*, the issue did not present itself in the same way. For those States, it must have been clear from the outset that the Community legal order was an autonomous legal order, inserted in the legal order of the Member States and to be enforced by the courts with precedence over conflicting national law. Admittedly, *Simmenthal* was not yet

---

[126] The analysis of the Member States acceding to the Communities and Union after *Van Gend en Loos* and *Costa v ENEL* will be limited to these countries. They acceded at a time when the Community doctrine, while it had been formulated by the ECJ, was still in a foundational stage. For the countries that joined later, the situation was entirely different as the foundational period had come to an end when they joined; *Simmenthal* had been handed to confirm the basic tenets of *Van Gend en Loos* and *Costa v ENEL*; the doctrine of the legal order was widespread and direct effect and supremacy were firmly established as principles of Community law. Denmark is left out due to language constraints, and apparently there has not, at least not in judicial decisions, been much debate on the issue. The Irish case is interesting as the Irish Constitution was amended to provide for the direct application and the supremacy of Community law; the English case is interesting since the most fundamental principles of British constitutional law on the one hand and those of Community law on the other seemed irreconcilable at the time of the accession.

decided when Ireland, the United Kingdom and Denmark[127] joined, but *Simmenthal* only restated *Costa v ENEL* in unequivocal terms emphasising the mandate of the courts resulting from the principle of supremacy.[128] They had the opportunity to brush up the national legal order before entering and to find a method to facilitate the application of Community law, and, if need be, to adjust the constitutional environment. Of those countries, the Irish and English case are especially interesting in the discussion of legal order thinking and its effects on judicial review powers. Both countries are devoted to radical dualism. Ireland is one of the rare countries in which the perception of the relation between legal orders is set out in the constitutional texts. According to Article 29.6 of the Irish Constitution *'No international agreement shall be part of the domestic law of the State save as may be determined by the Oireachtas'*.[129] In order to be enforceable by the courts, treaty provisions must be incorporated in Irish law; upon enactment, they have the status in Irish law of the incorporating measure.[130] The version of dualism prevailing in the United Kingdom is a direct repercussion of the cornerstone of constitutional law, the principle of parliamentary sovereignty. According to the doctrine of parliamentary sovereignty, all law derives from or under the authority of Parliament. Since the treaty making power rests with the Crown, treaties entered into cannot of their own force enter into the domestic legal order without impairing the legislative monopoly. In order to become operative in the domestic legal order and to affect the rights and obligations of individuals, treaty provisions must be incorporated by Parliament.[131] The status of the treaty provisions in the British legal order is

---

[127] During the legal constitutional debate on the Danish accession, it was asserted that the supremacy of Community law was unconceivable from a Danish perspective, and that it could only be achieved by constitutional amendment, see O Due and C Gulmann, 'Constitutional Implications of the Danish Accession to the European Communities', (1972) *CML Rev* 256; No constitutional amendment was however made, and Denmark joined on the basis of Article 20 of the Constitution, the transfer of powers provision. Denmark is a dualist country, see J Albaek Jensen, 'Human Rights in Danish Law', (2001) 7 *EPL*, 1; the Act of accession only provided for the direct applicability of Community law, without explicitly giving it supremacy; it seems however that there have not been cases of inconsistency and the courts have not had to pronounce themselves on the question of supremacy, see *eg* H Zahle, 'National constitutional law and the European Integration', *Le droit constitutionnel national et l'intégration européenne*, 17th FIDE Kongress (Berlin, 1996) 60, at 67.

[128] Even though it did cause an upheaval of doubts as to the compatibility of the supremacy of Community law and the sovereignty of Parliament, see JDB Mitchell, 'The Sovereignty of Parliament and Community Law: The Stumbling-Block that Isn't There', (1979) *International Affairs*, 33; O Hood Philips, 'Has the "incoming tide" reached the Palace of Westminster?' (1979) 95 *LQR*, 167.

[129] The Oireachtas is the Irish Parliament.

[130] CR Symmons, 'Ireland', in PM Eisemann (ed), *L'intégration du droit international et communautaire dans l'ordre juridique national* (Kluwer, 1996) 317, at 337ff.

[131] There are various ways in which this is done: Either the words of the treaty are repeated in a statute without reference to its source; or the statute may name the treaty and then enact all or part of the substance of the treaty; or, third, the statute sets out the text of the treaty in a schedule while giving effect to all or certain specified provisions thereof; see AW Bradley and KD Ewing, *Wade & Bradley, Constitutional and Administrative Law*, 11th edn (London, Longman, 1993) at 333.

determined by the act incorporating them, mostly in the form of an Act of Parliament. Under the principles of parliamentary sovereignty, a later Act always takes precedence over an earlier one, even if the latter incorporates a treaty. Parliament is supposed to have implicitly repealed the earlier Act by introducing another, contradictory Act. The courts acknowledge the fact that they have no business with treaties directly.[132] Both countries thus had to find a way to allow Community law to be effective in the national legal order, and to be given precedence over conflicting national law.

Bunreacht na héireann, the 1937 Constitution of Ireland, the youngest sovereign and independent State among the Members of the European Union, contains several elements that may be interpreted as opposing Irish membership of the European Communities and certain principles of Community law, such as direct effect, supremacy and the judicial enforcement of those principles. The notion of sovereignty and the problem of fundamental rights will be discussed in Part 2. What is of interest here is the supremacy of Community law and the *Simmenthal* mandate. The bulwark of the Irish Constitution was opened up to Community law by the introduction through a referendum of a new provision in the Constitution.[133] The new article[134] provided the constitutional authorisation to join the Communities, made Irish acts done pursuant to the obligations of membership lawful and granted constitutional immunity to Community law. Yet, it did not explicitly tackle the issue of ordinary supremacy[135] and, more importantly, of the power of all Irish courts to give effect to Community law over conflicting Acts. Within the dualist paradigm of the Irish Constitution, a further act incorporating the Treaties

---

[132] From among numerous examples, Lord Templeman in *Rayner (MIncing Lane) Ltd v Dept of Trade* [1989] 3 WLR 969; [1990] 2 AC 418, at 477: 'Except to the extent that a treaty becomes incorporated into the laws of the United Kingdom by statute, the courts (..) have no power to enforce treaty obligations (…)'.

[133] Known as the Third Amendment, adopted by the Oireachtas and approved by the People in a referendum. The Constitution was later amended, in relation to European Treaties amendments, by the Tenth Amendment of 1987 (SEA), the Eleventh Amendment of 1992 (Treaty of Maastricht); the Eighteenth Amendment of 1998 (Treaty of Amsterdam) and the Twenty-Sixth Amendment of 2002 (Treaty of Nice).

[134] The relevant provisions of article 29.4 of the Constitution now read: '(3) The State may become a Member of the ECSC (..), the EEC (..), and Euratom (..). The State may ratify the SEA (..). (4) The State may ratify the TEU signed at Maastricht (..) and may become a member of that Union. (5) The State may ratify the Treaty of Amsterdam (..) (6) The State may exercise the options or discretions [in the framework of flexibility] (..) subject to the prior approval of both Houses of the Oireachtas (7) No provision of this Constitution invalidates laws enacted, acts done or measures adopted by the State which are necessitated by the obligations of membership of the EU or of the Communities, or prevents laws enacted, acts done or measures adopted by the EU or by the Communities or by institutions thereof, or by bodies competent under the Treaties establishing the Communities, from having the force of law in the State'. [abbreviations added, place and date of signatures omitted].

[135] It seems, though, as a matter of common sense, that if Community law is supreme over the Constitution, it must also be supreme over primary legislation, inferior to the Constitution. 'Qui peut le plus, peut le moins'. It was not, however, stated in the Constitution.

and Community law was needed. This was the European Communities Act 1972.[136]

The constitutional and statutory provisions opened up the Irish legal order and introduced the Treaties and secondary law, granting them a special status over domestic law and even over the Constitution. Irish courts accept that they must, in accordance with the principles of Community law, apply Community law with precedence over competing Irish law.[137] That position has never been challenged judicially.[138] Irish judges accepted Community law , and its primacy, very easily and in a matter-of-fact way.[139] Community law must be enforced in the Irish courts on the terms dictated by the Treaties as interpreted by the Court of Justice. According to the Supreme Court in the *Meagher* case, '*Section 2 of the Act which provides for the application of the Community law and acts binding on the State and as part of the domestic law subject to the conditions laid down in the Treaty which, of course, include its primacy, is the major or fundamental obligation necessitated by membership of the Community*'.[140]

Diarmuid Rossa Phelan argues that the reasoning itself, which refers back to the constitutional and statutory provisions, does conflict with Community law, which in his view requires that the autonomy of Community law deriving from the Treaties as the constitutional charter must be respected also in national law.[141] The alternative view is that Community law makes no specific claim as to the source of its status within the domestic legal order as long as the results of its own conception, such

---

[136] A consolidated (until 1995) and annotated version of the Act can be found in G Hogan and A Whelan, *Ireland and the European Union: Constitutional and Statutory Texts and Commentary* (London, Sweet & Maxwell, 1995), at 166–81. Section 2(1) of the Act states: '(..) the treaties governing the EC and the existing and future acts adopted by the institutions of those Communities and by the bodies competent under the said treaties shall be binding on the State and shall be part of the domestic law thereof under the conditions laid down in those treaties'.

[137] *Pigs and Bacon Commission v McCarren* [1978] JISEL 87: '*If according to Community law the provisions of Community law take precedence over a provision of national law in conflict with it, an Irish court must give effect to the rule*'.

[138] Though there still is much debate, both judicially and scholarly, as to the exact meaning and impact of the constitutional and statutory provision. As the issues under debate do not concern the principle of ordinary supremacy and the judicial review powers, they will not be discussed here. The main points of contention are the meaning of 'necessitated' in article 29.4.5. of the Constitution, the question whether directives may be implemented by ministerial order, and the question of whether there is, despite the constitutional text, a nucleus in the Constitution which can never be overridden by Community law. See below.

[139] B Walsh, 'Reflections on the Effects of Membership of the European Communities in Irish Law', in F Capotorti *et al* (eds), *Du droit international au droit de l'intégration. Liber Amicorum Pierre Pescatore*, (Baden-Baden, Nomos, 1987), 805; J Temple Lang, 'European Community Law, Irish Law and the Irish Legal Profession', Frances E Moran Memorial Lecture 1982, at 23.

[140] *Supreme Court*, decision of 1 April 1993, *Meagher v Minister for Agriculture* [1994] 1 IR 329, at 350, *per* Finlay CJ; published on www.irlii.org.

[141] DR Phelan, *Revolt or Revolution. The Constitutional Boundaries of the European Community* (Dublin, Sweet & Maxwell, 1997), Chapter 27.

as primacy and direct effect are accepted.[142] The conception and terms of the effect and status of the Irish legal order may be different from those assumed by the Court of Justice, but they are not in practical terms inconsistent with them. Both conceptions lead to the same practical result, the courts awarding precedence to Community law over conflicting national law. Community law does not require the suppression of national constitutional conceptions of legal orders and of national constitutional and statutory techniques which are used as vehicles to make Community law operative.[143] In contrast to most of the founding Six, Ireland had brushed up its constitutional and statutory framework before entry to the Communities, with particular attention to the effect and primacy of Community law. The Irish way seems to be particularly recommendable since the statutory text refers back to the conditions laid down in the Treaty, it contains a *renvoi* to Community law.

In the United Kingdom, the same result was sanctioned *expressis verbis* only with the *Factortame* judgment of the House of Lords. Of course, the United Kingdom lacks a Constitution which could be brushed up. The British legal order was opened up for Community law by virtue of the European Communities Act 1972;[144] and Community law is accordingly given effect as a block, instead of each piece of Community legislation having to be transformed separately: '*It took only a few lines in an Act of Parliament to receive within the United Kingdom a massive body of Community law (..)*'.[145] Yet, the Act is not worded in the same clear terms[146] as its Irish equivalent, and more importantly, the fundamental question was whether the Act would be strong enough to break open the constraints of the principle of parliamentary sovereignty. Under the principle of sovereignty, no Parliament can bind its successor; there is no such thing as

---

[142] G Hogan and A Whelan, *Ireland and the European Union: Constitutional and Statutory Texts and Commentary* (Sweet & Maxwell, London, 1995) at 10ff For comments on the discussion DR Phelan and A Whelan, 'National Constitutional Law and European Integration', in *Le droit constitutionnel national et l'intégration européenne*, 17th FIDE Kongress, (Berlin, 1996) 292, at 313ff.

[143] See also G Hogan and A Whelan, op cit, at 13.

[144] The EC Act states, in relevant part: '2(1). All such rights, powers, liabilities, obligations and restrictions from time to time created or arising by or under the Treaties, and all such remedies and procedures from time to time provided for by or under the Treaties, as in accordance with the Treaties are without further enactment to be given legal effect or used in the United Kingdom shall be recognised and available in law, and be enforced, allowed and followed accordingly; and the expression "enforceable Community right" and similar expressions shall be read as referring to one to which this subsection applies ...

[145] AW Bradley, 'The Sovereignty of Parliament: Form or Substance?', in J Jowell and D Oliver (eds), *The Changing Constitution* (OUP, Oxford, 2000) 23, at 41.

[146] Different: JDB Mitchell, SA Kuipers and B Gall, 'Constitutional Aspects of the Treaty and Legislation relating to British Membership', (1972) *CMLRev* 134, at 149: '*From a legal point of view, the Bill is good. Indeed the draftsmen should be congratulated on producing an artistic piece of legislation which ingeniously achieves the desired results..*', it would however last until the 1989 *Factortame* judgment of the *House of Lords* for everyone to be convinced that the EC Act did have this result, and for the highest court of the land to acknowledge it in so many words; for another positive appraisal see J Jaconelli, 'Constitutional review and Section 2(4) of the European Communities Act 1972', (1979) 28 *ICLQ*, 65.

entrenched legislation. So, Community law was made part of English law by the EC Act of 1972, and would therefore override any existing rules of common law and conflicting Acts of Parliament passed before 1972, even under according to the traditional ides of parliamentary sovereignty. But, if an Act of Parliament passed after 1972 were to conflict with Community law, the traditional principle of parliamentary sovereignty would lead to results diametrically opposed to *Simmenthal*. Since the case law concentrated on the principle of parliamentary sovereignty and thus mostly on the constitutional position of the courts in relation to the primary legislature, the English solution will be discussed further in Chapter 8.

<h2 style="text-align:center">7.7. CLOSING REMARKS</h2>

The formulation of an adequate doctrine on the relation between national law and Community law has called for a good deal of judicial creativity, first from the Court of Justice itself, and later from the national courts. The building blocks were to be found in the Treaties and, for the national courts, in the Constitutions, and in constitutional principles, Acts of accession and the Treaties binding on the State. The Court of Justice has presented the national courts with a theory, qualifying the Community legal order as 'a new and autonomous legal order', 'integrated in the national legal orders', and applicable with precedence over conflicting national law. The national courts operate in that other, national legal order, based on the national Constitutions. Now, from an external point of view, it may not be so difficult to conceptualise the co-existence of these legal orders on the basis of theories of pluralism or mixity of legal orders. However, both the European Court and the national courts act *within* one of these orders. The relationship between the legal orders can only be approached from within one of the systems, and on the basis of the principles and rules prevailing within that order. The national views of the relation between the Community and the national legal order differ from State to State. Even Italy and Germany, which supposedly start from similar positions, arrive at different interpretations of the relationship between the national and Community legal order.

It is striking that the successive Treaty amendments and accessions have never been used to insert the basic doctrines of direct effect or supremacy or indeed a more general statement on the nature of the Community legal order in the text of the Treaties. Perhaps it was not considered necessary to insert them; it may have appeared the business of the courts, European and national. Perhaps, it was because these principles were so self-evident that they could go without saying.[147] Likewise, most

---

[147] B De Witte, 'Direct Effect, Supremacy and the Nature of the Legal Order', in P Craig and G de Búrca (eds), *The Evolution of EU Law* (Oxford, OUP, 1999) 177, at 194.

national Constitutions have not been amended to include the principles. However, in several Member States, the courts were left with far from ideal provisions and tools in the Constitution, or with nothing at all. The Italian and German constitutional provisions which were used as vehicles to accept the principles of direct effect and ordinary supremacy were not adopted with either of those in mind; in fact they had nothing to do with direct effect, and it requires a lot of creativity and even imagination to read into it what the constitutional courts have. One might have expected some co-operation from the constitutional legislature to assist the courts in this process. After all, the relationship between legal orders, the domestic effect of Community law and the consequences for conflicting national law do seem to be of huge constitutional importance. Why then was it left entirely to the courts? One element of the answer is probably that the courts apparently coped well despite the odds. They have been prepared to be creative, and while it has lasted somewhat longer for some than for others, there may have been no further need for constitutional amendment. At the very least, it was not high on some constitutional agendas. There have been proposals or suggestions in several countries to insert a constitutional provision to the effect that Community law or international law is to be directly effective and supreme, for instance in Belgium, Italy and recently in The Netherlands.[148] Yet, these have not been adopted. What is most remarkable is that supremacy and direct effect were not even included in the Europe Articles adopted in several Member States at the occasion of the Treaty of Maastricht (France, Germany and Spain). Possibly, the solution offered by the courts is considered the best one. For instance, it would be very difficult and hardly acceptable for the German constitutional legislature to insert in the Basic Law a provision explicitly stating what the *Bundesverfassungsgericht* has said about the limits on the supremacy of Community law. Such a clear and open statement would amount to a clear violation of Community law.

Nevertheless, almost all of the courts, with the notable exception of the Dutch courts, continue to use a constitutional foundation for the principles of direct effect and supremacy and an overall appreciation of the relationship between Community and national law. The view that Community law is different and is effective with primacy because of its very nature, is not the prevailing view among constitutional lawyers in most Member States. They would rather refer to a provision in the Constitution or to a decision of the supreme or constitutional court. The difficulty remains that both Community lawyers on the one hand and constitutional lawyers on the other, start from different premises, and view the relationship between two legal orders from essentially distinct perspectives.

---

[148] See LFM Besselink *et al*, *De Nederlandse Grondwet en de Europese Unie* (Groningen, Europa Law Publishing, 2002).

8

The Constitutional Limits
of the Judicial Function

THE SECOND CONSTITUTIONAL stumbling block many ordinary courts encountered was that of the predominant constitutional conception of the judicial function. The mandate to review legislation in the light of treaties was mostly not foreseen or recognised in the national mandate. But more importantly, the most fundamental canons of the judicial function were interpreted so that *any* judicial review of parliamentary legislation was excluded: it simply overstepped the limits of the judicial function. These canons were so deeply rooted that even in The Netherlands, where the Constitution made an express exception for treaty provisions, the courts did not immediately act upon it. In France, Article 55 of the Constitution was usually interpreted as not being addressed to the courts. Why, then, would the courts be willing to change the limits of the judicial function on request of the Court of Justice, when they were not willing when empowered to do so by their own Constitution, the direct source of their mandate?

This is the jurisdictional problem: for the supremacy of Community law to be judicially enforced by the ordinary courts, they must also set aside conflicting primary legislation, while they lack jurisdiction to do so. This is not to say that the courts would never take account of limitations imposed on the Legislature as a consequence of international obligations entered into by the State. In all countries under review the courts readily accept the duty to interpret Acts of Parliament as much as possible in line with Community law, as with other international treaties. Such a technique does not infringe the constitutional limits of the judicial function, since it is based on the assumption that the Legislature did not intend to violate international law and interpretation is the essence of the judicial function. To set aside an Act of Parliament is quite another thing.

In this chapter the phrase 'the place of the courts in the constitutional structure' is used to denote their position *vis-à-vis* the other state organs, and more in particular, the primary Legislature. It concerns mainly the issue of judicial review of parliamentary acts. Do the courts have the competence to review Acts of Parliament? If so, which courts? The place of the courts in the constitutional structure is a function of prevailing constitutional principles and doctrines, some of which are laid down in writing in constitutional documents, while many are to be found in unwritten principles and canons. The main doctrines which serve to define the place of the courts are the principle of a separation of powers[1] and a democracy principle.[2]

The actors under scrutiny in this chapter are the ordinary courts, excluding the constitutional courts, set up as specialised constitutional review courts. The latter are the central actors in this book's second Theme. Some Irish and all Danish[3] courts do have jurisdiction to review the constitutionality of statutes, in cases before them in the ordinary exercise of the judicial function. The ordinary courts in most other Member States are not competent to review the constitutionality of legislation passed by Parliament. The next section contains a short survey[4] of the position on constitutional review of primary legislation by ordinary courts in the Member States under review, in a purely national context.

8.1.1. Constitutional Review of Primary Legislation in the Original Six

8.1.1.1. The Netherlands

In The Netherlands, the prohibition of judicial review of the *constitutionality* of parliamentary legislation is laid down in Article 120 of the Constitution.[5] The courts have equally rejected the competence to review

---

[1]   Admittedly 'the' principle of separation of course does not exist; what defines the judicial position is a particular version of 'the' separation of powers doctrine. In addition, 'the' separation of powers argument is not conclusive for instance in defining whether or not courts have the power to review the validity of legislation: it can be used both in favour and against such review.

[2]   Again, 'the' democracy principle is not conclusive on the 'mighty problem of judicial review'. Is it the will of the current majority which is to be upheld by the courts, or the Will of the People expressed at a constitutional moment, 'We, the People'? What is meant here, again, is a particular version of the democracy principle.

[3]   O Due, 'Danish Preliminary References', in D O'Keeffe and A Bavasso (eds), *Judicial Review in European Union Law. Liber Amicorum in Honour of Lord Slynn of Hadley*, Vol I, (The Hague, Kluwer Law International 2000) 363.

[4]   Comparative literature on constitutional review of primary legislation includes C Grewe and H Ruiz Fabri, *Droits constitutionnels européens*, (Paris, PUF, 1995), 66ff, with references at 99; L.Favoreu and J-A Jolowicz, *Le contrôle jurisdictionnel des lois*, (Paris, Economica/PUAM, 1986); M Cappelletti, *Le pouvoir des juges*, (Paris, Economica/PUAM, 1990).

[5]   Article 120 of the Constitution states that *'No court shall enter into the review of the constitutionality of statutes and treaties'*; until 1983 the Constitution was even more radical stating in its Article 131 that *'Statutes are inviolable'*.

Statutes on their compatibility with the *Statuut van het Koninkrijk* and with general principles.[6] The *Hoge Raad* emphasised the fact that the Makers of the Constitution had during the revision of the Constitution in 1983, once again[7] rejected the power of the courts to review the constitutionality of statutes: it is a task which is reserved for Parliament and especially the First Chamber.[8] The most recent proposal for constitutional amendment was made in April 2002.[9] This context makes Article 94 of the Constitution,[10] which provides for the power of the courts to review 'conventionality' all the more noteworthy: the drafters of the Constitution give the courts jurisdiction to review the *conventionnalité* of statutes, but not their constitutionality, making the Constitution less enforceable than international agreements. The constitutional tradition of judicial deference to the primary legislature is probably the main reason why the Dutch courts did not feel inclined to make use of their review powers under Article 94 of the Constitution (then Articles 65 and/or 66) before *Van Gend en Loos*.

8.1.1.2. France

Since the Revolution, the French system has strongly repudiated constitutional review of Acts of Parliament by the courts. The *loi*, the expression of the sovereign will of the People, *l'expression de la volonté générale*, is not to be scrutinised by the courts. Judges are supposed to function as *la bouche qui prononce les paroles de la loi*, and must keep themselves far from the exercise of the legislative function.[11] The French dislike of judicial review is written

---

6 *Hoge Raad*, decision of 14 April 1989, *Harmonisatiewet*, NJ 1989/469.
7 The question as to whether some form of judicial constitutional review should be introduced is subject of an ongoing debate. Proposals for constitutional reform are introduced with regular intervals. The theme of constitutional review is discussed in MLP van Houten, *Meer zicht op wetgeving, Rechterlijke toetsing van wetgeving aan de Grondwet en fundamentele rechtsbeginselen*, (Zwolle, 1997).
8 The *Eerste Kamer* is the counterpart of the second chamber in many other countries; it has limited powers only; it cannot initiate or amend legislation, though it can reject it – on average only once a year; it meets only one day a week and is considered the constitutional conscience of the Netherlands Parliament. Dutch law students will often present the *Eerste Kamer* as an alternative for the lack of judicial constitutional review. On the Dutch *Eerste Kamer* in a comparative perspective, see ETC Knippenberg, *De Senaat. Rechtsvergelijkend onderzoek naar het House of Lords, de Sénat, de Eerste Kamer en de Bundesrat*, (De Haag, Sdu, 2002).
9 The Bill proposed to authorise decentralised judicial review of the compatibility of Acts of Parliament with certain specified fundamental rights contained in the Constitution; see Voorstel van wet van het lid Halsema houdende verklaring dat er grond bestaat een voorstel in overweging te nemen tot verandering in de Grondwet, strekkende tot invoering van de bevoegdheid tot toetsing van wetten aan een aantal bepalingen van de Grondwet door de rechter', Tweede Kamer, 2001–2, 28 331.
10 In 1953, then numbered Article 65; re-numbered (Article 66) and amended in 1956, and re-numbered in 1983.
11 There is a deep fear of what is referred to as a *'gouvernement des juges'*, after a book on judicial review by the US Supreme Court during a time when it interfered deeply in

down in revolutionary text which is still considered good law today: *'the judicial tribunals shall not take part, either directly or indirectly, in the exercise of the legislative power, nor impede or suspend the execution of the enactments of the legislative body'*.[12] The 1958 Constitution breaks with the tradition with the establishment of the *Conseil constitutionnel*.[13] Yet, even now constitutional review by the *Conseil constitutionnel* is rather limited,[14] [15] when compared to for instance the *Bundesverfassungsgericht* and the *Corte costituzionale*. Once in force, the constitutionality of statutes cannot be judicially reviewed, and *lois* remain inviolable when it comes to their constitutionality.

8.1.1.3. Belgium

The Belgian constitutional traditions are similar to the French. Ordinary courts are denied the competence to review the constitutionality of Acts of

---

political life, E Lambert, *Le gouvernement des juges et la lutte contre la législation sociale aux États-Unis. Expérience américaine du contrôle judiciaire de la constitutionnalité des lois*, 1921; on the notion of *'gouvernement des juges'*, see MH Davis, 'A Government of Judges: A Historical Re-view', (1987) *AJCL*, 559; the French rejection of any judicial interference in the legislative power goes back to pre-revolutionary France when the courts, (*'parlements'*) opposed social change by refusing to register laws adopted by the King.

[12]   Statutes of 16 and 24 August 1790, translation taken from M Cappelletti, *The Judicial Process in a Comparative Perspective* (Oxford, OUP, 1989) at 194.

[13]   The context surrounding the introduction of the 1958 Constitution and the establishment of the *Conseil constitutionnel* is described in J Bell, *French Constitutional Law*, (Oxford, Clarendon Press, 1992); see also A Stone Sweet, *The Birth of Judicial Politics in France: The Constitutional Council in Comparative Perspective* (Oxford, OUP, 1992); JH Reestman, *Constitutionele toesting in Frankrijk. De Conseil constitutionnel en de grondwettigheid van wetten en verdragen*, (Utrecht, Ars Aequi Libri, 1996) as well as French textbooks on constitutional law.

[14]   These limits were intentional, in line with the French aversion towards judicial review. Consider, for instance, the words of *Commissaire du gouvernement* Janot at the time of the creation of the *Conseil constitutionnel*, when discussing a type of constitutional court along the lines of the *Bundesverfassungsgericht* which can on a reference from ordinary courts review the constitutionality of a Statute in force: *'[Such] a system would be tempting intellectually, but it seemed to us that constitutional review through an action in the courts would conflict too much with the traditions of French public life. To give the members of the Conseil constitutionnel the power to oppose the promulgation of unconstitutional texts appeared sufficient to us. To go further would risk leading us to a kind of government by judges (gouvernement des juges), would reduce the legislative role of Parliament, and would hamper governmental action in a harmful way'*, cited in J Bell, *French Constitutional Law* (Oxford, Clarendon Press, 1992) at 27–28.

[15]   The *Conseil constitutionnel* can only review the constitutionality of bills, before promulgation. Once a *loi* has entered into force, it becomes inviolable, both before the *Conseil constitutionnel*, and before the ordinary courts. There is no cause of action available to individuals to bring an issue before the *Conseil*. Only political bodies can bring a bill before the *Conseil constitutionnel*. In addition, the *Conseil* must respect short and strict time limits. The other restrictions as to the grounds of review which did exist at the time of the creation of the *Conseil constitutionnel* have been transcended in the case law. The *Conseil* was established in order to police the boundaries of parliamentary powers, to prevent Parliament from interfering with the *'domaine du règlement'*. But this is no longer the main business of the *Conseil*. Most of its review concerns the content of Bills, rather than the question of competences. The standards for review, what the French call the *'bloc de constitutionnalité'* have been extended to include fundamental rights.

Parliament, on grounds of separation of powers and democracy arguments. An Act of Parliament[16] constitutes the expression of the sovereign will of the People, the courts which are not democratically elected, are not empowered to review their constitutionality. That is an issue for Parliament itself.

As in France, the traditional system has been modified. In 1983, an *Arbitragehof* or *Cour d'arbitrage* was established, to function as an independent 'arbitrator' supervising the division of powers between the federation and the federated entities and the respect for the principles of equality, non-discrimination and the freedom of education as laid down in the Constitution. Over the years, the *Cour d'arbitrage* has matured into a veritable constitutional court. Cases can be brought directly within a specified time-limit, or indirectly, by reference from ordinary courts. Direct actions can be instituted by the Council of Ministers and the governments of the federated entities, the Communities and the regions; by the presidents of all the legislative chambers at the request of two-thirds of their members; and by Belgian or foreign natural or legal persons, including both private law and public law corporations, provided that they have a justifiable interest. As a general rule, with certain exceptions, actions must be brought within six months of the publication of the challenged law in the *Moniteur belge/ Belgisch Staatsblad*. The ordinary courts may not themselves review the constitutionality of statutes, and are under an obligation to refer a question of unconstitutionality to the Court of arbitration. Should the *Cour d'arbitrage* find a statute unconstitutional on a reference from another court, courts delivering judgment in proceedings with the same litigants (including courts of appeal) must comply with the ruling given by the Court of Arbitration on the preliminary point of law in question. Moreover, where the Court finds a violation, the law will remain part of the system of law, but a new six-month term commences in which a direct action for annulment of the law in question can be brought, but only by the Council of Ministers or the governments of the Communities and Regions. So, in contrast to the French system, the constitutionality of statutes in force may now be judicially reviewed.

8.1.1.4. Luxembourg

Luxembourg has the same tradition of judicial deference to parliamentary legislation. Until the establishment of the *Cour constitutionnelle* in 1997, the constitutionality of statutes remained the province of Parliament itself.[17] However, the Luxembourg situation is special, given the traditional

---

[16] This applies both to Acts of the Federal Parliament and Decrees emanating from the Parliaments of the federated entities.

[17] See the Loi de révision constitutionnelle du 12 juillet 1997 introduisant dans la Constitution l'article 95 ter prévoyant une Cour constitutionnelle.

openness towards international treaties, which were enforced even as against Acts of Parliament from the 1950's. Luxembourg owes its very existence to international law, which is not regarded as a threat to the Luxembourg sovereignty: quite to the contrary, it is considered to consti-tute the source thereof.[18] So, while at the time of the formulation of the *Simmenthal* mandate the Luxembourg courts could not review the consti-tutionality of statutes, their *conventionnalité* could already be judicially reviewed, and the courts readily acted on this constitutional mandate.

8.1.1.5. Italy and Germany

As in the previous section on the relation between legal orders, the Italian and German context bear a lot of similarities. In both cases, the ordinary courts are precluded from giving a ruling on the constitutionality of Acts of Parliament. Both also possess a constitutional court at the apex of the constitutional system, which is considered to be the highest interpreter and guarantor of the Constitution: the *Corte costituzionale* and the *Bundesverfassungsgericht* respectively. Ordinary Italian and German courts must refer questions of unconstitutionality to these constitutional courts, which have a monopoly over constitutional review and strike down pri-mary legislation. Given the dualist tradition in both countries, the issue of the compatibility of statutes with higher law in the form of treaties does not arise.

8.1.2. 'New' Member States[19]

8.1.2.1. Ireland

In Ireland, constitutional review is entrusted to the High Court and Supreme Court in normal cases and controversies pending before the courts.[20] In addition, the President may under Article 26 refer a question to the Supreme Court whether a Bill, or any provision or provisions of it, which has been passed by both Houses of the *Oireachtas* and presented to the President of Ireland for signature, is repugnant to the Constitution. Other courts do not have jurisdiction to review the constitutionality of Statutes, even though they are under an obligation to uphold the Constitution. Neither the Constitution nor the case law is clear on the effects of a finding of unconstitutionality by the High Court or the Supreme

---

[18] See G Wivines, 'Le droit européen et les Constitutions nationales', FIDE 2002, (London).
[19] Again, the analysis will be limited to those countries which acceded during the 'foun-dational period', *i.e.* only the three that acceded in 1973.
[20] Article 34.3.2 of the Constitution.

Court.[21] The latter courts demonstrate judicial self-restraint in the exercise of the constitutional review of the validity of legislation, and will declare a statute unconstitutional only if this is unavoidable.[22]

8.1.2.2. The United Kingdom

In the United Kingdom the place of *all* courts in relation to Parliament is inherent in the doctrine of parliamentary sovereignty. According to the orthodox view, Parliament can make and unmake any law, and no person or body is recognised as having the right to override or set aside the legislation of Parliament.[23] The doctrine is under constant debate, and there are more modern versions of it.[24] But the main thrust, with respect to the power of the courts, is that they are precluded from reviewing parliamentary legislation: *'[T]he courts are subordinate to parliament. The task of law-making is the exclusive province of Parliament, and it would be undemocratic for the non-elected judiciary to act as law-makers. The judges' constitutional task is faithfully and strictly to interpret the will of Parliament, expressed in detailed legislation, to be read in accordance with its so-called 'plain meaning' and to declare the common law when it is incomplete or obscure.'*[25] The long standing tradition of immunity of parliamentary legislation from judicial scrutiny has, outside the context of EU law, only very recently undergone some changes with the adoption of the Human Rights Act, but even now the courts cannot annul or declare void an Act of Parliament, or even set its aside: it must be interpreted in conformity with the Convention rights as incorporated by the Human Rights Act,[26] and at the most it can be

---

[21] See G Hogan and G Whyte, *Kelly, The Irish Constitution*, 3rd edn, (Dublin, Butterworths, 1997), 479 *et seq.*

[22] *Ibidem*, at 449 *et seq.*

[23] The classic reference is to AV Dicey, ECS Wade (ed), *The Law of the Constitution*, 10th edn, (London, Macmillan 1959); and, since it is a common law principle, to several judgments of the House of Lords: *Matzimbamuto v Lardner* [1969] 1 AC 645; *Manuel v AG* [1983] Ch 77; *Vauxhall Estates Ltd v Liverpool Corporation* [1932] 1 KB 733l *Ellen Street Estates Ltd v Minister of Health* [1934] 1 KB 590; a comprehensive analysis of the traditional view is given in HRW Wade, 'The Basis of Legal Sovereignty', (1955) *CLJ*, 172; a recent study on the history of the principle of parliamentary sovereignty is J Goldsworthy, *The Sovereignty of Parliament. History and Philosophy*, (Oxford, Clarendon Press, 1999). Goldsworthy does not include a discussion of the impact of either the EU and the 1972 EC Act or the Human Rights Act.

[24] These more modern versions relate especially to the question as to whether Parliament can bind its successors, and whether it can prescribe manner and form of future legislation.

[25] Lord Lester of Herne Hill, 'Human Rights and the British Constitution', in J Jowell and D Oliver (eds), *The Changing Constitution* (Oxford, OUP, 2000) 89, at 91.

[26] The duty to interpret legislation in conformity with the Human Rights Act is however considered far-reaching, allowing the courts to give statutory provisions a meaning which was not in the minds of the legislator.'*So the judges need be under no inhibitions, on the grounds of Parliamentary sovereignty, about departing from what might be thought to have been the intention of parliament in their search for a possible meaning of the words used'*, Lord Hope of Craighead, 'The Human Rights Act 1998. The task of the Judges', in M Andenas and D Fairgrieve (eds), *Judicial Review in Comparative Perspective. Liber Amicorum in Honour of Lord Slynn of Hadley*, Vol II, (The Hague, Kluwer Law International, 2000), 415, at 417; see also AL Young, 'Judicial Sovereignty and the Human Rights Acts 1998', (2002) 61 *CLJ*, 53.

declared incompatible, triggering a special procedure for statutory amendment. The declaration of incompatibility cannot of itself provide an effective remedy for the victim of the effects of the incompatibility. The devolution Acts equally affect parliamentary sovereignty by transferring legislative powers to the parliaments of Northern Ireland and Scotland.[27] The devolution and Human Rights Acts affirm the ultimate sovereignty of the Westminster Parliament, in the sense that the latter may revoke them; but Parliament has exercised its sovereign legislative powers to give much greater powers to the judiciary, placing practical limits on its sovereign law-making powers.[28] When the United Kingdom joined the European Communities in 1973, however, the old principle of parliamentary sovereignty was unaffected.

8.1.2.3. Denmark

All Danish courts have jurisdiction, in theory, to review the constitutionality of Acts passed by Parliament. Yet, this power remains mostly theoretical, and courts will go out of their way to avoid any finding of unconstitutionality: until 1999 no statute had ever been declared unconstitutional and courts are in general very hesitant in their exercise of judicial review.[29] The ECHR was not incorporated until 1992, and has only since then started to play a role in the court rooms.[30]

8.1.3. Re-grouping

The survey demonstrates that none of the *ordinary* courts in the original six Member States were, under their constitutional mandate, empowered to review the *constitutionality* of statutes when the Court of Justice involved the national courts in the enforcement of Community law even as against conflicting national legislation. Constitutional review by a specialised constitutional court was provided for in Italy and Germany, where the ordinary courts must refer a suspicion of unconstitutionality to the constitutional court which has exclusive jurisdiction to set aside legislation. The French counterpart, the *Conseil constitutionnel* had, at that time even more so than today, much more restricted powers and could not, in

---

[27] Only regularity powers have been devolved to Wales.
[28] Lord Lester of Herne Hill, 'Developing Constitutional Principles of Public Law', (2001) *PL*, 684, at 689.
[29] P Biering, 'The Application of EU law in Denmark: 1986 to 2000', (2000) 37 *CML Rev* 925, at 934; *Højesteret*, decision of 19 February 1999, in re *Tvind*, UfR 1999, 227.
[30] J Albaek Jensen, 'Human Rights in Danish Law', (2001) 7 *EPL*, 1; O Due, 'Danish Preliminary References', in D O'Keeffe and A Bavasso (eds), *Judicial Review in European Union Law. Liber Amicorum in Honour of Lord Slynn of Hadley*, Vol I, (The Hague, Kluwer Law International) 363.

any case, be seized in the course of proceedings brought before an ordinary court. In Belgium, The Netherlands and Luxembourg, judicial review of the constitutionality of statutes was non-existent. Only in Luxembourg did the courts occasionally act upon their mandate to review the *compatibility of statutes with treaty provisions*. In The Netherlands, the power was explicitly provided but not used; in France, the general interpretation of Article 55 of the Constitution tended away from judicial review powers. In Belgium, Italy and Germany, international treaties could not serve as a standard for judicial review of parliamentary legislation, given the dualist tradition combined with the prevailing conception of the constitutional place of the courts and the limits of the judicial function.

It this context, it constituted a true novelty in every Member State for the Court of Justice to ask the national courts to review parliamentary legislation on its compatibility with Community law and set it aside in case of conflict. The natural task of the courts under the Constitution did not, at least in those days, include the duty to ensure that Parliament would comply with the Constitution or with the international treaty obligations of the State.

All Danish and some Irish ordinary courts are empowered to review the constitutionality of Acts of Parliament. However, in Denmark this power had remained purely theoretical; the Irish courts did act upon it. In both countries, however, treaties were unenforceable as such and could not serve as a reference standard to judge the validity of statutes, given the dualist attitude towards treaties. The United Kingdom, finally, combined the absence of constitutional review, with strict dualism, resulting in the complete absence of any higher law review of parliamentary legislation.

The jurisdictional problem arising from the *Simmenthal* mandate was most apparent in the case law of the French *Conseil d'état* until *Nicolo* and in the English courts until *Factortame*. In Italy, the jurisdictional problem was most acute during the intermediate phase between *Frontini* and *Granital*. But before looking into the national case law, it is interesting to see what the European Court's position is on the jurisdictional issue.

8.2. THE COURT OF JUSTICE AND THE JURISDICTIONAL ISSUE

The Court of Justice has shown little sympathy for national constitutional restrictions on the judicial function preventing the courts from ensuring the supremacy of Community law. Cases in point are *Simmenthal*, *Factortame* and *Brasserie du Pêcheur*.[31] The thrust of these judgment is that

---

[31] Case 106/77 *Simmenthal* [1978] ECR 585; Case C–213/89 *R v Secretary of State for Transport, ex parte Factortame Ltd and Others* [1990] *ECR* 2433; Joined Cases C–46/93 and C–48/93 *Brasserie du Pêcheur SA v Germany and The Queen v Secretary of State for Transport, ex parte Factortame Ltd and others* [1996] *ECR* 1029.

the constitutional limits on the judicial function arising from a certain conception of the place of the courts in relation to the other branches of government, cannot, as a matter of Community law, be opposed to their Community mandate.

In *Simmenthal* the *pretore di Susa* put the jurisdictional issue squarely in the hands of the Court of Justice. At that time, the Italian courts were obliged, under *Frontini*, to refer any incompatibilities between an Italian statute and Community law to the *Corte costituzionale* which could then declare the statute unconstitutional for violation of Article 11 of the Constitution.[32] While the *Corte costituzionale* had in *Frontini* accepted the normative supremacy of Community law, it denied the power of the ordinary courts to set aside primary legislation to give effect to Community law. The *pretore di Susa* asked the Court of Justice whether the route via the *Corte costituzionale* was in accordance with the requirements of Community law. The answer of the Court of Justice was square and simple: '*[A]ny provision of a national legal system and any legislative, administrative or judicial practice which might impair the effectiveness of Community law by withholding from the national court having jurisdiction to apply such law the power to do everything necessary at the moment of its application to set aside national legislative provisions which might prevent Community rules from having full force and effect are incompatible with those requirements which are the very essence of Community law*'. Consequently, '*[a] national court which is called upon, within the limits of its jurisdiction, to apply provisions of Community law is under a duty to give full effect to those provisions, if necessary refusing of its own motion to apply any conflicting provision of national legislation, even if adopted subsequently, and it is not necessary for the court to request or await the prior setting aside of such provision by legislative or other constitutional means*'.[33]

In application of structural supremacy, presented as a principle,[34] the Court of Justice thus commanded the lower courts to set aside the constitutional limitations on their function, and to give effect to Community law of their own motion, without awaiting the prior setting aside by a constitutionally competent instance, a constitutional court or Parliament itself, or presumably the Court of Justice. It is the instruction of the *Corte costituzionale* to refer incompatibilities between statutes and Community law itself which has to be set aside. Once that obstacle is removed, the Italian courts can proceed to enforce the normative supremacy of the Community rules at issue, and set aside conflicting Italian legislation of their own motion. While the wording of the reasoning is in the negative,

---

[32] *Frontini*, its reasoning and implications have been discussed *above* in Chapter 7.6.2.

[33] Case 106/77 *Simmenthal* [1978] ECR 585, paras 22 and 24.

[34] The question as to whether there is indeed a 'principle of structural supremacy' has been discussed in Chapter 5.2.

the effects are constructive: a new jurisdiction is created in the hands of the Italian courts.[35] They are empowered to review primary legislation themselves, without awaiting the decision of the *Corte costituzionale* on the constitutionality of the legislation at issue. The Community mandate to review legislation affects *all* courts, including those which do not have that power under their constitutional mandate.

The Court does recognise that there are limits to the application of Community law and its supremacy,[36] but not when these are found in the constitutional division of powers and prevent the courts from exercising the most fundamental duty under Community law to review that Parliament has acted in accordance with its Treaty obligations.

8.3. THE NATIONAL ANSWER

8.3.1. France

The French courts and especially the *Conseil d'État* had a real struggle overcoming the traditional conception of the judicial function and the courts' powers *vis-à-vis* Parliament. More than the issue of the relations between legal orders, this was the main problem for the French courts with the *Simmenthal*-mandate. For all French courts, constitutional, administrative and ordinary alike, to accept the Community mandate to review primary legislation, would constitute a *novum*. This may seem surprising as the constitutional texts since 1946 already seemed to break open the sovereignty of the *loi* with respect to international law. Article 55 of the 1958 French Constitution states that '*From their publication, duly ratified or approved treaties or agreements have a higher authority than lois, subject, for each treaty or agreement, to its implementation by the other party*'. Yet, since the article does not expressly mention the courts as its addressees and given the deeply rooted tradition against judicial review, the dominant position in the early years was that the provision only affected the legislature, and not the courts. In short, the dilemma facing the French courts was *une question de compétence*: '*(..) Aucune juridiction ne conteste et ne pourrait contester, l'idée même de la supériorité du traité sur la loi, qui est inscrite dans la Constitution. La difficulté réside donc pas dans la détermination de la hiérarchie juridique entre traités et lois, mais exclusivement dans une question de compétence (..). Dans tous les cas,*[37] *il s'agit bien de difficultés de compétence, non de fond.*' Under the rules and principles of French constitutional law, the French

---

[35] This is not conclusive on the source of the new powers *as a matter of Italian law*.

[36] See above, on national procedural law and the limits of 'structural' supremacy.

[37] Meaning, for all courts, *Conseil constitutionnel, Conseil d'État, Cour de cassation* and respective lower courts.

courts simply lacked jurisdiction to scrutinise legislation. Especially in the administrative courts there was the additional complication that at that time, the entire area of international relations was considered to be the business of the Government, in which the courts should not interfere.[38] The administrative courts would only concern themselves with international treaties in cases not related directly to the international relations of the French Republic with third countries. In addition, the act of interpreting a treaty was regarded as the responsibility of the Government, and until recently,[39] questions relating to the interpretation of treaties were submitted to the Ministry for Foreign Affairs.[40] It is clear that in this context where courts were extremely cautious in the application and interpretation of treaty law, and which were convinced of their incompetence to review primary legislation, the judges would not be too eager to embrace the Community mandate.[41]

On the other hand, even before *Van Gend en Loos* and *Costa v ENEL* were decided, French courts did not hesitate to apply treaty provisions directly.[42] Yet, where such treaty provision conflicted with a *loi*, they were willing to try and interpret the latter in accordance with the former, but if the conflict could not be by-passed by conform interpretation, precedence would have to be given to the *loi*. In the words of procureur général Matter, '*A supposer qu'il y ait conflit entre la loi et la Convention, quels seraient*

---

[38]   See J-L Delvolvé, 'Le pouvoir judiciaire et le Traité de Rome ou la diplomatie des juges', (1968) *JCP*, I, 2184; at marginal number 8, citing Odent: *'en un mot, le juge est incompétent pour connaître de toutes les questions qui se rattachent indissolublement aux rapports internationaux, qui sont des rapports de droit international'*; see also N Questiaux, 'L'application du droit conventionnel par le Conseil d'état', in P Reuter et al (eds), *L'application du droit international par le juge français*, (Paris, 1972) 63; and P Reuter, 'Le droit international et la place du juge français dans l'ordre constitutionnel national', above, 17; the more recent developments are commented in J Moreau, 'Internationalisation du droit administratif français et déclin de l'acte du gouvernement', in *L'internationalisation du droit. Mélanges en honneur de Yvon Loussouarn* (Paris, 1994) 293.

[39]   Only in 1990 did the *Conseil d'état* assume jurisdiction to interpret international treaties without reference to the Ministry for Foreign Affairs, *Conseil d'État*, 29 June 1990, *GISTI*, Rec. 171, conclusions Abraham; (1990) AJDA, 621, with annotation by G Teboul; (1990) RFDA, 923, with note JF Lachaume.

[40]   The civil courts submitted for interpretation only those treaties which involved public policy considerations; see A Blondeau, 'Application du droit conventionnel par les juridictions françaises de l'ordre judiciaire', in P Reuter et al (eds), *L'application du droit international par le juge français*, (Paris, 1972) 43.

[41]   As reported by RM Chevallier, 'Le juge français et le droit communautaire', in AM Donner *et al*, *Le juge national et le droit communautaire*, (Leiden, 1966) 2, at 2–3: *'Le juge français, (..) doit normalement connaître de très grandes difficultés. (..) [Il] aura du mal à se défaire des habitudes qu'il a prises en utilisant une mécanique qu'il connaît bien et dont les rouages lui sont familiers. (..) [Le droit communautaire] va bouleverser des conceptions reçues et heurter certaines dogmes judiciaires (..) les plus sacrés, (..) et sa conception presque religieuse du principe de la séparation des pouvoirs'.*

[42]   Generally, on the French position at that time see among others J Rideau, *Droit international et droit interne français'* (Paris, 1971); P Reuter (ed), *L' application du droit international par le juge français'* (Paris, 1972).

les devoirs du juge? Ici, aucun doute, vous ne connaissez et ne pouvez connaître d'autre volonté que celle de la loi. C'est le principe même sur lequel reposent nos institutions judiciaires'.[43] The *doctrine Matter* of conform interpretation where possible with ultimate precedence of the *loi*, was not modified after the adoption of the 1946 and the 1958 Constitutions. While Article 26 of the 1946 Constitution and Article 55 of the Constitution adopted in 1958 could be interpreted as departing from the prevailing principles and allowing for the courts to enforce the supremacy of treaties proclaimed in those articles, the *Matter* doctrine was so deeply rooted in the minds of French lawyers, that no change came about.[44] An express and explicit constitutional mandate was considered necessary to that effect.

The *Conseil d'état* was the first of the French highest courts to be confronted with a case involving a conflict between Community law and a *loi*, and awarded precedence to the *loi*.[45] *Commissaire du gouvernement* Questiaux admitted that Article 55 did grant treaties a higher authority than statutes, but that did not change the fact that the administrative courts were precluded from reviewing Acts done by Parliament: *'le juge administratif ne peut faire l'effort qui lui est demandé sans modifier, de sa seule volonté, sa place dans les institutions.(..) il ne peut ni censurer ni méconnaître une loi (..) sa mission (..) reste celle, subordonnée, d'appliquer la loi'.* The *Conseil d'État* could not review the compatibility of the statute with a Community regulation, since that would amount to a modification of its constitutional position, which could only be achieved by constitutional amendment, not on its own motion. The *Conseil d'État* was in this case confronted with the limits of its powers and could not give effect to the Community regulation.

There were probably other policy arguments for not assuming review powers in this case. First, there may be some legal nationalism in the

---

[43] Opinion of *Procureur général* Matter in *Cour de cassation*, 22 December 1931, Clunet, 1932, 687; *Gazette des tribunaux*, 14 January 1932; S 1932, I, 257, with note by Niboyet.

[44] Some commentators and courts did attempt to award precedence to Community law, see references in M Waelbroeck, *Traités internationaux et juridictions internes dans les pays du Marché commun* (Paris, Pedone, 1969) at 268; for court cases see L Constantinesco, 'Effets et rang des traités et du droit communautaire en France', (1968) *Riv.dir.civ.*, 259, at 271ff.

[45] *Conseil d'État*, decision of 1 March 1968, *Syndicat général de fabricants de semoules de France* (*semoules*), Rec., 149, with observations du Commissaire du gouvernement Questiaux; (1968) *RTDeur.*, 388, with annotation by C Constantinidès-Mégret; (1968) *AJDA*, 235; *Rev.crit.dr.int.pr.*, 1968, 516, with note by R Kovar; (1968) *RGDIP*, 1128, with note C Rousseau; *English translation in* [1970] CMLR 395; the case arose from a ministerial authorisation for the import of semolina from Algeria, founded on legislative provisions (in the form of an ordonnance issued by the President, but statutory in character) which were adopted after and in conflict with a Community regulation. French producers brought an action for annulment before the administrative court alleging that the ministerial authorization infringed Community law. The main legal issue was whether the theory of the *loi-écran* – the statute which is immune for review protects the administrative act covered by it – could apply in this context.

judgment,[46] and a concern for the fate of national sovereignty.[47] Second, the time may simply not have been ripe to change old habits for the sake of a new political and legal construct. The crisis in European decision making prompted by the French *politique de la chaise vide* had only recently come to an end with the Luxembourg Compromise, and President De Gaulle loathed the idea of a supranational Community. Third, the *Conseil d'État* may have been eager to resist all competition with the Court of Justice. In the *semoules* case, the applicant had asked for the case to be referred to the Court of Justice. The reluctance of the *Conseil d'État* to co-operate with the Court of Justice has been witnessed in other instances, such as the application of the theory of *acte clair* and the refusal of the *Conseil* to accord direct effect to directives in *Cohn-Bendit*.[48] In addition, when the *semoules* case arose, the *Conseil d'état* did not have much room for manoeuvre to oppose the President, since its powers had already come under attack in the *affaire Canal* a few years earlier.[49] Nevertheless, while all of these circumstances may help to explain the resistance of the *Conseil d'État* in the case at hand, they do not account for the fact that it would take the *Conseil* until 1989 to finally change its view.

From a formal legal point of view, review was excluded as exceeding the limits of the judicial function, imposing an obligation on the courts to respect the expression of the sovereignty of the People. Article 55 was held to be addressed to the Parliament, not to the courts. In addition, an incompatibility with a treaty provision would at the same time and for

---

[46]   R Abraham, *Droit international, droit communautaire et droit français*, (Paris, 1989), at 119; According to Ryziger the anti-European or nationalistic tendency in the *Conseil d'État* should not be overestimated, and was certainly not its position as a matter of principle, P-F Ryziger, 'Le Conseil d'état et le droit communautaire: de la continuité au change-ment', (1990) *RFDA*, 850, at 851; see also P Sabourin, 'Le Conseil d'état face au droit com-munautaire. Méthodes et raisonnements', (1993) *RDP*, 397 and J-Cl. Bonichot, 'Convergences et divergences entre le Conseil d'état et la Cour de justice des Communautés européennes', *RFDA*, 579.

[47]   Mme Questiaux in her Opinion in *semoules: 'Il est difficile d'imaginer que se créent, dans tous les domaines affectés par un traité international, des zones entières où les lois seraient privées d'ef-fet par le juge et justement sur la base des textes qu'il n'a même pas entière qualité pour interpréter. La thèse est séduisante pour encourager le développement d'un ordre juridique communautaire; l'évolution se conçoit moins facilement si elle fait échapper à l'action du législateur des pans entiers de la vie du pays parce que sont intervenus dans le domaine considéré des traités dont l'interpré-tation appartient au Ministre des Affaires étrangères'*, (1968) *RTDeur*, at 395.

[48]   *Conseil d'État*, 22 December 1978, *Cohn-Bendit*, (1979) *RTDeur*, 168 with note by L Dubouis; comments include G Isaac, 'Le juge administratif et les directives communau-taires', (1979) *CDE*, 591; Chr. Tomuschat, 'La justice c'est moi', (1979) *EuGRZ*, 257; A Barav, (1980) *RBDI*, 126 and more generally on the theory of *acte clair* in *Cohn-Bendit* and its ramifications, G Bebr, 'The Rambling Ghost of 'Cohn-Bendit': *Acte clair* and the Court of Justice', 20 (1983) *CML Rev* 439.

[49]   As recollected by L Dubouis, 'L'arrêt *Nicolo* et l'intégration de la règle internationale et communautaire dans l'ordre juridique français', (1989) *RFDA*, 1000, at 1001; and J-F Ryziger, 'Le Conseil d'état et le droit commuanautaire: de la continuité au changement', (1990) *RFDA*, 855, at 856.

that matter amount to an infringement of Article 55, and was accordingly a matter for the *Conseil constitutionnel* alone.

The *Conseil constitutionnel*, however, took a different view and ruled that a *loi* infringing a treaty provision was not for that matter unconstitutional.[50] The *Conseil constitutionnel* held that it only has attributed competences which derogate from the established principles of separation of powers and sovereignty of the *loi*, namely to review the *constitutionality* of Bills and not whether a *loi* infringes international treaties. From a policy point of view, for the *Conseil constitutionnel* to accept jurisdiction under Article 55 would grant it sole power to enforce the supremacy of Community law against conflicting statutes, to the exclusion of all other courts, and only within strict time limits and before the promulgation of the statute.

Shortly afterwards, the *Cour de cassation* did assume jurisdiction to review the compatibility of parliamentary legislation in the case *Jacques Vabre* in 1975.[51] In a wording reminiscent of *Van Gend en Loos* and *Costa v ENEL*, the *Cour de cassation* held that '*the Community Treaty which by virtue of Article 55 of the Constitution has an authority greater than that of statutes, institutes a different legal order integrated with that of the Member States. Because of that separateness, the legal order which it has created is directly applicable to the nationals of those States and is binding on their courts. Therefore the* Cour d'appel *was correct and did not exceed its powers in deciding that article 95 of the Treaty was to be applied in the instant case, and not [the* loi*], even though the latter was later in date'*.[52] In the view of *procureur général* Touffait, Article 55 established a hierarchy between treaties and statutes which the courts are to enforce, as in any other case of conflict between norms of a different rank: the superior norm is to be given effect, while the application of the lower provision is excluded in the particular case, without its validity being affected. To set aside a *loi* for conflicting with a treaty provision does not amount to a review of its constitutionality as the administrative courts would have it. It is a matter of comparing, by virtue of Article 55 of the Constitution, a *loi* with a treaty, not of testing its constitutionality. In addition, times had changed since *Matter* had in 1931 expressed the unanimous case law of his time, when apart from the Postal

---

[50] *Conseil constitutionnel*, decision of 15 January 1975, *Interruption volontaire de grossesse*, www. conseil-constitutionnel.fr. The *Conseil* declared that it was not, under Art. 55, competent to review the compatibility of bills with the ECHR or any other Treaty provisions. Art. 55 was not to be regarded as the infringed norm but as the provision empowering the ordinary courts to conduct review in the light of treaties.

[51] *Cour de cassation*, decision of 23 May 1975, *Cafés Jacques Vabre*, D, 1975, II, 497, *Conclusions* Touffait; *RTDeur*, 1975, 621, with note by R Kovar; (1975) CDE, 336; Oppenheimer, *The Cases*, 287.

[52] Translation taken from Oppenheimer, *The Cases*, 287, at 309.

Union and railways, international conventions related only to the war, the freedom of the sea and the safety of the State.[53] Times had changed, and these changes were witnessed in the post-war Constitutions of 1946 and 1958 declaring the superiority of treaties, with an international ethic in mind.[54] Yet, the *Procureur général* did urge the *Cour de cassation* not to take up the constitutional authorisation in the case of Community law. The precedence of Community law should not be based on Article 55 of the Constitution, he said, but be founded on the very nature of the legal order instituted by the Rome Treaty, so as not to tempt courts in other Member States with less internationally oriented Constitutions to do the same and arrive at the opposite solution.[55] The argument based on the very nature of Community law would recognise that the national judge is the common law judge of the application of Community law. He ended with a panoramic survey of the case law of the other Member States to prove the development of '*a European consciousness within all the national courts concerned to recognise the primacy of Community law without which there could not be created that unity of the market*'. However, the *Cour de cassation* did not follow and founded its jurisdiction on Article 55 of the French Constitution.

The *Conseil d'Etat* consequently became isolated in its refusal to assume review powers in the scope of Community law, both in France and in the Community. The *Conseil constitutionnel* from the mid-nineteen eighties sought to convince the *Conseil d'Etat* when it held more explicitly that '*il appartient aux divers organes de l'Etat de veiller à l'application des conventions internationales dans le cadre de leurs compétences*'. In addition, acting as an election court, in circumstances comparable to those of the *Conseil d'Etat*,[56] it did review the *conventionnalité* of a statute and set aside a *loi* in favour of a treaty.

---

[53] PG Touffait in *Jacques Vabres*, Oppenheimer, *The Cases*, at 299.
[54] Above, at 301.
[55] 'Indeed, in so far as you restricted yourselves to deriving from Article 55 of our Constitution the primacy in the French internal system of Community law over national law you would be explaining and justifying that action as regards our country, but such reasoning would let it be accepted that it is on our Constitution and on it alone that depends the ranking of Community law in our internal system. In doing so you would impliedly be supplying a far from negligible argument to the courts of the Member States which, lacking any affirmation in the Constitutions of the primacy of the Treaty, would be tempted to deduce therefrom the opposite solution, as the Italian Constitutional court did in 1962 when it claimed that it was for internal constitutional law to fix the ranking of Community law in the internal order of each Member State', Oppenheimer, *The Cases*, at 303.
[56] The *Conseil constitutionnel* acts as election court in national elections. In that capacity it does not have the characteristics of a constitutional court and cannot review the constitutionality of a *loi*; the *Conseil d'Etat* is the election court for local elections.

The *revirement* finally[57] came in the *Nicolo* decision of 1989, a case concerning elections to the European Parliament.[58] The reasoning of the *Conseil d'Etat* is concealed in the coded message that *'les règles (..) de la loi du 7 juillet 1977 ne sont pas incompatibles avec les stipulations claires (..) du Traité de Rome'*, implying that the *loi had* been reviewed, but no incompatibility had been found. *Commissaire du gouvernement* Frydman proposed a new interpretation of Article 55 of the Constitution as a constitutional exception to the prohibition of judicial review of the validity of statutes and containing an express authorisation: *'Sans doute y a-t-il bien ici contrôle de conformité des lois, mais cette atteinte au principe constitutionnel de séparation des pouvoirs trouve alors son fondement dans la Constitution elle-même'.*[59] In addition, Frydman pointed to the jurisdictional gap caused by the

---

[57] It was not a sudden and unexpected change of position. Several members of the *Conseil d'État* had announced their preference for a *revirement*. In addition, the *Conseil d'État* had already qualified the *'théorie de la loi-écran'*. Under the theory, the statute upon which an administrative act is based functions as a shield between the treaty and the administrative act. The act cannot be annulled for violation of the treaty if it is covered by the *loi*. Under the intermediate position, referred to as the *'loi-écran transparant'*, the *Conseil d'État* examined the scope of the underlying *loi*, to define the limits of the *loi-écran*, the shield. If the statute was limited to granting power to the Executive, the latter would be bound to respect treaty law when acting upon the powers granted. If the *loi* also imposed substantive rules, the administrative acts would be protected by the *loi* to that extent; On the intermediate position of the *Conseil d'Etat* just before *Nicolo*, see J-Cl. Bonichot, 'Convergences et divergences entre le Conseil d'État et la Cour de justice des Communautés européennes', (1989) *RFDA*, 579; R Abraham, *Droit international droit communautaire et droit français* (Paris, 1989) manuscript finished just before *Nicolo* was decided; the decision is discussed in a mise à jour of 1990; B Genevois, 'L droit international et le droit communautaire', in *Conseil constitutionnel et Conseil d' Etat* (Paris, 1988) 191. Also the doctrinal debate tended towards a modification, see references in J-F Lachaume, 'Une victoire de l'ordre juridique communautaire: l'arrêt *Nicolo* consacrant la supériorité des traités sur les lois postérieures', (1990) *RMC*, 384, at 388.

[58] Nicolo, a French voter, made an application for annulment of the 1989 French elections to the European Parliament alleging that the provisions of the 1977 Elections Act were incompatible with Art. 227(1) of the EEC Treaty. Similar actions had been brought equally alleging an infringement of EC law and of the ECHR In both cases the *Conseil d'État* rejected the claim, denying jurisdiction to review the compatibility of statutes with international treaties, *Conseil d'État*, decision of 22 October 1979, *RDP*, 1980, 541 and *Conseil dÉEtat*, decision of 27 April 1985, *Roujansky*, AJDA, 1985, 216; see C Haguenau, *L'application effective du droit communautaire en droit interne*, (Bruxelles, 1995), at 78. Roujansky also brought a case against the 1989 'Nicolo' elections, arguing this time that the statute was unconstitutional. The *Conseil d'Etat* rejected the claim unequivocally, on the same day as the *Nicolo* judgment, in *Conseil d'État*, decision of 20 October 1989, *Roujansky*.

[59] Opinion of *commissaire du gouvernement* Frydman in *Conseil d'Etat*, decision of 20 October 1989, *Nicolo*, RTDeur., 1989, 771, at 777; The other explanation of what a court really does when reviewing a *loi* in the light of a treaty is given by *Commissaire du gouvernement* Laroque in a later case: *'[Vous] n'avez dans votre décision Nicolo posé le principe d'un contrôle de légalité du juge sur la loi, qui pourrait aboutir à une censure de celle-ci. Vous avez en réalité révisé ou rétabli la hiérachie des normes jridiques, conformément à l'article 55 de la Constitution, en faisant prévaloir en cas de discordance (..) la norme internationale (..). Cela vous conduit non pas à vous prononcer sur la validité d'une loi postérieure à un traité internationale, mais sur son opposabilité ou son applicabilité à une situation donnée'*, Opinion of *commissaire du gouvernement* Laroque, in *Conseil d'Etat*, decision of 28 February 1992, *Philip Morris*, AJDA, 1992, 210, at 220.

denial of competence by both the *Conseil constitutionnel* and the *Conseil d'Etat*; to the new international environment, and the fact that all courts in the other Member States had assumed judicial review powers, including even the Italian and the German courts; and the fact that even lower civil courts in France controlled statutes on their compatibility with treaties. The foundation of the review powers was and could only be a constitutional one, Article 55. Since it does not distinguish between Community and other international law, there was no reason why Community law should be treated differently.

Since *Nicolo*, the review powers of the French courts in the light of international treaties, mostly Community law and the ECHR are firmly settled, and are often presented as an alternative of the judicial review of the constitutionality of statutes in force, which, as said, is still absent.

8.3.2. The United Kingdom

The British conception of the separation of powers between Parliament and the courts likewise seemed to make the acceptance of judicial control of the compatibility of Acts of Parliament with Community law impossible. The fundamental rules on the relationship between the courts and Parliament are contained in the basic constitutional doctrine of the Sovereignty of Parliament,[60] holding that the legislative acts of the Queen in Parliament are unassailable. The doctrine of the Supremacy or Sovereignty of Parliament consists of a dual proposition. The first one is positive and contends that Parliament can make and unmake any law whatever, that it can do anything,[61] 'except make a man a woman and a

---

[60] Also referred to as the doctrine of legislative supremacy, see ECS Wade and AW Bradley, *Constitutional and Administrative Law*, (Harlow, Pearson, 11th edn, 1993) at 68–69 and E Barendt, *An Introduction to Constitutional Law* (Oxford, Clarendon Press, 1998) 86 *et seq.*; see for the classic doctrine HRW Wade, 'The Basis of Legal Sovereignty', (1955) *CLJ*, 172 and of course the father of the doctrine AV Dicey's *The Law of the Constitution*, first published in 1885, AV Dicey, *An Introduction to the Study of the Law of the Constitution*, 10th edn, with an introduction by ECS Wade, (London, Macmillan 1959); the new view of parliamentary sovereignty as advocated by Jennings, Marshall and Heuston, is described in PP Craig, 'Sovereignty of the United Kingdom Parliament after Factortame', (1991) *YEL*, 221 and G Anav, 'Parliamentary sovereignty: An Anachronism?', (1989) *Colombia J Transnational L* 631; a recent study of the doctrine from a historic and philosophical perspective is J Goldsworthy, *The Sovereignty of Parliament. History and Philosophy* (Oxford, Clarendon Press, 1999).

[61] As Lord Reid put it: 'It is often said that it would be unconstitutional for the UK Parliament to do certain things, meaning that the moral, political and other reasons against doing them are so strong that most people would regard it as highly improper if Parliament did these things. But that does not mean that it is beyond the power of Parliament to do such things. If Parliament chose to do any of them, the courts could not hold the Act of Parliament invalid', in *Matzimbamuto v Lardner-Burke* [1969] 1 AC 645, 723 or as Dicey himself put it: ''Limited sovereignty', in short, is in the case of a Parliament as of any other sovereign, a contradiction in terms'.

woman a man'.[62] The second aspect of parliamentary sovereignty, put in the negative, states that no person or body outside the Legislature is recognised by the law of England as having the right to override or set aside the legislation of Parliament. No court can supervise Parliament or revise the legislation which it designs.[63] There are no legally enforceable limits to the legislative authority of the Westminster Parliament.[64] If Parliament speaks, the courts must obey. The courts readily accept this limitation of their jurisdiction,[65] in fact they are even at the source of it: the source of the principle of parliamentary sovereignty is to be found in common law: the doctrine is not laid down in any constitutional document, nor indeed in an Act of Parliament,[66] it is a common law rule.[67]

There is, however, under the traditional view,[68] one and only one limit to the omnipotence of Parliament: no Parliament can bind its successors. If Parliament legislates contrary to a previous statute, the courts will give effect to the later statute as the latest expression of the sovereign will, which impliedly repeals the previous statute. If Parliament would decree that a certain provision of a statute cannot be changed in future and a later Parliament *does* change the rule, the courts will apply the later provision. The courts thus act as guardians of the parliamentary sovereignty against Parliament itself: there is no such thing as entrenched legislation. Parliament cannot detract from its own continuing sovereignty.[69] The idea of Parliament's ability to bind its successors has not always been part of

---

[62] JL De Lolme, *The Rise and Process of the English Constitution*, (1838).

[63] The words of Lord Morris in *Pickin v British Railways Board* [1974] AC 765 at 789 are generally referred to as the essence of this aspect: 'It is the function of the courts to administer the laws which Parliament has enacted. In the processes of Parliament, there will be much consideration whether a bill should or should not in one form or another become an enactment. When an enactment is passed there is finality unless and until it is amended or repealed by Parliament. In the courts there may be argument as to the correct interpretation of the enactment: there must be none as to whether it should be on the statute book at all'.

[64] AW Bradley, 'The Sovereignty of Parliament – In Perpetuity?', in J Jowell and D Oliver (eds), *The Changing Constitution*, (2nd edn, 1989) 25, at 25.

[65] See *Harrison v Tew* [1990] 1 All ER 321 at 329.

[66] According to Salmond, this would have been impossible for reasons of logic: 'No statute can confer this power upon Parliament, for this would be to assume the very power to be conferred', in PJ Fitzgerald (ed), *Salmond on Jurisprudence* (12th edn, 1966) at 111.

[67] An alternative line of constitutional development was suggested by Lord Coke in the famous *Dr Bonham's Case*, arguing that the courts could in exceptional circumstances declare parliamentary acts void: *Dr. Bonham's Case* (1610) 8 Co Rep. 113b, 118a: '*When an Act of Parliament is against right and reason, or repugnant, or impossible to be performed, the common law will control it and adjudge that Act to be void*'. Yet, the doctrine of parliamentary sovereignty and the inability of the courts to supervise the Legislature was firmly established in British constitutional law since 1688.

[68] On the different views of the doctrine of parliamentary sovereignty, see PP Craig, 'Sovereignty of the United Kingdom Parliament after Factortame', (1991) *YEL*, 221.

[69] This does not howver reflect the view of Dicey who held that 'No principle of jurisprudence is more certain than that sovereignty implies the power of abdication', AV Dicey, *op.cit.*, at 68–69.

the orthodox doctrine: it does not appear in judicial opinions before the twentieth century.[70] Wade,[71] considered a proponent of the traditional view, supported the rule on reasons of logic, on several court decisions and on arguments of principle. First, the present holder of sovereignty cannot limit the sovereignty of the future holder, otherwise the future holder would no longer be sovereign. Second, there is case law proving that if Parliament introduces a statute prescribing a different procedure for future statutes changing the previous one, it is nevertheless impliedly changed by a later statute adopted by the normal procedure: the courts follow the latest expression of Parliament's will.[72] Wade's third argument is framed in answer to the proponents of the new view, who defend the view that since the rule of parliamentary sovereignty is a rule of common law, and since Parliament has the power to change common law rules, it could also change the rule of judicial obedience of parliamentary statutes. Wade rejected this argument by distinguishing between ordinary common law rules and the rule of legislative supremacy, which he described as 'the ultimate political fact' upon which the whole system of legislation hangs. Since no statute can establish the rule that the courts must obey Acts of Parliament – that would be to assume and act on the very power to be conferred – similarly no statute can alter or abolish that rule. Wade arrived at the conclusion that only the courts could change the top-rule: *'What Salmond calls the "ultimate legal principle" is a rule which is unique in being unchangeable by Parliament – it is changed by revolution, not by legislation; it lies in the keeping of the courts, and no Act of parliament can take it from them. This is only another way of saying that it is always for the courts, in the last resort, to say what is a valid Act of Parliament; and that the decision of this question is not determined by any rule of law which can be laid down or altered by any authority outside the courts It is simply a political fact'.*[73]

According to another and in my view more realistic view, the self-embracing view, Parliament can decide to restrict its own sovereignty, precisely because it is sovereign. Parliament has done so on several occasions, for instance by the 1707 Act of Union, or in Acts recognising the independence of former colonies. According to the 'manner and form'[74] school, Parliament can legislate effectively about the manner and form of future legislation, as it did for instance in the 1931 Act of Westminster or

---

[70] See G Anav, 'Parliamentary Sovereignty: An Anachronism?', (1989) *Colombia J of Transnational L*, 631, at 636.
[71] HWR Wade, 'The Basis of Legal Soevereignty', (1955) *CLJ*, 172.
[72] *Vauxhall Estates Ltd v Liverpool Corporation* [1932] 1 KB 733; *Ellen Street Estates Ltd v Minister of Health* [1934] 1 KB 590; *British Coal Corporation v R* [1935] AC 500.
[73] HWR Wade, 'The Basis of Legal Sovereignty', (1955) *CLJ*, 177, at 189.
[74] This is the name given to this school of thought by Wade; the terms 'continuing' and 'self-embracing are those of HLA Hart, see TRS Allan, 'Parliamentary Sovereignty: Lord Denning's Dexterous Revolution', (1983) 3 *Oxford Journal of Legal Studies*, 22, at 22.

the Parliament Acts of 1911 and 1949. The courts will give effect only to legislation which complies with whatever conditions are laid down at a moment in time required for valid legislation on the matter in question. Under this view, it *is* possible for Parliament to entrench legislation.

When Britain joined the EC it was questionable whether the supremacy of Community law would be accepted by British courts. It was widely agreed, when the EC Act 1972 was adopted, that Parliament could at any time repeal it and thus effectively prevent the continued operation of Community law within the United Kingdom.[75] But there was uncertainty about the less extreme situation, which was more likely to occur, of a post 1972 Act of Parliament containing a provision inconsistent with an established rule of Community law. In such a situation, the courts could go either way. One could imagine that they would give precedence to the provision of Community law, if not on the basis of the very nature of Community law, then on the basis of Sections 2(4) or 3 of the EC Act. Yet, it was also possible that, in application of the traditional rules of constitutional law and the continuing sovereignty of the UK parliament, they would assume that the inconsistent piece of primary legislation constituted an implied repeal of the 1972 EC Act, and apply the later Act.[76]

For many years, the question of the supremacy of Community law and the resulting review powers of the courts, was up in the air. In *Shields v Coomes* Lord Denning cited the decision of the Court of Justice in *Simmenthal* without criticism and stated that Parliament clearly intended to abide by the principles of direct effect and supremacy when it passed the 1972 Act. Consequently, the courts should resolve any inconsistencies with Community law so as to give primary effect to it.[77]

In *Macarthys v Smith* Lord Denning said *obiter*: '*It is important to note – and it must be made plain – that the provisions of Article 119 of the Treaty of Rome take priority over anything in our English statutes on equal pay which is inconsistent with Article 119. That priority is given by our own law. It is given by the EC Act 1972 itself. Community is now part of our law and, whenever there is any inconsistency, Community law has priority. It is not supplanting English law. It is part of our law which overrides any other part which is inconsistent with it.*'[78] However, in the earlier decision, Lord Denning held that if Parliament should pass an Act which was intended to repudiate the Treaty and said so

---

[75] See AW Bradley, 'The Sovereignty of Parliament – In Perpetuity?', in J Jowell and D Oliver (eds), *The Changing Constitution* (3rd edn, Oxford, 1994), 79, at 93.

[76] In *Felixtowe Dock v British Transport Docks Board* [1976] CMLR 655 Lord Denning stated obiter: '[I]t seems to me that once the bill is passed by Parliament and becomes a statute, that will dispose of all this discussion about the Treaty. These courts will then have to abide by the statute without regard to the Treaty at all'.

[77] *Shields v Coomes (Holdings) Ltd* [1978] 1 WLR 1408.

[78] *Court of Appeal*, decision of 17 April 1980, *Macarthys Ltd v Smith* [1980] 3 WLR 929; 2 [1980] CMLR 217, at 218.

in express terms, *'it would be the duty of our courts to follow the statute of our Parliament'*.[79] T.R.S. Allan has suggested that Lord Denning in *Macarthys Ltd v Smith* had effectively achieved a 'dexterous revolution', saving both parliamentary sovereignty and the supremacy of Community law.[80]

Yet, the courts remained cautious and bent backwards to escape direct and open conflicts between Community law and Acts of Parliament by taking recourse to what they referred to as the *rule of construction* contained in Section 2(4) of the EC Act 1972 and meaning that *'it is a principle of construction of United Kingdom statutes, now too well established to call for citation of authority, that the words of a statute passed after the treaty has been signed and dealing with the subject matter of the international obligation of the United Kingdom are to be construed, if they are reasonably capable of bearing such meaning, as intended to carry out the obligation and not to be inconsistent with it'*.[81] The courts then struggled with several difficulties such as the question relating to the extent of the rule of construction and appeared willing to go much further in the case of legislation passed in order specifically to comply with Treaty obligations,[82] as in the case of legislation implementing directives, than in the case of other legislation. In addition, Section 2(4) of the EC Act was considered only to apply where Community provisions were directly applicable.[83]

Then came the *Factortame* case[84] which unexpectedly would dispose rather easily of the problem of continuing parliamentary sovereignty in

---

[79] *Court of Appeal*, decision of 25 July 1979, *Macarthys v Smith* [1979] 3 All ER 325, at 329.

[80] TRS Allan, 'Parliamentary Sovereignty: Lord Denning's Dexterous Revolution', (1983) 3 *Oxford Journal of Legal Studies*, 22; *Court of Appeal*, decision of 25 July 1979, *Macarthys v Smith* [1979] 3 All ER 325.

[81] *House of Lords*, decision of 22 April 1982, *Garland v British Rail* [1983] 2 AC 751; [1982] 2 All ER 402; Oppenheimer, *The Cases*, 775, at 780, per Lord Diplock.

[82] *House of Lords*, decision of 30 June 1988, *Pickstone and Others v Freemans Plc* [1989] 1 AC 66; Oppenheimer, *The Cases*, 799; *House of Lords, Litster v Forth Dry Dock Co. Ltd* [1990] 1 AC 546;

[83] *House of Lords*, decision of 11 February 1988, *Duke v GEC Reliance Ltd* [1988] AC 618; Oppenheimer, *The Cases*, 783. After *Factortame*, the rule of construction was differently applied in *Webb v EMO* where the House of Lords gave an interpretation of the Act not intended to implement a directive and in a case between private individuals (no direct effect), which distorted the meaning of the Act, *House of Lords, Webb v EMO Air Cargo (UK) Ltd* [1992] 4 All ER 929.

[84] The saga of the Spanish fishermen has been long and complicated, involving many court proceedings before both the English and the European courts. The cases arose out of the 1988 Merchant Shipping Act, which limited the right to register fishing vessels, in order to stop the practice of quota-hopping by Spanish fishermen fishing in English waters, 'catching English fish'. The Spanish fishermen challenged the validity of the Act in the light of Community law (question referred for preliminary ruling). Pending the case on the compatibility of the Act with Community law, the fishermen applied for an interim injunction, ordering Ministers of the Crown to suspend application of the 1988 Act and to register the vessels under the old Act (question referred to the ECJ). Later, when the case was won on the merits, the fishermen applied for damages to compensate the damage caused to them during the time that their vessels were not registered (question referred to the ECJ). Parallel to these private proceedings, the Commission brought an enforcement action against the UK, including an application for interim measures.

the framework of Community law.[85] The central constitutional issue[86] in the case[87] was whether, unless and until it was established that a United Kingdom Act of Parliament was incompatible with Community law, the statute remained inviolable or could be 'disapplied' by the courts, even temporarily. In the words of Lord Bingham in the Court of Appeal, to disapply the Act or to restrain the Secretary of State from enforcing an Act of Parliament against the clearly expressed will of Parliament when the unlawfulness of that expression had not been established, would be 'a constitutional enormity'.[88] Lord Bridge in the House of Lords upheld the decision of the Court of Appeal and took the view that *as a matter of English law*, there were two jurisdictional obstacles to granting the interim relief sought by the Spanish fishermen. First, the presumption of validity of the Act of Parliament precluded the courts from ordering the disapplication of the Act. Second, the courts did not have jurisdiction to grant an interim injunction against the Crown. However, the House of Lords wondered whether *as a matter of Community law* there may be a duty or power to offer the relief sought, and referred a question for preliminary ruling to the Court of Justice. The Court held that there was such a duty.[89]

When the case on interim relief returned to the House of Lords, Lord Bridge had this to say on the issue of the impact of Community law on parliamentary sovereignty: *'Some public comments on the decision of the Court of Justice, affirming the jurisdiction of the courts of the Member States to override national legislation if necessary to enable interim relief to be granted in protection of rights under Community law, have suggested that this was a novel and dangerous invasion by the Community institution of the sovereignty of the United Kingdom Parliament. But such comments are based on a misconception. If the supremacy within the European Community of Community law over the national law of the Member States was not always inherent in the EEC Treaty it was certainly well established in the jurisprudence of the Court of Justice long*

---

[85] Among the many comments on the *Factortame* cases and parliamentary sovereignty see HWR Wade, 'What has Happened to the Sovereignty of Parliament?', *LQR*, 1991, 1; PP Craig, 'Sovereignty and the United Kingdom Parliament after Factortame', *YEL*, 1991, 221; G Anav, 'Parliamentary Sovereignty: An Anachronism?', *Columbia JTransnational L*, 1989, 631; M Akehurst, 'Parliamentary Sovereignty and the Supremacy of Community Law', *BYIL*, 1989, 351, and the more recent debate referred to in *below*.

[86] The arguments of the parties and of the English courts dealing with the constitutional issues are explained in NP Gravells, 'Disapplying an Act of Parliament Pending a Preliminary Ruling: Constitutional Enormity or Community Law Right?', *PL*, 1989, 568.

[87] A first question concerning the substantive compatibility of the 1988 Merchant Shipping Act had already been referred by the Divisional Court. The case which came up before the House of Lords concerned the issue of interim relief, in the form of an interim injunction ordering the Secretary of State for Transport to disapply the Act, pending the question of its compatibility with Community law.

[88] *Court of Appeal*, decision of 22 March 1989, *Regina v Secretary of State for Transport, ex parte Factortame Ltd and others* [1989] 2 CMLR 353, at 407.

[89] On the *Factortame* decision of the ECJ, see above, under Chapter 5.2.

before the United Kingdom joined the Community. Thus, whatever limitation of its sovereignty Parliament accepted when it enacted the European Communities Act 1972 was entirely voluntary. Under the terms of the 1972 Act it has always been clear that it was the duty of a United Kingdom court, when delivering final judgment, to override any rule of national law found to be in conflict with any directly enforceable rule of Community law. (..) Thus there is nothing in any way novel in according supremacy to rules of Community law in areas to which they apply and to insist that, in the protection of rights under Community law, national courts must not be prohibited by rules of national law from granting interim relief in appropriate cases is no more than a logical recognition of that supremacy.'[90] What is most striking is the ease with which Lord Bridge accepts the principle of supremacy of Community law: Lord Bridge 'passed on the puck' to Parliament itself: it was neither the English courts, nor the European Court which had invaded parliamentary sovereignty: Parliament itself had done so by passing the 1972 EC Act, thereby granting the power to the courts to accord precedence to directly enforceable rules of Community law over any rule of national law, including Acts of Parliament. Lord Bridge presented the judgment as a natural consequence of British membership and the EC Act, as if everything that had been written and all the problems the courts had experienced before had overlooked the mere fact that Parliament had passed the EC Act. However, one of the central issues was precisely what the effect of the Act would be and whether it would be powerful enough to allow for the courts to accept the *Simmenthal* mandate.

It would be mistaken to pretend that nothing has happened. The courts do now scrutinise parliamentary legislation, which was unheard of before, and considered 'a constitutional enormity'. The 1972 Parliament has apparently done what was considered impossible before, namely bind future Parliaments and make it difficult for the Crown in Parliament to legislate contrary to Community law, and convince the courts that this was indeed the effect sought. The question remains what would happen if Parliament should intentionally and openly legislate contrary to Community law. Most commentators would agree that in such a case, the courts would have to follow Parliament, which ultimately remains sovereign and can detract from the EC Act 1972, as long as it does so expressly and unequivocally. But exactly what has happened to the Sovereignty of Parliament in its relation to the courts in conceptual terms is still under debate among the most eminent constitutional lawyers.[91] Who has brought

---

[90]   *House of Lords*, decision of 11 October 1990, *Regina v Secretary of State for Transport, ex parte Factortame Ltd and others* [1991] 1 All ER 70, at 107–108; Oppenheimer, *The Cases*, 882, at 883.
[91]   HWR Wade, 'Sovereignty – Revolution or Evolution', *LQR* (1996) 568 maintains that a revolution *has* indeed occurred, since the courts have allowed the 1972 Parliament to bind the 1988 Parliament and to restrict its sovereignty. His article is a comment on PP Craig,

about that change? Was it the courts, who achieved some sort of legal revolution (Wade)? Was it the 1972 Parliament? Has the constitutional principle of parliamentary sovereignty itself been changed? If the 1972 Parliament has indeed achieved to limit the sovereignty of its successors, does this mean that the 1972 EC Act is in some way entrenched; that it is more than an ordinary Act of Parliament?[92] These questions were central in the case of the *metric martyrs*,[93] following an appeal by four greengrocers and a fishmonger against their conviction for breach, *inter alia*, of the Weights and Measures Act 1985 and several statutory instruments, by reason of their refusal to use metric measurements alongside the imperial pounds and ounces. Under a series of EU Council Directives, the sale of goods loose from bulk by the pound was to be prohibited from January 2000, although until 1 Januray 2010 imperial measurements could be used as supplementary indications. The directives were implemented in the United Kingdom by a series of subordinate instruments, amending among others the Weight and Measures Act 1985. The 'metric martyrs' had refused to use the new and continental measurements. They were backed by the UK Independence Party.

The metrication instruments were thus introduced by statutory instrument intended to amend an Act of Parliament. The 'metric martyrs'

'Sovereignty of the United Kingdom Parliament after *Factortame*', YEL (1991) 221 who suggested that there was another less revolutionary explanation holding that the disapplication of the 1988 Merchant Shipping Act was achieved merely by way of statutory construction under ordinary principles and was thus implicit in existing constitutional theory, not a departure from it. The discussion was carried on in J Eekelaar, 'The Death of Parliamentary Sovereignty – A Comment', *LQR* (1997) 185; TRS Allan, 'Parliamentary Sovereignty: Law, Politics and Revolution', *LQR* (1997) 443; PP Craig, 'Britain in the European Union', in J Jowell and D Oliver (eds), *The Changing Constitution*, 4th edn, (Oxford, OUP, 2000) 61.

[92] So eg Lord Lester of Herne Hill, 'Developing Constitutional Principles of Public Law', *PL* (2001) 684, at 689, according to whom the EC Act – and the Human Rights Act and Devolution Acts – are constitutional measures of a higher legal order, and to be treated as fundamental law unless and until a future Parliament clearly decides otherwise. This continues to be the main difference with 'real' entrenched constitutional rules in other systems, which cannot be amended following the ordinary legislative procedure, however clear, express and unequivocal Parliament is: these can only be amended following special procedures, which make it more difficult to amend the Constitution, requiring for instance special majorities, or new elections, or the approval of the majority of the people in a referendum.

[93] *High Court, Queen's Bench Division, Divisional Court*, decision of 18 February 2002, *Thoburn v Sunderland City Council; Hunt v London Borough of Hackney; Harman and Dove v Cornwall County Council* and *Collins v London Borough of Sutton* (metric martyrs) [2002] EWHC 195; available on www.bailii.org. This was a highly publicised case, which involved the establishment of a 'metric martyrs defence fund', selling christmas cards in support of the 'martyrs' etc. There was huge media coverage. For a discussion of the decision see A Perreau-Saussine, 'A tale of two supremacies, four greengrocers, a fishmonger, and the seeds of a constitutional court', *CLJ* (2002) 527.

argued[94] before the court that Parliament can only validly enact clauses empowering the executive to amend primary legislation ('Henry VIII clauses') – as the EC Act had allegedly done – to permit amendment of statutes already enrolled. A Henry VIII power could never bite on future statutes, otherwise they would amount to a constitutionally improper limitation on the sovereignty of subsequent Parliaments. Accordingly, the Henry VIII power attributed to the Government under Sections 2(2) and (4) of the EC Act could not lawfully be used to amend the 1985 Act. Therefore, the 1985 Act impliedly and *pro tanto* repealed Section 2(2) of the EC Act. The judgment in *Factortame* could not be used as a precedent in this case, as this point about implied repeal had not been argued before the courts.

Lord Justice Laws[95] stated that there was no inconsistency between the 1985 Act and the EC Act 1972: *'Generally, there is no* inconsistency *between a provision conferring a Henry VIII power to amend future legislation and the terms of any such future legislation. One might hold the conferment of such a power, and its use, objectionable on constitutional grounds as giving to the executive what belongs to the legislature (..) But points of that kind do not rest on the doctrine of implied repeal'.*[96] Consequently, there was no issue of implied repeal. Laws J attempted to steer between the traditional model of parliamentary sovereignty and the principle of European supremacy, and held that Parliament's sovereignty resided not in its continuing unlimited power, but in its capacity to alter the terms of its delegation of powers. Parliament always retains the power to pass a statute stipulating that its terms are not to be touched by older Henry VIII powers.

In case he was wrong on the issue of the Henry VIII powers, he added that the EC Act had special status in British law, which does not follow from Community law itself or from the case law of the Court of Justice, but was instead founded on English law. He stated that *'Parliament cannot bind its successors by stipulating against repeal, wholly or partly, of the ECA. It cannot stipulate as to the manner and form of any subsequent legislation. It cannot stipulate against implied repeal any more than it can stipulate against express repeal. Thus there is nothing in the ECA which allows the Court of Justice, or any other institutions of the EU, to touch or qualify the conditions of Parliament's legislative supremacy in the United Kingdom. Not because the legislature chose not to allow it;* because by our law it could not allow it. *That being so, the legislative and judicial institutions of the EU cannot intrude upon those conditions. The British Parliament has not the authority to authorise any such thing. Being sovereign, it cannot abandon its sovereignty.* Accordingly there are no

---

[94] See also the analysis by A Perreau-Saussine, 'A tale of two supremacies, four greengrocers, a fishmonger, and the seeds of a constitutional court', (2002) *CLJ*, 527.

[95] The judgment was written by Lord Justice Laws, Mr Justice Crane agreeing.

[96] Sir John Laws, *metric martyrs* case, at marginal number 50.

circumstances in which the jurisprudence of the Court of Justice can elevate Community law to a status within the corpus of English domestic law to which it could not aspire by any route of English law itself. *This is, of course, the traditional doctrine of sovereignty. If is to be modified, it certainly cannot be done by the incorporation of external texts. The conditions of Parliament's legislative supremacy in the United Kingdom necessarily remain in the United Kingdom's hands. But the traditional doctrine has in my judgment been modified. It has been done by the common law, wholly consistently with constitutional principle'.*

Laws LJ then proceeded to state that the EC Act could not be impliedly repealed, and held that in the present state of its maturity, the common law recognised a hierarchy of Acts of Parliament, between ordinary statutes and constitutional statutes. The latter category included the Magna Carta, the Bill of Rights 1689, the Act of Union, the Human Rights Act, the Scotland Act 1998 and the Government of Wales Act 1998. The EC Act 1972 clearly belonged in this family. Now, these constitutional Acts could not be impliedly repealed: they could only be amended or repealed by unambiguous words on the face of the later statute. This development, Laws LJ continued, was highly beneficial: it gave Britain the benefits of a written constitution, while preserving the sovereignty of the legislature and the flexibility of the uncodified constitution. It was for the courts, in interpreting statutes and applying the constitutional acts, to pay more or less deference to the legislature, according to the subject at hand. Finally, Laws LJ also commented on what would happen in the event *'which no doubt would never happen in the real world, that a European measure was seen to be repugnant to a fundamental or constitutional right guaranteed by the law of England, a question would arise whether the general words of the EC Act were sufficient to incorporate the measure and give it overriding effect in domestic law'*[97]

The judgment was handed down by the High Court; it would have been interesting to find out what the House of Lords had to say about the issue, but it refused leave to appeal. The judgment is remarkable as it expresses in clear terms the position of many other national courts: Community law cannot by and of itself impose the supremacy of Community law, without any basis in national law. If Community law is indeed to have precedence and the courts are to enforce it, this must be because there is a national constitutional foundation for it. In essence, constitutional law has developed, so as to comply with the requirements of the precedence of Community law as proclaimed by the Court of Justice. But this, Laws LJ claimed, was first and foremost an achievement of the courts, which *'have found their way through the impasse seemingly*

---

[97] At marginal number 69. This point, which has to do with the constitutional limits to supremacy, will be developed further below, in Part 2.

created between two supremacies, the supremacy of European law and the supremacy of Parliament'.[98]

8.3.3. Italy

In Italy, the jurisdictional issue was critical especially during the intermediate phase between *Frontini* and *Granital*. In *Frontini*, the normative supremacy of Community law was accepted, by virtue of a limitation of sovereignty theory based on Article 11 of the Constitution. But in *ICIC* it appeared that this did not entail review powers in the hands of the ordinary courts: the Italian courts were obliged to refer conflicts between Italian and Community law to the *Corte costituzionale*, since it was regarded as a constitutional issue. The Italian constitutional court thus took the same view as the *Conseil d'Etat* in *semoules*, namely that an infringement of Community law amounted to an infringement of the Constitution.

The jurisdictional issue disappeared in Italy when the conception of the relationship between the Community and domestic legal order was redefined, but in contrast to the Belgian scenario, it took two steps to arrive at the result sought. In *ICIC*, the *Corte costituzionale* failed to draw all the necessary consequences from its perception of a separate and autonomous but co-ordinated legal orders. The idea was the following: the transfer of powers to the Community did not imply, in the devolved spheres of competence, the radical abolition of State sovereignty. Consequently, it followed that the national judge did not have the power to establish and declare a provision of national law void in relation to the provisions enacted in a Community regulation in so far as there was 'an absolute lack of competence for the national legislation'. In such circumstances, the Italian courts were required to make a reference to the *Corte costituzionale* concerning the possible unconstitutionality by reason of the violation of Article 11 of the Constitution.

In *Granital*, the Court did draw the full logical conclusions from its new doctrine.[99] Where the Italian judge establishes that a Community regulation deriving from another, separate and autonomous legal order governs the case before him, he must apply its provisions by exclusive reference to the legal system of the supranational organisation. In relation to those provisions of Community law, municipal law forms an order that does not seek to superimpose its control over the rules produced by the separate and autonomous Community system. Municipal law simply does not operate in the domain covered by such regulations. Consequently, the

---

[98] At marginal number 60.
[99] Oppenheimer, *The Cases*, at 649.

courts are allowed to effectively set aside primary legislation. They do not in fact declare such conflicting legislation void or even inapplicable. It simply does not apply to the case before them. The applicability of the statute was restricted even before the court entered the arena. Obviously this is an enigmatic way of presenting things, based on a fiction. But apparently, this was the only way for the *Corte costituzionale* to allow for review powers in the hands of the lower courts while at the same time remaining loyal to the established constitutional principles, and without giving up the dualist dogma.

8.3.4. Belgium

The jurisdictional issue also arose in Belgium, where under the 1925 judgment of the *Cour de cassation*, '*il appartient au législateur belge, lorsqu'il édicte des dispositions en exécution d'une convention internationale, d'apprécier la conformité des règles qu'il adopte avec les obligations liant la Belgique par traité; (..) les tribunaux n'ont pas le pouvoir de refuser d'appliquer une loi pour le motif qu'elle ne serait pas conforme, prétendument, à ses obligations (..)*'.[100] The courts did not have the power to control statutes, neither in the light of the Constitution, nor in the light of treaty provisions. The supremacy of the legislative power resulted in a rejection of all review powers in the hands of the courts. In his 1963 *mercuriale* Hayoit de Termicourt criticised the analogy made between the control of the constitutionality of statutes and review of their *conventionnalité*. To his mind, these were two different issues. The control of the constitutionality of statutes was rejected because the Legislature, sovereign in its field of competence, solely decides on the constitutionality of statutes. Yet, in the field of treaties, the Legislature does not act as a sovereign in the same way; it merely approves a document concluded by the King, and the legal force of treaties derives from the agreement between States, not from Parliament. The Legislature is the sovereign interpreter of the Constitution, not of treaties.[101]

The jurisdictional problem vanished automatically when the relationship between international treaties and national law was redefined. It is not expressly dealt with in the *Le Ski* judgment of the *Cour de cassation*, nor is it analysed extensively by *Procureur général* Ganshof van der Meersch in his Opinion: both concentrate fully on the legal orders doctrine. How then can it be explained, that while the refusal of judicial review was first and

---

[100] *Cour de cassation (B)*, decision of 26 November 1925, *Schieble, Pas.*, 1926, I, 76.
[101] See R Hayoit de Termicourt, 'Conflict tussen het verdrag en de interne wet', mercuriale uitgesproken op de plechtige openingszitting van het Hof van Cassatie op 2 september (1963) *RW*, 73, at 77–79.

foremost a jurisdictional issue, that problem disappeared once the nature and effect of treaty provisions in the Belgian legal order had been re-construed? Or, to rephrase the question, why did the *Cour de cassation* in *Le Ski* not seem to feel the same reluctance in terms of jurisdiction as the French *Conseil d'Etat* or even the French *Cour de cassation*, while in 1925, the jurisdictional issue appeared to be the crux of the problem? The answer is probably to be found in the different foundations of the supremacy of international treaties. For the French courts, supremacy of treaties is dealt with under Article 55 of the Constitution, but that article was considered not capable of simultaneously solving the jurisdictional issue. The Belgian Constitution, however, was silent on the relationship between national law and international conventions. In *Le Ski*, the supremacy of international treaties was attained on the grounds of the very nature of international law itself, deriving, amongst other considerations, from the liability which would entail for the State, if the courts did not ensure that domestic law would be compatible with rules of treaty law. States have the duty to ensure that domestic law complies with the obligations entered into by treaty. *'This duty, sanctioned by liability under international law'*, Ganshof van der Meersch said in his Opinion in *Le Ski, 'binds the legislator. It also binds the judge.'*[102] The power of the courts to review the compliance of national law, including primary legislation, would thus derive immediately from international law. The subjection of the State, and therefore of its laws, to international law has its basis in the international legal system. This subjection implies the primacy of the rule of international law over that of domestic law.[103] Once this internationalist approach is accepted, the jurisdictional issue falls. And Ganshof van der Meersch added: *'It is above all in the very nature of international law, as the Cour supérieure de Justice of the Grand Duchy of Luxembourg has pointed out,*[104] *that the judiciary may find justification for this primacy'.* And since the Constitution, the ultimate source of the mandate of the courts, did not prohibit such review, it must be accepted.[105] The traditional tenet that the courts do not review parliamentary legislation no longer seemed to form an obstacle. In addition, the Belgian *Cour de cassation* did not have to confront the same problem as the *Corte costituzionale*, namely that of a review monopoly.

Le *Ski* was widely accepted, but its few critics mainly focussed on the jurisdictional issue, and argued that it infringed the fundamental principles

---

[102] Opinion of *Procureur général* Ganshof van der Meersch in *Cour de cassation (B)*, decision of 27 May 1971, *Franco-suisse le Ski*, in Oppenheimer, *The Cases*, 245, at 251.
[103] Above, at 252.
[104] In its *Pagani* judgment of 1954.
[105] There is an inconsistency in the fact that the statement on the Constitution is added: if the supremacy of international law and the courts' review powers are derived from international law itself, then it does not matter what the Constitution says. It has become irrelevant in this respect.

of Belgian constitutional law, or at least, that the jurisdictional dilemma had been neglected in the judgment.[106] What, then, is the basis for the courts' jurisdiction to review statutes in the light of directly effective provisions of the Constitution? Some argue that, since the *Cour de cassation* accepted supremacy on the basis of the very nature of international law, the mandate has its source in international law. However, attention was also paid to the fact that the Constitution did not prohibit treaty provisions from being awarded precedence. This should not however matter: if international law takes precedence of itself, and because of its very nature as higher law, what the Constitution says or does not say has become irrelevant. But at the end of the day, the *Cour de cassation* achieved a silent revision of the Constitution, which now includes a judicial mandate to review statutes in the light of treaties.

8.3.5. Final Remarks

The *Simmenthal* mandate was thus accepted in all Member States, but in some the process of acceptance was more difficult than in others. For instance, while in Belgium the jurisdictional issue appeared to evaporate in the face of a new conception of the relationship between the international legal order including Community law, and the national legal order, this was not the case in Italy, where the *Corte costituzionale* continued to struggle with the lack of jurisdiction for the ordinary courts reviewing primary legislation. The French *Conseil d'État* proved much less willing to co-operate than its counterparts in other countries, and what is more surprising, than its brethren in France, *Conseil constitutionnel* and *Cour de cassation*. Nevertheless, at the end of the day, all achieved the result required by the Court of Justice, at least in practical effect. All courts have achieved the result required on their own, without intervention from the political organs or the constitutional legislature.

As a result, all courts have now acquired judicial review powers, at least in the context of Community law. Yet, while this may have been new in most Member States, the acceptance of these review powers is often not restricted to Community law alone. In the Netherlands and France, Community law has triggered the application of the constitutional

[106] See *e.g.* R Senelle, 'De onschendbaarheid van de wet', (1971) *RW*, 641, and the ensuing discussion, H Rolin in (1971) *RW*, 876 and R Senelle, (1971) *RW*, 1127 and 1515; see also NJ Bricout, 'De l'ordre juridique européen', (1974) *JT*, 544; NJ Bricout, 'Blijft de wet onschendbaar?', (1974–75) *RW*, 2195; a Bill was tabled in Parliament to introduce a reference system to Parliament whenever a court was confronted with a conflict between a statute and a treaty, based on the assumption that it was Parliament, not the courts, who should control statutes and their compatibility with treaties, see for a discussion of the Bill, J-V Louis, 'Le droit belge et l'ordre juridique international', (1972) *JT*, 437.

provisions, which allow for judicial review in the light of directly effective treaty law. At the end of the day, the ECHR may even be more routinely applied than Community law. In both countries, review in the light of Community law, the ECHR and other international treaties operates as a substitute for full-fledged constitutional review, which is still considered to be outside the natural province of the courts. Hence, treaties are better enforced than the Constitution; vice versa, individuals may find better protection, even as before the domestic courts, in international documents, than in the national Constitution. In Belgium, where the Constitutional revision was not restricted to Community law, review in the light of the ECHR, Community law and other international treaties by all Belgian courts now operates alongside constitutional review by the *Cour d'arbitrage*. In Germany and Italy, the ECHR does not operate as a 'substitute-Constitution' or a basis for judicial review in the hands of the ordinary courts. These countries have a mature system of constitutional review by a constitutional court which acts as the guardian of the Constitution and protector of fundamental rights. The Simmenthal mandate remains restricted, in those systems, to Community law: the ECHR and other international documents do not play the same role as for instance in The Netherlands, France and Belgium.

9

Explaining Acceptance

IT HAS BEEN mentioned before that the Court of Justice may say what it wants, but the important question was why the courts would take heed. The national courts *have* heeded, and the ordinary supremacy of Community law and the *Simmenthal* mandate were widely accepted in all Member States by the late eighties, often requiring from the national courts a great deal of creativity, and sometimes even courage. *Why* have they done it? Why have they accepted the *Simmenthal* mandate if it was so difficult under national constitutional law? Why has it been so much more difficult for some courts than for others? There is almost twenty years between *Le Ski* and *Nicolo*, and even more between *Van Gend en Loos* and *Factortame*. And why are some better than others at complying with the Court's case law? Why do some courts accept supremacy unconditionally and on the basis of the very nature of Community law, while others continue to refer to a constitutional basis and impose limits on the supremacy of Community law? Several explanations have been suggested, all of which are particularly correct, and must be taken together in order to be convincing. In this Chapter, each of these explanations of acceptance will be considered and discussed in turn.

9.1. 'LEGALIST' EXPLANATIONS

'Legalist approaches explain judicial behaviour in legal integration based on legal logic and legal reasoning. EC law is seen as having an inherent legal logic which creates its own internal dynamic of expansion, compelling the ECJ to render legal decisions which promote integration, and compelling national courts to apply the ECJ's jurisprudence. . . . legalist approaches see national judiciaries as having been convinced by legal arguments of the validity of the supremacy of EC law over national law, and of the importance of national courts applying the supreme EC law in their own jurisprudence'.[1] These explanations have been criticised by sociologists and political

---

[1] This is how Karen Alter describes the essence of 'legalist explanations', in K Alter, 'Explaining National Court Acceptance of European Court Jurisprudence: A Critical Evaluation of Theories of Legal Integration', in A-M Slaugther *et al* (eds), *The European Court and National Courts – Doctrine and Jurisprudence. Legal Change in Its Social Context* (Oxford, Hart Publishing, 1998) 227, at 20.

scientists as naive and as being based on the short-sightedness of lawyers, who look at legal rules and legal logic only and turn a blind eye to the political and social context.[2] It is submitted that there is more truth in legalist explanations than political scientists want us to believe: legal argument is not simply there just to cover up policy arguments. In most cases where a court sets aside national legislation in favour of directly effective Community law, it is not concerned with higher goals of European integration, with keeping down the Government or with controlling Parliament: it is simply applying 'the law' *as it interprets it*. The sting is of course in the tail. Why did courts re-interpret the law so as to make it possible to comply with the case law of the Court of Justice? And why was that so much easier in some countries than in others? However, even this is not purely determined by non-legal arguments. Legal arguments are at least as important, and, it is submitted, are even central, albeit that they must be put in a wider legal and political and social context.

The main 'legalist' explanation is that the national courts were truly convinced by the Court of Justice that Community law should indeed be awarded precedence over conflicting parliamentary legislation, since Community law imposes it because of its very nature, and the aims of European integration, and because the Treaty implicitly says so. It is submitted that herein lies much of the explanation, perhaps not for the methods and techniques applied by the national courts to actually arrive at the conclusion, but in any case for the fact that they went out of their way to reach the result sought, *i.e.* the *Simmenthal*-mandate. Why might it not be true? Could the explanation not simply be that the Court of Justice indeed succeeded in convincing the national courts that Community law must be awarded precedence in order for the Community to have any chance of succeeding in achieving a common market? The Court was right or at least perceived to be right, and formulated its position in such convincing manner in well drafted decisions,[3] that its audience was swayed. After all, it was the first time that an international court – which the Court was and is – imposed the supremacy of a treaty and the law deriving from it and ordered all organs of the State including the courts to comply with the Treaty.[4] In con-

---

2   K Alter, *Establishing the Supremacy of European Law. The Making of an International Rule of Law in Europe* (Oxford, OUP, 2001); M Shapiro, 'Comparative law and Comparative Politics', (1980) 53 *Southern California Law Review*, 537.

3   At least at first sight. A thorough analysis of the judgments in questions may prove otherwise, but the critique of the landmark judgments will centre on the reasons adduced for the creation of the new legal order and the supremacy, not on the message contained in them that in order for the project to be successful, Community law must take precedence, and courts must be involved in the enforcement of Community law and the protection of individual rights. The Court was less successful, say, in the case of direct effect of directives, for which it had to find alternative reasoning since its first decisions were not convincing. This is developed further below.

4   E Stein, 'Toward Supremacy of Treaty – Constitution by Judicial Fiat in the European Economic Community', (1965) *Riv.dir.int.*, 3.

trast to classic international law, where infringements of international obligations may only lead to the liability of the State being established *ex post facto*, the Court of Justice could, by virtue of the preliminary rulings procedure, 'stop the clock' and intervene at an earlier stage, clarifying the obligations of all the State organs under the Community treaties. And if the Member States wanted to achieve a common market, they must comply with the obligations entered into by the Treaty: *Pacta sunt servanda*. The argument seems to imply that there was no need for the Court to insist on the special nature of the Community legal order and to contrast it to ordinary international treaties. The same is suggested by the reaction of some the national courts which accepted the *Simmenthal* mandate as part of a wider acceptance of judicial power to enforce all directly effective treaty provisions, as was the case in Belgium,[5] in France and in The Netherlands.[6] Nevertheless, even for those countries, it seems fair to say that the Court of Justice did convince the courts in the context of Community law to assume review powers, and triggered a wider revolution, which the courts, on the basis of their constitutional mandate (French *Cour de cassation* and much later also the *Conseil d'état* and The Netherlands) or the very nature of international law (Belgium), extended to treaties in general. These courts *were* convinced by the reasoning of the Court of Justice,[7] possibly in two ways: first, as the international court confirming that treaties take precedence and that it is indeed for courts to do what the Constitution (The Netherlands and France) or international law (Belgium) imply. And second, this is *a fortiori* (Belgium) the case for Community law, to an extent even that the Constitution no longer matters (The Netherlands).

Also for the courts in other countries, Germany and later the United Kingdom, it seems that the courts, including the *Bundesverfassungsgericht*, were convinced at least that Community law *should* be awarded precedence if European integration was to be a success. The same is true for several courts even before they did actually accept the full consequences of supremacy: the *Corte costituzionale*,[8] the French *Conseil d'État*[9] and the English courts did accept the normative supremacy of Community law (and acknowledged it) but there were other legal arguments which were in the beginning considered to form insurmountable obstacles preventing the acceptance of the *Simmenthal*-mandate.

Yet, there is an even simpler explanation, which has to do less with the actual content of case law of the Court and the quality of its decisions, and

---

[5]   *Le Ski* only happened to be an EC law case, but the acceptance of the review powers was wider.

[6]   In both countries, the *effective* acceptance of the constitutional mandate applied to all treaties, not only Community law.

[7]   Several courts have either explicitly referred to *Costa v ENEL* and *Simmenthal* or have paraphrased it.

[8]   In *Frontini*.

[9]   Mme Questiaux in *Semoules*.

rather with the mere fact that the Court has spoken. Indeed, under Article 220 EC (old Article 164) the Court of Justice has been given jurisdiction to interpret the Treaty and to ensure that in the interpretation and application of the Treaty the law is observed. Now, if this Court interprets the Treaty and Community law as able to produce direct effects and more importantly as being supreme over national law also before the national courts, that interpretation is binding on the national courts. Indeed, in *Van Gend en Loos* and *Costa v ENEL*, the Court referred to Article 5 of the EEC Treaty, and Articles 177 and 189 of the EEC Treaty, as grounds for the supremacy of Community law. It follows from the authoritative interpretation of those provisions, according to the Court, that Community law is to take precedence over conflicting legislation even before the domestic courts. Whether the latter agree with that interpretation or not, they are under the Treaty bound by the interpretation of the Court. This simple fact that national courts are bound by the case law of the Court of Justice and feel bound by it, also accounts for the rebellion of lower courts against their own national highest courts which did not respect the European Court, such as in the case of the *pretore* rebelling against the *Corte costituzionale* in *Simmenthal*.

9.2. JUDICIAL DIALOGUE

The preliminary rulings procedure and the judicial dialogue it generates provides many examples of how national courts are indeed convinced by the Court of Justice. The case law on the Community mandate is the result of a continuing dialogue between the national courts and the Court of Justice. The national courts make references, asking the Court to refine the mandate, to clarify what is required in a particular case, and often also indicate to the Court what constitutional problems they may experience in applying the mandate. *Simmenthal*, *Factortame* and *Brasserie* are the most obvious and famous examples, but there are many more, such as *Lück*, *IN.CO.GE '90* etc. The national courts participate in the formulation of the mandate, which may well make it easier to 'swallow'.

Vital in this dialogue (or multilogue)[10] is of course the preliminary rulings procedure. This procedure which was and is unique in international organisations, allows the national courts confronted with an issue of Community law to call in the assistance of the Court of Justice. In some cases, of courts of final instance or where the validity of a measure of Community law is doubted, a reference is even obligatory. Of course, the national courts must be willing to make these references. It is very easy to

---

[10] JHH Weiler, 'Journey to an Unknown Destination: A Retrospective and Prospective of the European Court of Justice in the Arena of Political Integration', (1993) 31 *JCMS*, 417, at 419.

duck the application of Community law by stating that Community law does not apply to the case, denying that it has direct effect, by simply not making the reference or even by making the issue of Community law disappear and solving the case on the basis of national law. It is a well-known fact that courts at times make an overly broad application of the theory of *acte clair*, or adduce other reasons why there is no need to refer a question for preliminary ruling. There may be several reasons for avoiding having to make a reference. First, it is a time consuming venture to suspend the case, make the reference and await the answer from Luxembourg: it will take on average almost two years for a case to return to the referring court.[11] Courts may feel that the reference to Luxembourg is excessively lengthy, and what is worse, they may be right. Second, it does happen at times that the answers from the Court of Justice are incomplete or cannot be used in the final judgment to be handed by the referring court. Sometimes the Court neglects to answer all questions.[12] Sometimes the answer does not entirely fit the case or does not take account of all the details of the national legal system; sometimes it is not sufficiently clear for the national court to solve the case at hand. All the court can do in such a case is make a new reference, or seek the correct answer of their own motion. But these courts may be less willing to make a reference the next time. In some cases, the Court of Justice is so complete in its answer that it solves the case for the national court: the Court does not always respect the principle that the application to the concrete case at hand is the responsibility of the national court. It does make it easier on national courts though, and some courts may even prefer over-complete answer. Furthermore, the Court has since the 1990's set out tougher standards of scrutiny when reviewing the appropriateness of references, and has posed conditions on the references made: they must contain adequate information, the procedure must not be diverted from its true purpose and must not be used to answer hypothetical or contrived disputes.[13] The Court has also declined jurisdiction in several cases. In the Information Note on References by

---

[11] According to the ECJ's Annual Reports, the average length for a preliminary rulings procedure before the ECJ was 22,7 months in 2001; 21,6 in 2000; 21,2 in 1999. These Reports are accessible on www.curia.eu.int.

[12] A famous example is Case C–213/89 *The Queen v Secretary of State for Transport, ex parte Factortame and Others* [1990] ECR I–2433 where the ECJ did not answer the question relating to the conditions for interim relief under Community law; see also Case C–65/98 *Safet Eyüp v Landesgeschäftsstelle des Arbeitsmarktservice Vorarlberg* [2000] ECR I–4747, as reported by the Austrian *Verwaltungsgerichtshof*, in General Report on the colloquium subject 'The Preliminary Reference to the Court of Justice of the European Communities', 18th Colloquium of the Association of the Councils of State and Supreme Administrative Jurisdictions of the European Union, Helsinki (May 2002), available on www.raadvst-consetat.be, at 37; the report also mentions other cases in which the national referring courts were not entirely satisfied with the answer from the ECJ.

[13] See C Barnard and E Sharpston, 'The Changing Face of Article 177 References', (1997) 34 *CMLRev* 1113.

National Courts for Preliminary Rulings, it is stated that the reference must contain a statement of reasons which is succinct but sufficiently complete to give the Court and all those involved a clear understanding of the legal and factual context of the main proceedings. It must include an account of the essential facts of the case, of the points of law which may apply, a statement of the reasons that prompted the court to make the reference and, if need be, a summary of the arguments of the parties. The reference must also be accompanied by documents needed for a proper understanding of the case, including the national legal texts involved. The reason why the Court has become more demanding is, so it says, because it wants to give an answer that is of assistance to the national court. But the Court has also become stricter in respect of its own jurisdiction in preliminary rulings, as an element of docket control. The Court is inundated with references, and this will for obvious reasons become worse after the accession of new members and with the ever growing area of Community and Union law. The stricter scrutiny of references may in itself have that effect, as national courts whose references are sent back as inadmissible will hardly be encouraged to make new references.

Sometimes there will be other reasons for not sending a reference. One has to do with control over a case: The refusal to make a reference may well be an indication of the national court's disagreement with the case law of the Court of Justice. The *Conseil d'État's* use of the *acte clair* doctrine is legendary.[14] But less well-known are some more recent instances. The House of Lords refusal in the *Three Rivers District Council* case may well have to do with the fear that under the strict application of the Community rules on State liability, the United Kingdom would have to pay the damage incurred by the investors.[15] And would the statement of the *Bundesgerichtshof* in the case of the *Fleischhygienegesetz*, that it did not concern a question of Community law but should be decided under national law, have been intended to circumvent the application of *Brasserie* and/or a reference to Luxembourg?[16]

The preliminary rulings procedure rests on a careful balance of competences and responsibilities between the Court of Justice and the national courts. The procedure appears to be successful since courts from all

---

[14] According to the report submitted to the Association of Councils of State and Supreme Administrative Jurisdictions of the European Union to the 2002 colloquium on preliminary references, the *Conseil d'état* applied the *acte clair* theory on 191 occasions between 1978 and 2001, see General Report on the colloquium subject 'The Preliminary Reference to the Court of Justice of the European Communities', 18th Colloquium of the Association of the Councils of State and Supreme Administrative Jurisdictions of the European Union, Helsinki, May 2002, available on www.raadvstconsetat.be, at 23.

[15] *House of Lords*, decision of 18 May 2000, *Three Rivers District Council and others v The Governor and Company of the Bank of England* [2000] CMLR 205; www.bailii.org. The case is discussed in Chapter 11.

[16] *Bundesgerichtshof*, decision of 14 December 2000, *Fleischhygienegesetz*, BGHZ 146, 153; available on www.bundesgerichtshof.de. The case is discussed in Chapter 11.

Member States and from all levels make use of it,[17] to an extent even that it has been said that the procedure is the victim of its own success, and is in need of reform.[18]

9.3. THE WIDER CONTEXT: NATIONAL CONSTITUTIONAL LAW ON TREATIES

It has already been demonstrated that when the Court of Justice handed down judgment in *Van Gend en Loos*, there was a changing mood in national constitutional law concerning the domestic effects of treaties. The Luxembourg courts had already gone all the way and accepted a *Simmenthal* type mandate for all international agreements. The Netherlands and French Constitutions had been amended to include constitutional provisions to that effect. In Belgium, the issue was debated in literature and by various successive *procureurs généraux*. The post-war Constitutions of Italy and Germany contained openness and transfer of powers provisions, which in their own way proved an increased awareness of international law in the domestic legal order.

The evolution has continued to date, though it is difficult to distinguish cause and effect: has Community law been accepted as part of a wider acceptance of the primordial effect of treaty law, or alternatively, has the wider acceptance been triggered by the 'example' of Community law. There is probably some truth in both propositions: it has been a mutually reinforcing development. Judicial review of primary legislation in the light of treaties, especially human rights treaties, by Netherlands, French and Belgian courts has even developed into an alternative (in The Netherlands) or an addition (Belgium and France) to constitutional review by a constitutional court. In The Netherlands, this type of review is even presented as the main reason why there is no need for the introduction of constitutional judicial review. In recent years, the ECHR has been given increased effect, by incorporation in the Human Rights Act 1998 in the United Kingdom and incorporation in Denmark in 1992,[19] and in Sweden in 1994.[20]

---

[17] This will not be further analysed. Studies have been conducted on the question as to which courts make references more frequently, and why and so on. See e.g. A Stone Sweet and TL Brunnell, 'The European Court of Justcie and the National Courts: A Statistical Analysis of Preliminary References, 1961–95'; J Golub, 'The Politics of Judicial Discretion: Rethinking the Interaction between National Courts and the European Court of Justice', (1996) 19 *West European Politics*, 360.

[18] See the official documents of the Court of Justice on www.curia.eu.int; see also H Rasmussen, 'Remedying the Crumbling Judicial System', (2000) 37 *CML Rev* 1071; G de Búrca and JHH Weiler (eds), *The European Court of Justice*, (Oxford, OUP, 2001); A Dashwood and A Johnston (eds), *The Future of the Judicial System of the European Union*, (Oxford, Hart Publishing, 2001).

[19] JA Jensen, 'Human Rights in Danish Law', (2001) 7 *EPL*, 1.

[20] See U Bernitz, 'Sweden and the European Union: On Sweden's Implementation and Application of European law', (2001) 38 *CML Rev* 903, at 929.

Courts have also in other respects become more involved with treaty law than before. Of course there is a proliferation of international treaties, and more and more areas of law are in addition (partly) regulated by international agreements. There is a general decline in the application of the one voice principle,[21] of the 'act of state' doctrine. Courts are no longer 'afraid' of international treaties, and are willing to interpret and apply them. Community law, for which the national courts can call in the assistance of the Court of Justice, has been a field for practice.[22]

9.4. THE WIDER CONTEXT: THE GENERAL INCREASE OF CONSTITUTIONAL REVIEW

When the Court of Justice handed down judgment in *Van Gend en Loos* and *Costa v ENEL*, only two out of six national systems contained a full-fledged constitutional court,[23] while in none of the Member States could the ordinary courts conduct constitutional review of primary legislation. Today, an additional three of the original six now have a constitutional court,[24] leaving only The Netherlands (of the Original Six) outside this evolution. Of the 'new' Member States, Ireland, Denmark, and later also Greece and Sweden[25] have a system of diffuse constitutional review.

---

[21] Under the one voice principle, in the field of foreign affairs the executive and the courts should speak with one voice; on the decline of the principle in English law, see L Collins, 'Foreign Relations and the Judiciary', (2002) 51 *ICLQ*, 85.

[22] See *eg* the statement by Lord Woolf in his Speech held at the Solemn hearing of the European Court of Human Rights on the occasion of the opening of the judicial year 2003, available on www.echr. coe.int, where he states that the application of the Human Rights Act and the case law of the ECtHR benefit from the practice the courts have had with Community law, with the support of the ECJ.

[23] By 1963–64 the *Conseil constitutionnel* had not yet developed into a 'real' constitutional court. It could only be seized preventively, by the President, the Prime Minister or the presidents of either chamber, and did not take into account fundamental rights. Milestones were the 1971 decision of the *Conseil constitutionnel* to include fundamental rights in the *bloc de constitutionalité, Conseil constitutionnel*, decision 71–44 of 16 July 1971, *liberté d'association*, www.conseil-constitutionnel.fr; and the 1974 constitutional amendment to allow a group of 60 deputies or senators to seize the *Conseil* (Article 61(2) of the Constitution).

[24] The *Conseil constitutionnel* has to a considerable extent developed into a constitutional court, be it still with certain limitations: for instance, it still does not deal with cases or controversies and cannot be seized by individuals. The Belgian *Cour d'arbitrage* was set up in 1983 as a 'semi-constitutional' court but would soon extend its jurisdiction; finally the Luxembourg *Cour constitutionnelle* was established in 1996. The constitutional courts and their relationship with Community law will be analysed in Part 2.

[25] Chapter 11, Section 14 of *Regeringsformen* states that 'If a court or other public body finds that a provision conflicts with a rule of fundamental law or other superior statute, or finds that a procedure laid down in law has been disregarded in any important respect when the provision was made, the provision may not be applied. If the provision has been approved by the Riksdag or by the Government, however, it shall be waived only if the error in manifest', translation taken from the official website of the Swedish Parliament www.riksdagen.se/english/work.fundamental/government/government/htm.

Spain and Portugal[26] set up a constitutional court as part of their new Constitutions after the fall of authoritarian regimes, while Austria has the oldest constitutional court in Europe. In the United Kingdom, the courts have been given a role in the Human Rights Act 1998, while the Privy Council has been modified in the context of Scottish devolution. In the new Finnish Constitution of 2000 responsibility for the supervision of constitutionality is shared between a special committee in Parliament,[27] and all courts.[28] At the end of the day, almost all of the national systems include some form of judicial review of primary legislation outside the framework of international law, with the sole exception of The Netherlands.[29] Looking at the *level of activity* of these constitutional courts and courts having constitutional jurisdiction, the past decades have shown an increase in cases being brought and being decided. The dockets of the constitutional courts are becoming crowded. Also in countries like Denmark[30] where the jurisdiction of the courts to review legislation existed for many years only in theory, it has started to be exercised effectively.

It is difficult to explain why there has been a general trend of increased constitutional review in Europe, and why there is an increase in the recourse to courts to decide constitutional issues. The following non-legal elements may help to explain this tendency. There is a wider and more general upgrade of the role of law *tout court* in society. There is an increase in legal norms and rules; entire new bodies of law have emerged over the past decades, or have made a quantum leap, such as environmental law, consumer protection as a species of contract law, and so on. Citizens have become much more litigious, they organise themselves in pressure groups

---

[26] This does not exclude constitutional review by the ordinary courts.

[27] Section 74 of the new Finnish Constitution of 1999 'supervision of constitutionality' states that 'The Constitutional Law Committee' [a parliamentary committee] shall issue statements on the constitutionality of legislative proposals and other matters brought for its consideration, as well as on their relation to international human rights treaties', translation taken from the official site of the Ministry of Justice www.om.fi/constitution/3340.htm. This is the old system, leaving responsibility for the constitutionality of Acts of Parliament with parliament itself. The Constitution entered into force on 1 March 2000.

[28] Section 106 'primacy of the Constitution' reads: 'If, in a matter being tried by a court of law, the application of an Act would be in evident conflict with the Constitution, the court of law shall give primacy to the provision of the Constitution', translation taken from www.om.fi/constitution/3340. htm. This new provision constitutes a break with the tradition of prohibiting the courts to pronounce themselves on the constitutionality of Acts of Parliament. The system chosen in Section 106 was considered to represent the least invasive break with this tradition; the courts cannot make a general assessment in principle as to whether an Act is unconstitutional, but they can now set it aside in a concrete case. The creation of a separate constitutional court was considered to constitute too great a departure from the prevailing principles, and was accordingly rejected. See the discussion of the New Constitution, its history and implications virtual.finland.fi.

[29] The issue of constitutional review of Acts of Parliament remains hotly disputed and is on the parliamentary agenda; see below on the proposal Halsema introduced in 2002.

[30] See the evidence presented in JA Jensen, 'Human Rights in Danish law', (2001) 7 *EPL*, 1.

and interest groups which bring cases. Human and/or fundamental rights have developed into judicially enforceable rights, in ever wider fields. At the same time, there is a general waning in confidence in government and in Parliaments. The role of Parliaments is declining:[31] they are controlled by government and pressure groups; they have lost powers to Europe; and in several countries recourse to governmental or subordinate legislation has increased accordingly. Several of the Member States have been federalised, requiring an independent arbitrator to supervise the division of powers between co-equal entities. Finally, the courts may simply have done a good job, or at least be perceived as having done so: even with respect to the most controversial political issues and the most sensitive societal problems, the courts operate and are perceived as operating as neutral and honourable institutions, which have probably retained much of their authority, more so, possibly, than governments and Parliaments.[32] These developments reflect or translate into an increase in the role of courts, and in the prestige and self-confidence of the judiciary.

9.5. THE EMPOWERMENT THESIS

According to the empowerment thesis, normative acceptance of the Court's constitutional construct, as well as the use of the preliminary rulings procedure which made it all possible, was rooted in plain and simple judicial empowerment: *'Lower courts and their judges were given the facility to engage with the highest jurisdiction in the Community and, even more remarkable, to gain the power of judicial review over the executive and legislative branches, even in those jurisdictions where such power was weak and non-existent'.*[33] It cannot be denied that empowerment *vis-à-vis* the legislature[34] has been the effect of the acceptance of the *Simmenthal* mandate.[35] Parliamentary legislation can be and is set aside even by the most inferior court. However,

---

[31] See for instance C Flinterman, AW Heringa and L Waddington (eds), *The Evolving Role of Parliaments in Europe* (Antwerp, Maklu, 1994).

[32] There are, obviously, some exceptions to this tendency, for instance, the Belgian courts suffered a serious blow in confidence after the *affaire* Dutroux. In addition, confidence in courts and their neutrality may suffer temporary lows after controversial decisions.

[33] JHH Weiler, 'Journey to an Unknown Destination: A Retrospective and Prospective of the European Court of Justice in the Arena of Political Integration', (1993) 31 *JCMS*, 417, at 425. Weiler's argument goes beyond the simple empowerment thesis and also includes a reference to the inter-court competition argument, see below.

[34] In the context of the *Simmenthal* mandate the executive is left out of the equation.

[35] This has been confirmed recently for one of the newest Member States, Sweden, in U Bernitz, 'Sweden and the European Union: On Sweden's Implementation and Application of European Law', (2001) 38 *CML Rev* 903, at 923: *'[T]he accession to the EU can be said to have upgraded the role of the law in Sweden and the importance of the judiciary. This is an important part of the explanation why judges, practising lawyers and academics in Sweden normally take a positive attitude towards Community law'*, thus accepting the explanatory strength of the argument.

even if empowerment may be the *consequence* of the acceptance of *Simmenthal*, it is submitted that in most cases it does not have a strong *explanatory* value of why the courts have accepted these review powers. There are several flaws in the argument.[36] The argument presumes that courts like power, and are eager to extend it, which, it is submitted, is not self-evident.[37] But would the courts, who have been educated in the orthodoxy of the supremacy of parliamentary legislation and the subordination of the courts to the primary legislature, really be eager to assume such radical new powers and responsibilities? Would not many judges feel rather uneasy about setting aside primary legislation? Even though the cases involving a Community law aspect are becoming more and more frequent, they continue to represent the minority of cases. In cases containing a Community law aspect, the European card is not always played, sometimes because the parties did not play it, at other times, because the courts prefer to solve the case on the basis of familiar national law.[38] Community law has its own logic, words have their own meaning, it may even disrupt the structure of the national system.[39] There are many reasons why a national court would rather shy away from this new 'power'. The responsibility that comes with power may not be such an attractive asset.

Second, the empowerment thesis fails to explain why 'power-minded' courts would grasp Community law as the means to expand their power *vis-à-vis* the legislature. There are other opportunities in systems lacking constitutional review of primary legislation to extend the involvement of courts by a judicial re-interpretation of their own powers: recourse to general principles, for instance, natural law, or, in the Netherlands, the *Statuut van het Koninkrijk*. If courts were so eager to expand their own powers, why choose Community law, which is mostly rather down-to-earth,

---

[36] See also K Alter, 'Explaining National Court Acceptance of European Court Jurisprudence: A Critical Evaluation of Theories of Legal Integration', in *The European Court and National Courts – Doctrine and Jurisprudence. Legal Change in Its Social Context* (Oxford, Hart Publishing, 1998) 227, at 20.

[37] Of course, again, it may well be true in some cases.

[38] See for instance the statement of Henchy J in *High Court (Ireland)*, decision of 26 April 1983, *Doyle v An Taoiseach* [1986] ILRM 693; available also on www.irlii.org: '*In my judgment the dispute between the parties is susceptible of a conclusive determination under the domestic law of this State. I consider that a decision on a question of Community law as envisaged by Article 177 of the Treaty of Rome is not necessary to enable this Court to give judgment in this case. Just as it is generally undesirable to decide a case by bringing provisions of the Constitution into play for the purpose of invalidating a impugned law when the case may be decided without [this], so also, in my opinion, should Community law, which also has the paramount force and effect of constitutional provisions, not be applied save where necessary for the decision of the case'*. The Court struck down the statutory instrument on the basis of unreasonableness without considering whether there was also a breach of Treaty obligations. See G Hogan and G Whyte, *Kelly's The Irish Constitution*, 3rd edn, (Dublin, Butterworths) 293–94.

[39] See for instance C Bollen, 'Verknoeit het Europees recht ook ons bestuursrecht? Terugvordering van in strijd met het Europese recht door de overheid verleende steun', in MA Heldeweg *et al* (eds), *Uit de school geklapt? Opstellen uit Maastricht* (Den Haag, Dsu, 1999) 39.

technical, and often does not ask from the courts a participation in the real shaping of society on fundamental areas of life? Community law, especially in the early days, was mainly about import duties and licences. The argument admittedly cuts both ways: the 'limited importance' of Community law in terms of subject matter in many concrete cases ('low politics') combined with its high impact on daily life may at the same time explain precisely why the courts chose Community law. However, this does not have to do with empowerment as an explanation. Rather, it explains how the courts were able to accept this type of empowerment precisely because it did not involve lofty principles and remained a fairly limited empowerment.

Finally, in many Member States, the courts were well aware of the empowerment accompanying the *Simmenthal* mandate. However, instead of convincing them to use these new powers, empowerment was precisely the reason why they did not act upon it, and went out of their way not to have to take it to its fullest consequences: conform interpretation, for example, is a natural reflex of courts attempting to avoid direct clashes and the need to actually interfere. It is a technique used in the context of Community law review and in the context of constitutional review alike, and is an expression of the supremacy of the Legislature. In many cases the ordinary courts waited for the blessing of the constitutional court (France)[40] or the supreme court (Belgium) before they assumed the new power under Community law, or continued to refer questions to the Court of Justice. It is as if they really had to be convinced to assume the review powers in the first place, and still are reluctant to 'go it alone' and refer questions to the Court of Justice.

9.6.   THE INTER-COURT COMPETITION ARGUMENT

The explanation favoured by Karen Alter is the notion of inter-court competition, whereby the lower courts use Community law and the preliminary rulings procedure to side-step the highest national court.[41] *'Lower courts can use EC law to get to legal outcomes which they prefer either for policy or*

---

[40]   In the extreme case, the *Bundesverfassungsgericht* has had to force Community law upon the *Bundesfinanzhof* by translating the duty to refer questions to the Court of Justice into a constitutional obligation.

[41]   For instance K Alter, 'Explaining National Court Acceptance of European Court Jurisprudence: A Critical Evaluation of Theories of Legal Integration', in A-M Slaughter et al (eds), *The European Court and National Courts – Doctrine and Jurisprudence. Legal Change in its Social Context* (Oxford, Hart Publishing, 1998) 227, at 241: *'The inter-court competition explanation claims that different courts have different interests vis-à-vis EC law, and that national courts use EC law in bureaucratic struggles between levels of judiciary and between the judiciary and political bodies, thereby inadvertently facilitating the process of legal integration'* see also her *Establishing the Supremacy of European Law. The Making of an International Rule of Law in Europe*, (Oxford, OUP, 2001).

257

for legal reasons, by using an appeal to the ECJ to challenge established jurisprudence and to circumvent higher court jurisprudence'.[42] There may be some truth in the argument, and there certainly have been instances, not least in the case of the *pretore* in *Costa v ENEL*, of lower courts who side-step the highest court, or even second guess it and align with the Court of Justice. The question in *Costa* was sent by the *pretore* after the *Corte costituzionale* had handed down its decision denying review powers for any Italian court in the light of Community law. *Van Gend en Loos* and *Simmenthal* were also sent by lower courts. *Factortame*, however, came from the House of Lords itself. And the reference in *Van Gend en Loos* can hardly be explained as an act of rebellion of a lower court against a higher court. *Costa v ENEL* and *Simmenthal*, on the other hand, do fit the inter-court competition explanation.

However, the inter-court competition argument has its flaws: it does not explain why the lower courts in other countries in many cases did *not* accept *Costa v ENEL* and *Simmenthal* until they had been accepted by the highest court. It does not take account of the fact that lower courts' decisions can still be overruled by higher courts, which the party losing the case would seek and which a lower court will usually seek to avoid. The argument cannot explain why, in those cases where the highest courts were reluctant to assume the review powers, for instance the French *Conseil d'État* or the House of Lords, the lower courts did not rebel against the highest courts and accept the *Simmenthal* mandate on their own motion.[43]

9.7. CROSS-FERTILISATION

National courts watch each others moves, both within the domestic legal system and across national boundaries. There are sufficient examples of courts referring to what happens in other countries, or in other branches of the judicial system. The French *Conseil d'État* was finally convinced in 1989 when it had become isolated in France and in Europe. While the European isolation may only have served to increase the peer pressure on the *Conseil d'État* to accept *Simmenthal*, the case law of the *Cour de cassation* and especially the *Cour constitutionnelle* proved that its position had become untenable not only from a policy point of view, but more importantly from a legal point of view. How could it maintain that the conflict statute-treaty amounted to a constitutional issue, when the *Cour constitutionnel* had declared several times that it did not and had denied jurisdiction; when all courts in the other Member States did accept review powers even as against their own State? The opinion of the *commissaire du gouvernement*

---

[42] *Ibidem*, at 242.
[43] An obvious example is Lord Denning in the Court of Appeal: he was ahead of his time in accepting the supremacy of Community law.

before the French *Conseil d'État* is telling: *'So far as foreign courts are concerned (..) all I would say is that your Court is now the last which formally refuses to apply Community measures which are contradicted by later laws. By way of example, it is sufficient to mention that the Constitutional Court of the Federal Republic of Germany for its part finally accepted the opposite principle no less than eighteen years ago, by a decision of 9 June 1971. And even more significant is the case of the Italian Constitutional Court which, although hindered by a dualistic legal tradition (..) finally went so far as to authorise the ordinary courts of their own motion not to apply laws contrary to Community regulations by an important judgment of 8 June 1984, Granital. The Conseil constitutionnel's attitude merits your attention just as much'.*[44] Likewise, the opinion of the *procureurs généraux* before the Belgian *Cour de cassation* and the judgment of Lord Bridge in *Factortame* demonstrate how the courts are influenced by what their brethren in other Member States do. Being part of a trend may facilitate acceptance of the Community mandate, and may convince the courts to comply with the Court of Justice. However, this also works the other way round: cross-fertilisation also works concerning the constitutional limits on supremacy: the German Court in *Solange I* was inspired by the *Frontini* judgment of the *Corte costituzionale*. Commentators have pointed to the resemblance between the *Maastricht* ruling of the *Højesteret* and the *Brunner* decision of the *Bundesverfassungsgericht*. More recently, Laws in the English High Court introduced a similar limit on the supremacy of Community law, made up by the fundamental or constitutional rights guaranteed by the law of England. He did not mention any of the foreign courts who do adopt such position. But the latter may well have been the source of inspiration for the judge, especially since the English do not have a tradition of 'fundamental constitutional rights guaranteed by the law of England' which would in some way be untouchable.[45]

Cross-fertilisation may display the need for better dissemination of information on national court cases involving European law. These cases are often sent to the Court of Justice,[46] which probably possesses the most

---

[44] Opinion of *Commissaire du gouvernement* Patrick Frydman in *Conseil d'État*, decision of 20 October 1989, *Nicolo*, Rec., 136, available also on www.conseil-etat.fr; *English translation taken from* [1990] 1 CMLR 173; see also Oppenheimer, *The Cases*, 335, at 348. Note that Frydman refers to the case law of constitutional courts, no less, of the large Member States, and not, for instance, to the *Le Ski* judgment of the Belgian *Cour de cassation*.

[45] *High Court, Queen's Bench Division, Divisional Court*, decision of 18 February 2002, *metric martyrs*, [2002] EWHC 195 (Admin); www.bailii.org.

[46] The Memorandum of the ECJ concerning references for preliminary ruling invites the national courts to notify to the ECJ how they have applied the judgment of the ECJ and to send their final judgments. Not all courts do send the final judgment. In addition, only few courts will inform the ECJ of other judgments of significance in which no preliminary reference was made. See General Report on the colloquium subject 'The Preliminary Reference to the Court of Justice of the European Communities', 18th Colloquium of the Association of the Councils of State and Supreme Administrative Jurisdictions of the European Union, Helsinki, May 2002, available on www.raadvst-consetat.be, at 39.

complete collection thereof. According to the Commission, some 1,600 new cases are sent to the Court annually. Each year the Commission is given access in order to prepare its survey on the application of Community law by national courts.[47] Why should these records not be accessible to the general public, and more importantly, to other courts, all over the Union? It may well be that a problem of European law arising before a French court has already been decided in a Belgian or Spanish court. A centralised database of national court cases might be a welcome source of information for other courts; it might even save on preliminary rulings. The downside of such a system is obvious as well: if one national court incorrectly applies Community law or gives it an interpretation which is different from what the Court of Justice would decide, this may spread all over Europe, and unless it is referred by a court that doubts the correctness of the approach of its brethren, the Court of Justice cannot of its own motion put it right. Against this, the Association of Councils of State and Supreme Administrative Jurisdictions of the European Union has reported difficulties in finding information to investigate the law or legal practice in other countries.[48] There does appear to be a need for such information exchange. The Association has recently set up a site, provisionally hosted by the Belgian Council of State, on which participating courts may inform their colleagues of noteworthy developments in their own case law. One may assume that the cases reported may at times touch upon Community law. The Court of Justice for its part does publish a *Bulletin Reflets* containing notable national cases; and the annual surveys by the Commission do mention the most important decisions.[49] But these sources cannot be searched easily, and it is unlikely that a judge will have the time to read all of these surveys just in case there might be a decision of interest to him.

9.8. NATIONAL LEGAL CULTURES

Differences in the speed of acceptance (there is almost twenty years between *Le Ski* and *Factortame*; there is even more between *Costa v ENEL* and *Nicolo*) lie to a certain extent in the diversity of legal systems, legal cultures and legal-constitutional sensitivities. The monism-dualism divide implies that the various Member State courts have encountered different

---

[47] Even though the Commission admits that it does not have the means to conduct an indepth study and analysis of all these cases.

[48] General Report on the colloquium subject 'The Preliminary Reference to the Court of Justice of the European Communities', 18th Colloquium of the Association of the Councils of State and Supreme Administrative Jurisdictions of the European Union, Helsinki, May 2002, available on www.raadvst-consetat.be, at 16–17.

[49] Both are available on the website of the ECJ, www.curia.eu.int.

obstacles. Likewise, the conception of the judicial function *vis-à-vis* the Legislature differs in the various Member States.[50] The Netherlands and France had a competitive advantage since their constitutional texts were easier to work with. Notions like 'transfer of sovereign power' or 'limitation of sovereignty' carry different weight in different Member States, as do notions of primacy, or legal hierarchy. Simply put, the *legal* answer was easier to give in some Member States than in others, since the legal tools available to the courts were more open to acceptance of the Court's message. In addition, there is an important difference in style of legal reasoning. A Netherlands or Scandinavian lawyer is more pragmatic while for instance Italian law is very principled and highly sophisticated. The development in the case law of the *Corte costituzionale* on the *Simmenthal*-mandate suffices to prove the point. The English method and style of reasoning appears to be particularly apt to absorb Community law and apply it in a manner conforming to the requirements of the Court of Justice.

The presence of a constitutional court does not in itself seem to have had an impact on the acceptance of ordinary supremacy in the hands of the ordinary courts. It does not of itself make acceptance any more difficult, or any easier. The German *Bundesverfassungsgericht* had no problem accepting it in *Lütticke,* and accordingly sharing review powers with the ordinary courts, while the Italian constitutional court struggled with the jurisdictional issue for ten years. The French *Conseil d'État* appeared more reluctant to accept the supremacy of Community law than the *Conseil constitutionnel.* On the other hand, the existence of a constitutional court will almost necessarily lead to constitutional limits being imposed on the supremacy of Community law. None of the constitutional courts has accepted the unconditional supremacy of Community law. Belgium may serve as an interesting example. After *Le Ski* and until the establishment of the *Cour d'arbitrage,* Belgium had converted to a monist approach and the supremacy of Community and international law over national law, without any limits being made explicit. When the *Cour d'arbitrage* was set up, it introduced a limit to the supremacy of international treaties: they would only be supreme over national law on condition that they could stand the constitutionality test: treaties infringing upon the Constitution – the highest norm of the land – would not take precedence.

---

[50] Karen Alter argues that legalist explanations do not suffice, because for instance monist France proved to encounter more problems than dualist Germany. However, the monism-dualism argument is only powerful when combined with other elements such as the jurisdictional issue: in France for instance the limited conception of the judicial function was much deeper rooted in the minds of the courts probably than in the other Member States; the *Conseil d'État* is the *juge de la légalité* and not of the *constitutionnalité*; it reviews secondary legislation routinely, but simply has (had) no jurisdiction to review primary legislation. The various legal elements must be seen together and carry different weight (alas, not measurable with precision) in the different Member States.

Explaining Acceptance

After all, *'la préférence donnée à la Constitution n'est pas chose étonnante de la part d'une juridiction constitutionnelle'.*[51] However, the *Cour d'arbitrage* may well find a way out of the dilemma – supremacy of the Constitution *and* supremacy of Community law – by declaring that it lacks jurisdiction to pronounce itself on the issue with reference to the transfer of powers provision contained in Article 34 of the Constitution.[52]

9.9. LA DOCTRINE AND PERSONALITIES ON THE BENCH...

There are other factors explaining the result (final acceptance of *Simmenthal*) and difference in ease and speed. There is, for instance, the input of *la doctrine*, of legal scholarship: did commentators side with the Court of Justice and seek to convince the courts of the need for acceptance; did they offer alternative modes of reasoning; were they, generally speaking, favourable to Community law? Who were those commentators? In several systems, individuals can be identified who have contributed much to the courts' acceptance of the *Simmenthal* mandate. Mostly they were not singled out in the relevant judgments, but some of the judgments were clearly inspired by specific scholars, such as Sorrentino in Italy.[53] Individual judges or advocates general of the national courts, some of whom later became or had already been members of the Court of Justice, have also been singled out: Ganshof van der Meersch in Belgium,[54] Galmot in the French *Conseil d'État*,[55] Lord Slynn of Hadley in the United Kingdom.[56]

---

[51] M Melchior and P Vandernoot, 'Controle de constitutionnalité et droit communautaire dérivé', (1998) *RBDC*, 3, at 11. The first author is president of the *Cour d'arbitrage*.
[52] *Ibidem*, at 12 *et seq*. The point is developed further *below*.
[53] So M Cartabia, 'Relationship between the Italian legal system and the EU', in A-M Slaughter *et al* (eds), *The European Court and National Courts – Doctrine and Jurisprudence. Legal Change in Its Social Context* (Oxford, Hart Publishing, 1998) 133, at 145. FP Ruggeri Laderchi adds the probable impact of La Pergola: FP Ruggeri Laderchi, 'Report on Italy', *Ibidem*, 147, at 154.
[54] H Bribosia, 'Report on Belgium', in A-M Slaughter et al (eds), *The European Court and National Courts – Doctrine and Jurisprudence. Legal Change in Its Social Context* (Oxford, Hart Publishing, 1998) 3, at 36.
[55] J Plötner has pointed out what may not be a simple coincidence: Yves Galmot was the first member of the *Conseil d'État* to be have been nominated judge at the ECJ. In his farewell speech after having served 6 years in Luxembourg, he announced that he would never again see French Public Law as before. One year after he had returned to the *Conseil d'État*, the latter court handed down its *Nicolo* decision: J Plötner, 'Report on France', in A-M Slaughter *et al* (eds), *The European Court and National Courts – Doctrine and Jurisprudence. Legal Change in Its Social Context* (Oxford, Hart Publishing, 1998) 41, at 68–69. Plötner names also Partick Frydman, Bruno Genevois and Marceau Long.
[56] PP Craig, 'Report on the United Kingdom', in A-M Slaughter *et al* (eds), *The European Court and National Courts – Doctrine and Jurisprudence. Legal Change in Its Social Context* (Oxford, Hart Publishing, 1998) 195, at 223–224.

Even today, many of the highest courts have within their ranks members who specialise in Community law, who co-ordinate matters of Community law and who are concerned with the acquisition of information on Community law and the preparation of cases. For example, a *'Cellule de droit communautaire'* was set up in the French *Conseil d'État*, led by a former Judge of the European Court of First Instance, and whose job it is to produce services related to Community law. The Netherlands *Raad van State* has formed a small group of members which can be consulted in matters related to Community law.[57]

9.10.   ...AND BEYOND

Another element is (or perhaps was) the attractiveness of Community law in itself as a new and exciting area of law, which in many countries attracted some of the best scholars. Practising lawyers and judges may also have been convinced by the attractiveness of a new legal system, if not of the idea of European integration as such. Judges who were given the competence to refer questions for preliminary rulings may have felt that they were truly involved in this new area, and were willing even to go against the most fundamental principles of constitutional law and against their own Government, Parliament or the highest courts. Perhaps they had *'une certaine idée de l'Europe'* of their own; maybe they were simply eager to participate in this new system and to explore new territory.

The 'newness' of Community law has diminished, and also possibly accordingly its attractiveness. In many areas, it is highly technical and complex, and difficult to understand. If Community law is to be enforced in the national courts as common courts of Community law, it is important that it should be sufficiently clear and of a high quality. What is more, and this is admittedly impossible to prove, national judges may well be prepared to cooperate in the enforcement and application of Community law if they believe in it, but their eagerness may well diminish if Europe is perceived as ill-functioning, as an undemocratic institute ran by technocrats, or as interfering intrusively not only in daily life but also in national law etc. In short, the Court of Justice and the European Union are dependent on the goodwill of the national authorities, including the courts, but they have a responsibility of their own to ensure a high level of quality and hence to earn legitimacy.

---

[57] See General Report on the colloquium subject 'The Preliminary Reference to the Court of Justice of the European Communities', 18th Colloquium of the Association of the Councils of State and Supreme Administrative Jurisdictions of the European Union, Helsinki, May 2002, available on www.raadvst-consetat.be, at 16–17.

9.11. THE CASES AT HAND

It is also important to look at the specific cases at hand. Are they politically sensitive cases,[58] do they involve 'defenceless individuals' desperate for judicial protection? Courts have first to wait for cases to be brought before them, and for 'good' cases to be brought before them.

9.12. THE PROPORTION OF COMMUNITY LAW CASES IN DOMESTIC PROCEEDINGS

It is difficult to find out how often and on what scale national courts are in practice confronted with Community law. There are not too many statistics available. According to a survey conducted by the final instance administrative courts of the Member States of the European Union, the proportion of Community law cases varies from one Member State to another.[59] The proportion is not very high. Some courts can present fairly precise figures; for instance the Belgian *Conseil d'État* stated that from 1991 to 2002, 2,560 decisions in a total of 68,100 cases concerned Community law, *i.e.* 3.8 per cent. Other courts stated that they had no statistics available, such as the Danish Supreme Court, or made a general estimate of the cases involving Community law. For instance, the Greek Council of State said that annually, some 15 cases out of a total of 4,500 to 5000 cases concerned Community law; the Portuguese *Supremo Tribunal Administrativo* spoke of some 20 to 40 cases out of approximately 3,500 annually. Some courts were vague, such as the Irish Supreme Court, which stated that the proportion of those cases was 'very small'; the qualification 'small' was used by the Luxembourg *Cour administrative*. Of the courts which made an educated guess, most estimated the proportion of Community law cases at about 5 per cent (Spanish *Tribunal Supremo*, Italian *Consiglio di Stato*; Netherlands *Raad van State* and *Centrale Raad van Beroep*; English *Court of Appeal*); some somewhat higher (8 per cent in English *House of Lords*; 5-20 per cent in the German *Bundesverwaltungsgericht*, depending on the division; 20 per cent *College van Beroep voor het Bedrijfsleven*). Remarkable is the response of the Finnish and Swedish final instance administrative courts who state that 25 per cent (Sweden) or as much as one third (Finland) of all cases involve Community law. The difficulty with these sorts of figures

---

[58] *Costa v ENEL* was a case involving an electricity bill of only a few euro's; but not a small case: the nationalisation of the ENEL, the electricity company, was claimed to infringe the Treaty!

[59] See General Report on the colloquium subject 'The Preliminary Reference to the Court of Justice of the European Communities', 18th Colloquium of the Association of the Councils of State and Supreme Administrative Jurisdictions of the European Union, Helsinki, May 2002, available on www.raadvst-consetat.be.

is of course that the jurisdiction of these courts varies a great deal. So the Swedish answer stated that the significance of Community law was especially considerable in taxation affairs, while in other countries these cases would come before separate courts. The English *Court of Appeal* and *House of Lords* seem to have given a general proportion of the cases decided by them, civil, criminal and administrative alike. But one conclusion which appears reasonable on the basis of this survey is that the average proportion of Community law cases is fairly limited, especially considering the fact that a great number of laws applied in the Member States have a European origin, and consist in the implementation of Directives etc.

9.13. FINAL REMARKS

It is very hard to say why the courts have heeded, and why the road to acceptance has proved so much longer for some courts than for others. The answer lies probably in a combination of all factors mentioned above, and perhaps others too. None of the elements taken on its own can explain acceptance and the differences in speed. It would require research of a different type, including interviews with the players involved to gain a better understanding of why particular courts have decided the way they have. Some patterns may appear from the actual decisions, as depicted above, but the full story cannot be discerned from the judgments alone.

10

Excursion:
The '*Costanzo* Mandate'
of Administrative Authorities

W HILE THIS ISSUE may go beyond the framework of this book, as it concerns the duties of the *administrative authorities* under Community law rather than the courts, a few thoughts will be spent on the *Costanzo* case law of the Court of Justice. In *Costanzo*,[1] the question was raised whether the national administrative authorities were under the same Community law mandate as the national courts to set aside national primary legislation in order to give effect to Community law. Italy had initially correctly implemented the Directive on public works contracts, but had subsequently adopted three decrees which turned out to be incompatible with the directive because they introduced additional conditions. The bid submitted by Costanzo for alteration work on a football stadium in preparation of the 1990 World Cup, was excluded from the tendering procedure because it did not comply with these latter conditions. Costanzo challenged the decision of the *Giunta municipale*, claiming *inter alia* that it was illegal since it was based on a decree law which was itself incompatible with the directive in question. The question was, therefore, whether the municipal authorities, *i.e.* administrative authorities, were under the same obligation as national courts to apply the provisions of a directive and to refrain from applying the provisions of national law which conflict with them; in other words, the referring court wanted to know whether there is a '*Simmenthal*-like mandate' for administrative authorities.

The Court held that administrative authorities including municipal authorities are indeed under the same obligations as national courts to refrain from applying provisions of national law which conflict with them. The duty of national courts was based on the fact that the provisions of a directive are considered to be binding on all the authorities of the State

---

[1]   Case 103/88 *Fratelli Costanzo SpA v Comune di Milano* [1989] ECR 1839.

(and thus also the courts), and including also administrative authorities. Moreover, the Court continued, it would be contradictory to rule that an individual may rely upon the provisions of a directive which fulfil the conditions defined above in proceedings before the national courts seeking an order against the administrative authorities, and yet to hold that those authorities are under no obligation to apply the provisions of the directive and to refrain from applying those provisions of national law which conflict with them. Consequently, when the conditions under which the Court has held that individuals may rely on the provisions of a directive before the national courts are met, *all organs of the administration*, including decentralised authorities such as municipalities, are obliged to apply those provisions, and to refrain from applying conflicting provisions of national law.

The reasoning is based on logic and appears convincing, and did not cause many reactions in scholarly writing at the time. The judgment is only mentioned in passing, if at all, and is often considered as a logical consequence of existing principles. However, the case is no less revolutionary than *Simmenthal*: national administrative authorities are under the most fundamental tenets of constitutional law, the principle of the rule of law and *Rechtsstaatlichkeit*, under an obligation to apply the law: they are subject to it and in no condition to set it aside. Primary legislation claimed to be unconstitutional cannot be set aside either:[2] its constitutionality can only be assessed by a constitutional court, or a court having constitutional jurisdiction where these courts exist; or by Parliament itself which can amend or repeal an Act that appears to be or to have become unconstitutional. Administrative authorities are subordinate to the legislative power and are accordingly prevented from refusing to apply the law adopted by it, particularly primary legislation. Advocate General Lenz did acknowledge these constitutional difficulties for the administrative authorities in his Opinion in *Costanzo*, and also pointed out that administrative authorities are not in a position to refer questions for preliminary ruling to the Court of Justice on the direct effect and exact meaning of directives or other provisions of Community law. He suggested therefore the following distinction: *'In the event that national implementing measures are incompatible with the directive, the administrative authorities are entitled – and, once the content and scope of the measures have been clarified in judicial proceedings, obliged – to refrain from applying national law. However, if the authority is in doubt as to*

---

[2] But see Article 1 of Chapter 11 of the Swedish *Regeringsformen*: 'If a court or other public body finds that a provision conflicts with a rule of fundamental law or other superior statute, or finds that a procedure laid down in law has been disregarded in any important respect when the provision was made, the provision may not be applied. If the provision has been approved by the Riksdag or by the Government, however, it shall be waived only if the error is manifest'. Under *Costanzo*, that last proviso is probably not to apply in the case of infringements of Community law!

the legal position it is quite at liberty to seek clarification from the courts, and in doing so may use any means available under national law'.[3] The Court did not follow its Advocate General and did not, at least not explicitly, distinguish between cases where there is a clear violation, possibly after a ruling of the Court, and other cases. Instead it imposed a general obligation on all administrative authorities to apply directly effective provisions of Community law and to refrain from applying conflicting provisions of national law.

Let us pause for a minute to see what actually happens here: national administrative authorities are under a Community obligation to set aside conflicting legislation, even though they have no direct relationship with the Court of Justice, and cannot therefore ascertain the correct interpretation and effect of a directive. Under the tenets of national constitutional law, these administrative authorities are bound by the law; where the law appears to conflict with a directly effective provision of Community law, they are no longer bound to apply it; on the contrary, they are under a Community obligation to set it aside. In *Costanzo*, the Court had already ruled in a previous case that a national rule of the kind at issue in *Costanzo* was unlawful. Yet, the Court did not consider this crucial: it is apparently irrelevant whether or not there has been a previous judgment of the Court of Justice. This *Costanzo* mandate conflicts with national constitutional law principles of *rule of law, legaliteitsbeginsel*[4] and *Rechtsstaat*, which despite their dissimilarities have in common that administrative authorities are bound by 'the law', and under national constitutional law, 'the law' used to be the law as laid down by the Legislature. Under national constitutional law, administrative authorities are not empowered to control for instance the constitutionality of primary legislation, nor is it accepted everywhere beyond doubt that they have an independent duty to control the conformity of Statutes with international treaties.

Administrative Authorities and Community Law in Other Situations

On the other hand, the *Costanzo* approach sits well with the Community law position in other situations. The Court has consistently held that a finding under Article 226 EC that a Member State has failed to fulfil its obligations under Community law entails, first, an automatic prohibition of the application by both the judicial *and the administrative authorities* of

---

[3] Case 103/88 *Fratelli Costanzo SpA v Comune di Milano* [1989] ECR 1839, at 1860.
[4] See for *Costanzo* in the Dutch context JH Jans et al, *Inleiding tot het Europees bestuursrecht*, Ars (Aequi Libri, 1999) 118 *et seq*, who also point out that some lower administrative organs may incur disciplinary measures where they fail to comply with the instructions of a hierarchically higher organ.

that State of the national rules in question, and secondly, an obligation on the part of those authorities to take all the appropriate measures to facilitate the full application of Community law.[5] In *Waterkeyn* the Court ruled that '*All the institutions of the Member State concerned must, in accordance with that provision [i.e.* Article 232 EC], *ensure within the fields covered by their respective powers, that judgments of the Court are complied with. If the judgment declares that certain legislative provisions of a Member State are contrary to the Treaty the authorities exercising legislative power are then under the duty to amend the provisions in question so as to make them conform with the requirements of Community law. For their part, the courts of the Member States concerned have an obligation to ensure, when performing their duties, that the Court's judgment is complied with'.*[6] The administrative authorities are not explicitly mentioned, but they appear to be included. At the end of the day, the statement is not surprising for an international court, that does not analyse the manner in which powers and responsibilities are divided within the constitutional set up of the State, or where the actual source of the infringement lies within the State: all that matters is that the obligations are fulfilled by 'the State'.

The case law on the direct effect of directives is also relevant in this respect. As is well known, non-implemented directives which are sufficiently clear, precise and unconditional, can be invoked by individuals before national courts in *vertical* relations, *i.e.* against the State (and not in *horizontal* relations between individuals).[7] In this context, the definition of what organs and entities belong to 'the State' is thus critical. Thus, in *Foster* the Court stated that '*unconditional and sufficiently precise provisions of a directive could be relied on against organisations or bodies which were subject to the authority or control of the State or had special powers beyond those which result from the normal rules applicable to relations between individuals'*, and further clarified that they could accordingly be relied on against tax authorities,[8] local or regional authorities,[9] or against constitutionally

---

5   Case 48/71 *Commission v Italy* [1972] ECR 527: '*In the present case the effect of Community law, declared as res judicata in respect of the Italian Republic, is a prohibition having full force of law on the competent national authorities against applying a national rule recognized as incompatible with the Treaty and, if the circumstances so require, an obligation on them to take all appropriate measures to enable Community law to be fully applied*'; Case C–101/91 *Commission v Italy* [1993] *ECR* 191. These effects seem to follow from the Treaty and Community law itself, rather than from the judgment of the ECJ.

6   Joined Cases 314–316/81 and 83/82 *Procureur de la République v Waterkeyn* [1982] ECR 4337.

7   See Case 152/84 *M H Marshall v Southampton and South-West Hampshire Area Health Authority (Teaching)* [1986] ECR 723; Case C–91/92 *Paola Faccini Dori v Recreb Srl* [1994] ECR I–3325.

8   As is Case 8/81 *Becker v Hauptzollamt Muenster-Innenstadt* [1982] ECR 53 and Case C–221/88 *ECSC v Acciaierie e Ferriere Busseni (in liquidation)* [1990] ECR I–495.

9   As is Case 103/88 *Fratelli Costanzo v Comune di Milano* [1989] ECR 1839.

independent authorities responsible for the maintenance of public order and safety,[10] and against and public authorities providing public health services.[11] In short, the Court concluded, '*a body, whatever its legal form, which has been made responsible, pursuant to a measure adopted by the State, for providing a public service under the control of the State and has for that purpose special powers beyond those which result from the normal rules applicable in relations between individuals is included in any event among the bodies against which the provisions of a directive capable of having direct effect may be relied upon*'.[12]

This definition is wide and appears to be open for other bodies as well. The Court seems to include all organs and bodies which exercise public authority in some way or other, or which are controlled by an organ exercising such jurisdiction. To this extent, the definition covers also bodies and organs for which the *estoppel* argument or the *nemo auditur turpitudinem suam allegans* principle, on which the vertical direct effect of directives is based since *Ratti*,[13] does not work in practical effect, as these authorities are often not under an obligation to implement the directive. However, and this follows from (a wide version) of *Costanzo*, they are under an obligation to do what is appropriate to comply with the State's obligations under the directive, and they must step in even where the organ or institution which has prime responsibility to implement the directive fails to do so.

Finally, the obligations of administrative organs under Community law, including their duty to set aside conflicting national legislation also have consequences in the context of governmental liability form infringement of Community law. This will be developed further in the chapter on governmental liability.[14]

Autonomous duties in the hands of the administrative authorities?

Under the principle of institutional and procedural autonomy, Community law respects the constitutional and institutional set up of the Member States, and does not in principle interfere in these matters. However, the Court does expect that the Member States make sure that the division of competences and responsibilities among national and subnational authorities and organs is such that '*the* Member State' as actor on

---

[10] Case 222/84 *Marguerite Johnston v Chief Constable of the Royal Ulster Constabulary* [1986] ECR 1651.

[11] Case 152/84 *M H Marshall v Southampton and South-West Hampshire Area Health Authority (Teaching)* [1986] ECR 723.

[12] Case C–188/89 *A Foster and others v British Gas plc* [1990] ECR I–3313, at para 20.

[13] Case 148/78 *Criminal proceedings against Tullio Ratti* [1979] ECR 1629.

[14] See Chapter 11.

the European field is in a position to comply with its obligations under Article 10 EC and other provisions of Community law. Problems arising from the federal structure of the State, from the decentralisation of the State or from the fact that specific functions have been devolved to independent and autonomous bodies cannot be invoked as a defence in infringement proceedings. The Court of Justice operates under the presumption that the Member States must organise themselves in such a way as to make it possible for them and all independent bodies and organs of the State to comply with Community law requirements.

Administrative authorities have independent and autonomous duties and responsibilities under Community law. This obligation is contained in Article 10 EC, and they are thus under an obligation to do what is appropriate to ensure the fulfilment of the obligations arising out of the Treaty, and to abstain from any measure which could jeopardise the objectives of the Treaty. Included in this obligation is also, under *Costanzo*, the duty to set aside any conflicting provisions of national primary legislation, and presumably even of constitutional law.[15]

In most cases, the focus will be on the possibility to rely on Community law as against the administrative authorities of the State *before the national courts* – those are indeed the cases which reach the Court of Justice, and on which it can give rulings. In *Costanzo*, the applicants claimed, before the Italian court, that it could invoke the directive before the municipality, which should accordingly have set aside the conflicting decrees. The Court agreed. In the context of directives, for instance, the Court held in the case of *Maria Luisa Jiménez Melgar* that *'It is settled case law that the Member States' obligation arising from a directive to achieve the result prescribed by the directive and their duty, under Article 5 of the EC Treaty (now Article 10 EC), to take all appropriate measures, whether general or particular, to ensure fulfilment of that obligation is binding on all authorities of the Member State* [reference to Faccini Dori and HI], *including decentralised authorities such as municipalities* [Costanzo and Ciola]'.

But more notable in this context is what principles apply where the national courts are left out of the equation and it is the individual invoking Community law before the administrative authorities. Or beyond that scenario, the case where there are no rights or obligations of individuals at stake.[16]

---

[15] For a discussion of the principles of legality (*'legaliteitsbeginsel'*) in Dutch law and the national duties of administrative organs in Community law, see J Jans *et al*, *Inleiding tot het Europees Bestuursrecht*, Ars (Aequi Libri, 2002) at 46 *et seq*.

[16] See P Van Nuffel, *De rechtsbescherming van nationale overheden in het Europees recht* (Deventer, Kluwer, 2000) at 70.

What obligations?

The issue of the obligations of administrative authorities under Community law arose in the case of *Ciola*. Ciola was the manager of a company which had been licensed to establish moorings for pleasure boats. The 1990 individual administrative decision ('*Bescheid*') of the *Bezirkhauptmannschaft* Bregenz (the administrative authority of first instance of the Land Vorarlberg), which had become final, included a condition in the licence that by 1996 a maximum of 60 boats whose owners were resident abroad could be accommodated. In August 1996, Ciola was prosecuted for committing an administrative offence[17] and fined accordingly. Ciola appealed against these fines, claiming that they constituted an infringement of Community law. The Austrian court asked the European Court whether Community law gave Ciola the rights to assert that the conditions contained in the 1990 decision should not be applied in decisions of the Austrian courts and administrative authorities adopted after the Austrian accession in 1995. The Court ruled: '*While the Court initially held that it is for the national court to refuse if necessary to apply any conflicting provision of national law* [Simmenthal], *it subsequently refined its case-law in two respects. Thus it appears from the case law, first, that* all administrative bodies, *including decentralised authorities, are subject to that obligation as to primacy, and individuals may therefore rely on such a provision of Community law against them* [Fratelli Costanzo]. *Second, provisions of national law which conflict with such a provision of Community law may be legislative or administrative* [butter-buying cruises]. *It is consistent with that case law that those administrative provisions of national law should include not only general abstract rules but also specific individual administrative decisions. It is inconsistent with that case law that those administrative provisions of national law should include not only general abstract rules but also specific individual administrative decision*'.[18] However, there were two particularities in the case: there did not seem to be a legislative provision obliging the Austrian authorities to impose the condition of residence; second, it is, again not clear whether the Court was speaking of a right to invoke Community law against a national authority before a national court; or of an independent duty on the part of administrative authority irrespective of any court intervention. Under the *Costanzo* reasoning, both should coincide, as it would be illogical if individuals could invoke it before the courts and against administrative bodies, and

---

[17] Ciola was found guilty of renting two (!) moorings to boat-owners who were resident abroad, namely in the Principality of Liechtenstein and in Germany, thus exceeding the limit of 60.

[18] Case C–224/97 *Erich Ciola v Land Vorarlberg* [1999] ECR I–2517.

hold at the same time that these bodies are not under an obligation to set aside conflicting legislation, or to set aside national administrative decisions (and presumably annul them).

National administrative organs cannot accordingly 'hide behind' national legislative norms, including primary legislation. They are under an obligation to check the compatibility of national norms with Community law, and if necessary, to set them aside. This obviously raises questions from the perspective of constitutional law, and in terms of equality before the law, legal certainty and uniformity. It would seem advisable, therefore, for the State to organise some form of co-ordinating procedure or instance, to ensure that where a problem is detected by the administrative authority, this is pointed out to the other organs and institutions responsible in that area, so that the infringement can be repaired.

In addition to setting aside conflicting legislation, administrative authorities appear to be under an obligation to interpret national law in accordance with Community law.[19] This obligation can generally be derived from the standard statement of the Court of Justice, reiterated on numerous occasions, *'the Member States' obligation arising from a directive to achieve the result envisaged by the directive and their duty under Article 5 of the EC Treaty to take all appropriate measures, whether general or particular, to ensure fulfilment of that obligation is* binding on all the authorities of Member States, including, for matters within their jurisdiction, the courts. *It follows that, when applying national law, whether adopted before or after the directive, the national court having to interpret that law must do so, as far as possible, in the light of the wording and the purpose of the directive so as to achieve the result it has in view and thereby comply with the third paragraph of Article 189 of the EC Treaty* [references omitted].[20] The obligation to take all measures necessary to ensure the result achieved by the directive thus also applies to the administrative authorities. However, the Court has never spelt out their obligation to interpret national law in conformity with Community law. This obligation must be limited to the extent that, presumably, the duty of conform interpretation on the part of national administrative authorities may not have as a consequence the reverse vertical direct effect of the directive.[21] A similar duty of conform obligation could only serve to the advantage of the individual concerned, not against him. Difficulties will of course then arise where there are also third parties involved.

Also, the State, or other public law bodies, may be held liable for infringements of Community law attributable to administrative authorities.

---

[19] So e.g. MH Wissink, *Richtlijnconforme interpretatie van burgerlijk recht* (Deventer, Kluwer, 2001) at 37.

[20] Taken from Case C–54/96 *Dorsch Consult Ingenieurgesellschaft mbH v Bundesbaugesellschaft Berlin mbH* [1997] ECR I–4961.

[21] Case 80/86 *Criminal proceedings against Kolpinghuis Nijmegen BV* [1987] ECR 3969.

It will depend on national law whether or not these administrative organs will have to pay compensation themselves, or whether it will be payable by the State.[22]

A case in which the Community obligations of administrative authorities appeared particularly wide is *Larsy*. *Larsy* was a governmental liability case, but its relevance reaches beyond the issue of governmental liability, and implies an extension of *Costanzo*, imposing also a form of structural supremacy on the administrative authorities.[23] Gervais Larsy and his brother Marius, of Belgian nationality and living in Belgium, had worked as self-employed nursery gardener in Belgium and France. When Gervais retired in 1985, he lodged an application for a self-employed worker's retirement pension with the Inasti (*Institut national d'assurances sociales pour travailleurs indépendants*). The full pension that was then awarded to him, was later reduced, when the Inasti became aware that Gervais was also paid a French retirement pension, where he had also paid social security contributions. Gervais Larsy brought an action against the decision before the *Tribunal du travail* (Labour Tribunal), Tournai, claiming that the original amount of the pension entitlement should be maintained, notwithstanding the grant of the French retirement pension, but the court dismissed the action as unfounded. Subsequently, Marius Larsy, Gervais' brother, who was in a similar factual and legal situation, brought an action before the Tribunal du Travail, Tournai. This time, the Tribunal du travail made a reference for preliminary ruling to the Court of Justice, which held, in short, that a national rule against overlapping benefits did not under the relevant Community Regulation apply where a person has worked in two Member States during one and the same period and has been obliged to pay old-age pension insurance contributions in those States during that period. The Belgian court thus upheld Marius' claim. On a new application, the Inasti awarded Gervais Larsy a full pension, but only with effect from the date of the new application. Before the *Cour du travail de Mons*, on appeal from the initial decision of the *Tribunal du travail*, Inasti acknowledged that Gervais Larsy was entitled to a full pension, with retroactive effect and that the original decision should be revised accordingly. However, the Inasti rejected the claim in damages which Gervais Larsy had equally brought, and argued that it had not committed a wrongful act. The case thus turned into a liability case. In the reference made by the *Cour du travail de Mons*, the Court of Justice was asked first, whether the Inasti had wrongly applied the Community Regulation; and second, whether the incorrect application of the Regulation was, in the circumstances of the case, a sufficiently serious

---

[22] See below in Chapter 11.
[23] Case C–118/00 *Gervais Larsy v Inasti* [2001] ECR I–5063.

breach of Community law so as to cause the liability of the Inasti to arise.[24] In answering the second question relating to the liability of the Inasti, the Court made some very interesting statements on the duties of administrative authorities in the context of Community law. Stating that it had all the necessary information to be able to assess whether the facts of the case must be considered to constitute a sufficiently serious breach, the Court answered the question which is normally for the national court to decide. The Court held that in the case, the competent authority had no substantive choice (and accordingly, the mere infringement *may* be sufficient to establish the existence of a sufficiently serious breach). In respect of both breaches (the initial failure to award a full pension, and the application of the Regulation, resulting in limiting the retroactive effect of the second decision) the Court held that they were sufficiently serious to the extent that the Inasti had failed to draw all the necessary consequences from a judgment of the Court of Justice, providing a clear answer to the issues before that institution, in other cases.

The Court then made a few statements on the defence of the Inasti to the effect that under national procedural law, it could not review the decision with full retroactive effect, and that accordingly the (incorrect) application of the Regulation was the only manner to review the decision at all. Neither the judgment or the opinion of Advocate General Léger are conclusive on the exact content of the defence of the Inasti, but it appears that it concerned the binding nature of the initial judgment of the *Tribunal du travail de Tournai*, upholding the initial decision reducing Larsy's pension, which was binding on the Inasti. The Court rejected the argument, strengthened by the fact that the Inasti had at least been prepared to review the decision with *partial* retroactive effect (and thus proving that the decision was not fully immune for review because of the binding nature of the judgment). Nevertheless, the statements of the Court are much wider, and are stated in very general terms. The Court held that '*Suffice it to observe in that regard that the Court has held that any provision of a national legal system and any legislative, administrative or judicial practice which might impair the effectiveness of Community law by withholding from the national court having jurisdiction to apply such law the power to do everything necessary at the moment of its application to set aside national legislative provisions which might prevent, even temporarily, Community rules from having full force and effect are incompatible with those requirements, which are the very essence of Community law (Cases 106/77*

---

[24] The case thus also concerned the question whether a national public authoity (instead of 'the State') could be liable in damages. The referring court did not raise the issue in the reference, but the Court of Justice repeated its statements in *Konle* and *Haim*, explained below in the chapter on governmental liability.

Simmenthal [1978] ECR 629, paragraph 22, and C-213/89 Factortame and Others [1990] ECR I-2433, paragraph 20)'. The reference to *Simmenthal* and *Factortame* appears to be nothing special, as the Court refers to these cases rather often, to support the principle that national courts are under an obligation to ensure the full effect of Community law. However, the particular paragraphs referred to are special: Paragraph 22 of *Simmenthal* is the expression of a principle of structural supremacy stating that anything in national law preventing the application of Community law must be set aside. It has been demonstrated that this is too bold a statement: there are limits to the full effect of Community law, in particular in national procedural law. The obligations imposed on national courts is not quite as stringent as the Court stated in paragraph 22 in *Simmenthal*, which is also why the Court has not – except in *Factortame* – made reference to that particular paragraph.

Yet, in this case, it reappears. The duty to set aside anything that prevents *the national court having jurisdiction* from doing everything necessary to set aside conflicting measures of national law, is then further extended. Indeed, in this case, the issue was not that a national court should be able to give full effect to Community law, but rather an administrative authority, the Inasti. The Court held that *'That principle of the primacy of Community law means that not only the lower courts but all the courts of the Member State are under a duty to give full effect to Community law (see, to that effect, Cases 48/71 Commission v Italy [1972] ECR 529, paragraph 7, and C-101/91 Commission v Italy [1993] ECR I-191, paragraph 24)'*. And it concluded: *'So, to the extent that national procedural rules precluded effective protection of Mr Larsy's rights derived under the direct effect of Community law, Inasti should have disapplied those provisions'*.

Now, the emphasis that that principle of supremacy applies not only to the lower but to all court does not make any sense, and the Inasti is not even a court. The French version of the paragraph at issue (which was also the language of the case), is clearer: *'Ce principe de primauté du droit communautaire impose non seulement aux juridictions, mais à toutes les instances de l'État membre de donner plein effet à la norme communautaire'*. It remains a very bold statement: it reinstates the 'principle of structural supremacy', which had been abandoned in the context of the duties of national courts, and in one move extends it to *all* public authorities, including administrative authorities. The statement is particularly crude, as it does not contain any reference to the principle of procedural autonomy applying in the context of the obligations of the national courts, or to the *Rewe* and *Comet* principles, or to any rule of reason. If these statements are to be understood in this way, the obligations imposed on the administrative authorities go far beyond those imposed on the national courts *à la Van Schijndel*. It may well be, however, that this is not what the Court implied: the decision was handed by a chamber of three judges, it can be explained by the peculiarities of the case and so forth.

Conclusion

While the Community obligations of the national courts are the subject of extensive doctrinal debate and dialogue between the national courts and the Court of Justice, the same cannot be said of the duties of the national administrative authorities. The picture concerning the mandate of the national administrative authorities is not yet complete. Some of the obligations are clear: as component parts of the State, they are under the obligation deriving from Article 10 EC to take all appropriate measures, whether general or particular, to ensure fulfilment of the obligations of membership, and to abstain from measures susceptible of jeopardising the attainment of the objectives of the Treaty. Yet, just how far these obligations reach is not yet clear. They must comply with decisions of the Court of Justice, and are obliged, for instance to refrain from applying legislation declared incompatible with Community law in enforcement actions; they have an independent duty to set aside conflicting national legislation (*Costanzo*); individuals can invoke directly effective provisions of Community law against them; they can even be held liable for their own infringements of Community law. But how far do these obligations reach? Presumably there will be limits arising from the principles of legal certainty and equality and so forth. Where exactly those limits are will require further clarification. Now, one factor delaying the clarification, and explaining why the duties of administrative authorities are much less developed until now than those of national courts, is the absence of a preliminary rulings procedure for those administrative authorities, after the example of the Article 234 EC procedure for courts. One could imagine a similar procedure for administrative authorities, either to the Commission which could assist these authorities in the execution of their Community mandate, or to the Court of Justice. The latter option would be preferable as it is the Court of Justice which has ultimate authority in interpreting the Treaty. Nevertheless, a reference procedure for administrative authorities, and independent of a concrete court case would lead the Court of Justice to become involved with theoretical questions or advisory opinions, in short, with non-contentious questions. It would be entirely novel. On the other hand, the fact that for a clarification of the autonomous duties of administrative authorities in the context of Community law, it is now necessary to await enforcement proceedings instituted by the Commission or national court cases slows down the process of clarification. In addition, in the last option, the issues involved will mostly be translated in questions concerning the duties of the national courts in deciding cases between individuals and administrative authorities. The issue of the autonomous Community mandate of administrative authorities remains, for the time being, incomplete.

11

The *'Francovich* Mandate': Jurisdiction to Hold the State Liable for Breach of Community Law

11.1. INTRODUCTION

IN FRANCOVICH,[1] the Court did not hide the fact that it created, or rather discovered,[2] a Community wide remedy.[3] It is a principle of Community law that the Member States are obliged to make good loss and damage caused to individuals by breaches of Community law for which they can be held responsible;[4] it is inherent in the system of the Treaty[5] and is required by Community law.[6] When the conditions for liability are fulfilled, the right to obtain compensation arises, a right founded directly on Community law.[7] It is a Community remedy for individuals and a Community sanction for breach of Community law, and accordingly, Community conditions are set for liability to arise. Other substantive conditions which may be set under national law do not apply.

---

[1] Joined Cases C–6/90 and C–9/90 *Francovich and Bonifaci v Italy* [1991] ECR I–5357.

[2] The ECJ claimed to have merely discovered it: it was inherent in the system of the Treaty. Upon criticism that it had 'invented' or created a new remedy not provided for by the Treaties *expressis verbis*, the Court stated in *Brasserie* that it alone has jurisdiction to interpret the Treaty in the light of fundamental principles of the Community legal system and, where necessary, general principles common to the legal systems of the Member States. The principle of State liability is known in some form or other in all the Member States as is reflected in Art. 235 EC, see Joined Cases C–46/93 and C–48/93 *Brasserie du Pêcheur v Germany and The Queen v Secretary of State for Transport, ex parte Factortame Ltd and Others* [1996] ECR I–1029, at para 27, see further *below*.

[3] See F Schockweiler, 'La responsabilité de l'autorité nationale en cas de violation du droit communautaire', *RTDeur* (1992) 27, at 42: 'Le droit à réparation trouvant directement son fondement dans le droit communautaire'; G Tesauro, 'La sanction des infractions au droit communautaire', *Rivista di diritto europeo* (1992) 477, at 492; see also D Curtin, 'State Liability Under Community Law: A New Remedy for Private Parties', *Industrial Law Journal* (1992) 74.

[4] *Francovich*, at para 37.

[5] *Francovich*, at para 35.

[6] *Francovich*, at para 38.

[7] *Francovich*, at para 41.

Moreover, it does not matter whether or not, as a matter of national law, the State may be held liable for particular acts: being a Community remedy, it is not dependent on national law concerning state liability, at least not as regards the availability of the remedy. The principle since *Francovich* has been firmly established in the case law of the Court of Justice has been further developed and clarified and the conditions are still being fine-tuned, but the basic principle itself is no longer questioned. As for the application in a concrete case, the general rule of national procedural and remedial autonomy applies, with the conditions of effectiveness and equality: national law designates the competent court, the time limits within which an action must be brought, the amount of the compensation and so forth. Community and national law are again intertwined in a complex manner. On the face of it, the separation of responsibilities seems obvious: liability for breach of Community law derives from Community law itself and the conditions for liability established by the Court of Justice are necessary and sufficient to give rise to a right to compensation. National law operates as the vehicle carrying the application of the action in damages. Yet in practice, the correlation and confrontation between national and Community law raises difficult issues.

Francovich and its progeny pose several problems of a constitutional nature when applied in the national context. First, and this will be the focus of this chapter, liability of the State for legislative acts, particularly for pieces of primary legislation, is excluded in most if not all of the Member States under review. While the notion of governmental liability for acts and omissions causing harm to individuals is known in each national system, and has been expanding gradually over the past decades, liability of the State for acts and omissions of *Parliament* is still a much debated issue, and appears to constitute one of the last bulwarks of State immunity in damages.[8] *Francovich* and *Brasserie du P êcheur/ Factortame III* break open these last immunities of the State. Second, in federal states and decentralised systems, questions of allocation of liability will arise: upon which level, body or organ will rest the final duty to compensate harm done? Third, questions of allocation will also arise in complex cases where, in contrast to *Francovich* which concerned a straightforward breach, the harm is caused by a series of infringements

---

[8] Also liability for judicial acts is often still excluded or has only recently started to develop in most Member States, see on this issue *eg* G Anagnostaras, 'The Principle of State Liability for Judicial Breaches: The Impact of European Community Law', *EPL* (2001) 281; SCJJ Kortmann, JS Kortmann and LP Kortmann, 'Nogmaals de aansprakelijkheid van de staat voor schade voortvloeiende uit rechterlijke uitspraken', *in Grensverleggend Staatsrecht. Opstellen aangeboden aan CAJM Kortmann*, (Deventer, Kluwer, 2001) 207; Toner, H, 'Thinking the Unthinkable? State Liability for Judicial Acts after Factortame (III)', *YEL* (1997) 165; liability for judicial acts infringing upon Community law has recently been developed in Case C–224/01 *Gerhard Köbler v Republik Österreich* [2003] ECRI-10239.

committed by several organs of the State: a conflicting primary law has not been amended to comply with Community law, the administration has not corrected the infringement and the courts have not repaired the breach either. These issues will be considered in turn. First, the pre-*Francovich* case law concerning the liability of the Member States for breach of Community law will be considered (under 11.2). Second, the state of national law relating to the liability of the legislating State will be analysed for several Member States (section 11.3). The next section analyses the specific case of State liability for breach of Community law (section 11.4). Section 11.5 looks into the case law of the Court of Justice concerning the liability of the Community for legislative wrong. The development of the *Francovich* mandate is discussed in section 11.6, with special attention to the elements in the case law raising constitutional questions from a national perspective. Finally, the response of the national courts is examined in section 11.7.

11.2. STATE LIABILITY FOR BREACH OF COMMUNITY LAW BEFORE *FRANCOVICH*

11.2.1. The Pre-*Francovich* Case Law of the Court of Justice[9]

There is only very little in the Treaty explaining what legal action individuals can take to protect their rights under Community law, and what remedies are available. In the case of an alleged infringement of the Treaty by the *institutions*, Article 230 EC provides that the individuals may bring an action for annulment before the European Court.[10] In addition, provision is made for an action in damages, in Article 288(2) EC (previously Article 215(2) of the EC Treaty) and Article 235 EC (previously Article 178 of the EC Treaty). When it comes to infringements committed by the *Member States* and causing harm to individuals, the Treaty is silent. The only remedy, or rather sanction, explicitly provided for infringements of Community law is to be found in Article 81(2) EC,[11] which states that anti-competitive agreements are null and void. However, this is a sanction for

---

[9]   For the state of the law before *Francovich,* see N Green and A Barav, 'Damages in National Courts for Breach of Community Law', *YEL* (1986) 55; D Simon and A Barav, 'La responsabilité de l'administration nationale en cas de violation du droit communautaire', *RMC* (1987) 165; A Barav, 'Damages in the Domestic Courts for Breach of Community Law by National Public Authorities', in HG Schermers, T Heukels and P Mead (eds), *Non-Contractual Liability of the European Communities,* (Dordrecht, Kluwer Law International, 1988) 149; G Whyte, 'State responsibility in the context of European Community Law', in *Contemporary Problems of International Law. Essays in Honour of G Schwarzenberger,* (London, Stevens and Sons, 1988) 301; F Schockweiler, G Wivines and JM Godart, 'Le régime de la responsabilité extra-contractuelle du fait d'actes juridiques dans la Communauté européenne', *RDTeur* (1990) 27.

[10]   Access for individuals is however very limited and generally does not lie against legislative acts, such as directives or (veritable) regulations.

[11]   Previously Art. 85(2) of the EC Treaty.

violations committed by individuals. No remedies or sanctions have been provided for violations by Member States. The public enforcement mechanism of Article 226 EC does not take account of the damage done to individuals as a consequence of those violations, and is not intended to protect their rights. Until *Francovich* the Court never explicitly stated that national courts were under an obligation or had jurisdiction as a matter of Community law to hold the State liable in damages upon a declaration under Article 226 EC that a Member State had failed to fulfil its obligations under the Treaty. Yet, the Court at several occasions had implied that there was such an obligation, when it held that a judgment delivered in an enforcement action was important, even if the violation had been amended before the case actually reached the Court, on the ground that the interest of having a judgment *'may consist in establishing a basis for the liability which a Member State may incur, in particular, towards individuals as a result of the breach of its obligations'*.[12] The existence of a right to damages in national courts as a consequence of a judgment of the Court derived more clearly from the 1960 *Humblet* case, in the context of the ECSC Treaty, but readily transposable to the EC Treaty, where the Court held that *'if the Court rules in a judgment that a legislative or administrative measure adopted by the authorities of a Member State is contrary to Community law, that Member State is obliged, by virtue of Article 86 of the ECSC Treaty, to rescind the measure in question and to make reparation for any unlawful consequences which may have ensued'*.[13]

However, none of these cases explicitly stated that *the national courts* must have jurisdiction *as a matter of Community law* to declare the State liable in damages under conditions to be set *by Community law*, independent of a judgment of the Court declaring that there had been a violation. Compensation was apparently a matter for national law.

The Commission was recorded as stating that although Community law did not make specific provision for such right, Member State were, on grounds of Article 10 EC (previously Article 5 of the Treaty) and the general principles of Community law obliged to provide for a system of compensation of individuals adversely affected by public authorities actions incompatible with the free movement of goods.[14] The question was, however,

---

[12] Case 309/84 *Commission v Italy* [1986] 599, at para 18; see also Case 39/72 *Commission v Italy (premiums for slaughtering cows)* [1973] ECR 101, at para 11: 'Moreover, in the face of both a delay in the performance of an obligation and a definite refusal, a judgment by the court under Articles 169 and 171 of the Treaty may be of substantive interest as establishing the basis of a responsibility that a Member State can incur as a result of its default, as regards other Member States, the Community or private parties'; Case 103/84 *Commission v Italy* [1986] ECR 1759; and Case 154/85 *Commission v Italy* [1987] 2717, at para 6: 'That object may consist in particular in establishing the basis of the liability that a Member State could incur towards those who acquire rights as a result of its default'.

[13] Case 6/60 *Humblet v Belgium* [1960] ECR 559, at 569.

[14] References in A Barav, 'State liability in damages for breach of Community law in the national courts', in T Heukels and A McDonnell (eds), *The Action for Damages in Community Law* (The Hague, Kluwer, 1997) 363, at 364.

who was responsible for installing the system: the national legislatures acting for each State individually adapting the national rules on state liability, as the Commission seemed to indicate? Or rather the Member States acting together as the Community legislature, introducing a special provision in the Treaties providing for a Community system of State liability, to be applied by the Court of Justice or the national courts? Or did the Court of Justice have jurisdiction to create a new remedy to be awarded by the national courts? The Court of Justice appeared to be of the opinion, for a long time, that it did not have that power: in *Russo v AIMA*, the Court held that *'If such damage has been caused through an infringement of Community law the State is liable to the injured party of the consequences* in the context of the provisions of national law on the liability of the State'.[15] And in *Granaria*, the Court held that *'the question of compensation by a national agency for damage caused to private individuals by the agencies and servants of Member States, either by reason of infringement of Community law or by an act or omission contrary to national law, in the application of Community law does not fall within the second paragraph of Article 215 of the Treaty and must be determined by the national courts* in accordance with the national law of the Member State concerned'.[16] In a letter to the Chairman of the Permanent Representatives Committee, recommending the introduction into the Treaty of the provision providing for the liability of the Member States for infringement of Community law, the Court stated that such provision would require legislative Community rules harmonising the criteria and detailed conditions governing the right to compensation. It is clear that the Member States, during the negotiations concerning the Treaty of Maastricht recognised and discussed the problem of the liability of Member States towards individuals, but they did not lay down any rules to that effect, and instead, introduced the mechanism of Article 228(2) EC (old Article 171(2) of the Treaty).

In short, the case law before 1991 concerning liability of the Member States for infringement of Community law indicated that there was probably a duty incumbent on the State to make good the damage incurred by individuals, but that this must be applied in accordance with the national rules concerning State liability.

11.2.2. Strengthening Member State Compliance

By the end of the 1980's and the beginning of the 1990's, it became apparent that some new mechanism must be introduced to improve the observance and enforcement of Community law by the Member States. The failure on the part of the Member States to implement directives

---

[15] Case 60/75 *Carmine Antonio Russo v AIMA* [1976] ECR 45, at para 9, emphasis added.
[16] Case 101/78 *Granaria BV v Hoofdproduktschap voor Akkerbouwprodukten* [1979] ECR 623, at 14, emphasis added.

timely and correctly had reached a level of intolerance and irritation.[17] Until the amendment of Article 228(2) EC by the Treaty of Maastricht, there was no procedure available for the Commission and the Court to force a disobedient State which persisted in a violation of Community law even upon a declaration made by the Court under Article 226 EC.[18] In 1990 the number of judgments of the Court rendered under Articles 226 and 227 EC with which Member States failed to comply was 83, most involving the failure to implement directives and more than one third concerning one particular Member State, Italy.[19] The legal weakness of directives, *i.e.* their dependence on national implementation, was not overcome by means explicitly provided for in the Treaty and while the doctrines developed by the Court, direct effect and conform interpretation, did bring some relief to protect individual rights and to reinforce effectiveness of Community law, there continued to be gaps in the system. The failure to implement directives continued to pose problems of uniformity, of effectiveness, and of effective protection of individual rights. The Court of Justice itself had also pointed to the gap in the Community enforcement system due to the absence of a mechanism effectively forcing Member State compliance with Community obligations.[20] At the 1991 Intergovernmental Conference which would lead to the adoption of the Maastricht Treaty, one of the amendments under consideration was the introduction of a new paragraph in Article 171 of the Treaty (now Article 228 EC).[21] The proposal was

---

[17] So G Tesauro, 'La sanction des infractions au droit communautaire', *Rivista di diritto europeo* (1992) 477, at 480–81.

[18] Art. 171 of the Treaty (now Art. 228(1) EC) did provide that the Member States were under an obligation to comply with a judgment of the European Court; and where a Member State failed to do so, the Commission could bring new proceedings before the Court for failure of the Member State to comply with its obligation under Art. 171 of the Treaty. But that was the end of it. If the State still did not comply, there was nothing more the Commission and the Court could do.

[19] See C Plaza Martin, 'Furthering the Effectiveness of EC Directives and the Judicial Protection of Individual Rights Thereunder', 43 *ICLQ* (1994) 26, at 35.

[20] See reference in G Tesauro, 'La sanction des des infractions au droit communautaire', *Rivista di diritto europeo* (1992) 477, at 480–81. The Court at the time apparently was awaiting legislative intervention by the Member States to introduce a new procedure. The concern was shared also by the Parliament and the Commission. The Commission sought to involve the national courts, stating that '*enforcement through the national courts is of great importance to the proper functioning of the rules in a system ensuring that competition in the Common market is not distorted…The possibility of being awarded damages would be an incentive to turn to national courts, and the Commission is therefore, in particular, studying the possibility of further legislative action to strengthen enforcement by private damages actions*', Answer given on 27 March 1984 by Mr Andriessen on behalf of the Commission to written question no. 1935/83, OJ 1984 C 144/14, cited in N Green and A Barav, 'Damages in National Courts for Breach of Community Law', *YEL* (1986) 55, at 57.

[21] See also the Declaration annexed to the Treaty of Maastricht, stating that 'la Conférence souligne qu'il est essentiel, pour la cohérence et l'unité du processus de construction européenne, que chaque État membre transpose intégralement et fidèlement dans son droit national les directives communautaires dont il est destinataire, dans les délais impartis par celle-ci'.

to authorise the Commission, where a Member State persisted in a violation of Community law, to ask the Court to impose a lump sum or penalty payments on a defaulting Member State. While this system may well help to force the Member States to comply with their Community obligations in the long run – the procedure may be rather long and can only be brought where a State fails to comply with a judgment already rendered by the Court – it does nothing to protect the Community rights of individuals: it is a sanction on the defaulting Member State and presumably a deterrent preventing it and other Member States from violating their obligations; it does not however provide a remedy for individuals. Before the Treaty of Maastricht was even agreed, the Court of Justice found its own way to increase the effectiveness of Community law while at the same time protecting the Community rights of individuals, in the *Francovich* judgment.

11.2.3. Article 228(2) EC: Financial Sanctions for Infringements of Community Law

The second and third paragraph of Article 228 EC have not, so far, given rise to much litigation,[22] and only twice has the Court imposed penalty payments on a defaulting Member State.[23] There have been other cases in which the procedure was initiated, but the infringements were ended

---

[22] For a discussion of the legal and policy issues involved, see J Candela and B Mongin, 'La loi européenne, désormais mieux protégée. Quelques réflexions sur la première décision de la Commission demandant à la Cour de justice de prononcer une sanction pécuniaire au sens de l'article 171 du Traité à l'encontre de certains États membres pour violation du droit communautaire', *RMUE* (1997) 9.

[23] Case C–278/01 *Commission v Spain*, decision of 25 November 2003, nyr; and Case C–387/97 *Commission v Greece* [2000] ECR I–5047. Concerning the latter case: in a Communication of 21 August 1996 the Commission established the criteria according to which it would set the amount of the financial penalty, *i.e.* seriousness and length of the infringement and dissuasive nature of the sanction. In a further Communication of 28 February 1997 the Commission set out more explicitly the method of calculating the penalty payment. In Case C–387/97 *Commission v Greece* [2000] ECR I–5047, concerning Council Directive 75/442/EEC of 15 July 1975 on waste (OJ 1975 L 194, 39) and Council Directive 78/319/EEC of 20 March 1978 on toxic and dangerous waste (OJ 1978 L 84, 43), the Court ordered the Greek State *'to pay to the Commission, into the account EC own resources, a penalty payment of EUR 20 000 for each day of delay in implementing the measures necessary to comply with the judgment in Case C–45/91, from delivery of the present judgment until the judgment in Case C–45/ 91 has been complied with'*. The Commission sent periodically to the Greek authorities letters requesting the payment of the daily penalty of £20,000 for the months of July 2000 to February 2001 included which Greece paid within the deadlines foreseen. This represented a total amount of £ 5 400 000 paid to the Commission by Greece. By successive letters sent in July 2000, October 2000 and March 2001, the Greek authorities communicated to the Commission information concerning the measures taken in order to fulfil the Treaty obligations. With the purpose of verifying the technical and factual dimension of this information, the Commission selected two independent experts, who, after inspecting the site area, produced a report (July 2001) accompanied with photographic evidence. In the light of the above, the Commission con-

before the Court could hand a decision imposing penalty payments. The threat of such decision in itself appears to constitute a powerful incentive for Member States to comply with their Community obligations.[24] The main difference with *Francovich* liability is that individuals receive no compensation: the payments must be made to the Community's own resources.

11.3. LIABILITY OF THE LEGISLATING STATE IN NATIONAL LAW

Government liability is, in many legal systems, one of the most controversial issues of tort law. It is a complex area of law, combining questions of constitutional, administrative and tort law.[25] All Member States know some form or other of liability of the State or public authorities. The idea of absolute State immunity in damages has been overcome. The old adage that 'the King can do no wrong' is no longer valid. In most Member States, the immunity has been overcome through judicial decision, and is an ongoing evolution of extending liability to ever more fields. The crumbling off of full State immunity typically started in the area of illegal individual administrative acts, moving into areas where discretion has been wrongfully used, perhaps even accepting also liability for secondary legislation.[26] Nevertheless, the idea that the State could not be held liable in damages for acts or omissions of the primary Legislature was, and still is, a widespread dogma. The immunity of the King as Sovereign has been taken over by the State acting as the primary legislature, the expression of the Sovereign Will of the People, or by Parliament itself. Among the argu-

cluded that Greece complied with the requirements of the Court of Justice's judgement. Because of the particularity and the unique character of this case, the Commission handled it in a very careful way, which necessitated the involvement of many officials and a great investment in terms of time. The procedure aiming to ensure that Greece had undertaken measures to conform to the Community environmental law on waste commenced in 1989; Greece was considered to fulfil its obligations under the relevant directives in July 2001. The introduction of this new procedure by the Maastricht Treaty was considered to be successful, mainly because of its preventing effect; see Answer by Mrs Wallström on behalf of the Commission to written question by MEP Chris Davies, OJ 2002 C 134/98. Other cases have been brought, but have not led to a judgment of the ECJ, *e.g.* Case C–85/01 *Commission v UK*, concerning the UK's continued failure to implement correctly the bathing water directive after a judgment of the ECJ The case was brought before the Court in February 2001, but removed from the register in February 2002.

[24] For an overall view of the various procedures before national and European courts see D Simon, 'The Sanction of Member States' Serious Violations of Community Law', in D O'Keeffe and A Bavasso (eds), *Judicial Review in European Union Law. Liber Amicorum in Honour of Lord Slynn of Hadley*, (The Hague, Kluwer Law International, 2000) 275.

[25] In some systems that recognise a division between public and private law, it may not be clear whether governmental liability should be treated as private or as public law. The public law–private law divide is not very useful in this area.

[26] A form of governmental action that is often excluded is that of *'acts of State'*.

ments against liability of the State for acts or omissions by Parliament are the most fundamental principles of democracy, separation of powers, absence of judicial review of primary legislation, and the notion that the courts should not interfere with law-making. Other arguments include the more practical idea that the law-making power must not be hindered by the threat of damage claims, the idea that Acts of Parliament are general and abstract, or the claim that primary legislation will hardly ever directly cause damage to individuals, and finally the floodgate argument. The risk for wrongful legislation, or legislation which otherwise causes damage,[27] thus lies not with the State, but with the individuals or companies suffering harm.[28] In some systems, liability for legislative wrong may be excluded on grounds of a theoretical conception of rights which the citizen may have against the legislating State or of the duties which the legislating State has *vis-à-vis* individual citizens; or the fact that the legislative State acts in the 'general interest'.

Francovich concerned the issue of liability of the State for a failure to implement a directive, *i.e.* a failure to adopt legislation. Liability of the State for acts or omissions attributable to the legislature, and especially the primary legislature, Parliament, was excluded in most national systems.[29] Several of the intervening Member States pointed to the principle of immunity of the legislating State. Advocate General Mischo examined the objection, but emphasised the fact that the context of Community law was entirely different from that in which the theory of the immunity of the State as legislator was developed in certain Member States. In the context of Community law, the national legislature was under an obligation to enact a law, it is possible to determine with a sufficient degree of precision what it must do, and it must act within a certain period of time. *'In my view'*, he concluded, *'it is not excessive to say that in relation to the transposition of directives the legislature is in a situation close to that of the administration responsible for the implementation of the law'.*[30] While this may be true and almost self-evident from a Community perspective, it would not be so simple for a national court to actually hold the State liable in damages in situations where it had been excluded on grounds that it would run

---

[27] Except in those systems recognising some form of no-fault liability on grounds of *'égalité devant les charges publiques'* and the like.

[28] Obviously, Parliament may decide to repair damage; but it is not for the courts to order it.

[29] Comparative analyses of the state of the law in various Member States available at the time when *Francovich* was decided are J Bell and AW Bradley (eds), *Governmental Liability: A Comparative Study* (Glasgow, UK Comparative Law Series, 1991); F Schockweiler, G Wivines and JM Godart, 'Le régime de la responsabilité extra-contractualle du fait d'actes juridiques dans la Communauté européenne', *RTDeur* (1990) 27 (Schockweiler was one of the judges on the bench in *Francovich*; one can assume that the article was known to the bench).

[30] Opinion of AG Mischo in Joined Cases C–6/90 and C–9/90 *Andrea Francovich and Danila Bonifaci v Italian Republic* [1991] ECR I–5357, at marginal number 47.

against the most fundamental principles of constitutional law. In the following pages, a short insight will be given in the principles governing the national law on liability of the State, in particular the legislating State, before *Francovich*.

11.3.1. Belgium

Under Belgian law,[31] the law of governmental liability has developed from the *Flandria* judgment of the *Cour de cassation* in 1920 onwards.[32] The principles and rules governing governmental liability for administrative acts and omissions are the same as those applying to liability of private persons under civil law. Governmental liability for administrative acts and omissions,[33] whether individual or general – in the form of secondary legislation – and including physical acts, is based on Articles 1382 *et seq.* of the Belgian Civil Code, and applies under the usual three basic conditions: the existence of a wrongful act or omission ('fault'),[34] damage and causal link. However, the State was traditionally considered immune for acts and omissions of the primary legislature,[35] on grounds of consideration of parliamentary sovereignty, of the theory that the Act of Parliament represents the will of the people, and of the principle of the separation of powers; also, until the establishment of the *Cour d'arbitrage* no court was competent to rule on the legality of Acts of Parliament. Additional arguments were found in the fact that Acts of Parliament are gen-

---

[31] See for general overviews of the state of the law before *Francovich*: M Leroy, 'La responsabilité de l'État législateur', *JT* (1978) 321; W Van Gerven, *Hoe blauw is het bloed van de prins? De overheid in het verbintenissenrecht*, (Antwerpen, Kluwer, 1984); I Cornelis, *Beginselen van het Belgische buitencontractuele aansprakelijkheidsrecht*, (Antwerpen, Maklu, 1989); LP Suetens, 'The Law of Belgium', in J Bell and AW Bradley (eds), *Governmental Liability: A Comparative Study*, (London, UK Comparative Law Series, 1991); M Leroy, 'Responsabilité des pouvoirs public du chef de méconnaissance des normes supérieures de droit national par un pouvoir législatif', in *La responsabilité des pouvoirs publics*, (Bruxelles, Bruylant, 1991) 299.

[32] *Cour de cassation*, decision of 5 November 1920, *Flandria*, Pas (1920) I, 193.

[33] Including the failure to adopt secondary legislation on the part of the Executive, see *Cour de cassation (B)*, decision of 23 April 1971, *postontvangers*, Arr. Cass., 1971, 786; see A Van Oevelen, 'De materiële voorwaarden voor de aansprakelijkheid van de Staat voor de niet-uitvoering van zijn regelgevende bevoegdheid: een vergelijking tussen de rechtspraak van het Europese Hof van Justitie en die van het Hof van Cassatie', in Publiek recht, ruim bekeken *Opstellen aangeboden aan Prof. J Gijssels* (Antwerp, Maklu, 1994) 427, at 431 *et seq.*

[34] Acts which are unconstitutional or otherwise illegal are considered wrongful and constitute a fault, except if there is a justification, for instance a justifiable error. The breach of the general duty of care may equally constitute a fault.

[35] See *eg* M Leroy, 'La responsabilité de l'État législateur', *JT* (1978) 321; M Leroy, 'Responsabilité des pouvoirs publics du chef de méconnaissance des normes supérieures de droit national par un pouvoir législatif', in *Le responsabilité des pouvoirs publics* (Bruylant, 1991) 299, with many references.

eral and abstract in nature and are not directed to particular individuals,[36] and the fact that the legislative function would be paralysed by the threat of having to indemnify persons harmed by a law. The immunity of the State extended also to the State acting in its judicial capacity.[37]

Even before *Francovich*, the case against liability of the legislating State became weaker.[38] It was argued in the literature that it should be possible for the State to be held liable in damages for wrongful primary legislation adopted in breach of higher national constitutional law, and for infringement of international norms:[39]Parliament could no longer be considered sovereign to the same extent and the principle of separation of powers had been given a different meaning, to include judicial checks and balances: courts had jurisdiction since *Le Ski* to set aside primary legislation conflicting with directly effective treaty provisions,[40] and the *Cour d'arbitrage* could even annul primary legislation adopted by the national or regional

---

[36] The argument is akin to the concept of *'Drittbezogenheit'* in Germany. However, the argument is difficult to maintain in Belgian law, since the liability for secondary legislation has been accepted by the *Cour de cassation*.

[37] The immunity of the State acting in its judicial capacity would be finally given up one month after *Francovich* in the *Anca* judgment of the *Cour de cassation* of 19 December 1991, see below.

[38] Van Oevelen argued, soon after *Francovich*, that the liability of the State for failure to adopt legislation had already been accepted by the *Cour de cassation* in the 1971 *postontvangers* case, and maintained that there was therefore nothing revolutionary in *Francovich* from the point of view of Belgian law, and then proceeded to compare the conditions put forward by the *Cour de cassation* in the context of liability for secondary legislation, and those of the ECJ He did not enter into the preliminary discussion of whether the two cases were indeed comparable: as a matter of constitutional law, there is an important difference, in the sense that in the judgment of the *Cour de cassation*, it was not Parliament which had failed to introduce the relevant legislation, the case concerned a failure to introduce secondary legislation. It may well be that at the end of the day the *Francovich*-type situation of an omission of Parliament to implement a Community directive is comparable to that of a lower legislator to adopt secondary legislation; this is indeed a widely held view, see *supra* the Opinion of AG Mischo in *Francovich*. It is submitted that this may be true for the simple and straightforward violations of clear obligations under Community law, the position is much more difficult to maintain where there is still a lot of discretion on the part of the Member States, and while limited by Community law, Parliament retains much (or some) of its original freedom of choice. This is a gliding scale: from which point onwards is the national Parliament to be compared to a secondary legislature on the national level? Van Oevelen's position resembles the view prevailing in The Netherlands, see *below*. A Van Oevelen, 'De materiële voorwaarden voor de aansprakelijkheid van de Staat voor de niet-uitvoering van zijn regelgevende bevoegdheid: een vergelijking tussen de rechtspraak van het Europees Hof van Justitie en die van het Hof van Cassatie', in *Publiek recht ruim bekeken. Opstellen aangeboden aan Prof. J Gijssels* (Antwerp, Maklu, 1994) 429.

[39] See M Leroy, 'Responsabilité des pouvoirs publics du chef de méconnaissance des normes supérieures de droit national par un pouvoir législatif', in *La responsabilité des pouvoirs publics* (Bruylant, 1991) 299; H Simonart, 'La responsabilité du législateur en raison de la méconnaissance de normes supérieures de droit international', above., 343; see also P Van Ommeslaghe, 'La responsabilité des pouvoirs publics en droit interne', in M Storme (ed), *Recht halen uit aansprakelijkheid. Willy Delva Cyclus 1992–1993*, (Gent, Mys & Breesch, 1993), 415.

[40] Since the *Le Ski* judgment of the *Cour de cassation*, discussed *above*.

parliaments. The power of the court to hold the State liable in damages was considered to follow automatically. In short, Belgian law on the issue was in flux.[41]

11.3.2. France

The French fundamental conceptions of the separation of powers and the ensuing powers of the courts *vis-à-vis* primary legislation were similar to those prevailing in Belgium: *'La loi est un acte de souveraineté et le propre de la souveraineté est de s'imposer à tous sans qu'on puisse réclamer d'elle aucune compensation'.*[42] And further: *'La loi n'est pas fautive par définition car la représentation nationale ne peut pas être accusée de commettre des fautes'.*[43] The French system of governmental liability is rather well developed and fairly complete, and is built on two strands: liability for fault, which follows in case of illegality of an administrative act,[44] and no-fault liability, which is based on the principle of *égalité devant les charges publiques*. As for acts and omissions of Parliament, the application of the system of fault-liability was excluded on constitutional grounds, as it was impossible for the courts to establish the illegality, unlawfulness or wrongfulness of *lois*.[45] A failure to act on the part of the legislature could never cause the liability of the State to arise, in the absence of a suitable cause of action.[46] On the other hand, it was accepted that the State could be under an obligation to compensate harm caused by primary legislation on the basis of no-fault liability, built on the principle of *'égalité devant les charges publiques'*. As early as 1938 the *Conseil d'État* accepted the no-fault liability of the legislating State, subject to the very strict conditions that the harm suffered is abnormal and special (*anormal et spécial*), and that the

[41] This is exemplified by the decision of a lower court concerning the failure of the Belgian State to adapt the legislation on pension schemes in favour of Community officials, see *below*.

[42] E Laferrière, *Traité de la juridiction administrative et des recours contentieux*, (Berger-Levrault, 1887), tôme 2, at 183.

[43] G Braibant, *Le droit administratif français*, 3rd edn (Paris, Dalloz, 1992) at 285.

[44] An illegal act is by and of itself wrongful, but this wrongfulness may not always be sufficient to establish the duty to pay compensation, see G Alberton, 'Le régime de la responsabilité du fait des lois confronté au droit communautaire: de la contradiction à la conciliation?', *RFDA* (1997) 1017, at 1026.

[45] In contrast to the Belgian situation after the establishment of the *Cour d'arbitrage*, the immunity for constitutional review of statutes in force remained in existence even after the establishment of the *Conseil constitutionnel*.

[46] It was also not possible to bring an action against the government for failure to table proposals for legislation, since the decision to introduce or not to introduce legislation is considered to constitute *'un acte de gouvernement'* not subject to judicial review, see M Dony, Le droit français', in G Vandersanden and M Dony (eds), *La responsabilité des Etats membres en cas de violation du droit communautaire. Etudes de droit communautaire et de droit national comparé* (Brussels, Bruylant, 1997) 235, at 252.

Legislature had not excluded the existence of a duty to compensate.[47] These conditions are so restrictive, that the no-fault liability of the legislating State for breach of the principle of the *égalité devant les charges publiques* had only been successfully invoked on three occasions prior to *Francovich*.[48]

Now, it was only two years before *Francovich* was decided, that the *Conseil d'État* had handed its decision in *Nicolo*, assuming jurisdiction to declare that the Legislature had infringed the hierarchy of norms imposed by Article 55 of the Constitution by adopting a *loi* conflicting with treaty provisions or provisions of Community law.[49] Would it follow automatically that the courts would now also assume jurisdiction to hold the State liable for legislative wrong, under the French adage that *responsabilité suit illégalité*? It is one thing to declare that a *loi* is inapplicable in a particular case because it infringes the duty to respect treaties as laid down in the Constitution; it is quite another to hold the State liable in damages. It was not clear whether the courts would be so inclined.

11.3.3. Germany

In the light of what has been said about the French and the Belgian arguments against public liability for legislative wrong, focussing on the inability of the courts to declare that the legislature has committed a wrong, it might have been expected that given the existence of a constitutional court in Germany with competence to declare primary legislation unconstitutional, it would also be acceptable that the State be held liable in damages. Not so. It was impossible before *Francovich* to hold the State liable for legislative acts or omissions, but on rather different grounds. German law on state liability developed along several lines.[50] Liability of

---

[47] *'Il faut que rien, ni dans le texte même de la loi ou dans les travaux préparatoires, ni dans l'ensemble des circonstances de l'affaire, ne permette de penser que le législateur a entendu faire supporter à l'intéressé une charge qui ne lui incombe pas normalement'*, Conseil d'État, decision of 14 January 1938, *Société des produits laitiers La Fleurette*, Rec., 25.

[48] Beside the *La Fleurette* decision in which the principle was first stated, also *Conseil d'État*, decision of 21 January 1944, *Caucheteux et Desmonts*, Rec., 222 and *Conseil d'État*, decision of 25 January 1963, *Bovero*, Rec., 53, see G Alberton, 'Le régime de la responsabilité du fait des lois confronté au droit communautaire: de la contradiction à la conciliation?', *RFDA* (1997) 1017, at 1018.

[49] As Denys Simon would put it, *'le caractère irréprochable de la loi était le corollaire de son caractère incontestable'*, D Simon, 'Droit communautaire et responsabilité de la puissance publique. Glissement progressifs ou révolution tranquille?', *AJDA* (1993) 235, at 242.

[50] German law on non-contractual liability is not founded on one conceptual rule, which applies to all situations, but on several different heads of liability. In every case, the correct applicable 'tort' has to be found, in order to assess whether there exists a right to compensation. The system aims to limit liability in respect of classes of claimants and the kinds of damage eligible for compensation, see W van Gerven, *Cases, Materials and Text on National Supranational and International Tort Law* (Oxford, Hart Publishing, 2000).

the State for unlawful acts derives on the one hand from the specific tort of unlawful acts committed by a public authority (*'Amtshaftung'*) provided for in Paragraph 839 of the *Bürgerliches Gesetzbuch*,[51] in conjunction with Article 34 of the Basic Law,[52] and from the notion of *Enteignungsgleichen Eingriff* (expropriation). In the context of liability for legislative acts and omissions, a distinction is often made between *legislatives Unrecht*, which refers to acts and omissions imputable directly to the primary Legislature, and *normatives Unrecht*, which relates to secondary legislation.[53]

Paragraph 839 of the *Bürgerliches Gesetzbuch* (BGB) allows claims against organs and officials of the State who, in violation of their official duty (*Amtspflicht*), have intentionally or negligently caused damage. The provision is read in the light of Article 34 of the Basic Law shifting liability from the official to the State or the public body which employs him. Article 34 of the Basic Law only comes into effect when the conditions set out in paragraph 839 BGB are fulfilled.[54] For governmental liability to arise three conditions must be fulfilled. First, the official was exercising a public office and has acted in violation of an official duty; second, the breach of official duty was committed intentionally or negligently; and third, the official duty breached was 'referable to the third party' (*'Drittbezogen'*), which means that the State is only responsible for breaches of official duties, the exercise of which is expressly directed at a

---

[51] Paragraph 839 of the German Bürgerliches Gesetzbuch (BGB) reads: '(1) If an official wilfully or negligently commits a breach of official duty incumbent upon him as against a third party, he shall compensate the third party for any damage arising therefrom. If only negligence is imputable to the official, he may be held liable only if the injured party is unable to obtain compensation elsewhere. (2) If an official commits a breach of his official duty in giving judgment in an action, he is not responsible for any damage arising therefrom, unless the breach of duty is punished with a public penalty to be enforced by criminal proceedings. This provision does not apply to a breach of duty consisting of refusal or delay in the exercise of the office. (3) The duty to make compensation does not arise if the injured party has wilfully or negligently omitted to avert the injury by making use of a legal remedy'.

[52] Art. 34 of the Basic Law reads: 'Where any person, in the exercise of a public office entrusted to him, violates his official obligations to a third party, liability shall rest in principle on the State or the public body which employs him. In the event of wilful intent or gross negligence, the right of recourse against the holder of a public office shall be reserved. In respect of the claim for compensation or the right of recourse, the jurisdiction of the ordinary courts shall not be excluded'.

[53] See K Boujoung, 'Staatshaftung für legislatives und normatives Unrecht in der neueren Rechtsprechung des Bundesgerichtshofes', in HJ Faller, P Kirchhof and E Träger (eds), *Verantwortlichkeit und Freiheit. Festschrift für Willi Geiger zum 80. Geburtstag*, 1989, 430, at 430; the distinction is also taken over by F Ossenbühl, even though he deems it not fully correct from a linguistic point of view: F Ossenbühl, *Staatshaftungsrecht*, 5th edn (München, Beck, 1998) at 104, fn 134.

[54] H-J Papier, 'Staatshaftung', in J Isensee and P Kirchhof (eds), Handbuch *des Staatsrechts der Bundesrepublik Deutschlands*, Vol VI, 1989, 1353, at 1358, with references to the relevant case law.

third party and has the aim of protecting a right of the third party.[55] However, it is precisely that requirement which is normally absent in the case of a legislative wrong. In the case law of the *Bundesgerichtshof*[56], the application of Paragraph 839 BGB and Article 34 GG to legislative wrongs, *i.e.* to legislative actions or omissions by Parliament, leads to denial of any liability on the part of the State, since Parliament and its members do not act under an official duty which is *drittbezogen*: *i.e.* the official was not under an obligation *vis-à-vis* the applicant *in particular*.[57] The application of these same principles to legislative wrong thus amounts to excluding in practice almost all liability for damage caused by the legislature. According to the case law of the *Bundesgerichtshof* the *Amtspflichten* of the Legislature are not 'referable to third parties', since the Legislature takes general and abstract measures and only has statutory duties *vis-à-vis* the public in general, not *vis-à-vis* specific persons or groups of individuals. The only possible exceptions are *Maßnahme-oder Einzelfallgesetzen*[58] (Acts relating to specific cases) which directly affect a defined individual or group of individuals, who can thus be considered *'Dritten'* in the sense of Paragraph 839 BGB. But in principle no compensation can be obtained for damage inflicted by statutes, even if they are and have been declared unconstitutional.[59] Furthermore, no distinction is made between simple or qualified infringements of higher law.

Special attention should be paid to a specific form of legislative wrong, namely inaction or the failure to legislate. In such cases an additional difficulty is that liability can only arise if there is a breach of a *precise* duty to legislate, also indicating *which* statute should be adopted.[60] Instructions to the Legislature are hardly ever specified in the Basic Law, and accordingly, liability for failure to act is also generally excluded for this reason.[61]

---

[55] See Opinion of Advocate-General Tesauro in Joined Cases C–46/93 and C–48/93, *Brasserie du Pêcheur SA v Germany and The Queen v Secretary of State for Transport, ex parte Factortame Ltd and Others* [1996] ECR I–1029, at marginal number 4.

[56] See *e.g. Bundesgerichtshof*, decision of 29 March 1971, BGHZ 56, 40; see also BGHZ 84, 292; BGHZ 87, 321; NJW 1988, 478.

[57] *'Drittbezogenheit'* is interpreted to mean something more than *'Drittschutz'*; if *Drittbezogenheit* would be taken in the latter sense, this would imply that liability for legislative wrong would be possible if the plaintiff would be part of an identifiable group of persons which the Act aims to protect; however, in the meaning generally given to it – and this cannot be changed by judicial interpretation – denotes something more that mere *Drittschutz* is needed, namely *an 'Individualisierbare Beziehung'*; see F Ossenbühl, *Staatshaftungsrecht*, 5th edn, (München, Beck, 1998) at 105.

[58] *Bundesgerichtshof*, decision of 29 March 1971, BGHZ 56, 40; see also BGHZ 87, 321; and BGHZ 91, 243.

[59] See *e.g.* S Detterbeck, 'Staatshaftung für die Missachtung von EG-Recht', *Verwaltungsarchiv* (1994) 159, at 163; see BGHZ 56, 40; BGHZ 87, 321; BGHZ 84, 292; [1988] NJW 478.

[60] See F Ossenbühl, *Staatshaftungsrecht*, 5th edn, (München, Beck, 1998) at 106.

[61] See H-J Papier, 'Staatshaftung', in J Isensee and P Kirchhof (eds), *Handbuch des Staatsrecht der Bundesrepublik Deutschlands*, Vol VI (1989) 1353, at 1371, with references to the relevant case law.

The second strand in the case law is based on the notions of *Aufopferung*[62] and *enteignungsgleichen Eingriff,* linked with Article 14 of the Basic Law as developed by the *Bundesgerichtshof*. The origins of this ground of liability are to be found in liability for lawful encroachments upon individual rights, but it was also extended to cover unlawful acts.[63] The claim is not based on fault, however. The most important element of a claim based on quasi-expropriatory encroachment is the 'special sacrifice' which is to be made good through the compensation. In principle, all unlawful encroachments upon actual rights and assets have to be regarded as quasi-expropriatory. Omissions to act are regarded as an encroachment.[64] In addition, the claim can only be justified if *actual* rights or assets are encroached; impairment of earning capacity or the prevention of future activities and earnings can never be regarded as being of expropriatory character.[65] Finally, intention has been omitted as a constitutive condition for liability; immediacy is required. *Enteignungsgleicher Eingriff* does apply to *normatives Unrecht* attributable to *lower* legislating bodies, other than Parliament,[66] but it did not encompass legislative wrong. In a 1987 decision,[67] the *Bundesgerichtshof* rejected a claim for damages for harm caused by an unconstitutional law.[68] The

---

[62] Compensation for *Aufopferung* is based on the general rule that the State is bound to compensate for the deprivation of private rights and assets. Since the eighteenth century this rule, which became codified by §§ 74 and 75 of the Introduction to the Prussian General Land Law, was part of the general common law in the German legal system. Compensation for expropriation has to be regarded only as a special application of this general principle, see W Rüfner, 'Basic Elements of German Law on State Liability', in J Bell and W Bradley (eds), *Governmental Liability: A Comparative Study* (Glasgow, UK Comparative Law Series, 1991) 249, at 259.

[63] In principle, compensation for expropriation and sacrifical encroachement had to be paid for lawful encroachments upon individual rights, the redress for unlawful acts being left to the area of tortious governmental liability of officials or the State (§ 839 BGB). The *Reichsgericht* and the *Bundesgerichtshof* extended the claims to unlawful action, arguing that if compensation was due for damage which had lawfully been inflicted, it would *a fortiori* have to be paid for harm done unlawfully; RGZ 140, 276; BGHZ 6, 270; BGHZ 13, 88, see W Rüfner, 'Basic Elements of German Law on State Liability', in J Bell and W Bradley (eds), *Governmental Liability: A Comparative Study* (Glasgow, UK Comparative Law Series, 1991) 249, at 260.

[64] BGH DVBl. 1971, 464.

[65] For an overview of the case law, see W Hüfner, 'Basic Elements of German Law of State Liability, in J Bell and AW Bradley (eds), *Governmental Liability: A Comparative Study*, (Glasgow, UK Comparative Law Series, 1991), 249, at 264–265; F Ossenbühl, *Staatshaftungsrecht*, 5th ed. (München, Beck, 1998) at 214 *et seq.*

[66] See *e.g.* W-R Schenke and U Guttenberg, 'Rechtsprobleme einer Haftung bei normativem Unrecht', *DÖV*, 1991, 945; F Ossenbühl, *Staatshaftungsrecht*, 5th ed, (München, Beck, 1998) at 235 *et seq.* (critically).

[67] *Bundesgerichtshof*, decision of 12 March 1987, *Kleingarten*, BGHZ 100, 136; NJW 1987, 1875; confirmed in *Bundesgerichtshof*, decision of 10 December 1987, *Waldschäden*, BGHZ 102, 350.

[68] Prior to that the BGH had indicated that the judge made concept of *enteignungsgleichen Eingriff* could be applied to the adoption of an unlawful statute, not for a failure to act, BGHZ 56, 40.

Bundesgerichtshof held, first, that the award of damages would appear to validate an unconstitutional law. However the main argument was that the *Bundesgerichtshof* denied jurisdiction to create governmental liability for legislative wrong judicially, in the absence of legislation to the effect. The award of compensation for unconstitutional statutes could upset the budget and therefore was to be reserved for Parliament itself.[69] Moreover, several solutions could be contemplated, so it was not the jurisdiction of the court to decide. Finally, the *Staatshaftungsgesetz*, which had been adopted in 1981 to reform the system of state liability, but was declared unconstitutional by the *Bundesverfassungsgericht*,[70] had provided in its Paragraph 5 that the liability of the State for legislative wrong would arise only in so far as an Act of Parliament would so provide.[71] The principles of separation of powers and of democracy prevented the *Bundesgerichtshof* to decide the matter; instead, it left the question for Parliament itself to decide. In other words, the development of governmental liability was considered to fall outside the limits of the judicial function.[72] The *Bundesverfassungsgericht* did not take the action brought against this decision, but it did hold that the opinion of the *Bundesgerichtshof* that the development of a system of governmental liability for legislative wrong was beyond the limits of the judicial function was sustainable.

The *Staatshaftungsgesetz* which had been adopted in 1981 but declared unconstitutional in 1982 did not provide for a general system of liability for legislative wrong committed by the primary legislature. Compensation would only be obtainable if and in so far as was provided for expressly by statute.[73] The *Bundesverfassungsgericht* declared the Act unconstitutional and void on the ground that the *Bund* lacked legislative

[69]   W Rüfner, 'Basic Elements of German Law on State Liability', in J Bell and AW Bradley (eds), *Governmental Liability: A Comparative Study* (Glasgow, UK Comparative Law Series, 1991) 249, at 263; the argument relates to the *'Haushaltsprerogative'* of Parliament.

[70]   *Bundesverfassungsgericht*, decision of 19 October 1982, *Staatshaftungsgesetz*, BVerfGE 61, 149. The unconstitutionality was due to the lack of competence of the federal legislature, see F Ossenbühl, *Staatshaftungsrecht*, 5th edn, (München, Beck, 1998) at 455.

[71]   See H Dohmold, 'Die Haftung des Staates für legislatives und normatives Unrecht in der neueren Rechtsprechung des Bundesgerichtshofes', *DÖV* (1991) 152, at 155; the *Staatshaftungkommission* which had prepared the *Staatshaftungsgesetz* had stated that liability for unconstitutional Acts of Parliament should only arise in cases where the Legislature had not regulated the matter within 18 months after the judgment declaring the unconstitutionality.

[72]   This is probably also why it was stated later in German literature that the ECJ could not develop State liability without legislative intervention, and that accordingly *Francovich* amounted to an *ultra vires* development of the law.

[73]   K Boujoung, 'Staatshaftung für legislatives und normatives Unrecht', in HJ Faller, P Kirchhof und E Träger (eds), *Verantwortlichkeit und Freiheit. Festschrift für Willi Geiger zum 80. Geburtstag* (1989) 430, at 436–37; H-J Papier, 'Staatshaftung', in J Isensee and P Kirchhof (eds), *Handbuch des Staatsrecht der Bundesrepublik Deutschlands*, Vol VI (1989) 1353, at 1388 ff.

competence in this field. A proposed amendment of the Basic Law to overcome this lack of competence failed.[74]

11.3.4. Italy

The main reasons why the Italian legal system did not recognise the liability of the State for legislative acts or omissions are not unrelated to the considerations relating to *'Drittbezogenheit'* in Germany.[75]The main problem in Italy is the distinction between *diritti soggetivi*, infringement of which can give rise to liability and a duty to pay compensation, and *interessi legitimi*, an infringement of which cannot. Now, with respect to legislation, an individual only has *interessi semplici* which can never give rise to a right to be compensated.

Under Italian law prevailing at the time,[76] the State could not be held liable for acts or omissions on the part of the primary legislature. The same rules of non-contractual liability apply to governmental organs as to private individuals, namely those based on the *Code napoléon*, and contained in Article 2043 of the Italian Civil Code.[77] The provision has traditionally been interpreted narrowly concerning the liability of public authorities.[78] The liability in damages of public authorities in general is a matter for the civil courts,[79] and the *Corte di cassazione* has always held that Article 2043 can be

---

[74] See W Rüfner, 'Basic Elements of German Law on State Liability', in J Bell and W Bradley (eds), *Governmental Liability: A Comparative Study* (Glascow, UK Comparative Law Series, 1991) 249, at 272–73.

[75] So also AG Tesauro in his Opinion in Joined Cases C–46/93 and C–48/93 *Brasserie du Pêcheur SA v Germany and The Queen v Secretary of State for Transport, ex parte Factortame Ltd and Others* [1996] ECR I–1029, at fn 5.

[76] See M Clarich, 'The Liability of Public Authorities in Italian Law', in J Bell and W Bradley (eds), *Governmental Liability: A Comparative Study* (Glasgow, UK Comparative Law Series, 1991) 225; L Daniele, 'Italian Report', *The Imposition of Sanctions for Breach of Community Law. XVth FIDE Congress*, Lisbon, 1992, 259; R Caranta, 'Governmental Liability after Francovich', 52 *CLJ* (1993) 272; F Zampini, 'Responsabilité de l'État pour violation du droit communautaire: l'exemple de l'Italie', *RFDA* (1997) 1039; L Malferrari, 'State Liability for Violation of EC Law in Italy: The Reaction of the Corte di Cassazione to *Francovich* and Future Prospects in Lights of its Decision of July 22, 1999, No. 500', *ZaORV* (1999) 809.

[77] 'Any fraudulent, malicious, or negligent act that causes an unjustified injury to another obliges the person who has committed the act to pay damages', translation taken from M Beltramo, GE Longo and JH Merryman, *The Italian Civil Code and complementary legislation*, (Dobbs Ferry, NY, Oceana, 1996).

[78] R Caranta, 'Governmental Liability after Francovich', 52 *CLJ* (1993) 272, at 287.

[79] Article 28 of the Italian Constitution stating that 'Officials and employees of the State and public entities are directly responsible, according to criminal, civil and administrative laws, for acts committed in violation of rights. In such cases liability extends to the State and the public entities' is considered to concern only the issue of the distribution of liability among the public auhorities and the public agents. It has not radically altered the model of civil liability of public authorities, see M Clarich, 'The Liability of Public Authorities in Italian Law', in J Bell and W Bradley (eds), *Governmental Liability: A Comparative Study* (Glasgow, UK Comparative Law Series, 1991) 225, at 227 *et seq*.

applied to public authorities only when they violate a subjective right (*diritto soggettivo*) and not a mere legitimate interest (*interesse legittimo*). As a general rule, citizens do not have subjective rights where the public authority has discretionary powers. Nor is the rule that there is no liability altered by the fact that an administrative decision has been annulled, in contrast to for instance Belgian or French law. Illegality is not equated with the unlawfulness which gives rise to a right to compensation. When it comes to legislation, an individual does not even have a legitimate interest: he has only a simple interest (*interesse semplice*), and he cannot avail himself of any personal right in relation to activities and omissions on the part of the legislature. He cannot therefore claim compensation for damage incurred due to legislative acts or omissions. The principle of legislative liability was, accordingly, completely unknown as such.[80] Likewise, a declaration by the *Corte costituzionale* that a statute is unconstitutional does not give rise to a right to compensation. While the exclusion of the right to compensation of damage suffered as a consequence of legislative activities or omissions is directly founded on the distinction between *interesse legitimi* and *diritti soggettivi*, there may also have been an underlying constitutional argument, based on the separation of powers and the respective functions of the state organs. It is this argument which would re-surface in the post-*Francovich* judgment of the *Corte di cassazione*, where it held that in the Italian constitutional system legislation is a manifestation of the political function of government, *i.e.* free in setting its aims and thus immune from control by the judiciary.[81] Accordingly, the principle that the sovereign Parliament can do no wrong and that courts cannot hold the State liable in damages for legislative wrong was firmly established in Italian law.[82]

11.3.5. The United Kingdom

English tort law is based on specific heads of tort; each case must be fitted into the pigeon-hole of a specific head of tort, such as negligence (the most general tort), nuisance, breach of statutory duty and so forth.[83] The same rules generally apply equally to tortious conduct by individuals and

---

[80] So L Daniele, 'Italian Report', The Imposition of Sanctions for Breach of Community Law. XVth FIDE Congress, Lisbon, 1992, 259, at 266.

[81] *Corte di cassazione*, decision n. 7832 of 19 July 1995, Il Fallimento, 1996, 137; see L Malferrari, 'State Liability for Violation of EC Law in Italy: The Reaction of the Corte di Cassazione to *Francovich* and Future Prospects in Lights of its Decision of July 22, 1999, No. 500', *ZaORV* (1999) 809, at 818–19.

[82] See E Zampini, 'Responsabilité de l'État pour violation du droit communautaire: l'exemple de l'Italie', *RFDA* (1997) 1039.

[83] A brief and general overview of the various systems of tort law is given in W van Gerven, *Cases, Materials and Text on National, Supranational and International Tort Law*, (Oxford, Hart Publishing, 2000) at 1 *et seq.*

public authorities, with the exception of the tort of misfeasance in public office, applicable to public authorities alone.[84] The tort of misfeasance in public office applies only under very limited circumstances, even though it was recently expanded in *Three Rivers District Council v Bank of England*.[85] It requires that there has been intentional unlawful conduct, whereby the decision-maker knew that he was acting unlawfully as he did and knew that his act would injure the plaintiff. The other, general, torts applied to public authorities, create varying degrees of liability depending on the degree of discretion, the seriousness of the fault on their part and the nature of the interest affected.[86] At the time when *Francovich* was decided, liability of public authorities was usually assessed on the basis of the torts of negligence and breach of statutory duty.[87] Liability for exercise of a statutory duty was extremely limited.[88]

Yet, there were also special immunities: there was no liability for judicial acts,[89] and Acts of Parliament could never give rise to the liability of the State, since this would require the courts to declare that the Sovereign Parliament had infringed a rule of higher law, which they cannot. No cause of action is known in English law capable of fastening on 'wrongs' attributable to the primary Legislature. In the case of the tort of negligence for instance, it would be required to show that there was a duty of care on the part of Parliament *vis-à-vis* the applicant, which is rejected. Holding the State[90] liable in damages would require the courts to declare that the Queen in Parliament has acted *ultra vires*, or declare that its Acts were invalid. Under the doctrine of parliamentary sovereignty, English courts do not possess that jurisdiction: even after *Factortame*, the language is of 'compatibility' rather than 'validity'.[91] In addition, a public authority cannot be held liable in tort for valid acts.

---

[84] See W van Gerven *et al*, *Cases, Materials and Text on National, Supranational and International Tort Law*, (Oxford, Hart Publishing, 2000), at 358.

[85] *House of Lords*, decision of 15 May 2000, *Three Rivers District Council and Others v The Governor and Company of the Bank of England* [2000] 2 WLR 1220; [2002] UKHL 33; [2000] 3 All ER 1; [2000] CMLR 205; discussed in M Andenas and D Fairgrieve, 'Misfeasance in Public Office, Governmental Liability, and European Influences', 51 *ICLQ* (2002) 757.

[86] See J Bell, 'The Law of England and Wales', in J Bell and W Bradley (eds), *Governmental Liability: A Comparative Study* (Glasgow, UK Comparative Law Series, 1991).

[87] W van Gerven *et al*, *Cases, Materials and Text on National, Supranational and International Tort Law*, (Oxford, Hart Publishing, 2000), at 358 et seq;

[88] See *e.g.* PP Craig, 'Compensation in Public Law', *LQR* (1980) 413.

[89] J Bell, 'The Law of England and Wales', in J Bell and W Bradley (eds), *Governmental Liability: A Comparative Study* (Glasgow, UK Comparative Law Series, 1991).

[90] Actions in damages are instituted against the competent Secretary of State, rather than against the State. It is unclear who should be sued when the author of the wrong is the Legislature itself, *i.e.* the Queen in Parliament. Neither of the Houses has legal personality. See J Convery, 'State Liability in the United Kingdom after *Brasserie du Pêcheur*', 34 *CML Rev* (1997) 603, at 619.

[91] See J Convery, 'State Liability in the United Kingdom after *Brasserie du Pêcheur*', 34 *CML Rev* (1997) 603, at 620.

11.3.6. The Netherlands

As in France and Belgium, governmental liability is governed by the rules of civil law applying to private individuals.[92] Liability of the State for legislative acts had been accepted, but the relevant case law applied only to acts and omissions of secondary legislation.[93] Liability of the State for secondary legislation is readily accepted, and there is no requirement of a qualified breach or a grave and manifest infringement of the limits of discretion when the secondary legislature makes legislative choices.[94] In principle, liability of the State arises when the unlawfulness of the legislative measure has been established.[95] With respect to primary legislation, the rule contained in Article 120 of the Constitution that the courts do not control the constitutionality of primary legislation, seems to exclude the possibility of the courts holding primary legislation illegal and wrongful. The same provision would equally prevent the courts from holding the State liable for harm caused due to a failure of the *Staten Generaal* (the Netherlands primary legislature) to adopt primary legislation (*wet in formele zin*).[96] However, the *Hoge Raad* had not ruled on this issue.[97] The position may be different in the case of a violation by the primary Legislature of international treaties and directly effective Community

---

[92] In addition to specific provisions in the context of administrative law, but these do not apply to the specific case of legislative wrong.

[93] *Hoge Raad*, decision of 24 January 1969, *Pocketbooks II*, NJ 1969, 316; *Hoge Raad*, decision of 9 May 1986, *Van Gelder-Papier*, AB 1986, 429; *Hoge Raad*, decision of 26 September 1986, *Hoffmann-La Roche*, AB 1987, 70; see *e.g.* PJJ van Buuren and JEM Polak, De rechter en onrechtmatige wetgeving, (Zwolle, WEJ Tjeenk Willink, 1987); AJ Bok, 'Het Francovich-arrest en onrechtmatige wetgeving naar Nederlands recht', *TPR* (1993) 27; RM van Male, *Gevolgen van onrechtmatige regelgeving in Nederland*, (Zwolle, WEJ Tjeenk Willink, 1995); and more recently GE van Maanen and R de Lange, *Onrechtmatige Overheidsdaad*, (Deventer, WEJ Tjeenk Willink, 2000), 126 *et seq.*; HPh.JAM Hennekens, *Overheidsaansprakelijkheid op de weegschaal*, (Deventer, WEJ Tjeenk Willink, 2001).

[94] In fact, in *Van Gelder Papier*, the State had argued that it could only be held liable on those restrictive conditions, under express reference to the case law of the ECJ on liability of the Community for normative acts involving choices of economic policy. The *Hoge Raad* rejected the analogy and held that a simple infringement of the limits would suffice to establish liability.

[95] Under the adage that '*schuld is in beginsel gegeven*', implying the the illegality of the act as pronounced by an administrative court proves its wrongfulness in the tort liability case before the civil courts.

[96] See JCM Montijn-Swinkels *et al*, 'The imposition of sanctions for breaches of Community law. Report of the Netherlands Association for European Law for the FIDE Congress 1992', *SEW* (1992) 256, at 265; S Prechal, 'Onrechtmatige (niet) wetgeving: nu procederen!', *NJB* (1992) 1138, at 1138; T Koopmans, 'Liability of Member States for legislative Omissions. The consequences of Francovich for national law', presentation at the Conference on *The Liability of Member States for legislative Omissions – The Case Law of the Court of Justice following the Francovich Judgment, Trier, ERA*, 1996, resumé on file with the author.

[97] See the Opinion of Procureur Generaal Langemijer in *Hoge Raad*, decision of 21 March 2003, *Stichting Waterpakt et al v Staat der Nederlanden*, NJ 2003/691, at marginal number 2.18. Yet, by 2003 the PG argued that it would only be natural, given the gradual extension of the liability of the State, to also include liability for primary legislation.

law.[98] Primary legislation *can* be reviewed in the light of provisions of international treaties that are binding on anyone under Article 94 of the Constitution, and in the light of directly effective Community law.[99] It can be argued that the case of the primary legislature acting or failing to act in violation of such provisions, is comparable to the situation of a secondary legislature violating primary legislation or the Constitution, particularly where the primary legislature is not left any freedom of discretion: the prohibition to judicially review primary legislation is then left out of the equation.[100] However, the State had never actually been held liable to compensate damage caused by an action or inaction attributable to the primary legislature. Also, it must be stressed that in the case of *Francovich*, the provisions of the directive were *not* directly effective, and the analogy with Article 94 of the Constitution is accordingly limited. Finally, it must be stressed that Netherlands courts are generally very reluctant to interfere in the legislative activity of Parliament, especially where it is in the course of preparing the relevant legislation.

11.3.7. Final Remarks

Of the legal systems analysed above, none were unproblematic with regard to the liability in damages of the State for legislative wrongs, acts or omissions, attributable to Parliament itself. In fact there appears to be no 'constitutional tort' available in any of the legal systems under review.[101] In most Member States, the exclusion of liability for legislative wrong follows from a number of arguments, most of which are of a

---

[98] So *e.g.* JCM Montijn-Swinkels *et al*, 'The imposition of sanctions for breaches of Community law. Report of the Netherlands Association for European Law for the FIDE Congress 1992', SEW (1992) 256, at 265. But see recently *Hoge Raad*, decision of 21 March 2003, *Stichting Waterpakt e.a. v Staat der Nederlanden*, NJ 2003/691; discussed *below*.

[99] Some will argue that this type of review is equally based on Art. 94 of the Constitution; others found it on the special nature of Community law, and on the ECJ's judgments in *Van Gend en Loos* and *Costa v ENEL*.

[100] So already *e.g.* Alkema, *Een meerkeuzetoets* (Zwolle, WEJ Tjeenk Willink, 1985) and see S Prechal, 'Onrechtmatige (niet) wetgeving: nu proceberen', *NJB* (1992) 1138, at 1138; AJ Bok, 'Het Francovich-arrest en onrechtmatige wetgeving naar Nederlands recht', *TPR* (1993) 37, at 47; and later G Betlem, 'Onrechtmatige Wetgeving: Overheidsaansprakelijkheid voor Schending van EG recht in het post-Francovich Tijdperk', *RegelMaat* (1996) 128, at 138; MH Wissink, 'De Nederlandse rechter en overheidsaansprakelijkheid krachtens Francovich en Brasserie du Pêcheur', SEW (1997) 78, at 81.

[101] As stated by IB Lee: *'In fact, there are very few legal systems in which constitutional torts of this kind* [a system of liability in which the violation of constitutional rights by any State organ could result in the liability of the State for the harm caused, MC] *are recognised. While all of the Member States of the EU recognise liability for unconstitutional administrative action, I have found none that recognize liability for unconstitutional legislative or judicial conduct'*, IB Lee, 'In Search of a Theory of State Liability in the European Union', Harvard Jean Monnet Working Paper 9/99, available on www.jean monnetprogram.org/papers/99/990901.html, at 14. (the statement may not be wholly correct in respect of liability for judicial acts, which was

constitutional nature: the principle of separation of powers, the limits of the judicial function, the argument that Parliament has no obligations *vis-à-vis* particular individuals but only in relation to the public at large, and, closely related to it, that individuals cannot invoke subjective rights against Parliament and primary legislation. The argument that the courts could not review the validity of primary legislation was used against liability in France, Belgium, The Netherlands and the United Kingdom. The argument lost strength once it was accepted that the courts could review primary legislation in the light of higher law. Nevertheless, while the notion of liability of the State for legislative wrong was developing in literature, there were no cases accepting it *expressis verbis*. In Germany and Italy, the denial of the liability of the legislating State results from a specific conception of the subjective rights of individuals *vis-à-vis* the Legislature and, conversely, of the duty of care imposed on Parliament in its relations to specific individuals. It is striking that in both countries, there is a constitutional court with jurisdiction to declare primary legislation unconstitutional and invalid. Yet, as in the other Member States, the State cannot be held liable in damages for the harm caused by an unconstitutional statute: there is accordingly no tort of unconstitutional behaviour of Parliament.[102] The immunity of the State for legislative acts is even wider than in France, Belgium and The Netherlands, and extends also to pieces of secondary legislation.

11.4. THE CASE OF INFRINGEMENTS OF COMMUNITY LAW: PRE-*FRANCOVICH* DECISIONS OF NATIONAL COURTS

As has been demonstrated in section 11.2 above, before *Francovich*, under *Russo v AIMA*, it was for national law to rule on the issue of compensation of individuals for harm done as a consequence of the State's infringement of Community law. It is impossible to give a full and complete survey of the national cases concerning liability for breach of Community law,[103] but a brief overview of some of the most marked cases reported may expose

---

in certain Member States subject to special Acts providing for liability in specified and restricted cases; in Belgium it was even judge-made). The author adds that the tort of unconstitutional behaviour does not exist either in the United States or in Canada. In his opinion, what comes closest to a constitutional tort, is the liability of the State for infringement of the ECHR imposed by the ECtHR.

[102] On the tort of unconstitutional behaviour and its relevance for Community law see IB Lee, 'In Search of a Theory of State Liability in the European Union', Harvard Jean Monnet Working Paper 9/99, available on www.jeanmonnetprogram.org/papers/99/990901.html. On the development of such a tort in the UK see D Fairgreave, 'The Human Rights Act 1998, Damages and Tort Law', *PL* (2001) 695.

[103] Only reported cases and cases commented in the literature can be included in the survey.

the issues which the Court would have to solve in *Francovich,* and demonstrates the constitutional sensitivities encountered by the national courts.[104]

11.4.1. France

France is probably the Member State where most actions for compensation for harm caused by infringement of Community law by public authorities have been brought. The leading case was *Alivar,* decided by the *Conseil d'État* in 1984.[105] Alivar, an Italian company, had concluded an agreement with a French company to import potatoes from France. Due to a scarcity of potatoes in France the Government introduced the requirement of an export licence, which was refused in this case. Alivar sued the French State for compensation, relying mainly on the judgment of the Court of Justice,[106] declaring that France had failed to fulfil its obligations under Article 34 of the EC Treaty (now Article 29 EC) by introducing the system of licences. The Paris administrative court held that the infringement of Community law constituted a fault and awarded damages to Alivar.[107] The *Conseil d'État* confirmed the decision and increased the amount of damages, but on different grounds. It did cite the judgment of the Court of Justice but immediately added that it was for the French administrative courts to decide whether the refusal of a licence entailed the liability of the State. Since the licence had been refused on grounds of public interest *(intéret général)* no fault could have been committed and the State could only be held liable on grounds of no-fault liability: accordingly, compensation could only be awarded if a special and abnormal loss existed, which it did, and damages were indeed awarded.

Most striking in the judgment is the statement that the infringement of the Treaty was regarded as neither unlawful or wrongful,[108] while under French law as it stood, a failure to fulfil a treaty obligation constituted an illegality and any illegality constitutes a fault giving rise to compensation, even if it was caused by a simple error of judgment.[109] The decision was heavily criticised, mostly because it upset the rather systematic approach

---

[104] Not all cases mentioned involve the liability of the State for acts and omissions on the part of the primary legislature. They may however still be included since they contribute to forming an idea of the position of the national courts concerning the liability of the State for violation *of Community law* (so considering the nature of the infringed rule, rather that the organ responsible organ).

[105] *Conseil d'État,* decision of 2 March 1984, *Ministre du Commerce extérieur v Société Alivar,* RTDeur., 1984, 341; AJDA, 1984, 396.

[106] Case 68/76 *Commission v France (pommes de terre)* [1977] ECR 515.

[107] *Tribunal administratif de Paris,* decision of 2 April 1980, *Société Alivar v Ministre du Commerce extérieur,* unreported.

[108] Compare with the similar position of the Court of Appeal in *Bourgoin* where it stated that not every infringement of Community law constituted a wrongful act, see *below.*

[109] See R Errera, 'The Scope and Meaning of No-fault Liability', 157, at 170.

prevailing under French administrative law.[110] Compensation is hardly ever awarded on the basis of no-fault liability precisely in the context of economic choices to be made; in addition, it is difficult to maintain that an infringement of the Treaty does not constitute an illegality (and accordingly, in French law, a wrongful act). While in this case the *Conseil d'État* it was accepted that the damage was special and abnormal and even increased compensation was awarded. In most cases, the application of no-fault liability rules to infringements of Community law by the national authorities would make it more difficult for citizens to obtain damages for harm incurred.[111]

In addition, the *Conseil d'État* refused to draw the consequences from the judgment of the Court of Justice, which had established with binding effect *erga omnes* that the French State had infringed its obligations under the Treaty. The *Conseil* on the other hand attempted to justify the acts of the French Minister by reference to the public interest. However, the public interest should always underlie the acts of the administration,[112] and these motives cannot reverse the unlawfulness of these acts as established by the Court of Justice.[113] The *Conseil d'État* did not want to be seen to be declaring that an infringement of Community law by and of itself constituted an illegality from the point of view of French law, or that a judgment of the Court of Justice would allow for damages to be obtained before the national courts.[114]

---

[110] R Errera, 'The Scope and Meaning of No-fault Liability', 157, at 170 *et seq.*; B Genevois, 'Responsabilité de la puissance publique', *AJDA* (1984) 396, esp. 399; A Barav, 'Damages in the Domestic Courts for Breach of Community Law by National Public Authorities', in HG Schermers, T Heukels and Ph Mead (eds), *Non-Contractual Liability of the European Communities*, (Dordrecht, Kluwer Law International, 1988) 149, at 161; a different view, defending the position of the *Conseil d'État* was presented in J Moreau, 'L'influence du développement de la construction européenne sur le droit français de la responsabilité de la puissance publique', in *L'Europe et le droit. Mélanges offertes à Jean Boulouis*, (Paris, Dalloz, 1991), 409.

[111] See N Dantonel-Cor, 'La mise en jeu de la respnsabilité de l'État français pour violation du droit communautaire', *RTDeur* (1995) 471, at 500; M Dony, 'Le droit français', in G Vandersanden and M Dony (eds), *La responsabilité des États membres en cas de violation du droit communautaire. Études de droit communautair et de droit national comparé*, (Bruxelles, Bruylant, 1997), 235, at 259.

[112] As noted by R Errera, 'The Scope and Meaning of No-fault Liability in French Administrative Law', 157, at 171: '*the public interest is a condition of the legality of any administrative decision*'.

[113] D Simon and A Barav, 'La responsabilité de l'administration nationale en cas de violation du droit communautaire', *RMC* (1987) 165, at 168.

[114] It would later appear in *Francovich* and its progeny, that the liability of the State does not derive from a judgment of the Court declaring that there has been an infringement, but from the infringement itself, while such judgment does play a role in establishing whether or not there has been a *serious* breach. See already D Simon and A Barav, above, at 168 *et seq*, who derived the obligation of the Member State to compensate damages sustained as a consequence of infringements of Community law from the principle of direct effect. Under the current case law of the Court, while the right to damages is viewed as a necessary corollary of the direct effect of the provision infringed (*Brasserie du Pêcheur/Factortame III*, at 22), it does not depend on it. The Francovich directive for instance did not produce direct effects. In those cases State liability serves as a substitute for direct effect and specific performance.

In three earlier cases concerning similar factual situations,[115] the *Tribunal administratif de Rennes* held the State liable in damages for breach of Article 34 of the EC Treaty (Article 29 EC) that was declared by the Court of Justice, any general public interest considerations notwithstanding, apparently on the basis of fault liability. Also in later cases,[116] several lower administrative courts *did* declare that an act was wrongful because of its infringement of Community law and accordingly held the State liable. Some of these decisions referred to a judgment of the Court of Justice decided in infringement proceedings and declaring the French State in violation of Community law as the ground for accepting fault; others pointed to the direct effect of a provision of the Treaty, mostly Articles 30 and 34 of the Treaty; or to both. But in all cases, the administrative courts applied the principle of fault liability on violations of Community law committed by French administrative authorities.[117] There were other cases holding the State liable to pay compensation for damages caused by infringements of Community law, several of which were decided in the context of the *'guerre vini-viticole franco-italianne'*. Due to an increase of the imports of Italian wines into France, the prices on the market decreased, causing violent demonstrations of French wine producers. The French authorities sided with these producers and subjected all bulk imports of wine from Italy to systematic oenological analysis, causing substantial delays, and inflicting damage to the importers of the Italian wines. The Court of Justice in an interim judgment ordered France to limit these checks to 15% of the wine imported, restricted the delay to a maximum of 21 days, and later declared that France had violated its obligations under Article 28 EC (then Article 30 of the EC Treaty). In the actions for damages, most of the administrative courts hearing the cases decided that there had been an illegality, either consisting of an infringement of Article 30 of the Treaty and Community regulations on wine, or because of the judgment of the Court, or because the time limit imposed by

---

[115] Judgments not reported, mentioned in A Barav, 'State liability in damages for breach of Community law in the national courts', in T Heukels and A McDonnell (eds), *The Action for Damages in Community Law* (The Hague, Kluwer, 1997) 363, at 394. Since the appeal had been brought out of time, the *Conseil d'État* did not rule on them, and the decisions stood.

[116] M Dony, 'Le droit français', in G Vandersanden and M Dony (eds), *La responsabilité des Etats membres en cas de violation du droit communautaire. Études de droit communautaire et de droit national comparé* (Brussels, Bruylant, 1997) 235, at 259 *et seq.*; see also A Barav, 'State liability in damages for breach of Community law in the national courts', in T Heukels and A McDonnell (eds), *The Action for Damages in Community Law* (The Hague, Kluwer, 1997) 363, at 394 *et seq.*

[117] In *Cour administrative d'appel de Nantes*, decision of 20 June 1991, *SA Duault*, AJDA, 1992, 172, a case decided in the aftermath of the wine war, the *Cour* attempted to bring this approach in line with *Alivar*. The *Cour* declared that a wrong had been committed causing the liability for fault to arise and that the State had not invoked a general public interest which presumably might have prevented the automatic liability of the State, and restricted it to cases of special and abnormal losses; see N Dantonel-Cor, 'Mise en jeu de la responsabilité de l'État français pour violation du croit communautaire', 31 *RTDeur* (1995) 471, at 501; see also M Dony, *art. cit.*; and A Barav, *art. cit.*

the Court in the interim order had been exceeded. Other cases dealt with the refusal to issue licences for the import of bananas; with the exclusion on grounds of nationality from a tender for public works, or the failure to provide correct information.[118]

There was, however, no case law relating to the question of liability of the State for harm caused directly by a *loi* violating Community law, or for a failure on the part of Parliament to comply with it. Nevertheless, it is highly likely that the courts would have denied liability for acts or omissions of Parliament, given the state of French law on state liability, and the reluctance of the *Conseil d'État* to hold the State liable in damages for infringements of Community law even on the part of the Executive, deviating from the more generous rules applying in purely French cases.

11.4.2. The United Kingdom

Also in the United Kingdom, there were several cases dealing with the issue of the liability of the State for violations of Community law, but none did concern the liability of the State for harm attributable to an Act of Parliament.

A preliminary question which the English courts had to decide was the appropriate qualification of the rights which individuals derive from Community law in order to assess the appropriate remedy in the English courts. Public law rights were enforceable only by way of judicial review under Order 53 of the Rules of the Supreme Court, under the authority of Section 31 of the Supreme Court Act 1981. Conversely, private law rights are enforceable as of right, without leave, and they may give rise to private law remedies, such as compensation.[119] In *An Bord Bainne Co-operative Ltd v The Milk Marketing Board*[120] the Court of Appeal held that

---

[118] References to cases can be found in A Barav, 'Damages in the domestic courts for breach of Community law by national public authorities', in HG Schermers, T Heukels and Ph Mead (eds), *Non-contractual Liability of the European Communities* (Kluwer, Dordrecht, 1988) 149, at 158 *et seq.*; M Dony, 'Le droit français', in G Vandersanden and M Dony (eds), *La responsabilité des Etats membres en cas de violation du droit communautaire. Études de droit communauatire et de droit national comparé* (Brussels, Bruylant, 1997) 235; J Moreau, 'L'influence du développement de la construction européenne sur le droit français de la responsabilité de la puissance publique', in *L'Europe et le droit*. Mélanges offertes à Jean Boulouis, (Paris, Dalloz, 1991), 409.

[119] For this distinction, and the difficulties in the English courts relating to the classification of Community law rights, see N Green and A Barav, 'Damages in the National Courts for Breach of Community Law', *YEL* (1986) 55, at 83 *et seq*; see also M Friend, 'Judicial Review, Private Rights and Community Law', *PL* (1985) 21.

[120] *Court of Appeal*, decision of 18 May 1984, *An Bord Bainne Co-operative Ltd v The Milk Marketing Board* [1984] 2 CMLR 584; the decision was remarkable, since the House of Lords had recently held that in English law, private law actions would not lie for the protection of public law rights, if the applicant was entitled to protection under public law and tried to evade the provisions of Order 53, see House of Lords, *O'Reilly v Mackman* [1983] 2 AC 237.

although the Milk Marketing Board was a public authority adopting decisions in the public sphere, its decisions might give rise to private law actions, in case of an alleged breach of directly effective rights deriving from Community law which the national courts must protect. A private law action in damages was therefore available, irrespective of whether or not it was possible to institute an action for judicial review of the decision. The latter remedy alone was considered inappropriate for the protection of the rights derived from Article 86 of the Treaty (Article 82 EC). By virtue of the EC Act 1972 directly effective Community law rights are converted into enforceable rights in the United Kingdom legal system, and it was established that there may be tortious liability to compensate harm caused by breach of statutory duty where it is apparent that the obligation or prohibition was imposed for the benefit or protection of a particular class of individuals or where the statute created a public right and a particular member of the public suffers particular direct and substantial damage other and different from that which is common to the rest of the public.[121] Lord Denning in *Falks Veritas* suggested that breach of Community law might, under English law, constitute a new head of tort.[122]

In *Garden Cottage Foods*,[123] an action for damages was brought against the Milk Marketing Board, claiming compensation for the damage caused by an infringement of Article 86 of the Treaty (now Article 82 EC). The issue in this case was the choice of the relevant tort. Lord Diplock found it *'difficult to see how it can ultimately be successfully argued (..) that a contravention of Article 86 which causes damage to an individual citizen does not give rise to a cause of action in English law of the nature of a breach of statutory duty'.* However, the tort of breach of statutory duty cannot be brought against the State for Parliamentary Acts or omissions in English law, because of the principle of parliamentary sovereignty.

The issue of state liability presented itself squarely in *Bourgoin*, concerning a breach of Article 30 of the Treaty (now Article 28 EC).[124] The Minister, acting under statutory powers enabling him to order the exclusion from the

---

121 See J A Usher, 'The imposition of sanctions for breaches of Community law', Lisbon, UK Report, FIDE 1992, 391, at 392, *under reference to Lohnro v Shell* [1982] AC 173.

122 *Court of Appeal*, decision of 22 May 1974, *Application des gaz v Falks Veritas Ltd.* [1974] Ch 381; [1974] 2 CMLR 75. *Falks Veritas* did not concern a claim for damages, but Lord Denning did make a few statements *obiter*.

123 *House of Lords*, decision of 23 June 1983, *Garden Cottage Foods v Milk Marketing Board* [1984] AC 130; [1983] 3 CMLR 43, commented in F Jacobs, 'Damages for breach of Article 86 EEC', *ELRev* 1983, 353.

124 *Court of Appeal*, decision of 19 July 1985, *Bourgoin SA v Ministry of Agriculture, Fisheries and Food* [1985] 3 WLR 1027; [1986] 1 CMLR 267 (Lords Parker and Nourse, Lord Oliver dissenting). The case was appealed to the House of Lords, but it was settled before the appeal was heard, see P Oliver, 'Enforcing Community rights in the English Courts', *MLR* (1987) 881, at 904.

United Kingdom of specified animals or carcasses for the purpose of preventing the introduction of disease into Great Britain, ordered the exclusion of turkeys and turkey parts. The Court of Justice held that the United Kingdom had infringed its obligations under Article 30 of the Treaty (Article 28 EC) in June 1982, but the import ban was not in fact repealed until November of that year. The loss of the Christmas trade that the embargo entailed, hit French exporters deep in their pockets, and they brought claims for compensation against the Minister. The case turned on the appropriate heads of claim. Three torts were put forward: breach of statutory duty, the innominate tort – as suggested by Lord Denning in *Falks Veritas* – and the tort of misfeasance in public office. The innominate tort was discarded in the High Court and was not subject of the appeal.

The majority in the Court of Appeal distinguished *Garden Cottage* and rejected the tort of breach of statutory duty. *Bourgoin* was a public law case, they said, concerned with public authorities as defendants while *Garden Cottage* concerned a private law situation.[125] They emphasised that the Court of Justice adopted a similar approach when deciding on the liability of the Community, where it holds that the latter can only in very restricted circumstances be held liable for legislative acts, namely only where the breach of Community law constitutes a manifest and grave violation of discretionary powers. Conduct that would render a private individual liable in damages might not suffice to render a public authority liable. When it came to actions in damages against the State, the appropriate tort would consequently be misfeasance in public office, which requires that the decision maker has knowingly infringed the law and was aware that he was causing injury to the claimant.[126] The Crown could not be liable for an infringement of Article 30 of the Treaty through an honest error.[127]

Apparently, the appropriate tort for breach of Community law by the State would be the tort of misfeasance in public office, making it almost impossible for the liability of the State to arise for parliamentary acts and omissions.

---

[125] In the High Court, Mann J had extrapolated the judgment of the House of Lords in *Garden Cottage* and held that the violation of Art. 30 of the Treaty by the minister did give rise to an action in damages in private law for breach of statutory duty; *High Court, Queens Bench Division*, decision of 1 October 1984, *Bourgoin SA v Ministry of Agriculture, Fisheries and Food* [1985] 1 CMLR 528.

[126] The additional condition that the decision-maker intentionally caused harm to the claimant was dropped.

[127] Critically *e.g.* Y Cripps, 'European 'rights', invalid actions and denial of damages', *CLJ* (1986) 165, at 167, who states that the situation of the revocation of an import licence should not be equated with the case of Community legislation. In addition, the Court of Appeal had introduced a test or standard which had neither been described in the Treaty, identified by the ECJ or required by pre-existing English law on the tort of breach of statutory duty.

11.4.3. Italy

In the case of *Biscotti Panettoni Colussi*,[128] the applicant company had been refused an import licence which it was required to obtain on grounds of a ministerial circular which appeared to violate the provisions on the free movement of goods. In its defence, the State argued that the company did not have a subjective right to the licence, but only a legitimate interest, and accordingly no damages lay. The Rome *Corte d'appello* held the State liable in damages on grounds of a violation of Community law. The *Corte di Cassazione* confirmed the decision declaring that the legal position of the company did not constitute a legitimate interest, given the fact that the mere requirement of a licence constituted a breach of Community law, which must accordingly be set aside, making the requirement null and void. Since a licence was no longer required, the company's position was to be qualified as a subjective right, the exercise of which could not be limited by public authorities. Since the Community rights infringed were directly effective, the company had a right to compensation.[129] The case is based on the assumption that there is a subjective right, which cannot exist in relation to legislation.

11.4.4. The Netherlands

In 1984 the Hague District Court[130] declared the State liable to compensate all the damages, past, present and future, which the plaintiffs – Dutch pharmaceutical undertakings – suffered as a result of the 1982 Prices of Registered Medicines Decree (a piece of secondary legislation) which was illegitimately enacted and implemented as regards its effects on the plaintiffs. The relevant Decree authorised the competent Minister to fix maximum prices and prohibited the sale of imported medicinal products at a price above a certain threshold. Upon a reference for preliminary ruling, the Court of Justice held that national legislation differentiating between home produced and imported medicinal products

---

[128] *Corte di Cassazione*, decision n. 3458 of 4 August 1977, *Biscotti Panettoni Colussi snc*, mentioned in M Merola and M Beretta, 'Le droit italien', in G Vandersanden and M Dony (eds), *La responsabilité des États membres en cas de violation du droit communautaire. Études de droit communautaire et de droit national comparé* (Brussels, Bruylant, 1997) 289.

[129] The direct effect of the infringed provision appears to be required; after *Francovich* this can no longer be required, see also M Merola and M Beretta, 'Le droit italien', in G Vandersanden and M Dony (eds), *La responsabilité des États membres en cas de violation du droit communautaire. Études de droit communautaire et de droit national comparé* (Brussels, Bruylant, 1997) 289, at 321.

[130] *Arrondissementsrechtbank 's Gravenhage*, decision of 18 July 1984, *Roussel*, unpublished, reported in A Barav, 'Damages in the Domestic Courts for Breach of Community Law by National Public Authorities', in HG Schermers, T Heukels and Ph. Mead (eds), *Non-Contractual Liability of the European Communities* (Dordrecht, Nijhoff, 1988) 149, at 156–157.

was incompatible with Article 28 EC (then Article 30 of the EC Treaty).[131] The Dutch courts accordingly set aside the relevant Decree, but then went on to discuss the liability of the State for the damage incurred by the applicants, more particularly the question whether mere illegality would suffice to create liability, or whether something more was needed such as a gross error, as the defendant State argued. The court held that in this case, the State should in any case have known that similar practices had been declared in breach of the Treaty by the Court of Justice, and that the State could and must consequently have understood that it was treading on a very thin ice from the point of view of Community law when enacting the Decree. While the State was held liable in this case, a mere breach of the Treaty by the legislator would not suffice to create liability.[132]

Particular to the Dutch context, is the fact that the general tort liability provisions contained in the Civil Code are used quite often in order to obtain a remedy other than damages, but rather in order to declare a lower legislative act or decree inapplicable (*'buitenwerkingstelling'*); in order to prohibit the application of such decree; or to order that a particular decree be adopted; or, finally, in order to be granted a declaration that a particular decree is unlawful.[133] This peculiar role of the general tort provision of the Dutch Civil Code in public law has to do with the fact that there are no causes of action available to have regulations and decrees (legislative acts issued by authorities lower than the primary legislature) reviewed judicially. There is no action for annulment, no action for judicial review against general acts. Even before *Francovich*, the general tort of Article 6:612 of the Civil Code had been applied in the context of Community law. In an early case[134] environmental organisations had argued that the State had acted in contrary to a Euratom directive and accordingly wrongfully under the general rules governing liability for wrongful acts by allowing an infringement of the radiation standards. The court accepted the position of the applicants that an infringement of international norms constituted a wrongful act under national law, but rejected the claim because the applicants failed to show that the standards had been surpassed. In the *WWV* case (the *'Wet Werkloosheidsvoorziening'*, the Act on Unemployment benefits), the President of the Hague Court ordered the State to adapt the Act (a piece of primary legislation) so as to

---

[131] Case 181/83 *Roussel Laboratoria BV v The Netherlands* [1983] ECR 3849.

[132] So A Barav, 'Damages in the Domestic Courts for Breach of Community Law by National Public Authorities', in HG Schermers, T Heukels and Ph. Mead (eds), *Non-Contractual Liability of the European Communities* (Dordrecht, Nijhoff, 1988) 149, at 157.

[133] For examples see AJ Bok, 'Het Francovich-arrest en onrechtmatige wetgeving naar Nederlands recht', *TPR* (1993) 37, at 44 *et seq.*

[134] *Arrondissementsrechtbank 's Gravenhage*, decision of 23 October 1974, *Kerncentrale Borssele*, NJ, 1975, 115; reported in JH Jans et al, *Inleiding tot het Europees Bestuursrecht* (Ars Aequi Libri, 2002) at 394–95.

comply with the relevant directive.[135] The president stated that in the Netherlands legal order, courts were in principle precluded from interfering in any way in the process of law-making. However, given the specific circumstances of the case, he considered it lawful and warranted in practice to diverge from that rule. The special circumstances consisted in the fact that the case concerned a fundamental principle (equal treatment); that the State had allowed the wide time-limit of 6 years to pass without any justification; that if the Commission were to initiate proceedings, the ECJ would most likely impose a deadline while an order of a national court to the same effect could be considered a speedy variant of that procedure.[136] However, the Hague Court of Appeal quashed the decision, holding that the Constitution did not empower the courts to order the primary legislature to adopt legislation before a specified date, as the President had done.[137] It argued on grounds of the separation of powers: it was not for the courts to order the primary legislature to adopt legislation.[138]

11.4.5. Belgium

Before *Francovich*, the State had in several decisions of lower courts been held liable to compensate harm incurred as a consequence of an infringement of Community law by an administrative authority. A

---

[135] *President Arrondissementsrechtbank 's Gravenhage*, decision of 17 January 1985, *FNV v Staat der Nederlanden (WWV)*, NJ, 1985, 262; AB 1985, 154; The procedure was founded on the general liability provision of Art. 1401 of the Civil code (Art. 6:162 of the new Civil code).

[136] Compare with the order issued by the Belgian court in the case of the Community officials and the Belgian pensions scheme. The Belgian court not only ordered the Belgian State to adopt the necessary measures, but even imposed penalty payments.

[137] *Gerechtshof 's Gravenhage*, decision of 13 March 1985, *Staat der Nederlanden v FNV (WWV)*, AB, 1985, 253, note FHvdB.

[138] In Germany for instance, judicial protection against failure to act on the part of the legislature is approached under Art. 19(4) of the Basic Law (the constitutional right to judicial protection). Actions at law are available even as against a failure to act on the part of the primary legislature in order to force it to adopt legislation. See W-R Schenke, 'Rechtsschutz gegen das Unterlassen von Rechtsnormen', *VerwArch* (1991) 307. The issue has arisen once again in The Netherlands, almost 20 years later, in the *Waterpakt* case. In the first instance, the *Arrondissementsrechtbank 's Gravenhage* ordered the State to take appropriate action within a specified time limit so as to make an end to unlawful inaction of the State leading to an infringement of the standards set in European legislation, *Arrondissementsrechtbank 's Gravenhage*, decision of 24 November 1999, *Stichting Waterpakt et al v Staat der Nederlanden*, M & R, 2000, 24, note Jans and Verschuuren. On appeal, the *Hof 's Gravenhage* quashed the decision of the lower court, holding that the constitutional position of Dutch courts prevented them from interfering in the process of primary legislation, *Gerechtshof 's Gravenhage*, decision of 2 August 2001, *Staat der Nederlanden v Stichting Waterpakt et al*, M & R, 2001, 95, note Jans and De Jong. The case then came before the *Hoge Raad*, which had to decide whether in the event that the failure to adopt legislation with a view to implement a directive was unlawful, Netherlands law would preclude the courts from ordering the State to adopt primary legislation; and in the alternative, whether Community law would lead to a different position. The case is discussed below.

breach of Community law constituted an illegality, in the same way as an infringement of a higher norm of internal law, and the same conditions were to be applied.[139] The case of the Belgian Community *fonctionnaires* and the omission of the Belgian State to adopt measures for the transfer to the Community pension scheme of sums due to be repaid under the Belgian pension scheme probably comes closest to the issue of the liability of the legislative State for infringements of Community law. Following consecutive judgments of the Court of Justice declaring the Belgian State in breach of its obligations under the Treaty, the Brussels court of first instance[140] condemned the Belgian State to adopt the necessary measures, and imposed periodic penalty payments unless the measures were adopted within a six-months time limit. After that judgment, it took the Belgian State exactly six months to adopt the measures, 27 years (!) after the beginning of the infringement. The Brussels court did not consider the defence based on the immunity of the legislating State justified in the circumstances of the case. After having referred to the principle of the precedence of international law provisions, the court stated that *'c'est l'État en tant que tel, valablement représenté par le pouvoir exécutif, qui doit supporter les conséquences de cette négligence, sans pouvoir invoquer les carences voire l'indépendance du pouvoir législatif'*.[141] The court did accept that it could not issue an order against the primary legislature to adopt the necessary measures on grounds of the latter's sovereignty, but it considered that it did have the power and the obligation to declare that the Belgian legislation was not in conformity with an international provision having precedence over national law, and accordingly to draw the legal consequences therefrom in favour of the individuals harmed by that situation.

Two courts were asked to pronounce themselves on the liability of the legislative State concerning the *minerval*, the additional enrolment fees to be paid to universities by non-Belgian students.[142] When the Court of Justice declared in *Gravier* that the *minerval* constituted a discrimination contrary to Community law in the context of vocational training,[143] a

---

[139] See references in M Dony, 'Le droit belge', in G Vandersanden and M Dony (eds), *La responsabilité des États membres en cas de violation du droit communautaire. Études de droit communautaire et de droit national comparé* (Brussels, Bruylant, 1997) 149, at 164.

[140] *Tribunal de première instance de Bruxelles*, decision of 9 February 1990, *Michel*, unpublished, reported in DF Waelbroeck, 'Treaty Violations and Liability of Member States: The Effect of the Francovich Case Law', in *The Action for Damages in Community Law* (The Hague, Kluwer, 1997) 311, at fn. 17; see also M Dony, 'Le droit belge', in G Vandersanden and M Dony (eds), *La responsabilité des États membres en cas de violation du droit communautaire. Études de droit communautaire et de droit national comparé* (Brussels, Bruylant, 1997) 149, at 171–73.

[141] Quotation taken from M Dony, above, at 172.

[142] See M Dony, 'Le droit belge', in G Vandersanden and M Dony (eds), *La responsabilité des États membres en cas de violation du droit communautaire. Études de droit communautaire et de droit national comparé* (Brussels, Bruylant, 1997) 149, at 173–76.

[143] Case 293/83 *Françoise Gravier v City of Liège* [1985] ECR 593.

number of foreign university students applied for a reimbursement of the *minerval* paid in application of the *loi de financement des universités*. In these cases, a new reference was made to the Court of Justice, which applied the same principle to university students, but limited the judgment in time, since the inclusion of university students was a result of an gradual development of the case law, and secondly, because the Belgian authorities could reasonably have believed that the *minerval* was compatible with Community law.[144] The court cases in Belgium continued, against the universities, against the Belgian State and against the *Communauté française*, which had become the State's successor in these matters after the constitutional reform of the State.[145] The actions against the *Communauté française* were not considered as actions for restitution of undue payments, since the defendant had never received these payments, but rather as actions for damages. The *Cour d'appel de Liège* held the Belgian State, and not the *Communauté française*,[146] liable to pay back the sums paid. Under reference to the landmark judgments of the Court of Justice in *Van Gend en Loos*, *Costa v ENEL* and *Francovich*, which had by then been decided, and to the *Le Ski* judgment of the *Cour de cassation*, the State was ordered to compensate the harm done to the applicants.[147]

11.4.6. Final Observations

Only a few of the cases discussed above concerned the issue of liability for parliamentary acts or omissions. The Belgian case concerning the pension rights of Community fonctionnaires probably comes closest, but it is an a typical case, since the remedy sought was not compensation, but an injunction addressed to the State to adopt the relevant legislation. The vehicle used under Belgian law, however, was the general tort provision, since the failure to act on the part of the legislature was considered to constitute a wrongful act. The court granted the injunction, in the form of an order to adopt legislation before the expiry of a specified deadline, upon the expiry of which penalty payments would become due.

On the other hand, liability of the State for administrative acts infringing Community law was accepted under the same conditions and rules as for comparable violations of domestic higher norms in Belgium and The Netherlands. This was not so however in France and the United Kingdom, where under *Alivar* and *Bourgoin* respectively, it was held that infringements of Community law did not automatically constitute an

---

[144] Case 24/86 *Vincent Blaizot and others v University of Liège and others* [1988] ECR 379.

[145] Competence on education was transferred from the federal State to the Communities.

[146] The judgment would be quashed on this point in *Cour de cassation (B)*, decision of 26 January 1995, *minerval*, JMLB (1995) 425.

[147] Since the case had by then become post-*Francovich*, it will be analysed below.

illegality or an unlawfulness giving rise to a right to compensation. Something more was needed: in France, the damage must be special and abnormal since these cases were considered as instances of no-fault liability; in the United Kingdom, the State would only be liable if the restrictive conditions of misfeasance in public office were fulfilled. In both countries however, there were doubts as to the correctness of these decisions, both in literature and in decisions of lower courts. The cases at issue are similar in that they both concern a policitally sensitive issue going to the heart of the limits of the judicial function: while it was obvious that both States had infringed Community law, both had done so not by oversight or imprudence, but in the framework of an intentionally protectionist national economic policy. Holding the State liable to protect the interests of a foreign company (in the case of *Bourgoin*) or its contract party (in the case of *Alivar*) would involve an interference into economic policy on the part of the courts.[148] In addition, the choice of the relevant test (no-fault liability) or tort (misfeasance in public office) made liability of the State for legislative acts or omissions highly unlikely. In Belgium and The Netherlands, acceptance of the liability for acts or omissions of the primary legislature was prepared in the literature. There is not sufficient case law from Italian courts and no case law from German courts to make confident statements about the position in German and Italian law. However, given the national starting points and the absence of liability of the State even for unconstitutional primary legislation, it is highly likely that the same would apply for infringements of Community law and consequently for liability for legislative wrong to be excluded.

11.5. NON-CONTRACTUAL LIABILITY OF THE COMMUNITY

11.5.1. Introduction

In contrast to the absence of explicit liability of the Member States for harm done due to violations of Community law, the Treaty does provide for a regime regulating the liability of the Community, under reference to the general principles prevailing in the national legal systems.[149] Under

---

[148] This is most obvious in the decision of the *Cour administrative d'appel de Nantes* in the case *SA Duault*, where it held that infringements of Community law would have to be decided under the rules governing fault-liability, unless the State had invoked a general public interest, causing liability to arise only under the test applicable for no-fault liability.

[149] See most recently J Wakefield, *Judicial Protection through the Use of Article 288(2) EC*, (The Hague, Kluwer Law International, 2002) see also E Grabitz, 'Liability for Legislative Acts', in HG Schermers, T Heukels and Ph Mead (eds), *Non-contractual Liability of the European Communities* (Dordrecht, Martinus Nijhoff, 1988) 1; more recently, A Arnull, 'Liability for Legislative Acts under Article 215(2) EC', in T Heukels and A McDonnell (eds), *The Action for Damages in Community Law* (Antwerpen, Kluwer, 1997) 129.

Article 235 EC (old Article 178) the Court of Justice has jurisdiction to hear disputes concerning the compensation for damage provided for in Article 288(2) EC (old Article 215(2)). Under the latter provision, the Community shall, in accordance with the general principles common to the laws of the Member States, make good any damage caused by its institutions or by its servants in the performance of their duties. By reference to these common principles, the Court has held that the Community shall be liable in damages in the presence of a wrongful act or omission, actual damage, and a causal link between the damage claimed and the conduct alleged against the institution.[150] The Court is much more restrictive when it comes to claims for compensation of harm caused by *legislative* action involving a choice of economic policy. In those cases, the Community will under the *Schöppenstedt* formula, only be held liable if there has been a sufficiently serious violation of a superior rule of law for the protection of the individual.[151] This should come as no surprise given the reference in Article 288 EC to the common principles prevailing in the Member States and the restrictive approach to liability of the legislating State under national law.

11.5.2. The *Schöppenstedt* Formula

The first issue to be decided in *Schöppenstedt* was whether there was any immunity for legislative harm. Was liability for legislative acts or omissions excluded as a matter of principle; or could the Community incur liability of this type? Advocate General Roemer briefly examined the principles prevailing in the Member States concerning the liability of the legislative State, and found that it was not entirely excluded. He chose as the parameter for comparison not only the liability for primary legislation, but also included the liability for secondary legislative measures.[152] Roemer made a few comments about his *method* of defining the applicable rules, which must under Article 288(2) EC be found with reference to the general principles common to the laws of the Member States.[153] He

---

[150] Case 4/69 *Lütticke v Commission* [1971] ECR 325.
[151] Case 5/71 *Schöppenstedt v Council* [1971] ECR 975; see also Joined Cases 83–94/76, 4–15 and 40/77 *HNL v Council and Commission* [1978] *ECR* 1209 and many other cases.
[152] Opinion of AG Roemer in Case 5/71 *Schöppenstedt v Council* [1971] ECR 975, at 989–990.
[153] See on the comparative method in the context of 288(2) EC and beyond W van Gerven, 'Comparative Law in a Texture of Communitarization of National Laws and Europeanization of Community Law', in D O'Keeffe and A Bavasso (eds), *Judicial Review in European Union Law. Liber Amicorum in Honour of Lord Slynn of Hedley*, Vol. I, (The Hague, Kluwer Law International, 2000), 433; and by the same author 'From Communitarisation of National Tort Rules to Europeanisation of Community Tort Law: The Invader Invaded', in R Scholz (ed), *Auslegung europäischen Privatrechts und angeglichenen Rechts*, (Baden-Baden, Nomos, 1999) 179.

stated that the provision should not be taken too literally: the criterion would not be only rules which exist in all Member States (the maximum standard), nor the lowest common denominator. What was indicative was a process of assessment in which above all the particular objectives of the Treaty and the peculiarities of the Community structure must be taken into account (and in which perhaps it was appropriate that the guideline be the best elaborated national rules). Roemer referred to the deficient parliamentary control in the Community; the fact that Article 34 ECSC did provide for liability for legislative acts; the fact that general acts are not completely removed from challenge by individuals affected under Articles 177 and 184 of the Treaty. Finally, the principle stressed in the case law should be remembered that provisions concerning the protection of individuals should not be interpreted restrictively. Accordingly, liability for general acts should not be excluded as a matter of principle. There was thus no immunity of the legislative Community. Some of the arguments brought against the liability of the State for primary legislative acts and omissions under national law, could not be transposed to Community law. Most importantly, the argument that an Act of Parliament represents the 'sovereign expression of the general will of the People' could not seriously be invoked to deny liability for, say, a Community regulation in the area of agriculture, where Parliament has hardly any say at all. On the contrary, Roemer pointed to the rudimentary nature of democratic legitimation at the Community level in 1971 as an argument in favour of at least some form of liability for legislative acts involving economic policy, however limited.[154] With respect to the argument relating to the wide measure of discretion which the Council has in adopting legislative measures, the Court[155] held that this did not exclude liability as a matter of principle, but would be relevant in determining the applicable test. The fact that the Council has a wide discretion in adopting a particular measure did not make it immune for claim in damages; it merely meant that liability could only be incurred under strict conditions.[156]

11.5.3. 'A Sufficiently Serious Breach…'

The condition that there must be a sufficiently serious breach was developed in the 1978 *Bayerische HNL* decision, where the Court held that the finding that a legislative measure is null and void is insufficient by itself

---

[154] Opinion of AG Roemer in Case 5/71 *Schöppenstedt v Council* [1971] ECR 975, at 989.

[155] The restrictive conditions accepted by the ECJ (sufficiently serious breach of a superior rule of law for the protection of the individual) was not proposed by the AG (who did not propose any coherent test).

[156] Case 5/71 *Schöppenstedt v Council* [1971] ECR 975, at para 7.

for the Community to incur liability. Individuals may be required with respect to the economic policy of the Community, to accept within reasonable limits certain harmful effects on their economic interests as a result of a legislative measure without being able to obtain compensation from public funds, even if that measure has been declared null and void. In a legislative field, in which one of the chief features was the exercise of a wide discretion essential for the implementation of the common agricultural policy, the Community did not incur liability unless the institution concerned had 'manifestly and gravely disregarded the limits on the exercise of its powers'.[157] The Court defended its restrictive approach with reference to the principles prevailing in the Member States: '*Although these principles vary considerably from one Member State to another, it is however possible to state that the public authorities can only exceptionally and in special circumstances incur liability for legislative measures which are the result of choices of economic policy. This restrictive view is explained by the consideration that the legislative authority, even where the validity of its measures is subject to judicial review, cannot always be hindered in making its Decisions by the prospect of applications for damages whenever it has occasion to adopt legislative measures in the public interest which may adversely affect the interests of individuals*'.[158] In *Amylum* the Court added another consideration, noting that an individual who had suffered loss as a result of a legislative measure of the Community which had been implemented as the national level, could challenge the validity of the measure in proceedings before the national courts against the national competent authorities. The question of the validity of the underlying Community measure could or must then be referred to the Court of Justice. The existence of such an action, the Court held, was by itself of such a nature as to ensure the efficient protection of the individuals concerned.[159] Liability in damages should consequently be restrictive.

In the application of the test, the Court in *HNL* focussed on the effects of the decision on the claimants and decided that these did not exceed the bounds of economic risks inherent in the activities of the agricultural sectors concerned. In the *Amylum* case the Court stated that 'grave disregard'

---

[157] Above, at para 6.
[158] Joined Cases 83 and 94/76, 4, 15 and 40/77 *Bayerische HNL Vermehrungsbetriebe GmbH & Co KG and others v Council and Commission* [1978] ECR 1209, at para 5. See also the considerations of AG Darmon in Vreugdenhill II: 'In many, if not all, Member States the conditions for liability for legislative action are appreciably different from those concerning administrative action. (..) liability of the legislative authorities, however, is governed by stricter rules, with in particular a requirement of unusual and specific damage, or is quite simply non-existent', Case C–282/90 *Vreugdenhill v Commission (Vreugdenhill II)* [1992] ECR I–1937, at marginal number 43.
[159] Joined Cases 116/77 and 124/77 *Amylum v Council and Commission* [1979] ECR 3497, at para 14.

was to be understood as meaning conduct verging on the arbitrary.[160] It follows that liability of the legislating Community would not be easily accepted for this type of breach: it would arise only exceptionally.

11.5.4. '...of a Superior Rule of Law'

The condition seems to presuppose a hierarchy of norms, which is a difficult issue in Community law. It appears that both the importance of the rule and its formal status may be relevant for a rule to be considered a superior rule of law.[161] Certain Treaty provisions are in any case included, but it is as yet unclear whether all are, or only those considered to constitute rules of a fundamental nature, such as the rules on free movement. General principles of law, such as proportionality, legal certainty or legitimate expectations also form superior rules of law in this respect.

11.5.5. '...for the Protection of the Indivual'

A manifest and flagrant breach of a higher norm will only give a right to compensation if the infringed norm was intended to protect the claimant. The condition is inspired by the German *'Schutznormtheorie'* and its application to the liability of the State under *'Amtshaftung'*.[162] However, it is not entirely the same and is certainly less restrictive than its German pendant. In Germany the condition leads to the exclusion of liability for legislative wrong. In the case law of the Court of Justice, the condition has been applied rather liberally. The fact that a regulation is not considered to be of direct and individual concern to a particular undertaking, for instance, does not mean that the regulation was not intended to protect its rights. Neither does the condition require that the infringed norm was *exclusively* intended to protect the claimants.

---

[160] Joined cases 116 and 124/77 *G R Amylum NV and Tunnel Refineries Limited v Council and Commission* [1979] ECR 3497.

[161] A Arnull, 'Liability for Legislative Acts under Article 215(2) EC', in T Heukels and A McDonnell (eds), *The Action for Damages in Community Law*, (The Hague, Kluwer Law International, 1997), 129, at 138 and P Craig and G de Búrca, *EU Law. Text, Cases and Materials*, 3rd ed, (Oxford, OUP, 2002), at 550.

[162] So E Grabitz, 'Liability for Legislative Acts', in HG Schermers, T Heukels and Ph Mead (eds), *Non-Contractual Liability of the European Communities*, (Dordrecht, Martinus Nijhoff, 1988), 1, at 6.

11.5.6. Closing Remarks

With respect to legislative acts involving a wide discretion, liability of the Community does not easily arise.[163] In itself, this should not come as a surprise given also the limited availability of damages for legislative action and inaction, especially when attributable to the primary legislature, in national law. Similar arguments apply in the context of Community law. On the other hand, the protective approach of the Court of Justice with respect to the legislating Community, and its more strict approach with respect to the liability of the Member States has lead to serious criticism. While it may be reasonable that the Member States would in practical effect incur liability more easily than the Community because the Member States will often have less discretionary powers, and their margin for manoeuvre will be rather more limited than that of the Community, it should not be so as a matter of principle. In other words, the conditions under which liability is incurred should not be any different, even if in practical effect, it may be harder to obtain damages from the Community where the limits on its action are less strict. The parallel between liability of the Community and of the Member States would become an important element in the development of case law.

11.6. THE EUROPEAN PERSPECTIVE: THE COURT'S CASE LAW ON GOVERNMENTAL LIABILITY FOR BREACH OF COMMUNITY LAW

11.6.1. *Francovich* and *Bonifaci*

11.6.1.1. *Facts and Issues*

Francovich does not need much of an introduction, but it may be useful for the occasional uninformed reader to repeat some of the issues. It is no coincidence that the case was referred from Italy and concerned a particular type of infringement, namely the failure to implement a directive.[164] The Court of Justice had already declared that Italy had infringed its treaty obligations by failing to implement directive 80/987/EEC on the approximation of the laws of the Member States relating to the protection of employees in the event of the insolvency of their employer.[165] Under

---

[163] Successful cases are listed in A Arnull, 'Liability for Legislative Acts under Article 215(2) EC', in T Heukels and A McDonnell (eds), *The Action for Damages in Community Law*, (The Hague, Kluwer Law International, 1997), 129, at 142–46.

[164] See above, section 11.2.2..

[165] Case 22/87 *Commission v Italy* [1989] ECR 163.

the directive,[166] the Member States were obliged to introduce a system guaranteeing employees the payment of outstanding claims in the event of insolvency of their employer. When their employer went bankrupt and their outstanding wage claims were not paid, Francovich and Bonifaci, in the absence of Italian implementation of the directive, brought proceedings before the *pretore di Vicenza* and the *pretore di Bassano del Grappa* against the Italian State, claiming the payment of unpaid wages; or in the alternative, compensation of the loss incurred by failure to timely and correctly implement the directive. The Italian tribunals referred two main questions, one relating to the direct effect of the directive, the other concerning the liability of the Italian State. The second question, concerning the claim in damages, was therefore formulated as an alternative, in case the directive could not be invoked against the State directly and the due payments could not be claimed on the basis of the directive directly.

11.6.1.2. The Court's Judgment

The first question was concerned with the direct effect of the directive at hand. The Court analysed in great detail whether the provisions were sufficiently clear and precise to produce direct effect as against the State, and held that they were, first, with respect to the identity of the employees entitled to the guarantee, and second, with respect to the content of the guarantee.[167] However, the relevant provisions were not sufficiently unconditional concerning the identity of the person liable to provide the guarantee: while the directive required the States to organise an appropriate institutional guarantee system, it left them a broad discretion with regard to the organisation, operation and financing of the guarantee institutions. Accordingly, the applicants could not enforce the rights, which the directive intended to confer upon them, against the State where no implementation measures were adopted within the prescribed period.

The second question was whether there was a right to compensation for the legislature's failure to implement a directive *as a matter of Community law*, and despite the prevailing Italian rules and principles against this type of liability. The Court held, under reference to *Van Gend*

---

[166] Council Directive 80/987/EEC of 20 October 1980 on the approximation of the laws of the Member States relating to the protection of employees in the event of the insolvency of their employer, OJ 1980 L 283/23.

[167] In this respect, the ECJ developed the so-called minimum direct effect: the directive left to the Member States the possibility to set a ceiling. However, the State which had failed to implement the directive could not defeat the rights which the directive creates by relying on the option of limiting the amount of the guarantee which it could have exercised if it had taken the measures necessary to implement the directive, see Joined Cases C–6/90 and C–9/90 *Francovich and Bonifaci v Italy* [1991] ECR I–5357, at paras 15–22.

en Loos[168] and *Costa v ENEL*, that the Community had created its own legal system, giving rise to rights for individuals. It then turned to the obligation of the national courts whose task it is to apply the provisions of Community law to ensure that those rules take full effect and to protect the rights which they confer on individuals (*Simmenthal* and *Factortame*). The full effectiveness of Community rules would be impaired, and the protection of the rights of individuals would be weakened if individuals were unable to obtain redress from the Member States when their rights are infringed by the Member State. It followed, that the principle whereby a State must be liable for loss and damage caused to individuals as a result of breaches of Community law for which the State can be held responsible was inherent in the system of the Treaty. In support of this conclusion, the Court further pointed to Article 5 of the Treaty (now Article 10 EC), requiring the State to take all appropriate measures, whether general or particular, to fulfil their obligations under Community law, among which the obligation to nullify all consequences of a breach of Community law. Contrary to its Advocate General, the Court did not explicitly deal with the national constitutional issues involved in the case, namely the absence of possibility of the State being liable for legislative actions or omissions in several Member States.[169]

Turning to the conditions for liability, the Court held that these would depend on the nature of the breach. In the case of a failure to implement a directive, the right to compensation would arise when three conditions were fulfilled. First, the result prescribed in the directive should entail the grant of rights to individuals; second, it should be possible to identify the content of those rights on the basis of the provisions of the directive; and third, there must be a causal link between the Member State's breach and the damage incurred. Those conditions were sufficient to give rise to a right to obtain reparation, a right founded directly on Community law. Subject to that reservation, it was for national law to designate the competent courts and to lay down the substantive and procedural conditions and rules, subject to the principles of equivalence and effectiveness (the *Rewe* and *Comet* rules).

---

[168] The reference to *Van Gend en Loos* does not however mean that the principle of State liability derives from direct effect and should therefore be limited to infringements of directly effective provisions. Indeed, the *Francovich* directive itself lacked direct effect, and liability served as a substitute for direct effect. However, in *Brasserie du Pêcheur/Factortame III* the ECJ stated that the right to reparation was a corollary of direct effect, see Joined Cases C–46/93 and C–48/93 *Brasserie du Pêcheur SA v Germany and The Queen v Secretary of State for Transport, ex parte Factortame and Others* [1996] ECR I–1029, at para 22. The reference to *Van Gend en Loos* in *Francovich* is rather to the concept of the new legal order creating rights for individuals.

[169] This is all the more striking since one of the members of the bench had just published a comparative survey of the national systems relating to governmental liability and stated that there was no general acceptance of liability for legislative acts, F Schockweiler, G Wivines and JM Godart, 'Le régime de la responsabilité extra-contractuelle du fait d'actes juridiques dans la Communauté européenne', *RTDeur* (1990) 27.

Community and national law are thus interwoven in a complex manner. While on the face of it, the separation between Community law (substantive conditions) and national law (procedural and remedial issues, subject to *Rewe* and *Comet*) appears to be fairly straightforward,[170] the practical application would appear very difficult.[171]

11.6.1.3. *The Impact of* Francovich

The *Francovich* judgment evoked many reactions, some negative,[172] many positive. Most commentators saw *Francovich* as the *'aboutissement final et logique d'une évolution jurisprudentielle qui a affirmé les principes de la spécificité de l'ordre juridique communautaire, de la primauté et de l'effet direct du droit communautaire'*.[173] The case was considered as the final piece completing the 'judge-made jigsaw of protection',[174] filling the gap due mainly to the lack of horizontal direct effect of directives and the national constitutional limits on the judicial function and the national courts' duty to interpret national law in conformity with Community law. It is in this context that the Court first made reference to the principle of State liability in subsequent cases, such as *Faccini Dori*,[175] *Wagner Miret*,[176] and *El Corte Inglés*:[177] *Francovich* liability would constitute the third route, where direct effect and the duty of conform legislation fails to ensure the effective protection of individual rights under Community law in general and

---

[170] Another way of presenting it is that national law provides the vehicle to make the claim based on Community law effective.

[171] Many national courts and commentators start with the question whether *Francovich* constitutes a separate Euro-tort, or rather qualifies national tort rules (on the condition that they do not go beyond what is required under Community law), see *e.g.* in the English courts (choice of the relevant tort or innominate tort); in the Netherlands (the question whether conditions of '*schuld*' and '*relativiteit*' must be fulfilled). The question may sometimes appear more academic than practical, but it may cause a lot of confusion.

[172] So for example W Dänzer-Vanotti, 'Unzulässige Rechtsfortbildung des Europäischen Gerichtshofs', *RIW* (1992) 733, at 740, who argued that the ECJ had overstepped the limits of the judicial function by creating a rule which even the Community legislature could not have adopted, but rather required the intervention of the Member States and a Treaty revision. Whether or not the ECJ had crossed the line was hotly debated in Germany, much more than in other Member States, see also C Tomuschat, 'Das Francovich-Urteil des EuGH – Ein Lehrstück zum Europarecht', in O Due, M Lutter and J Schwarze (eds), *Festschrift für Ulrich Everling* (Baden, Nomos, 1995) 1585; S Schlemmer-Schulte and J Ükrow, 'Haftung des Staates gegenüber dem Marktbürger für gemeinschaftsrechtswidriges Verhalten', *EuR* (1992) 82, at 90 *et seq.*; M Nettesheim, 'Gemeinschaftsrechtliche Vorgaben für das deutsche Staatshaftungsrecht', *DÖV* (1992) 999, at 1000; F Ossenbühl, 'Der gemeinschaftsrechtliche Staatshaftungsanspruch', *DVBl* (1992) 993.

[173] F Schockweiler, 'La responsabilité de l' autorité nationale en cas de violation du droit communautaire', *RTDeur* (1992) 27, at 46.

[174] So M Ross, 'Beyond Francovich', 56 *MLR* (1993) 55, at 55.

[175] Case C–91/91 *Paula Faccini Dori v Recreb Srl* [1994] ECR I–3325.

[176] Case C–334/92 *Wagner Miret v Fondo de Garantía Salarial* [1993] ECR I–6911.

[177] Case C–192/94 *El Corte Inglés v Cristina Blázques Rivero* [1996] ECR I–1281.

directives in particular.[178] Furthermore, the expectation was that the prospect of the State being held liable in damages would constitute an effective deterrent for States with a notoriously bad track record concerning implementation of directives.[179] Denis Waelbroeck has demonstrated that the remedy in damages may indeed be very efficient to force the State to comply with its obligations under the Treaty by reference to the Belgian case of the pension scheme for Community officials of Belgian origin.[180] The case once again proved the relative weakness of infringement proceedings, and the fact that national courts may be much more effective in forcing the State to comply with its Treaty obligations. Where direct effect already involved private applicants and national courts in the enforcement of Community law complementing the defective system of public enforcement, state liability could reinforce private enforcement and replace it in cases where there was no direct effect.[181]

The introduction of the remedy in damages may also have an impact on the readiness of national courts to extend reliance on their duty to conform interpretation.[182] The applicant may then, instead of being awarded the financial alternative of his right by way of damages, enjoy the substantive rights which the Community provision intended to create, such as the issuance of a licence. It may also incite the courts to find additional remedies, or to further extend them to new cases, assuming that they want to limit the liability in damages imposed as a sanction on the disobedient State. One may expect, for instance, that courts may be more willing to issue a declaration that there has been an infringement of Community law,[183] or even to order the State to introduce the required measures, so as to comply with Community obligations in order to avoid liability, possibly even under the threat of penalty payments. Retroactive

---

[178] See among the many examples J Steiner, 'From direct effects to Francovich: Shifting means of enforcement of Community law', 18 *ELR* 1993, 3; C Plaza Martin, 'Furthering the Effectiveness of EC Directives and the Judicial Protection of Individual Rights Thereunder', 43 *ICLQ*, 1994, 26; E Szyszczak, 'Making Europe More Relevant To Its Citizens: Effective Judicial Process', 21 *ELR* 1996, 351. On the relationship between direct effect, conform interpretation and State liability, see M H Wissink, *Richtlijnconforme interpretatie van burgerlijk recht* (Deventer, 2001) ch 8.

[179] DF Waelbroeck, 'Treaty violations and liability of Member States: The effect of the *Francovich* case law', in T Heukels and A McDonnell (eds), *The Action for Damages in Community Law* (The Hague, Kluwer, 1997) 311, at 316, fn. 17.

[180] As reported above, under Section 11.4.5.

[181] *Francovich* liability is not dependent on a previous finding by the ECJ that there has indeed been a violation of Community obligations on the part of the Member State. The availability of case law of the ECJ on Community obligations will however contribute to the establishment of a sufficiently serious breach of Community law, see *below*.

[182] On this issue see the dissertation by HM Wissink, *Richtlijnconforme interpretatie van burgerlijk recht* (Deventer, Kluwer, 2001) chapter 8.

[183] See the declaration issued in the *EOC* case: House of Lords, decision of 3 March 1994, *Equal Opportunities Commission and another v Secretary of State for Employment* [1994] 1 All ER 910; [1994] 2 WLR 409; [1995] 1 AC 1.

application of belated implementing measures would be an example.[184] *Francovich* liability offers the courts and applicants a new type of remedies and sanctions, and may lead to a different use of existing remedies and methods of enforcement.[185] On the other hand, *Francovich* liability may also push the duty to conform interpretation into a retreat.[186]

The *Francovich* judgment left many questions unanswered. Would liability arise only in cases of non-implementation of directives or also in respect of other violations of Community law? Would it arise in case of infringement of directly effective provisions, or was State liability rather an alternative to direct effect; Or for infringements made by the legislatures even in cases not related to the implementation of directives? What about judicial acts? What would the conditions be for liability to arise in case of violations by national administrative organs, public authorities, or even public undertakings? How about violations by federated entities, where the federation (the Member State) has no jurisdiction? Who would have to pay the damage? Would the courts also have jurisdiction to impose other sanctions on the defaulting State, for instance, order it to implement a directive (correctly)? These are only some of the questions, relating to public law aspects.[187] Private law aspects[188] concern the question of the amount of damages, the existence of a right to compensation of immaterial damage, questions of causation, ceilings etc. Finally, it was not

---

[184] G Anagnostaras, 'State liability v Retroactive application of belated implementing measures: Seeking the optimum means in terms of effectiveness of EC law', webjcli.ncl.ac.uk/2000/issue1/anagnostaras1.html.

[185] See also E Deards, "Curiouser and Curiouser'? The Development of Member State Liability in the Court of Justice', 3 *EPL* (1997) 117 at 141; see also P Eeckhout, 'Liability of Member States in Damages and the Community System of Remedies', in J Beatson and T Tridimas (eds), *New Directions in European Public Law* (Oxford, Hart Publishing, 1998) 63, and P Oliver, 'State Liability in Damages following *Factortame III*: A Remedy Seen in Context', above, 49.

[186] It is not clear whether direct effect, conform interpretation and State liability are mere alternatives, or whether there is a strict order between them. It would seem that the ECJ is of the opinion that the national courts would first try to achieve the result intended in a directive through conform interpretation, and only then move on to the alternative remedy of State liability. The advantage of conform interpretation certainly is that the primary result of the directive can be achieved, while state liability will only lead to the payment of a sum of money. However, the availability of an alternative remedy may influence the judge in his decision whether or not he can achieve the result prescribed by the directive through conform interpretation, and it may be sufficient to convince him not to venture on dubious paths, or to decide that the interpretation required cannot be achieved without overstepping the boundaries of the judicial function. See on this question, among others, MH Wissink, *Richtlijnconforme interpretatie van burgerlijk recht*, (Deventer, Kluwer, 2001) 341 *et seq*.

[187] It is admittedly a dangerous venture to use the 'public law – private law divide' (even irrespective of the question whether or not the division is relevant at all in general, but that is a different question altogether) in a comparative perspective, or in the context of Community law in domestic legal orders. Especially in the area of governmental liability the division between public law and private law aspects the division is notoriously difficult.

[188] Again, this is an overly general qualification, that does not apply to all legal systems.

clear whether the same principles would apply to breaches of Community law committed by individuals.[189]

In what follows, the focus will be on three fundamental issues that under national law involve questions of a constitutional nature. Firstly, and central to the remainder of the chapter, is the issue of the liability of the State for legislative actions or omissions. The second issue is that of State liability for infringements attributed to decentralised, federated or independent public authorities, and, directly related to the latter issue, that of the liability *of* those public authorities themselves and the ensuing duty to compensate. Thirdly, the question of complex cases will be touched upon, *i.e.* the question of imputablility, applicable test and allocation of liability, in cases where the State has contributed in several capacities to the infliction of harm: for instance by failure to implement on the part of the primary legislature, the absence of a rectifying intervention on the part of the administration, and failure of the courts to remedy the wrongful situation in conformity with the requirements of Community law.

11.6.2. Liability of the Legislating State

11.6.2.1. Brasserie du Pêcheur *and* Factortame III: *Facts and National Background*

The 1996 judgment of the Court of Justice in *Brasserie/Factortame III* is, again, a widely commented case, and does not need much of an introduction. The cases were joined as they raised similar questions though there are some differences also. *Brasserie du Pêcheur* derived from the German beer cases, concerning the German *Biersteuergesetz* which contained a prohibition against the marketing of beers lawfully manufactured in, and imported from other Member States, but which did not comply with requirements of the *Biersteuergesetz* under the designation of *'Bier'*, and against the importation of beers containing certain additives. Brasserie du Pêcheur, a French brewery exporting beer to Germany, was forced to discontinue these exports since the German authorities objected that its beers did not comply with the German purity law. When the Court of Justice declared that the prohibition contained in the *Biersteuergesetz* was incompatible with Article 30 of the Treaty (now Article 28 EC),[190] Brasserie du Pêcheur brought an action against the German State for compensation of the loss suffered. Given that the infringement, the failure to adapt primary legislation to

---

[189] This has finally been resolved in Case C–453/99 *Courage Ltd v Bernard Crehan and Bernard Crehan v Courage Ltd and Others* [2001] ECR I–06297; before that comments to the same effect had been made by AG van Gerven in Case C–128/92 *HJ Banks & Co Ltd v British Coal Corporation* [1994] ECR I–1209.

[190] Case 178/84 *Commission v Germany (German purity of beer law)* [1987] ECR 1227.

conform to Community law was attributable to the legislature, and given the denial of the liability of the legislating State in German law, the *Bundesgerichtshof* referred several questions for preliminary ruling.

It must be recalled that liability for legislative wrong is excluded under German law for several reasons. One reason lies in the limits of the judicial power, excluding the extension of the procedure of *enteignungsgleichen Eingriff* to legislative wrong attributable to Parliament itself. The other, of *Drittbezogenheit* does not lie in constitutional law,[191] but it has the effect of excluding the liability of the State, for legislative wrong committed both through primary and secondary legislation. Both the *Landesgericht* and the *Oberlandesgericht Köln*[192] rejected the claim of Brasserie de Pêcheur. The *Oberlandesgericht* checked all possible manners available under German law for compensation to be granted. It rejected in very simple terms the claims based on Community law itself: all consequences of a breach of Community law by the State had to be assessed in accordance with national law,[193] which did not allow damages to be granted. First, the claim based on Paragraph 839 BGB *juncto* Article 34 GG failed because under constant case law of the *Bundesgerichtshof*, a failure to legislate does not amount to a breach of an official duty which is referable to the applicant. There would be no reason to adapt this case law to the requirements of Community law, since the effectiveness of Community law could not be more important than that of constitutionally guaranteed fundamental rights, the infringement of which, by Statute does not give rise to damages. Second, recourse to § 823(2) BGB[194] *juncto* Article 171 EC could bring no relief, since Paragraph 839 BGB, as *lex specialis*, takes precedence over the more general Paragraph 823(2) BGB. Thirdly, claims based on the procedure of *enteignungsgleichen Eingriff* failed because it applies only to *lawful* acts, whereas in this case the unlawfulness of the Statute with respect to Community law was not in dispute. In addition, the extension of this principle to legislative wrong would overstep the limits of the judicial function, and breach the principles of separation of powers and democracy. Whether and to what extent the breach of

---

[191] F Ossenbühl, 'Staatshaftung zwischen Europarecht und nationalem Recht', in O Due, M Lutter and J Schwarze (eds), *Festschrift für Everling* (Baden, Nomos, 1995) 1031, at 1043.

[192] *Oberlandesgericht Köln*, decision of 20 June 1991, *Brasserie du Pêcheur*, EuZW, 1991, 574.

[193] *Oberlandesgericht Köln*, decision of 20 June 1991, *Brasserie du Pêcheur*, EuZW, 1991, 574, at 575.

[194] The general tort provisions §§ 823 (1) and (2) of the BGB provide that '(1) Anyone who intentionally or negligently injures life, body, health, freedom, ownership or any other right of another in a manner contrary to law shall be obliged to compensate the other for the loss arising. (2) The same liability is incurred by a person who infringes a law intended to protect another person. If such a law may be infringed without culpability, liability to compensate shall be incurred only in the event of culpability', translation taken from W van Gerven, *Cases, Materials and Text on National, Supranational and International Tort Law*, (Oxford, Hart Publishing, 2000), at 63, containing also a general introduction on the provision and its application in practice.

Community law by the Legislature proper would create a right to compensation was for the Legislature to decide, and had nothing to do with the relation between national law and Community law. The *Bundesgerichtshof*[195] confirmed the decision of the *Oberlandesgericht* Köln as concerns German law, adding that a claim on the basis of *enteignungs-gleichen Eingriff* would in any case fail, since the case did not concern a breach of a protected property right. However, the *Bundesgerichtshof* doubted that a right *based in Community law* would exist in this case.

The *Factortame III* reference was a sequel to the saga of the Spanish fishermen who were excluded from the British fishing quota. It will be remembered that the Spanish fishermen objected to the new Merchant Shipping Act 1988, which introduced a new system of registration of fishing vessels, imposing certain conditions relating to nationality, domicile and residence, depriving the Spanish fishermen, in practical effect, of their right to fish in British waters. The Spanish fishermen had been prevented from fishing during the interval between the entry into force of the Merchant Shipping Act (1 April 1989) and the application of the Order of the President of the Court of Justice ordering the British authorities to suspend the application of the Merchant Shipping Act (2 November 1989).[196] When the Court of Justice decided that the United Kingdom had indeed failed to fulfil its Treaty obligations by imposing conditions as to nationality,[197] the Divisional Court made an order giving effect to the judgment in respect of the registration of the Spanish vessels, and directed the applicants to give detailed particulars of their claims for damages against the Secretary of State for Transport. The Divisional Court considered that if English law were to be applied, there would be no remedy in damages under *Bourgoin*, but doubted whether *Francovich* liability would lie.

In both cases, the infringement of a directly effective provision of the Treaty was imputable to Parliament itself – as had been the case in *Francovich*. In contrast to *Francovich*, the infringement did not consist of the failure to implement a directive – a clear and simple breach of a positive obligation – but of the adoption of primary legislation contrary to directly effective provisions of the Treaty, from which individuals may derive directly effective rights, enforceable in the national courts. Several fundamental points of a constitutional nature were argued before the Court, relating to the jurisdiction of the Court of Justice and the liability of the legislating State.[198]

---

[195] *Bundesgerichtshof*, decision of 28 January 1993, *Brasserie du Pêcheur* NVwZ 1993, 601.

[196] Case 246/89 R *Commission v United Kingdom (Merchant Shipping Act)* [1989] ECR 3125. The United Kingdom partially amended the Merchant Shipping Act with effect from 2 November 1989.

[197] Case C–221/89 *The Queen v Secretary of State for Transport, ex parte Factortame (Factortame I)* [1991] ECR I–3905, on reference from the Divisional Court, relating to the compatibility of the Merchant Shipping Act with the Treaty.

[198] No fewer than seven Member States intervened.

11.6.2.2. The Constitutional Issues

The first point, and a crucial one indeed, concerned the competence of the Court of Justice, and its jurisdiction to create a principle of State liability for legislative acts infringing Community law. Several Member States, among which most prominently Germany, argued that the Court of Justice did not have jurisdiction to develop such principle in the absence of a Treaty provision to that effect, and given that the Member States had rejected the introduction of such provision during the latest revision of the Treaties. According to the German Government,[199] the extension of State liability to legislative wrong would constitute a revolution in many legal systems, would have an important impact on the financial situation of the Member States, and would have to be approved by the national Parliaments. Secondly, both referring courts had emphasised that prevailing national constitutional law prevented the State from being held liable in damages for this particular type of infringement directly attributable to the primary Legislature. Furthermore, it was argued, the Community itself would not be held liable in parallel cases, given the restrictive approach of the Court to liability for normative acts under *Schöppenstedt*. Why, then, should the Member States be so liable?

The first issue was probably the most difficult for the Court to answer, because it was crucial to convince its audience that *Francovich* liability constituted a lawful development of Community law, and a justified piece of judge-made law. If the national courts or other members of the audience were not convinced of the legitimacy of the Court's case law, *Francovich* could die a sudden death, and the Court's legitimacy could be seriously damaged even beyond the issue of state liability.

The second issue was a difficult one to argue for the German government: The Court of Justice, an international Court, never accepts arguments in defence based on the constitutional set-up of the State, or on constitutional principles.[200] In that sense, and raised before the Court of Justice, the argument is not a very strong one. The Member States as a whole are under an obligation to comply with Community law, and to

---

[199] Supported by the Netherlands and Irish Governments, see Opinion of AG Tesauro, Joined Cases C–46/93 and C–48/93 *Brasserie/Factortame III*, at marginal number 24.

[200] The Court consistently rejects arguments based on constitutional division of powers within the State. The Court knows only the States as monolithic blocks (the unitary principle), and does not look beyond the State boundaries. Member States as such are declared to have infringed Community law, not a particular constituent part thereof, and independent of the organ to which the breach is attributable. Horizontal or vertical separation of powers cannot serve as a valid defence in enforcement procedures, see *e.g.* Case 77/69 *Commission v Belgium* [1970] ECR 237; Case 8/70 *Commission v Italy* [1970] ECR 961; Case 100/77 *Commission v Italy* [1978] ECR 879;Case 239/85 *Commission v Belgium* [1986] ECR 3645; Case C–85/89 *Commission v Germany* [1991] ECR I–4983; see also Case 9/74 *Casagrande v Munich* [1974] ECR 773.

organise their institutions and organs in such a way that Community obligations are met. On the other hand, the second argument helped to reinforce the first argument. To hold the State liable in damages for harm caused by the primary legislature in cases before national courts, where they could not be so held in national law, constituted such a constitutional revolution, that it could not be carried out by the Court of Justice, but required the intervention of the Member States acting as Community legislature or constitutional legislature. The argument based on the parallel between liability of the Member States on the one hand and of the Community on the other touched upon a very sensitive issue, and the Court would have to be very careful not to displease the Member States and to retain the goodwill of the national courts. The way it would handle the question of parallellism would contribute to convincing the audience of the first point, *i.e.* that this constituted a lawful development of Community law in the hands of the Court.

11.6.2.3. The Court's Judgment[201]

Liability of the Legislating State

Under the heading '*State liability for acts or omissions of the national legislature contrary to Community law*' the Court combined several fundamental issues, not all of which concern the question of liability of the legislating State. Firstly, the Court discussed the issue of the relationship between direct effect and State liability, and held that direct effect and State liability are not mutually exclusive: where there is no direct effect, as in the case of the failure to transpose a directive, *Francovich* liability serves to provide reparation for the injurious consequences of the failure to implement, in so far as the beneficiaries are concerned. However, in the event of infringement of a directly effective provision of Community law, the right to reparation is *the necessary corollary* of direct effect. Secondly, the Court entered into the most sensitive issue concerning its legitimacy and jurisdiction to introduce a general right to reparation for individuals.[202] The Court held, firstly, that it did have subject matter competence: the question had been referred by national courts under the preliminary rulings procedure and concerned a question of interpretation relating to the consequences under Community law of a State's infringement of Community law. Secondly, as there is no specific provision dealing with the issue in the Treaty, it is for the Court under Article 164 of the Treaty (now Article

---

[201] It took the Court 3 years to answer the questions referred. The references were received at the Court in February 1993; the judgment was delivered on 5 March 1996.

[202] The question of whether or not the Court was right to develop the doctrine of State liability is discussed in D Wyatt, 'Injunctions and Damages against the State for Breach of Community Law – A Legitimate Judicial Development', in M Andenas and F Jacobs (eds), *European Community Law in the English Courts* (Oxford, Clarendon Press, 1998) 87.

220 EC) to rule on it, in accordance with generally accepted methods of interpretation, *i.e.* by reference to fundamental principles of Community law and general principles common to the legal systems of the Member States, also reflected in Article 215 of the Treaty (now Article 288 EC). In many Member States the essentials of the legal rules governing state liability are judge-made. There was, it was implied, nothing in any way novel in a court developing a system of state liability. Moving on to the *third* fundamental issue, concerning liability of the legislating State, the Court inferred from the fact that the principle of State liability is inherent in the Treaty, that it must hold good regardless of the organ whose act or omission was responsible for the breach. In addition, the Court went on, it was a fundamental requirement that Community law be uniformly applied, and accordingly, that the obligation to pay damages could not depend on domestic rules as to the division of powers between constitutional authorities. Finally, the Court drew on international law, where the State is viewed as a single entity, whose liability arises irrespective of whether the breach is attributable to the legislature, the judiciary or the executive. This must apply *a fortiori* in Community law, since all national authorities, including the legislature, are bound to perform their task to comply with Community law.

By combining distinct issues, the Court conceals the weakness of some of the arguments. The reference to Article 288(2) EC (then Article 215 of the Treaty) is hardly convincing when it comes to the liability of the legislating State. Indeed, any comparative survey — a method which appears to be assumed under Article 288 EC — demonstrates that it is *not* in accordance with the general principles common to the Member States to recognise liability for legislative wrongs committed by the legislature proper.[203] Reference to Article 288 EC does not give much support to an extension of the principle to legislative wrong attributable to the legislature proper. On the other hand, the Court had to deal with the critique, justified it is submitted, that it was applying a double standard requiring a more stringent approach to Member State infringements and infringements by the Community institutions, without offering a satisfactory explanation.

---

[203] See W van Gerven, 'Taking Article 215(2) EC Seriously', in J Beatson and T Tridimas (eds), *New Directions in European Public Law*, (Oxford, Hart Publishing, 1998), 35, at 36; When the ECJ had to rule on the issue of the liability of the Community for normative acts, the AG's in the landmark cases did enter into a comparative study of the national law. Their main conclusion was, that there was not much of a common approach in the Member States which could be transposed to the liability of the Community. See AG Roemer in Case 5/71 *Aktien-Zuckerfabrik Schöppenstedt v Council* [1971] ECR 975; Opinion of AG Capotorti in Joined Cases 83 and 94/76, 4, 15 and 40/77 *Bayerische HNL v Council and Commission* [1978] ECR 1209: Capotorti pointed out that the issue of the liability of the legislating State for Acts deriving from the sovereign parliaments was, in national law, very disparate, and far from settled even in those Member States where these acts could be reviewed in the light of higher national principles, Italy and Germany.

Double standards are always difficult to justify,[204] and cause resentment on the part of national courts, as is exemplified by the judgment of the Court of Appeal in *Bourgoin*.[205] The reference to Article 288 EC in the judgment is misleading.

The analogy with international liability of the State seems an obvious one given that the European Court is an international court, which views the State as a single entity. However, *Brasserie* and *Factortame III* originated in national courts, which form part of the State, and do not normally view the State as a single entity. To require the national courts not to distinguish as to the organ responsible for the infringement, is an intrusion *par excellence* in the national constitutional system, whereby the national courts are elevated to the level of international courts, standing, as it were, outside the constitutional system which has instated them. One can imagine the schizophrenia on the part of the national courts. It must be recalled that the liability must be assessed in accordance with the national rules, subject to the conditions of equivalence and effectiveness. Furthermore, liability in international law does not intend to protect individuals; it involves interstate relationships. International liability may not be a well chosen standard of reference.[206]

Conditions for Liability

Turning then to the conditions for liability, the Court followed the path set out in *Francovich*, that the conditions would depend on the type of the breach. It then sought to relate the conditions of the liability of the State to those applying to similar situations of Community liability. One of the most serious and consistent critiques of *Francovich* had been that the Court was more severe on the Member States – *Francovich* almost constituted a form of strict liability – than on the Community institutions, which in many cases escape liability. The difficulty was, then, to find a common denominator: which types of acts and omissions in the field of Community law by Community institutions and Member States should be treated in the same way and be decided under similar conditions? It could not be an institutional denominator, as is the case in many national

---

[204] See however the Opinion of AG Léger in *Hedley Lomas* who insisted that State liability and liability of the Community should not be treated along the same lines. Member States, he said, are subject to a hierarchy of legal norms which does not exist in the Community, and moreover, it would seem paradoxical to align state liability for breach of Community law with Article 215 of the Treaty which was considered to afford insufficient protection to individuals', see Opinion of AG Léger in Case C–5/94 *The Queen v Ministry of Agriculture, Fisheries and Food, ex parte Hedley Lomas (Ireland) Ltd* [1996] ECR I–2553, at paras 138 *et seq*.

[205] See P Oliver, 'State Liability in Damages following *Factortame III*', in J Beatson and T Tridimas (eds), *New Directions in European Public Law* (Oxford, Hart Publishing, 1998) 49, at 53.

[206] Also the statement that this must *a fortiori* be true for Community law makes one wonder.

constitutional sysems, where the State could be held liable for legislative wrong committed by lower or secondary legislating bodies, such as for ministerial decrees or municipal regulations, but not for Acts adopted by or omissions attributable to the primary legislature, *i.e.* Parliament itself. Community institutional law does not make the same constitutional division along the lines of *trias politica* as the Member States do. There is no body comparable to a national Parliament, expressing the *volonté générale* in the legislation it adopts; there is, furthermore, not a type of act comparable to Acts of Parliament. In its case law under Article 288 EC, the Court chose as the decisive criterion the amount of discretion enjoyed by the Community institutions when adopting a particular act. This resulted in the *Schöppenstedt* denomination of 'normative or legislative measures involving choices as to economic policy'. Presumably, these are not limited to *economic* policy; what is crucial, is the wide discretion enjoyed by the institutions involved. The limited liability of the Community for this type of act misses one element which is also present in several national systems, namely that the immunity for legislative wrong is also due to the fact that Parliament represents the sovereign will of the people.[207] The main argument for a strict approach to liability for legislative wrong of the Community was that the exercise of legislative functions must not be hindered by the prospect of actions for damages whenever the general interest requires the institutions to adopt measures which may adversely affect individual interests.

Decisive, thus, is the measure of discretion enjoyed by the national authority, which must be comparable to that of the Community institutions when they adopt legislative measures pursuant to a Community policy.[208] The Court added that the national legislatures do not always have a wide discretion in the context of Community law. Discretion is a gliding scale; and the issue of the measure of discretion cuts across functional borders and competent authorities.[209]

Where there is wide discretion, Community law confers a right to reparation where three conditions are met: the rule infringed must be intended to confer rights on individuals, the breach must be sufficiently serious and there must be a direct and causal link between the breach of the obligation resting on the State and the damage sustained by the injured party. The second of these conditions, of a sufficiently serious breach, is the most dif-

---

[207] 'The "power to express the sovereignty of the people" justifies the legislature's immunity in relation to the general rules of liability', see AG Léger, in his Opinion in Case C–5/94 *The Queen v Ministry of Agriculture, Fisheries and Food, ex parte Hedley Lomas* [1996] ECR I–2553, at marginal number 96.

[208] This appears to be an extension from *Schöppenstedt* where the Court spoke only of legislative measures involving choices as to *economic* policy; this is extended here to *a* Community policy, whatever its nature.

[209] A Minister may be have a wider discretion in adopting certain measures than the legislature when making other decisions.

ficult to apply. In *Brasserie/Factortame III* the Court explained that a breach is sufficiently serious when the Member State (or the institution concerned) manifestly and gravely disregarded the limits on its discretion.[210] The factors which the national courts may take into consideration include the clarity and precision of the rule breached, the measure of discretion left by that rule to the national or Community authorities, whether the infringement and the damage caused was intentional or involuntary,[211] whether any error of law was excusable or inexcusable, the fact that the position taken by a Community institution may have contributed towards the omission and the adoption or retention of national measures or practices contrary to Community law. A breach will be sufficiently serious if it has persisted despite a judgment declaring the infringement, or a preliminary ruling or settled case law of the Court of Justice on the matter from which it is clear that the conduct in question constituted an infringement.

National Law is the Vehicle

These conditions constitute a minimum level of liability: they are necessary and sufficient to found a right in damages, but where the national rules governing State liability are more generous towards injured individuals, these national rules should apply. Apart from the substantive conditions giving rise to a right to reparation, the additional procedural and remedial conditions are set by national law, subject to the normal *Rewe* and *Comet* provisos of equivalence and effectiveness. The exclusion of liability of the legislating State in general, and the German rule of *Drittbezogenheit* which in practical effect excludes the liability of the legislating State, make the recovery of damages impossible or excessively difficult and are therefore not to be applied in the context of liability of Community law. The same goes for the requirement of misfeasance in public office, where an abuse of power is inconceivable in the case of the legislature.[212]

11.6.3. Drawing the Lines Together: towards *Dillenkofer*

After *Brasserie*, there seemed to be at least two sets of conditions for State liability to arise: the *Francovich* conditions for cases of failure to implement directives to the detriment of individuals, where a mere

---

[210] Clearly inspired by the case law under Article 288(2) EC.

[211] Fault is thus not a constitutive condition for liability to arise, but fault-like considerations do play a role in the assessment of the seriousness of the infringement. For the rejection of fault as a condition, see *Brasserie/Factortame III*, at paras 75–80.

[212] It is striking that these issues are dealt with at this stage, which appears only to concern 'the details', once the substantive conditions which are necessary and sufficient to establish liability have been established. In the German case, *Dirttbezogenheit* normally forms one of the substantive conditions for the application of § 839 BGB in conjunction with Art. 34 of the Basic Law; the requirement of misfeasance in public office concerns the preliminary question of the choice of the approporiate tort, and hardly relates to a secondary issue.

infringement would appear to suffice, and the *Brasserie* conditions applying to cases where the State has wide discretion making legislative
choices, where it would be much more difficult to recover damages.
Discretion seemed to be decisive in order to choose the applicable test.

Only three weeks after the ruling in *Brasserie*, the Court gave judgment
in its third State liability case, *British Telecommunications*, where a third type
of infringement appeared to have been committed, namely the incorrect
implementation of a directive.[213] The Court decided the case under
Brasserie, because in this case also, the State should not be hindered by the
prospect of actions in damages. It did not however inquire whether the
State did indeed have wide discretion implementing the relevant directive.
While it may well be true that some directive provisions allow the State a
wide margin, in other cases the discretion will be extremely limited. In
British Telecom, the Court held that in this case there had been no sufficiently
serious breach, but rather an excusable error.[214] The directive lacked precision, and was reasonably capable of bearing the interpretation given to it by
the United Kingdom in good faith: it was wrong, but not manifestly contrary to the wording of the directive, and there was no guidance from the
case-law of the Court, nor clarification from the Commission.

A few months later, the Court decided *Hedley Lomas*, again referred to
it by an English court,[215] concerning a refusal of the English authorities to
issue an export licence for live sheep to Spain. At the time when the
licence was requested and denied, the United Kingdom had imposed a
general ban on the export to Spain of livestock arguing that Spanish
slaughter-houses did not comply with the rules laid down in the relevant
directive. The exporters sought a declaration that the refusal constituted
an infringement of Community law and claimed damages. Once again the
Court of Justice decided the case under the conditions set forth in
Brasserie/Factortame III, *i.e.* the conditions applying to cases of breach of
Community law attributable to a Member State acting in a field in which
it has a wide discretion to make legislative choices. This is striking, since
the Minister was not making a 'legislative' choice,[216] which the Court did

---

[213] Case C–392/93 *The Queen v HM Treasury, ex parte British Telecommunications* [1996] ECR
I–1631.
[214] In fact, the assessment whether there has been a sufficiently serious breach is a matter for
the national court to decide. However, the Court may, when it considers that it has all the
relevant information, decide the case for the national court, see e.g. *British
Telecommunications, Hedley Lomas, Larsy.*
[215] Case C–5/94 *R v Ministry of Agriculture, Fisheries and Food, ex parte Hedley Lomas (Ireland)
Ltd* [1996] ECR I–2553.
[216] This is not to imply that it should matter from a Community law perspective which
organ was responsible for the breach. However, in *Brasserie/Factortame III* and in *British
Telecommunications*, the Court itself had insisted that the infringements were attributable
to the legislative organs, making legislative policy choices. It is hard to see why in this
case the authorities were making legislative policy choices.

admit when assessing whether there had been a sufficiently serious breach: *'where, at the time when it committed the infringement, the Member State in question was not called upon to make any legislative choices and had only considerably reduced, or even no, discretion, the mere infringement of Community law may be sufficient to establish the existence of a sufficiently serious breach'*. However, the requirement that a breach should be sufficiently serious had been developed precisely for cases where the State *does* have a wide discretion to make legislative choices. Why the infringement at issue should, in the system of the Court, come under the *Brasserie/Factortame III* category of cases is not clear. In addition, while the Court claimed to be applying the *Brasserie/ Factortame III* test, it did not mention the condition that there should be a manifest and grave disregard of the limits of discretion allowed, and instead held that the mere infringement sufficed to give rise to liability, apparently under a test similar to the basic test under Article 215 of the Treaty (damage, causation and wrongful act)[217] or a *Francovich*-type test.[218] The Court was blurring its new system.[219]

In *Dillenkofer*, the Court re-arranged the system and drew the lines together in what may be described as the general tort of infringement of Community law by a public authority.[220] *Dillenkofer* concerned the failure of the German State to implement the package travel directive within the prescribed time limits. The referring court stated that under German law, damages would not lie, but it doubted whether damages would be available as a matter of Community law. The question was whether failure to transpose a directive within the prescribed period is sufficient *per se* to afford individuals a right to reparation if the other conditions are fulfilled. This would appear to follow from *Francovich*. However, the German government argued that liability for belated transposition would only be incurred if there had been a serious, that is, a manifest and grave breach of Community law. The Court re-iterated its double standard system – the distinction between two sets of conditions applying to different types of infringements – but it then stated that *'In substance, the conditions laid down in that group of judgments are the same, since the condition that there should be*

---

[217] See E Deards, "Curiouser and Curiouser'? The Development of Member State Liability in the Court of Justice', 3 *EPL* (1997) 117, at 128.

[218] Also in *Francovich*, no mention was made of a fault requirement: the mere failure to implement would suffice to constitute a wrongful act, which then gives rise to a right to reparation where three conditions are fulfilled, relating the type of directive and causation: the directive is intended to confer rights on individuals, those rights can be identified on the basis of the directive, and there is a causal link.

[219] See also L Goffin, 'A propos des principes régissant la responsabilité non contractuelle des États membres en cas de violation du droit communautaire', *CDE* (1997) 531, at 535.

[220] Joined Cases C–178/94, C–179/94, C–189/94 and C–190/94 *Erich Dillenkofer and Others v Germany* [1996] ECR I–4845.

a sufficiently serious breach, although not expressly mentioned in Francovich, *was nevertheless evident from the circumstances of that case.*

When the Court held that the conditions under which State liability gives rise to a right to reparation depended on the nature of the breach of Community law causing the damage, that meant that those conditions are to be applied according to each type of situation.

On the one hand, a breach of Community law is sufficiently serious if a Community institution or a Member State, in the exercise of its rule-making powers, manifestly and gravely disregards the limits on those powers. On the other hand, if, at the time when it committed the infringement, the Member State in question was not called upon to make any legislative choices and had only considerably reduced, or even no, discretion, the mere infringement of Community law may be sufficient to establish the existence of a sufficiently serious breach'.[221] Failure to implement a directive in time constitutes by and of itself a sufficiently serious breach of Community law and gives rise to a right in damages, if the directive was of a particular type, *i.e.* it was intended to create rights for individuals which are identifiable on the basis of the directive, and there is a causal link.

11.6.4. 'Second Generation' Governmental Liability Cases: Allocation of Liability in Federal and Decentralised States

After *Dillenkofer*, the system appeared to be in place: the principle was firmly established, and now constituted a single tort of infringement of Community law, governed by a single set of conditions (sufficiently serious breach of a rule of law intended to confer rights on individuals, and causal link). The cases following *Dillenkofer* have been described as 'second generation'. While these may not contain any innovations and merely develop and refine the remedy[222]with respect to the private law aspects of liability,[223] some decisions did touch upon important national constitutional issues.[224]

---

[221] Joined Cases C–178/94, C–179/94, C–189/94 and C–190/94 *Erich Dillenkofer and Others v Germany* [1996] ECR I–4845, at paras 23–25.

[222] So T Tridimas, 'Liability for Breach of Community Law: Growing up and Mellowing down?' (2001) 38 *CML Rev* 301, at 303.

[223] It is again admitted that it is precarious to distinguish between public and private law aspects, especially in this context where both Community law and 15 national systems are involved, all of which have their own conception of the division, and some of which may not even recognise the distinction. What is meant here with the notion 'private law aspects' are those relating to type of damage for which compensation can be obtained, quantum, causal link, etc.

[224] See *e.g.* G Anagnostaras, 'The allocation of responsibility in State liability actions for breach of Community law: a modern gordian knot?', 26 *ELR* (2001) 139.

All of the actions referred to the Court so far, had been brought against the State, a Minister of the State, or both.[225] The question had already arisen, however, before several national courts, and was discussed in scholarly writing, whether liability cases could also have been brought against 'State emanations', public authorities which form part of, or are related to the State as such, while being distinct from it. As has already been explained, the Court of Justice being an international court adopts a unitary concept of 'the State',[226] and does not distinguish as to which authority within the State was responsible for the breach, and which authority will be liable to pay damages. But until the references made in *Konle*,[227] *Haim*[228] and *Larsy*,[229] all cases had concerned the *central* State, and infringements had been attributable to central organs of the State, whether acting in their legislative[230] or administrative capacity.[231] The question of what constitutes *the State*[232] has been discussed in various other fields, mostly in enforcement proceedings, where the Court consistently holds that it does not see to the constitutional separation of powers

---

[225] The choice of the defendant is a matter of national procedural law, and will typically involve issues of legal personality and so forth. The following defendants had, until *Haim*, been addressed in cases which reached the ECJ: the State itself (the Italian Republic in *Francovich*, the Federal Republic of Germany in *Brasserie* and *Dillenkofer*, the Republic of Austria in *Konle*, the Swedish State in Case C–150/99 *Svenska Staten v Stockholm Lindöpark AB and Stockholm Lindöpark AB v Svenska Staten* [2001] I–493); a Minister of the State (a UK Secretary of State, in *Factortame III*, *British Telecommunications* and *Hedley Lomas*); a Ministry (in Case C–319/96 *Brinkmann Tabakfabriken GmbH v Skatteministeriet* [1998] 5255 and Case C–127/95 *Norbrook Laboratories Ltd v Ministry of Agriculture, Fisheries and Food* [1998] ECR 1531); and a joint action was brought against the Commissioners of Inland Revenue and HM Attorney General (Joined Cases C–397/98 and C–410/98 *Metallgesellschaft Ltd, Hoechst AG and Hoechst (UK) Ltd v Commissioners of Inland Revenue and HM Attorney General* [2000] ECR I–1727.

[226] Hence also its straigthforward analogy with the liability of the State in international law, which does not seem so appropriate to cases to be decided by national courts.

[227] Case C–302/97 *Klaus Konle v Republic of Austria* [1999] ECR I–3099. While the action was brought against the State, the issues involved concerned the constitutional distribution of powers between the federation and the federated entities, and the question whether the State could avoid liability by referring to the obligations imposed on the federated entities.

[228] Case C–2/97 *Salomone Haim v Kassenzahnärztliche Vereinigung Nordrhein* [2000] ECR I–512; the defendant was, as is clear from the reference, *'a legally independent public-law body of the Member State'*, which was responsible for the registration of dental practitioners.

[229] Case C–118/00 *Gervais Larsy v Inasti* [2001] ECR I–5063; the defendant was the Institut national d'assurances sociales pour travailleurs indépendants.

[230] As in *Francovich*, *Brasserie/Factortame III*, *British Telecom*, or *Dillenkofer*.

[231] As in *Hedley Lomas*. The fact that more cases have been referred concerning infringement attributable to the legislating State should not be taken to imply that this is where most violations occur. Rather, it is probably the area where national courts find most legal issues which they cannot solve on their own and invoke the help from the ECJ For the liability of the State for acts and omissions of courts see Case C–224/01 *Gerhard Köbler v Republik Österreich*, decision of 30 September 2003, nyr.

[232] See MP Chiti, 'The EC Notion of Public Administration: The Case of the Bodies Governed by Public Law', 8 *EPL* (2002) 473; Kvjatkovski, 'What is an 'Emanation of the State'? An Educated Guess', 3 *EPL* (1997) 329; Hecquard-Theron, 'La notion d'État en droit communautaire', 26 *RTDeur* (1990) 693; D Curtin, 'The Province of Government: Delimiting the Direct Effect of Directives in the Common Law Context', 15 *ELRev* 1990, 195.

in the State or at which organ or institution has been responsible for the violation.[233] A second area in which the Court has elaborated on the meaning of the notion 'State', with many more difficulties than in the area of enforcement actions, is that of the direct effect of directives, and the possibility of individuals to invoke Community law against organs of the State. Given the absence of full-fledged horizontal effect of directives, and the acceptance of vertical direct effect of directives even as against State organs that were not under an obligation to implement, it is crucial to know what constitutes a public authority.[234]

Two related questions arose in these cases: whether the State can also be held liable for infringements attributable to an independent public law authority (allocation of responsibility); and whether an action in damages can also be brought directly against such authority or must be addressed against the State (allocation of liability). In the discussion of a third issue, the nature and measure of discretion which the State or authority in question enjoys, the two become intertwined, causing additional problems of application. The decisions in *Konle*, *Haim* and *Larsy* will first be explained, before entering into a discussion of the national constitutional issues they raise.

11.6.4.1. Konle[235]

Konle, a German national, attempted to obtain a plot of land in the Tyrol in the context of a procedure for compulsory sale by auction. Under the Tyrol law on the transfer of land, authorisation was required to obtain such land, which was virtually impossible to receive for foreigners, and Konle's application was denied. The Tyrol Law was later declared unconstitutional by the Austrian *Verfassungsgerichtshof*, on grounds that it involved an excessive infringement of the fundamental right to property.[236] In a later procedure, the decision of the administrative authority denying the authorisation was quashed, and remanded to it. Without awaiting a new decision, Konle also brought an action for damages against the Republic of Austria to establish the liability of the State for breach of Community law. The referring court explained that under Austrian law, in case of infringements attributable to a federated entity of

---

[233] So for instance Case 77/69 *Commission v Belgium* [1970] ECR 237; Case 93/71 *Leonesio* [1972] *ECR* 287.

[234] See Case C–188/89 *Foster v British Gas plc* [1990] ECR I–3313.

[235] Case C–302/97 *Klaus Konle v Republic of Austria* [1999] ECR 3099.

[236] *Verfassungsgerichtshof*, decision of 10 December 1996, *Tiroler Grundverkehrsgesetz*, VfSlg, 1996, 14701. The law was declared unconstitutional because the rules on the publication of laws had not been complied with; in addition, the rules effectively precluding the acquisition of secondary residences were declared unconstitutional as infringing the right to sell and acquire property, the right to establishment and the right to property, see A Lengauer, Casenote in 37 *CML Rev* 2000, 181, at 183.

the State, the injured party may claim damages only against that part of the State, not the State as a whole, and asked what the position under Community law was. The Court held that it was for each Member State to ensure that individuals obtain reparation for damage caused to them by non-compliance with Community law, whichever public authority was responsible for the breach and whichever public authority was in principle, under the law of the Member State concerned, responsible for making reparation. A Member State could not, therefore, plead the distribution of powers and responsibilities between the bodies existing in its national legal order in order to free itself from liability. One might deduce from that statement that in any case, the (federal or central) State could be held liable, since it has final responsibility.[237] However, the Court went on to say that *'subject to that reservation, Community law does not require Member States to make any change in the distribution of powers and responsibilities between the public bodies which exist on their territory. So long as the procedural arrangements in the domestic system enable the rights which individuals derive from the Community legal system to be effectively protected and it is not more difficult to assert those rights than the rights which they derive from the domestic legal system, the requirements of Community law are fulfilled. The answer to the fourth question must therefore be that, in Member States with a federal structure, reparation for damage caused to individuals by national measures taken in breach of Community law need not necessarily be provided by the federal State in order for the obligations of the Member State concerned under Community law to be fulfilled.'*[238]

These paragraphs are not easy to understand, as there seems to be a tension between both assertions: on the one hand, that the State cannot invoke national rules to avoid liability (implying that the action could be brought against the Austrian State), and on on the other hand that Community law does not require any change in the distribution of powers and responsibilities, and that so long as the procedural arrangements in the domestic system enable Community rights to be protected effectively and in a manner equivalent to similar national situations, the requirements of Community law are fulfilled (meaning that Konle should have brought his action against the Tyrol). The passage could be interpreted as meaning that at the least, it must be possible for individuals to claim damages from the central State which is as such responsible: it is the State which carries ultimate (international) responsibility as a Member State, and it may not, in accordance with the consistent case law in other areas, invoke its constitutional rules to free itself from liability. This position would be consistent with the idea that this type of liability is based on the international liability of the State.[239] On the other hand, if it is possible under national law for an

---

[237] So also J Jans *et al, Inleiding tot het Europees bestuursrecht,* Ars Aequi Libri, 2002, at 376–77.
[238] Case C–302/97 *Klaus Konle v Republic of Austria* [1999] ECR I–3099, at para 63.
[239] As the ECJ implied in *Brasserie,* at para 34.

individual to claim compensation from other public authorities, who are as a matter of national law responsible in the last resort to pay the compensation,[240] it must at least be possible to bring an action in damages against these public authorities in question.[241] The statements of the Court probably go further, and indicate that an action *must* be brought in accordance with national law, and other actions can be dismissed. If the appropriate defendant under national law is another entity, such as a federated entity, the action against the State can[242] be dismissed also in the context of an action based on Community law,[243] if this would be the position under national law in similar national proceedings.

Accordingly, it seems that the Community stance is that national law defines the appropriate defendant, under the conditions of equivalence and effectiveness.[244] If no other action is available, it must at the least be possible to bring it against the State. The option chosen makes it more difficult for the individual to obtain compensation, since he will have to decide who the appropriate defendant is. It would have been preferrable if the Court would have decided that in any case at least the Member State as such or a central authority can be held liable, as is the case in enforcement actions.[245] Once the individual has been awarded damages, it is then for the State and the public authorities involved to settle who is ultimately liable to pay under national law, possibly after new court cases.

---

[240] If the State were held liable in damages for breach of Community law and under national law, the federated entities should be held responsible, the State would have to recover the damages paid from the authority in question. This issue does not concern Community law, and is a matter for national law to decide.

[241] It is certain that it must be possible, under the principle of equivalence (para 63 of the judgment). It is not entirely clear whether it is the only possibility, at the exclusion of a separate action brought against the State, which also seems possible, under para 62 of the judgment.

[242] It would go too far to conclude that the action must, as a matter of Community law be denied; and this derives also from *Konle* where the ECJ held that reparation need *not necessarily* be provided by the federal State. As always, the ECJ is concerned mainly with the result, *i.e.* the effective protection of the individual.

[243] This was also the final decision of the Austrian courts in *Konle*, see *Oberster Gerichtshof*, decision of 25 July 2000, *Klaus Konle v Republik Österreich*, available on www.ris.bka.gv.at/jus. Since the transfer of land was a *Länder* competence, the claim against the Austrian State was dismissed. Konle tried to 'save' his claim against the federation by stating that the federal State should at least be held liable for the failure of the *Verwaltungsgerichtshof* to send a question for preliminary ruling to the ECJ This was rejected. His request to the *OGH* to send a new reference on grounds that the judgment of the ECJ on the first reference was not sufficiently clear and could be interpreted as meaning that a case against the federal State should as a matter of Community law also be admissible, was equally denied.

[244] M Dony argued before *Konle* that the action against the federal State should always be admissible for reasons of judicial protection of the individual, because especially in cases of failure to act and legislative omissions, it may be extremely difficult to establish where liability lies, see M Dony, 'Le droit belge', in *La responsabilité des Etats membres en cas de violation du droit communautaire. Etudes de droit communautaire et de droit national comparé* (Bruylant, 1997) 149, at 180–181.

[245] The safest option for the individual may be to bring a joint action against several defendants – assuming that these can be brought before the same court and on the same conditions, see *e.g.* the Dutch *Lubsen* case below.

11.6.4.2. Haim II

In *Haim*, the action was not brought against the central State or a federated entity, but against an autonomous public law body, the Nordrhein
Association of Dental Practitioners of Social Security Schemes
(*Kassenzahnärztliche Vereinigung Nordrhein*). Haim, an Italian national
holding a Turkish diploma that had previously been declared equivalent
to a Belgian diploma, applied to this public law body for enrolment on the
register of dental practitioners so that he could treat patients affiliated to
social security schemes. When his application was denied, he brought an
action before the German court, which, upon a reference to the Court of
Justice,[246] decided that the *Vereinigung* must enrol Haim. He then sued the
Vereingigung for compensation for loss of earnings. The German court
dealing with the case was of the opinion that Haim did not have a right
to compensation under German law, but made a reference concerning a
potential right to reparation under Community law.

The decision inflicting the damage was adopted by a public law
body, legally independent not only of the German Federal Government
but also of the Land of Nordrhein, on the basis of an instrument, the
Zulassungsordnung für Zahnärzte, which, according to the national court,
had legislative force. The German court wanted to know how the case
must be decided: Should the individual sue the autonomous public law
body which had issued the decision, or rather, as the latter was only
applying the (conflicting) legislation in force, the State, which is
answerable for any breaches of Community law committed by its legislature, or, the third option, could he bring a claim against both of them
cumulatively?

The Court of Justice first re-called the principle of liability inherent in
the system of the Treaty – as it usually does in liability cases, under reference to *Francovich, Brasserie/ Factortame III* and other cases – but this time
it spoke not of the principle of liability of the *State*: it did not fill in as to
whose liability it would be, and referred to breaches attributable to '*a
national public authority*': '*it should be recalled that* liability *for loss and damage caused to individuals as a result of breaches of Community law* attributable
to a national public authority *constitutes a principle, inherent in the system of
the Treaty, which gives rise to obligations on the part of the Member States* [fol-
low the usual references, MC]'.[247] It then referred to the principle stated
in *Konle* that it is for each Member State to ensure that individuals obtain
reparation for loss and damage caused to them by non-compliance with
Community law, whichever public authority is responsible for the breach

---

[246] Case C–319/92 *Salomone Haim v Kassenzahnärtztiche Vereinigung Nordrhein (Haim I)* [1994]
I–425.
[247] Case C–424/97 *Salomone Haim v Kassenzahnärtztiche Vereinigung Nordrhein (Haim II)* [2000]
I–5123, at para 26.

and whichever public authority is in principle, under the law of the Member State concerned, responsible for making reparation. The internal distribution of powers and responsibilities cannot be pleaded in defence; but damages need not necessarily be provided by the federal State. The Court now added that this was also true for those Member States, federal or not, in which certain legislative or administrative tasks are devolved to territorial bodies with a certain degree of autonomy or to any other public law body legally distinct from the State. Reparation for loss and damage caused to individuals by national measures taken in breach of Community law by a public law body *may* therefore be made by that body.[248] '*Nor does Community law preclude a public-law body, in addition to the Member State itself, from being liable to make reparation for loss and damage caused to individuals as a result of measures which it took in breach of Community law*'.[249] The Court then added its usual reference to the principle of procedural autonomy. Consequently, the Court merely confirmed the various possibilities under national law, without imposing a particular stance from the point of view of Community law: subject to the existence of a right to obtain damages it is for the Member States to make sure that individuals obtain reparation, but it is left to national law which organ is to be held liable in final instance, and against which organ the action is to be brought.

In itself, this position may not be so remarkable. In the case law of the Court, all national authorities, at whatever level and whatever their status under national (constitutional) law, have autonomous obligations under Article 10 EC to comply with Community law. It is only logical that they can also be held liable for the damage they cause by not complying with the obligations. However, the position deviates from the principles of international law where '*the*' State is liable, whichever organ committed the breach and whichever organ will finally be held responsible to bear the financial loss. In *Brasserie/Factortame III* the Court had referred to the principle of State liability in international law as an argument in favour of accepting liability of the State for legislative acts. If the same analogy would be made in the case of the independent liability of the decentralised and independent public law bodies, the outcome would have been different: while an infringement of international law which has been caused by an act of a decentralised body does give rise to the liability of the State as a subject of international law, there is no independent liability under international law of this body. The difference is that in the context of Community law, liability cases are to be decided by the national courts, which obviously do look beyond the limits of the State and do allocate responsibility within it.

---

[248] Above, at para 31.
[249] Above, at para 33.

11.6.5. Complex Cases: Allocation of Imputability and the Intensity of the Test

From the foregoing, it follows that the liability of the State, of federated entities or of public law bodies arises irrespective of the nature and function of the body responsible for the breach, and irrespective of the body which will ultimately be responsible to pay. Neither horizontal nor vertical separation of powers and division of competences matters in this respect: a right to reparation may arise for administrative, regulatory, legislative and judicial acts of public authorities, operating at any level in the State, whether at the federal level, the level of federated entities, decentralised authorities such as municipalities or provinces, but also for harm caused by public-law bodies independent of the State. It is when these main principles are combined that complex issues arise, which must in most cases be solved on the basis of national law, and the Court of Justice takes its hands off. Difficult issues arise for instance where the damage is caused by a combination of breaches of Community law, attributable to various instances within the State, both horizontally and vertically, for instance, where a directive has been incorrectly implemented, on top of that, it has been wrongly applied (either directly or indirectly by way of application of the incorrect national implementation of the directive) and the harm has not been repaired because a court has not repaired the breach, by incorrectly applying Community law to the case at hand.

In this type of situation, several questions arise: where does liability lie? Who will have to pay in ultimate analysis? Most importantly, who should the individual sue in damages? And, which test should apply: should the test be applied in cases where there is a wide discretion? Or where the administrative authorities do not have a wide discretion, should the mere infringement suffice? Whose discretion matters? It appears that in each case, all the elements involved should be considered by the court deciding the case. The Court has lifted an edge of the veil in *Brinkmann Tabakfabriken, Haim II* and *Larsy*.

11.6.5.1. *Brinkmann Tabakfabriken*

In *Brinkmann Tabakfabriken*,[250] the relevant directive[251] had not been implemented. Failure to implement a directive is a *per se* serious breach of Community law. However, in the case, the Danish administrative authorities had attempted to mend the breach by giving direct effect to the directive. The Court held that this attempt of the administrative authorities in the application of Community law breached the causal link between

---

[250] Case C–319/96 *Brinkmann Tabakfabriken GmbH v Skatteministeriet* [1998] ECR I–5255.
[251] Second Council Directive 79/32/EEC of 18 December 1978 on taxes other than turnover taxes which affect the consumption of manufactured tobacco, OJ 1979 L 10/8.

the breach consisting of non-implementation of the directive, and the damage suffered by the applicant. The non-implementation in itself did not accordingly give rise to liability on the part of the State. Now, the administrative authorities had not made a correct application of the directive: there was, accordingly, a second breach of the directive. It must then be determined whether the incorrect application constituted a sufficiently serious breach of the directive, having regard to the degree of clarity and precision of the relevant provisions. The Court ruled[252] that the breach was not sufficiently serious, as the interpretation given by the Danish authorities was not manifestly contrary to the wording of the directive.

It is striking that in this case, the Court again did not assess whether the responsible authorities had wide discretion or not, and accordingly, whether the mere breach would suffice for liability to arise or whether something more was needed. It is difficult to assess what the exact measure of discretion is in a particular case, but since the Court appears to give much weight to the notion in the application of the test and the strictness of its conditions for liability, it was an important element. Where there is no or very little discretion, a mere infringement will be sufficiently serious to establish liability; where there is wide discretion, something more is needed. It must be recalled where the notion comes from. It was introduced in the context of governmental liability in *Brasserie/Factortame III*, when the Court had to convincingly state the principle of state liability also for legislative acts. Since the legitimacy of its *Francovich* judgment had been questioned as an overly activist form of judicial law-making, and it had been criticised for applying double standards to the Member States on the one hand, and the Community institutions on the other, the Court in that case drew an analogy with liability under Article 288(2) EC. In that context, the Court distinguishes between 'normal' cases of liability, and certain legislative fields where the relevant institution has a wide discretion. In *Brasserie*, the Court had to rule on the question whether liability could also be incurred for breaches imputable to the national legislature. *Francovich* had also been concerned with legislative breaches, namely the failure to implement. The difference between *Brasserie* and *Francovich* was not that the breach was imputable to the legislature, but the measure of discretion left to the Member State. In *Francovich*, there was no discretion as to whether or not to implement. The normal objections of a constitutional nature against liability for legislative actions or omissions carry little weight in those circumstances. The courts are not asked to interfere with the content of legislation, or with the choices made by the legislature. In *Brasserie*, the Court stated that the breach had been

---

[252] This should normally be the responsibility of the national court, but the ECJ held that it had all the necessary information to judge whether the facts presented were to be characterised as a sufficiently serious breach, at para 26.

committed in an area where the legislature *did* have wide discretion, to distinguish *Francovich* and to allign State liability with the liability of the Community institutions. But the notion of discretion would come back to haunt the Court.

11.6.5.2. Haim II

In *Haim II*, a legislative act was incompatible with Community law, and the public-law body had merely applied it: it did not *under national law* have any discretion in taking its decision. Would a mere infringement suffice?[253] The referring court put the issue of discretion squarely before the Court. The Court insisted that the same conditions applied to all cases, but that they must be applied according to each type of situation.[254] The Court then reiterated the distinction between cases in which there is only considerably limited or no discretion, where a mere infringement may suffice, and cases where there is wide discretion and something more is needed. It then continued to explain the notion of discretion saying: *'The discretion referred to (..) above is that enjoyed by the Member State concerned. Its existence and its scope are determined by reference to Community law and not by reference to national law. The discretion which may be conferred by national law on the official or the institution responsible for the breach of Community law is therefore irrelevant in this respect',*[255] and *'It is also clear from the case-law cited (..) above that a mere infringement of Community law by a Member State may, but does not necessarily, constitute a sufficiently serious breach'.*[256] In order to determine whether an infringement constitutes a sufficiently serious breach, all factors which characterise the situation as a whole must be taken into account. The Court left the application of these principles to the case at hand for the national court – it was a difficult case, given that there had been a dual breach, by the German legislature which had adopted the law and the public law body which had applied it. Whose discretion was relevant? That of 'the State' taken as a whole; but how should the respective discretion of the legislature and the *Vereinigung* be measured: should

---

[253] The test in itself is the same: the three conditions mentioned in *Brasserie/Factortame*, as came to the fore in *Dillenkofer*. But the intensity of the test differs, depending on whether there was no discretion (mere infringement suffices, *Hedley Lomas*) or not (more is required to make up a qualified breach, e.g. clarity of the norm infringed, previous case law of the ECJ etc).

[254] *'Those three conditions must be satisfied both where the loss or damage for which reparation is sought is the result of a failure to act on the part of the Member State, for example in the event of a failure to implement a Community directive, and where it is the result of the adoption of a legislative or administrative act in breach of Community law, whether it was adopted by the Member State itself or by a public-law body which is legally independent from the State'*, Case C–424/97 *Salomone Haim v Kassenzahnärztliche Vereinigung Nordrhein (Haim II)* [2000] ECR I–5123, at para 37.

[255] Case C–424/97 *Haim II*, at para 40.

[256] Above, at para 41.

they be added up? The Court only drew attention to the fact that when the legislature adopted the law and the *Vereinigung* applied it, the Court had not yet handed its decision in *Vlassopoulou*.[257] But even with the explanation of the Court, the question of discretion remains difficult to apply; what would have been the correct answer, for instance, had the law been adopted before *Vlassopoulou*, but had the *Vereinigung* applied it thereafter?

The Court also made a small correction to the system, when it held that a where there is only limited discretion, a mere infringement *may* suffice to establish liability; even in this type of cases, the mere infringement may not always lead to a right to compensation.

11.6.5.3. Final Remarks

Governmental liability for breach of Community law before the national courts is trapped between international law and national law. It has in common with State liability under international law that the liability arises irrespective of which organ was responsible for the breach. Whether or not particular action or inaction, or rather 'situation', is unlawful is to be decided from the point of view of Community law. Also the strictness of the applicable test will be decided looking at the wrongful situation as a whole. Decisive is not the identity, the nature or constitutional position of the organ or organs responsible for the breach, but their discretion from the point of view of Community law.

On the other hand, the system of governmental liability is also fully dependent on national law, with respect to the question of which enitity, central, federated, decentralised, or which public body is to be held liable to pay compensation; to indicate the competent court, and to define the conditions of causal effect and so forth. Community law remains important to patrol the *Rewe* and *Comet* minumum conditions.

The system of governmental liability for breach of Community law is very complex and requires the national courts to 'step out' of their national legal order and to judge the 'unlawful situation' taken as a whole from the perspective of Community law, in order to decide the strictness of the test. They must then step in again and decide which organ or institution will be liable to actually pay compensation and so forth. The Community rules governing governmental liability for breach of Community law and their intertwinement with national law result in a system that leaves a lot to the national courts, asking them to behave as Community law courts, and to relinquish some of the most fundamental principles of national constitutional law. This cannot be an easy task for the national courts.

[257] Case C–340/89 *Irène Vlassopoulou v Ministerium für Justiz, Bundes- und Europaangelegenheiten Baden-Württemberg* [1991] ECR I–2357.

11.7. LIABILITY OF THE STATE: THE NATIONAL ANSWER

In analysing the national answer to *Francovich* and its progeny, the focus will be on constitutional questions, mainly the liability of the legislating State, and the allocation of liability within the State. A preliminary remark concerns the method. The research is limited to cases which have been published or which have at the least been recounted in scholarly writing. A good – though not complete – source of cases is the annual survey of the Commission on the application of Community law by national courts, which is published as an annex to the Annual report on monitoring the application of Community law.[258] One of the traditional questions in the *questionnaire* is whether there were any decisions applying the rulings of the Court of Justice in *Francovich*, *Factortame* and *Brasserie du Pêcheur*. The discussion will be fairly extensive, since there is not yet, in the literature, an overall account of the national case law on the topic.

11.7.1. France

Several decisions of the *Conseil d'État* demonstrate its reluctance to over-come the deeply rooted principle of immunity of the legislating State.[259] One author spoke of *'une acrobatique "délocalisation" de l'imputation de la responsabilité'*[260] in an effort to prevent the *'désacralisation de la fonction lég-islative'*.[261] The use of avoidance mechanisms may be understandable from the point of view of a national court with a traditional extreme def-erence towards the *loi* as the expression of the sovereign will of the peo-ple, as exemplified by the long and difficult road to *Nicolo*, but it could also be argued that even on the basis of the principles of French law alone[262]it would be fairly simple for the *Conseil d'État* to take it one step further and hold the State liable for legislative wrong. Indeed it is only one step: once it is accepted that the Legislature can act unlawfully, under the adage that *responsabilité suit illégalité*: *'De là à engager la responsabilité il n'y a qu'un pas'*.[263] Nonetheless, it has not been so easy.

---

[258] The most recent of these reports are also available on the ECJ's website. Another source of information of this type is the ECJ's Bulletin 'Reflèts'.

[259] So also F Fines, 'Quelle obligation de réparer pour la violation du droit communautaire? Nouveaux développements jurisprudentiels sur la responsabilité de 'l'État normateur'', *RTDeur*, 1997, 69, at 79.

[260] D Simon, 'Droit communautaire et responsabilité de la puissance publique, glissements progressifs ou révolution tranquille?' *AJDA*, 1993, 235, at 241.

[261] Above, at 242.

[262] Under the assumption that the *Conseil d'État* would not think it sufficient to 'simply' fol-low the instructions of the ECJ (*'les oukases de la Cour de justice'*), and would want to find a basis in national law for its jurisdiction to hold the State liable to pay compensation, see also G Alberton, 'Le régime de la responsabilité du fait des lois confronté au droit com-munautaire: de la contradiction à la conciliation?', *RFDA*, 1997, 1017, at 1019.

[263] Above, at 1019.

Shortly after *Francovich* had been decided and long before the judgments of the Court of Justice in *Basserie/Factortame III* and *British Telecommunications*, the *Conseil d'État* decided two cases in which it was asked to condemn the French State to pay compensation to tobacco importers. A 1976 *loi*, adopted with a view to implement a Community directive, suppressed the State monopoly on the importation and wholesale of tobacco products originating from other Member States, but maintained the State monopoly on the importation from third States, and for the retail sales in France of all tobacco products. The retail price of those products was decided by the Minister of Finance. This full discretionary power of the Minister had been the cause of many difficulties between importers and the French authorities, as price increases had been denied. The French system was for the first time condemned by the Court of Justice in an enforcement action in 1983;[264] but the French authorities did not comply with it. Some time later, the *Conseil d'État* rejected an action for annulment against the decision of the Minister, and did not allow damages, despite the declaration of the Court of Justice. It stated that the refusal of the Minister to accept an increase in retail prices was not wrongful as it was motivated by the desire to control inflation.[265] In 1988 the French State was condemned once again by the Court of Justice, for failure to implement the previous judgment.[266]

In *Rothmans, Arizona Tobacco and Philip Morris*,[267] finally, the *Assemblée* of the *Conseil d'État* awarded compensation to importers of tobacco of the

---

[264] Case 90/82 *Commission v France* [1983] ECR 2011. The Court held that the power to fix tobacco prices reserved to the government by national legislation within the scope of the provisions organizing the national monopoly of retail sales of manufactured tobacco, was incompatible with the scheme and objective of the Directive and the interpretation of Article 5 (1) thereof to the extent to which that power, by altering the selling price determined by the manufacturer or importer, allows the competitive relationship between imported tobacco and tobacco marketed by the national monopoly to be adversely affected. The exercise of that power was also contrary to Article 28 EC inasmuch as it allowed the public authority, by a selective intervention as regards tobacco prices, to restrict the freedom of importation of tobacco originating in other Member States. It was furthermore contrary to Article 31 EC inasmuch as the fixing of a price other than that determined by the manufacturer or importer constituted an extension to imported tobacco of a prerogative typical of the national monopoly, of such a nature as adversely to affect the marketing of imported tobacco under normal conditions of competition.

[265] *Conseil d'État*, decision of 13 December 1985, *Société International Sales and Import Corporation BV*, Rec., 377; in line with *Alivar*.

[266] Case 169/87 *Commission v France* [1988] ECR 4093.

[267] *Conseil d'État*, decisions of 28 February 1992, *SA Rothmans International France and SA Philip Morris France and Société Arizona Tobacco Products and SA Philip Morris France*, Rec., 78; AJDA, 1992, 210 with conclusions of Commissaire du gouvernement Laroque; [1993] 1 CMLR 25; comments in R Kovar, 'Le Conseil d'État et le droit communautaire: des progrès mais peut mieux faire', D 1992, chron., 207; L Dubouis, 'Directive communautaire et loi française: primauté de la directive et respect de l'interprétation que la Cour de justice a donnée de ses dispositions', *RFDA*, 1992, 425; D Simon, 'Le Conseil d'État et les directives communautaires: du gallicisme à l'orthodoxie?', *RTDeur.*, 1992, 265; J Dutheil de la Rochère (1993) 30 *CMLRev* 187; D Simon, 'Droit communautaire et responsabilité de la puissance publique, glissements progressifs ou révolution tranquille?', *AJDA*, 1993, 235.

damage they claimed to have sustained as a consequence of the application of the ministerial *décret* fixing the retail prices in a way that was incompatible with the objectives of the directive. There had been an infringement
of Community law, but the *Conseil d'État* was not confident to attribute the
infringement and the ensuing liability to the Legislature. It preferred to
identify the ministerial decree as the infringement of Community law causing the damage, even though the *loi* itself violated the directive, which had
been established by the Court of Justice on two occasions,[268] and the
infringement committed in the decree followed automatically from it.[269]

The decision of the *Conseil d'État* follows a *Costanzo*-type reasoning: the
damage was imputable to the ministerial decisions applying the decree
which was *ultra vires (dépourvu de base légale)* because the underlying *loi*
was incompatible with the directive. Put differently, the *loi* was incompatible with the directive and it was for the minister not to apply it; since
he did apply the *loi* he committed a violation of Community law, which
caused harm to individuals. By imputing the violation to the minister
instead of the primary legislature, the *Conseil* avoided the difficulty that
under French law, the State can only be held liable for legislative acts on
grounds of the extremely strict conditions of disruption of the *egalité
devant les charges publiques*. The conditions for such no-fault liability to
arise are difficult to transpose to infringements of Community law attributable to the legislature. The *Conseil d'État* clearly refused to declare the

---

[268] The Court of Justice does not decide which organ has infringed Community law; that is
not its task: it merely decides whether or not the State as a whole has infringed its obligations under Community law. However, it followed from the judgments that the directive had been incorrectly transposed, therefore that the infringement had been
committed by Parliament.

[269] Irrespective of the issue of liability, it was the first time that the *Conseil d'État* would have
to decide on this type of conflict between a *loi* and a directive after *Nicolo*. The case thus
concerned first of all the question of whether the French administrative courts had jurisdiction to review whether the *loi* correctly implemented a directive. *Nicolo* had concerned
a conflict between a *loi* and a provision of the Treaty, while in *Boisdet*, the *Conseil d'État*
had already accepted to review the compatibility between a *loi* and a regulation, *Conseil
d'État*, decision of 24 September 1990, *Boisdet*, Rec., 250. The *Conseil d'État* has a notoriously reluctant attitude towards the direct effect of directives. In *Conseil d'État*, decision
of 22 December 1978, *Cohn-Bendit*, Rec., 524; *RTDeur*, 1979, 168 with note by L Dubouis,
the *Conseil* refused to accept that provisions contained in non-implemented directives
could produce direct effects. This blunt refusal had been mellowed, and directives could
now be invoked in various circumstances, but the *Conseil d'État* continued to deny that
individuals could invoke a directive in the absence of any implementing national measure, in order to have an individual decision annulled, *Conseil d'État*, decision of 13
December 1985, *Zakine*, Rec., 515; and decision of 23 July 1993, *Compagnie générale des
Eaux v Lechat*; Directives therefore only produced a restricted direct effect. See on the case
law of the *Conseil d'État* concerning directives: P-F Ryziger, 'Le Conseil d'État et le droit
communautaire: de la continuité au changement', *RFDA* (1990) 164; AFT Tatham, 'Effect
of European Community Directives in France: The Development of the *Cohn-Bendit*
Jurisprudence', 40 *ICLQ* (1991) 907; R Kovar, 'Le Conseil d'État et le droit communautaire: des progrès mais peut mieux faire', *D* (1992) *chron.*, 207; F Hervouet, 'Politique
jurisprudentielle de la Cour de Justice et des jurisdictions nationales. Réception du droit
communautaire par le droit interne des États', *RDP* (1992) 1257.

'illegality' of the *loi*,[270] and opted for the indirect route via the *Costanzo* obligations imposed on all public authorities to correct the infringements of Community law in legislation over the more straightforward imputation to the legislature. *Commissaire du gouvernement* Laroque had pointed out that it would take *Nicolo* one step too far, and suggested this indirect route. *'(..) vous n'avez dans votre décision Nicolo posé le principe d'un contrôle de légalité du juge sur la loi, qui pourrait aboutir à une censure de celle-ci. Vous avez en réalité révisé ou rétabli la hiérarchie des normes juridiques, conformément à l'article 55 de la Constitution, en faisant prévaloir en cas de discordance entre une norme internationale et une norme nationale, fût-elle législative, la norme internationale, en excluant le facteur temps. Cela vous conduit non pas à vous prononcer sur la validité d'une loi postérieure à un traité international, mais sur son opposabilité ou son applicabilité à une situation donnée. En décidant d'écarter l'application d'une loi qui ne serait pas compatible avec un traité international et, au besoin aujourd'hui avec le droit communautaire dérivé, vous créez une obligation qui ne s'impose pas seulement au juge lors de l'examen d'un litige, mais au pouvoir exécutif, c'est à dire à l'autorité administrative. Contrairement aux apparances, il ne s'agit pas pour cette autorité de désobéissance à la loi, mais au contraire – au non du principe de la légalité – du devoir de respect de l'ordre constitutionnel des règles de droit. L'autorité gouvernementale ou administrative qui se voit attribuer, comme en l'espèce, par le législateur un pouvoir réglementaire, qui n'est pas compatible avec une norme internationale, et que, de surcroît, elle n'est pas tenue d'utiliser dans un sens contraire à cette norme, ne peut légalement en user dès lors qu'elle doit, d'elle-même, faire prévaloir la norme internationale sur la loi interne. L'illégalité de la décision administrative du dommage ne procède donc pas dans ce cas directement de la loi, mais du comportement de l'autorité administrative.'* And she concluded: *'C'est donc l'acte réglementaire illégal lui-même, qui s'est interposé entre le loi et l'administré, qui est le fait générateur direct du préjudice de ce dernier'.*[271]

The theory of the *'loi écran'* which used to protect the Executive against judicial scrutiny in the light of Community law was thus replaced by a *'règlement-écran'*: the administrative act is placed between the *loi* and the citizen and prevents the problem of the liability of the *État législateur* to arise.[272] Since fault was attributed to the minister, the principles of the

---

[270] This is the general appreciation of the decision, see *e.g.* R Kovar, 'Le Conseil d'État et le droit communautaire: des progrès mais peut mieux faire', *D* (1992) *chron.*, 207, at 212; H Calvet, 'Droit administratif de la responsabilité et droit communautaire' *AJDA* (1996); M Dony, 'Le droit français', in G Vandersanden and M Dony (eds), *La responsabilité des États membres en cas de violation du droit communautaire. Études de droit communautaire et de droit national comparé*, (Bruxelles, Bruylant, 1997), 235, at 279; see also Opinion of AG Tesauro in Joined Cases C–46/93 and C–48/93 *Brasserie du Pêcheur/Factortame III* [1996] ECR I-1029, at marginal number 42 *et seq.*

[271] Conclusions of *Commissaire du gouvernement* Mme Laroque, *AJDA* (1992) at 220, emphases added.

[272] L Dubouis, 'Directive communautaire et loi française: primauté de la directive et respect de l'interprétation que la Cour de justice a donnée de ses dispositions', *RFDA* (1992) 425, at 428.

responsabilité pour faute simple could be applied,[273] and the cohesion of the national system could be preserved. It allowed the *Conseil d'Etat* to hold the State liable for damages which were originally caused by the primary legislature without questioning the fundamental principles of French constitutional law.[274] The technique has certain flaws:[275] one of the main fields in which State liability is useful, is in the area of directives, which have not (timely) or incorrectly been implemented. In those cases, the detour via an administrative decision may not always be available, for instance in relations between two individuals or where the harm has been caused by a failure to act, a pure *Francovich*-type situation.[276]

The *Cour administrative d'appel de Paris* was less reluctant to attribute the damage to the legislating State. In *Dangeville*[277] and *John Walker*,[278] the appeal court was confronted with a multiple infringement: the legislature had failed to implement a directive; the minister had applied the existing (conflicting) legislation, and the courts had not rectified this 'situation'.

---

[273] In *Brasserie/Factortame III* the Court of Justice would be less severe and under Community law, the legislating State would be liable only in case of a qualified infringement of Community law; the condition of fault was expressly omitted. However, the Community law conditions are only minimum conditions, and where national law is more severe than Community law, the national rules must apply under the *Rewe* and *Comet* condition of equivalence. The question is then whether, if the *Conseil d'État* would have followed the direct route and held the State liable for the *loi* infringing Community law, under the Community conditions (which would apply since the parallel in French law would be the *liability sans faute*, and was considered to be insufficient, as was admitted by Mme Laroque), liability would only arise in case of a manifest and flagrant breach; while in the indirect option chosen by the *Conseil d'État*, the State would have to pay any time the Minister declines to set aside an incompatible *loi* (constituting a fault under French law).

[274] The *Conseil d'État* did not refer a question for preliminary ruling to the ECJ The issues were however comparable to those arising later before the *Bundesgerichtshof* in *Brasserie* and the High Court in *Factortame III*, *i.e.* the possible inadequacy of the national law of State liability for legislative wrongs. The latter two courts chose to involve the ECJ, while the *Conseil d'État* decided the case on its own, finding a way to make existing national law to fit the case. However, a reference to the ECJ would have made it clear to the *Conseil d'État* that fault is not required under Community law, and that there was accordingly no need to declare that the legislature had acted wrongfully.

[275] See also H Calvet, 'Droit administratif de la responsabilité et droit communautaire' *AJDA* (1996).

[276] It could be argued that in such case, the individual would have to provoke a (negative) decision of the Minister refusing to introduce legislation (which is however considered an *acte de gouvernement*) or refusing to apply the directive directly.

[277] *Cour administrative d'appel*, decision of 1 July 1992, *Sté Dangeville, AJDA* (1992) 768; Droit fiscal, 1992, n. 1665; The SA Cabinet Jacques Dangeville had in the 1970's claimed restitution of taxes which it had paid, allegedly in conflict with the 6th VAT Directive. The claims were rejected by the fiscal authorities and the administrative courts, including, in last resort, the *Conseil d'Etat*. Dangeville then claimed compensation for the damage sustained caused by the undue payment of taxes. In first instance, the claims were rejected on the basis of the then prevailing principles on the relations between national law and Community law.

[278] *Cour administrative d'appel*, decision of 12 November 1992, *Sté John Walker*, Dr. Adm., mars 1993, n. 130; RJF 3/93, n. 469. The applicants claimed damages for failed profits caused by the imposition of taxes between 1975 and 1983 which had proved to be incompatible with the Treaty in *Case 168/78 Commission v France* [1980] ECR 347.

When the case had to be decided by the *Cour administrative d'appel*, both *Nicolo* and the *tobacco* cases had been handed. However, the *'règlement écran'* or *'décret-écran'* was lacking. Instead of skating on thin ice and analysing whether the unlawfulness was to be imputed to Parliament, to the Government, or even to the courts,[279] the *Cour administrative d'appel* held *the State as a whole*[280] liable for the *'situation illicite'*, as would be the approach of the Court of Justice or of any other international tribunal for that matter[281] and accordingly acted as a veritable *'juge communautaire'*. Moreover, no reference was made to the French notion of fault: instead it was held that the relevant provisions were incompatible with the directive and that the *'situation illicite'*[282] arising from the imposition of the taxes.[283]

The Minister appealed to the *Conseil d'État*.[284] The *Commissaire du gouvernement* stated that the *Conseil d'État* had in the *tobacco* decisions made an application *avant la lettre* of *Brasserie*, since the failure to implement had been clearly imputable to the legislature, and it had even applied it without reference to the very restrictive condition of sufficiently serious breach. In this case *Dangeville*, he said, the *Conseil d'État* was invited to extend it to a case where there was no administrative regulation imposing itself between the *loi* and the individual decision. He suggested that all administrative decisions applying a *loi* which is incompatible with a directive would be wrongful and would accordingly provoke the liability of the State. But again, the *Commissaire du gouvernement* was eager to

---

279 The *Commissaire du gouvernement* spoke of *'une faute commise par l'Etat, à un niveau qu'il n'y a pas lieu d'identifier'*, Opinion of *Commissaire du gouvernement* Bernault, Droit Fiscal, 1992, n. 1665, 1420, at 1427.

280 See also the opinion of AG Léger in Case C–5/94 *Hedley Lomas* [1996] ECR 2553, at marginal number 126: *'The requirements of Community law are identical in any event: it sees only one liable party (the State), just as, in proceedings for failure to fulfil Treaty obligations, it sees only one defendant (the State)'.*

281 See also the analogy drawn by the ECJ in *Brasserie/Factortame III* with the liability of the State under international law.

282 '[C]ompte tenu des normes en cause et de la prudence rédactionnelle du Conseil d'Etat, qu'il faut imiter, vous ne devriez pas (..) employer le terme 'faute' dans votre arrêt, non plus que celui d'illégalité ou d'irrégularité, s'agissant d'une loi incompatible avec les objectifs fixés par une directive et de décisions d'imposition conformes à cette loi. Le terme plus neutre d''illicéité' ou l'expression 'situation illicite à réparer' nous paraissent de nature à faire ressortir très exactement l'idée de responsabilité pour faute à raison de l'application d'une loi incompatible que nous tendons à faire valoir; en outre, cette notion d'illicéité a le mérite d'avoir été consacrée par [l'arrêt Francovich de la CJCE]', conclusions of the *Commissaire du gouvernement* in *Dangeville*, Droit Fiscal, 1992, n. 1665, 1420, at 1427, emphases added.

283 In the words of the *Commissaire du gouvernement*: *'L'illégalité du décret d'application ne tient pas, en effet, d'après les termes des arrêts ['tobacco'], à sa contrariété directe avec le droit communautaire, mais à ce que ses auteurs ont fait application d'une loi incompatible avec une directive. L'illicéité est radicale, elle touche la loi elle-même: c'est la loi qui est déclarée incompatible, et le décret n'est finalement illégal, d'un point de vue logique, que par voie de conséquence même si, juridiquement, son interposition permet d'innocenter la loi'*, Droit Fiscal, 1992, no 1665, 1420, at 1426.

284 *Conseil d'État*, decision of 30 October 1996, *Ministre du Budget v Sté Jacques Dangeville*, with conclusions of *Commissaire du gouvernement* Goulard, *RFDA* (1997) 1056; RTDeur (1997) 171.

move responsibility away from the primary legislature: *'il ne s'agit pas là d'une véritable responsabilité pour faute du législateur, dans la mesure où l'existence d'une décision individuelle d'imposition permettait encore d'imputer la faute à l'autorité administrative'.*[285] Even after *Brasserie/Factortame III*, and despite the recognition that also the *tobacco* cases in fact concerned breaches imputable to the legislature, liability for legislative wrong remains difficult to acknowledge.[286] The *commissaire du gouvernement* condoned the approach of the *Cour administrative d'appel* which declined to identify the level responsible for the failure, and allowed to evade the issue of the liability of the legislature proper.

The decision of the appeal court was quashed but on entirely different grounds. The *Conseil d'État* held that the case should have been held inadmissible because the claim for compensation in fact constituted the same claim as for restitution of taxes unduly paid, which should have been claimed from the tax authorities.[287] The state of the law appears to remain as it resulted from the *tobacco* cases, and demonstrates the *Conseil*'s reluctance to declare the liability of the legislating State.[288]

The *Tribunal administratif de Rennes* did hold the State liable on account of belated transposal of the nitrates directive.[289] In 1995 the Société Suez Lyonnaise des Eaux had been held liable to pay compensation to 176 subscribers to its drinking water network on account of the excessive nitrate content of the water it distributed. The company was successful in its claim in recovery against the State which had been late implementing the directive late.[290]

---

[285] *Conclusions* of *commissaire du gouvernement* Goulard, *RFDA* (1997) 1056, at 1059.

[286] See also G Alberton, 'Le régime de responsabilité du fait des lois confronté au droit communautaire: de la contradiction à la conciliation?', *RFDA* (1997) 1017, 1019.

[287] However, the previous actions for restitution had been rejected on grounds contrary to Community law, namely the refusal to accept the direct effect of directives in this type of cases. The CAA and its *Commissaire du gouvernement* had accepted that given this treatment of the actions in restitution, the action in damages should be declared admissible, in accordance with the ratio of *Francovich* liability which is to remove the consequences of failure to implement. The *Conseil d'État* did not follow. see M Dony, 'Le droit français', in G Vandersanden and M Dony (eds), La responsabilité *des États membres en cas de violation du droit communautaire. Études de droit communautaire et de droit national comparé* (Brussels, Bruylant, 1997) 235, at 286–288. The applicant complained to the ECtHR in Stasbourg which held the French State in breach of Art. 1 of the First Protocol; *European Court of Human Rights*, decision of 16 April 2002, *SA Dangeville v France*, which can be found on www.echr.coe.int.

[288] G Alberton, 'Le régime de responsabilité du fait des lois confronté au droit communautaire: de la contradiction à la conciliation?', *RFDA* (1997) 1017; see also W van Gerven, Cases, Materials and Text on National *Supranational and International Tort Law* (Oxford, Hart Publishing, 2000) at 382–83.

[289] Council Directive 91/676/EEC of 12 December 1991 concerning the protection of waters against pollution caused by nitrates from agricultural sources, OJ L 375, 1.

[290] *Tribunal administratif de Rennes*, decision of 2 May 2001, *Société Suez Lyonnaise des Eaux*, unpublished; recounted in the Commission's survey of the application of Community law by national courts in 2001, at 49.

To sum up, most striking in the French case is on the one hand the fact that the *Conseil d'État*, in contrast to several *Commissaires du gouvernement* and lower courts, still avoids to pronounce the liability of the State for action or inaction attributable to the primary legislature. On the other hand, while equally avoiding to pronounce the liability for primary legislation, the lower courts view the situation as a whole, as an international court would do. The *Costanzo*-type reasoning of the *Conseil d'État* may be very helpful as it allows to shift liability, in practical effect, from one organ to the other, but it will not be of help in all types of cases, and it will lead to budgetary questions: where does the risk lie, and which institution is liable to pay the damages awarded to the individuals? But presumably, as long as the individual is paid the compensation due, Community law is complied with.

11.7.2. Germany

When *Brasserie du Pêcheur* returned from the Court of Justice, no damages were awarded to the French brewery. The *Bundesgerichtshof*[291] repeated its previous statement that because it was a case of legislative wrong,[292] the State could not be held liable under German law. It then considered whether a right to compensation would arise under Community law, *i.e.* in application of the conditions and principles as set out by the Court of Justice. With respect to the breach consisting in excluding the use of the name *'Bier'*, which in accordance with the judgment of the European Court was considered to constitute a sufficiently serious breach, the *Bundesgerichtshof* held that the condition of a direct causal link was not fulfilled: The German implementation of the Community condition of causation required a necessary and sufficient causation, which was absent in the case. As regards the breach consisting in the prohibition to use certain additives, the German court held that the infringement may well have caused the damage incurred by Brasserie, but it was not sufficiently serious to entail the liability of the German State. While the Court of Justice had rejected the arguments of the German State[293], based on the protection of public health in assessing whether the German legislation

---

[291] *Bundesgerichtshof*, decision of 24 October 1996, *Brasserie du Pêcheur SA v Germany*, BGHZ 134,3; DVBl., 1997, 124; [1997] 1 CMLR 971; commented in E Deards, *'Brasserie du Pêcheur*: Snatching Defeat from the Jaws of Victory?', 22 *ELR* (1997) 620.

[292] In contrast to the French cases, there was no possibility in this case to attribute the violation to an administrative authority, as there had been no (individual) administrative decisions interposed between the relevant statute and the applicant: all proceedings and fines had been against the plaintiffs contracting party; the plaintiff company had never been the actual addressee of the relevant executive acts taken to its disadvantage, see *Bundesgerichtshof*, decision of 24 October 1996, *Brasserie du Pêcheur SA v Germany* [1997] 1 CMLR 971, at 976.

[293] In the enforcement action, Case 187/84 *Commission v Germany (Biersteuergesetz)* [1987] ECR 1226.

could be justified under Article 30 EC (then Article 36 of the Treaty), there was nothing in the judgment to indicate that the German legal position was so far removed from the requirements of Community law that it was necessary to hold that there was a manifest and grave transgression of the boundaries placed on the discretion of the national legislature. As for the damage which may have been incurred after the European Court's judgment of 1987, this could not be considered to be attributable to the German State.[294] Accordingly, the action in damages was denied. The decision of the Court of Justice in *Brasserie* proved to be a hollow victory for the applicant.[295]

In a case concerning the levels of fees to be charged for health inspections and controls of fresh meat, the *Landgericht* Mosbach and the *Oberlandesgericht* Karlsruhe did award damages for a legislative omission, but the *Bundesgerichtshof*[296] quashed the decision for incorrect application of the Community law on liability of the State. It held that there had not been a sufficiently serious infringement of Community law giving rise to a duty to compensate the applicant. The case accordingly had to be decided on grounds on national law.

11.7.3. Italy

Andrea Francovich's name will forever remain linked up with the principle of State liability for breach of Community law, but Andrea Francovich never received a euro or lira, since his case appeared not to be covered by the directive, and his losses were accordingly not attributable to the failure of the Italian State to implement the directive.[297]

The implementation law of the *Francovich* directive gave rise to a whole series of new references to the Court. On 27 January 1992, the Italian Government adopted Decree-Law No 80, transposing the directive into national law,[298] which did not only implement the directive *strictu senso*,

---

[294] The German State immediately complied with the ECJ decision. However, Brasserie contended it had to build up a new distribution network and suffered damages even after the judgment of the ECJ The BGH held that the profits lost in that period were not attributable to the defendant State but rather constituted the late consequences of the State's earlier actions, for which no liability lay, see *Bundesgerichtshof*, decision of 24 October 1996, *Brasserie du Pêcheur SA v Germany* [1997] 1 CMLR 971, at 982.

[295] So E Deards, '*Brasserie du Pêcheur*: Snatching Defeat from the Jaws of Victory?', 22 *ELR* (1997) 620, at 623.

[296] *Bundesgerichtshof*, decision of 14 December 2000, *Fleischhygienegesetz*, BGHZ 146, 153; available on www.bundesgerichtshof.de.

[297] The *pretore* referred a new set of questions to the ECJ, asking *inter alia* whether the exclusion in the directive of certain categories of workers was valid. The ECJ held that it was, Case C–479/93 *Andrea Francovich v Italian Republic (Francovich II)* [1995] I–3843.

[298] Legislative-decree no. 80/1992, transposing Council Directive 80/987 on the protection of employees in the event of the insovency of their employer, GURI No 36, 13 February 1992.

but also contained provisions relating to actions in damages arising from the late transposal of the directive, and limited the retroactive effect of the possibility of receiving compensation for loss and damage caused by the delay to employees whose employers were subject to proceedings to satisfy collectively the claims of creditors. As regards future cases, it guaranteed payment for work done during the last three months of their contract of employment to the employees of all insolvent employers, whether or not subject to proceedings to satisfy collectively the claims of creditors. The INPS was designated as debtor of these claims.[299] It is reportedly a unique piece of legislation in Italy, prescribing that damages must be paid as a consequence of belated implementation.[300] The *Corte costituzionale* reviewed its compatibility with the constitutional principles of formal and substantial equality, access to courts, *juge légal* and the need for public expenses to be covered by the budget,[301] and upheld the law.[302] In several cases before various courts questions were referred to the Court of Justice, inquiring especially about the limitations and their compatibility with Community law.[303]

---

[299] The *Istituto Nazionale della Previdenza Sociale* ('INPS'), is the public body responsible for the payment of pensions and other social welfare benefits, see L Malferrari, 'State Liability for Violation of EC Law in Italy: The Reaction of the Corte di Cassazione to *Francovich* and Future Prospects in Light of its Decision of July 22, 1999, No. 500', *ZaöRV* (1999) 809, at fn. 34.

[300] M Merola and M Beretta, 'Le droit italien', in G Vandersanden and M Dony (eds), *La responsabilité des États membres en cas de violation du droit communautaire. Études de droit communautaire et de droit national comparé* (Brussels, Bruylant, 1997) 289, at 334.

[301] *Corte costituzionale*, decision n. 285/93 of 16 June 1993, *Paolo Bracaglia and Others v INPS*, www.giurcost.org; and decision n. 512/93 of 31 December 1993, *Daniele Assoni v INPS*, www. giurcost.org. The constitutional court upheld the constitutional validity of the Act and declared that the legislature had intended to impute damages to an institution of the State, in this case INPS.

[302] The decisions did not focus on the issue of the liability of the legislating State, see L Malferrari, 'State Liability for Violation of EC Law in Italy: The Reaction of the Corte di Cassazione to *Francovich* and Future Prospects in Light of its Decision of July 22, 1999, No. 500', *ZaöRV* (1999) 809, at 822.

[303] Danila Bonifaci (Francovich's partner in the groundbreaking case) brought an action before the *Pretura Circondariale, Bassano del Grappa*, pursuant to Article 2(7) of that Decree, seeking compensation from the INPS Many other applications to the INPS for compensation had been rejected altogether because none of the periods of work fell within the 12-months preceding the judicial declaration of insolvency. In other cases, the applications had been partly accepted, inasmuch as the compensation awarded to the applicants for work within the 12-months period had either been limited to three months' remuneration in accordance with Article 2(1) of Decreto Legislativo No 80/1992 or had been reduced because of the ceiling set in Article 2(2) of that Decree. The national court before which the cases were brought had serious doubts as to whether the rules contained in the Decreto Legislativo were consistent with the provisions of the Directive and the principles stated in the Court's judgment in *Francovich I* The ECJ held that it was for the national court to ensure that reparation of the loss or damage sustained by the beneficiaries is adequate. Retroactive and proper application in full of the measures implementing the directive will suffice for that purpose unless the beneficiaries establish the existence of complementary loss sustained on account of the fact that they were unable to benefit at the appropriate time from the financial advantages guaranteed by the direc-

The central issue in many cases was whether compensation should be claimed from the State on the basis of the *Francovich* doctrine, or whether these claims should be brought against the INPS on the basis of the Legislative Decree.[304] The decisions of lower courts following *Francovich* and the Italian implementing Act went in different directions. The *Corte di Cassazione* focussed on the procedural autonomy which *Francovich* left to the Member States, confirmed the Italian principle of the immunity of the legislating State, and stated that the legislature constitutes the sovereign expression of the political power.[305] It declared that '(..) *la Constitution (..) règle la fonction législative en répartissant celle-ci entre le gouvernement et le parlement, expression du pouvoir politique. Ce pouvoir est, par définition, libre dans ses buts et donc soustrait à toute sorte de controle juridictionnel; face à son exercice, les particuliers ne sauraient se prévaloir de situations subjectives protégées (..). Par conséquent, il faut exclure que des normes communautaires, telles qu'elles sont interprétées par la Cour de justice, puisse dériver, dans l'ordre juridique italien, un droit subjectif du particulier vis-à-vis du pouvoir législatif,*

tive with the result that such loss must also be made good, Joined Cases C–94/95 and C–95/95 *Danila Bonifaci and Others and Wanda Berto and Others v INPS* [1997] ECR I–3969. In *Palmisani*, the ECJ held that Community law, as it stood, did not preclude a Member State from requiring that actions for reparation of the loss or damage sustained as a result of the belated transposition of the relevant directive to be brought within a limitation period of one year from the date of its transposition into national law, provided that that procedural requirement is no less favourable than procedural requirements in respect of similar actions of a domestic nature (which was for the national court to assess. The ECJ stated that if no similar action were available under Italian law, the principle of equivalence was complied with). Such procedural requirements could not make the reparation of damages virtually impossible or excessively difficult, which they did not, Case C–261/95 *Rosalba Palmisani v INPS* [1997] ECR I–4025. See also Case C–373/95 *Federica Maso and Others and Graziano Gazzetta and Others v INPS* [1997] ECR I–4051; these cases were all handed on the same day, 11 July 1997. In practical effect, the ECJ thus upheld the passing on of liability to a public law body when it held that retroactive and proper application in full of the measures implementing the directive suffices in principle for reparation of the damage incurred, see *infra*. The ECJ's approach is highly pragmatic and focusses on the practical result, *i.e.* compensation of the individual who suffered harm imputable to the State.

[304] See references in M Merola and M Beretta, 'Le droit italien', in G Vandersanden and M Dony (eds), *La responsabilité des États membres en cas de violation du droit communautaire. Études de droit communautaire et de droit national comparé* (Brussels, Bruylant, 1997) 289, at 335 et seq; L Malferrari, 'State Liability for Violation of EC Law in Italy: The Reaction of the Corte di Cassazione to Francovich and Future Prospects in Light of its Decision of July 22, 1999, No. 500', *ZaöRV* (1999) 809 and G Anagnostaras, 'State Liability v Retroactive application of belated implementing measures: Seeking the optimum means in terms of effectiveness of EC law', 1 Web J, 2000, webjcli. ncl.ac.uk/200/issue1/anagnostaras1.html, at 4.

[305] In several decisions handed in 1995, *Corte di cassazione*, decision n. 7832 of 19 July 1995, 2 Il Fallimento, 1996, 137; decision n. 9547 of 9 September 1995, I Giustizia Civile, 1996, 1383; decision n. 10617 of 11 October 1995, Il Foro Italiano, I, 1996, 503; references to and discussion of these decisions in L Malferrari, 'State Liability for Violation of EC Law in Italy: The Reaction of the Corte di Cassazione to *Francovich* and Future Prospects in Light of its Decision of July 22, 1999, No. 500', *ZaöRV* (1999) 809, at 814.

ainsi qu'une responsabilité de l'État au sens de l'article 2043 du code civil (..)'.[306]
The break between Community law and the principles of national law
appeared too great to be overcome by judicial decision. However, the
Legislative Decree had been adopted with a view to bridge this divergence, and actions in damages must be brought not against the legislature
proper or the State, but against the INPS[307] which had been made responsible for the payment of outstanding wage claims in the Decree. While
this solution may help to protect individuals who had suffered harm as a
consequence of the belated implementation of the *Francovich* directive, it
does not work in cases where such a corrective implementing law is not
adopted, or for other types of breaches.[308] In the case of the *Francovich*
directive, the Court of Justice, in practical effect, accepted the Italian solution, and declared that provided that the directive had been properly
transposed, the retroactive application in full of the belated implementing
measures would in principle remedy the loss suffered by individuals due
to the violation of the obligation to implement timely and correctly.[309]
However, any further damage which may exist must be made good also,
presumably on the basis of *Francovich*.

In another set of cases,[310] relating to the issue of interest due for late
payments, the *Corte di Cassazione* made an interesting statement with
respect to the separation and autonomy of the Italian and Community
legal orders. The separation of both legal orders is a recurrent theme in
Italian law and in the case law of the *Corte costituzionale*.[311] In the context
of governmental liability, the *Corte di Cassazione* concluded from this separation that the illegality of State action under Community law does not

---

[306] Translation taken from M Merola and M Beretta, 'Le droit italien', in G Vandersanden
and M Dony (eds), *La responsabilité des États membres en cas de violation du droit communautaire. Études de droit communautaire et de droit national comparé* (Brussels, Bruylant, 1997)
289, at 339.

[307] The reasoning of the *Corte di Cassazione* to pass on the liability of the State to the INPS is
explained and criticised at 815 *et seq*. As pointed out by Malferrari, passing on liability of
the State to INPS, is tantamount to passing on liability of the negligent legislating State
to the employers, given the fact that the INPS is financed through contributions of the
employers, at 821.

[308] See also G Anagnostaras, 'State Liability v Retroactive application of belated implementing measures: Seeking the optimum means in terms of effectiveness of EC law', 1 Web J,
2000, webjcli. ncl.ac.uk/200/issue1/anagnostaras1.html, at 7–8.

[309] It is remarkable, tough, that while the solution does contribute to protect the right of
individuals, it does not contribute to achieving the other aim pursued by *Francovich*,
namely to force the *State* to comply with its Community law obligations. The INPS,
which is now under an obligation to pay compensation was not the public body responsible to implement the directive. In this context, even *Costanzo* cannot be of any help,
since Community law in this context required the active intervention of the public
authorities (in this case the legislature) to make legislative choices, and not the mere
leaving inapplied conflicting national law.

[310] *Corte di cassazione*, decision n. 133 of 9 January 1999, *Campanelli*, Il Foro Italiano I, 1998,
1469; decision n. 1366 of 10 February 1998, *Pacifico*, Il Foro Italiano I, 1998, 1476.

[311] As discussed above in Chapter 7.6.2.

entail its illegality under national law.[312] A failure to implement a directive does not constitute a wrongful act under Article 2043 of the *Codice Civile*: national rules which do not comply with Community law must simply be set aside. The emphasis on the separateness of the two legal orders and the differences between *Francovich* liability under Community law and Italian rules on liability, is probably explained by an attempt on the part of the *Corte di Cassazione* to limit the impact of Community law[313] to those cases carrying a Community law component; and reversely to make it possible to comply with the case law of the Court of Justice without dramatically altering Italian law on governmental liability.

Finally, a 1999 decision of the *Corte di Cassazione*[314] introduced a new and revolutionary interpretation of Article 2043 of the Italian Civil Code which can now be used as the basis for a right to compensation to protect *interessi legittimi* violated by public authorities, and which is no longer restricted to protect subjective rights.[315] However, the court came up with a new type of 'rights', namely *interessi rilevanti per l'ordinamento* (individual legal interests significant for the legal order), which may include not only subjective rights, but also legitimate and other interests. The individual's factual interest is significant for the legal order, only if its sacrifice is not justified by the purpose of an overriding objective by the public authorities. It is not yet clear how this criterion will be applied in practice, and it is not clear whether *Francovich*-type cases, and indeed other types of violations of Community law will indeed give rise to a right to compensation. The 1999 decision did not refer to *Francovich* as a reason for the *revirement*, which is remarkable given the fact that in order to comply with *Francovich*, the restrictive traditional approach must be abandoned.[316] It seems that the revirement reaches far beyond *Francovich*, and applies to other areas than Community law as well. Nevertheless, it appears that *Francovich* has contributed to bringing about a revolution in Italian law, and that it will now be possible to receive compensation in cases where it used to be unheard of before.

---

[312] The reasoning is heavily criticised in L Malferrari, 'State Liability for Violation of EC Law in Italy: The Reaction of the Corte di Cassazione to *Francovich* and Future Prospects in Light of its Decision of July 22, 1999, No. 500', *ZaöRV* (1999) 809, at 827–29. The argumentation is comparable in practical effect to that of the *Conseil d'État* in *Alivar* prior to *Francovich*, and the Court of Appeal in *Bourgoin*.

[313] Other explanations of the more Euro-friendly attitude in the second set of cases offered by Malferrari are the ECJ's decision in *Brasserie/Factortame III* and the fact that the central issue in the second set of cases was not the liability of the State for a failure to enact legislation.

[314] *Corte di cassazione (Sezione Unite)*, decision n. 500 of 22 July 1999, *Comune di Fiesole v Vitali*, available on www.giust.it.

[315] Remember that the main ground for rejecting State liability for legislative wrong had been that no individual has a 'subjective right to particular legislation', or vice versa, Parliament does not have an obligation *vis-à-vis* a particular individual.

[316] See L Malferrari, 'State Liability for Violation of EC Law in Italy: The Reaction of the Corte di Cassazione to *Francovich* and Future Prospects in Light of its Decision of July 22, 1999, No. 500', *ZaöRV* (1999) 809, at 836–7.

11.7.4. The United Kingdom

In *Kirklees Borough Council v Wickes Building Supplies Ltd*, a Sunday trading case, Lord Goff said that in the light of *Francovich*, there must be doubt whether *Bourgoin*, where a mere violation of Article 28 EC would be sanctioned only by proceedings for judicial review while damages could only be obtained under the tort of misfeasance in public office, was correctly decided.[317] In *Factortame III* the Court of Justice held that the requirement of proof of misfeasance in public office could indeed not be applied in the case, since such abuse of power was considered inconceivable in the case of the legislature, and would therefore make it impossible or extremely difficult in practice to obtain effective reparation for loss or damage resulting from a breach of Community law where the breach was attributable to the legislature.[318]

In another case, damages were claimed for the harm caused by the failure to implement the Equal treatment Directive. Mrs. Porter had been employed by Cannon Hygiene Ltd, but was dismissed on reaching her 60th birthday. Male employees were allowed to continue working until they reached the age of 65, while the normal retirement age for women was 60. The facts of the case resemble those in Mrs. Marshall's case, who was allowed to invoke the Equal Treatment Directive against her employer, a public authority. Following the judgment of the Court of Justice in Marshall, the Sex Discrimination Act was amended to comply with the directive. However, the relevant legislation for Northern Ireland only took effect in January 1989, and was not given retroactive effect, so that it did not cover Mrs. Porter's dismissal. Mrs. Porter, however, had been employed by a private company, and could not, accordingly, invoke the directive directly. Her actions were dismissed by the Industrial Tribunal and the Northern Ireland Court of Appeal. In the meantime, *Francovich* was decided by the Court of Justice, and counsel for Mrs. Porter prepared a case against the State to claim compensation.[319] However, the case was settled out of court, and Mrs. Porter was paid a sum representing 5 years' loss of earnings plus interest, *i.e.* what she would have been paid had the directive been implemented correctly and timely.

The issue of liability of the State for legislative breaches of Community law arose before the Court of Appeal in the case of *John Gallagher*, an Irish

---

[317] *House of Lords*, decision of 25 June 1992, *Kirklees Borough Council v Wickes Building Supplies Ltd* [1992] 2 CMLR 765, commented in A Robertson, 'Effective Remedies in EEC Law before the House of Lords?', 109 *LQR* (1993) 27.
[318] Joined Cases C–46/93 and C–48/93 *Brasserie du Pêcheur v Germany and The Queen v Secretary of State for Transport, ex parte Factortame and Others (Factortame III)* [1996] ECR I–1029, at para 73.
[319] As set out in E McCaffrey, 'Equal Treatment, Unequal Retirement Ages and the *Francovich* Claim', 25 *Industrial Law Journal* (1996) 144.

national who was served an exclusion order on grounds of the Prevention of Terrorism (Temporary Provisions) Act 1989.[320] On a reference for preliminary ruling, the Court of Justice had declared that the Act was contrary to certain provisions of Council Directive 64/221, as his right to be heard had not been complied with.[321] Gallagher then sought to obtain compensation from the Home Secretary. The case would fail on the issue of causation, but Lord Bingham in the Court of Appeal took the opportunity to make some statements about the principle of liability of the legislative State for breaches of Community law, citing extensively from the decisions of the Court of Justice in *Francovich, Faccini Dori, Brasserie/Factortame III, British Telecom*. He held that in *Gallagher* the United Kingdom was called upon to make a legislative choice, and certainly did enjoy a measure of discretion;[322] the choice made was wrong, but it was not obviously wrong in substance: there was no blatant breach of Community law. It is striking that Lord Bingham did not attempt to fit the case into any of the existing torts under English law, nor did he explicitly seek to define it as an innominate or Community tort. Implicitly, however, the case seems to have been treated as a *sui generis* tort, following the conditions of Community law.[323] Lord Bingham did not designate the source of the breach, nor did he attribute the breach to a particular institution or organ of the State. At various occasions he spoke of the duties of 'the United Kingdom' under Community law, and of 'the United Kingdom's violation'. It is as if *Gallagher* was persuaded by an outside court, not part of the English legal order: a veritable Community court?

When *Factortame III* returned from the Court of Justice, the Divisional Court did accept that there had been a sufficiently serious breach of Community law on the part of the United Kingdom, since there had been

---

[320] *Court of Appeal*, decision of 10 June 1996, *Regina v Secretary of State for the Home Department, ex parte John Gallagher* [1996] 2 CMLR 951.

[321] Case C–175/94, *The Queen v Secretary of State for the Home Department, ex parte John Gallagher* [1995] ECR I–4253.

[322] See critically Barav, who argues that under Directive 64/221 the State did not have any discretion in respect of the point in time in which the opinion of the competent authority should be sought, namely prior to the making of the exclusion order and not after. Such clarity was missing *British Telecom*. Barav argues that this was a *Hedley Lomas* type infringement, namely one where there was no discretion on the part of the member State, and where, therefore, a mere infringement may be sufficient to establish liability. Such a serious breach would also have been found, he argues, in accordance with *British Telecom*, on grounds of the clarity of the provisions of the directive. However, it was not yet clear whether the infringement, however serious, of a procedural as distinguished from a substantive right under Community law could be sufficient to create liability, see A Barav, 'State Liability in Damages for Breach of Community Law in the National Courts', in T Heukels and A McDonnell, *The Action for Damages in Community Law* (The Hague, Kluwer, 1997) 363, at 387 *et seq.*

[323] So also J Convery, 'State Liability in the United Kingdom after *Brasserie du Pêcheur*', 34 *CML Rev* (1997) 603, at 621.

a grave and manifest disregard of the discretion allowed.[324] Two sets of breaches were identified: the infringement of the Treaty by the adoption of the Merchant Shipping Act,[325] and the failure to comply immediately with the order of the President of the Court of Justice. As for the qualification of the action and its classification in English law, the court held that *'whilst it can be said that the cause of action is* sui generis, *it is of the character of a breach of statutory duty. The United Kingdom and its organs and agencies have not performed a duty they were statutorily required to perform'*.[326] Only compensatory damages were awarded, no penal or exemplary damages, since there was no express statutory provision for the award of the latter damages in this case.[327] As in *Gallagher*, the judges did not dwell much on the issue of imputability of the breach to one particular organ: the breach appears to have been committed by the 'United Kingdom, its organs and agencies'; on many occasions, the judges speak of the actions of 'the Government'. The decision of the High Court was upheld on appeal in the Court of Appeal[328] and the House of Lords.[329] The Law Lords also

---

[324] *High Court, Queen's Bench Division (Divisional Court)*, decision of 31 July 1997, *Regina v Secretary of State for Transport, ex parte Factortame and Others (Factortame III)*, [1997] EWHC Admin 755; available on bailii.org; commented in NP Gravells, 'Part II of the Merchant Shipping Act 1988: A Sufficiently serious breach of European Community Law?', *PL* (1998) 8.

[325] For this breach, the Divisional Court took into consideration the fact that (1) discrimination on the ground of nationality was the intended effect of the conditions; (2) in law, the respondent intended to injure the applicants (because he was aware that the imposition of the conditions must necessarily injure them); (3) the Government decided to achieve its objective by means of primary legislation, so as to make it impossible for interim relief to be obtained without the intervention of the ECJ, hoping that no damages could be awarded in respect of any breach of Community law if it were to be established, following the Court of Appeal's decision in *Bourgoin*; and (4) the attitude of the Commission was hostile to the proposed legislation, *High Court, Queen's Bench Division (Divisional Court)*, decision of 31 July 1997, *Regina v Secretary of State for Transport, ex parte Factortame and Others (Factortame III)*, [1997] EWHC Admin 755; available on bailii.org, at marginal number 152.

[326] *High Court, Queen's Bench Division (Divisional Court)*, decision of 31 July 1997, *Regina v Secretary of State for Transport, ex parte Factortame and Others (Factortame III)*, [1997] EWHC Admin 755; available on www.bailii.org, at marginal number 212. This approach had also been suggested in the literature, e.g. 'The national action for breach of statutory duty operates as the vehicle through which the EC principle of state liability is applied at national level. (..) This (..) means that the three key elements of the Community test for liability must be met before the national action can be sustained', see PP Craig, 'The Domestic Liability of Public Authorities in Damages: Lessons from the European Community?', in J Beatson and T Tridimas (eds), *New Directions in European Public Law* (Oxford, Hart Publishing, 1998) 75. In the same book, Mark Hoskins pleaded for the innominate tort: M Hoskins, 'Rebirth of the Innominate Tort?', above, 91.

[327] The relevant statute, in this case, was the EC Act 1972. The principle of equivalence or non-discrimination was not infinged, according to the High Court. Further explained in NP Gravells, 'Part II of the Merchant Shipping Act 1988: A Sufficiently Serious Breach of European Community Law?', *PL* (1998) 8, at 18.

[328] *Court of Appeal*, decision of 8 April 1998, *Regina v Secretary of State for Transport, ex parte Factortame and Others (Factortame III)* [1998] 3 CMLR 192.

[329] *House of Lords*, decision of 28 October 1999, *Regina v Secretary of State for Transport, ex parte Factortame and Others (Factortame III)*, [1999] UKHL 44; [1999] 3 WLR 1062; [1999] All ER 906; [2000] 1 AC 524.

referred to 'the actions of the United Kingdom', the 'United Kingdom's breach', but also to the actions of 'officials and ministers'[330] or 'the Government'. Lord Hoffman in the House of Lords was most explicit on the issue of imputability, when he stated, discussing the defence of the Solicitor General that the government had acted upon legal advice and that the breach should therefore be excused, that *'It is a basic principle of Community law that in considering the liabilities of a Member State, all its various organs of government are treated as a single aggregate entity. It does not matter how their responsibilities are divided under domestic law or what passed between them'*. Nevertheless, he did not conceal the fact that the violation was attributable to the legislature: *'There is no doubt that (..) the legislature was prima facie flouting one of the most basic principles of Community law. (..) the Divisional Court has held that the* Government *acted* bona fide. *But they could have been in no doubt that there was a substantial risk that they were wrong. (..) I do not think that* the United Kingdom, *having deliberately decided to run the risk, can say that the losses caused by the legislation should lie where they fell. Justice requires that the wrong should be made good'*.

In the case of *JH Mann and others* the question arose as to which court had jurisdiction to hear cases in damages against the State, and who should be the correct respondent. The applicants had been summarily dismissed for redundancy, and it was argued before the Industrial Tribunal that the *Francovich* directive had been wrongly interpreted and applied. The case turned on several issues of interpretation and application of the directive, and on *Francovich* liability.[331] The Industrial Tribunal had assumed jurisdiction, but on appeal the Employment Appeals Tribunal rejected jurisdiction of the industrial tribunals: the latter courts can only exercise the jurisdiction conferred on them by statute, and no provision of Community law conferred jurisdiction in this case or required *Francovich* claims to be determined by them. An effective remedy was available in the High Court, and the correct respondent would be the Attorney General and not the Secretary of State for Employment.[332] This position was upheld by the Court of Appeal:[333] claims in damages against the State

---

[330] For instance: 'Officials and ministers were clearly aware that there was a risk that if the legislation was adopted it would be held contrary to Community law', *per* Lord Slynn of Hadley.

[331] Compensation was claimed for the losses suffered as a result of the alleged misapplication of the relevant English application and the directive.

[332] *Employment Appeals Tribunal, JH Mann and others v Secretary of State for Employment* [1996] ICR 197.

[333] It was agued on behalf of the applicants *inter alia* that under *Simmenthal*, which may grant courts powers which they do not possess under national law, all courts should have jurisdiction to award damages; that a *Francovich* claim would most often be bought as an alternative to a claim based on the direct effect of the relevant Community provisions, and that accordingly it would be more efficient for *Francovich* claims to be decided by the same courts. The case on behalf of the Secretary of State was based on the principle of procedural autonomy.

for violation of Community law must be pursued in the same way as any other claim for damages in the ordinary courts, but the question was moot in this case, since there had been no infringement of Community law in the first place.[334]

The case of *Mrs Scullion*[335] concerned a failure to correctly and timely implement the Equal Treatment Directive.[336] The infringement was probably imputable to Parliament, but the imputability of the violation to a particular institution was not explicitly disputed in the High Court.

[334] *Court of Appeal*, decision of 30 September 1996, *JH Mann and Others v Secretary of State for Employment*, [1996] EWCA Cv 617; www.bailii.org; confirmed in the *House of Lords*, decision of 8 July 1999, *JH Mann and Others v Secretary of State for Employment*, available on www. bailii.org.

[335] *High Court, Queen's Bench Division*, decision of 30 July 1999, *R v Department of Social Security, ex parte Scullion* [1999] EWHC Admin 767; www.bailii.org. Mrs. Scullion was a 63-year-old woman who in 1986 had been refused the invalid care allowance ('ICA'). In order to be eligible, the person concerned had to have been entitled to this benefit before reaching the retirement age, 60 for women and 65 for men. Together with other persons in her position, she appealed against the decision. In the meantime, following the ruling of the ECJ in Case C–328/91 *Secretary of State for Social Security v Evelyn Thomas and Others* [1993] ECR I–1247 that such discrimination could not be justified under Art. 7(1)(a) of Directive 79/7, the House of Lords had held that the age difference provided for by the national regulations with respect to this benefit was contrary to the directive. Thereupon, Mrs. Scullion's case was reviewed and she was awarded the benefit as from 1985. However, since she also received an old-age pension, she was not allowed the ICA at the same time, but was entitled to the carer's premium introduced in 1990. She then sought compensation for injury suffered as a result of the failure to implement the directive. She was then paid premium arears from 1990, but the Secretary of State refused to pay interest on this sum. Accordingly, an application for judicial review was brought in the High Court.

[336] The case of Mrs Scullion was very similar to that of Mrs Sutton, in whose case references were made to Luxembourg, Case C–66/95 *The Queen v Secretary of State for Social Security, ex parte Eunice Sutton* [1997] ECR I–2163, regarding the payment of interest on arrears of a social security benefit known as invalid care allowance ('ICA'). Under English law, no interest was payable on arrears of social security benefits in respect of a period prior to the decision of the competent body in favour of the claimant on the basis of the Equal treatment Directive. Mrs Sutton brought an action before the High Court of Justice, Queen's Bench Division, claiming that on the basis of *Francovich*, she was entitled to compensation for the loss suffered as a result of the infringement of the directive by the United Kingdom. Questions were referred asking essentially to ascertain whether Community law requires that an individual should be able to obtain interest on arrears of a social security benefit, such as ICA, when the delay in payment of the benefit is the result of discrimination prohibited by Directive 7/79. The Court held that Article 6 of Directive 79/7 did not require that an individual should be able to obtain interest on arrears of a social security benefit such as invalid care allowance, when the delay in payment of the benefit was the result of discrimination prohibited by Directive 79/7. However, a Member State was required to make reparation for the loss and damage caused to an individual as a result of the breach of Community law. The Court, under reference to its previous cases on State liability, stated that it was for the national court to assess, in the light of the foregoing, whether in the context of the dispute before it and of the national procedure, Mrs Sutton was entitled to reparation for the loss which she claimed to have suffered as a result of the breach of Community law by the Member State concerned, and, if appropriate, to determine the amount of such reparation. Mrs. Eunice Sutton had died by the time of the Court's judgment, so it was for the High Court in *Scullion* to answer the questions left open in *Sutton*.

Justice Sullivan applied what he called a *'basket or global approach'*, weighing various factors including the clarity of the directive, the fact that the view of the Commission had not been sought nor legal advice from any other quarter. He further stated that the Government had been *'swimming against the tide'*, and that *'one was left with the impression that (..) successive UK Governments have been fighting a series of rearguard actions to delay or minimise the effect of inevitable defeat. They have not been pursuing a convincing, coherent strategy with a real hope of victory'*. Damages were awarded, which had major financial implications for the State finances, because of the number of persons concerned.[337]

Shirley Burns[338] sought declarations to the effect that the United Kingdom Government had been in breach of its obligation to transpose the Working Time Directive, and claimed damages for loss and damage which she had allegedly suffered as a result of the failure of the Government to enact legislation giving effect to the directive. The High Court decided, under reference to *Dillenkofer*, that the failure to implement the directive constituted a serious breach *per se*, and that the United Kingdom should be held liable for injury suffered in consequence. However, Mrs. Burns could not show that there was a causal link between her dismissal and the failure to implement. She was, accordingly, entitled to the declarations sought,[339] but not to damages.[340]

Three Rivers District Council and Others v The Governor and Company of the Bank of England[341] arose out of alleged misfeasance by the Bank of England in supervising the Bank of Credit and Commerce International, the BCCI.[342] The Bank of England had, acting as the supervisory authority for the purpose of the Banking Act 1979 transposing the First Banking Directive[343], and authorised the BCCI to carry on the business of

---

[337] See J Convery, 'State Liability in the United Kingdom after Brasserie du Pêcheur' (1997) 34 *CML Rev* 603.

[338] Shirley Burns had, under threat of redundancy, agreed to work night shifts. Since she disliked night shifts, and was under severe stress as a result of it, she applied for the day shift, but was not successful. Her employment was terminated. The United Kingdom had not implemented the Working Time Directive, and had brought an annulment action against it. The implementation procedure was started when the ECJ had given judgment in that action in Case C–84/94 *United Kingdom v Council (Working Time Directive)* [1996] ECR I–5755, annulling only one sentence, and dismissing the application otherwise.

[339] Compare with the Dutch *Waterpakt* case discussed *below*.

[340] *High Court (Northern Ireland), Queen's Bench Division*, decision of 15 March 1999, *In Re Burns's Application for Judicial Review*, [1999] NIEHC 5; [1999] NI 175; www.bailii.org.

[341] *House of Lords*, decision of 15 May 2000, *Three Rivers District Council and Others v The Governor and Company of the Bank of England* [2000] UKHL 33; [2000] 3 All ER 1; [2000] 2 WLR 1220; [2000] CMLR 205.

[342] On the facts of the case and the judgment in the first instance, see J Lever, 'Aspects of Liability for the State and Public Bodies in English and Community Law', in M Andenas and F Jacobs (eds), *European Community Law in the English Courts* (Oxford, Clarendon Press, 1998) 67.

[343] First Council Directive 77/780/EEC of 12 December 1977 on the coordination of the laws, regulations and administrative provisions relating to the taking up and pursuit of the business of credit institutions, OJ 1977 L 322/30.

a licensed deposit taking institution. After the BCCI went into liquidation mainly due to fraud on a vast scale perpetrated at senior level, some six thousand depositors brought proceedings against the Bank of England. The claim was based first on alleged misfeasance in public office claiming that certain senior officials had acted in bad faith by giving authorisation to the BCCI when it was illegal, and by not interfering when they should have. The second claim was that the Bank of England was liable for violation of Community law as laid down in the First Banking Directive. Under provisions introduced in the Banking Act 1987, liability on the part of the Bank of England could only arise if the impugned act or omission was in bad faith; accordingly, there was statutory immunity against actions based on negligence or breach of statutory duty. It would thus have been attractive for the applicants if the courts would accept a Euro-tort, as it would avoid many of the restrictive elements of the tort of misfeasance in public office. However, it was decided that the directive did not intend to create rights for the benefit of individuals,[344] but was rather meant as a first step towards harmonisation of treatment of banks. The House of Lords escaped the obligation to make a reference for preliminary ruling on the issue, stating that it was *acte clair*.[345]

Final remarks

The English courts do appear to be prepared to relinquish the traditional principles of constitutional law and to hold the State liable in damages for various types of breaches of Community law, including breaches which are ultimately attributable to the primary legislature. Typical is the statement by Lord Hoffmann in the House of Lords in *Factortame III*, that in considering the liability of the State in Community law, the various

---

[344] Particularly striking in the judgment given by the Court of Appeal and by Lord Hope of Craighead, who wrote the leading speech on Community issues in the House of Lords, is the discussion of what is termed '*Becker* liability' and '*Francovich* liability'. However, *Becker* in Community law is concerned with the direct effect of directives in judial review cases (*applicabilité d'exclusion*); where the issue is the liability of the State, direct effect is not a condition. Lord Hope did not accept the difference between both types of liability and stated that the conditions were so analogous that they could be taken to be the same. However, it is submitted that the conditions as to clarity are more restrictive to establish direct effect (even of the *Becker*-type), than they are for the fulfilment of the first condition for liability under *Francovich*. See also M Andenas and D Fairgrieve, 'Misfeasance in Public Office, Governmental Liability and European Influences', 51 *ICLQ* (2002) 757, at 768.

[345] Lord Hope took account of the fact that in the courts below neither of the parties had asked for a preliminary reference; Clarke J had said that he would have made a reference had the parties not requested to give judgment without doing so. In the Court of Appeal, the majority said that they did not regard the issue of the *Becker*-type liability *acte clair*, but that as a matter of discretion they had chosen not to make a reference. In the House of Lords, the appellants did ask for a reference to be made. However, Lord Hope said referring also to the unanimous position of the Lords themselves on the issue, the matter was *acte clair*.

organs of government are treated as a single aggregate entity. The courts have even held the State liable in cases which had severe financial consequences on the State, as in the case of *Mrs Scullion*. However, the House of Lords appeared extremely reluctant in the *Three Rivers District Council* case. Several of the statements made by the Lords in that case are disputable from a Community law perspective, and the clear refusal on the part of the House of Lords to make a reference, on grounds of *acte clair* which there was not, demonstrates that the House was, probably on policy grounds not prepared to hold the State liable in this case.

The law of public tort liability is rapidly evolving, also outside the area of Community law. Under the Human Rights Act 1998, for instance, the courts have acquired jurisdiction to award damages as a remedy for the breach of a Convention right by a public authority.[346] The power to award damages is discretionary, and financial compensation constitutes a residual remedy which may only be awarded if, after consideration of the effects of any other relief or remedy granted, or order made, in relation to the act in question, the award of damages is necessary to afford just satisfaction. The courts are statutorily obliged to take account of the principles of the European Court of Human Rights in making reparation.

11.7.5. Belgium

One month after *Francovich* was decided, the Belgian *Cour de cassation* decided a purely national case concerning the liability of the State for judicial acts.[347] The *Cour* held that disputes concerning civil rights came within the exclusive jurisdiction of the ordinary courts, and that the Constitution did not distinguish as to the nature of the defendant or the capacity in which it was acting. The State was subject to the law, including the rules concerning liability for harm done to the subjective rights and legitimate interests of individuals. The principles of separation of powers, independence of the judicial branch and the courts, and the principle of finality (*gezag van rechterlijk gewijsde*) could not result in an absolute immunity of the State.[348] The decision was later confirmed and clarified.[349]

---

[346] See on this development D Fairgrieve, 'The Human Rights Act 1998, Damages and Tort Law', in *PL* (2001) 695.

[347] *Cour de cassation (B)*, decision of 19 December 1991, *PVBA Anderlecht Café (Anca) v Belgian State*, Pas., 1992, I, 316; JT, 1992, 142; commented *inter alia* in A Van Oevelen, 'De aansprakelijkheid van de Staat voor ambtsfouten van migistraten en de orgaantheorie na het Anca-arrest van het Hof van Cassatie van 19 december 1991', *RW* (1992) 377; M Storme, 'De rechterlijke macht', *NJB* (1993) 917; SCJJ Kortmann, 'Wie betaalt de rekening?', *NJB* (1993) 921; see also W van Gerven, 'De normatieve en rechterlijke aansprakelijkheid naar Europees en Belgisch recht', in M Storme (ed), *Recht halen uit aansprakelijkheid*, (Gent, Mys en Breesch, 1993), 396.

[348] A right to compensation can arise only if the injurious decision has been revoked, varied, quashed or retracted (*retiré, réformé, annulé ou rétracté*).

[349] *Cour de cassation (B)*, decision of 8 December 1994, *Anca II*, RW 1995, 180–81; JT, 1995, 497, available on www.cass.be.

One of the first cases concerning liability under Community law to be decided after *Francovich*[350] concerned the *minerval*.[351] The *Liège* Court of Appeal,[352] in application of the principle of procedural autonomy in *Francovich*, decided the case under Articles 1382 and 1383 of the Civil Code, containing the general tort liability provisions applying to both private persons and public authorities. In the case of the *minerval*, the harm was caused by an infringement of Community law imputable to the primary legislature. The Court of Appeal stated that the general tort rules also applied to acts of the primary legislature, provided that where fault consisted of *excès de compétence* or an unconstitutionality committed by the legislature, there had been a prior declaration by the *Cour d'arbitrage* to that effect. Under those conditions, it would not be contrary to the Constitution nor against the principle of separation of powers for a court to hold the State liable in damages for primary legislative acts. In the case at hand, the irregularity had been declared by the Court of Justice. Accordingly, in the absence of an excusable error or other justification, the court had to decide that the legislating State had committed a fault and award damages if the condition of causality was also complied with.

After *Brasserie/Factortame III*, it appears that the *Cour d'appel* may have gone beyond what is required under Community law. Indeed, the Court of Justice had stated in *Blaizot* that the Belgian authorities *could* reasonably have believed that the law was compatible with Community law; for the Court of Justice this was sufficient to limit the retroactive effect of its judgment under Article 234 EC, which it does not often do. It is submitted that accordingly, the infringement would not constitute a sufficiently serious breach under *Brasserie/Factortame III*.[353] In the test applied by the *Liège Cour d'appel*, the State would only be exonerated if the error was excusable, which was not accepted. The statement of the Court of Justice as to the reasonable interpretation of Community law by the Belgian authorities did not, in the eyes of the *Cour d'appel* exonerate the State. Under *British Telecom* it can be argued that the error on the part of the Belgian authorities would not constitute a sufficiently serious breach entailing the liability of the State as a matter of Community law. *Francovich* actions in damages must be brought in accordance with national law, subject to the

---

[350] But prior to *Brasserie/Factortame III*; the *minerval* cases originated from before *Francovich*.

[351] The facts of the case are set out above in Section 11.4.5.

[352] *Cour d'appel de Liège*, decision of 25 January 1994, *minerval*, unreported, explained in M Dony, 'Le droit belge', in G Vandersanden and M Dony (eds), *La responsabilité des États membres en cas de violation du droit communautaire. Études de droit communautaire et de droit national comparé* (Brussels, Bruylant, 1997) 149, at 161–62 and 173 et seq.

[353] Given the fact that in this area the Belgian legislature had a wide margin of discretion, a mere infringement would not suffice for a right to compensation to arise, and more was required. The statement of the ECJ in Blaizot implies that the legislature had not gravely and manifestly disregarded the limits of its discretion, and hence that there was no sufficiently serious breach.

condition that the substantive requirements introduced by the Court are sufficient to establish liability and subject to the requirements of equivalence and effectiveness. The difficulty in this case is the application of the principle of equivalence: the national rules applying to the liability of the legislative State for primary legislation was not at all clear before *Francovich* was decided: the law was in flux. While the case law and literature had consistently rejected this type of liability, it was argued in legal writing that the State could be held liable under the same conditions as for any other type of infringements.[354] The judgment of the *Cour de cassation* concerning the liability of the State for judicial acts points in the same direction. However, no court decisions had been handed in purely domestic cases. It may well be that without the judgment of the Court of Justice in *Brasserie*, the Belgian case law would have developed in the direction of a more generous acceptance of liability for primary legislation, following the pattern of liability in all other areas, *i.e.* liability of the State for administrative acts and omissions including of a legislative nature (*i.e.* secondary legislation) and for judicial acts.[355]

The Brussels Court of appeal decided a similar case relating to the *minerval*, holding the *Communauté française* and the *Université libre de Bruxelles* liable *in solidum* to pay the damage suffered by the applicants.[356] Thus, while the Liège court held the federal State liable, the Brussels court ordered the French Community, which had succeeded the federal State by the constitutional reform of 1988 in the area of education, to compensate the damage. The *Cour de cassation* quashed the judgment of the Liège court because it did not comply with the law governing the rights and obligations of the Regions and Communities succeeding to the federal State, which prescribed that the federated entities would also succeed to the federal State in this type of case.[357]

In a case concerning the equal treatment of men and women, the *Cour du travail de Liège* allowed an action brought by an employer against the State for the harm caused as a consequence of the failure of the legislature to adapt the legislation to the requirements of Community law.[358] The

---

[354] After the establishment of the *Cour d'arbitrage* and after the *Le Ski* judgment.

[355] This is confirmed by the judgment in *Tribunal de première instance de Bruxelles*, decision of 17 March 1997, *NV Spaas Industrie v Belgian State*, RW, 1997, 257, note P Popelier discussed below.

[356] *Cour d'appel de Bruxelles*, decision reported in in M Dony, 'Le droit belge', in La responsabilité des États membres en cas de violation du droit communautaire. Études de droit communautaire et de droit national comparés, (Bruxelles, Bruylant, 1997), 149, at 161–62 and 173 et seq.

[357] *Cour de cassation (B)*, decision of 26 January 1995, *minerval*, JMLB, 1995, 425; available on www. cass.be/juris/jucn/htm.

[358] *Cour du travail de Liège*, decision of 6 April 1995, Chronique Droit social, 1995, 7, reported in in M Dony, 'Le droit belge', in La responsabilité des États membres en cas de violation du droit communautaire. Études de droit communautaire et de droit national comparés, (Bruxelles, Bruylant, 1997), 149, at 177.

employer had been ordered by the court to pay compensation to a female employee who had been dismissed upon reaching the age of 60. Under the Belgian law implementing the Equal Treatment Directive, the dismissal was null and void, and accordingly, the employer had to pay compensation in the amount of the missed earnings. The employer thereupon sued the State. The *cour* apparently did not accept the immunity of the legislating State and awarded compensation.

The *Tribunal de première instance de Bruxelles* analysed the issue of the liability of the legislating State in more detail.[359] The applicant was a company established under a special legal regime designed to promote investments in certain specified regions (*'reconversiezones'*). When the legislature modified the system and withdrew the benefits provided to the companies in question, the applicant sued the State in damages. It was disputed before the court whether, as a matter of principle, the State could be held liable for damage incurred due directly to primary legislation. The court stated first, that there was no reason why the ordinary rules on tort liability should not apply to the legislating State also for acts of primary legislation. Under the principle of the Rule of Law, the State was bound by the law,[360] also when acting as legislature. This would only be otherwise if immunity was especially provided for by (constitutional) legislation. Second, the principles of separation of powers and of the independence of the legislative power did not prevent a court from holding the legislating State liable in damages. Separation of powers, the court stated, was to be understood as an equilibrium a system of checks of balances rather than a strict separation. There was no reason to exclude liability for legislative acts, from the general system of liability, which was already applied to administrative and judicial acts. Third, there was no trace of a 'principle of sovereignty of the legislative power' in legal or constitutional texts. Legislation was not as a matter of principle 'sovereign', immune or 'free from judicial control'. Fourth, the court rejected the argument that damage could not be caused by legislation directly because of its general and abstract character. Acts of Parliament could indeed directly and without intervention of implementing acts, cause harm. Last, even the legislature had recognised that Acts of Parliament could cause harm, since the Act on the *Cour d'arbitrage* gave that Court jurisdiction to suspend pieces of primary legislation challenged before it where the latter could cause 'severe and irreparable damage'. There was, accordingly, no reason why the State could not be held liable for Acts of the primary legislature.

The next question to be decided was whether the primary legislature had actually committed a fault, which is one of the substantive conditions

---

[359] *Tribunal de première instance de Bruxelles*, decision of 17 March 1997, *NV Spaas Industrie v Belgian State*, RW, 1997, 257, note P Popelier.
[360] Under the adage *'Patere legem quam ipse fecisti'*.

for liability to arise under Articles 1382–83 of the Belgian Civil Code. The court accepted that there had been a violation of the principle of legal certainty contained in the Belgian Constitution. However, the court could not review the constitutionality of Acts of Parliament, since that function is exclusively attributed to the *Cour d'arbitrage*. Therefore, if the court was convinced that there had been an unconstitutional infringement of the principle of legal certainty in combination with the principles of non-discrimination and equality, a question must be referred to the *Cour d' arbitrage*. Nevertheless, the court considered that there had clearly been no violation of the latter two principles, and under the theory of *acte clair*, no reference was made. As for the infringement of the principle of legal certainty as a general principle of Community law, the court pointed out that the case did not come within the scope of application of Community law. On the other hand, the court *ex proprio motu* stated that there might have been an infringement of the right to property under Article 1 of the First Protocol to the ECHR and accordingly re-opened the proceedings.[361]

Several decisions handed in 1998 concerned liability of the legislating State for the damage incurred as a consequence of the parliamentary Act of 10 December 1997 adopted by the federal Parliament, prohibiting advertising for tobacco and tobacco products. The Act, which has created severe political problems and has given rise to several court actions, prohibits almost all types of advertising for tobacco products, also for sports events such as the Grand Prix de Belgique held annually at the race-track of Francorchamps. Bernie Ecclestone, president of the Formula One Administration Ltd (FOA) announced that the Grand Prix de Belgique would be cancelled from the World Championship calandar in favour of another country if the Act be adopted without providing for an exception for Formula one. Members of Parliament attempted to block the adoption of the Act, delay its entry into force or to provide for transitory measures. A number of applicants, both private persons and public bodies,[362] brought an action in interlocutory proceedings before an ordinary court[363] claiming that the Act would cause a grave and irreparable damage to each of them. They asked for a suspension of the Act, arguing that the State was acting wrongfully harming their rights and legitimate

---

[361] No trace has been found of subsequent decisions in the case.
[362] Among which the Walloon region, one of the federated entities of the federal State of Belgium.
[363] The choice of forum seems remarkable, but in fact, it appeared to be the only route available judicially: the FOA and the *Fédération internationale de l'automobile* (FIA) had posed an ultimatum, saying that they would revoke their decision to withdraw the championship from Belgium on the condition that the relevant provisions of the Act were suspended before 31 December 1997. Proceedings before the *Cour d'arbitrage* (including interlocutory proceedings requesting suspension of the Act) were however not available since the Act had not yet been published (and the time limit for bringing an action for annulment of an Act before the *Cour d'arbitrage* commences on the day of the publication).

interests, by infringing higher norms of national and supranational law, in particular Articles 10 and 11 of the Constitution, the Community provisions on free movement of goods and the freedom to provide services, Article 10 of the ECHR and Article 1 of the First Protocol to the ECHR. In the alternative, they requested the disapplication of the Act[364] until the outcome of references to be made to the *Cour d'arbitrage* and to the Court of Justice. The first instance court denied jurisdiction to suspend the Act,[365] as did the Court of Appeal of Liège[366] because to hold otherwise would infringe the principle of the separation of powers and would violate the exclusive competence of the *Cour d'arbitrage* to rule on the compatibility of an Act with the Constitution. This would not be otherwise in the case of Community law, since the *Simmenthal* mandate applied in the context of national procedural law, and as long as it was possible in practice for the result of direct and effective protection to be attained, Community law accepted that the application of Community law before the national courts was not entirely uniform.

It is not clear that the requirement of immediate effective protection was met in the light of *Factortame*, since access to the *Cour d'arbitrage* was equally blocked as the Act had not yet entered into force. In *Factortame*, private individuals invoke *putative* Community rights against a national Act of Parliament.[367] However, in contrast to *Factortame*, where the applicants requested the disapplication of the Act, the applicants in this case requested its *suspension* or an order *preventing the entry into force of the Act*. While Community law requires the national courts to have jurisdiction to *disapply* an Act of Parliament in concrete cases for an alleged violation of Community law rights under certain specified conditions, it is not clear whether there must be jurisdiction to *prevent the adoption* of legislation allegedly conflicting with Community law.

Turning to the claim for *non-application* of the Act in respect of the applicants, the court confirmed what it had said on the issue of suspension. The court added an analysis of the nature of the rights protection of which was sought. Some applicants claimed that their fundamental rights

---

[364] As opposed to suspension, which would have an *erga omnes* effect, the non-application would be restricted to the applicants, while the Act could lawfully enter into force.

[365] *Président du tribunal de première instance de Verviers*, decision of 30 December 1997, *in re Spa Francorchamps*, unpublished.

[366] *Cour d'appel de Liège*, decision of 12 February 1998, *in re Spa Francorchamps*, Jurisprudence de Liège, Mons et Bruxelles, 1998, 502, commented by F Abu Dalu.

[367] In this case however, it was obvious that there was no infringement of Community law. It is doubtful whether the court was correct in holding that Community law did not require it to assume jurisdiction under *Simmenthal*. *Simmenthal* is notoriously difficult as it combines jurisdiction under national law and jurisdiction under Community law. The ECJ held, in practical effect that national courts must have jurisdiction to set aside conflicting legislation (even where this is excluded under national (procedural) law; *but that this jurisdiction must exist in cases 'within their jurisdiction'*, Case 106/77 *Simmenthal* [1978] ECR 629, at paras 21 and 24.

were threatened; others spoke of their rights and legitimate interests to be able to organise races. Under Belgian law, the ordinary courts have jurisdiction only to protect subjective rights,[368] and there was, according to the *Cour d'appel*, no right to have legislation maintained in force: it is for the legislature to make legislative choices. In this case, the court said, the real object of the case was the organisation of specified events at a specified location, which did not constitute a subjective right, but rather an economic interest. The ordinary courts could not therefore interfere. If it *were* accepted that the case did concern a violation of a subjective right and the court did have jurisdiction, the merits of the allegations – that the challenged Act infringed constitutional and supra-national norms – had to be examined: *'il est constant, en droit interne, que l'État est soumis, notamment dans sa fonction législative, aux règles de droit et notamment à celles qui régissent le réparation des dommages'*.[369] However, the court could not check the conformity of the Act with the Constitution. As for the alleged liability of the State for infringement of Community law, the court applied the conditions as set forth by the Court of Justice in *Brasserie/Factortame III*, and held that the condition of a sufficiently serious breach of Community law was not complied with.[370]

While the conclusion is certainly correct in the sense that there clearly was no infringement of Community law, especially not a qualified breach, several statements seem hardly convincing from the point of view of Community law.[371] The denial of jurisdiction on grounds that there was

---

[368] Arts. 144 and 145 of the Constitution deal with disputes over so-called subjective rights. A subjective right is the object of a dispute whenever a plaintiff alleges that the defendant refuses to fulfil a precise obligation, which is directly imposed upon him by a statute or a regulation. The essential feature is that for the fulfilment of the obligation, the law leaves no room for any discretion. Within the category of subjective rights, a distinction is made between civil rights, which belong to the exclusive competence of the ordinary courts, and political rights, which in principle also belong to the competence of the ordinary courts, but which can be subject to exceptions provided by Act of Parliament; disputes concerning these rights can be endowed to administrative courts; see on this issue P Lemmens, 'The impact of Article 6, § 1, of the European Convention on Human Rights on the proceedings before the Belgian Council of State, available on the website of the Association of Councils of State, www.raadvst-consetat.be/colloquia/2000/ Belgium.pdf, at 1–5.

[369] Without however referring to Arts. 1382–83 of the Civil Code, see also F Abu Dalu, 'Francorchamps, le juge et la loi', note under *Cour d'appel de Liège*, decision of 12 February 1998, *in re Spa Francorchamps*, Jurisprudence de Liège, Mons et Bruxelles, 1998, 513, at 516.

[370] The prohibition could not constitute an infringement of Community law given the fact that the Community had just adopted a directive to the same effect. Even though the directive provided that the prohibition only had to be applied from 1 October 2006, it also allowed for stricter national rules adopted in order to protect national health.

[371] Should the court have referred a question for preliminary ruling to the Court of Justice? It would seem not. Even if the ECJ would hold that a national court must have jurisdiction to suspend the application of an Act of Parliament or prevent its adoption for imminent breach of directly effective Community law rights, it would not have to be ordered in the case as there clearly was no infringement as yet, and the Act would not constitute an infringement when passed. A decision on a question of interpretation of Community law thus did not seem necessary to resolve the dispute.

no subjective right involved, is based purely on Belgian law, and must comply with the conditions of effectiveness under *Rewe* and *Comet*. It is submitted that in order to lawfully deny jurisdiction in the context of Community law, the courts should have checked if there were other routes available to the individuals in order to have their Community law rights protected.

When the Act was finally passed and published, the *tribunal de première instance de Verviers* had to rule on an action in damages against the State.[372] The court held that the applicable test was the one established by the Court of Justice, since in this case the legislature had a wide discretionary power. Accordingly a mere infringement would not entail the State's liability. In this case however, there was no infringement and *a fortiori* no qualified breach of Community law. Compensation was denied accordingly.[373] It is not clear however why the *cour* added that the application of Article 1382 of the Civil Code would constitute a refutation of the system established by the ECJ (*'la négation même de tout ce qu'a voulu la Cour de justice'*), and even a violation of the Treaty. The *cour* seemed to be of the opinion that the State could not be held liable for simple breach because this would not be the case either for the Community institutions. However, the matter is not that simple. If national law *does* provide for the liability of the State for primary legislation infringing upon higher norms under conditions more protective of the individual than *Brasserie*, the former would have to apply under the *Rewe* principle of equivalence. On the

---

[372] *Tribunal de première instance de Verviers*, decision of 26 June 1998, *Sc. Association pour l'exploitation du circuit de Francorchamps et al v État belge*, JTDE, 1998, 210.

[373] The Act was challenged finally before the *Cour d'arbitrage*, which annulled two provisions of the Act. The *Cour* held that it was unconstitutional to apply the Act to events with worldwide relevance (such as the Formula One races at Spa-Francorchamps) before 31 July 2003. Since the Community directive provided for a suspension of the prohibition for that type of events until that date and most Member States would make use of the possibility left open in the directive, there was a risk of the events being moved to locations in other Member States, and more spectators would still be confronted with advertising, as people would be watching the races on TV Accordingly, it would be disproportionate to prohibit tobacco advertising at events with worldwide relevance before 31 July 2003. *Cour d'arbitrage*, decision n. 102/99 of 30 September 1999, *in re tobacco advertising*, available on www.arbitrage.be. This was not the end of the conflict. The Walloon Region adopted a legislative decree (*'decreet'* or *'decrèt'*, i.e. a legislative act adopted by the Parliament of one of the federated entities, having the same force and rank as a federal Act of Parliament), which allowed sponsoring of all events organised on locations owned or sponsored by the Walloon Region; sponsoring that contributed to the promotion of tobacco products was allowed until 30 July 2003, while it was allowed until 1 October 2006 for events with worldwide effect if it could be shown that the survival of the event depended on it and that the event had a positive effect on the local economy, the local and regional tax revenues and the tourist industry in the region. The Flemish Government brought an action for annulment for lack of competence, and succeeded. Arguments brought forward by the Walloon Region based on the Community Directive carried no effect, as it had in the meantime been annulled by the ECJ, see *Cour d'arbitrage*, decision n. 36/2001of 13 March 2001, *in re sponsoring of events in the Walloon Region*, available on www.arbitrage.be.

other hand, if it is accepted that liability of the State for harm caused by primary legislative acts is not available under Belgian law, the minimum conditions of *Brasserie* must apply. The difficulty is that it is not yet clear whether liability of the State can arise in case of harm caused directly by a primary legislature under Belgian law as it stands. So, while it may well be correct that the applicable test is *Brasserie* (in the absence of national rules governing the liability of the legislative State), this cannot be so for the reasons stated by the *tribunal*, where it holds that the Court of Justice's test must apply since it alone has competence to interpret Community law.

On other occasions the State was held liable in damages for a failure on the part of the State for a correct and timely implemention of a directive.[374] Notable is also a decision of the *Cour de cassation* quashing a judgment which applied the restrictive *Brasserie/Factortame III* conditions for liability of the State for breach of Community law to a breach of Article 28 EC committed by a piece of secondary legislation adopted by the Government (*'Koninklijk Besluit'* or royal decree).[375] The Brussels Court of Appeal had held, under reference to *Brasserie*, that such infringement would give rise to a duty to pay compensation only if there had been a sufficiently serious, manifest and grave breach. However, Belgian law governing the liability of the State for secondary normative acts is less restrictive than is required under Community law: a mere breach suffices, except in the case of excusable error or in the presence of an other ground of exoneration. Since the *Cour d'appel* had not established that the grounds to deny the existence of a manifest and serious breach would also constitute a ground of exoneration under the Belgian rules, its judgment was quashed. The judgment of the *Cour de cassation* is in perfect harmony with the case law of the Court of Justice, since Community law only sets minimum conditions for the protection of individuals and national law

---

[374] *Tribunal de première instance de Bruxelles*, decision of 13 February 1998, *Delsa v SPRL Rovi and État belge, Ministre de la Justice*, Revue de jurisprudence de Liège, Mons et Bruxelles, 1998, 1261, confirmed on appeal in *Cour d'appel de Bruxelles*, decision of 6 September 2000, *contrat d'agence*, available on www.cass.be. The case against the private defendant was declared inadmissible. The court rejected the argument that the Belgian law should be interpreted in conformity with the directive, since this would amount to the horizontal application of a non-implemented directive (Council Directive 86/653/EEC on self-employed commercial agents, OJ 1986 L 382, 17). Another case concerned the *Dillenkofer* directive on package travel (Directive 90/314 on package travel, package holidays and package tours, OJ 1990 L , 158/59). While a law had been adopted to implement the directive, the secondary legislation laying down the practical arrangements had not been issued. Referring to *Francovich*, the *tribunal de première instance* found that the failure to implement the directive fully by the due date constituted a breach entailing the liability of the State. *Tribunal de première instance de Bruxelles*, decision of 9 September 1999, *in re NV Abba Travel* Consumentenrecht, 1999, 305.
[375] *Cour de cassation (B)*, decision of 14 January 2000, *rayon de braquage*, available on www.cass.be.

continues to apply (because of the principle of equivalence) where it is more generous to the individuals or companies who have suffered harm.[376]

Final remarks

It appears, thus, that Belgian courts no longer consider the State immune for legislative wrong. It is as yet unclear, however, whether the liability of the State for acts of primary legislation or omissions of the primary legislature (and there are many in federal Belgium!) follows the *Brasserie* pattern or whether it may be wider and follow the same pattern as applies to any other type of State liability under national law. The Belgian courts do not share the tendency of the French courts to avoid holding the State liable for acts or omissions attributable to Parliament. As for the allocation of liability, it appears that this will have to be decided in accordance with the Law on the rights and obligations of the federated entities succeeding the federal State. This appears to be in conformity with *Konle*: applicants will have to decide on who the appropriate defendant is in accordance with national law.

11.7.6. The Netherlands

The general appreciation in Dutch legal community was that *Francovich* constituted no novelty relevant to Netherlands law, as liability for legislative acts had long been accepted, and the *Francovich* conditions were rather less than more severe on the State.[377] The reaction to *Brasserie* was similar. Nevertheless, there had been no cases in which the State had actually been held liable to compensate harm done to individuals as a consequence of acts or omissions on the part of the primary legislature considered as 'wrongful'.[378]

---

[376] Joined Cases C–46/93 and C–48/93 *Brasserie du Pêcheur v Germany and The Queen v Secretary of State for Transport, ex parte Factortame Ltd and Others* [1996] ECR I–1029, at para 74.

[377] So G Betlem and E Rood, 'Francovich-aansprakelijkheid. Schadevergoeding wegens schending van het gemeenschapsrecht', *NJB* (1992) 250, at 254. more cautious is AJ Bok, 'Het Francovich-arrest en onrechtmatige wetgeving naar Nederlands recht', *TPR* (1993) 37; G Betlem, 'Onrechtmatige wetgeving: Overheidsaansprakelijkheid voor Schending van EG-recht in het post-Francovich Tijdperk', *RegelMaat* (1996) 128, at 139 ('As concerns wrongful legislation and wrongful administration, the influence of *Brasserie* on the Dutch tort law seems to me to be 0,0', my tanslation); A de Moor-van Vugt and EM Vermeulen, *Europees Bestuursrecht*, (Deventer, WEJ Tjeenk Willink, 1998), at 108; GE van Maanen and R de Lange, *Onrechtmatige Overheidsdaad*, 3rd. edn, (Deventer, WEJ Tjeenk Willink, 2000), at 194; JH Jans et al, *Inleiding tot het Europees bestuursrecht*, 2nd edn, (Nijmegen, Ars Aequi Libri, 2002), at 399. Nevertheless, it was generally agreed that, should the ECJ accept that liability also arises as a matter of Community law for infringements of Community law by judicial organs, this would certainly be novel for the Dutch legal order, given the case law of the *Hoge Raad* in the matter.

[378] See also AG Langemijer in *Hoge Raad*, decision of 21 March 2003, *Waterpakt*, NJ 2003/691, at marginal number 2.18. However, the AG argued that it would be in line with the evolution so far to accept that primary legislation can also be 'wrongful'.

Maria *Lubsen-Brandsma* was successful in her action against the municipality of Abcoude and the Netherlands State.[379] The plaintiff, a gynaecologist, had not been awarded certain grants of money since the relevant Act of Parliament excluded from the benefit married women who did not earn the main income (*'kostwinner'*), while that condition was not set for men. The exclusion appeared to conflict with the Equal Treatment Directive 79/7 which was to be adapted before 23 December 1984.[380] The implementing Act was passed late, but with retroactive effect from the expiry of the time limit set forth in the directive. However, the exclusion remained in force for women who had become unemployed before that date. When the Court of Justice declared this provision to be contrary to Community law, the Junior Minister (*'staatssecretaris'*) sent a circular to the municipal authorities competent to award the benefits. Put simply, Lubsen claimed the relevant benefits with retroactive effect including interests. She based the claim against the State on the wrongful belated implementation of the directive, and argued that the action must be governed by Community law alone. The claim against the municipal authorities was based on a *Costanzo*-type reasoning, that even in the absence of correct implementation by the State authorities, the municipal authorities should have applied the directive. The court applied the *Francovich* conditions and held both the State and municipality liable *in solidum*. The State had acted wrongfully by not implementing the directive in time; the municipality was held liable because it had infringed its independent duty to apply national law in conformity with Community law.

The court deciding the case of *Genaro Acciardi* against the municipality of Amsterdam approached the issue of the allocation of liability differently.[381] Acciardi's social security benefits had been reduced on grounds that his wife and child were living abroad; he was therefore treated as a single person. When the Court of Justice decided that it should not matter that the family was living in another Member State,[382] the decision of the municipality was quashed, and Acciardi was paid the difference between the amounts due and the amounts that had already been paid. In the current proceedings, he claimed interests on the amounts paid and compensation for the costs of legal assistance. The court awarded the claim against the municipality: as the decision had been quashed, there

---

[379] *Arrondissementsrechtbank Utrecht*, decision of 25 October 1995, *Lubsen-Brandsma v Staat der Nederlanden and Gemeente Abcoude*, JB 1995, 305; Rawb 1996, 24.

[380] As apparent from the ECJ's decision in Case 80/87 *A Dik, A Menkutos-Demirci and HGW Laar-Vreeman v College van Burgemeester en Wethouders Arnhem and Winterswijk* [1988] ECR I–1601.

[381] *Arrondissementsrechtbank Amsterdam*, decision of 11 September 1996, *Genaro Acciardi v Gemeente Amsterdam and Gemeente Amsterdam v Staat der Nederlanden*, JB 1996, 237; Rawb, 1997, 23.

[382] Case C–66/92 *Genaro Acciardi v Commissie Beroepszaken Administratieve Geschillen in de Provincie Noord-Holland* [1993] ECR I–4567.

was under Dutch liability law no further requirement of 'fault' or 'culpability'. Nevertheless, the municipality was of the opinion that the State was ultimately responsible for the lawfulness of legislation to be applied by municipalities and brought an action in recovery against the State. In its defence, the State argued that the municipality had an independent obligation to act in conformity with Community law (a *Costanzo*-type reasoning). In addition, it argued, because the relevant measure constituted a *'wet in formele zin'* (an Act of Parliament), the only remedy available in case of unlawfulness (*'onrechtmatigheid'*) was its disapplication on the basis of Article 94 of the Constitution. In the alternative, the State contended that the Dutch condition of relativity was not complied with, since the relevant provision of Community law was not intended to protect the municipality. Finally, it argued that the European Court's decision could easily have been different and hence the infringement was not suffiently serious to cause the liability of the State to arise (as the defence would probably have been after *Factortame III*), and constituted an excusable error on the part of the legislature (see also *British Telecom*). The court – explicitly exercising its Community duty to give full effect to Community law – held that the Act did constitute a wrongful act both as against individuals who could derive rights from the relevant provision of Community law, and in relation to the municipality, and held that 'wrongful' primary legislation could cause the liability of the State. It rejected the *Costanzo*-argument of the State and held the State had acted wrongfully *vis-à-vis* the municipality. The court concluded that the State had acted wrongfully by adopting legislation instructing the municipality to refuse to Acciardi the payment of benefits he was entitled to under Community law. It thus ordered the municipality to compensate Acciardi, but also ordered the State to pay the same amount to the municipality.

Both the *Lubsen* and *Acciardi* courts accepted liability of the State despite the fact that the breach was (partly or ultimately) due to an action or inaction on the part of the primary legislature. But they differ in outcome and approach: the *Lubsen* court applied *Francovich* directly, as a separate tort, while the *Acciardi* court applied the usual tort provisions and conditions under Dutch law, adapted to the Community law context.

Also in the case of Boris *Shapiro*, Dutch tort provisions were applied.[383] Boris Shapiro, a scientist, claimed compensation for the damage suffered allegedly as a result of the failure on the part of the Netherlands to implement a Euratom Directive. The Netherlands State was seven years late in implementing the directive. Shapiro sued the State for compensation of the loss suffered as a result of the belated implementation: he claimed that as a consequence of the delay there was only limited demand

---

[383] *Arrondissementsrechtbank Den Haag*, decision of 14 February 1996, *Boris Shapiro v Staat der Nederlanden*, RAwb 1996, 90.

for employees with his expertise and he had not accordingly found a job in The Netherlands. The damage suffered was the loss of earnings, consisting of the difference in the salary which he would have earned and the salary actually received in the same period. The court rejected the claim since Shapiro had not showed that the State had acted wrongfully *in his respect*.[384] The court thus applied a condition of Netherlands tort law to the facts of the case, which is debatable under *Francovich*, if it would have been the only reason why the case should fail. On the other hand, the condition of relativity is similar to the *Francovich* conditions that the infringed norm intended to create rights for individuals, which were clearly identifiable on the basis of the directive. But the case would have been unsuccessful on other counts also: it is unlikely that a court (national or European) would have accepted that the directive intended to create rights for the applicant (a right to a job as expert);[385] and more importantly, it is difficult to establish a direct causal link between the failure to implement the directive, and the loss of earnings (Shapiro would have had to prove that if the directive had been implemented he would necessarily have been given the position).

Particularly striking is the recent *Waterpakt* decision of the *Hoge Raad* to which reference has already been made on several occasions, and which raises a few interesting point relevant to Community law.[386] While the case did not directly concern a claim in damages, it was decided under the Dutch rules on tort liability for breach of Community law, and will accordingly be discussed here. As explained before, the general tort liability provisions of the Civil Code can be invoked before Dutch courts to various ends: in order to obtain damages, but also to request the disapplication of legislation, or to obtain an injunction against the State in the form of an order to do or to refrain from doing something. In the case of *Waterpakt*, several environmental organisations brought an action to obtain a declaration that the State had acted wrongfully *vis-à-vis* the applicants by not implementing the nitrates directive;[387] and secondly, to order the State to take appropriate action to comply with the directive before a specified deadline. The first instance court gave a declaration that the failure to implement (part of) the directive timely and correctly was

---

[384] The condition of relativity (*'relativiteitseis'*) under Netherlands liability law requires that the act was wrongful with respect to the applicant, in that the infringed norm was intended to protect the applicant.

[385] This may have been different if a claim had been brought by victims for harm caused directly by the absence of the prescribed tests.

[386] *Hoge Raad*, decision of 21 March 2003, *Stichting Waterpakt et al v Staat der Nederlanden*, NJ 2003/691; see also *Gerechtshof 's Gravenhage*, decision of 2 August 2001, *Staat der Nederlanden v Stichting Waterpakt et al*, M & R, 2001, 95; *Arrondissementsrechtbank*, decision of 24 November 1999, *Stichting Waterpakt et al v Staat der Nederlanden*, M & R, 2000, 24.

[387] Council Directive 91/676/EEC of 12 December 1991 concerning the protection of waters against pollution caused by nitrates from agricultural sources, OJ 1991 L 375/1.

wrongful,[388] and issued an order to take appropriate action so as to ensure that for the year 2002 the directive was complied with. The court ruled that if it should not have jurisdiction to give such order, judicial protection of the applicants would be severely limited. It further emphasised that it did not order the State to adopt primary legislation – an order which is very debatable in Dutch constitutional law and had been rejected in the *WWV* case[389] – but merely to 'take appropriate action to make an end to the wrongful act'. On appeal the *Gerechtshof 's Gravenhage* quashed the decision, on grounds that are debatable from the point of view of Community law. First, the appeal court held that it would not give the declaration asked for, as an infringement action was pending before the Court of Justice. In order to prevent conflicting judgments, it suspended its decision on the claim for a declaration that the State had acted wrongfully. However, there is nothing in Community law to prevent national courts from ruling on national acts while an enforcement action is pending before the Court of Justice. Indeed, enforcement actions before the European Court and proceedings before the national courts are complementary, and they may serve different purposes (public enforcement versus private enforcement). As for the second claim, the appeal court held that it had no jurisdiction to grant the injunction: in order to comply with the directive, the State would have to adopt primary legislation, and the Dutch courts are not, in the Dutch constitutional system, in a position to make an order to the primary legislature. It would have been interesting to find out what the Court of Justice had to say on the issue from a Community perspective, but no reference was made under Article 234 EC.

The case then came before the *Hoge Raad*, which upheld the decision of the appeal court. The *Hoge Raad* stated that under the Dutch Constitution, the courts may not interfere in the essentially political process of making primary legislation, which is constitutionally endowed to the Government and Parliament together. This was the same in the context of Community law, for instance when legislation is to be adopted in order to achieve a result prescribed in a directive within a prescribed time limit. According to the *Hoge Raad*, even in cases where the State had not complied with its obligations under the directive, and even if it had accordingly acted wrongfully, the courts did not have jurisdiction to issue an order to adopt legislation before a specified date: the questions as to whether legislation would have to be adopted, and if so, with which

---

[388] *'Dat het nalaten van de Staat (..) onrechtmatig is jegens Waterpakt'*. The claim that the State had acted wrongfully by infringing the duty to protect the environment as laid down in Art. 21 of the Constitution was rejected as the State has a very wide margin of discretion in the area, and the applicants had not proven that the State had not complied with the constitutional duty. Claims based on the London and Rio Declarations were equally not accepted.

[389] See *above*.

content, would require a political decision which is not for the courts to decide: it would also be a matter for the political organs to choose not to comply with the Community obligations and to risk enforcement actions. The jurisdiction to grant an order to adopt legislation could not be derived from Article 94 of the Constitution which is limited to allowing the courts to set aside conflicting legislation, which is quite different from ordering the adoption of legislation, as it operates only with respect to the applicants in the case. The *Hoge Raad* finally stated that there were other means to have Community rights protected: the courts would be obliged to conform interpretation, to hold the State liable in damages, and where the directive had direct effect, individuals could rely on it to protect their rights.[390]

The *Hoge Raad* then turned to the question whether Community law would impose a different approach, *i.e.* whether there would be a duty (or jurisdiction?) to grant an order to adopt primary legislation. The *Hoge Raad* cited from *Francovich* the duty of national courts to guarantee the *effet utile* of Community law and to protect the rights of individuals deriving from it. However, the *Hoge Raad* went on to say under reference to *Van Schijndel*, that this duty existed only within the scope of competences and jurisdiction as defined under national law, while under Netherlands law the courts did not have jurisdiction to order the adoption of primary legislation. In addition, the *Hoge Raad* stated, the Court of Justice is equally precluded from ordering the Member States to adopt primary legislation, and accordingly, Community law cannot impose such duty on national courts.

The *Hoge Raad* decided the case without making a reference to the Court of Justice, while, it is submitted, it had every reason to do so. It may well be argued that there must be jurisdiction under Community law to order the State to do what is required to comply with Treaty obligations, even if such injunction would imply that an order is issued for primary legislation to be adopted. The difficulty, as in *Simmenthal* and in other cases, is in the delimitation between 'jurisdiction' under national law and Community 'jurisdiction'. The fact that a court does not have 'jurisdiction' to award a particular remedy or to adopt a specific decision under national law does not imply that it does not have that 'jurisdiction' under Community law. The *Simmenthal* court did not have 'jurisdiction' to set aside a national Act of Parliament, but that did not prevent it from having jurisdiction as a matter of Community law. It may well be argued that a similar reasoning could be applied in this case. Likewise, arguments based on national constitutional law and the national separation of powers have not proven very strong in cases like *Simmenthal*, *Factortame*,

---

[390] It seems that the *Hoge Raad* started from a very limited interpretation of the notion 'direct effect', limited to those cases where rights of individuals are created and leaving aside the *Becker*-type situations.

Francovich and *Brasserie/Factortame III*. In any case, the discretion of the primary legislature in the *Waterpakt* case is not as wide as the *Hoge Raad* wanted its audience to believe: the position of the primary legislature when implementing Community law is rather comparable to that of a secondary legislature in the national context, and the powers and competences of the national courts could be adapted accordingly.[391] The argument that it is a political choice on the part of the primary legislature to prefer enforcement proceedings (and thus to delay the obligation to comply with the directive) is shocking from a Community law perspective and proves once again the inadequacy of the procedure as a means to ensure compliance with Community law obligations. This was precisely the reason why the Court of Justice involved the national courts in the enforcement of Community law in cases like *Van Gend en Loos* and *Francovich*. Furthermore, the fact that the Court of Justice does not have jurisdiction to order the adoption of primary legislation has nothing to do with the question as to whether national courts should have such power. The Court of Justice essentially remains an international court, and can only declare that 'the State' has infringed its obligations under the Treaty, but the national courts are national courts, operating within the State, and their competences *vis-à-vis* the various State organs are very different from those of the Court of Justice. The argument carries no weight in this case, just as it cannot be convincing in other cases: the Court of Justice cannot set aside national legislation, but that is no reason why the national courts would not be so empowered (*Simmenthal*); the Court of Justice cannot suspend the application of national law allegedly in conflicting with Community law, the national courts can or must (*Factortame*); the Court of Justice cannot hold the State liable to pay damages to an individual for damage caused by an infringement of Community law, the national courts can or must (*Francovich* etc). Reference can also be made to court decisions in other Member States. So the Belgian court in the pensions case ordered the State to comply with its Community law obligations, under the threat even of penalty payments! The *House of Lords* did give a declaration that the United Kingdom was in breach of the equal treatment directive in the *EOC* case. The latter case was not decided as a tort case, but that is not relevant as a matter of Community law. Whether or not it should be decided as a tort case or differently, is a matter of national law; whether the national court must have jurisdiction to issue a declaration or even an order, may well be a matter of Community law. The decision of the *Hoge Raad* that it is beyond all reasonable doubt that Community law would not give jurisdiction to the national courts to order the State to comply with a directive, is rather doubtful, and a reference *was* in place.

---

[391] This is the argument which has often be used in legal literature, see above.

11.8. CONCLUSION

Even more so than the *Simmenthal* mandate, the *Francovich* mandate requires the national courts to step outside the national context and to let go of fundamental principles of constitutional law in order to decide cases as veritable Community law courts. The national courts in this context operate both as 'international courts' and as national courts simultaneously. As international courts, they are required to view an alleged infringement of Community law from the outside, approaching the State as one entity. But at the same time, they remain national courts, and they may have to allocate liability to the correct level and instance within the State. Community law and national law are hence intertwined and blurred in a very complex manner. National law decides the competent court, and in essence also the appropriate defendant (while it appears that 'the State' as such – as an actor in Community law at the Community level – cannot escape liability by recourse to constitutional provisions concerning the separation of powers, a particular public organ or entity can, even if it is the central State itself). Community law imposes the substantive conditions for liability; national law further implements the technical and procedural conditions, as long as these comply with the *Rewe* and *Comet* conditions.

One could even go further and argue that the national courts in this context act more as a Community court than the Court of Justice would ever be able to. The Court of Justice essentially remains an international court, viewing the State as one entity, making no distinction as to the identity, nature and constitutional position of the organs involved. The national courts, on the other hand, are required not only to decide the cases between the individual applicant and 'the State', but also between the various entities and organs making up the State, allocating responsibility and liability within the State. In doing so, the courts must comply with the requirements of Community law, but will at the same time manoeuvre so as to upset the constitutional principles as little as possible. The survey of the national court cases shows a disparate image. While most courts do attempt to apply the case law of the Court of Justice, they encounter very difficult issues of national law, and it is too early to say whether the Court of Justice has been as successful in turning the national courts into Community courts in this type of cases, as in the case of the *Simmenthal* mandate.

The national courts cases show different sensitivities in different Member States. For instance, the French *Conseil d'État* does not appear convinced that it can actually impute liability to the primary legislature and applies *Costanzo* to shift liability from the latter to the Executive. The old ghosts of national constitutional law keep showing their faces: so the Dutch court claimed that it had no jurisdiction, under Dutch constitutional law, to order the State to adopt primary legislation – but would it have jurisdiction under Community law? The German courts appear to be very reluctant to hold the State liable for damage caused by infringement of Community law on the part of the State, especially where it is attributable to the legislature. Other courts have not experienced the same reluctance to hold the State liable in damages for primary legislation, such as the Belgian and the English courts. Italy has altered its system, which may lead to a very new approach to the liability of the legislating State, also in purely domestic cases. In the latter three systems, the law of State liability is in flux, and Community law may well have worked as a catalyst for change in other areas as well. Nevertheless, it appears from the survey that the Court of Justice has not (yet) been very successful in achieving a level of uniformity. Much of this is due to the complexity of the issues involved and the inevitable intertwinement – in the absence of harmonising legislation – between national and Community law in this context.

In any case, *Francovich* has not, contrary to what may have been expected at the time, caused a floodgate of liability cases. Apparently, it is one thing to set aside conflicting national law, but quite another to hold the State liable in damages for breach of Community law. Most cases fail on the condition that the infringement should be sufficiently serious on causation, or on some form of relativity. It would be interesting, however, to find out whether there is Community jurisdiction for national courts to order the State, including the primary legislature, to comply with its Treaty obligations. In my view there is a strong case to argue that such jurisdiction should indeed be inherent in the Treaty, and that the conditions could well be less restrictive than for a simple damages case. There should not be a condition that the infringement of an obligations arising from the Treaty is sufficiently serious; the only requirement should be that the obligation follows sufficiently clearly from Community law itself. Such an order would obviously not directly compensate the individual who suffered damage as a consequence of the infringement. On the other hand, liability in damages could follow much more easily if the State should not comply with an order issued by its own courts.

Part 2

The Court of Justice and National Constitutional Jurisdiction: *La Guerre des Juges?*

12

Introduction

EUROPEAN LAW AND the case law of the Court of Justice on the mandate of national courts have had quite a different effect on the constitutional position of national courts having a constitutional jurisdiction. Part 1 in practical effect demonstrated an overall empowerment of national courts *vis-à-vis* the other state organs, through the case law of the Court of Justice, be it directly by the endowment of a Community mandate or indirectly through an adjustment of the constitutional mandate of the courts. It was, in essence, a success story for the Court of Justice and its national allies, the courts: all national courts have on the whole accepted the duty to enforce and administer Community law, with precedence over national law, even primary legislation of a later date, thereby reinforcing their powers towards the other State organs, and particularly, the national Parliaments. As a result they have all, be it only within the scope of Community law, become review courts. The Court of Justice and the national courts have become 'brothers in arms', in enforcing Community law against the Member States, even the national Parliaments.

For the constitutional courts and the courts having constitutional jurisdiction, the effect of the Court's case law is dramatically less constructive and congenial. In essence, the case law of the Court of Justice implies a curtailment of some of the powers they possess under their constitutional mandate. Take the Community doctrine of supremacy: the Court's version of supremacy is unconditional and absolute: Community law must be awarded precedence even against the very national Constitution. As a direct consequence, the constitutional courts are asked to refrain from enforcing the constitutional provisions that they have a sworn duty to uphold and protect, in favour of any act of Community law, whatever its form, rank or content.

The dilemma for the constitutional courts is obvious: their natural function, their mission is to guarantee observance for the State's fundamental rules and principles laid down in the Constitution. Yet, since their State is a Member of the Union and must hence comply with its Treaty obligations, the constitutional courts must also comply with the Treaty obligations and ensure respect for Community law. At the Rome conference of constitutional courts Antonio Baldassarre, then president of the Corte costituzionale, put it this way: *'[la Corte costituzionale si muove fra due padroni. L'importante è che le Corti costituzionale non facciano come la maschera italiana di Arlecchino tra due padroni. L'importante è saper trovare l'equilibrio giusto nel servire l'uno e l'altro ideale: entrambi si muovono in una direzione che, se non è collimante, comunque non è divergente'.*[1] The image is that of a servant of two masters, whose duty it is to achieve a balance between two ideals. But even that image was contested by the not so European minded Member of the *Bundesverfassungsgericht* who also wrote the judgment in the *Brunner* case,[2] Paul Kirchhof: *'Wir haben nur die Aufgabe,* einem Herren *zu dienen, nämlich dem deutschen Grundgesetz.'*

The *discourse* between the Court of Justice and the national constitutional courts has been much more strenuous than with the ordinary courts, so much so, that there has been word of a *guerre des juges*, in which the Court of Justice has been diametrically opposed to the constitutional courts, notably the German, but the Italian and other courts as well. The provisional outcome of this battle, according to the conventional presentation of facts, has been that the constitutional courts have, rightly or wrongly depending on the perspective assumed, not surrendered, and have introduced exceptions to the principle of supremacy, thus threatening the uniformity and full effectiveness of Community law.

In the framework of Community law the constitutional courts thus seem to have an impossible choice to make: either they accept the mandate from the Court of Justice and consequently partly renounce their constitutional mandate to uphold the Constitution; or they continue to protect the fundamental values enshrined in the Constitution and consequently are unable to guarantee, in all cases, the supremacy of Community law. Most of the constitutional courts and courts having jurisdiction have assumed the latter position and ultimately grant precedence to the Constitution. Hailed as protectors of the national sovereignty, national fundamental rights or the Nation State by some, they have been accused by others of interfering with European integration, of jeopardising the uniform application of Community law and of provoking the Court of Justice.

Yet, envision their case. Only a few national Constitutions provide Community-proof rules governing a conflict between the Constitution and Community law, and present the constitutional courts with the

---

[1] A Baldassarre in *Diritto comunitario europeo e diritto nazionale,* Atti del seminario internazionale Roma 1995, Milano (Giuffrè, 1997) at 57.

[2] *Bundesverfassungsgericht,* decision of 12 October 1993, *Treaty of Maastricht,* 89 BverfGE 155; [1994] 1 CMLR 57; Oppenheimer, *The Cases,* 526.

necessary tools to deviate from their natural task to protect the Constitution. The Irish Constitution provides constitutional immunity for Community law and national law covered by it, and since the 11th Amendment, even for Union law and the national law necessitated thereby. The Luxembourg Constitution seems to start from the same premises and excludes treaties from constitutional review by the newly established constitutional court.[3] The Netherlands Constitution is even more generous and awards precedence over the Constitution even to all treaties.[4] That is the combined effect of Articles 94 (precedence of treaties which are 'binding on anyone' over legislation in force in Kingdom) and 120 (the courts do not rule on the constitutionality of statutes and treaties) of the Constitution. However, there is no constitutional court in The Netherlands and none of its highest courts has ever presented an over all theory of the relation between legal orders and between the European Treaties and the Constitution. Other Constitutions are not explicit as to the tasks of the (constitutional) courts in this particular framework and at most proclaim general principles which govern European integration and membership to the Union.[5] Ultimately it is for them to settle possible inconsistencies or conflicts between the Constitution and Community law on the basis of very open provisions and general principles of law.

And is there really a *guerre des juges*? At the end of the day, the focus should not be on the dispute between the European Court of Justice and the national constitutional courts, on any 'imminent collision' or inevitable discord. What is crucial are the statements these constitutional courts have made on the constitutional limitations of European integration, on the problems with the European construct and the way things work in Europe from a constitutional perspective. The national constitutional courts' audience is not first and foremost the Court of Justice. The message is addressed primarily to those who are responsible for the constitutional foundations of the State and of the European Union, let there be no mistake. Obviously, the relationship with the Court of Justice is complicated by some of these courts' pronouncements. Yet, none of these courts, even the most confident and resilient, oppose the Court of Justice

---

[3] Under Article 95ter of the Constitution inserted in 1996 the *Cour constitutionnelle* rules on the constitutionality of statutes, with the exception of statutes whereby a treaty is approved. The *Cour constitutionnelle* is seized by way of preliminary references from the ordinary courts when the issue of constitutionality is raised by one of the parties or by the court *ex officio*.

[4] M Slaughter, *et al* (eds), *The European Court and National Courts—Doctrine and Jurisprudence. Legal Change in Its Social Context* (Oxford, Hart Publishing, 1998) 171.

[5] See for instance Art. 23 of the German Basic Law (since 1992; until then German membership and the effect of Community law in the internal legal order were considered to be sufficiently regulated by the general provision of Art. 24). 'Europe provisions' were also inserted in the French Constitution at the occasion of the ratification of the Maastricht Treaty. The Italian and the Belgian Constitutions do not contain any specific 'Europe provisions'.

for the sake of it, and while there may be ego issues involved, these cannot account for all of the statements made and positions taken. There are important lessons to be learned from the case law of the constitutional courts, and now is the time to be aware of them. This point will be further developed in Part 3, the position of the national constitutional courts will first be analysed, as will their relationship with the European Court of Justice.

13

Introducing the Actors: 'Courts Having Constitutional Jurisdiction'

WHAT IS IT that makes the relationship between the European Court of Justice and the constitutional courts and courts with constitutional jurisdictions so much more complicated than the relationship with the 'ordinary' national courts discussed in the previous section? Who are these courts? The mandate of the national constitutional courts, their function and mission are very different from those of ordinary courts. Within the national order, constitutional courts function mostly as the ultimate guardians of the integrity of the Constitution. Their duty is to uphold the Constitution and to ensure its supremacy. Admittedly, *all* courts owe allegiance to the Constitution, as do all other State organs, but for the constitutional courts, the function of upholding the Constitution is their very *raison d'être*. They protect the constitutional values and principles against infringements, as the case may be, by legislative, executive and judicial action, thereby upholding the internal rules of law. In the framework of Community law, these constitutional courts may be confronted with challenges to the constitutional rules and the constitutional integrity from outside the national legal order, in particular by the Community institutions, or by the national organs operating under their Community mandate.

Some of these courts are key players in the national constitutional dialogue and decide issues which in other States are considered to belong to the political branches which directly represent the people. The impact of the constitutional courts and courts having jurisdiction on the constitutional and political debate is not the same for each of the courts under review, but some effects and functions can, generally, be detected.[1] The presence of a court having the power to review the constitutionality of primary legislation may translate political issues into legal ones, which contributes to pacify the debate, as in the case of abortion laws.

---

[1] The following are drawn from L Favoreu, 'La légitimité du juge constitutionnel', *RIDC*, 1994, 557, at 567ff.

Constitutional jurisdiction may contribute to achieving acceptance of controversial legislation and of political changes, for instance after a change in government.[2] And the prestige of the Constitution and the awareness of and respect for its values are re-enforced by the existence of a constitutional court guarding it. In addition, constitutional case law may promote the respect for and the debate on fundamental rights and values.[3]

The Court of Justice is equally often referred to as a constitutional court for the Community legal order. Under Article 220 EC the Court of Justice shall ensure that in the interpretation and application of this Treaty the law is observed. In its role of highest court of the Community legal order, the Court has gradually revealed itself as akin to a constitutional court, by developing fundamental principles such as direct effect, supremacy, implied powers and the like, by introducing fundamental rights as general principles of Community law and by *behaving* as a constitutional court in interpreting and developing Community law.

13.1. DEFINING THE ACTORS: NATIONAL COURTS HAVING CONSTITUTIONAL JURISDICTION

In national and comparative legal literature on constitutional courts and courts having constitutional jurisdiction,[4] the focus is mainly on the power of judicial review of primary legislation in the light of the Constitution. In essence, constitutional jurisdiction protects the consensus of the Constitution against the majority of the day,[5] thus enforcing the provisions and principles of the Constitution against Parliament. Constitutional courts may also have additional roles and competences, such as controlling the boundaries between the federation and the feder-

---

2   A wellknown example is the case law of the *Conseil constitutionnel* after the *alternance* of 1981, see L Favoreu, 'Le Conseil constitutionnel et l'alternance', *RFSP*, 1984, 1002 or FL Morton, 'Judicial Review in France: A Comparative Analysis', *AJCL*, 1988, 89.

3   On the respect for the Basic Law in Germany and the role of the *Bundesverfassungsgericht*, see J Limbach, 'The Effects of the Jurisdiction of the German Federal Constitutional Court', EVI Distinguished Lectures of the Law Department, 99/5.

4   Alternative methods of upholding the Constitution, other than by courts, are not considered. The role of institutions like the Belgian, Luxembourg or Dutch *Raad van State* or *Conseil d'Etat* in their advisory capacity is also to guard the Constitution against violations, by the primary Legislature, but they can only give advice, and not block legislation which they consider to be unconstitutional. Also left to the side is the Finnish system in which constitutional control is endowed to a parliamentary organ, and in which the public authorities may ask the advice of the Supreme Court. See also C Grewe and H Ruiz, *Droits constitutionnels européens* (Paris, PUF, 1995) at 66–67.

5   The Constitution operates as the norm of reference. This distinguishes constitutional jurisdiction from other forms of scrutiny of primary legislation, such as review in the light of international treaties. In The Netherlands, constitutional review is expressly excluded by the Constitution itself, while primary legislation can be reviewed in the light of international treaties. This way, the majority of the day can judicially be restricted, but not by the Constitution itself.

ated entities in a federal system,[6] or between Parliament and the Executive,[7] acting as an election court[8] or settling conflicts between different state organs. But in any case, the review of the constitutional validity of primary legislation is what they all have in common. Ordinary courts do not have that power: they may pronounce occasionally on constitutional issues, but the scrutiny of the constitutionality of parliamentary legislation is not within their province.

A further distinction can be made between constitutional courts and other courts having constitutional jurisdiction. Constitutional courts are set up as separate courts, outside the ordinary judicial branch or at least not forming part of the ordinary judicial hierarchy, and enjoy a monopoly in judging the constitutionality of primary legislation. As such, a constitutional court is a veritable constitutional power, supervising the legislative, administrative and the judicial branches, in some cases even the constitutional legislature. Courts having constitutional jurisdiction are those courts belonging to the ordinary judicial branch which may decide constitutional issues, and have particular attributes, including most importantly the power to review primary legislation, which the other ordinary courts do not share. Finally, other ordinary courts may also pronounce on constitutional issues, and some have done so on the issue of the relation between European and constitutional law. They are not however covered by the notion of 'courts having constitutional jurisdiction'.

13.1.1. Constitutional Courts

Constitutional courts are those courts of law that have been established with a view to dealing specifically and exclusively with constitutional cases. They are not part of the ordinary judicial organisation, and are independent from it and from the other State organs.[9] To Louis Favoreu, *'une Cour constitutionnelle est une juridiction créée pour connaitre spécialement et exclusivement du contentieux constitutionnel, situé hors de l'appareil juridictionnel ordinaire et indépendante de celui-ci comme des pouvoirs publics. Une Cour suprême ou un Tribunal suprême, ou même le chambre constitutionnelle d'une Cour suprême peuvent être des juridictions constitutionnelles mais*

---

6   So the German *Bundesverfassungsgericht* (see Art. 93(1) of the Basic Law) and the Belgian *Arbitragehof* (Art. 142 of the Constitution).
7   The French *Conseil constitutionnel* patrols the limits of the legislative powers of Parliament *(domaine de la loi)*: Arts. 61, 41 and 37 of the Constitution.
8   For the French *Conseil constitutionnel*, Arts. 58–60 (presidential and national elections, and referendums).
9   L Favoreu, 'La notion de Cour constitutionnelle', in *De la Constitution. Etudes en l'honneur de J-F Aubert*, P Zen-Ruffinen and A Auer, (Basel, Helbing, 1996) 15.

ne sont pas des Cours constitutionnelles'.[10] At a 1981 *colloque* organised at Aix en Provence on constitutional courts and the protection of fundamental rights in Europe, the five constitutional courts studied were the Austrian *Verfassungsgericht*, the German *Bundesverfassungsgericht*, the Italian *Corte costituzionale*, the French *Conseil constitutionnel* and the Spanish *Tribunal constitucional*.[11] Several years later, at the occasion of the Uppsala conference on constitutional review in continental Europe, Favoreu added to the list of 'separate constitutional courts or tribunals', the Portuguese *Tribunal constitucional* and the Belgian *Cour d'arbitrage*, while describing the Greek supreme court as *'les juges habituellement chargés de juger le contentieux constitutionnel'*.[18]

The separate constitutional courts are the German *Bundesverfassungsgericht*, the Italian *Corte costituzionale*, the French *Conseil constitutionnel*,[12] the Spanish *Tribunal constitucional*, the Portuguese *Tribunal constitucional*, the Belgian *Cour d'arbitrage* or *Arbitragehof*, the Austrian *Verfassungsgerichtshof* and the newly established Luxembourg *Cour constitutionnelle*.[13]

13.1.2. Courts Having Constitutional Jurisdiction

In their discussion of judicial review of the constitutionality of primary legislation, Grewe and Fabri[14] follow the functional/organisational distinction made by Cappelletti between the Austrian or European model in which constitutional is endowed to a separate jurisdiction situated outside the ordinary judicial organisation (the 'constitutional courts' of the previous section), and the American model in which constitutional justice and review is integrated in the ordinary judicial organisation and ensured by all courts of law. The latter system exists in Sweden, Denmark, Greece, and recently Finland. The Greek system is particular in the sense that a special supreme court has been created by the 1975 Constitution, in order to settle diverging case law between the ordinary courts. In Denmark, the courts have repeatedly asserted that they are empowered to perform constitutional review, but they have not yet actually decided to repeal a

---

10 L Favoreu, *Les cours constitutionnelles*, 2nd edn, (Paris, PUF, 1992) at 93.
11 L Favoreu (ed), *Cours constitutionnelles européennes et droits fondamentaux* (Paris, Economica, 1982). The Spanish Court was not included in the in depth analysis due to its short existence.
12 There is a still on-going debate in France on whether or not the *Conseil constitutionnel* qualifies as a constitutional court.
13 The Luxemburg constitutional court was established in 1996. Under the new article 95ter of the Luxembourg Constitution the constitutional court decides on the conformity of Acts of Parliament, at the exclusion of Acts by which treaties are assented to. The *Cour constitutionnelle* is seized by way of preliminary references from the ordinary courts; see the *Loi du 27 juillet portant organisation de la Cour constitutionnelle*.
14 C Grewe and H Ruiz Fabri, *Droits constitutionnels européens* (Paris, PUF, 1995) at 66ff.

statute for the reason that it was unconstitutional.[15] Danish courts generally show great judicial restraint when reviewing the constitutionality of acts of Parliament,[16] though this may be changing as a consequence of the incorporation of the European Convention on Human Rights in 1992, the influence of judicial activism in the Court of Justice, the European Court of Human Rights and the German Constitutional Court and an increased focus on the role of the courts as the ultimate protection of the citizens towards an ever growing State.[17] In Sweden, the courts will only interfere in the case of manifest infringements. Recently, the Finnish courts have been empowered to set aside unconstitutional legislation, in the new Finnish Constitution adopted in 2000. The European model was opted for in Austria, Germany, Italy, Spain, France, and Belgium and recently in Luxembourg. In the classification by Grewe and Ruiz Fabri, Ireland and Portugal are among those having a mixed system. In Ireland, constitutional control is entrusted to the ordinary courts, but not to all of them: Only the High Court and the Supreme Court are competent to pronounce themselves on the constitutionality of statutes. Portugal does possess a constitutional *Tribunal*, but this does not exclude the exercise of constitutional review by the ordinary courts. The latter conduct constitutional review in first instance, while in specific cases, the case can be referred to the *Tribunal*.

Separate constitutional courts are not at the top of the ordinary judicial hierarchy. They usually only decide cases containing a constitutional element. Ordinary (supreme) courts which are empowered to control the constitutionality of primary legislation could then be described as 'part–time constitutional courts'.[18] In this book, these courts would then fit both in the first section on ordinary courts and in this section on courts having constitutional jurisdiction, depending on the case at hand, and the issues raised in it.

13.1.3. Ordinary Courts Pronouncing on Constitutional Issues

The foregoing observations should not be understood as implying that ordinary courts, which have no powers of constitutional review of primary legislation, can never pronounce on constitutional issues. Any court

---

[15] H Rasmussen, 'Confrontation or Peaceful Co-existence? On the Danish Supreme Court's Maastricht Ratification Judgment', in D O'Keeffe and A Bavasso (eds), *Judicial Review in European Union Law. Liber Amicorum in Honour of Lord Slynn of Hadley*, Vol I, (The Hague, Kluwer Law International, 2000), 377, at 381.

[16] O Due, 'Danish Preliminary References', in D O'Keeffe and A Bavasso (eds), *Judicial Review in European Union Law. Liber Amicorum in Honour of Lord Slynn of Hadley*, Vol I, (The Hague, Kluwer Law International, 2000), 363, at 368.

[17] So J A Jensen, 'Human Rights in Denmark', 7 *EPL*, 2001, 1, at 9.

[18] L Favoreu, above, at 21.

may be confronted with constitutional issues in some form, and will apply constitutional provisions, conventions and principles. The Netherlands *Hoge Raad*[19] for instance does not have the power of constitutional review of primary legislation,[20] but it too is at times confronted with issues of a constitutional nature, and its decisions may have constitutional implications. Yet, these cases are dealt with in a different form, under the guise of ordinary judicial activity. On the other hand, as was expounded by Favoreu, *'il y a là (..) dans cette allusion au charactère 'politique' des cours constitutionnelles l'intuition de ce que sont les cours constitutionnelles vues comme pouvoir constitutionnel'*.[21] Constitutional courts in the strict sense do not decide cases in the same way as ordinary courts. Whatever their competences, the way in which they can be seized, and even if they can be seized directly by individual citizens, they are not there to decide individual cases as such.. Every case decided by a constitutional court has much wider ramifications on the legal and political order, beyond the limits of the specific case.[22]

The Netherlands and the United Kingdom do not have a constitutional court or courts having jurisdiction to review the constitutionality of statutes and to invalidate them. In the Netherlands none of the highest courts have pronounced themselves on the constitutional issues of Dutch membership to the European Union or have offered a coherent doctrine of the relationship between national constitutional and European law in general or on issues of fundamental rights, *Kompetenz Kompetenz*, democracy and the like. In the United Kingdom on the other hand, it is the courts and especially, though not exclusively, the House of Lords which has taken the lead in conceptualising the repercussions of British membership on issues of national law. The recognition of the power to set aside parliamentary legislation in *Factortame* and to issue a declaration of incompatibility in the *Equal Opportunities Commission* case may well have contributed to the introduction of similar powers in the context of the Human Rights Act. However, at least for the time being, the competences under the Human Rights Act are more restrictive than those which have been derived from the European Communities Act 1972.[23] While it is now established that *all* courts have jurisdiction to disapply conflicting Acts of Parliament for breach of Community law, under the Human Rights Act *all*

---

[19] The same goes for any lower court, but, given their place in the judicial hierarchy, the pronouncements of the highest courts on constitutional issues are much more influential.

[20] There is an ongoing debate in The Netherlands on the introduction of constitutional review.

[21] L Favoreu, 'La notion de Cour constitutionnelle', in P Zen-Ruffmen and A Auer (eds), *De la Constitution. Etudes en l'honneur de J-F Aubert* (Basel, Helbing, 1996) 15, at 19.

[22] L Favoreu, above, at 20.

[23] On the Human Rights Act, see *in lieu* of many others Lord Lester of Herne Hill, 'Human Rights and the British Constitution', in J Jowell and D Oliver (eds), *The Changing Constitution* (Oxford, OUP, 2000) 89.

courts have a duty of consistent interpretation, but no jurisdiction to set aside or disapply is granted and only specified higher courts[24] may issue a declaration of incompatibility under Section 4 of the Human Rights Act, which is thus less intrusive in the principle of parliamentary sovereignty. A declaration is not binding on the parties involved; it acts as trigger for amending legislation by means of a remedial order. Devolution also has its effects on the principle. Under the Scotland Act, devolution issues arising when the Scottish Parliament has issued an Act that is claimed to exceed its competences, are to be decided by the superior courts, and ultimately by the Judicial Committee of the Privy Council.[25] Acts of the Scottish Parliament are accordingly not sovereign in the same way, and may be set aside by the courts if they exceed legislative competence.[26]

But even in Member States where there is a constitutional court, other highest courts have participated in the debate on constitutional issues of membership. Notable examples are the French *Conseil d'État*, which has decided the issue of the relationship between the Constitution and Treaty law in favour of precedence for the latter and the Belgian *Conseil d'État*, which accorded precedence to treaties over the Constitution. Some of these courts will therefore from time to time be incorporated in the discussion.

13.1.4. Self-Perception of Constitutional Courts and Courts Having Constitutional Jurisdiction

All of the courts just mentioned have different functions, competences and prestige, so that any generalisation is precarious. Yet, they have a few fundamental characteristics in common. All of them review the constitutionality of primary legislation, in order to make sure that the majority of the day does not impair the terms of the Constitution. All perceive themselves as the ultimate guardians of the Constitution, both against internal and external challenges.

Members of constitutional courts gather occasionally to discuss issues of common concern. These meetings were formalised in the *Conférence des Cours constitutionnelles européennes*, established in 1972 by the constitutional courts of Austria, Germany, Italy, Switzerland and Yugoslavia. Several constitutional courts joined later, including the Portuguese, Spanish and French in 1987 and the Belgian in 1990.[27] But other courts

---

24 The House of Lords; the Judicial Committee of the Privy Council; the Courts-Martial Appeal Court; in Scotland, the High Court of Justiciary sitting otherwise than as a trial court, or the Court of Session; in England and Wales or Northern Ireland, The High Court or the Court of Appeal, see Section 4(5) of the Human Rights Act.

25 Schedule 6, Parts II–V of the Scotland Act 1998.

26 AW Bradley, 'The Sovereignty of parliament – Form or Substance?', in J Jowell and D Oliver (eds), *The Changing Constitution* (Oxford, OUP, 2000) 23, at 49.

27 In addition to the Turkish (1987) and Hungarian (1991) constitutional courts.

have also been invited to the meetings in this framework. The Paris Conference of 1993 was attended also by representatives from *'cours européennes ayant compétence en matière constitutionnelle'*, among which representatives from Ireland and Luxemburg.[28] In addition, several supreme courts were invited as 'observers': the Belgian *Cour de cassation*, the Danish and Swedish Supreme courts,[29] the *Cour supérieure de Justice de Luxembourg*, and the Netherlands *Hoge Raad*. Finally, the European Court of Justice and the European Commission for the Protection for Fundamental Rights also attended.

Other meetings have been held outside the framework of the *Conférence*. At the 'International Seminar' held in Rome in 1995 concerning the relation between European Community law and national law,[30] participation was limited to 'real' constitutional courts, excluding courts which may sometimes decide constitutional issues, such as the Irish and Danish courts.[31] The French *Conseil constitutionnel* in turn organised a conference on constitutional review of secondary Community law in 1997.[32] Present were delegations from 'courts having constitutional jurisdiction' from all 15 Member States, and from the Court of Justice. It included also the Netherlands *Hoge Raad* and *Raad van State*, two of the highest courts, which do not however have jurisdiction to review the constitutionality of primary legislation. Obviously, the constitutional texts are relevant to these courts. They apply them, and use them as a standard for revision of secondary legislation, individual decisions and so on. But, in contrast to other 'constitutional courts or courts having constitutional jurisdiction' attending, these Dutch courts do not enforce the Constitution against Parliament. The same goes for the English courts, including the House of Lords which, given the unique character of the British Constitution, contributes in forming the Constitution: the principle of parliamentary

---

[28] And from Bosnia Herzegovina, Bulgaria, Cyprus, Croatia, Liechtenstein, Lithuania, Norway, Romania, Russia, Slovakia and Slovenia.

[29] In addition to those from Hungary and the Czeck Republic.

[30] The proceedings have been published in *Diritto comunitario europeo e diritto nazionale*, Atti del seminario internazionale, Roma 1995 (Milan, Giuffrè, 1997).

[31] The conference convened Presidents and Members of the constitutional and supreme courts of the Member States of the EU, of several Central and Eastern European countries, from the US and from several Latin American countries. Of the Member States of the Union attended the Italian *Corte costituzionale*, the German *Bundesverfassungsgericht*, the Belgian *Cour d'arbitrage*, the Spanish *Tribunal Constitucional*, the Austrian *Verfassungsgerichtshof* and the Portuguese *Tribunal Constitucional*. The president of the French *Conseil constitutionnel* was invited but did not attend due to the celebrations surrounding the *fête nationale*. Both Italian Advocates General of the ECJ also attended. In addition, there were representatives from constitutional or supreme courts from Argentina, Brazil, Canada, Czech Republic, Cyprus, the Central American Court of Justice, Costa Rica, Croatia, Poland, Romania, the Russian Federation, Slovakia, Slovenia, the United States, Switzerland and Hungary.

[32] The *Conseil constitutionnel* has made several reports available on its website, www.conseil-constitutionnel.fr.

sovereignty is, after all, a common law principle. Nevertheless, the House of Lords would not perceive of itself as a court having constitutional jurisdiction even today, since it lacks certain attributes, especially, the power of review of Acts of Parliament.

What is decisive, ultimately, is the competence to rule on the constitutionality of primary legislation, and the existence of certain tools or attributes to censure infringements of the Constitution by the direct representation of the majority of the people, represented in Parliament.

13.1.5. Delimitation of the Research Field

Decisive elements are the respective court's mission, its role and function, and its attributes, powers and competences *vis-à-vis* the other State organs, in particular the Parliament and sometimes also those responsible for a revision of the Constitution. This Theme focuses on the German *Bundesverfassungsgericht*, the Italian *Corte costituzionale*, the Belgian *Arbitragehof* and the French *Conseil constitutionnel*. The Spanish *Tribunal constitucional* and the Austrian *Verfassungsgerichthof* will be considered from time to time. The case law of the Irish *High Court* and *Supreme Court*, and of the Danish *Højesteret* will also be discussed. The Portuguese and the Luxembourg constitutional courts are left out, as are the Greek, Swedish and Finnish courts.

13.2. THE EUROPEAN COURT OF JUSTICE AS A RIVAL CONSTITUTIONAL COURT

It is a precarious venture to pigeonhole the Court of Justice along classical lines and in existing categories of national and international law. The Court combines features of an international jurisdiction, with those of national constitutional and administrative courts. The easy way out is to characterise the Court as *hybrid* or *atypical*, as the Community legal order is often described as *sui generis*. The Court of Justice unmistakably has features of an *international* court: it was established by an international treaty; the enforcement procedure of Article 231 EC is a typical international procedure brought by one State against another.[33] The fact that the Commission may bring similar procedures under article 230 EC is more uncommon, but not entirely unheard of,[34] and the outcome remains the same, declaratory, judgment. The Member States, before the Court, continue to be considered single and unitary entities and the Court cannot

---

[33] Of course, the procedure has hardly ever been used; but it shows that the Court was meant to be inter alia an international court settling disputes between Member States.

[34] So for instance the procedure brought by the former European Commission for the Protection of Human Rights in Strasbourg (under the old rules).

directly interfere in national law: It cannot itself invalidate or annul national law; it can merely declare that a State has breached its obligations under the Treaty and it is then up to the State and the national institutions to remedy the breach. Also in other procedures, even the preliminary rulings procedure in which the Court's co-operation is requested in the course of litigation before a national court, the Court is not able to become involved directly in national law: It is dependent on the co-operation of national authorities, and the national courts.

Yet, the international dimension of the Court is often ignored, and eclipsed by its dimension as constitutional court. There is a wide measure of agreement these days that the European Court of Justice has the role of a constitutional court.[35] In the popular view the process of transformation of the Court of Justice into a court akin to a federal constitutional court, complements the constitutionalisation of the Treaties, put in motion by the Court itself. Along with the transformation and constitutionalisation of the Treaties the Court is said to have developed into more than an international court,[36] more than an administrative court[37] and to have transformed into a constitutional-type court. In its *Report of the Court of Justice on certain aspects of the application of the Treaty on European Union* of May 1995 the European Court itself put it this way: '*the Court thus carries out tasks which, in the legal systems of the Member States are those of the* constitutional *courts, the courts of general jurisdiction or the administrative tribunals as the case may be*'.[38]

---

[35] See for instance. A Dashwood and A Johnston, 'Synthesis of the Debate', in A Dashwood and A Johnston (eds), *The Future of the Judicial System of the European Union* (Oxford, Hart Publishing, 2001) 55, at 59.

[36] So R Dehousse, *The European Court of Justice* (New York, St Martin's Press, 1998) at 16ff, 'From international to constitutional justice'; the author underscores the 'hybrid' nature of the ECJ's tasks, some of which are similar to those of international jurisdictions, others resemble those of constitutional courts, and a third role is similar to that of administrative courts at a national level. See also M Shapiro, 'The European Court of Justice', in P Craig and G de Búrca (eds), *The Evolution of EU Law* (Oxford, OUP, 1999) 321, at 330, who stresses however that the story is more complicated that that of an international court transforming itself into a constitutional court. After all, the Treaty writers explicitly gave the Court judicial review powers to enforce the Treaty, thus bringing it into the category of judicial review courts. It was to be expected that the Court would consider the treaties supreme over conflicting acts of the Member States. Shapiro sees as 'the Court's great bootstrapping operation' the case law on direct effect and supremacy which exists in federal constitutional states, rather than in international organisations operating under international law.

[37] A O'Neill, *Decisions of the European Court of Justice and their Constitutional Implications* (London, Butterworths, 1994) at 8: 'The history of the European Court of Justice shows a development of the role of the Court from being a purely administrative court modelled on the French Conseil d'État into a Constitutional court, apparently inspired by the activism of the American Supreme Court. This development is not one which was specifically envisaged in the Treaties, but it has instead resulted from the Court's repeated claims about its own role in promoting 'an ever closer union of the peoples of Europe and ensuring that 'in the interpretation and application of the Treaty the law is observed'.

[38] Report of the Court of Justice on certain Aspects of the Application of the Treaty on European Union, May 1995.

The characterisation of the European Court as a constitutional court has an immediate complicating effect on the dialogue with national constitutional courts and may have its impact on their acceptance of the Court's case law.[39] As nicely put by Joseph Weiler, the national challenges to the case law of the Court of Justice are a paradoxical sign of an acknowledgement by national courts of the constitutional nature of the Court's posture: it is easier to deal with the doctrinal elements of constitutionalism if they can be pigeonholed as international law. A constitutional-constitutional dialogue has inbuilt conflictual elements.[40]

In this section it will first be analysed *how* the Court of Justice became a constitutional court. Subsequently, a few observations will be made on the orthodox view of the Court as a constitutional court.

13.2.1. Positioning of the Court of Justice as a Constitutional Court

While it is the national constitutional courts' mission to guarantee respect for the Constitution, the Court of Justice has a mandate under the Treaty to preserve the integrity of the Treaty and of Community law.[41] The Court is often labelled a constitutional court, and the Court itself perceives part of its tasks as 'those which, in the legal systems of the Member States, are those of the constitutional courts'. In its Report on Certain Aspects of the Application of the Treaty on European Union drafted in preparation for the 1996 Intergovernmental Conference preparing the Treaty of Amsterdam, the Court stated:

> In its constitutional role, the Court rules on the respective powers of the Communities and of the Member States, on those of the Communities in relation to other forms of co-operation in the framework of the Union and, generally, determines the scope of the provisions of the Treaties whose observance it is its duty to ensure. It ensures that the delimitation of powers between the institutions is safeguarded, thereby helping to maintain the institutional balance. It examines whether fundamental rights have been observed by the institutions, and by the Member States when their actions fall within the scope of Community law. It rules on the relationship between Community law and national law and on the reciprocal obligations between the Member States and the Community institutions. Finally, it

---

[39] In the early days, when it was not yet common to speak of the Treaties in constitutional terms, the *Bundesverfassungsgericht* had no problem holding that 'The EEC Treaty to a certain extent constitutes the Constitution of the Community', in *Bundesverfassungsgericht*, decision of 18 October 1967, *EEC Regulations constitutionality case*, 22 BverfGE 293, English version in Oppenheimer, *The Cases*, 410, at 413. This constitutional language has not been used by the same court in later times.

[40] JHH Weiler, 'The European Court of Justice: Beyond "Beyond Doctrine" or the Legitimacy Crisis of European Constitutionalism', in *The European Court and National Courts. Doctrine and Jurisprudence* (Oxford, Hart Publishing, 1998) 365, at 368.

[41] 'The Court of Justice shall ensure that in the interpretation and application of this Treaty the law is observed', Art. 220 EC (old Art. 164 of the EC Treaty).

may be called upon to judge whether international commitments envisaged by the Communities are compatible with the Treaties.

But it is mostly in legal writing about the Court and its case law that the idea of the Court as a constitutional court has developed,[42] not least in the writings of members of the Court themselves.[43] The transformation of the Court of Justice into a constitutional court goes hand in hand with the constitutionalisation of Europe.

13.2.1.1. The Making of a Constitution for Europe[44]

There is nowadays a wide array of scholarly writing taking recourse to constitutional language to describe the Union and Communities. This

[42] For instance J Rinze, 'The Role of the European Court of Justice as a Federal Constitutional Court', *PL*, 1993, 426; R Dehousse, *La Cour de justice des Communautés européennes*, (Paris, Montchrestien, 1994); also published in English, R Dehousse, *The European Court of Justice*, (New York, St Martin's Press, 1998); M Poiares Maduro, *We, The Court. The European Court of Justice and the European Economic Constitution*, (Oxford, Hart Publishing, 1998).

[43] Many members of the Court of Justice have contributed to divulging the message. See amongst many others, P Pescatore, 'La Cour en tant que juridiction fédérale et constitutionnelle', in *Zehn Jahre Rechtsprechuhg des EuGH*, Kölner Schriften zum Europarecht, Band 1, 1965, 520; AM Donner, 'The Constitutional Powers of the Court of Justice of the European Communities', *CML Rev*, 1974, 127; AM Donner, 'The Court of Justice as a Constitutional Court of the Communities', in *Tussen het echte en het gemaakte*, 1986, 343; GF Mancini, 'The Making of a Constitution for Europe', *CML Rev*, 1989, 595; J Mischo, 'Un rôle nouveau pour la Cour de justice?', *RMC*, 1990, 681; GF Mancini and DT Keeling, 'From CILFIT to ERT: the Constitutional Challenge facing the European Court', 11 *YBEL*, 1991, 1, reprinted in CF Mancini, *Democracy and Constitutionalism in the European Union. Collected Essays*, (Oxford, Hart Publishing, 2000), 17; F Jacobs, 'Is the Court of Justice of the European Communities a Constitutional Court?', in D Curtin and D O'Keeffe (eds), *Constitutional Adjudication in the European Community and National law, Essays for the Hon Mr Justice TF O'Higgins*, (Dublin, Butterworth Ltd 1992) 25; O Due, 'A Constitutional Court for the European Communities', above, 2; GC Rodriguez Iglesias, 'Der Gerichtshof der Europäischen Gemeinschaften als Verfassungsgericht', *EuR*, 1992, 225; G Slynn of Hadley, 'What is a European Community Judge', 52 *CLJ*, 1993, 234; M Zuleeg, 'Die Verfassung der Europäischen Gemeinschaft in der Rechtsprechung des EuGH, *Betriebs-Berater*, 1994, 581; W van Gerven, 'Toward a Coherent Constitutional System within the European Union', *EPL*, 1996, 81; FG Jacobs, 'The Community Legal Order—A Constitutional Order? A Perspective from the European Court of Justice', in J-D Mouton and Th Stein (eds), *Towards a New Constitution for the European Uhion? The Intergovernmental Conference 1996* (Köln, 1997) 31.

[44] Beside the contributions mentioned above, publications include E Stein, 'Lawyers, Judges and the Making of a Transnational Constitution', *Am J Int L*, 1981, 1; JHH Weiler, 'The Transformation of Europe, *Yale LJ*, 1991, 2403; J Temple Lang, 'The Development of European Community Constitutional Law', *The International Lawyer*, 1991, 455; the constitutionalization of Community law is also discussed in the broader analysis by J Gerkrath, *L'émergence d'un droit constitutionnel pour l'Europe* (Brussels, Editions de I'Université de Bruxelles, 1997). Snyder's 'Constitutional Law of the European Union' takes a different approach, applying constitutional language to the EU rather than focussing on the EC as most authors do, see F Snyder, 'Constitutional Law of the European Union', *Collected Courses of the Academy of European Law 1995*, Vol VI-1 (The Hague, Kluwer, 1998) 41; see also and J-C Piris, 'L' Union européenne a-t-elle une constitution? Lui en faut-il une?', *RTDeur*, 1999, 599.

constitutional narrative deals with a variety of related issues, all of which touch upon topics labelled 'constitutional'. The notion of 'European constitutional law' is a chameleon concept,[45] which changes its skin, body and even its existence, according to the perspective and the politics or beliefs of the observer. Moreover, there seems to be a linguistic and national preconditioning in the tendency to describe the Community legal system and its development in constitutional terms. As Jacqué has indicated, the concept of constitutionalisation *'est d'origine anglo-saxonne'*,[46] but it has been embraced by others, possibly mostly by German scholarship.[47]

Most often the notion of *constitutionalisation* of European law is used to denote the process of the transformation of the Treaties into a charter of a constitutional nature governed by a form of constitutional law rather than by the tenets of classic international law. The constitutional language then reaches far beyond the idea that the Treaties form the constitutional charter of an international organisation, in the sense that, say, the UN Charter constitutes the constituent document of the UN. The European Constitution not only deals with the European level of the European construct as the Community's *internal* Constitution,[48] but also with the relationship between the European level and the Member States, and with the effects of Community law within the constitutional order of the Member States. The making of a Constitution for Europe includes, amongst other things, the emergence of European law as a constitutionally superior law with immediate effects within the legal space of the Community, and therefore also doctrines as direct effect, supremacy and the protection of fundamental rights.[49]

More recently, the discussion has changed: the drafting of the Constitution for Europe has become the talk of the day. It has become *bon ton*. But where the notion of 'Constitution' used to be common to Community lawyers and denote an integration friendly attitude, it is now often used with the opposite reflex to protect State sovereignty and establish legally enforceable limits to European integration. The discussion on the drafting of that European Constitution will be discussed in Part 3.

---

[45] See F Snyder, 'Constitutional law of the European Union', *in Collected Courses of the Academy of European Law*, Vol IV-I, (The Hague, Kluwer International Law, 1998) 41, at 47. While most commentators use constitutional language only in the domain of Community law, Snyder is concerned with EU constitutional law.

[46] J-P Jacqué, 'Cours général de droit communautaire', *Collected Courses of the Academy of European Law*, Vol I, Book I, 1992, 49, at 265.

[47] See A von Bogdandy, 'A Bird's Eye View on the Science of European Law: Structures, Debates and Development Prospects of Basic Research on the Law of the European Union in a German Perspective', *ELJ*, 2000, 208.

[48] Relating to, for instance, the relationship between the European institutions or the protection of fundamental rights against abuse from the European institutions.

[49] JHH Weiler, *The Constitution of Europe* (Cambridge, CUP, 1999) at 4, and more elaborate in his 'The Transformation of Europe', *Yale LJ*, 1991, 100, also in *The Constitution of Europe*, 10.

13.2.1.2. Constitutional Language in Legal Writing[50]

The initial view of constitutionalisation in Community law stems from the distinction between treaty and constitution, between international organisation regimes and constitutional federal systems.[51] These authors stress the fact that the Court of Justice has taken recourse to methods of interpretation which resemble those of a constitutional court, rather than of an international court. Other elements of the constitutionalisation process are the development of legal principles such as direct effect, supremacy and the protection of fundamental rights. The result is that the Community resembles more a federal type constitutional construct than an international organisation.

This element of constitutionalisation is not limited to the Treaty alone. If the term constitutionalisation is appropriate in this sense, it is better to speak of constitutionalisation of Community law or the Community legal order than of the Treaty alone. All of the elements brought forward to describe the process of constitutionalisation relate to the whole of Community law, and not only the Treaty, even though within the body of Community law the Treaty serves as the basic norm, or in kelsinian parlance, as the highest norm in the pyramid.

Constitutionalisation, in a formal and positivist sense, means that the founding Treaties, like a veritable Constitution, have been placed at the top of the legal hierarchy. Like national Constitutions, they serve as the highest norm and define the conditions for the exercise of political power. Community constitutional law, in this sense, is the internal constitution of the Community legal order at the Community level: it contains rules on the division of powers between the Community institutions, the decision making processes, the principles governing the relations between the institutions and so on. But from the point of view of Community law, the Treaty is also the highest norm of the entire polity which includes the national legal systems in so far as they come within the scope of Community law. Also the Member States and their organs are subject to

---

[50] For a detailed analysis of the notion of 'European constitutional law' see J Gerkrath, *L'émergence d'un droit constitutionnel pour l'Europe*, (Brussels, Editions de l'Université de Bruxelles, 1997), 27–143; for a brief introduction see P Craig, 'Constitutions, Constitutionalism and the European Union', *ELJ*, 2001, 125, at 126–28.

[51] JHH Weiler defines the 'constitutionalism thesis' as claiming 'that in critical aspects the Community has evolved and behaves as if its founding instrument were not a treaty governed by international law but, to use the language of the European Court of Justice, a constitutional charter governed by a form of constitutional law. Constitutionalism, more than anything else, differentiates the Community from other transnational systems and, within the Union, from the other "pillars"', in 'The Reformation of European Constitutionalism', *JCMS*, 1997, 97, at 97–98; in this sense also E Stein, 'Lawyers, Judges, and the Making of a Transnational Constitution', *AJIL*, 1981, 1; GF Mancini, 'The Making of a Constitution for Europe', *CML Rev*, 1989, 595; JHH Weiler, 'The Transformation of Europe', *Yale LJ*, 1991, 2403.

the Treaties, just as the Community institutions. They too are bound by the highest norm of the polity, the founding Treaties. Yet, if European constitutional law is limited to this, is the constitutionalisation of the Treaties anything other than a re-statement, in constitutional terms, of the principle that *pacta sunt servanda*? It would appear that constitutionalisation is more. It means that, even *within* the national legal orders of the Member States, the Treaties and Community law in its entirely are to be applied by all the organs of the State with precedence over national law. The national courts are under a European constitutional obligation to enforce Community law against the other organs of the State, notwithstanding the national Constitutions. The constitutionalisation of the Treaties is accordingly often identified with unconditional supremacy, the positioning of the Treaties as the highest norm of the Community polity, over and above the national Constitutions.

The notion of *European constitutional law*, then, is used with various meanings. First, and adopting a broad perspective and fusing different layers, national and supra- or international, the notion may be used to denote the fertilisation and cross-fertilisation of principles of a constitutional nature in Europe and the emergence and development of a common constitutional tradition. It then focuses on the common constitutional principles that exist or develop through the working of the Council of Europe, the EU/EC and the relations between their Member States. It describes the process of the infusion of constitutional values and principles into constitutional documents, or in the case law of (constitutional) courts. 'The European Constitution' or 'European constitutional law' then contains not only the principles common to the European States, which move back and forth from one system to the other, but also the principles deriving from common membership of international organisations. It contains the ECHR and the practice and case law of the Strasbourg organs, the case law of the Community organs and the principles deriving from national constitutions.

Even leaving aside the Council of Europe and its legal heritage, and remaining within the framework of the European Union and Communities, the notion has varying meanings. National constitutional law, whether purely national or related to European law is often entirely excluded. The focus then is on the European level and no account is taken of the other, national, side of the coin. 'European constitutional law' would then mainly concentrate on institutional law (composition and organisation of the institutions, competences, decision making procedures and the like). The protection of fundamental rights against abuse by the European institutions is often included, as are issues as direct effect, supremacy and fundamental rights protection against the Member States in the scope of Community law. These issues are concerned with the relationship between European and national law, but only from a Community law angle. While a complete picture of this mutual relationship can only be acquired by looking at both perspectives, the European and national perspectives, a discussion of this aspect is often limited to the one, European, perspective, thus omitting part of the reality.

Conversely, the notion of *European constitutional law* is sometimes, primarily in French doctrine,[52] used to indicate those principles and provisions of *national* constitutional law which concern European law, transfer of powers arrangements, rules on effectiveness and hierarchy of norms and so on. Again, this is too narrow a perspective to grasp the reality. Constitutionalism then is a consequence only of the fact that international law is recognised by the national Constitution and given its place in the national constitutional legal order.

The notion *European constitutional law* may also be used to describe the image of a co–existence of Constitutions, the existence of two, or rather 16 Constitutions, side by side, which 'constitute' the legal order(s) in the European area. When considering 'the European Constitution', the national Constitutions cannot simply be left out. Whatever the nature of the Treaties and the legal order they establish, they do not make *tabula rasa* of the national Constitutions, which continue to be critical not only in those areas which have not been transferred to the European institutions, but also within the scope of the Community and the Union. Ingolf Pernice names this presentation of European integration as a dynamic process of constitution-making instead of a sequence of international treaties establishing an organisation of international co-operation *multilevel constitutionalism*.[53] According to this strand the European Union already has a multilevel Constitution, made up of the Constitutions of the Member States bound together by a complementary constitutional body consisting of the European Treaties, a *Verfassungsverbund*.[54] Others too have used the idea of complementary constitutions, or of a multi-layered Constitution. It presupposes cutting the umbilical cord connecting the Constitution and

---

[52] It forms, then, part of 'le droit constitutionnel international' which denotes 'les dispositions consacrées aux relations internationales et au droit international par les Constitutions', see J Rideau, 'Constitution et droit international dans les Etats membres des Communautés européennes. Réflexions générales et situation française', *RFDC*, 1990, 259; the term was proposed by L Favoreu at the 1988 Colloque sur l'Ecriture de la Constitution, see L Favoreu, 'Le contrôle de la constitutionnalité du Traité de Maastricht et le développement du "droit constitutionnel international"', 92 *RGDIP*, 1993, 39.

[53] I Pernice, 'Multilevel Constitutionalism and the Treaty of Amsterdam: European Constitution-making Revisited?', 36 *CML Rev*, 1999, 703; I Pernice, 'De la constitution composée de l'Europe', *RTD Eur*, 2000, 623. This conception is related to the idea of constitutional pluralism put forward by Neil Walker, 'The Idea of Constitutional Pluralism', *MLR*, 2002, 317.

[54] I Pernice, 'Multilevel Constitutionalism and the Treaty of Amsterdam: European Constitution-making Revisited?', 36 *CML Rev*, 1999, 703, at 707.

the Nation-State[55] and it requires taking a step back from the realm of the national or European legal order[56] in order to obtain a broad view of the entire constitutional landscape.

And then, all of a sudden,[57] constitutional language sprang up in political circles and is now very much *en vogue*.[58] Nevertheless, it is not the same as the one which had become common among EC lawyers. Indeed, the talk of the day is the drafting and adopting of a constitutional document. In other words, the Constitution is not yet in place; it does not yet exist: it is constitution-making 'in its true sense'. The European Parliament had already made efforts to draft a Constitution for the European Union, but those were, after having been adopted by a vast majority in the European Parliament, disposed of easily and quickly forgotten.[59] This time, '*there is a political and intellectual stampede to embrace the idea of a constitution for Europe*'.[60] The debate was initiated in the speech made by Joshka Fisher in May 2000 at the Berlin Humboldt University,[61] and followed by speeches of Chirac, Ciampi and others. Following a declaration on the future of the Union, adopted at the occasion of the adoption of the Treaty of Nice in December of the same year, [62] the European Council adopted the so-called Laeken Declaration, in which the fundamental constitutional questions facing the Union were set out and which stated, under the heading '*Towards a Constitution for European Citizens*' that '*The question ultimately arises as to whether this simplification and reorganisation might not lead in the long run to the adoption of a constitutional text in the Union. What might the basic features of such a constitution be? The values which the Union cherishes, the fundamental rights and obligations of its citizens, the relationship between Member States in the Union?*' The European Council

---

[55]   See eg B de Witte, 'The Closest Thing to a Constitutional Conversation in Europe: The Semi-Permanent Treaty Revision Process', in P Beaumont, C Lyons and N Walker (eds), *Convergence and Divergence in European Public Law* (Oxford, Hart Publishing, 2002), 39; J Gerkrath, *L'émergence d'un droit constitutionnel pour l'Europe*, (Brussels, Editions de l'Université de Bruxelles, 1997), at 117: 'L'édifice constitutionnel européen se construit en effet simultanément au niveau européen et au niveau national'.

[56]   Even the 'European' legal order is multi-layered, consisting of different forms of cooperation in one organisation, each having their own intensity of constitutionalism.

[57]   'All of a sudden' is a bit of an overstatement. The debate was prepared for instance by the Convention on the Charter of Fundamental Rights, in various statements of European institutions, in legal writing etc, see A Verhoeven, *The European Union in Search of a Democratic and Constitutional Theory* (The Hague, Kluwer, 2002) at 75 *et seq*.

[58]   A Verhoeven, *The European Union in Search of a Democratic and Constitutional Theory*, (The Hague, Kluwer Law International, 2002), at 75.

[59]   Draft Treaty on European Union, approved on 14 February 1984, [1984] OJ C 77/33; Draft Constitution, adopted on 10 February 1994, [1994] OJ C 61/156.

[60]   JHH Weiler, 'A Constitution for Europe? Some Hard Choices', 40 *JCMS*, 2002, 563, at 563.

[61]   J Fischer, 'From Confederacy to Federation. Thoughts on the finality of European integration', 12 May 2000, Humboldt Universität, Berlin.

[62]   Declaration on the Future of Europe, included in the Final Act of the Conference that adopted the Treaty of Nice on 11 December 2000,

convened a Convention to consider the key issues and to try to identify the various possible responses.[63]

This meaning of the term constitutionalisation is entirely different from those listed before, and relates to the adoption of a constitutional document, treaty or constitution. It is distinct from the process of constitutionalisation led by the Court of Justice. It will therefore not be further pursued in this Part, and instead be dealt with in Part 3.

13.2.1.3. *Constitutional Rhetoric of the Court of Justice*

If today one can speak of a European Constitution or a European constitutional charter,[64] it is largely attributable to the case law of the Court of Justice which has, by virtue of methods and techniques familiar to constitutional courts, transformed the Treaty into a document resembling a Constitution with superior force rather than an ordinary international convention. The Court of Justice has judicially adopted the language of constitutionalism first in 1977, with regard to the Community's 'internal constitution'.[65] Its most famous assertions of the constitutional character of the Treaties are its judgments in *Les Verts* and *Opinion 1/91 on the EEA Agreement*. All in all, the Court has only on a few occasions qualified the Treaties as a constitutional charter. There have been many more cases, of a constitutional nature, in which the Court has omitted to use the same constitutional language, even if its Advocates General did use constitutional rhetoric in their Opinion.[66]

---

[63] See www.europa.eu.int/futurum.

[64] The notion is here used to refer to the existing constitutional charter and not to the Treaty establishing a Constitution for Europe signed in November 2004.

[65] *Opinion 1/76 Laying-up Fund* [1977] ECR 741, para 12: 'Thus it appears that the Statute (..) constitutes (..) a change in the internal Constitution of the Community by the alteration of essential elements of the Community structure as regards both the prerogatives of the institutions and the position of the Member States vis-à-vis one another'.

[66] See for instance Opinion of AG Lenz in Joined cases 31 and 35/86 *Levantina Agricola Industrial SA (LAISA) and CPC Espana SA v Council of the EC* [1988] ECR 2285 (conditions of accession can only be amended in the ponderous procedure for revising the Treaties, that is to say, the basic constitutional charter of the Community, *ie* unanimously and with the approval of the national parliaments.); Opinion of AG Darmon in Case 302/87 *European Parliament v Council of the EC (Comitology)* [1988] ECR 5615 (reference *to Les Verts* to argue in favour of *légitimation active* of the European Parliament along the Same lines as in *Les Verts*; Opinion of AG Darmon in Joined cases 193 and 194/87 *Maurissen and EPSU v Court of Auditors of the EC* [1989] ECR 1045 (*légitimation passive* of the Court of Auditors); Opinion of AG van Gerven in Case C–70/88 *European Parliament v Council of the EC (Chernobyl)* [1990] ECR I–2041 (*légitimation active* of the EP); Opinion of AG Jacobs in Joined cases C–181/91 and C–248/91 *European Parliament v Council of the EC and Commission* of the EC [1993] ECR I–3685 (whether a decision presented as a decision of the Member States meeting in Council can be challenged under art. 173 *(old)* of the Treaty. The AG referred to the ECJ's statement in *Les Verts* and argued that `this fundamental principle would be violated if it were to be accepted that an act is not susceptible to judicial review solely on the basis that it has been characterised as an act of the Member States meeting in Council').

Les Verts,[67] in fact related to the internal Constitution of the Communities, focusing on the rights and obligations of the European Parliament, its legal status and right of standing before the European Court. The case dealt with the issue of *légitimation passive* of the European Parliament under Article 230 EC (then Article 173), that is, of its *locus standi* before the Court of Justice as a defendant. Until the amendments to Article 230 with the Treaty of Maastricht, the provision did not mention the European Parliament, either as an applicant or as a defendant. But the Court drew on the Rule of Law, which in the European context applies to all Community institutions which make decisions producing legal effects and to the Member States, thereby expanding the reach of the principle beyond the issues of the case at hand. According to the Court '*it must first be emphasised in this regard that the European Economic Community is a Community based on the rule of law, in as much as neither its Member States nor its institutions can avoid a review of the question whether the measures adopted by them are in conformity with the basic constitutional charter, the Treaty*'. The notion was thus used in relation to the principle of the Rule of Law, which the Court saw as being intimately linked with judicial review. Both the Member States and the Community institutions are bound by the Treaty, and in a Community based on the principle of the rule of law, judicial review must be available. The Treaty has, according to the Court, established in its Articles 230, 241 and 234 EC a complete system of legal remedies and procedures designed to permit it to review the legality of Community measures. The use of the constitutional language by the Court of Justice was rather limited. The Court was dealing with another aspect of European constitutionalism than the one that is mostly stressed in legal writings: It related to inter-institutional relations rather than the relationship between the Community and the Member States.

While several Advocates General did take recourse to the notion in the years following *Les Verts*, the Court would use it again only in 1990, in the case of *Zwartveld*.[68] *Zwartveld* is an unusual case, which was referred to the Court not by a veritable national court, but a Dutch court–like organ, the *rechter-commissaris*. The latter was hearing proceedings on an alleged infringement of Community rules in the course of which he sought to obtain certain documents from the Commission, which refused to produce them. Thereupon, the *rechter-commissaris* submitted to the Court a request for judicial co–operation that could not – owing to his function, and the content of the request – be fitted within the preliminary rulings procedure of Article 234 EC. In assessing the objection of inadmissibility, the Court first recalled its statement in *Costa v ENEL* that the EEC Treaty has created its own legal system, which has become an integral part of the

---

[67]   Case 294/83 *Les Verts* [1986] ECR 1339.
[68]   Case C–2/88 Imm. *Zwartveld* [1990] ECR I–3365.

legal systems of the Member States. It then repeated the statement in *Les Verts* that the Community is a Community based on the rule of law in as much as neither its Member States nor its institutions can avoid a review of whether measures adopted by them are in conformity with the basic constitutional charter, the Treaty. And the Court added: *'The EEC Treaty established the Court of Justice as the judicial body responsible for ensuring that both the Member States and the Community institutions comply with the law. In that community subject to the rule of law, relations between the Member States and the Community institutions are governed, according to Article 5 of the EEC Treaty, by a principle of sincere co-operation.'* And: *'this duty of sincere co-operation imposed on Community institutions is of particular importance vis-à-vis the judicial authorities of the Member States, who are responsible for ensuring that Community law is applied and respected in the national legal system.'* While, again, the ruling aims at the rule of law and the duties of the Community institutions, the link with the 'traditional' constitutional themes of direct effect and supremacy and hence the relationship between Community and national law, is more obvious. The duty of co-operation included the duty of the Commission to co-operate with the national organs which, under the principles of direct effect and supremacy, are under an obligation to uphold Community law.

The most sweeping assertion, by the Court of Justice, of the constitutional character of the Treaty came in *Opinion 1/91*.[69] The relevant paragraphs contain a characterisation of the Treaty and the Community legal order in very general terms, and oppose it to the EEA Agreement. In assessing the objectives and the context of the agreement on the one hand and those of Community law on the other, the Court held that *'In contrast, [to the EEA which constitutes a treaty of the classical type, not containing any transfer of sovereign rights] the EEC Treaty, albeit concluded in the form of an international agreement, none the less constitutes the constitutional charter of a Community based on the rule of law. As the Court of Justice has consistently held, the Community Treaties established a new legal order for the benefit of which the States have limited their sovereign rights, in ever wider fields, and the subjects of which comprise not only Member States but also their nationals (see, in particular in Case 26/62, Van Gend en Loos [1963] ECR 1). The essential characteristics of the Community legal order which has thus been established are in particular its primacy over the law of the Member States and the direct effect of a whole series of provisions which are applicable to their nationals and to the Member States themselves.'*

Identity in content and wording of the provisions of the EEA Agreement and Community law could not secure homogeneity of the rules of law throughout the EEA. *Opinion 1/91* demonstrates also that the Court's assertion of a constitutional charter reaches beyond the rather

---

[69] Opinion 1/91 *on the EEA Agreement (no. 1)* [1991] ECR I–6079.

restricted meaning that it seemed to have in *Les Verts* and *Zwartveld*. Yet, the paragraph contains distinctive elements, which must not be confused. Firstly, the Treaty is the constitutional charter of a Community based on the rule of law. Remarkably, the Court omits the epithet 'in as much as neither its Member States nor its institutions can avoid a review of whether the measures adopted by them are in conformity with the basic constitutional charter'. That was indeed not the point in *Opinion 1/91*. The *Opinion* was not about the fact that the Member States and the institutions are bound by the Treaty and that their acts are subject to judicial review. The qualification of the Community legal order is much more crucial and aims to characterise the entire Community construct. The first sentence is not a re-iteration of *Les Verts*. It has an entirely different meaning, which must be read in relation to the second and the third sentence, dealing with the establishment of a new legal order and primacy of the Community legal order (and not only the Treaty). The constitutional rhetoric does not aim to underscore the principle of the rule of law. It underscores the fact that the Community legal order is a new legal order, characterised by the direct effect of a whole series of provisions, and the unconditional primacy of Community law over the law of the Member States. That is what distinguishes Community law from ordinary international law.

After *Opinion 1/91*, the Court has on only one occasion taken recourse to the notion of a constitutional charter, in the case of *Beate Weber*.[70] In that case, a former MEP brought an action under Article 230 EC for the annulment of the Parliament's decision to grant her a transitional end-of-service allowance. The Parliament contested the admissibility of the claim on the ground that the contested measure related to the internal organisation of its work and did not have legal effects *vis-à-vis* third parties. The Court repeated its *Les Verts* position that '(..) *the EEC is based on the rule of law inasmuch as neither its Member States nor its institutions can avoid a review of the question whether the measures adopted by them are in conformity with the basic constitutional charter the Treaty, which established a complete system of legal remedies and procedures designed to permit the Court of Justice to review the legality of measures adopted by the institutions'.* Beate Weber thus falls in the *Les Verts* and *Zwartveld* line of cases.

---

70 Case C–314/91 *Beate Weber* [1993] ECR I–1093, at para 8; The Court referred to its judgements in Case 294/83 *Les Verts* [1986] ECR 1339; Case 314/85 *Foto-Frost* [1987] ECR 4199; Case C–2/88 *Imm. Zwartveld* [1990] ECR I–3365 and *Opinion 1/91* [1991] ECR I–6079. The Court apparently does not distinguish between the various meanings of the 'constitutional charter'. The reference to the judgment in *Foto-Frost* is striking since, while it did concern the need for a coherent system of judicial protection, no mention was made in that case of a constitutional charter. This was a different type of case since, in contrast to the other cases, *Foto-Frost* directly concerned the jurisdiction of the national courts by adding a duty to refer under Art. 177 (now Art. 234) in cases where the validity of Community measures is at stake.

The Court of First Instance has over the past years referred to the notion of the basic constitutional charter in at least three decisions, all concerning actions for annulment brought by Members of the European Parliament against the European Parliament under Article 230 EC.[71] *Willy Rothley* and 70 other Members sought annulment and suspension of the Decision of the European Parliament amending its Rules of Procedure pursuant to the Interinstitutional Agreement concerning internal investigations conducted by the European Anti-Fraud Office (OLAF), alleging, first, infringement of legislative procedure and, second, breach of parliamentary immunity and of the independence of their mandate. The President of the Court of First Instance declared the application for interim relief admissible, stating that the decision was one challengeable by the applicants, who may well be directly and individually concerned by the decision.[72] He merely added that account must also be taken of the case law of the Court of Justice according to which the European Community is a community based on the rule of law 'inasmuch as neither its Member States nor its institutions could avoid a review of the question whether the measures adopted by them were in conformity with the basic constitutional charter, the Treaty', etc.[73] It is, thus, a classic *Les Verts* type of case.

The case of *Jean-Claude Martinez, Charles de Gaulle, Front national, Emma Bonino and Others* chiefly concerned the decision of the European Parliament dissolving with retro-active effect the 'Groupe technique des députés indépendants (TDI) – Groupe mixte', which had been set up as a political group within the European Parliament, even though the members had affirmed their total political independence of one another. Later, the constitution of the group was considered not in conformity with the Rules of Procedure, as it excluded any political affiliation, and the group was dissolved. Before the Court of First Instance, the European Parliament claimed that its acts were not capable of forming the subject matter of an action of annulment before the Community judicature, since it was only concerned with the internal organisation of its work and produced no legal effects in regard to third parties. As a preliminary point, the Court of First Instance repeated the statement that 'the European Community is based on the rule of law inasmuch as neither its Member States nor its institutions could avoid a review of the question whether their acts were in conformity

---

[71] Case T–17/00 R *Willy Rothley and Others v European Parliament* [2000] ECR II-2085; Joined Cases T–222/99, T–327/99 and T–329/99 *Jean-Claude Martinez, Charles de Gaulle and Others v European Parliament* [2001] ECR II-2823; Case T–236/00 *Gabriele Stauner and Others v European Parliament and Commission* [2002] ECR II-135.

[72] In the main action, the Court of First Instance held the action inadmissible, since the applicants were not individually concerned, as the decision affected them in the same way as any other present or future MEP, Case T–17/00 *Willy Rothley and Others v European Parliament* [2002] ECR II-579.

[73] Case T–17/00 R *Willy Rothley and Others v European Parliament* [2000] ECR II-2085, at para 54. The appeal is currently pending before the ECJ as Case C–167/02 P *Willy Rothley and Others v European Parliament*.

with the basic constitutional charter, the Treaty, which established a complete system of legal remedies and procedures designed to permit the Court of Justice to review the legality of acts of the institutions'.[74] Given that the relevant acts did affect the manner in which the applicants could exercise their parliamentary functions, the Court held that it did produce legal effects to third parties and rejected this plea of inadmissibility. The action was declared admissible, but was dismissed on the merits.

And in the case of *Gabriele Stauner and others*, a group of Members of the European Parliament sought annulment of the Framework Agreement on Relations between the European Parliament and the Commission.[75] The Court of First Instance began by recalling that the European Community is based on the rule of law and so forth,[76] but this could not help the case of the applicants. The Court dismissed the case as inadmissible, because the Agreement was limited to governing the relations between the Commission and the Parliament and did not alter the legal position of the Members of the Parliament acting individually.

To sum up, all of these cases thus dealt with the duties and obligations of the Community institutions, rather than those of the Member State organs, which are usually implied in legal writing on the constitutionalisation of the Treaties. *Les Verts* dealt with the Parliament's standing before the Court of Justice, *Zwartveld* with the duty of co-operation with the national authorities imposed on the Commission; and *Beate Weber* had to do with the internal workings of the European Parliament and its relations to its members. *Opinion 1/91* contains the most striking statement since it uses the notion of constitutional charter when describing the Community legal order as such. Yet, even that case does not deal primarily with the relationship between Community law and the national legal orders of the Member States. And that is where the focus is in the legal literature on constitutionalisation of the Treaties, namely on the positioning of the Treaties (or the entirety of Community law?) at the top of the legal hierarchy over and above national law, including the national constitutions, through the principles of direct effect, supremacy and fundamental rights. This is not the context in which the Court of Justice has, in its case law, used the concept. It is striking that the Court of Justice[77] has not used the term since the entry into force of the Treaty of Maastricht and the establishment

---

[74] Joined Cases T–222/99, T–327/99 and T–329/99 *Jean-Claude Martinez, Charles de Gaulle and Others v European Parliament* [2001] ECR II-2823, at para 48.

[75] Framework Agreement on Relations between the European Parliament and the Commission, [2001] OJ C 121/122.

[76] Case T–236/00 *Gabriele Stauner and Others v European Parliament and Commission* [2002] ECR II-135, at para 50.

[77] AG Tesauro made reference to the constitutional charter in Case C–65/93 *European Parliament v Council* [1995] ECR I–643 on an application for annulment of a Council Decision on the ground that it had been adopted without awaiting the Parliament's advice as required by the Treaty. '*The rules on the relations between the institutions and on the corresponding distribution of powers clearly constitute one of the essential components of that*

of the European Union. The context has, since then, changed and become far more complex than before. Should the Court continue to refer to the Community Treaties as its constitutional charter, or rather to the Union Treaty? And could the notion, in the latter case, still have the same meaning as before? The Court can hardly maintain that the *Union* is based on the rule of law 'in the sense that nor its institutions nor the Member States can avoid judicial review of the question whether their acts are in conformity with the constitutional charter of the Union, the Treaty', when the Court itself is excluded from a large part of the second and third pillar. The Court of First Instance has mentioned the constitutional charter since the establishment of the European Union, but only in the context of the European Community, and only in cases concerning the relations between the European Parliament and its members.

As a final point, it must be stressed that the Court of Justice is not and should not be the only institution and not even the most instrumental in the making of a European Constitution. Constitutions have been created in different ways, by a constitutional assembly or convention, by way of referendum, but never before has a Constitution been created by a court. The making of a Constitution is not essentially a judicial but rather a political exercise. The main responsibility lies with the Member States who, at times of consecutive Treaty revision have the responsibility of Masters of the Treaties and makers of the Constitution, or even beyond the Member States, with the People or Peoples of Europe.[78] Obviously, courts interpreting constitutions are instrumental in further developing constitutional law. They put the flesh and blood on the constitutional bones contained in the basic texts. Yet, it is quite another thing to leave the responsibility for the creation of a Constitution entirely on the doorstep of the Court of Justice.[79] It is quite

---

constitution', he said, 'and derogations from them cannot be made without thereby altering the characteristics of the system'. An alteration of these rules was a matter for the constitutional legislature clone. The AG thus used the qualification constitutional as denoting the fundamental rules that can only be altered following prescribed procedures. The Court of Justice did not follow its AG and rejected the Parliament's application with reference to the principle of sincere co-operation, which the Parliament was said to have broken by not acting promptly as the Council had requested.

[78] For a similar view see B de Witte, 'The Closest Thing to a Constitutional Conversation in Europe: The Semi-Permanent Treaty Revision Process', in P Beaumont, C Lyons and N Walker (eds), *Convergence and Divergence in European Public Law*, (Oxford, Hart Publishing, 2002), 39, who rightly stresses the fact that the constitutional nature of the judicial dialogue between the ECJ and the national courts should not be overrated and who instead focuses on the political constitutional conversations taking place in the framework of the successive IGC's.

[79] H Schepel and R Wesseling, 'The Legal Community: Judges, Lawyers, Officials and Clerks in the Writing of Europe', *ELJ*, 1997, 165, at 166; see also the fierce critique of M. Shapiro on the dominant orthodoxy of Community law that the EC legal system as a supranational legal Community is above all a product of the case law of the ECJ ('constitutional law without politics): M Shapiro, 'Comparative Law and Comparative Politics', 53 *Southern California Law Review*, 1980, 537; and J Weiler, 'European Neo-Constitutionalism: In Search of Foundations for the European Constitutional Order', 44 *Political Studies*, 1996, 517.

remarkable that a constitutional document refers to general principles elaborated by a court when it comes to the protection of fundamental rights, rather than vice versa. It is striking that the relation between the Treaties and the law stemming from them on the one hand and national law and constitutions on the other hand are left undecided in the constitutional texts of a multi-level polity.[80] These issues will be developed further in Part 3 of this book.

13.2.2. The Court of Justice as a Constitutional Court

13.2.2.1. The Court of Justice's Functions as a Constitutional Court

It may be useful to recapitulate what exactly it is that makes the Court of Justice a constitutional court in the general perception. Several of the Court's *functions* are similar to those of constitutional courts, or of constitutional or higher law judicial review courts.[81] As is usual in division of powers systems, the Court resolves conflicts between the central level and the lower levels (vertical division of powers)[82] and within the central level between the various institutions (horizontal division of powers). In preliminary rulings the Court rules on the validity of secondary Community law and ensures that Community law is interpreted uniformly throughout the Community. Attaining uniformity is a function of supreme courts in general, not only of constitutional courts. Perhaps it is the system of preliminary rulings itself that is crucial in the case of the Court of Justice. Indeed, the landmark cases constitutionalising the Treaties are all cases referred to the Court by national courts, cases sometimes of a seemingly limited importance, but containing fundamental issues of constitutional significance. In addition, and again in common with most higher law judicial review courts,[83] the Court has declared to be a guardian of *fundamental rights*. Yet, in contrast to many of its counterparts, human rights are not the main area of concern for the Court.[84]

---

[80] For the view that these issues should be included in a basic document see P Craig, 'Constitutions, Constitutionalism and the European Union', *ELJ*, 2001, 125, esp at 143–45. The point is developed further in Part 3.

[81] See M Shapiro, 'The European Court of Justice', in P Craig and G de Búrca (eds), *The Evolution of EU Law* (Oxford, OUP, 1999) 321.

[82] For instance the American Supreme Court, the German *Bundesverfassungsgericht* and the Belgian *Cour d'arbitrage*; for a comparison between the Supreme Court and the Court of Justice see PR Dubinsky, 'The Essential Function of Federal Courts: The European Union and the United States Compared', *Am J Comp L*, 1994, 295.

[83] This is true even for constitutional review courts which have not expressly been established with a view to protect fundamental rights (the *Conseil constitutionnel*) or only to a limited extent (the *Arbitragehof*).

[84] The US Supreme Court's judicial review powers are now largely exercised in the realm of the Bill of Rights. Fundamental rights cases also make out the bulk of the case load of the *Bundesverfassungsgericht*.

All of these functions correspond to what (federal) constitutional courts do in national systems.

13.2.2.2. The Court of Justice's Methods

Judicial review entails interpreting and developing the law, and announcing, formulating or refining the rules in order to resolve cases. It is a truism to state that in *interpreting* and *applying* legal rules in order to decide cases, any court contributes to *making* the law. This is even more so for constitutional – or higher law – review courts.[85] As is the case with Constitutions, while the European Treaties may be detailed and technical in some areas, they also contain many clauses in general language. Moreover, the Treaties are difficult to amend which gives their interpreter more discretion and the political actors less inclination to initiate amendment procedures. In interpreting and applying the Treaties the Court of Justice has transformed the Treaty text into a self-generating body of case law, which states what the Treaties say at a given moment in time. It has turned the Constitution into constitutional law.[86]

The *methods of interpretation* used by the Court resemble those of constitutional courts.[87] The Court has a preference for the teleological and contextual approaches to interpretation, sometimes straining the limits of the ordinary meaning of the words. In addition, the Court frequently takes recourse to *general principles of Community law* which it 'discovers' and builds on fundamental doctrines to find new principles 'inherent in the Treaty'. The Court has on a regular basis been under attack for being overly active and has been accused of inventing rather than interpreting legal texts.[88] Of course the Court has done more than apply text. It has developed new legal rules and principles which have helped at shaping Europe. It is not an exaggeration to state that Europe would have looked quite differently without the principles of direct effect and supremacy, the

---

[85] As pointed out by M Shapiro, 'The European Court of Justice', *art.cit.*, at 323–24.

[86] Above, at 324.

[87] This is of course a rather general statement and I am not going to develop it further, but see for a theoretical analysis of this and related issues J Bengoetxea, *The Legal Reasoning of the Court of Justice: Towards a European Jurisprudence*, (Oxford, Clarendon Press, 1993); see also A Arnull, *The European Union and its Court of Justice*, (Oxford, OUP, 1999) Ch 14; L Neville Brown and T Kennedy, *The Court of Justice of the European Communities*, 5th edn (London, Sweet & Maxwell, 2000), Ch 14–15; J Bengoetxea, N MacCormick and L Moral Soriano, 'Integration and Integrity in the Legal Reasoning of the Court of Justice', in G de Búrca and JHH Weiler (eds), *The European Court of Justice*, (Oxford, OUP, 2001), 43; for a very balanced and realistic view see T Koopmans, 'The theory of interpretation and the Court of Justice', in D O'Keeffe and A Bavasso (eds), *Judicial Review in European Union Law. Liber Amicorum in Honour of Lord Slynn of Hadley*, Vol I, (The Hague, Kluwer Law International, 2000), 45.

[88] Most notoriously H Rasmussen, *On Law and Policy in the European Court of Justice: A Comparative Study in Judicial Policymaking* (Nijhoff, Dordrecht, 1987) and P Neil, *The European Court of Justice: A Case Study in Judicial Activism* (London, European Policy Forum, 1995).

general principles of Community law protecting the fundamental rights of the citizens and institutional principles such as institutional balance and the duty of sincere co-operation and the like, which were not as such included in the text of the Treaty but rather 'discovered' by the Court. The Court may have crossed the lines between interpretation and creation;[89] some of its decisions are better than others; it has been creative and activist on some occasions, conservative and restrictive in its interpretation of the Treaty and its underlying principles on others. Yet, the *modus operandi* resembles that of other courts dealing with legal issues that have important political ramifications, most notably constitutional courts.[90]

13.2.2.3. The Court of Justice as Guardian of Fundamental Rights

The story of how the Court developed the general principles of Community law protecting fundamental rights is well known and a lot has been written about it. A few comments are in place here. Firstly, in creating for itself the role of protecting fundamental rights where such role has not expressly been given, the Court of Justice is in the company of other constitutional courts, like the Belgian *Cour d'arbitrage* and the French *Conseil constitutionnel*. These courts too were given a rather limited constitutional role but developed into real constitutional courts, *inter alia* by developing and elaborating their role of protector of fundamental rights. Even courts set up as judicial review courts in the context of fundamental rights are most successful in mobilising support for and legitimising their power in the context of human rights.[91] Courts are most audacious in asserting their power when they serve as guardians of fundamental rights, but the good of the cause, the protection of fundamental rights, eclipses the empowerment of the courts. It is in the area of fundamental right protection that the review powers of courts are most accepted even in the absence of democratic legitimation. After all, who could be opposed to enhancing protection of fundamental rights? While fundamental rights as standards for review of Community action may not have altered the role of the Court of Justice dramatically in that they merely confirmed and added to its existing jurisdiction to review Community action,[92] they do give it the allure of a constitutional court, and this has been picked up by many commentators. Many national

---

[89] It is of course a matter of interpretation or taste where the line is, and therefore also to find out whether or not it has been crossed.

[90] B De Witte, 'Interpreting the EC Treaty like a Constitution: The Role of the European Constitution in Comparative Perspective', in R Bakker, AW Heringa and F Stroink (eds), *Judicial Control. Comparative Essays on Judicial Review* (Antwerp, Maklu, 1995) 133.

[91] See J Weiler, 'Human Rights, Constitutionalism and Integration: Iconography and Fetishism', *International Law FORUM du droit international*, 2001, 227, at 228.

[92] B De Witte, 'The Past and Future Role of the European Court of Justice in the Protection of Human Rights', in P Alston (ed), *The EU and Human Rights* (Oxford, OUP, 1999) 859, at 866.

courts have expressed their agreement with the fact that the Court of Justice has assumed jurisdiction in the area of fundamental rights.[93]

Secondly, it has often been argued that the Court's track record as guarantor of fundamental rights is not very impressive. The *number* of cases decided in the field of fundamental rights is much more limited than, say, those decided by the German, Italian or Belgian constitutional courts. The Court of Justice has also been accused of applying *a low standard of review* to Community action; some have even argued that the Court is not really interested in protecting fundamental rights, but that it merely uses them to promote the supremacy of Community law,[94] or that it gives greater weight to the economic value of achieving the internal market over fundamental rights, including even the most basic right to life.[95] Certainly, the fundamental rights jurisprudence of the Court of Justice has not matured to the standards of for instance that of the Italian or the German constitutional courts. Yet, it should be remembered that at the outset, the drafters of the Treaties had overlooked fundamental rights completely and that the Court has developed them from scratch.

Thirdly, the fundamental rights case law of the Court of Justice has also met with the approval of the political institutions[96] and the Member States who have codified it at the occasion of the revision of the Treaties in Maastricht and Amsterdam. Article 6(2) EU now states that *'The Union shall respect fundamental rights, as guaranteed by the European Convention for the Protection of Human Rights and Fundamental Freedoms signed in Rome on 4 November 1950 and as they result from the constitutional traditions common to the Member States, as general principles of Community law'.* But the Member States have at times hampered and obstructed the fundamental rights case law of the Court of Justice: it was they who excluded the Court of Justice from the second and third pillar in Maastricht and left those areas without a real and effective judicial review at the European level.[97] In the absence of a real judicial protection from the Court of Justice, the question will arise sooner or later whether it must instead be offered by the national courts or by the Strasbourg Court of Human Rights.[98] With respect to accession to

---

[93] Examples are *Conseil constitutionnel*, decision n. 92–308 DC of 9 April 1992, *Treaty on European Union (Maastricht I)*, Oppenheimer, *The Cases*, 384, at 390; the position of the *Bundesverfassungsgericht* has varied over time. Its most recent position is that the protection offered by the Court of Justice is sufficient, *Bundesverfassungsgericht*, decision of 7 June 2000, *EC Regulation on Bananas*, BverfGE 102,147; in *Solange II* the case law of the Court of Justice was the reason for the Court to put on hold its power of review of Community law, even if in *Solange I* it seemed to require the introduction of a European Bill of Rights.

[94] *Eg.* J Coppel and A O'Neill, 'The European Court of Justice: Taking Rights Seriously?', *CML Rev*, 1992, 669.

[95] DR Phelan, 'Right to Life of the Unborn v Promotion of Trade in Services: The European Court of Justice and the Normative Shaping of the European Union', 55 *MLR*, 1992, 670.

[96] Already Joint Declaration by the European Parliament, the Council and the Commission on Fundamental Rights of 5 April 1977, [1977] *OJC* 103/1.

[97] See *eg* S Peers, 'Human Rights and the Third Pillar', in Ph Alston (ed), *The EU and Human Rights* (Oxford, OUP, 1999) 167.

[98] This question will be discussed further below.

the European Convention on Human Rights, the decision of the Court of Justice that the Communities could not, under the Treaties as they stood, adhere to the Convention may raise eyebrows, but the Member States did not mend that defect by adding a provision to that end in the Treaties.

Fourthly, by treading on the area of fundamental rights the Court enters one of the main fields of action of the national constitutional courts. It is a generally accepted theory that the Court introduced fundamental rights as general principles of Community law in order to convince the national courts, mainly the German and Italian constitutional courts, to embrace unconditional supremacy of Community law. At the end of the day, the constitutional courts have enticed the Court of Justice to develop into a constitutional court in the context of fundamental rights.[99] With the introduction of the Court to the area of fundamental rights protection, the threat of a positive conflict of jurisdiction transpired, with both the Court of Justice and the constitutional courts possibly claiming jurisdiction in a particular case, and it is likely that there will be divergences of interpretation of rights and levels of protection. As said, a constitutional–constitutional dialogue has inbuilt conflictual elements. No real and lasting conflicts have occurred in practice, with either or both sides yielding in the end.[100]

A final remark concerns the way in which the Court of Justice approaches the main European codifications of fundamental rights, namely the ECHR and the newly adopted EU Charter on Fundamental Rights. The ECHR was for the first time mentioned *expressis verbis* by the Court in the *Nold* judgment of 1974,[101] and is now considered as having special significance as a source of inspiration for the formulation and definition of the general principles of Community law, whose observance the Court guarantees.[102] Reference to the provisions of the ECHR is now standard. It was thus inevitable that divergent or inconsistent interpretations between the two European Courts would emerge.[103] Legally, the Court of Justice is not obliged to follow the interpretation of the European Court of Human Rights. Indeed, the Community, and the Union for that matter, are

---

[99] In fact, in *Solange I* the BVerfG still required the adoption of a European codified catalogue of fundamental rights, the substance of which would be reliable and unambiguously fixed for the future in the same way as the substance of the German Basic Law and which would be adequate measured by the standard of the German Constitution, see *Bundesverfassungsgericht*, decision of 29 May 1974, *Internationale Handelsgesellschaft (Solange I)*, 37 BverfGE 271, Oppenheimer, *The Cases*, 419, at 447–48. The BVerfG possibly did not expect the ECJ to come up with fundamental rights itself, but so it did. The BVerfG approved of that step in *Solange II*.

[100] See *eg* the Irish abortion issue, discussed below; and the German *bananas* saga.

[101] *Case 4/73 Nold v Commission* [1974] ECR 491; see also Case 44/79 *Liselotte Hauer v Rheinland Pfalz* [1979] ECR 3727.

[102] So for instance Case C–299/95 *Friedrich Kremzow v Austrian State* [1997] ECR I–2629, at para 14.

[103] D Spielmann, 'Human Rights Case Law in the Strasbourg and Luxembourg Courts: Conflicts, Inconsistencies, and Complementarities', in Ph Alston (ed), *The EU and Human Rights* (Oxford, OUP, 1999) 757.

not party to the Convention. In its *Opinion 2/94 on Accession to the ECHR*[104] the Court of Justice held that the Community did not have competence to adhere to the ECHR: no Treaty provision conferred on the Community institutions any general power to enact rules on human rights or to conclude international agreements in this field; in the absence of express or implied powers for this purpose, the Court also analysed whether Article 235 of the EC Treaty might be used. The Court gave a conveniently limited application of the provision, also in the light of the Maastricht decision of the *Bundesverfassungsgericht* rendered not long before, which had criticised the extensive use of that provision in the past, and stated that it could not serve as the basis for the accession. Such would amount to an amendment of the Treaty without following the appropriate procedures, and furthermore, did not appear necessary after all. The Opinion was heavily criticised and many commentators accused the Court of seeking to escape the supervision of a higher court.[105] Indeed, before that time, no reference had been made to the case law of the Strasbourg Court, which is the flesh and blood of the Convention,[106] and the Court of Justice seemed to develop its own autonomous fundamental rights case law. However, the Court of Justice has, possibly as a reaction to the fierce comments on *Opinion 2/94*,[107] made references to the case law of the Court of Human Rights.[108] In recent cases, it has stated that for the purposes of determining the scope of general principles, regard must be had to the case law of the European Court of Human Rights, and that it may have to adjust its case law to align with decisions of the Strasbourg Court.[109]

With respect to the European Charter of Fundamental Rights solemnly proclaimed by the European Parliament, the Council and the Commission at Nice in December 2000, there is a striking discrepancy between the Court of Justice on the one hand and the Court of First Instance and several Advocates General on the other. So far, the former has never made any reference to the Charter, while the latter have on several occasions. Obviously, the Charter is not a legally binding document. One British

---

[104] Opinion 2/94 *Accession by the Community to the ECHR* [1996] ECR I–1759.

[105] See e.g. P Wachsmann, 'L'avis 2/94 de la Cour de justice relatif à l'adhésion de la Communauté européenne à la Convention de sauvegarde des droits de l'homme et des libertés fondamentales', *RTDeur*, 1996, 467; L Mathieu, 'L'adhésion de la Communauté à la CDEH: un problème de compétence ou un problème de soumission?', *RMUE*, 1998, 31.

[106] So B De Witte, 'The Past and Future Role of the European Court of Justice in the Protection of Human Rights', in Ph Alston (ed), *The EU and Human Rights* (Oxford, OUP, 1999) 859, at 878.

[107] Above, at 878.

[108] The reverse is true also: in *European Court of Human Rights*, decision of 24 September 2002, *Posti and Rahko v Finland*; where the ECtHR referred to the case law of the ECJ as an additional argument.

[109] Case C–94/00 *Roquette Frères SA v Directeur général de la concurrence, de la consommation et de la répression des fraudes* [2002] ECR I–9011; Joined Cases C–238/99 P, C–244/99 P, C–245/99 P, C–247/99 P, C–250/99 P to C–252/99 P and C–254/99 P *Limburgse Vinyl Maatschappij (LVM) and Others v Commission* [2002] ECR I–8375; see also Case C–270/99 Z *v Parliament* [2001] ECR I–9197.

Minister was reported saying that for a lawyer to cite the Charter before the Court would be like coming to the Court with a copy of *The Beano* (a children's comic).[110] And yet, the Court of First Instance has been willing to cite the Charter as a source of inspiration, or as proof of the existence of a common or general principle,[111] and so have several Advocates General.[112] The Court has opted to ignore the Charter. It consistently

---

[110] See FG Jacobs, 'Human Rights in the European Union: the role of the Court of Justice', 26 *ELR*, 2001, 331, at 338.

[111] Case T–211/02 *Tideland Signal Ltd v Commission* [2002] ECR II-3781 (Art. 41 of the Charter, right to sound administration); Case T–177/01 *Jégo-Quéré et Cie SA v Commission* [2002] ECR II-2365 (Art. 47 of the Charter, right to an effective remedy for everyone whose rights and freedoms guaranteed by the law of the Union are violated); Case T–54/99 *max.mobil Telekommunikation Service GmbH v Commission* [2002] ECR II-313 (Art. 41 of the Charter, the right to sound administration).

[112] AG Léger in Case C-353/99 P *Council v Heidi Hautala* [2001] ECR I-9565 (Art. 42, right of access to European Parliament, Council and Commission documents): 'Naturally, the clearly-expressed wish of the authors of the Charter not to endow it with binding legal force should not be overlooked. However, aside from any consideration regarding its legislative scope, the nature of the rights set down in the Charter of Fundamental Rights precludes it from being regarded as a mere list of purely moral principles without any consequences. It should be noted that those values have in common the fact of being unanimously shared by the Member States, which have chosen to make them more visible by placing them in a charter in order to increase their protection. The Charter has undeniably placed the rights which form its subject-matter at the highest level of values common to the Member States'; see also Opinion of AG Tizzano in Case C-173/99 *Broadcasting, Entertainment, Cinematographic and Theatre Union (BECTU) v Secretary of State for Trade and Industry* [2001] ECR I-4881, at marginal numbers 27–28: 'Admittedly, like some of the instruments cited above, the Charter of Fundamental Rights of the European Union has not been recognised as having genuine legislative scope in the strict sense. In other words, formally, it is not in itself legally binding. However, without wishing to participate here in the wide-ranging debate now going on as to the effects which, in other forms and by other means, the Charter may nevertheless produce, the fact remains that it includes statements which appear in large measure to reaffirm rights which are enshrined in other instruments. In its preamble, it is moreover stated that 'this Charter reaffirms, with due regard for the powers and tasks of the Community and the Union and the principle of subsidiarity, the rights as they result, in particular, from the constitutional traditions and international obligations common to the Member States, the Treaty on European Union, the Community Treaties, the European Convention for the Protection of Human Rights and Fundamental Freedoms, the Social Charters adopted by the Community and by the Council of Europe and the case-law of the Court of Justice of the European Communities and of the European Court of Human Rights. I think therefore that, in proceedings concerned with the nature and scope of a fundamental right, the relevant statements of the Charter cannot be ignored; in particular, we cannot ignore its clear purpose of serving, where its provisions so allow, as a substantive point of reference for all those involved – Member States, institutions, natural and legal persons – in the Community context. Accordingly, I consider that the Charter provides us with the most reliable and definitive confirmation of the fact that the right to paid annual leave constitutes a fundamental right'. See also AG Jacobs in Case C-377/98 *The Netherlands v European Parliament and Council (Biotechnology)* [2001] ECR I-7079 (Art. 1, right to human dignity) and AG Jacobs in Case C-50/00 P *Unión de Pequeños Agricultores v Council* [2002] ECR I-6677 (Art. 47); AG Jacobs has also expressed his views extra-judicially, see FG Jacobs, 'Human Rights in the European Union: the role of the Court of Justice', 26 *ELR*, 2001, 331. While he admitted that there was no real need for the Charter, and that it may at times be misleadingly formulated, he did see it as a useful instrument, providing a convenient point of reference to identify the rights, to give them a lapidary formulation, and to set out the permissible limitations, and being more up to date than the ECHR.

omits all references suggested by its Advocates General and made by the Court of First Instance. Probably the Court does not want to go against the clear will of the *pouvoir constitutant*, the Member States, not to give the Charter binding force.[113]

13.2.2.4. *The European Court of Justice and the Economic Constitution*

The crucial role of the Court in the completion of the common market, 'the heart of the material constitution of the Community'[114] can hardly be overstated. Obviously the goal of the internal market and the methods to achieve it were comprised in the original Treaties. Yet, the Court has played a decisive role in preserving the ideal of the common market, re-launching it in the late seventies, mid-eighties, and has determined the pace of completing the internal market.[115] One needs only to point at those few landmark cases *Dassonville*,[116] *Cassis de Dijon*,[117] and *Keck*,[118]

---

[113] This point is further developed in Part 3.

[114] JHH Weiler, 'The Constitution of the Common Market Place: Text and Context in the Evolution of the Free Movement of Goods', in P Craig and G de Búrca (eds), *The Evolution of EU Law* (Oxford, OUP, 1999) 349, at 350.

[115] See on this topic M Poiares Maduro, *We The Court. The European Court of Justice and the European Economic Constitution* (Oxford, Hart Publishing, 1998); JHH Weiler, 'The Constitution of the Common Market Place: Text and Context in the Evolution of the Free Movement of Goods', in P Craig and G de Búrca (eds), *The Evolution of EU Law* (Oxford, OUP, 1999) 349 and references.

[116] Case 8/74 *Dassonville* [1974] ECR 837. In *Dassonville*, the Court held that the prohibition of Article 28 EC (then Article 30 of the EC Treaty) applied to any obstacle to free movement rather than only to discriminatory measures and thus took a clear stand in favour of free trade and against protectionism, extending the reach of Article 28 EC to any national measure which could actually or potentially have hinder intra-Community trade. *Dassonville* would prove to be overly broad, for example in the *Sunday trading* cases, but when it was handed, it put its mark on the field in its clear and unambiguous choice for the need to accomplish the internal market.

[117] Case 120/78 *Rewe-Zentral AG v Bundesmonopolverwaltung für Branntwein (Cassis de Dijon)* [1979] ECR 649. *Cassis de Dijon* introduced the doctrine of mandatory requirements, which may under conditions outweigh the interest of achieving a common market. The Court became the ultimate judge of the national measures, balancing national socio-economic policies against the internal market and testing their proportionality. This gave the Court tremendous discretion and it became enmeshed in national policies. The second doctrine contained in *Cassis*, of mutual recognition or functional parallelism, changed the legislative approach to harmonisation, and, more importantly, put the Court of Justice on the map as a major political actor for everyone to see. See on the *Cassis* case and its political consequences KJ Alter and S Meunier-Aitsahalia, 'Judicial Politics in the European Community: European Integration and the Pathbreaking *Cassis de Dijon* Decision', *Comparative Political Studies*, 1994, 535.

[118] Joined Cases C–267 and C–268/91 *Keck and Mithouard* [1993] ECR I–6097. *Keck* represented a departure from *Dassonville*, which had proved to be too inclusive. *Keck* limited the reach of the prohibition contained in Article 30 of the EC Treaty (now Article 28 EC) and excluded national selling arrangements from its scope. Given that selling arrangements are no longer caught by Article 28 EC and are retracted from the legislative competences of the Community, the case led to a more limited form of Community governance. *Keck* may be seen to represent a new, more tolerant and mature attitude to national measures and a new phase in the balancing of Community and Member State competences.

which have shaped the field. In all of these cases, the Court of Justice proved to be a decisive political player in the relations with the political institutions and between the Community and the Member States; it made and shaped policy, and was instrumental in the making of the European economic Constitution. The case law of the Court of Justice has in a decisive way contributed to constituting the European internal market, in the same way as its most eminent national counterparts play a part in building and moulding the social and economic constitution within the Member States.[119]

13.3. A STRENUOUS CONSTITUTIONAL DIALOGUE

13.3.1. Opposite Mandates

The problem of the language of constitutionalism as employed by the Court and by commentators is that the Member States already have constitutions, and, in some cases constitutional courts to guarantee the supremacy of those constitutions. The Court of Justice and the national constitutional courts are, by nature, in a difficult mutual relationship. A constitutional–constitutional dialogue has inbuilt conflictual elements. Imagine a constitutional court which is confronted with the mere existence of the Court of Justice. Such a court is likely not opposed to an international court ruling on the interpretation of Community law, the observance of the rule of law by the Community institutions, the institutional balance between the various institutions and so on, in other words, the internal Constitution of the Communities. It will, arguably, also accept that an international court can declare that the State has failed to fulfil its Treaty obligations, even if the breach was (also) attributable to it. But the picture changes when that 'international' Court of Justice begins to mingle in the national legal order, which is exactly the consequence of the Court's case law on direct effect, supremacy, full effect and so forth. The judgments in *Van Gend en Loos*, *Costa v ENEL*, *Simmenthal*, *Internationale Handellsgesellschaft*, *ERT* and the like concern issues containing a double dimension. From the perspective of Community law, they concern the interpretation of Community law and thus fall to be dealt with by the Court of Justice; yet from a national constitutional perspective, they concern constitutional issues, which traditionally belonged to the province of the Constitution.[120] One would assume that constitutional jurisdictions would not be pleased with a rival treading on the same ground.

---

[119] See, for Germany, J Limbach, 'Das Bundesverfassungsgericht als politischer Machtsfaktor', *Humboldt Forum Recht*, 1996, Beitrag 12, www.rewi.hu-berlin.de/HFR/12–1996.

[120] This became obvious already in the interventions of the Netherlands and Belgian Governments in Case 26/62 *Van Gend en Loos* [1963] ECR 1 (though both countries lacked a veritable constitutional jurisdiction at the time) and of the Italian Government in Case 6/64 *Costa v ENEL* [1964] *ECR* 585.

To return to the description of its own role by the Court of Justice: 'In its constitutional role, the Court rules *on the respective powers of the Communities and of the Member States,* on those of the Communities in relation to other forms of co-operation in the framework of the Union and, generally, determines the scope of the provisions whose duty it is to ensure. It ensures that the delimitation of powers between the institutions is safeguarded, thereby helping to maintain the institutional balance. It examines whether *fundamental rights* have been observed by the institutions, and by the Member States when their actions fall within the scope of Community law and on *the reciprocal obligations between the Member States and the Community institutions.* Finally, it may be called upon to judge whether international commitments envisaged by the Communities are compatible with the Treaties'.

All of the marked passages involve a task that may oppose the Court to the national courts having constitutional jurisdiction, since both assume the same task from a different perspective. A first possible area of contention is the delimitation of the respective powers of the Communities and the Member States. The constitutional courts equally assume that power, but looking from the perspective of the national Constitution. One author, coming from a country lacking a constitutional court, put it this way: *'The jurisdiction of the national governmental institutions – legislative, judicial and executive – must, under national law, be determined by national constitutional law except to the extent that national constitutional law determines otherwise. The Member States assented to the Treaties and the Treaties are part of the national legal system. As such, the Treaties can transfer powers from the national governmental institutions to the Community. However, they can do this only to the extent that they are valid law in the national legal systems and they are valid only to the extent permitted by national constitutional law. In the final analysis, therefore, national law determines the extent to which the Treaties can transfer powers from the Member States to the Community. In most, if not all, Member States there are significant limits to such transfer. Only the national courts have jurisdiction to decide what these limits are'.*[121] While his words may not be sufficiently accurate to reflect the exact legal reasoning of the constitutional courts, they do pinpoint the essence of the problem. Since the issue is the division of powers between two polities, each of them comprising a court assuming the power to control the limits of the powers of the other polity from their own perspective, there is a deep-seated positive conflict of jurisdiction.

Second, the Court examines whether fundamental rights and general principles of law have been observed by the Community institutions and

---

[121] TC Hartley, 'The Community Legal Order: A British View', in J-D Mouton and Th Stein (eds), *Towards a New Constitution for the European Union? The Intergovernmental Conference 1996* (Köln 1997) 57, at 59–60, my emphases.

by the Member States acting within the scope of Community law. This is precisely one of the main responsibilities of constitutional jurisdictions. Even the French and Belgian constitutional courts,[122] which had not or only to a limited extent been charged by the Constitution to protect fundamental rights, have extended their own jurisdiction and added fundamental rights protection to their mandate.[123] The Court of Justice made a similar move. Faced with the silence of the Treaties in the field of fundamental rights, it developed its own fundamental rights jurisprudence, by recourse to the notion of general principles of Community law. Yet, the Court did not simply add another layer of protection: The implication of the Court assuming fundamental rights protection was, in the light of the supremacy of Community law, that the constitutional courts must not review acts of the Community institutions and of the Member States covered by Community law for violation of the constitutionally protected fundamental rights. In addition, the Court mandated all the national courts, including all ordinary courts, to offer fundamental rights protection against Member State action in the scope of Community law.[124] Fundamental rights protection is a function that the constitutional courts are unlikely to relinquish.

Third, 'the Court rules on the relationship between Community law and national law', an area which has always been, from the national and even the international perspective, part of national constitutional law. The Court has assumed the power to decide on the effect of Community law in the legal orders of the Member States and on its status within those orders. In doing so, it has acted less like an international court, and more like the constitutional court of a federal-type construct. Acting in this field, the Court of Justice has developed the direct effect and supremacy doctrines, involving all the national courts in the enforcement of Community law against the national authorities, altering the powers of the national courts, and upsetting the constitutional balance between national organs. In other words, the Court of Justice has meddled in a national constitutional issue of fundamental importance, and accordingly in one of the chief responsibilities of the constitutional courts.

[122] The French Constitutional Court was set up primarily to patrol the boundaries of the legislative powers of Parliament. But already in 1971 did the *Conseil constitutionnel* extend the *bloc de constitutionnalité* so as to include fundamental rights. The Belgian *Cour d'arbitrage* was only given the task of protecting three of the fundamental rights contained in the Constitution, the rights of equality and non-discrimination and the freedom of education. Yet, it soon extended those rights to include, indirectly, all other rights contained in the Constitution.

[123] See also J Robert, 'Constitutional and International Protection of Human Rights: Competing or Complementary Systems? General Report to the IXth Conference of European Constitutional Courts', *HRLJ*, 1994, 1, at 4.

[124] Case C–260/89 *Elliniki Radiophonia Tiléorassi* (ERT) [1991] ECR I–2925.

Another aspect of the Court's case law in this area is its assumption that Community law takes precedence over the national Constitution. This assumption will not lightly be embraced by the constitutional courts whose duty it is to preserve the integrity of the Constitution. Francis Jacobs, Advocate General at the Court of Justice acknowledged extra-judicially that *'It is quite understandable that from the point of view of a constitutional court, which has a special duty to protect the national constitution, there may be difficulties in giving unlimited primacy to Community law'*.[125] This concern is shared also by other members of the Court. At the occasion of the 1997 Paris *Conférence des Cours ayant compétence constitutionnelle des Etats membres de l'Union européenne*, President of the Court Rodriguez Iglesias and Judge Puissochet wrote: *'On comprend cependant bien la réticence qu'une cour constitutionnelle peut éprouver d' assumer le principe de primauté ainsi conçu si l'on tient compte du fait que la suprematie de la Constitution est le présupposé existentiel d'une cour de ce type. En fait, au stade actuel de l'intégration, caractérisée sur le plan juridique par la relative autonomie réciproque des ordres communautaire et nationaux, malgré leurs multiples imbrications, et par la séparation de leurs systèmes jurisdictionnels, entre lesquels n'existe pas de relation hiérarchique, un conflit radical entre les exigences de l'ordre communautaire et celles de la Constitution d'un Etat membre n'est pas susceptible de recevoir une solution logique satisfaisante.'*

However, they added that in the unlikely event of a conflict, both the constitutional courts and the Court of Justice would have the possibility and the duty to avoid an impasse, through the preliminary reference procedure and the duty of conform interpretation.

13.3.2 The Court of Justice in National Constitutional Law: The Court of Justice as 'gesetzlicher Richter'

This section will attempt to depict the stance of the constitutional courts towards the Court of Justice. Clearly, it is impossible to detect with precision how the constitutional courts truly appreciate the Court of Justice. The only source of information available consists of comments and remarks made by these courts in their judgments, and sometimes by the judges extra-judicially. The likes and dislikes of a court are hardly ever explicit, especially for those tribunals whose judicial decisions are brief and concise. Furthermore, judges speak not only through what they say but also through what they omit. It is easy for a court to escape a situation in which it would have to give a statement on the Court of Justice. Not to

[125] FG Jacobs, 'The Community Legal Order – A Constitutional Order? A Perspective from the European Court of Justice', in *Towards a New Constitution for the European Union? The Intergovernmental Conference 1996* (Köln, 1997) 31, at 34.

refer a question to Luxembourg is easier than to refer it and then to challenge or reject the answer from the European Court. Or simpler even, the court in question could ignore questions of Community law and solve the issues raised before it, purely on the basis of national law. This section will give an impression of some of the statements made *en banc* on the Court of Justice, its role and function.

The German constitutional court has given the Court of Justice a place in the German constitutional structure as *gesetzlicher Richter* in the sense of Article 101(1)(2) of the Basic Law, which provides for access to a 'lawful court' as a fundamental right.[126] If a party is denied access to such a lawful court in an arbitrary manner, the party may bring a petition for review on constitutional grounds (*Verfassungsbeschwerde*) to the *Bundesverfassungsgericht*. In the national constitutional context, the arbitrary failure to refer a question on the constitutionality of a measure to the *Bundesverfassungsgericht* constitutes an infringement of the right to a lawful judge. The question whether the Court of Justice could equally be considered as a lawful court in the sense of Article 101(1)(2) of the German Constitution was first raised in the case of *Alphons Lütticke GmbH*.[127] The *Bundesverfassungsgericht* did not rule on the question of whether the Court of Justice was to be regarded as a lawful judge under Article 101(1)(2) of the Basic Law. It held that the right to a lawful judge could only be infringed if the refusal to refer was arbitrary which it clearly was not in the case at hand.

In the *Solange II* decision the Constitutional Court did qualify the Court of Justice as a lawful court within the meaning of Article 101(1)(2) of the Basic Law.[128] 'There can be no doubt', the *Bundesverfassungsgericht* held, 'of

---

[126] Art. 101(1)(2) reads: '*Niemand darf seinem gesetzlichen Richter entzogen werden*'; 'No one may be removed from the jurisdiction of his lawful judge', translation taken from SE Finer *et al*, *Comparing Constitutions* (Oxford, Clarendon Press, 1995).

[127] *Bundesverfassungsgericht*, decision of 9 June 1971, *Alphons Lütticke*, BVerfGE 31, 145; Oppenheimer, *The Cases*, at 415. Alphons Lütticke was involved in a long and complicated dispute with the tax authorities over a turnover equalisation tax on milk powder which the firm had imported from Luxembourg. The Fiscal Court of Saarland had sought and obtained a preliminary ruling from the ECJ on the interpretation of Art. 95 of the EEC Treaty and remitted the case to the local customs office. On appeal to the *Bundesfinanzhof* the judgment of the fiscal court was quashed and the *Bundesfinanzhof* fixed itself the average rate of the turnover tax in deviation from the German *Umsatzsteuergesetz* (Turnover Tax Code). The company then lodged a complaint before the *Bundesverfassungsgericht*, arguing that its right to a *gesetzliche Richter* under Art. 101(1)(2) GG had been infringed by the failure of the *Bundesfinanzhof* to make a further reference for a preliminary ruling by the ECJ pursuant to Art. 234 EC.

[128] *Bundesverfassungsgericht*, decision of 22 October 1986, *Wünsche Handelsgesellschaft (Solange II)*, BverfGE 73, 339; [1987] 3 CMLR 225; Oppenheimer, *The Cases*, 461. The applicant company, Wünsche, was refused a licence for the importation of mushrooms which was required under certain Commission Regulations. In proceedings before the administrative courts and finally the Federal Administrative Court (*Bundesverwaltungsgericht*), the question of the validity of the Regulations was referred to the ECJ Following the European Court's decision to uphold the validity of the Commission Regulations, the applicant company argued before the Federal Administrative Court that there had been a violation

the European Court's character as a court within the meaning of Article 101(1)(2) of the Constitution'.[129] The Court of Justice was a sovereign organ of the judicature established by the Community Treaties, functionally interlocked with the institutions of the Member States. This functional interlocking together with the fact that the Community Treaties were, by virtue of Articles 24(1) and 59(2)(1) of the Basic Law part of the legal order which applies in Germany, gave the European Court the character of a lawful court under Article 101(1)(2) of the Basic Law in so far as the legislation ratifying the Treaties confers on the Court judicial functions contained therein, including the conclusive authority to make decisions on the interpretation of the Treaties and on the validity of Community law derived therefrom.

The classification of the Court of Justice as a statutory court 'translates' the Community obligations of the German courts deriving from Article 234 EC into constitutional obligations. An arbitrary refusal to refer a question for preliminary ruling to the Court of Justice of itself amounts to a violation of the German Constitution, in particular the right to a lawful court. This conclusion, the *Bundesverfassungsgericht* underlined, corresponds to the international law obligation on the Federal Republic arising under Article 5(1) of the EEC Treaty (now Article 10 EC) to take all appropriate measures to fulfil the obligations arising from the Treaty. The conclusion is all the more important since there is hardly a Community law sanction of the (arbitrary) refusal of a court of final instance (or any other court for that matter) to refer a question for preliminary ruling to the European Court: an infraction procedure will not be instituted, and by and of itself, the failure to make a reference will not suffice for the liability of the State to be established under *Köbler*.[130] In Germany there is now a national constitutional means to enforce the duty to refer questions for preliminary ruling, even if it is restricted to

of various constitutional rules and requested that the proceedings be suspended and that either the question should be referred to the Constitutional Court whether the relevant regulations as interpreted by the ECJ could be applied in the Federal Republic, or a fresh reference should be made to the European Court under Art. 234 EC In breach of the constitutional principle of a right to a hearing the ECJ had allegedly failed to appraise a large part of the arguments put forward by the parties. The Federal Administrative Court dismissed the appeal as unfounded without making a further reference to the ECJ or the Constitutional Court, the first because the appellant had not given any occasion to doubt the correctness or clarity of the European Court's judgment; the latter since the Basic Law gave the Constitutional Court a power of review over the Legislature, but not over courts and therefore not over the European Court either. Wünsche then brought an appeal on constitutional grounds before the Federal Constitutional Court arguing that the judgment of the Bundesverwaltungsgericht disregarded its procedural and substantial rights under several Articles of the Basic Law in conjunction with Art. 234(3) EC.

[129] *Bundesverfassungsgericht*, decision of 22 October 1986, *Wünsche Handelsgesellschaft (Solange II)*, BverfGE 73, 339, under BI[4](aa), Oppenheimer, *The Cases*, at 477.
[130] Case C–224/01 *Köbler v Austrian Republic*, decision of 30 September 2003, nyr in ECR.

cases of arbitrary refusal. One such instance is where a court of last resort deviates from a ruling of the Court of Justice on a particular question without making a new reference.

This is what occurred in the *Kloppenburg* case, where the *Bundesverfassungsgericht* brought an end to the 'rebellion' of the *Bundesfinanzhof* against the Court of Justice on the issue of the direct effect of directives. In 1981 the *Bundesfinanzhof* had ruled that a directive was beyond any reasonable doubt binding on the Member States, but that it could not create directly applicable law in those States. Individuals could not therefore rely on the provisions of a directive which had not been implemented, in other words, directives lacked direct effect.[131] The Federal Fiscal Court saw no reason to refer the matter to the Court of Justice under Article 234(3) EC.[132] The rebellion in the 1985 *Kloppenburg* decision[133] was even more blatant since the Court of Justice had already handed a preliminary ruling in the very case at hand, upon reference by the *Finanzgericht Niedersachsen*.[134] The *Finanzgericht* followed the ruling of the Court of Justice, but on appeal the *Bundesfinanzhof* quashed the decision and dismissed the application. The *Bundesfinanzhof* explained its rebellion on the basis of German constitutional law. The thrust of the argument was that the Court of Justice had transgressed the proper limits of interpretation of Article 189(3) of the EC Treaty (now Article 249 EC) and had extended the effect of directives in a way which was no longer covered by the German legislation enacting the Treaty. In other words, the Court of Justice was accused of having made an *ultra vires* interpretation of the Treaty, which could not be binding on national courts. This is, in fact, an application *avant la lettre*, by the *Bundesfinanzhof*, of the *Maastricht Urteil* of the Constitutional Court holding that should the Court develop

---

[131] *Bundesfinanzhof*, decision of 16 July 1981, *Kloppenburg*, V B 51/80, BFHE 133, 470; [1982] 1 CMLR 527. The *Bundesfinanzhof* expressed its concurrence with the *Cohn-Bendit* decision of the *Conseil d'État*, decision of 22 December 1978, *Cohn-Bendit*, Rec. 524; [1980] 1 CMLR 543. As the reader will be aware, the Court of Justice had held in 1974 that directives could, under specific conditions, be relied upon by individuals before their national courts, *Case 41/74 Van Duyn v Home Office* [1974] ECR 1337. Due to the peculiarities of the French system of constitutional review, the *Conseil constitutionnel* could not play a similar role as arbiter between the *Conseil d'État* and the Court of Justice in the parallel rebellion of the *Conseil d'État* in the case of the direct effect of directives.

[132] Exactly the same question on the direct effect of art. 13 B (d) 1 of the Sixth Council Directive 77/388/EEC of 17 May 1977 on the harmonization of the laws of the Member States relating to turn-over tax, [1977] OJ L 145/1 was already pending before the Court of Justice upon reference by the *Finanzgericht* Münster, *Case 8/81 Ursula Becker v Finanzamt Münster-Innenstadt* [1982] ECR 53, decided on 19 January 1982.

[133] *Bundesfinanzhof*, decision of 25 April 1985, *Kloppenburg*, V R 123/84, BFHE 143, 383; [1989] 1 CMLR 873, see comments Th Stein, *CML Rev*, 1986, 727; X, 'The Bundesfinanzhof rebels again', *ELR*, 1985, 303; Chr Tomuschat, 'Nein, und abermals Nein! Zum Urteil des BFH vom 25. April 1985', *EuR*, 1985, 346; G Meier, 'Krieg der Richter – Was nun?', *RIW*, 1985, 748.

[134] Case 70/83 *Kloppenburg v Finanzamt Leer* [1984] ECR 1075.

Community law beyond what had been agreed in the Treaties and enacted by the German Legislature, such rulings would be considered as *ultra vires* and therefore be inapplicable in Germany.

It was the *Bundesverfassungsgericht* who put the *'Krieg der Richter'* to rest,[135] holding that Article 234 EC conferred upon the Court of Justice the power of final decision over the interpretation of the Treaty and the interpretation and validity of Community law deriving from it. Judgments of the Court under Article 234 EC were binding on the national courts deciding the same issue. However, the jurisdiction granted by Article 234 EC was not unlimited, and the limits imposed on it by the Basic Law were ultimately subject to the jurisdiction of the *Bundesverfassungsgericht*. But the Court held that in the case at hand, the Court of Justice had stayed within the bounds of the powers assigned to it. It was within the bounds of Article 24(1) of the Constitution to grant the Court of Justice an authority to develop the law, within the limits to the scope of the Community's authority. Therefore, the *Bundesfinanzhof* was bound by the preliminary ruling handed by the Court of Justice. If it had not wished to follow the view of the law stated by the Court of Justice, it should have made a fresh reference. And the Constitutional Court concluded: *'The Federal Supreme Fiscal Court avoided in an objectively arbitrary way the obligation to request a further preliminary ruling from the Court of Justice pursuant to Article 177(3) EEC. It a court of final appeal refuses to fulfil this obligation regarding questions of law which have already been subject of a preliminary ruling by the European Court of Justice in the same proceedings, that constitutes a violation of Article 101(1), sentence 2 of the Constitution, regardless of how the criterion of arbitrariness is construed in relation to violations of the obligation to obtain a preliminary ruling pursuant to Article 177'.*[136] In the case at hand the Constitutional Court in practical effect strengthened the authority of the Court of Justice. Yet, the decision also contains an important warning, which it repeated in stronger terms in the *Maastricht Urteil*: the *Bundesverfassungsgericht* will check the development of Community law by the Court of Justice.

The *Bundesverfassungsgericht* defined the notion of arbitrariness in a decision of 1990, where it detected three sets of cases that amount to an infringement of Article 101 of the *Grundgesetz*:[137] first, cases where the relevant court does not at all consider referring a question, even though

---

[135] *Bundesverfassungsgericht*, decision of 8 April 1987, *Kloppenburg*, BverfGE 75, 223; [1988] 3 CMLR 1; Oppenheimer, *The Cases*, 497; see *e.g.* M Zuleeg, 'Bundesfinanzhof und Gemeinschaftsrecht', *in 75 Jahre Reichsfinanzhof – Bundesfinanzhof – Festschrift*, Der Präsident des Bundesfinanzhofs (ed) Bonn, Stv, 1993) 115; CO Lenz and G Grill, 'Zum Verhältnis zwischen dem Bundesfinanzhof und dem Gerichtshof der Europäischen Gemeinschaften', in P Kirchhof *et al* (eds), *Steuerrecht – Verfassungsrecht – Finanzpolitik – Festschrift für Franz Klein*, (Köln, Otto Schmidt Verlag, 1994), 103.
[136] Translation taken from Oppenheimer, *The Cases*, 496, at 518.
[137] *Bundesverfassungsgericht*, decision of 31 May 1990, *Absatzfonds*, BVerfGE 82, 159.

that court itself has doubts about how to answer the question at issue correctly; second, where the court deliberately departs from the case law of the Court of Justice without making a reference. The third set of cases, and the most difficult to decide in practice, were those where the case law of the Court of Justice was not entirely clear or open for development, and the court of final instance decided the case in one way, while the opposing opinions on the Community issue would evidently have to be given priority.[138] The second case in which the right to a lawful judge was successfully pleaded against a failure to refer under Article 234(3) EC was handed in 2001,[139] when the *Bundesverfassungsgericht* made the test even stricter on the final instance courts: where the position of the Court of Justice was not entirely clear on a particular topic, any failure to refer would constitute a violation of Article 101 of the Basic Law, even absent any 'incorrect' decision of the final instance court, or any arbitrariness.

When it comes to its own relationship with the Court of Justice, the *Bundesverfassungsgericht* speaks of a *'Kooperationsverhältnis'*, a relation of co-operation. This relationship is however not the relation of co-operation which one would expect on the basis of the text of the Treaties, whereby the application of Community law is left to the national courts, while the European Court deals with the interpretation and validity thereof, with the preliminary rulings procedure as the means of communication between both levels. The relation of co-operation described by the *Bundesverfassungsgericht*, most notoriously in its *Maastricht Urteil*, is one in which, in practical effect, the Constitutional Court supervises the Court of Justice, in the area of fundamental rights and with respect to the limits of the Community competences. The *Maastricht* judgment must be put in perspective since the *Alcan* decision[140] and the final decision in the banana saga,[141] but in any case, the *Bundesverfassungsgericht* does not display the same strictness when it comes to its own duty to refer.

The characterisation of the Court of Justice as a *gesetzliche Richter* has been taken over in Austria.[142] But most systems do not know any similar rule or provision. In fact, the Spanish *Tribunal constitucional* has announced that it had no business with the way in which the lower courts did or did not refer questions to Luxembourg. In the *FOGASA* case, a complainant claimed that his right to effective judicial protection under

---

[138] See also CD Classen, Case comment, 'German Bundesvergfassungsgericht: Medical training, Decision of 9 January 2001', 39 *CML Rev*, 2002, 641, at 644–45.

[139] *Bundesverfassungsgericht*, decision of 9 January 2001, *Medical training*, available on www.bverfg. de; commented in 39 *CML Rev*, 2002, 641.

[140] *Bundesverfassungsgericht*, decision of 17 February 2000, *Alcan*, available on www.bverfg.de.

[141] *Bundesverfassungsgericht*, decision of 7 June 2000, *Bananas III (Atlanta)*, BVerfGE 102, 147.

[142] See P Fischer and A Lengauer, 'The Adaptation of the Austrian legal system following EU membership', *CML Rev*, 2000, 763, at 779, reference to *Verfassungsgericht*, decision B 3067/95 of 30 September 1996.

the Spanish Constitution had been infringed, because the court of final instance hearing his case had not referred a question to the European Court. The *Tribunal constitucional* answered that *'the decision not to ask for a preliminary ruling from the European Court of Justice may not,* per se, *result in a violation of the Constitution (..) This decision belongs exclusively to the ordinary judge and may not be subject to review by this Court'*.[143]

13.3.3. Are the Constitutional Courts under an Obligation to Make References for Preliminary Ruling?

The main avenue for judicial dialogue between the European Court of Justice and the national courts is the preliminary rulings procedure of Article 234 EC.[144] Article 234 provides for a mechanism, previously unknown in international organisations,[145] that serves as the direct link between the European Court of Justice and the first in line Community courts, the national courts of the Member States. The aim of Article 234 EC', as is well known, is to facilitate the tasks of the national courts when confronted with Community law and to ensure the uniform interpretation and application of Community law throughout the Community. The procedure has played a pivotal role in the establishment and the development of the Community legal order as it stands. The concepts of direct effect, supremacy, the protection of fundamental rights and the like which have been instrumental in what is generally called the constitutionalisation of Europe have all been developed in the context of references from national courts. The procedure of Article 234 EC has provided the basis for the European judicial system. Yet, it has not created an open forum for discussion or direct and open link between the constitutional

---

[143] *Tribunal constitucional*, decision 180/93 of 31 May 1993, *FOGASA, BOE* 5 July 1993, also available on www.boe.es; translation and comments taken from A Estella de Noriega, 'A Dissident Voice: The Spanish Constitutional Court Case Law on European Integration', 5 *EPL*, 1999, 269, at 281.

[144] See generally e.g. D Anderson, *References to the European Court of Justice* (London, Sweet & Maxwell, 1995); D Edward, *Article 177 References to the European Court – Policy and Practice* (Butterworths, 1994); C Barnard and E Sharpston, 'The Changing Face of Article 177 References', 34 *CML Rev* (1997) 1113;

[145] There are several national courts structures which do provide for similar preliminary references to a higher specialized court, mainly concerning questions of constitutionality. The German *Vorlageverfahren* before the *Bundesverfassungsgericht* and the Italian procedure of *questione incidentale di legittimità costituzionale* referred to the *Corte costituzionale* have served as examples for the preliminary rulings procedure under the founding Treaties, see P Pescatore, 'De werkzaamheden van de "juridische groep" bij de onderhandelingen over de Verdragen van Rome', *Studia Diplomatica*, 1981, 167, at 181 who believes that it was Catalano who suggested to introduce a system of preliminary questions on interpretation to be added to the reference procedure on validity already existing under the ECSC Treaty. The preliminary reference procedure exists also in the Belgian system of constitutional review by the *Arbitragehof*.

courts and the Court of Justice. References by constitutional courts are extremely exceptional. To this day only the Belgian *Arbitragehof* and the Austrian *Verfassungsgericht* have made references to Luxembourg, and they have done so only very recently. The Italian *Corte costituzionale* has even expressly ruled out the possibility of sending questions to the Kirchberg.

Why does Article 234 EC not play the same pivotal role in the relationship between constitutional courts and the European Court? Why does it not function as the obvious vehicle for a direct judicial constitutional dialogue? Are the constitutional courts comprised in the notion of 'court or tribunal' in Article 234 EC? If so, are they not necessarily under an obligation to refer, given the fact that there is no appeal against decisions of constitutional courts?

13.3.3.1.   Article 234 EC

The basic principles governing the operation of Article 234 EC are familiar. The system is based on co-operation entailing a division of duties between the national courts and the Court of Justice in the interest of the proper application and uniform interpretation of Community law throughout the Community. It is jurisdictional exclusivity rather than hierarchical superiority.[146] It is for the national court to assess the relevance of Community law with regard to the outcome of the case and to decide whether a reference is necessary. The national court decides what questions to refer[147] and when to refer them.[148] The national court also bears the responsibility for the subsequent judicial decision. Thus: application to the facts of the case is for the national court, interpretation and decision on the validity of Community law for the European Court of Justice. While the general rule is that the need for and appropriateness of a reference are at the discretion of the national court, the European Court has made some exceptions for manufactured, hypothetical and moot questions, for manifestly irrelevant questions and for incomprehensible questions.

For the first category, manufactured, hypothetical and moot questions, the Court held first in *Foglia v Novello* that there must be a genuine dispute involving an issue of Community law for the Court to have jurisdiction to

---

[146] It is however correctly pointed out that the relationship between the ECJ and the national courts has developed from the original horizontal and bilateral relation, to a more vertical and multilateral relationship, see P Craig and G de Búrca, *EU Law, Text, Cases and Materials*, 3rd edn, (Oxford, OUP, 2003), Chapter 11.

[147] The Court does make a habit of rephrasing questions. In some instances, rewriting the questions leaves the referring national court with an answer that does not make the resolution of the case any easier, *e.g.* in the Sunday trading cases, see J Steiner, 'Drawing the line: Uses and Abuses of Article 30 EEC', 29 *CML Rev*, 1992, 749.

[148] Joined Cases C–320/90, C–321/90 and C–322/90 *Telemarsicabruzzo SpA v Circostel and Ministero delle Poste e Telecomunicazioni and Ministero della Difesa* [1993] I–393.

answer a question.[149] The Court does not deliver advisory opinions.[150] *Foglia and Novello* was heavily criticised in the literature and has not often been applied. Secondly, the Court will not give a ruling where the questions raised are not relevant to the resolution of the substantive action.[151] And third, the Court does not answer questions which are unintelligible or where the national court fails to define the factual and legislative context to allow the Court to be able to give a meaningful answer.[152] These instances are still the exception: under the general stance it is for the referring court to decide whether and what to refer.[153]

13.3.3.2. *Article 234(3) EC*

Where a national court or tribunal considers that a decision on the interpretation or the validity of the Treaty and specified Community acts is necessary to give judgment, such a court may request the Court of Justice to give a ruling thereon. If such question is raised in a case pending before a court or tribunal against whose decisions there is no judicial remedy under national law, that court or tribunal *shall* bring the matter before the Court of Justice. Thus, lower courts may refer; courts of final instance are under an obligation to refer. Several exceptions have been made to the rule. First, an additional duty to refer has been introduced for lower courts also. Where a lower court maintains doubts about the validity of Community law, it *must* refer the issue to the Court in Luxembourg, since that Court has exclusive jurisdiction to hold a Community act

---

[149] As the Court held in *Foglia v Novello* 'the duty assigned to the Court by article 177 is not that of delivering advisory opinions on general or hypothetical questions but of assisting in the administration of justice in the Member States'. It accordingly does not have jurisdiction to reply to questions of interpretation which are submitted to it within the framework of precedural devices arranged by the parties in order to induce the Court to give its view on certain problems of Community law which do not correspond to an objective requirement inherent in the resolution of a dispute', Case 244/80 *Foglia v Novello (No* [1981] 2 ECR 3045, para 16. The parties had fabricated a dispute in order to obtain a ruling from the Court.

[150] Case 244/80 *Foglia v Novello (No* [1981] 2 ECR 3045, para 18.

[151] Examples are Case C–343/90 *Lourenco Dias v Director da Alfandega do Porto* [1992] ECR I–4673; C–83/91 *Wienand Meilicke v ADV/ORGA FA Meyer AG* [1992] ECR I–4871C-18/93 *Corsica Ferries Italia Srl v Corpo dei Piloti del Porto di Genova* [1994] ECR I–1783.

[152] Most famously in Case C–320–322/90 *Telemarsicabruzzo SpA v Circostel, Ministero delle Poste e Telecommunicazioni e Ministero della Difesa* [1993] ECR I–393, at para 5: 'the need to provide an interpretation of Community law which will be of use to the national court makes it necessary that the national court define the factual and legislative context of the questions it is asking or, at the very least, explain the factual circumstances on which those questions are based'; see also Case C–157/92 *Pretore di Genova v Giorgio Banchero* [1993] ECR I–1085.

[153] According to Judge D Edward, only 27 references have been rejected as inadmissible over 9 years until 2000, on average around one per cent per year, D Edward, 'Reform of Article 234 Procedure: The Limits of the Possible', in D O'Keeffe and A Bavasso (eds), *Judicial Review in European Union Law. Liber Amicorum in Honour of Lord Slynn of Hadley*, Vol I, (The Hague, Kluwer Law International, 2000), 119, at 122.

invalid.[154] The text of Article 234 EC may have suggested otherwise, but the Court drew on the requirements of uniform application and of legal certainty and the coherence of the system of judicial review. In addition, the Court has introduced two exceptions to the duty to refer imposed on the courts of final instance, known as *acte clair* and *acte éclairé*. Under the *acte éclairé* exception, national courts falling under the scope of Article 234(3) EC are not under an obligation to refer when the same point of law has been addressed in a previous case, irrespective of the type of proceedings that led to those decisions and even though the questions at issue are not strictly identical.[155] This precedent type rule applies both for rulings on the interpretation of Community law and for judgments upholding the validity of a Community act. In both cases, while the national courts are left with the discretion to raise once again a question which has already been answered, they are not under an obligation to do so and may rely on the authority of the previous case. The second exception to the obligation to refer, *acte clair*, has been much more problematic and has given rise to several cases of abuse.[156] Courts of final instance are no longer under an obligation to refer when it is established that the correct application of Community law is so obvious as to leave no scope for any reasonable doubt, in the light of the specific characteristics of Community law, the particular difficulties to which its interpretation gives rise and the risk of divergences in judicial decisions within the Community.[157] *Acte clair* was for the first time accepted by the Court in *CILFIT*, possibly as an answer to several 'unwilling' national courts of final instance which had on several occasions refused to refer questions to Luxembourg and had answered them on their own motion, most notoriously the French *Conseil d'État* in *Cohn-Bendit*.[158] Under that analysis of *CILFIT*, the judgment was based on a strategy of 'give and take'. The Court, unable to coerce the national courts of final instance to act on their obligation to refer, concedes something to the professional or national pride of the municipal judge, but restricts the circumstances in which the

---

[154] Case 314/85 *Foto-Frost v Hauptzollamt Lübeck-Ost* [1987] ECR 4199.

[155] Cases 28–30/62 *Da Costa and Schaake NV v Nederlandse Belastingadministratie* [1963] ECR 31; Case 283/81 *CILFIT* [1982] ECR 3415.

[156] See e.g. G Bebr, 'The Rambling Ghost of "Cohn-Bendit": *Acte Clair* and the Court of Justice', 20 *CML Rev*, 1983, 439; H Rasmussen, 'The European Court's Acte Clair Strategy in CILFIT, 9 *ELR*, 1984, 242; A Arnull, 'The Use and Abuse of Article 177', 52 *MLR*, 1989, 622; F Mancini and DT Keeling, 'From CILFIT to ERT: the Constitutional Challenge facing the European Court', 11 *YEL*, 1991, 1.

[157] Case 283/81 *CILFIT* [1982] ECR 3415.

[158] *Conseil d'État*, decision of 22 December 1978, *Cohn-Bendit*, Rec. 524; in the case the *Conseil d'État* refused to grant direct effect to directives on the ground that the text of article 189 EEC clearly excluded such effect for directives. The decision of the *Conseil d'État* was cited in approval by the German *Bundesfinanzhof* when it rejected direct effect of directives in *Kloppenburg, Bundesfinanzhof*, decision of 16 July 1981, *Kloppenburg*, BFHE 133, 47; *EuR*, 1981, 442; English translation in [1982] CMLR 527.

clarity of the provision may legitimately be sustained to cases so rare that the nucleus of its own authority is preserved intact.[159] Indeed the conditions are extremely restrictive, to the extent even that a correct application of *acte clair* is extremely rare. The Court expects the national courts also to look into the different language versions of the provisions under interpretation, they must be convinced that the matter is equally obvious to the courts of other Member States and to the Court of Justice, bearing in mind the peculiarity of Community law terminology and in keeping with the context of Community law as a whole, regard being had to the objectives thereof and to its state of evolution at the date on which the provision in question is to be applied.[160]

13.3.3.3. Are the National Constitutional Courts to be Considered 'Courts and Tribunals' in the Sense of Article 234 EC?

It is settled case law that the question of whether a body making a reference is a court or tribunal for the purposes of Article 234 EC is governed by Community law alone.[161] It does not matter therefore whether or not the instance is under its own national law considered as such or not. In deciding the question the Court takes account of a number of factors, such as whether the body is established by law, whether it is permanent, whether its jurisdiction is compulsory, whether its procedure is inter partes, whether it applies rules of law and whether it is independent.[162] Are the constitutional courts to be considered 'courts or tribunals' in the sense of Article 234 EC?

A distinction must be made between the separate constitutional courts, *Bundesverfassungsgericht, Corte costituzionale, Arbitragehof, Tribunal constitucional, Verfassungsgerichtshof* and *Conseil constitutionnel* on the one hand and the supreme courts having constitutional jurisdiction on the other: the Irish Supreme Court and the Danish *Højesteret*. There is no reason why

---

[159] F Mancini and DT Keeling, 'From CILFIT to ERT: the Constitutional Challenge facing the European Court', 11 *YEL*, 1991, 1, at 4.

[160] Case 283/81 *CILFIT* [1982] ECR 3415, paras 16–20.

[161] For instance Case C–17/00 *De Coster v College van Burgemeester en Schepenen van Watermaal-Bosvoorde* [2001] ECR I–9445, para 10.

[162] Case C–54/96 *Dorsch Consult* [1997] ECR I–4961; Joined Cases C–110/98 to C–147/98 *Gabalfrisa and Others* [2000] ECR I–1577; Case C–17/00 *De Coster* [2001] ECR I–9445. In his Opinion in the latter case. AG Ruiz-Jarabo Colomer asked the ECJ to reconsider its case law on the notion of 'court or tribunal' for want of clarity. He said that the notion had been so extended as to allow Sancho Panza to refer a question for preliminary ruling as governor of the Isle of Barataria, Opinion of AG Ruiz-Jarabo-Colomer in Case C–17/00 *De Coster* [2001] ECR I–9445, at marginal number 14. In the concrete case he came to the conclusion that the '*Raadsprekend college van het Brussels Hoofdstedelijk Gewest*' did not constitute a 'court or tribunal' in the sense of Art. 234 EC and that therefore the ECJ should decline jurisdiction. The ECJ did not follow its AG and maintained the existing definition and accepted jurisdiction to answer the question in the case at hand.

the latter courts should not be included in the notion of 'court or tribunal' in the sense of Article 234 EC. They are courts of final instance in the
judicial hierarchy, and always rule in concrete cases. Both the
Højesteret[163] and the Irish Supreme Court have referred questions to
Luxembourg in the past.[164]

The issue may be less clear in the case of separate constitutional courts.
The Court of Justice has never pronounced on the question. In the first
case ever to be referred by a veritable, *i.e.* separate constitutional court, the
issue of admissibility and of jurisdiction of the Court of Justice was not
discussed.[165] The Court answered the question without much ado. In the
case referred by the Austrian *Verfassungsgerichtshof*, it was the Austrian
Government who questioned the validity of the questions for the purposes of the main proceedings, having regard to the division of powers
between the Austrian courts.[166] Repeating the settled case law the Court
held that except where it is quite obvious that the interpretation of
Community law sought bears no relation to the actual facts of the main

---

[163] See O Due, 'Danish Preliminary References', in D O'Keeffe and A Bavasso (eds), *Judicial Review in European Union Law. Liber Amicorum in Honour of Lord Slynn of Hadley*, Vol I, (The Hague, Kluwer Law International, 2000), 363, who states there are probably no cases where Danish courts of last instance have clearly violated their obligation to refer questions to the ECJ The *Højesteret* has also held that before a Danish court may declare a Community act inapplicable in Denmark under its Maastricht decision, it must obtain a ruling from the ECJ on the validity of the act according to Community law, see Højesteret, decision of 6 April 1998, *Treaty of Maastricht*, UfR 1998.800 H; unofficial trans-lation available on the internet: www.um.dk/udenrigs-politik/europa/domeng.

[164] There have been cases where the Irish Supreme Court may have declined to refer a ques-tion to Luxembourg where it should have, see G Hogan and G Whyte, *Kelly's The Irish Constitution*, 3rd edn, (London, Butterworths, 1994) at 392, referring to *Supreme Court*, decision of 6 March 1997, *Society for the Protection of Unborn Children (Ire.) Ltd v Open Door Counselling Ltd* [1989] IR 593; [1989] ILRM 19; avaialable on www.irlii.org; *Supreme Court*, decision of 5 March 1992, *Attorney General v X* [1992] 1 IR 1; [1992] 2 CMLR 277; www.irlii.org; in the latter case there were of course practical time scale difficulties, as was pointed out by Finlay CJ.

[165] Case C–93/97 *Fédération belge des Chambres Syndicales de Médecins ASBL* [1998] ECR I–4837. The questions were raised in proceedings brought before the *Cour d'Arbitrage* seeking annulment of a Decree (regional equivalent of a loi) of the Flemish Community. The question of admissibility was probably not raised before the ECJ and the latter chose not to go into the issue. The question inquired about the interpretation of Art. 31 of Council Directive 93/16/EEC of 5 April 1993 to facilitate the free movement of doctors and the mutual recognition of their diplomas, certificates and other evidence of formal qualifications, OJ 1993 L 165/ 1. For the decision to suspend proceedings and refer a question to the ECJ see Arbitragehof, decision n. 6/97 of 19 February 1997, *Fédération belge des Chambres Syndicales de Médecins ASBL*, available on www.arbitrage.be; final deci-sion in *Arbitragehof*, decision n. 120/98 of 3 December 1998, *Fédération belge des Chambres Syndicales de Médecins ASBL*, available on www.arbitrage.be.

[166] The case turned on the constitutionality of an administrative decision. Under the Austrian Constitution, judicial review of administrative decisions is divided between the VGH and the *Verwaltungsgerichtshof*. The VGH may hear cases alleging infringements of the Constitution only if there has been a sufficiently serious and therefore also manifest breach. Except in those cases, it must leave judicial review to the *Verwaltungsgerichtshof*, see Opinion of AG Mischo in Case C–143/99 *Adria-Wien Pipeline GmbH v Finanzlandesdirektion für Kärnten* [2001] ECR I–8365, para 14.

action, it is for the national court hearing a dispute to determine both the need for a reference and the relevance of the questions. Moreover, it was not for the Court to determine whether the decision whereby a matter is brought before it was taken in accordance with the rules of national law governing the organisation of the courts and their procedure. The questions submitted by the *Verfassungsgerichtshof* were allowed.[167]

Writing extra-judicially, Gil Carlos Rodriguez Iglesias and Jean-Pierre Puissochet, President and Judge of the Court of Justice respectively, stated that the constitutional courts *did* constitute a court in the sense of Article 177 (old) of the EC Treaty, and that accordingly, references would be admissible. As any other court, they said, courts having constitutional jurisdiction would have to request a preliminary ruling from the European Court when they doubted the validity of an act of secondary Community law. And *'elle pourrait également, de la même manière, poser à la Cour une question portant sur l'interprétation de telle ou telle disposition pouvant ou non fonder la compétence de l'institution communautaire auteur de l'acte en cause'*.[168] The mere faculty to refer which they seem to suggest is striking: if the courts are indeed included in Article 234 EC, they must necessarily come under the last sentence of the Article and the faculty converts into an obligation.

In the absence of any Court decisions, it is not entirely clear whether the constitutional courts must make references for preliminary rulings, but it would seem that they are indeed included in the notion 'courts and tribunals' in Article 234 EC.[169] The fact that constitutional courts are sometimes not considered, under national law, to belong to the judicial organisation or to constitute veritable courts is not relevant:[170] The notion has a Community meaning. Constitutional courts are established by law, they are permanent, and have compulsory jurisdiction; they are independent and apply rules of law. The fact that they have jurisdiction exclusively to rule on the constitutionality of national law does not exclude the possibility of questions of interpretation or validity of Community law

---

[167] Case C–143/99 *Adria-Wien Pipeline GmbH v Finanzlandesdirection für Kärnten* [2001] ECR I–8365 paras 14–20.

[168] GC Rodriguez Iglesias and J-P Puissochet, 'Rapport de la Cour de Justice des Communautés europénnes', report for the conference of constitutional courts on 'Droit communautaire dérivé et droit constitutionnel' organised by the *Conseil constitutionnel* in 1997, published on www.conseil-constitutionnel.fr/cahiers/ccc4/ccc4aver.htm; my emphasis.

[169] The Court has traditionally been extremely generous in accepting instances as 'courts and tribunals'; this generosity has been criticised given the ECJ's workload, see e.g. Opinion of AG Ruiz-Jarabo Colomer in Case C–17/00 *De Coster v College van Burgemeester en Schepenen van Watermaal-Bosvoorde* [2001] ECR I–9445. If references from an administrative organ acting in a non-adversarial procedure are admissible (Case C–54/96 *Dorsch Consult* [1997] ECR I–4961) why not those from a constitutional court?

[170] See e.g. JE Schoettl, *Rapport général* drafted for the Conference of constitutional courts held in Paris, 1997, www.conseil-constitutionnel.fr/cahiers/ccc4/ccc4rage.htm, at 8.

arising. For instance, it may be that the correct interpretation of a Statute in accordance with Community law must be ascertained first.[171] Nevertheless, some criteria may argue against the qualification of constitutional courts as 'courts or tribunals': the procedure may not be *inter partes*[172] and there may not be a real conflict, in other words, a case or controversy. There are two situations where it is not so clear that the constitutional courts should make references. The first situation is where a constitutional court decides on a proposed Treaty amendment, as the *Conseil constitutionnel* and the *Bundesverfassungsgericht* in the case of the Treaty of Maastricht. The second is where the courts decide on preliminary references from ordinary courts.

In the first situation, where a constitutional court is asked to control the constitutionality of a proposed Treaty that has not yet entered into force, a reference would not be admissible. The Court of Justice has no jurisdiction to decide on questions dealing with a Treaty not yet in force. Therefore the *Conseil constitutionnel*, the *Bundesverfassungsgericht* and the Irish Supreme Court had no possibility, if they would have wanted to, to invoke the help from the Court of Justice, when deciding on the Maastricht Treaty or the Single European Act respectively. Yet, it is highly unlikely that they would have done so. In the instances mentioned the cases turned on the very heart of constitutional jurisdiction, on the most fundamental questions of constitutional interpretation. In these instances, the constitutional courts will go it alone.

The second area is that of constitutional courts deciding on preliminary reference from an ordinary court. The *Corte costituzionale*, the *Arbitragehof* and the *Bundesverfassungsgericht* have jurisdiction to rule on questions of constitutionality on preliminary reference from ordinary courts. It could be argued that in those circumstances it is the judge *a quo* who is responsible for referring questions to Luxembourg, while the constitutional court has to deal with constitutional issues exclusively. This seems to be the approach of the Italian *Corte costituzionale*. While in 1991 the *Corte* had in an *obiter* accepted that it had the possibility[173] of seizing the Court of Justice, it in 1995 *expressis verbis* excluded the possibility of it making a preliminary reference to the Court of Justice, because it lacked the quality of court or tribunal in the sense of Article 234 EC.[174] The case at hand was

---

[171] Moreover, are not all courts under an obligation in cases within their jurisdiction, enforce Community rights and set aside contrary legislation?

[172] The requirement that the procedure be *inter partes* is however not an absolute criterion, see Case C–54/96 *Dorsch Consult* [1997] ECR I–4961, para 31; Joined Cases C–110/98 to C–147/98 *Gabalfrisa* [2000] ECR I–1577, para 37; Case C–17/00 *De Coster* [2001] ECR I–9445, para14.

[173] '*la facoltà*', in *Corte costituzionale*, decision n. 168/91 of 18 April 1991, *Giampaoli, Foro italiano*, 1992, I, 660; published also on www.giurcost.org.

[174] *Corte costituzionale*, decision n. 536/95 of 15 December 1995, *s.r.l. Messaggero Servizi*, available on www.giurcost.org.

one in which the *Corte costituzionale* itself was adhered as *giudice incidentale di costituzionalità*, in other words, on a reference from a lower court. It
seems that in the opinion of the *Corte costituzionale*, it would be the judge
a quo who may refer a question to the Court in Luxembourg and the ordinary court of final instance in the case, the *Corte di cassazione*, which
would be obliged to refer, so that a question could in any case reach the
Court of Justice, even if the *Corte* did not itself make the reference. This
interpretation of the judgment is confirmed by another decision of the
Corte in which it held that it had no jurisdiction to rule on preliminary
references from ordinary courts if the latter had not ascertained the compatibility of the relevant law with Community law first. Community law,
including references to the Kirchberg, is in principle a matter for the
ordinary courts; the *Corte costituzionale* only deals with questions of constitutionality.[175] While this may make the entire process burdensome and
needlessly lengthy, it would still make a reference to the Court of Justice
possible at some moment in time.[176]

An additional argument against references could be the time restraints
imposed on the constitutional courts especially when dealing with *a priori*
questions of constitutionality.[177] The national courts act under strict time
limits in these cases, while it takes the Court of Justice almost two years
to deliver judgment in an Article 234 procedure. The new provisions on
an accelerated procedure most likely rule out this argument.[178]

13.3.3.4. An Obligation to Refer?

If the constitutional courts are considered courts and tribunals for the
purposes of Article 234 EC, they must also be *obliged* to refer questions,
given the fact that they always rule in final instance. Several cases of the
Court of Justice discuss the issue as to which courts are to be regarded as
covered by the third paragraph of Article 234 EC. Crucial in the case law

---

[175] This is different in the case of direct actions. Where the *Corte costituzionale* is the only
judge in the case, it will enforce Community law and annul legislation contrary to
Community law for breach of Art. 11 of the Constitution; see *Corte costituzionale*, decision
n. 384/94 of 7 November 1994, *Regione Umbria*, [1995] *Gazzetta Ufficiale*, I, Special Series,
no. 47; www.giurcost.org.

[176] See further below.

[177] As was stated by the Irish Supreme Court in the *fiches nationales synthétiques* at the occasion of the Conference of constitutional courts on the control of constitutionality of secondary Community law in Paris, 1997. The Supreme Court answered on the question of
preliminary reference to the ECJ: '*incompatible avec les délais du controle a priori, sauf à con-
sidérer que l'article 29 de la Constitution permet une dérogation aux règles de délai*'; the argument was raised at the meeting also by the Italian constitutional court and the *French
Conseil constitutionnel*.

[178] Under Art. 104(5) of the Rules of Procedure of the ECJ a national court may request the
President of the Court to decide to apply an accelerated procedure to a reference for a
preliminary ruling where the circumstances referred by the national court establish that
a ruling on the questions put to the ECJ is a matter of exceptional urgency.

is the aim of the obligation to refer: *'the obligation to refer is based on cooperation, with a view to ensuring the proper application and uniform interpretation of Community law in all the Member States, between national courts, in their capacity as courts responsible for the application of Community law, and the Court of Justice (..); the particular purpose of the third paragraph of Article 177 is to prevent a body of national case-law that is not in accord with the rules of Community law from coming into existence in any Member State'.*[179] It is clear that the Court rejects the view according to which only the courts at the top of the judicial pyramid are considered to be included: whether a court must be regarded as final instance court depends may differ from case to case. What is crucial is the aim of Article 234 EC namely to prevent any national decisions having force of *res judicata* and which would lead to divergences in the application of Community law. Accordingly, if the court decides a particular case in final instance, whether or not it is at the top of the judicial hierarchy, it is under an obligation to refer.[180] On the other hand, it appears that courts which are at the top of the judicial hierarchy and/or against whose decisions no remedy lies in national law, are automatically included in the third paragraph of Article 234 EC.[181] Sometimes two courts may be considered final instance courts in one case, but the obligation to refer will be adjusted, so that the reference made by the first court hearing the case dissolves the obligation of the court which comes in second. In *Parfums Christian Dior*,[182] the Dutch *Hoge Raad* (against whose decisions there is no remedy under national law) asked whether it was under an obligation to refer despite the fact that it was bound by the decisions of the Benelux court. The Court of Justice first confirmed that the Benelux court could indeed send questions for preliminary ruling to Luxembourg, and that it was obliged to do so since no appeal lies against its decisions. With respect to the *Hoge Raad* itself, the Court stated that *'there is no question that such a national supreme court, against whose decisions likewise no appeal lies under national law, may not give judgment without first making a reference to this Court under the third paragraph of Article 177 of the Treaty when a question relating to the interpretation of Community law is raised before it'.* However, it did not follow that both courts would actually be obliged to make a reference. In application of the principle of *acte éclairé*, the Court held that *'if, prior to making a reference to*

---

[179] Case C–337/95 *Parfums Christian Dior SA and Parfums Christian Dior BV v Evora BV* [1997] ECR I–6013, at para 25; see also Case C–99/00 *Criminal proceedings against Kenny Roland Lyckeskog* [2002] ECR I- 4839; at para 14.

[180] *So already Case 6/64 Costa v ENEL* [1964] ECR 585 (*giudice conciliatore* as final instance court); Case 107/76 *Hoffmann-La Roche* [1977] *ECR* 957; Joined Cases 35/82 and 36/82 *Morson and Jhanjan* [1982] *ECR* 3723.

[181] See Case C–99/00 *Criminal proceedings against Kenny Roland Lyckeskog* [2002] ECR I–4839; at para 15.

[182] Case C–337/95 *Parfums Christian Dior SA and Parfums Christian Dior BV v Evora BV* [1997] ECR I–6013.

the Benelux Court, a court like the Hoge Raad has made use of its power to sub-mit the question raised to the Court of Justice, the authority of the interpretation given by the latter may remove from a court like the Benelux Court its obligation to submit a question in substantially the same terms before giving its judgment. Conversely, if no reference has been made to the Court of Justice by a court like the Hoge Raad, a court like the Benelux Court must submit the question to the Court of Justice, whose ruling may then remove from the Hoge Raad the obligation to submit a question in substantially the same terms before giving its judgment'.

It would appear that national constitutional courts against whose deci-sions no appeal lies under national law are covered by Article 234(3) EC.[183] Nevertheless, it may not automatically follow that they are actually obliged to make a reference in a concrete case. Indeed, the reference by another final instance court deciding in the same case could dissolve the constitutional court from its obligation. In other words, if the *Bundesverfassungsgericht* accomplishes full respect of Article 234(3) EC on the part of the final instance *Fachgerichte*, as it attempts to do, it will hardly ever be left with a unresolved question, which it must refer. This applies only to those cases, of course, where others courts are involved in the same case.

Nevertheless, the constitutional courts do not usually figure in the answer to question one in Annual Reports of the application of Community law by national courts. Traditionally, question one in those reports asks whether there were cases 'where decisions against which there was no appeal were taken without a reference for preliminary ruling even though they turned on a point of Community law whose interpreta-tion was less than perfectly obvious'. The answers are drawn up by the Commission which has had access to data gathered by the Research and Documentation Department of the Court of Justice. The answers cite deci-sions of several courts of final instance every year, such as the Dutch *Hoge Raad*, the French *Cour de cassation*, the Italian *Consiglio di Stato* or the like. But separate constitutional courts did not, until very recently, figure in the reports. There was one remarkable exception: the Belgian *Arbitragehof*, the first one to have referred a question for preliminary ruling, has been cited in the answer to question one, even before it made its first reference.[184] The *Bundesverfassungsgericht* was mentioned in the answer to the first question, but only in the context of the question whether there were other decisions relevant in the context of the preliminary rulings procedure. The cases referred to concerned the right to a lawful judge and the failure of other courts of final instance to make a reference to the European Court.

---

[183] Case 337/95 *Parfums Christian Dior* [1997] ECR I–6013; at para 27.
[184] For the year 1995: *Annex IV – Application of Community law by National Courts in Thirteenth Annual Report on monitoring the Application of Community law – 1995*, OJ C 303, 14.10.1996, 178; For the year 1999: *Annex VI – Application of Community law by National Courts: A Survey*, published on the ECJ's website.

There may be several explanations for the fact that the Belgian Court is the only one ever to have been mentioned. One would be that none of the other courts[185] has ever ruled a case that turned on a point of Community law whose interpretation was less than perfectly obvious. This explanation is questionable: these cases do exist. A second explanation would be that only the Belgian *Arbitragehof* is considered a court or tribunal in the sense of Article 234 EC. This too is highly unlikely. The jurisdiction of the *Cour d'Arbitrage*, which decides on the constitutionality of primary legislation in direct actions and on preliminary reference, is similar to that of for instance the German or the Italian constitutional courts.[186]

Then, the 2001 Annual Report suddenly mentioned the *Bundesverfassungsgericht* and its decision not to refer a question for preliminary ruling in the case concerning the ban on the *Nationaldemokratische Partei Deutschlands (NPD)*.[187] The NPD had asked the *Bundesverfassungsgericht* to suspend the proceedings and refer several questions to the Court of Justice for preliminary ruling, whether Community law precluded a Member State from prohibiting a political party which stood not only at national elections but also at elections for the European Parliament. The claimant had asked the *Bundesverfassungsgericht* to refer questions under Article 234(3) EC, under the presumption that it was to be regarded as a final instance court. Nevertheless in its answer the *Bundesverfassungsgericht* stated that there were no grounds to make a reference under Article 234(1) EC, indicating that it did not consider itself covered by Article 234(3) EC. The case will be discussed further below. What is particularly striking here is the very mention in the annual report, while previously failures to refer, or the suggestion by a constitutional court that it would not in future make a reference such as in the case of the Italian *Corte costituzionale*, were never mentioned. Of course, the *NPD* decision dealt with the issue of the preliminary reference exclusively, and it would have been hard to miss it,

---

[185] Except for the Austrian *Verfassungsgerichtshof*.

[186] The German *Bundesverfassungsgericht* is mentioned several times in the answer to question one, but relating then to the second limb of the question 'Were there any other decisions regarding preliminary rulings that merit attention?'. The decisions of the *BVerfG* that are referred to are those on the right to a lawful judge under Article 101(1)(2) of the German Basic Law which is interpreted as containing for the German courts of final instance an obligation to refer under the German Constitution. The *BVerfG* does not seem to hold itself obliged under Art. 234 or Art. 101(1)(2) Basic Law, *infra*. The Austrian *Verfassungsgericht* has a similar stance: failure to discharge the obligation to refer questions incumbent on courts of final instance is a violation of the principle that nobody may be deprived of access to a lawful court enshrined in Art. 83(2) of the Austrian Federal Constitution; see *Verfassungsgerichtshof*, decision of 11 December 1995, Case B 2300/95–18, available on www.ris.bka.gv.at/vfgh.

[187] *Bundesverfassungsgericht*, decision of 22 December 2001, *Nationaldemokratische Partei Deutschlands (NPD)*, available on www.bundesverfassungsgericht.de.

while in most other cases the question of whether or not to refer is only one element of the case: this case could not be omitted.[188]

13.3.3.5. *The National Answer*

The Austrian *Verfassungsgericht* is the only one to have *expressis verbis* accepted to be under an obligation to refer questions for preliminary ruling to the Court of Justice.[189] The Court simply stated that since its decisions were final under domestic law, it was to be considered as a court in the sense of Article 177(3) of the EC Treaty. Consequently, a reference to the Court of Justice was obligatory. It then went on the check whether the conditions for application *CILFIT* were met, and found that they were not. The proceedings were suspended and the questions referred. The Belgian *Arbitragehof* made the reference without questioning its nature as 'court or tribunal' in the sense of Article 234 EC.[190] Writing extra-judicially, Michel Melchior, president of the *Cour d'arbitrage* attempted to minimise the importance of the reference, insisting that it should not be inferred that the *Cour d'arbitrage* did now recognise the primacy of Community law over the Belgian Constitution, or that it accepted any supervision from the Court of Justice. The *Cour d'arbitrage* merely asked about the exact interpretation and meaning of the relevant directive.[191]

The German *Bundesverfassungsgericht* has never referred questions for preliminary ruling to the Court in Luxembourg, even though it is

---

[188] It must be remembered that these reports are drawn up by the Commission, not by the Court of Justice. They contain only a brief description of the issues of the case and of the decision itself, and do not give an appreciation thereof.

[189] *Verfassungsgericht*, decision B 2251, 2594/ 97 of 10 March 1999, *Adria-Wien Pipeline GmbH v Finanzlandesdirection für Kärnten*; available on www.ris.bka.gv.at/vfgh; unofficial French translation of extracts on www.conseil-constitutionnel.fr/cahiers/ccc7/autext.htm. A new reference was made in Case C–171/01 *Wählergruppe 'Gemeinsam Zajedno/Birlikte Alternative und Grüne Gewerkschafter Innen/UG'*, pending, Opinion of AG Jacobs delivered on 12 December 2002.

[190] *Arbitragehof*, decision n. 6/97 of 19 February 1997, *Fédération belge des Chambres Syndicales de Médecins ASBL*, available on www.arbitrage.be, at marginal number B10. There are reasons to doubt whether it was necessary in the case to refer the question to the ECJ The applicants had argued before the *Arbitragehof* that the Flemish provision in question, whose interpretation was not entirely clear given the difficulty to interpret the Directive, infringed a Royal Decree; alternatively, that the violation of the Directive created an unconstitutional discrimination, given that it was violated only in one part of the country. The *Arbitragehof* sent questions to Luxembourg in order to find out the correct interpretation of the Directive and, by consequence, of the Flemish Decree that had to be interpreted accordingly. However, the *Arbitragehof* then held that a) it had no jurisdiction to ensure compliance with European Directives and with Royal Decrees and b) that a difference in legislation between the Regions could never constitute a form of unconstitutional discrimination, since that was the essence of regional autonomy. The outcome did not seem to depend on the interpretation of the Directive.

[191] See M Melchior and P Vandernoot, 'Controle de constitutionnalité et droit communautaire dérivé', *RBDC*, 1998, 3, at 32–36.

extremely helpful to the Court in obliging the other German courts of final instance to make references, and the duty to refer imposed on the final *Fachgerichte* is constitutionally enforced. But the *Bundesverfassungsgericht* abstains from seizing the Court of Justice itself, even though in *Solange I* it admitted that Article 177 of the Treaty also applied to it, and that it would be bound by rulings of the Court of Justice,[192] and despite its claim of having a relationship based on co-operation.[193]

There are cases in which the *Bundesverfassungsgericht* could or should have made a reference to the Kirchberg. The banana saga is a case in point. Instead of having an indirect and long dialogue with the Court of Justice, the Constitutional Court could have referred questions to Luxembourg, which would certainly have made the process shorter. Would it have been better? There are factors pointing in the opposite direction. The manner in which the dispute was solved was long and cumbersome for the parties in the case. But the courts involved in the process and especially the Court of Justice and the *Bundesverfassungsgericht* had the advantage of time, and a head-on collision was avoided in the end.

In the 2001 *Nationaldemokratische Partei Deutschlands* the Federal Constitutional Court did reveal its position on whether or not it might be covered by Article 234(3) EC. The claimant had asked the *Bundesverfassungsgericht* to suspend the proceedings to ban it[194] and to ask the Court of Justice whether a Member State would be precluded from banning a political party, since it also stood in the elections for the European Parliament. The question was framed on the basis of Article 234(3) EC, thus presuming that if the conditions were fulfilled, the *Bundesverfassungsgericht* would be obliged to make the reference. Nevertheless, the Constitutional Court answered that there were no grounds to make a reference *under Article 234(1) EC*. It was of the opinion that the Community did not have competence to make rules on political

---

[192] '(..) the BVerfG never rules on the validity or invalidity of a rule of Community law. (..) It can (just like, vice versa, the European Court) itself decide incidental questions of Community law in so far as the requirements of Article 177 of the Treaty, which are also binding on the Bundesverfassungsgericht, are not present or a ruling of the European Court, binding under Community law on the Bundesverfassungsgericht, does not supervene', *Bundesverfassungsgericht*, decision of 29 May 1974, *Internationale Handelsgesellschaft (Solange I)*, BVerfGE 37, 271; English translation in Oppenheimer, *The Cases*, 419, at 449.

[193] In the *questionnaire* drawn up at the occasion of the conference of constitutional courts on the issue of constitutional control of secondary Community law organised by *the Conseil constitutionnel* the German answer – drawn up by the *BVerfG* – to the question of references for preliminary rulings to the ECJ reads: '*Le tribunal constitutionnel s'abstient de saisir lui-même le juge communautaire, mais il s'estime lié par les arrêts préjudicials de la Cour de justice intervenus dans le case d'espèce dont il a à connaître*'.

[194] Under Article 21(2) of the German Basic Law. The procedure was brought by the Federal Government, the *Bundestag* and the *Bundesrat*; under § 43 of the *Bundesverfassungsgerichtsgesetz* the application may also be brought by any of the three separately or by the Government of a Land where the relevant party is restricted to its territory.

parties. In addition, the claims made on the basis of principles of *rechtsstaatlichkeit, Demokratie* and *Grundrechtsschutz* would not lead to a different conclusion, as these Community principles applied only where the Community itself or the Member States had acted in the scope of application of Community law. Beyond that, Member States were not bound by the constitutional norms of Union and Community law, as was clear from the *ERT* decision of the Court of Justice and Article 51 of the EU Charter of Fundamental Rights.[195] A reference on validity on the basis of Article 234(1)(b) EC did not lie either given that the relevant decisions in this context were not acts adopted by the Community institutions, but agreements in public international law within the field of application of Community law, as the European Court of Human Rights had held in the *Matthews* case.[196] The *Bundesverfassungsgericht* also stated that there was no ground for a reference under Article 68(1) EU on the preliminary rulings procedure under Title IV of the EC Treaty, since there was no issue of the free movement of persons involved. Finally, the Court of Justice would not have jurisdiction in the absence of a Community act, and Articles 46(d) and 6(2) EU read in conjunction with Article 234 EC could not be of any avail.

Now, while it may well be true that the case fell outside the scope of Community and Union law, and a reference was indeed not in place, it is striking that the *Bundesverfassungsgericht* considered its own position under Article 234(1) EC, while clearly under German law, there is no remedy against a decision of the *Bundesverfassungsgericht*, especially in a case of this type, *i.e.* the banning of a political party. The decision of the *Bundesverfassungsgericht* that a political party is unconstitutional is final and leads to its dissolution.[197] It is hard to see how the *Bundesverfassungsgericht* would not be covered by the third paragraph of Article 234 EC. Nevertheless, even then, the outcome of the case would not have been different since a reference would still not have been necessary to decide the case. This is an obvious attempt of the *Bundesverfassungsgericht* to free itself from any obligations to refer in other cases as well.

The French *Conseil constitutionnel* equally has never made a reference to the Court of Justice, nor does it seem to feel obliged to.[198] One can imagine situations in which the interpretation or validity of a Community act is of interest for a decision. Yet, it is unlikely that the *Conseil* will make such reference if only for the very strict time constraints. In addition, the *Conseil* does not decide actual disputes between parties.

---

[195] Note that the *Bundesverfassungsgericht* make reference to the Charter before the ECJ, be it to confirm the limited impact of fundamental principles on the Member States.
[196] European Court of Human Rights, decision of 18 February 1999, *Matthews v United Kingdom*.
[197] See § 46 Bundesverfassungsgerichtsgesetz.
[198] In the report to the 1997 Paris Conference of constitutional courts, it was considered '*douteux*' that the *Conseil constitutionnel* would make reference, '*ne serait-ce que du fait des contraintes de délais qui s'imposent à lui*', Rapport français, www.conseil-constitutionnel.fr /cahiers/ccc4/ccc4 fran.htm.

The Italian *Corte costituzionale* has stated that it will *not* refer questions for preliminary ruling when seized by an ordinary court on an exception of constitutionality. While it had accepted in *Giampaoli*[199] that it had the *possibility* – though not an obligation – to make a reference, it later held that it could not, since the *Corte costituzionale* was not to be considered a 'court or tribunal' in the sense of Article 234 EC. In that case, *Messaggero Servizi*,[200] the *Corte* was deciding a case upon reference from a lower court: it was itself seized by way of preliminary reference. The *Corte* held that the ordinary courts could and should – depending on whether an appeal lay against their decisions – make the reference, not the *Corte* itself. The up-side of that position is that the question may reach the Court of Justice at some point. But it would seem that insome cases it would be more efficient and logical for the *Corte costituzionale* to refer the question itself. As for the denial of its character as a 'court or tribunal', it should be kept in mind that it is a Community law notion, and must if necessary be interpreted by the Court of Justice, possibly upon a reference... from the *Corte costituzionale*? The *Corte costituzionale* also decides cases in direct actions, where it is the only and final judge. If the rationale for excluding the possibility of preliminary references to the European Court is the lack of quality of court or tribunal, this would seem to imply that the possibility (or obligation) of sending questions would also be absent in case of a direct action.[201] The result would then be that the European Court is in those cases definitively denied an interpretative role.[202] In that case, the violation of Article 234 EC is more obvious.

The Spanish *Tribunal constitucional* is equally unwilling to make references to the Court of Justice. Its dislike of the preliminary rulings procedure transpires from its position on references made by ordinary courts.[203] The *Tribunal* is unwilling to send questions itself: in its decision on the constitutionality of the Organic Law on the *General Electoral System*,[204] it denied a request by the Basque Parliament to refer a question.

---

[199] *Corte costituzionale*, decision n. 168/91 of 18 April 1991, *Giampaoli*, Foto italiano, 1992, I, 660, see also www.giurcost.org.

[200] *Corte costituzionale*, decision n. 536/95, *s.r.l. Messaggero Servizi*, available on www.giurcost. org.

[201] The Italian answer in the *questionnaire* of the *Conseil constitutionnel* seems to imply that is restricted to cases decided on reference: it is stated that the question of preliminary references to the Court of Justice is '*sans objet dans le cadre du controle a posteriori (question préjudicielle): c'est au juge a quo de renvoyer, le cas échéant, à la CJCE Jugement sur recours principal: renvoi logique en théorie, mais situation non encore rencontrée*'.

[202] See also G Tesauro, 'Community Law and National Courts – An Italian Perspective', in D O'Keeffe and A Bavasso (eds), *Judicial Review in European Union Law. Liber Amicorum in Honour of Lord Slynn of Hadley*, Vol I, (The Hague, Kluwer Law International, 2000), 391, at 398.

[203] A Estella de Noriega, 'A Dissident Voice: The Spanish Constitutional Court Case Law on European Integration', 5 *EPL*, 1999, 269, at 284ff.

[204] *Tribunal constitucional*, decision n. 28/91 of 14 February 1991, *General Electoral System*, Oppenheimer, *The Cases*, 702.

The *Tribunal* seemed to imply that references were a matter for the ordinary courts alone, and that it did not have anything to do with it.[205] In the *Lao* case, the Court again refused to make a reference and stated that *'the Community legal order has its own organs of control, among which this Court is not included. The verification of the fit of a Community and a national norm is a function therefore of the ordinary Spanish courts, with the assistance of the ECJ. This excludes, consequently, that this Court may make Article 177 references'.*[206] To say the least, this is a very dubious interpretation of Article 234 EC.

13.3.3.6. An Appraisal

References to the European Court could have important advantages in the relationship with constitutional courts. First, the Court of Justice could be alerted directly in a specific case that a constitutional court has its doubts about a particular Community act, for example, if it infringes fundamental rights or may be considered *ultra vires.* If references are left to the ordinary courts in such instance, the communication is only indirect. Secondly, and this is a point made by Dieter Grimm in the context of the German Federal Constitutional Court but which may apply to other courts as well, references also provide the Constitutional Court with important information. If a constitutional court doubts the validity (or applicability) of a Community act because the Community institutions have usurped powers, which have not been transferred, or because the act infringes fundamental rights. In such a case, the other Member States are also affected. If a reference is made, all the Member States can make their positions known. If the Court of Justice would still hold that there has been no violation of the Treaties and the Constitutional Court would want to exercise its competence to hold the act *ultra vires* and inapplicable in German, it would do so in full knowledge of the position of the other Member States.[207] The question is whether this scenario pleads for or against a reference. For example, if the *Bundesverfassungsgericht* has doubts on the validity of a Regulation for breach of fundamental rights, and the European Court has already ruled that there was no such breach. If the Constitutional Court would then make a reference, either the Court of Justice will take up the warning, change its opinion and declare the act invalid for breach of higher Community law. Or, and this seems more

---

[205] See also D Liñan Nogueras and J Roldán Barbero, 'The Judicial Application of Community Law in Spain', *CML Rev*, 1993, 1135, at 1150.

[206] *Tribunal constitucional*, decision n. 372/93 of 13 December 1993, *Lao*, *BOE* 19 January 1994; translation taken from Estella de Noriega, at 285–6.

[207] D Grimm, La Cour européenne de justice et les Juridictions nationales, vues sous l'angle du droit constitutionnel allemand. Situation après la 'Décision Maastricht' de la Cour Constitutionnelle fédérale d'Allemagne', drawn up for the 1997 Paris Conference of Constitutional Courts, www. conseil-constitutionnel.fr/cahiers/ccc4/ccc4grim.htm.

likely, it sticks to its case law and upholds the validity of the act, thus intensifying the conflict between the two courts. Indeed, it is even worse to declare a Community act inapplicable without asking than to ask first and then still do it when told not to. In both cases, there is a violation of Community law, including in any case of Article 234 EC, but the latter alternative is even more damaging for the Court of Justice, as it implies not only a denial of a duty to refer on the part of the constitutional court and of jurisdiction of the Court Justice, but also a clear rejection of the solution found by the Court of Justice and accordingly of its authority as the supreme interpreter of Community law. Psychologically and politically it is not acceptable first to ask the Court of Justice for a preliminary ruling and then to ignore it.[208] Such a scenario would be even more destructive for the Community judicial system based on mutual trust and co-operation. Not making a reference, while contrary to Article 234 EC, is less damaging to the system as a whole.

A case in point is the dispute over the Banana Regulation.[209] This long and complicated dispute lead to many judgments of the Court of Justice, three decisions of the *Bundesverfassungsgericht* and numerous decisions of ordinary courts not only in Germany but also in other Member States, and the WTO dispute settlement bodies. When the *Bundesverfassungsgericht* was confronted with the Bananas Regulation for the first time, the Court of Justice had already confirmed its legality in a severely criticised judgment[210] on an application for annulment brought by Germany.[211] In its order of 25 January 1995, the *Bundesverfassungsgericht* ordered the referring *Verwaltungsgerichtshof Kassel*[212] to re-examine the case. It insisted that German courts must protect the property rights of an importer if the latter risks going bankrupt because of an EC Regulation and that they must offer effective judicial protection including provisional measures. The Federal Constitutional Court found the EC Regulation open enough to allow for transitory measures and referred to the Government's obligation to use the possibilities in the Regulation to seek for an increase of the quota. It did so without referring the case to the European Court even though there were certainly questions relating to the interpretation and validity of the Regulation and the granting of interim relief in the case. The *Verwaltungsgerichtshof*, which was ordered to reconsider the case, found itself trapped between the demands of supremacy of Community

---

[208] CU Schmid, 'All Bark and No Bite: Notes on the Federal Constitutional Court's "*Banana* Decision"', *ELJ*, 2001, 95, at 110.

[209] Council Regulation 404/93 of 13 February 1993 on the common organisation of the market in bananas, OJ 1993 L 47, p 1. The saga is discussed further below.

[210] See for instance U Everling, 'Will Europe Slip on Bananas? The *Bananas* Judgment of the Court of Justice and the National Courts', *CML Rev*, 1996, 401.

[211] Case C–280/93 *Germany v Council* [1994] ECR I–4973.

[212] Verwaltungsgerichtshof Kassel = Verwaltungsgerichtshof Hesse.

law and the constitutional protection of fundamental rights, between the Court of Justice and the *Bundesverfassungsgericht*. It awarded additional licences provisionally and referred questions to the European Court.[213]

Sending a reference to the European Court was thus left to the ordinary courts, while there are sufficient reasons to argue that the *Bundesverfassungsgericht* should have done it itself.[214] There may, however, also be advantages to that approach: the dialogue remains indirect and consequently it does not lead to a head on collision. Conversation through intermediaries may be less confronting and therefore smoother. The European Court's real interlocutor was in fact still the *Bundesverfassungsgericht*.[215]

It is difficult to see how the national constitutional courts would not be included in the text of Article 234(3) EC. But how should the obligation be enforced? Enforcement proceedings under Article 226 EC are not very likely. Cases that reach the constitutional courts are mostly the difficult and sensitive cases, involving fundamental rights and national sensitivities, such as the Irish abortion cases, the German NPD case or the Belgian case concerning the prohibition of tobacco advertising and the Formula I races at Spa Francorchamps. Nevertheless, they may have an important impact on the internal market, as exemplified by the German bananas cases. But for the Commission to commence proceedings would stir up national hostility towards the Court of Justice and the Community rather than reinforce co-operation. In addition, courts are independent, and to sue the State for a failure to refer on the part of its constitutional court would be like suing the innocent. National actions, under *Köbler*,[216] seem even more unlikely, as it is difficult to see how an ordinary court could stand up against a constitutional court. It remains an obligation that is difficult to enforce.

13.3.3.7. *Alternative Modes of Communication*

Article 234 EC is not the main avenue for dialogue between the constitutional courts and the Court of Justice. Most constitutional courts do not make use of the direct channel to the Court of Justice, and rather communicate indirectly, by making other courts refer questions or by sending

---

[213] Case 68/95 *T Port GmbH Co KG v Bundesanstalt für Landwirtschaft und Ernährung* [1996] ECR I–6065.

[214] See *e.g.* N Reich, 'Judge-made 'Europe à la carte': Some Remarks on Recent Conflicts between European and German Constitutional Law Provoked by the Banana litigation', 7 *EJIL*, 1996, 103, at 108; U Everling, 'Will Europe Slip over Bananas? The Bananas Judgment of the Court of Justice and the National Courts', *CML Rev*, 1996, 401, at 434.

[215] Or, as Steve Peers has it, 'this reference was very crowded: there were three courts in it right from the beginning', S Peers, 'Taking Supremacy Seriously', 23 *ELR*, 1998, 146, at 154.

[216] Case C–224/01 *Köbler v Austrian Republic* [2003] ECR I-10239.

'messages' to Luxembourg in decisions relating to Community law from time to time.[217] There may be several reasons for the unwillingness to refer questions for preliminary ruling. There are procedural constraints and time limits; there may be legal constraints as the interpretation of the notion of court or tribunal. It may be that the constitutional courts view the preliminary reference procedure as *'une tutelle inacceptable'*;[218] there may even be an issue of ego. On the other hand, the Belgian *Arbitragehof* and the Austrian *Verfassungsgericht* have shown that referring questions is not 'such a big deal'.

There are, however, alternative forms of communication between the Court of Justice and the constitutional courts. There are regular visits of constitutional judges to the Court of Justice in Luxembourg[219] and *vice versa*. The European Court sponsors at regular intervals judicial conferences bringing together judges from throughout the Community,[220] in order to become better informed about the Court and to improve mutual understanding *'under the mellowing influence of wine and good cheer'*.[221] In turn, Members of the European Court are invited to meetings of the constitutional courts.[222] These meetings are invaluable for the development of mutual understanding between the Court of Justice and the national courts. The Court of Justice remains dependent on the goodwill of the national courts, and a pleasant relationship is, accordingly, vital.

---

[217] The *BVerfG* is considered to have this type of indirect dialogue with the ECJ The *Maastricht Urteil* for instance has often been interpreted as a warning addressed to the ECJ; the banana saga also contains elements of an indirect conversation with Luxembourg.

[218] O Dord, 'Le controle de constitutionnalité des actes communautaires dérivés: De la nécessité d'un dialogue entre les juridictions suprèmes de l'Union européenne', www.conseil-constitutionnel.fr/cahiers/ccc4/ccc4dord.htm, at 7.

[219] These vitis are reported on www.curia.eu.int.

[220] See R Dehousse, *The European Court of Justice. The Politics of Judicial Integration* (New York, St. Martin, 1998) at 139.

[221] So LN Brown and T Kennedy, Brown & Jacobs *The Court of Justice of the European Communities, 5th edn* (London, Sweet & Maxwell, 2000) at 401.

[222] For instance at the meeting of presidents of Constitutional Courts in Rome 1995, reported in *Diritto comunitario europeo e diritto nazionale. Atti del seminario internazionale*, Roma, Palazzo della Consulta, 14–15 Luglio 1995, (Milano, Giuffrè, 1997).

14

La Guerre des Juges?

14.1. CONSTITUTIONAL COURTS AND THE '*SIMMENTHAL* MANDATE':
ARE THE CONSTITUTIONAL COURTS UNDER THE SAME MANDATE
AS ORDINARY COURTS?

THIS SECTION SEEKS to ascertain whether the constitutional courts are under Community law to be considered as '*juges communs de droit communautaire*' in exactly the same way as the ordinary courts discussed in Part 1. The primacy of Community law, formulated in terms of the mandate of national judges as ordinary judges of Community law,[1] seems to imply that *all* courts must in cases within their jurisdiction award precedence to Community law and accordingly set aside any conflicting act of national law, including Acts of Parliament or Statutes.[2] Are the constitutional courts under the same Community law obligation to apply Community law, to enforce it against contrary acts of national law and to set aside those aside? And if so, what does 'to set aside' or 'disapply' mean in the case of constitutional courts? Are they under a Community obligation to declare conflicting legislation null and void?

14.1.1. The Community Duty to Set Aside Conflicting Legislation

The primacy of Community law entails duties for *all* national authorities. For the Legislature primacy entails the obligation to ensure that conflicting legislation is repealed, that inconsistencies are removed and, for the future, that inconsistent legislation is not adopted.[3] Secondly, all

---

[1] See Part 1.

[2] This section centres around the issue of '*ordinary supremacy*', the precedence of Community law over national legislation and more in particular primary legislation; the relationship between Community law and national constitutional law, which is even more complicated, is central in the remainder of this Part.

[3] *Eg,* Case 104/86 *Commission v Italy* [1988] ECR 1799; Case C–307/89 *Commission v France* [1991] ECR I–2903; Case 74/86 *Commission v Germany* [1988] ECR 2139. The fact that Community law precludes the valid adoption of new national legislative measures which would be incompatible with Community law does not however mean that such measures would have to be treated as non-existent. It simply implies that they cannot be applied, see Joined Cases C–10/97 to C–22/97 *Ministero delle Finanze v INCOGE '90 Srl* [1998] ECR I–6307.

administrative bodies, including decentralised authorities, are under the obligation to refuse to apply any conflicting provision of national law and individuals may rely on directly effective provisions of Community law against them.[4] And thirdly, under *Simmenthal*, 'every court *must, in a case within its jurisdiction, apply Community law in its entirety and protect rights which the latter confers on individuals and must accordingly set aside any provision of national law which may conflict with it, whether prior or subsequent to the Community rule'*;[5] *'a national court which is called upon, within the limits of its jurisdiction, to apply provisions of Community law is under a duty to give full effect to those provisions, if necessary refusing of its own motion to apply any conflicting provision of national legislation, even if adopted subsequently, and it is not necessary for the court to request or await the prior setting aside of such provision by legislative or other constitutional means'*.[6] These statements are broad enough to include courts having constitutional jurisdiction, including constitutional courts.

The question can also be turned around: why would constitutional courts *not* be under a Community law obligation to enforce Community law against conflicting legislation? It is sometimes argued that constitutional courts are not under an obligation to enforce Community law since they only have jurisdiction to review the *constitutionality* of legislation, not its compatibility with treaties or Community law.[7] Yet, this argument does not seem very convincing given the fact that the lack of jurisdiction under the national Constitution does not free the *ordinary* courts from a duty to review national law for compatibility with Community law. On the contrary, ordinary courts often have no jurisdiction to review primary legislation at all, whether on constitutionality or compatibility with treaty law. And yet, Community law gives them the mandate to review national primary legislation on its compatibility with Community law, irrespective of their jurisdiction under national law.[8] That is precisely the essence of *Simmenthal*: *'Every national court* must, *in a case within its jurisdiction, apply*

---

[4]   Case 103/88 *Fratelli Costanzo v Comune di Milano* [1989] ECR 1805; Case C–224/97 *Erich Ciola v Land Vorarlberg* [1999] ECR I–2517.

[5]   *Case 106/77 Simmenthal* [1978] ECR 629, para 21 (my italics).

[6]   Case 106/77 *Simmenthal* [1978] ECR 629, at para 24. In *Larsy*, the Court recently stated that 'that 'principle of the primacy of Community law means that not only the lower courts but all the courts of the Member State are under a duty to give full effect to Community law. If this were indeed the correct version of the ECJ's judgment, it would be a clear indication that also the constitutional courts were under such obligation. However, the French version (the language of the case) states that *'Ce principe de primauté du droit communautaire impose non seulement aux juridictions, mais à toutes les instances de l'État membre de donner plein effet à la norme communautaire'*. Given the context of the case, the ECJ must have been referring to the duties imposed on administrative authorities not to enforce conflicting national law; Case C–118/00 *Gervais Larsy v Institut national d'assurances socials pour travailleurs indépendants (Inasti)* [2001] ECR I–5063, at para 52.

[7]   See *infra* with respect to the French and Belgian situation.

[8]   See Part 1.

Community law in its entirety and protect rights which the latter confers on individuals and must accordingly set aside any provision of national law which may conflict with it, whether prior or subsequent to the Community rule'.[9] *Simmenthal* applies to all national courts irrespective of the domestic definition of their jurisdiction, so why not constitutional courts as well?

Simmenthal was concerned with an ordinary court which did not have jurisdiction to review primary legislation and which, under Italian constitutional law, had to refer an incompatibility between an Italian Statute and Community law to the *Corte costituzionale* by way of preliminary ruling. The Court of Justice freed the Italian courts from the obligation to make that detour via the *Corte costituzionale* and held that the direct applicability of Community law implied the power and obligation to all courts to give effect to such provisions of Community law if necessary refusing of its own motion to apply any conflicting provision of national law without awaiting the prior setting aside of such provision by another authority, in this case the *Corte costituzionale*. The ruling in *Simmenthal* seems broad enough to also include constitutional courts. There certainly are situations in which constitutional courts may be confronted with questions of 'ordinary supremacy', *i.e.* a conflict between a statute and Community law. A private applicant may then, in some systems, in a direct action[10] challenge the validity of a statute for violation of the Constitution and, in the alternative, for infringement of Community law. Does not *Simmenthal* give the constitutional court sufficient authority to rule on that second allegation?

The issue may be more complicated for the other main avenue for cases to reach the constitutional court, *i.e.* references for preliminary rulings coming from ordinary courts.[11] Say that an ordinary court is confronted with a question of validity of a statute, again for reason of compatibility with the Constitution and, in the alternative, with Community law. The first issue obviously is one for the constitutional court and for the constitutional court alone to decide. It alone has competence to rule on the constitutional validity of statutes. Yet, the question of the compatibility of the statute with Community law is one that can, again under *Simmenthal*, be decided by the *a quo* judge. Nevertheless, it is submitted that the competence of the referring court does not necessarily entail the lack of competence on the part of the constitutional court. From a Community law perspective it would seem that constitutional courts, as any other court, are under a *Simmenthal* obligation to ensure that Community law is applied even as against conflicting national law, especially where the

---

9   *Simmenthal*, para 21.
10 Such direct actions exist, in several varieties, for instance in Germany and Belgium.
11 For instance in Belgium, Germany or Italy.

constitutional court is the only court in the procedure, but even where there are other courts involved.

14.1.2. 'Disapplication' in the Hands of the Constitutional Courts

If the constitutional courts are, as any other judicial authority, under an obligation to enforce Community law even as against conflicting national law, what is expected of them? Most of these courts have the competence under national law to declare legislation unconstitutional and void. Are they also expected to annul primary legislation for violation of Community law, or does the direct applicability and primacy of Community law simply require the constitutional courts to merely 'disapply' the conflicting national provision in the case at hand as is the case for ordinary courts?[12]

As a general rule, the principle of primacy of Community law implies for the national courts a duty to set aside conflicting legislation. Statutes will most often simply not be applied to the case at hand. In practical effect disapplication will often lead to the same result as invalidation or annulment. But there are important differences. Provisions that are simply disapplied are not annulled or declared invalid; they remain on the law books, but are simply not applied to the extent of their inconsistency. They may continue to be applied in cases which are not in the scope of Community law or in cases where it is not inconsistent. This is different where the Community legislation seeks to harmonise legislation. In that case inconsistencies must be removed from the law books: there simply are no situations left in which the conflicting rule may be applied lawfully. Disapplication by the courts and administrative practices of not applying the rule do not suffice. It is what is expected of the courts in a particular case, but it does not take away the infringement of Community law. The Court has repeatedly held that the mere existence of conflicting legislation, even if the State acts in conformity with Community law in practical effect, creates an ambiguous situation causing uncertainty for individuals as to their rights under Community law. The State is required to do everything necessary to comply with Community law by repealing or modifying the conflicting norm. If not, the State fails to fulfil its obligations under Community law.[13]

---

[12] Joined Cases C–10/97 to 22/97 *Ministero delle Finanze v INCOGE '90 Srl* [1998] ECR I–6307, where the ECJ held that it could not be inferred from *Simmenthal* that the incompatibility with Community law of a subsequently adopted rule of national law has the effect of rendering that rule of national law non-existent. The national court must *disapply* that rule, *'provided always that this obligation does not restrict the power of the competent national courts to apply from among the various procedures available under national law, those which are appropriate for protecting the individual rights conferred by Community law'.*

[13] See *e.g.* Case C–307/89 *Commission v France* [1991] ECR I–2903.

The duty to disapply is only a minimum requirement. In *Lück* the Court of Justice was asked about the consequences of the precedence of Community law, in particular whether a national court must hold conflicting national provisions *inapplicable* to the extent to which they are incompatible with Community law or whether it must declare them *null and void*. The Court ruled that *'Although Article 95 of the Treaty has the effect of excluding the application of any national measure incompatible with it, the Article does not restrict the powers of the competent national courts to apply, from among the various procedures available under national law, those which are appropriate for the purpose of protecting the individual rights conferred by Community law'.*[14] Thus, individual administrative decisions based on conflicting national legislation will usually be annulled.[15] Does this also imply that a court having competence to annul primary legislation under national law must do so also in case of violation of Community law?[16]

An argument in favour of such obligation may be found in the *Rewe and Comet principle of non-discrimination or equivalence,* which provides that the forms of action, procedures and remedies available to ensure the observance of national law must be available in the same way to ensure the observance of Community law.[17] As is sufficiently known,[18] under *the principle of national procedural autonomy* it is for the national legal system to determine how the Community rights of individuals are to be protected, subject to the two conditions of *non-discrimination or equivalence* and *effectiveness*. The Court of Justice has intruded in this autonomy and has tightened the requirements of national procedural law. In essence, the obligation imposed on the national courts to enforce Community rights is

---

[14] Case 34/67 *Firma Gebrüder Lück v Hauptzollamt Köln-Rheinau* [1968] ECR 245, at 251.

[15] See recently Case C–224/97 *Erich Ciola v Land Vorarlberg* [1999] ECR I–2517.

[16] In this sense see *e.g.* D Simon, 'Les exigences de la primauté du droit communautaire: continuité ou métamorphoses?', in *L'Europe et le droit. Mélanges en hommage à Jean Boulouis* (Paris, Dalloz, 1991) 481, at 483.

[17] As laid down in Case 33/76 *Rewe Zentralfinanz eG and Rewe-Zentral AG v Landwirtschaftskammer für das Saarland* [1976] ECR 1989 and Case 45/76 *Comet BV v Produktschap voor Siergewassen* [1976] ECR 2043 where the ECJ held that 'In the absence of Community rules on this subject, it is for the domestic legal system of each Member State to designate the courts having jurisdiction and to determine the procedural conditions governing actions at law intended to ensure the protection of the rights which citizens have from the direct effect of Community law, it being understood that such conditions cannot be less favourable than those relating to similar actions of a domestic nature nor render virtually impossible or excessively difficult the exercise of rights conferred by Community law'.

[18] See above Chapter 5 in Part 1. P Craig and G de Búca, *EU Law. Text, Cases and Materials*, 2nd edn, (Oxford, OUP, 1998), Chapter 5; on the difficult issue of national procedural autonomy and the ECJ's interference therein see e.g. A Biondi, 'The European Court of Justice and Certain National Procedural Limitations: Not Such a Tough Relationship', 36 *CML Rev*, 1999, 1271; F Jacobs, 'Enforcing Community Rights and Obligations in National Courts: Striking the Balance', in M Lonbay and A Biondi (eds), *Remedies for Breach of EC Law*, (Chichester, Wiley, 1997), 25; S Prechal, 'Community Law in National Courts: The Lessons from *Van Schijndel*', 35 *CML Rev* (1998) 681.

an *obligation de résultat* to ensure that the directly enforceable rights, which individuals derive from Community law are protected in each case.

In the *Butter-buying Cruises* ruling the European Court held that although Community law was not intended to create new remedies in the national courts, to ensure the observance of Community law other than those already laid down by national law, *'it must be possible for every type of action provided for by national law to be available for the purpose of ensuring observance of Community provisions having direct effect, on the same conditions concerning the admissibility and procedure as would apply were it a question of ensuring the observance of national law'*.[19] The principle of equivalence suggests that if a court has jurisdiction to declare legislation void under national law, it should equally exercise that competence in order to ensure the observance of rights under Community law. Accordingly, a constitutional court that has jurisdiction to hold a statute null and void for unconstitutionality, must also have jurisdiction to declare it null and void for breach of Community law.

The difference between declaring a conflicting Act void and setting it aside in a concrete case is that in the former situation the Act completely disappears and the violation of Community law is removed; the decision has *erga omnes* effect. In the latter situation, Community law is effectively applied in the case at hand but there may be future infringements and the mere existence of the conflicting Act may create a diffuse situation, which makes it more difficult for the citizens to know their Community rights. The annulment of conflicting legislation certainly has important advantages: it disappears from the law books, and the constitutional courts thus protect the State from violating Community law.

14.1.3. The Practice of Constitutional Courts

14.1.3.1. The Conseil constitutionnel

The *Conseil constitutionnel* refuses to review primary legislation in the light of Community law. A distinction is made between review of constitutionality, which is reserved for the *Conseil constitutionnel* and the compatibility with treaties, the *conventionnalité*, which is the province of the ordinary courts.[20] In its decision *IVG* of 15 January 1975 the *Conseil constitutionnel* decided that it had no jurisdiction to review the conformity of

---

[19] Case 158/80 *Rewe-Handelsgesellschaft Nord mbH and Rewe-Markt Steffen v Hauptzollamt Kiel (butter-buying cruises)* [1981] ECR 1805, paragraph 44.

[20] For a critique of this '*dédoublement discret de la justice constitutionnelle*' D de Béchillon, 'De quelques incidences du controle de la conventionnalité internationale des lois par le juge ordinaire. (Malaise dans la Constitution)', *RFDA*, 1998, 225.

a pending bill with a treaty provision, in this case the ECHR.[21] The *Conseil constitutionnel* held that *'une loi contraire à un traité n'est pas, pour autant, contraire à la Constitution'*. Its decisions on the constitutionality of *lois* had an absolute and final character, while the supremacy of treaties over *lois* was of a relative and contingent nature. Relative, because the supremacy would be limited to the sphere of the Treaty, and contingent, because Article 55 of the Constitution submits supremacy to the condition of reciprocity. Consequently, the ordinary courts, first the *Cour de cassation* and later the *Conseil d'État* assumed jurisdiction under Article 55 to ensure the primacy of treaties and, if necessary, to set aside conflicting legislation.[22] The French system thus distinguishes between the *contrôle de constitutionnalité concentré a priori* and the *contrôle de conventionnalité diffus a postériori*. The distinction applies also to Community law which is not considered to be included in the *bloc de constitutionnalité* protected by the *Conseil constitutionnel*. Bills are not reviewed on their compatibility with Community law; the ordinary courts ensure the observance and application of Community law on a case-by-case basis, once the bill has become a *loi* and in the context of a concrete case or controversy.

Obviously the case of the *Conseil constitutionnel* is special: the *Conseil* only reviews Bills before their promulgation, and not those related to a particular case; the time limit is extremely short (1 month) and the bulk of treaty and Community law is enormous for the *Conseil* to exercise a full review. In addition, if the assumption of jurisdiction by the constitutional judge entails a denial of jurisdiction on the part of the ordinary courts, which is not excluded given the history of the case law of the *Conseil d'État*, the effectiveness of Community law would gain nothing. But why cannot both the constitutional council *and* the ordinary courts, each within their jurisdiction, ensure that Community law is observed: the *Conseil constitutionnel* a priori and in general; the ordinary courts a posteriori and on a case-by-case basis? The text of the Constitution does not seem to exclude that possibility: Article 55 does not attribute jurisdiction to the *Conseil constitutionnel* to review the *conventionnalité*, but it does not attribute it to the ordinary courts either.[23] There is no reason why not both

---

[21] *Conseil constitutionnel*, decision n. 74–54 DC of 15 January 1975, *Interruption volontaire de grossesse (IVG)*, published on www.conseil-constitutionnel.fr ; confirmed on numerous occasions since.

[22] See Part 1. When the *Conseil constitutionnel* acts as an election court, thus as an ordinary court, it does award precedence to treaty provisions over conflicting legislation, *Conseil constitutionnel*, decision n. 88–1082/1117 AN of 21 October 1988, *Val d'Oise*, RFDA, 1988, 908; AJDA, 1989, 128; published on www.conseil-constitutionnel.fr.

[23] De Béchillon proposes the introduction of an *exception d'inconventionnalité* before the *Conseil constitutionnel* whereby an ordinary court, confronted with a conflict between a *loi* and a treaty provision would have to refer to the constitutional council, so that the control of the *loi* would be in the hands of one court; D de Béchillon, *art. cit.*; Obviously, such a procedure would for Community law amount to an infringement of the basic principles of direct effect and supremacy as laid down in *Simmenthal*.

the *Conseil constitutionnel* and the ordinary courts could assume jurisdiction, each with distinct legal effects.

14.1.3.2. The Bundesverfassungsgericht

The German Federal Constitutional Court has, since 1971, rejected jurisdiction to review the compatibility of national law with Community law: *'The Federal Constitutional Court is not competent to answer the question of whether a norm of ordinary municipal law is incompatible with a provision of Community law invested with priority. The settlement of such a conflict of norms is a matter left to the courts with competence over the trial proceedings'.*[24] However, it is submitted that the jurisdiction of the ordinary courts should not exclude jurisdiction of the Constitutional Court. In cases coming within its jurisdiction, *i.e.* cases brought before it regularly and in accordance with the procedural requirements, the *Bundesverfassungsgericht* should also review the compatibility of German law with Community law and possibly annul legislation, or otherwise set aside this legislation.[25]

14.1.3.3. The Arbitragehof

The Belgian *Arbitragehof* denies jurisdiction to review the compatibility on Statutes and Decrees[26] with treaties *directly*, arguing that it has only been given jurisdiction, under Article 142 of the Constitution and the Special Act on the Court of Arbitration, to review the compatibility of Statutes with certain specified provisions of the Constitution.[27] This is not different for Community law, even if the jurisdiction could in this case be derived directly from Community law itself under *Simmenthal*. On the other hand, the *Arbitragehof* does review the compatibility with treaties

---

[24] *Bundesverfassungsgericht*, decision of 9 June 1971, *Alphons Lütticke*, BverfGE 31, 145; Oppenheimer, *The Cases*, 415, at 418.

[25] The *Bundesverfassungsgericht* does not only annul legislation and declare it void. It may also arrive at other conclusions, for instance declare that a particular rule may become unconstitutional in time, or that a particular situation is in fact unconstitutional, but that reparation is left to the legislature. Some of these decisions may also apply in the context of Community law. However, the last example may not pass the standards imposed by the Court of Justice, which requires the absolute unenforceability of conflicting national law. On the various types of decisions of the *Bundesverfassungsgericht*, see W Rupp-von Brünneck, 'Admonitory Functions of Constitutional Courts. Germany: The Federal Constitutional Court', 20 *AJCL*, 1972, 387.

[26] Primary legislation deriving from the federated entities.

[27] Twice, in 1983 and 1989, has a proposal been tabled to give the *Arbitragehof* jurisdiction to annul legislation for violation of Community law, in a direct action for annulment, alongside the competence of all the ordinary courts to review legislation in the case at hand, see H Bribosia, 'Applicabilité directe et primauté des traités internationaux et du droit communautaire. Réflexions générales sur le point de vue de l'ordre juridique belge', *RBDI*, 1996, 33, at 70.

and Community law *indirectly*, through violation of the reference standards in the Constitution. As the Court has held on numerous occasions, Articles 10 and 11 of the Constitution[28] have general scope in that they forbid all discrimination irrespective of its nature, so that the constitutional rules of equality and non-discrimination apply with respect to all rights and liberties that have been granted to Belgian citizens, either by the Constitution or by directly applicable rules of international treaties. The latter category also includes the directly applicable provisions of Community law, including secondary Community law.[29]

The technique of reviewing the respect for Community law through the constitutional principles of non-discrimination and equality aims at ensuring the primacy, at least in practice, of Community law. But it is artificial and sometimes far-fetched. The *Cour d'arbitrage* does not want to be seen as assuming new competences which it has not been given in the Constitution or in the Special Act on the Court of Arbitration. The technique of indirect control does attain the effects required by Community law, and it does imply that a statute or decree could be declared unconstitutional and be annulled accordingly, since it infringes Community law and therefore also Articles 10 and 11 of the Constitution.

14.1.3.4. *The Corte costituzionale*

In the case of the Italian *Corte costituzionale* a distinction is made between direct actions and preliminary rulings.[30] In the latter case, the review of the compatibility of an Italian Act is a matter for the referring court. As has been discussed,[31] since *Granital*[32] the *Corte costituzionale* has accepted that

---

[28] The Articles on equal treatment and the prohibition of discrimination, which do operate as constitutional reference standards.

[29] See e.g. *Arbitragehof*, decision n. 13/2000 of 2 February 2000, *Radio Flandria SA et al*, www. arbitrage.be; Arbitragehof, decision n. 7/95 of 2 February 1995, *NV Solvay and NV Bru Chevron et al*, www.arbitrage.be. The condition that the provision is directly effective does not require it to create rights for individuals; the *Cour d'arbitrage* controls whether the authorities under scrutiny have complied with their obligations. See M Melchior and P Vandernoot, 'Controle de constitutionnalité et droit communautaire dérivé', *RBDC*, 1998, 3, at 4–5.

[30] The functions of the *Corte costituzionale* are described in Art. 134 of the Constitution. The Court reviews the constitutionality of national and regional statutes and settles jurisdictional conflicts (conflicts over the attribution of competence) between the different branches of the State; between the State and the Regions and between the Regions. Review cases can be brought directly by specified applicants (roughly State and Regions), not by individuals; or indirectly, by way of a reference for preliminary ruling from an ordinary court. The latter category counts for three quarters of the Court's workload. (In addition, under Art. 134 the *Corte costituzionale* rules on impeachments of the President according to the norms of the Constitution).

[31] See Part 1.

[32] *Corte costituzionale*, decision n. 170/84 of 8 June 1984, *Granital*, Giur. Cost. I 1098; English translation in Oppenheimer, *The Cases*, at 642.

Community law is given effect directly and immediately as against conflicting Italian law by all the ordinary courts, without the need to refer the issue to the *Corte* first. Thus every Italian court reviews the compatibility of national and regional statutes with Community law and sets them aside in case of a conflict with directly effective provisions of Community law. The courts consider the conflicting Italian measures inapplicable. The *Corte costituzionale* denies jurisdiction to review such statutes and leaves the issue entirely to the referring court, including, in a relevant case, the reference for a preliminary ruling to the European Court. References to the *Corte* from ordinary courts are declared inadmissible.

On the other hand, where it is the only and principal judge, the Constitutional Court does review the compatibility with Community law, in terms of the constitutionality of the act under revision, through the parameter of Article 11 of the Constitution.[33] In decision n. 384/94,[34] in the context of a direct procedure brought by the State against a regional statute before its entry into force, the *Corte costituzionale* declared that the regional act infringed a Community Regulation and that therefore there was a violation of Article 11 of the Constitution.[35] This way, the violation of Community law by a regional entity of the State – which entails the liability of the State under Community law – is prevented. As explained extra judicially by a former President of the *Corte costituzionale*, Renato Granata, the main reason for the difference in approach between direct actions against regional statutes and cases brought before the *Corte* by way of preliminary reference, is that in the former case there simply is no referring court which could disapply the Italian norm conflicting with Community law.[36] The role of guardian of correct adaptation of national law to Community law can only be assumed by the Constitutional Court itself.[37] With the declaration of unconstitutionality conflicting regional

---

[33] This used to be the stance of the *Corte costituzionale* before *Granital* in relation to every case of conflict between an Italian statute and a provision of Community law: a breach of Community law was considered to constitute a violation of Art. 11 of the Constitution, see *Corte costituzionale*, decision n. 183/73 of 27 December 1973, *Frontini*, 18 Giur. Cost. I 2401; English translation in Oppenheimer, *The Cases*, 629; [1974] 2 CMLR 372; French version in *RDI*, 1989, 64 and *Corte costituzionale*, decision n. 232/75 of 30 October 1975, *ICIC*, 20 Giur. Cost. I 2211; English summary in *CML Rev* (1975) 439.

[34] *Corte costituzionale*, decision n. 384/94 of 10 November 1994, *Regione Umbria, Foro italiano*, 1994, I, 3289, available on www.giurcost.org.

[35] On this case law see *e.g.* G Amoroso, 'La giurisprudenza costituzionale nell'anno 1995 in terme di rapporto tra ordinamento comunitario e ordinamento nazionale: verso una "quarta" fase?', *Foro italiano*, 1996, V, 73; see also G Tesauro, 'Community law and national courts – An Italian Perspective', in D O'Keeffe and A Bavasso (eds), *Judicial Review in European Union Law. Liber Amicorum in Honour of Lord Slynn of Hadley*, Vol I, (The Hague, Kluwer Law International, 2000), 391, at 394–95.

[36] See B Genevois, 'Entretien avec le Président de la Cour constitutionnelle italienne: Renato Granata', www.conseil-constitutionnel.fr/cahiers/ccc6/entretien.htm.

[37] See G Tesauro, 'Community law and national courts – An Italian perpective', in D O'Keeffe and A Bavasso (eds), *Judicial Review in European Union Law. Liber Amicorum in Honour of Lord Slynn of Hadley*, Vol I, (The Hague, Kluwer Law International, 2000), 391, at 394.

legislation does not come into existence and the State complies with its obligation under Community law to remove inconsistencies and with the constitutional principle of legal certainty.

In decision 94/95 this position was extended and now applies to all direct actions brought either against regional acts or acts adopted by the Provinces or against national statutes in so far as the infringement of Community law entails a violation of the constitutionally guaranteed competences of the regions.[38] Since, in these cases, the *Corte costituzionale* is the only court involved in the procedure, the question of the possibility – or duty – of sending references for preliminary ruling to the Court of Justice becomes even more acute.[39] While this stance may be difficult to understand in the light of the position of the Court in indirect procedures, it does make perfect sense in practical effect. The mere 'non-application' of the conflicting norm would in this type of case before the constitutional court not comply with the duty imposed on the State to do everything necessary to give full and correct effect to Community law, and, in the Italian logic, with the obligation under Article 11 of the Constitution, to give full and correct effect to the Community obligations.[40] In addition, it does not conflict with the *Simmenthal* duty of ordinary courts to disapply conflicting national law in cases coming within their jurisdiction. However, it is submitted that also in cases on reference from an ordinary court, the Corte should review the compatibility of Italian law with Community law, as it is 'a court' under the *Simmenthal* mandate.

14.1.3.5. Concluding Remarks

It thus appears that only in Belgium and in certain cases in Italy, the constitutional court may actually annul legislation on grounds of incompatibility with Community law. Nevertheless, it is submitted that *all* constitutional courts are under a Community obligation to include Community law in their control of the lawfulness of acts submitted to them. Under the principle of equivalence, and assuming that the constitutional courts fall under the notion 'all courts' in *Simmenthal*, the constitutional courts must in cases coming within their jurisdiction also include Community law in their review, and where they have competence to annul legislation, the minimum requirement of disapplication would in their case transform into an obligation to annul. Most constitutional

---

[38] *Corte costituzionale*, decision n. 94/95 of 30 March 1995, *Regione Siciliana*, Foro italiano, 1995, I, 1081; confirmed in Corte costituzionale, decision n. 482/95 of 7 November 1995, *Regione Emilia Romagna et al*, Rivista italiana di diritto pubblico comunitario, 1996, 749 and decision n. 520/95 of 28 December 1995, *Regioni Lombardia e Veneto*, Rivista italiana di diritto pubblico comunitario, 1996, 768, see G Amoroso, *art. cit.*, at 81–82.

[39] See *supra*.

[40] See *Corte costituzionale*, decision n. 94/95 of 30 March 1995, *Regione Siciliana*, Foro italiano, 1995, I, 1081.

courts have not followed suit and refute the *Simmenthal* mandate for themselves.

14.2. COMMUNITY LAW AND THE NATIONAL CONSTITUTIONAL
COURTS' MANDATE

It has been demonstrated that the national constitutional courts do not, or only to a limited extent, act upon the *Simmenthal* mandate themselves, even if they expect the ordinary courts to do so. However, the direct effect and supremacy of Community law have additional consequences on the constitutional courts, at least in the Community orthodoxy. Let us again very shortly revise the Community doctrines of direct effect and supremacy of Community law. Community law that is directly effective must be given effect and be applied in the courts of the Member States, with priority over national law, however framed and including, even, the national Constitution. In *Internationale Handelsgesellschaft* the Court expressly established the precedence of Community law over Member States' national constitutions, considering that '*the validity of a Community measure or its effect within a Member State cannot be affected by allegations that it runs counter to either fundamental rights as formulated by the constitution of that State or the principles of a national constitutional structure*'.[41] It follows that the national constitutionality of rules of primary and secondary Community law cannot be examined. In addition, under *Foto-Frost*, all national courts, including the national constitutional courts are precluded from declaring acts of the Community institutions invalid. The Court of Justice has exclusive jurisdiction to declare void an act of a Community institution, and the coherence of the Community legal system requires that where the validity of a Community act is challenged before a national court the power to declare the act invalid must also be reserved to the Court of Justice.[42]

The consequences for the mandate of the national constitutional courts are straightforward from the point of view of Community law: they too must give effect to Community law, whether primary or secondary, with precedence over national law, including the Constitution. They may not, therefore, review the validity of the Treaties, or of secondary Community law, and must, where necessary, set aside or disapply national constitutional provisions in order to give full effect to Community law. To put it bluntly: national constitutional values, fundamental rights and core principles of the Constitution must all give way to Community law; and

---

[41] Case 11/70 *International Handelsgesellschaft v Einfuhr- und Vorratstelle für Getreide und Futtermittel* [1970] ECR 1125, paragraph 3.
[42] Case 314/85 *Firma Foto-Frost v Hauptzollamt Lübeck-Ost* [1987] ECR 4199, paragraphs 15 and 17.

their natural guardians, the constitutional courts, must suspend the exercise of their usual function when it comes to Community law.[43]

Now, while this picture may represent the strict Community orthodoxy, it does not do justice to reality. National constitutional values and fundamental rights are not simply deleted when Community law comes on their path. Community law does not make *tabula rasa*. These constitutional values may have their corollary in the Treaties or may be protected by the Court of Justice and national courts as general principles of Community law. As is well known, the common constitutional heritage of the Member States serves as a source of inspiration for the Court, so it claims, in developing its case law on the general principles of Community law and in interpreting rules and principles already established in Community law. It does mean, however, that the national principles and values are replaced by Community counterparts.

When it comes to the mandate of the constitutional courts therefore, the direct effect and supremacy of Community law entail primarily a negative command not to enforce the Constitution and constitutional norms as against Community law. The impact of Community law on the national constitutional courts' mandate may be broken up into four elements. Firstly, Community law does not prevent the prior review of the constitutionality of the Treaties, *i.e.* the scrutiny of the compatibility with the Constitution of the Treaties *before* their ratification. Secondly, Community law does prevent the review of the constitutionality of the Treaties and of membership upon the entry into force of the Treaties. Thirdly, and coming to secondary Community law, *ex ante* scrutiny of secondary Community law will be considered. And fourthly, in the same way as review of the constitutionality of the Treaties is prohibited upon their entry into force, so can secondary Community law never be reviewed on its constitutionality. These elements will be considered in turn. For each case, the issue of the mandate of the constitutional courts will be considered first from a European angle. Subsequently, the perspective will change to that of the national constitutional courts.

---

[43] For a nuance of the classic approach to supremacy, defending the position of the ECJ see J Wouters, 'National Constitutions and the European Union', *LIEI*, 2000, 1, esp at 46ff.

15

Prior Review of the Constitutionality of Treaties

15.1. THE EUROPEAN PERSPECTIVE

THERE IS NOTHING in European law to preclude national courts from reviewing the constitutionality of Treaties *before* their ratification. Given that the Treaties themselves state that they must be ratified by every Member State 'in accordance with their respective constitutional requirements', it could even be argued that they encourage such review where there is a court that is so competent.

Review of the constitutionality of a Treaty before its ratification certainly has its advantages. It allows the court having jurisdiction to verify if any conflict exists, and if so, to bring into motion a process of adaptation, either of the treaty or of the Constitution. It makes it less conceivable for any serious and obvious conflicts to arise after the Treaty has been ratified and entered into force. The objective of preventive judicial review of the constitutionality of a treaty is thus to avert the situation where international commitments and constitutional obligations cannot be reconciled, provoking either the international liability of the State[1] or the infringement of constitutional provisions.[2] Prior review certainly seems to contribute to achieving harmony between the various constitutional texts and the Treaties. In an era where the 'constitutional reality' of the Member States is no longer exclusively to be found in the Constitution itself, but also in its participation in international organisations and most conspicuously the European Union, it seems careless or at least inelegant not to aim at achieving harmony between the constitutive texts. Preventive control further contributes to making the treaty-making powers, the *Herren der Verträge*, aware of any legal constitutional prerequisites which they should bear in mind at the time of future negotiations, in order to avoid

---

[1] A State cannot invoke its own constitutional provisions to escape treaty obligations.

[2] Depending on whether at a later stage precedence is given to the treaty or the Constitution. If inconsistencies are removed from the outset, the difficult issue of the hierarchy between the international and the constitutional norms becomes less acute.

any difficulties at a later stage.[3] Given the fact that the judges having constitutional jurisdiction are inquired about the constitutionality of the treaty *in tempore non suspectu*, before it has entered into force, they may feel that they still have some leeway to ensure that the State's constitutional and international obligations do not conflict. Such freedom is absent when a constitutional court has a case to decide *after* the entry into force of the Treaty, in which case the pressure is high to conform to the international obligations of the State and the judges are easily constrained to compromise the content of constitutional law.[4] Nevertheless, the constitutional courts' intervention would be most useful and unconstrained if it were to take place even before signature. While it may well be a useful exercise to ask a constitutional court to draft a report in the preparation of an Intergovernmental Conference, possibly of the kind submitted by the Court of Justice, it is not likely to happen. It simply is not the place of a constitutional court to participate in this type of negotiations.

A wide interpretation of Article 48 of the EU Treaty seems to commend *a priori* review: If the provision is given a *substantive* meaning, it may be taken to require the Member States to ensure consonance between the Treaty and the Constitution before ratification. On this interpretation, the Member States would be under an obligation under the Treaty to tune in the Constitution with the intended Treaty obligations and to make sure that the Treaty is in accordance with the constitutional requirements. The Member States would be obliged by the Treaty itself to verify and guarantee that the Treaty proposed for ratification meets 'the constitutional purity standard'.[5] The constitutional courts would be the appropriate instances to rule on the constitutional compliance. Yet, the better view seems to be that Article 48 TEU merely obliges the Member States to ensure the democratic legitimisation of the basic Treaties: they must make it possible for the national parliaments or, where applicable, the people in a referendum, to exert their influence in the way prescribed for each Member State by the relevant constitutional rules. In other words, it orders the Member States to follow the appropriate constitutional *procedures* prescribed for the approval and ratification of Treaties. It does not oblige the Member States to guarantee that the Treaty meets the constitutional purity standard on the substance. If on the other hand the intervention of a constitutional court were required by the constitutional provisions in a Member State, such intervention would also be obligatory from a European perspective. This is however not the case, and European

---

[3] See also J Rideau, 'Aspects constitutionnels comparés de l'évolution vers l'Union européenne', in *La Constitution et l'Europe* (Paris, Montchrestien, 1992) 67, at 85.

[4] See A Whelan, 'National Sovereignty in the European Union', in T Murphy and P Twomey (eds), *Irelands evolving Constitution 1937–1997: Collected Essays* (Oxford, Hart Publishing, 1998) 277, at 288.

[5] See J Wouters, 'National Constitutions and the European Union', *LIEI*, 2000, 25, at 76.

law is, in fact, neutral to prior judicial review of the constitutionality of
the Treaties.

Nonetheless, it seems only natural that consonance is guaranteed
between the various levels. It is commendable that the bodies responsible
for the interpretation of constitutional texts and respect for constitutional
rules, are involved in the process of Treaty and/or constitutional amendment. In several of the Member States this could or should be the constitutional court. Many Member States do not seem to be very consistent in
their dealing with Treaty amendments. Maastricht, Amsterdam and Nice
have not, in many Member States, had the same constitutional treatment.
To a cynic, it may even seem that the question whether a referendum must
be held, whether special majorities are required in Parliament and
whether the Treaty is put before the constitutional court are even left to
political coincidence and opportunism rather than constitutional prudence. Only in Ireland has a referendum been held for all Treaties. In none
of the Member States has the constitutional court been involved in the
case of all three Treaties. In France, only the Treaties of Maastricht and
Amsterdam were put before the *Conseil constitutionnel*, Nice was not. The
Bundesverfassungsgericht only had to pronounce itself on the Treaty of
Maastricht. Obviously, it is much more burdensome to follow special
procedures, putting the Treaty before the people, a special majority in
Parliament or going through judicial proceedings before ratifying the
Treaty, but some consistency may be warranted.

The relationship between the Constitution and the European Treaties
as basic documents is an extremely difficult and sensitive one, since it
touches upon the most fundamental questions of the organisation of society from a legal and political perspective. It is impossible to grant priority
to one or the other on the basis of logical argument. The ideal solution
seems to be to combine the principle of supremacy of the national
Constitution as the basic document with that of the precedence of
European law in the legal order, which can best be done at the national
constitutional level, by introducing a provision to that effect in the
Constitution itself,[6] and by ensuring, as far as possible, consonance
between the foundational texts. Yet, even if consonance is achieved at the
normative level, the question of who has the final say over the relationship between both texts, the Court of Justice or national constitutional
court, remains. Both are embedded in their own legal order, and are
bound to protect it. As a matter of prudence, the national court having

---

[6]   As it has been done in The Netherlands (Articles 94 and 120 of the Constitution); the
      Netherlands situation is of course peculiar since it lacks a court having constitutional
      jurisdiction in the sense described above. The Irish Constitution comes closest to the ideal
      situation (through the provisions of Article 29.4 of the Constitution), but it will be shown
      that even then it is difficult for the courts to take the solution to the extreme, see below.

constitutional jurisdiction should assess the constitutionality of the treaties prior to their ratification, while the constitutional texts should grant it immunity from constitutional review upon ratification.[7] Obviously, the difficulty with the European Treaties is that they are living documents, which are interpreted by the Court of Justice as they go along and serve as the basis for Acts adopted and decisions made in the framework of the evolving European integration. No constitutional court has the ability to see what the future will bring, and it is difficult to foresee all possible frictions between the constitutional principles and the treaties beforehand.[8]

Prior review is also permissible, from the European perspective, for implementing agreements, *i.e.* decisions which are adopted by the European Council or the Council to elaborate or complete the Treaty or which concern important issues and for their entry into force require ratification by the Member States in accordance with their respective constitutional requirements.[9] This has been done: The decision on own resources[10] and on direct elections of the European Parliament[11] were submitted for review to the French *Conseil constitutionnel*, as was the French statute approving the Convention for the Application of the Schengen Agreement.[12]

Judicial review of the constitutionality of treaties before ratification is expressly provided for in the French and the Spanish Constitutions. In Spain it was maintained even when prior constitutional review of national legislation was abolished. In Germany, prior constitutional review is not in so many words contained in the constitutional texts, but it has developed in practice. It is the *Zustimmungsgesetz* which, after the parliamentary vote, is put before the Constitutional Court. The German President will suspend the ratification of the underlying treaty until it has passed the constitutionality test of the constitutional court. In practical effect the procedure leads to the same result as the French and Spanish situation, be it that the German President is not under a formal legal obligation to suspend ratification. In other countries also, most notably Ireland

---

7   M Fromont, 'Le droit constitutionnel national et l'intégration européenne', in *Ergebnisse und Perspektiven, 17. FIDE Kongress* (Berlin, 1996) 29, at 54.

8   It did not seem probable for instance that the common market would have an impact on the Irish constitutional stance on abortion.

9   For an overview of the various references to ratification in accordance with the constitutional requirements, see J Wouters, 'National Constitutions and the European Union', *LIEI*, 2000, 1, at 28ff.

10 *Conseil constitutionnel*, decision n. 70–39 DC of 19 June 1970, *ressources propres*, available on www.conseil-constitutionnel.fr.

11 *Conseil constitutionnel*, decision n. 76–71 DC of 29–30 December 1976, *Parlement européen*, available on www.conseil-constitutionnel.fr.

12 *Conseil constitutionnel*, decision n. 91–294 DC of 25 July 1991, *Schengen*, www.conseil-constitutionnel.fr.

and the United Kingdom, the Community and Union treaties have given rise to court proceedings. These will be considered in turn.

15.2. THE NATIONAL PERSPECTIVE

15.2.1. France

15.2.1.1. The Constitutional System

In the French system, an international commitment can be referred to the *Conseil constitutionnel* for prior review either directly, on the basis of Article 54 of the Constitution,[13] or through the *'loi d'approbation'* or the *'loi autorisant la ratification'* on the basis of the 'ordinary' provision on constitutional review of bills, Article 61 (2).[14] The decision is final and binding and if the *Conseil constitutionnel* finds that there is an incompatibility between the international agreement and the French Constitution, the agreement cannot be ratified without prior amendment of the Constitution.

Prior to its first decision on the Treaty of Maastricht, the *Conseil constitutionnel* had never held an international commitment[15] to require constitutional amendment. Since then, it has done so on several occasions.[16] The *Conseil constitutionnel* must decide the case within the very short time limit of one month, which may be reduced to eight days in the case of urgency.[17] The constitutional scrutiny concerns the entire treaty as submitted. In the case of the Treaty of Maastricht, for instance, the President submitted for review *'l'ensemble des engagements souscrits par la France, tels qu'ils résultent du traité lui-même, des protocols qui lui sont annexés et des déclarations de la conférence des ministres'*. Once ratified, the treaty enjoys constitutional immunity: the *Conseil constitutionnel* will not review its constitutionality at a later

---

[13] *'If, on a reference by the President of the Republic, the Prime Minister, the President of either House, or sixty deputies or sixty senators, the Constitutional Council rules that an international agreement contains a clause contrary to the Constitution, its ratification or approval may be authorized only after amendment of the Constitution'*, Art. 54 of the Constitution as amended by the constitutional law of 25 June 1992 (which added to the list of applicants the 60 deputies or senators).

[14] *'[for a ruling on their conformity to the Constitution], before promulgation, legislation may be referred to the Constitutional Council by the President of the Republic, the Prime Minister, the President of the National Assembly, the President of the Senate, or sixty deputies or sixty senators'*.

[15] *'un engagement international'*.

[16] Namely in the case of the Treaty of Maastricht (decision n. 92–308 DC of 9 April 1992), the Treaty of Amsterdam (decision n. 97–394 DC of 31 December 1997), the Treaty establishing the International Penal Court (decision n. 98–408 DC of 22 January 1999) and the European Charter of regional and minority languages (decision n. 99–412 DC of 15 June 1999). All decisions can be found on www. conseil-constitutionnel.fr.

[17] B Genevois, 'Le Traité sur l'Union européenne et la Constitution', *RFDA*, 1992, 373, at 376–77.

stage, for instance when an amending treaty is brought before it.[18] The *Conseil constitutionnel* respects the principle that *pacta sunt servanda*.

15.2.1.2. *The Conseil constitutionnel and Preventive Review of the Constitutionality in the Context of European Integration*

The proceedings relating to the Treaty of Maastricht provide a nice illustration of the role of the *Conseil constitutionnel*.[19] President Mitterrand seized the *Conseil* under Article 54 of the Constitution and asked it to determine whether the ratification of the Treaty of Maastricht must be preceded by a constitutional amendment. In its decision of April 1992, the *Conseil constitutionnel* indicated that there were three inconsistencies between the Treaty and the Constitution.[20] As a consequence, the Constitution was revised.[21] On 1 July the President decided to put the Treaty before the French People in a referendum, on 20 September 1992. In the meantime, a group of seventy senators seized the *Conseil constitutionnel* under their newly attributed power under Article 54.[22] They requested an assessment of the Treaty in the light of the revised Constitution. A second scrutiny may demonstrate that the constitutional revision has not been sufficient to eliminate the inconsistencies or has added a new one. This time, the *Conseil constitutionnel* ruled that it did not and that the Treaty could be ratified by virtue of an ordinary *loi*.[23] On 20 September sixty three deputies challenged the *loi référendaire* authorising the President to ratify the Treaty. This time the *Conseil constitutionnel* was

---

[18] See *Conseil constitutionnel*, decision n. 70–39 DC of 19 June 1970, *Parlement européen*, www. conseil-constitutionnel.fr; confirmed in *Conseil constitutionnel*, decision n. 92–308 DC of 9 April 1992, *Treaty of Maastricht I*, www.conseil-constitutionnel.fr.

[19] An account and analysis of the three decisions can be found for instance in S Boyron, 'The Conseil constitutionnel and the European Union', *PL*, 1993, 30; P Oliver, 'The French Constitution and the Treaty of Maastricht', *ICLQ*, 1994, 1; F Luchaire, 'L'Union européenne et la Constitution', *RDP*, 1992, 589, 933, 956 and 1587; L Favoreu, 'Le contrôle de constitutionnalité du Traité de Maastricht et le développement du 'droit constitutionnel international', *RGDIP*, 1993, 39.

[20] *Conseil constitutionnel*, decision n. 92–308 DC of 9 April 1992, *Treaty of Maastricht I*; the *Conseil* found three inconsistencies: (1) article 8 B which aimed to introduce for Community nationals a right to vote and stand as a candidate in municipal elections conflicted with arts. 3, 24 and 72 of the Constitution; (2) the provisions relating to the establishment of the EMU violated the 'essential conditions of the exercise of national sovereignty'; (3) so did art. 100 C which provided for the abolishment of unanimity as of January 1996 concerning decisions in the Council on visas.

[21] The *loi constitutionnelle* n. 92–554 of 25 June 1992 added a new Title IV 'On the European Communities and the European Union'. It introduced Articles 88–1 to 88–4 into the Constitution. In addition, arts 2, 54 and 74 were amended; The text of the constitutional amendment is also reproduced in F Luchaire, *art. cit.*, *RDP*, 1992, at 980–81.

[22] The constitutional amendment of 25 June 1992 had added to the list of those who can challenge the constitutionality of a treaty before ratification 60 deputies or 60 senators.

[23] *Conseil constitutionnel*, decision n. 92–312 DC of 2 September 1992, *Treaty of Maastricht II*, www. conseil-constitutionnel.fr.

seized under Article 61 of the Constitution.[24] However, the Council declined jurisdiction to review the constitutionality of the content of a *loi référendaire* containing the direct expression of the national sovereignty.[25]

The Treaty of Amsterdam was also submitted to the scrutiny of the Constitutional Council, by the President and the Prime Minister acting jointly. Again the *Conseil constitutionnel* detected several inconsistencies between the Treaty and the Constitution, which caused a constitutional revision before France could ratify.

The *Conseil constitutionnel* has on two occasions also reviewed the constitutionality of other acts adopted in the framework of the European Communities. In 1970, the *Conseil constitutionnel* was seized by the Prime Minister in order to review both the Treaty modifying certain budgetary provisions of the Treaties establishing the European Communities and the Merger Treaty and the Council Decision on the Communities' own resources.[26] The *Conseil* assumed jurisdiction, given that it was a decision of a special nature, adopted on the basis of the Community Treaties and whose entry into force was subject to adoption by the Member States in accordance with their constitutional requirements. It was not, therefore, a normal decision adopted by the Community institutions, but constituted an *'engagement international'* under Article 54. That was the case also for the Decision of the representatives of the Member States meeting in the Council relating to the election of the representatives of the Assembly by direct universal suffrage[27] and the Act annexed to it. The procedure under Article 54 of the French Constitution is not available for secondary Community law.[28] But it seems that it could be used for other types of decisions requiring further adoption or ratification on the part of the Member States.

15.2.1.3.   The Conseil constitutionnel and les conditions essentielles de la souveraineté nationale

In theory, the entire *bloc de constitutionnalité* can serve as a ground for review, consisting of the 1958 Constitution, its Preamble, and, by reference,

---

[24] *Conseil constitutionnel*, decision n. 92–313 DC of 23 September 1992, *Treaty of Maastricht III*, www. conseil-constitutionnel.fr.

[25] If however the Treaty had been approved by an ordinary statute rather than through a referendum, that statute could have been subject, presumably, to a third procedure of revision, see L Favoreu, RGDIP, 39, at 50.

[26] Council Decision of 21 April 1970 on the replacement of financial contributions from member States by the Communities' own resources, [1970] OJ L 94, 19.

[27] Decision 76/787/ECSC/EEC/Euratom of 20 September 1976 of the representatives of the Member States meeting in the council relating to the Act concerning the election of the representatives of the Assembly by direct universal suffrage [1976] OJ L 278, 1 and Act concerning the election of the representatives of the Assembly by direct universal suffrage [1976] OJ l 278, 5.

[28] See below.

the Preamble of the 1946 Constitution, and rules and principles of a constitutional nature.[29] Since its decision concerning the Maastricht Treaty the *a priori* review of the constitutionality of an international commitment turns on two issues. The *Conseil constitutionnel* controls first whether the treaty is consistent with specific provisions of the Constitution, and secondly, it rules on whether its provisions infringe the essential conditions of the national sovereignty, *'les conditions essentielles de la souveraineté nationale'*. This notion does not appear in the constitutional texts, but was 'discovered' so as to reconcile the several meanings of 'sovereignty' in the French Constitution.[30] The principle of national sovereignty which appears several times in the constitutional texts,[31] serves both as a concept to internally establish the holder of sovereignty and to give guidelines as to its exercise, and as the notion of sovereignty on the international plane.[32] In both respects, it may be affected by international treaties. On the *Conseil constitutionnel* weighs the task of reconciling both versions of sovereignty. It took the *Conseil* many years to formulate a suitable theory of sovereignty and limitations thereof. In 1976 the *Conseil constitutionnel* had specified that the Constitution only authorises *limitations* of sovereignty, but not *transfers* of part or the totality of sovereignty.[33] Apart from the fact that the distinction is very difficult to make[34] – where

[29] J Rideau, 'Aspects constitutionnels comparés de l'évolution vers l'Union européenne', in *La Constitution et l'Europe* (Paris, Montchrestien, 1992) 67, at 142; some of these provision are neutralised by nature when it comes to international treaties, since they merely relate to the French institutions, see *Conseil constitutionnel*, decision n. 76–71 DC of 29–30 December 1976, *Parlement européen*, www.conseil-constitutionnel.fr.

[30] See for instance F Luchaire, 'Le Conseil constitutionnel et la souveraineté nationale', *RDP*, 1991, 1499; J Rideau, *La Constitution et l'Europe* (Paris, Montchrestien, 1992) 137 ff., and the literature on the Maastricht decisions referred to above.

[31] The preamble of the 1958 Constitution refers to the *'droits de l'homme et aux principes de la souveraineté nationale tels qu'ils ont été définis par la Déclaration de 1789 confirmée et complétée par le préambule de la Constitution de 1946'*. Art. 3 of the 1789 Declaration states that *'le principe de toute souveraineté réside essentiellement dans la Nation'*. The Preamble of the 1946 Constitution allows for limitations of sovereignty: *'sous réserve de réciprocité, la France consent aux limitations de souveraineté nécessaires à l'organisation et à la défense de la paix'*. Art. 3 of the 1958 Constitution holds that *'La souveraineté nationale appartient au peuple, qui l'exerce par ses représentants et par la voie de référendum'*. And Art. 4 obliges political parties and groups to respect *'les principes de la souveraineté nationale et de la démocratie'*.
Also relevant in this respect is Art. 5 which makes the President of the Republic the guardian of the national independence and Art. 16 which grants him emergency powers in order to protect that independence.

[32] See J Rideau, 'Aspects constitutionnels comparés de l'évolution vers l'Union européenne', in La Constitution et l'*Europe* (Paris, Montchrestien, 1992) 67, at 143.

[33] *'Considérant que si le préambule de la Constitution de 1946, confirmé par celui de la Constitution de 1958, dispose que, sous réserve de réciprocité, la France consent aux limitations de souveraineté nécessairea à l'organisation et à la défense de la paix, aucune disposition de nature constitutionnelle n'autorise des transferts de toute ou partie de la souveraineté nationale à quelque organisation internationale que ce soit'*, *Conseil constitutionnel*, decision n. 71–76 of 29–30 December 1976, *Parlement européen*, available on www.conseil-constitutionnel.fr.

[34] For an overview of the critique of the case law see T de Berranger, *Constitutions nationales et construction communautaire* (Paris, LGDJ, 1995) at 257ff.

does the *limitation* of sovereignty, which is constitutionally allowed, end to become a *transfer* of sovereignty, which is prohibited under the Constitution? – it does not exist in the case law of the Court of Justice.[35] The decision was interpreted as giving proof of *'une volonté jalouse de préservation de la souveraineté'*[36] of the *Conseil constitutionnel* and it was understood as a warning that further developments within the European Communities towards closer political integration could only take place after a revision of the Constitution and that there may well be constitutional limits to further integration.[37] There was apparently a nucleus of sovereignty which could only be national and which was inalienable and inalterable.

On other occasions however, the *Conseil* did not make that distinction, and instead examined whether agreements submitted to it for review did not infringe the *'conditions essentielles d'exercice de la souveraineté nationale'*. It distinguished between constitutionally acceptable limitations of sovereignty and limitations infringing upon the essential conditions for the exercise of national sovereignty, which would be unacceptable under the prevailing Constitution. These 'essential conditions' were not defined by the *Conseil*, but in the 1985 decision on the protocol to the ECHR relating to the death penalty, the constitutional council revealed that it included at least the principles *'continuité de la vie de la Nation'*, *'le respect des institutions de la République'* and the *'droits et libertés du citoyen'*. In any case, the notion gave the *Conseil constitutionnel* an unlimited margin of appreciation in the examination of the constitutionality of a proposed treaty. Since the principle of national sovereignty is not defined in the Constitution in strict legal terms, the construction and interpretation thereof by the Conseil constitutionnel and its application to specific treaties, is critical and decisive. It is the *Conseil constitutionnel* which puts flesh on the bones of sovereignty.

Both stances combined provided, at that stage, a double constitutional threshold for international treaties: they could not infringe the essential

---

[35] In *Costa v ENEL* the Court spoke of both a limitation of sovereignty and a transfer of powers from the States to the Community. The ECJ stated that *'by creating a Community of unlimited duration, having its own institutions, its own personality, its own legal capacity and capacity of representation on the international plane and, more particularly, real powers stemming from a limitation of sovereignty or a transfer of powers from the States to the Community, the Member States have limited their sovereign right and have thus created a body of law which binds both their nationals and themselves'*, Case 6/64 *Costa v ENEL* [1964] ECR 585, at 593–594.

[36] See J Rideau, 'Constitution et droit international dans les Etats membres des Communautés européennes. Réflexions générales et situation française', *RFDC*, 1990, 259, at 280.

[37] See L Favoreu and L Philip, *Les grandes décisions du conseil constitutionnel*, 6th edn (Paris, Sirey, 1991) 331, at 346.

conditions for the exercise of national sovereignty or amount to a transfer of sovereignty.[38]

In *Maastricht I*, the *Conseil constitutionnel* definitively moved away from the distinction between *transfer* and *limitation*, and held that the Constitution allowed France to be a part of a permanent international organisation with legal personality and powers of decision due to a *transfer* of *powers*, rather than of sovereignty itself, agreed to by the Member States. A distinction is now made between constitutional and unconstitutional limitations of sovereignty, the latter being those which affect the *'conditions essentielles d'exercice de la souveraineté nationale'*.[39] The *Conseil constitutionnel* at the same time de-mystified the concept of national sovereignty.[40] Indeed, if the *Conseil* finds that certain provisions of the treaty would infringe the core of national sovereignty, as laid down in the Constitution, all it takes to remedy that situation, is an amendment of the Constitution. Thus, it seems that ultimately there are no limitations as a matter of principle to European integration contained in the constitutional concept of sovereignty. Sovereignty does not have an inalterable and supra-constitutional status. If the *Conseil constitutionnel* finds that certain provisions of a treaty do affect *'les conditions essentielles d'exercice de la souveraineté nationale'*, it puts the matter into the hands of the constitutional legislature.[41] The *Conseil* merely identifies the areas of friction, and makes ratification of the treaty conditional upon adaptation of the Constitutions by the organs responsible to that end. Thus, the principle of

---

[38] At the occasion of the Schengen Agreement, the *loi d'autorisation* was brought before the *Conseil constitutionnel* for constitutional review based on both approaches. The applicants contended that the Schengen Agreements on the one hand, constituted an *atteinte aux conditions essentielles d'exercice de la souveraineté nationale* and on the other hand, amounted to a transfer or even a surrender *(abandon)* of sovereignty. The *Conseil constitutionnel* rejected both contentions, *Conseil constitutionnel*, decision n. 91–294 DC of 25 July 1991, *Schengen*, www.conseil-constitutionnel.fr. It did investigate whether or not the Agreement constituted a transfer of sovereignty, but without reiterating its 1976 statement that while the Constitution allowed for limitations of sovereignty, no constitutional article provided for a transfer. It came to the conclusion that no such transfer was effectuated. The *Conseil constitutionnel* did however indicate that a certain interpretation must be given to the Agreement so as to make it constitutional, see F Luchaire, 'Le Conseil constitutionnel et la souveraineté nationale', *RDP*, 1991, 1499, at 1506–1507. As concerns the second claim, that the Agreement infringed the essential conditions for the exercise of national sovereignty, the applicants followed the clarifications which the *Conseil constitutionnel* had given in its decision on the Sixth Protocol to the ECHR with respect to the death penalty, and copied its pattern. They asserted that the Agreement was incompatible with the duty to ensure respect for the institutions of the Republic, the *'continuité de la Vie de la Nation'* and the basic rights and freedoms. These arguments were likewise rejected.

[39] See, with respect to the same wording in article 88–1 which was subsequently inserted in the Constitution, J Gerkrath, *L'émergence d'un droit constitutionnel pour l'Europe* (Brussels, Editions de l'Université de Bruxelles, 1997) at 277–278.

[40] In this sense, see F Luchaire, 'L'Union européenne et la Constitution', *RDP*, 1992, 589, at 606.

[41] In the same sense F Luchaire, 'L'Union européenne et la Constitution', *RDP*, 1992, 589, 933, 956, 1587, at 605–6.

sovereignty is, in the hands of the *Conseil constitutionnel*, merely a temporary barrier for integration, which can be removed by the Constituent power, *i.e.* the People who decide directly by referendum or indirectly through their representation in *Congrès*. The *Conseil* respects the *'pouvoir souverain d'appréciation du constituant'*. But obviously, the role of the *Conseil constitutionnel*, even if it refers back to the Nation or to the *Congrès* is crucial: it is the *Conseil*, when seized, which decides whether recourse is to be taken to constitutional amendment, and which may indicate the margins for revision and future negotiations. But the *Conseil constitutionnel* does not perform the role of guardian of the Nation and its sovereignty, it merely acts as guardian of the existing Constitution. In other words, it uses the notion of sovereignty as an instrument to regulate the pace of European integration,[42] but only within the context of the current Constitution, not as a matter of principle. Rather than preserving to itself the competence to restrict European integration, it is for the constitutional legislature or ultimately the People as the seat of sovereignty to decide.

The *Conseil constitutionnel* refused to answer theoretical questions on possible limits to constitutional revision. What the senators were in fact asking in *Maastricht III* was where, from the point of view of French constitutional law, the limits to European integration lie, and how far the Constitution can be revised time and again in order to allow for further transfers. The *Conseil constitutionnel* declined to answer, stating that its mission under Article 54 was merely to find out whether a particular treaty contains unconstitutional provisions.

There is still a great deal of confusion on the hierarchical relation between treaty provisions and the Constitution.[43] Most commentators argue that Article 54 builds on the postulate that the Constitution is superior to treaty provisions, since the *Conseil constitutionnel* examines the latters' constitutionality. The standard of reference thus is the Constitution. According to others Article 54 underscores the superiority of treaties over the Constitution since it is the latter which must be amended and give way. An alternative view is that the Article does not determine any hierarchical relationship between the two. In fact, there is only one norm, the Constitution, and one proposed obligation, the treaty in question. Article 54 merely institutes a procedural mechanism to prevent conflicts from arising, but it is not conclusive on the hierarchical relation between the

---

[42]   B De Witte, 'Sovereignty and European Integration: The Weight of Legal Tradition', *MJ*, 1995, 145, at 149.

[43]   See further below; on the subject see among many others O Cayla, 'Lire l'article 55: Comment comprendre un texte établissant une hiérarchie des normes comme étant lui-même le texte d'une norme?', www.conseil-constitutionnel.fr/cahiers/ccc7/cayla.htm; B Mathieu and M Verpeaux, 'À propos de l'arrêt du Conseil d'Etat du 30 octobre 1998, *Sarran et autres*: le point de vue du constitutionnaliste', *RFDA*, 1999, 67; C Richards, 'Sarran et Levacher: ranking legal norms in the French Republic', *ELR*, 2000, 192.

Constitution and treaties.[44] In fact, the *Conseil constitutionnel* has never had to pronounce itself directly on the issue of the hierarchical relationship between the Constitution and treaties.[45]

Once in force, a treaty enjoys constitutional immunity before the *Conseil constitutionnel*. It points at the international law principle that *pacta sunt servanda*.[46] While this seems to be the position of the *Conseil constitutionnel*,[47] it has not been taken over by the *Conseil d'État*. In the *Koné* [48]and *Sarran et Levacher*[49] decisions the *Conseil d'État* has stated that the Constitution remains the highest norm in the land, and that treaties must at all times conform to it. The *Conseil d'État* assumes jurisdiction to review the applicability from the point of view of the French Constitution of treaties in force. The implications seem to be that a finding of the *Conseil constitutionnel* that a treaty that is constitutional is not necessarily final: the *Conseil d'État* can at a later stage consider the treaty to be unconstitutional and hence inapplicable in France. As a result, the *Conseil d'État* enters in competition with the *Conseil constitutionnel* over the constitutionality of treaties.

15.2.2. Spain

Article 95(2) of the Spanish Constitution provides for the preventive control of the constitutionality of treaties by the *Tribunal Constitucional*.[50] While the constitutionality of treaty provisions can at all times be disputed

---

[44] See C Blaizot-Hazard, 'Les contradictions des articles 54 et 55 de la Constitution face à la hiérachie des normes', *RDP*, 1992, 1293.

[45] See the Report of the *Conseil constitutionnel* presented at the occasion of the *Conférence des Cours ayant compétence constitutionnelle des États membres de l'Union européenne*, at 5; some decisions of the *Conseil constitutionnel* have been read as sanctioning the supremacy of treaties over the Constitution; the *Conseil's* opinion, expressed extra-judicially, seems to go in the direction of the primacy of the Constitution in the internal legal order.

[46] Already held in *Conseil constitutionnel*, decision n. 70–39 DC of 9 June 1970, *ressources propres* www.conseil-constitutionnel.fr; confirmed in decision n. 92–308 DC of 9 April 1992, *Treaty of Maastricht I*, www.conseil-constitutionnel.fr.

[47] Yet, it seems to be based on jurisdictional restrictions, not on a principled acceptance of the supremacy of treaties over the Constitution.

[48] *Conseil d'État*, decision of 3 July 1996, *Koné*, AJDA, 1996, 722; RGDIP, 1997, 237.

[49] *Conseil d'État*, decision of 30 October 1998, *Sarran, Levacher et autres*, RFDA, 1998, 1081; AJDA, 1998, 1039, commented in, among many others, Chr. Maugüé, 'L'arrêt Sarran, entre apparance et réalité', www.conseil-constitutionnel.fr/cahiers/ccc7/maugue.htm; D Alland, 'Consécration d'un paradoxe: primauté du droit interne sur le droit international', *RFDA*, 1998, 1094; D Simon, 'L'arrêt Sarran: Dualisme incompressible ou monisme inversé', *Europe*, 1999, 4; L Dubouis, 'Les trois logiques de la jurisprudence Sarran', *RFDA*, 1999, 57.

[50] Article 95 provides: '*(1) The conclusion of an international treaty which contains stipulations contrary to the Constitution shall require a prior constitutional revision. (2) The Government or either of the Chambers may request the Constitutional Court to declare whether or not such a contradiction exists*'. Originally, the Constitution also provided for such preventive review of the constitutionality of statutes, but that type of preventive review was abolished in 1985.

before the *Tribunal Constitucional*, this procedure has for specific effect that inconsistencies are removed *before* the treaty is ratified so as to avert any disturbances involved for foreign policy and the international relations of the State in a possible declaration of lack of constitutionality of the treaty. A finding of unconstitutionality of a treaty in this procedure is binding and produces *erga omnes* all the effects of *res judicata*. The matter to which the declaration relates cannot again be brought before the Court. In addition, the decision requires all public authorities to respect and comply with it, and the Constitution must, in the case of a finding of unconstitutionality, be amended before the Treaty concerned is ratified.

The Maastricht Treaty was the first convention ever to be put before the *Tribunal Constitucional*. It gave the *Tribunal* the opportunity to elaborate on its duties in this field and on the relationship between the Constitution and the European Treaties.[51] The *Tribunal* attempted, to use its own words, to combine both functions as guarantor of the Constitution and as guarantor of the safety and stability of the commitments to be entered into by Spain at the international level.[52]

The Constitutional court explored whether Article 93 of the Constitution[53], which allows for the transfer of powers to an international organisation or institution dissipated the incompatibility found between the Constitution and the Treaty so that there was no need to proceed to a constitutional amendment involving a three fifth majority in both

[51] *Tribunal constitucional*, decision n. 1236/92 of 1 July 1992, *Treaty of Maastricht*, Rev. Inst. Eur., 1992, 633; *English translation in* [1994] 3 *CML Rev* 101; Oppenheimer, *The Cases*, 712; commented in A López Castillo and J Polakiewicz, 'Verfassung und Gemeinschaftsrecht in Spanien. Zur Maastricht-Erklärung des Spanischen Verfassungsgerichts', *EuGRZ*, 1993, 277; A Estella de Noriega, 'A Dissident Voice: The Spanish Constitutional Court Case Law on European Integration', 5 *EPL*, 1999, 269; see also V Ferreres Comella, 'Souveraineté nationale et intégration européenne dans le droit constitutionnel espagnol', www.conseil-constitutionnel.fr/cahiers/ccc9/comella.htm; A Mangas Martín, 'Le droit constitutionnel espagnol et l'intégration européenne', in *Le droit constitutionnel national et l'intérgation européenne. 17. FIDE Kongress, Berlin*, 1996, 206.

[52] *Tribunal constitucional*, decision n. 1236/92 of 1 July 1992, *Treaty of Maastricht*, Oppenheimer, *The Cases*, 712, at 720: 'As supreme interpreter of the Constitution, the Court is called upon to rule on the possible contradiction between it and a Treaty, the text of which, already finally fixed, has not yet received the consent of the State (section 78.1 of the Organic Law on the Supreme Court). Should the doubt as to the constitutionality be confirmed, the Treaty will not be able to be ratified without a prior constitutional amendment (Art. 95.1 of the Constitution). In this way the primacy of the Constitution is guaranteed through the procedure provided for in Part X, and at the same time the Treaty acquires, as regards that part of it undergoing examination, full legal status by reason of the binding nature of the declaration of the Court (section 78.2 of the Organic Law on the Supreme Court), which is the reason for this precautionary examination'.

[53] Article 93 reads: 'By means of an organic law, authorization may be granted for including treaties by which powers derived from the Constitution shall be vested in an international organisation or institution. It is incumbent on the Cortes Generales or the Government, as the case may be, to guarantee compliance with these treaties and with the resolutions emanating from the international and supranational organisations upon whom the powers have been conferred'.

Chambers of Parliament.[54] The Government had maintained that by virtue of Article 93 an exception could be made, by Organic law, to other provisions of the Constitution, such as Article 13.2 on the right to stand as a candidate in elections. The Constitutional court did not follow that line of reasoning: Article 93 of the Constitution could not be used as a legitimate vehicle for tacit or implicit constitutional reform; it did not permit a constitutional 'self-rupture'. Since the Treaty did contain a provision which conflicted with a provision of the Constitution, the latter must be amended before the Treaty could be ratified. This way, the *Tribunal* achieved the best possible conciliation between the text of the Constitution and the Treaty.[55] Yet, the case also contains an *obiter*, which suggests that should an incompatibility between the Treaty and the Constitution not be remedied before the Treaty is ratified, the constitutional norm will still take precedence. In the Court's reasoning, Article 93 and 95 had to be interpreted in conformity, and Article 93 could not be understood as providing for the supremacy of Community law over the Constitution.[56]

15.2.3. Germany

15.2.3.1. The Constitutional System

The German Constitution does not explicitly provide for preventive constitutional review of treaties by the *Bundesverfassungsgericht*. Yet, the Federal Constitutional Court has attained the same result in practice, by allowing for an exception, in respect of Acts approving an international treaty, to the rule that Acts may only be challenged *upon* promulgation.[57] If an Act approving a treaty for ratification is challenged, the President will suspend ratification until the *Bundesverfassungsgericht* has decided the case. He is not, however, under a legal or constitutional obligation to do so.

In the case of the Treaty of Maastricht, the German Constitution had already been amended and the *Zustimmungsgesetz* had been voted with

---

[54] Art. 167.1 of the Constitution.

[55] DJ Liñán Nogueras and J Roldán Barbero, 'The Judicial Application of Community law in Spain', *CML Rev* (1993) 1135, at 1138.

[56] Critically commented in A Estella de Noriega, 'A Dissident Voice: The Spanish Constitutional Court Case Law on European Integration', 5 *EPL*, 1999, 269; however, the Court also seemed to imply that a treaty which had been considered constitutional in a procedure under Art. 95 cannot later be reviewed as to its constitutionality.

[57] For ordinary Acts, a procedure can only be brought upon promulgation of the Act. Acts of assent can be submitted for review upon the parliamentary vote, even before promulgation, see JA Frowein and K Oellers-Frahm, 'German Report', in PM Eisemann (ed), *L'intégration du droit international et communautaire dans l'ordre juridique national* (The Hague, Kluwer, 1996) 69, at 72.

an overwhelming majority[58] before the Constitutional Court was seized, while its French and Spanish counterparts were in fact asked whether the Constitution needed amendment and to what extent. There was political agreement that Article 24(1) of the Constitution was too slim a basis for the quality leap which the transition of the Communities to the Union was considered to constitute. The constitutional amendment was adopted in Parliament without much debate, and the Treaty was approved with an overwhelming majority in the *Bundestag* and a unanimous *Bundesrat*. The judgment may confirm the German tendency of constitutionalising foreign policy issues, which in most countries are considered outside the realm of the courts.[59] The German constitutional court did not deny jurisdiction on grounds of political question: it analysed the Treaty and the wider issue of European integration in much detail, seriously criticising it from a German constitutional perspective, but at the end of the day, the Court yielded to the will of Parliament, be it reluctantly.

Another remarkable difference with the French and Spanish cases concerns the question as to *who* can bring a treaty before the constitutional courts. In the French and Spanish context, the constitutionality of a treaty can only be challenged by a limited number of constitutional organs.[60] In Germany, the Treaty on European Union was put before the *Bundesverfassungsgericht* by way of a *Verfassungsbeschwerde*, brought by individuals who argued that their fundamental rights were infringed by the Act approving the Treaty on European Union.[61] The challenge was declared admissible with respect to an alleged violation of Article 38 of the Constitution which was for the first time interpreted as containing an individual right to participation in the democratic process of elections of the Federal Parliament as the manifestation of the sovereignty of the People. For the future, it seems that there is now an *actio popularis* against any treaty that transfer substantial competences.[62] The entire Treaty on European Union could be tested via the individual right contained in the Court's interpretation of Article 38.

---

[58] In the *Bundestag* the TEU was approved with 543 votes in favour out of 568 votes cast, and all the *Länder* voted in favour in the *Bundesrat*.

[59] See J Kokott, 'Report on Germany', in A-M Slaughter, A Stone Sweet and JHH Weiler (eds), *The European Court and National Courts – Doctrine and Jurisprudence. Legal Change in Its Social Context* (Oxford, Hart Publishing, 1998) 77, at 111.

[60] In Spain, by the Government or either of the Chambers (Art. 95.2); the French *Conseil constitutionnel can be seized by the President, the Prime Minister, the President of the Assemblée, the* President of the Senate, 60 deputies or 60 senators (Art. 54).

[61] The claim was brought by Manfred Brunner, former *chef de Cabinet* of EC Commissioner Martin Bangemann, and four members of the faction of the Green Party in the European Parliament. Only the first claim was – partially – admissible.

[62] See *e.g.* J Kokott, 'Deutschland im Rahmen der Europäischen Union. Zum Vertrag von Maastricht', *AÖR*, 1994, 207, at 210ff; very critical in this respect is also J Schwarze, 'Europapolitik unter deutschem Verfassungsrichtervorbehalt', *NJ*, 1994, 1, who points at the many extraordinary elements relating to standing and admissibility, which constitute a breach with existing case law.

The act under review, in the German case, was the Act approving the Treaty and authorising its ratification and, secondly, the Act amending the Basic Law.[63] In France and Spain, it was the Treaty itself which came directly under review. This formal difference does not seem so important in practical effect. All three courts conducted a constitutional review of the Treaty texts.

A last difference concerns the length of the procedure. In France and Spain there are strict time limits so that any inconsistencies are readily identified and can be corrected by the responsible organs in time for ratification at the agreed time. In the German case, there is no such strict time schedule. It took the *Bundesverfassungsgericht* nine months to give judgment, causing a delay of the German ratification and thus, of the entry into force of the Treaty on European Union.[64]

15.2.3.2. *The Bundesverfassungsgericht and the Treaty of Maastricht*

The *Bundesverfassungsgericht* was eager to take the case and express its position on various issues of the Treaty on European Union and areas of Community law.[65] It could have decided not to take the case, for instance for lack of standing or for containing a political question. But on the contrary, the Court bent the existing case law as it stood so as to make the challenge admissible. Its French and Spanish counterparts limited their role to indicating the inconsistencies between the Constitution and the Treaty from a legal point of view, thus assisting the political organs responsible for constitutional amendments, in both cases Parliament acting under special majority, and leaving the ultimate decision to them. The German Constitutional Court intervened at a time when the constitutional amendment had been adopted and the Act of Assent had been passed in

---

[63] The constitutional complaint against the Act of 21 December 1992 amending the Constitution was dismissed as inadmissible. The Act inserted *inter alia* Art. 23, Art. 28(1), third sentence, Art. 52(3)(a) and Article 88, second sentence into the Basic Law.

[64] See Schwarze, who commented cynically that '*alle anderen gespannt warten müssen, ob das BVerfG als Wächter über nationale Verfassungsgrundsätze höhere demokratische und rechtsstaatliche Anforderungen stellen würde als alle anderen ebenso demokratisch und rechtsstaatlich verfaßten Staaten*', J Schwarze, 'Europapolitik unter deutschem Verfassungsrichtervorbehalt', NJ, 1994, 1, at 2; see also U Everling, 'The Maastricht Judgment of the German Federal Constitutional Court and its Significance for the Development of the European Union', YEL, 1994, 1, at 1.

[65] The judgment is not restricted to the Treaty of Maastricht, but relates also to the past and to existing Community law and case law of the ECJ, which does not relate to the TEU strictly speaking. For instance, the Court's criticism of the ECJ's case law on article 235 (*old*) of the EC Treaty or on implied powers does not relate to the TEU The *Conseil constitutionnel* for instance has declared that it will not consider the constitutionality of treaties in force, not even at the time of a treaty amendment. These have acquired constitutional immunity. The Court in Karlsruhe does not adopt such a position of judicial restraint. It seizes the challenge of the TEU as an opportunity to discuss many various aspects of areas of Community law which were not amended or affected by the TEU.

Parliament. And yet, this was no reason for the *Bundesverfassungsgericht* to limit its role to restrain itself and the newly inserted Article 23 of the Constitution was taken into account only marginally.[66] The Court scrutinised the Treaty very thoroughly, much more, so it seems, than the French and Spanish courts. Even more so, the Court seemed to impose conditions and limits to what had been done by the Member States who negotiated the Treaty and by the German organs which proceeded to a constitutional amendment and approval of the Treaty.[67] It is common knowledge that the decision reflects the views Judge Kirchhof, not only on the Treaty under review, but also on the entire construct of European integration.[68] The Court gave its views on the legal nature of the European Union,[69] and on the right to withdrawal of the Member States.[70] It evaluated the level of democracy of the European Union[71] and 'explained' the division of powers between the Member States and the Union.[72] It stressed the fact that the establishment of the Monetary Union was not an automatic matter. As concerns future treaty amendments, it held that these must not go so far as to evacuate German sovereignty or statehood. With respect to fundamental rights, the Federal Constitutional Court indicated that the Court of Justice must in individual cases offer sufficient protection or else, it would feel bound to step in.

While the Court in Karlsruhe rejected the complaint and endorsed the ratification of the Treaty on European Union, the judgment contained important messages and warnings, which were certainly heard all over

---

[66]   So C Tomuschat, 'Die Europäische Union unter der Aufsicht des Bundesverfassungsgericht', *EuGRZ*, 1993, 489, at 492.

[67]   In one of the many highly critical comments, Tomuschat wrote: '*[Das Urteil] enthält zahlreiche prinzipielle Aussagen über das Verhältnis der jetzt geschaffenen EU nicht nur zur BRD, sondern zur Gesamtheit der Mitgliedstaaten, verbunden mit Einschränkungen, Vorbehalten und Mahnungen*', and further: '*Insgesamt müsste der uneingeweihte Beobachter, der sich nur Anhalt des Urteils über den Stand der Dinge informieren wollte, den Eindruck gewinnen, dass die Verfassungssubstanz der BDR von einem hinterhälrigen Angriff bedroht gewesen sei, dessen verletzungsträchtige Aspekte nur dank des BVerfG noch in letzter Minute hätten abgewendet werden können*', C Tomuschat, 'Die Europäische Union unter der Aufsicht des Bundesverfassungsgerichts', *EuGRZ*, 1993, 489.

[68]   P Kirchhof, 'Deutsches Verfassungsrecht und Europäisches Gemeinschaftsrecht', *EuR*, 1991, 11; P Kirchhof, in P Kirchhof and J Isensee (eds), *Handbuch des Staatsrecht der Bundesrepublik Deutschland*, 1993, 855.

[69]   It is not a State relying on a European federal people, but rather a Community of States ('*Staatenverbund*'); it has no sovereign powers of its own, but only powers that derive from the Member States.

[70]   Germany is one of the '*Herren der Verträge*'. In the last resort they may revoke their membership.

[71]   European democracy does not have to comply with the same standards as German democracy. But for the time being, while the European Parliament may offer additional democratic legitimacy, the citizens supply democratic legitimacy via their national parliaments, which must therefore be left with a substantial level of tasks and authority.

[72]   Under the principle of limited specific attribution of powers, the Union and Community cannot determine or extend their own powers. The Community institutions must keep within the boundaries of their powers; *ultra vires* acts will not be applicable in Germany.

Europe: the decision caused vehement reactions both inside Germany and throughout Europe. With the benefit of hindsight, some tentative appreciation may be made on the repercussions of the decision. As was the case with *Solange*, the 'threats' expressed by the *Bundesverfassungsgericht* at the address of the Court of Justice have not materialised, and *Maastricht* was followed by a 'peace offering' in the case of the *TV Broadcasting Directive*[73] and by much gentler versions in the 2000 *Alcan* decision[74] and the final *Bananas*[75] judgment which even contained an express retreat from the Maastricht decision, or at least, from the common understanding thereof.[76] One factor accounting for the softening of the *Bundesverfassungsgericht* was the fact that Judge Kirchhof had left the Bench.[77] Other factors may have been the new efforts at the European level to enhance the protection of fundamental rights,[78] and a renewed trust in the Court of Justice. In addition, and this is impossible to back up, the *Bundesverfassungsgericht* had to demonstrate its good will and benevolence with respect to Europe and its Court of Justice. Indeed, the decision was in 1993 hailed as arrogant, as revealing a fundamental distrust against Europe and its Court of Justice, as being excessively patriotic and downright nationalistic.[79] The decision and its underlying beliefs were criticised from all sides, German and European alike, including voices close to the Court of Justice[80] and the brethren in other constitutional courts.[81]

---

[73] *Bundesverfassungsgericht*, decision of 22 March 1995, *TV Broadcasting directive*, BVerfGE 92, 203; See K Alter, *Establishing the Supremacy of European law. The Making of an International Rule of Law in Europe* (Oxford, OUP, 2001) at 109; see also infra.

[74] *Bundesverfassungsgericht*, decision of 17 February 2000, *Alcan*, available on the Court's own website www.bundesverfassungsgericht.de.

[75] *Bundesverfassungsgericht*, decision of 7 June 2000, *Bananas III (Atlanta)*, BVerfGE 102, 147; In the first and second *Bananas* rulings the *Bundesverfassungsgericht* had showed that is was still quite willing to challenge European law and the case law of the Court of Justice; *Bundesverfassungsgericht*, decision of 25 January 1995, *Bananas I (TPort)*, NJW 1995, 950; EuZW 1995, 126; *Bundesverfassungsgericht*, decision of 26 April 1995, *Bananas II (TPort)*, EuZW 1995, 412.

[76] At least one commentator has expressed his disappointment about the Federal Court's retreat: CU Schmid, 'All Bark and No Bite: Notes on the Federal Constitutional Court's 'Banana Decision'', 7 *ELJ*, 2001, 95. In his opinion, review by the national constitutional courts is among the essential vertical 'checks and balances' in the European multi-level system.

[77] F Hoffmeister, Case note on the *Alcan* and *EC Regulation on Bananas* decisions of the Bundesverfassungsgericht, 38 *CML Rev* (2001) 791, at 801, who seems to imply that the departure of Kirchhof from the Bench suffices to explain the retreat of the *Bundesverfassungsgericht*. This does not seem to do much justice to the other members of the Bench; see also KJ Alter, *Establishing the Supremacy of European Law. The Making of an International Rule of Law in Europe* (Oxford, OUP, 2001) at 115.

[78] The EU Charter of Fundamental Rights was about to be adopted in December 2000 in Nice.

[79] Not to mention some comparisons with the ugliest periods in Germany's history.

[80] So G Hirsch, 'Europäischer Gerichtshof und Bundesverfassungsgericht – Kooperation oder Konfrontation', *NJW*, 1996, 2457.

[81] At the 1995 Meeting of Presidents of Constitutional Courts, Kirchhof was sharply criticised, see *Diritto Comunitario Europeo e Diritto Nazionale* (Milano, Giuffrè, 1997) at 62.

Nevertheless, in all the *Brunner Urteil*, together with the near-defeat of the Treaty on European Union after the Danish referendum and the narrow escape in the French referendum, functioned as a 'wake up call'. After the first fierce and critical reactions about the 'arrogance' of the *Bundesverfassungsgericht* had faded, it triggered a real constitutional debate in Europe. After all, even if one disagrees with much that the Constitutional Court had to say, the European construct does struggle with some of the most fundamental issues of national constitutional law: democracy, fundamental rights, checks and balances, the division of powers.[82] These issues were at the heart of the constitutional debate in the Convention drawing up a Constitution for Europe. On the other hand, the decision demonstrated the inaptness of national constitutional theory to account for the European process. The *Bundesverfassungsgericht* used outworn constitutional tools to tackle the challenges of the European Union. While the decision and the most important views of the *Bundesverfassungsgericht* expressed in it are sufficiently known, it may be helpful to shortly repeat some of the judgment's main themes.[83]

The Legal Nature of the European Union

The Union was not a European State, but a *Staatenverbund* of independent and sovereign States, who exercised in common some of their competences in the area of an economic community. The States remained the *Herren der Verträge* and could at all times decide to withdraw. The European Union was not a State based on a European People. Germany

---

[82] 'See also M Everson, 'Beyond the Bundesverfassungsgericht: On the Necessary Cunning of Constitutional Reasoning', 4 *ELJ*, 1998, 389, at 391.

[83] It is impossible to give a full overview of the doctrinal comments on the decision. These are only a few: U Everling, 'The Maastricht Judgment of the German Federal Constitutional Court and its Significance for the Development of the European Union', *YEL*, 1994, 1; JA Frowein, 'Das Maastricht-Urteil und die Grenzen der Verfassungsgerichtsbarkeit', *ZaöVR*, 1994, 1; J Schwarze, 'Europapolitik unter deutschem Verfassungsrichtervorbehalt', *NJ*, 1994, 1; C Tomuschat, 'Die Europäische Union unter der Aufsicht des Bundesverfassungsgericht', *EuGR*, 1993, 489; M Herdegen, 'Maastricht and the German Constitutional Court: Constitutional Restraints for an "Ever Closer Union"', 31 *CML Rev*, 1994, 235; J Kokott, 'Deutschland im Rahmen der Europäischen Union – Zum Vertrag von Maastricht', *AÖR*, 1994, 207; NG Foster, 'The German Constitution and EC Membership', *PL*, 1994, 392; P Kirchhof, 'Das Maastricht-Urteil des Bundesverfassungsgerichts', in P Hommelhoff and P Kirchhof (eds), *Der Staatenverbund der Europäischen Union*, (Heidelberg, Müller, 1994); D Hanf, 'Le jugement de la Cour constitutionnelle fédérale allemande sur la constitutionnalité du Traité de Maastricht', *RTDE*, 1994, 391; A Bleckmann and SU Pieper, 'Maastricht, die grundgesetzliche Ordnung und die "Superrevisionsinstanz"', *RIW*, 1993, 971; D Köning, 'Das Urteil des Bundesverfassungsgerichts zum Vertrag von Maastricht – Ein Stolperstein auf dem Weg in die europäische Integration?', *ZaöVR*, 1994, 17; R Streinz, 'Das Maastricht-Urteil des Bundesverfassungsgerichts', *EuZW*, 1994, 329; W Schroeder, 'Alles unter Karlsruher Kontrolle? Die Souveränitätsfrage im Maastricht-Urteil des BverfG', *ZfRV*, 1994, 143; JHH Weiler, 'Does Europe Need a Constitution? Demos, Telos and the German Maastricht Decision', 1 *ELJ*, 1995, 219; J Wieland, 'Germany in the European Union – The Maastricht Decision of the Bundesverfassungsgericht', 5 *EJIL*, 1994, 259.

still retained the quality of a sovereign State in its own right on the basis of sovereign equality with the other Member States.

Democracy in Europe

Given the immaturity of a genuine democracy[84] at a European level, and the fact that the European Parliament only had a supporting role, democratic legitimacy in the European Union was necessarily conferred by the national parliaments. Limits must therefore be set to the extension of the tasks and powers of the European Communities.

The Division of Power between the Member States and the European Institutions

The Union did not have the power to determine its own powers. The Treaties were based on the principle of limited specific attribution of powers. Any interpretation by the European institutions of their powers must not amount in practical effect, to an extension of those powers. In addition, the principle of subsidiarity limited the exercise of powers granted to the European Community, in order to protect the national identities of the Member States and safeguard their powers. The Court of Justice must monitor respect for the principle of subsidiarity. *Ultra vires* acts of the institutions were not covered by the German consent to the Treaties and were therefore not applicable on the German territory.

Fundamental Rights

The Federal Constitutional Court safeguarded the substance of the constitutional basic rights also *vis-à-vis* the sovereign powers of the Community. However, the Constitutional Court exercised its jurisdiction over the applicability of secondary Community law in Germany in a relationship of co-operation with the Court of Justice, which guaranteed protection in each individual case, while the Federal Court confined itself to providing a general guarantee of the unalterable standard of basic rights. The exclusion of the Court of Justice from the second and third pillar did not create a gap in the legal protection, since measures adopted in that framework would require a further law of approval which may then be examined for any gaps in legal protection.

Constitutionality of Membership

Article 23(1) of the Basic Law constituted special authorisation to participate in the development of the European Union for the purpose of creating a United Europe.

---

[84] Characterised by a constant free exchange of views between social forces, interests and ideas, in the course of which political objectives also become clear and change and from which public opinion gives initial shape to the political will; and in which decision making processes are generally clear and understandable.

15.2.4. Ireland

15.2.4.1. The Constitutional System

Constitutional review in Ireland is the competence of the highest instances of the ordinary court structure, High Court and Supreme Court, and constitutional review occurs in the context of cases brought under the existing causes of action. Preventive judicial review of the constitutionality of treaties is not specifically foreseen in the Irish Constitution, but there are two ways in which the courts may be seized with a question of constitutionality of a treaty. First, where the *Dáil* passes legislation, the President has express power under Article 26.1 of the Constitution to refer the Bill to the Supreme Court to test its constitutionality. This could be done also where the possible unconstitutionality is connected directly with treaty law,[85] but it has never been done.[86] Secondly, there is a possibility for a question to arise before a court in the framework of 'ordinary' actions at law, as was the case for the Single European Act.[87]

15.2.4.2. The Irish Courts and the Single European Act

When the Bill authorising ratification of the Act was passed by both Houses and signed by the President, Mr Crotty sought an injunction restraining the Government from depositing the instrument of ratification alleging that the agreement infringed various articles of the Constitution. The High Court declared that the courts would only be free, under the Irish Constitution, to consider the constitutionality of the Treaty *before* Ireland ratified it. The Third Amendment to the Constitution,[88] adopted

---

[85] CR Symmons, 'Irlande', in PM Eisemann (ed), L'intégration du droit international et communautaire dans l'*ordre juridique national* (The Hague, Kluwer, 1996) 317, at 320.

[86] For a discussion of the procedure and an overview of the decisions held under Art. 26, see J Casey, *Constitutional Law in Ireland*, 3rd edn, (Dublin, Round Hall Sweet & Maxwell, 2000), at 332–38.

[87] *Supreme Court*, decision of 18 February and 9 April 1987, *Crotty v An Taoiseach* [1987] ILRM 400; [1987] IR 713; Oppenheimer, *The Cases*, 594; available also on www.irlii.org; for an analysis of the *Crotty* case see J Temple Lang, 'The Irish Court Case which Delayed the Single European Act: *Crotty v. an Taoiseach and Others*', 24 *CML Rev*, 1989, 709; G Hogan and A Whelan, *Ireland and the European Union: Constitutional and Statutory Texts and Commentary*, (London, Sweet & Maxwell, 1995), Ch. 3; D R Phelan, *Revolt or Revolution. The Constitutional Boundaries of the European Community*, (Dublin, Round Hall Sweet & Maxwell, 1997), Ch. 27; G Hogan, 'The Nice Treaty and the Irish Constitution', *EPL*, 2001, 565.

[88] The Third Amendment to the Constitution (1972) introduced Art. 29.4.3 into the Constitution specifically authorizing the State to join the Communities, providing for the supremacy of Community law and supplying constitutional immunity to Community law and Irish laws, acts and measures necessitated by the obligations of membership of the Communities. What was originally Art. 29.4.3 from 1973 until the coming into force of the Maastricht Treaty in 1993 was re-numbered Art. 29.4.5 from November 1993 until the coming into force of the Treaty of Amsterdam. It has since been re-numbered Art. 29.4.7.

at the occasion of the Irish accession to the European Communities, declared that '*no provision of the Constitution invalidates laws enacted, acts done or measures adopted by the State necessitated by the obligations of member-ship of the Communities or prevents laws enacted, acts done or measures adopted by the Communities, or institutions thereof, from having the force of law in the State.*' The High Court stated that ratification of the Single European Act was not necessitated by the obligations of Community membership, since the Act would only come in force once all the Member States had ratified it in accordance with their constitutional requirements. If it would have been so necessitated, Article 29.4.3 of the Constitution would have con-ferred on it immunity against constitutional attack, and the courts would not have been able to check its constitutionality.

The High Court held that it would be embarrassing for the Irish Government not to be able to ratify before 31 December 1986, as had been agreed between the Contracting States. Yet, the Court wished to safeguard the citizen's right to raise constitutional issues, and it was not clear whether these could still be raised after ratification. In addition, if after rat-ification the Single Act *were* to be held unconstitutional, there would be a conflict between the requirements of the Irish Constitution on the one hand and Community law on the other. The embarrassment of the Irish Government would then be complete. The Court decided that the balance of convenience made it appropriate to order the Government not to ratify the Single Act until the case had been decided. Ratification was suspended.

In its final judgment however, the High Court dismissed Crotty's case. He appealed to the Supreme Court, which held that the Single European Act could not be ratified by the Irish Government before prior amend-ment of the Constitution, and thus made it subject to prior authorisation by the People.[89] Not all amendments to the Treaties necessitate an amend-ment of the Constitution passed by referendum. The majority in the Supreme Court held that the constitutional permission of Article 29.4.3. (as it then stood) covered '*amendments of the Treaties as long as such amend-ments do not alter the essential scope or objectives of the Communities. To hold that the first sentence of Article 29.4.3. does not authorise any form of amendment to the treaties after 1973 without a further amendment of the Constitution would be too narrow a construction; to construe it as an open ended authority to agree, without further amendment of the Constitution, to any amendment of the treaties would be too broad*'. The Supreme Court adopted a double standard. Title III of the Single European Act on European Political Union was considered to constitute such an alteration of the essential

---

[89] Under Art. 46 of *Bunreacht na hÉireann* (the Irish Constitution) amendments are initiated as a Bill in *Dáil Éireann* (the House of Representatives), and upon having been passed by both Houses of the *Oireachtas* (Parliament), are submitted to the decision of the People in a ref-erendum. Once approved by the People, the Bill is promulgated by the President as a law.

scope and objectives of the Treaty and its constitutionality must therefore be assessed. Title III was found to be unconstitutional as it interfered with the power of the Government contained in Article 29.4 of the Constitution to conduct foreign affairs freely. The other parts of the Single Act, containing amendments to the original treaties were considered as covered by the constitutional authorisation. Following the judgment of the Supreme Court in *Crotty*, the Tenth Amendment of the Constitution Act 1987 was passed which permitted the State to ratify the Single European Act.[90]

Under the *'essential scope and objectives'* test introduced by the Supreme Court in *Crotty* not all Treaty amendments warrant further amendment of the Constitution. If they were 'pre-figured' by the scheme of the existing treaties, they are considered as covered by the constitutional authorisation.[91] The test is obviously very vague, and seems to warrant close scrutiny of any Treaty amendment, in final analysis, by the courts. However, the Treaties of Maastricht, Amsterdam and Nice were all put before the people in a referendum with a view to amend the Constitution, without court cases arising. The Government has never awaited legal challenges to find itself forced to hold a referendum following a successful *Crotty*-type challenge, it prefers to secure constitutional endorsement of any major Treaty amendments.[92] It could be argued that since the Nice Treaty did not itself seek to effectuate any further substantial transfer of sovereignty away from the Member States that a referendum was not necessary under *Crotty*.[93] However, the Nice Treaty itself sought to amend some of the provisions of the Amsterdam Treaty which are specifically referred to in Article 29.4.6 of the Constitution and therefore a constitutional amendment and thus, a referendum, was inevitable. As a result of *Crotty*, the Irish people enjoy the luxury[94] as of right, to approve further transfers of sovereign powers to the European Union. This is due to the specific procedure to amend the Constitution: all constitutional amendments are to be enacted by referendum.

It was suggested that *Crotty* blurred the line between executive and judicial power and that it constituted a summit in the range of judicial activism, the traditional view being that external affairs were a matter for the Government under supervision of the *Dáil*.[95] In response to the

---

[90] It added to the text of Art. 29.4.3 the sentence that the State may ratify the Single European Act.

[91] D Rossa Phelan and A Whelan, 'National constitutional law and European integration', in *Le droit constitutionnel national et l'intégration européenne*, 17. *FIDE Kongress*, Berlin, 1996, 292, at 312.

[92] See G Hogan, 'The Nice Treaty and the Irish Constitution', *EPL*, 2001, 565, at 570–71.

[93] See G Hogan, 'The Nice Treaty and the Irish Constitution', at 570.

[94] So F Murphy, 'Maastricht: Implementation in Ireland', 19 *ELR*, 1994, 94.

[95] J Casey, *Constitutional Law in Ireland* (London, Sweet and Maxwell, 1992) at 175.

contention that the courts could not interfere with the Government's treaty-making power, the Supreme Court majority in *Crotty* stated that intervention was permissible here, given the courts' function of upholding the primacy of the Constitution.

15.2.5. The United Kingdom

15.2.5.1. The Constitutional System

For obvious reasons there is no specific procedure allowing for treaties or Acts incorporating them to be challenged before a court. Acts of Parliament are immune for judicial review, due to the constitutional principle of parliamentary sovereignty. The immunity from judicial review of treaties derives from the fact that the treaty making power, that is the power to negotiate, sign and ratify treaties,[96] lies with the Crown as part of the royal prerogative. It is not for the courts to interfere with the treaty making power. Yet, there have been attempts, in the framework of British membership to the European Union, to challenge the ratification of the Treaty in a court of law. The ordinary causes of action apply. The common approach would be to bring an application for judicial review of the Government's action.

15.2.5.2. The English Courts and the European Treaties

The accession to the European Communities was the direct object of a challenge brought before ratification of the Treaty while the negotiations were still in progress. Mr Blackburn sought a declaration that signature of the Treaty by the Government would be in breach of English law because it would amount to a partial surrender of the sovereignty of the Queen in Parliament and would be irreversible. The case was dismissed in the Court of Appeal, on grounds of lack of jurisdiction of the courts to scrutinise treaties: the courts had no power to interfere with the royal prerogative to make treaties. But Lord Denning did express some views on what was about to happen if Britain would sign and ratify the Treaty: '*Much of what Mr Blackburn says is quite correct. It does appear that if this country should go into the Common Market and sign the Treaty of Rome, it means that we will have taken a step which is irreversible. The sovereignty of these islands will thenceforth be limited. It will not be ours alone but will be shared with others. Mr Blackburn referred us to [Costa v ENEL]*'. And: '*What are the realities*

---

[96] There is no rule that Parliament must be involved in the treaty making procedure. However, a treaty can only produce effects in the internal legal order if and in so far as it has been incorporated by Act of Parliament. But it is the Government that has the power and competence to assume international obligations and to enter into treaties.

here? If Her Majesty's Ministers sign this treaty and Parliament enacts provisions to implement it, I do not envisage that Parliament would afterwards go back on it and try to withdraw from it. (..) But we must wait to see what happens before we pronounce on sovereignty in the Common Market'.[97]

The ratification of the Treaty of Maastricht was equally challenged before the courts, or at least so were the parliamentary proceedings relating to it. Lord Rees-Mogg sought a declaration that the United Kingdom could not lawfully ratify the Treaty of Maastricht. The application was based on three grounds. First, by ratifying the Protocol on Social Policy, the Government would be in breach of the 1978 European Parliamentary Elections Act which requires parliamentary approval before ratification of any treaty providing for an increase in the powers of the European Parliament. Secondly, by ratifying the Protocol, the Government would be altering the content of Community law without parliamentary approval. And finally, by ratifying Title V of the Treaty, containing the second pillar, the Government would be transferring to Community institutions, without statutory authority, part of the Crown prerogative power to conduct foreign and security policy.

Lloyd LJ in the Divisional Court allowed the case, but emphasised that it was restricted to the legality of government actions and intentions, not with events which occurred in Parliament. However, the application was refused. Although leave to appeal was granted, Lord Rees-Mogg announced that he would not appeal against the judgment of the Divisional Court. The United Kingdom Government lodged the instrument of ratification on the same day.[98] The rule that the Crown has exclusive control over foreign relations and accordingly, that the treaty-making power belongs to the executive and is beyond judicial control was still very strong.[99] So, whether or not it would be constitutional for a particular treaty to be concluded and ratified was not a matter to be decided by the courts. It fell entirely to the Executive. Constitutional issues will be raised, discussed and decided in Parliament, not by the courts.[100]

---

[97]   *Court of Appeal*, decision of 10 May 1971, *Blackburn v AG* [1971] 1 WLR 1037; [1971] 2 All ER 1380; reprinted also in Oppenheimer, *The Cases*, at 735.

[98]   *High Court, Queen's Bench Division, Divisional Court*, decision of 30 July 1993, *Regina v Secretary of State for Foreign and Commonwealth Affairs, ex parte Lord Rees-Mogg* [1994] 1 All ER 457; reprinted in Oppenheimer, *The Cases*, 911; the case and the parliamentary proceedings surrounding it are commented in R Rawlings, 'Legal Politics: The United Kingdom and Ratification of the Treaty on European Union', *PL*, 1994, 254 and 367; see also G Marshall, 'The Maastricht Proceedings', *PL*, 1993, 402.

[99]   L Collins, 'Foreign Relations and the Judiciary', 51 *ICLQ*, 2002, 485, at 497.

[100] The question of what would happen to the sovereignty of the Queen in Parliament was hotly debated. The Government assured the House that nothing would happen! In the debates on the EC Bill 1972 Ministers assured the Members of Parliament that the sovereignty of Parliament would remain intact because it was legally indestructible: whatever was enacted could always be repealed and the freedom of future Parliaments would remain untrammelled. See HWR Wade, 'Sovereignty – Revolution or Evolution?', 112 *LQR*, 1996, 568, at 573, with references.

15.2.6. Other Member States

In Italy the Constitutional Court has no jurisdiction to consider the compatibility with the Constitution of international treaties *before* their approval or ratification. Since treaties are given effect in the Italian legal order by way of ordinary statutes, the question of their constitutionality can arise *after* ratification. Likewise, there is no procedure providing for preventive constitutional review of proposed treaties by the *Cour d'arbitrage* in Belgium. Again, the issue of the constitutionality of treaties may come up upon ratification, bringing the constitutional court in the difficult position of having to decide on the compatibility with the Constitution of a treaty in force.[101]

In Denmark too, where constitutional review is in theory conducted by all courts, there is no specific procedure for preventive constitutional control of treaties. In 1972, an action was brought by an individual, Grønborg, who argued that Article 20 of the Danish Constitution did not offer a substantive basis for Danish accession to the European Communities, and that the procedure for constitutional amendment under Article 88 of the Constitution was required. The case was declared inadmissible, on the ground that the courts do not have jurisdiction to assess the constitutionality of Bills that have not yet been passed by the *Folketing*.[102] With respect to the Treaty on European Union, an action was brought by twelve citizens against the Prime Minister arguing that the 1993 Act approving the Treaty of Maastricht[103] infringed the Constitution and that the Prime Minister could not ratify the Treaty. The next day, the Danish people voted in favour of the Treaty of Maastricht in the second referendum and the Government subsequently ratified the Treaty.[104] The

---

[101] Both systems are discussed further below.

[102] *Østre Landsret*, decision of 19 June 1972, *Grønborg*, UfR 1972, 903 H; [1972] CMLR 903; see O Due and C Gulmann, 'Constitutional Implications of the Danish Accession to the European Communities', *CMLRev* 1972, 256; Th. De Berranger, 'Danemark', in J Rideau (ed), *Les Etats membres de l'Union européenne. Adaptations – Mutations – Résistances*, Paris, LGDJ, 97, at 105–106. Art. 20 (2) requires a five sixth majority in Parliament or, if that majority is not obtained, approval by a majority of the voters in a referendum, for a transfer of powers to an international organisation. It was debated in Denmark whether Art. 20 provided sufficient authority for a Danish accession. The procedure for constitutional review of Art. 88 requires a vote in the *Folketing*, new elections, the passing of the same Bill in the newly elected *Folketing* and a referendum requiring a vote in favour of a majority of the people voting and at least forty percent of the Electorate. It is needless to say that amendments to the Danish Constitution are not a common occurrence.

[103] Act no. 281 of 28 April 1993, 1993 *Lotvidende* 1157.

[104] Transfers of powers to the EU must, under Art. 20 of the Danish Constitution, enacted either by a five-sixth majority in the *Folketing* or a simple majority combined with the approval of the electorate in a binding referendum. In the first (binding) referendum on 2 June 1992 the Danish people voted 'no'. After negotiations with the other Member States the Treaty of Maastricht including the Edinburgh agreement obtained the requisite five-sixth in the Folketing in 1993. The Government nevertheless decided for political reasons to hold a new referendum, resulting this time in a 'yes'. The Danish Government subsequently ratified the Treaty which was then incorporated into Danish law; see S Harck and H Palmer Olsen, 'Decision concerning the Maastricht Treaty', *AJIL*, 1999, 209.

final decision in the case was handed down only on 6 April 1998[105] – well after the entry into force of the Treaty of Maastricht[106] and therefore it will be discussed in the next chapter.

15.3. PREVENTIVE CONSTITUTIONAL REVIEW OF THE TREATIES: A FEW OBSERVATIONS

European law does not alter the constitutional position of the constitutional courts in respect of the prior review of the constitutionality of treaties. Where it is available, it can be carried out in respect of the European Treaties. Genuine prior review of the European treaties has taken place on a few occasions. The Single European Act was, prior to ratification, reviewed by the Irish Supreme Court, delaying the entry into force of the Treaty. The Maastricht Treaty was reviewed, again prior to ratification, by the French and Spanish constitutional courts, and by the German *Bundesverfassungsgericht*. The Amsterdam Treaty was put before the *Conseil constitutionnel* only. In fact, only the French and Spanish courts have explicit constitutional jurisdiction to review the treaties before they are put before Parliament, which then decides for approval or constitutional amendment. These courts can thus steer the process of adapting the Constitution to the requirements of the Treaties. The German constitutional court came in action only after the Constitution had been amended and the law approving the Treaty had been voted in Parliament. It was not given the opportunity to have a direct and immediate say in the national constitutional process, but its influence on the entire European integration process was much bigger than that of its French or Spanish counterparts and its echoes can still be heard today.

Preventive judicial review of the constitutionality of treaties is a technique with many advantages. It contributes to reducing legal doubts as to the compatibility between constitutional and treaty texts and gives the courts the opportunity to signal those issues which have to be resolved if

---

[105] *Højesteret*, decision of 6 April 1998, *Treaty of Maastricht*, UfR 1998, 800; an unofficial translation is available on www.um.dk/udenrigspolitik/europa/domeng. Comments in H Rasmussen, 'Confrontation or peaceful co-existence? On the Danish Supreme Court's Maastricht ratification judgment', in *Judicial Review in European Union Law. Liber Amicorum in Honour of Lord Slynn of Hadley*, Vol. 1 (The Hague, Kluwer, 2000) 377; S Harck and H Palmer Olsen, 'Decision concerning the Maastricht Treaty', *AJIL*, 1999, 209. In a previous decision the Supreme Court had quashed a judgment of the *Østre Landsret* which dismissed a claim of twelve citizens that they had standing to bring an action against the Prime Minister claiming that ratification infringed Section 20 of the Constitution. The case was then remanded to the *Østre Landsret* which dismissed the claim on the merits. The 1998 Maastricht judgment of the *Højesteret* was handed on appeal from that decision; see *infra*.

[106] In fact, the date for the referendum on the Amsterdam Treaty was set so as to allow the Supreme Court to hand its final judgment on the Maastricht Treaty first. The referendum on Amsterdam was held one month later, on 28 May 1998.

the process of integration is to continue in a manner compatible with the national Constitutions, and, in the long run, to influence future European integration from a national constitutional perspective, by unveiling its weaknesses in the light of fundamental principles which have matured in the national constitutional systems, much more than in the European context. Evident examples are the principles of the rule of law, the protection of fundamental rights, and the principle of democracy.

The *Conseil constitutionnel*, the Spanish *Tribunal constitucional* and the Irish Supreme Court were able to reveal inadequacies of the constitutional texts, which were subsequently refurbished to meet the requirements of the new environment. In their decisions, these courts participated in the national constitutional debate and contributed to shaping the multi-level Constitution from a national perspective. One critique could be that they do not seem to be very principled: the *Conseil constitutionnel*, for example, speaks of the *'conditions essentielles de l'exercice de la souveraineté nationale'*, which ultimately appear to be only so 'essential' that a 'plain' revision of the Constitution is sufficient to repair the flaws. At the end of the day, the decisions did not provoke major innovations from a constitutional law perspective: 'simple' adjustments of the constitutional texts sufficed to overcome their objections to the Treaties. Yet, these courts understood their role as guarantors of the Constitution of the day, pointing out the flaws in the current constitutional texts and referring the final questions back to where they belong: with the constituent power.[107] The law is for the courts to decide; politics are for the people and the politicians.

The *Brunner* judgment is the odd one out. The judgment is only in part addressed to the German constitutional organs. To put it bluntly and, at the risk of being unfair, the Court barely looked at the Treaty on European Union before putting it up for review. It looked backwards, at what had been done in the past by the European institutions, including the Court of Justice, in order to issue warnings and threats[108] as to how it should be done in the future, and, ultimately, under its own supervision. At the end of the day, one would almost forget that the Court did agree to German ratification of the Treaty on European Union, which may even seem astonishing given the fundamental nature and severity of its critique. Yet, it did not do so without giving instructions to the European institutions to guarantee respect for the vertical division of powers in the Union; and especially to the European Court of Justice to protect fundamental rights to a standard acceptable to the *Bundesverfassungsgericht*; to patrol the boundaries of Community competences and respect for the principle of subsidiarity. As for the German organs, they were warned that they should

---

[107] The People itself in the Irish case, the Parliament convening as the constituent power under more rigorous rules in Spain and France.
[108] At least, that is how the judgment was generally perceived.

take their roles in the European construct seriously, and to bear in mind that their participation in the European institutions must meet the conditions of the German Constitution.

Whatever its merits,[109] the Constitutional Court did not play the game of European integration 'one step at a time'. What is the use of pointing out what will be problematic in the future[110] other than spoiling the atmosphere of the moment? Surely, European integration is not an aim in itself, one that should be achieved at all costs including sacrificing all that has been achieved in national constitutional law. Yet, the reverse is true as well. Must national constitutional principles and certainties be defended at all costs? Are there really no valuable alternatives to the basic constitutional principles as they have been laid down at present in the national Constitutions? Is it not possible to develop a European version of democracy, for instance? The decision prompts the eternal question of the role of (constitutional) courts in society. Who has authority, for instance, to decide whether or not Germany can decide to cease to exist and evaporate to become part of a European Super State.[111] Is it really up to a Court to decide?

In the countries lacking preventive constitutional review by a constitutional court, it is missed.[112] In Belgium and Denmark, in the case of the Treaty on European Union, and in Italy, in the case of the original treaties, questions as to the constitutionality of the Treaties and of membership itself were raised at a later stage after entry into force. By then, it is too late for a court to make a valuable contribution to the constitutional debate. A finding of unconstitutionality is without effect from an international and Community law point of view, and is unworkable from a national constitutional and political point of view. Italy still has to live with the consequences

---

[109] The 'wake up call' referred to above: the decision contributed to intensify the debate on a European Constitution; and more directly, it urged the institutions and the ECJ to take the principle of limited competences seriously.

[110] Especially the passages on the evaporation of Statehood, and on the possibility of a real democracy at the European level, given the absence of a European People.

[111] This should not be understood as a plea for such a Super State! I am merely posing the question as to who is to decide.

[112] Also in The Netherlands where there is no constitutional court, questions were raised as to the compatibility of the Treaty on European Union with the Constitution, and it was convincingly argued that a special procedure had to be followed to be able to ratify it –if not this Treaty, which Treaty will ever need a special majority in Parliament, one may wonder. See AW Heringa, 'De verdragen van Maastricht in strijd met de Nederlandse Grondwet. Goedkeuring met twee derde meerderheid?', *NJB*, 1992, 749. Most commentators did not agree, and thought that the Treaty could be ratified in accordance with the normal procedure, and with a normal majority, see *Ibidem*, at 861 *et seq*. The Government took note of the issue, but proceeded under the ordinary procedure for the ratification of Treaties. Maybe it would have been more elegant to have given it more thought and modernise the Netherlands Constitution at that time. See also JG Brouwer, 'Wijkt het Unie-Verdrag van Maastricht af van de Grondwet of van het Statuut?', *NJB*, 1992, 1045. For the current debate see LFM Besselink *et al*, *De Nederlandse Grondwet en de Europese Unie* (Groningen, Europa Law Publishing, 2002).

of the then unresolved question whether Article 11 of the Constitution offered a sufficient basis for membership and whether the Constitution should not be adapted to the requirements of membership. Belgium, despite the warnings of the Advisory Division of the Council of State, ratified the Treaty on European Union knowing that it infringed certain provisions of the Constitution with respect to citizenship and the right to vote. The contention that 'it doesn't matter, since in any case the Treaty will have precedence over the Constitution' just will not do, irrespective the question of as to whether the Belgian courts would accept it. Such an attitude exhibits a lack of respect for the national Constitution, and for the significance of the Treaty as part of the constitutional set up of the polity. They are not just texts and articles, they are supposed to represent the basic legal documents constituting the polity representing fundamental choices as to how to organise society.

Preventive constitutional review does not offer a guarantee that constitutional issues will not emerge once the Treaties have been ratified and are operational. Their interpretation by the Court may reveal[113] or create[114] inconsistencies. Moreover, the Treaties serve as the basis for secondary law, which, in turn appears to be at odds with the requirements of the national Constitution.[115] Yet, at the time of a major Treaty amendment, after all a 'constitutional moment', it seems a logical technique.

---

[113] 'The Court of Justice merely interprets the Treaty and unveils its true meaning'.
[114] 'Interpretation amounts to law-making'.
[115] These issues will be discussed in Chapters 16 and 18.

16

A Posteriori Constitutional Review of the Treaties

16.1. THE EUROPEAN PERSPECTIVE

FROM A EUROPEAN LAW perspective, the constitutionality of the Treaties can be reviewed *prior* to their ratification and entry into force, and it has been argued in the previous section that such review is to be recommended. However, once ratified, the European Treaties must enjoy full immunity from judicial review, by any national court. There is simply no room for judicial review upon ratification.[1] Already under the rules of classic international law, immunity from constitutional review follows from the principle that *pacta sunt servanda*.[2] A State may not invoke its constitutional rules to escape its obligations freely entered into in an international agreement.[3] If a State would, as a consequence of its constitutional court's decision that a treaty is unconstitutional, not comply with its treaty obligations, this would have to be considered an unlawful violation of these obligations.

In addition, the immunity from constitutional review is a direct consequence of the European principles of the *autonomy* of the Community

---

[1] For a very European discussion of *a posteriori* constitutional review of the Treaties, J Wouters, 'National Constitutions and the European Union', *LIEI*, 2000, 25, at 72ff.

[2] In the formulation of Art. 26 of the Vienna Convention on the Law of Treaties: *'Every treaty in force is binding upon the parties to it and must be performed by them in good faith'*.

[3] Under Art. 27 of the Vienna Convention on the Law of Treaties *'A Party may not invoke the provisions of its internal law as justification for its failure to perform a treaty. This rule is without prejudice to article 46'*. Under Art. 45 of the same Convention a State may no longer invoke the various grounds for invalidating, terminating, withdrawing from or suspending the operation of a treaty (as contained in Arts. 46 to 50 or Arts. 60 to 62, among which the provisions of internal law regarding the competence to conclude treaties) if, after becoming aware of the facts (a) it has expressly agreed that the treaty is valid or remains in force or continues in operation, as the case may be; or (b) it must by reason of its conduct be considered as having acquiesced in the validity of the treaty or in its maintenance in force or in operation, as the case may be. Art. 46 states: *'(1) A State may not invoke the fact that its consent to be bound by a treaty has been expressed in violation of a provision of its internal law regarding competence to conclude treaties as invalidating its consent unless that violation was manifest and concerned a rule of its internal law of fundamental importance. (2) A violation is manifest if it would be objectively evident to any State conducting itself in the manner in accordance with normal practice and in good faith'*.

legal order, its *supremacy* and of the principle of *loyalty* as laid down in
Article 10 of the Treaty. The immunity commences immediately upon
entry into force. From that moment onwards, the Treaties have force of
law in the Member States and take precedence over national law. As soon
as 1960, four years before *Costa v ENEL* did the Court give its view in
Humblet: '*In fact, if the Court holds in a judgment that a legislative or administrative measure adopted by the authorities of a Member State is contrary to
Community law, that Member State is obliged, by virtue of article 86 of the ECSC
Treaty, to rescind the measure in question and to make reparation for any unlawful consequences which may have ensued. This obligation is evident from the
Treaty and from the Protocol* which have the force of law *in* the Member
States following their ratification and which take precedence over
national law'.[4] Strictly speaking, the Court's position was little more than
a restatement of the international law principle that *pacta sunt servanda*.
Contracting Parties must comply with their treaty obligations and should
an international court or tribunal hold them in breach of those obligations,
they are under an obligation to comply with the judgment and do all that
is necessary to eliminate the breach. Yet there is also a hint that there is
more: the Court held that the Treaty has force of law *in* the Member States
– it has become clear what that means in *Van Gend en Loos* and its progeny
– and that it takes precedence over national law; since *Costa ENEL* it has
become apparent that this is more than the principle of international law
that treaties take precedence *on the international plane.*

The immunity from constitutional review also follows from *Costa v
ENEL*, in which the Court held that the Treaty took precedence over
national law, *however framed*, which must include the Constitution. As a
consequence, the national Constitution could never serve as a standard of
reference. But the clearest assertion came in 1967 in *San Michele*,[5] where

---

4   Case 6/60 *Humblet* [1960] ECR 559, at 569 (my emphasis).
5   San Michele, an Italian steel firm, was imposed a fine by the High Authority, as a result
     of a judgment of the Court of Justice. The company objected to the implementation of
     that decision and brought the matter before the *Tribunale di Torino*, on the ground that
     the introduction of certain provisions of the Treaty into the Italian legal system by an
     ordinary law and not in accordance with the procedure for constitutional amendment,
     was constitutionally invalid and could thus not be opposed to it. In addition, it was
     argued that the reference to the jurisdiction of the Court of Justice was contrary to the
     constitutional Arts. 102 (stating that the judicial function is to be exercised by ordinary
     judges in accordance with and controlled by the provisions on the judiciary and pro-
     hibits the creation of extraordinary or special judges) and 113 (ensuring to every citi-
     zen full protection of his rights and other legitimate interests as against the executive).
     The constitutional uncertainties were increased by the fact that the *Corte costituzionale*
     had held, in its *Costa ENEL* decision (*Corte costituzionale*, decision n. 14/64 of 24
     February 1964, *Costa v ENEL*, Foto italiano, 1964, I, 30; 1 *CML Rev* (1963–64) 463) that
     Art. 11 of the Constitution did not grant an ordinary law by which effect is given to a
     treaty which limits the national sovereignty, any greater force than the Constitution.
     The *Tribunale* referred the matter to the *Corte costituzionale*. When the High Authority
     issued a new decision against San Michele, the company brought an action for annul-

the Court held that *'Whereas the Court of Justice, as the institution entrusted with ensuring that in the interpretation and application of the Treaty the law is observed, can only take into consideration the instrument of ratification, which itself was deposited on behalf of Italy on 22 July 1952 and which, together with the other instruments of ratification, brought the Treaty into force; Whereas it is clear from the instruments of ratification, whereby the Member States bound themselves in an identical manner, that all States have adhered to the Treaty on the same conditions, definitively and without any reservations other than those set out in the supplementary protocols, and that therefore* any claim by a national of a Member State questioning such adherence would be contrary to the system of Community law. *Whereas such a claim is all the more inadmissible in that, in this case, any decision to suspend judgment would be tantamount to reducing the Community to a cipher by regarding the instrument of ratification either as only partially accepting the Treaty, or as a means of according it different legal consequences, varying with the Member State concerned, or as the means whereby some nationals might evade its rules.'*[6]

The ratification of the Treaty by the Member States is the alpha for the Court of Justice. Any constitutional quandaries must have been solved before that time. Upon ratification, any claims questioning the adherence of the State should be inadmissible before the national courts.

The European logic was perfected in *Internationale Handelsgesellschaft: 'The validity of a Community measure or its effects within a Member State cannot be affected by the constitution of that State or the principles of the national constitutional structure'.*[7] This principle applies not only to secondary Community law but also to the Treaties themselves. It is clear that constitutional provisions cannot serve as standards of reference to control the legality of the Treaties. The principles of Community law thus oppose the jurisdiction of national courts to review the constitutionality of the Treaties. The Community mandate of the national courts contains a negative duty not to exercise any jurisdiction they may have to review the constitutionality of the Treaties in force.

Like the national courts, the *Court of Justice* itself equally lacks jurisdiction to review the validity of the Treaties *in force*.[8] Under Article 220 EC *'the Court shall ensure that in the interpretation and application of this Treaty the law is observed'*. While the provision does not grant the Court jurisdiction

---

ment before the European Court. Pending that case, the company applied for interim measures suspending judgment of the Court until the *Corte costituzionale* had decided on whether various provisions of the ECSC Treaty were unconstitutional. In support of its application, San Michele alleged that the judgment of the *Corte costituzionale* carried absolute authority and that any court having jurisdiction over Italian citizens was obliged to suspend judgment.

6 Case 9/65 *Acciaierie San Michele SpA v High Authority* [1967] ECR 27, at 30.
7 Case 11/70 *Internationale Handelsgesellschaft* [1970] ECR 1125.
8 The issue here is the *validity* of a treaty provision, which is not the same as its *constitutionality* from a national perspective.

to review the validity of the treaties themselves, it does not expressly exclude it either. One could think of a treaty provision conflicting with other provisions of the Treaty; of a clause alleged to infringe higher principles of law; or of an inconsistency between provisions of the Treaty on European Union of the one hand and the Treaty on the European Community on the other. But the provisions on the Court's jurisdiction seem to point in the direction of a denial of that competence. Article 230 EC is limited to specified categories of secondary Community law. In the case of *LAISA*,[9] a Spanish company brought an action for the annulment of certain provisions contained in an Annex to the Accession Treaties of Spain and Portugal, and alternatively, it sought a declaration that the EEC, represented by the Council, was liable for the damage suffered as a result of their adoption. The Court held that the contested provisions contained in the Act annexed to the Act of Accession formed an integral part of the Act; and that they were accordingly provisions of primary law and not acts of the Council which could be submitted for review. As for the action in damages, the Court declared that while it was directed in form against the Council, compensation was sought for damage allegedly caused by an agreement concluded between the Member States, the Kingdom of Spain and the Portuguese Republic, and the Court declined jurisdiction. This was confirmed in the recent *Roujansky* case, where a French national brought an application for a finding that the Declaration of the European Council of 29 October 1993 purporting to inform the citizens of the Union that the Treaty of Maastricht was to enter into force on 1 November 1993 was non-existent or at least void; and for a finding that the Treaty on European Union in the version of 7 February 1992 and the Treaty on European Union as amended by the Declarations of Denmark were void. The Court of First Instance declined jurisdiction to take cognisance of the action for annulment and dismissed it as inadmissible, mainly because both the declaration of the European Council and the Treaty itself did not constitute an act of a Community institution within the meaning of articles 4 and 173 (old) of the EC Treaty.[10] In the case of *Dubois*,[11] a customs agent asked the Court to declare the Council and the Commission liable for the damage caused by the repercussions on his activities as a customs agent of the implementation of the Single Act establishing an area without frontiers between the Member States of the Community from 1 January 1993. The Court of First Instance held that the Treaties, including the Single Act, constituted agreements concluded

---

9   Joined Cases 31 and 35/86 *Levantina Agricola Industrial SA (LAISA) and CPC España SA v Council* [1988] ECR 2285.
10   Order of the CFI in Case T–584/93 *Roujansky* [1994] ECR II-585; the appeal to the ECJ was dismissed as being clearly unfounded; Order of the Court in Case C–253/94 P *Roujansky* [1995] I–7.
11   Case T–113/96 *Dubois et Fils v Council and Commission* [1998] ECR II-125.

between the Member States in order to establish or modify the European Communities. The Single Act thus constituted neither an act of the institutions or an act of the servants of the Community. It could not, therefore, give rise to non-contractual liability on the part of the Community. Likewise, a Member State could not plead in defence in an enforcement action that the period set by the Act of Accession was unfair or inappropriate: Acts of Accession were not acts of the institutions, the validity of whose provisions could be challenged before the Court.[12]

Article 234 EC makes a clear distinction between questions concerning the *interpretation* of the Treaty, the *validity and interpretation* of acts of the institutions of the Community and of the ECB and the *interpretation* of the statutes of bodies established by an act of the Council, where those statutes so provide. Questions concerning the validity of Community law are restricted to secondary Community law only and cannot concern the validity of the Treaties themselves.

Could it be argued that the Commission can undertake infringements proceedings under Article 226 EC against the Member States acting jointly for having adopted a treaty provision infringing a higher principle of Union law?[13] This is a highly unlikely situation, and it remains to be seen whether the Court of Justice would take the risk of engaging in battle with all the Member States acting jointly. I assume that it would not. In addition, Article 226 EC speaks of a failure 'to fulfil an obligation under this Treaty'.[14] Nevertheless, with the increasing complexity of the Treaties it

---

[12] Case C–313/89 *Commission v Spain* [1991] ECR I–5231.

[13] Jan Wouters' hypothesis is where a Member State has ratified the Treaty in manifest violation of its constitutional rules and procedures purporting to a violation of the purpose of Art. 52 TEU, see J Wouters, *art. cit.*, at 78, footnote 220. His hypothesis is therefore extremely complex: the violation by a Member State of its constitutional requirements amounts to a violation of a treaty provision. In our case a Treaty provision would allegedly violate another provision in the Treaty or a 'higher principle of Community law'.

[14] Another question concerns the issue of whether an infringement of a national constitutional requirement for the ratification of the Treaty could affect the validity, the operation and/or the application of the Treaty from a European perspective. According to Article 52 EU, the Treaty must be ratified by all Member States *in accordance with their respective constitutional requirements*'. What happens if it appears after the entry into force of the Treaty that one Member State has violated one of its constitutional requirements? Say that the Danish Government had ratified the Treaty of Maastricht despite the negative outcome of the first referendum and without holding a new one? Would the validity of the Treaty be affected, and would the ECJ have jurisdiction to decide on the issue? Jan Wouters claims that the Court does have a part to play in reviewing the degree of democratic legitimation of a national ratification procedure – thus of its national constitutionality, for instance where a Member State would manifestly violate its constitutional rules and procedures when ratifying a new Treaty, *e.g.* by denying the negative outcome of a binding referendum. Such a frustration of the purpose of Art. 52 EU would have to lead the ECJ to answer that the conditions for the coming into effect of the Treaty had not been met, and that therefore the Treaty. Wouters does admit that the question arises what legal avenues are available to make this possible. See J Wouters, 'National Constitutions and the European Union', *LIEI*, 2000, 25, at 72ff, particularly 75–79.

does become more and more likely that there may be conflicting Treaty provisions where one seems to invalidate the other. Evidently, in such a case the most obvious technique for the Court is that of conform interpretation. Yet, it is uncertain what is to be done in the case of manifest inconsistencies.

16.2. THE NATIONAL PERSPECTIVE

Despite the fact that Community law rules out the possibility, the constitutionality of the Treaties has been challenged before the constitutional courts upon ratification in several Member States. The constitutionality of the original treaties was challenged notably before the Italian and the German constitutional courts; the constitutionality of the Treaty of Maastricht was questioned before the Danish *Hø jesteret* and the Belgian *Arbitragehof*. The Irish Supreme Court was confronted with a near clash between substantive provisions of the Constitution and the Treaty in force. These cases will be analysed in turn, but a word of caution must precede the analysis. A distinction must be made between a veritable review of the validity of a treaty that has entered into force and a form of *Constitution-écran*. In the first situation, a decision that the treaty is unconstitutional will imply that the State in question will have to withdraw or re-negotiate. The declaration that the Treaty or the Act assenting to is unconstitutional does not automatically rescind it. The State is still bound internationally, and the declaration of unconstitutionality may lead to the international liability of the State to arise. Yet the declaration of the constitutional court would imply that it is unconstitutional for the State to be bound by the relevant treaty. In the case of *Constitution-écran*, the objections of the constitutional court to a treaty will be more limited and relate only to a limited aspect of the treaty. It means that the Constitution is considered to operate as a shield and allows for an exception to the treaty.

16.2.1. Italy

Judicial review of the constitutionality of treaties is not *expressis verbis* foreseen in the Italian Constitution. As a general rule, treaties acquire the status and rank of the act by which they are introduced in the Italian legal order. Since they are mostly given effect to by ordinary statute, they have the same status and rank, and the *Corte costituzionale* assumes jurisdiction to review their constitutionality indirectly through the act of assent. This is a direct consequence of the dualistic approach to the effect and rank of treaties in the Italian legal order. If the Court finds that the treaty is unconstitutional, the Act assenting to it is annulled and loses its legal force 24 hours after the publication of the decision. Such a decision of the Court does not of course annul the treaty or affect its legal force on the international plane. Yet, it ceases to produce effects in the Italian legal order, which may lead to the international liability of the Italian State. A finding of unconstitutionality may thus have an enormous impact and the *Corte costituzionale* has shown great restraint in the exercise of its review powers when it comes to international treaties. There are however a few cases in which the *Corte costituzionale* has actually declared unconstitutional the Act giving effect to a treaty.[15]

Despite some doubts as to the constitutionality of the ECSC Treaty, there was agreement that the Treaties could, as any other 'ordinary international treaty', be ratified by means of an ordinary law.[16] This initial choice of setting the European Community Treaties in the frame of classic international law has influenced the constitutional jurisprudence with respect to the effect of Community law in the Italian legal order and its relation to the Constitution. In its 1964 *Costa v ENEL* decision,[17] the Constitutional Court held that it was lawful under Article 11 of the Constitution to give effect to treaties imposing a limitation on Italian sovereignty by means of an ordinary Statute. This did not however confer upon the ordinary law any special effect. The normal rules and principles of constitutional law relating to international treaties would thus apply, and the *Corte costituzionale* presumably retained the power to at any time review the constitutionality of the Act of assent to the Community Treaties and to declare it void.[18] The *Corte* even held that it would be constitutional for the Italian State to pass an ordinary Statute withdrawing the limitations of sovereignty agreed to in the Community Treaties. '*The international obligation of the State in respect of the Treaty is another matter, but this must not interfere with the precedence of subsequent laws in time*', it declared, thereby showing a remarkable lack of understanding of the innovative nature of the European enterprise.

---

[15] *Corte costituzionale*, decision n. 54/76, *Italo-French Extradition Treaty*; decision no. 128/87 of 8 April 1987, *US-Italian Extradition Treaty*; decision n. 132/85 of 2 May 1985, *Convention of Warsaw on International Air Transport*; decision n. 210/86 of 9 July 1986, *ILO Convention no. 89 on night labour for women*, all available on www.giurcost.org; see references in T Treves and M Frigessi di Rattalma, 'Italie', in PM Eisemann (ed), *L'Intégration du droit international et communautaire dans l'ordre juridique national. Etude de la pratique en Europe*, (The Hague, Kluwer Law International, 1996) 365, at 385.

[16] As reported by C Maestripieri, 'The Application of Community Law in Italy in 1973', *CML Rev*, 1975, 431, at 431.

[17] The case concerned the issue of a conflict between an Italian Statute adopted after the entry into force of the Treaty and the Treaty, and not directly the issue of the constitutionality of the Treaty itself. That question would be put squarely in *San Michele*.

[18] *Corte costituzionale*, decision n. 14/64 of 24 February 1964, *Costa v ENEL*; English translation in 1 *CML Rev*, 1963–4, 363, 365; see also *CML Rev* (1964–5) 224, with critical note by N Catalano.

The constitutionality of the Italian law giving effect to the ECSC Treaty was explicitly challenged in the *San Michele* case of 1965.[19] The applicant company which was fined by the High Authority,[20] argued that the introduction into the Italian legal order of a number of provisions of the ECSC Treaty was unconstitutional alleging that the exclusive jurisdiction of the Court of Justice to review the legality of Community acts was contrary to Articles 102 and 113 of the Italian Constitution, which exclude the creation of extraordinary courts and ensure the full protection of individual rights and legitimate interests against the executive. This time the *Corte costituzionale* showed itself much more integration friendly. While confirming the view that the Act of assent did not produce any greater force than an ordinary Act, it now introduced the theory of the separateness between the Italian and the Community legal order. As a consequence of that separation, the Constitution must not in its entirety be upheld against the Community and its acts, since, belonging to a distinct legal order, are not subject to it. However, there are certain fundamental principles of the Constitution which must be upheld even against the Community and its institutions.

This theory of *controlimiti* was further developed in *Frontini*,[21] the decision in which the Court also finally admitted to the normative ordinary precedence of Community law on the basis of Article 11 of the Italian Constitution. The reasoning, highly abstract and difficult to grasp, is explained as follows. Article 11 of the Constitution allows for limitations of sovereignty, which are given effect by means of an ordinary law. By virtue of such a limitation through a treaty approved by a law, the Italian institutions withdraw from certain specified areas. This may even bring about some modifications to the Constitution, which is thus not upheld fully. But Article 11 also has its limits: the core principles of the Italian constitutional order and the inalienable rights of man cannot be affected by virtue of a limitation of sovereignty. If ever the Treaty were to be given such 'an aberrant interpretation', the *Corte costituzionale* will control the continuing compatibility of the Treaty with the fundamental principles. In such a case, the Act by which the Treaty is given effect in the internal legal order may be declared unconstitutional. This limit to the precedence of Community law has been repeated since.[22] As a consequence, the *'copertura costituzionale'*[23] offered by Article 11

---

[19] *Corte costituzionale*, decision n. 98/65 of 16 December 1965, *San Michele; English version in* [1967] CMLR 160; 4 *CMLRev* (1966) 81; S Neri, 'Le droit communautaire et l'ordre constitutionnel italien', CDE, 1966, 363.

[20] Confirmed by the ECJ in Case 2/63 *Acciaierie San Michele v High Authority* [1963] ECR 661.

[21] *Corte costituzionale*, decision n. 183/73 of 27 December 1973, *Frontini, English version in* [1974] 2 CMLR 372; Oppenheimer, *The Cases*, 629.

[22] Most notably *Corte costituzionale*, decision n. 170/1984 of 8 June 1984, *Granital*, Oppenheimer, *The Cases*, at 642 and decision n. 232/1989 of 21 April 1989, *Fragd*, Oppenheimer, *The Cases*, at 653.

[23] M Luciani, 'La Costituzione italiana e gli ostacoli all'integrazione europea', *Politica del diritto*, 1992, 557, at 571.

of the Constitution is incomplete, and does not cover potential infringements of the most fundamental values of the Italian constitutional system.

To summarise, whilst the Treaties establish an entirely separate sphere of law from the Italian legal order and to which the constitutional rules do not usually apply, in exceptional cases, the Treaty may again come up for review. This may happen in the unlikely event[24] of an act of secondary Community law infringing upon a fundamental principle of the constitutional order or of an inalienable right of man. The issue under review would then be the Italian Act in its entirety, and the constitutionality of continued Italian membership would be put in question. The *Corte costituzionale* was anxious to emphasise that it would not examine individual acts of Community law, but rather cases concerned with in the evolution of the Communities at the macroscopic level, of such magnitude that they called into question Italian membership. There is therefore a difference with ordinary international treaties: their constitutionality can judicially be reviewed by the *Corte costituzionale* at any time, via the Act of assent, with the entire Constitution serving as a review standard. In the case of the European Treaties, the *Corte costituzionale* will only offer protection against a violation of the fundamental principles of the constitutional order and of the inalienable rights of man.[25]

Obviously the entire construction is a fiction, but it is one with drastic consequences: it brings on an all or nothing situation: if an act of Community law is found to violate the core principles of the Italian Constitution, this may lead to the unconstitutionality of continuing Italian membership and may provoke the Italian withdrawal from the Communities. Cases that are really about an inconsistency between secondary European law and the core values of the Constitution, are handled under the guise of a review of the Act of assent of the Treaty on the basis of which the European acts have been adopted, which must, if it allows for these acts to be adopted, be unconstitutional. While the Treaty seems constitutional now,[26] it may appear to be unconstitutional later if it allows for such acts.[27]

---

[24]   As the Court qualified it: it is clear from both *Frontini* ('an aberrant interpretation') and *Granital* ('the albeit unlikely possibility') that the *Corte* considered the likelihood of an act of Community law violating the *controlimiti* in the Italian Constitution extremely remote, and appeared surprised when such unlikely situation did occur after all in *Fragd*: 'Such a conflict, whilst being highly unlikely, could still happen'. In *Fragd*, the Court avoided the dilemma by declaring the reference inadmissible for lack of relevance.

[25]   The *Corte costituzionale* has never drawn up a list of which principles qualify as fundamental, though it has named a few; On this see M Cartabia, *Principi inviolabili e integrazione europea* (Milan, Giuffrè, 1995); see also M Luciani, 'La Constitution italienne et les obstacles à l'intégration européenne', *RFDC*, 1990, 663, at 666.

[26]   Or better, the Act assenting to it.

[27]   In *Fragd*, it appeared that a finding of inconsistency can now be restricted to some articles, interpretations or applications, without necessarily putting the entire Treaty at risk, see M Cartabia, 'The Italian Constitutional Court and the Relationship between the Italian Legal System and the European Community', *Michigan J Int L*, 1990, 173, at 182 *et seq*.

16.2.2. Germany

The Basic Law does not regulate the jurisdiction of the *Bundesverfassungsgericht* to review the constitutionality of treaties. However, the Constitutional Court assumes jurisdiction to review the constitutionality of the German Act of assent, which can be submitted for review in the same way as any other Statute. Any treaty can therefore be declared unconstitutional via its Act of assent. The Constitutional Court has only once actually declared a treaty unconstitutional, and as a general rule it exercises great restraint when it comes to the constitutionality of international treaties.[28]

During the first decade or so after the establishment of the European Communities, there was a fierce discussion in German legal literature as to whether German membership violated the German constitutional law.[29] The central issue of contention was that the institutional set up of the Communities did in several respects not comply with the most fundamental and unalterable requirements of the German Basic Law, such as the separation of powers and the principle of the rule of law.[30] The *Finanzgericht Rheinland Pfalz* raised similar doubts as to the validity under the German Basic Law of German membership. It challenged the entire political structure of the Communities, which it considered to be so '*incongruous*' with the requirements of division of powers contained in the German Constitution, that the Community structure violated essential and inviolable provisions of the Constitution. The *Finanzgericht* had been asked about the validity of Regulation 19, but rather than sending the question to the Court of Justice, it took the view that Article 189 of the Treaty itself was unconstitutional. The court considered the political structure of the Community, in which a purely executive organ, the Council, was given legislative powers, so incongruous with the requirement of division of powers, that the transfer could not be covered by Article 24(1) of the Basic Law, and violated the delegation of powers restrictions of Article 80 of the Basic Law. Regulations could only be constitutionally sound if they were issued through the regular channels of German parliamentary procedure or if the Member States were to establish a full and

---

[28] See JA Frowein and K Oellers-Frahm, 'Allemagne', in P M Eisemann (ed), *L'Intégration du droit international et communautaire dans l'ordre juridique national* (Deventer, Kluwer, 1996) 69, at 85–86.

[29] The discussion surrounding the court cases is reported in CJ Mann, *The Function of Judicial Decision in European Economic Integration*, (The Hague, Nijhoff, 1972), 418ff; references to the doctrinal debate can be found in K Hopt, 'Report on Recent German Decisions'. 4 *CML Rev* (1966) 93; see also K Alter, *Establishing the Supremacy of European Law. The Making of an International Rule of Law* (Oxford, OUP, 2001) 71–80.

[30] The central issue was that of structural congruence or '*strukturelle Kongruenz*': the question whether the Communities had to comply with the same basic requirements as the German institutions.

operational European Parliament with legislative power. Yet, as it stood, the Community political structure was unconstitutional.[31]

The *Finanzgericht* suspended the proceedings and referred the case to the *Bundesverfassungsgericht*.[32] The conclusions of the *Finanzgericht* were sharply attacked in legal literature, and repudiated by a Resolution of the *Bundestag*.[33] At a 1964 Conference of public lawyers, there was wide agreement that Community law should be given a status independent of the Constitutions of the Member States and must be understood in terms of its own needs and conceptions.[34] Pending the case before the Federal Constitutional Court, the *Finanzgericht* maintained its defiant position in another case concerning the application of the same regulation one year later, and continued to attack the structure of the Communities, calling for a reform of the Community system. In 1967, the *Bundesfinanzhof* rejected the contentions of the *Finanzgericht*, arguing that Article 24 of the Basic Law should be interpreted to mean that the transfer of powers to the Communities could not be measured by the strict standards which apply to the exercise of these sovereign powers by the constitutional authorities within the State itself. Whatever questions might arise as to the constitutionality of a Community norm under German law, there was no doubt as to the constitutionality of the Treaty itself. Two months later the *Bundesverfassungsgericht* finally gave judgment in the case referred to it by the *Finanzgericht*. It had taken four years to answer the question referred to it, biding its time for decision until the issue had been discussed in the literature and legal opinion had consolidated.[35] During that time, 'almost a full generation in the life of the EEC',[36] the Court of Justice rendered its *Costa v ENEL* decision, while the Communities had passed a point of no-return. It had become unthinkable that the *Bundesverfassungsgericht* would hold German membership of the Communities unconstitutional. Even so, it rejected the claim of the *Finanzgericht* on procedural grounds, rather than on the merits and by a very slim majority of 4 to 3.[37] It side-stepped

---

[31]   This critique of the Community system by the *Finanzgericht* would much later re-emerge in the *Maastricht Urteil*. The principal issue was therefore whether the German ratification of the Treaty on European Union would violate the constitutional requirements of democracy; see also A Bleckmann and SU Pieper, 'Maastricht, die grundgesetzliche Ordnung und die 'Superrevisionsinstanz'. Die Maastricht-Entscheidung des Bundesverfassungsgerichts', *RIW*, 1993, 969, at 974ff.

[32]   *Finanzgericht Rheinland Pfalz*, decision of 14 November 1963, FGE 22,17; *CML Rev* (1963–64) 463.

[33]   See CJ Mann, *The Function of Judicial Decision in European Economic Integration*, (The Hague, Nijhoff, 1972), at 419, with references.

[34]   Kiel Conference of German public lawyers, October 1964, reported in CJ Mann, *The Function of Judicial Decision in European Economic Integration*, (The Hague, Nijhoff, 1972), at 419–20.

[35]   CJ Mann, at 420.

[36]   See CJ Mann, at 420.

[37]   *Bundesverfassungsgericht*, decision of 5 July 1967, *EEC Treaty Constitutionality Case*, BVerfGE 22, 134.

the constitutional issue, by holding that there was no conflict between the Community and the national provisions at issue in the case. A potentially embarrassing conflict with the Treaty was averted; but the outcome was unsatisfactory since the question of the constitutionality of the Treaties and of German participation was not answered definitively.

It did so in another case decided later that year. The *Bundesverfassungsgerich* – this time the first chamber, denied jurisdiction to review the constitutionality of EEC regulations, because of the autonomous nature of the Community legal order.[38] While the case formally concerned the issue of the constitutionality of regulations, it ended for the time being the judicial discussion about the constitutionality of the Treaties and of German membership, but the issue of the constitutionality of the Treaties re-appeared in the *Maastricht Urteil*, where, even though it was only the Treaty of Maastricht that was under review, the entire system was again looked into.

16.2.3. Belgium

As in Germany and Italy the Constitution is not explicit on the jurisdiction of the Constitutional Court, the *Cour d'arbitrage*, to review the compatibility of treaties with the Constitution. In the Belgian case there is also a question of chronology. When the original treaties were ratified, the *Arbitragehof* had not yet been established. The position under Belgian law to the effect and rank of treaties in the internal legal order and the power of the courts in this respect was to a large extent determined by the *Cour de cassation* in its famous *Le Ski* judgment of 1971. The *Cour de cassation* did not, in that case or later on, have to pronounce itself on the issue of the relation between treaties and the Constitution. The question as to the hierarchy between treaty and Constitution was left unresolved.[39]

It re-surfaced with the establishment of the *Arbitragehof*, which was given the competence to review the compatibility of statutes with specified provisions of the Constitution, including Acts assenting to treaties. Consequently, the *Arbitragehof* is empowered to indirectly verify the compatibility of treaties with certain constitutional provisions.[40] It has done so on several occasions, and each time it was decided that the Act and thus

---

[38] *Bundesverfassungsgericht*, decision of 18 October 1967, *EEC Regulations Constitutionality case*, BVerfGE 22, 293; Oppenheimer, *The Cases*, at 410.

[39] For references to the debate see J Velu, 'Toetsing van de grondwettigheid en toetsing van de verenigbaarheid met de verdragen', *RW*, 1992–93, 481, at 487–93.

[40] The Special Act on the *Arbitragehof* expressly restricts the time-limit for direct actions brought before it against Acts assenting to a treaty; those acts are therefore within the control of the *Arbitragehof*. There is no provision excluding Acts assenting to a treaty from the application of the preliminary rulings, so they must be included also.

the treaty it assented to were constitutional.[41] The position of the *Arbitragehof* was condemned by Velu, *procureur général* of the *Cour de cassation*. He maintained that the *Arbitragehof* could only review the constitutionality of treaties *before* their entry into force on the international plane. Once entered into force, they would assume a higher rank than the Constitution and thus be immune from review. The *Arbitragehof* holds differently,[42] starting from the premise that the Constitution is the highest norm of the land, and that accordingly no organ or authority, deriving its authority from the Constitution, can deviate from it, even when concluding treaties. The Constitution prohibits the legislature to adopt Acts conflicting with the constitutional provisions the protection of which is entrusted to the *Cour d'arbitrage*, and accordingly, it cannot be right that the Constitution would allow the legislature to do just that by assenting to a treaty. Furthermore, the *Cour d'arbitrage* stated, there is no norm of international law, not even Article 27 of the Vienna Convention on the Law of Treaties, which grants States the power to conclude treaties contrary to their Constitutions.[43]

The situation seems to be that the European Treaties are to be considered as any other international treaty and can, at any time via the Acts of assent, be submitted to the *Cour d'arbitrage* for constitutional review.[44] However, it is to be expected that the *Cour* will be extremely restrictive, and it is highly unlikely that it will ever come to the decision that the Act of assent violates the Constitution and must partly be held

---

[41] On reference from ordinary courts: *Arbitragehof*, decision n. 26/91 of 16 October 1991, *Commune de Lanaken*; decision no. 12/94 of 3 February 1994, *European School*; decision n. 33/94 of 26 April 1994, *Van Damme*; commented in Y Lejeune and Ph. Brouwers, 'La Cour d'arbitrage face au controle de la constitutionnalité des traités', *JT*, 1992, 671; C Naômé, 'Les relations entre le droit international et le droit interne belge après l'arrêt de la Cour d'arbitrage du 16 octobre 1991', *RDIDC*, 1994, 24; H Bribosia, 'Applicabilité directe et primauté des traités internationaux et du droit communautaire. Réflexions générales sur le point de vue de l'ordre juridique belge', *RBDI*, 1996, 33; and see M Melchior and P Vandernoot, 'Contrôle de constitutionnalité et droit communautaire dérivé', *RBDC*, 1998, 3. In addition, the *Cour d'arbitrage* has on one occasion had to decide on a direct action brought against the Act assenting to a treaty, *i.e.* in the case of the Treaty of Maastricht, see *below*.

[42] However, in their report to the IXth Conference of constitutional courts the presidents of the *Arbitragehof* did agree that the drafters of the Special Act on the *Cour d'arbitrage* probably intended the Court to verify the constitutionality of treaties *before* their entry into force. Yet, they went on to say, that is not what the texts say; see L De Greve and M Melchior, *Constitutionele bescherming en internationale bescherming van de mensenrechten: concurrentie of complementariteit*, Report to the IXth Conference of European Constitutional Courts held in Paris, 1993.

[43] *Cour d'arbitrage*, decision n. 12/94 of 3 February 1994, *European School*, published on www. arbitrage.be, at B4.

[44] So M Melchior and P Vandernoot, 'Contrôle de constitutionnalité et droit communautaire dérivé', *RBDC*, 1998, 3, at 12. M Melchior is president of the *Cour d'arbitrage*.

unconstitutional.[45] In a report drafted for the 1997 Conference of Constitutional Courts held in Paris, President of the *Cour d'arbitrage* Michel Melchior suggested that the *Cour d'arbitrage*, in order to prevent the difficulties that would follow from a partial declaration of unconstitutionality, would seek to distinguish the Community Treaties from ordinary treaties. This specificity of Community law[46] could either be based on an acceptance of the case law of the Court of Justice, or be 'created' by the *Cour d'arbitrage*, with reference to the transfer of powers provision of Article 34 of the Constitution.[47] In this manner, the Community treaties would acquire a status at the least equal to the Constitution, and accordingly, the *Cour d'arbitrage* would have to decline jurisdiction to review their constitutionality.[48]

In a 1994 decision, the *Cour d'arbitrage* declined the opportunity to express itself on the constitutionality of the Treaty of Maastricht.[49] The Treaty had already entered into force when the *Cour d'arbitrage* was seized,[50] and if the Belgian Act of assent were unconstitutional, the con-

---

[45] See also the report written by the then presidents of the Arbitragehof to the IXth Conference of European constitutional courts: L De Greve and M Melchior, *Constitutionele bescherming en internationale bescherming van de mensenrechten: concurrentie of complementariteit*, Report to the IXth Conference of European Constitutional Courts, held in Paris, 1993.

[46] Melchior stated that also the German and Italian constitutional courts had already accepted the specificity of Community law. What he did not say, however, was that the Italian and German specificity are used to disinguish Community law from ordinary international treaties so as to be able to leave aside the normal rules concerning the effect of treaties in the domestic legal order, and to conceptualise direct effect and ordinary supremacy of Community law. The specificity is not recognised with the effect of allowing for a total and absolute supremacy of Community law over the Constitution: some deviation from some constitutional provisions is allowed, but not from the most vital principles. Melchior does not seem to distinguish between a nucleus and other provisions, see M Melchior and P Vandernoot, 'Contrôle de constitutionnalité et droit communautaire dérivé', *RBDC*, 1998, 3, at 13.

[47] The question is, then, whether Art. 34 could serve as a basis for the hierarchy of the European Treaties as well as secondary Community law; see H Bribosia, *art. cit.*, at 64–65; this is probably why the *Conseil d'État* in its *Orfinger* decision insisted that it was not dealing with a conflict between the ECT and the Constitution, but rather with an interpretation of the ECT handed well after the entry into force of the ECT and the Constitution, see *below*.

[48] M Melchior and P Vandernoot, 'Contrôle de constitutionnalité et droit communautaire dérivé', *RBDC*, 1998, 3, at 13–14. See also L De Greve and M Melchior, *Constitutionele bescherming en internationale bescherming van de mensenrechten: concurrentie of complementariteit*, Report to the IXth Conference of European Constitutional Courts held in Paris, 1993, at 47.

[49] *Cour d'arbitrage*, decision n. 76/94 of 18 October 1994, *Treaty of Maastricht*, www.arbitrage.be.

[50] The Act of assent was voted on 26 November 1992, but it was not published until 30 October 1993, only one day before the Treaty entered into force. The action was brought in December 1993, so within the time limit of 60 days after the day of publication, which applies to Acts whereby an international treaty is given assent to; the decision was handed almost one year later, on 18 October 1994. Formally, and in contrast to comparable cases in Spain, France and Germany, this did not amount to *a priori* review; but on the substance, the issues were virtually identical.

sequences would have been dramatic both legally and politically. In the case, two individuals brought an action for annulment of the Act approving the Treaty of Maastricht, in so far as it gave its assent to Article 8B of the EC Treaty (now Article 19 EC) relating to the right of non-Belgian European citizens to vote and stand as a candidate in municipal elections and the election of the European Parliament. They claimed that these provisions infringed the principles of equality and non-discrimination contained in Articles 6 and 6b to be of the Constitution, in conjunction with Article 4, their right to vote, which they considered to be part of their 'national personality'.[51] Moreover, they said, Article 8B of the EC Treaty infringed the supra-constitutional decrees of the National Congress of 1830 and 1831 which state that *'The political rights associated with nationality are essentially connected with the very principle of the nation and even more so with the independence of the State'*.[52] In their opinion, Article 8B of the EC Treaty compromised the national independence. Under Special Act on the Court of Arbitration, individuals who bring an action for annulment against an Act of Parliament, must prove a legal interest in order to have standing. Only individuals who whose legal position could directly and adversely be affected by the Act brought for review are considered to have such interest. The applicants claimed that their action should be held admissible, since Article 8B of the EC Treaty would infringe the prerogative deriving from their basic right to nationality,[53] which reserves the right to vote to Belgians only, and because it would reduce the weight of their vote and would alter the composition of the corps of voters and candidates.

The *Cour d'arbitrage* denied standing to the applicants. It held that the right to vote and to stand as a candidate was not infringed. While Article 8B of the EC Treaty could influence the outcome of elections, *'the interest which the applicants have to express such criticism, is not different from the interest which any individual could have to challenge the rules on the basis of which European integration rests'*. Therefore, the *Cour* held, the necessary interest had not been proven, and the action was inadmissible since it would constitute an *actio popularis*.

When analysed in the light of the prevailing case law on standing and sufficient legal interest, the Court was unusually restrictive on standing of the applicants. One reason must be that, since the Treaty already in was effect, a finding of unconstitutionality, which was highly conceivable given the textual discrepancies, would have had dramatic consequences. Beyond that, the *Cour d'arbitrage* was probably reluctant to reverse the

---

[51] As opposed to the 'human personality' *(menselijke persoonlijkheid)* which relates to civil rights.

[52] *'De aan de nationaliteit verbonden politieke rechten (hangen) onlosmakelijk samen met het beginsel zelf van de natie en, meer nog, met de onafhankelijkheid van het land'*.

[53] *'grondrecht van nationaliteit'*.

decision of a vast majority in Parliament which, even if unconstitutionally,[54] had given its assent to the Treaty.

The *Conseil d'État*[55] has decided in favour of the supremacy of Community law, including the Treaty, over the Constitution. The case before the *Conseil d'État* concerned specifically Article 39 EC (then Article 48 of the EC Treaty) as interpreted by the Court of Justice. The applicant brought an action for annulment of the Royal Decree fixing the general principles on the administrative and pecuniary status of civil servants[56] arguing, *inter alia*, that it infringed Article 10 of the Constitution. The Royal Decree authorised access to the civil service, under certain conditions, to EU citizens – in accordance with Article 39 EC (then 48 of the EC Treaty) as interpreted by the Court of Justice – while Article 10 of the Constitution reserves access to the civil and military service to Belgians, except in cases established by an Act of Parliament. The applicant referred to the case law of the *Cour d'arbitrage* which awards precedence to the Constitution over international treaties,[57] and argued that it would be unacceptable to award precedence to the Treaty over the Constitution, since the Treaty derives its binding force from the assent in accordance with the formal and substantive constitutional norms. In other words, the Constitution is the source of the binding force of the Treaties in the Belgian legal order and must therefore be considered the supreme norm and to take precedence over the Treaty. In addition, the Court of Justice cannot, through an interpretation of the Treaties, achieve an amendment of the Belgian Constitution. Such would imply that the European Court would have the last say, rather than the Belgian or European Legislature, which would violate the principle of the Rule of Law.

The *Conseil d'État* took a different view. To begin with, it insisted that the case did not concern a clash between the Constitution and a directly effective provision of a Treaty, but rather between the Constitution and the interpretation of the Treaty by the Court of Justice in 1980, well after the entry into force of the Treaty. This statement may surprise anyone familiar with Community law, and with judicial interpretation in general.

---

[54] The Council of State had in its advice on the Act approving the TEU recommended a prior amendment of the Constitution since Art. 8B TEU conflicted with the provision in the Belgian Constitution relating to the right to vote. However, Parliament proceeded to approving the TEU without such constitutional amendment, for political reasons: constitutional amendment requires the dissolution of the Chambers, elections and after that, a two-thirds majority. In addition, Prime Minister Dehaene had stated that there was no urgent need for constitutional amendment: once in force, he said, the Treaty would in any case have precedence over the Constitution.

[55] *Conseil d'État (B)*, decision of 5 November 1996, *Orfinger*, JT, 1997, 254, with note R Ergec.

[56] Arrêté royal du 26 septembre 1994 fixant les principes généraux du statut administratif et pécuniaire des agents de l'Etat.

[57] More specifically, to *Cour d'arbitrage*, decision n. 12/94 of 3 February 1994, *European School*, discussed above.

Indeed, the interpretation of the Treaty by the Court of Justice is considered simply 'to make plain what has always been'; the Court of Justice declares what is considered to be the correct interpretation of the relevant provision since the entry into force of the Treaty.[58] This may be a fiction, in that the Court, as any other court, makes law when it interprets it. It is clear that under the prevailing doctrine, what came before the *Conseil d'État*, was a conflict between the Treaty of Rome and the Belgian Constitution.[59] The *Conseil d'État* had to make this side step because it was going to take recourse to Article 34 of the Constitution, which allows for the transfer of competences to international organisations, and this, as the *Conseil* stressed, *without limitations*.[60]

It held: '*Lorsqu'un conflit existe entre une norme de droit interne et une norme de droit international, qui a des effets directs dans l'ordre juridique interne, la règle établie par le traité doit prévaloir; (..) du point de vue constitutionnel belge, l'autorité de l'interprétation donnée au Traité de Rome par la Cour de justice repose sur l'article 34 de la Constitution, quand bien même cette interprétation aboutirait à arrêter les effets d'une partie des articles 8 et 10 de la Constitution'.* If supremacy of the constitutional principles was to be achieved, it would be up to the Belgian State to re-negotiate the conditions of membership. It may be desirable that the constitutional texts are revised so as to be in compliance with the requirements of European law. Yet, such amendment could not constitute a condition for the application of European law, even in conflict with the constitutional texts. Since the Royal Decree was in conformity with the case law of the Court of Justice, it could not be unconstitutional. On the basis of Article 34 of the Constitution, Article 8 and 10 of the Constitution thus had to cede to the interpretation of the Court of Justice.

Firstly, it is striking that the *Conseil d'État* resolved the issue without making a reference to the *Cour d'arbitrage*, the more so since in the same case it did send several other questions.[61] Secondly, while the decision may be in line with Community law, it raises questions from a constitutional point of view. The *Conseil d'État* accepts that on the basis of Article 34 of the Constitution powers can be attributed to the European institutions with *no further restrictions*. This means that, firstly, the Belgian State can transfer *all* powers to the European Union, which would, in the end, result in the 'evaporation' of the Belgian State altogether. There appear to

---

[58] L Neville Brown and T Kennedy, *The Court of Justice of the European Communities*, 5th edn (London, Sweet & Maxwell, 2000) at 234; the Court may in exceptional cases limit the retroactive effect of its rulings.

[59] See also R Ergec, 'La consécration jurisprudentielle de la primauté du droit supranational de la Constitution', *JT*, 1997, 256, at 256.

[60] This is where the *Conseil d'état* differs with other courts, such as the Italian *Corte costituzionale* and the German *Bundesverfassungsgericht* which hold that the transfer of powers provisions in the Constitution are limited by the other provisions of the Constitution.

[61] See *Arbitragehof*, decision n. 78/97 of 17 December 1997, *Orfinger*, www.arbitrage.be.

be no core competences or principles which cannot be given up. Secondly, even if only limited powers have been transferred in a particular Treaty, the institutions set up under that Treaty apparently may develop the law further beyond what has been agreed under the Treaty, to an extent even that infringes the Constitution. This stands in stark contrast with the position adopted by the *Bundesverfassungsgericht,* the *Corte costituzionale* and the *Hø jesteret,* who take the view that the institutions must remain within the limits of the powers transferred, and that any *ultra vires* acts are at least suspicious, and probably inapplicable. Third, there is an odd twist in the reasoning, which can only be explained by the result that the *Conseil d'État* wished to achieve, namely to avoid an open clash between the Constitution and Community law and ultimately perhaps the international responsibility of the Belgian State. The *Conseil d'État* started from the premise that when the Treaty was ratified, there was no conflict between the Treaty and the constitutional texts: The Treaty that was ratified was constitutional. That, the *Conseil* held, was not the issue: It was the Court of Justice which with its interpretation of Article 39(4) EC created a conflict with the Constitution. One would think that this would make the situation worse, not better: the Court of Justice transformed a constitutional treaty into an unconstitutional one. The *Bundesverfassungsgericht* and the *Hø jesteret,* to name only the two most obvious examples, have expressed their concerns about the expansionist interpretation of the Court and the Community institutions. Yet, the *Conseil d'État* seemed to argue the other way around: since there was no conflict between the Treaty and the Constitution – so it said – but rather between the case law of the Court of Justice and the Constitution which emerged long after the entry into force, there was no problem from a constitutional point of view, given that under Article 34 of the Constitution, the Court of Justice had been awarded the power to interpret the Treaty *without any constitutional restrictions.* The *Conseil d'État* seemed however to prefer this position, probably because it gives the impression to combine compliance with the result required by Community law[62] with observance of the Constitution: if Articles 8 and 10 of the Constitution are not upheld in the case, it is because Article 34 of the Constitution permits it.

Finally, the *Conseil d'État* achieved what the Community orthodoxy and the Court of Justice require of the national courts: the constitutionality

---

[62] Although some may argue that it does not fully meet the conditions of the Community orthodoxy since Article 34 is given as the basis for the precedence of the case law of the ECJ over the rest of the Constitution. In my opinion, the position of the *Conseil d'État* is in line with the requirements of Community law, since recourse to Art. 34 does not, in the approach of the *Conseil d'État,* lead to constitutional limitations on the supremacy of Community law, as is the case in Italy and Germany where Arts. 11 (Italy) and 23 and 24 (Germany) have been interpreted as limited by the core of the constitutional principles (the theory of *controlimiti* in Italy and the *Solange* case law in Germany. The ECJ case law of the does not prohibit recourse to the constitutional articles as a basis for supremacy; it does, however, preclude constitutional exceptions to that supremacy.

of the Treaty is not questioned. It is striking that, again, the grounds for not exercising any mandate that they may have under national law, is not found in the supremacy of Community law over the national Constitution or the autonomy of the Community legal order. It is based on an interpretation of the Article 34 of the Constitution, which according to the *Conseil* allows for exceptions to the Constitution, which must therefore not be upheld as against the Treaty or the interpretation thereof by the Court of Justice.

The case does not give a conclusive answer to the issue of infringements of the Constitution by the Treaty itself. It is still unclear whether in such a case, the court will still award precedence to the Treaty and suspend the application of the Constitution.

16.2.4. Denmark

In Denmark, all courts are competent to review the constitutionality of Acts of Parliament, and to assess whether they comply with the formal or substantive requirements of the Constitution; this includes Acts whereby a Treaty is incorporated into domestic law. However, the requirement of legal interest to be awarded standing, and the reluctance of the judiciary to assess the constitutionality of statutes in general and to find legislation unconstitutional made it unlikely that a Danish court would actually find a treaty or the Act incorporating it unconstitutional.[63]

In 1973 the *Østre Landsret* found an action brought against the Danish accession to the European Communities inadmissible for lack of legal interest, and refused to take the case.[64] Natural or legal persons could only bring a case before the courts in order to determine whether a parliamentary act was in conformity with the Constitution if they could prove that the act affected them in a sufficiently concrete and direct way, which they could not.[65]

---

[63] So F Harhoff, 'Danemark', in PM Eisemann (ed), *L'intégration du droit international et communautaire dans l'ordre juridique national* (The Hague, Kluwer, 1996) at 165.

[64] *Østre Landsret*, decision of 4 December 1972, *Helge Tegen v The Prime Minister*, UfR 1973, 694; [1973] CMLR 1.

[65] So J Svenningsen, 'The Danish Supreme Court Puts the Maastricht Treaty on Trial', 4 MJ, 1997, 101, at 101; see also *Østre Landsret*, decision of 19 June 1972, *Grønborg v Prime Minister*, UfR 1972, 903 H; [1972] CMLR 516 and *Højesteret*, decision of 27 September 1972, *Grønborg v Prime Minister* [1972] CMLR 516. Both decisions are reprinted in Oppenheimer, *The Cases*, at 268. Grønborg tried to block the Danish accession before the courts and sought a declaration that the procedure followed for the accession was unconstitutional. Since the accession required Denmark to surrender sovereignty to the EEC institutions, he said, a specific constitutional amendment was needed. The courts denied jurisdiction, stating that they could not rule on the provisions of a Bill before it had been enacted, or on the procedure laid down by the Government and Parliament for ratification. The *Østre Landsret* did hold that a procedure could be brought once the Act was adopted, provided that an action was brought by an plaintiff who could demonstrate a concrete and present interest.

The Danish Supreme Court did however accord *locus standi* to a group of individuals without an apparent direct legal interest in the case of the Treaty of Maastricht, but ultimately rejected the claim of unconstitutionality. The case arose following the second referendum on ratification of the Treaty on European Union. A majority of the electorate voted in favour and the Danish Government ratified the Treaty, which was then incorporated into Danish law.[66] Prior to the ratification, a group of eleven Danish citizens challenged the parliamentary act of approval before the *Østre Landsret* arguing that it violated several articles of the Constitution and that the Treaty could not be ratified.[67] More than one year later, and well after the Treaty had entered into force, the court rejected the challenge as inadmissible for lack of standing. On appeal, the *Højesteret* declared that the individuals did have sufficient legal interest in having their allegations tried.[68] The Supreme Court applied a more lenient test of admissibility than usual and explained that *'the accession to the Treaty on European Union implies a transfer of legislative competences within a range of common and essential areas of life and therefore on its own is of far-reaching importance for the Danish population generally speaking. By this, the case differs from ordinary cases concerning the examination of an act's conformity with the Constitution'.*[69] It was therefore not necessary for the appellants to prove that a legal act had been adopted with a concrete and direct influence on their situation. It was considered that *'such condition would not be suitable for securing better information concerning the question on the limits for the application of article 20 of the Constitution, which is the question raised by the appellants'.*[70]

In contrast to the Belgian *Cour d'arbitrage*, the *Højesteret* obviously was eager to take the case. While the Belgian court was unusually strict in

---

[66] Even before the second referendum the Treaty, including the Edinburgh agreement, had obtained the requisite majority of five-sixths in the *Folketing*, the Danish Parliament. It was however thought politically desirable to put the Treaty before the People in a second referendum.

[67] The proceedings are explained in R Hofmann, 'Der Oberste Gerichtsh of Dänemarks und die europäische Integration', *EuGRZ*, 1999, 1.

[68] *Højesteret*, decision of 12 August 1996, *Treaty of Maastricht (admissibility)*, UfR 1996, 302, commented in J Svenningsen, 'The Danish Supreme Court Puts the Maastricht Treaty on Trial', *MJ*, 1997, 101; H Rasmussen, 'Denmark's *Maastricht Ratification* Case: The Constitutional Dimension', in A Jyränki (ed), *National Constitutions in the Era of Integration* (The Hague, Kluwer, 1999) 87.

[69] Translation taken from J Svenningsen, above, at 103.

[70] Above. Art. 20 of the Constitution provides that *'(1) Powers vested in the authorities of the Realm under this Constitution Act may, to such extent as shall be provided by Statute, be delegated to international authorities set up by mutual agreement with other States for the promotion of international rules of law and co-operation. (2) For the passing of a Bill dealing with the above a majority of five-sixths of the Members of the Parliament shall be required. If this majority is not obtained, whereas the majority required for the passing of ordinary Bills is obtained, and if the Government maintains it, the Bill shall be submitted to the electorate for approval or rejection in accordance with the rules for referenda laid down in Section 42'*, translation from www.uni-wuerzburg.de/law.

applying the conditions for standing, the Danish court was unusually lenient in allowing the case. The case was referred back to the *Østre Landsret* which rejected the claim on its merits, and the *Højesteret* had to decide the case on its substance after all. Thus, when the Treaty came up for review before the Supreme Court, it had long been ratified, and judgment was given only in April 1998, almost five years after the entry into force of the Treaty.[71]

The appellants brought two main claims against the Act approving the Treaty on European Union. Firstly, they argued that the Act could not be based on Article 20 of the Constitution and should have been preceded by a constitutional revision. They pointed out that Article 20 authorises transfers of sovereignty 'to a specified extent',[72] and that the Treaties lacked the necessary precision, given Article 308 EC (then Article 235 of the EC Treaty) and the law-making activities of the Court of Justice. Secondly, they contended that the delegation of sovereignty was on such a scale and of such nature that it was inconsistent with the Constitution's premise of a democratic form of government. The complaints of the Danish applicants were similar to those of Dr Brunner and his fellow-applicants in the German case.

The *Højesteret* started from the premise that an international organisation cannot under Article 20 of the Danish Constitution be entrusted with the making of decisions which infringe the Constitution including fundamental rights, since the authorities of the Realm do not have those powers themselves. It also stated the ground rule that international organisations cannot be left to make their own specification of powers. It then explicitly restricted the claim to the Treaty as amended by the Treaty of Maastricht, and therefore, to the new Article 235 of the Treaty (now re-numbered as Article 308 EC), which was presumed to have been adjusted since the entry into force of the Treaty on European Union since some of the areas in which the provision had been used before had now been inserted in the

---

71 *Højesteret*, 6 April 1998, *Treaty of Maastricht*, UfR 1998, H 800; English translation on www.um.dk/udenrigspolitik/euorpa/domeng/; commented in K Høegh, 'The Danish Maastricht Judgment', *ELR*, 1999, 80; S Harck and HP Olsen, 'Decision concerning the Maastricht Treaty', *AJIL*, 1999, 209; R Hofmann, 'Der Oberste Gerichtsh of Dänemarks und die europäische Integration', *EuGRZ*, 1999, 1; H Rasmussen, 'Confrontation or Peaceful Co-existence? On the Danish Supreme Court's Maastricht Ratification Judgment', in D O'Keeffe and A Bavasso (eds), *Judicial Review in European Union Law. Liber Amicorum in Honour of Lord Slynn of Hadley*, Vol I, (The Hague, Kluwer Law International, 2000), 377; P Biering, 'The Application of EU Law in Denmark: 1986 to 2000', 37 *CML Rev* (2000) 925, at 928–932.

72 In Danish '*i noermere bestemt omfang*'; the translation in English is disputed. Propositions are 'to a specified extent', 'to a more specified extent' and 'specified in some detail', see S Harck and HP Olsen, 'Decision concerning the Maastricht Treaty', *AJIL*, 1999, 209, footnote 6; the English version of the decision found on the homepage of the Danish Foreign Ministry uses the notion 'to an extent specified by statute', see www.um.dk/udenrigspolitik/europa/domeng/.

Treaty.[73] The Supreme Court found support for that interpretation in a Government's note to Parliament, and in *Opinion 2/94* of the European Court of Justice on accession of the European Communities to the European Convention on the Protection of Fundamental Rights.[74]

Now, given the fact that the Danish Government had its say in any decision taken under Article 308 EC and thus had the power to block decisions, and since the Court of Justice would ensure that the scope of operation of the Community is observed, it could not be held that the determination of powers in the Treaties, albeit giving rise to doubts at times, and the transfer of jurisdiction to rule on the interpretation of such questions to the Court of Justice, were *per se* incompatible with the requirement for specification of Article 20 of the Constitution. The Supreme Court thus accepted that there might be some doubts at times about the limits of Community competences. It also accepted that it was for the Court of Justice and not for the Danish courts to decide on the interpretation of the validity and legality of Community acts. However, in the exceptional case where it should arise with the required certainty that a Community act which had been upheld by the Court of Justice was based on an application of the Treaty which lay beyond the surrender of sovereignty according to the Act of accession, the Danish courts must come to the conclusion that such act is inapplicable in Denmark. In sum, given the supervision of the Danish Government, the Court of Justice and ultimately the Danish courts, the Treaty could not, at this stage, be considered contrary to the requirement of precision laid down in Article 20 of the Constitution.

The Supreme Court went on to state that Article 20 must be considered as implying that the transfers authorised under it could not take place to such an extent that Denmark could no longer be considered to be an independent state. The Court only said that it was beyond doubt that the limit

---

[73] The Supreme Court let it be understood that it disagreed with some previous use of the Art. 235 of the Treaty. The applicants had selected instances of dubious use of the article, based on partly confidential materials concerning the Danish decision making procedure with respect to proposals based on Art. 235, which illustrated the Danish Government's approach to that use in the past. The applicants were only given that information following an order of the Supreme Court. The materials indicated that the Government had given in to pressure from other Member States and from the Commission and had accepted Community competence, for political reasons, and in spite of its own initial doubts as to whether the demand for specification under Art. 20(1) of the Constitution would be fulfilled. The examples also suggested that the control exercised by the Danish Parliament was insufficient and that the Europe Committee never refused to give the Government a mandate to vote in favour of doubtful proposals; see K Høegh,' The Danish Maastricht Judgment', *ELR*, 1999, 80, at 82ff These elements contribute to explaining the judgment: the Supreme Court did not 'put the blame' on Europe exclusively, but also warned the Government and Parliament to take their role in European affairs seriously. Only then could the conditions of specificity in Art. 20(1), and of the principle of democracy in the Danish Constitution be complied with.

[74] Opinion 2/94 *Accession to the ECHR* [1996] ECR I–1788.

had not been reached in the Treaty on European Union, without specifying where that limit was. Finally, on the issue of democracy, the *Højesteret* held that any delegation of legislative powers would involve a certain encroachment on the Danish democratic system of government, but that this had been taken into consideration when drawing up the rigorous requirements for adoption under Article 20(2) of the Constitution.[75] The Court pointed at the indirect democratic control of the Danish Parliament over the Danish representation in the Council of Ministers and it added that '*it is reasonable to assume that the* Folketing *has been entrusted to consider whether participation in the EC co-operation should be conditional upon any additional democratic control*'. It saw no grounds for holding the Act of Accession unconstitutional.

The *Højesteret* thus held the Act of accession constitutional, but issued a number of instructions and warnings to various addressees. The Government must, in the Council, pay due regard to the condition of specificity in the Danish Constitution, and block a decision when it cannot be considered to be covered by the Treaty. The Danish Parliament must, for the sake of democracy, control the Government as participant in decision making in the Council. The Court of Justice, as interpreter of the Treaty, must patrol the boundaries of the transferred powers. And in the last instance, the Danish courts must control the applicability of Community acts that clearly go beyond the powers transferred. Nevertheless, at the end of the day, the Danish ratification of the Treaty was constitutional. Could the Supreme Court have held otherwise? A contrary decision would have entailed the international liability of the Danish State: it would have been impossible to execute. A court cannot in actual fact decide after five years that the ratification of the Treaty on European Union was unconstitutional. It certainly is to be preferred to involve a constitutional court *before* ratification, not afterwards.

Since the *Maastricht Ratification* case, other actions have been brought before the Danish courts. The Act on Accession to the Schengen Agreement was brought before the High Court, Western Division, especially since the agreements conferred rights on foreign police officers concerning the investigation of crimes in Denmark, which allegedly violated the Constitution. The High Court repeated the statement of the Supreme Court in *Maastricht* that in cases concerning issues of general and vital importance for the Danish population, applicants may have a right to obtain constitutional review of an Act of Parliament without being required to show that it is of immediate and specific interest to them. However, none of the provisions invoked in the case were considered to

---

[75]   Article 20(2) requires a five-sixths majority of the members of Parliament, or, where this majority is not obtained whereas the majority required for the passing of ordinary bills is, and the Government maintains it, the Bill is submitted to the People in a referendum.

have such importance and the case was held inadmissible.[76] On appeal, the *Højesteret* rejected the case as inadmissible on grounds that the applicants did not have sufficient legal interest in the case, since Schengen did not transfer sovereignty on vital areas of life.[77]

16.2.5. France

The French constitutional system builds on the prevention of conflicts between the Constitution and treaties by the *Conseil constitutionnel* under Article 54 of the Constitution. The system is not watertight: not all treaties are submitted for review; the law deriving from a treaty may, after the entry into force of the treaty, appear to conflict the constitutional provisions; or the Constitution may be changed. What happens then? There is much debate about the combined constitutional provisions Articles 54 and 55, and the ensuing hierarchical relationship between the Constitution and provisions of international agreements, and about the courts having jurisdiction to uphold the higher norm.[78]

The French Constitutional Council has in principle refused jurisdiction to pronounce on the constitutionality of the treaties in force.[79] Once in force, the treaty enjoys constitutional immunity.[80] The *Conseil* referred to the fourteenth paragraph of the Preamble of the 1946 Constitution to which the 1958 Constitution refers and which proclaims that the French Republic shall conform to the rules of public international law. Amongst those rules, the *Conseil constitutionnel* continued, is the rule that *pacta sunt*

---

[76] A case has also been brought against the Prime Minister accusing the Government of having misused civil servants during the election campaign before the referendum on the Amsterdam Treaty, see P Biering, *art.cit.*, at 932; the claim was rejected since, it was held, Danish Ministers could advocate a 'yes' and be helped to that effect by civil servants, as long as this was done with consideration; *Højesteret*, decision of 29 November 2001, *Folkebevaegelsen mod EU v the Prime Minister, Poul Nyrup Rasmussen*, UfR 2002, 418 H.

[77] *Højesteret*, decision of 26 June 2001, *Foreningen Grundlaovsvoern 1977 for Susanne Tiggelsen v the Prime Minister, Poul Nyrup Rasmussen*, UfR 2001, 2065 H.

[78] See for instance D de Béchillon, 'De quelques incidences du contrôle de la conventionnalité internationale des lois par le juge ordinaire. *(Malaise dans la Constitution)*', RFDA, 1998, 225.

[79] *Conseil constitutionnel*, decision n. 92–308 DC of 9 April 1992, *Treaty of Maastricht I*, www.conseil-constitutionnel.fr; the *Conseil* declared that it would only rule on those elements of the TEU that were new, and did not yet exist under the existing Treaties. A constitutional challenge against a Treaty amendment could not be used to attack existing provisions. See also decision n. 97–394 DC of 31 December 1997, *Treaty of Amsterdam*, www.conseil-constitutionnel.fr where the *Conseil* specifically restricted its review to the revisions of Amsterdam.

[80] Perhaps it is better to speak of *'une immunité contentieuse'*: it is the consequence of a specific system of constitutional review as provided in the French Constitution and which provides only for *a priori* constitutional review. In fact, that does not decide the issue of the hierarchy between the constitutional and treaty norms, see the *Conclusions* of *Commissaire du gouvernement* Christine Maugüé in *Conseil d'État*, decision of 30 October 1998, *Sarran et Levacher*, RFDA, 1998, 1081, at 1086.

servanda, meaning that every treaty in force binds the parties to it and must be performed in good faith. In addition, Article 55 of the Constitution provides that treaties properly ratified have superior authority to laws. Therefore, the *Conseil constitutionnel* concluded, where a reference is made to it pursuant to Article 54 concerning a treaty which supplements or modifies an existing treaty already inserted in the domestic legal order, the *Conseil* must determine the scope of the treaty submitted for its examination in relation to the international agreements which that treaty seeks to modify or supplement.[81]

The position of the *Conseil constitutionnel* thus seems to be that once ratified and published, the treaty takes precedence in the national legal order. Yet, there are some decisions which have created uncertainty, and which seem to imply that the *Conseil constitutionnel* may award precedence to the Constitution over treaty provisions. In a decision relating to the Convention on the Application of the Schengen Agreement, the *Conseil* stated that the legislature had to respect the fourth paragraph of the 1946 Preamble also in statutes restating what was agreed in treaties.[82] On the other hand, in a cryptic and difficult to read decision of May 1998 the *Conseil constitutionnel* seemed to take the opposite view when it held that it was possible to derogate from a constitutional principle *'dans la mesure nécessaire à la mise en oeuvre d'un engagement international de la France et sous réserve qu'il ne soit pas porté atteinte aux conditions essentielles d'exercice de la souveraineté nationale'*.[83] The decision seemed to imply that only the most essential principles of the Constitution would be at the top of the pyramid of norms, while the remaining part of the Constitution would have to give way to treaties. But the case law of the *Conseil constitutionnel* is too ambiguous to determine definitively its position in clear terms.[84]

Another question concerns the role and position of the ordinary courts on the relationship between the Constitution and international treaties. In its report to the 1997 Conference of constitutional courts held in Paris, the *Conseil constitutionnel* expressed the opinion that it had exclusive competence concerning the judicial control of the constitutionality of international agreements, at the exclusion of the ordinary civil and administrative

---

[81] The decision confirms the 1970 decision in which the *Conseil* had stated that the Treaties of Rome had been duly ratified and published and had hence entered into the scope of application of Art. 55 of the Constitution, *Conseil constitutionnel*, decision n. 70–39 DC of 19 June 1970, *ressources propres des Communautés*.

[82] *Conseil constitutionnel*, decision n. 93–325 DC of 13 August 1993, *Maîtrise de l'immigration*.

[83] *Conseil constitutionnel*, decision n. 98–399 DC of 5 May 1998, *Séjour des étrangers et droit d'asile*.

[84] See on the contradictions in the jurisprudence of the *Conseil constitutionnel* E Picard, 'Petite exercice pratique de logique juridique. A propos de la décision du Conseil constitutionnel no. 98–399 DC du 5 mai 1998 'Séjour des étrangers et droit d'asile'', RFDA, 1998, 620; see also D Alland, 'Le droit international 'sous' la Constitution de la Ve République', *RDP*, 1998, 1649, esp. at 1660ff.

courts. The treaty once ratified or approved by statute imposed itself on the courts, which could not substitute the *Conseil constitutionnel*.[85] At that time the *Conseil d'État* had already given judgment in the *Koné* case, but the members of the *Conseil constitutionnel* maintained that the decision should not be interpreted as conveying to the ordinary courts the jurisdiction to control the applicability of treaties in force. *'Cette interprétation parraît aventurée puisqu'elle donne à penser qu'une exception de constitutionnalité pourrait s'exercer à l'encontre du traité, alors qu'elle ne s'exerce pas à l'encontre de la loi pourtant située, en vertu de l'article 55 de la Constitution, une place inférieure dans la hiérarchie des normes.'* According to the constitutional council, the ordinary courts did not have jurisdiction to rule on the constitutionality, or even the applicability, of treaties in force.

In *Koné*[86] the *Conseil d'État*, asked to control the legality of the ministerial decree ordering extradition, interpreted the 1962 Franco-Malian Extradition Agreement[87] so as to conform to a 'fundamental principle recognised by the laws of the Republic' according to which, the State must refuse extradition of an alien when it is requested for a political aim.[88] Apparently, in case of a direct conflict between a treaty provision in force and the Constitution, the latter would take precedence.[89] Finally, in *Sarran et Levacher*[90] the *Conseil d'État* unequivocally stated that the precedence of

---

[85] See Report of the *Conseil constitutionnel*, published in *Cahiers du Conseil constitutionnel* no. 4 and www.conseil-constitutionnel.fr/cahiers/ccc4/ccc4fran.htm, at 5.

[86] In short, the relevant facts are as follows. Mr Koné, a national from Mali, was living in France when the Malian Government accused him of embezzlement of public funds and unjust enrichment and requested his extradition. When a ministerial decree ordered the extradition, Koné challenged the decree before the *Conseil d'Etat* arguing that the request had a political aim since he was close to the former leaders of Mali. The 1962 Franco-Malian Convention made no reference to the political aim of an extradition request. The decision of the *Conseil d'État* and the Opinion of *Commissaire du gouvernement* Delarue are published in RFDA, 1996, 870; comments by L Favoreu, P Gaïa and H Labayle in RFDA, 1996, 882ff; D Alland, RGDIP, 1997, 237; X Prétot, JCP, 1996, 22720.

[87] The Agreement stipulated that there would be no extradition when requested for offences considered by the requested State as political or as related to a political offence. The *Conseil d'État* interpreted the provision extensively as applying also to cases where extradition is requested with a political aim.

[88] However, Koné's application was rejected on grounds of substance because there was no evidence that the Government of Mali had a political aim in requesting his extradition.

[89] See *e.g.* P Gaïa, 'Normes constitutionnelles et normes internationales', RFDA, 1996, 885.

[90] *Conseil d'Etat*, decision of 30 October 1998, *Sarran et Levacher*, RFDA, 1998, 1081; AJDA, 1998, 1039; see C Maugüe (*commissaire du gouvernement* in the case), 'L'auît Sarran, entre apparence et réalité', www.conseil-constitutionnel.fr/ cahiers/ccc7/maugue.htm; further commented in D Alland, 'Consécration d'un paradoxe: primauté du droit interne sur le droit international', *RFDA*, 1998, 1094; L Dubouis, 'Les trois logiques de la jurisprudence *Sarran*', RFDA, 1999, 57; B Mathieu and M Verpeaux, 'A propos de l'arrêt du Conseil d'Etat du 30 octobre 1998, *Sarran et autres*: le point de vue constitutionnaliste', *RFDA*, 1999, 67; O Gohin, 'La Constitution française et le droit d'origine externe', *RFDA*, 1999, 77; D Simon, 'L'arrêt Sarran: dualisme incompressible ou monisme inversé?', *Europe*, no 3, 1999, 4; J Dehaussy, 'La Constitution, les traités et les lois: à propos de la nouvelle jurisprudence du Conseil d'Etat sur les traités', *JDI*, 1999, 675, at 675; C Richards, '*Sarran et Levacher*: Ranking Legal Norms in the French Republic', *ELR*, 2000, 192.

treaty provisions over *lois* contained in Article 55 of the Constitution does not apply to provisions of a constitutional nature. The applicants, Sarran, Levacher and others brought proceedings for judicial review seeking annulment of a decree adopted by the French Government under Article 76 of the Constitution[91] which provides for consultation of the population of New Caledonia on the terms of the 1998 Nouméa Agreements.[92] The Decree set out the detailed measures required to organise the vote, reproducing the terms of the *loi* that was referred to in the Constitution.[93] The applicants claimed that the decree infringed several international provisions on the right to vote and equality of citizens.[94] Given the fact that the decree reproduced the provisions of the loi referred to expressly in the Constitution, the *conventionnalité* of the constitutional provision itself was at stake. The *Conseil d'État* stated the supremacy of the Constitution over treaty law: *'La suprématie conférée aux engagements internationaux (par l'article 55 de la Constitution) ne s'applique pas, dans l'ordre interne,[95] aux dispositions de nature constitutionnelle'*. Yet, the *Conseil d'État* did not actually review the constitutionality of the treaty: it merely stated that in the case at hand the Constitution formed a shield between the administrative act under review and the international conventions invoked in the case.[96] The

---

91 Article 76 of the Constitution, introduced by *loi constitutionnelle* no. 98–610 of 20 July 1998 reads: 'The poulation of New Caledonia is called upon to vote by 31 December 1998 on the provisions of the Agreement signed at Nouméa on 5 May 1998(..). Persons satisfying the criteria laid down in Article 2 of loi no. 88–1028 of 23 November 1988 shall be eligible to take part in the vote. The measures required to organise the ballot shall be taken by decree adopted after consultation with the Conseil d'État and discussion in the Council of Ministers'.

92 The Nouméa Agreements provide for the definitive transfer of certain powers from the French State to the authorities of New Caledonia. See JY Faberon, 'Nouvelle Calédonie et Constitution: La révision constitutionnelle du 20 juillet 1998', *RDP*, 1999, 113.

93 The normative system applying here was compared to the Russian doll *('les poupées gigognes')*: the *décret* reproduced the provisions of a *loi*, which is referred to in Art. 76 of the Constitution. A challenge of the legality of the *décret* thus amounts to challenging the Constitution itself, see B Mathieu and M Verpeaux, 'À propos de l'arrêt du Conseil d'état du 30 Octobre 1998, Sarran et autres: le point de vue du constitutionnaliste', *RFDA*, 1999, 67, at 72.

94 More particularly Arts. 2, 25 and 26 of the International Covenant on Civil and Political Rights, Art. 14 of the ECHR and Art. 3 of the First Protocol to the ECHR; in addition, the décret was alleged to violate Arts. 3, 55 and 76 of the Constitution, Arts. 1 and 6 of the *Déclaration des droits de l'homme et du citoyen*, and several provisions of the Electoral Code and of the Civil Code.

95 The *Conseil d'État* accepts that its position may entail the *international* liability of France, if its decision should lead the French State to infringe its international obligations. Yet, this does not lead the *Conseil* to draw consequences for its jurisdiction on the internal plane.

96 That is the explanation of the case offered by *Commissaire du gouvernement* Christine Maugüé in 'L'arrêt Sarran, entre apparence et réalité', www.conseil constitutionnel.fr/cahiers/ccc7/maugue. htm, at 4. Denis Alland in his comment to the *Sarran* case speaks of a new application of the theory of the *écran*: 'Constitution-écran', D Alland, 'Consécration d'un paradoxe: primauté du droit interne sur le droit international', *RFDA*, 1998, 1094. The Constitution operates as a shield between the decree and the treaty, preventing the court from reviewing the decree. The original image was that of the *'loi-écran'*: in so far as an administrative act is based on and covered by a statute,

Conseil proceeded on the basis of a literal interpretation of the text of Article 55 which speaks of *'une autorité supérieure à celle des* lois', and which thus does not apply to provisions of a constitutional nature. The *commissaire du gouvernement* stated: *'La hiérarchie des normes juridiques qui découle en France des articles 54 et 55 de la Constitution est telle que l'insertion d'une disposition dans la Constitution confère aux mesures qui reprennent cette disposition une immunité contentieuse par rapport au droit international'*. The supremacy of the Constitution has been confirmed, since *Sarran*, in the case *Blotzheim*.[97]

The *commissaire du gouvernement* writing extra-judicially, emphasised that the case must not be understood as creating jurisdiction for the ordinary courts to review the constitutionality of treaties, or of statutes. Firstly, the Constitution had organised the review of the constitutionality of treaties and statutes and laid it in the hands of the *Conseil constitutionnel*, which should decide *a priori*. While this system did leave *'un angle mort'*,[98] it was not for the ordinary courts to change the constitutional system of their own motion. Secondly, a dual system – *a priori* review by the *Conseil constitutionnel* and *a posteriori* review by the ordinary courts – could create inconsistencies in the case law; and it would create an untenable situation for secondary Community law: secondary Community law cannot be reviewed by the *Conseil constitutionnel*, and yet it would be reviewable by the ordinary courts. And third, the issue of the incompatibility Constitution-international norm would be so exceptional that it was not worth disturbing the equilibrium attained between the mission of the constitutional judge on the one hand and the ordinary courts on the other.[99] *Sarran and Levacher* was exceptional due to the fact that the decree

its constitutionality cannot be reviewed, since that would amount to a judicial review of the constitutionality of the statute, which is excluded. The theory was applied also before *Nicolo* with respect to treaties: the statute operated as a shield, protecting the administrative act from review in the light of a treaty. Denys Simon equally suggested that it was restricted to a jurisdictional issue, the *Conseil d'État* merely holding that it had no jurisdiction to disapply provisions of a constitutional nature in favour of treaty provisions; such would not be included in the *habilitation* of Art. 55 of the Constitution. This reading builds on *Nicolo*, where the *Conseil d'État* accepted that Art. 55 contained the mandate for the courts to give effect to the supremacy of treaties and thus to review the constitutionality of statutes. What happened in *Sarran* is merely a refusal to extend *Nicolo* to *lois constitutionnelles*. *Sarran* states the new limit for the ordinary courts, the *non possumus*, D Simon, 'L'arrêt Sarran: dualisme incompressible ou monisme inversé?', *Europe*, 1999, 4, at 5–6.

[97] *Conseil d'État*, decision of 18 December 1998, *SARL du Parc d'activités de Blotzheim et SCI Haselaecker*, AJDA, 1999, 127; the *Conseil d'état* assumed jurisdiction, by virtue of Arts. 53 and 55 of the Constitution and contrary to its previous position, to review whether a treaty has been *duly* ratified, i.e. whether the ratification of a treaty within the scope of Art. 53 of the Constitution has been approved by Parliament.

[98] Statutes and treaties cannot be reviewed on the compatibility with the Constitution after promulgation or ratification.

[99] Chr. Maugüé, 'L'arrêt Sarran: entre apparence et réalité', www.conseil-constitutionnel.fr/cahiers/ccc7/maugue.htm, at 2–3.

in effect reproduced the contents of the constitutional provision. *'L'écran que forme la Constitution entre l'acte administratif et des traités internationaux est ainsi d'une très grande densité'.*[100]

Nevertheless, the *Cour de cassation* has followed the *Conseil d'état* in another case concerning the elections in New Caledonia.[101] Pauline Fraisse had not been granted the right to vote under the *loi organique* of 18 March 1999. Before the *Cour de cassation*, she argued that the *loi organique* infringed various provisions contained in international conventions, among which Article 6 EU, and that the courts should have controlled the conventionality of the *loi organique*; in the alternative, a question should be referred to the European Court of Justice for a preliminary ruling. The *Cour de cassation* quickly disposed of the EU law issues by stating that the case did not come within the scope of Community law. As for the other claims, the *Cour de cassation* stated that the *loi organique* had constitutional value and that the supremacy conferred to international conventions did not apply in the internal legal order with respect to provisions that are constitutional in nature.

16.2.6. Ireland

On at least two occasions the Irish Supreme Court has reviewed the constitutionality of the State's adherence to international treaties, post ratification:[102] in *Gilliland*,[103] and in *Mc Gimpsey*.[104] Things appear in a different light when it comes to the Treaties on the European Communities and the European Union. The Irish constitutional answer to potential conflicts

---

[100] B Mathieu and M Verpeaux, 'øAGraveø propos de l'arrêt du Conseil d'état du 30 Octobre 1998, *Sarran et autres*: le point de vue du constitutionnaliste', *RFDA*, 1999, 67, at 76.

[101] *Cour de cassation*, decision 450 of 2 June 2000, *Pauline Fraisse*, Bull., Ass. plén., no. 4, 7.

[102] The statement of Walsh J in *Crotty* that post ratification litigation would be ineffective to challenge the validity of an international agreement, seems to have been implicitly overruled, G Hogan and G Whyte, *JM Kelly, The Irish Constitution*, 3rd ed, (Dublin, Butterworths, 1994), at 299–300; see also C Symmons, 'International Treaty Obligations and the Irish Constitution: The McGimpsey Case', 41 *ICLQ*, 1992, 311.

[103] *Supreme Court*, decision of 24 July 1986, *State (Gilliland) v Governor of Montjoy Prison* [1987] IR 201; [1987] ILRM 278; www.irlii.org; the Supreme Court was asked whether the Extradition Act 1965 was invalid having regard to the provisions of Art. 29.5.2 of the Constitution by reason of the fact that the terms of the US-Irish Extradition Treaty (which was the subject matter of the order) were not approved by *Dáil Éireann*. The Court held that it was indeed invalid; the effect on the legal status of the Treaty itself remained unclear, see CR Symmons, 'International Treaty Obligations and the Irish Constitution: The McGimpsey Case', 41 *ICLQ*, 1992, 311, at 326–327 and references.

[104] *Supreme Court*, decision of 1 March 1990, *McGimpsey v Ireland* [1990] 1 IR 110; [1990] ILRM 441; www.irlii.org. The applicants sought a declaration that the provisions of the 1985 Anglo-Irish Agreement were contrary to certain provisions in the Constitution, more particularly the principle of the reintegration of the national territory contained in Arts. 2 and 3 of the Constitution. The Supreme Court held that they were not.

between the Constitution and European Community and later Union law was pre-emptive, in the shape of constitutional (and legislative) provisions adopted with a view to the Irish accession to the Communities in 1973, which have been amended several times since. Article 29.4 of the Constitution explicitly authorises ratification of the Community Treaties, the Single European Act and the Treaties of Maastricht and Amsterdam on the European Union (Articles 29.4.3–5) and further states that *'no provision of this Constitution invalidates laws enacted, acts done or measures adopted by the State which are necessitated by the obligations of membership of the European Union or of the Communities, or prevent laws enacted, acts done or measures adopted by the European Union or by the Communities or by the institutions thereof, or by bodies competent under the Treaties establishing the Communities, from having the force of law in the State'* (Article 29.4.7). The latter provision is stated in the negative and *prima facie* provides for constitutional immunity, while the former are enabling, and were inserted because membership of the European Communities was considered inconsistent with several constitutional provisions and principles.[105] Yet, despite the apparently carefully drafted provisions in the Constitution, questions have arisen before the Courts as to the constitutionality of the Treaties.

Crotty has been considered above in the section on preventive review of the constitutionality, since it was decided before the Single European Act was ratified. As the Act had not yet been ratified and would enter into force when ratified in accordance with the constitutional requirements of the Member States, the Supreme Court held that ratification was not 'necessitated by the obligations of membership of the Communities' for the purposes of Article [29.4.7] of the Constitution.[106] It was not therefore covered by the constitutional immunity provided by that Article. The wording of Article [29.4.7] has thus been interpreted as containing a *legal* obligation. Given the fact that upon ratification there is a legal obligation to comply with the Treaty, it is implicit that the Irish courts will not normally question the constitutional validity of adherence of the State to an amendment of the Treaty or the incorporation thereof in Irish law, even in the absence of specific constitutional authorisation.[107]

The Irish Constitution thus seems to restrict the jurisdiction of the courts to uphold the Constitution against the Treaties once ratified. The Irish

---

[105] Such as the retention of exclusive national legislative, executive and judicial power; the sovereignty and independence of the State. In addition, a way had to be found to allow for the direct effect and supremacy of Community law over national law including the Constitution.

[106] Then numbered Article 29.4.5.

[107] So DR Phelan and A Whelan, 'National constitutional law and European integration', in *Le droit constitutionnel national et l'intégration européenne*, 17th FIDE Kongress, Berlin, 1996, 292, at 299; G Hogan and A Whelan, *Ireland and the European Union: Constitutional and Statutory Texts and Commentary* (London, Sweet & Maxwell, 1995) at 32ff; see also the statement of Walsh J that once ratified it would no longer be possible to have the validity of an international agreement questioned before the courts; this statement does no longer seem to be good law.

Constitution is the only of the Constitutions considered here which contains provisions specifically limiting the mandate of the courts to uphold the Constitution against the European Treaties. This way, it achieves compliance with the requirements of Community law,[108] while allowing the courts to continue to observe the Constitution. This approach is commendable. It is the constitutional Legislature who has put the system in place, rather than leaving this thorny issue for judicial decision. Yet, although the constitutional provisions of Article 29 seem to dispose of the problem, there still is reluctance on the part of the Irish courts to carry it to the extreme and to completely give up the mandate to uphold the Constitution against the Treaty duly ratified and covered, *prima facie*, by the constitutional immunity awarded by Article 29.4.7. After all, while the provision is receptive to Community law and even provides constitutional immunity, it remains an *Irish* constitutional provision, and is part of the Constitution that the Irish courts have an obligation to uphold.

The question as to what extent Article 29.4.[7] may be taken to qualify another provision of the Constitution arose for the first time in the *Campus Oil* case.[109] The issue was whether an appeal lay to the Supreme Court against a decision of the High Court to refer a question for preliminary ruling to the Court of Justice. Under Article 34.4.3 of the Irish Constitution there is a right of appeal from every decision of the High Court save in cases provided by law. The Supreme Court held that a decision to refer a question for preliminary ruling to the Court of Justice was not a decision in the sense of the Constitution and ruled that it was not permissible to appeal to the Supreme Court against it. Yet, Walsh J also added an obiter that even if it did constitute a decision of the High Court for the purposes of Article 34.4.3 of the Constitution, the right of appeal must by virtue of Article 29.4.[7] yield to the primacy of Article 177 of the Treaty (Article 234 EC). The statement is remarkable, since the Court of Justice had indicated that it was permissible for national procedural rules to provide for such appeals.[110] In that sense, Walsh J seemed to be *plus royalist que le roi*,[111] or, if you will, *plus communautaire que la Communauté*.[112] Yet, at the same time, it has the effect of scheduling every Article of the Treaty to the text of the Constitution.[113] Walsh J's statement indicates that it is for the Irish courts

---

108 *Internationale Handelsgesellschaft* and *Foto-Frost*.

109 *Supreme Court*, decision of 17 June 1983, *Campus Oil Ltd v Minister for Industry and Energy* [1983] IR 82; [1984] 1 CMLR 479; commented in D O'Keeffe, 'Appeals Against an Order to Refer under Article 177 of the EEC Treaty', *ELR*, 1984, 87.

110 *Cases 146 and 166/73 Rheinmühlen Düsseldorf v Einfuhr-und Vorratsstelle für Getreide und Futtermütte (II)* [1974] ECR 33.

111 O'Keeffe, 'Appeals Against an Order to Refer under Article 177 of the EEC Treaty', *ELR*, 1984, 87, at 97.

112 DR Phelan and A Whelan, 'National constitutional law and European integration', in *Le droit constitutionnel national et l'intégration européenne*, 17th FIDE Kongress, Berlin, 1996, 292, at 304.

113 So G Hogan and G Whyte, *JM Kelly, The Irish Constitution*, 3rd. edn. (Dublin, Butterworths, 1994) at 285.

to decide what are the obligations of membership of the Communities which under Article 29.4.7 qualify the other terms of the Constitution.[114]

Both in *Campus Oil*, and in *Meagher*[115] and other cases[116] the Irish Courts gave proof of a generous interpretation[117] of the constitutional immunity provision in the Constitution. It seemed therefore that the courts would take Article 29.4.7 at its word, and refrain from upholding the Constitution against the Treaties, possibly even beyond what was strictly required by the immunity clause of Article 29.4.7 of the Constitution.

Then, in *SPUC*[118] *v Grogan*, a direct conflict was looming between the Community Treaty and one of the most sensitive substantive provisions of the Irish Constitution, Article 40.3.3,[119] protecting the right of the unborn. The provision was introduced in the Irish Constitution by the 1983 Eighth Amendment of the Constitution Act,[120] and is therefore subsequent in time to the Third Amendment introducing Articles 29.4.3–5.[121] The issue was whether the procedural constitutional provision contained in Article 29.4.5 (now 29.4.7) of the Constitution would serve to solve a potential conflict between the Treaty and a subsequent substantive provision in the Constitution. What was at stake was one of the most sensitive issues of Irish constitutional law and indeed of the Irish society as a whole, in the context of European integration. A year before proceedings were initiated in the High Court in *SPUC v Grogan*, the Supreme Court had ruled on the Eighth Amendment in another case *Open Door*[122] and held that the freedom of expression and privacy of women's health clinics to provide non-directive

---

[114] See B Walsh, 'Reflections of the Effects of Membership of the European Communities in Irish Law', in F Capotorti *et al* (eds), *Du droit international au droit de l'intégration. Liber Amicorum P Pescatore* (Baden, Nomos, 1987) 805, at 809, where he states that the Supreme Court had noted the case law of the ECJ on the possibility to appeal against decisions to refer, but did not seek to rely on it since it took the view that the matter must be decided as a question of Irish law. The Supreme Court after all was not so *communautaire* as the outcome gave reason to believe.

[115] Supreme Court, decision of 1 April 1993, *Meagher v Minister for Agriculture and Food* [1994] 1 IR 329; [1994] ILRM 1; www.irlii.org. The case is discussed further below.

[116] *High Court (Ireland)*, decision of 2 October 1987, *Lawlor v Minister for Agriculture* [1988] ILRM 400; [1990] 1 IR 356; www.irlii.org.; *High Court (Ireland)*, decision of 4 April 1989, *Greene v Minister for Agriculture* [1990] 2 IR 17; [1990] ILRM 364; www.irlii.org.

[117] Or as Phelan and Whelan argue, a 'disturbing' generosity.

[118] SPUC is the Society for the Protection of Unborn Children.

[119] For a discussion of the issue in a comparative and European context see CJ Forder, 'Abortion: A Constitutional Problem in European Perspective', 1 *MJ*, 1994, 56.

[120] It was later, after the constitutional quandaries caused by the *SPUC v Grogan* and *AG v X* cases, complemented by the Twelfth and Thirteenth Amendments of the Constitution adopted in 1992. Art. 40.3.3. now reads: '*The State acknowledges the right to life of the unborn and, with due regard to the equal right to life of the mother, guarantees in its laws to respect, and, as far as practicable, by its laws to vindicate that right*' (adopted in 1983). *This subsection shall not limit the freedom to travel between the State and another State* (adopted in 1992). *This subsection shall not limit freedom to obtain or make available, in the State, subject to such conditions as may be laid down by law, information relating to services lawfully available in another State* (adopted in 1992)'.

[121] Now Articles 29.4.3.-7.

[122] *Supreme Court*, decision of 16 March 1988, *Attorney General v Open Door Counselling and Dublin Well Woman* [1988] IR 593.

counselling regarding abortion was inferior to the right to life of the unborn in Article 40.3.3 of the Constitution. The Supreme Court issued an injunction prohibiting the clinics to give information on abortion abroad. The defendants in the case appealed the decision to the European Commission on Human Rights on the grounds that it violated the freedom of expression (Article 10 ECHR), the right to privacy (Article 8 ECHR) and the principle of non-discrimination on Article 14 ECHR. Pending that case, and strengthened by the decision of the Supreme Court, SPUC commenced proceedings in *Grogan* against students' unions to obtain an injunction restraining the publication of information about abortion clinics abroad. This time, the defendants sought to argue the case on the basis of Community law, claiming that a pregnant woman had a right to travel to another Member State to obtain an abortion and that, as a corollary, she had a right to obtain the necessary information about the location of clinics and thus, that they had a right to publish and distribute the information. In the High Court Carroll J stayed the proceedings and referred a question to the Court of Justice asking whether abortion did constitute a service under the Treaty and if so, whether Ireland could still impose restrictions on the distribution of information on the availability of abortion abroad.[123] On appeal against the failure of the High Court to grant an interlocutory injunction pending the case in Luxembourg, the Supreme Court balanced the constitutional prohibition on the dissemination of abortion information under *Open Door* against a possible or putative right to disseminate which may exist in European law as a corollary to a right to travel and to obtain services abroad, and granted an injunction. It did however grant liberty to any party to apply to the High Court for a variation of the order in the light of the preliminary ruling of the Court of Justice.

There was, when the case came before the Supreme Court, only a possible conflict between Article 40.3.3 of the Constitution and the Treaty, since the Court of Justice had not yet decided whether the Treaty did indeed grant a right to provide the relevant information. Nevertheless, two Justices commented on the position of the Irish courts should a conflict occur. Walsh J's statement was most specific.[124] He said: '*It was sought to be argued in the present case that the effect of [Article 29.4.7] is to qualify all rights, including fundamental rights, guaranteed by the Constitution. The Eighth Amendment of the Constitution [Article 40.3.3] is subsequent in time, by several years, to the amendment of Article 29. That fact may give rise to the consideration of the question whether or not the Eighth Amendment itself qualifies*

---

[123] *High Court (Ireland)*, decision of 11 October 1989, *SPUC v Grogan* [1989] IR 753.

[124] McCarthy J said that '*The sole authority for the construction of the Constitution lies in the Irish Courts, the final authority being this court*'. And: '*Article [29.4.7] may exclude from constitutional invalidation some provisions of the Treaty of Rome the enforcement of which is necessitated by the obligations of membership of the European Communities; it may be that in enacting the Eighth Amendment to the Constitution as explained by this Court in the* Open Door Counselling *case, the people of Ireland did so in breach of the Treaty to which Ireland had acceded in 1973*'. The statement is not explicit as to what would happen if the Treaty as interpreted would indeed appear to conflict with the Eighth Amendment as interpreted by the Supreme Court.

the Amendment to Article 29. Be that as it may, any answer to the reference from the Court of Justice will have to be considered in the light of our own constitutional provisions. In the last analysis only this court can decide finally what are the effects of the interaction of the Eighth Amendment and the Third Amendment [Article 29.4.3-7] of the Constitution'. And he added: *'It cannot be one of the objectives of the European Communities that a Member State should be obliged to set at nought the constitutional guarantees for the protection within the State of a fundamental human right'*. These statements were *obiter*, since there was, as yet, no direct conflict between the Treaty and the Constitution, but they demonstrate that Article 29.4.7 of the Constitution may not in the most sensitive cases, achieve what it aims to do, namely ensure the full precedence of Community law in the Irish legal system.

The crisis was averted. Firstly, the Court of Justice[125] ruled that abortion did constitute a service under the Treaty, but that the link between the students' organisations disseminating information on abortion abroad and the clinics providing the service was too tenuous, and the case fell outside the scope of Community law. The Court did not therefore have to consider whether a restriction to the freedom to provide information on a service was lawful under Community law.[126] The judgment did not forestall the re-emergence of the conflict in further cases, since it is based on the 'coincidence' that the information was disseminated by a student's organisation whose link with the provider of the service was too remote.

Two months after the judgment of the Court of Justice had been handed, the Irish Government asked a Protocol to be added to the Treaty of Maastricht,[127] to guarantee that nothing in the Treaty would be so construed

---

[125] Case C–159/90 *The Society for the Protection of Unborn Children Ireland Ltd v Grogan* [1991] ECR I–4685; for a highly critical analysis of the case from an Irish perspective, see DR Phelan, 'Right to Life of the Unborn v Promotion of Trade in Services: The European Court of Justice and the Normative Shaping of the European Union', 55 *MLR* 1992, 670. He argues cogently that the *Grogan* case represents the low watermark of the Court's regard for national constitutional law; also, in the wider perspective of the Court's general human rights jurisprudence at the time, J Coppel and A O'Neill' The European Court of Justice: Taking Rights Seriously?', 29 *CML Rev* (1992) 669; but see the severe critique of that article in JHH Weiler and NJS Lockhart, '"Taking Rights Seriously" Seriously: The European Court and its Fundamental Rights Jurisprudence', 32 *CML Rev* (1995) 51–94 and 579–627.

[126] AG van Gerven did go into the question, since he was of the opinion that the case did fall within the scope of Community law. He concluded that the information ban constituted a permissible derogation from the Treaty, including the general principles of Community law. He accepted that the ban interfered with the freedom of expression under Art. 10 ECHR, but he felt that the States had a margin of discretion and were entitled to consider that an information ban as the one under scrutiny was necessary in a democratic society to protect the life of the unborn and was a proportionate derogation from Art. 10. On this point he was contradicted by the decision of the *European Court of Human Rights*, decision of 29 October 1992, *Open Door Counselling Ltd and Dublin Well Woman v Ireland*, Series A, no 246.

[127] Protocol 17 provides that 'Nothing in the Treaty on European Union, or in the Treaties establishing the European Communities, or in the Treaties or Acts modifying or supplementing those Treaties, shall affect the application in Ireland or Article 40.3.3 of the Constitution of Ireland'; on the Protocol see G Hogan and A Whelan, *Ireland and the European Union: Constitutional and Statutory Texts and Commentary*, (London, Sweet & Maxwell, 1995), Ch 9, 'Renvoi in Reverse? Protocol No. 17 to the Maastricht Treaty'.

as to interfere with Ireland's domestic law regarding abortion. The aim was to avert any conflict between Community law and Irish constitutional law in respect of abortion information and assistance, as well as anxiety among the Irish people on possible future effects of Irish membership to the Communities and the Union relating to abortion. During that time, facts occurred that would give rise to yet another case before the Irish courts, which this time concerned the right to travel abroad to obtain an abortion.

Attorney General v X, concerned the horrific case of a 14-year-old girl who had been raped and impregnated by her friend's father. She left the country with her parents to travel to England to obtain an abortion. The Attorney General obtained an order of interim injunction from the High Court restraining them leaving the country or arranging or carrying out an abortion, and they returned to Ireland, to argue the case in court. During that time the girl manifested an intention to end her own life if she was not allowed to terminate her pregnancy. The defendants argued their case *inter alia* on the basis of the right to travel and the right to obtain an abortion, that is, to receive a service under Community law. The High Court nevertheless granted the injunction, finding that the right to travel must be subordinated to the right to life of the unborn. On the issue of Community law, the Court held that although the European Court had held that abortion constituted a service under the Treaty, it was unlikely to interfere with the Irish abortion issue given its tendency to defer to Member States regarding issues of public security and public health.

On appeal from the defendants, the majority in the Supreme Court reversed the decision and held that under the Constitution and having regard to the specific circumstances of the case, given that she had threatened to take her own life, she was permitted to have an abortion in the country. Article 40.3.3 was interpreted as providing for a right to an abortion where this is necessary to avert a real and substantial risk to the life of the mother. The Supreme Court decided the case under Irish law and did not consider the issues that might have arisen under Community law, but some judges did make obiter statements on the question of the right to travel under the Irish Constitution. Three out of five judges indicated that the right to travel to obtain an abortion would, irrespective of the special circumstances, be overridden by the right to life of the unborn. Shortly after the judgment of the Supreme Court, the Irish Government sought to have Protocol 17 amended and proposed an addendum stating that *'This Protocol shall not limit the freedom to travel between Member States or to make available in Ireland, in accordance with conditions which may be laid down by Irish legislation, information relating to services lawfully provided in other Member States'.*[128] A majority of Member States refused Ireland's request, fearing the opening of Pandora's box in the IGC. Instead, the

---

[128] See D Curtin, Case note under Case C-159/90 *SPUC v Grogan*, 29 *CML Rev* (1992) 585, at 602.

High Contracting Parties adopted a Solemn Declaration *'That it was and is their intention that the protocol shall not limit freedom to travel between Member States or, in accordance with conditions which may be laid down, in conformity with Community law, by Irish legislation, to obtain or make available in Ireland information relating to services lawfully available in Member States'*. The exact meaning and effect of the Declaration is not entirely clear.

Instead, the Irish Government decided to hold a referendum to change the Constitution in order to guarantee the right to travel and to be informed about abortions abroad as a matter of Irish law.[129] In December 1992 the 13th[130] and 14th[131] Amendment to the Constitution were incorporated into Article 40.3.3 of the Irish Constitution. The European Court of Justice and the Irish Supreme Court are no longer 'on a collision course' on the issue.[132] Nevertheless, as Phelan and Whelan suggest, 'it is difficult to summarise the state of Irish law on substantive constitutional conflicts with Community law'. Normally the Irish courts will give effect to and accord primacy to Community law on its own terms, and in the words of Temple Lang, *'Article 29.4.7 constitutes a renvoi from the Constitution of Ireland to the constitutional law of the Community'*.[133] The direct effect and supremacy of Community law over Irish law including the Constitution are accepted on

---

[129] Three proposed amendments were submitted to the people. The first of the three, which would have confirmed the holding of the Supreme Court that abortion be allowed only where the pregnancy posed a real and substantial risk to the life of the mother was overwhelmingly defeated (by 34,6% for and 65,4% against), due to a bizarre alliance of pro-life activists (who thought it went too far) and pro-choice activists (who believed that it did not go far enough). The second (the right of the woman to travel abroad to terminate her pregnancy) and third (the freedom to obtain or make available information relating to services lawfully available in another State) passed easily (62,3% and 59,8% in favour respectively); see KS Koegler, 'Ireland's Abortion Information Act of 1995', 29 *Vanderbilt J of Transnational L*, 1996, 1117, at 1134–1137.

[130] '[Art. 40.3.3 (1)] shall not limit the freedom to travel between the State and another State'.

[131] '[Art. 40.3.3 (1)] shall not limit freedom to obtain or make available, in the State, subject to such conditions as may be laid down by law, information relating to services lawfully available in another State'. The conditions referred to were laid down in the Abortion Information Act of 1995, which was under Article 26.1.1 of the Constitution referred to the Supreme Court by the President for a determination as to their constitutionality. The Supreme Court upheld the 1995 Act: Supreme Court, decision of 12 May 1995, In the Matter of the Abortion Information Act [1995] 2 ILRM 81, see K S Koegler, 'Ireland's Abortion Information Ats of 1995', 29 *Vanderbilt J of Transnational L*, 1996, 1117, at 1139–1142.

[132] DR Phelan, 'Right to Life of the Unborn v Promotion of Trade in Services: The European Court of Justice and the Normative Shaping of the European Union', 55 *MLR*, 1992, 670, at 687.

[133] J Temple Lang, 'The Widening Scope of Community Law', in D Curtin and D O'Keeffe (eds), *Constitutional Adjudication in European Community and national law. Essays for the Hon. Mr. Justice TF O'Higgins*, (Dublin, Butterworth, 1992) 229, at 231; he argued, though, that to interpret the provision a reference to Luxemburg might be necessary. The Irish courts have taken the opposite position that it ultimately remains a provision of the Irish Constitution and falls to be interpreted by the Irish court. In the final analysis they may limit its effects and 'accept on the terms of the Irish Constitution the effects of Community law on its own terms'. This stands in contrast with the Dutch approach which is that in the context of Community law Article 93 and 94 of the Constitution are applied in accordance with the case law of the Court of Justice and the reference made in *Van Gend en Loos* was considered as a question of interpretation of the Netherlands Constitution.

the conditions of the Court of Justice on the basis of Article 29.3.7. Nonetheless, in situations of profound normative conflict that concern the most fundamental values of society and of the Constitution, the Irish courts may consider the non-application of a Community law rule as part of domestic law. To again cite Phelan and Whelan, *'It is difficult to place total reliance in such situations on a provision, like Article 29.4.[7] of the very Constitution which is felt to be fundamentally threatened'.*[134]

16.2.7. The Netherlands

In The Netherlands, the jurisdiction of the courts to review the constitutionality of Treaties is expressly excluded in Article 120 of the Constitution, as it is for Acts of Parliament.[135] Under Article 94 there is absolute judicial supremacy of treaties over the Constitution.[136] The notion of 'statutory regulations in force in the Kingdom' was intended to include the Constitution.[137] The courts have no constitutional mandate to review the constitutionality of Treaties. Community law therefore brings about no change. Furthermore, Article 91(3) of the Constitution allows for the conclusion of treaties that deviate from the Constitution. All that is required is a two thirds majority in both Chambers of Parliament. Once entered into force, such treaty takes precedence over the Constitution.[138] However, even if the procedure was not followed, as in the case of the Treaty of Maastricht or the other European Treaties for that matter, the (unconstitutional) treaty will still take precedence over the Constitution at

---

[134] DR Phelan and A Whelan, 'National constitutional law and European integration', in *Le droit constitutionnel national et l'intégration européenne*, 17. FIDE Kongress, Berlin, 1996, 292, at 311. Both authors have analysed what Irish courts may do in such case, see DR Phelan, *Revolt of Revolution. The Constitutional Boundaries of the European Community*, (Round Hall, Sweet & Maxwell, 1997); G Hogan and A Whelan, *Ireland and the European Union: Constitutional Texts and Statutory Texts and Commentary*, (London, Sweet & Maxwell, 1995), Ch. 8, '"The mirror crack'd from side to side" Normative Conflict and Constitutional Interpretation', 121.

[135] 'The constitutionality of Acts of Parliament and treaties shall not be reviewed by the courts', translation by the Foreign Office, available on www.minbuz.nl. Original version: *'De rechter treedt niet in de beoordeling van de grondwettigheid van wetten en verdragen'.*

[136] 'Statutory regulations in force in the Kingdom shall not be applicable if such application is in conflict with provisions of treaties that are binding on all persons or of resolutions by international institutions', translation by the Foreign Office, available on www.minbuz.nl. *'Binnen het Koninkrijk geldende wettelijke voorschriften vinden geen toepassing indien deze toepassing niet verenigbaar is met een ieder verbindende bepalingen van verdragen en van besluiten van volkenrechtelijke organisaties'.*

[137] Handelingen EK, 1952–1953, 2700, n. 63a (Memorie van Antwoord).

[138] However, even if the procedure has not been followed, the (unconstitutional) treaty will still take precedence over the Constitution at least in practical effect: the courts cannot under Art. 120 of the Constitution enter into the constitutionality of treaties and review whether they have been concluded in accordance with the procedural requirements laid down in the Constitution.

least in practical effect: the courts cannot, under Article 120 of the Constitution, enter into the constitutionality of treaties and review whether they have been concluded in accordance with the procedural requirements laid down in the Constitution.

The absolute precedence of treaties over national law including the Constitution, may be explained by the fact that historically the Kingdom of the Netherlands – then still including Belgium – owes its existence to an international treaty, the 1815 Vienna Peace Treaty.[139] In addition, the country of Grotius, has always wanted to play an significant role in international relations, and is extremely dependent on these relations.[140] The courts will not review whether a treaty has been concluded in accordance with the constitutionally prescribed procedural requirements.[141] Likewise, they will not hold that a treaty conflicts with a substantive provision in the Constitution.[142]

16.3. CONCLUDING REMARKS

Community law precludes the national courts from exercising a mandate that they may have under national law to review the constitutionality of the Treaty in force. Of all the courts under review in this section, none have *expressis verbis* accepted these implications of the Community orthodoxy for their mandate. While in none of the Member States under review, a court has actually declared a provision of the EC and EU Treaty, or its country's membership to the Community or the Union unconstitutional, this was not because of the case law of the Court of Justice. Some of the courts have commented expressly on the discomfort of their position. Walsh J was most explicit in his elaboration in *Crotty*.[143] He did not draw on the specific character of the Community Treaties, but rather on the duties of States under the rules of international law in general and said: '*If some part or all of the Treaty was subsequently translated into domestic legislation and found to be unconstitutional it would avail the State nothing in its obligations to its fellow members. It would still be bound by the Treaty (..) in international law (..). It is not for the other Member States to satisfy themselves that the*

---

[139] JG Brouwer, 'Nederlandse gedachten over de Grondwet en het Verdrag', *RW*, 1992–1993, 1366, at 1368, with references to the relevant literature in the late 19th Century.

[140] So L Erades, 'Enige vragen betreffende de artikelen 65 en 66 van de Grondwet', *NJB*, 1962, 357, at 390–391.

[141] The courts may however review the international validity of the treaty, see *Hoge Raad*, decision of 31 August 1972, *Uitleveringsverdrag met Zuid-Slavië*, NJ, 1973, 4.

[142] The statement that a treaty provision conflicts with a provision in the Constitution would imply that there is also a procedural defect: treaties which do not conform to the Constitution must be approved with a two thirds majority in Parliament.

[143] To be sure, *Crotty* concerned a preventive review of the constitutionality of the Irish ratification of the SEA. In his judgment, however, Walsh J elaborated on the questions as to whether post ratification, the constitutionality of the Treaty could come up for review.

Government of Ireland observed its own constitutional requirements. It is solely a matter for the Government of Ireland and if it fails to take the necessary steps, the State cannot afterwards be heard to plead that it is not bound by the Treaty'.

When confronted precisely with the issue of the constitutionality of their country's accession to the Treaties, there was not much that the *Corte costituzionale* and the *Bundesverfassungsgericht* (with respect to the original treaties) or the *Højesteret* and the *Cour d'arbitrage* (with respect to the Treaty on European Union) could do. A declaration of unconstitutionality would not be viable; the State would still be bound under international and Community law. A declaration of unconstitutionality of a treaty in force is a decision with ambiguous legal consequences: it does not 'free' the State from the unconstitutional treaty: the State continues to be bound on the international level. On the other hand, the domestic impact of the treaty may be affected. Yet, the non application of the Treaty domestically may cause the international liability of the State to arise. In practical effect, a decision of unconstitutionality pronounced by a national court would not, to say the least, enhance its credibility, and indeed, it may raise questions as to its legitimacy.

Nevertheless, these actions did present an opportunity for the courts to elaborate on the relationship between Community law and national law, on the applicability of Community law and the constitutional limits to integration in the future. But with respect to the constitutionality of the Treaties and of membership itself, it is hard to envisage a case of a court actually declaring the unconstitutionality of the Treaty.

The *Cour d'arbitrage* was the only court to shy away from this opportunity by declaring the applications inadmissible. There *was* in this case an overt inconsistency between the texts of the Treaty and the Constitution, one that was known already when the Treaty was negotiated. but which would have been difficult to ease without being pushed to say what a constitutional The Court probably did not want to be forced to be saying that the Treaty takes precedence over the Constitution. If, on the other hand, it would have opted for the primacy of the Constitution, it would have had to pronounce the unconstitutionality of the Treaty, and risk that its judgment would carry no real effect. Perhaps one could even say that more than anything, such a decision would have demonstrated the ineffectiveness of the decision of the *Cour d'arbitrage* itself.

Constitutional provisions may however operate as shields against the operation and effect of Union law in the domestic legal order. The Constitution may serve as a counter-limit in isolated cases, which do not put the State's continued membership at stake. It is striking that it was the French *Conseil d'État*, and not a veritable constitutional court, which opposed a constitutional provision against the application of a Treaty provision.

Finally, even an express constitutional immunity provision appears to be ineffective in the case of a direct conflict of the most sensitive kind between a constitutional provision and a provision in the Treaties. The Irish Supreme Court was confronted with a potential conflict between a provision of the Constitution and a Treaty provision in *Grogan*, but suggested that if the conflict materialised, the Treaty may have to give way. The Irish case indicates the boundaries of the supremacy of Community law over the national Constitutions. Probably it has to be accepted that there are areas in which a hierarchical solution simply does not work.[144] Those may be the true limits of integration.

The courts featuring in this chapter have shown restraint in the exercise of their review of the constitutionality of the treaties. None has, in so many words, declared the Treaties, or a provision thereof, unconstitutional; nor have any of them declared that State membership conflicted with the Constitution. But none has in so many words declined jurisdiction on grounds of the supremacy of Community law or the case law of the Court of Justice.

---

[144] This will be developed further in Part 3.

17

Preventive Constitutional Review of the Constitutionality of Secondary Law

17.1.1. General Considerations

CAN THE NATIONAL constitutionality of secondary Union law be judicially reviewed by national courts *before* its adoption? Is it at all possible for constitutional courts[1] to become involved in the Community legislative process and have their say on the constitutionality of secondary legislation *before* it is adopted? Is such prior review lawful under Community law? Is it viable?

During the stage of drafting and negotiating Community legislation, there is not yet an act which is supreme over national Constitutions: the principle of supremacy comes into play as soon as the act is adopted, but only from that time onwards. One only needs to read the text of the *Simmenthal* judgment of the Court of Justice: '(..) *in accordance with the principle of the precedence of Community law, the relationship between [Community law] and the national law of the Member States is such that those measures and provisions [of Community law] not only* by their entry into force *render automatically inapplicable any conflicting provision of current national law but (..) also preclude the valid adoption of new national legislative measures to the extent to which they would be incompatible with Community provisions*' etc.[2] But what rules and principles of European law govern the situation *before* the entry into force of the Community act? The Community legislature consists, amongst others, of representatives of the Member States, acting together in the Council of Ministers. The 'two hats' tale is a familiar and helpful way of presenting the position of the government representatives in the Council: as members of the Council,

---

[1]   Or other courts, see further the discussion on the Netherlands *Emesa* cases.
[2]   *Case 106/77 Simmenthal* [1978] ECR 629, at para 17, my emphasis.

they form part of the Community decision-making process; nevertheless, as representatives of their government and State, they are still bound by the constitutional provisions of their State. It is to be expected that they should, when drafting and negotiating Community legislation, display a *vigilance spontanée*,[3] a natural concern not to violate any national constitutional principles. If a particular proposal for a Community measure should infringe upon national constitutional principles or provisions, these objections will be presented during the negotiations and be taken into account, and an alternative solution should be sought, possibly in the form of a derogation clause.[4] Reverting to the 'two-hat' metaphor, it could be said that the representatives in the Council are wearing two hats at the same time: they do not set aside their duties under the national Constitution, when assuming their role as part of the Union decision-making machinery.

It may not be considered sufficient to leave the vigilance over the national constitutional requirements in Community decision-making to the national representatives at the Community level. At the national level, some of the Member States have instituted mechanisms to examine proposals for Community legislation on their constitutionality. As Rodriguez Iglesias, President of the Court of Justice and Puissochet, member of the Court of First Instance explained in their paper submitted to the 1997 Paris Conference of Courts having Constitutional Jurisdiction: '*De tels examens n'ont rien de répréhensible au regard de l'orthodoxie, aussi longtemps bien entendu qu'il est accepté qu'une incompatibilité avec l'ordre constitutionnel national ne constitue pas,* ipso jure, *une violation du droit communautaire. Ce qu'on pourrait appeler 'l'organisation de la veille national' peut avoir des effets très positifs. Encore une fois, si un Etat constate, avant l'aboutissement du processus législatif, l'existence d'une difficulté, il est bien compréhensible qu'il en fasse part à ses partenaires au sein du Conseil, tout comme aux autres acteurs de la procédure, de façon à ce que compte puisse en être tenu. Ce n'est pas une question de 'Compromis de Luxembourg', mais une simple considération des problèmes que peut rencontrer un Etat et de recherche d'une solution appropriée dans le plus strict esprit communautaire*'.[5]

---

3   GC Rodriguez Iglesias and J-P Puissochet, 'Rapport de la Cour de Justice des Communautés européennes', report to the Conférence des Cours ayant compétence constitutionnelle des Etats membres de l'Union européenne, www.conseil-constitutionnel. fr/cahiers/ccc4/ccc4cjce.htm at 3.
4   See in the context of the third pillar for instance in the Council Framework Decision of 13 June 2002 on the European Arrest Warrant and the Surrender Procedures between Member States, OJ 2002, L 190/1, which contains, among a provision providing for an exception applying to Austria and Gibraltar, a series of statements made by certain Member States on the adoption of the Framework Decision.
5   GC Rodriguez Iglesias and J-P Puissochet, 'Rapport de la Cour de Justice des Communautés européennes', report to the Conférence des Cours ayant compétence constitutionnelle des Etats membres de l'Union européenne, www.conseil-constitutionnel.fr/cahiers/ccc4/ccc4cjce.htm at 3.

Rodriguez Iglesias was apparently referring to national systems in which proposals of Community legislation are examined either in a committee in Parliament, such as the *'Europaudvalget'* in the Danish Folketing, or by a consultative body such as the French *Conseil d'Etat, Section administrative* and its counterparts in other countries. Would it make a difference, from a Community perspective, if it were a *court* signalling an incompatibility between a proposal of Community legislation and a constitutional principle? There seems to be no legal reason why it should matter which instance draws attention to constitutional issues. On the other hand, if a court should find that there is an incompatibility, it is for the national representative in the Council to convince his colleagues to adapt the proposal. If that does not happen, and the proposal is adopted after all in the form that was considered unconstitutional, [6] that is the end of it. From that time onwards, there *is* a piece of Community legislation against which national law, however framed and including the Constitution, cannot be invoked, neither before the European Court of Justice,[7] nor before the national courts.[8]

Obviously, there are practical difficulties if it is accepted that national courts may become involved during the elaboration of Community legislation. What, if in all Member States, attempts are made to block proposals of Community legislation before the courts? It would imply opening Pandora's box, and would complicate decision-making even further. In addition, if a national court had to consider the constitutionality of a proposal of Community law, questions of interpretation of the proposal are very likely to arise. Yet, no reference can be made to the Court of Justice which can only itself pronounce on the interpretation and validity of acts of the institutions, and preparatory acts are not among those which are susceptible for review.[9] Furthermore, the Community decision-making process is not transparent: proposals are discussed and amended until they are adopted. What would be the appropriate time for a court to intervene? On the other hand, the complexity and lack of transparency of

---

[6]   Where the act is to be adopted by unanimity, the Member State can block the decision; if only a qualified majority is required, the State cannot block the adoption of the decision on its own; another case in point would be where the national representatives in the Council ignores a decision of the national court; the State remains bound in the same way on the Community level.

[7]   Case 48/71 *Commission v Italy* [1972] ECR 529; Case 102/79 *Commission v Belgium* [1980] ECR 1473; Case 149/79 *Commission v Belgium* [1980] ECR 3881; Case C–473/93 *Commission v Luxemburg* [1996] ECR I–3207; Case C–290/94 *Commission v Greece* [1996] ECR I–3285.

[8]   Case 11/70 *Internationale Handelsgesellschaft* [1970] ECR 1125; Case 106/77 *Simmenthal* [1978] ECR 629.

[9]   Other questions, relating to the interpretation of the Treaty e.g. may be made; if however the alleged unlawfulness of the proposed Community measure is based solely on the claim that it infringes the national Constitution (and not at the same time also 'higher' Community law such as the Treaties or general principles of Community law), it will be difficult to involve the ECJ.

the decision-making process, and the lack of democratic control may argue in favour of intervention by the courts by way of compensation. Nevertheless, it will be extremely difficult and delicate for a court to get involved in decision-making at the European level.

Another, more universal issue, is whether it is desirable that courts, at whatever level, become involved in a process which is essentially political. In most constitutional systems, it is not considered the natural role for the courts to interfere with law making in Parliament. Court intervention is considered undemocratic. Should that be different at the Community level? There is an important difference with one-tier systems: due to the supremacy of Community law, once a Community measure is adopted, it is too late to discuss its compatibility with the national Constitution. *Preventive* review of the constitutionality of secondary measures is the only form of judicial review which is not contrary to the principles of Community law.

If there is a cause of action available in national law, *national* preparatory acts done during the process at the Community level may be justiciable before national courts. Indeed, these acts and decisions constitute the exercise of national authority, and while they may be preparatory in the decision-making at a European level, they remain national acts. On the other hand, the decision of the Government whereby it agrees with a proposal in the Council is no longer *preparatory*, but is *constitutive* of the Council decision. From a Community perspective, it is too late to challenge that act, since such a challenge would at the same time address the Council decision, which is immune from constitutional challenge.

17.1.2. A Role for the Court of Justice?

If a State, an institution or a legal or natural person is of the opinion that a project or proposal for Community legislation infringes *national* constitutional provisions, fundamental rights, for instance, or that the Community does not have competence to adopt the decision, is there a cause of action available before the Court of Justice in order to prevent the adoption of the decision? It would seem not: the Court of Justice has jurisdiction only to review the validity of binding acts of the Community institutions[10] which are intended to produce legal effects,[11] by bringing a

---

[10] The ECJ only reviews *Community* acts and denies competence to review the validity of decisions and agreements adopted by the Representatives of the Governments of the Member States meeting within the Council. The representatives are then considered to act not in their capacity as members of the Council but as representatives of their governments and thus collectively exercising the powers of the Member States. This may be otherwise if it can be shown that they in reality constitute acts of the Council; *cf* Joined Cases C–181/91 and C–248/91, *European Parliament v Council and Commission* [1993] ECR I–3685.

[11] Case 22/70 *Commission v Council (ERTA)* [1971] ECR 263.

distinct change in the legal position of the applicant.[12] Only final acts are susceptible to review, at the exclusion of preparatory acts: before adoption, there simply is no act to be challenged. The Court of First Instance has dismissed as manifestly inadmissible an action for annulment brought against a Commission proposal for a Council Regulation replacing the term 'ECU' by 'Euro'.[13] The Court held that a proposal for regulation submitted by the Commission to the Council under the procedure described in Article 235 of the EC Treaty (now Article 308 EC) was part of a legislative process involving several stages, and was only an intermediate measure solely intended to pave the way for the final measure, the Council Regulation, without definitively determining the position that the Council will adopt. Consequently, it may not form the subject of an action for annulment. When the Regulation was finally adopted,[14] the same applicant, a French Member of the European Parliament, in his private capacity brought a new action for annulment under Article 173(4) of the EC Treaty (now Article 230(4) EC), which was again dismissed as manifestly inadmissible, this time on grounds that the applicant could not prove direct and individual concern in order to have standing. Remarkable was the applicant's reference to the decision of the Danish *Højesteret* of 12 August 1996 on the ratification of the Treaty of Maastricht:[15] Berthu claimed *inter alia* that the change in the name of the European currency, carried out in breach of the provisions of the Treaty, affected the exercise of national sovereignty in such a serious manner that it was of direct and individual concern to him as a citizen. He argued that the decision of the Danish Supreme Court, which held admissible an action brought by natural persons challenging the legality of certain provisions of the Treaty on the ground that infringement of national sovereignty constituted such serious harm that each citizen was directly and individually concerned, should be transposed to Community law. The Court analysed the applicant's standing under the normal Community law conditions for standing under Article 230(4) EC, found that there was nothing to differentiate Berthu from other citizens in the Union, and denied standing.[16]

In the case of actions for annulment, a further complicating factor is the fact that individuals are not normally entitled to challenge general acts, except under strict conditions that they are directly and individually concerned: is no such thing as an *actio populari* before the European Courts, *a fortiori* not before the act has been adopted. Class actions, public interest

---

[12]   The ECJ does also control whether an act based on the EU Treaty should instead have been based on the EC Treaty, Case C–170/96 *Commission v Council* [1998] ECR I–2763.

[13]   Order of the CFI in Case T–175/96, *Georges Berthu v Commission* [1997] ECR I–811.

[14]   Council Regulation (EC) No 1103/97 of 17 June 1997 on certain provisions relating to the introduction of the Euro, OJ 1997 L 162/ 1.

[15]   Discussed above in Chapter 5.

[16]   Case T–207/97 *Georges Berthu v Council* [1998] ECR II-509, in particular paras 19 and 28.

litigation, popular constitutional complaints are all excluded due to the restrictive approach on standing under Article 230 EC. In addition, time limits[17] for bringing an action for annulment begin to run from the 14th day after the publication of regulations and other measures that have to be published in the Official Journal. Publication of those acts has constitutive effect.[18] Until they have been published, they do not exist and cannot be challenged.[19]

Furthermore, the Court of Justice has in various judgments shown that it does not want to 'have its courtroom transformed into a legislative assembly'.[20] In annulment actions the Court generally exercises mere judicial review functions, and rather marginally: as long as Community law is not infringed there is no illegality. In the area of review of Community action, the Court will not easily be accused of being overly strict. On the contrary, the Court's track record in this context may rather be described as one of 'passive activism': by refraining from scrutinising Community legislation thoroughly and by allowing the Community institutions to make extensive use of Community competences and of Article Article 308 EC, the Court has contributed to the expansion of Community law. More than the issue of fundamental rights, this attitude of passive cooperation was what set off the distrust of some of the national courts, most notably the *Bundesverfassungsgericht*. When the Court reviews Community acts in which the Community legislator or executive exercises political responsibility, the Court only exercises marginal review, and generally allows the institutions wide discretionary powers.[21] Also in the context of actions for damages, the Court shows great reluctance to hold that the Community should compensate for damages caused by wrongful normative acts. When the Community institutions have adopted legislative measures involving choices as to economic policy, damages are only awarded if there is a sufficiently serious breach of a superior rule of law for the protection of individuals.[22] The Court of Justice does not want to been seen to be interfering in the legislative activity.

---

[17] Two months for the action for annulment under the EC and Euratom Treaties, Arts 230(3) EC and 146(3) Euratom Treaty.

[18] Case 185/73 *König* [1974] ECR 616.

[19] Cf HG Schermers and DF Waelbroeck, *Judicial Protection in the European Union*, 6th edn, (The Hague, Kluwer Law International, 2001), at 687.

[20] H Schepel and E Blankenburg, 'Mobilizing the European Court of Justice', in G de Búrca and JHH Weiler (eds) *The European Court of Justice* (Oxford, OUP, 2001) 9, at 41.

[21] A case in point is Case C–280/93 *Germany v Council* [1994] ECR I–4973, on which one commentator and former member of the Court said that the Court almost granted the institutions *carte blanche* and reduced judicial control to a minimum, see U Everling, 'Will Europe slip on Bananas? The Bananas Judgment of the Court of Justice and National Courts', 33 *CML Rev*, 1996, 401, at 419.

[22] Case 5/71 *Schöppenstedt* [1971] ECR 984; Liability of the State for normative action was at the time, and is still not, knwon in every national system. AG Roemer in the case argued in favour of accepting it for the Community to increase judicial control as compensation for the lack of democratic control of the Community's legislative action.

The Court of Justice does not review *national* acts done or measures adopted in the framework of the preparation of a Community measure. Under Article 230 EC the Court does not control the legality of national measures.[23] Nor does it, in the framework of questions for preliminary ruling, rule on the validity of national law; it may however give an interpretation of Community law so as to allow the national court to draw conclusions on the validity of the relevant national acts. In addition, the Court of Justice does not look beyond Community law: as long as Community law is not infringed, there is no illegality. The Court does not review whether national constitutional provisions have been observed.[24]

It thus seems that under Community law as it stands it is not possible to have the validity or lawfulness of secondary Community law reviewed *a priori* by the Court of Justice, either directly or indirectly via the national preparatory acts.

17.2. THE NATIONAL PERSPECTIVE

17.2.1. France

The *Conseil constitutionnel*, which in the national context scrutinises the constitutionality of *lois*[25] and treaties[26] only after they have been passed in Parliament but *before* promulgation or ratification respectively, and is thus familiar with preventive review, has reviewed, *a priori*, the constitutionality of the decision concerning the resources of the Communities[27] and the decision on the direct election of the European Parliament.[28] Under the Treaty these acts were subject to ratification in accordance with national constitutional rules, and did not therefore constitute 'ordinary'

---

[23] See Case C–97/91 *Oleificio Borelli SpA v Commission* [1992] ECR I–6313, paras 10–11: '*It should be pointed out that in an action brought under Article 173 of the Treaty the Court has no jurisdiction to rule on the lawfulness of a measure adopted by a national authority. That position cannot be altered by the fact that the measure in question forms part of the Community decision-making procedure, since it clearly follows from the division of powers in the field in question between the national authorities and the Community institutions that the measure adopted by the national authority is binding on the Community decision-taking authority and therefore determines the terms of the Community decision to be adopted'*. The field in question was the administration of the EAGGF, where the Commission adopted decisions on the basis of binding opinions of national authorities.
[24] Constitutional fundamental rights may however be protected not as such, but as general principles of Community law.
[25] Art. 61(2) of the Constitution.
[26] Art. 54 of the Constitution.
[27] *Conseil constitutionnel*, decision n. 70–39 DC of 19 June 1970, *ressources propres*; available on www.conseil-constitutionnel.fr; English translation in Oppenheimer, *The Cases*, 275.
[28] *Conseil constitutionnel*, decision n. 76–71 DC of 30 December 1976, *Parlement européen*; available on www.conseil-constitutionnel.fr; English translation in Oppenheimer, *The Cases*, 313.

decisions of secondary law.[29] The *Conseil constitutionnel* has never had to pronounce on the availability of the procedure under Article 54 of the Constitution in the case of proposed secondary legislation.[30] The procedure applies to *'engagements internationaux'*, and it has been argued by some commentators that this could also include secondary Community legislation.[31] However, the provision concerns *engagements internationaux* that are subject to ratification or approval, which is not the case for secondary Community legislation.[32] Members of the *Conseil constitutionnel*, writing extra-judicially, have denied the possibility of submitting proposed secondary legislation before it on the basis of Article 54.[33]

Several proposals[34] have been tabled in the French Parliament to amend the Constitution in order to provide for preventive constitutional review of secondary legislation. The key motive for the proposal was the alleged lacuna in the system of constitutional review, given that once a Community measure is adopted, it enjoys constitutional immunity in France at least before the *Conseil constitutionnel*, who refuses jurisdiction to conduct direct review of the constitutionality of secondary Community

---

[29] *'Ni l'un ni l'autre de ces actes ne mérite la qualification de décision puisque dans l'un et l'autre cas le traité prévoit que le Conseil arrête "les dispositions dont il recommande l'adoption par les Etats membres, conformément à leurs règles constitutionnelles respectives". L'Etat n'est donc juridiquement lié que s'il donne cette acceptation, tout comme pour une convention internationale (..)'*, L Dubois, 'Le controle de la compatibilité des décisions de l'Union européenne avec la Constitution française', in J-F Flauss and P Wachsmann (eds), *Le droit des organisations internationales. Recueil d'études à la mémoire de Jacques Schwob* (Brussels, Bruylant, 1997) 331, at 341. The 1970 and 1976 decisions of the *Conseil constitutionnel* have been discussed in the chapter on preventive review of the constitutionality of treaties, supra.

[30] *'Peut-être à tort'*, Mme Lenoir, member of the *Conseil constitutionnel*, stated during a debate on the preventive review of the constitutionality of secondary law, in 'Les constitutions nationales face au droit européen. Conférence-débat - 12 juin 1996', *RFDC*, 1996, 675, at 698.

[31] See L Favoreu and L Philip, *Les grandes décisions du Conseil cotitutionnel*, 11th edn, (Paris, Dalloz, 2001) at 800.

[32] J Rideau, 'Constitution et droit international dans les Etats membres des Communautés européennes. Réflexions générales et situation française', *RFDC*, 1990, 259, at 270; T Meindl, 'Le controle de constitutionnalité des actes de droit communautaire dérivé en France. La possibilité d'une jurisprudence Solange II', *RDP*, 1997, 1665, at 1676.

[33] 'Rapport français', in *Droit communautaire et droit dérivé*, report submitted to the Conference of courts having constitutional jurisdiction in the Member States of the European Union, Paris, 1997, www.conseil-constitutionnel.fr/cahiers/ccc4/ccc4fran.htm, at 7.

[34] In 1992, a proposal was made for constitutional amendment of Article 54, to include Community directives. The proposal was not discussed, see 'rapport français', cited above, at 7. In 1993 and 1996 proposals were made io introduce a new provision in the chapter on the European Union, to provide for a similar procedure; discussed in O Passelecq *et al*, 'Les constitutions nationales face au droit européen. Conférence-débat, 12 juin 1996', *RFDC*, 1996, 675; T Meindl, 'Le controle de constitutionnalité des actes de droit communautaire dérivé en France. La possibilité d'une jurisprudence Solange II', *RDP*, 1997, 1665; L Dubois, 'Le controle de la compatibilité des décisions de l'Union européenne avec la Constitution française', in J-F Flauss and P Wachsmann (eds), *Le droit des organsiations internationales. Recueil d'études à la mémoire de Jacques Schwob* (Brussels, Bruylant, 1997) 330, at 344–352.

law in force.[35] Under the proposal Mazeaud, if the *Conseil constitutionnel* were to consider a proposed piece of secondary legislation to conflict with the French Constitution, the Government could vote in favour of the proposal only after constitutional amendment, in order to *'redonner à la Constitution son rang de norme supérieure'*.[36] The proposed article read: *'Art. 88-5 - Si le Conseil constitutionnel, saisi par le Président de la République, par le Premier ministre, par le président de l'une ou l'autre Assemblée ou par soixante députés ou soixante sénateurs, a constaté qu'un projet ou une proposition d'acte des Communautés européennes ou de l'Union européenne comporte une disposition contraire à la Constitution, le Gouvernement ne peut l'approuver qu'après révision de la Constitution'*.[37]

The report annexed to the proposal[38] further explained that the Government would, if the *Conseil constitutionnel* was indeed seized, have to invoke a sort of *'réserve d'examen constitutionnel'* in the Council, in order to allow the *Conseil constitutionnel* to assess the constitutionality of the proposed act; and, if need be to allow the constitutional organs to complete the procedure for constitutional amendment. If the *Conseil constitutionnel* should find an incompatibility, either the Government could negotiate a modification of the project or proposal in the Council of Ministers, or, in the alternative, the Constitution would have to be revised following the procedure for constitutional amendment. If neither solution could be attained, the French Government would have to invoke the Luxembourg compromise.

The aim was thus *'to restore the pre-eminence of the Constitution'*,[39] even if the Constitution had to be adapted to conform to a proposal for Community legislation allegedly conflicting with it, in order to remain the principal norm in the land. There are several practical difficulties with the solution: the final piece of legislation adopted may not contain the allegedly unconstitutional provisions; or it may, at a later point in time, be repealed or amended. Furthermore, the procedural difficulties are not easy to surmount: At what time, for instance, would a proposal have to be submitted for review? In addition, the decision-making procedure at the

---

[35] This point will be developped in the next chapter on posterior review of the constitutionality of secondary Community law.

[36] Taken from T Meindl, 'Le contrôle de constitutionnalité des actes de droit communautaire dérivé en France. La possibilité d'une jurisprudence *Solange II*', RDP, 1997, 1665, at 1680, who cites from the report drafted by the members of the *Assemblée générale* who tabled the proposal.

[37] Assemblée nationale, *Documents parlementaires*, Xe Législative, no. 2641; reproduced in O Passelecq *et al*, 'Les constitutions nationales face au droit européen. Conférence-débat, 12 Juin 1996', RFDC, 1996, 675, at 706.

[38] Reported in T Meindl, 'Le contrôle de la constitutionnalité des actes de droit communautaire dérivé en France. La possiblité d'une jurisprudence *Solange II*', RDP, 1997, 1665, at 1677 *et seq.*

[39] *'Redonner à la Constitution son rang de norme supérieure'*.

Community level is opaque and complex.[40] There is the element of time limits within which the *Conseil constitutionnel* would have to pronounce on questions of incompatibility,[41] and, as the case may be, for the constitutional organs to review the Constitution.

The proposal was never adopted. Instead, on the basis of the new Article 88(4) of the Constitution, introduced in 1992, proposals for Community legislation which are legislative in nature[42] are submitted by the Government to Parliament.[43] Since 1993, the *Conseil d'État* has been involved in its consultative capacity, and has pronounced on the nature of the acts,[44] and on other legal issues, notably their constitutionality. The procedure has been extended to acts adopted in the second and third pillar and to decisions in the framework of Schengen. In one case,[45] the *Conseil d'État* found an incompatibility between a proposed directive and the fundamental rights protected under the French Constitution. The French Government took account of the advice during the rest of the negotiations and sought to have the directive amended.[46]

17.2.2. The Netherlands

In the Netherlands judicial proceedings were brought during the Community decision-making process in the *Emesa Sugar saga*, which generated a whole series of decisions of both Netherlands and European Courts, a 'veritable legal guerrilla'.[47] A sugar company sought an order

---

[40] The obscurity of the decision-making process and the democratic deficit were, however, put forward as arguments in favour of involvement of the courts by way of compensation.

[41] This applies *a fortiori* for frivolous actions, brought with the sole aim to slow down the process.

[42] From a French constitutional perspective, *i.e.* areas which come in the competence of Parliament, as opposed to those in which the legislative competence lies with the Executive; on the division of law-making power under the French Constitution see J Bell, *French Constitutional Law* (Oxford, Clarendon Press, 1992) 78 ff.

[43] A similar procedure was inserted in Art. 23 of the German Basic Law. In Denmark, the Danish representative in the Council receives a negociation mandate from the special committee of European affairs of the Folketing, see T de Berranger, 'Danemark' in J Rideau (ed), *Les Etats membres de l'Union européenne. Adaptations – mutations – résistances*, (Paris, LGDJ, 1997), 97, at 124ff; in the United Kingdom it is the Select Committee on the European Union which follows the European decision-making procedure.

[44] Whether they come within the legislative or executive domain, in other words, whether they are *'de nature législative ou réglementaire'*.

[45] In the case of the proposal for a directive on data protection, Directive 95/46/EC of the European Parliament and of the Council of 24 October 1995 on the protection of individuals with regard to the processing of personal data and on the free movement of such data, OJ L 1995, 181/31.

[46] See 'Rapport français', art. cit., at 8.

from a Dutch court to prevent the Government from voting in favour of a Council Decision amending at mid-term Decision 91/482/EEC on the association of overseas countries and territories with the Community, the 'OCT Decision'.[48] Under the 1991 OCT Decision products originating in the OCT benefited from favourable treatment under Community customs rules; furthermore, a product was also considered as originating in the OCT if it was the result of the processing there of products wholly obtained in the Community or the ACP States. Mesa established a sugar factory in Aruba,[49] where it processed sugar originating in Trinidad and Tobago. In 1997 the Council intended to modify the Decision at mid-term in order to restrict the advantageous rule to a limited quantity annually. The Netherlands Government had been opposed to the mid-term revision of the Decision, but withdrew its objections in October 1997. This was, of course, against the wishes of the Netherlands, Antilles and Aruba. Under Article 25 of the Charter for the Kingdom of the Netherlands (*'Statuut voor het Koninkrijk der Nederlanden'*) overseas countries enjoy a power of veto with respect to certain international economic or financial agreements. This special power of veto of the overseas countries had even been notified to the other Member States in an annex to the OCT Decision. However,

---

[47] As the French Government termed it in its submissions to Case C-17/98 *Emesa Sugar (Free Zone) NV v Aruba* [2000] ECR I-675; For an overview of the cases brought before the European Court of Justice (including the Court of First Instance) see the case note by P Oliver to Cases C-390/95 P *Antillean Rice Mills NV v Commission* [1999] ECR I-769; C-17/98 *Emesa Sugar (Free Zone) NV v Aruba* [2000] ECR I-675; T-32 and 41/98 *Netherlands Antilles v Commission* [2000] ECR II-201; C-110/97 *Netherlands v Council* (judgment of 22 November 2001); C-301/97 *Netherlands v Council* (judgment of 22 November 2001); and C-452/98 *Netherlands Antilles v Council* (judgment of 22 November 2001), 39 *CML Rev*, 2002, 337, with references, in particular in footnote 6; An overview of the case until the judgment of the ECJ in Case C-17/98 *Emesa Sugar (Free Zone) NV v Staat der Nederlanden, Hoofdproductschap voor Akkerbouwproducten and Land Aruba* [2000] ECR I-675 can alo be found in the Opinion of AG Ruiz-Jarabo Colomer in that case, in particular footnote 5; The main Netherlands decisions are *President Arrondissementsrechtsbank 's Gravenhage*, decision of 6 October 1997, *Emesa Sugar (Free Zone) BV v Kingdom of the Netherlands, State of the Netherlands, the Netherlands Antilles and Aruba*, JB, 1997, 248, note AWH; *President Arrondissementsrechtsbank 's Gravenhage*, decision of 17 October 1997, JB, 1997, 259, note AWH; *Gerechtshof 's Gravenhage*, decision of 20 November 1997, JB, 1997, 272, note AWH; *President Arrondissementsrechtsbank 's Gravenhage*, decision of 16 December 1997, KG, 1997, 1657; *President College van Beroep voor het Bedrijfsleven*, decision of 12 February 1998, AWB, 1998, 12 and AWB, 1998, 65; *Hoge Raad*, decisions of 10 September 1999, *Emesa Sugar (Free Zone) NV v Staat der Nederlanden*, RVDW, 1999, 122 c and 123 c; AB, 1999, 462, note by FHvdB; commented in LFM. Besselink, 'Suiker en rijst uit de West – over Europees recht en de Koninkrijksverhoudingen', *NJB*, 1998, 1291; LFM. Besselink, 'Community Loyalty and Constitutional Loyalty', *EPL*, 2000, 169.

[48] Council Decision 91/482/EEC of 25 July 1991 on the association of of the overseas countries and territories with the EEC, OJ 1991 L 263, p.1 ('the OCT decision').

[49] The Kingdom of the Netherlands comprises three countries: The Country in Europe (the Netherlands) and the two overseas countries in the Carribean, the Netherlands Antilles and Aruba. The relationship between the countries in governed by the Charter for the Kingdom of the Netherlands (*'Statuut voor het Koninkrijk der Nederlanden'*) which is hierarchically superior to the Constitution of the Netherlands (*'Grondwet'*).

the Government of the Netherlands intended to agree with the amendment of the OCT Decision against the express wishes of the overseas countries, thus ignoring their veto. There was thus a clear constitutional issue in the case at hand, namely whether it fell within the ambit of Article 25 of the Charter.[50] If it did, the decision of the Netherlands Government to participate in the revision of the Council Decision would be in breach of the Charter.[51]

The company brought interlocutory proceedings in order to obtain an order against the Government not to participate in the adoption of a political agreement for the Council Decision, which it considered to be in breach of Article 132(1) (old) of the EC Treaty.[52] The President of the Hague court granted the injunction, ordering the Government not to vote in favour of the proposal until the Court of Justice had ruled on the questions which he, the President, was about to send.[53] Yet, on the same day, shortly before the *President van de Rechtbank Den Haag* handed down his decision, the

---

[50] Art. 25 of the Charter states that *'(1) The King shall not bind the Netherlands Antilles or Aruba to international economic or financial agreements if the Government of the Country, indicating the reasons for considering that this would be detrimental to the Country, has declared that the Country should not be bound by them. (2) The King shall not denounce international economic or financial agreements in respect of the Netherlands Antilles or Aruba if the Government of the Country, indicating the reasons for considering that a denunciation would be detrimental to the Country, has declared that denunciation should not take place with respect to that Country. An agreement may nevertheless be denounced if exclusion of the Country concerned from the denunciation is incompatible with the provisions of the agreement'*, translation taken from LFM Besselink, 'Community Loyalty and Constitutional Loyalty', *EPL*, 2000, 169, at 177.

[51] These issues are explained in LFM Besselink, 'Community Loyalty and Constitutional Loyalty', *EPL*, 2000, 169; LFM Besselink, 'Suiker en rijst uit de West – over Europees recht en de Koninkrijksverhoudingen', *NJB*, 1998, 1291.

[52] Now Art. 183 concerning the preferential treatment of overseas countries and territories.

[53] *President Arrondissementsrechtbank 's Gravenhage*, 6 October 1997, *Emesa Sugar (Free Zone) NV v The Netherlands*, JB 1997, 248. The President seems to have been of the opinion that the ECJ had jurisdiction to pronounce itself on the validity of a proposal for secondary legislation, which it most likely does not have, see Case T-175/96 *Georges Berthu v Commission* [1997] ECR II-811 in which the ECJ dismissed as manifestly inadmissible an action for annulment against a Commission proposal. Actions must be brought against the final decision adopted. While the category of acts on which preliminary questions can be asked under Art. 234 EC is wider than that of acts challengeable under Art. 230 EC and also includes non-binding acts (Cf HG Schermers and DF Waelbroeck, *Judicial Protection in the European Union*, 6th edn, (The Hague, Kluwer Law International, 2001), at 289 *et seq.*) it seems unlikely that the Court would assume jurisdiction. This was also the position of the Gerechtshof Den Haag in the case at hand. The reference for a preliminary ruling in this case apparently also concerned questions as to the possibility of national courts preventing the national authorities of a Member States from participating in the adoption of Community acts (According to AG Ruiz-Jarabo Colomer in his Opinion in another Case C-17/98 *Emesa Sugar (Free Zone) NV v Staat der Nederlanden, Hoofdproductschap voor Akkerbouwproducten en Land Aruba* [2000] ECR I-675. If the reference should concern the interpretation of the existing Decision or other provisions in force, it would be admissible, see further below. The first reference, made before the Decision was adopted, was removed from the Court's register on 20 January 2000 (Case C-380/97).

Government representative informed the Council of the European Union that of the Council of Ministers of the Kingdom[54] had agreed to the proposal. The Netherlands Government *did* thus co-operate in the adoption of a political agreement on the proposal. In a further action, instigated a few days later, the same President of the *Arrondissementsrechtbank's Gravenhage* ordered the Government not to co-operate, actively or passively,[55] in the final adoption of the decision, and even imposed penalty payments in the amount of 500.000.000 FL![56] Before the Council Decision was tabled for formal adoption, the decisions of the President were overruled by the *Gerechtshof's Gravenhage*, which was of the opinion that under Community law a national court did not have jurisdiction to prevent the adoption of Community acts. The *Gerechtshof* held that the validity of Community acts could only be reviewed by the Court of Justice and only after they had been adopted and published in the Official Journal; the Court of Justice could not rule on the preparation of the relevant act in the Council or on the position of the Member States. Accordingly, the national court would also have to await the adoption and publication of the act to have competence to suspend the application of the act and send questions on the validity of the act to the Court of Justice.[57] Only a few days later, the Netherlands representative in the Council voted in favour of the proposal, and the Council Decision was definitively adopted.[58] The judgment of the *Gerechtshof* seems to blur the distinction between final decisions of Community law and national decisions adopted in the preparation of those Community decisions, which are governed not by Community law, but rather by national constitutional law.

[54] The *'Koninkrijksministerraad'*.
[55] By abstaining. Abstentions do not prevent the adoption of acts for which unanimity is required, Art. 205(3) ECT.
[56] Over 225.000.000 euro; the President was of the opinion that only an exceptionally high amount could produce a preventive effect *vis-à-vis* the State; *President Rechtbank Den Haag*, 17 October 1997, *Emesa Sugar (Free Zone) NV v Kingdom of the the Netherlands and State of the Netherlands*, JB, 1997, 259, annotation by AW Heringa.
[57] *Gerechtshof Den Haag*, decision of 20 November 1997, *Staat der Nederlanden v Emesa Sugar (Free Zone) BV* , JB, 1997, 272, annotated by AW Heringa.
[58] Council Decision 97/803/EC of 24 November 1997 amending at mid-term Decision 91/482/EEC on the association of the overseas countries and territories with the European Economic Community, OJ 1997 L 329, 50. When the decision was adopted, the company brought proceedings before the European Courts, and before several Netherlands courts, among those the same President of the Court of The Hague, who referred 13 questions for preliminary ruling. These were decided in Case C–17/98 *Emesa Sugar (Free Zone) NV v Staat der Nederlanden, Hoofdproductschap voor Akkerbouwproducten en Land Aruba*. LFM Besselink, 'Suiker en rijst uit de West – over Europees recht en Koninkrijksverhoudingen', NJB, 1998, 1291 focusses on the merits of the case and on constitutional aspects concerning the relations between the Kingdom of the Netherlands, The Antilles and Aruba and the Netherlands State, see also MFJM de Werd, 'Een Grafschrift op de Grondwet: de gebrekkige privaatrechtelijke rechtspersoonlijkheid van de Nederlandse Staat', *NJB*, 1998, 213. I do not enter into the discussion of the Netherlands constitutional issues.

The additional claim, that the position of the Council of Ministers of the Kingdom was adopted in violation of the Charter of the Kingdom was not considered.[59]

The cases reached the *Hoge Raad* only after the adoption of the final Council Decision. The *Hoge Raad* upheld the decision of the *Gerechtshof* and ruled that the 'decision' of the *Rijksministerraad* was not to be considered a national administrative act since it constituted a preparatory act in the context of decision-making at the Community level. The case, so the *Hoge Raad* held, turned on the validity of the Council Decision, and held that national courts had no power to rule on the validity of Community law; in addition, preparatory acts could not be challenged before the European Courts: only the final act could be the subject of an action for annulment. There was, under Community law, only a very limited role for interim measures imposed by national courts, which could only suspend the application of national implementing measures. '*In this system*', the *Hoge Raad* concluded, '*there is no room for the jurisdiction of national courts to grant interim measures based on infringements of Community law in the course of the decision-making procedure which precedes the making of a Community act such as the disputed Council Decision*'.[60] With respect to the allegation that the decision of the *Rijksministerraad* was in conflict with the Charter of the Kingdom, the *Hoge Raad* held *obiter* that even if the *Gerechtshof* had considered it and had held it well founded, this could not have led to any different decision, given that the President lacked the competence to intervene in the decision-making process of the Council of the European Union by means of interim injunctions.

The issues in the case are complex and must be carefully distinguished. It seems that the *Gerechtshof* and the *Hoge Raad* have confused issues, and have arrived at a conclusion which does not seem warranted by Community law and to infringe national constitutional law. First, it is important to distinguish the acts under review. What was brought before the Netherlands courts was not the Council Decision or *Community* preparatory acts, but acts of the national authorities.[61] The *Hoge Raad* was correct to point out that the validity of Community acts can only be reviewed by the Court of Justice and that national courts are under an obligation to refer questions as to their validity to the Kirchberg. It was also correct in saying that the Court of Justice only has jurisdiction under Article 230 EC to review final acts. Yet, to conclude from this that *therefore* the national courts are precluded, *by Community law*, from reviewing

---

[59] Despite the fact that such a claim will not be considered by the ECJ, which only rules on the validity of Community decisions under Community law.

[60] *Hoge Raad*, decision of 10 September 1999, *Emesa Sugar (Free Zone) NV v The Netherlands*, AB 1999/462, annotated by FHvdB, my translation.

[61] The decision of the *Koninkrijksministerraad* and the position which the Netherlands was to take in the Council of the European Union.

national preparatory acts, seems rash. The fact that national measures are adopted in the framework of decision-making at the Community level, does not transform them into Community measures which are reviewable only by the Court of Justice.[62] It is a matter of national constitutional law whether these acts are reviewable by national courts. One may doubt whether it is at all opportune for a national court to become involved,[63] i.e. whether it is appropriate for courts to intervene in the political process of adopting legislation.[64] Nevertheless, it does not seem correct to state that the *Community* system of judicial protection prevents the national courts from assessing the validity of *national* measures taken in the preparation of Community legislation.[65] Or does the principle of Community loyalty of Article 10 EC come into play here? The Government had argued before the President of the *Rechtbank Den Haag* that once the Netherlands Government had notified its intention of agreeing with the proposal in the Council, it was under the duty of Community loyalty under Article 5 of the EC Treaty (new Article 10 EC) bound to act in accordance with it. Blocking the formal adoption of a political agreement would be contrary to Article 10 EC since it would jeopardise the internal functioning of the Council, and the national court could not force the Government to infringe the Treaty. The President of the court simply responded that in

---

[62] The ECJ does not consider the validity of national acts done in the framework of the preparation of a Community act, see in the context of administrative law, *Case 97/91 Oleificio Borelli SpA v Commission* [1992] ECR 63313, paras 9 and 10.

[63] Cf below, the decision of the *Bundesverfassungsgericht* in the case of the *TV Broadcasting Directive*. However, the German Court chose not to grant an injunction against the Government to vote against the Directive because such injunction would limit the scope for manoeuvre in the negotiations for the adoption of a Directive under qualified majority voting. In the Netherlands case, since the Decision was to be adopted by unanimity, the Netherlands Government could effectively prevent its adoption.

[64] Cf the theory of *'acte de gouvernement'*; in the Netherlands context see *President Rechtbank Den Haag*, decision of 21 May 1984, *Samenwerkingsverdrag Ems-Dollard*, AB, 1985, 12, where the court held that 'In the Netherlands constitutional system, the competence to conclude treaties is confined to the King and the Parliament. The courts have no role in it. An injunction prohibiting signature or court order to suspend signature has the character of interference by a court in the elaboration of a treaty, to an extent which is not appropriate in our constitutional system' (my translation), see also *Gerechtshof Den Haag*, decision of 27 September 1990, *Samenwerkingsverdrag Ems-Dollard*, AB, 1991, 85. In his decision in the *Emesa* case, the President of the *Rechtbank Den Haag* considered that while the courts must show (great) restraint in blocking the adoption of legislative measures, and the scope for judicial intervention was small, it was not non-existent.

[65] In the context of administrative law, the Court of Justice has even held that where a measure adopted by the national authorities is binding on the Community decision-making authority – in the relevant case the Commission – it was for the national courts, where appropriate after obtaining a preliminary ruling from the Court, to rule on the lawfulness of the natial preparatory act, and to regard an action brought for that purpose as admissible even if the domestic rules of procedure do not provide this in such a case. The Member States were obliged to comply with the Community law principle of judicial control, Case C–97/91 *Oleificio Borelli SpA v Commission* [1992] ECR I–6313, paras 10–15.

the first place Article 10 required that the Treaties were complied with.[66] It could be argued that the duty of sincere co-operation, contained in Article 10 EC and which under the prevailing case law works both ways,[67] includes the duty to respect each others constitutional requirements.

A further complicating factor was that the Netherlands' participation in the adoption of a Community measure was claimed to be unlawful because the outcome, the Council Decision, allegedly infringed Community law. If the national court is granted competence to rule on the lawfulness of national preparatory measures, and the grounds for review are to be found in Community law, it should be possible for the national court to refer a question for preliminary ruling to the Court of Justice, which is alone competent to rule on the validity of a Community measure,[68] and which has the ultimate authority to rule on the interpretation of Community law. The latter possibility was available, so it seems: the national court could have asked the Court of Justice what was the correct interpretation of Articles 132 and 136 of the EC Treaty and of the existing OCT Decision.[69]

Another distinction that must clearly be held in mind concerns the standards for review. Two main arguments were put before the Netherlands courts: the first claim, which was given the most weight, was that the amendment would infringe primary Community law; the second claim was that the decision of the *Koninkrijksministerraad* and the position of the Netherlands Government were adopted in violation of the constitutional rules concerning the relations between the countries of the Kingdom as laid down in the Charter for the Kingdom of the Netherlands. That latter claim concerns national constitutional law, not Community law, and is not for the Court of Justice to decide. The *obiter dictum* of the *Hoge Raad* that even if the mandate of the Government to consent was in conflict with the Charter and Article 18 of the Vienna Convention of the Law of Treaties[70] this could not have led to the competence of the *President Rechtbank Den Haag* to issue the injunctions, because 'the President lacks the

---

[66] Note that the main claim of the applicants was that the Council Decision would infringe Article 132 of the Treaty.

[67] See Case C–2/88 Imm, *Zwartveld* [1990] ECR I–3365.

[68] Which does not yet exist, since it has not yet been adopted.

[69] It was claimed that the mid-term amendment was unlawful under the terms of the existing OCT Decision; The *President of the Rechtbank Den Haag* did send questions for preliminary ruling to the Court of Justice. The case was registered as Case C–380/97, and removed from the register on 20 January 2000.

[70] 'A State is obliged to refrain from acts which would defeat the object and purpose of a treaty when: (a) it has signed the treaty or has exchanged instruments constituting the treaty subject to ratification, acceptance or approval, until it shall have made its intention clear not to become a party to the treaty; or (2) it has expressed its consent to be bound by the treaty, pending the entry into force of the treaty and provided that such entry into force is not unduly delayed'. It is difficult to understand why there would be an infringement of this provision.

competence to intervene in the decision-making process of the Council of the European Union by means of interim injunction' seems rash. The *Hoge Raad* did not explain this further, but presumably the lack of competence of the President was based on the same reasons as mentioned before, namely that it is for the Court of Justice to review the validity of Community law, and that it only has competence to do so once the Decision has been adopted. If that was indeed the reasoning of the *Hoge Raad*, it overlooks the fact that the question of the validity of national acts in the light of the national Constitution is a matter which is not governed by Community law,[71] and that the Court will not review the validity, *under Netherlands constitutional law*, of the *national* preparatory acts which preceded the adoption of the Council Decision. Once the Community act has been adopted, national court actions can be of no avail due to the supremacy of Community law; nor is it the business of the Court of Justice to ensure that national constitutional rules have been observed in the creation of a Community act. That is the responsibility of the national organs, including, possibly, the courts.

17.2.3. Germany

The German Constitutional Court does accept that where a Council measure takes effect without separate domestic implementation, the vote of the German executive authority in the Council is open to judicial challenge, as it is the final act of co-operation in the production of a measure which may infringe constitutional rights, and which is itself no longer subject to constitutional standards, as it is an act of Community legislation. The most notable case, on the transborder television Directive, related to the legislative competences of the *Länder* and the duty of the Federal Government to take these to heart in the decision-making process at a European level. The decision has to some extent been superseded by the new Article 23 of the Constitution, which establishes a new equilibrium of powers within the federal structure of Germany in the European context. But the interest of the case is not restricted to the controversy at hand and may have effects beyond the issue of federalism, more particularly in the area of constitutional restraints imposed of the Government flowing from fundamental rights.[72]

---

[71] See also LFM Besselink, 'Community Loyalty and Constitutional Loyalty', *EPL*, 2000, 169, at 179.

[72] So M Herdegen, 'After the TV Judgment of the German Constitutional Court: Decision-making within the EU Council and the German Länder', 32 *CML Rev*, 1995, 1369; for comments on the final decision see also J Gerkrath, 'L'arrêt du Bundesverfassungsgericht du 22 mars 1995 sur la directive 'télévision sans frontières'. Les difficultés de la répartition des compétences entre trois niveaux de législation', *RTDeur*, 1995, 539 and G Ress, 'Die Rundfunkfreiheit als Problem der europäischen Integration', *ZfRV*, 1992, 434.

The case arose from a Commission proposal for a Council Directive on transborder television.[73] The matter was subject to majority voting in the Council and consequently, single Member State possessed the power of veto. Under the German Basic Law, television broadcasting is a matter for the *Länder*, but Germany was represented in the Council by the Federal Government.[74] The *Länder* had from the beginning been opposed to the Community's competence in the field of television broadcasting. When the Commission first made a proposal for a directive in 1986, the *Bundesrat* adopted a resolution stating the objections held by the *Länder* in February 1987, mainly that the EC Treaty did not provide for Community competence in the area of culture and that the freedom of services did not offer a sufficient legal basis for Community legislation. The Federal Government shared some of these objections, but when the Commission presented an alternative proposal, it stated that it would vote in favour, provided that some changes be made. This decision of the Federal Government however did not respond adequately to the concerns of the *Länder*. The Government of Bavaria challenged the Federal Government's decision before the *Bundesverfassungsgericht*, maintaining that it violated the constitutional division of powers, and applied for an interim injunction preventing the Federal Government giving assent to the TV Directive.

The *Bundesverfassungsgericht* accepted that it had jurisdiction to provisionally regulate the situation by way of an interim injunction in a *Bund-Länder-Streit* under Article 93(1)(3) of the Basic Law, if there was an urgent need to avoid a threat of force or for any other major reason of public interest. The Court made a balance of convenience, and weighed the consequences which would follow if no interim measures were granted but the main action were to succeed against the disadvantages which would arise if the interim injunction were granted as asked but the application in the main action had to be refused. It rejected the application on grounds that an interim order would deprive the Government of the freedom of negotiation in the Council necessary for bringing the Directive as far as possible in line with the Basic Law. If interim measures were granted, the Federal Government would lose all opportunity to influence the content of the Directive, having regard to the federal state principle of the Constitution and the restrictions contained therein. *'Thus it is possible'*, the Court continued, *'that in the event of the main action failing, the consequence of the making of an interim injunction would be to bring about precisely what has to be prevented as far as possible in the interest of the applicant Länder*

---

[73] The decision of the *Bundesverfassungsgericht* on interim measures was published in *Bundesverfassungsgericht*, decision of 11 March 1989, *TV Broadcasting Directive - interim measures*, BVerfGE 80, 74; *English version in* [1990] 1 CMLR 649.

[74] The new Article 23 of the Basic Law, inserted on the occasion of the Treaty of Maastricht, has altered the basic rules under German constitutional law on the division of powers between the *Länder* and the *Bund* in respect of the European Union.

and others, that is, the passing of secondary legislation which is incompatible with German constitutional law (and would not have come about without the interim injunction). The conflict which would then result between Community law and German constitutional law is a major disadvantage which alone is good reason for the interim order sought not to be made. The Federal Constitutional Court may not lend its aid in such a way that its intervention causes a constitutional conflict to arise which would otherwise be averted'.[75] The Government had indicated that it was aware of the constitutional significance of the Directive's provisions for the legislative jurisdiction of the *Länder*. In contrast with the *Hoge Raad*, the position of the *Bundesverfassungsgericht* is thus that it does have jurisdiction to interfere, but in the relevant case it took a rather realistic approach and chose not to interfere at that stage.

The Federal Government's efforts to modify the Commission's proposals were not very successful, and a Directive was finally adopted that seemingly encroached on the *Länder'* competences.[76] The context was now very different from a Community law perspective. There now *was* a piece of secondary legislation, which from a Community point of view, is immune from constitutional challenge. The Bavarian Government requested a declaration from the *Bundesverfassungsgericht* that the Government's decision to approve the proposal and its assent to the Directive constituted a violation of its rights under the Basic law and a declaration that the Directive must be treated as inapplicable. The *Bundesverfassungsgericht* dismissed the latter claim for lack of standing. The requests relating to the declaration of unconstitutionality of the decision and the assent to the Directive partially succeeded on grounds that the Federal Government had given its assent to the Directive without previously informing the *Bundesrat* about the results of the negotiations within the Council and without further consultations. The judgment thus turned on German constitutional issues, and the *Bundesverfassungsgericht* did not rule on the constitutionality or applicability of the Directive itself.[77]

In another case,[78] relating to the draft Directive on the labelling of tobacco products, German tobacco companies sought an interim injunction

---

75   [1990] 1 CMLR 649, at 654.

76   The Directive was adopted on 3 October 1989 on the basis of qualified majority, only Belgium and Denmark voting against it. Germany voted in favour; Council Directive 89/552/EEC of 3 October 1989, OJ 1989 L 289, 23.

77   *Bundesverfassungsgericht*, decision of 22 March 1995, *TV Broadcasting Directive*, BVerfGE 92, 203; commented in J Gerkrath, 'L'arrêt du Bundesverfassungsgericht du 22 mars 1995 sur la directive "télévision sans frontières"', *RTDeur*, 1995, 539; M Herdegen, 'After the TV Judgment of the German Constitutional Court: Decision-Making within the EU Council and the German Länder', 32 *CML Rev*, 1995, 1369.

78   *Bundesverfassungsgericht*, decision of 12 May 1989, *M GmbH and others v Bundesregierung*, BverfGE 80, 74; *published in English in* [1990] 1 CMLR 570; see also G Nicolaysen, 'Tabakrauch, Gemeinschaftsrecht und Grundgesetz. Zum BVerfG-Beschluß vom 12.5.1989', *EuR*, 1989, 215; R Scholz, 'Wie lange bis "Solange III"', *NJW*, 1990, 941.

requiring the German Federal Government to vote against the proposal in the Council and to urge the other Member States to reject the proposal. The applicants argued that the Directive would infringe their fundamental rights under the German Constitution, more particularly the fundamental right of freedom of expression (Article 5(1) of the Basic Law), their right of self-determination (under Article 2(1) in conjunction with Article 1(1) of the Basic Law) and right to property under Article 14(1) of the Constitution, as the directive would constitute an interference with get up and visibility of trademark. The *Bundesverfassungsgericht* refused the application for an interim injunction since the main action would be inadmissible. The applicants could not challenge the Federal Government's participation in the adoption of secondary Community law because an agreement of the Government to the common position of the Council did not constitute a sovereign act with direct adverse effects on the applicants. The Federal Government's participation was not an exercise of executive powers as regards the applicants but was only a contribution to the creation of a directive which did not adversely affect the applicants until it had come into force and was implemented into national law. The condition of 'direct adverse effect on the applicant' which conditions an application for constitutional review was not met. Furthermore, the *Bundesverfassungsgericht* held, the vote in favour of the Directive would not be the decisive cause of the alleged infringement of constitutional rights. That would be the German implementation, which was open to independent challenge. In the process of implementation the German legislature would be subject to the restrictions imposed by the Constitution. The question whether the applicants' constitutional or equivalent rights were infringed in the implementation of the directive within the scope allowed to the legislature was open to constitutional judicial review. Finally, in so far as the directive may infringe the basic constitutional standards of Community law, the Court of Justice ensured legal protection of rights. If the constitutional standards laid down as unconditional by the German Constitution should not be satisfied by this route, recourse could then still be had to the Federal Constitutional Court.

Implicit in the judgment is that where a Community measure does take effect without separate domestic implementation, the vote of the the German executive authority may be reviewable, as it does constitute the final act of co-operation in the production of a measure which may affect constitutional rights directly. According to Nicolaysen, the *Bundesverfassungsgericht* should have added that the vote of the German member in the Council is an act of co-operation in the Community, not the German, decision-making process. *'Denn wenn die Türen sich hinter den Ministern zur Ratssitzung geschlossen haben, sind diese nichts anderes als Mitglieder des Organs Rat und aktiv und passiv nur noch in die Rechtsordnung der Gemeinschaften eingebunden'.*[79] In its decision in the case of the TV Broadcasting Directive which was decided in a procedure concerning a *Bund-Länder-Streit*, the *Bundesverfassungsgericht* took the view that it did have jurisdiction to issue an interim injunction and it did start from the premise that in the Council the Government representative had to bear the constitutional rights of the *Länder* in mind. This seems the better view, one which is not opposed by the principles of Community law, namely that the representatives in the Council remain bound by their national Constitutions, and that due regard must be had to national constitutional requirements. In the words of Rodriguez Iglesias and Puissochet: *'Toute situation de conflit entre le droit communautaire et une norme constitutionnelle nationale d'un Etat membre est, en premier lieu, imputable à un probable manque de vigilance de la part du législateur communautaire en général, et des représentants de l'Etat membre concerné en particulier. Sauf cas exceptionnel, qui ne vient guère à l'esprit, on peut en effet présumer que le législateur communautaire souhaiterait éviter de violer les dispositions constitutionnelles d'un Etat membre (sauf éventuellement si le traité l'y contraignait) et que si un Etat membre invoque le risque d'une telle violation, le Conseil fera son possible pour trouver une solution alternative* (my emphasis)'.[80] With reference to the two-hat theory, the representatives do not take off their national hat when they put on their Community hat; they two hats at the same time.

The dismissal of the case by the Constitutional Court was based on the assumption that fundamental rights can be protected at a later stage *after* the adoption of the directive, either by scrutiny of the directive itself by the Court of Justice, or of the implementing German legislation by the German Constitutional Court. Yet, individuals have no direct access to the Court of Justice against a directive to have their Community fundamental rights protected. They have no standing under Article 230 EC, since directives are not among those acts that can usually be challenged by individuals. The case would have to be brought by one of the privilieged applicants under Article 230 EC, or reach the Court of Justice via the detour of the national courts. The latter type of indirect challenge of the validity of secondary Community law, it is submitted, is not the most efficient, or the most adequate, even if it has now also been advanced by the Court of Justice.[81] The second assumption that in the process of implementation the national legislature is subject to the restrictions imposed by

---

[79] G Nicolaysen, 'Tabakrauch, gemeinschaftsrecht und Grundgesetz', *EuR*, 1989, 215, at 218–9.

[80] GC Rodriguez Iglesias and J-P Puissochet, 'Rapport de la Cour de Justice des Communautés européennes' to the 1997 Paris Conférence des Cours ayant compétence constitutionnelle des États membres de l'Union européenne on *Droit communautaire dérivé et droit constitutionnel,* which can be found on the internet, www.conseil-constitutionnel.fr/cahiers/ccc4/ccc4cjce.htm. at 9.

[81] Case C–50/00 P *Unión de Pequeños Agricultores* [2002] ECR I–6677, discussed further *below.*

the Constitution is only true within the scope allowed to the Member State. To the extent that the implementing legislation is covered by the directive, it is immune from constitutional review. Should the *Bundesverfassungsgericht* accept jurisdiction to review the compatibility of national legislation fully covered by the directive, it would in effect review the directive itself, and thus act in violation of the principle of the supremacy and constitutional immunity of Community law. Constitutional fundamental rights are, at that stage, replaced by general principles of Community law, the scope and interpretation of which is to be decided by the Court of Justice.

Following these two decisions, the discussion on the role of the *Bundesverfassungsgericht* with respect to Community law was renewed in Germany, in the discussion of the need for a so-called *Solange III*.[82] Scholz suggested that the *Bundesverfassungsgericht* had missed an opportunity in both cases to timely ensure that Community measures comply with the German Constitution. It is agreed that it is better to prevent the adoption of unconstitutional Community legislation, than to review it at a later stage, as the *Bundesverfassungsgericht* seemed to have it. Once a Community act is adopted it simply is too late for a national court to question its validity from a national constitutional perspective, and it is, needless to say, unacceptable from the point of view of Community law.

17.2.4. Ireland

While there are no court cases as yet, it has been argued that the Irish courts might reserve, at least in principle, the right to restrain approval by the Government of any 'unconstitutional' decision in the Council.[83] Given the constitutional immunity clause contained in Article 29.4.7 of the Irish Constitution, such preventive intervention of the courts would be the only avenue to uphold the Constitution in the context of Community law. In the context of the second and third pillar, the same argument can be made, given that the Constitution extends the immunity from constitutional review to laws enacted, acts done or measures adopted by the European Union or laws enacted, acts done or measures adopted by the State which are necessitated by the obligations of membership of the Union.

---

[82] R Scholz, 'Wie lange bis "Solange III"', *NJW*, 1990, 941; Chr. Tomuschat, 'Aller guten Dinge sind III?', *EuR*, 1990, 340; U Everling, 'Brauchen wir "Solange III" — Zu den Forderungen nach Revision der Rechtsprechung des Bundesverfassungsgerichts', *EuR*, 1990, 195.

[83] G Hogan and A Whelan, *Ireland and the European Union: Constitutional and Statutory Texts and Commentary* (London, Sweet & Maxwell, 1995) 110–13.

17.3. CONCLUDING REMARKS

So far, the few actions brought before national courts to prevent the adoption of Community measures that allegedly violate national constitutional requirements have proved unsuccessful. The courts that have been seized appear reluctant to restrain Government participation in the adoption of Community legislation. It is often considered an unlawful intervention in what is essentially a political process, one that does not come within the province or natural duty of the courts to assist in the adoption of legislation. In addition, there are many practical difficulties, such as finding the appropriate moment for court actions, the fact that it may not be possible to refer questions for preliminary ruling to the Court of Justice and so on. Furthermore, the credibility of the national courts themselves is at stake. If a court should find that it is unconstitutional for the national Government to co-operate in the adoption of a particular decision, and the State is out-voted in the Council, it is still bound by the decision. It is then part of Community law and accordingly takes precedence over national (constitutional) law.

It is first and foremost the responsibility of the national representatives in the Community organs to make constitutional objections heard in the Council and for the Commission and the other members of the Council to hear them. The Community organs, and the Member States represented in them should be careful not to cause constitutional problems for Member States, also where decisions are adopted by majority voting. It may even be considered an element of the duty of sincere co-operation imposed both on the Member States and the Community institutions[84] under Article 10 EC.[85] Non-judicial methods, such as the vigilance by a Committee in Parliament or an independent body, may be preferred over the intervention by national courts. Where a national representative in the Council knowingly infringes constitutional rules and procedures, as it seems to have been the case in *Emesa*, there is little a court, national or European, may do.

If it is accepted that there is indeed a role for the national courts prior to the coming into existence of Community law, a distinction may have to be made between the cases analysed. With respect to fundamental rights protection under the national Constitution, it may be argued that in most cases, the Court of Justice will offer protection after the adoption of the Community measure by recourse to the general principles of Community law. However, national constitutional rights and the fundamental rights

---

[84] Case C–2/88 *Imm. Zwartveld* [1990] ECR 3365; Case C–234/89 *Delimitis v Henninger Bräu AG* [1990] *AG ECR* 35.

[85] See also G Hogan and A Whelan, *Ireland and the European Union: Constitutional and Statutory Texts and Commentary* (London, Sweet & Maxwell, 1995) at 113.

as general principles of Community law do not always coincide. More importantly, there are cases where the constitutional issue is of a strictly national nature, as in *Emesa*. With respect to the constitutional question of the *Statuut voor het Koninkrijk* no assistance could be expected from the Court of Justice, either before or after the adoption of the measure. The national courts could no longer uphold the *Statuut* against the final Decision, due to the supremacy of Community law. There is then a veritable lacuna in the system of review. In such cases, the option of preventive review is least harmful to the Community principles, and is probably allowed under prevailing Community law. But also in other cases, from a Community law perspective, it is better to have any constitutional quandaries solved before the measure becomes final. Nevertheless, it seems that courts are reluctant to interfere at that stage, for reasons of separation of powers and because they do not want to be seen to be interfering in what is essentially the business of the political organs.

18

Judicial Review of Secondary European Union Law by National Courts?

ITH THE EXPANSION of the scope of Community and Union law, it has become more likely that a provision of secondary law will be claimed to infringe upon national constitutional provisions or principles. A confrontation between a national constitutional provision and a provision of secondary law, including judgments of the Court of Justice, may arise before a national court in several ways. A piece of secondary legislation may be brought directly before a national court on grounds that it is unconstitutional or otherwise invalid. For technical reasons, this type of action is not widespread, since it is assumed that acts of the Union institutions are not among those that may be challenged before national courts. Another possibility is where a *national* measure, whatever its nature, whether legislative or executive, implementing or applying Union law is brought before a national court on grounds that it infringes the Constitution. If and in so far as the national measure is covered by the underlying European act, such procedure amounts to indirect scrutiny of European law.

18.1. THE EUROPEAN PERSPECTIVE

18.1.1. The First Pillar: Community Law

18.1.1.1. General Considerations

In the context of Community law and from a Community law perspective, national courts are precluded from reviewing the validity or applicability of Community law. The ban on such review stems first, from the principle of supremacy of Community law, and secondly, and independent from the principle of supremacy, from the lack of jurisdiction on the part of the national courts to rule on the validity of Community law on whatever ground. First, under the principle of supremacy, precedence must always be given to Community law over conflicting national law however framed and including national constitutional provisions. The validity of Community law can only be reviewed in the light of the Treaties and higher Community law,[1] the general principles of Community law, including fundamental rights, and in the light of international law,[2] but not in the light of national constitutional principles *qua* national principles.[3] The exclusion of national constitutional provisions is crystalline: they can never be invoked, before a Community court or a national court. Things are more complicated when it comes to the validity of measures of Community law in the light of international law. The case law of the Court of Justice on its own jurisdiction and that of national courts in this area may be perceived as leaving a gap in the system of judicial review, which some national courts may want to fill.[4]

Secondly, *the Court of Justice has exclusive jurisdiction* to declare secondary Community law invalid, at the exclusion of the national courts.[5] In the case law of the Court of Justice a dual system of judicial protection has developed involving both the European and national courts. The Treaties have, according to the Court, established a complete system of legal remedies and procedures designed to ensure the legality of acts of the institutions, and has entrusted such review to the Community courts. Where natural or legal persons cannot, by reason of the conditions for admissibility laid down in Article 230(4) EC directly challenge Community measures of general application, they must plead the invalidity of such acts before the national courts. The national courts play a central role in the Community system of judicial protection, even when it comes to review of the validity of Community law.[6] Yet, the national courts lack the competence to hold Community law invalid themselves: if they are convinced that a provision of secondary law may well be invalid, they must make a reference to the Court of Justice which alone has jurisdiction to declare those measures invalid.

---

[1] For a discussion on the relationship between primary and secondary law in the context of the internal market, see K Mortelmans, 'The Relationship between the Treaty Rules and Community Measures for the Establishment and Functioning of the Internal Market. Towards a Concordance Rule', 39 *CML Rev*, 2002, 1303.

[2] Case C–162/96 *A Racke GmbH v Hauptzollamt Mainz* [1998] ECR I–3655.

[3] Case 11/70 *Internationale Handelsgesellschaft* [1970] ECR 1125.

[4] See below.

[5] In the wording of the ECJ, the national courts '*may consider the validity of a Community act*' and may, if they consider that the grounds of invalidity put forward before them by the parties are unfounded, reject them and conclude that the measure is completely valid. On the other hand, they '*do not have the power to declare acts of the Community institutions invalid*', Case 314/85 *Foto-Frost v Hauptzollamt Lübeck-Ost* [1987] ECR 4199, at paras 14 and 15; Case C–27/95 *Woodspring District Council v Bakers of Nailsea Ltd* [1997] ECR I–1847, at paras 19–20.

[6] See lastly, Case C–50/00 P *Unión de Pequeños Agricultores v Council* [2002] ECR I–6677.

The combined effect of the principle of supremacy of Community law over national law however framed and the lack of jurisdiction on the part of the national courts to review the validity of Community law is that national (constitutional) courts may not uphold the national Constitution or indeed any other rule of national law[7] against conflicting Community law. The Court of Justice has taken over the ultimate responsibility to ensure judicial review of the legality of acts of the Community institutions, either directly in an action for annulment or indirectly on a reference from national courts. National constitutional principles are not protected as such in the context of Community law, but are replaced, where relevant, by Community principles, such as fundamental rights as general principles of Community law, derived from the common constitutional traditions of the Member States, the ECHR and, possibly,[8] the Charter of Fundamental Rights of the European Union.

To sum up, the denial of the competence of national courts to rule on the validity of secondary Community law results from the supremacy of Community law (there simply is no national standard for review since Community law always ranks higher) and the lack of jurisdiction of the national courts under *Foto-Frost*.

18.1.1.2. The Ultimate Supremacy of Community Law

A distinction has been made between 'ordinary supremacy'[9] and 'ultimate supremacy' over the national Constitutions.[10] Formally, there may not be a major difference between the two types of supremacy: in both cases Community law prevails and must be enforced against conflicting measures of national law. Yet, looking at it from the perspective of the

---

[7]   The exclusive jurisdiction of the ECJ extends to all grounds allegedly capable of invalidating them, including 'higher' Community law, principles found in national law and including also rules of international law; see e.g. Case C–162/96 *Racke v Hauptzollamt Mainz* [1998] ECR I–3655, cf. *below*.

[8]   See *e.g.* the reference to Art. 47 of the Charter of Fundamental Rights of the European Union by the CFI in Case T–177/01 *Jégo-Quéré v Commission* [2002] ECR II-2365; the judgment was 'reversed' by the ECJ in Case C–50/00 P *Unión de Pequeños Agricultores v Council* [2002] ECR I–6677, the reference to the Charter was omitted.

[9]   The supremacy of Community law over 'ordinary' statutes and anything inferior to the Constitution, but including Acts of Parliament (*Costa v ENEL*). In the framework of this book 'ordinary supremacy' was the central theme of the first Theme on the ordinary courts, since it corresponds to the mandate of the national courts to ensure that Community law is applied and enforced even as against conflicting national law, including Acts of Parliament. The national courts are so involved in the (private) enforcement of Community law as against the Member States.

[10] Deriving from *Internationale Handelsgesellschaft*. The consequence of this supremacy is a denial on the part of the European Court for the national (mostly constitutional) courts to review the constitutionality of Community law. National courts may not enforce the Constitution (or indeed any other 'higher norm') as against Community law. This area of supremacy is central in this Theme on courts having constitutional jurisdiction.

national courts and their mandate, there is an important difference in that 'ordinary supremacy' endows the court (mostly an 'ordinary court') with the mandate to enforce Community law and to set aside any conflicting norm of national law, while the second type of supremacy precludes the national court (mostly a court having constitutional jurisdiction) from exercising its national mandate to uphold the Constitution. Since *Internationale Handelsgesellschaft* it is undisputed under Community law that *'recourse to the legal rules or concepts of national law in order to judge the validity of measures adopted by the institutions of the Community would have an adverse effect on the uniformity and efficacy of Community law. The validity of such measures can only be judged in the light of Community law'. '[T]he valid-ity of a Community measure or its effect within a Member State cannot be affected by allegations that it runs counter to either fundamental rights as for-mulated by the Constitution of that State or the principles of a national constitu-tional structure'.*[11] The validity of secondary Community law or its effects in the internal legal order cannot be questioned on the basis of national constitutional law. It should be emphasised that *Internationale Handelsgesellschaft* rules out the possibility not only that national courts hold Community law invalid, but also that they decide on its effects within a Member State, and accordingly, its applicability.[12]

18.1.1.3. *Jurisdiction to Declare Community Law Invalid:* the Foto-Frost *Principle*

In addition, there is a jurisdictional issue: the Court has held in *Foto-Frost*[13] that it has exclusive jurisdiction to rule on the validity of Community law. This principle is independent of the principle of supremacy of Community law: even if the alleged invalidity follows from an infringement of the Treaties,[14] the national court is under an obligation to refer the case to the European Court which alone has competence to actually declare Community law invalid. This is not evident from the text of the Treaties.[15] Article 230 EC (old Article 173 of the EC Treaty) provides for an action for annulment of specified Community acts to the Court of

---

[11] Case 11/70 *Internationale Handelsgesellschaft* [1970] ECR 1125, at para 3.
[12] This is developed further below.
[13] Case 314/85 *Foto-Frost v Hauptzollamt Lübeck-Ost* [1987] ECR 4199; see also Case C–27/95 *Woodspring District Council v Bakers of Nailsea Ltd* [1997] ECR I–1847.
[14] Which is an accepted ground for illegality or invalidity under Community law and expressly provided for in the text of Art. 230 EC.
[15] AG Mancini stated, in his Opinion in *Foto-Frost*, that the 'eliptical' wording of Art. 177 was attributable to 'a singular but not impossible oversight' on the part of the authors of the Treaty. In his view the textual interpretation would lead to such 'dangerous and anomalous results as to overshadow the undeniable uneasiness which one feels in reject-ing them', Opinion of AG Mancini in Case 314/85 *Foto-Frost v Hauptzollamt Lübeck-Ost* [1987] ECR 4199, at 4218.

Justice. Yet the wording of Article 234 EC (old Article 177 of the EC Treaty) seems to allow the lower national courts to rule on the validity of Community law themselves. Indeed, according to the text of Article 234 EC, the lower courts *may* refer questions as to the interpretation *and the validity* of Community law to the Court of Justice.[16] The text does not make such reference obligatory.[17] Nevertheless, the Court held in *Foto-Frost* that the national courts have no jurisdiction to declare that acts of Community institutions invalid. Consequently, if a court doubts the validity of a Community act, it is under an obligation to refer it to the Court of Justice. The Court held that the lower courts *'may consider the validity of a Community act and, if they consider that the grounds put forward before them by the parties in support of invalidity are unfounded, they may reject them, concluding that the measure is completely valid. By taking that action they are not calling into question the existence of the Community measure. On the other hand, those courts do not have the power to declare acts of the Community institutions invalid'.*[18] Accordingly, the Community position is straightforward: national courts, in all instances,[19] are precluded from holding Community law invalid. There is only one exception. Already in *Foto-Frost* itself, the Court held that *'it should be added that the rule that national courts may not themselves declare Community acts invalid may have to be qualified in certain circumstances in the case of proceedings relating to an application for interim measures'.*[20] Such circumstances occurred in *Zuckerfabrik Süderdithmarschen,*[21] where the Court held that where a national measure based on a Community regulation is challenged before a national court on grounds that the validity of the Community measure itself is contested, interim relief may be granted. The national court may suspend application of the national measure and therefore also of the underlying Community act, but only if strict conditions are met. These conditions

---

[16] The ECJ was of the opinion that *'in enabling the national courts against whose decisions there is a judicial remedy under national law, to refer to the Court for a preliminary ruling questions on interpretation or validity, Article 177 did not settle the question whether those courts themselves may declare that acts of the Community institutions are invalid'*, Case 314/85 *Foto-Frost v Hauptzollamt Lübeck-Ost* [1987] ECR 4199, at para 13.

[17] In contrast, Art. 41 ECSC expressly gave the Court exclusive jurisdiction over questions of validity, see Case C–221/88 *Busseni* [1990] ECR I–495, at para 14.

[18] Case 314/85 *Foto-Frost v Hauptzollamt Lübeck-Ost* [1987] ECR 4199, at para 14–5; see also Case C–27/95 *Woodspring District Council v Bakers of Nailsea Ltd* [1997] ECR I–1847; Case C–6/99 *Association Greenpeace France v Ministère de l'Agriculture et de la Pêche* [2000] ECR I–1651.

[19] Courts against whose decisions there is no remedy under national law, are under an obligation to refer questions concerning the validity of Community law under Art. 234 (3) EC They are by consequence precluded from ruling themselves on the validity of Community law.

[20] Case 314/85 *Foto-Frost* [1987] ECR 4199, at para 19.

[21] Case C–143/88 and 92/89 *Zuckerfabrik Süderdithmarschen AG v Hauptzollamt Itzehoe* [1991] ECR I–415.

were refined in *Atlanta*[22] and have been repeated since.[23] Interim relief can only be granted if the court entertains serious doubts as to the validity of the Community act and, should the question of the validity of the contested measure not already have been brought before the Court of Justice, it must be referred. Secondly, there must be urgency and the interim relief must be necessary to avoid serious and irreparable damage being caused to the party seeking the relief. Third, the court must take due account of the Community's interests. Lastly, in its assessment of all those conditions, the court must respect any decision of the Court of Justice or the Court of First Instance ruling on the lawfulness of the regulation or on the application of interim measures seeking similar interim relief at Community level.[24]

An issue which at first sight appears merely technical-judicial, but one with far-reaching consequences, is the distinction which is sometimes made between *validity* of Community law and its *applicability* in the national legal order. In line with the wording of Article 234 EC, *Foto-Frost* deals with the issue of the *validity* of a measure of Community law.[25] As will be demonstrated further in the discussion of the national positions, some national courts have added another issue, namely that of the *applicability* of a Community measure in the national legal order. The *Bundesverfassungsgericht* for instance in *Brunner* stated that Community measures which are *ultra vires* are not applicable on German territory, and it is for the German Court to rule on the question whether or not a particular measure is *ultra vires*.[26] It allegedly does not rule on the *validity* of the Community act, but merely on its *applicability* on German territory. Nonetheless, such a view is merely a consequence of a certain conception about the nature of the Community legal order and its relationship with the national legal order. While Article 234 EC refers only to the *interpretation* and *validity* of Community law and not its *applicability*, this 'shrewd' distinction carries no weight from the point of view of Community law:

---

[22] Case C–465/93 *Atlanta Fruchthandelsgesellschaft* [1995] ECR I–3761.

[23] Case C–68/95 *T Port v Bundesanstalt für Landwirtschaft und Ernährung* [1996] ECR I–6065; Case C–334/95 *Krüger GmbH & Co KG v Hauptzollamt Hamburg-Jonas* [1997] ECR I–4517; Case C–17/98 *Emesa Sugar (Free Zone) NV v Aruba* [2000] ECR I–675.

[24] Case C–465/93 *Atlanta Fruchthandelsgesellschaft* [1995] ECR I–3761, at para 51.

[25] In contrast, Internationale Handelsgesellschaft says that *'the validity of a Community measure or its effect within a Member State cannot be affected by allegations that it runs counter to either fundamental rights as formulated by the Constitution of that State or the principles of a national constitutional structure'*, Case 11/70 *Internationale Handelsgesellschaft* [1970] ECR 1125, at para 3, emphasis added.

[26] This will be explained below. In short, the BVerfG argues that Community law becomes effective in the German legal order thanks to the German Act adopted under the Constitution and giving effect to the Treaty. If a measure of Community law is *ultra vires* it does not become effective in the German legal order. In the BVerfG's reasoning, this is a question of its *applicability*, not of its *validity*.

Indeed, the question of the applicability and effectiveness of Community law in the national legal order is one for the Court of Justice to decide, and has ever since *Van Gend en Loos* been considered an issue of *interpretation* of Community law, which ultimately falls to be decided by the Court of Justice.

While *Foto-Frost* is one of the Court's most important constitutional decisions, and continues the line of *Van Gend en Loos, Costa v ENEL, Internationale Handelsgesellschaft, Simmenthal*, it is a fairly sober decision and lacks references to the autonomous nature of the Community legal order,[27] to transfers of sovereignty and similar doctrines. While the case seems restricted to an interpretation of the powers of the lower courts under Article 234 EC and in textbooks often figures in the discussion of the preliminary rulings procedures, its importance in the building of the Community constitutional structure and the division of labour between the Community and national courts, can hardly be overstated. Beyond imposing a duty to refer a question for preliminary ruling on the lower courts, it states the fundamental principle that national courts, including those against whose decisions there is no judicial remedy under national law, do not have jurisdiction to hold secondary Community law invalid, *for whatever reason*. While this could, with respect to the highest courts, already be derived from the text of Article 234(3) EC, it is now clear for all courts alike and beyond all possible doubt, and placed in the context of the entire Community system of judicial protection.

The Court built its decision first, on the principle that Community law should be uniformly applied by all national courts, second, on the coherence of the Community system of judicial protection,[28] and third, on the fact that the Court is in the best position to decide on the validity of Community acts.[29] In addition, it has rightly been noted that it is important that Community provisions should only be declared invalid by a court whose decisions may be treated as authoritative by the European and national political institutions and courts in all the Member States, *i.e.* the European Court itself.[30] As the Court explained, although a declaration

---

[27] As pointed out in G Bebr, 'The Reinforcement of the Constitutional Review of Community Acts under Article 177 EEC Treaty', 25 *CML Rev*, 1988, 667, at 678.

[28] The ECJ reasoned that since it had exclusive jurisdiction under Art. 173 of the EC Treaty (now Art. 230 EC) to annul measures of the Community institutions, the cohesion of the Community system of legal protection required that it also had exclusive jurisdiction to declare a Community act invalid under Art. 177 of the EC Treaty (now Art. 234 EC).

[29] Moreover, the ECJ observed, the reference procedure enabled the Community institutions involved to 'defend' the act in question, and the ECJ to request all necessary information from them. The ECJ implicitly suggested that the national courts simply were not equipped to rule on the validity of Community law, see G Bebr, 'The Reinforcement of the Constitutional Review of Community Acts under Article 177 EEC Treaty', 25 *CML Rev*, 1988, 667, at 670.

[30] A Arnull, 'National courts and the validity of Community acts', *ELR*, 1988, 125, at 126.

of invalidity delivered on a preliminary reference is directly addressed to the national court which brought the matter before the Court, it is sufficient reason for any national court to regard that act as void for the purposes of a judgment which it has to give. That is simply not the case with judgments delivered by national courts. The grounds which the Court invoked for asserting its exclusive jurisdiction seem powerful and their logic unassailable from the point of view of Community law.[31] According to one commentator, *'the Court could not have ruled otherwise if it wished to do justice to the nature of the Community legal order and respect the fundamental principles and requirements it has developed'.*[32] Nonetheless, the exclusive jurisdiction of the Court to rule on the validity of Community law puts a huge responsibility on its shoulders and its record as watchman of the Community institutions will be closely scrutinised, not so much by the lower courts to whom *Foto-Frost* is addressed, but even more so by the highest courts, especially the constitutional courts, who in the framework of Community law must not exercise their constitutional role as protectors of the constitutional rule of law and fundamental rights. To put it bluntly: the Court will have to earn legitimacy as sole judge of the validity of Community law; it will need to build credibility and deserve confidence as guarantor of the legality of Community law.[33]

The judgment of the Court in *Foto-Frost* must be put in the context of the entire Community system of judicial protection of Community law rights as against the Community institutions, and the restrictive rules on standing for individuals under Article 230 EC. The Community system of judicial review has recently been described by the Court of Justice in the following terms: *'By Article 173 and Article 184 (now Article 241), on the one hand, and by Article 177, on the other, the Treaty has established a complete system of legal remedies and procedures designed to ensure judicial review of the legality of acts of the institutions, and has entrusted such review to the Community courts (see, to that effect,* Les Verts v Parliament, *paragraph 23). Under that system, where natural or legal persons cannot, by reason of the conditions for admissibility laid down in the fourth paragraph of Article 173 of the Treaty, directly challenge Community measures of general application, they are able, depending on the case, either indirectly to plead the invalidity of such acts before the Community Courts under Article 184 of the Treaty or to do so before the national courts and ask them, since they have no jurisdiction themselves to*

---

[31] The judgment was however criticised by those who saw in it an attempt by the ECJ to obtain omnipotence, see e.g. TC Hartley, *Constitutional Problems of the European Union* (Oxford, Hart Publishing, 1999) at 31–35.

[32] G Bebr, 'The Reinforcement of the Constitutional Review of Community Acts under Article 177 EEC Treaty', 25 *CML Rev*, 1988, 667, at 678.

[33] See U Everling, 'Will Europe Slip on Bananas? The Bananas Judgment of the Court of Justice and National Courts', 33 *CML Rev*, 1996, 401, at 435–37.

declare those measures invalid (see Case 314/85 Foto-Frost *[1987] ECR 4199, paragraph 20), to make a reference to the Court of Justice for a preliminary ruling on validity'.*[34] Contrary to what might have been anticipated following the *Jégo-Quéré* judgment of the Court of First Instance decided three months earlier, and in line with the prevailing case law, the Court thus confirmed its restrictive stance on standing for private applicants under Article 230 EC. This time, however, the Court emphasised the role of national courts in the judicial review of acts of the Community institutions, despite the obvious disadvantages of the detour via national courts.[35] The Court's position assumes that there *is* access to a court in national law, which must then refer the question to the European Court, when there is a *prima facie* case. In *Unión de Pequeños Agricultores* (UPA) it was argued by the applicant that its fundamental right to judicial protection, as a recognised principle of Community law and inherent in the system of remedies established by the Treaties, would be infringed if standing was not allowed since it did not have access to a national court. The Court of Justice simply stated: *'Thus it is for the Member States to establish a system of legal remedies and pro-cedures which ensure respect for the right to effective judicial protection. In that context, in accordance with the principle of sincere co-operation laid down in Article 5 of the Treaty, national courts are required, so far as possible, to interpret and apply national procedural rules governing the exercise of rights of action in a way that enables natural and legal persons to challenge before the courts the legality of any decision or other national measure relative to the application to them of a Community act of general application, by pleading the invalidity of such an act'.*[36] The reference to the national legal systems and to Article 5 of the Treaty (now Article 10 EC) sounds familiar and has antecedents in the case law on the enforcement of Community law before national courts

---

[34] Case C–50/00 P *Unión de Pequeños Agricultores v Council* [2002] ECR I–6677, at para 40.
[35] Examples are: Case C–70/97 P *Kruidvat BVBA v Commission* [1998] ECR I–7183, where the applicant argued that if its action before the European Court was not declared admissible, it would not be accorded adequate legal protection and submitted that the CFI was best competent to determine direct actions concerning the lawfulness of exemtpions under Art. 85 of the Treaty. Legal protection before a national court, in conjunction with a pre-liminary reference was not sufficient. The Court dismissed the argument by reference to the 'complete system of legal remedies and procedures' based on Arts. 173, 177 and 184 of the EC Treaty and designed to permit the ECJ to review the legality of Community meas-ures; In Case C–87/95 P *CNPAAP v Council* [1996] ECR I–2003, the Court rejected argu-ment based on the possible length of proceedings under Art. 177; Other disadvantages are: Access to the ECJ via Art. 234 EC is not a remedy available to individual applicants as of right: national courts may refuse to refer questions; the act to be challenged before the national court is the national act implementing or applying the Community measure; yet, some Community measures do not require any acts of implementation by national authorities; the only way to bring the validity of the Community measure before a court is by violating the measure! Or as AG Jacobs put it: *'Individuals clearly cannot be required to breach the law in order to gain access to justice'* Opinion of AG Jacobs in Case C–50/00 P *Unión de Pequeños Agricultores v Council* [2002] I–6677, at para 43.
[36] Case C–50/00 P *Unión de Pequeños Agricultores v Council* [2002] ECR I–6677, at paras 41–42.

against the Member States. However, in this case what is at stake is the judicial protection of the rights of *individuals as against acts of the Community institutions* and the ways to seize the Court as sole judge of the validity of Community law. While it may have seemed 'natural' and efficient to involve the national courts as common courts of Community law to ensure the application and enforcement of Community law by the Member States, it is much more artificial to make the national courts the ordinary courts of Community law when the validity *of Community law* is at stake. *Foto-Frost* proves that the national courts are not the correct forum for such cases. And yet the Court is keen to divert these cases via the national courts. It was probably concerned most with the problem of managing its own workload, but it is rather cynical for a court to prefer what appears almost a denial of justice over its own workload. It seems slightly paradoxical to oblige the parties to seize the national courts while at the same time prohibiting the national courts from ruling on the validity of Community law.[37] Since the question has necessarily to be referred back to the Court of Justice,[38] the argument of the floodgate is not so convincing. Even if opening up Article 230 EC did lead to an increase in the number of cases to be decided by the Court of Justice, the problem of back-log should be solved by other means, not by denying the applicants direct access to the European Courts.

Another case which sits ill with the 'complete system of judicial review' designed by the Court, is *TWD Textilwerke Deggendorf.*[39] In that case the Court ruled, in the context of state aids, that where an individual has not challenged the validity of a Commission decision within the time-limit, although he could have done so and was aware of that fact, the national court is bound by the Commission decision on grounds of legal certainty and cannot make a reference questioning its validity. The validity of the Commission decision could only be challenged directly before the European Courts and within the prescribed time limits; afterwards, an indirect challenge was to be dismissed by the national court. The preference for the indirect route via the national courts thus has an exception where there is a direct action available and the applicant was or should have been aware of that possibility. The scope of *TWD* is, however, limited.[40] It applies only where it is clear beyond doubt that the applicant did have standing under Article 230 EC and that he was or should have been aware

---

[37] So HG Schermers and DF Waelbroeck, *Judicial Protection in the European Union*, 6th edn, (The Hague, Kluwer Law International, 2001), at 501.

[38] And not to the Court of First Instance which would be competent in first instance were direct actions held to be admissible.

[39] Case C–188/92 *TWD Textilwerke Deggendorf GmbH v Germany* [1994] ECR I–833.

[40] Case C–241/95 *The Queen v Intervention Board for Agricultural Products*, ex parte *Accrington Beef* [1996] ECR I–6699 (concerning a regulation) and Case C–408/95 *Eurotunnel v SeaFrance* [1997] ECR I–6315 (concerning a directive).

of that fact.[41] In such cases, the expiry of the time limit of Article 230 EC makes the measure final.[42]

18.1.1.4. The Validity of Community Measures in the Light of International Law[43]

In its *Racke* judgment[44] the Court held that 'the European Community must respect international law in the exercise of its powers. It is therefore required to comply with the rules of customary international law when adopting a regulation suspending the trade concessions granted by, or by virtue of, an agreement which it has concluded with a non-member country'. In addition, the Court has held in *International Fruit*[45] and repeated since, that the jurisdiction of the Court to rule on the validity of acts of the Community institutions cannot be limited in respect of the grounds on which the validity of those measures may be contested. Since such jurisdiction extends to all grounds capable of invalidating those measures, the Court is obliged to examine whether their validity may be affected by reason of the fact that they are contrary to a rule of international

---

41　Case C–188/92 *TWD Textilwerke Deggendorf GmbH v Germany* [1994] ECR I–833 (recipient of state aid; decision addressed to a Member State, but the applicant had been sent a copy of the decision and its attention had been drawn to the fact that it had two months time to attack it); confirmed in Case C–178/95 *Wiljo v Belgian State* [1997] ECR I–585 (concerning a decision addressed to the applicant); Case C–239/99 *Nachi Europe GmbH v Hauptzollamt Krefeld* [2001] ECR I–1197 (Council regulation modifying anti-dumping duties; importer of the relevant goods). The *TWD* principle applies in any case to Member States, who are precluded from pleading before a national court the unlawfulness of a Community decision addressed to them in respect of which no action for annulment was borught within the two months time limit, see Case C–241/01 *National Farmers' Union v Sécretariat général du gouvernement* [2002] ECR I–9079.

42　In other cases, Community measures can be challenged via the national courts beyond the expiry of the two months time limit; there simply is no time limit, Case 216/82 *Universität Hamburg v Hauptzollamt Hamburg-Kehrwieder* [1983] 2771.

43　On the relationship between international and Community law see e.g. K Lenaerts and E De Smijter, 'The European Union as an Actor under International Law', *YEL*, 1999, 95; J Vanhamme, *Volkenrechtelijke beginselen in het Europees recht* (Groningen, Europa Law Publishing, 2001).

44　Case C–162/96 *A Racke GmbH v Hauptzollamt Mainz* [1998] ECR I–3655; in the case, the ECJ examined whether the validity of the Council decision suspending the Cooperation Agreement with Yugoslavia was affected by reason of the fact that it was contrary to a rule of international law. Racke, a private company, was allowed to challenge the validity under customary international law rules of a regulation suspending the trade concessions granted under that Agreement. The ECJ held that in this case, 'an individual relying in legal proceedings on rights which he derives directly from an agreement with a non-member country may not be denied the possibility of challenging the validity of a regulation which, by suspending the trade concessions granted by that agreement, prevents him from relying on it, and of invoking, in order to challenge the validity of the suspending regulation, obligations deriving from rules of customary international law which govern the termination and suspension of treaty relations', at para 51.

45　Joined Cases 21/72 to 24/72 *International Fruit Company v Produktschap voor Groenten en Fruit* [1972] ECR 1219, at para 5; see also Case C–162/96 *A Racke GmbH v Hauptzollamt Mainz* [1998] ECR I–3655, at para 26.

law.[46]Given that *Foto-Frost* equally does not distinguish as to the nature of the grounds of invalidity invoked before the national court, but concerns the issue of jurisdiction to review the validity irrespective of the grounds for invalidity, it follows that the compatibility of Community measures with international law is a matter for the Court alone to decide. National courts may confirm the validity of a Community measure and reject arguments based on international law, but they may not hold a Community measure invalid for infringement of international law.

However, the Court held in *International Fruit*, before the incompatibility of a Community measure with a provision of a treaty can affect the validity of that measure, the Community must first be bound by that provision,[47] and secondly, before invalidity can be relied upon before a national court, that provision of international law must also be capable of conferring rights on citizens of the Community which they can invoke before the courts.[48] In other words, it must have direct effect, and that was where the old GATT failed. The Court refused to grant direct effect to the provisions of GATT and therefore the validity of Community law could not be affected by GATT.[49] In *Germany v Council*, also referred to as the *Bananas* judgment, the Court extended its case law to direct annulment actions. It held that *'Those features of GATT from which the Court concluded that an individual within the Community cannot invoke it in a court to challenge the lawfulness of a Community act, also preclude the Court from taking provisions of GATT into consideration to assess the lawfulness of a regulation in an action brought by a Member State under the first paragraph of Article 173 of the Treaty'.*[50] Germany could not therefore invoke the provisions of GATT to challenge the lawfulness of the Community regulation at issue. Only if the Community intended to implement a particular obligation entered into within the framework of GATT (the *Nakajima* doctrine),[51] or if the Community act expressly refers to specific provisions of GATT (the *Fediol* doctrine),[52] the Court can review the lawfulness of the Community act in

---

[46] Above, at paras 6 and 27 respectively.

[47] *International Fruit*, at para 7.

[48] Above, at para 8.

[49] See Joined Cases 21 to 24/72 *International Fruit Company v Produktschap voor Groenten en Fruit* [1972] ECR 1219, confirmed on numerous occasions since; an odd case out is Case 112/80 *Firma Anton Dürbeck v Hauptzollamt Frankfurt am Main-Flughafen* [1981] ECR 1095, in which the Court did control the validity of Commission regulation in the light of GATT without entering into the discussion of the direct effect of the relevant GATT provisions. The judgments may be explained by the specific circumstances: a special GATT group had examined the conformity of Community measures with GATT and concluded that the Commission had not infringed Arts. I and II of GATT.

[50] Case C–280/93 *Germany v Council (Bananas)* [1994] ECR I–4973, at para 109.

[51] Case C–69/89 *Nakajima All Precision Co Ltd v Council* [1991] ECR I–2069; applied in Case C–352/96 *Italy v Council* [1998] ECR I–6937.

[52] Case 70/87 *Fediol v Commission* [1989] ECR 1781.

question in the light of the GATT rules.[53] Finally, in the *Portuguese Textiles* case,[54] the Court extended its old case law to WTO law and held that the WTO Agreements could not in principle be used as a standard for reviewing the legality of Community acts. The Court based its decision on the principle of reciprocity and the dispute settlement system contained in the WTO Agreements, especially the possibility provided therein that WTO inconsistent rules of domestic law are maintained if mutually acceptable compensation is agreed on.[55]The rationale is explained better in a later case, on a reference from English and Irish courts,[56] where the Court stated that *'the decisive factor here is that the resolution of disputes concerning WTO law is based, in part, on negotiations between the contracting parties. Withdrawal of unlawful measures is indeed the resolution recommended by WTO law, but other resolutions are also authorised, for example settlement, payment of compensation or suspension of concessions (..). In those circumstances, to require the judicial organs to refrain from applying rules of domestic law which are inconsistent with the WTO Agreements would have the consequence of depriving the legislative or executive organs of the contracting parties of the possibility of finding negotiated solutions, even on a temporary basis'.*[57]Nevertheless, it is also important to note that in its decision on the conclusion of the WTO Agreement, the Council expressly stated that by its nature, the Agreement establishing the WTO was not susceptible of being directly invoked in Community or Member State courts. The Council accordingly

---

[53] See also Case C–149/96 *Portugal v Council (Portugal Textiles)* [1999] ECR I–8395, at para 27.

[54] Case C–149/96 *Portugal v Council (Portuguese Textiles)* [1999] ECR I–8395; commented in G Zonnekeyn, 'The status of WTO law in the Community legal order: some comments in the light of the Portuguese Textiles case', 25 *ELR*, 2000, 293; A Desmedt, 'European Court of Justice on the Effect of WTO Agreements in the EC Legal Order', *LIEI*, 2000, 93; S Griller, 'Judicial Enforceability of WTO Law in the European Union. Annotation to Case C–149/96, *Portugal v Council'*, *JIEL*, 2000, 441; F Berrod, 'La Cour de justice refuse l'invocabilité des accords OMC: essai de la régulation de la mondialisation', *RTDeur* 2000, 419; repeated on many occasions since, *e.g.* Joined Cases C–27/00 and C–122/00 *Omega Air Ltd* [2002] ECR I–2569, where the GATT inconsistency had been pleaded before national courts; it was extended equally to actions in damages under based on Arts. 235 and 288 EC, see *e.g.* Case T–174/00 *Biret International SA v Council* [2002] II-17, and references in para 61.

[55] Case C–149/96 *Portugal v Council* [1999] ECR I–8395, at paras 36–41; the Court concluded from the specific provisions of the DSU that the WTO Agreements themselves did not determine the appropriate legal means of ensuring that they were applied in good faith in the legal order of the contracting parties'. In other words, the WTO Agreements themselves did not force to accept the classic direct effect-supremacy tandem which would lead always to the 'setting aside' of the contrary provision of Community law; for a contrary view see P Eeckhout, 'The Domestic Legal Status of the WTO Agreement: Interconnecting Legal Systems', 34 *CML Rev*, 1997, 11, at 54–55.

[56] See also Joined Cases C–300/98 and C–392/98 *Dior* [2000] ECR I–11307, where the principle of the *Portuguese Textiles* case was applied in a case which arose before a national court and referred under Art. 234 EC The Court held that for the same reasons as those put forward in the Portuguese case the provisions of TRIPs, an annex to the WTO Agreement were not such as to create rights upon which individuals may rely directly before the courts by virtue of Community law, at para 44.

[57] Joined Cases C–27/00 and C–122/00, *Omega Air Ltd* [2002] ECR I–2569, at paras 89–90.

intended to limit the effects of the Agreement and to follow the approach of the other contracting parties, who made it quite clear that they wished to limit the possibility of relying on provisions of that agreement before national courts.[58]

Accordingly, the WTO Agreement and the Annexes thereto are not in principle among the rules in the light of which the Court reviews measures of the Community institutions in direct actions. Also, they are not such as to create rights which individuals may rely upon directly before the courts by virtue of Community law.[59] However, the Court in *Dior* went further and stated that the finding that the relevant provisions did not produce direct effect *in that sense*[60] did not fully resolve the issue. It stated that within the scope of Community law, the national courts were obliged, when called upon to apply national rules with a view to ordering provisional protection of Community law rights, to do so as far as possible in the light and the wording of Article 50 of TRIPs. In cases falling within the competence of the Member States, Community law neither requires nor forbids that the legal order of a Member State should accord to individuals the right to rely directly on a TRIPs rule or that it should oblige the courts to apply that rules of their own motion.[61] In other words, outside the scope of Community law, the effect of provisions of the WTO Agreement or their Annexes was a matter for national law.

The Court of Justice adopts a different approach when it comes to rules of international law other than GATT.[62] Other international agreements have been granted direct effect. This is the case for instance with the Europe Agreements concluded in the 1990's with former Central and Eastern European Countries,[63] free trade agreements,[64] with Association Agreements and co-operation agreements concluded with third countries,[65]

---

[58] Contrary to the Opinion of AG Saggio in the *Portuguese Textiles* case, at para 20, who argued that the jurisdiction of the ECJ and of the national courts to interpret and apply the WTO Agreements was not affected by the unilateral Council declaration in the preamble to the decision; see also AG Tesauro in his Opinion to Case C–53/96 *Hermès International v FTH Marketing Choice BV* [1998] ECR I–3603, at para 25; for an opposite view Opinion of AG Cosmas in Case C–183/95 *Affish* [1997] ECR I–4315 and Opinion of AG Elmer in Joined Cases 364/95 and 365/95 *T Port v Hauptzollamt Hamburg-Jonas* [1998] ECR I–1023.

[59] Joined Cases C–300/98 and C–392/98 *Dior* [2000] ECR I–11307, at para 44.

[60] The Court thus distinguishes between different types of direct effect, even if it does not, in this case or other cases, make them explicit.

[61] Joined Cases C–300/98 and C–392/98 *Dior* [2000] ECR I–11307, at para 49.

[62] See AG Saggio in his Opinion to Case C–149/96 *Portugal v Council (Portuguese Textiles)* [1999] ECR I–8395, at para 18.

[63] See e.g. Case C–63/99 *R v Secretary of State for the Home Department, ex parte Gloszczuk and Gloszczuk* [2001] ECR I–6369; Case C–235/99 *R v Secretary of State for the Home Department, ex parte Kondova* [2001] ECR I–6427.

[64] Case 270/80 *Hauptzollamt Mainz v Kupferberg* [1982] ECR 3641.

[65] So for instance Case C–18/90 *Onem v Kziber* [1991] ECR I–199; C–37/98 *The Queen v Secretary of State for the Home Department, ex parte Abdulnasir Savas* [2000] ECR I–2927.

and with decisions adopted by association councils or bodies set up under those agreements.[66]

Now, the issue of the lawfulness of Community law in the light of GATT becomes even more complex when it is realised that GATT and the WTO Agreements bind not only the Community but also its Member States, and that the issue of an alleged incompatibility of Community law with GATT provisions, can raise similar questions before different courts. One question, dealt with before, is whether GATT can serve as a standard to review the legality of Community law before the Court of Justice. The other related question is whether the obligations imposed by GATT and the WTO Agreements on the Member States may entitle the national courts not to apply provisions of Community law that infringe them. In the bananas saga, several German courts[67] adopted the view that even if the 'Bananas Regulation'[68] was to be considered valid under Community law,[69] it was contrary to certain fundamental GATT rules which Germany, as a contracting party to GATT was required to observe. The question arose, therefore, whether having regard to Article 234 of the EC Treaty (now Article 307 EC) the application of the relevant GATT rules must take precedence over that of the Community bananas regulations.[70] The question was referred by the *Finanzgericht Hamburg* which gave a veritable ultimatum to the European Court. It held[71] that the bananas regulations, by reason of their incompatibility with GATT, must be considered as *ultra vires* acts (*'ausbrechende Rechtsakte'*), adopted outside the scope of Community competence and would, therefore, not be applicable in Germany. The same would be true for the judgment of the Court in *Germany v Council (bananas)*.[72] It also gave it to be understood to the Court that it would itself consider the relevant GATT provisions as directly effective.

---

[66] Case 12/86 *Demirel v Stadt Schwäbisch Gmümd* [1987] ECR 3719; C–192/89 *Sevince v Staatssecretaris van Justitie* [1990] ECR I3461; C–262/96 *Sema Sürül v Bundesanstalt für Arbeit* [1999] ECR I–2685.

[67] The BVerfG equally appears to have had doubts as to the compatibility of the EC regulations with GATT In an obiter dictum, the BVerfG stated that it was not impossible that the (German lower) court hearing the application for interim relief might, in view of the inconsistency between Council Regulation 404/93 and the obligations incumbent on Germany under GATT decide not to apply that regulation for the time being, see *Bundesverfassungsgericht*, decision of 26 April 1995, *Bananas II (TPort)*, EuZW, 1995, 412.

[68] Council Regulation (EEC) No 404/93 of 13 February 1993 on the common organisation of the market in bananas, OJ 1993 L 47/1.

[69] As the Court had held in Case C–280/93 *Germany v Council (Bananas)* [1994] ECR I–4973, see *supra*.

[70] The German side of the story will be told and analysed in the next chapter.

[71] *Finanzgericht Hamburg*, decision of 19 May 1995, *T Port v Hauptzollamt Hamburg-Jonas*, EuZW, 1995, 413; the judgment was confirmed by the *Bundesfinanzhof*, decision of 9 January 1996, *Hauptzollamt Hamburg-Jonas v T Port*, NJW, 1996, 1367; see also N Reich, 'Judge-made Europe à la carte': Some Remarks on Recent Conflicts between European and German Constitutional Law Provoked by the Banana Litigation', 7 *EJIL*, 1996, 103, at 109–111.

[72] Case C–280/93 *Germany v Council (bananas)* [1994] ECR I–4973.

Article 307 EC deals with a situation in which there is a conflict between an obligation incumbent upon a Member State under an earlier agreement and its obligation to apply Community legislation. In accordance with the principles of international law, the Article provides that application of the EC Treaty does not affect the commitment of the Member State concerned to respect the rights of third countries under an earlier agreement and to comply with its corresponding obligations. Accordingly, a Community rule may be deprived of effect by an earlier international agreement; in other words, there may be an exception to the principle of supremacy of Community law in a Member State, on grounds of a pre-existing agreement concluded with third States. It is for the national courts to determine which obligations are imposed by an earlier international agreement on the Member State concerned and to ascertain their ambit so as to be able to determine the extent to which they constitute an obstacle to the application of conflicting measures of Community law. The obligation to apply Community law with precedence over national law may thus suffer an exception and applies *unless* the application of a provision of national law conflicting with Community law is necessary in order to ensure the performance by the Member State concerned of obligations arising under an agreement concluded with non-member countries prior to the entry into force of the Treaty.[73]

In the context of WTO and GATT, Article 307 EC can be of no avail to private applicants seeking to challenge Community law before the national courts, or the European Courts. In *T. Port*,[74] the Court of Justice first turned to the interpretation of Article 307 EC (then Article 234 of the Treaty) and stated that for a Community provision to be deprived of effect as a result of an international agreement, two conditions must be fulfilled: the agreement must have been concluded before the entry into force of the Treaty and the third country concerned must derive from it rights which it can require the Member State concerned to respect. This was not the case here.[75] The issue of the direct effect of GATT did not have to be answered. In later cases, *T. Port* and *Bananatrading*, the Court of First Instance held that the GATT Agreement which applied at the time of the facts was GATT 1994, which had replaced GATT 1947 and which was not a pre-existing treaty, and furthermore that the obligations arising from GATT 1994 fell not on the Member States but on the Community, which had exclusive competence, pursuant to Article 113 of the EC Treaty, to

---

[73] See Case C–158/91 *Criminal proceedings against Jean-Claude Levy* [1993] I–4287.
[74] Joined Cases C–364 and 365/95 *T Port v Hauptzollamt Hamburg-Jonas* [1998] ECR I–1023.
[75] Ecuador, from which T Port imported its bananas, was not a contracting party to GATT 1947 and only became a member of the WTO and party to GATT 1994 in 1996 (so post-EC Treaty), while the case concerned customs duties payable on bananas imported in 1995.

conclude that agreement.[76] Finally, in the event that the applicant was basing its case directly on the alleged breach of the first paragraph of Article 307 EC, the Court of First Instance held that that provision was not intended to confer rights on individuals, while in actions for damages it is required that there is a sufficiently serious infringement of a higher rule of law intended to confer rights on the applicant. Neither could the reference to Article 307 EC be used as a means to allow individuals to rely in legal proceedings in breach of the provisions of GATT 1994: the latter do not have direct effect and do not, as a general rule, come within the body of rules by reference to which the legality of acts of the Community institutions will be reviewed by the Court.

The issue of the relation between Community law and international treaties will not be further analysed here. What is important is that it is for the Court alone to review the validity of Community law, even in the context of international treaties. Only in the case of international treaties concluded before the Community Treaties were signed and from which third States may derive obligations imposed on Community Member States can there be an exception to the supremacy of Community law. In those cases, it is for the national courts to decide whether the conditions for the application of Article 307 EC are fulfilled. Nevertheless, it must also be remembered that under the second paragraph of Article 307 EC *'to the extent that such agreements are not compatible with this Treaty, the Member State or States concerned shall take all appropriate steps to eliminate the incompatibilities established'.*

18.1.2. Title IV on Visas, Asylum, Immigration and Other Policies Related to Free Movement of Persons

18.1.2.1. *General Considerations*

The uniformity of the Community legal order characterised by a system of uniform and coherent remedies and a complete system of judicial protection suffered a serious blow with the Treaty of Maastricht. The Court of Justice was excluded from the second and third pillars on Common Foreign and Security Policy and on Justice and Home Affairs. The impact of the measures adopted thereunder, and their interpretation was accordingly left to be determined, presumably, by the national courts. The Court of Justice demonstrated its concern over effective judicial protection and uniformity in its report in the run-up to the Amsterdam

---

[76] Case T–2/99 *T Port v Council* [2001] ECR II-2093; T–3/99 *Bananatrading GmbH v Council* [2001] ECR II-2123.

Intergovernmental Conference. While some improvements were achieved in respect of judicial protection in Amsterdam, further damage was done to the uniformity of the system of protection. With the Treaty of Amsterdam, part of the third pillar was moved to the first pillar to form a separate 'ghetto'[77] within the system of Community law.[78] The transfer to the first pillar, or 'communitarization', implies a fundamental change:[79] co-operation of Member States is replaced by action by the Community institutions by means of Community legislation,[80] in the form of regulations, directives, decisions and recommendations. The system of judicial review operating under Title IV differs from the system governing the rest of the first pillar, 'mainstream Community law'.

It would appear that the Treaty provisions regarding the jurisdiction of the Court of Justice apply to Title IV,[81] but the jurisdiction of the Court has been modified on three counts: Under Article 68(1) EC only courts or tribunals against whose decisions there is no judicial remedy under national law can, and must, refer questions for preliminary ruling on the

---

[77] For the first five years after the entry into force of the Treaty of Amsterdam, the Title is only partly under the Community umbrella and still forms a 'ghetto' since in some important respects, it diverges from mainstream Community law: the Commission shares inititatives with the Member States, decisions are all unanimous, the European Parliament is not directly involved in the decision-making: it is only consulted. These restrictions will be removed or re-analysed after this period of five years (Art. 67 EC).

[78] On Title IV and the jurisdiction of the ECJ in it see *inter alia* P Eeckhout, 'The European Court of Justice and the 'Area or Freedom, Security and Justice': Challenges and Problems', in *Judicial Review in European Union Law. Liber Amicorum in Honour of Lord Slynn of Hadley*, Vol. I, (The Hague, Kluwer Law International, 2000), 153; N Fennelly, 'The Area of "Freedom, Security and Justice" and the European Court of Justice – A Personal View', 49 *ICLQ*, 2000, 1; A Arnull, 'Taming the Beast? The Treaty of Amsterdam and the Court of Justice', in D O'Keeffe and P Twomey (eds), *Legal Issues of the Amsterdam Treaty*, (Oxford, Hart Publishing, 1999), 109; D O'Keeffe, 'Can the Leopard Change its Spots? Visas, Immigration and Asylum – Following Amsterdam,' above, 271; K Hailbronner, 'European Immigration and Asylum Law under the Amsterdam Treaty', 35 *CML Rev*, 1998, 1047; A Albors-Llorens, 'Changes in the Jurisdiction of the European Court of Justice under the Treaty of Amsterdam', 35 *CML Rev*, 1998, 1273; N Fennelly, 'Preserving the Legal Coherence within the New Treaty. The European Court of Justice after the Treaty of Amsterdam', 5 *MJ*, 1998, 185; J Monar, 'Justice and Home Affairs in the Treaty of Amsterdam: Reform at the Price of Fragmentation', *ELR*, 1998, 320; A Ward, 'The Limits of Uniform Application of Community Law and Effective Judicial Review: A Look Post-Amsterdam', in C Kilpatrick, T Novitz and P Skidmore (eds), *The Future of Remedies in Europe*, (Oxford, Hart Publishing, 2000), 213.

[79] Since the transfer does not amount to a full communitarization given the special provisions referred to above, there is a major disadvantage: it adds to the fragmentation of the system and increases its complexity. Since communitarization is not complete, it has a pendant in the form of the introduction of more 'intergovernmental' elements in a predominantly 'supra-national' pillar.

[80] See K Hailbronner, 'European Immigration and Asylum Law under the Amsterdam Treaty', 35 *CML Rev*, 1998, 1047, at 1047.

[81] See e.g. P Eeckhout, *art. cit.*, at 155.

interpretation and validity of acts of the institutions based on Title IV.[82] The route of Article 234 EC is not open to lower courts. Second, jurisdiction of the Court to rule on any measure or decision adopted pursuant to Article 62(1) relating to the maintenance of law and order and the safeguarding of internal security is excluded under Article 68(2) EC.[83] And third, Article 68(3) EC has introduced a new procedural route to the Court: The Council, the Commission or a Member State may ask the Court to give a ruling on a question of interpretation of Title IV or acts adopted by the Community institutions based on it.[84] Domestic judgments which have become *res judicata* are not to be affected by Article 68(3) EC rulings of the Court.

The restriction of the preliminary rulings procedure to final instance courts is said to be inspired by a concern for the potentially high number of cases at national level involving a point of Community law under Title IV and aimed to avoid a flood of cases in Luxembourg. There may also have been an issue of expediency: Member States governments were seeking a swift resolution of disputes, especially in the area of asylum and immigration, and references to the European Court could be used as a delaying tactic.[85] It is deplorable, however, that the possibility of sending references to the Court of Justice should be restricted in exactly the area where the need for judicial protection and concern for fundamental rights seem greater than in any other area of Community law: Title IV is after all the area of the Schengen acquis and of the evolving common immigration policy.

As mentioned, the other provisions concerning the jurisdiction of the Court of Justice in the first pillar will apply. Accordingly, actions for annulment, for damages and actions for failure to act will be available, possibly subject also to the Article 68(2) EC exclusion of decisions concerning maintenance of law and order and the safeguarding of internal security.[86]

---

[82]   Art. 68 EC reads: '1. *Article 234 shall apply to this Title under the following circumstances and condition: where a question on the interpretation of this Title or on the validity or interpretation of acts of the institutions of the Community based on this Title is raised in a case pending before a court or a tribunal of a Member State against whose decisions there is no judicial remedy under national law, that court or tribunal shall, if it considers that a decision on the question is necessary to enable it to give judgment, request the Court of Justice to give a ruling thereon'.*

[83]   '2. *In any event, the Court of Justice shall not have jurisdiction to rule on any measure or decision taken pursuant to Article 62(1) relating to the maintenace of law and order and the safeguarding of internal security'.*

[84]   '3. *The Council, the Commission or a Member State may request the Court of Justice to give a ruling on a question of interpretation of this Title or of acts of the institutions of the Community based on this Title. The ruling given by the Court of Justice in response to such a request shall not apply to judgments of courts or tribunals of the Member States which have become* res judicata'.

[85]   So P Eeckhout, *art. cit.*, at 155.

[86]   See also A Ward, 'The Limits of Uniform Application of Community Law and Effective Judicial Review: A Look Post-Amsterdam', in C Kilpatrick, T Novitz and P Skidmore (eds), *The Future of Remedies in Europe* (Oxford, Hart Publishing, 2000) 213, at 218.

18.1.2.2. Supremacy of Title IV Acts

In principle, decisions adopted by the Community under Title IV are binding, and capable of having direct effect within the national legal orders.[87] Given that Title IV is part of the first pillar, and does not make special provision with respect to the direct effect or supremacy of measures adopted under it, there seems to be no reason why they should not produce direct effects and be superior over conflicting national legislation. *Van Gend en Loos, Costa ENEL, Simmenthal,* and *Internationale Handelsgesellschaft* will likely apply to measures adopted under Title IV.

18.1.2.3. Title IV and Foto-Frost

A difficult question concerns the applicability of the *Foto-Frost* principle in the context of Title IV of the EC Treaty post-Amsterdam. The question is whether *Foto-Frost* applies at all: The prohibition imposed on the national courts to hold a Community measure invalid was concomitant with the duty to refer a question on the validity of the measure to the Court of Justice, which has sole power to declare Community measures invalid. In the context of Title IV, however, the lower courts do not even have the option of referring the issue to the Kirchberg. On the other hand, the same three arguments that led the Court to decide *Foto-Frost* are pertinent here as well. First, the need for uniform application of Community law: divergences between national courts as to the validity of Community law would be liable to place in jeopardy the very unity of the Community legal order and detract from the fundamental requirement of legal certainty. These considerations impose themselves with the same force in the context of Title IV. The third argument is likewise relevant in the context of Title IV: The Court of Justice is better equipped to rule on the validity of Community law, and the institutions and the Member States are entitled to participate in the proceedings. However, the second limb of the Court's reasoning in *Foto-Frost*, the 'coherent system of legal remedies and procedures' established by Articles 230 EC and 241 EC on the one hand and Article 234 EC on the other hand which is designed to permit the Court of Justice to review the legality of measures adopted by the institutions is devoid of its persuasive force. As for mainstream Community law, the Court has exclusive competence to declare void a Title IV act under Article 230 EC. Nonetheless, it becomes, therefore, an uneasy position to maintain that the power to declare such act invalid must also be reserved to it, since there is a problem of access. If lower national courts are precluded from holding a Title IV act invalid, they must be in a position to

---

[87] K Hailbronner, above, at 1048.

pass the issue on the a competent court. Under the principle of the rule of law and the right to effective judicial protection, which have both been embraced by the Court, there must be a cause of action to bring the case before a competent court. Regard must also be had to the wider context of the 'complete system of judicial protection designed by the Treaty': The Court finds support for a restrictive interpretation of standing for private applicants under Article 230 EC in the alternative route via the national courts, *in combination with Article 234 EC*.[88] The latter clarification is crucial because the reference to the preliminary rulings procedure includes the *Foto-Frost* obligation imposed on national courts to refer the case in case of *prima facie* invalidity. However, this argument cannot apply to Title IV cases since there simply is no recourse to Article 234 EC for lower courts. Does this mean that the European Courts would have to relax the conditions for standing under Article 230 EC within the scope of Title IV?[89]

Several options have been suggested to resolve the dilemma. A first position is that *Foto-Frost*[90] should apply with the same force in the context of Title IV measures as for mainstream Community measures: the Court of Justice has exclusive power to rule on the validity of Community law, and national courts may not hold a Community measure invalid. Given that lower courts are not entitled to make referrals in the context of Title IV, they must consider the relevant act as valid. Various suggestions have been made to have the questions referred by the courts of final instance in the case, but these seem convoluted and are hardly realistic.[91] The (partial) application of *Foto-Frost* does justice to concerns of uniformity and legal certainty, but it flies in the face of the principle of the rule of

---

[88] See for instance Case C–231/95 P *Greenpeace v Commission* [1998] ECR I–1651; Case C–70/97 P *Kruidvat BVBA v Commission* [1998] ECR I–7183; Case C–50/00 P *Unión de Pequeños Agricultores* [2002] I–6677.

[89] This has been suggested by Arnull who argues that *Foto-Frost* does not apply to Title IV and national courts are free to declare invalid acts adopted under Title IV (including those covered by Article 68(2) EC). Only if standing for non-privileged applicants under Article 230 EC is relaxed would the opposite be acceptable, A Arnull, 'Taming the Beast? The Treaty of Amsterdam and the Court of Justice', in D O'Keeffe and P Twomey (eds), *Legal Issues of the Amsterdam Treaty* (Oxford, Hart Publishing, 1999) 109, at 117.

[90] Or at least: the principle that national courts do not have jurisdiction to declare Community measures invalid; the second limb of *Foto-Frost*, that 'may' in Art. 234 EC must be read as 'must', is not so easy to extend to Title IV.

[91] Steve Peers has suggested, roughly, that the lower court could grant interim measures under *Atlanta*, on the condition that appeals would be made until the final court which would then be under an obligation to refer, S Peers, 'Who's Judging the Watchmen? The Judicial System of the 'Area of Freedom Security and Justice', *YEL*, 1998, 337, at 354–55. It is hard to imagine that a national court would actually impose as a condition that its decision is appealed; one may even wonder whether it is at all possible under national law.

law,[92] the right to effective judicial protection[93] and poses questions of fundamental rights protection.[94]

Another option would be that, in the absence of the possibility of engaging the Court of Justice, the lower national courts *would* be competent to hold a Community measure invalid or inapplicable, and that accordingly *Foto-Frost* would not apply to its full extent in the context of Title IV.[95] Gaja, for instance, stated: *'When, by contrast, courts are not entitled to make a referral, they should not be regarded as barred from ruling on the validity of Community acts. The existence of an exclusive power of the Court presupposes first of all that a power is granted – which is not the case with regard to the Community acts mentioned in Article 68(2) – and then that the national courts can engage the Court'.*[96] The peculiarity of this position is that the power to declare a Community measure invalid would only lie with the lower courts, while the highest courts would be under an obligation to refer the matter to the Court of Justice for decision. A declaration made by a national court that a Title IV measure is invalid can only have limited effect: it is restricted to the Member State of the court making the declara-

---

92 As expressed in Art. 6(1) EU and in *Case 294/83 Les Verts v European Parliament* [1986] ECR 1365.

93 See e.g. Case 222/84 *Johnston v Chief Constable of the RUC* [1986] ECR I1651; Case 222/86 *Heylens v UNCTEF* [1987] ECR 4097; Case 213/89 *R v Secretary of State for Transport*, ex parte *Factortame (Factortame I)* [1990] ECR I–2433, all in the context of judicial protection against the Member States before national courts. In the context of its own jurisdiction and review of acts of the Community institutions, the ECJ has extended its jurisdiction in order to fill a lacuna in 'the complete system of legal remedies and procedures designed to permit the Court to review the legality of acts adopted by the institutions', for instance in Case 294/83 *Les Verts v European Parliament* [1986] ECR 1365; note, however, that the decision is not phrased in terms of the right to effective judicial protection of individuals, but rather in terms of the system of remedies and procedures. On the contrary, in Case T–398/94 *Kahn Scheepvaart BV v Commission* [1996] ECR II–477, at para 50, the CFI held that the absence of a cause of action under national law was no reason for the Court to extend its jurisdiction under Article 230(4) EC, even if that would not amount to an interpretation *contra legem* of the Treaty, as the Court wants us to believe: it is for the Court to interpret 'direct and individual concern'; in Case C–50/00 P *Unión de Pequeños Agricultores* [2002] ECR I–6677, at para 41 and 42, the ECJ turned the reasoning around: given that there was no access to the European Court, the Member States must ensure that there is a cause of action under national law and it is for the national courts to interpret national procedural rules so as to allow individuals to challenge the legality of national implementing measures.

94 Art. 6(2) EU states that 'the Union shall respect fundamental rights' etc.

95 There does not appear to be a legal difference in practical effect between a declaration made by a national court that a measure is *invalid* or *inapplicable*. In both cases the measure remains in existence and both declarations are necessarily limited to one Member State.

96 G Gaja, 'The Growing Variety of Procedures concerning Preliminary Rulings', in D O'Keeffe and A Bavasso (eds), *Judicial Review in European Union Law. Liber Amicorum in Honour of Lord Slynn of Hadley*, Vol. I, (The Hague, Kluwer Law International, 2000), 143, at 148; see also A Arnull, 'Taming the Beast? The Treaty of Amsterdam and the Court of Justice', in D O'Keeffe and P Twomey (eds), *Legal Issues of the Amsterdam Treaty*, (Oxford, Hart Publishing, 1999), 109, at 117, who suggests that *Foto-Frost* can only apply if the conditions for standing of private applicants under Art. 230 EC are relaxed.

tion, and the measure remains in existence and remains binding. The uniform application of the measure would be in jeopardy. The decision of a lower court to hold a Title IV measure invalid could be appealed ultimately to the final instance court, which would then be under an obligation to refer the case to Luxembourg. Yet, what if no appeal is made? Probably, the time limit for a Member State or an institution to bring an action for annulment of the measure will have passed. The Council, the Commission or a Member State may, then, request the Court to give a ruling on a question of *interpretation*[97] of the relevant act under Article 68(3) EC. Such a ruling does not apply to national judgments that have become *res judicata*,[98] but they do carry effect as for the future, and are binding on the national courts.

A third solution would be for the Court to accept references by lower courts on validity issues, contrary to the text of Article 68(1) EC. There have been instances in the past where the Court has extended its own jurisdiction contrary to the text of the Treaty: *Foto-Frost* itself, remember, sits ill with the wording of Article 234 EC; other examples are *Les Verts*[99] and *Chernobyl*.[100] Yet, in the context of Title IV it seems unlikely that the Court will extend its jurisdiction *contra legem*: Article 67 EC provides that after the initial period of five years, the Council shall take a decision with a view to adapting the provisions relating to the powers of the Court of Justice. If the Court aspires a change in its jurisdiction,[101] it should not cause annoyance on the part of the Member States in the Council. It may well be that the issue never comes up in real terms before the end of the five-year period. Yet, one would hope that the Council would make use of

---

[97] Apparently, the Court cannot hold a measure invalid under this procedure.

[98] Article 68(3), second sentence EC.

[99] Case 294/83 *Les Verts v European Parliament* [1986] ECR 1339 where the ECJ held that acts of the European Parliament were susceptible to review by the ECJ.

[100] Case C–70/88 *European Parliament v Council* [1990] ECR I–2041 where the ECJ held that despite the 'procedural gap' resulting from the fact that the EP was not among the institutions mentioned in Article 173, the Parliament could bring an action for annulment against acts of the Council or the Commission in order to safeguard its prerogatives.

[101] It is not certain that it does: in the context of Art. 230 EC the Court goes out of its way to prevent more cases being brought to it by refusing to extend standing for private applicants. The Courts' Paper and the Due Report – also referred to as the Report by the Working Party on the Future of the European Communities' Court System or the 'Wise Persons' Report – drafted in the run-up to the Nice IGC focus almost exclusively on the problem of the workload of the European Courts. However, both reports argue against the extension of the limitation to final instance courts in Art. 68(1) EC as a method of limiting the ECJ's case law under Art. 234 EC. See A Dashwood and A Johnston, *The Future of the Judicial System of the European Union* (Oxford, Hart Publishing, 2001) where both reports are re-printed and discussed; see on this issue also G de Búrca and JHH Weiler, *The European Court of Justice* (Oxford, OUP, 2001), H Rasmussen, 'Remedying the Crumbling EC Judicial System', 37 *CML Rev*, 2000, 1071; A Arnull, 'Judicial architecture or judicial folly? The challenge facing the European Union', 24 *ELR*, 1999, 516.

the opportunity of Article 67(2) EC to extend the preliminary rulings procedure to all national courts.[102]

Fenelly has suggested that any jurisdictional gap or delays consequent on the reservation of the referring functions to the courts of final instance is to be compensated by the provision on requests of interpretation under Article 68(3) EC.[103] However, while such procedure may be beneficial in clarifying obscurities, it is restricted to questions of interpretation, and does not apply to questions about the validity of Community measures. Moreover, only the Council, Commission and a Member State may make a request to the Court to give a ruling. And finally, they 'shall not apply to judgments of courts or tribunals of the Member States which have become res judicata'. Article 68(3) EC is not conclusive on the question whether national courts may declare Title IV acts invalid.[104]

With respect to the exclusion of the Court of Justice from the area of maintenance or law and order and the safeguarding of internal security, in Article 68(2) EC, Fenelly has suggested that the removal of any judicial review at the Community level, or even interpretation of a Community measure seemed very far-reaching, especially in the light of Article 6(2) EU which obliges the Union to respect fundamental rights, as guaranteed by the ECHR and as general principles of Community law. *'In the result'*, he concluded, *'the judicial review function would devolve on the national courts'*.[105] Angela Ward, on the other hand, has stated that it may well be that with respect to decisions or measures relating to the maintenance of law and order and the safeguarding of internal security, there will be no avenue of judicial review to assess the validity of these decisions, given *Foto-Frost* and the exclusion of the jurisdiction of the European Court. She argues that the latter may have to accept jurisdiction irrespective of Article 68(2) EC, on grounds of the fundamental right of access to an effective judicial remedy stated in *Johnston*.[106] Given the Court of Justice's track record in the context of mainstream first-pillar law and its refusal to re-intepret standing for private applicants to review the validity of general Community acts under Article 230(4) EC in *Unión de Pequeños Agricultores*,

---

[102] A compromise would be to restrict lower courts' preliminary references to questions concerning the validity of Title IV acts, which could then be made obligatory. (For the sake of clarity and coherence, the text of Art. 234 EC may also have to be adapted to include the *Foto-Frost* principle. However, that would require a fully-fledged Treaty amendment).

[103] N Fennelly, 'The Area of "Freedom, Security and Justice" and The European Court of Justice – A Personal View', *ICLQ*, 2000, 1, at 5.

[104] So S Peers, *art.cit.*, at 354.

[105] N Fennelly, 'The Area of "Freedom, Security and Justice" and the European Court of Justice – A Personal View', *ICLQ*, 2000, 1, at 6.

[106] A Ward, 'Limits of the Uniform Application of Community Law and Effective Judicial Review: A Look Post-Amsterdam, in C Kilpatrick, T Novitz and P Skidmore (eds), *The Future of Remedies in Europe*, (Oxford, Hart Publishing, 2000), 213, at 221–22.

it is unlikely that the Court will go this far. The fundamental principle of a right of access to a competent court seems much less powerful in the context of review of Community legislation than in the context of the review conducted by the national courts of the compatibility of national law with Community law. There is, however, an important difference with the case of *Unión de Pequeños Agricultores* where *Foto-Frost* applies without any doubt and national courts all have access to the Court of Justice. In the case of Title IV the Treaty itself excludes *expressis verbis* the jurisdiction of the Court of Justice and it is highly unlikely that it will assume jurisdiction irrespective. The national courts will have to fill the gap, at the expense of the uniformity of Title IV law. Indeed, if a national court should find that there are serious doubts about the validity of the measure in question, it will have to make the decision without the help of the Court of Justice, and with effects in its Member State only.

18.1.3. Title VI: Provisions on Police and Judicial Co-operation in Criminal Matters (PJCC)

18.1.3.1. General Considerations

In the context of Title VI, the third pillar,[107] the measures that may be adopted by the Council are listed in Article 34 EU. The Council may adopt *common positions, framework decisions* and *decisions*, and may establish *conventions* which it shall recommend to the Member States for adoption. *Framework decisions* are adopted for the purpose of approximation of the laws and regulations of the Member States and are binding upon the Member States as to the result to be achieved but shall leave to the national authorities the choice of methods and form. They are, if you will, the third

---

[107] It is, I agree, not correct to speak of 'pillars' as in the pillar structure of a Greek temple, since the image over-emphasises the separation and distinctiveness of the pillars, rather than the unity of the entire construct. If an image must be used – images, even if they are never perfect, do make a theory visible – those of the 'Gothic cathedral' or the 'holy trinity' are to be preferred, as they reflect better the complex reality, the unity and interwovenness of the 'sub-organisations' in one European Union. See JHH Weiler, 'Neither Unity nor Three Pillars. The Trinity Structure of the Treaty on European Union', in J Monar, *et al*, (eds), *The Maastricht Treaty on European Union. Legal Complexity and Political Dynamic* (Brussels, EIP, 1993) 49; B De Witte, 'The Pillar Structure and the Nature of the European Union: Greek Temple or French Gothic Cathedral', in T Heukels, *et al*, (eds), *The European Union After Amsterdam* (Deventer, Kluwer, 1998) 51; The image of the Russian doll is less well chosen since it seems to presume that the various sub-organisations are fitted one inside the other; it does have the advantage of being less 'architecturally ambitious', see D Curtin and I Dekker, 'The EU as a "Layered" International Organization: Institutional Unity in Disguise', in P Craig and G de Búrca (eds), *The Evolution of EU Law* (Oxford, OUP, 1999) 83, at 132. However, in EU law parlance, it is still common to speak of the 'third pillar', more than of 'Title VI' or PJCC, for instance, terms which are known almost only to 'insiders'. I will therefore, also use the notion of 'second and third pillar'.

pillar version of directives. They shall not, according to Article 34(2)(b) EU, entail direct effect. *Decisions* are binding, but, again, they shall not entail direct effect according to Article 34(2)(c). The Council shall, acting by qualified majority, adopt measures necessary to implement those decisions at the level of the Union. *Conventions* established by the Council within Title VI shall be recommended for adoption to the Member States, in accordance with their respective constitutional requirements.

In contrast to Title IV, the mainstream Community provisions on the Court's jurisdiction do not apply in Title VI. The jurisdiction of the Court in the context of Title VI is limited to what is specifically provided for in Article 35 EU. Under that provision, the Court of Justice has jurisdiction to give preliminary rulings on the validity and interpretation of framework decisions and decisions on the interpretation of conventions established under Title VI and on the validity and interpretation of measures implementing them,[108] *if* the Member State has agreed accept jurisdiction of the Court of Justice to give these preliminary rulings. Member States are not obliged to accept the jurisdiction of the Court of Justice to give preliminary rulings. Under Article 35(2) EU, the Member States *may*, at the time of signing the Treaty of Amsterdam or any time thereafter make a declaration accepting the jurisdiction of the Court of Justice to give preliminary rulings. Under Article 35(3) EU a State making a declaration must specify whether (a) any court or tribunal of that State *against whose decisions there is no judicial remedy* under national law *may* request the Court of Justice to give a preliminary ruling on a question raised in a case pending before it and concerning the validity or interpretation of an act referred to in paragraph 1 if that court or tribunal considers that a decision on the question is necessary to enable it to give judgment; or (b) *any* court or tribunal of that State *may* request the Court of Justice to give a preliminary ruling on a question raised in a case pending before it and concerning the validity or interpretation of an act referred to in paragraph 1 if that court or tribunal considers that a decision on the question is necessary to enable it to give judgment. Several Member States have opted for a third version: they have reserved the right to make it obligatory for the courts of final instance to

---

[108] Note that Art. 35 EU does not give the Court jurisdiction to rule on the interpretation of Title VI itself, in contrast to Art. 68(1) EC on Title IV. Yet, it seems impossible to refrain from interpreting the basis of an act when interpreting the act itself. Say that the validity of a decision is challenged on grounds of lack of competence: in order to assess the validity the Court will have to interpret the text of the Title to be able to decide the case. Any doubts are removed by Art. 46 EU (former Art. L) which provides that the provisions of the Community Treaties on the powers of the ECJ and the exercise thereof shall apply (b) to the provisions of Title VI under the conditions provided for in Art. 35 EU, see also S Peers, *art. cit.*, at 376.

refer. This possibility is not provided for in Article 35(3) EU but is clearly inspired by the system of Article 234 EC and was also mentioned as a possible choice in the Declaration on Article K7 of the Treaty on European Union adopted at Amsterdam.[109]

Under Article 35(5) EU the Court has no jurisdiction to review the validity or proportionality of operations carried out by the police or other law enforcement services of a Member State or the exercise of the responsibilities incumbent on Member State with regard to the maintenance of law and order and the safeguarding of internal security. There is also a parallel with actions for annulment: under Article 35(6) EU the Court has jurisdiction to review the legality of framework decisions and decisions in actions brought by a Member State or the Commission, but not by private applicants, on the same four grounds as provided for in Article 230 EC. Finally, Article 35(7) EU creates a dispute settlement mechanism for disputes between Member States regarding the application or interpretation of all types of acts which may be adopted under this Title: if such dispute cannot be settled by the Council within six months, the Court has jurisdiction to rule on it. The Court also has jurisdiction to rule on any dispute between Member States and the Commission regarding the interpretation or the application of conventions established under Article 34(2)(d) EU.[110] Private applicants and the European Parliament remain completely absent from these procedures.

Before the entry into force of the Amsterdam Treaty, the Court of Justice has on one occasion ruled on the validity of a Council act adopted under Title VI in an action brought under Article 173 of the EC Treaty (now Article 230 EC).[111] The Commission brought an action for annulment challenging the validity of the Council Joint Action regarding air transit visas on grounds that the act should not have been adopted on the basis of the provisions of Title VI, but rather on Article 100(c) of the EC Treaty (old).

---

[109] On 1 May 1999, the state of the declarations made under Art. 35 EU was the following: Spain has recognised jurisdiction of the ECJ on references made by courts of final instance (Art. 35(3)(a) EU); Belgium, Germany, Luxembourg, Italy, the Netherlands, Austria have recognised jurisdiction of the ECJ on references from any court (Art. 35(3)(b) EU) and reserved the right to make provisions in national law to make references compulsory for highest courts (as did Spain); Greece, Portugal, Finland and Sweden have recognised jurisdiction of the ECJ on references from any court (Art. 35(3)(b) EU); OJ 1999 L 114/56. Ireland, Denmark, the United Kingdom and France had accordingly made no declaration by the time the Treaty of Amsterdam entered into force. The ECJ has handed its first decision under Art. 35 EU references on 11 February 2003 concerning the interpretation of Art. 54 of the Convention implementing the Schengen Agreement, in Joined Cases C–187/01 and C–385/01 *Criminal proceedings against Hüseyin Gözütok and against Klaus Brügge* [2003] ECR I–1345, on references from the *Oberlandesgericht Köln* and the *Rechtbank van eerste aanleg Veurne* respectively. Neither was a final instance court.

[110] By virtue of Art. 35(7) second sentence EU.

[111] Case C–170/96 *Commission v Council (airport transit visas)* [1998] I–2763.

The Court accepted jurisdiction[112] with reference to Articles L and M of the EU Treaty.[113]

The issue of the competences of the *national courts* in the context of Title VI is even more critical than in the context of Title IV, given the restricted competences of the Court of Justice. The prohibition of national courts to rule on the validity of secondary Community law derives from the principle of supremacy of Community law and the *Foto-Frost* principle concerning the jurisdiction of national courts. Two central issues thus also arise to answer the question whether national courts have jurisdiction to rule on the validity of acts under the third pillar: the first relates to the effect of the decisions adopted in the context of Title VI in the national legal order, the second to the possibility of transposing *Foto-Frost* to Title VI. The *Foto-Frost* issue arises with even more force given the complicating element that the competence of the lower (and the highest) courts to refer a question for preliminary ruling to the Kirchberg varies in accordance with the declaration made by the Member State. It is hard to believe that whether or not a national court has the competence to rule on the validity of a decision adopted in the context of Title VI could depend on whether or not its Member State has accepted the jurisdiction of the Court, and in what form. These issues will be analysed in turn.

18.1.3.2. *The Supremacy of Acts Adopted under Title VI*

No special provision is made on the *supremacy* of framework decisions and decisions, and indeed, of other acts adopted in the framework of Title VI. Article 34(2)(b) and (c) EU denies direct effect of framework decisions and decisions, but says nothing about their relation to national law. The absence of direct effect does not imply the absence of supremacy. There is no reason why that should automatically follow: Indeed, for Community law also, there is no conclusive link between direct effect and supremacy: also provisions lacking direct effect are supreme over conflicting national law. What is different, however, is what the court can do with a non-directly effective supreme provision of Community law, and this is

---

[112] In Case C–167/94 *Grau Gomis and Others* [1995] I–1023 where a request for a preliminary ruling which was clearly intended to obtain a ruling on the obligations of the Member States under Art. B EU was dismissed as inadmissible, the Court held that by virtue of Art. L, it *'clearly has no jurisdiction to interpret that article in the context of such proceedings'*.

[113] Art. L provided that the Court had jurisdiction with respect to Arts. L to S of the EU; Art. M stated that apart from the provisions of the EU Treaty which expressly amend the Community Treaties, *'nothing in [the TEU] shall affect the Treaties establishing the European Communities or the subsequent Treaties and Acts modifying or supplementing them'*. On 'border disputes' see S Peers, 'Who's Judging the Watchmen? The Judicial System of the 'Area of Freedom, Security and Justice', *YEL*, 1998, 337, at 393 *et seq*; RA Wessel, 'The Inside Looking Out: Consistency and Delimitation in EU External Relations', 37 *CML Rev*, 2000, 1135, at 1151.

substantially different from the case of a directly effective provision. On the other hand, is not self-evident that the supremacy of Title VI acts should be accepted. The Court of Justice does have jurisdiction to give preliminary rulings on the interpretation of framework decisions and decisions, of conventions and of implementing measures. The question of supremacy of these acts may come up before a national court and be referred to the Court of Justice. While the Court may not grant direct effect to framework decisions and decisions, it may nevertheless declare them, and other Title VI measures, supreme over conflicting national measures. Will it? Given that whatever the exact nature of the Court of Justice, it is at least an international court, it seems that it will in any case hold Title VI measures superior over national law *in cases before it*. Any international court gives priority to international law over national law and the general principle that a State cannot plead its own domestic law as a justification for non-compliance with a Treaty obligation applies here.[114]

Yet, the real question is whether the Court will also award '*internal supremacy*' to decisions and framework decisions and oblige national courts to grant them precedence over conflicting national law. The first difficulty then is that the Treaty denies direct effect to these acts. In the easiest direct effect – supremacy cases in Community law, supremacy and direct effect operate as a conflict of laws rule:[115] in the case of a conflict between Community law and national law, the directly effective Community norm should apply. Yet, the superiority of a framework decision over conflicting national legislation cannot operate as a conflict of laws rule: the provision of the framework decision 'shall not entail direct effect', and for the time being, that seems to mean that 'individuals cannot derive rights from them and that national courts are not bound to apply them'. What else could be the practical consequence of a declaration that the provision is supreme, given the absence of direct effect? The parallel with prevailing Community law would lead one to come up with the doctrines of 'indirect effect' or conform interpretation,[116] and State liability, the 'other ways to give effect to Community law'. Even in the absence of direct effect,[117] the supremacy issue is highly relevant.

---

[114] See also JHH Weiler, 'Neither Unity nor Three Pillars. The Trinity Structure of the Treaty on European Union', in J Monar *et al, The Maastricht Treaty on European Union. Legal Complexity and Political Dynamic* (Brussels, EIP, 1993) 49, at 55.

[115] A rule of conflict decides a case where there are two conflicting applicable norms, whether the court should choose the later, more specific, or higher norm as the case may be.

[116] Which is in fact also a 'natural' reflex of courts confronted with conflicts of norms, including conflicts with treaty provisions, even, or perhaps even mostly so, in dualist systems.

[117] There are many provisions of Community law which equally lack direct effect, either because of the nature of the norm, its wording or the nature of the parties in the legal dispute.

In *Costa v ENEL* the Court based the supremacy of Community law over national law on an amalgam of reasons and arguments,[118] particularly the *'special and original nature'* of Community law, distinguishing it from classic international law, which did not, according to the Court,[119] by and of itself impose supremacy.[120] In *Internationale Handelsgesellschaft* the main ground was again 'the very nature' of the law stemming from the Treaty and its character as Community law, and, in addition, the uniformity and efficacy of Community law. Now, what does all this say about Community law which cannot be said of the law stemming from the Treaty on European Union in the context of Title VI? According to the unity thesis, which rejects the 'classic' presentation of the European Union as a three-pillared Greek temple, the European Union forms one entity from the point of view of the organisation, its actions and its laws. It has been argued[121] that the same principles on the relationship with national law, including its supremacy, apply to what is known as the second and third pillar. Yet, there are differences between Community law on the one hand and Title V and VI on the other. The very fact that these matters are not inserted in the Community law pillar proves the point. However, several

---

[118] To cite the Court, once again: 'It follows from all these observations that the law stemming from the Treaty, an independent source of law, could not, because of its special and original nature, be [judicially] overridden by domestic legal provisions, however framed, without being deprived of its character as Community law and without the legal basis of the Community itself being called into question. The transfer by the States from their domestic legal system to the Community legal system of the rights and obligations arising under the Treaty carries with it a permanent limitation of their sovereign rights, against which a subsequent unilateral act incompatible with the concept of the Community cannot prevail', Case 6/64 *Costa v ENEL* [1964] ECR 585, at 593, my addition, see French version: '(..) se voir judiciairement opposer (..)'.

[119] The Belgian *Cour de cassation* took a different stance and argued that the very nature of international law commanded its supremacy, and that this applied *a fortiori* for Community law, *Cour de cassation (B)*, decision of 27 May 1971, *Franco-suisse le Ski*, JT, 1971, 460; [1972] CMLR 330; Oppenheimer, *The Cases*, 245, at 266: 'The primacy of the treaty results from the very nature of international treaty law'.

[120] Though this may have been a mistaken position at the time as has been argued by O Spiermann, 'The Other Side of the Story: An Unpopular Essay on the Making a the European Community Legal Order', 10 *EJIL*, 1999, 763.

[121] A von Bogdandy and M Nettesheim, 'Ex Pluribus Unum: Fusion of the European Communities into the European Union', 2 *ELJ*, 1996, 267, at 283–4; see also A von Bogdandy, 'The Legal Case for Unity: The European Union as a Single Organization with a Single Legal System', 36 *CML Rev*, 1999, 887; for a more nuanced view, see B De Witte, 'The Pillar Structure and the nature of the European Union: Greek Temple or French Gothic Cathedral', in T Heukels *et al*, *The European Union After Amsterdam*, (The Hague, Kluwer, 1998) 51. De Witte considers the Communities as sub-organisations which have their own legal existence, while Nettesheim and von Bogdandy take it one step further and argue that the Communities are completely encapsulated within the one entity of the European Union while the European Community no longer has a legal existence but is merely a separate legal regime; for a similar view see also D Curtin and I Dekker, 'The EU as a "Layered" International Organization: Institutional Unity in Disguise', in P Craig and G de Búrca (eds), *The Evolution of EU Law* (Oxford, OUP, 1999) 55; RA Wessel, 'The Inside Looking Out: Consistency and Delimitation in EU External Relations', 37 *CML Rev*, 2000, 1135.

of the elements mentioned by the Court in *Costa v ENEL* apply to measures under Title V and VI as they did in the first pillar, albeit not with the same force.[122] At the end of the day, it would seem anomalous for the Court *not* to grant supremacy to Title V and VI measures. Paraphrasing the Court in *Costa*, a denial of supremacy would imply that Member States could, by a unilateral act, detract from measures commonly adopted under the Treaty. It would mean that the executive force of the Treaty was allowed to vary from one State to another. The obligations undertaken under the Treaty would become merely contingent, instead of unconditional. It all boils down to the binding force of the measures adopted under Title VI: *'Nier sa supériorité revient à nier son existence'*, said Virally in 1954, in the context of classic international treaty law.[123] From the point of view of an international court, there is nothing more to it.

In the context of the Brussels Convention,[124] the Court equally held that it took priority over conflicting national law. The Court first looked at the aims of the Convention to strengthen the legal protection of persons established in the Community. It then stated that the principle of legal certainty and the aims of the Convention required that the equality and uniformity of rights and obligations arising from it for the Contracting States and the persons concerned must be ensured, regardless of the rules laid down in that regard in the laws of those States. As a consequence, the Convention must override incompatible national provisions.[125]

One textual argument may be added: Article 34(2)(b) and (c) EU expressly denies direct effect of framework decisions and decisions. *A contrario*, one may argue, since the principle of supremacy is not excluded, it applies.[126]

---

[122] See above, Part 1. Chapter 4.2.4.; see also C Timmermans, 'The Constitutiuonalization of the European Union', *YEL*, 2002, 1, at 9.

[123] M Virally, 'Sur un pont aux ânes: Les rapports entre le droit international et ldroit interne', in *Mélanges offertes à Henri Rolin. Problèmes de droit des gens*, (Paris, Pédone, 1964), 488, at 497; in the context of Community law, Lord Mackenzie-Stuart formulated it this way: *'There is here no question of Community supremacy, of a command by the Austenian (sic) superior, of liege-lord and lackey, of de haut en bas or however you care to pharse it. The so-called supremacy of Community law is no more than a rule founded on necessity. Far from necessity knowing no law, necessity is the law. The Community would fall to bits if it were otherwise'*, cited in AIL Campbell, 'Introduction', in AIL Campbell and M Voyatzi (eds), *Legal Reasoning and Judicial Interpretation of European Law. Essays in Honour of Lord Mackenzie-Stuart*, (London, Trenton Publishing, 1996), at xxx.

[124] The Brussels Convention no longer exists as a Convention, but has been transformed into secondary Community law by Council Regulation 44/2001 of 22 December 2000, OJ 2001 L 12/1; as a consequence, the preliminary rulings reference procedure is restricted, here too, to final instance courts.

[125] Case 288/82 *Ferdinand Duijnstee v Lodewijk Goderbauer* [1983] ECR 3663, at para 12–14; see also Case 25/79 *Sanicentral GmbH v Réné Collin* [1979] ECR 3423.

[126] So A von Bogdandy, 'The Legal Case for unity: The European Union as a Single Organization with a Single Legal System', 36 *CML Rev*, 1999, 887, at 909; '[A]s a presumption' von Bogdandy argues, *'the legal principles developed in the context of the EC Treaty can be extended to the EU Treaty as long as they are not expressly excluded'*.

If Title VI measures are indeed given priority over conflicting measures of national law, there is no apparent reason why, *from the perspective of Union law,* a distinction should be made between 'ordinary supremacy' and 'ultimate supremacy', that is, according to the nature of the national provision which is inconsistent with the relevant measure. If it is accepted that Title VI measures are supreme over conflicting national law, they are also supreme over the Constitution. The Court of Justice does not pay regard to the nature of national law: it treats it as one piece, and, as an international court, does not look inside.

Nevertheless, this is exactly the point where the differences between mainstream Community law and the law deriving from the second and third pillar are most evident, which may lead to a rejection of an absolute version of supremacy. Consider the dispute between the Court of Justice and the German constitutional court in *Internationale Handelsgesellschaft*: the German court first stated that it retained jurisdiction to review the compatibility of Community law with German fundamental rights, due to the absence of a sufficient level of protection at the European level. In *Solange II*, the *Bundesverfassungsgericht* was convinced by the case law of the Court of Justice, which replaced the protection offered at the national level with protection at the Community level under the general principles to be guaranteed by the Court of Justice and the national courts. In the context of the second and third pillar, the Court of Justice cannot offer the same guarantee due to the restrictions on its jurisdiction under those pillars. In addition, the lack of democratic legitimation under these second and third pillars equally argue against the acceptance of the same unconditional and absolute version of supremacy. It remains to be seen what the Court will do, if it is referred the question about the supremacy of Title VI acts.

18.1.3.3. *Title VI and* Foto-Frost

The same considerations on *Foto-Frost* apply as in the context of Title IV, and these will not be repeated here. However, there are some factors that complicate matters further in the context of Title VI. First, courts in different Member States have different rights and obligations to refer questions for preliminary rulings to the Court, depending on their State's declaration. It is difficult to accept that as a consequence, the jurisdiction of national courts to rule on the validity of Title VI measure would vary. On the other hand, given the content of the declarations made by several Member States accepting jurisdiction of the Court along the patterns of Article 234 EC, it may well be that cases will reach the Court much easier and sooner in the context of Title VI than in the context of Title IV. Nevertheless, Member States are even entitled under Article 35 EU to exclude preliminary references. Second, there is no parallel to Article 67 EC concerning adaptation of the jurisdiction of the Court by the Council after five years. Title VI seems stuck with the restrictions on preliminary references. Third, the Court is vested, under Article 35(1) with jurisdiction to rule on the validity of framework decisions, decisions and of measures implementing conventions established under Title VI, as is the case for the validity of Community law under Article 230 EC, which was one of the main arguments for the Court of Justice to hold that its jurisdiction must be exclusive in *Foto-Frost*. Add the concern for uniformity, and the parallel with *Foto-Frost* is easily made. Yet, to extend *Foto-Frost*, at least its first limb that national courts may not review them, to Title VI instruments would in many cases render them immune for judicial review, since they cannot reach the Court of Justice. The national courts should fill the gap.

18.1.4. Title V: Provisions on a Common Foreign and Security Policy (CFSP)

18.1.4.1. General Considerations

The *Court of Justice* has, under Article 46 EU, no jurisdiction under Title V: Acts adopted under the second pillar are not subject to judicial review by the Court of Justice. The exclusion of the Court of Justice is related to the political nature of the second pillar, Common Foreign and Security Policy (CFSP), and is not unusual. Foreign affairs and especially defence and security matters are in most countries considered not to be the business of the courts; even democratic control frequently suffers in these areas.[127] It is an area characterised by judicial deference to political decisions.

Will there be a role for the *national courts*? If national courts should be confronted with acts adopted in the context of CFSP, they will be on their own. The Court of Justice cannot be seized or asked for judicial assistance.[128]

---

[127] See also JW de Zwaan, 'Community Dimensions of the Second Pillar', in T Heukels, N Blokker and M Brus (eds), *The European Union After Amsterdam* (Kluwer, Deventer 1998) 179, at 188.

[128] The CFI has assumed jurisdiction to rule on public access to measures adopted under Title V, on grounds that Decision 93/731 on public access to Council documents applies to all Council documents regardless their contents. The fact that the Court does not have jurisdiction under Art. L of the EU Treaty (now Art. 46 EU) to assess the lawfulness of acts falling within Title V does not exclude its jurisdiction to rule on public access to those acts, Case T–14/98 *Hautala v Council* [1999] ECR II-2489; see, in the context of Title VI, Case T–174/95 *Svenska Journalistförbundet v Council* [1998] ECR II-2289.

18.1.4.2. Internal Effects of CFSP Acts

Acts which may be adopted in the framework of the 'second pillar', are joint actions,[129] common positions,[130] common strategies[131] and systematic co-operation.[132] In contrast to what the Treaty says about decisions and framework decisions in the context of the third pillar, no special provision is made with respect to the direct effect of these measures. The Court cannot express itself on the issue, nor on that of supremacy. It would appear that these questions will have to be decided by the national courts on the basis of the usual principles of international law, such as *pacta sunt servanda* and so forth. However, it may well be that many national courts will decline jurisdiction to decide cases in the area of CFSP, or that they will apply avoidance techniques so as not to answer difficult questions, such as *acte du gouvernement*, political question, separation of powers and the like.

18.1.4.3. CFPS and Foto-Frost

The *Foto-Frost* principle cannot, as such, apply in the context of the second pillar, given the exclusion of the Court of Justice. The prohibition on the national courts to pronounce themselves on the lawfulness of Community law was based on the exclusive competence of the Court of Justice to rule on their validity. Since the Court of Justice has no jurisdiction at all in the second pillar and cannot rule on the validity of acts adopted in the second pillar, that cannot be the ground for excluding the national courts' competence.

Nonetheless, legal issues may arise, for instance in relation to fundamental rights. Perhaps unexpectedly, it is the Human Rights Court that has been asked about judicial protection in the context of the second pillar.[133]In the light of the fight against terrorism in the aftermath of 9-11, the Council of the European Union adopted two common positions under the second

---

[129] Art. 14 EU.

[130] Art. 15 EU.

[131] Art. 13 EU.

[132] Art. 16 EU.

[133] *European Court of Human Rights*, admissibility decision of 23 May 2002, *Segi and Gestoras Pro Amnistia and others v Germany, Austria, Belgium, Denmark, Spain, Finland, France, Greece, Ireland, Italy, Luxembourg, the Netherlands, Portugal, the United Kingdom and Sweden*, available on www. echr.coe.int.

[134] Council common position 2001/930/CFSP of 27 December 2001 on combating terrorism, OJ 2001, L 344/90, contained statements of principle on the fight against terrorism and contained measures to be adopted by the Union and the Member States, and urged the Member States to accede to a number of international treaties against terrorism. Council common position 2001/ 931/CFSP of 27 December 2001 on the application of specific measures to combat terrorism, OJ 2001 L 344/93 instructed the Community to adopt measures concerning the freezing of funds, and ordered the Member States to afford each other the widest possible assistance in preventing and combating terrorist acts.

pillar.[134] In December 2001 and February 2002 the activities of the organ-isations Segi and Gestoras Pro-Amnistia, which figured in the list annexed to Common position 2001/931/CFSP, were prohibited by court order, on the grounds that they were linked to the Basque terrorist move-ment ETA. Eleven members of Segi were placed in custody. Before the Strasbourg Court, the applicant associations brought a case against all 15 Member States of the Union, alleging infringements of several Convention rights. They stated that their rights had been infringed as they had not been able to challenge before the Court of Justice the meas-ures adopted by the 15 Member States in the framework of these common positions.

The Court held that it did not have to rule on the question whether the applicants had exhausted all legal remedies under Union law, such as the action in damages or even the action for annulment, in the light of the judgment *Jégo-Quéré* that had been handed down by the Court of First Instance only a few days before:[135] the complaints were in any case inad-missible, since the applicants could not be considered direct victims of the Common positions. Common position 2001/930/CFSP was not directly applicable and merely urged the Union and the Member State to adopt measures against terrorism. The measure could not serve as a legal basis for criminal or administrative actions adopted against private persons. Common position 2001/931/CFSP did not concern the applicants directly either. Articles 2 and 3 were addressed to the Community, which had sub-sequently adopted Council regulation 2580/2001 of 27 December 2001. However, this regulation did not concern the applicants either; to the extent that it did, they could seize the Court of Justice. Article 4 of the Common position was addressed to the Member States and was intended to improve co-operation in the fight against terrorism, in the context of Title VI of the EU Treaty. To that end, the Member States could fully exploit their existing powers in accordance with acts of the Union and other international agreements binding on the Member States. The Strasbourg Court stated that Article 4 of the Common position could serve as a legal basis for concrete measures liable to affect the applicants, especially in the context of police co-operation and Europol. However, the provision did not add any new powers that could be used to the detri-ment of the applicants. It only contained an obligation for Member States to co-operate, which did not address private individuals or affect them directly.

The Court of Human Rights added that concrete measures implement-ing the Common positions would be susceptible to judicial review in each

---

[135] It is striking that the Strasbourg Court reacted so swiftly to a revolutionary judgment of the CFI intended to reverse a longstanding position of the ECJ The judgment was soon 'reversed' by the ECJ in *Unión de Pequeños Agricultores*. The remark of the Strasbourg Court seemingly contained an approval of the position of the CFI.

legal order concerned, whether national or international. The fact that the organisations figured on the list annexed to the position might be embarrassing, but was not sufficient to justify an application of the Convention. Consequently, the Court did not consider the applicants victims of a violation of the Convention as is required under Article 34 ECHR, and declared the complaints inadmissible.

The Court of Human Rights thus seemed to start from the premise that Common positions do not, by nature, affect individuals directly, and require further implementation before they take effect. Accordingly, it is not the Common position itself that is to be regarded as directly infringing the rights of individuals, but rather the national or Community measures implementing them. These should however be open to judicial review either before the national or the European Courts as the case may be; the Common positions themselves must not.

Segi and Gestoras Pro Amnistia did however bring actions before the Court of First Instance, seeking compensation for the damage allegedly suffered as a result of their name having been included in the list of terrorist groups pursuant to Common position 2001/931/CFSP. In support of their arguments, the applicants claimed that the Common position was vitiated by a number of irregularities, among them breach of fundamental rights and principles as protected by the ECHR and the Charter of Fundamental Rights, the right to the presumption of innocence and the right to a proper hearing in so far as there was no means of challenging the common position through the courts, and several other fundamental rights.[136] The cases are still pending, but given that the Luxembourg Courts have no jurisdiction in the second pillar, it is not very likely that the applicants will be awarded damages.[137]

18.2. THE NATIONAL PERSPECTIVE

In several Member States the constitutional court or a court having constitutional jurisdiction has announced that it does retain the right to review the constitutionality of secondary law, either directly, or indirectly, through the national implementation or application. The German *Bundesverfassungsgericht* and the Italian *Corte costituzionale* have announced that they have reserved this power to themselves since the nineteen seventies in the *Solange* and *Frontini* cases and their progeny, in

---

[136] See pending cases T–333/02 *Gestoras Pro Amnistía association and others v Council* and T–338/02 *Segi association and others v Council*.

[137] In Case T–228/02 *Organisation des Modjahedines du Peuple d'Iran (OMPI) v Council*, pending, the applicants sought annulment of several decisions, among which two common positions updating the Common position 2001/931/CFSP, arguing that the measures infringed their fundamental rights by including them in the lists. The CFI does not however have jurisdiction.

the area of fundamental rights. The principles enunciated in those cases still exist, even if they have been somewhat adjusted overtime. While these cases were and are the subject of fierce criticism, as being nationalist and hostile to the uniformity of Community law, their merit has been that they have played a part in the development of a fundamental rights case law of the Court of Justice. Indeed, with these cases, the Italian and German constitutional courts have contributed to exposing the lack of fundamental rights protection in the project of European integration.[138] And as a consequence, one may assume that their case law has contributed to convincing the Court of Justice to fill the gap in fundamental rights protection under the Treaties, and to actually enforce these principles against the Community institutions, as it did for instance in the *T Port* banana cases.

It is no coincidence that it is the area of fundamental rights where the constitutional courts reserve control functions. The area of fundamental rights is their single most significant domain, the area that they consider to be their chief responsibility. While the German and Italian court accepted that Community law might infringe on certain constitutional principles, such as the division of powers between the State organs and the exercise of the legislative, executive and judicial function, fundamental rights are sacred. More recently, other courts have joined the Italian and German courts and have refused to hand over ultimate responsibility for fundamental rights. The president of the Belgian *Arbitragehof* was reported stating that secondary Community law would not escape review of its constitutionality, be it indirectly through the national implementation, as long as there was no European Court which would effectively ensure the respect of the fundamental rights as it exists in the national systems. As long as that was not the case and in the absence of a catalogue of fundamental rights, he said, *'il me paraît que la limitation du respect des droits fondamentaux est encore justifiable'*.[139] The analogy with the *Solange* case

---

[138] That is at least common perception. In contrast Everling, a former German ECJ Judge wrote: *'This is historically not correct since the relevant jurisdiction began long before. Above all it is certainly an odd supposition that the personalities who were or are judges of the Court of Justice are squinting timidly at the judgment of a German or other national court and that they can be influenced by pressures of national institutions. According to the author's experience, the judges are never impressed if national courts even of the highest level threaten to ignore their obligations under the Treaty. But of course, they are highly interested in their opinions and they are always ready to be convinced by better arguments'*, U Everling, 'The Maastricht Judgment of the German Federal Constitutional Court and its Significance for the Development of the European Union', YEL, 1994, 1, at 14–15.

[139] M Melchior, in *Diritto comunitario europeo e diritto nazionale*, (Milano, Giuffrè, 1997), 233, at 236; It must be stressed however, that the position of the president of the *Arbitragehof* did not coincide with the view of the *procureur général* of the *Cour de cassation* who in his 1992 mercuriale enounced the superiority of all treaties over the national Constitution, J Velu, 'Contrôle de constitutionnalité et contrôle de compatibilité avec les traités', JT, 1992, 729 and 749; In addition, the case in which the Belgian *Conseil d'Etat* awarded precedence to the interpretation of the Treaty by the ECJ over the Constitution, concerned fundamental rights, namely Art. 8 of the Constitution on Belgian nationality and Art. 10 (principle of equality); see *Conseil d'Etat*, 5 November 1996, *Orfinger v Etat belge*, JT, 1997, 253.

law of the *Bundesverfassungsgericht* is obvious. The Danish *Højesteret* also retains the right for Danish courts to control the respect for fundamental rights by the Community institutions, but it follows a different reasoning. In its decision on the constitutionality of the Treaty of Maastricht, the *Højesteret* announced that the Danish courts could not be deprived of their right to try questions as to whether a Community act which is upheld by the Court of Justice exceeds the limits for the surrender of sovereignty under the Act of Accession. *'Therefore, Danish courts must rule that an EC act is inapplicable in Denmark if the extraordinary situation should arise that with the required certainty it can be established that an EC act which has been upheld by the Court of Justice is based on an application of the Treaty which lies beyond the surrender of sovereignty according to the Act of Accession'*. This is a variation of the German *Maastricht Urteil* with respect to *Kompetenz Kompetenz*, but for the Danish courts the same reasoning applies to conflicts with Danish fundamental rights. The *Højesteret* held that *'Section 20 of the Danish Constitution does not permit that an international organisation is entrusted with the issuance of acts of law or the making of decisions that are contrary to provisions in the Constitution, including its rights of freedom. Indeed, the authorities of Realm have themselves no such power'*.[140] It therefore seems that should the Community act in conflict with Danish constitutionally-protected fundamental rights, it is considered to be acting *ultra vires*, and as a consequence, the Danish courts must hold such act to be inapplicable in Denmark.

The second area of contention between the *Bundesverfassungsgericht* and the Court of Justice is precisely that of *Kompetenz-Kompetenz*. In the *Brunner* decision, the *Bundesverfassungsgericht* announced that it would control whether specific Community measures were *ultra vires*. If they were, they would be inapplicable in Germany. The decision conflicts with the principle of supremacy and with the exclusive jurisdiction of the Court of Justice to review the validity of Community law.[141]

Before making a cross-national appraisal, it may be useful to examine the positions of various national courts on their jurisdiction to review secondary law on a country by country basis.

18.2.1. Germany

In Germany, the question whether the courts or the *Bundesverfassungsgericht* have jurisdiction to review secondary Community law has been the subject of debate from the beginning of European integration, and has been answered differently at different

---

[140] *Højesteret*, decision of 6 April 1998, *Treaty of Maastricht*, UfR, 1998, 800; English version can be found in www.um.dk/udenrigspolitik/europa/domeng.
[141] Even though the *Bundesverfassungsgericht* claims that it rules only the applicability of a Community measure in Germany rather than its validity. This is a false distinction.

points in time. Under the current state of the law, the *Bundesverfassungsgericht* assumes jurisdiction, in theory and only in exceptional, and even improbable cases, to review the compatibility of secondary Community law with the constitutionally protected fundamental rights. In addition, it may review whether a particular Community act is *ultra vires,* and if it is, declare it inapplicable on German soil.[142] It is not entirely clear whether German courts may, under German law, review Community legislation in the light of WTO law. With respect to acts adopted under CFSP and PJCC, the powers of the *Bundesverfassungsgericht* seem more extensive. Given the complexity of the case law and the adjustments made therein over time, the position of the Constitutional Court will first be presented in a chronological order. Due to the importance and intricacy of the *Bananas* saga, a road map will be presented.

18.2.1.1. *The* EEC Regulations Constitutionality *Case: the Autonomy of the Community Legal Order*

In the early *EEC Regulations constitutionality* case,[143] German companies instituted a *Verfassungsbeschwerde* against two regulations issued by the Council and the Commission, arguing that they violated their fundamental rights as enshrined in the German Basic Law. The complainants argued that their case should be admissible, because legislative acts adopted by the Community institutions were to be considered acts of the German public authorities since those organs derive their basic competence from Article 24(1) of the Basic Law. The Constitutional Court denied jurisdiction to review the constitutionality of EEC regulations, under reference to the autonomous nature of the Community legal order. The complaints were inadmissible: in constitutional complaint proceedings, the Court could only review acts of public authority emanating from German public authorities. *'Regulations of the Council and the Commission are acts of a special 'supranational' public authority created by the treaty and clearly distinguished from the public authorities of the Member States.'* And: *'Consequently its acts do not require approval ('ratification') by the Member States, nor can they be annulled by those States.'*[144]

The *Bundesverfassungsgericht* distinguished the own legal order established by the Treaty from public international law and from the national

---

[142] Such finding would not amount to a direct infringement of the Basic law. Instead an *ultra vires* act is not covered by the German Act assenting and giving effect to the Treaties, and is not, therefore, effective in the German legal order.

[143] *Bundesverfassungsgericht,* decision of 18 October 1967, *EEC Regulations Constitutionality case,* BVerfGE 22, 293; Oppenheimer, *The Cases,* 410.

[144] *Bundesverfassungsgericht,* decision of 18 October 1967, *EEC Regulations Constitutionality case,* BVerfGE 22, 293; Oppenheimer, *The Cases,* 410, at 412–13.

law of the Member States. *'Community law and the municipal law of the Member States are two internal legal orders which are distinct and different from each other'*. The Court pointed to the system of legal protection provided for by the Treaty in the hands of the Court of Justice. Moreover, Article 24(1) of the Basic Law could not be used as an excuse to regard acts of the Community institutions as measures taken by German public authorities. It also rejected the contention that it had residual competence to review Community regulations, in case of an urgent need for constitutional protection, on the basis that the Community system of judicial protection did not provide sufficient guarantees. In its view, this would amount to an extension of the jurisdiction of the *Bundesverfassungsgericht*; it would blur the demarcation between the national and the supranational competence and lead to unequal protection in the Member States.

The *Bundesverfassungsgericht* thus gave proof of a remarkably integration-friendly attitude and showed absolutely no jealousy with regard to the jurisdiction of the Court of Justice. Yet, it added a footnote to its judgment, expressly limiting it to *Verfassungsbeschwerden* instituted directly against Community regulations, but it did not exclude the possibility that the Court may, in proceedings properly brought before it, examine the compatibility of Community law with the fundamental rights as enshrined in the Basic Law. The answer would depend on whether and to what extent the institutions of the European Communities might be subject to a system of basic rights in Germany or to what extent Germany had been able to exempt the Community organs from being bound by German basic rights when it transferred *Hoheitsrechte* under Article 24(1) of the Constitution. Nevertheless and overall, the decision was favourable towards Community law, which was recognised as an autonomous and independent legal system, which could not be directly challenged before the Constitutional Court.[145] This qualification the Community would, as an autonomous legal order, erode in later cases and it would finally disappear.[146]

18.2.1.2. Solange I: *Protection of German Fundamental Rights*

It was in the case *Internationale Handelsgesellschaft*,[147] the very case which from the point of view of Community law is the leading case on the ultimate supremacy of Community law over the national constitutions,[148]

---

[145] See J Kokott, 'German Constitutional Jurisprudence and European Integration', 2 *EPL*, 1996, 237 and 413, at 246.

[146] J Kokott, 'German Constitutional Jurisprudence and European Integration', 2 *EPL*, 1996, 237, at 246.

[147] *Bundesverfassungsgericht*, decision of 27 May 1974, *Internationale Handelsgesellschaft mbH v Einfuhr- und Vorratsstelle für Getreide und Futtermittel (Solange I)*, BverGE 37, 271; [1974] 2 CMLR 540; Oppenheimer, *The Cases*, 419.

[148] Case 11/70 *International Handelsgesellschaft* [1970] ECR 1125.

that the *Bundesverfassungsgericht* revolted against the Court of Justice and proclaimed that it retained jurisdiction to ensure the protection of constitutional fundamental rights in Germany.[149] The case is well-known, and the whole story will not be repeated here,[150] but some comments may be made. First, it should be noted that the judgment did not come as a complete surprise: it had been announced in the *EEC Regulations Constitutionality case*; it was also prepared in the German political community, uneasy about the lack of basic rights protection and of democracy at the Community level.[151] Second, it is fascinating to see the role of instigator, played by the referring court, the *Verwaltungsgericht Frankfurt*, which 'orchestrated' the entire conflict. The *Verwaltungsgericht* referred the issue of the validity of the system of export licences and deposits provided for in a Council regulation on the common organisation of the market in cereals to the Court of Justice, indicating that it had never, itself, accepted the legality of the provisions at issue. It stated that although Community law was not German law, it must nevertheless respect the elementary, fundamental rights guaranteed by the German Constitution and the essential structural principles of national law. The Court of Justice, in a short and lucid judgment, asserted the priority of Community law over the national Constitutions, but replaced the protection offered by the German Constitution by the general principles of Community law.[152] In the case at hand, however, fundamental rights were not infringed, and the validity of the regulation was upheld. Dissatisfied by the answer of the Court of Justice, the *Verwaltungsgericht* brought the case before the *Bundesverfassungsgericht*, and urged the Constitutional Court to assume jurisdiction.

---

[149] The case goes under the nickname *Solange I*, 'Solange', after the promise of the Constitutional Court that it only provisionally stepped in in order to protect fundamental rights *as long as* the protection of fundamental rights was not sufficient under Community law, 'I', because it was the first in a line of cases. *Solange I* was followed by *Solange II, Vielleicht*, a discussion calling for *Solange III*, a *Wenn-nicht-Beschluss* aso.

[150] For those who are not familiar with the case, this was the conclusion drawn by the BVerfG: 'The result is: As long as the integration process has not progressed so far that Community law also receives a catalogue of fundamental rights decided on by a parliament and of settled validity, which is adequate in comparison with the catalogue of fundamental rights contained in the Constitution, a reference by a court in the Federal Republic of Germany to the Bundesverfassungsgericht in judicial review proceedings, following the obtaining of a ruling of the European Court under Art. 177 of the Treaty, is admissible and necessary if the German court regards the rule of Community law which is relevant to its decision as inapplicable in the interpretation given by the European Court, because and in so far as it conflicts with one of the fundamental rights in the Constitution', translation taken from Oppenheimer, The Cases, 401, at 452.

[151] See K Alter, *Establishing the Supremacy of European Law. The Making of an International Rule of Law in Europe* (Oxford, OUP, 2001) at 87 *et seq.*

[152] It has been argued that by asserting the supremacy of Community law over the national Constitutions the way it did in *International Handelsgesellschaft*, the Court had gone too far and had stepped onto the Constitutional Court's own turf. *Solange I* was designed to let the ECJ know that the BVerfG would not see its authority subjugated. See K Alter, *Establishing the Supremacy of European Law. The Making of an International Rule of Law in Europe* (Oxford, OUP, 2001) at 91.

The *Bundesverfassungsgericht* grasped the opportunity to limit the 'ultimate supremacy' of Community law over the German Constitution. Yet, the Court was keen to point to the limited effect of its judgment. First, it stressed that the decision concerned only conflicts between the fundamental rights contained in the Constitution (not the entire Constitution) and rules of secondary Community law (not the Treaty). Second, in principle, each court was competent in its own field, and they would concern themselves with the concordance of the two systems. Only where this would be unsuccessful, would a conflict arise. Third, the *Bundesverfassungsgericht* stated that it would never rule on the *validity* of a rule of Community law, but only on its *applicability* in the German legal order by the German authorities.[153] Yet, its message was clear: Fundamental rights could be protected in many ways, and the European Court may also claim jurisdiction: *'On the other hand, only the Bundesverfassungsgericht is entitled, within the framework of the powers granted to it in the Constitution, to protect the fundamental rights guaranteed in the Constitution. No other court can deprive it of this duty imposed by constitutional law'*.[154] Four, the Constitutional Court insisted that the assumption that Community law must always be supreme, otherwise its very existence would be at stake, was exaggerated: Community law was not put in question, when it was, in exceptional cases, not permitted to prevail over entrenched constitutional law. Finally, the national courts would always first have to refer the issue to the Kirchberg, and the Constitutional Court equally considered itself subject to Article 177 of the Treaty (Article 234 EC) and bound by the case law of the Court of Justice.[155] The reasoning of the Court was based on an interpretation of Article 24 of the Basic Law read in the context of the entire Constitution, and more specifically, the fundamental rights, which form an inalienable essential feature of the German Basic Law. Article 24 could not allow for transfers of *Hoheitsrechte* that would infringe upon fundamental rights contained in the Constitution.

Three judges dissented. They considered the decision of the majority to be wrong under the German Constitution and argued that it constituted an inadmissible trespass on the jurisdiction reserved to the European Court, the recognition of which was dictated by Article 24 of the Constitution.[156] While the majority in the *Bundesverfassungsgericht* had tried to demonstrate the limited nature of the German constitutional exceptions to the ultimate supremacy of Community law, the judgment

---

[153] For a critique of this distinction from the point of view of Community law, see *above*.
[154] Oppenheimer, *The Cases*, 401, at 449.
[155] This is no longer the case, see Chapter 13 above.
[156] Dissenting opinion of Judges Rupp, Hirsch and Wand, in Oppenheimer, *The Cases*, 452, at 460.

was considered as disloyal, a betrayal, a threat to the primacy of Community law.[157] The Commission even asked the German Government to distance itself from the judgment, under the threat of commencing infringement proceedings against the Government.[158]

18.2.1.3. Solange II: *Jurisdiction Suspended*

In the *Solange II* decision,[159] handed down twelve years later,[160] the *Bundesverfassungsgericht* recognised the European Court as an effective guardian of fundamental rights, and while not giving up its own jurisdiction to review the applicability of Community law in Germany entirely, it stated that it would not exercise it *as long as* ('solange') the Communities, and in particular the Court of Justice, would generally ensure an effective protection of the basic rights against acts of the Communities, which was to be regarded as substantially similar to the protection of fundamental rights required unconditionally by the Basic Law, and so far as the essential content of fundamental rights would generally be safeguarded.[161]

---

[157] Among many others M Zuleeg, 'Das Bundesverfassungsgericht als Hüter der Grundrechte gegenüber der Gemeinschaftsgewalt', *DÖV*, 1975, 44; G Cohen Jonathan, 'Cour constitutionnelle allemande et règlements communautaires', *CDE*, 1975, 173; D Soulas de Russel and U Engles, 'L'intégration de l'Europe à l'heure de la décision de la Cour constitutionnelle fédérale du 24 mai 1974', *RIDC*, 1975, 377; CD Ehlermann, 'Primauté du droit communautaire mise en danger par la Cour constitutionnelle fédérale allemande', *RMC* 1975, 10; Darras and Pirotte, 'La Cour constitutionnelle allemande a-t-elle mise en danger la primauté du droit communautaire?', *RTDeur*, 1976, 415.

[158] On the basis of interviews with current and former officials at the German Ministry of Justice and of Economics, Karen Alter claims that in exchange for dropping the infringement proceedings, the German Government promised to work to ensure that the Constitutional Court did not carry out its threat; K Alter, *op. cit.*, at 93; see also CD Ehlermann, 'Primauté du droit communautaire maise en danger par la Cour constitutionnelle fédérale allemande', *RMC*, 1975, 10, at 17–19.

[159] *Bundesverfassungsgericht*, decision of 22 October 1986, *Wünsche Handelsgesellschaft (Solange II)*, 73 BVerfGE 339; [1987] 3 CMLR 225; Oppenheimer, *The Cases*, 461.

[160] The decision was prepared in other decisions, such as *Bundesverfassungsgericht*, decision of 25 July 1979, *Vielleicht ('maybe')*, BVerfGE 52, 187; [1980] 2 CMLR 531 (the *Bundesverfassungsgericht* does not have jurisdiction of declare provisions of primary Community law inapplicable in Germany in contradiction to an interpretation by the European Court; the question whether and to what extent, having regard to legal and political developments in the Community, the principles laid down in *Solange I* still applied, was expressly left open). The case was seen as a reaction to the criticism of *Solange I*, see J Kokott, 'German Constitutional Jurisprudence and European Integration: Part I', *EPL*, 1996, 237, at 248; and *Bundesverfassungsgericht*, decision of 23 June 1981, *Eurocontrol*, BVerf GE 58, 1 (this decision did not concern Community law, but it did demonstrate the willingness of the Constitutional Court to relax the requirements for the protection of fundamental rights offered by an international organisation).

[161] *Bundesverfassungsgericht*, decision of 22 October 1986, *Solange II*, Oppenheimer, *The Cases*, 462 at 494.

What had changed during the twelve years between *Solange I* and *Solange II*?[162] The Constitutional Court stated that in the meantime a measure of protection of fundamental rights had been established which in its conception, substance and manner of implementation was essentially comparable with the standards provided for in the Constitution.[163] All the main institutions had since then acknowledged in a legally, significant manner that they would be guided by respect for fundamental rights, as established by the constitutions of the Member States and by the ECHR. The Court of Justice had done a good job in formulating, consolidating and adequately guaranteeing this standard of fundamental rights,[164] all Member States had, since 1974 acceded to the ECHR and the accessions had been approved by their Parliaments. In those circumstances, the prerequisite of a catalogue of fundamental rights decreed by a Parliament could be dropped. Although the *Bundesverfassungsgericht* took a step back and promised that it would not in each and every case determine whether fundamental rights had been infringed, it could not resist urging the Court of Justice to pursue a high level of protection,[165] and insisted that in exceptional cases it could step in again, if protection of fundamental rights were to decline generally.[166]

---

[162] Other factors, not mentioned by the *Bundesverfassungsgericht*, but which may have influenced the Court in changing its position are mentioned by J Kokott, 'German Constitutional Jurisprudence and European Integration II', 2 *EPL*, 1996, 413, at 422–23, such as the change in the composition of the Bench; the changed mood in European integration by the mid-eigthies and in the doctrinal debate.

[163] *Ibidem*, at 487.

[164] The Bundesverfassungsgericht paid particular attention to the Nold judgment of the ECJ, Case 4/73 *Nold* [1974] ECR 491, where, so it said, the ECJ took a crucial step from the viewpoint of the Constitution where it stated that it had to start from the common constitutional traditions of the Member States. This is an odd remark. What was new in *Nold* was not the reference to the common constitutional traditions of the Member States (that had also been done before, for instance in the ECJ's judgment in *Internationale Handelsgesellschaft*, in the very case which led the BVerfG to decide *Solange I*). New, in *Nold*, was the reference to international treaties on fundamental rights as an additional source of inspiration. In addition, *Nold* was decided two weeks before the BVerfG handed its *Solange I* decision. The minority, in its dissenting, opinion knew the decision of the ECJ and referred to it in its dissenting opinion. Or did *Nold* come too late to change the opinion of the majority? Did they not trust the good intentions of the ECJ?

[165] Above, at 493.

[166] This 'threat' was repeated in other cases, so *Bundesverfassungsgericht*, decision of 12 May 1989, *M GmbH and other v Bundesregierung (tobacco labelling directive)*, BVerfGE 80, 74; [1990] 1 CMLR 570, discussed before in Chapter 15; '*In so far as the directive may infringe the basic constitutional standards of Community law the European Court of Justice ensures legal protection of rights. If the constitutional standards laid down as unconditional by the German Constitution should not be satisfied by this route, recourse can be had to the Federal Constitutional Court*'. The BVerfG did not deal with the difficulty that under Community law, individuals cannot directly challenge the legality of directives under the restrictive case law on Article 230(4) EC (that was, of course, not the issue in this case). In addition, and in contrast to what it had said in *Solange II*, the BVerfG implied that it would assume competence to protect fundamental rights in individual cases, see also G Nicolaysen, 'Tabakrauch, Gemeinschaftsrecht und Grundgesetz', *EuR*, 1989, 215. The case is also referred to as the '*Wenn-nicht-beschluss*', see J Kokott, 'German Constitutional Jurisprudence and European Integration', 2 *EPL*, 1996, 237, at 250.

18.2.1.4. Kloppenburg: Kompetenz Kompetenz *Announced*

The peace-offering to the Court of Justice, and the solution to the conflict resulting from *Solange I* was a procedural one, and was not based on a new approach on substance where, in fact, *Solange II* does not differ from *Solange I*.[167] Between I and II lies only the goodwill of the *Bundesverfassungsgericht* not to exercise its jurisdiction. This friendly attitude of the German Court was even more obvious, at first sight, in *Kloppenburg*, where it forced the recalcitrant *Bundesfinanzhof* to accept the case law of the Court of Justice on the direct effect of directives, and accepted that the Court of Justice could develop the law and confirmed and the European Court's position as a lawful judge under the German Constitution.[168] Yet, the case also sowed the seeds for its *Kompetenz-Kompetenz* doctrine, which would be developed in the *Maastricht Urteil* only a few years later. In *Kloppenburg*, the *Bundesfinanzhof* had been of the opinion that the case law of the European Court on the direct effect of directives transgressed its powers under Article 24(1) of the Basic Law and was therefore not covered by the German law giving effect to the Treaty. The Federal Constitutional Court reviewed whether the Court of Justice had, by granting direct effect to directives, developed the law to the effect of exceeding its sovereign rights assigned to it, and found that it had not. It stated: '(..) *Zwar ist es auch verfassungsrechtlich erheblich, ob eine zwischenstaatliche Einrichtung im Sinne des Art. 24 Abs. 1 GG sich in den Grenzen der ihr übertragenen Hoheitsrechte hält oder aus ihnen ausbricht* [references to Solange I, Eurocontrol, and Solange II, MC]. *Der Gemeinschaft ist durch den EWG-Vertrag nicht eine Rechtsprechungsgewalt zur unbegrenzten Kompetenzerweiterung übertragen worden. Die Gemeinschaft ist kein souveräner Staat im Sinne des Völkerrechts* [reference omitted, MC], *dem eine Kompetenz-Kompetenz über innere Angelegenheiten zukäme. (..) Nach wie vor sind die Mitgliedstaaten im Rahmen des allgemeinen Völkervertragsrechts die Herren der Gemeinschaftsrechtsverträge, wie nicht zuletzt* [the SEA, MC] *belegt'.*[169]

---

[167] *Bundesverfassungsgericht, Solange II*, Oppenheimer, *The Cases*, 461, at 485: 'The power conferred by Article 24(1) of the Constitution, however, is not without limits under constitutional law. The provision does not confer a power to surrender by way of ceding sovereign rights to international institutions the identity of the prevailing constitutional order of the Federal Republic by breaking into its basic framework, that is, into the structure which makes it up'. That basic framework in any case contained the legal principles underlying the constitutional provisions on fundamental rights. The Court found support in the similar position adopted by the Italian *Corte costituzionale*.

[168] Discussed in Chapter 13 above.

[169] *Bundesverfassungsgericht*, decision of 8 April 1987, *Kloppenburg*, BVerfGE 75, 223; [1988] 3 CMLR 1; Oppenheimer, *The Cases*, 496.

18.2.1.5. *The* Maastricht Urteil: *Judicial Review of Secondary European Law*

Doctrinal reactions to *Solange II* were predominantly positive,[170] but by the end of the nineteen eighties and in the beginning of the nineties,[171] there was a call for a *Solange III* decision, for a renewed activity of the *Bundesverfassungsgericht* in the protection of fundamental rights within the scope of Community law. Then came the *Maastricht-Urteil*,[172] which has become known as the German Constitutional Court's most defiant and critical commentary on the case law of the Court of Justice,[173] and on the European Union taken as a whole. Formally, the case was concerned with the question of the constitutionality of the Treaty of Maastricht,[174] but the Court also seized the opportunity to elaborate on a series of other issues, among which its own jurisdiction to review the validity[175] of secondary Community law[176] in two areas, one concerning the protection of fundamental rights (the line of *Solange I* and *II*),[177] the second relating to *Kompetenz Kompetenz* (a sequel to *Kloppenburg*). What is striking is that in both cases, the intervention of the *Bundesverfassungsgericht* appears no longer to be restricted to an indirect review of secondary law through the national application, but the Court equally perceives direct review of the European measure itself as a possibility.

---

[170] See J Kokott, 'German Constitutional Jurisprudence and European Integration II', 2 *EPL*, 1996, 413, at 427–8;

[171] What instigated the renewed call for constitutional protection were two decisions of the BVerfG, one concerning the tobacco labelling directive case and the other relating to the TV broadcasting directive, discussed above under Chapter 17, which left a gap in the judicial review system given the alleged insufficient protection offered by the ECJ, see e.g. R Scholz, 'Wie lange bis Solange III?', *NJW*, 1990, 941; R Streinz, '*Bundesverfassungsrechtlicher Grundrechtsschutz und Europäisches Gemeinschaftsrecht*, 1989; reactions by U Everling, 'Brauchen wir "Solange III"? Zu den Forderungen nach Revision der rechtsprechung des Bundesverfassungsgerichts', *EuR*, 1990, 195 and C Tomuschat, 'Aller guten Dinge sind III?', *EuR*, 1990, 340; C-D Ehlermann, 'Zur Diskussion um einen "Solange III" – Beschluss: Rechtspolitische Pesrpektiven aus der Sicht des Gemeinschaftsrechts', *EuR*, 1991, 27, in answer to P Kirchhof, 'Deutsches Verfassungsrecht und Europäisches Gemeinschaftsrecht', *EuR*, 1991, 11 (He concluded: '*dreimal solange, aber nicht "Solange III"'*, at 25, suggesting that, besides the fundamental rights issue, there were more conditions, more 'solanges', relating to the principle of enumerated powers and the question of *ultra vires* acts).

[172] *Bundesverfassungsgericht*, decision of 12 October 1993, *Maastricht Urteil*, BVerfGE 89, 155; [1994] 1 CMLR 57; Oppenheimer, *The Cases*, 526.

[173] K Alter, *Establishing the Supremacy of European Law. The Making of an International Rule of Law in Europe*, (Oxford, OUP, 2001), at 105.

[174] It has therefore been considered above in Chapter 4.

[175] Or applicability; however, while the distinction may make sense from a specific national perception of the relationship between national and Community law, it does not make any difference in practical effect and from the point of view of Community law, whether a national court declares a Community rule inapplicable or invalid.

[176] Only this aspect of the case is discussed here.

[177] The *Maastricht Urteil* is sometimes referred to as *Solange III* and much of the debate on the passages concerning fundamental rights in the judgment centre around the question whether *Maastricht* was a retreat from *Solange II* to *Solange I*, and whether it confirmed or distinguished *Solange II*.

18.2.1.5.1. Judicial Protection of Basic Rights against Secondary Community Law

With respect to the fundamental rights issue, the constitutional environment had changed since *Solange II* in that the new Article 23 now proclaimed that Germany participated in the development of a European Union which guarantees a protection of basic rights essentially comparable to that of the Basic Law. Nevertheless, the *Bundesverfassungsgericht* did not pay much attention to the newly inserted Article, and proceeded as if the Basic Law had not been amended. The *Bundesverfassungsgericht* confirmed its *Solange* case law stating that it may exercise its jurisdiction over the applicability of secondary Community law, in the light of the basic rights enshrined in the German Constitution. The passage is not entirely clear: what exactly did the Constitutional Court mean when it spoke of a relationship of co-operation with the Court of Justice? Would it offer protection in each and every case, or only guard the general level of protection? What exactly did the German Constitutional Court imply when it said that it would protect fundamental rights, not only as against acts of the German authorities implementing or applying Community law which allegedly infringes basic rights? Much ink has been spilt on it, but, given the 2000 *Bananas* and *Alcan* decisions, there is not much point dwelling on it here.

18.2.1.5.2. Judicial Protection of Basic Rights against Acts Adopted in the Framework of the Second and Third Pillar

With respect to acts adopted in the framework of CFSP and JHA, the *Bundesverfassungsgericht* in its *Maastricht Urteil* stated that the exclusion of the Court of Justice from the second and third pillar in Article L of the Treaty of Maastricht did not lead to any gaps in judicial protection. Articles A through F of the Treaty did not contain any basis for actions of any kind affecting fundamental rights. Defining *common positions* under CFSP and JHA in no way imposed on the individual binding obligations which could affect their fundamental rights. Joint actions and measures adopted to implement co-operation in the field of JHA could not have direct effect and claim supremacy over national law. Conventions adopted in the framework of JHA could give the Court of Justice jurisdiction and in addition, their ratification may also be examined by the *Bundesverfassungsgericht*. If joint actions and measures under the second and third pillar would commit the Member States to interfere with basic rights, all such interferences carried out in Germany would be subject to full scrutiny by the German courts. The protection of fundamental rights in Germany would not be interfered with by any supranational or international law claiming precedence. If implementation nationally would violate fundamental rights, constitutional law would prohibit it. Finally, where second or third pillar decisions were transposed by a Community act, for instance in the case of economic sanctions, and basic rights were interfered with, the Court of Justice, or failing that, the *Bundesverfassungsgericht* would provide adequate protection of fundamental rights. In sum, the *Bundesverfassungsgericht* and the Court of Justice would complement one another in a relationship of co-operation designed to guarantee protection of basic rights.[178]

18.2.1.5.3. Kompetenz Kompetenz

The issue of *Kompetenz Kompetenz* is a complicated one and may need some explanation,[179] especially since the notion is, throughout the judgment, used in two related but different meanings. Simply put, *Kompetenz Kompetenz* is the 'competence to decide on competences'. A further distinction must be made between constitutional *Kompetenz Kompetenz*[180] and judicial *Kompetenz Kompetenz*. The former relates to the ultimate authority to distribute competences in a division of powers structure. The latter relates to the question as to which court has ultimate judicial authority to decide disputes concerning the extent of competences in such structure. These questions, which emerge in any vertical division of powers system at some stage, had been dormant in the Community, but they were out there and had been signalled by some.[181] Nevertheless, it will not have been clear to everyone that the issue in the *Foto-Frost* decision of the Court of Justice, decided already in 1987, was really about judicial *Kompetenz Kompetenz*: The Court ruled that it had exclusive jurisdiction to rule on the legality and validity of Community law, and under Article 230 EC one of the grounds of invalidity is precisely the lack of competence.[182]

---

[178] Paraphrased from the *Maastricht Urteil*, Oppenheimer, *The Cases*, 526, at 546–8.

[179] An analysis in German historical context is offered by P Lerche, '"Kompetenz-Kompetenz" und das Maastricht-Urteil des Bundesverfassungsgerichts', in *Verfassungsrecht im Wandel. Wiedervereinigung Deutschlands, Deutschland in der Europäischen Union Verfassungsstaat und Föderalismus* (Stuttgart, Carl Heymanns, 1995) 409; the focus is not on judicial *Kompetenz-Kompetenz*.

[180] Weiler has termed this 'legislative' *Kompetenz-Kompetenz* and described it as the power to determine and extend its own jurisdiction, see JHH Weiler, 'The Autonomy of the Community Legal Order: Through the Looking Glass, in his *The Constitution of Europe*, (Cambridge, CUP, 1999) 286, at 312. I prefer the notion 'constitutional' over 'legislative', since it better reflects the fundamental nature of the issue and the level at which these decisions are made.

[181] From the German perspective: P Kirchhof, 'Deutsches Verfassungsrecht und Europäisches Gemeinschaftsrecht', *EuR*, 1991, 11; T Schilling, 'Die deutsche Verfassung und die Europäische Einigung', *AÖR*, 1991, 32; PM Huber, 'Bundesverfassungsgericht und Europäischer Gerichtshof als Hüter der Gemeinschaftsrechtlichen Kompetenzordnung', *AÖR*, 1991, 210; from the European perspective, see JHH Weiler, 'Journey to an Unknown Destination: A Retrospective and Prospective of the European Court of Justice in the Arena of Political Integration', *JCMS*, 1993, 417.

[182] 'Legality' is the language of Art. 230 EC; 'validity' is the notion used in Art. 234 EC. From its exclusive jurisdiction to rule on the legality of Community law in direct actions under Art. 230 EC the ECJ concluded that it must also have exclusive jurisdiction to rule on the validity of Community law and that therefore national courts must refer these questions to it, even the lower courts. The BVerfG would try to find a way out of the conflict by

One *caveat* is in place concerning the relationship between *Kompetenz Kompetenz* and supremacy. Supremacy implies that European law takes precedence over national law. However, it only does so when it has been validly adopted and is *intra vires*: An *ultra vires* European act cannot claim supremacy over national law.[183] The issue of judicial *Kompetenz Kompetenz* deals with the question who has jurisdiction to decide that an act is indeed *intra vires* and therefore supreme over conflicting national law.

From the point of view of European law, it appears to be accepted that the European Union and the Communities do not possess constitutional *Kompetenz Kompetenz*:[184] they have only enumerated powers, powers attributed to them, explicitly or implicitly,[185] by the Member States. They do not possess original jurisdiction: their powers derive from the Member States. In order for the powers of the Union and the Communities to be extended, a new transfer must take place from the Member States, through a Treaty amendment, following the prescribed procedure. On the other hand, the Court of Justice does possess judicial *Kompetenz Kompetenz*: it has been attributed jurisdiction, under Articles 220 EC[186]

---

indicating that it would not decide on the validity or legality of secondary law, but only on its *applicability* in Germany. From the point of view of European law, and in practical effect, there is no real distindtion between the two. The distinction only makes sense in from the national perspective, given a specific perception of the relationship between legal orders.

[183] In *Costa v ENEL* the Court held the Member States had limited their sovereign rights 'within limited fields'. Within those fields, Community law was to be supreme in the national legal order, but not outside these fields. That the Community had been expanding its 'fields' became clear in the changed language of the familiar passage in *Opinion 1/91 on the EEA Agreement* [1991] ECR I–6079, where the Court held that the member States had limited their sovereign rights 'in ever wider fields', at para 21.

[184] See also JHH Weiler, 'The Autonomy of the Community Legal Order: Through the Looking Glass', in JHH Weiler, *The Constitution of Europe* (CUP, Cambridge, 1999) 286, at 311–12; originally published as JHH Weiler and U Haltern, 'The Autonomy of the Community Legal Order Through the Looking Glass', 37 *Harvard Int Law J*, 1996, 411.

[185] The issue of implied powers will undoubtedly lie at the heart of the competence issue. It is accepted under international law that international organisations may have implied powers. In its Advisory Opinion in *International Court of Justice*, decision of 11 April 1949, *Reparations for Injuries Suffered in the Service of the UN*, [1949] ICJ 182, the ICJ stated that 'Under international law, the Organisation must be deemed to have those powers which, though not explitily provided in the Charter, are conferred upon it by necessary implication as being essential to the performance of its duties'. For Community law, the ECJ has accepted implied powers in Case 8/55 *Fédéchar* [1956] ECR 299 where it held that '*without having to take recourse to a wide interpretation it is possible to apply a rule of interpretation generally accepted in both international and national law, according to which the rules laid down by an international treaty or law presuppose the rules without which that treaty or law would have no meaning or could not be reasonably and usefully applied*'; implied treaty-making powers were accepted in Case 22/70 *Commission v Council (ERTA)* [1971] ECR 274; see also Case C–295/90 *European Parliament v Council* [1992] ECR I–4193; Joined Cases 281/85, 283–285/85 and 287/85, *Germany, France, The Netherlands, Denmark and United Kingdom v Commission* [1987] ECR 3203.

[186] Old Article 164 of the Treaty.

and Articles 230 and 234 EC to rule on the legality or validity of secondary European law, and, as the Court of Justice has emphasised in *Foto-Frost*, this jurisdiction is exclusive. Only the Court of Justice has jurisdiction to declare secondary law void or invalid, at the exclusion of national courts, of whatever rank. This is not an issue of supremacy, but one of jurisdiction. The Court of Justice possesses this exclusive jurisdiction because the Member States have attributed it in the Treaties, in Articles 220, 230 and 234 EC.

The *Bundesverfassungsgericht* in the *Maastricht Urteil* took a different approach.[187] It held, first, that Article F(3) of the EU Treaty (now Article 6(4) EU)[188] was not to be interpreted in the sense that the Union was granted (constitutional) *Kompetenz Kompetenz* and was therefore not unconstitutional. The ideas behind this view are present throughout the judgment, and, in my view, they are not problematic from the point of view of European law.[189] However, when it comes to the second issue, of judicial *Kompetenz Kompetenz*, the *Bundesverfassungsgericht* adopts a stance opposite to that of the European Court. The German Court, starting from the principles of enumerated powers and the dividing line between judicial development of the law – which it accepts[190] – and Treaty amendment, made it clear that should the Community institutions interpret rules conferring competence so as to extend the powers granted on a limited basis, amounting in effect to a Treaty amendment, rather than an interpretation thereof, such extension would not give rise to any binding effect for Germany. If the European institutions were to apply or extend the Union Treaty in some way which was no longer covered by the Treaty in the form which constituted the basis of the German law approving it, the resulting legal acts would not be binding on German

---

[187] Among the many comments, here are some that concentrate on the *Kompetenz-Kompetenz* issue: M Heintzen, 'Die "Herrschaft" über die Europäische Gemeinschaftsverträge – Bundesverfassungsgericht und Europäischer Gerichtshof auf Konfliktkurs?', *AÖR*, 1994, 564; F Schokweiler, 'Zur Kontrolle der Zuständigkeitsgrenzen der Gemeinschaft', *EuR*, 1996, 123; A Weber, 'Zur Kontrolle grundrechts – bzw. Kompetenzwidriger Rechtsakte der EG durch national Verfassungsgerichte, in O Due, M Lutter and J Schwarze (eds), *Festschrift für Ulrich Everling*, (Baden-Baden, Nomos, 1995), 1625; and, in a wider pespective, see M Kumm, 'Who is the Final Arbiter of Constitutionality in Europe? Three Conceptions of the Relationship Between the German Federal Constitutional Court and the European Court of Justice', 36 *CML Rev*, 1999, 351; CU Schmid, 'From Pont d'Avignon to Ponte Vecchio: The Resolution of Constitutional Conflicts between the European Union and the Member States through the Principles of Public International Law', *YEL*, 1998, 415.

[188] Now Art. 6(4) EU, which (then and now) provides: 'The Union shall provide itself with the means necessary to attain its objectives and carry though its policies'.

[189] The Member States as *Herren der Verträge*, the principle of enumerated powers, the qualification of the Union as a '*Staatenverbund*', the emphasis on the right to withdraw. What is disturbing is the tone, rather than the content.

[190] Under reference to its *Kloppenburg* decision, where it held that the ECJ had not transgressed its jurisdiction by granting direct effect to directives. It had developed the law, but within the limits of the powers conferred in the Treaties.

sovereign territory. The German legal order was opened up for European law, by virtue of Article 24(2) and now Article 23 of the German Basic Law, via the German Act approving and giving effect to the Treaty. *Ultra vires* acts, *'Ausbrechende Rechtsakte'*, could not be effective in the German legal order since they were not covered by the Act giving effect to the Treaty. The act concerned does not necessarily directly infringe the Constitution, and it is not clear, whether such act would also be unconstitutional.[191] But the German organs of State would be prevented, on constitutional ground, from applying those legal acts in Germany.[192] Accordingly, the Federal Constitutional Court could and would examine whether legal acts of the European institutions and bodies kept within or exceeded the limits of the sovereign rights granted to them.[193] The *Bundesverfassungsgericht* thus denied the exclusive jurisdiction of the Court of Justice to decide whether a particular measure had been validly adopted or was invalid for lack of competence. And the Court of Justice was warned: in the future, doctrines such as implied powers, *effet utile* or an extended use of Article 308 EC (then Article 235 of the EC Treaty), would not be acceptable where they would amount to an extension of transferred powers. Judge Kirchhof, who, as is well known, masterminded the judgment, further explained this element of the judgment extra-judicially. The German law approving and giving effect to the Treaty under Article 23 of the Basic Law operated as the bridge between the European and the German legal order, and all European measures would have to cross over the bridge in order to be effective in the German legal order. However, at the German end of the bridge, *'steht in einem kleinen Häuschen ein Wächter. Unauffällig und bescheiden freut er sich, dass auf dieser Brücke ein lebhafter Verkehr stattfindet, dass die Menschen sich begegnen, das die Wahren getauscht werden, dass Meinungen, Ideen und Kultur über diese Brücke laufen. Er wacht aber darüber, dass die Tragfähigkeit dieser Brücke nicht*

---

[191] See R Streinz, 'Das Maastricht-Urteil des Bundesverfassungsgericht', *EuZW*, 1994, 329, at 331. As a consequence, it is not clear whether only the BVerfG or all authorities should have jurisdiction to declare an act inapplicable.

[192] It was argued by some that since the BVerfG held that such acts were to be considered not to be binding and since the German organs would be prevented from applying them, all courts and all other authorities could make that decision unilaterally, without intervention of the BVerfG. Günter Hirsch referred to several instances where 'ordinary' courts had reviewed whether Community acts were *intra vires* and ironically stated, building on the image of the bridge: *'es herrscht in dem Brückenhäuschen ein ziemliches Gedränge, da dort nicht nur das BVerfG sitzt, sondern auch sämtliche deutschen Gerichte, vielleicht auch noch das Heer der deutschen Beamten, um zu prüfen, ob ein Gemeinschaftsrechtsakt passieren darf'*, G Hirsch, 'Europäischer Gerichtshof und Bundesverfassungsgericht – Kooperation oder Konfrontation', *NJW*, 1996, 2457, at 2461.

[193] Whether they are *'ausbrechende Rechtsakte'*; for a critique of the dramatic term, which, by and of itself would already make the jurisdiction of the BVerfG acceptable to prevent 'evil acts breaking out', see M Kumm, 'Who is the Final Arbiter of Constitutionality in Europe? Three Conceptions of the Relationship between the German Federal Constitutional Court and the European Court of Justice', 36 *CML Rev*, 1999, 351, at 364.

überfordert wird, dass die Brücke nicht zum Schaden der Mitgliedstaaten und zum Schaden des Europäisches Gemeinschaftsrechts zusammenbricht. In einigen Staaten ist dieser Wächter das Parlament. In Deutschland ist er in Letztverantwortung das Bundesverfassungsgericht'.[194]

Under European law, however, there must not, at the national end be a guardian of whatever kind.[195] Under the prevalent doctrines of direct effect, supremacy and given the exclusive jurisdiction of the Court of Justice, the guardian sits at the European end in the form of the Court of Justice which has sole jurisdiction to rule on the validity of Community law. The *Bundesverfassungsgericht* accepted the exclusive jurisdiction of the Court of Justice only within the limits of the powers transferred, thus only for those acts for which the bridge is *'tragfähig'*. Whether or not an act crosses the bridge was, according to the *Bundesverfassungsgericht*, a matter of German law.

18.2.1.6. *Television and Bananas I and II*

Going back to the period immediately after *Maastricht*, there were several cases that appeared to provide occasions for the Federal Constitutional Court to apply *Maastricht*. In the dispute surrounding the TV broadcasting directive, the *Land* Bavaria attempted to block the adoption of the Community Directive before the *Bundesverfassungsgericht* in interlocutory proceedings.[196] The final decision was handed down only in 1995, after the introduction of the new Article 23 of the Basic Law[197] and the ruling in *Maastricht*.[198] The dispute was related to the issue of competence, in the relation Member States–Community, but was further complicated by an

---

[194] P Kirchhof, in *Diritto comunitario europeo e diritto nazionale*. Atti del Seminario internazionale, Roma, Palazzo della Consulta, 14–15 Luglio 1995 (Milano, Giuffrè, 1997) at 62. During this session of the Conference of Constitutional Courts, Judge Kirchhof defended the position adopted by the Bundesverfassungsgericht. Most of the other Judges present disagreed with the view of the BVerfG on Kompetenz Kompetenz.

[195] It is not clear which system Kirchhof is referring to when he argues that in some Member States Parliament sits as guardian. That may be true before the adoption of a European act, but not afterwards (this is different only in the case of conventions or other decisions which need ratification, but that is not apparently what Kirchhof was referring to).

[196] *Bundesverfassungsgericht*, decision of 11 April 1989, *TV broadcasting directive – interim measures*, BVerfGE 80, 74; [1990] 1 CMLR 649, discussed in Chapter 15.

[197] On the problem of German federalism in the context of European integration after the adoption of Art. 23 GG, see J Kokott, 'Federal States in Federal Europe: The German Länder and Problems of European Integration', in A Jyränki (ed), *National Constitutions in the Era of Integration* (The Hague, Kluwer, 1999) 175.

[198] *Bundesverfassungsgericht*, decision of 22 March 1995, *TV broadcasting directive*, BVerfGE 92, 203; the case had been pending for six years; comments in M Herdegen, 'After the TV Judgment of the German Constitutional Court: Decision-Making within the EU Council and the German *Länder*', 32 *CML Rev*, 1995, 1369; J Gerkrath, 'L'arrêt du Bundesverfassungsgericht du 22 mars 1995 sur la directive "télévision sans frontières". Les difficultés de la répartition des compétences entre trois niveaux de législation', *RTDeur*, 1995, 539.

internal federal issue. It concerned the question of the responsibilities of the federal Government where the Community claims jurisdiction in a matter falling within the province of the *Länder* on the domestic plane, where the existence or the extent of the Community jurisdiction is in dispute between the Federation and the *Länder*.[199] The *Bundesverfassungsgericht* decided the case on the basis of German constitutional law, and did not address the issue of the *Kompetenz* of the Community. The silence of the Constitutional Court may be seen as a voluntary retreat and an attempt to harmonise relations with the Court of Justice,[200] or at the least to reduce the tension.

In the *Bananas I* and *II* decisions the *Bundesverfassungsgericht* avoided an open and direct conflict with the Court of Justice, but it did incite the German courts to offer judicial protection in cases where national courts were not so empowered under Community law, and insisted that German courts may find the *Bananas* regulation contrary to WTO law and therefore inapplicable in Germany for the time being. The Constitutional Court even interfered without controlling whether the general standard of protection in the Community had fallen. In *Bananas I* and *II* the *Bundesverfassungsgericht* directed the German ordinary courts in their dispute with the Court of Justice, in the area of basic rights and WTO law.

18.2.1.7. *Excursion:* Bananas, *a Road Map*

Reference has been made on several occasions to the banana saga. The *'feuilleton de la banane'*[201] has given rise to a plethora of court proceedings before numerous courts in various Member States, before the European Courts and the GATT and WTO dispute settlement bodies. For the sake of clarity, it may be helpful to present a road map of the court decisions handed in the dispute,[202] which raises so many fundamental issues of European constitutional law, that an entire course on Community law could be built on it. The now more than ten-year-old dispute arose from Council Regulation 404/93 introducing a common organisation of the market in bananas.[203] The Regulation that, in short, provided protection

---

[199] The *Land* Bavaria requested a declaration to the effect that the decision of the Government to vote in favour of the directive, as well as the consent itself violated its rights under the Basic Law. Furthermore, it requested that the directive be treated as inapplicable within Germany, or, alternatively, that the Federation must recognise such inapplicability. Several *Länder* joined the Bavarian action.

[200] So M Herdegen, 'After the TV Judgment of the German Constitutional Court: Decision-Making within the EU Council and the German Länder', 32 *CML Rev*, 1995, 1369, at 1379.

[201] C Grewe, 'Le "traité de paix" avec la Cour de Luxembourg: l'arrêt de la Cour constitutionnelle allemande du 7 juin 2000 relatif au règlement du marché de la banane', 37 *RTDeur*, 2001, 1, at 1.

[202] Space precludes a complete overview of all the national, European and WTO decisions relating to the regulation. The road map is restricted to the general decisions and the cases relating to German importers, especially *Atlanta* and *T Port* and their allies, in a more or less chronological way.

for the Community and ACP bananas at the expense of the so-called dollar-bananas, was adopted by qualified majority against the votes of Belgium, The Netherlands and Germany. Its validity in Community, national constitutional, GATT 1947 and WTO law would be challenged, before judicial instances at national, Community and WTO level.

Both the German importers and the German Government brought actions for the annulment of the Regulation before the Court of Justice. The former actions were considered inadmissible for lack of standing;[204] in the case brought by Germany, the Court upheld the regulation's legality.[205] German importers also brought proceedings before German courts, against the application of the Regulation in Germany, claiming infringements of their fundamental rights[206] and WTO law. Initially the applicants were unsuccessful. The *Verwaltungsgericht Frankfurt* made a reference to the European Court, asking whether the regulation was valid, and whether it was allowed under Community law to suspend the application of the regulation.[207] Yet, the applicants then called upon the *Bundesverfassungsgericht* against the decision of the *Verwaltungsgerichtshof Kassel* that had rejected the allegation that the regulation should be considered inapplicable.[208] The *Bundesverfassungsgericht*[209] dismissed the

---

[203] Council Regulation 404/93 on the common organisation of the market in bananas OJ 1993 L 47/1; on the circumstances surrounding the adoption of the regulation, see W Wessels, *Das Bananendiktat* (Campus, 1995).

[204] By Order of of 21 June 1993, the ECJ dismissed the application for annulment as inadmissible, Case C–286/93 *Atlanta v Council and Commission*. The action was allowed to continue with respect to the action in damages, OJ 1993 C 215/13. That part of the case was transferred to the CFI by order of 27 September 1993, OJ 1993 C 303/6. On 11 December 1996, the CFI dismissed the case in damages, Case T–521/93 *Atlanta v Council and Commission* [1996] ECR II-1707, declaring that no illegality imposing non-contractual liability could be found, under reference to the judgments handed down before, and upholding the legality of the Regulation. The applicants appealed the decision to the ECJ, which in essence upheld the judgment of the CFI, Case C–104/97 P *Atlanta at al. v Commission and Council* [1999] ECR I–6983.

[205] Previously, the ECJ had, by Order of 29 June 1993, dismissed the application for interim measures, Case C–230/93 R *Germany v Council* [1993] ECR I–3667. In Case C–280/93 *Germany v Council* [1994] ECR I–4973 the ECJ upheld the Regulation's legality and rejected claims based *inter alia* on infringement of legal basis requirement, breach of fundamental rights and general principles of law, infringement of international obligations under the Lomé Convention, infringement of GATT rules and infringement of the Banana Protocol annexed to the Treaty in 1958; very critical U Everling, 'Will Europe Slip on Bananas? The Bananas Judgment of the Court of Justice and National Courts', 33 *CML Rev*, 1996, 401.

[206] Mostly the right to property, right to conduct a business, right to legitimate expectations.

[207] Cases C–465/93 *Atlanta and others v Bundesamt für Ernährung und Forstwirtschaft* [1995] ECR I–3761 (interim measures) and C–466/93 *Atlanta and others v Bundesamt für Ernährung und Forstwirtschaft* [1995] ECR I–3799 (validity of regulation 404/93 upheld), both decided on 9 November 1995.

[208] The VHG Kassel had ruled that while it had jurisdiction to offer interim relief where the validity of Community law was in doubt, that was not the case in this instance, since the ECJ had upheld the validity of the Regulation in Case C–280/93 *Germany v Council* [1994] ECR I–4973, see NJW, 1995, at 950.

[209] *Bundesverfassungsgericht*, decision of 25 January 1995, *Bananas I (T Port)*, NJW, 1995, 950; EuZW, 1995, 126, commented in M Nettesheim, 'Art. 23 GG, nationale Grundrechte und

application as inadmissible, and remanded the case to the *Verwaltungsgerichtshof Kassel*. It held that the German courts must protect the fundamental rights of individual importers threatened by bankruptcy, and that the regulation was open enough to allow for transitory measures in hardship cases, and instructed the administrative courts to grant interim relief under the German Constitution. Particularly striking is what is missing: the Court did not make a reference under Article 234(3) EC; it did not mention its decision in *Maastricht*, even though this must have been a case of the kind contemplated in that decision; the Court did not mention the case law of the Court of Justice relating to interim relief involving the suspension of the application of Community law; and finally, the Court did not control whether the essence of the fundamental right had been infringed and whether the fundamental rights protection in the Community was no longer in general sufficient. The *Verwaltungsgerichtshof* granted interim relief, granting additional licences, and referred questions to the Court of Justice relating to the powers of the national courts to grant interim relief and the validity of the regulation.[210]

Strengthened by that success, the plaintiffs requested clearance from the customs authorities for a consignment of bananas from Ecuador, without producing import licences or paying the customs duty due. Against the refusal of the Hauptzollamt Hamburg-Jonas, T. Port instituted a *Verfassungsbeschwerde* before the *Bundesverfassungsgericht*, which dismissed the case as inadmissible for lack of exhaustion of remedies.[211] It held that the plaintiffs must first make an application before the ordinary courts in order to safeguard their rights. Yet, it also stated that it was not impossible that the German court hearing the case for interim measures might, in view of the inconsistency of Regulation 404/93 and the obligations incumbent on Germany under GATT, decide not to apply the Regulation for the time being. It also pointed out that the validity of Commission regulation 478/95 had not yet been examined. The case then came before the *Finanzgericht Hamburg*, where T. Port argued that, although valid under Community law, Regulations 404/93 and 478/95 should be regarded as *ausbrechende Rechtsakte*, because of their violation of GATT. The same was also true for the judgment of the Court of Justice in *Germany v Council* upholding the validity of Regulation 404/93.[212] Those

EU-Recht', *NJW*, 1995, 2083; E Pache, 'Das Ende der Bananenmarktordnung?', *EuR*, 1995, 95; D Besse, 'Die Bananenmarktordung im Lichte deutscher Grundrechte und das Kooperationsverhältnis zwischen BVerfG und EuGH, *Juristische Schulung*, 1996, 396.

[210] Case C–68/95 *T Port v Bundesanstalt für Landwirtschaft und Ernährung (T Port I)* [1996] ECR I–6065; judgment would be handed on 26 November 1996.

[211] *Bundesverfassungsgericht*, decision of 26 April 1995, *Bananas II (T Port)*, EuZW, 1995, 412; the *Verfassungsbeschwerde* was directed against the negative decision of the customs authority and against Commission Regulation (EC) 478/95 of 1 March 1995 on additional rules for the application of Council Regulation (EEC) 404/93, OJ 1995 L 49/13.

[212] Case C–280/93 *Germany v Council* [1994] ECR II–4973.

legal measures, which undermined the substance of T. Port's fundamental rights, were thus not applicable in Germany. The *Finanzgericht Hamburg* referred several questions for preliminary ruling to the Court of Justice.[213] Shortly thereafter the European Court handed down judgment in two of the *Atlanta* cases, referred to it by the *Verwaltungsgericht Frankfurt*. The validity of Regulation 404/93 was, again, upheld,[214] as the referring court had not, according to the Court, raised any grounds of invalidity altering the Court's assessment in *Germany v Council*. The Court also elaborated on national courts' jurisdiction to grant interim relief, effectively suspending the application of a Community regulation.[215]

In the next judgment handed down one year later,[216] the first *T. Port* decision,[217] the Court of Justice openly showed its annoyance with the German courts,[218] which continued to dispute the validity of the Regulation, thereby effectively challenging the authority of the European Court, and offering protection to companies in ways it no longer considered acceptable under Community law, as they threatened the uniform

[213] The actual procedure was more complex: in a first case, the *FG Hamburg* referred questions for preliminary ruling to the ECJ (Case C–182/95 *T Port v Hauptzollamt Hamburg-Jonas*), *Finanzgericht Hamburg*, decision of 19 May 1995, EuZW, 1995, 413, insisting that the obligations imposed by GATT on Germany must, in accordance with Art. 234 of the Treaty (*old*, now Art. 308 EC), lead to the inapplicability of the Community Regulations. In addition, the court again referred the issue of the direct effect of GATT, indicating that under German law, GATT could most likely be invoked before the courts. Finally, the *Finanzgericht* added an ultimatum, indicating that after the case returned to it, it could seize the *Bundesverfassungsgericht*, which would then review whether there was indeed an *ausbrechende Rechtsakt* or whether the plaintiff's basic rights had been infringed. The decision was however overruled by the *Bundesfinanzhof*. The proceedings were stayed in Case C–182/95. Yet, in a decision handed down only a few months later the *Finanzgericht Hamburg* referred the same questions (Joined Cases C–364/95 and C–365/95 *T Port v Hauptzollamt Hamburg-Jonas*). This time the *Bundesfinanzhof* upheld the decision. Judgment would be handed down on 10 March 1998. Case C–182/93 was removed from the Court's register on 12 March 2001.

[214] Case C–466/93 *Atlanta and others v Bundesamt für Ernährung und Forstwirtschaft* [1995] ECR I–3799.

[215] Case C–465/93 *Atlanta and others v Bundesamt für Ernährung und Forstwirtschaft* [1995] ECR I–3761. The Court stated that interim measures could include the making of an order to the domestic authorities to provisionally disapply a regulation; it also insisted that the national courts must comply with the decisions of the European Courts.

[216] Case C–68/95 *T Port v Bundesanstalt für Landwirtschaft und Ernährung* [1996] ECR I–6065; commented in S Peers, 'Taking Supremacy Seriously', 23 *ELR*, 1998, 146.

[217] Numbering the *T Port* cases may give rise to confusion: they are not handed down in order of reference; they have been referred by different courts; some *T Port* cases were brought directly and at least one has been removed from the register.

[218] And the *Bundesverfassungsgericht*! Remember that the administrative courts had initially rejected all claims, and had only ordered the authorities to supply additional licences after the intervention of the *Bundesverfassungsgericht*, ordering the courts to offer interim relief in compliance with the right to effective judicial protection under the German Basic Law. The Constitutional Court had referred the case back to the VGH Kassel, which granted additional licences by way of interim relief, thereby suspending the application of Regulation 404/93, referring questions for preliminary ruling to the ECJ This was a very crowded reference: there were three courts in it right from the beginning, see S Peers, 'Taking Supremacy Seriously', 23 *ELR*, 1998, 146, at 154.

application of Community law and the exclusive jurisdiction of the Community institutions. Throughout the judgment the Court emphasised its exclusive jurisdiction to rule on the lawfulness of the Community institutions' action or failure to act. The Community institutions were required to act and provide transitory measures where the introduction of the common organisation of the market infringes certain traders' fundamental rights (and not the national courts or the national authorities), under supervision only of the Court of Justice.[219] Where the Commission had not yet acted, only the Court of Justice or the Court of First Instance could review an alleged failure to act. The Treaty did not provide for a reference for preliminary ruling by which a national court asks the Court of Justice to rule that an institution has failed to act. The individuals must turn to the Commission or the Court of First Instance, not to the national courts.[220]

A few weeks later, the Court of First Instance[221] dismissed the action for damages in the *Atlanta* line of cases and ruled that no illegality had been found so as to impose the non-contractual liability of the Community. The Court referred extensively to the judgments of the Court of Justice, in particular those upholding the validity of the Regulation.[222]

In the meantime, decisions had also been handed at GATT and WTO level. A GATT Panel had already on 18 November 1994,[223] so just after the Court of Justice had dismissed the claim brought by Germany, found the Community regulation of the banana market contrary to GATT rules. However, under the old GATT, the Community could effectively block the adoption of the decision. However, on 9 September 1997 the Appellate Body handed down a report[224] finding a substantive part of the regulation contrary to WTO rules.

---

[219] Paras. 39–40.

[220] By letter of 16 December 1996 the applicant requested the Commission rapidly to adopt measures applicable to cases of hardship and sought the allocation of additional import licences. The Commission did not define its position within two months following the request. T Port then brought an action for failure to act under Art. 175 of the Treaty (*old*, now Art. 232 EC). Since the Commission did issue a decision before the CFI could hand judgment, the case became without object, and the CFI held in an Order of 26 November 1997 that there was no need to adjudicate, Case T–39/97 *T Port v Commission* [1997] ECR II-2125. In its decision, the Commission rejected the requests made by T Port, which then instituted proceedings requesting the annulment of the Commission decision (Case T–251/97 *T Port v Commission*).

[221] Case T–521/93 *Atlanta and others v Council and Commission* [1996] ECR II-1707, judgment of 11 December 1996; the case was appealed to the Court of Justice, as Case C–104/97 P.

[222] Case C–280/93 *Germany v Council* [1994] ECR I- 4973 and Case 466/93 *Atlanta v Bundesamt für Ernährung und Forstwirtschaft* [1995] ECR I–3799.

[223] On 3 June 1993 a GATT Panel report had already found against prior national policies of various Member States, *DS* 23 /R, 3 June 1993; *DS* 38 /R of 18 November 1994 found against the Community system.

[224] WT/DS27/AB/R European Communities – Regime for the Importation, Sale and Distribution of Bananas, report of the Appellate Body of 9 September 1997, adopted by the Dispute Settlement Body on 25 September 1997; see WTO Panel report of 22 May 1997, WT/DS27/R European Communities – Regime for the Importation, Sale and Distribution of Bananas.

Yet, in the decision of 10 March 1998 handed down in the *T. Port* case[225] referred by the *Finanzgericht Hamburg*, the Court of Justice did not make any reference to the Appellate Body Report.[226] Nevertheless, the Court came to the same conclusions as the WTO Panel and the Appellate Body and found Commission Regulation 478/95 partially invalid.[227] Yet, the Court circumvented the problem of Article 234 of the EC Treaty (now Article 308 EC) in relation to GATT, which was the bottom line of the threatening reference by the *Finanzgericht*, by pointing to the (coincidental) fact that Ecuador was not a Party to GATT 1947 and had not become Party to GATT 1994 and Member of the WTO until 1996. It therefore did not have to enter into the issue of the direct effect of GATT. Yet, the WTO decision was there. In the appeal against the decision of the Court of First Instance in the case for compensation,[228] Atlanta's first plea was based on the decision of the WTO Dispute Settlement Body arguing that the decision placed beyond doubt the illegality of the common organisation of the market under Community law. However, as the plea was only raised before the Court at the stage of the reply before the Court, it was dismissed as inadmissible.[229] In the *T. Port* line of cases, the Court of First Instance rejected the action for annulment brought against the decision of the Commission refusing to grant additional import licences.[230]

On 7 June 2000, then, the *Bundesverfassungsgericht*[231] handed its third (and final?) *Bananas* judgment,[232] and held that the referring

[225] Joined Cases C–364/95 and C–365/95 *T Port v Hauptzollamt Hamburg-Jonas* [1998] ECR I–1023. On the same day, the Court also handed down judgment in Case C–122/95 *Germany v Council* [1998] I–973 in which Germany had sought the annulment of certain provisions of the decision of the Council concerning the conclusion on behalf of the European Community as regards matters within its competence of the agreements reached in the Uruguay Round multilateral negotiations (1986–1994) (OJ 1994 L 336, p 1), to the extent that the Council thereby approved the conclusion of the Framework Agreement on Bananas with the Republic of Costa Rica, the Republic of Colombia, the Republic of Nicaragua and the Republic of Venezuela. The ECJ partially annulled the decision.

[226] The Court of Justice was now under pressure from the German courts and from the WTO Appellate Body.

[227] See G Zonnekeyn, 'The Status of Adopted Panel and Appellate Body Reports in the European Court of Justice and the European Court of First Instance', 34(2) *JWT*, 2000, 93, at 103; see on this issue also N Lavranos, 'Die Rechtswirkung von WTO panel reports im Europäischen Gemeinschaftsrecht sowie im deutschen Verfassungsrecht', *EuR*, 1999, 289.

[228] Case C–104/97 P *Atlanta and others v Council and Commission* [1999] ECR I–6983, appeal against the decision in T–521/93 *Atlanta and Others v European Community* [1996] ECR II–1707.

[229] Paras. 17–23. The Court held that there was an inescapable and direct link between the WTO decision and the plea of breach of GATT raised before the CFI Yet, *'such a decision could only be taken into consideration if the Court of Justice had found GATT to have direct effect in the context of a plea alleging the invalidity of the common organisation of the market'*.

[230] Case T–251/97 *T Port v Commission* [2000] ECR II–1775.

[231] The judgment will be analysed further under Section 18.2.1.8. The focus here is on the effect of the judgment on the bananas saga itself, and less on the wider perspective.

[232] *Bundesverfassungsgericht*, decision of 7 June 2000, *Bananas III (Atlanta)*, see www .bundesverfassungsgericht.de; *EuZW*, 2000, 702; French version in 37 *RTDeur*, 2001, 155;

court[233] had not demonstrated that the protection of fundamental right in general had fallen below an acceptable standard. On the contrary, in the case at hand, the Court of Justice had in the *T. Port III* judgment[234] instructed the Commission to deal with transitory measures in hardship cases.[235] There was, therefore, no proof of a gap in the protection of basic rights. The *Bananas III* judgment is limited to the fundamental rights aspects of the case: it does not concern the issue of the *ausbrechende Rechtsakt* put forward by some of the other lower courts,[236] nor the issue of the obligations imposed on Germany under the WTO Agreements.

And so the tale continues.[237] T. Port continues to seek to rely on WTO rules in order to claim compensation for the loss suffered by the intro-

comments in F Mayer, 'Grundrechtsschutz gegen europäische Rechtsakte durch das BverfG: Zur Verfassungsmässigkeit der Bananenmarktordnung', *EuZW*, 2000, 685; A Peters, 'The Bananas Decision (2000) of the German Federal Constitutional Court: Towards Reconciliation with the European Court of Justice as regards Fundamental Rights Protection in Europe', 43 *German Yearbook of International Law*, 2000, 276; C Grewe, 'Le "traité de paix" avec la Cour de Luxembourg: L'arrêt de la Cour constitutionnelle allemande du 7 juin 2000 relatif au règlement du marché de la banane', 37 *RTDeur*, 2001, 1; U Elbers and N Urban, 'The Order of the German Federal Constitutional Court of 7 June 2000 and the Kompetenz Kompetenz in the European Judicial System', 7 *EPL*, 2001, 21; F Hoffmeister, case note Alcan and EC regulation on bananas, 38 *CML Rev*, 2001, 791; CU Schmidt, 'All Bark and No Bite: Notes on the federal Constitutional Court's 'Banana Decision'', 7 *ELJ*, 2001, 95.

[233] The *Verwaltungsgericht Frankfurt*.

[234] Case C–68/95 *T Port v Bundesanstalt für Landwirtschaft und Ernährung* [1996] ECR I–6065. In her comments on the *Bananas III* judgment, President Jutta Limbach of the *Bundesverfassungsgericht* emphasised the fact that the *T Port* judgment followed the *Bananas I* decision of the *Bundesverfassungsgericht*, and considered it an example of the '*konstruktive Gedankenaustausch im Kooperationsverhältnis*' between the ECJ and the national constitutional courts, J Limbach. *art. cit.*, at marginal number 26.

[235] The *Bundesverfassungsgericht* stated that the referring court should have recognised this and withdrawn the reference to the Constitutional Court, since its allegation that the regulation was unconstitutional related in particular to the absence of transitory measures in hardship cases. In any case, the court should have realised that the *T Port III* judgment of the ECJ proved it impossible to argue '*ein generelles Absinken des Grundrechtsstandards*' in the case law of the ECJ.

[236] These allegations are false: the Community did have jurisdiction to introduce the common organisation of the market in bananas (see also Case C–280/93 *Germany v Council* [1994] ECR I–4973). It was claimed that the regulation constituted an *ausbrechende rechtsakt* because it infringed GATT or WTO law. These are, however, distinct issues. An *intra vires* Community act may infringe GATT; an *ultra vires* act may comply with GATT; an *ultra vires* act may infringe GATT In the case of Regulation 404/93 an *intra vires* act allegedly infringed GATT and WTO rules; see also F Mayer, 'Grundrechtsschutz gegen europäische Rechtsakte durch das BverfG: Zur Verfassungsmässigkeit der Bananenmarktordnung', *EuZW*, 2000, 685, at 688–9.

[237] On the next day, 8 June 2000, the CFI handed judgment in another, related series of cases brought by Italian importers of bananas against the Commission's failure to take measures in hardship cases (caused by civil war and flood in Somalia), or against negative decisions, and actions in damages. The CFI annul the Commission decisions and declared that it had failed to act in one case. Yet, most of the actions for damages were declared inadmissible, as they were not sufficiently substantiated, or alleged future damage. Only in one case did the CFI award damages; Joined Cases T–79/96, T–260/97 and T–117/98 *Camar srl and Tico srl v Commission and Council* [2000] ECR II-2193.

duction of the export licence system itself, or implementing regulations adopted by the Commission. The actions have, so far been dismissed.[238]

18.2.1.8. *Alcan and Bananas III: No Bark?*

In *Alcan*,[239] the petitioner claimed, *inter alia*, that the judgment of the Court of Justice decided earlier in the case, constituted an *ausbrechender Rechtsakt*, by creating far-reaching procedural rules. The complainant claimed infringements of the *Rechtsstaatsprinzip* (based on Article 14(1)(2) of the Basic Law) and the principle of democracy (Articles 20 and 38 of the Basic Law). By creating procedural rules, the European Court and, by applying the preliminary ruling also the *Bundesverwaltungsgericht*, had encroached upon the jurisdiction of the national and of the Community legislature. The judgment was not, therefore, covered by the Act of assent. The *Bundesverfassungsgericht* stated that the question of an *ausbrechende Rechtsakt* did not arise in the case, since the relevant judgment of the Court of Justice only took effect for a specific case and did not generate general Community procedural rules with direct effect. The doctrine of *'ausbrechende Rechtsakte'* seemed to remain intact.

In its *Bananas III* decision,[240] the *Bundesverfassungsgericht* dismissed as inadmissible the reference by the *Verwaltungsgericht Frankfurt*, because the special conditions for submitting provisions of secondary Community law for constitutional review had not been met. Only then would the reserve-jurisdiction of the Constitutional Court revive if it was demonstrated in detail that the present evolution of the law concerning the protection of fundamental right in Community law, including the case law of the Court of Justice, does not generally ensure the protection of fundamental rights

---

[238] Case T–1/99 *T Port v Commission* [2001] ECR II-465 (no sufficient proof of damage; no need to rule on the legality of the conduct of the Commission); Case T–52/99 *T Port v Commission* [2001] ECR II-981 *'It is clear from* [the *Portuguese Textitles case,* Case C–149/96 *Portugal v Council* [1999] ECR I–8395] *that as the WTO rules are not in principle intended to confer rights on individuals, the Community cannot incur non-contractual liability as a result of infringement of them'*, at para 51; no existence of unlawful conduct on the part of the Commission established); Case T–2/99 *T Port v Council* [2001] ECR II-2093 (Art. 234 of the Treaty (Art. 308 EC) does not apply to the facts of the case due to the chronology of treaties); see also, on the same day, Case T–3/99 *Bananatrading v Council* [2001] ECR II-2123.

[239] *Bundesverfassungsgericht*, decision of 17 February 2000, *Alcan*, available on www.bundesverfassungsgericht.de.

[240] It took the BVerfG almost four years to declare the reference to be manifestly inadmissible. One can only speculate as to why it took so long. Possibly, the Court waited because it hoped for a solution at the WTO level or by political means; perhaps the delay had to do with the imminent retirement of Paul Kirchhof. Maybe the prospects of the European Charter of Fundamental Rights, which could strengthen the confidence in the European system of fundamental rights protection and could favour a retreat of the BVerfG, were also taken into account, see A Peters, 'The Bananas Decision (2000) of the German Federal Constitutional Court: Towards Reconciliation with the European Court of Justice as regards Fundamental Rights Protection in Europe', 43 *German Yearbook of International Law*, 2000, 276, at 277.

required unconditionally. The jurisdiction of the *Bundesverfassungsgericht* was restricted, in practical effect, to what the then President of the *Bundesverfassungsgericht* Jutta Limbach termed *'eine sehr theoretische Reservekompetenz'*, which did not pose a threat against Luxembourg, but merely underscored the significance of the appreciation common in modern democratic constitutions that all public power is obliged to respect fundamental rights.[241] In the system based on an interlocking of national and Community systems, the original jurisdiction to protect fundamental rights within Community law lay with the European Court.

What Jutta Limbach appeared to be saying is that the *Bundesverfassungsgericht* in its *Bananas I* judgment pointed out that there was a gap in the protection of fundamental rights of individuals because of the lack of transitory measures in hardship cases. If necessary, the German courts would step in. In its *T. Port I* judgment,[242] however, the European Court pointed out that there was no such gap, since the Commission was obliged to provide for the relevant measures, under the supervision of the European Courts. In *Bananas III* the *Bundesverfassungsgericht* accepted this as a sufficient form of protection, and stepped back again. There is no power struggle: the *Bundesverfassungsgericht* does not want to retain for itself jurisdiction to protect; as long as rights are protected, it is willing to step back.

18.2.1.9. Final Remarks

The *Bananas III* judgment of the *Bundesverfassungsgericht* marks a new era[243] of *pax germana* between the Constitutional Court and the Court of Justice. The power struggle in the field of fundamental right seems to be over, or at least suspended indefinitely. However, there remains the issue of *Kompetenz-Kompetenz* and of WTO law and its effects before the European and national courts.[244] In addition, the *Bundesverfassungsgericht* seems to reserve the power to review acts adopted under the second and the third pillars. Conflicts may still occur, and if a new critical case should

---

[241] So J Limbach, 'Die Kooperation der Gerichte in der zukünftigen europäischen Grundrechtsarchitektur', at www.rewi.hu-berlin.de, marginal number 27. Jutta Limbach was President of the *Bundesverfassungsgericht* and was Member of the Bench in the *Bananas III* judgment; see also CU Schmid, 'All Bark and No Bite: Notes on the Federal Constitutional Court's "Banana Decision"' 7 *ELJ*, 2001, at 105–6.

[242] Case C–68/95 *T Port v Bundesanstalt für Landwirtschaft und Ernährung* [1996] ECR I–6065.

[243] Eventhough he *Bundesverfassungsgericht* contended that *Maastricht* did not differ from *Solange II* It is easier to say 'we never said that' than to alter a position taken and be expected to explain the U-turn. Grewe speaks of a *'toilettage'* of the Maastricht jurisprudence, C Grewe, 'Le "traité de paix" avec la Cour de Luxembourg: l'arrêt de la Cour constitutionnelle allemande du 7 juin 2000 relatif au règlement du marché de la banane', 37 *RTDeur*, 2001, 1, at 12.

[244] See CU Schmid, 'All Bark and No Bite: Notes on the Federal Constitutional Court's 'Banana Decision'', 7 *ELJ*, 2001, 95.

arise, involving issues of fundamental rights, but more importantly competence issues, or questions of the compatibility of Community law with international treaties, or questions of all three types in the framework of the second and the third pillar, the *Bundesverfassungsgericht* may return to its old position. For the time being, however, the pressure seems to be off.

18.2.2. Italy

In Italy, the *Corte costituzionale* has denied jurisdiction to review the constitutionality of an EC regulation directly: it could only, under the Italian Constitution, review the constitutionality of statutes and of acts having statutory force of the State and of the Regions, and Community regulations were not among those.[245] However, there may be cases where Community law is not given effect in the Italian legal order, for breach of the core values of the Constitution including fundamental rights.

18.2.2.1. Frontini

In *Frontini*[246] the *Corte costituzionale* reserved for itself jurisdiction to review, in exceptional cases, the compatibility of secondary Community law with certain fundamental principles of the Italian constitutional order and the inalienable rights of man. The reserve of competence was a consequence of the Italian conception of the relationship between the European legal order. European law, it is recalled, is given effect in the Italian legal order by virtue of the Italian Act assenting to the Treaties on the basis of Article 11 of the Constitution, which must, says the *Corte*, be read in context. So, while Article 11 may allow Community law, primary or secondary, to derogate from certain national norms having constitutional rank,[247] it could not allow a violation of the core values recognised in the Constitution. In fact, the *Corte costituzionale* preceded the

---

[245] *Corte costituzionale*, decision n. 183/73 of 27 December 1973, *Frontini* [1974] 2 CMLR 372; Oppenheimer, *The Cases*, 629, at 640; see also decision n. 509/95 of 11 December 1995, *Zandonà Albano v INPS*, on www.giurcost.org.

[246] Note that before *Frontini*, the *Corte Costituzionale* did not recognise the direct applicability and supremacy of Community law *qua* Community law, see above Part 1, Chapter 7. In *Frontini*, the *Corte costituzionale* presented a new theory about the relationship between the Community and national legal orders, which allowed for the ordinary supremacy of Community law (which was not however to be enforced by the ordinary courts), and partial ultimate supremacy (not over the core values of the Constitution). It is the latter stipulation which is of interest here.

[247] Very explicit in *Corte costituzionale*, decision n. 117/94 of 31 March 1994, *Fabrizio Zerini*, *Foro it.*, 1995, I, 1077; www.giurcost.org; which did not directly concern the question of review of the validity of Community law. On the contrary, the *Corte de cassazione* alleged that an Italian norm violated a Community directive. The *Corte* held that it did not have jurisdiction to rule on these cases stating that Community law could not constitute stan-

Bundesverfassungsgericht in formulating these exceptions to the supremacy of Community law.

It is not entirely clear how the Court distinguishes between 'ordinary' constitutional norms, from which Community law may diverge on the one hand, and the fundamental principles of the Italian constitutional order and the inalienable rights of man,[248] the *principi inviolabili*[249] operating as *controlimiti*, on the other.[250]

The legal technique designed to allow for such review while permitting the direct application and supremacy of Community law in 'ordinary cases' is highly remarkable.[251] It had been argued that Article 189 of the Treaty (*rectius*: the Italian Act assenting to the Treaty) was unconstitutional since it allowed the Community institutions to issue directly applicable acts. This violated, among others, the constitutional guarantee of judicial review of constitutionality and the protection of fundamental rights. The *Corte costituzionale* dismissed the claim, stating that the Court of Justice carried out review of the lawfulness of secondary law. It was difficult to imagine that an essentially economic organisation would affect civil, ethico-social or political relations conflicting with the Constitution. Moreover, under Article 11 limitations of sovereignty were only allowed for the purposes mentioned therein, and it would be unacceptable that the Community institutions be given the power to violate fundamental principles of the Italian constitutional order, or the inalienable rights of man. If ever Article 189 of the Treaties were given such 'an aberrant interpretation', the *Corte costituzionale* would step in again, and control the continuing compatibility of the Treaty with the core values of the Constitution. In other cases, however, it should be excluded that that it could control individual

---

dards for reference for the *Corte costituzionale*, since even though it may derogate from national law having a constitutional rank (except those containing fundamental principles or inalienable rights of man), it belonged to a distinct, be it coordinated, legal order, and could not therefore be qualified as norms of constitutional value.

[248] Also referred to as 'supra-constitutional' norms, see R Guastini, 'La primauté du droit communautaire: une révision tacite de la Constitution italienne', www.conseil-constitutionnel.fr/cahiers/ccc9/ guastini.htm, at 4.

[249] The *Corte costituzionale* has held, in another context. that the fundamental principles of the constitutional order and the inalienable rights of man cannot be modified by constitutional revision, see *Corte costituzionale*, decision n. 1146/88 of 15 December 1988, *Criminal proceedings against Franz Pahl*, available on www.giurcost.org.

[250] On this issue, M Cartabia, *Principe inviolabili e integrazione europea* (Milano, Giuffrè, 1995); Schermers suggested to replace the notion with that of 'peremptory norms' under international law, and, for th sake of uniformity of Community law, replace the additional protection offered by the national constitutional courts–in additional to the original jurisdiction of the Court of Justice- by supervision by the Stasbourg organs, HG Schermers 'The Scales in Balance: National Constitutional Court v Court of Justice', 27 *CMLRev* 1990, 97.

[251] For a fierce criticism of the (lack of) logic in the approach of the *Corte costituzionale*, R Guastini, 'La primauté du droit communautaire: une révision tacite de la Constitution italienne', www.conseil-constitutionnel.fr/cahiers/ccc9/guastini.htm.

regulations, given that they did not constitute Italian statutes subject to constitutional review under Article 134 of the Italian Constitution.[252] If therefore, a regulation would ever be found to conflict with the core principles of the Constitution, the constitutionality of the Treaty itself, or better even, the Act assenting to it could come up for review.

18.2.2.2. Fragd

In *Fragd*,[253] the norm under review became 'the treaty norm as interpreted and applied by the institutions and organs of the EEC' and the constitutional court retained jurisdiction to verify the constitutionality of the laws implementing such norms. This has been interpreted as implying that a finding of inconsistency does no longer necessarily imply the invalidation of the entire ratification law, but only some of the Treaty's articles, interpretations or applications.[254] In *Fragd*, the *Corte* re-stated *Frontini* in an attempt to convince the audience that its position was appropriate. It said: *'It is true that Community law, (..), provides an ample and effective system of judicial protection for the rights and interests of individuals. The procedure for requesting a preliminary ruling from the Court of Justice under Article 177 of the EEC Treaty, is the most important instrument of that system. On the other hand, it is equally true that the fundamental rights guaranteed by the legal systems of the Member States constitute, according to the jurisprudence of the Court of Justice, an essential and integral part of the Community legal order. It cannot therefore be stated that the Constitutional Court has no competence to verify whether or not a treaty norm, as interpreted and applied by the institutions and organs of the EEC, is in conflict with the fundamental principles of the Italian Constitution or violates the inalienable rights of man'.*[255] The *Corte costituzionale* thus sought to justify its jurisdiction on the basis of Community law itself. However, the conclusion drawn from the starting point that the constitutional conditions matter to Community law is obviously wrong from the point of view of Community law. It negates *Foto-Frost*, and overlooks the fact that the constitutional fundamental rights bind the

---

[252] See also *Corte costituzionale*, decision n. 509/95 of 11 December 1995, *Zandonà Albano v INPS*, *Riv. It. dir. Pubbl. com.*, 1996, 764; www.giurcost.org.
[253] *Corte costituzionale*, decision n. 232/89 of 21 April 1989, *Fragd*, *Riv. Dir. Int.*, 1989, 103; www.giur.cost.org; Oppenheimer, *The Cases*, 653; commented in G Gaja, 'New Developments in a Continuing Story: The Relationship between EEC Law and Italian Law', 27 *CML Rev*, 1990, 83; L Daniele, 'Après l'arrêt Granital: Droit communautaire et droit national dans la jurisprudence récente de la Cour constitutionnelle italienne', *CDE*, 1992, 3, at 15 *et seq*.
[254] See M Cartabia, 'The Italian Constitutional Court and the Relationship between the Italian Legal System and the European Community', *Michigan J Int L*, 1990, 173, at 182 et seq.
[255] Cited from Oppenheimer, *The Cases*, 653, at 657.

Community not as such, but only in so far as they define general principles of Community law under *Internationale Handeslgesellschaft*.

The *Corte costituzionale* further explained that it had jurisdiction to examine the constitutionality of laws implementing treaty norms as interpreted and implemented by the Community institutions. Whilst being highly unlikely such a conflict could still happen. Moreover, it may well be that not all fundamental principles of the Italian constitutional order were to be found among those common to the legal orders of the other Member States and included in the Community legal order. For all these reasons, the *Corte costituzionale* reserved jurisdiction to intervene in exceptional cases.

Fragd was important since it was the first time that the *Corte costituzionale* was referred an exception of unconstitutionality on the ground that Community law, in this case a judgment of the Court of Justice,[256] actually infringed a fundamental principle of the Italian Constitution, *i.e.* the situation described as 'aberrant' in *Frontini*. The tribunal of Venice was confronted with the situation where a preliminary ruling of the Court of Justice could not be applied in the very case it was handed in, since that Court had limited its temporal effects, which according to the Italian tribunal violated the constitutional principle of judicial protection. The *Corte costituzionale* held that if a judgment of the Court of Justice went as far as ruling that a finding of invalidity would not apply in the case that led to the preliminary ruling, serious doubts would arise as to the consistency of the rule that allows this type of judgment with the essential elements of the right to judicial protection. The right to a judge and a decision would be emptied if the preliminary ruling of the Court were not to apply in the very case in which the reference was made. In the presence of a possible infringement of a fundamental principle, it was impossible to invoke the overriding considerations of the uniform application of Community law and the principle of legal certainty. Nevertheless, at the end of the day the Court declared it irrelevant in the case at hand and dismissed the reference as inadmissible. Probably, the *Corte* tried to persuade the Court of Justice to change its view on a particular issue,[257] without going it all the way and declaring the (partial) unconstitutionality of the Act asserting to the Treaty.

---

[256] *Frontini* dealt with regulations adopted under Art. 189 of the Treaty, but may be applied to secondary Community law taken as a whole.

[257] So R Gaja, 'New Developments in a Continuing Story: The Relationship between EEC law and Italian law', 27 *CML Rev* (1990) 83, at 94–95; L Daniele, 'Áprès l'arrêt Granital: Droit communautaire et droit national dans la jurisprudence récente de la Cour constitutionnelle italienne', *CDE*, 1992, 1, at 17; M Cartabia, 'The Italian Constitutional Court and the Relationship between the Italian legal system and the European Union', in *The European Court and National Courts – Doctrine and Jurisprudence. Legal Change in its Social Context* (Oxford, Hart Publishing, 1998) 133, at 138–39.

It was willing, thus, to test the consistency of individual rules of Community law with the *principi fondamentali*,[258] and showed its eagerness to play an effective role in controlling the conformity of Community norms with fundamental principles.[259] Nevertheless, it avoided a head-on collision with the Court of Justice. In fact, the Court has never actually exercised its jurisdiction to annul the Act of ratification or parts thereof or otherwise limit the application of Community law for reasons of infringements of the core values of the Constitution. In addition, it seems that the lower courts must, before referring the issue of an alleged unconstitutionality to the *Corte costituzionale*, first seize the Court of Justice.[260] The jurisdiction of the *Corte costituzionale* thus seems restricted only to those cases where Community law infringes the core principles of the Italian constitutional order, and the Court of Justice does not declare it unlawful.[261]

It is not entirely clear what the position of the *Corte costituzionale* will be on *Kompetenz* issues. Nevertheless, given the importance of the limitation of sovereignty and counterlimits and the central role of the 'competence' in the entire theoretical framework of the *Corte costituzionale*, it appears probable that the *Corte* will, from the constitutional perspective, assume competence to interpret the Italian Act assenting to the Treaties in order to set the limits of the competences of the European institutions.[262]

---

[258] Note that the decision was handed during the *pax germana*, after the *Solange II* judgment, where the *Bundesverfassungsgericht* had held that it would not, for the time being, exercise its jurisdiction in concrete cases.

[259] A Adinolfi, 'The Judicial Application of Community Law in Italy (1981–97)', 35 *CML Rev* (1998) 1313, at 1324.

[260] So A Adinolfi, 'The Judicial Application of Community Law in Italy (1981–97)', 35 *CML Rev* (1998) 1313, at 1324–5.

[261] In addition, speaking extra-judicially, Justice Onida of the *Corte costituzionale*, argued that a veritable conflict had become less likely given the adoption of the EU Charter of fundamental rights. On the other hand, the extension of areas in which the European institutions operate, among which justice and ordre public did make it more probable that conflicts may occur in future. This seems to imply that the *Corte* may also assume jurisdiction to verify the constitutionality of acts adopted outside the framework of 'pure' Community law. V Onida, 'L'état de la jurisprudence constitutionnelle sur les rapports entre le système juridique national et le système juridique communautaire: "harmonie dans la diversité" et questions ouvertes', paper on file with the author, also published in V Onida, '"Armonia tra diversi" e problemi aperti. La giurisprudenza costituzionale sui rapporti tra ordinamento interno e ordinamento comunitario', *Quaderni costituzionali*, 2002, 549.

[262] So Justice Onida, art. cit., at 7; see also M Cartabia, 'Report on Italy', in A-M Burley *et al* (eds), *The European Court and National Courts – Doctrine and Jurisprudence. Legal Change in Its Social Context* (Oxford, Hart Publishing, 1998) 133, at 142–44; FP Ruggeri Laderchi is of the opinion that a question concerning the validity of Community law deriving from a lack of competence will be solved by the *Corte costituzionale* on the basis of the *Frontini-Granital* doctrine, FP Ruggeri Laderchi, 'Report on Italy', in A-M Burley *et al* (eds), *The European Court and National Courts – Doctrine and Jurisprudence. Legal Change in Its Social Context* (Oxford, Hart Publishing, 1998) 147, at 169–70.

18.2.3. Denmark

The Danish *Højesteret* has never been asked to rule on the lawfulness of secondary European law. Nevertheless, in its judgment on the constitutionality of the Treaty of Maastricht it has expounded its views on the matter.[263] The applicants had argued that the Act approving the Treaty of Maastricht could not have been based on Article 20 of the Constitution, which only allows for transfers of sovereignty 'to a specified extent'[264] while the transfers in the Treaty of Maastricht were not sufficiently specified. Secondly, they contended that the transfers were on such a scale that they were inconsistent with the Constitution's premise of a democratic form of government.

In its final ruling in the case the *Højesteret* held that Article 20 did not permit that an international organisation is entrusted with the issuance of acts of law or the making of decisions that are contrary to provisions in the Constitution, including its fundamental rights.[265] Indeed, the authorities of the realm have themselves no such powers. It is implied that Community law infringing upon Danish fundamental rights would be unconstitutional. In addition, Community law must remain within the limits of the powers transferred in the Treaties as assented to by the Danish Act of assent and the *Højesteret* found that it did: the Community is based on the principle of enumerated powers; Article 235 of the Treaty (now Article 308 EC) does not violate this constitutional requirement of itself, given the new powers and competences provisions introduced by the Treaty of Maastricht and the newest case law of the Court of Justice[266] and the fact that Denmark retains a veto right under the provision.[267] The fact that the Court of Justice rules on the interpretation of Article 235 of the Treaty and on the detailed interpretation of the powers vested in the Community institutions, including the European Court, was not by and of itself unconstitutional.

---

[263] *Højesteret*, decision of 6 April 1998, *Treaty of Maastricht*, UfR 1998, 800; www.um.dk/udenrigspolitik/europa/domeng/; discussed in K Høegh, 'The Danish maastricht Judgment', *ELR* 1999, 80; S Harck and HP Olsen, 'Decision concerning the Maastricht Treaty', *AJIL*, 1999, 209; R Hofmann, 'Der Oberste Gerichtshof Dänemarks und die europäische Integration', *EuGRZ*, 1999, 1; H Rasmussen, 'Confrontation or Peaceful Coexistence? On the Danish Supreme Court's Maastricht Ratification Judgment', in D O'Keeffe and A Bavasso (eds), *Judicial Review in European Union Law. Liber Amicorum in Honour of Lord Slynn of Hadley*, Vol I, (The Hague, Kluwer Law International, 2000), 377; P Biering, 'The Judicial Application of EU Law in Denmark: 1986 to 2000', 37 *CML Rev*, 2000, 925, at 928–32; the decision has been discussed in Chapter 5 above.

[264] '*i noermere bestemt omfang*'.

[265] The unofficial translation of the Forein Office uses the notion 'rights of freedom'.

[266] The *Højesteret* approvingly cited *Opinion 2/94 on accession to the ECHR* [1996] ECR I–1788.

[267] The *Højesteret* expressly stated that it was not ruling on any previous use of Art 308 EC since it could only pronounce itself on the Treaty of Maastricht and not on Community law as such. Yet, it made it clear that it did not agree with some of the previous expansion of Community competences.

The *Højesteret* then retained some jurisdiction for the Danish courts to review whether Community acts exceed the limits of the powers surrendered by the Act of Accession under Article 20 of the Constitution. It ruled that by adopting the Act of Accession it had been recognised that the power to test the validity and legality of EC acts of law lies with the European Court of Justice, so that Danish courts of law could not hold an EC act inapplicable in Denmark without first having referred the question of its compatibility with the Treaty to the Court of Justice. Danish courts of law could generally base their decision on the decisions of the Court of Justice. Nevertheless, given the requirement of specification in Article 20 of the Constitution and the Danish courts' jurisdiction to review the constitutionality of acts, Danish courts could not be deprived of their right to consider questions as to whether a Community act exceeds the limits of the surrender of sovereignty made by the Act of Accession. *'Therefore, Danish courts must rule that an EC act is inapplicable in Denmark if the extraordinary situation should arise that with the required certainty it can be established that an EC act which has been upheld by the Court of Justice is based on an application of the Treaty which lies beyond the surrender of sovereignty according to the Act of Accession. Similar interpretations apply with regard to Community law rules and legal principles which are based on the practice of the EC Court of Justice'.*[268]

All Danish courts thus retain jurisdiction to review the applicability[269] of secondary Community law, but this jurisdiction is confined by several restrictions: the case must first be referred to the *Court of Justice*, it must be established *with the required certainty* that despite the fact that the Court of Justice has *upheld* it, the act is *ultra vires* of the Danish Act of Accession. Given the record of the Danish courts when considering the constitutionality of Acts of the Danish Parliament, it does not seem probable that the Danish courts will make such decision lightly.[270] It is striking that the issue of fundamental rights violations is treated essentially as a competence issue: under Article 20 of the Constitution, the Community institutions have not been transferred the power to violate the constitutional provisions, including fundamental right. In addition, no distinction is made among constitutional provisions, as does for instance the *Corte costituzionale* and the *Bundesverfassungsgericht*: none can be infringed by Community law. The Supreme Court drew attention to the fact that the applicants had restricted their claim to those parts of the Treaty of

---

[268] *Højesteret*, decision of 6 April 1998, *Treaty of Maastricht*, UfR 1998, H 800; cited from unofficial translation of the Foreign Office, www.um.dk/udenrigspolitik/europa/domeg/, at para 9.6.

[269] The *Højesteret* plays with the same distinction between *validity* and *legality* on the one hand and the *applicability* of secondary Community law on the other as the *Bundesverfassungsgericht*. It is submitted that from the European perspective, all three types of declaration by a national court – invalidity, illegality or inapplicability – amount to a violation of Community law and fall within the exclusive jurisdiction of the ECJ.

[270] Different: H Rasmussen, *art. cit.*, at 389.

Maastricht relating to Community law,[271] which almost seemed to surprise it. Second and third pillar and the passages on EMU were not
included in the judgment.

18.2.4. France

In France it is not entirely clear what the position on conflicts between the
Constitution and secondary European law is, and what the courts will do
should such conflict come to the fore. The theme is in flux.[272] The *Conseil
constitutionnel* and *Conseil d'État* appear to diverge on the wider issue of
the hierarchical relationship between the Constitution and International
and European law.

18.2.4.1. The Conseil constitutionnel

The jurisdiction of the *Conseil constitutionnel* is unusual when compared to
the other courts analysed so far, in that its review applies to acts adopted,
but not promulgated.[273] Nevertheless, in theory, the *Conseil constitutionnel*
can be confronted with the constitutionality of Community law *indirectly*,[274] via the *loi* adopted to apply or implement secondary Community
law, and be asked to assess indirectly whether, the underlying norm of
Community law is unconstitutional. Until now, the *Conseil constitutionnel*
has avoided to pronounce itself clearly on these questions in particular,
and on the wider issue of the hierarchical relationship between
the Constitution and secondary European law generally.[275] There have,

---

[271] First pillar law in temple-parlance.

[272] The *Conseil constitutionnel* chose as topic for the Conference of constitutional courts
organised in Paris in 1997 'Droit communautaire dérivé et droit constitutionnel. Coopération
internationale et juridictions constitutionnelles étrangères', see www.conseil-
constitutionnel.fr/cahiers/ccc4.

[273] In the case of *lois* (Art. 61(2) of the Constitution) the *Conseil constitutionnel's* review is situated between the parliamentary vote and the promulgation; in the case of international
agreements (Art. 54 of the Constitution) the review takes place during the time between
signature and ratification or approval. It is not likely that the *Conseil constitutionnel* could
assume jurisdiction to control the validity of a proposal for secondary Community law
directly, since Art. 54 relates to *'engagements internationaux'* subject to ratification or
approval, which secondary European law normally is not. This question has been discussed in Chapter 16.

[274] As the French would have it: *'le controle par voie d'exception d'inconstitutionnalité'*. This is
where a *loi* applying or implementing a secondary Union act is alleged to infringe the
Constitution and the unconstitutionality is in fact imputed to the Union act. This is the
case where the provisions under attack are imposed by the underlying Union act. It is
submitted that where the provisions under attack are not so imposed, and they are not
covered by the underlying Union act, Union law does not oppose any judicial review of
the implementing national law.

[275] F Chaltiel, 'Droit constitutionnel et droit communautaire', *RTDeur*, 1999, 395, at 398.

however, been cases where it was given the opportunity to do so. In a 1977 decision,[276] the *loi de finance rectificative* was alleged to infringe the Constitution[277] on grounds that the French Parliament had not co-operated in its adoption. The *Conseil* stated that the division of competences between the national and Community institutions in the matter of taxes was only *'la conséquence d'engagements internationaux souscrits par la France qui sont entrés dans la champ de l'article 55 de la Constitution'*. In those circumstances, the act could not be unconstitutional. The decision has been interpreted as implying a denial of jurisdiction on the part of the *Conseil constitutionnel* to review the constitutionality, even indirectly, of secondary Community law.[278] It has even been described as sanctioning the 'constitutional immunity of Community law'.[279]

In cases involving French acts implementing Community directives, claims of unconstitutionality has always been rejected, but always on procedural grounds, and without the *Conseil constitutionnel* giving a clear statement about its jurisdiction to review (indirectly) the constitutionality of the directives.[280]

In a 1991 decision,[281] the *Conseil constitutionnel* reviewed the constitutionality of the *loi* adopted in order to bring French law in line with the case law of the Court of Justice on Article 48(4) of the Treaty (now Article 39(4) EC) concerning the access of Union citizens to employment in the public sector.[282] The applicants argued *inter alia*[283] that the loi infringed the constitutional principle that access to *'des fonctions qui intéressent la*

---

[276] *Conseil constitutionnel*, decision n. 77–90 DC of 30 December 1977, *Loi de finance rectificative pour 1977*, Rec. 44; See also *Conseil constitutionnel*, decision n. 77/89 DC of 30 December 1977, *Loi de finance pour 1978*, Rec. 46.

[277] More precisely the principle of national sovereignty (Art. 3) and the legislative power of Parliament in tax matters (Art. 34).

[278] So L Dubouis, 'Le juge français et le conflit entre norme constitutionnelle et norme européenne', in *L'Europe et le droit. Mélange en hommage à Jean Boulouis* (Paris, Dalloz, 1991) 205, at 208; however, Boulouis also suggests that the passage may imply that the *Conseil constitutionnel* reserves for itself *Kompetenz-Kompetenz*, above, at 209.

[279] D Simon, *Le système juridique communautaire*, (Paris, PUF, 1997), at 290; see also L Dubouis, 'Le juge français et le conflit entre norme constitutionnelle et norme européenne', in *L'Europe et le droit. Mélange offertes à J. Boulouis*, (Paris, Dalloz, 1991), 204.

[280] *Conseil constitutionnel*, decision n. 78-100 DC of 29 December 1978, *Loi de finance rectificative pour 1978 (sixième directive TVA)*, Rec., 36; *Conseil constitutionnel*, decision 94-348 DC of 3 August 1994, *Loi relative à la protection sociale complémentaire des salariés (transposition des directives 92/49 et 92/96)*; *Conseil constitutionnel*, decision n. 96-383 of 6 November 1996, *Loi relative à l'information et à la consultation des salariés dans les entreprises et les groupes d'entreprises de dimension communautaire*; *Conseil constitutionnel*, decision n. 2000-440 DC of 10 January 2001, *Loi portant diverses dipositions d'adaptation au droit communautaire dans le domaine des transports*; all decisions can be found on the website of the *Conseil constitutionnel*.

[281] *Conseil constitutionnel*, decision n. 91–293 DC of 21 July 1991, *loi sur la fonction publique*.

[282] Compare *Conseil constitutionnel*, decision n. 80–126 DC of 30 december 1980, *Loi de finance pour 1981*, where the *Conseil constitutionnel* held in relation to a provision adopted with a view to bring French law in line with the case law of the ECJ, that the condition of reciprocity did not constitute a condition for the constitutionality of statutes.

[283] The applicants also argued that the *loi* infringed Art. 48 of the Treaty and consequently Art. 55 of the French Constitution. The *Conseil constitutionnel* dismissed the claim holding

souveraineté de la Nation' was restricted to French nationals. The *Conseil constitutionnel* rejected the claim, finding that the *loi* did not infringe the essential conditions of the exercise of national sovereignty, because functions involving the exercise of sovereign power continued to be reserved to French nationals. What is striking, though, is that the *Conseil constitutionnel* did consider the claim and did not rule that the law was constitutional simply because it was the inevitable consequence of obligations flowing from a Treaty falling under Article 55 of the Constitution, in the same vein as it had done in the case of the *loi de finance rectificative de 1977*.[284]

The *Maastricht I* decision[285] contains a very unclear passage, where the *Conseil constitutionnel* claimed that the rights and freedoms of citizens were sufficiently guaranteed under Article F(2) of the Treaty of Maastricht, and respect for these principles was ensured by the Court of Justice 'in particular though proceedings instituted at the initiative of individuals'. This was blatantly untrue: the Court of Justice was by virtue of Article L of the Treaty of Maastricht excluded from Article F(2)[286] and, more importantly, direct access of individuals to the Court of Justice is extremely restricted, and there is no such thing as a European *amparo*.[287] Yet, the *Conseil* continued to say that the provisions of Article F(2), *taken in conjunction with the intervention of national courts rendering decisions in the exercise of their jurisdiction*, enabled the rights and freedoms of citizens to be guaranteed. The marked passage is not clear: the *Conseil constitutionnel* did not make any pronouncements as to its own jurisdiction in the matter, nor that of the ordinary courts.[288]

However, it is not excluded that secondary law could be found to conflict with norms of constitutional law. In the 1997 report to the Conference

that it did not come within its jurisdiction to review the compatibility of a loi to a treaty. That was the province of the other organs.

[284] See also P Oliver, 'The French Constitution and the Treaty of Maastricht', 43 *ICLQ*, 1994, 1 at 9.

[285] *Conseil constitutionnel*, decision n. 92–308 DC of 9 April 1992, *Treaty of Maastricht I*, www.conseil-constitutionnel.fr.

[286] It was generally accepted that this did not matter so much, since Art. F(2) reflected the case law of the ECJ on the general principles, which could continue to be applied.

[287] For a discussion of the idea of introducing a 'European *amparo*' on grounds of violation of fundamental rights, B De Witte, 'The Past and Future Role of the European Court of Justice in the Protection of Human Rights', in Ph Alston (ed), *The EU and Human Rights*, (Oxford, OUP, 2000), at 893 *et seq*.

[288] As stated in the 1997 report to the Conference of Courts having constitutional jurisdiction on the issue: *'Toutefois, le Conseil constitutionnel n'a pas eu l'occasion à l'instar des cours constitutionnelles allemande et italienne par exemple, de se prononcer sur ce qui serait son attitude dans l'hypothèse, heureusement imporable, d'une défaillance des organes communautaires dans le domaine du respect des droits fondamentaux'*, www.conseil-constitutionnel.fr/cahiers/ccc4/ccc4 fran.htm, at 11.

of courts having constitutional jurisdiction, it was stated that in the area of fundamental rights, a conflict was rather unlikely, given the fact that the Court of Justice was to protect fundamental rights on the basis of common constitutional traditions and the ECHR under Article F of the EU Treaty (now Article 6 EU). The *Conseil constitutionnel* had not yet had the opportunity to clarify what it would do in the event that the Community institutions would fall below a particular standard, but the hypothesis was also considered *'heureusement improbable'*. It was, however, in the context of other constitutional norms and values that conflicts could arise. In the context of Title IV (ex-pillar three) questions could arise as to the compatibility of secondary law and the essential conditions of the exercise of the national sovereignty. Yet, the report was mostly apprehensive about certain fundamental principles and values inherent in the French constitutional traditions. The following principles were indicated as 'hazardous' and likely to cause conflicts: the principle of the indivisibility of the Republic (should a Community decision ever impose direct co-operation between Community organs and *'les collectivités territoriales françaises'*), the right to asylum (should the right to asylum be restricted for Union citizens), the principle of the independence of the judicial function (which was considered to be affected directly by the communitarization of the third pillar), and the rules on the *'service public'*.[289]

In a 1998 decision concerning the *Loi relative à l'entrée et au séjour des étrangers en France et au droit d'asile*[290] the *Conseil constitutionnel* failed to clarify its position and held that it was constitutional to derogate from a constitutional principle insofar as was necessary for the implementation of international obligations and on the condition that the essential conditions of the exercise of national sovereignty were not violated.[291] It thus seems that there are two types of constitutional provisions: those which may have to cede to international law (*'les principes constitutionnelles infra-conventionnelles'*) and those which do not give way to international obligations (*'les principes constitutionnelles supra-conventionnelles'*).

18.2.4.2. The Conseil d'État

The *Conseil d'État* appears to apply the principles of *Foto-Frost* in its case law. It considers whether the question of the validity of a Community acts has a direct link with the case, whether the answer to the question of

---

[289] www.conseil-constitutionnel.fr/cahiers/ccc4/ccc4fran.htm, at 11.
[290] *Conseil constitutionnel*, decision n. 98–399 DC of 5 May 1998, *Loi relative à l'entrée et au séjour des étrangers en France et au droit d'asile*; on the difficulties interpreting the decision see E Picard, 'Petit excercice de logique juridique. à propos de la décision du Conseil constitutionnel no 98–399 du 5 mai 1998 "Séjour des étragers et droit d'asile', *RFDA*, 1998, 620.
[291] The case did not concern Union law, but seems to apply to any international obligation.

validity is necessary to decide the case, and whether there is a *prima facie* case for invalidity.[292] If not, it rejects the claim and upholds the validity of the Community act. There are no examples of the *Conseil d'État* reviewing the *constitutionality* of secondary Union law. Doubts may have arisen after the *Sarran* decision where the *Conseil d'État* established the hierarchically higher place of the Constitution over international treaties and ruled that the supremacy of treaties over *lois* did not, in the French legal order, apply to provisions of a constitutional nature. Under French law, no distinction is made between types of international treaties, and the specificity of Community law is not accepted. If *Sarran* were to be applied to Community law, and if it were taken to imply that the *Conseil d'État* accepts jurisdiction to review the constitutionality of treaties,[293] that would imply that the *Conseil d'État* assumes jurisdiction to review the constitutionality of Union law and not of *lois*, while it does accept that in the hierarchy of norms Union law (and other treaty provisions duly ratified etc) precedes *lois*, and it does assume jurisdiction to review the compatibility of *lois* with treaty provisions. This would create a highly paradoxical situation.

In the 2001 *SNIP* decision,[294] the *Conseil d'État* has, in what seems to be an *obiter dictum*, stated that *'le principe de primauté, (..) au demeurant ne saurait conduire, dans l'ordre interne, à remettre en cause la suprématie de la Constitution'*, thereby seemingly implying that the primacy of Community law would have to yield to constitutional norms. Nevertheless, it appears that in this case, there was no conflict between Community law and a *loi*. The *loi* had been held constitutional in a decision of the *Conseil constitutionnel*, but that did not affect the issue of any conflict between the *loi* and Community law. It was not claimed, however, that there was a conflict between the constitutional provisions and Community law.[295]

---

[292] See P Cassia, 'Le juge administratif français et la validité des actes communautaires', *RTDeur*, 1999, 409, with references to the case law. One example is *Conseil d'État*, decision of 18 September 1998, *Société Demesa*, available on www.légifrance.fr: *'Considérant qu'il résulte de tout ce qui précède, et sans qu'il y ait lieu, en absence de difficulté sérieuse quant à la validité de la décision de la Commission (..) de saisir, sur ce point, la Cour de justice des Communautés européennes en application de l'article 177 du traité CEE'*.

[293] Though many have considered that this is a consequence of *Sarran*, it is submitted that *Sarran* is restricted to the situation where the *Conseil* is asked to review the *conventionnalité* of a constitutional provision as reproduced in a decree/loi, see supra, and C Maugüé, 'L'arrêt Sarran, entre apparence et réalité', www.conseil-constitutionnel.fr/cahiers/ccc7/maugue.htm; D Simon, 'L'arrêt Sarran: dualisme incompressible ou monisme inversé?', *Europe*, March 1999, 4; both refer to the interpretation of the majority of commentators that *Sarran* means that the *Conseil d'État* will review the applicability of treaty provisions in the light of the Constitution.

[294] *Conseil d'État*, decision of 3 December 2001, *SNIP*, available on www.legifrance.gouv.fr.

[295] See A Rigaux and D Simon, '"Summum jus, summa injuria…" À propos de l'arrêt du Conseil d'État du 3 décembre 2001 SNIP', *Europe*, April 2002, 6; see also F Chaltiel, 'La boîte de Pandore des relations entre la Constitution française et le droit comunautaire. À propos de l'arrêt SNIP du Conseil d'État du 3 décembre 2001', *RMCUE*, 2002, 595.

18.2.5. Ireland

When Ireland joined the European Communities in 1973, Article 29 of the Constitution was amended in order to permit Ireland to join the Communities and, more importantly in this context, to provide a large measure of constitutional immunity to the Treaties and to Community measures, laws and acts.[296] Article 29.4.7 of *Bunreacht na hÉireann* now reads:[297] '*No provision of this Constitution invalidates laws enacted, acts done or measures adopted by the State which are necessitated by the obligations of membership of the European Union or of the Communities, or prevents laws enacted, acts done, or measures adopted by the European Union or by the Communities or by institutions thereof, or by bodies competent under the Treaties establishing the Communities, from having the force of law in the State*', and provides the most elaborate consideration, in constitutional text, of the issue of the relation between constitutional and Community and Union norms of all Member States. The provision constitutes a bar to constitutional challenges to Community law rules themselves and to Irish implementing measures necessitated by the obligations of membership. Nonetheless, the provision is not sufficient of itself to dispose of all problems. Within the dualist paradigm of the Irish Constitution, a further act of domestic incorporation was deemed necessary in order to make the Treaties and the laws deriving from them effective in the Irish legal order and to allow them to benefit from the constitutional immunity of Article 29.4.7 This was the 1972 European Communities Act, which has been amended many times since.

Article 29.4.7 does not distinguish between primary and secondary Community law. It would therefore seem that what has been said about the *a posteriori* review of the Treaties, should also apply to this chapter on secondary law. Yet, an attempt has been made to break up the case law and consider in turn review of the constitutionality of primary law,[298] of secondary Community law, of implementing Irish law and of non-Community Union law.

18.2.5.1. Article 29.4.7 and Secondary Community Law

Laws enacted, acts done and measures adopted by Community institutions cannot be made subject of constitutional challenge in the Irish

---

[296] See above in Chapter 4; for a short overview see G Hogan, 'The Nice Treaty and the Irish Constitution', *EPL*, 2001, 565; a wider perspective is offered in DR Phelan, *Revolt or Revolution. The Constitutional Boundaries of the European Community*, (Dublin, Round Hall, Sweet & Maxwell, 1997), 328 *et seq.*; G Hogan and A Whelan, *Ireland and the European Union: Constitutional and Statutory Texts and Commentary*, (London, Sweet & Maxwell, 1995), Chapter 1.

[297] This provision is not subject to the proposed Nice Treaty amendment.

[298] This has been done in Chapter 16 above.

courts, without any conditions of necessity or otherwise applying. Their constitutional validity or applicability[299] cannot be challenged in the Irish courts. This was accepted for instance by the High Court in *Lawlor*[300] where it was held (per Murphy J) that *'Whilst it is no part of the function of this court to determine whether or not any part of the EEC regulation is invalid, it would be open to this court to refer the matter to the [Court of Justice] if I considered that a decision of that court was necessary to enable me to give judgment to these proceedings'*. However, the judge did not consider such a reference to be necessary.

18.2.5.2.   Article 29.4.7 and Irish Law Necessitated by the Obligations of Membership of the Communities

Most cases concern not the constitutionality of Community law itself, but of Irish law adopted with a view to give effect to or to implement it. Under Article 29.4.[7] constitutional immunity is granted to Irish laws enacted, acts done or measures adopted by the State which are necessitated by the obligations of membership of the Communities. The notion *'necessitated by membership'* is therefore crucial: if Irish law is not so necessitated, it must, as usual, fully comply with all the instructions of the Constitution; if it is so necessitated, Article 29.6.7 permits derogation from other constitutional provisions.

The interpretation of the notion 'necessitated by the obligations of membership' was central in the cases *Lawlor, Greene, Meagher and Maher*. In *Lawlor*[301] the constitutional validity of both the Community superlevy on milk regulation and the Irish ministerial regulation giving effect to it was challenged. The applicant argued that they infringed his right to property as protected under the Constitution. Murphy J. first rejected the constitutional claim against the ministerial regulations on the substance and only then did he proceed to point out that they came under the protection of Article 29.4.[7]. He adopted a flexible and loose interpretation of the words 'necessitated': *'It seems to me that the word 'necessitated' (..) could not be limited in its construction to laws, acts or measures all of which are in all their parts required to be enacted, done or adopted by the obligations of membership of the Community. It seems to me that the word 'necessitated' in this context must extend to and include all acts or measures which are consequent upon membership of the Community, and even where there may be a choice or degree of discretion vested in the State as to the particular manner in which it would*

---

[299] In accordance with the constitutional text: constitutional barries may not prevent [Community law] from having the force of law in the State.

[300] High Court (Ireland), decision of 2 October 1987, *Lawlor v Minister for Agriculture* [1990] 1 IR 356; [1988] ILRM 400; www.irlii.org.

[301] High Court (Ireland), decision of 2 October 1987, *Lawlor v Minister for Agriculture* [1990] 1 IR 356; [1988] ILRM 400; www.irlii.org.

meet the general spirit of its obligations of membership'.[302] The choice of words was unfortunate:[303] the notion 'consequent upon' had precisely been replaced at the time of drafting of the constitutional provision, because it was both too wide and imprecise. It would have validated otherwise unconstitutional measures adopted by Irish authorities on their own initiative to deal with issues within the scope of the Treaties.[304] Murphy J elaborated on the definition of 'necessity' in *Greene,*[305] finding that the notion did apply even where the actions of the State involved a certain measure of choice, selection or discretion. If there were no such flexibility, it would hardly be necessary to say that the particular actions were adopted by the State at all: presumably, they would have operated as a Community regulation rather than as a directive by it. Yet, there is a point where the protection of Article 29.4.7 ends: *'On the other hand, there must be a point at which the discretion exercised by the State or the national authority is so far-reaching or so detached from the result to be achieved by the directive, that it cannot be said to have been necessitated by it'.* The word 'necessitated' in Article 29.4.[7] involved a question of degree. In finding that point, it seemed to be for the Irish courts to strike a balance between not needlessly thwarting the reception of Community measures into Irish law, and not needlessly restricting the scope of application of the Constitution.[306] In *Greene*, the ministerial regulations passed that point. Murphy J paid particular attention to the fact that the directive merely *authorised* the Member States to introduce restrictive conditions: the Irish State decided to do so and chose a particular means test. Other Member States had not introduced any restrictive conditions. In most cases it will be much more difficult to decide whether or not a particular act was necessitated by the obligations of membership.

---

[302] My emphasis.

[303] So A Whelan, 'Article 29.4.3. and the Meaning of :"Necessity", 2 *Irish Student Law Review*, 1992, 60, at 65; compare also, in another context, the definition of necessity in *Crotty*, dicussed above, where necessity implies the absence of choice.

[304] See J Temple Lang, 'Legal and Constitutional Implications for Ireland of Adhesion to the EEC Treaty', *CML Rev* (1972) 167, at 169–70.

[305] High Court (Ireland), decision of 4 April 1989, *Greene v Minister for Agriculture* [1990] 2 IR 17; [1990] ILRM 364; www.irlii.org. It is interesting to note the particularities of the case: The relevant Council Directive authorised the Member States to introduce a special system of aids in respect of mountain and hill farming, and allowed them to lay down restrictive conditions for granting the allowance. The ministerial regulations did insert a means test: they would benefit only farmers whose off-farm income combined with that of their spouses did not exceed a specified amount. The plaintiffs argued that the ministerial regulation treated married couples less favourable than unmarried couples living together, thus violating the State's constitutional pledge to guard with special care the institution of Marriage, on which the Family is founded, and to protect it against attack, as laid down in Article 41.3.1 of *Bunreacht na hÉireann*.

[306] So A Whelan, 'Article 29.4.3 and the Meaning of "Necessity", 2 *Irish Student Law Review*, 1992, 60, at 60; see however the position of Temple Lang discussed *below*.

A rather different decision was handed in *Condon*[307] where Lynch J held: 'The fact that a scheme under [a Council regulation] is optional and mandatory does not mean that it must remain a dead letter. It is for the competent authority to decide if it should be activated and implemented and once the competent authority so decides then that necessitates details of how the scheme should work. These details are determined by the Minister as competent authority not directly by the European Community and therefore their constitutional validity arises for consideration under the first part of [Article 29.4.3]. Insofar as such details of implementation are reasonable they must be regarded as necessitated by the obligations of membership of the Communities and cannot therefore be unconstitutional. If however the details were unreasonable or unfair then they could hardly be said to be necessitated by the obligations of membership of the Communities and they would be open to constitutional challenge'.

In all of these cases, the Irish courts attempt to define the notion 'necessitated' from an Irish perspective, finding a balance between the constitutional and Community obligations imposed on the State. Temple Lang has, nevertheless, argued that Article 29.4.7 must mean that measures which would otherwise be unconstitutional are authorised, if they are necessitated *objectively* by the obligations of membership *as determined by Community law,* and it should not be interpreted as meaning 'necessitated by the obligations of membership of the Communities *as ultimately judged subjectively by the Irish courts'.*[308] He suggested that Article 29.4.[7] constitutes a *renvoi* from the Constitution of Ireland to the constitutional law of the Community, and in particular to Article 5 of the Treaty (now Article 10 EC). To interpret Article 29.4.[7], a reference to Luxembourg under Article 234 EC might be necessary.

The meaning of Article 26.4.[7] of the Constitution was also explored in another case, which did not directly concern an inconsistency between the Community law and the Constitution, but rather the Irish implementation methods in answer to Article 189(3) of the Treaty (now Article 249 EC). It concerned, therefore, not the constitutional scrutiny of the content of implementing measures, but of the implementing mechanism itself as provided for in Section 3 of the 1972 EC Act. In *Meagher*,[309] the question

---

[307] High Court (Ireland), decision of 12 October 1990, *Condon v Minister for Agriculture*, commented in A Whelan, 'Article 29.4.3. and the Meaning of "Necessity"', 2 *Irish Student Law review*, 1992, 60, at 66 *et seq.*

[308] J Temple Lang, 'The Widening Scope of Constitutional law', in D Curtin and D O'Keeffe (eds), *Constitutional Adjudication in European Community and National Law. Essays for the Honorable Mr Justice TF O'Higgins* (Dublin, Butterworth, 1992), 229, at 231, my emphasis.

[309] Supreme Court, decision of 1 April 1993, *Meagher v Minister for Agriculture and Food* [1994] 1 IR 329; [1994] ILRM 1; commented in A Whelan, 'Constitutional Law – *Meagher v Minister for Agriculture*', 15 *Dublin University Law Journal*, 1993, 152; G Hogan, 'The Implementation of European Union Law in Ireland: The *Meagher* case and the Democratic Deficit', 1 *Irish Journal of European Law*, 1994, 190; G Hogan, 'The *Meagher* Case and the Executive Implementation of European Directives in Ireland', 2 *MJ*, 1995, 174; N Travers, 'The implementation of directives into Irish law', 20 *ELR*, 1995, 103.

was whether a Minister could validly amend Irish primary legislation in order to give effect to an EC Directive. Section 3 of the 1972 EC Act allows for the implementation of non-directly applicable Community legislation by statutory instrument in the form of ministerial orders. Were it not for the Community dimension such procedure would be unconstitutional under Article 15 of the Irish Constitution, reserving to the *Oireachtas* the sole and exclusive power of making laws for the State. The essence of the case therefore was whether Article 29.4.[7] could be called in aid to justify a procedure of implementing directives which would otherwise be in breach of Article 15 of the Constitution.[310] Prior to *Meagher*, it had been argued that it was unconstitutional to transpose directives by way of ministerial orders where this involved legislative repeal or amendment, since Article 189 of the Treaty (now Article 249 EC) does not prescribe any particular method of implementation and the immunity clause in Article 29.4.[7] of the Constitution rescues only those national measures which are 'necessitated' by membership of the European Communities. Since Section 3 of the 1972 EC Act was not so necessitated, it was subject to the full rigours of the Constitution, including Article 15.[311] The scope of application of the Constitution should not needlessly be restricted and due regard should still be had to the separation of powers and the constitutional principle of democracy.

The High Court, in *Meagher*, held that at least part of Section 3 of the 1972 EC Act was indeed not shielded by the constitutional immunity provision of Article 29.4 and that a ministerial order could only be used constitutionally where the transposition of a directive did not require the amendment of existing primary legislation.[312] On appeal from the Government, however, the Supreme Court upheld the constitutionality of the 1972 Act, and effectively saved the practice of implementing directives by way of ministerial order even in ways that would ordinarily conflict with the Constitution. It adopted a broad and generous interpretation of the 'necessity' clause in Article 29.4.[7] and allowed not only what is necessary as a matter of strict law, but also what was *justified and appropriate* to comply with the obligation of implementing non-directly effective Community law fully, efficiently and timely. It held that having regard to the number of Community laws, acts done and measures adopted which need further implementation or whose application must be facilitated by State action, the obligations of membership would necessitate facilitating

[310] G Hogan, 2 *MJ*, 1995, at 177.
[311] Among others A Whelan, 'Art. 29.3.4 and the Meaning of "Necessity"', *Irish Student Law Review*, 1992, 60.
[312] As a result, several hundred ministerial orders adopted with a view to transpose directives appeared to be on shaky grounds. The European Communities (Amendment) Act 1993 was adopted to confirm all existing measures, see N Travers, 'The implementation of directives into Irish law', 20 *ELR*, 1995, 103, at 107–8.

these activities, in some instances at least, and possibly in the great majority of instances, by the making of ministerial regulation rather than legislation of the *Oireachtas*. The Supreme Court was criticised for having unduly sacrificed on the altar of administrative efficiency the traditional separation of powers doctrine recognised expressly in the Constitution.[313] Indeed, the particular machinery chosen in Section 3 of the EC Act is not, as a matter of Community law, necessitated by membership. Phelan suggests that what is considered by the Supreme Court as being necessitated by the obligations of membership is again more *communautaire* than Community law itself, while being an Irish interpretation of it.[314] As to the ministerial regulation in question, it was considered to be *intra vires* of the ministerial powers, and was thus upheld.

The issue was again brought before the Supreme Court in *Maher*,[315] which again concerned a milk quota case. The applicants challenged the validity of a ministerial regulation made in pursuance of a Community regulation on grounds that it constituted the exercise of legislative power by the Minister contrary to Article 15.2.1 of the Constitution, violated the property rights of the applicants guaranteed by the Constitution and was not offered immunity by Article 29.4.7 of the Constitution. The case was dismissed in the High Court, and appealed to the Supreme Court. Before the Supreme Court the case did not turn on the constitutionality of Section 3 of the EC Act which had been upheld in *Meagher*, but rather on the question whether a particular ministerial regulation was *ultra vires* of the powers conferred on Ministers by Section 3 of the EC Act. Keane CJ explained that there were two broad categories of cases in which a regulation adopted pursuant to Section 3 might be found *ultra vires*: firstly, if the making of the regulation was not necessitated by the obligations of membership and violated some constitutional rights of the plaintiff; secondly, where the implementation of Community law by ministerial regulation rather than by an Act of the *Oireachtas* would be in conflict with the exclusive legislative role of the *Oireachtas* under Article 15.2.1 of the Constitution and would not be saved by Article 29.4.7. That would be the case where the ministerial implementation went further than simply implementing details of principles or policies to be found in the Community Directive or Regulation in question and determined such principles or policies itself and the making of the ministerial regulation in that form, rather than an Act of the *Oireachtas* could not be regarded as necessitated by the obligations of membership.[316]

---

[313] N Travers, 'The implementation of directives into Irish law', 20 *ELR*, 1995, 103, at 104.
[314] DR Phelan, *Revolt or Revolution. The Constitutional Boundaries of the European Community* (Dublin, Round Hall, 1997) at 344.
[315] Supreme Court, decision of 30 March 2001, *Maher v Minister for Agriculture*, [2001] 2 ILRM 481; www.bailii.org/ie/cases.
[316] Supreme Court, decision of 30 March 2001, *Maher v Minister for Agriculture*, [2001] ILRM 481; www.bailii.org/ie/cases, at marginal number 82.

The test of 'necessity' is applied at different levels: Keane CJ first established that implementation itself of the Community regulation (in whatever form) was indeed necessitated by the obligations of membership. Then, he inquired whether the particular form, ministerial regulation rather than Act of the *Oireachtas* was in conflict with the exclusive legislative role of the *Oireachtas* as was not necessitated by the obligations of membership.[317] He held that it was not, under reference to the *Eridania* judgment of the Court of Justice.[318] He then proceeded to review whether the making of the ministerial regulation was an impermissible exercise of the legislative role of the *Oireachtas*. The appropriate test here was whether the ministerial regulation did more than giving effect to principles and policies contained in the Community regulation.[319] Keane CJ found that it did not. Furthermore, there was no violation of any property rights under the Constitution and accordingly it was irrelevant in this context whether it was necessitated by the obligations of membership. Finally, there was no infringement of the rights of property under Community law. The appeal was dismissed.

18.2.5.3. Article 29.4.7 and Secondary (Non-Community) Union Law

At the occasion of the Treaty of Maastricht, the text of the constitutional immunity clause of Article 29.4.[7] was amended so as to include a reference to (non-Community) Union law and decisions by other organs than the Community institutions. The constitutional immunity now extends to

---

[317] Kearne CJ explained that there were two routes by which a conclusion could be reached on this issue: One could start by first considering the issue of whether it was necessitated, and if it was, it would be unnecessary to consider whether there was a conflict with Art. 15.2 or private property rights; or, alternatively, one could first determine whether it violates Art. 15.2 or the private property rights or both. If no breach was found, then it would be unnecessary to found out whether enactment in the form of a regulation rather than an Act was necessitated by the obligations of membership. He decided that it was immaterial which route was chosen because it was clear that the particular choice of form (a ministerial regulation rather than an Act) was not necessitated by the obligations of memberhip.

[318] Case 230/78 *SpA Eridania-Zuccherifici nazionali v Minister for Agriculture and Forestry* [1979] ECR 2749, where the Court held that the fact that a regulation is directly applicable does not prevent the provision of that regulation from empowering a Community institution or a Member State to take implementing measures.In the latter case the detailed rules for the exercise of that power are governed by the public law of the Member State. However, the direct applicability of the regulation empowering the Member State to take the national measure in question will mean that the national court may ascertain whether such national measures are in accordance with the content of the Community regulation.

[319] This 'principles and policies' test was an application of the test applied in strictly national cases to review whether delegated legislation constitutes an unauthorised delegation of parliamentary power. If it does more than merely giving effect to principles and policies contained in the parent statute, it is not authorised and constitutes a violation of Art. 15 of the Constitution. Applied to the case of ministerial regulations implementing Community law, the 'parent statute' was the Community directive or regulation which the ministerial regulation intended to implement.

'laws enacted, acts done and measures adopted by the State which are *necessitated by the obligations of membership of the European Union* or of the Communities' and to 'laws enacted, acts done or measures adopted *by the European Union* or by the Communities or by institutions thereof, or *by bodies competent under the Treaties establishing the Communities'*.[320] It has been pointed out[321] that in at least three respects the provision was revolutionary and problematic: first, it assumed that the Union would be able to adopt, in its own right, acts which can have force of law in the State. Ireland had thus prepared itself constitutionally for an ambitious Union competence. However, it is not at all clear that the Union may legislate with force of law in the Member States. In the case of Title VI, direct effect of decisions and framework decisions is expressly excluded. In addition, and from an Irish perspective, there is no parallel to the EC Act for Union law. Union law is therefore not made effective in the Irish legal order, and it has no force of law in the State in the first place. Second, it extends immunity from constitutional scrutiny to acts that are not subject to scrutiny from the European Court of Justice. Indeed, the provision appears to say that acts adopted by the Union or acts done by the Irish authorities applying or implementing Union law falls outside the scope of the Irish courts and the Irish judicial protection of fundamental rights and other constitutional interests, and this, despite the fact that judicial protection offered at the Union level is very limited and often non-existent.[322] And third, there is no possibility of referring to the Court of Justice the necessity test with respect to all cases on Union law.[323] Article 29.4.7 will accordingly operate differently in the context of non-Community Union law: the Court of Justice cannot in all cases be seized to assist the Irish courts on deciding what is necessitated by the obligations of membership.

18.2.6. Belgium

There are no cases, in Belgium, of the applicability of Community or Union law being questioned by the constitutional court or the ordinary

---

[320] My emphasis.

[321] DR Phelan and A Whelan, 'National Constitutional Law and European Integration', in *Le droit constitutionnel national et l'intégration européenne. 17. FIDE Kongress*, Berlin, 1996, 292, at 322–24; G Hogan and A Whelan, *Ireland and the European Union: Constitutional and Statutory Texts and Commentary*, (Dublin, Sweet & Maxwell), at 90.

[322] This is diametrically opposed to the position of the *Bundesverfassungsgericht* which did not find the absence of a role for the ECJ in the second and the third pillar unconstitutional, precisely because the German courts would offer judicial protection and uphold the constitutional fundamental rights. The Irish constitutional provision adds to the lack of judicial control in the second and third pillar (or, since Amsterdam, the limited role of the ECJ in Titles V and VI and the restrictions in Title IV) by granting immunity to Union acts and national acts necessitated by them.

[323] This is important if it is accepted that the necessity test refers back to Community law, which is not accepted by all, see e.g. DR Phelan, *Revolt or Revolution*, at 347.

courts. Nor has there been an open 'threat' to the supremacy of Community law comparable to that of the *Bundesverfassungsgericht*, the *Corte costituzionale* or the *Højesteret*. And yet, Belgium is sometimes mentioned among those Member States where the supremacy of Community may be limited or may suffer counterlimits based on the national constitution. The position of the ordinary civil and administrative highest courts and of the *Cour d'arbitrage* will be discussed in turn.

18.2.6.1. The Ordinary Courts: the Cour de cassation

For a long time, the 1971 *Le Ski* judgment of the *Cour de cassation* was considered to dispose conclusively of the question of the supremacy of international law in general and Community law specifically. *Le Ski*, it will be remembered, was one of the most pro-Community pronouncements of supremacy over national law. Acceptance of supremacy was not restricted to Community law, but applied to the entirety of directly effective international law, and was founded on the full consequences drawn from the *pacta sunt servanda* principle of international law, which applied, *a fortiori*, to Community law, a new legal order for the benefit of which the Member States had restricted the exercise of their sovereign powers. The judgment did not distinguish between types or ranks of national law. It did not mention the Constitution, but its logic, that international law takes precedence by its very nature, implies that even constitutional provisions would have to give way to international and Community law. Yet, the issue never arose before the ordinary courts, until 1996.

18.2.6.2. The Ordinary Courts: the Conseil d'État

The question of the relationship between the Constitution and Community law came up before the *Conseil d'État* in *Orfinger*.[324] The case concerned an alleged conflict between Article 48 of the EC Treaty (old) and several constitutional provisions. Yet, the *Conseil d'État* approached the case as one of a conflict between an interpretation of the Treaty by the Court of Justice, rather than the Treaty itself, on the one hand, and the Constitution on the other.[325] Yet, the *Conseil d'État* probably assumed this

---

[324] *Conseil d'État* (B), decision of 5 November 1996, *Orfinger*, JT, 1997, 254, note R Ergec; the decision has been discussed in the chapter on constitutional review of the Treaties themselves, since the alleged conflict, in the case, was between several articles of the Constitution, and Art. 48 of the Treaty, as interpreted by the ECJ From a Community point of view, it would have to be accepted that the interpretation by the Court of Justice is considered to form part of the Treaty itself; it remains primary Community law. Yet, the *Conseil d'État* put emphasis on the fact that it was not, in its view, a conflict between the Treaty and the Constitution, but 'only' between an interpretation of the constitutional treaty with the Constitution.

[325] This position has been criticised above in Chapter 16.

position so as to make its technique acceptable: it found the basis for the precedence of the interpretation by the Court of Justice over the constitutional norms not in the 'very nature' of international or Community law (as the *Cour de cassation* had done in *Le Ski*), but rather in Article 34 of the Constitution which authorises the transfer of the exercise of sovereign powers, including the power to interpret the Treaty, and without any limitations. On the basis of Article 34 of the Constitution, the interpretation by the Court of Justice would have to be applied, even if such implied that constitutional norms could not be upheld. This type of reasoning may work for secondary Community law; it is not however convincing in order to argue the case for the supremacy of the Treaties themselves.[326] The *Conseil d'État* thus arrived at the position imposed by Community law and the Court of Justice, albeit on different, constitutional, grounds.

18.2.6.3. The Cour d'arbitrage

The issue of constitutional review of treaties re-appeared when the *Cour d'arbitrage* was created. The constitutional court was established essentially to supervise the division of competences between the federation and the federated entities, and also has jurisdiction to review the constitutionality of Acts assenting to treaties.[327] Indirectly it can thus review the constitutionality of treaties. The principle of supremacy of treaties over national law, which was firmly established in Belgian law since *Le Ski*, now suffers an exception: it does not apply to treaties which do not pass the constitutionality test.[328] Now, does this apply also to secondary Community law? Can or will the Cour d'arbitrage review its constitutionality?

On the basis of the existing case law it is difficult to predict what the position of the *Cour d'arbitrage* will be, should it be confronted with, for instance, a Belgian statute implementing a Community directive alleged to conflict with the Constitution. The *Cour d'arbitrage* may well be the least protective and most *communautaire* of all constitutional courts: it refers questions for preliminary ruling; it has obviously shied away from obstructing

---

[326] It is, however, the route followed by the *Corte costituzionale* to accept the ordinary supremacy of Community law, and even the ultimate supremacy over the non-core constitutional provisions (the reference to Art. 11 of the Constitution).

[327] The Special Act on the *Cour d'arbitrage* expressly restricts the time limit for direct actions against Acts assenting to a treaty; these acts are therefore within the control of the *Arbitragehof*; no special provision is made with respect to questions for preliminary ruling on the constitutionality of Acts assenting to a treaty; accordingly, the common rules apply and the constitutional ity of Acts assenting to a treaty, and therefore indirectly of the treaty itself, can at all times be put before the *Cour d'arbitrage*.

[328] See M Melchior, in *Diritto comunitario europeo e diritto nazionale. Atti del seminario internazionale*, (Milano, Giuffrè, 1997), at 233; Melchior is president of the Cour d'arbitrage; he further explained: '*L'idée de base est que le législateur ne peut faire indirectement par la voie de traités ce qu'il ne peut pas faire directement par voie de lois nationales*'.

the Belgian membership of the European Union which seemed defective for a direct conflict with a constitutional provision. The same prudence may be expected where the constitutionality of secondary Community law is at issue.

In an article published on the occasion of the 1997 Paris Colloque of Constitutional Courts of the Member States of the Union, organised by the *Conseil constitutionnel*, the French-speaking president of the *Cour d'arbitrage*[329] Michel Melchior predicted what the stance of the *Cour d'arbitrage* would be, in the absence of any case law.[330] In his opinion, a *direct* challenge of the constitutionality of a piece of secondary Community law would be inadmissible, since the *Cour* had jurisdiction only to review the constitutionality of Acts adopted by one of the Parliaments, federal and regional. He rejected the parallel with the position of the *Bundesverfassungsgericht* in *Maastricht*, that all laws applicable in Belgium – including Community law – should be subject to constitutional review, on grounds that Article 34 of the Constitution authorises the transfer of the exercise of powers to international organisations. Nevertheless, the Act assenting to the Treaties could be brought for review, and regulations and directives produce effects in the Belgian legal order on grounds of Article 249 EC, and accordingly by virtue of the Acts assenting to the Treaties. Consequently, through the Acts assenting to the Treaties, the content of regulations or directives could indirectly come up for constitutional review: an allegedly unconstitutional directive would make the Treaty allowing for it to be adopted unconstitutional, and accordingly also the Acts assenting to the Treaties. This is what could be termed the Italian type situation, after *Fragd*. However, Melchior continued, such indirect review of the content of regulations and directives themselves would in any event result in an infringement by Belgium of the obligations resulting from membership, and would jeopardise the effectiveness and uniformity of secondary Community law; in addition, it would be contrary to the case law of the Court of Justice as espoused in *Foto-Frost*.[331] Melchior therefore suggested that the intervention by the *Cour d'arbitrage* would have to be mitigated, and this was possible on the basis of the transfer of powers provision contained in Article 34

---

[329] The *Cour d'arbitrage* has two presidents, one from the Dutch language group and one from the French language group. The judges of each linguistic group elect a president, who presides over the Court for a term of one year, commencing on 1 September, in rotation with the other president: the president from the Dutch language group in the even years, the president from the French language group in the odd years.

[330] M Melchior and P Vandernoot, 'Controle de constitutionnalité et droit communautaire dérivé', *RBDC*, 1998, 3.

[331] Melchior noted that there was one important difference at least from a national perspective: in *Foto-Frost* what was at stake was the Community validity; while in the hypothesis under analysis, it was the national constitutional validity which was at issue. However, for the ECJ this would not make any difference. One may add the reference to *Internationale Handelsgesellschaft* and the principle of ultimate supremacy.

of the Constitution: Belgium has transferred legislative, executive *and judicial powers* (Article 220 EC) to the Communities, and has accordingly agreed not to exercise these powers unilaterally. Belgium has thus agreed not to conduct any judicial review of secondary Community law: *'Donner et retenir ne vaut'*.[332]

Matters are somewhat more complicated when it comes the Belgian acts implementing or applying secondary Community law. Melchior did accept the possibility that *national or regional acts implementing Community law* could be brought for review of their compatibility with the Constitution. Nevertheless, Melchior and Vandernoot stated, in such case the *Cour d'arbitrage* would always first make a reference to the Court of Justice, or try to conciliate Community law and national constitutional provisions through conform interpretation. If these methods did not resolve the issue, and a conflict continued to exist, Melchior drew a distinction between the two types of standards of reference the *Cour* was established to protect. With respect to the constitutional provisions concerning the division of competences between the federation and the federated entities, there was noting in European Union law to prevent the *Cour d'arbitrage* from conducting its constitutional review: indeed, the annulled measure could be re-adopted by the competent authority.[333] In contrast, in the second situation, of an alleged infringement of the constitutional principles of equality and non-discrimination, the challenged provision could not, when declared unconstitutional, as such be reinstated. *'Ainsi, si ces actes établissent des discriminations, même en application du droit communautaire, et même si cette discrimination est contenue dans une directive, ils devraient, à mon sens, être annullés. En effet, si les traités sont inférieurs à la Constitution, alors le droit dérivé l'est aussi.'*[334] In this case also, Melchior suggested that the solution could be found in Article 34 of the Constitution, so as to allow a national provision implementing a secondary Community measure contrary to the Constitution to subsist, because this infringement of the Constitution was in some way covered by Article 34 of the Constitution.[335]

Melchior rejected the view that Article 34 of the Constitution excluded any (indirect) judicial review of the constitutionality of secondary Community law, at least as long as there was not at the European level a Court of Justice which would effectively protect fundamental rights as the

---

[332] M Melchior and P Vandernoot, 'Controle de constitutionnalité et droit communautaire dérivé', *RBDC*, 1998, 3, at 38.

[333] In addition, the *Cour d'arbitrage* has jurisdiction to maintain the effects of the annulled measure even for the period after the annulment, in order to avoid a legal vacuum, and to give the competent legislature the opportunity to intervene.

[334] Above, at 234.

[335] M Melchior and P Vandernoot, 'Controle de constitutionnalité et droit communautaire dérivé', *RBDC*, 1998, 3, at 39.

constitutional courts did at the national level. As long as there was no catalogue of fundamental rights, the constitutional courts were justified in maintaining a limit on the supremacy of Community law in the area of fundamental rights and not leaving it entirely to the Court of Justice. He explicitly agreed with the *Bundesverfassungsgericht* and the *Corte costituzionale* on the issue of fundamental rights protection. However he did not agree with the position of the *Bundesverfassungsgericht* on the issue of *Kompetenz Kompetenz*: a similar position would be unconstitutional in the light of Article 34 of the Constitution, which allows for the transfer of judicial power, and the Treaties granted the Court of Justice jurisdiction to review the legality of Community law, inter alia on grounds of competence. Moreover, it violated the principles of international law, more particularly the principle of good faith in the application of Treaties; and it was tantamount to introducing a reservation in an existing treaty in force. And finally, it conflicted with the Community Treaties where the Member States have recognised the judicial *Kompetenz Kompetenz* of the Court of Justice. One could hope that the Court of Justice would adopt a position of *self-restraint*, but national courts should not take matters in their own hands.[336]

Melchior's solutions are exceptionally Community friendly, and go beyond the most integrationist decisions of the other Constitutional courts. He proposes to use the transfer of powers provision of Article 34 of the Constitution as a *'soupape de sécurité'*[337] in order to circumvent potential conflicts between secondary Community law and the Constitution. The provision would thus allow for a deviation from the Constitution. Melchior does not seem to distinguish to this effect between core principles and other provisions of the Constitution. This extremely generous use of Article 34 of the Constitution is all the more remarkable since the provision says nothing more than, say, Article 24 of the German Constitution. In contrast, the German Constitutional Court has used Article 24 of the German Basic Law precisely to limit the effects of Community law in the German legal order. In addition, it is striking that Melchior seems to go further than the Irish Supreme Court, which does have an express constitutional provision providing Community law and Irish acts adopted under it immunity for constitutional review. The position of the Irish

---

[336] President Melchior's critique of the German Court's position was particularly harsh: it was not only wrong, it was also dangerous for a Member State, even the most powerful economically and politically, to defy Community law, it would have *'un effet destructeur'*, *'ce serait établir le système de la tour de Babel dans le droit communautaire et revenir à un système de droit international tout à fait primitif'*. And: *'Par ailleurs, il ne paraît pas admissible de justifier un tel comportement en se voilant du drapeau des exigences de la démocratie. Je crois quíl s'agit là d'un alibi'...*, above, at 240.

[337] M Melchior and P Vandernoot, 'Controle de constitutionnalité et droit communautaire dérivé', *RBDC*, 1998, 3, at 40.

Courts in the abortion cases is probably to be explained by the sensitivity of the subject concerned, and it is not clear what the *Cour d'arbitrage* would do in a case of similar importance for Belgium. But for the time being, it seems that the Belgian *Cour d'arbitrage* may well accept the full and ultimate supremacy of both primary and secondary Community law on the basis of the transfer of powers provision, which 'neutralises' any alleged conflict with constitutional provisions.

18.3. CONCLUDING REMARKS

In all of the member States discussed in the present chapter, some 'pockets of resistance' have been detected. In order to come to an overall conclusion it may be helpful first to draw the lines together and make a cross-national analysis, in order to find out what the main areas of contention are.

18.3.1. Non-core Constitutional Norms

In most of the Member States it is accepted, either by constitutional provision or by the judicial decision, that Union law may deviate from certain constitutional provisions. It is difficult to maintain otherwise: the very existence and effect of secondary law is at odds with principles of national sovereignty, exclusive legislative powers for the national (or regional) Parliament and the like. The Italian *Corte costituzionale* was first to distinguish between those constitutional norms which ceded in the face of Community law, and the core principles of the Constitution which operate as counterlimits to the supremacy of Community law. Other courts have followed suit.

The *Bundesverfassungsgericht* in *Solange I* desiganted constitutional fundamental rights as entrenched,[338] but left open the question as to whether there would be more of these core principles.[339] In *Solange II*, and under explicit reference to similar limits under the Italian Constitution and the decisions of the *Corte costituzionale*, it spoke of 'essential structural parts of the Constitution' or 'the identity of the prevailing constitutional order' and, in particular, the legal principles underlying the constitutional provisions on fundamental rights.[340] In *Maastricht*, the link was made with the

---

[338] *Bundesverfassungsgericht*, decision of 29 May 1974, *Internationale Handelsgesellschaft (Solange I)*, Oppenheimer, *The Cases*, at 446.

[339] Above, at 445.

[340] *Bundesverfassungsgericht*, decision of 22 October 1986, *Wünsche Handelsgesellschaft (Solange II)*, Oppenheimer, *The Cases*, at 485.

Ewigkeitsklausel of Article 79(3) of the German Basic Law, in the discussion of the claim that the democratic principle was violated. It is as yet unclear whether the *Cour d'arbitrage* will distinguish between fundamental rights and other principles which it protects. It may well be that it accepts full constitutional immunity of Comunity law.

18.3.2. Fundamental Rights

The protection of fundamental rights has been a bone of contention between several national courts and the Court of Justice, ever since the seventies and continuing to this date. The Italian and German constitutional courts were first to doubt that the protection of fundamental rights at the Community level was sufficient, and accordingly made exceptions to the principle of supremacy and the effect of Community law in that area. To be more precise, they threatened to step in where the protection at the Community level would fall short, with varying degrees of intention to actually intervene if need be, but neither ever did.

In the meantime, the Danish *Højesteret* has joined the Italian and German courts and warned that should Community law infringe upon fundamental rights and the Court of Justice did not correct it, such provisions would not be applicable in Denmark. The Danish version is an application of *Kompetenz Kompetenz*, applied in the area of fundamental rights: should the Community infringe upon Danish rights, and this would be considered lawful under Community law, this would imply that the Danish Government has transferred powers to Europe than it does not retain: Danish authorities do not have to competence to infringe fundamental rights. Accordingly, such Act would be inapplicable in Denmark. However, the Danish version does appear to be a rather soft version, which leaves much to be decided by the Court of Justice. The Irish Supreme Court equally may reserve the right to make an exception to the supremacy of Community law, where the most fundamental of fundamental rights are at stake, despite what the Constitution itself seems to provide. It is not as yet clear what the position will be of the Belgian *Cour d'arbitrage*, but it may well follow the lines set out by the Court of Justice, on the basis of Article 34 of the Belgian Constitution.

The differences in stance of the national constitutional courts may be explained by the difference in prestige, the varying traditions relating to the (judicial) protection of fundamental rights, and indeed the dissimilar national perceptions of the relationship between European law and national (constitutional) law, including fundamental rights. The *Bundesverfassungsgericht*, for instance, is on the national plane one of the main constitutional actors, which regularly decides difficult and controversial issues that politics may not be able to answer. By translating them into legal questions and answering them by reference to the dictates of the *Grundgesetz*, the *Bundesverfassungsgericht* has on occasions solved critical controversies. The Belgian *Cour d'arbitrage*, to mention an example at the other end, is much younger than its Italian and German counterparts, and has not (yet) achieved the same position, certainly not in the area of fundamental rights. And *'courts are most audacious in asserting their power when they garb themselves in the mantle of guardians of the human rights guaranteed by constitutional documents. They are, too, most successful in mobilizing support for and legitimising their power in the context of human rights'*.[341] But there are great differences between the Member States not only with respect to the actual rights and their content but also with respect to the degree to which legislative choices may be scrutinised on their compatibility with fundamental rights by the courts.[342] It is a reflection of the national interpretation of the separation of powers principle.

None of the constitutional courts has actually intervened, though the conflict surrounding the bananas cases came close. The fact that there have been no head on collisions cannot be explained by the fact that there have been no appropriate cases: the bananas case is a perfect example a Community regulation that could (with good reason) be declared unconstitutional. Even so, it is of course not a small matter for a court to actually hold that a measure of Community law infringes national constitutional fundamental rights, where the Court of Justice has held differently, and subsequently to hold that Community law cannot be applied. If the German Court would have so decided in the bananas cases, that would have been the end of the regulation. In the context of *Kompetenz Kompetenz*, but applicable also to the area of fundamental rights or indeed any case in which a Community act is declared unconstitutional, Weiler has described the relationship between the *Bundesverfassungsgericht* and the Court of Justice in terms of the dynamics of the Cold War, with its paradoxical guarantee of co-existence following the MAD (Mutual Assured Destruction) logic.[343] For the German court or indeed any constitutional court to actually declare a Community norm unconstitutional would be an extremely hazardous move so as to make its usage unlikely. And yet, the constitutional courts continue from time to time to reiterate the threat. While believers in the Community orthodoxy may be scandalised by the mere warnings of the constitutional courts – indeed, the position is contrary to *Internationale Handelsgesellschaft* – many have pointed out that the

---

[341] So JHH Weiler, 'Human Rights, Constitutionalism and Integration: Iconography and Fetishism', 3 *International Law FORUM du droit international*, 2001, 227, at 228.

[342] See B De Witte, 'The Past and Future Role of the European Court of Justice in the Protection of Human Rights', in P Alston (ed), *The EU and Human Rights* (Oxford, OUP, 1999) 859, at 881.

[343] See *e.g.* JHH Weiler, 'The Autonomy of the Community Legal Order: Through the Looking Glass', in *The Constitution of Europe* (Cambridge, CUP, 1999) 286, at 320 *et seq*.

position of the Italian and German courts has triggered the Court of Justice's fundamental rights jurisprudence. The Court was forced by the national courts to recognise fundamental rights as limits on Community competence in order to achieve full acceptance by those national courts of ultimate supremacy. In general opinion, the national courts were indeed persuaded by the efforts of the Court of Justice: in *Solange II* the *Bundesverfassungsgericht* backed away from its most radical position adopted in *Solange I*, and withdrew to an almost symbolic position of watchdog in unlikely cases where the Court of Justice did not in general offer sufficient protection. The *Bundesverfassungsgericht* even dropped some of the conditions it had posed in *Solange I*: there still was no catalogue of human rights, but it no longer appeared necessary. In the same line, the apparent move back into the direction of *Solange I* in *Maastricht*, was explained by the fact that despite the appearances the Court of Justice had not done a sufficiently good job in protecting fundamental rights. The Court had been accused of merely paying lip-service to the protection of fundamental rights without taking them seriously. The final position (for the time being) in the *Bananas III* decision could then be explained by the fact that a Convention presided over by the former president of the *Bundesverfassungsgericht* Roman Herzog was drafting the EU Charter on Fundamental Rights to be adopted only a few months later. Of course, these explanations can only account for part of the story: there are other elements, such as the influence of individual members on the Bench and so forth. Finally, the refusal of the constitutional courts to give up the last say over fundamental rights may be explained by the fact that fundamental rights constitute the area in which their legitimacy pull is strong; where they mobilise support. Constitutional courts take pride in their roles of guardians of fundamental rights. Fundamental rights and the judicial protection of those rights signify an increasing acceptance of the central role of courts and judges in the public discourse.[344] There is an inevitable tension between judicial power and democracy, but judicial protection of fundamental rights 'against the tyranny of the majority' (or, in this context against the tyranny of Brussels?) does increase legitimacy of non-elected judges.

There is accordingly an interesting paradox in the rationale. The German and Italian, and to a lesser extent, other constitutional courts, in an attempt to retain control, may have forced the Court of Justice into judicial activism and to start reviewing Community acts in the light of unwritten higher principles. At a later stage, the Court would be condemned for its activism in other areas, especially for having extended the competences of the Community at the expense of the Member States. Yet,

---

[344] JHH Weiler, 'Human Rights, Constitutionalism and Integration: Iconography and Fetishism', 3 *International Law FORUM du droit international*, 2001, 227, at 228.

in the area of fundamental rights, judicial activism of the European Court is what the constitutional courts achieved, and in that sense, they enticed the Court of Justice to transform into a rival constitutional court.

18.3.3. *Kompetenz Kompetenz*

Judicial *Kompetenz Kompetenz* was a dormant problem for what appears, with the benefit of hindsight, a remarkably long time. Since the *Maastricht* decision of the *Bundesverfassungsgericht* it has become one of the main constitutional quandaries in the relationship between the Union and the Member States, and between the European and the national constitutional courts. At least the Danish *Højesteret* has followed the German example. The doctrine created an outcry when it was first handed down,[345] but the critique of the European institutions expanding their powers and usurping competences not transferred by the Member States, and the Court of Justice standing by and watching, was, when the dust settled, shared by many. Nevertheless, not many would agree with the conclusion of the *Bundesverfassungsgericht* that it – and possibly other national courts – had jurisdiction to step in where the Court of Justice failed.

As was the case with fundamental rights, the threat has never materialised to this date. Some have made the parallel with the human rights tale where the warning issued by national courts encouraged the Court of Justice to protect human rights. So too, the statements of national courts concerning limited competences and the reservation of judicial *Kompetenz Kompetenz* would compel the Court of Justice to take competences seriously. Some decisions of the Court of Justice have been explained on the ground that the Court had become more active in reviewing acts of the institutions.[346] On the other hand, others have signalled that the episode marks the beginning of a period of judicial restraint on the part of the Court of Justice in the development of Community law, for instance in the area of judicial protection of individuals before national courts.

Overall, it does not seem that the position of the *Bundesverfassungsgericht* is shared by many courts. This is problematic, in the sense that it allows only some representatives in the Community decision making a competitive advantage: 'this decision cannot be adopted because our constitutional court will strike it down'.

---

[345] See M Kumm, 'Who is the Final Arbiter of Constitutionality in Europe? Three Conceptions of the Relationship between the German Federal Constitutional Court and the European Court of Justice', 36 *CML Rev* (1999) 351, at 364.

[346] So for instance *Opinion 2/94 on Accession to the ECHR* [1996] ECR I–1759; Case C–376/98 *Germany v European Parliament and Council of the European Union (tobacco advertising and sponsoring)* [2000] ECR I–8419.

18.3.4. Drawing the Lines Together

Where does all this leave us? It does appear that total and ultimate supremacy of Community law is not fully accepted in all Member States, to different extents. The statement that Community law always takes precedence over national law however framed is only true from a strict European perspective, and may not be true if a wider perspective is adopted. In addition, it may be less true in some countries than in others. Some constitutional courts continue to watch the Community and its Court, and keep up the pressure on the Court by at least threatening to step in where it leaves off. While this situation certainly has its downsides – breach of uniformity, national courts assuming jurisdiction over Community law, or even worse, one or two courts controlling the European Court, and 'spoiling of the atmosphere' – some good may also come out of it. Indeed, one may assume that it forces the Court to take fundamental rights and competences seriously. More generally and more importantly, these decisions of constitutional courts may contribute to keeping the Community institutions and the Member States and national institutions alert. It has been mentioned before: even if these cases seem to concern first and foremost the national courts and the Court of Justice, and there has been word of a *guerre des juges*, there is much more to it: in final analysis, these constitutional courts do not intend to control the Court of Justice: this is all about controlling the Community institutions and the Member States acting in the field of Community law. The Member States and their national institutions, legislative and administrative at all levels, should not, by transferring powers to Europe, be able to escape scrutiny under the Constitution. As long as the protection offered by the national Constitution is not substituted, in the European context, with comparable protection at that level, the national courts will not fully retreat. It is inconvenient, impracticable and simply unfair for a national court to exercise review powers over Community legislation, and as soon as the Community and Union encompass similar protection mechanisms and comply with what may be termed the constitutional *ius commune* – democracy, fundamental rights, rule of law etc – it seems downright wrong, but for the time being, it seems that we will have to live at least with the threat of national review. Whether this may change after the adoption of a European Constitution will be discussed in Part 3.

Part 3

The National Courts' Mandate
and the Future of the European Union

19

Introduction

THE ISSUES CENTRAL in the relationship between the national courts and the Court of Justice, which have been discussed so far in this book, will now be considered again, placed in the context of the current discussion on the European Constitution. Comments will be made on the principle of supremacy, on formalising the mandate of the national courts, on the judicial protection of fundamental rights, the Union Charter of Fundamental Rights, on accession of the Union to the ECHR, and on the judicial patrolling of the division of powers between the Member States and the Union. These general topics will be analysed from a specific perspective, namely that of the national courts, and their relationship with the Court of Justice.

To begin with, some more general remarks will be made on the current discussion on the European Constitution. The debate on the adoption of a 'veritable' European Constitution is for the time being the last stage in an ongoing process. First, there was the period of constitutionalisation, leading to the Court of Justice's description of the EC Treaty as the constitutional charter, and comprising the national courts' acceptance – to a considerable extent – of the central features of constitutionalisation, direct effect, (ordinary) supremacy and the like. Central in that phase was the issue of the relationship with national law and the national Constitutions, with the focus mostly on the judicial dialogue between national courts and the Court of Justice. In the aftermath of the Maastricht Treaty, which established the Union and sanctioned the development of the Communities beyond an internal market, but damaged the existing constitutional coherence,[1] the question was discussed whether the constitutional language that had been developed could be applied to the new circumstances, or should be limited to the first pillar. In addition, the discussion of the nature of the Union (a federation, an international organisation, a *sui generis* autonomous legal order, a *Staatenverbund*?) was taken up again, encompassing also the issue of whether the Union, if it was not a State, could actually have a Constitution. This is also when the discrepancy between the legal science – there already is a European Constitution, as pronounced by the Court of Justice – and

---

[1] See for instance D Curtin, 'The Constitutional Structure of the European Union: A Europe of Bits and Pieces', 30 *CML Rev* (1993) 17.

Introduction

political science – does Europe need a Constitution? – became apparent, and where the lack of a constitutional foundation of Europe, 'constitutionalism without a constitution', was described: the constitutionalisation of the Treaties, so it was argued, had created a constitutional body without discussing its soul.[2] With respect to the court-to-court dialogue, this is the period when the focus was mostly on the unresolved conflicts between the constitutional courts and the Court of Justice, a relationship which was often described as a *guerre des juges* heading towards inevitable collision.

In the running up to the IGC preparing the Amsterdam Treaty, the question was raised whether the next Treaty amendment should follow the 'usual' pattern or should be conceptualised as a constitutional moment, and a Constitution should be drafted.[3] After Amsterdam, which can hardly be described as a success in outcome, method or procedure alike, that discussion was intensified. The questions whether the European Union had a Constitution, whether it needed one[4] and if so, which type of Constitution ('for what type of polity') were hotly debated and new concepts were proposed to merge traditional constitutional principles and the realities of European integration.[5]

But more importantly, the discussion on the adoption of a European Constitution was embraced by politicians, and rather than an argument among lawyers, it became a political debate. The concern for the need of institutional reform in the light of future enlargement and the growing public disenchantment with the European Union set in motion the Future of Europe debate. Romano Prodi's White Paper on European Governance, Joschka Fischer's speech at the Humboldt University in Berlin and the open debate they occasioned went far beyond the Nice leftovers, and prepared for the Laeken Declaration on the Future of Europe.

---

[2] See JHH Weiler, '"...We Will Do, and Hearken" (Ex. XXIV:7) Reflections on a Common Constitutional Law for the European Union', in R Bieber and P Widmer (eds), *The European Constitutional Area*, (Zurich, Schulthess, 1995), 413, and other essays, published in JHH Weiler, *The Constitution of Europe.'Do the new clothes have an emperor' and other essays on European integration* (Cambridge, CUP, 1999); also e.g. M Poiares Maduro, *We, The Court The European Court of Justice and the European Economic Constitution* (Oxford, Hart Publishing, 1998).

[3] B De Witte, 'International Agreement or European Constitution?', in J Winter, D Curtin, A Kellermann and B De Witte (eds), *Reforming the Treaty on European Union: The Legal Debate*, (The Hague, Kluwer Law International, 1996) 1.

[4] See for example JHH Weiler, 'Does Europe Need a Constitution? Demos, Telos and the German *Maastricht* Decision', 1 *ELJ*, 1995, 230; D Grimm, 'Does Europe Need a Constitution?', 1 *ELJ*, 1995, 282, commented on by J Habermas, 'Remarks on Dieter Grimm's 'Does Europe Need a Constitution'', 1 *ELJ*, 1995, 303; N Reich, 'A European Constitution for Citizens: Reflections on the Rethinking of Union and Community Law', 3 *ELJ*, 1997, 131; J Gerkrath, *L'émergence d'un droit constitutionnel pour l'Europe*, (Brussels, Éditions de l'Université de Bruxelles, 1997); J-Cl Piris, 'Does the European Union have a Constitution? Does it Need One?', Harvard Jean Monnet Working Paper, 5/00.

[5] I Pernice, 'Multi-level Constitutionalism and the Treaty of Amsterdam: European Constitution-making Revisited?', 36 *CML Rev*, 1999; I Pernice and F Mayer, 'De la Constitution composée de l'Europe', HWI Paper 1/2001; N MacCormick, *Questioning Sovereignty. Law, State and Nation in the European Commonwealth*, (Oxford, OUP, 1999); N Walker, 'The Idea of Constitutional Pluralism', 65 *MLR*, 2002, 317.

20

Towards a European Constitution

20.1. PAST CONSTITUTION BUILDING: THE IGC MODEL

O NLY A FEW years ago, it was not common to speak of the drafting of a veritable European Constitution. Certainly, the language of constitutionalisation and constitutionalism was used long before, in the case law of the Court of Justice and by many commentators. The tone and nature of the debate changed, and started to turn on the drawing up of a single document type Constitution. The Convention on the Future of the European Union opened in Brussels on 28 February 2002. The decision to establish a Convention to consider the Future of Europe reflected the failure of past IGC's to deal with some of the constitutional problems affecting the Union.[1] Development towards a European Constitution began at Maastricht, when it appeared that European citizens – 'citizenship' was introduced at Maastricht precisely in order to make Europe a reality to its citizens – had become estranged from the European project. Maastricht was designed to constitute a giant step forward in the direction of an ever closer union, and established the European Union, encompassing the existing Communities (including EMU and the euro-project) and two new pillars, organised, however, on a different, intergovernmental basis. Scholars in European law and political studies were irritated mostly about the three pillar structure and the technical hitches it entailed. Nevertheless, the outcome of the first Danish and French referendum demonstrated that citizens had lost touch with the European project. The *Bundesverfassungsgericht* pointed out the weaknesses of the European project from a German constitutional perspective, some of which were controversial even from a national constitutional perspective, but others identified open wounds in the European

---

[1] See for instance, B De Witte, 'The Closest Thing to a Constitutional Conversation in Europe: The Semi-Permanent Treaty Revision Process', in P Beaumont, C Lyons and N Walker (eds), *Convergence and Divergence in European Public Law* (Oxford, Hart Publishing, 2002) 39.

construct as it existed: there *were* (and remain) problems of democracy (even if one removes the specific interpretation thereof by the Constitutional Court suggesting that democracy must necessarily ultimately be based nationally); there *were* issues concerning fundamental rights protection; the division of competences between the Union and the Member States was not sufficiently clear.

The successive IGC's at Amsterdam and Nice were, to say the least, not able to satisfactorily address the more fundamental questions of how to make the Union more effective, and, more important still, to make it more legitimate in the eyes of European citizens. Public disenchantment with an ever more powerful yet opaque Union increased further. It was not only the disappointing *content* of the successive treaties which caused the dismay. The IGC *method* of meeting behind closed doors, of solving fundamental issues during marathon sessions lasting well into the night, the horse-trading, had had its day. Probably also the *density* of IGC's over the past decade had affected their legitimacy and ability to mobilise support. IGC's had developed from exceptional events to an institutionalised element.[2]

20.2. THE CONVENTION MODEL: THE CONVENTION PREPARING THE EU CHARTER ON FUNDAMENTAL RIGHTS

In the meantime, an alternative method had been used for the drafting of the EU Charter of Fundamental Rights: the Convention model. The idea of drafting a European Bill of Rights was not new. Already in *Solange I*, the *Bundesverfassungsgericht* requested the drafting of a catalogue of fundamental rights. Frequently, the issue of a Bill of Rights was presented as an alternative to accession to the ECHR. Yet, it did not happen and for a long time, the protection of fundamental rights developed in the case law of the Court of Justice as general principles of Community law was widely considered sufficient; it was sanctioned by the Member States in the Treaty of Maastricht. The *Maastricht* decisions of the *Bundesverfassungsgericht* and later the *Højesteret* demonstrated that the issue of fundamental rights protection was *not* settled. Also in scholarly writing the protection offered in the case law of the Court of Justice was, by some, considered insufficient.[3] Some commentators argued that the Court did nothing or little more than

---

[2] BPG Smith, *Constitution Building in the European Union. The Process of Treaty Reforms*, (The Hague, Kluwer Law International, 2002), at 208. In fact, during sixteen years between 1984 and 2000, from the initiation of the ICG leading up to the Single European Act signed in 1986 and the Nice IGC, there were only nineteen months free from treaty amendment linked activities, see Ph De Schoutheete, 'Guest Editorial: the Intergovernmental Conference', 37 *CML Rev*, (2000) 845, at fn 1.

[3] See *e.g.* J Coppel and A O'Neill, 'The European Court of Justice: Taking Rights Seriously?', 29 *CML Rev* (1992) 669; but see the fierce and extensive reaction of JHH Weiler and NJS Lockhart, '"Taking Rights Seriously": The European Court of Justice and its Fundamental Rights Jurisprudence', 32 *CML Rev* (1995) 51 and 579.

paying mere lip-service to the protection of fundamental rights. The Court of Justice then in *Opinion 2/94* denied competence of the Communities to access to the ECHR, stating that such decision of constitutional importance would require an express legal basis in the Treaties. Nevertheless, in Amsterdam there was a clear absence of political will to include such provision in the Treaty permitting accession.[4] The idea of a bill re-surfaced.

The actual initiative for the drafting of the Charter lay with the German Presidency of the Union in the first half of 1999, and the Convention was launched at the Cologne European Council meeting. The Charter itself was an exercise in visibility, clarity, and consequently, legitimacy. A Charter of Fundamental Rights for the citizens was seen as a tool to re-build the bridge between the EU and its citizens: *'there appears to be a need at the present stage of the Union's development'*, the Presidency concluded at Cologne, *'to establish a Charter of Fundamental Rights in order to make their overriding importance and relevance more visible to the Union's citizens'*.[5] The Charter would be an important symbol; it would make visible what supposedly already existed in the case law of the Court of Justice but was known only to specialists. In addition, it could facilitate the work of the Court of Justice, which would no longer have to seek human rights in other international documents and common constitutional traditions, but could simply refer to the EU's own Charter. Some influential commentators and actors however questioned the usefulness and desirability of drafting a Charter and suggested that the Union should instead develop a veritable human rights policy (complete with a Commissioner, a Directorate-General, a budget and a horizontal action plan for making the rights already listed elsewhere effective)[6] or accede to the ECHR.[7] Nevertheless, the choice was for a Charter.

What is of interest here is the process and method of the Convention rather than the content of the Charter. The Charter was drafted by a 'Body' which would soon call itself 'Convention', a reference to a constitutional convention at the example of the Philadelphia Convention; it was

---

[4]   See *e.g.* G de Búrca, 'The Drafting of the European Union Charter of Fundamental Rights', 26 *ELR*, 2001, 126, at 129–30.

[5]   European Council Decision on the drawing up of a Charter of Fundamental Rights of the European Union, Annex IV to the Conclusions of the Presidency of the Cologne European Council of 3 and 4 June 1999.

[6]   See *e.g.* JHH Weiler, 'Editorial: Does the European Union Truly Need a Charter of Rights?', 5 *ELJ*, 2000, 95; Ph Alston and JHH Weiler, 'An 'Ever Closer Union' in Need of a Human Rights Policy: The European Union and Human Rights', in Ph Alston (ed), *The EU and Human Rights* (Oxford, OUP, 1999) 3; and see 'Leading by Example: A Human Rights Agenda for the European Union for the Year 2000', Florence, EUI, 1998, report for the *ComitúeAcuteú des Sages*.

[7]   D Curtin, 'The EU Human Rights Charter and the Union Legal Order: the "Banns" before the Marriage?', in D O'Keeffe and A Bavasso (eds), *Judicial Review in European Union Law. Liber Amicorum in Honour of Lord Slynn of Hadley*, (The Hague, Kluwer Law International, 2000), 303.

an 'embryonic constitutional assembly'.[8] The representative character of the Convention was intended to restore the confidence of the Peoples of Europe and to increase Europe's legitimacy. As for the working methods, the Convention would have to constitute a response to the major criticisms of the IGC method: lack of transparency, secrecy, non-consultation of civil society, social groups and experts. This time, there was an open debate, and there was room for participation of civil society. There are down-sides to this method: the reactions, interventions and comments made by 'civil society' are often one-sided, may be of little relevance, politically unrealistic and of a poor quality from a technical legal point of view. And yet, if the openness and invitation to the public to participate is to have any value other than merely giving the impression of participation, the members of the Convention will at least have to take notice of them, which may take up valuable time. The pluralistic process for the drafting of the Charter has much to be said for, especially when compared to the traditionally secretive horse-trading during the classic IGC's. However, the process may also enhance and disguise the power of the draftsmen who *'lurk behind the piles of drafts and amendments, and may thus paradoxically produce less, rather than more, accountability'.*[9] The process may not necessarily be better suited than traditional diplomacy, in terms of legal certainty and quality of the end result, and possibly even in terms of participation.

20.3. THE CONVENTION ON THE FUTURE OF EUROPE

20.3.1. The Inception

In December 2001 the issue of a Convention to prepare for the next and vital IGC was finally decided in the Laeken Declaration.[10] The Declaration described the European Union as a success story, bringing peace and prosperity to Europe. However, it also recognised the challenges of the future: internally, such as the need to bring the Union closer to the citizen, the need for efficiency and transparency, the call for enhanced democratic control and containment of the Union within the limits of its functions; and externally in the redefinition of the Union's role in a globalized world. The Laeken Declaration posed a total of 54

---

8   B De Witte, 'The Closest Thing to a Constitutional Conversation in Europe: The Semi-Permanent Treaty Revision Process', in P Beaumont, C Lyons and N Walker (eds), *Convergence and Divergence in European Public Law* (Oxford, Hart Publishing, 2002) 39.

9   So JB Liisberg, 'Does the EU Charter of Fundamental Rights Threaten the Supremacy of Community Law? Article 53 of the Charter: a fountain of law or just an inkblot?', Harvard Jean Monnet Working Paper 04/01, at 18.

10 The Laeken Declaration, Annex I to the Presidency Conclusions on the Laeken European Council, 14–15 December 2001.

questions for the Convention to answer, under four headings: a better division and definition of the competencies of the European Union, simplification of the Treaties, more democracy, transparency and efficiency in the Union and finally, examining the case for a Constitution for Europe. The Laeken Declaration convened a Convention, in order to pave the way for the next Intergovernmental Conference as broadly and openly as possible and asked it to consider the key issues arising for the Union's future development and try to identify the various possible responses.

20.3.2. The Convention Model

While the EU Charter on Fundamental Rights in itself has not unanimously been regarded a success, the Convention *method* met with general approval, and in the search for democratic legitimation, the choice for the Convention model also for the broader project of a European Constitution seemed self-evident.[11] Nevertheless, this is not a veritable Convention such as the Philadelphia Convention. This Convention prepares the work of an IGC, which will take the ultimate decisions. However, if the Convention does succeed to make a realistic and high-quality proposal for a Constitutional Treaty or Constitution, it will not be simple for the IGC to discard it. If the proposals of the Convention do indeed meet with the approval of the IGC, this will also increase acceptance of the outcome by the general public. In the best possible scenario, if the Convention is indeed successful, it can rightly be said that both the peoples and the Member States of the European Union have acted as constituent authority. Indeed, both in the preparatory Convention phase – through their elected representatives in the national and European Parliaments and through the participation of civil society in the Forum-and in the ratification phase – either directly (through referendum) or indirectly (ratification by national Parliament) the citizens are involved alongside the Government authorities of the Member States.[12] If that would be the case, this participation of the People or Peoples of Europe could be proclaimed and adopted in the text of the Constitution. Such a 'We, The People...' could have a tremendous legitimating effect, it could even be a self-fulfilling prophecy.

[11] See, for a highly favourable discussion of the Convention-model L Hoffmann, 'The Convention on the Future of Europe – Thoughts on the Convention Model', Jean Monnet Working Paper 11/02, who even looks ahead of this Convention and sees a future for the Convention as a semi-permanent institution to solve institutional and constitutional challenges still laying ahead. The current Convention is the test for the model.

[12] See K Lenaerts and M Desomer, 'New Models of Constitution-making in Europe: The Quest for Legitimacy', 39 *CML Rev* (2002) 1217, at 1251–1252. I do not enter into the debate of the European referendum and/or national referendums, and certainly not of the issue of whether there is a European *demos*.

20.3.3. Drafting a Constitution

The task of constitutionalisation, while it aims at the establishment of a Constitution, a Constitutional Treaty or a Treaty establishing a Constitution for Europe, does not necessarily mean that the wheel is invented all over again, or that Europe is for the first time constitutionally established: Europe already had a Constitution, it simply lacked a single constitutional document titled Constitution. Europe's Constitution is scattered around in the consecutive Treaties, in principles developed in practice and recognised in the case law of the Court of Justice, such as the principle of institutional balance, and including the general principles of Community law as derived from the ECHR and the common constitutional traditions of the Member States; and last but not least, it is completed with the national Constitutions of the Member States. What emerges is a multilevel Constitution; a *Constitution composée*, a *Verfassungsverbund*. This is not to say that this Constitution is finished and perfect: it is a developing Constitution of an evolving polity, of an 'ever closer Union among the peoples of Europe'. This view of the European Constitution, of European constitutionalism, requires that traditional models are abandoned, such as the equation Volk or Nation = State = Constitution, and so forth. The old models of statal constitutionalism are not adequate to describe and organise a multi-layered polity such as the European Union. But there is a danger in this view of the European Constitution: namely that when it is accepted that the European Constitution cannot and must not be measured to the classic standards, it will not be measured at all. It can no longer be maintained that since Europe is not a State, it must not comply with the same fundamental requirements of democracy, rule of law, fundamental rights protection etc. The time has come for a fundamental re-thinking of the constitutional foundations of Europe.

The work of the Convention should not be regarded as being limited to a rephrasing of the existing situation. The very term chosen to describe the outcome of the Convention is not innocent:[13] it aims to prepare for a 'Constitutional Moment',[14] confirming and reinforcing the existing Constitution, making it visible to its citizens, their Member States, and to the world. To that effect, it should be more than conceptual constitutional

---

[13] A Vitorino, 'The Convention as a Model for European Constitutionalisation', Vortrag am Walter Hallstein-Institut für Europäisches Verfassungsrecht der Humboldt Universität zu Berlin am 14 Juni 2001, FCE 6/01, at marginal number 27.

[14] See B Ackerman, 'Constitutional Politics/Constitutional Law', 99 *Yale LJ*, 1989, 453; and his *We the People: Foundations*, (Cambridge, MA, Harvard University Press, 1991); *We The People: Transformations*, (Cambridge, MA, Harvard University Press, 1998). In the context of the Convention and the EU Draft Constitutional Treaty, see N Walker, 'After the Constitutional Moment', in I Pernice and M Poiares Maduro (eds), *A Constitution for the European Union: First Comments on the 2003-Draft of the European Convention*, (Baden Baden, Nomos, 2003).

clarification, and should make a break with the past, and mark the beginning of a new constitutional era.

20.3.4. Constitution or Basic Treaty?

What exactly is meant by the adoption of 'a European Constitution'? What would make it different from the past, international treaties considered as the constitutional charter? What would be the hallmarks of a veritable Constitution? I only want to make a few comments. First, it is assumed here that the umbilical cord between State and Constitution is cut. While it is usual currently that Constitutions constitute States, there does not appear to be any reason why it should be absolutely excluded that non-statal entities can also have a Constitution. Hence, the debate on a European Constitution does not coincide with that concerning the statal qualities of the Union, on whether it is or is heading towards a federal State or not; these issues should not be confused. I do not agree with the well-known statement by Kirchhof, that *'Wo kein Staat, da keine Verfassung'*.[15] In my opinion, the Union is not a State, and is not heading in that direction, at least not for the time being.[16] It may also be true that there is no European Nation-State, and no European Nation or European People; it may even be true that it will never exist to the same extent as it exists currently in many States. Nevertheless, this does not exclude the possibility of the Union having a proper Constitution. Nonetheless, the fact that the Union is not a State and for the time being is not intended to become a State, and that the Member States do remain independent States under international law does raise questions as to the relationship between a European Constitution and the national Constitutions. The creation of a European Constitution does not preclude the continuing existence of national Constitutions: many federal States know the existence of Constitutions at different levels, such as in Germany and the United States. Yet the emergence of a formal European Constitution makes the question of the relation between Constitutions at the European and national levels acute. The question already existed, and was raised long before the Court of Justice termed the Treaty the constitutional charter of the Community. But labelling the next document a 'Constitution' makes the issue more visible, and its answer more critical.

---

[15] And he continued: *'wo kein Staatsvolk, da kein Staat'*, as cited in J Gerkrath, *L'émergence d'un droit constitutionnel pour l'Europe*, (Brussels, Éditions de l'UniversitéeAcuteú de Bruxelles, 1997), at 89.

[16] See on this issue for instance J-Cl Piris, 'L'Union europúeAcuteúenne a-t-elle une constitution? Lui en faut-il une?', 35 RTDeur., 1999, 599, at 610 *et seq.*; and J Gerkrath, *L'émergence d'un droit constitutionnel pour l'Europe*, (Brussels, Éditions de l'UniversitéeAcuteú de Bruxelles), esp. at 85 *et seq.*

Secondly, and this is a hotly debated topic, it may be asked whether there is a European *demos* to legitimise a European Constitution, and if not, whether it is possible to adopt a Constitution without it. The *demos* issue does not relate to the question of *Volk*. It would be clear that there is no European *Volk* if the term is taken in its narrow sense. That, however, is not, or should not be the issue. The question is whether the European 'People or Peoples' can establish a Constitution and constitute the constitutional *demos*, the *pouvoir constituant* in whose supreme authority the Constitution is rooted. There does not seem to be a reason why it or they cannot. The only question is *how* it can be done, and this concerns the question of the type and measure of popular involvement in the adoption process.[17] If this Constitution is indeed intended to signify a 'constitutional moment', a break with the past, if its legitimacy is to be increased, including also a 'We the People' message, there is a need for intensified popular involvement in the adoption of the document, possibly though a referendum. One could object that most of the prevailing Constitutions in Europe have not been adopted with much popular involvement: most of them were 'imposed' by a constitutional convention, many were approved by (a special majority) in Parliament. Why then should a European Constitution involve a higher degree of popular involvement, preferably in the form of a European-wide referendum? The importance of the question probably lies in the fact that a constitutional moment would symbolise a shift in the '*Grundnorm*', a constitutional revolution, or the formal sanctioning thereof, and that such endeavour would arguably require an active participation of the people or peoples of Europe. Also, the most obvious alternative for the adoption of the Constitution by the *pouvoir constituant* itself, is the adoption through ratification by the Member States in accordance with their constitutional requirements. If that should be the procedure, what would be the difference with the past? The validity of the Constitution is then derived from the contract between the Member States. The consent of the People(s) is mediated by the States and the *pouvoir constitutant* rests with the Member States. The outcome would be a Constitutional Treaty rather than a Constitution. Again, the relationship between the European and national Constitutions and the national and European *demos* will have to be made explicit. Nevertheless, there does not seem to be a reason why a *demos* cannot constitute a polity at various levels.

Thirdly, the control of the Member States over the European Constitution remains complete if the procedure for amendment is not amended. At the moment, the Treaties are amended following the procedure provided in Article 48 EU, providing that an IGC shall be convened and that amendments shall enter into force after having been ratified by

---

[17] See JHH Weiler, 'A Constitution for Europe? Some Hard Choices', 40 *JCMS*, 2002, 563, at 566.

all the Member States in accordance with their respective constitutional requirements. Constitutional *Kompetenz Kompetenz* thus remains with the Member States acting unanimously and the powers of the Union and Community derive from the States who are the original holders of those powers. The unanimity among the Member States as required by Article 48 EU embodies the principle of sovereign equality and consent is typically a hallmark of internationalism, not constitutionalism.[18] As long as this is the case, the Constitution will, in that respect, remain a Treaty, it will be a 'Treaty masquerading as a Constitution', a Treaty establishing a Constitution.

Finally, a few comments on the name of the document. The use of constitutional language in the title of the document, whether 'Treaty Establishing the Constitution of Europe', the 'Constitutional Treaty' or simply the 'Constitution of Europe' sends a powerful symbolic message to the Member States, their Parliaments and courts, to the outside world and not least to the citizens of Europe.[19] In that respect, a title which leaves out the international treaty aspect, carries more weight than a title combining elements of a Constitution and a Treaty (which is on the other hand probably closer to the truth). Also for national constitutional and supreme courts, constitutional language adds legitimacy to the case law of the Court of Justice and its position as a constitutional court. It may even be helpful to overcome some of the supremacy issues which currently still divide some national constitutional courts and the European Courts.[20] The term 'Constitution' by and of itself may operate as a self-fulfilling prophecy, and transform a Treaty into a real Constitution.

20.3.5. The European Constitutional Treaty and National Constitutions

In a multi-level polity, a pluralist system governed by a mixed or multi-level Constitution, the constitutional reality rests on multiple foundations. The European Constitution comprises the European Treaties (in future the 'Constitutional Treaty' or 'Constitution'?) as interpreted by the European Court, viewed together with the national constitutions as interpreted by their supreme guardians, often with Courts having constitutional jurisdiction. In order to understand the constitutional reality of Europe, the polity as a whole must be considered objectively, without selecting one particular perspective, European or national (which is by nature restricted to the

---

[18] So JHH Weiler, 'A Constitution for Europe? Some Hard Choices', 40 *JCMS*, 2002, 563, at 565.
[19] See also 'The sixteen articles: On the way to a European Constitution', Editorial Comments, 40 *CML Rev* (2003) 267, at 268.
[20] 'The sixteen articles: On the way to a European Constitution', Editorial Comments, 40 *CML Rev* (2003) 267, at 268.

perspective of one Member State). Nevertheless, while this may be a comfortable position for an academic, it is not a position which can be assumed by a judicial organ, which by nature belongs to either the Union or a Member State. The Court of Justice can invite (or order?) the national courts to become Community courts, and to disregard the constraints of the national Constitution that might hinder their acting as *juge commun de droit communautaire*. Nevertheless, the national courts and especially the national constitutional courts will not easily shrug off their national constitutional mandates. Likewise, the Court of Justice may attempt to pay due regard to the national constitutional identity of the Member States,[21] but the Court essentially remains an organ of the Communities (and soon of the Union), and will act as such. Given the reality of a pluralist or mixed Constitution, which also comprises the national Constitutions, there may be a need to complete 'the European Constitutional Moment' with so many national 'Constitutional Moments', possibly adjusting the national Constitution to the reality of the European Constitution. Now, whether there is indeed a need to adapt the national Constitution, and what these modifications and improvements should encompass, will be different for each Member State. Nevertheless, constitutional modernisation in a multi-level Constitution where the hierarchical relation between the various level is not conclusively resolved, seems to require an effort at all levels involved. There does seem to be a lacuna there in the debate on and the preparation of the new European Constitution.[22]

---

[21] And it is so obliged under Art. I–5 of the TCE.

[22] Surely, there are national civil society debates; there is some academic debate, see for instance for the Netherlands LFM Besselink *et al*, *De Nederlandse Grondwet en de Europese Unie*, (Groningen, Europa Law Publishing, 2002); commented in JWL Broeksteeg et al, *De Nederlandese Grondwet en de Europese Unie*, (Publikaties van de Staatsrechtkring, Deventer, Kluwer, 2003). However, with a touch of malice it could be argued that these volumes are in themselves already old-fashioned, since they still deal with adapting the Netherlands Constitution to the 'old' European Constitution, and not directly, or only to a limited extent with the question whether the new Draft Constitution would require a fundamental re-thinking of the Netherlands Constitution (the answer may be 'no', but the question must now be asked). In contrast, J Pelckmans, M Sie Dhian Ho and B Limonard (eds), *Nederland en de Europese grondwet*, (Amsterdam, Amsterdam University Press, 2003) does deal with the Convention and the Netherlands position in the debate, but it does not concern itself with the national constitutional issues which may arise. For instance, the question of EU accession to the ECHR and incorporation of the Charter and the difficulties which may arise if both it indeed brought into effect – relation between ECJ and ECtHR, diverging interpretation also – are only discussed at the European level. No account is taken of the national constitutional issues which may arise. There is, in some countries, also political debate on the Convention and the consequences it may have at the national constitutional level, so for instance in the UK However, most Member States do not seem to be heading towards a national 'Constitutional Moment' other than the adoption of the European Constitution, in the form of the signing of the Draft Treaty.

20.3.6. From Communities and Union to Union

The division in pillars has been abandoned in the context of the Constitutional Treaty. This merger of the Communities and the Union will have tremendous repercussions also for the duties and competences of the national courts. Indeed it has been pointed out in the book that the Community mandate of the national courts does not necessarily apply outside the first pillar, given the different status and jurisdiction of the Court of Justice in the three pillars and within the first pillar in Title IV of the Community Treaty. Outside the hardcore first pillar, the general principles of Community law, direct effect and supremacy do not necessarily apply with the same force and effect, and this implies that the European mandate of the national courts which is grafted on those principles, is not the same in those areas. If the Communities and the Union are indeed to merge into an overarching Union, the same principles will apply, unless special provision is made to the contrary. However, despite appearances, and despite the formal removal of the pillar structure, the pillars continue to loom even within the unified Union. Especially Common Foreign and Security Policy in particular continue to have a separate place in the unity. It may even be argued that the removal of the pillars also removes their explanatory value, and may add to the complexity of the unified structure: indeed, diversity no longer follows the clear pattern of the pillars, but is scattered around in the Constitution. It remains to be seen how this will develop.

20.4. CONCLUDING REMARKS

The aim of this Part is not to provide a thorough examination of the Convention, its method, and the Constitutional Treaty. Such an enterprise is clearly beyond the scope of this book on national courts. The Convention, the Constitutional Treaty and the debate surrounding them will rather serve as the context to discuss the loose ends and unresolved issues between the national courts and the Court of Justice. Indeed some of the Convention and the Constitutional Treaty are related to these issues; some may even find their origin in the past judicial dialogue. Much of the discussion will consist in highlighting the issues involved, and elements of available solutions will be adduced, but it is not intended to be condusive.[23]

---

[23] This part was originally drafted when the debate about the Convention was still on going. It has been updated, but the debate, which started after the signing of the TCE and continued during the process of ratification, has not been included.

21

The Principle of Primacy

21.1. THE CURRENT SITUATION: REVOLT OR REVOLUTION, OR COEXISTENCE?

THROUGHOUT THE BOOK, the principle of supremacy or primacy has played a prominent part: the judicial dialogue between the national courts and the Court of Justice is framed in terms of the principle: the Court of Justice has put it forward as an axiom, and the national courts have accepted it to a large extent but they have in many cases adopted their own, national constitutional version of it, and in several cases rejected it as an absolute and unconditional principle. In the Community version, the Member States have transferred competences – 'sovereign rights' – to the Communities and have thus created an autonomous legal order, which is now separate from that of the Member States, but is integrated in the national legal orders, and applies with precedence over national law. All Community law enjoys supremacy over all domestic law. This supremacy is unconditional and absolute and its acceptance is often presented as vital for the continuing existence and functioning of the Communities. The basis of the principle lies in the very nature of the Community legal order, as a separate and autonomous legal order. Member States have transferred powers, they have agreed to accomplish specified functions together. It is, in essence, contractarian: the Member States have signed the Treaties, and the necessary consequence is that they must now accept that they cannot derive unilaterally from what they have agreed in common.

While the national courts have gradually and on the whole accepted at least ordinary supremacy and in some cases even ultimate supremacy, they have done so, in many cases, on entirely different grounds, seeking the foundation for the supremacy of Community law in their national Constitutions. This has allowed some of the national constitutional courts to make reservations and footnotes to the unconditional and absolute version of supremacy as put forward by the Court of Justice. Indeed, while the relevant provisions of the national Constitution may be interpreted as allowing for a transfer of powers – or a retreat from certain areas – they do form part of the Constitution and must be read in context: they cannot be read as allowing for unconditional surrender to the Communities, and accordingly, Community law will not take precedence over the most fundamental precepts of the Constitution, its core principles, such as fundamental rights.[1]

The reason why the Court of Justice and several of the national courts cannot agree is that they each start from their own, distinct, premises. After all, the question of supremacy is one of the relation between two norms, or between two legal orders, and since conflicts must be resolved and it must be clear which provision must be applied in a particular case where they would arrive at different conclusion, the question is ultimately phrased in terms of which one is higher in rank, has higher authority, or applies with precedence. Both the Court of Justice and the national courts apply their own logic and beliefs since they each reason from within their own legal order, and accordingly they may arrive at different solutions. The national courts regard their Constitution as the highest norm, from which all authority derives and which also contains the limits imposed on the exercise of public authority. Community law applies only by virtue of national constitutional law to which it is in essence subordinate. It is accordingly not surprising that some of these courts are not prepared to go it all the way and open up the domestic legal order unconditionally to Community law. The Court of Justice, on the other hand, is not, formally speaking, bound by the national Constitutions and starts from a different premise and with a different aim in view: the Member States have agreed to decide and regulate certain issues in common and they cannot accordingly, unilaterally diverge from what they have agreed jointly. If supremacy were not accepted a common market could never really be achieved. In order to be effective, Community law must be supreme over national law, of whatever rank.

For the courts involved, there is a problem of allegiance and of ultimate authority. The constitutional courts have a responsibility to uphold constitutional principles; the Court of Justice is under an obligation to ensure that the law is observed in the interpretation and application of the Treaty. Both the constitutional courts and the Court of Justice claim ultimate authority. Which one is right?[2] And which one will win?

Diarmuid Rossa Phelan in his *Revolt or Revolution* has suggested that the current legal situation cannot last forever. A time may – or as Phelan seems to imply, will – come that a national court will be driven to the point where one or other of two paths must be chosen. Either, loyalty to the Community will force that court to sanction a *revolution* in its own State, a constitutionally unauthorised change of the Constitution that would effectively transfer sovereignty to the Union. Or, loyalty to the

---

[1]   To paraphrase roughly the German and Italian positions.

[2]   For an attempt to answer the question, see CU Schmidt, 'From Pont d'Avignon to Ponte Vecchio: The Resolution of Constitutional Conflicts between the European Union and the Member States through Principles of Public International Law', *YEL*, 1998, 415. In my view, there is no answer: both a 'right' from their own perspective.

Constitution will sanction a *revolt* against the Court of Justice and the Community constitution created by it. He suggests the following remedy: *'A European Community law constitutional rule* [ought to be] *adopted to the effect that the integration of European Community law into national law is limited to the extent necessary to avoid a legal revolution in national law. The extent to which such limitation is necessary is to be finally determined by national constitutional authorities (such as the* Supreme Court [of Ireland] *or the* Conseil constitutionnel) *in accordance with the essential commitments of the national legal order, not by the Court of Justice. The rule does not relieve the Member States from the obligation to satisfy, short of causing a legal revolution European Community law wants'.*[3]

However, Phelan's thesis is certainly open to critique. Firstly, as has been pointed out,[4] Phelan's argument is firmly premised on an absence of explicit Member State consent to the Court of Justice's doctrines of supremacy, direct effect and so forth. However, especially with respect to the Member States acceding after 1963–1964, this is not convincing: by the time they acceded, direct effect and supremacy had become part of the *acquis communautaire*: these Member States knew what they were getting into. Even so, with respect to the six original Member States, there was no vehement reaction of the national political organs. In addition, there have been numerous occasions for the Member States to turn back time and to revert to the pre-*Van Gend en Loos* and *Costa v ENEL* era, by inserting a specific Treaty provision. The jurisprudence of the Court of Justice has not been repealed. The Member States have, on the other hand, in Maastricht and Amsterdam refused to extend the competences of the Court of Justice in the second and third pillar to the same level as within the first pillar; they have not been clear on the jurisdiction of the Court of Justice in the area of fundamental rights, and in Amsterdam they have explicitly denied direct effect of certain acts adopted within the third pillar. In other words: if there would have been the will and agreement among the Member States to limit the effects of the Court's case law also within mainstream first pillar law, they would have done so in a more general manner. However, they have not done so, and on the contrary, they have sanctioned the Court's case law in the Protocol on the application of the principles of subsidiarity and proportionality. The Member States recognise the advantages of the doctrine of ordinary supremacy within the first pillar: it forces not only themselves, but more importantly the other Member States to comply with Community law and obliges their courts to enforce Community law against an unwilling State.

---

[3] DR Phelan, *Revolt or Revolution. The Constitutional Boundaries of the European Community*, (Dublin, Round Hall Sweet & Maxwell, 1997), at 417.

[4] N MacCormick, *Questioning Sovereignty. Law State and Nation in the European Commonwealth* (Oxford, OUP, 1999) ch 7, 'Juridical Pluralism and the Risk of Constitutional Conflict', at 112.

Phelan seems to get carried away in his analysis. Reality shows that, while on paper the positions of the Court of Justice and the national constitutional courts may be diametrically opposed and there appears to be a threat of head-on collision, the actual situation is not that desperate. Even in the few concrete cases where it seemed most likely that the national constitutional courts would make use of their self-professed power, such as the bananas cases or the Irish abortion case, a collision was ultimately avoided by restraint on the part of the Court of Justice or the national courts, or both. In other words, the legal problem of applicability of one norm over another was not decided legally in the concrete cases; precedence was not awarded to one rule over the other. Rather, the courts found a way to settle the issue by other means, declaring that a case fell outside the scope of Community law, by shelving a case until the circumstances had changed and the imminent danger of crisis was averted. By declining to answer the question, no one overtly wins but no one loses either, and both parties maintain their own position to mutual advantage.[5] The fact that a concrete case of conflict has not occurred to date does not seem to be merely good fortune, it rather seems to be part and parcel of a strategy. There seems to be judicial agreement to disagree. In addition, it should be stressed that it is not likely that, should a national court ever actually decline to give precedence to Community law over national law, that should mean the end of the Community or the Union. Supremacy as a general rule is indeed vital for the day to day effective functioning of the Communities, but one incident of a court failing to award precedence to Community law in a particular case does not imply the collapse of the internal market and the end of the European Union.[6] At the end of the day, the situation does not seem to be so threatening that there will be revolt *or* revolution. The Court of Justice and the national constitutional courts have attained a state of peaceful coexistence, of a careful balance, an equilibrium.

In contrast to Phelan, the *pluralist thesis* suggests that neither Community law or Member State law can or should claim ultimate supremacy over the other. A proposal like the one made by Phelan places too much emphasis on the apparent superiority of State Constitutions over Community law by explicitly granting ultimate authority to the national courts, and would incite them to 'use the bomb' rather than to avert collision by other means. On the other hand, in the present situation of

---

5   So S Weatherill, 'Is constitutional finality feasible or desirable? On the cases for European constitutionalism and a European Constitution', ConWEB 7/2002, at 12.

6   Much more pessimistic is for instance CU Schmid, 'From Pont d'Avignon to Ponte Vecchio: The Resolution of Constitutional Conflicts between the European Union and the Member States through Principles of Public International Law" *YEL*, 1998, 415, at 447: '..*even issues of minor economic concern for the whole of the Community, like the banana conflict, are capable of destroying its legal unity and, thus, of endangering the European peace system in the last instance'.*

peaceful coexistence, the Court of Justice also must be aware, and demonstrate this awareness, of the national constitutional core principles of the Member States in order to convince them that there is no need for them to interfere. Perhaps, the inconsistency between the European Court's and the national constitutional courts' positions is a fact which academics will have to learn to live with. In the absence of a single authority over and above the rivalling courts,[7] the conflict may be unresolvable by imposition of a clear-cut and absolute rule. The conflict may however be mitigated by converging the positions.[8] There have been signs over the past years of supportive respectful interaction between the European and national courts, underpinned by an anxiety on both sides to avoid direct confrontation in which there must be winners and losers.[9]

If this is indeed true, then the reality of the supremacy of Community law escapes the either/or assumption of constitutional hierarchy or absolute precedence as put forward in the orthodox doctrine. The principle of supremacy remains essentially 'two-dimensional':[10] it is a complex, layered reality of dialogue and persuasion.[11] Perhaps it must be concluded that neither the assertion of supremacy of national constitutional law nor of Community law by national courts and the European Courts respectively is supreme over the other?

Obviously, the answer that there is no final resolution in the sense that one order has absolute supreme authority over the other, is not a solution which lawyers, especially those educated in systems based on clear-cut Kelsenian hierarchy of norms and straightforward rules of conflict, will find particularly satisfying. Nevertheless, this may well be 'as good as it gets'.[12] Any writing down of the current situation in constitutional text may well lead to no more than opening old wounds.

---

[7] Could there be an independent adjudicator at the international level? See CU Schmid, 'From Pont d'Avignon to Ponte Vecchio: The Resolution of Constitutional Conflicts between the European Union and the Member States through Principles of Public International Law" *YEL*, 1998, 415.

[8] Some of these have been mentioned before, see for instance the statements of Gil Carlos Rodrigues Iglesias and Jean Pierre Puissochet at the 1997 Paris meeting of constitutional courts, referred to above in Part 2, Chapter 13.3.1, and the statements of Jutta Limbach on the *Bananas III* judgment of the *BVerfG* See also A Peters, 'The Bananas Decision (2000) of the German Federal Constitutional Court: Towards Reconciliation with the European Court of Justice as Regards Fundamental Rights Protection in Europe', 43 *German Yearbook of International Law*, 2000, 276, at 281–82.

[9] So S Weatherill, 'Is constitutional finality feasible or desirable? On the cases for European constitutionalism and a European Constitution', ConWEB 7/2002, at 14.

[10] So B De Witte, 'Direct Effect, Supremacy, and the Nature of the Legal Order', in P Craig and G de Búrca (eds), *The Evolution of EU Law* (Oxford, OUP, 1999) 177, at 209.

[11] S Weatherill, 'Is constitutional finality feasible or desirable? On the cases for European constitutionalism and a European Constitution', ConWEB 7/2002, at 14.

[12] See M Poiares Maduro, 'Europe and the Constitution: What if this is as good as it gets?', Con WEB 5/2000, les1.man.ac.uk/conweb.

21.2. PRIMACY IN THE EUROPEAN CONSTITUTION?

It has been argued that it is now time for the principle of supremacy to be inserted in the Constitutional Treaty. The Constitution of many federal States does contain a supremacy clause. Article 31 of the German Basic Law states that *'Bundesrecht bricht Landesrecht'*; likewise, Section 2 of Article VI of the Constitution of the United States provides that *'This Constitution and the Laws of the United States which shall be made in pursuance thereof (..) shall be the supreme Law of the Land; and the Judges in every State shall be bound thereby, any Thing in the Constitution or Laws of any State to the Contrary notwithstanding'*. The US Constitution is accordingly even more complete, and also contains an express mandate for all courts to apply federal law with precedence, even over national constitutional law. Nevertheless, not all Constitutions of federal States contain supremacy clauses. Belgian federalism for instance is not based on a notion of supremacy: the division of competences between the Federation and the federated entities is such that in case of conflict, either one of the legislative bodies, federal or federated, has overstepped the limits of its powers. Both federal and regional law are supreme in their own sphere of application.

The supremacy of Community law is a legal reality only to the extent that the national courts have accepted their Community mandate, which is mostly based on the national courts' own constitutional terms. This fact distinguishes Community supremacy from analogous federal principles.[13] While supremacy was developed at the central, Community level by the Court of Justice, its actual application depends on the willingness of the national courts to cooperate. In federal States, the relations between central and regional law is a matter for central, federal constitutional law. The issue is decided in the federal Constitution, whose primacy is beyond dispute. In contrast, the Community claim of autonomous validity and absolute supremacy of the Community's constitutional charter was and is not uncontested. The foundation for the supremacy of Community law, in so far as it has been accepted, lies, in the view of many national courts, in the national Constitutions, not in the Community Treaty itself, at least not explicitly. It may be implied in it as the Court of Justice would have it; it may be one of the most important elements of the *'acquis communautaire'*; its existence will not seriously be contested at least not by lawyers;[14] but its formal legal foundation will mostly be found in national law.

The closest thing to an explicit supremacy clause in the Treaties is the Protocol on the Application of the Principles of Subsidiarity and

---

[13] See B De Witte, 'Direct Effect, Supremacy, and the Nature of the Legal Order', in P Craig and G de Búrca (eds), *The Evolution of EU Law* (Oxford, OUP, 1999) 177, at 209.
[14] But see the heated debate in the framework of the Convention, infra.

Proportionality annexed to the Treaty of Amsterdam, stating that it *'shall not affect the principles developed by the Court of Justice regarding the relationship between national and Community law'*. The principle of supremacy is thus not even mentioned in so many words, but it must now be presumed to be confirmed by the Member States. This would imply that the Member States as High Contracting Parties have agreed to accept the absolute and unconditional version of supremacy, since such is the 'principle developed by the Court of Justice regarding the relationship between national and Community law'. In German literature it was argued that the provision was meant to limit the competence of control exercised by national constitutional courts by virtue of their Constitutions.[15] Rupp even argued that the Protocol would dilute the position of the *Bundesverfassungsgericht* and recommended that ratification of the Amsterdam Treaty be postponed until the provision was amended.

Will the inclusion of the principle of supremacy or primacy in the Treaty establishing a Constitution for Europe solve the dispute between the European and national courts and make it clear once and for all that Union law always prevails over national law, including national Constitutions? Will it make supremacy truly unconditional,[16] as is the case in many federal systems?[17]

Will inclusion of the principle of primacy be effective solving the conflicts? Will it 'do the trick'? Will the inclusion of primacy in article I-6 of TCE necessarily imply the end of the counterlimits jurisprudence of the national constitutional courts? If the State does ratify a Treaty stating that it has primacy over national law (including the Constitution), this does confirm beyond any doubt an obligation imposed on all Sate organs at all levels, including legislatures, government and administrative bodies and courts, to comply with the law deriving from the Treaty with precedence over national law. Looking at the relationship from the outside it seems hardly conceivable that a national court could continue to deny absolute supremacy. Looking at it from the perspective of the Court of Justice, the inclusion of primacy in the TCE does not make much of a difference

---

[15] See for instance K Hasselbach, 'Der Voorrang des Gemeinschaftsrechts vor dem nationalen Verfassungsrecht nach dem Vertrag von Amsterdam', 52 *JZ*, 1997, 942; H Rupp, 'Die Ausschaltung des Bundesverfassungsgerichts durch den Amsterdamer Vertrag', 53 *JZ*, 1998, 213.

[16] Of course, the answer depends to a great extent on how the principle is formulated. If it states that 'the Constitutional Treaty and the law deriving from it takes precedence over national law', it is stated as an unconditional principle. But it is also possible to include escapes from the absoluteness of the principle, for instance with reference to the ECHR, or even, as in the proposal made by Phelan, with reference to national Constitutions. That would truly be a novelty, especially where the adjudication in concrete cases would be left to national courts rather than the ECJ. Yet, it does not seem wise to pose the principle of supremacy and then to include exceptions.

[17] For a more moderate position concerning the federal nature of the principle of supremacy, see B De Witte, 'The Primacy of Community Law: A Not-so-federal Principle?', unpublished paper, on file with the author.

(except for the fact that the Court itself could not allow for limited exceptions, for instance in the context of international treaty law?). From the very beginning, the Court of Justice has stated that the principle of supremacy is inherent in the very nature of Community law: while the Treaty does not mention supremacy, it is implied, underlying several provisions expressly stated in the Treaty. Inclusion in the text of the Constitution-Treaty only confirms what the Court has said in 1964; it is only declaratory. This is confirmed by the Declaration on Artice I-6, annexed to the TCE.

How about the national perspective? Would it make a difference for the *Bundesverfassungsgericht* that the Treaty contains the principle of supremacy? Schmid claims that *'even an express statement by the Community legislator about the unlimited primacy of European law would not change the constitutional conflict in any way, since its origin in national constitutional law would remain unaffected'*.[18] It must be emphasised that the principle included in the Constitutional Treaty is not a *'statement by the Community legislator'*, but the result of an agreement between the High Contracting Parties, the Member States acting as *Herren der Verträge*, as the *pouvoir constituant*. If the German State would ratify a Treaty containing the provision that European law takes precedence over national law, it could not at a later stage claim that the provision could not operate for Germany, not even on constitutional grounds: *Pacta sunt servanda*. If it were indeed the case that the German Constitution would appear to object to such provision in a Treaty, the German State would have to seek amendment, or in the extreme case, termination of the Treaty, in accordance with the rules of international law. The primacy provision in the Treaty means that in each case as provided in the Treaty, European law takes precedence, and it imposes an obligation on the German State to make the necessary adjustments in the national (constitutional) system so that the treaty provision is complied with. If so required, the constitutional system would have to be adapted. Based on pure logic, the *Bundesverfassungsgericht* could maintain its current position and hold that supremacy in the European Constitution only applies in so far as it does not conflict with the national Constitution: it would apply only to the extent that the German Constitution allows for it. Nevertheless, the express statement that the European Constitution and the law deriving from it is supreme removes the force of the argument, and the interpretation of the German Court would have to be considered as infringing the principle of good faith.

Now, is it *feasible* to include the principle of primacy in the *Constitutional Treaty*? First, such endeavour will certainly be extremely delicate indeed. It

---

[18]   CU Schmid, 'From Pont d'Avignon to Ponte Vecchio: The Resolution of Constitutional Conflicts between the European Union and the Member States through Principles of Public International Law', *YEL*, 1998, 415, at 422.

has been pointed out that the concept is difficult to define: there does not seem to be a generally accepted principle of supremacy: does it imply a general hierarchical relationship between Community law and national law? Or is it merely a rule of conflict, to be applied by courts and limited to directly effective provisions of Community law? Does it apply to other Community measures as well? Does it apply also to national procedural rules, in other words would it also comprise structural supremacy? Are there any exceptions to supremacy, in the area of fundamental rights, core principles of national constitutional law, or in the light of international treaty provisions? Does the principle apply with the same force to what is now the second and third pillar, to non-Community Union law? Will the principle of supremacy be affected should the Union accede to the ECHR, in the sense that in cases where the Human Rights Court declares a particular Community measure to infringe the ECHR while the Court of Justice has upheld it, the national courts are allowed to set aside that provision of Community law in favour of a national measure which does not infringe the ECHR? These and other questions will require answers before the principle is stated.

Is it *desirable* to include the principle of primacy in the Constitutional Treaty? For the sake of constitutional 'purity' and clarity, it does seem that the principle of supremacy cannot remain absent from the Constitutional Treaty. Indeed, it is probably the single most important principle of Community law,[19] which makes the Community legal order different from ordinary international law, and distinguishes the Community from any other international organisation, so the story goes. Why then not include it in the Basic Constitutional Document? What could justify not including it? Indeed, the principle is so fundamental that there must be good arguments to leave it unwritten. One argument could be that there is *no need* for the principle to be included: the Community has functioned well without any formalisation of the principle, so why bother at all? Nevertheless, formalisation would serve the purpose of clarification and would appear elegant. Also, while it may be true that the Community functions well without a formal provision, there still is a fair amount of resistance against the absolute and unconditional version of supremacy as pronounced by the Court of Justice. Formalisation may well be the only way to remove this resistance on the part of the constitutional courts and their equivalents. It places the decision over this fundamental issue in the hands of those who are responsible for it, the *pouvoir constituant*, rather than in the hands of the courts. If their own Member State agrees to bind itself to a principle of primacy, it would be very difficult for the courts to reject it. On the other hand, formalising the principle at Treaty level may well evoke powerful opposition, as was proven in the context of the Convention.

---

[19] The use of the notion 'Community law' rather than Union law is intentional. For a discussion of the supremacy of non-Community Union law, see supra.

Codifying the principle of primacy as a general and absolute principle, applying to the whole of Union law, irrespective of whether the Court of Justice has jurisdiction to review the validity of the relevant provision, irrespective of whether it has direct effect, irrespective the issues involved, does not, despite its appearances, consist of a pure and simple codification. It goes beyond the limits of the principle as they currently exist even in the case law of the Court of Justice which is limited to the areas where the Court has jurisdiction. It definitely goes beyond the current reality, where absolute and ultimate supremacy exists from the perspective of the Court of Justice, but not in most Member States in the case law of the constitutional courts and their equivalents. Presently, the principle is two-dimensional, it is a legal reality only to the extent that national courts accept their mandate.[20] And while the latter subscribe to it to a large extent, they maintain, at least in theory, reservations to unconditional acceptance. The Court of Justice and the national courts have proven that this is not an unworkable situation. On the contrary, this coexistence, including the threat of exceptions to the absolute supremacy of Community law, may well add to the legitimacy of Community law in the domestic legal order: the mere possibility that in exceptional cases, Community law may not be supreme before the national courts, contributes to its acceptance in all other cases. To include supremacy in the text of the Constitutional Treaty does more than simply codify an existing principle. It changes the current situation to the extent that it removes the limitations (or conditions for its acceptance) on the part of national constitutional law and the national courts, and makes it a one-dimensional principle. And as said, it applies to the bulk of Union law, rather than being restricted to mainstream first pillar law.

All in all, it may have been better to leave the principle unwritten, and to leave it in the hands of the courts, at the European and national level. From the perspective of constitutional purity, this may not be the most elegant position. However, I believe that it is not possible to formulate the principle in manner that takes into account all its niceties and subtleties, and that reflects its present two-dimensional nature which currently gives it legitimacy. The footnotes to the principles, the subtleties and niceties will still have to be added by the Court of Justice which will mould the constitutional text to constitutional law.

21.3.   THE TREATY ESTABLISHING A CONSTITUTION FOR EUROPE

Article I-10 of the Convention Draft read '*The Constitution and law adopted by the Union institutions in exercising competences conferred on it by the Constitution, shall have primacy over the law of the Member States*'. As drafted,

---

[20]   B De Witte, 'Direct Effect, Supremacy and the Nature of the Legal Order', in P Craig and G de Búrca (eds), *The Evolution of EU Law* (Oxford, OUP, 1999) 177, at 209.

the provision may appear overly bold; for example it does not distinguish between what is currently mainstream Community law, and non-Community Union law, which is now contained in the second and third pillar. Even if the pillars are to be merged, it remains to be seen whether the aim is really that the law deriving from the provisions on what is now second and third pillar should have the same status as what is now mainstream Community law. Yet, it is striking that the reaction to the proposed article in the Convention even questioned the basic idea of primacy, and doubted whether it would have sufficient legitimacy and support from the citizens.[21]

The place of the provision in the Title on competences was rather peculiar, since primacy is does not relate to the division of competences and the way in which competences are divided: it means that Community/Union law that has been lawfully adopted takes precedence. In the November Draft the provision was moved to a separate Article I-5a entitled 'Union law', after the provision on Relations between the Union and the Member States (respect for national identities and loyal co-operation). Article I-6 TCE now states that ' *The Constitution and law adopted by the institutions of the Union in exercising competences conferred on it shall have primacy over the law of the Member States'*. The Declaration on Article I-6 annexed to the TCE clarifies that '*The Conference notes that Article I-6 reflects existing case-law of the Court of Justice of the European Communities and of the Court of First Instance'*. Nevertheless, while this may give the impression that there is nothing new to it, many issues remain unclear, and these will need to be addressed by the Court of Justice and the national courts.

21.4. NATIONAL PRIMACY PROVISIONS

It is commendable, in order to make the provision on primacy fully effective, and to prevent the type of reasoning as suggested by Schmid, to complete any primacy provision in the Treaty with a provision to the same effect in the national Constitutions. Examples can be found in the Dutch and the Irish Constitutions. The Netherlands Constitution does not distinguish between European law and international treaties is general: all treaties take precedence over the bulk of national law, including the Netherlands Constitution. The Constitution itself accordingly provides for the precedence of treaties: it cedes before treaties: under Article 94 of the Constitution '*Legislation in force in the Kingdom shall not apply if this application would be incompatible with provisions of agreements which are binding on anyone (..)'*, and the notion 'legislation in force in the Kingdom' is taken to include the Constitution. This view of the primacy of international treaties over the

---

[21] See 'The sixteen articles: On the way to a European Constitution', Editorial Comments, 40 *CML Rev* (2003) 267, at 275, with reference.

Constitution is unchallenged in The Netherlands. The ease with which this primacy is accepted is to a large extent explained by the fact that The Netherlands lack a system of judicial review of primary legislation and/or a constitutional court. Courts cannot review the constitutionality of parliamentary acts and of treaties. As a result, treaties play a very important role before the courts, especially in the context of fundamental rights protection. Before the courts, fundamental rights as contained in international treaties such as the ECHR are more effectively enforced than their constitutional equivalents.[22] Now, for European law the situation may be different, as the majority of commentators are of the opinion that Article 94 of the Constitution does not even come into play in the context of Community law, and find the basis in the very nature of the Community legal order and the transfer of sovereign rights to the Community. The case law of the Court of Justice is accepted without any objection, and accordingly, the absolute and unconditional version of supremacy as espoused by the Court of Justice is unchallenged. It is questionable however whether most other Member States would go so far and follow the Netherlands pattern.

The Irish example is different. Ireland is a dualist State and thus the law contained in the Treaties and deriving from them had to be given effect by a national act. This is done in special provisions in the Constitution. Article 29.6.10 of the Irish Constitution further states that *'No provision of this Constitution invalidates laws enacted, acts done or measures adopted by the State which are necessitated by the obligations of membership of the European Union or of the Communities, or prevents laws enacted, acts done or measures adopted by the European Union or by the Communities or by institutions thereof, or by bodies competent under the Treaties establishing the Communities, from having the force of law in the State'*. The aim of the provision was to forestall questions about the compatibility of Community rules with the substantive provisions of the Constitution.[23] Irish courts are normally content to take the provision at its word and to accord primacy in domestic law to Community law as interpreted by the Court of Justice. Nevertheless, the possibility of direct conflict did arise, in the context of one of the most sensitive provisions of the Irish Constitution, Article 40.3.3. protecting the life of the unborn. That the conflict should arise in this area is not accidental. Conversely, in exceptional cases of profound normative conflict which threatens directly the Constitution's fundamental principles, even a constitutional provision does not seem to suffice to prevent courts from protecting the Constitution against infringements from outside.[24]

---

[22] M Claes and B De Witte, 'Report on the Netherlands', in A-M Slaughter, A Stone Sweet and JHH Weiler (eds), *The European Court and National Courts – Doctrine and Jurisprudence. Legal Change in its Social Context* (Oxford, Hart Publishing, 1998) 171, at 174.

[23] DR Phelan and A Whelan, 'National constitutional law and European integration', in *Le droit constitutionnel national et l'intégration européenne. 17. Fide Kongress* (Berlin, 1996) 292, at 306.

[24] DR Phelan and A Whelan, 'National constitutional law and European integration', in *Le droit constitutionnel national et l'intégration européenne. 17. Fide Kongress* (Berlin, 1996) 292, at 310–11.

The constitutional provision seems to have worked better in the Netherlands than in Ireland. This may be only appearance: A concrete case of the extreme sensitivity as the Irish abortion case has not arisen in the Netherlands. And yet, it seems also less likely for such case to arise and for the courts to 'rebel' against Community law and the constitutional provisions contained in Article 94 and 120, which are not contested and apply also beyond the scope of Community law. The Irish and Dutch experience demonstrate that a constitutional provision can reinforce the theory as stated by the Court of Justice. The Irish example proves that this type of provision may be effective also in dualist States, with constitutional jurisdiction. Nevertheless, it also proves that even a constitutional provision may not be sufficient to guarantee the primacy of European law even in the most sensitive cases. But to a great extent, it will, and it will certainly contribute to limiting conflict to extremely sensitive cases. The inclusion of a primacy provision in the national Constitution is at least elegant: supremacy is about the relationship between legal orders and texts which currently both claim primacy for themselves; if a resolution is required, it will have to be found on both sides.

There are no specific rules as to how the *national* constitutional provision should be phrased. It could be a general provision like the Dutch Article 94, or a provision specifically drafted for European law, or a provision making reference to the case law of the Court of Justice. If the Member States would be required to make the necessary constitutional arrangements to provide for the absolute and unconditional supremacy of European law, it should be agreed in advance whether any exceptions could be allowed, whether it would apply for all Union law (including what is now second and third pillar) or be restricted to certain categories etc.

In conclusion, if the aim is indeed to ensure the primacy of European law as much as possible, the best route is twofold, and would combine the provision contained in the Constitutional Treaty with a national constitutional provision to the effect that European law must take precedence. In a multi-tier system governed by a mixed Constitution, consisting of constitutions both of which claim ultimate authority, a rule concerning a hierarchical relationship between rules originating from both orders can best be incorporated at both levels. If it must be incorporated, it should be incorporated at both levels.

21.5. THE CONCEPT OF DIRECT EFFECT

Should the concept of direct effect be incorporated in the Treaties? It has been argued elsewhere in this book that the principle of supremacy is an autonomous principle, independent of that other notion 'direct effect'. However, it is in the presence of a directly effective provision of Community law that supremacy is most 'powerful' and that the obligations of the national courts are most dramatic in the domestic context. If supremacy is included, should 'direct effect' also be? In contrast to supremacy or primacy, direct effect already appears in the current Treaty: in the context of what is now the third pillar, direct effect is denied to certain types of Union acts. Direct effect may also be considered to be present in Article 249 EC which states that regulations are 'directly applicable', if it is indeed accepted that direct effect and direct applicability coincide. But the inclusion of direct effect in the Treaty establishing a Constitution for Europe would be far more difficult than incorporation of supremacy, and it does not seem desirable at this stage to include it. It would be much more complicated for several reasons. First, as opposed to the principle of supremacy, direct effect is not a general 'principle' which applies to the whole of Community law (and much less even to non-Community Union law). A statement that 'Union law has direct effect' would not make any sense, as direct effect is not a general characteristic of all Community acts, let alone the bulk of Union law, and possibly not even of a particular provision in all types of cases and in all circumstances alike. In addition, the notion of direct effect is much more complicated than that of supremacy. 'Direct effect' has come to mean many things, depending on the type of act, the type of procedure and even the national law of the court using the term. There are as many interpretations and meanings of 'direct effect' as there are Member States, and even more.[25]These and other arguments have also been brought against maintaining the concept for mainstream Community law altogether. I do not agree with this position, and in the light of the imminent amplification of non-Community Union law, where the concept of direct effect will likely prove renewed significance, and in the context of the accession of new Member States, I would argue to preserve the concept. Nevertheless, it should not be included in the Treaty as a rule. It is a judge-made concept, which has operated as the foundation of the national courts' involvement in the enforcement and application of Community law, and has grown and developed to a point that it has almost (but not completely) become redundant. It is best to leave it in the hands of the courts, for them to mould and develop it. And when the time is ripe, it may well become superfluous, and disappear. To incorporate it in the Constitutional Treaty would be impossible, redundant and would hamper the development of Union law and its application in domestic law.[26]

---

[25] See S Prechal, 'Direct Effect Reconsidered, Redefined and Rejected', in *Direct Effect. Rethinking a Classic of EC Legal Doctrine*, (Groningen, Europa Law Publishing, 2002), 15, at 20.
[26] The TCE does still contain the notion of direct applicability to define European laws and European regulations and distinguish them from framework laws, see Art. I–33TCE. It coincides with the use of the notion in the current Treaty.

22

Incorporation of the National Courts' Mandate?

THE NATIONAL COURTS' European mandate was developed entirely in the case law of the Court of Justice, on the basis of fundamental principles: direct effect, supremacy, *effet utile* and the like. National courts feature in the current Treaties only in the provisions on preliminary rulings procedures. For the remainder, the mandate is the product of the case law of the Court of Justice. It has been demonstrated that on the whole, the national courts have heeded and accepted their European mandate, albeit mostly in a different form and on different grounds than provided for in the case law of the Court of Justice, by adapting the national constitutional mandate. Should the 'Constitutional Moment' be seized to introduce the national courts' role as ordinary courts of Community law in the text of the Constitutional Treaty? National courts form a relatively blank spot in the debate on the European Constitution in general and the reform of the European judicial architecture in particular.[1] Where national courts do appear in the debate, the discussion focuses on management on the Community's side of the preliminary reference flood, not the wider issue of their mandate as Community courts. Is it desirable to include the national courts' mandate in the Constitutional Treaty? From the European perspective, the recognition of the role of national courts by inserting it in the Treaty would change nothing but appearances: Indeed, the national courts' mandate is already inherent in the Treaty and derives inter alia from Article 10 EC. Nevertheless, it was suggested by Ziller and Lotarski, who proposed the introduction of the national courts as 'associates' of the Court of Justice, the Court of First Instance and the judicial panels introduced by the Treaty of Nice. In their opinion, the national courts are the *de facto* common courts of Union law and their absence from the Constitutional

---

[1] So A WH Meij, 'Guest Editorial: Architects or Judges? Some Comments in relation to the Current Debate', 37 *CML Rev* (2000) 1039, at 1044.

Treaty can no longer be justified.[2] Accordingly, they proposed a provision reading *'Dans le cadre de leurs compétences respectives, les autorités juridictionnelles des États membres sont associées à la mission de la Cour de justice'*. In addition, they would include a general provision obliging the national courts to apply Union law: *'La Cour de justice, le Tribunal de première instance, les chambres juridictionnelles* ainsi que les autorités juridictionnelles des États membres *sont tenues d'appliquer, dans le cadre de leurs compétences respectives, le droit de l'Union, y compris le droit international qui lie l'Union'*.

It is agreed that the absence of the national courts in the text of the Constitutional Treaty does not do justice to reality, where the national courts are first in line to enforce Community law in the Member States. However, this is true for all national organs, including national Parliaments and other bodies implementing directives, customs authorities and all other national administrative authorities, which apply and administer Community law on a daily basis. They too are absent as such from the Treaties, while in reality the Community could not function without them. It could even be argued that the national courts are about the only national authorities which are *qualitate qua*[3] mentioned in the Treaties already in Article 234 EC on preliminary references. On the other hand, *all* national authorities taken as a whole are already in the Treaties: they appear most prominently in Article 10 EC and in other provisions of the Treaty, but hide behind the notion 'Member State'. Given the origins of the Communities and the Union as international organisations based on international treaties, and given the disparities in the national constitutional and administrative organisations of each of the Member States, it is not helpful to mention particular organs in so many words.

The inclusion of the second provision, obliging the national courts to apply Union law, would operate as an additional (or separate) guarantee at Treaty level against constitutional restrictions on the principle of primacy since the provision is stated as a general obligation. It would not be a very forceful brake on national courts claiming *Kompetenz Kompetenz*, as these courts would, in line with the theoretical underpinnings of their retained powers, argue that the duty to apply Union law would only apply in so far as this Union law was *intra vires*, and, in the German context, would fit over the bridge of the Act of assent. The same argument could, with some malice, be used to oppose the supremacy principle: the duty to apply Union law applies only in so far as it does not conflict with the core principles of the national Constitution... It would appear,

---

[2]   J Ziller and J Lotarski, 'Institutions et organes judiciaires', in *Ten Reflections on the Constitutional Treaty for Europe*, (Florence, EUI, 2003), 67, at 70, available on www.iue.it.

[3]   As opposed to for instance government representatives acting as part of a Community organ.

accordingly, that the force of a similar provision would again be dependent on a pendant in the national Constitution or national Act governing the duties and obligations of national courts.

On the other hand, inclusion of the national courts would set the tone, and would be useful to clarify the constitutional setting. If that is the purpose of the exercise, there is no reason why only courts should be mentioned: it would also apply to national Parliaments and administrative authorities. Such an exercise would however prove to be challenging, given the disparities between Member States, the national constitutional issues involved, etc.

22.2. THE TREATY ESTABLISHING A CONSTITUTION FOR EUROPE

The TCE does not contain a provision on national courts as suggested above. Nevertheless, hidden in Article I-29 (1) 2nd sentence they must be considered to be included. Article I-29 states: *'(1) The Court of Justice of the European Union shall include the General Court of Justice, the General Court and specialised courts. It shall ensure that in the interpretation and application of the Constitution the law is observed. Member States shall provide remedies sufficient to ensure effective legal protection in the fields covered by Union law'.*[4] The first two sentences seem clear, and will not be further discussed here. It is the third sentence which is of interest. The sentence is probably inspired by the *UPA* judgment of the Court of Justice where it held, in the context of standing for private applicants that *'Thus it is for the Member States to establish a system of legal remedies and procedures which ensure respect for the right to effective judicial protection'.*[5] If that is indeed the case, and if that is the meaning of the provision, then it is meant to provide for the Member States' obligation to provide for judicial protection (a competent court, access to justice, causes of action, legal remedies) of private individuals claiming that their rights have been infringed by acts of the Community (Union) institutions which they cannot challenge directly before the Court of Justice. The Court favours the indirect route via the national courts which must, where necessary, make a reference to the Court of Justice under *Foto-Frost*. In that sense, the provision must probably be read in conjunction with the new Article III-365 (4) TCE which

---

[4]   The French version which is authentic at the moment provides that *'Les États membres établissent les voies de recours nécessaires pour assurer une protection juridictionnelle effective dans le domaine du droit de l'Union'.*

[5]   Case C–50/00 P *Unión de Pequeños Agricultores v Council of the European Union* [2002] ECR I–6677, at para 41. The French version states that *'Ainsi, il incombe aux États membres de prévoir un système de voies de recours et de procédures permettant d'assurer le respect du droit à une protection juridictionnelle effective'.*

relaxes only to a very limited extent the conditions for standing for private applicants, and presumably continues to rely on the indirect route via the national courts.

What then, does the provision say? What is required is that the Member States provide the necessary causes of action and legal remedies. They must make sure that private individuals always have access to a national court in order to challenge the validity of Union acts where they do not have standing before the European Courts. Who, within the unitary notion of 'Member States' is under such obligation? First and foremost it will of course be the (constitutional) legislature. Yet, what should a national court do when it claims not to have jurisdiction to take a case which is essentially brought against a Union act? The notion 'Member State' in Article I-29 TCE must be interpreted as also be addressed to the national courts, so they must assume jurisdiction on the basis of Article I-29 TCE even in the absence of national causes of action or national remedies. It is probably the first time that the notion of effective judicial protection which is so central in the case law of the Court of Justice on the national courts' mandate, is mentioned in the text of the Treaties.

Finally, the provision obliges the Member States to provide legal remedies to ensure effective legal protection *'in the field covered by Union law'*. This is broad enough to include not only the *UPA* type of cases, where effective judicial protection must be ensured against Community (in future: Union) acts, but more importantly, all cases where national courts ensure judicial protection of individuals against the Member States. This therefore encompasses the entire case law, presumably, on the Community mandate of the national courts: *Van Gend en Loos, Costa v ENEL, Simmenthal, Factortame, Francovich, Johnston, Rewe, Comet*. If that is indeed the case, this means that the national courts' mandate in now included in the text of the Constitution. It is therefore regrettable that the mandate is hidden in a cryptic and ill-drafted provision. It would be preferable to be more straightforward, and mention the national courts as 'common courts of Union law' in so many words.

23

Fundamental Rights

23.1. REMINDER: THE CURRENT SITUATION

FUNDAMENTAL RIGHTS PROTECTION has been a bone of contention between several national courts and the European Court since the early seventies, and this situation has continued to date. The current state of affairs is as follows: According to Article 6 EU the Union is founded on, among other principles, respect for human rights and fundamental freedoms; the Union shall respect fundamental rights, as guaranteed by the ECHR and as they result from the constitutional traditions common to the Member States, as general principles of Community law.[1] The Court can only enforce these rights in so far as it has jurisdiction in a particular area, as stated in Article 46 EU, *i.e.* with regard to action of the institutions, and only insofar as the Court has jurisdiction under the EC and EU Treaties. Member State action is not mentioned. Nevertheless, under its general principles case law, the European Court protects fundamental rights as against the Community institutions.[2] General principles of Community law also restrict the exercise of public power by the Member States (national measures) when they act 'within the scope of Community law',[3] *i.e.* when they implement or apply

---

[1] With respect to the relationship between the ECHR and the common constitutional traditions of the Member States, Koen Lenaerts states that the ECHR functions as the primary source, while it is only in so far as the Member States of the Union have enough in common to add to the ECHR, that the Union is also bound, to require its institutions to respect additional protection from common constitutional traditions, see K Lenaerts, 'Fundamental Rights in the European Union', 25 *ELR*, 2000, 575, at 578.

[2] See generally, FG Jacobs, 'Human Rights in the European Union: the Role of the Court of Justice', 26 *ELR*, 2001, 331; B De Witte, 'The Past and Future Role of the European Court of Justice in the Protection of Human Rights', in Ph Alston (ed), *The EU and Human Rights* (Oxford, OUP, 1999) 859.

[3] On the notion 'scope of Community law' see *e.g.* J Temple Lang, 'The Sphere in which Member States are Obliged to Comply with the General Principles of Law and Community Fundamental Rights Principles', 2 *LIEI*, 1991, 34; K Lenaerts, 'Fundamental Rights in the European Union, 25 *ELR*, 2000, 575; B De Witte, 'The Past and Future Role of the European Court of Justice in the Protection of Human Rights', in Ph Alston (ed), *The EU and Human Rights* (Oxford, OUP, 1999) 859; K Lenaerts, 'Fundamental Rights in the European Union', 25 *ELR*, 2000, 575, at 590 *et seq.*; FG Jacobs, 'Human Rights in the European Union: the Role of the Court of Justcie', 26 *ELR*, 2001, 331.

Community law,[4] or when they rely on an exception contained in a provision of the Community Treaty[5] or in the case law of the Court of Justice[6] to justify national law likely to obstruct the exercise of free movement within the common market. In practice, this means that when national authorities act within the scope of Community law, the Court of Justice provides the national courts with the necessary guidance to enable them to assess the compatibility of those measures with the fundamental rights as general principles of Community law. The Court does not assume jurisdiction where national law falls outside the scope of Community law.[7]

Expressly excluded from the protection by the Court of Justice are 'operations carried out by the police or other law enforcement services of a Member State or the exercise of the responsibilities incumbent upon member States with regard to the maintenance of law and order and the safeguarding of internal security' under Article 35 EU (Title VI or third pillar). Similarly, within Title IV of the first pillar (visas, asylum, immigration and other policies related to the free movement of persons) the Court does not have jurisdiction to rule on measures relating to the maintenance of law and order and the safeguarding of internal security. In these areas, fundamental rights protection does not lie before the Court of Justice.

National courts are under a Community mandate (the *ERT* mandate) to protect Community fundamental rights – as general principles of Community law – as against national measures falling within the scope of Community law, if necessary with the help of the Court of Justice. Conversely, several constitutional court have threatened that they may, in exceptional cases, review national measures within the scope of Community law in the light of *national* constitutional fundamental rights. There is thus a potential for conflict, even if it has never materialised, and even if it is by the constitutional courts themselves characterised as 'highly unlikely', or 'exceptional', a *'Reservezuständigkeit'*.[8] Jutta Limbach has explained the position of the *Bundesverfassungsgericht* in a manner which probably also applies to the other constitutional courts which have expressed the fundamental rights counter-limit: It is not to be considered a threat to the Court of Justice, but underscores the importance of the understanding common to all modern democratic Constitutions, that any public authority is restricted by fundamental rights.[9]

---

4 Case 5/88 *Wachauf* [1989] ECR 2609.
5 Case C–260/89 *ERT* [1991] ECR I–2925.
6 Case C–368/95 *Familiapress* [1997] ECR I–3689.
7 Case C–299/95 *Kremzow* [1997] ECR I–2629.
8 J Limbach, 'Die Kooperation der Gerichte in der zukünftigen europäischen Grundrechtsarchitektur', FCE, 7/00, available at www.rewi.hu-berlin.de/WHI/deutsch/fce/fce700/limbach. htm.
9 J Limbach, 'Die Kooperation der Gerichte in der zukünftigen europäischen Grundrechtsarchitektur', FCE, 7/00, available at www.rewi.hu-berlin.de/WHI/deutsch/fce/fce700/limbach.htm, at 6.

Other conflicts which may occur before national courts are those between Community (or Union) fundamental rights and those contained in other international treaties, most prominently the ECHR. In countries like the Netherlands, France, and Belgium, ordinary courts are empowered by the Constitution to review national law, including primary legislation, in the light of directly effective provisions of international treaties. The ECHR plays an important role in this respect, and especially in the Netherlands and France, the ECHR as enforced by the national courts replaces fundamental rights contained in the Constitution by a court having constitutional jurisdiction. In Belgium it adds to the constitutional protection offered by the *Cour d'arbitrage*. Now, these courts may accordingly be confronted with conflicting obligations deriving from different treaties. It may happen that the national court is obliged to apply a specific provision of Community law, which the national court considers to infringe the State's obligations under the ECHR. Certainly, the Court of Justice 'applies' the ECHR and seeks to comply with the case law of the Strasbourg Court. But there is a risk of diverging case law between the Court of Justice and the Human Rights Court, with the national courts caught in the middle.

Will the potential of conflict be removed by (1) the incorporation of the EU Charter on Fundamental Rights in the Constitutional Treaty and/or (2) the accession of the Union to the European Convention of Fundamental Rights?

23.2. THE EU CHARTER OF FUNDAMENTAL RIGHTS

23.2.1. The Current Position

23.2.1.1. *Legal Status*

At the moment, the Charter does not have the status of a legally binding document: it was solemnly proclaimed by the Council, the Commission and the European Parliament at the Nice European Council in December 2000. The Member States have accordingly not participated in the proclamation, although members of the European Council were present during the ceremony, standing behind the signatories, presumably so as to indicate their approval.[10] The Presidency Conclusions of the Nice European Council did welcome the proclamation by the three political institutions of the Union and repeated that *'in accordance with the Cologne conclusions, the question of the Charter's force will be considered later'*.[11] The

---

[10] So B De Witte, 'The Legal Status of the Charter: Vital Question or Non-issue?', 8 *MJ*, 2001, 81, at 82.

[11] Conclusions of the Presidency, Nice European Council of 7, 8 and 9 December 2000, at para 2.

Charter was published in the C part of the Official Journal, indicating that it was indeed not a legally binding document.

The lack of binding force of course does not mean that the Charter has no legal value at all. Lawyers may well prefer legally binding texts: if it is not binding and justiciable, why adopt it at all? However, the Charter was in the eyes of its supporters, mostly an exercise in visibility and identity: it was to make fundamental rights – already protected by the national Constitutions, general principles of Community law and the ECHR – visible at a Union level to its citizens. It was meant to have a symbolic function in order to increase the legitimacy of the European project. In addition, it was to assist the Court and political actors by bringing clarity: instead of finding and constructing fundamental rights as general principles of Community law from disparate sources, the Court could now simply draw on the Charter. Even without it being legally binding, the Charter was to be of great symbolic, political and legal value. Yet, the possible effects of a non-binding document on the activity of the European Court is not necessarily positive from the point of view of increased protection:[12] the Charter could also have the effect of *freezing* the existing case law to the effect that some provisions are expressly founded on the case-law of the Court of Justice, which will thus feel less inclined to further develop or overrule these judgments. It may have an *inhibiting* effect on the general principles case law, while it other cases it may encourage the Court to *expand* the existing case law, supported as it may feel by the language of the Charter. In other words, there is no imperative for increased protection in future case law: the influence of the Charter could go either way.

The expectation of many[13] was that the Court would soon start to refer to the Charter, and 'incorporate' it into the legal order by judicial activity. It would not be the first time for the Court to give some legal authority to formally non-binding instruments. Several Advocates General and the Court of First Instance have indeed in various cases made reference to the Charter. However, the Court of Justice has itself remained silent and refused to take note of the Charter. Why has it done so? One reason could lie in the quality of the text of the Charter, which at times does not meet the highest standards of clarity. Secondly, if the Court were to draw from the Charter instead of its usual sources, it may come under pressure to reject any progressive interpretations and to stick to what the political

---

[12] See for further explanation and examples B De Witte, 'The Legal Status of the Charter: Vital Question or Non-issue?', 8 *MJ*, 2001, 81, at 84 *et seq.*

[13] Not in the least the Commission, which stated that it 'can reasonably be expected that the Charter will become mandatory through the Court's interpretation of it as belonging to the general principles of Community law', Commission's Communication on the legal nature of the Charter of fundamental rights of the European Union, COM (2000) 644 of 11 October 2000.

constituent assembly, the Convention, has stated, decided and rejected with respect to specific rights.[14] The Court may well prefer the existing situation where it can use the ECHR and the constitutional system of the Member States as an organic and living laboratory of human rights protection which can be adopted and adapted to the needs of the European Union.[15] Thirdly, and most importantly, one may wonder whether it would be proper for the Court to go very far with judicial incorporation of the Charter, given the fact that it was constitutionally rejected as a binding and integral part of the Union legal order. If the Court were to garb the Charter with any derived legal force, it would be going against the clear will of the Member States as constituent power, which was not to make it a binding document. As Weiler has put it: *'One cannot chant odes to democracy and constitutionalism and then flout them when it does not suit one's human rights agenda'*.[16] The stony silence of the Court of Justice is not to be explained by its lack of interest or respect for the Charter and the fundamental rights proclaimed therein, but as an act of judicial restraint of a Court that is well aware of the intention of constituent powers and of its own place in the constitutional construct. The restraint on the part of the Court of Justice may also hide a long term strategy and policy of the Court: its silence will force the Member States to make up their minds as to the formal legal status of the Charter in the framework of the Convention. Had the Court jumped to award the Charter indirect legal force, the Member States could have decided to let 'nature have its course' and leave it to the Court of Justice (and to criticise it later for judicial activism?).

23.2.1.2. *Content*

The Charter may well be the most complete and up-to-date catalogue of fundamental rights. Yet, the Charter seems to be more than that: it contains not only those rights which are traditionally considered to constitute fundamental rights, but also provisions which are not usually so considered, and which before the Charter were traditionally 'rights of the citizens of the Union under Community law', and are not exactly human rights in the classic sense. Nevertheless, and despite its apparent completeness, much of the Charter may prove to be deceptive and may raise expectations it cannot meet. *'The sting is always in the tail'*, wrote Deirdre Curtin and Ronald van Ooik: upon a first reading the Charter seems very promising, to offer a very wide and general protection, to remove much of it in the final provisions. In addition, many specific provisions

---

[14] See JHH Weiler, 'A Constitution for Europe? Some Hard Choices?', 40 *JCMS*, 2002, 563, at 576–77. See also his 'Human Rights, Constitutionalism and Integration: Iconography and Fetishism', 3 *International Law FORUM du droit international*, 2001, 227, at 232–34.

[15] Above, at 576.

[16] Above, at 575.

are very unclear and imprecise, as they result from a compromise between divergent aims and beliefs.[17]

23.2.1.3. *General Provisions*

According to its Preamble, 'the Charter reaffirms the rights as they result, in particular, *from the constitutional traditions* and international obligations *common to the Member States*, the Treaty on European Union, the Community Treaties, the ECHR, the Social Charters adopted by the Community and by the Council of Europe and the case law of the Court of Justice and of the European Court of Human Rights'. It is, thus, not intended to constitute a break with the past, or to limit the protection offered by other documents.

Article 51(1) of the Charter states that *'The provisions of this Charter are addressed to the institutions and bodies of the Union with due regard for the principle of subsidiarity and to the Member States only when they are implementing Union law'.*[18] At first sight, the provision does not constitute the full confirmation of the case law of the Court of Justice which applies in cases falling within the scope of Community law, also where the Member States are derogating from the free movement provisions under the Treaty. To limit the application of the Charter to national measures implementing Union law, especially with the emphasis 'only', appears to restrict the case law of the Court of Justice. The Charter would appear to be about more than mere action by the Union institutions (and the Member States only within limited scope): the Charter prohibits torture (by the Commission?); it includes rights of the child and the elderly, rights of access to placement services... It gives the impression therefore that it aims at Member States action in a much broader way. This makes the Charter paradoxical and it appears to promise more than it can deliver: it makes bold claims, states very general rights, contains all types of fundamental rights, but then in Article 51 appears to retreat from them, and to be of a fairly limited scope.[19]

Article 52 states the scope of the rights guaranteed. Paragraph 1 defines the conditions for limitations on the exercise of rights and freedoms to be lawful. Paragraph 2 declares that the rights based on the Community and Union Treaties shall be exercised under the conditions and within the limits defined by those Treaties. And under the third paragraph, *'In so far as this Charter contains rights which correspond to rights guaranteed by the [ECHR], the*

---

[17] As McCrudden formulates it: '*[The Charter] is elegantly conceived, beautifully drafted, and a masterly combination of pastiche, compromise and studied ambiguity'*, Chr. McCrudden, 'The Future of the EU Charter of Fundamental Rights', Jean Monnet Working Paper, 10/01, at 7.

[18] For a discussion of the provision see P Eeckhout, 'The EU Charter of Fundamental Rights and the Federal Question', 39 *CML Rev* (2002) 945.

[19] P Eeckhout, 'The EU Charter of Fundamental Rights and the Federal Question', 39 *CML Rev* (2002) 945, at 957–58.

meaning and scope of those rights shall be the same as those laid down by the said Convention. This provision shall not prevent Union law providing more extensive protection.' According to the Explanatory Note, the provision intends to ensure consistency between the Charter, and the ECHR: insofar as the rights in the Charter also correspond to rights guaranteed by the ECHR, the meaning and scope of those rights, and the authorised limitations, are the same as those laid down by the ECHR, and as determined by the case law of the European Court of Human Rights, and the Court of Justice.

Article 53 'Level of Protection' states that *'Nothing in this Charter shall be interpreted as restricting or adversely affecting human rights and fundamental freedoms as recognised, in their respective fields of application, by Union law and international law and by international agreements to which the Union, the Community or all the Member States are party, including the [ECHR], and by the Member States' constitutions'.* According to the Explanatory Note, the provision is intended to maintain the level of protection currently afforded by Union law, national law and international law. Owing to its importance, mention is made of the ECHR. The level of protection afforded by the Charter may not, in any instance, be lower than that guaranteed by the ECHR, with the result that the arrangements for limitations may not fall below the level provided for by the ECHR.

23.2.2. The Charter and National Constitutional Rights

It is a public secret that the Convention was 'if not a child, at least a god-child'[20] of Germany. Concern for the lack of sufficient fundamental rights protection has been a constitutional issue since *Solange*, and made explicit in the new Article 23 inserted in the Basic Law at the occasion of the Maastricht Treaty. Article 23 of the Basic Law states *inter alia* that Germany is under a *'duty to participate in the development of the European Union which (..) provides a protection of fundamental rights equivalent to that of this Constitution'.* It was thought that the provision required more than the open statement contained in Article 6 EU and the case law of the Court of Justice, which could, after all, be overruled, and which had been open to the critique – rightly or wrongly – that the level of protection offered by the Court was not sufficient. In *Solange I*, the German Constitutional Court had specifically requested a catalogue of fundamental rights as a prerequisite for its unconditional acceptance of supremacy of Community law. That claim was dropped in *Solange II*, when the *Bundesverfassungsgericht* appeared to be satisfied, at least on a

---

[20] See LFM Besselink, 'The Member States, the National Constitutions and the Scope of the Charter', 8 *MJ*, 2002, 68, at 68.

general level, by the general principles case law of the Court of Justice.[21] Nevertheless, the *Bundesverfassungsgericht*, but also its brethren in other Member States, such as the *Corte costituzionale*, the *Højesteret* and possibly the *Cour d'arbitrage*, remain wary of the protection offered by the European institutions and the supervision of the Court of Justice.

Will this Charter dispose of all the remaining doubts concerning the protection of fundamental rights from the point of view of national law and the national courts?

23.2.2.1. 'Common Constitutional Traditions' in the Charter

The notion of 'constitutional traditions common to the Member States' appears on several occasions in the text of the Charter. It is stated in the Preamble that the Charter *'reaffirms the rights as they result, in particular, from the constitutional traditions and international obligations common to the Member States'*, after which follows the reference also to a series of specified international treaties and the case law of the two European Courts (Luxembourg and Strasbourg). The statement may be considered an affirmation of the theory of equivalent protection as propounded by the German Constitutional Court and as laid down in the German Constitution. The reference does not re-appear in the specific provisions, but it is used at several instances in the Explanatory Note. It has however been pointed out that these references do not succeed in establishing that these rights are in fact common to all the Member States.[22]

The notion of 'constitutional traditions common to the Member States' in the Charter suffers the same deficiencies and weaknesses as in the case law of the Court of Justice. Firstly, and without looking at specific rights, constitutional rights have a very different status in the various Member States. In Italy and Germany, both dualist and both comprising a constitutional court with jurisdiction in the area of fundamental rights, constitutional fundamental rights possess a much more privileged role than in countries like the Netherlands and France, where much of the judicial human rights protection depends on the ECHR and its application by the national courts. Secondly, even in countries where the judicial protection of constitutional rights exists, its prominence will vary, depending on the means of judicial enforcement of those rights, for instance the availability of a constitutional complaint procedure such as *Verfassungsbeschwerde* or *amparo*. Turning to specific rights, it is extremely difficult to detect the

---

[21] Of course, this is only a partial explanation of why the Charter was adopted, see for a 'plethora of justification', Chr., McCrudden, 'The Future of the EU Charter of Fundamental Rights', Jean Monnet Working Paper, 10/01, at 7.

[22] SeeLFM Besselink, 'The Member States, the National Constitutions and the Scope of the Charter', 8 *MJ*, 2002, 68, at 70 *et seq*.

'common constitutional tradition' with respect to a particular right. This has to do with definition of a particular right, scope of protection, level of protection, possible limitations and so forth. These difficulties have been described in the literature on the standard of protection which the Court of Justice is to offer in the context of its general principles case law.

23.2.2.2. *Article 53 of the Charter*[23]

Article 53[24] relates to the situation where the protection offered by the Charter does not meet the standard of protection offered by the Member States' constitutions in their respective fields of application. The provision is much wider, and also (or perhaps more importantly) refers to the situation where the level of protection offered by the Charter appears lower than that of treaties in their respective fields of application. Its relevance will concern mostly the Charter–ECHR relationship. This aspect of Article 53 will not be discussed here.

The aim of Article 53 is to make clear that the Charter can only serve as minimum protection, and will not stand in the way of further protection offered by other human rights documents. Charter protection cannot be inferior to that afforded by those other documents. In the original version of the provision,[25] mention was made only of the ECHR. From the outset there had been a concern within the Council of Europe and in other quarters that the Charter would dilute the protection offered by the ECHR,[26] and Article 53 was intended to remove any doubt about this matter. Article 53 was clearly inspired by Article 53 of the ECHR,[27] and the Council of Europe observers in the Convention have apparently contributed much to the provision.

---

[23] This section draws heavily on JB Liisberg, 'Does the EU Charter of Fundamental Rights Threaten the Supremacy of Community Law?', 38 *CML Rev* (2001) 1171, at 1172 *et seq.*, and the somewhat more complete version 'Does the EU Charter of Fundamental Rights Threaten the Supremacy of Community Law? Article 53 of the Charter: a fountain of law or just an inkblot?', Harvard Jean Monnet Working Paper 04/01.

[24] Article 53 provides that *'Nothing in this Charter shall be interpreted as restricting or adversely affecting human rights and fundamental freedoms as recognised, in their respective fields of application, by Union law and international law and by international agreements to which the Union, the Community or all the Member States are party, including the European Convention for the Protection of Human Rights and Fundamental Freedoms, and by the Member States' Constitutions'.*

[25] On the drafting history of Article 53 see JB Liisberg, 'Does the EU Charter of Fundamental Rights Threaten the Supremacy of Community Law?' 38 *CML Rev* (2001) 1171, at 1172 *et seq.*, and the somewhat more complete version 'Does the EU Charter of Fundamental Rights Threaten the Supremacy of Community Law? Article 53 of the Charter: a fountain of law or just an inkblot?', Harvard Jean Monnet Working Paper 04/01.

[26] See on this, and on the question whether the Charter has avoided the risk of dilution or duplication feared within the Council of Europe, P Lemmens, 'The Relation between the Charter of Fundamental Rights of the European Union and the European Convention on Human Rights – Substantive Aspects', 8 *MJ*, 2001, 49.

[27] *'Nothing in this Convention shall be construed as limiting or derogating from any of the human rights and fundamental freedoms which may be ensured under the laws of any High Contracting Party or under any other agreement to which it is a Party'.*

Comparable provisions can be found also in other international texts, and in earlier human rights draft catalogues drawn up previously by the European Parliament. Article 27 of the European Parliament's Declaration of Fundamental Rights and Freedoms of 12 April 1989 provided that *'No provision in this Declaration shall be interpreted as restricting the protection afforded by Community law, the law of the Member States, international law and international conventions and accords on fundamental rights and freedoms or as standing in the way of its development'.*[28] The European Parliament's Draft Constitution for the European Union, adopted on the basis of the Herman report, contained a revised version of Article 27 (point 24 of Title VII): *'No provision in this Constitution may be interpreted as restricting the protection afforded by the law of the Union, the law of the Member States, and international law'.*[29] Accordingly, the reference was not only to international treaties, but to international law generally. More importantly, the provisions stated that 'nothing in this Constitution' could restrict protection afforded elsewhere, and was thus not restricted to the provisions relating to fundamental rights. The text appeared to challenge the supremacy of Union law. Yet, the Draft also contained a supremacy clause in Article 1(6) stating that *'The law of the Union takes precedence over the law of the Member States'.* It was not however clear how both provisions were to be read in conjunction.

23.2.2.2.1. '...in their Respective Fields of Application...'

The phrase 'in their respective fields of application' is not clear on a first reading of the provision. Apparently, it was inserted at a rather late stage of the drafting of the provision, and without explicit explanation from the Secretariat. According to Liisberg, who bases his information on *'information from EU officials closely involved in the drafting'*, the proviso was inserted as a result of extensive consultations between the Legal Service of the Commission and the Secretariat (*i.e.* members of the Legal Service of the Council). The intention was apparently was to foreclose any doubt about the supremacy of Community law over national Constitutions, and the understanding of the two Legal Services was that the revised wording would make it clear that national Constitutions could only prevail in the limited sphere of exclusive national competence.[30] If that is the intended meaning of Article 53, it is rather peculiar, given the fact that the Charter

---

[28] Declaration of Fundamental Rights and Freedoms of the European Parliament of 12 April 1989 [1989] OJ C 120/51. Note that Article 27 refers to 'the law of the Member States' in general and not to the Constitutions; it does not contain the 'in their respective fields of application' proviso, and is not restricted to international conventions to which *all* the Member States are party.

[29] European Parliament's Draft Constitution for the European Union of 10 Ferbuary 1994 [1994] OJ C 61/155.

[30] JB Liisberg, 'Does the EU Charter of Fundamental Rights Threaten the Supremacy of Community Law? Article 53 of the Charter: a Fountain of Law or just an Inkblot?', Harvard Jean Monnet Working Paper 04/01, at 11.

is addressed to the Member States only insofar as they are implementing Union law (Article 51(2) Charter), and in the sphere of exclusive national competence the Charter does not apply at all.

23.2.2.2.2. '...by the Member States Constitutions...'

In an early draft of the provision, the reference to national law was broader and was more general to 'the law of the Member States'. Later, the reference to national law was limited to national Constitutions. During the discussion on the draft provision in the Convention, it appeared that one of the main goals of the reference to national Constitutions would be to emphasise that the Charter would not necessitate a constitutional amendment in the Member States, and that national Constitutions would not be replaced by the Charter.[31] However, the text at first sight seems to threaten the supremacy of Community law.

The plural in the final phrasing may cause problems of interpretation: Does it refer only to rights recognised by *all* Member States' Constitutions? This interpretation does seem to be supported by the reference to 'international agreements to which (..) *all* the Member States are party'. However, neither the drafting history, nor the aim of the provision seems to warrant such a strict interpretation.[32] The intention was to make clear that the Charter only provides minimum protection, and the reference to national Constitutions was inserted to make clear beyond a doubt that the national Constitutions need not be adapted and are not replaced by the Charter.

23.2.2.2.3. Does Article 53 Challenge the Supremacy of Community Law?

The aim of the provision clearly was not to introduce an explicit exception to the general principle of supremacy, or to sanction the case law of some of the constitutional courts. Yet, a national constitutional court could well find support in the text of Article 53 of the Charter to maintain its case law limiting the supremacy of Community law by national fundamental rights protection.

Liisberg has argued that Article 53 does not threaten the supremacy of Community law. While he does accept that Article 53 might be sufficiently ambiguous or difficult to understand to attract attention from national judges protective of national fundamental rights,[33] he argues that a close reading of the text ('nothing in this Charter'), its political purpose (to send the signal that the Charter is not intended to replace national Constitutions) and perhaps most importantly, its source of inspiration

---

[31] *Ibidem*, at 15–17, and 35.

[32] See also LFM Besselink, 'The Member States, the National Constitutions and the Scope of the Charter', 8 *MJ*, 2001, 68, at 74.

[33] JB Liisberg, 'Does the EU Charter of Fundamental Rights Threaten the Supremacy of Community Law? Article 53 of the Charter: a Fountain of Law or just an Inkblot?', Harvard Jean Monnet Working Paper 04/01, at 40.

(Article 53 ECHR), all confirm that Article 53 and its reference to constitutions of the Member States leave the principle of supremacy of Community law intact.[34]

The first argument states that since the provision is limited to the Charter itself and not Union law in general, the Charter does not rule out that other Community instruments may have such an effect of restricting or adversely affecting human rights as recognised by *inter alia* the Member States' Constitutions. However, that appears to be the very purpose of the provision, namely to guarantee that the level of protection will not be decreased, that the advent of the Charter cannot be used as an argument to restrict protection offered elsewhere, including the national Constitutions. It contains at least a hint – even if mistaken – that the supremacy of Community law may not be absolute.

Liisberg's second argument (the political intention of the provision) is a strong one at face value. However, if the Charter does become a binding document and the Court of Justice is to interpret it, it is unlikely that the Court of Justice will look into the drafting history of the provision. The Court does not look at 'original intent', it starts from the text, and mostly interprets Community law teleologically. It is on the other hand to be expected that the Court will interpret in favour of the absolute principle of ultimate supremacy. The argument would then be that Article 53 cannot be considered as an exception to the principle of supremacy because such a far-reaching and revolutionary modification of a constitutional principle would at least have to be stated explicitly in clear and ambiguous terms and could not be brought about by accident and in an almost creeping manner. However, 'malignant' national courts do not start from the premise of absolute supremacy, and they may abuse the provision to their advantage.

Thirdly, Liisberg states that Article 53 of the Charter is entirely inspired by its equivalent in the ECHR, Article 53 ECHR, and accordingly, that the only natural meaning of Article 53 of the Charter is to see it as the equivalent of Article 53 ECHR. As such, the provision is simply a politically valuable safeguard, found in almost all human rights instruments, which serves to calm any concerns that the Charter could be used as a pretext to cut down protection enjoyed on the basis of existing rules. Nevertheless, Liisberg does recognise that the Community (and should one add Union) legal order is completely different from the legal order devised by the ECHR within the Council of Europe. One might even take it a step further and argue that the ECHR is not concerned with the creation of a legal order. It is concerned only with human rights protection, and controls that the human rights protection in the Contracting States does not fall below the standard set out

---

[34]   JB Liisberg, 'Does the EU Charter of Fundamental Rights Threaten the Supremacy of Community Law?' 38 *CML Rev* (2001) 1171, at 1191.

in the ECHR, which is considered a minimum standard. The ECHR allows for Contracting Parties to award a higher level of protection, unless that protection would entail the violation of another right protected under the Convention. The ECHR does not concern itself with creating uniformity of any kind.[35] Under current Union law, however, the principle of supremacy was introduced in order to ensure that Member States cannot unilaterally deviate from what has been agreed in common, and this is so whatever the grounds that a Member State would invoke to escape the application of Community law, including national fundamental rights.[36] A similar provision in the Charter, if it were to become binding, does not necessarily have the same meaning as Article 53 of the ECHR: under the current position, Community law *does* prevent a Member State, in specific cases, to grant a 'higher' level of protection, if this should imply that Community law is not applied within that Member State. Say that Germany had been allowed in the bananas cases to offer a 'higher level of protection' to the importers of bananas as prevailing under the German Constitution and had been allowed to protect their right to conduct their business in German style, that would have seriously affected the application of the Bananas regulation in Germany. The parallel with Article 53 of the ECHR is thus only partially correct, and does not pay due regard to the principle of supremacy of Community law.

The least one can conclude is that Article 53 is not well drafted, and while it may be intended as merely giving a political signal to ease any concerns about lowering the existing standards of protection in general, it is at least ambiguous and may be open to abuse. The text should have been revised, but has not been done and the text of Article 53 has not been touched. However, the provision must now be read in conjunction with the primacy provision of Article I-6 of the TCE.[37]

23.2.3. The Charter and the ECHR

According to Article 52 of the Charter *'In so far as this Charter contains rights which correspond to rights guaranteed by the [ECHR], the meaning and scope of those rights shall be the same as those laid down by the said Convention. This provision shall not prevent Union law providing more extensive protection.'*

---

[35] 'Common principles' do play a role in the case law of the Court of Human Rights, but only in order to define the minimum standard.
[36] Case 11/70 *Internationale Handelsgesellschaft* [1971] ECR.
[37] Nevertheless, could it also be argued that Article I-6 TCE must be read in context, and that Article II-113TCE contains an exception to the general rule?

The Charter may offer wider protection than the ECHR, but not a narrower one. The protection offered by the ECHR serves as a minimum. According to the Explanations, the meaning and scope of the Convention and its Protocols is to be determined not only by the text but also by the case law of the European Court of Human Rights, and by the Court of Justice. The Explanation further contains two lists of rights, one of corresponding Charter and ECHR rights; and a list of Charter rights having a wider scope than the corresponding ECHR rights. Article 53 is intended to remove all doubts that may still remain and declares that the Charter cannot be interpreted as lowering the level of protection currently afforded by Union law, national law and international law, including the ECHR. The ECHR is thus clearly intended to be the minimum, the Charter may only afford more, not less protection.

As to the respective positions of the Luxembourg and Strasbourg Courts, Article 52 does not mention the case law of the Human Rights Court. However, since the Human Rights Court is established on the basis of the ECHR and interprets the ECHR rights *ex tunc*, it must be assumed that the case law of the Human Rights Court forms an integral part of the meaning and scope of these rights.[38] This is also made explicit in the Explanations, which refer to the case law of the Court of Justice. It appears that there is a hierarchy in the authority between both Courts, and that the Court of Justice will have to follow the interpretation by the Human Rights Court. This would also be in line with the current practice of the Court of Justice. Yet, incorporation of the Charter alone will not guarantee that protection offered by the Court of Justice will in all cases be equivalent with that offered by the Strasbourg Court: divergent case law may continue to arise, if only because a question may arise in Luxembourg before it has been decided in Strasbourg, and because the Court of Justice interprets fundamental rights through the prism of Community law and may strike different balances to those struck by the Strasbourg Court.[39] Accession to the ECHR *would* achieve that result, as the Strasbourg Court would ultimately have supervision over the case law of the Court of Justice.

23.2.4 Incorporation of the Charter

When the Charter was drafted, its legal status was not yet entirely clear, and the final document was not adopted as a binding instrument but

---

[38] See K Lenaerts and E De Smijter, 'The Charter and the Role of the European Courts', 8 *MJ*, 2001, 90, at 98.

[39] So also R Harmsen, 'National Responsibility for European Community Acts Under the European Convention on Human Rights: Recasting the Accession Debate', 7 *EPL*, 2001, 625, at 627.

solemnly proclaimed. The question of its binding force was transferred to the Constitutional Convention, which would study whether the Charter was to be incorporated, and if so, how and in what form. Article I-9 of the Treaty establishing a Constitution for Europe refers to the Charter which is incorporated as Part II. The content of the Charter was left untouched. The Working Group II 'Incorporation of the Charter/ Accession to the ECHR' stated in its final report that its starting point had been that the content of the Charter represented a consensus reached by the previous Convention, *'a body which had special expertise in fundamental rights and served as a model for the present Convention, and endorsed by the Nice European Council. The whole Charter – including its statements of rights and principles, its preamble and, as a crucial element, its 'general provisions' – should be respected by this Convention and not be re-opened by it'.*[40] Nevertheless, the Group did recognise that certain technical 'drafting adjustments' in the Charter's 'general provisions' were possible and appropriate. These adjustments did not however concern Article 53.

Incorporation of the Charter did not have priority, in my view, for the national courts. Incorporation will mostly serve symbolic purposes: to bring the Union closer to its citizens, demonstrate to the outside world (including the national constitutional courts) and the candidate Members that the Union does take fundamental rights seriously. In itself, this may be important: it increases visibility, adds legitimacy to the Constitutional Document, and constitutes an important element for building confidence of the European citizens. It may well give the Treaty establishing a Constitution for Europe an added, 'constitutional' value: it represents one of the constitutional elements of the Constitutional Treaty. Indeed, it is these days common opinion that a proper Constitution includes or even starts with a Bill of Rights.

What will incorporation do for the national courts? It could be argued that yet another catalogue does not necessarily contribute to more and improved protection. What it is liable to result in, is an enhanced role of the courts, both European and national, in the protection of fundamental rights, if only to clarify the interpretation of the various documents and to decide whether a particular right may be better protected under one document than under the other, and thus to clarify the relationship between them. Nevertheless, any added value of the Charter will be found more in increased awareness of fundamental rights on the part of political organs and better visibility for the citizens than with the courts, which already have several catalogues at their disposal, and also work with general principles and unwritten norms. If the Charter is indeed incorporated in the Treaty, as Part II inconsistencies, overlaps etc, become more problematic.

---

[40] Final Report of Working Group II, CONV 352/02, at 4.

Various overlaps, tensions and inconsistencies may occur: between the other Parts of the Constitutional Treaty and the Charter, between the Charter and the ECHR, between the Charter and national constitutional fundamental rights, between the Charter and other human rights conventions. It will be for the courts to solve them.

Will Part II convince the national (constitutional) courts which currently retain fundamental rights jurisdiction in the scope of Union law to abandon it? It could be argued that the Charter finally meets the requirements formulated by the German Constitutional Court in *Solange I*, where it held that as long as there was no catalogue at the European level, it would not give up jurisdiction over Community law. The requirement had been dropped already in *Solange II*, and even absent a catalogue had the German Court retreated from the area, to an almost theoretical and symbolic position in *Bananas III*. It is to be expected that incorporation in itself does not alter that position. The German *Bundesverfassungsgericht* has made mention of the Charter in the case concerning the prohibition of the Nationaldemokratische Partei Deutschlands (NPD). It accordingly did take judicial note of it before the Court of Justice! Yet, the provision referred to was Article 51 of the Charter, and it was mentioned in order to prove the limited effect and field of application of the Charter and to support the statement that *'Eine allgemeine Bindung der Mitgliedstaaten des Unions- und Gemeinschaftsrechts besteht nicht'*.[41] The case did not come within the scope of Community law and accordingly, general principles of Community law did not apply to the case, according to the *Bundesverfassungsgericht*. It is difficult to predict what the reaction of the court will be in cases which do come within the scope of application of Community law, but much will depend on the supervision by the Court of Justice.

What will incorporation do for the courts which, as has been described, apply the ECHR as a Bill of Rights? Will not the addition of yet another catalogue further complicate the problems which for instance the Netherlands, French and Belgian courts may incur, when confronted with conflicting treaty obligations under the ECHR and Union law? At first sight this risk is real. The situation does become more complicated as yet another document is added, but this merely complicates the definition of the obligations imposed on the State by Union law: There are no additional obligations imposed on the Member States, the manner in which they are defined changed. Under the current situation, *i.e.* before incorporation of the Charter or adoption thereof as binding document, and absent accession to the ECHR, the Court of Justice defines European fundamental rights as general principles of Community law on the basis of the common constitutional traditions of the Member States and international

---

[41] *Bundesverfassungsgericht*, decision of 22 November 2001, *Nationaldemokratische Partei Deutschlands (NPD)*, available on www.bverfg.de.

documents, especially the ECHR. In practice, the Court adopts a fairly open approach to fundamental rights. It does aim to follow the Human Rights Court in the interpretation of actual provisions, but for the rest, it can adopt a relatively open-ended and non-exhaustive approach, using the common constitutional traditions as 'an organic and living laboratory of rights protection' which case by case and in permanent dialogue with its national counterparts can be adopted and adapted for the European Union.[42] Incorporation of the Charter into the Constitutional Treaty may have the effect of 'chilling the constitutional dialogue'.[43] But combined with accession and the maintenance of the reference to the general principles as derived from the common constitutional traditions of the Member States and from the ECHR, may make it more difficult for the Court of Justice to define the obligations imposed on the Member States, and to avoid inconsistencies and loyalty conflicts for itself and for the national courts. The issue will be taken up again in the next section.

23.3. ACCESSION TO THE EUROPEAN CONVENTION ON HUMAN RIGHTS

23.3.1. Background

The question of accession to the ECHR has been debated for a very long time, and much has been written about the issues involved in accession to the ECHR, both from the point of view of Union law and of the ECHR. These will not be pursued here. From the point of view of national law and the national courts, accession of the EC or EU to the ECHR has important implications, especially for those countries where judicial fundamental rights protection is to a large extent based on the application of the ECHR, such as the Netherlands, France, and Belgium, and recently also the United Kingdom through the Human Rights Act. As for Germany and Italy, the conflict between the constitutional courts and the Court of Justice concerns mainly the relationship between the protection offered by the Court of Justice under its case law and protection offered by the constitutional courts under the national Constitutions. To those courts, accession will mostly be important from the point of view of binding the Union institutions themselves, including the Court of Justice.

The ECHR has played a crucial role in the development of the human rights case law of the Court of Justice. An explicit reference to the ECHR

---

[42] JHH Weiler, 'Editorial: Does the European Union Truly Need a Charter of Rights?', 6 *ELJ*, 2000, 95, at 96.
[43] *Ibidem*, at 96.

appeared for the first time in *Rutili*,[44] while the Court had already before made mention more generally of international human rights treaties on which the Member States had participated. In the position of the Court, respect for human rights is a condition for the lawfulness of acts of the Community institutions. The ECHR is a chief source of inspiration for the Court of Justice to formulate fundamental rights, and over the past years, the Court has demonstrated its willingness to follow the jurisprudence of the Strasbourg Court.[45]

Yet, the 1978 Commission proposal to begin a process which would lead to the accession of the EC to the ECHR, was not taken up by the Council and the Member States.[46] At the occasion of the Treaty of Maastricht, Article F(2) was included in the Treaty on European Union stating that '*The Union shall respect fundamental rights, as guaranteed by the European Convention for the Protection of Human Rights and Fundamental Freedoms signed in Rome on 4 November 1950 and as they result from the constitutional traditions common to the Member States, as general principles of Community law*'. The provision sanctioned and confirmed the case law of the Court of Justice, but a lot of confusion was caused by the fact that at the same time, Article F(2) of the EU Treaty was not among the provisions with regard to which the Court of Justice was competent. At the end of the day, this did not alter the existing situation as the Court continued to develop its case law outside the framework of the Treaty, on the basis of its general principles case law; accession was not part of the parcel.

In its *Opinion 2/94* the Court of Justice held that accession of the Communities was not possible under the existing Treaties, and that it would require an express provision granting the Communities competence to do so. The reasoning of the Court in its decision is not entirely convincing.[47] One can only hope that the Court did not find a perverse satisfaction in the decision, as one could cynically suspect: the decision could be interpreted as a *male fide* response of the Court to the *Maastricht* judgment of the *Bundesverfassungsgericht*: you want us to be serious about the Community's competences? There you have it, and it is only a coincidence that the outcome saves the Court from outside control by the

---

44 Case 36/75 *Rutili v République française (Ministre de l'intérieur)* [1975] ECR 1219.
45 See for insatnce Case C–185/95 *Baustahlgewerbe GmbH v Commission* [1998] ECR I–8417.
46 See Ph Alston and JHH Weiler, 'An "Ever Closer Union" in Need of a Human Rights Policy: The European Union and Human Rights', in Ph Alston (ed), *The EU and Human Rights*, (Oxford, OUP, 1999), 3, at 10–11 with reference. The proposal was relaunched in 1990, see on the proposal and its implications FG Jacobs, 'European Community Law and the European Convention on Human Rights', in D Curtin and T Heukels (eds), *Institutional Dynamics of European Integration. Essays in Honour of Henry G Schermers*, (Dordrecht, Nijhoff, 1994), 564.
47 See P Eeckhout, 'The EU Charter of Fundamental Rights and the federal Question', 39 *CML Rev* (2002) 945, at 981 *et seq*.

European Court of Human Rights, or that the subject matter of the competence at issue happened to be fundamental rights, the other concern of the *Bundesverfassungsgericht*. Yet, the Member States did not take up the invitation and did not make the necessary arrangements in Amsterdam or Nice. Instead, Amsterdam did correct what appeared to be a drafting error in the Treaty of Maastricht concerning the jurisdiction of the Court of Justice concerning fundamental rights (in Article 46 EU). Veritable membership, including a clear position on the jurisdiction of the Strasbourg Court to review respect for the ECHR by the Union institutions, remains absent.

23.3.2. The Current Situation

23.3.2.1. *Supervision by the Strasbourg Court*

It is in the interest of ensuring credibility that protection is ensured under the supervision of an external institution. The Court of Justice cannot perform this function of third party where Union acts are concerned, as it belongs to the Union system. Under the current case law of the Court of Human Rights, no complaints can be brought *against the Communities or the Union directly*, as they are not party to the Convention.[48]

However, complaints may be brought *against the Member States* for the execution of Community acts alleged to be contrary to the ECHR.[49] The Member States are responsible for all acts and omissions of their domestic organs allegedly violating the Convention irrespective of whether the act or omission in question is a consequence of domestic law or of the necessity to comply with international obligations. A transfer of powers does not necessarily exclude a State's responsibility under the Convention with regard to the exercise of the transferred powers, otherwise the guarantees of the Convention could be limited and thus be deprived of their peremptory character. It was stated that the transfer to an international

---

[48] For instance *European Commission of Human Rights*, decision of 10 July 1978 as to the admissibility of application n. 8030/77, *CFDT v European Communities and its Member States*, see also *European Commission of Human Rights*, decision of 9 February 1990 as to the admissibility of application n. 13258/87, *M&Co. v Germany*, [1990] 64 DR 138. The company M & Co. brought a complaint against Germany for having issued a writ for the execution of a judgment of the ECJ which the applicant claimed to infringe its rights under Art. 6 ECHR See on these cases RA Lawson, *Het EVRM en de Europese Gemeenschappen. Bouwstenen voor een aansprakelijkheidsregime voor het optreden van internationale organisaties* (Deventer, 1999) Chapter 2.

[49] See e.g. *European Court of Human Rights*, decision of 15 November 1996, *Cantoni v France*, where the ECtHR held that 'The fact, pointed to by the Government, that Article L 511 of the Public Health Code is based almost word for word on Community Directive 65/65 (see paragraph 12 above) does not remove it from the ambit of Art. 7 of the Convention (art. 7)'.

organisation was not incompatible with the ECHR provided that within that organisation fundamental rights would receive an equivalent protection, and noted that the legal system of the European Communities not only secured fundamental rights, but also provided for control of their observance. Since the Communities were based on the rule of law, the Member States would not incur individual liability in assisting in the implementation of Community law in their territory. This demonstrates restraint *vis-à-vis* the Member States acting in the implementation of Community law.

In *Pafitis v Greece*, the Court of Human Rights equally seemed committed to self-restraint,[50] when it held that the period during which a case had been pending before the Court of Justice on a reference for preliminary ruling should not be taken into account to determine whether the proceedings before the Greek courts was to be considered as infringing the reasonable time provision contained in Article 6 ECHR.[51] However, the Member States must earn the restraint of the European Court of Human Rights, and where the system would fall below the standard, the Court may well hold the Member States individually or jointly liable for infringement of the ECHR.

Finally, in *Matthews v United Kingdom*, the Strasbourg Court indicated that it is likely to scrutinise transfer of power to international organisations more closely than in the past, and that *Member States* may be held responsible for acts adopted in the context of international organisations. Yet, the alleged violation in *Matthews* flowed not from acts adopted by the Community or Union institutions, but from international instruments which were freely entered into by the United Kingdom, and which could not be challenged before the Court of Justice. Accordingly, The United Kingdom was held responsible for securing the Convention rights.[52] The Court of Human Rights thus appears to accept competence to check acts

---

[50]   So K Lenaerts, 'Fundamental Rights in the European Union', 25 *ELR*, 2000, 575, at 583.

[51]   'The Court cannot, however, take this period into consideration in its assessment of the length of each particular set of proceedings: even though it might at first sight appear reltaively long, to take it into account would adversely affect the system instituted by Article 177 of the EEC Treaty and work against the aim pursued in substance in that Article', *European Court of Human Rights*, decision of 26 February 1998 in Case 163/1996/782/983, *Pafitis and Others v Greece*, at marginal number 95. This is not the only decision in which the ECtHR appears to be protective of the special position of the ECJ, see also *European Court of Human Rights*, decision of 19 March 1997, *Hornsby v Greece*, where the ECtHR stated that the delay by the Greek administrative authorities in taking the appropriate measures to comply with two judgments of the Supreme Administrative Court implementing a decision of the ECJ constituted an infringement of Art. 6 ECHR It has also been argued that a refusal to make a reference for preliminary ruling could constitute an infringement of Art. 6 ECHR, see D Spielmann, 'Human Rights Case Law in the Strasbourg and Luxembourg Courts: Conflicts, Inconsistencies, and Complementarities', in Ph Alston (ed), *The EU and Human Rights* (Oxford, OUP, 1999) 757, at 779, with references.

[52]   *European Court of Human Rights*, decision of 18 February 1999, *Matthews v United Kingdom*, at marginal nrs 26–35.

of the Community institutions in case brought against one or all Member States[53] insofar as the Community or the Union[54] do not provide equivalent protection where the Court of Justice does not have jurisdiction to hear the case.[55] It is not clear however, whether the Court of Human Rights will control 'real' Community acts, and whether it will indeed interfere if it considers the level of protection offered by the Court of Justice insufficient.[56] Nevertheless, the fact that the EU Member States may find themselves in the dock at Strasbourg for Community or Union acts may influence the Member States' position on accession.

23.3.2.2. *Divergent Case Law between Court of Justice and the Court of Human Rights*[57]

The Court of Justice protects fundamental rights as general principles of Community law as they arise from the ECHR and the common constitutional traditions of the Member States, as against actions of the Community institutions and against national authorities acting within the scope of Community law. The involvement of the Court of Justice with the ECHR raises questions of compatibility between the case law of the Court of Justice and that of the authority ultimately responsible for the interpretation of the ECHR, the Court of Human Rights. The Court of Justice is called upon to interpret rights guaranteed by the ECHR in a Union legal context, and it may occur that its interpretation deviates from the interpretation given – mostly later – by the Court of Human Rights. Now, in and of itself, this is not an exceptional situation: national courts applying the Convention may find themselves in a similar position, and there is no such thing as a preliminary reference procedure under the Convention, not for the national courts, nor for the Court of Justice. The system of the

---

[53] So for instance *Segi*; and pending case *Senator Lines*.
[54] As seems to follow from *European Court of Human Rights*, decision of 23 May 2002 on the admissibility of applications 6422/02 and 9916/02, *Segi and others and Gestoras Pro-Amnistia and Others v Germany, Austria, Belgium, Denmark, Spain, Finland, France, Greece, Ireland, Italy, Luxembourg, the Netherlands, Portugal, the United Kingdom and Sweden*, available on www.echr.coe.int.
[55] So also K Lenaerts and E De Smijter, 'A "Bill of Rights" for the European Union', 38 *CMLR*, 2001, 273, at 291.
[56] For an argument in favour of the the development of a de facto vertical relationship between the ECtHR and the ECJ, see I Canor, '*Primus inter pares*. Who is the ultimate guardian of fundamental rights in Europe?', 25 *ELR*, 2000, 3.
[57] On the general issue of divergent case law, see D Spielmann, 'Human Rights Case Law in the Strasbourg and Luxembourg Courts: Conflicts, Inconsistencies, and Complementarities', in Ph Alston (ed), *The EU and Human Rights*, (Oxford, OUP, 1999), 757; R Lawson, 'Confusion and Conflict? Divergent Interpretations of the European Convention on Human Rights in Strasbourg and Luxembourg', in R Lawson and M de Bloijs (eds), *The Dynamics of the Protection of Human Rights in Europe. Essays in Honour of HG Schermers*, Vol III, (Dordrecht, Nijhoff, 1994), 219.

ECHR supposes that there are many (national) courts implicated in the protection of human rights, and hence it is inevitable that there will at times be different interpretations of the rights and principles involved.[58] This is not different for the Court of Justice. Yet, at the difference with national courts, there is no correction system for the Court of Justice: absent accession, the Strasbourg Court cannot directly handle complaints against the Union or Communities. Nevertheless, on the whole the Court of Justice usually draws inspiration from the case law of the Strasbourg court with a view to the application of the ECHR as part of the general principles of Community law, and more and more, the Court of Justice makes explicit reference to the case law of Strasbourg.[59] In addition, the Court of Justice has made it a guiding principle that should the Court of Human Rights interpret rights protected under the ECHR differently in a later decision, it will adapt its case law accordingly. However, what makes the situation more complex in the context of the Community legal order is that the *national courts* may get stuck between the principle of the supremacy of Community law on the one hand and the obligations flowing from the ECHR on the other hand.

Indeed, the fundamental rights contained in the ECHR may be protected at various levels:[60] in some Member States, the domestic courts test the compatibility of acts of the national authorities (also where they are implementing or applying Community law) on their compatibility with the ECHR. In some of the Member States,[61] for instance The Netherlands and France, and to a lesser extent Belgium, this is even the only way available to have fundamental rights protected against primary legislation in force, and the ECHR functions as the Bill of Rights for practical purposes. These national courts may make a reference to the Court of Justice, whose decision they are bound by, including on the interpretation of the ECHR as part of the general principles of Community law.[62] Yet, upon exhaustion of all

---

[58] See RA Lawson, 'Confusion and Conflict? Diverging Interpretations of the European Convention on Human Rights in Strasbourg and Luxembourg', in R Lawson and M de Bloijs (eds), *The Dynamics of the Protection of Human Rights in Europe. Essays in Honour of HG Schermers*, Vol III, (Dordrecht, Nijhoff, 1994), 219, at 229.

[59] See examples in D Spielmann, 'Human Rights Case Law in the Strasbourg and Luxembourg Courts: Conflicts, Inconsistencies, and Complementarities', in Ph Alston (ed), *The EU and Human Rights* (Oxford, OUP, 1999) 757, at 772 et seq.;

[60] See *e.g.* K Lenaerts and E De Smijter, 'The Charter and the Role of the European Courts', 8 *MJ*, 2001, 90, at 92.

[61] All of the Member States are party to the ECHR; given the dualist position of some of the Member States, individuals cannot invoke the ECHR *directly* before the domestic courts, where the Convention has not been incorporated into national law Incorporation of the Convention has recently occurred in Denmark, and in the United Kingdom (in the Human Rights Act 1998).

[62] The decision of the ECJ need not even have been handed in the same case. While the judgments of the ECJ in Art. 234 references are binding only on the court that made the reference, the interpretation given by the ECJ is considered to be part of the interpreted text, and in that sense it has binding force also for other courts in other cases.

national remedies, the case may also be brought before the Court of Human Rights, adding a third layer of protection, and using the same document as the standard, the ECHR. Now, *quid*, if these court should all arrive at a different conclusion? The State is bound to comply both with the ECHR and with EU law. The interpretation of Community law, including general principles of Community law, by the Court of Justice is binding on the national courts. A judgment of the Court of Human Rights is equally binding on the Member States. What should the national court do where the decisions of both European Courts diverge? It is then caught between the principle of supremacy of Community law on the one hand, and the obligation to comply with the Convention and the decisions of the Strasbourg Court on the other hand, and thus with conflicting treaty obligations.

Also in cases concerning an alleged infringement of ECHR rights *by the Community institutions*, is there a risk of divergent case law of the Court of Justice, the Court of Human Rights and the national courts. The Court of Human Rights may rule on the compatibility with the ECHR of Union law where no equivalent protection is or can be offered by the Court of Justice in cases brought against one or more Member States. From the Community law perspective, only the Court of Justice is competent to rule on the validity of Community law, including its compatibility with fundamental rights. But what will a national court do when it feels that a measure of Community law which has been held valid by the Court of Justice, does infringe the ECHR? The national court is then caught, again, between the supremacy of Community law and its lack of jurisdiction to rule on the validity of Community law under *Foto-Frost* on the one hand, and its obligation to comply with the ECHR on the other. The national court is again confronted with conflicting treaty obligations. The difficulty is that in most legal systems, there is no hierarchy between treaties, and it will be up to the courts to balance the conflicting obligations, possibly also to give precedence to one over the other, which necessarily entails the infringement of at least one treaty obligation. Can accession of the Union to the ECHR serve to avoid or solve these loyalty conflicts for the national courts?

23.3.3. Should the EC/EU Accede?

Accession is considered an important signal that the Union is willing to submit to outside control, in other words, that it is confident about its fundamental rights situation. In addition, it had become almost a disgrace that the Union would not want to become a party to the ECHR while at the same time requiring all candidate Member States to accede. Obviously, accession does raise a number of important and difficult legal issues, but these can be resolved, by making the necessary arrangements both on the side of the Council of Europe and in the text of the future EU Constitutional Treaty. Accession does seem to be a very attractive option (whether alongside the incorporation of the Charter or not), since it would contribute to solving the issue of divergent case law. As mentioned, I do not consider divergent case law an evil in and of itself.[63] But from the perspective of the national courts, central in this book, divergent interpretation of the ECHR by the Strasbourg and Luxembourg courts will put them in the uncomfortable position of having to choose between infringing obligations under the Convention or violating the Community principle of supremacy. Accession would make it possible to solve questions of divergent case law in a more concrete and straightforward manner. As a consequence of accession, the Union will be formally subject to outside control by a third party, which should not matter: it brings the Court of Justice a similar position as the national constitutional courts, who have been subject to the scrutiny of the Court of Human Rights ever since their State ratified the ECHR. Consequently, the Court of Justice will be subject to the case law of the Court of Strasbourg.

In addition, it is in the interest of the Member States to enable accession to the European Convention. It is the only manner to ensure that they will not be held responsible for infringement of the ECHR on the part of the Union institutions.

23.4. ACCESSION AND/OR CHARTER?

One option does not exclude the other. The incorporation of the Charter does not render accession to the ECHR obsolete, as the Charter does not provide for third party control. Nor does it exclude accession. Conversely, accession to the Convention system may be considered as insufficient: some argue that protection offered by the new Court of Human Rights belonging to a Council of Europe of 40 States can never reach the highest level of protection that would be appropriate for the European Union, which should aim for a higher standard. The options are not mutually exclusive.[64] A combination of both incorporation and accession may well be considered the best route to an improved human rights protection system. From the point of view of the national courts, I believe that accession is more important than the incorporation of (yet another) human rights document. The Charter raises new questions of consistency and convergence in standards, which accession attempts to answer. It adds an additional standard, beside the existing standards: national

---

[63] Of course, divergent case law may be frustrating if the Court deciding your case offers you a lower level of protection than the other court would. But divergence may be the expression of a constitutional dialogue, of searching the optimal position in the case law, where one court can learn from and be inspired by the other.

[64] See also K Lenaerts and E De Smijter, 'The Charter and the Role of the European Courts', 8 *MJ*, 2001, 90, at 100–1.

Constitutions, common constitutional traditions, general provisions of Community law, the ECHR and other international documents. The ambiguity of the horizontal provisions relating to the relation between the ECHR and the Charter, and the case law of the respective courts is a cause for concern.

In addition to incorporation and accession, the maintenance of the reference to general principles, as deriving from the ECHR and the common constitutional traditions is envisaged. Preserving the reference has the advantage that it confirms the current position of the Court of Justice. Yet, it again demonstrates the need for clarifying the relation or hierarchy between the various sources and catalogues of fundamental rights.

23.5. THE TREATY ESTABLISHING A CONSTITUTION FOR EUROPE

The Constitutional Treaty comprises all three elements: incorporation, accession and reference to the general principles. The Charter is incorporated as Part II of the Constitutional Treaty, including its Preamble and General Provisions. Reference is already made to Part II in Part I, which states in its Article I-9 that *'The Union shall recognise the rights, freedoms and principles set out in the Charter of Fundamental Rights which constitutes Part II'*. Article 53 now numbered Article II-113 is kept intact, while Article 52, now Article II-112 has undergone some changes. Paragraph 4 now states that *'Insofar as this Charter recognises fundamental rights as they result from the constitutional traditions common to the Member States, those rights shall be interpreted in harmony with those traditions'*.

Article I-9 states that *'The Union shall seek accession to the [ECHR]. Such accession shall not affect the Union's competences as defined in the Constitution'*. The third paragraph of Article I-9 repeats the reference to fundamental rights as general principles, this time of the Union's law: *'Fundamental rights, as guaranteed by the [ECHR], and as they result from the constitutional traditions common to the Member States, shall constitute general principles of the Union's law'*.

The choice for a triple form of protection is probably, from the perspective of the individuals whose rights are protected, to be preferred, as it seems likely at first sight that the highest level of protection can thereby be reached. However, it does increase the likelihood of divergences of interpretation and of clashes of rights contained in different catalogues, and it may well prove to be a very difficult task for the courts, both national and European, to achieve consistency.

24

Kompetenz Kompetenz

THE SECOND CURRENT sticking point between the national constitutional courts and the European Court of Justice is the issue of judicial *Kompetenz Kompetenz*. Which court has ultimate authority to decide *Kompetenz* issues between the Member States and the Union?

24.1. THE CURRENT SITUATION

24.1.1. Judicial Kompetenz Kompetenz

From the perspective of Community law, the Court of Justice has sole jurisdiction to review the validity of Community law, and thus to hold it invalid for lack of competence.[1] Nevertheless, this position is challenged by several constitutional courts, most notably the *Bundesverfassungsgericht*, the *Corte costituzionale* and the *Højesteret*. As in the case of the fundamental rights conflict, there have only been mere warnings, and there has not been an actual decision of a constitutional court declaring a Community measure inapplicable. The situation is different in respect of those areas of non-Community Union law (and even under Title IV of the EC Treaty), where the Court of Justice has no or only limited jurisdiction to rule on conflicts of competence, since it may not have jurisdiction to review Union acts at all. In those cases, there is no positive conflict of jurisdiction between courts claiming *Kompetenz-Kompetenz*, as the Court of Justice cannot claim *sole* jurisdiction: it has no jurisdiction at all.

The *Bundesverfassungsgericht* has criticised the attitude of the Court of Justice with respect to the alleged practice of the Union institutions to usurp more powers than had been transferred to the Union, through Article 308 EC, and through the theories of *effet utile* and implied powers. The German Constitutional Court in *Maastricht* at first sight accused the Court of Justice of judicial activism. But on closer inspection, it appears that at least with respect to the 'extensive' use of Article 308 EU and the

---

[1] Case 314/85 *Foto-Frost v Hauptzollamt Lübeck-Ost* [1987] ECR 4199.

theory of implied powers, what bothered the German Court is not an activist attitude of the Court of Justice, but rather a lack of supervision by that Court of the Union's political institutions. The latter have adopted decisions on the basis of Article 308 EU on a wide scale; they have adopted decisions which the Court has tolerated and failed to annul, inventing the theory of implied powers to 'cover up' an usurpation of new powers. The Court has given proof of judicial restraint *vis-à-vis* the Union institutions, at the expense of the Member States. This is not activism, at the most it could be termed 'passive activism', or 'activism through passivism' or even 'active passivism'.[2] In contrast, the Court's case law on *effet utile* is entirely attributable to the Court of Justice and can surely be termed activist. While it has led to the empowerment of the national courts in many respects, developing a veritable Community mandate for them, it is ultimately applied to the detriment of the Member States and to the advantage of the Union. The *effet utile* case law has resulted in formulating the mandate of national courts, of how they should ensure Community rights of individuals as against national authorities; of how national authorities should be forced to comply with their Community obligations. Nevertheless, it could be argued that the Court has not, in the *effet utile* case law extended the powers transferred to the Union and created new obligations for the Member States: it has merely developed ways to enforce the obligations deriving from the Treaties and from Community law, and thus to make Community law more effective. This was conceded by the *Bundesverfassungsgericht* in its *Kloppenburg* decision on the direct effect of directives, where the German court agreed that the relevant jurisprudence of the Court of Justice did amount to a development of the law, but not to an unjustified expansion of the competences of the Communities. It merely made Community law more effective where it had been validly adopted.

Yet, the judicial *Kompetenz Kompetenz* position of the *Bundesverfassungsgericht* in *Maastricht* – and there are no signs of any retreat of the *Bundesverfassungsgericht* on this point – gives proof of considerable mistrust on the part of the German court *vis-à-vis* the Court of Justice, of the manner in which it controls the Union institutions. It demonstrates the apprehension of the Constitutional Court that the Court of Justice functions as an ally of the Union institutions. The critique of the *Bundesverfassungsgericht* was aimed more against the way in which the Court of Justice had until then exercised its jurisdiction, than against the exclusive power of the Court of Justice *per se*.[3] Quite on the

---

[2]   So JHH Weiler, *The Constitution of Europe*. 'Do the new clothes have an emperor?' *and other essays on European integration* (Cambridge, CUP, 1999) at 320.

[3]   So JHH Weiler, *The Constitution of Europe*. 'Do the new clothes have an emperor?' *and other essays on European integration* (Cambridge, CUP, 1999) at 317–318. See for instance U Goll and M Kenntner, 'Brauchen wir ein Europäisches Kompetenzgericht? Vorschlage zur Sicherung der mitgliedstaatlichen Zuständigkeiten', *EuZW*, 2002, 101, at 101, who state that given the ECJ's record, it must be doubted that the ECJ can be considered a neutral arbiter for this type of conflict.

contrary, the German Constitutional Court expects the Court of Justice to behave more like an active or activist (constitutional) court.

24.1.2. The Political Issue: in Search of a Balance of Power between the Member States and the Union

Underlying the judicial *Kompetenz Kompetenz* issue is of course the wider and more fundamental issue of the separation and balance of power between the Union and its Member States. Any multi-level polity where powers are divided between several levels is confronted with problems of delimitation. This is not different in the European Union. The European Union possesses those powers which have been conferred to it by the Member States – Masters of the Treaties – in the founding Treaties,[4] and cannot transgress the limits of the powers attributed. In the exercise of the powers transferred, the Union institutions must respect the principles of subsidiarity and proportionality. These basic principles (of conferred powers, and particularly of subsidiarity and proportionality), in their exquisite vagueness, are extremely difficult to apply. Moreover, the competence issue and the power struggle between the Union and the Member States hide issues of democracy and legitimacy. A transfer to the Union institutions entails a reduction of democratic legitimation on the national plane, a shift in the domestic balance of powers from Parliament to Government, and adds new levels in the democratic legitimation. Over the past two decades, and starting more particularly with the move to qualified majority voting, there is a growing impression of an over-ambitious Community and Union liable to damage national and local identity, and a feeling of a creeping expansion of Union competences at the expense of the Member States.[5]

24.2. SOLVING THE COMPETENCE ISSUE

24.2.1. A Better Division and Definition of Competences between the Member States and the European Union

It is often argued that the Union is centralising competences, and that in order the protect the Member States and their federated or decentralised

---

[4]   On the principle of conferred or attributed powers see A G Soares, 'The Principle of Conferred Powers and the Division of Powers between the European Community and the Member States', 23 *Liverpool Law Review*, 2001, 57.

[5]   See for instance S Weatherill, 'Competence', in B De Witte (ed), *Ten Reflections on the Constitutional Treaty for Europe*, EUI, 2003, 45, at 46 *et seq.*; B De Witte, 'Clarifying the Delimitation of Powers. A Proposal with Comments', paper delivered at the Conference of the Jean Monnet Group on the Future of Europe, *Europe 2004, Le Grand Débat, Setting the Agenda and Outlining the Options*, available on www.ecsanet.org.

entities, there is a need for a more precise delimitation of powers between the Union and its Members. From some quarters, particularly the German *Länder*, there has even been a call for a re-nationalisation of certain powers already transferred. The Declaration attached to the Nice Treaty and the Laeken Declaration was more neutral. The starting point for the paragraphs on '*A better division and definition of competences in the European Union*' in the latter Declaration was, that citizens may sometimes hold expectations of the Union that are not always fulfilled, and *vice versa* that sometimes they have the impression that the Union takes on too much in areas where its involvement is not always essential. The starting point was accordingly mostly the ambiguity in the current situation, but also the claim that the current choices in division of powers were not always the best. Accordingly, the Declaration stated that '*[t]he important thing is to clarify, simplify and adjust the division of competence between the Union and the Member States in the light of the new challenges facing the Union. This can lead both to restoring tasks to the Member States, and to assigning new missions to the Union, or to the extension of existing powers, while constantly bearing in mind the equality of the Member States and their mutual solidarity*'.

The Declaration did not say *how* the delimitation of competences should be improved: whether a catalogue of competences of the Union should be drawn up as the German *Länder* requested, or whether a list should be outlined of areas where Union action is excluded,[6] whether it should be a bipolar system, or a flexible mechanism, or whether it should rather proceed on the basis of an 'intermediate description' of Union powers.[7] The work in the Convention seemed to proceed on the basis of the notion of an 'intermediate article', defining the main categories of Union powers, describing their nature and indicating which Union power belongs to which category.

A thorough analysis of the delimitation of competences between the Member States and the Union would go beyond the scope of this book. Nevertheless, I would like to highlight some considerations made by others which are important to grasp the complexity of the issue. Firstly,[8] as most powers are shared powers, it is important to avoid the mistaken

---

6   A 'nucleus of sovereignty that the Member States can invoke, as such, against the [Union]'?, see K Lenaerts, 'Constitutionalism and the many Faces of Federalism', 38 *AJCL*, 1990, 205, at 220.

7   See e.g. B De Witte, 'Clarifying the Delimitation of powers. A Proposal with Comments', paper delivered at the Conference of the Jean Monnet Group on the Future of Europe, *Europe 2004, Le Grand Débat, Setting the Agenda and Outlining the Options*, available on www.ecsanet.org. For an overview of these possible approaches see I Pernice, 'Rethinking the Methods of Dividing and Controlling the Competencies of the Union', paper delivered at the Conference of the Jean Monnet Group on the Future of Europe, *Europe 2004, Le Grand Débat, Setting the Agenda and Outlining the Options*, available on www.ecsanet.org.

8   See S Weatherill, 'Competence', in B De Witte (ed), *Ten Reflections on the Constitutional Treaty for Europe, EUI*, 2003, available on www.iue.it, 45, at 46.

assumption that power is held *either* by the Union *or* by the Member States and that arguments about power are arguments about who wins and who loses. It is accordingly not commendable to impose a rigid division between Union and State competences, as it misleadingly portrays the relationship between Union and State as confrontational rather than cooperational.[9] It is erroneous to enter the debate about the allocation of powers of competences by treating the vice to be a long-term power grab by the Union and the virtue an entrenchment of State power (or *vice versa!*) Secondly, 'golden or magic formulae' cannot capture the complexity of the issues at stake. They promise more than can be delivered. In addition, they rob the system of its capacity for dynamism and adaptability. Thirdly, the rise of Qualified Majority Voting has altered the dynamics of the system; it has removed the protection of the veto and accordingly increased anxiety on the part of the Member States about 'creeping' Community and Union competences. It has given rise to the introduction of the principles of subsidiarity and proportionality, Treaty amendments to adjust the delimitation of competences, etc, which all reflect the concern of the Member States to protect their national prerogatives.[10] On the other hand, there must also be the consideration that the system should not be rigid and must not bring to halt the European dynamic.[11]

Whichever method is chosen to formulate the division of competences between the Member States and the Union, and whatever the essentially political choice of competences belonging to the Union, competence conflicts will continue to occur, presumably with increasing frequency. Now, in the search for a stable balance of powers between the Member States and the Union and in order to reduce the risk of conflict, two procedural devices come to the fore. One is situated at the level of decision-making, and involves the national Parliaments. The other relates to the judicial control of the division, and concerns the question *quis judicabit?*

24.2.2. Non-judicial Procedural Safeguards

24.2.2.1. The Choice of a System

Several proposals were made to monitor observance of the division of powers, and the principle of subsidiarity. One was to involve the national Parliaments, who really have an interest in preserving room for national

---

9   See also B De Witte, 'Clarifying the Delimitation of Powers. A Proposal with Comments', paper delivered at the Conference of the Jean Monnet Group on the Future of Europe, *Europe 2004, Le Grand Débat, Setting the Agenda and Outlining the Options*, available on www.ecsanet.org.

10   S Weatherill, 'Competence', in B De Witte (ed), *Ten Reflections on the Constitutional Treaty for Europe, EUI*, 2003, available on www.iue.it, 45, at 49–51.

11   See the Laeken Declaration.

legislation, in the decision-making process at the European level. This involvement may assume many different appearances: participation of representatives of the national parliaments in a Second Chamber at the European level as the federal chamber, similar at least in purpose to the American Senate and the German *Bundesrat*; the convening of interparliamentary conferences; the idea of a Congress involving both national parliaments and the European Parliament. In the framework of the Convention Working Group I on the Principle of Subsidiarity, proposed the setting up of an 'early warning system' allowing national Parliaments to participate directly in monitoring compliance with the principle of subsidiarity, which would enable them to ensure correct application of the principle. They would be informed, at the same time as the Union legislators (Council and European Parliament), of the Commission's proposals of a legislative nature, and would have the possibility of issuing a reasoned opinion regarding compliance with the principle of subsidiarity by the proposal concerned. The consequences of such opinions for the continuation of the legislative process could include a duty imposed on the Commission to clarify its position with respect to subsidiarity, and, in the presence of an opinion from for instance one third of national parliaments, the Commission would re-examine its proposal, leading either to maintenance of the proposal, to its amendment or its withdrawal. This 'early warning system' would place all national Parliaments on an equal footing and have the advantage of not making the institutional architecture more cumbersome, as it would not require the establishment of a new body or institution. This system of *ex ante* involvement of the national parliaments would be completed with *ex post* judicial review by the Court of Justice.

24.2.2.2. The Draft Protocol on the Application of the Principles of Subsidiarity and Proportionality: The Early Warning System

The early warning mechanism constitutes a novelty in European constitutional law. National Parliaments are for the first time included in the decision making process *qua* national organs. It is exceptional for any particular national organs to be mentioned at Treaty level[12] given their status as international agreements the Treaties mostly refer to 'the Member States' without specifying the specific organ. Some comments may briefly be made. Firstly, it seems rather restrictive to limit the intervention of the national Parliaments to the principle of subsidiarity. Issues concerning the delimitation of powers do not only concern subsidiarity. Obviously, it is one of the most politically sensitive issues with respect to the delimitation, but it is submitted that the

---

[12] The fact that the procedure figures in a Protocol rather than in the main body of the Constitution does not seem to matter. It has the same force as the Constitution. It is probably only due to historic accident: the Protocol was already there.

system should be more extensive and should also encompass for instance the monitoring of the principle of attributed competences. The intervention should not be restricted to subsidiarity, but involve all types of issues concerning the division of competences, and be included in a more general *Kompetenz* monitoring system so as to contribute also to mitigate the judicial *Kompetenz Kompetenz* issue. Indeed, the involvement of the national Parliaments in the general monitoring of the delimitation of powers would make the reservation of judicial *Kompetenz Kompetenz* in the hands of the national courts less critical, and could diminish the legitimacy of a claim of ultimate authority on the part of the national courts. There is a question, then, why the early warning system should be restricted to matters of competence, and why it should not relate to substantive issues also, for instance to questions of fundamental rights. Lack of competence is after all, in the current state of affairs, only one ground of invalidity of Community acts, beside other grounds as the infringement of an essential procedural requirement, infringement of the Treaty or any rule of law relating to its application, or misuse of power.[13] However, it does make sense to restrict the *ex ante* control to competence issues given the highly political nature of the issue of delimitation of competences between the Union and the Member States. This is especially so for the principle of subsidiarity, but the experience in federal type systems reveals that any division of competence between the central and decentralised or federated entities may fluctuate over time and that conflicts over competences often hide other political conflicts, for instance the distribution of economic resources.[14] As Weiler has noted, *'the very language of law, and of legal interpretation, suggests that practically no language in a constitutional document can guarantee a truly fundamental boundary between, say, the central power and that of the constituent units. The extent to which a system will veer toward one pole or another depends much more on the political and legal ethos which animates those who exercise legislative competencies and those who control it'.*[15] The European example is but an instance of that more general experience. A role for national Parliaments would reflect, it is submitted, not only the current concern at Member State level over the impression that the Union usurps powers that have not been transferred, but also a concern for more popular legitimacy of the decision, and for an improved balance, not only in the distribution of competences, but also in the monitoring thereof. Indeed, if the decision to adopt a particular act is made exclusively by the political organs at the central level, and controlled by a constitutional court belonging to that same level, there will at least be an impression that

---

[13] See the text of the current Art. 230 EC.
[14] See W Lehmann, 'Attribution of Powers and Dispute Resolution in Selected Federal Systems', European Parliament Working Paper AFCO 103 EN, at 61.
[15] See European parliament DG IV Working Paper, The Division of Competences in the European Union, Working Paper W–26, www.europarl.eu.int/workingpapers/poli/w26/default_en.htm, at 4.

the federated or decentralised units are left unprotected and that the central level will usually be favoured.[16] There is much to be said for restricting the involvement of national Parliaments to competence issues. However, competence issues may be intertwined with other issues; the competence issue may be abused to cover other grounds for opposing a particular proposal.

Secondly, there is a danger that the transmission of all legislative proposals to the national parliaments for competence scrutiny would submerge national parliaments with a vast volume of drafts and documents, to an extent that sight of the truly controversial minority of proposals may be lost. One may wonder whether members of national parliaments – or the relevant Committees in Parliament – will be prepared to or have time to study and analyse each and every proposal. Nevertheless, it could be argued that it is up to the national Parliaments to organise themselves in such a manner that the controversial cases are filtered out in a Committee or by a Secretariat, so that the assembly is not concerned with other proposals. One side effect of the involvement for competence issues is that national Parliaments, which are willing to be interested, will be involved in a much earlier stage in decision making at the European level than is the case in most national Parliaments today. This would encourage them to seek to influence decision making at the European level through the national representative in the Council – which is under the current system also presumed as an element of European democracy, but is not always the case in practice. It could accordingly have the effect of extending the Danish or British model of parliamentary involvement to other Member States and Parliaments, and cure the currently poor participation of national and sub-national Parliaments in the discussions about European legislative proposals.[17] Furthermore, it would supposedly also improve and facilitate implementation by national Parliaments given that they are aware of what a particular European measure requires at an earlier stage.

Thirdly, one may wonder whether the 'red flag' raised by one third of national Parliaments should not entail a formal veto power and imply the end for the proposal at issue. Making it binding would however implicate a new form of veto, coming not from the Member State as such, but from a group of national Parliaments. The competence issue can be misused for other purposes, and the procedure would be open to easy abuse. It is assumed that the Commission will be politically obliged to take the process of explanation and persuasion seriously. It will be aware that ex post facto review by the Court of Justice is feasible.[18]

Fourthly, there is a problem in certain federal Member States where the scrutiny of Union proposals would have to be divided between several

---

[16] *Ibidem*, at 63.

[17] See also S Weatherill, 'Competence', in B De Witte (ed), *Ten Reflections on the Constitutional Treaty for Europe, EUI*, 2003, available on www.iue.it, 45, at 63.

[18] See also S Weatherill, 'Competence', in B De Witte (ed), *Ten Reflections on the Constitutional Treaty for Europe, EUI*, 2003, available on www.iue.it, 45, at 64–65.

parliaments. Indeed, for instance for Belgium it would not be coherent to endow the competence scrutiny at the European level to the national Parliament also in areas which belong exclusively to the parliaments of the federated entities, and where, accordingly, the national Parliament does not have jurisdiction. It could be argued that no account should be taken of that problem at the European level under the assumption that it is essentially a national constitutional issue which must be solved at that level. The national constitutional system must find a method to ensure that the concerns of the federated Parliaments are transmitted through the national parliament, which must waive the red flag for a Parliament (or all, or a majority thereof, that would be a matter of national constitutional law) of a federated entity having competence concerns. Such a substitution mechanism would be a matter entirely of the constitutional law of the Member State. Consequently, should the national Parliament fail to act for a federated Parliament within the prescribed period, this would carry no consequences at the European level. It would have to be resolved at the national level. It would also be a matter for national constitutional law to find a method to force the national Parliament to act on behalf of a parliament of a federated entity. These arguments will mostly be based on the presumption that it would not be reasonable for one Member State to hold several 'red flags', while most States would only have one (or two, should it be decided that each Chamber would be given a flag). Nevertheless, these Member States would not have more flags in a particular case, depending on the topic, at least assuming that the early warning can be given only if the majority (or..) of the sub-national Parliament competent in the relevant area want to use it (which is difficult where there would be only two..).

Fifthly, there is the issue of linking the early warning mechanism to the ex post scrutiny by the Court of Justice. This will be considered under the following heading.

24.2.3. Solving the Issue of Judicial *Kompetenz Kompetenz*

Whichever system is chosen to clarify the division of competences between the Union and the Member States, and even encompassing an early warning system, it will continue to raise problems of patrolling the division of powers *ex post*. Despite the 'clarified' division of competences, and even in the presence of procedural safeguards discussed above, decisions may still be adopted whose validity is challenged on the basis of the competence question. *'Since, from a material point of view, the question of boundaries has a built-in indeterminacy, the critical issue is not what the boundaries are, but* who gets to decide'.[19] And this is where the problem lies: both

---

[19] JHH Weiler, 'Conclusions' of the Conference of the Jean Monnet Group on the Future of Europe, Europe 2004, *Le Grand Débat, Setting the Agenda and Outlining the Options*, available on www.ecsanet.org, at 13, my emphasis.

the Court of Justice and some of the constitutional courts now claim ultimate authority, each from their own perspective. And at the moment, it can
be argued that both the European and the national position on judicial
Kompetenz Kompetenz are coherent and cogent, each from their own perspective. Can this dissonance be solved legally?

24.2.3.1. Weiler's European Constitutional Council

Several authors and groups have suggested the setting up of a separate
competence court, which in most cases would decide cases *ex post* facto.
An overview of these proposals can be found elsewhere.[20] Most of them
have in common that the European Constitutional Court, Union Court of
Review, European Conflicts Tribunal etc., would consist both of members
of the Court of Justice and of the national constitutional courts, possibly
on an equal basis (*paritaire*). One of the most noted suggestions is the one
made by Weiler, for a Constitutional Council for the Community, modelled in some ways after the French *Conseil constitutionnel*.[21] It would consist of sitting members of the constitutional courts or their equivalents in
the Member States, and be presided over by the President of the Court of
Justice. Within the Constitutional Council, no single member would have
a veto power. The Council would have jurisdiction only over issues of
competences (including subsidiarity) and would decide cases submitted
to it after a law had been adopted but before its coming into force. It could
be seized by any Member State or the European Parliament acting on a
majority of its members. In Weiler and Haltern's view, the principal merit
of the proposal would be that it addresses the concern for fundamental

---

[20] See F C Mayer, 'Die drei Dimensionen der Europäischen Kompetenzdebatte', *ZaöRV*,
2001, 577, at 602 *et seq.*, and see for instance the debate in *EuZW*, 2002: U Goll and M
Kenntner, 'Brauchen wir ein Europäisches Kompetenzgericht? Vorschlage zur Sicherung
der mitgliedstaatlichen Zuständigkeiten', *EuZW*, 2002, 101; N Reich, 'Brauchen wir eine
Diskussion um eine Europäische Kompetenzgericht?', *EuZW*, 2002, 257; U Everling,
'Quis custodiet custodies ipsos? Zur Diskussion über die Kompetenzordnung der
Europäischen Union und ein europäisches Kompetenzgericht', *EuZW*, 2002, 357.

[21] JHH Weiler and U Haltern, 'The Autonomy of the Community Legal Order – Through the
Looking Glass', 37 *Harvard Int LJ*, 1996, 411; also published in JHH Weiler, *The Constitution
of Europe*. 'Do the new clothes have an emperor?'*and other essays on European integration*
(Cambridge, CUP, 1999) at 322–323; see also JHH Weiler and U Haltern, 'Constitutional or
International? The Foundations of the Community Legal Order and the Question of
Judicial Kompetenz Kompetenz', in A-M Slaughter, A Stone Sweet and JHH Weiler (eds),
*The European Court and National Courts – Doctrine and Jurisprudence. Legal Change in Its
Social Context* (Oxford, Hart Publishing, 1998) 331; JHH Weiler, 'The European Union
Belongs to its Citizens: Three Immodest Proposals', 22 *ELR*, 1997, 150; The proposal for a
Constitutional Council was originally made in a study commissioned by the
European Parliament, JHH Weiler, A Ballbaum, U Haltern, H Hofmann, F Mayer and S
Schreiner-Linford, *Certain Rectangular Problems of European Integration*, (Luxembourg,
European Parliament, Political Series W–24, 1996). See also, available on the internet,
The Division of Competences in the European Union, Working Paper W–26,
www.europarl.eu.int/working papers/poli/w26/default_en.htm. See more recently JHH
Weiler, 'A Constitution for Europe? Some Hard Choices', 40 *JCMS*, 2002, 563, at 573–574.

jurisdictional boundaries without compromising the constitutional integrity of the Community, as do the national constitutional courts claiming *Kompetenz Kompetenz*. The composition of the body would underscore that the question of competences is fundamentally also one of national constitutional norms, and it would enjoy far greater measure of public confidence than the Court of Justice, which after all, is part of the Communities.

While the authors agree that the proposal is not fully worked out, some critical observations can be made. First, it may be asked why a new institution should be set up, when the Union already has an institution which has been endowed with jurisdiction to rule on competence issues, the Court of Justice. Certainly, this position is not accepted by all constitutional courts, but should – and would – they be convinced by simply setting up another institution? Why would they abide by the decisions of this Constitutional Council if they do not follow the decisions of the Court of Justice? The obvious answer would be: because the Court of Justice cannot act as a neutral arbiter as it belongs to the Union, and given its track record. It is agreed that the Court has not, in the past, given proof of strict scrutiny of the Union institutions, and has not always been strict on competences. Yet, why would the constitutional courts comply with the decisions of this Constitutional Council – irrespective of their content? Why would it have more legitimacy than the Court of Justice? Weiler claims that the 'composition of the Council is the key to its legitimacy': it would help restore confidence in the ability to have effective policing of the boundaries as well as underscore that the question of competencies is fundamentally also one of national constitutional norms, but still subject to a binding and uniform solution by a Union institution. For each Member State, one member of the constitutional court (or its equivalent) has taken part in the decision and in the deliberations within the Constitutional Council. However, he has had no veto power, and may not have been able to convince his colleagues on the Council. Would, in such a situation, the decision of the Constitutional Council be more convincing than the decision of the Court of Justice?[22] Even where the own member of the Constitutional Council ruled in favour of competence of the Union or Communities, the national constitutional courts as a whole (or a different composition thereof) could arrive at a different conclusion. *'Letztentscheidungsansprüche nationaler Gerichte lassen sich nicht ausschliessen'.*[23]

---

[22] See the reluctant reaction of Paul Kirchhof in the dicussion on a European Constitutional Court consisting of an equal number of judges from the ECJ and the national constitutional courts. He argued, typically, that such an institution could not guarantee the German constitutional legal order, see D Merten (ed), *Föderalismus und Europäische Gemeinschaften unter besondere Berücksichtigung von Umwelt und Gesundheit Kultur und Bindung* (Berlin, Duncker & Humblot, 1990) at 127.

[23] FC Mayer, 'Die drei Dimensionen der Europäischen Kompetenzdebatte', *ZaöRV*, 2001, 577, at 609.

Second, and related to the last issue, it is important to take notice, once again, of the composition of the Council: 'sitting members of the constitutional courts *or their equivalents'*. In some Member States there is no equivalent. The most extreme example is probably the Netherlands. There is no constitutional court; there is no diffuse constitutional review either. Highly controversial issues are not normally decided by the courts, but by Parliament. In addition, and more importantly, the 'mighty problem' of *Kompetenz Kompetenz* has not yet been raised in the Netherlands, and I believe that it is fair to say that it would by and large be agreed in the Netherlands that the Court of Justice has ultimate authority to rule on questions of competence *de lege lata*, as an element of the validity of Community law.[24] Were the Dutch asked to send a representative of 'the equivalent of a constitutional court' to the European Constitutional Council, they would without a doubt send a member from the *Hoge Raad*, even though it does not have constitutional jurisdiction in the sense that constitutional courts do, and even if it is not even the only court of final instance in The Netherlands. Yet, this member will, from his background, have a very different position with respect to the issue of competence than, say, his German colleague who will approach cases from a German constitutional perspective. The Dutch member will not have the same experience, he will not share any of the sensitivities of the German member. At the end of the day, it may well be that only the Italian, the German and Danish members will, from the outset, share concern for the *Kompetenz Kompetenz* issue. The proposal cannot solve the crux of the competence issue: namely that in many cases, the conflict will be over the interpretation of Treaty provisions, which may differ *depending on the perspective taken*. The position of the Constitutional Council will likely be that of the majority of the constitutional courts, and not a common position from a national perspective. It is of course true that the question of division of competences and of boundaries of competencies is as much a question of national constitutional law. But there is not one 'national constitutional law' perspective, there are currently 15, and many more in the future. Even with a Constitutional Council the fact will remain that a particular decision may appear *ultra vires* from the point of view of one, two or even seven national courts (and their Member States?). To prove the point: it seems that the Danish *Højesteret* approaches Community measures which infringe upon Danish fundamental rights from a competence perspective, while most courts and commentators do make a clear distinction between fundamental rights issues and competence issues.

Third, it is very difficult to predict how these judges will decide cases. Weiler and his collaborators seemed concerned to demonstrate that the

---

24 See M Claes and B De Witte, 'Report on the Netherlands', in A-M Slaughter, A Stone Sweet and JHH Weiler (eds), *The European Court and National Courts – Doctrine and Jurisprudence. Legal Change in Its Social Context* (Oxford, Hart Publishing, 1998) 171, at 187.

division of competences is also a matter of national constitutional law. Nevertheless, it should be pointed out that it is at least to the same extent a matter of Community law (and indeed, of Union law). Members of national constitutional courts are exactly that: they are *national* courts, and decide cases from the perspective of national constitutional law. It should be assumed, however, that the cases submitted to the Constitutional Council would, in the first place, have to be answered on the basis of Community or Union law. Must this or that provision of the Treaty be interpreted as empowering the Union to adopt a particular decision? To say the least, this is not their expertise.

Fourth, there may be a danger, that members of the Constitutional Council give in to political concerns of their colleagues on the Bench – except where it is clearly an abuse of procedure – to block a particular decision. Indeed, next time it may be their State opposing a decision, and the members of the Constitutional Council will then need the support of the majority of their brethren. Given the composition of the Council, it may have a natural tendency towards a restrictive interpretation of the Union's competences (similar to the belief that the Court of Justice has a natural tendency *pro Comunitate*),[25] and to protect national constitutional interests.

Fifth, there is a flaw in the argument where it is claimed that the question of competences has become so politicised that the European Court of Justice should welcome having this hot potato removed from its plate by an *ex ante* decision of a body with a jurisdiction limited to that preliminary issue. Yet, if it has become such a politicised issue that it would be good to remove it from the Court of Justice, why then pass it on to another body consisting of judges? Admittedly, it would decide cases *ex ante*, but that does not suffice to remove its nature of a judicial body. On the other hand, Weiler is concerned to remove the conflict from the purely political arena, which is precisely why the Council should consist of (constitutional) judges. And would the members of the Constitutional Council be pleased to be passed the hot potato? As already mentioned, these remain highly politicised issues.

Sixth, the attribution of this task of monitoring the division of powers to a separate body poses difficult questions with respect to the existing jurisdiction of the Court of Justice.[26] Will it require an amendment of the Treaty, deleting the words 'on grounds of lack of competence' from the

---

[25] Mayer argues that the involvement of the ECJ would guarantee neutrality of the Constitutional Council, FC Mayer, 'Die drei Dimensionen der Europäischen Kompetenzdebatte', *ZaöRV*, 2001, 577, at 608. He is not clear however as to the required participation of the ECJ to guarantee neutrality. Would neutrality be guaranteed by participation of only the ECJ President? I would think not. On the other hand, would it make much sense to have a Constitutional Council consisting of 30 members, 15 from the Member State courts and 15 from the ECJ?

[26] See also JHH Weiler, 'The European Union Belongs to its Citizens: Three Immodest Proposals', 22 *ELR*, 1997, 150, at 156. He argues that the potential of conflict can be dealt with by competent drafting.

text of Article 230 EC? Probably not. Even if a Constitutional Council is set up, questions of competence will still arise *ex post*: it is to be expected that only a limited number of acts will be submitted to the Constitutional Council. In addition, the phrase 'lack of competence' in Article 230 EC is broader and does not only encompass the question of the separation of powers between the Union and the Member States. Furthermore, the question of competence can also arise in preliminary rulings references (unless this too should be explicitly excluded). Yet, if it remains in the text of Article 230 EC (and by analogy, in the spirit of Article 234 EC) there is a possibility that the Court of Justice will be asked to rule on the validity of a decision which had been submitted to the Constitutional Council and passed: a Member State which is opposed to a particular decision on grounds of competence, and does not obtain the result sought from the Constitutional Council will institute annulment proceedings before the Court of Justice (unless this is explicitly excluded in the Treaty).

Seventh, and this is also pointed out by Weiler in some of the publications,[27] the potential applicants may have to include not only the Member States, but also their Parliaments who stand to lose most if the Union should usurp powers which have not been attributed in the Treaties. Building on this idea, it should be considered whether Parliaments or legislative chambers of federated entities should also not be granted standing. This will be considered in the next section.

Eighth, the proposal is necessarily limited to acts adopted by the political organs, excluding decisions of the Court of Justice, while these are certainly included in the position on *ultra vires* acts of the *Bundesverfassungsgericht*, and of the *Højesteret*. Consequently, the Constitutional Council will not have jurisdiction for some of the most sensitive conflicts between the Court of Justice and the national constitutional courts (*'effet utile'*), and in this respect does nothing to resolve the Cold War situation to use Weiler's terminology. The most it may do is avert and reduce situations of conflict, but it cannot rule them out.

By way of conclusion, I am not convinced that the Constitutional Council would have more legitimacy than the Court of Justice in deciding competence issues. I fail to see the added value of a Council consisting of representatives of national constitutional courts. The mere fact that it consists of representatives of national courts does not, in my view, suffice to give it more legitimacy. It will all depend, again, on the way in which it decides disputes. Surely it will have legitimacy in cases where the decision goes in the direction of the State's position. Yet, that may easily change when the Constitutional Council fails to follow the position of, say, Germany and the German member in the Constitutional Council.

[27] JHH Weiler, 'The European Union Belongs to its Citizens: Three Immodest Proposals', 22 *ELR*, 1997, 150, at 155. In JHH Weiler, 'A Constitution for Europe: Some Hard Choices', 40 *JCMS*, 2002, 563, at 574, he insists on standing for national parliaments, as typical losers from expansion of European competences.

24.2.3.2. Ultimate Authority of the European Court of Justice

24.2.3.2.1. Why the Court of Justice?

There are several reasons why the Court of Justice and not the national courts should have jurisdiction to review whether Union acts are *intra vires*. The main argument is of course the need for uniformity. To allow national courts, even in exceptional cases, to hold Community acts inapplicable in the domestic legal order, would entail too serious a blow to the principle of uniformity. It must be remembered, in addition, that *Kompetenz Kompetenz* has been claimed only by the German constitutional court, possibly its Italian counterpart, and by the Danish *Højesteret*. It simply cannot be that only a few Member States may, in some cases, have the benefit of a national court releasing the Member State from an obligation under the Treaty. The easiest argument against any judicial *Kompetenz Kompetenz* in the hands of the national courts is the fact that at least for Community law, it constitutes a violation of Community law and the case law of the Court of Justice, which is binding on the Member States. The Court of Justice has held that it has ultimate authority over the division of competences as it involves the interpretation of the Treaty, endowed to it. Any exercise of the *Kompetenz Kompetenz* jurisdiction by a national court implies a violation of Community law. Indeed the decision that a particular decision is not applicable in the domestic legal order constitutes a violation of the binding character of the decision in question and thus a violation of the Treaty obligations imposed on the Member State. National courts simply cannot be the correct forum for this type of cases.

Why should the Court of Justice have jurisdiction, rather than a new and separate body? The European Court of Justice already has exclusive[28] jurisdiction to rule on the validity of Community law because the Member States have endowed the Court with that competence, even if they have not been very explicit on the exclusive nature of the Court's jurisdiction to decide competence issues. In this context, it must be emphasised that the fact that the Union currently lacks constitutional *Kompetenz Kompetenz* as all competences derive from the Member States as *Herren der Verträge*, does not prevent an institution of the Union to possess judicial *Kompetenz Kompetenz*. There does not seem to be a rule of principle as to why constitutional and judicial *Kompetenz Kompetenz* should reside in the same level. As the *tobacco* decision demonstrates, the Court is prepared to guard the delimitation of competences between the Community and the Member States.[29] Of course, one case does not make case law, and the Court of Justice will have to continue to earn the confidence of the constitutional courts, and indeed of the Member States.

---

[28] Case 314/85 *Foto-Frost* [1987] ECR 4199.
[29] So FC Mayer, 'Die drei Dimensionen der Europäische Kompetenzdebatte', *ZaöRV*, 2001, 577, at 612.

Nevertheless, the decision has been perceived as a signal by the Court of Justice that it is well aware of its role as adjudicator of competences, and that it intends to take that role seriously.[30] It is only if the Court of Justice does take its function to protect the Member States and their Parliaments against unlawful Community measures seriously, that the call for a European Constitutional Court will abate.[31]

24.2.3.2.2. *Incorporating the Exclusive Competence of the Court of Justice in the Treaty?*

Now, would it help to inscribe the exclusive role of the Court of Justice as Ultimate Umpire of the division of competences in the Constitutional Treaty? From the point of view of the Community orthodoxy, inclusion in the Treaty would not alter the current position and would only amount to codification: Under the current position, the exclusivity of the Court of Justice is part of the complete system of judicial protection provided by the Treaty; in other words, it is already in there. Nevertheless, incorporation certainly would remove credibility from the national courts claiming judicial *Kompetenz Kompetenz* for themselves. Obviously, on the basis of pure logic, nothing much would change: the explicit exclusive jurisdiction of the Court of Justice to rule on competence issues would only be awarded within the limits of the powers transferred, and it could still be argued that from the national point of view, it remains the constitutional duty of the constitutional court to guard the limits of the powers transferred from the national angle. Should the exclusive jurisdiction of the Court of Justice be incorporated in the Constitutional Treaty, it would only apply within the limits of the powers transferred, and the limits thereof should be guarded by the constitutional court. However, such an argument would loose much of its force. Indeed, why else would the provision be included if not to empower the Court to decide exclusively on where the limits of the transferred powers are? If not for these cases, it would be a redundant provision. It would accordingly, in order to avoid any misunderstanding, be useful to include in the Constitutional Treaty that the Court of Justice does indeed have exclusive jurisdiction to rule on the division of competence between the Member States and the Union.

---

[30] See 'Editorial Comments. Taking (the Limits of) Competences Seriously?', 37 *CML Rev* (2000) 1301, qualifying the decision as 'one of the most important judgments of the decade', and insisting that the Court of Justice has resisted to practice judicial restraint *vis-à-vis* the Council and the Parliament, and actually exercised its powers to check whether the conditions for the power to enact legislation were actually met; see also PJ Slot, 'A Contribution to the Constitutional Debate in the EU in the Light of the Tobacco Judgment. What can be learned from the USA?', *European Business Law Review*, 2002, 3; YS Tolias, 'Has the Problem concerning the Delimitation of the Community's Competence been Resolved since the Maastricht Judgment of the Bundesverfassungsgericht?', *European Business Law review*, 2002, 267.

[31] 'Editorial Comments. Taking (the Limits of) Competences Seriously?', 37 *CML Rev* (2000) 1301, at 1305.

How and where should it be included in the Treaty? One possibility would be a separate provision providing that the Court of Justice has exclusive competence. In addition, or in the alternative, the exclusive nature of the jurisdiction of the Court could be included in the existing provisions. Article 230 EC could be rephrased to include the exclusivity of the mandate of the Court of Justice to review the validity of measures of Community law. In addition, it is commendable to formalise *Foto-Frost* and adopt it in the text of Article 234 EC,[32] so that there is a clear Treaty basis for the obligation of each national court to make a reference where the validity of a provision of Community or Union law is in doubt. Every national court, including the constitutional courts, will in any case be under an obligation to refer, and cannot claim *Kompetenz Kompetenz* without making a reference first. To do so would then without a doubt entail a direct breach of the Treaty.

The Treaty establishing a Constitution for Europe does not include any of the suggestions made.

24.2.3.2.3. *Preventive Review by the Court of Justice*

The *'Lamassoure proposal'* contained in the Report of the Committee on Constitutional Affairs of the European Parliament on the delimitation of competences between the European Union and the Members States,[33]proposed to introduce a new procedure for *partial preventive review by the Court of Justice*. The suggestion was to give the Court of Justice jurisdiction to review European legislative acts[34] on request by a qualified minority in the Council, by the European Parliament or the Commission. The request could be brought within a month after the final adoption of the legislative act, and the Court would have to hand a judgment within a one-month time limit. The only grounds for review would be the principles of subsidiarity and of proportionality. The possibility of one Member State bringing an action was rejected because in a Union of twenty-five or thirty Member States, it was considered too great a risk that virtually every decision would be subject to a Court case and the decision-making process would become even more laborious.[35] The proposal, inspired by the

---

[32] See also J Ziller and J Lotarski, 'Institutions et organes judiciaires', in B De Witte (ed), *Ten Reflections on the Constitutional Treaty for Europe, EUI*, 2003, 67, at 79.

[33] PE 304.276.

[34] It is not clear whether the proposal is restricted to the Communities or extends also to the Union. Given the context of the Report as a whole, which promotes the transformation of the ECJ into a real Constitutional Court of the Union, it seems that it would apply also to acts done in the framework of what is now the second and third pillar.

[35] The 1990 Report Giscard d'Estaing did contain the proposal that any Member State, as well as the Council, the Commission and the European Parliament could bring a similar action, within a twenty days time limit, to request the ECJ to verify that a Community act did not exceed the limits of Community competences, having regard to the principles of subsidiarity and proportionality.

procedure for preventive constitutional review before the *Conseil constitutionnel* had the advantage that *ultra vires* acts could at an early stage be detected and withdrawn.[36] However, the Convention Working Group on Subsidiarity saw as its main disadvantage that it lay an essentially political question in the hands of a court, rather than a political body. Accordingly, it chose for a two tier system, in which national parliaments are involved during the legislative procedure, with the Court of Justice operating *ex post*.

24.2.3.2.4. *Relation between the Early Warning System and* ex post *Judicial Control by the Court of Justice*

If the Court of Justice is to be the sole guardian, judicially, of the division of competences, and the role of the national parliaments in the decision making process is recognised with respect to competence issues, at least subsidiarity, should the national parliaments be able to raise competence issues before it? Under the law as it stands, national or regional parliaments do not have standing under Article 230 EC to bring an autonomous application for annulment of a Community measure which in their opinion is *ultra vires*. Indeed, the parliaments, national or regional, are as organs of the State dependent on the will of their Member State government to bring the claim on their behalf. Only the Member States as such are recognised as privileged applicants under Article 230 EC, at the exclusion of regions or federated entities, and at the exclusion of parliamentary organs. Should the provision be amended so as to include national and regional parliaments?

24.2.3.2.5. *Standing for National and Regional Parliaments?*

First consider the current position. National and regional parliaments which consider a particular measure *ultra vires* of the Union competences and a breach of their own powers, have to ask the national government to bring an action for annulment on their behalf. Member States as privileged applicants under Article 230 EC are represented by the national government. Federated entities or national organs such as parliaments do not have the same privileged standing as the Member States. A Member State may nevertheless bring an action on behalf of the federated entity, or of an organ of the State requesting action, for instance parliament. Under prevailing Community law, Member States as privileged applicants do not have to prove legal interest, and do not accordingly have to prove that they are acting on their own behalf and for themselves. This is different only for interim measures under Article 242 and 243 EC, where the State requesting suspension or interim measures must demonstrate *personal*

---

[36] The Report is not clear as to the effects of a finding that the act under scrutiny is *ultra vires*. It is not clear whether the entry into force is suspended until the delay for bringing the action has passed, and whether an action brought has suspensive effects.

imminent and irreparable damage.[37] In Germany, the federal government can be forced to bring an action or to intervene in cases touching upon the exclusive competences of the *Länder*.[38] Likewise, the Belgian Government is obliged to bring actions before the Court on request of a region or a community in matters relating to their respective competences.[39]

Can federated entities bring an action on their own behalf? Do they have an independent right of action before the Court? Until 1977, actions had always been brought by the national government on behalf of the Member State.[40] Nevertheless, the Court had already made it clear implicitly that regional and local authorities were considered as private applicants, and accordingly have to bring the claim before the Court of First Instance and prove direct and individual concern.[41] In the 1997 case brought by the *Walloon region*,[42] the Court of Justice held that it clearly had no jurisdiction under Article 230(1) EC in a case brought by *'a legal person such as a regional federated authority'*: The jurisdiction of the Court of Justice had been limited to actions brought by Member States and Community institutions, other actions were transferred to the Court of First Instance. An action brought by a regional federated authority could not be considered an action brought by a Member State. The term 'Member State' in respect of proceedings before the Court of Justice did not include governments of regions or autonomous communities, irrespective of the powers they may have. The contrary would undermine the institutional balance provided for by the Treaties: the Communities could not comprise a greater number of Member States than the number of States between which they were established. Consequently, the case was referred to the Court of First Instance, and the Walloon region was treated as a private applicant.[43] The Court of Justice apparently started from the

---

[37] For instance, imminent damage to one company does not suffice, see Case 142/87 R *Belgium v Commission* [1987] ECR 2589.

[38] P Van Nuffel, *De rechtsbescherming van nationale overheden in het Europees recht*, (Deventer, Kluwer, 2000) at 551, with references.

[39] Where the issue involves both the regional and the federal level, consensus is required, implying that the federal Government may refuse to bring the claim.

[40] So P Van Nuffel, *De rechtsbescherming van nationale overheden in het Europees recht* (Deventer, Kluwer, 2000) at 548.

[41] See Joined Cases 62 and 72/87 *Exécutif régional wallon and Glaverbel SA v Commission* [1988] ECR 1573 (standing under Article 230 (4) EC not disputed); Case C–213/87 *Gemeente Amsterdam and (Stichting Vrouwenvakschool voor Informatica Amsterdam (VIA) v Commission* [1990] ECR I–221; Case 222/83 *Municipality of Differdange v Commission* [1984] ECR 2889.

[42] One of the federated entities of the federal State Belgium. Belgium is divided in regions and communities.

[43] This has been confirmed since in Case C–180/97 *Regione Toscana v Commission* [1997] ECR I–5245; Case T–214/95 *Vlaams Gewest v Commission* [1998] ECR II-717; Case T–238/97 *Comunidad Autónoma de Cantabria v Council* [1998] ECR II-2271; Case T–609/97 *Regione Puglia v Commission and Spain* [1998] ECR II-4051; Joined Cases T–32/98 and 41/98 *Government of the Netherlands Antilles v Commission* [2000] ECR II-201.

premise that to allow for the federated entities to bring an action under Article 230 EC would rupture the balance between the Member States and favour some more than others: indeed, action could not, for instance, be brought only by Germany, but also by each of the *Länder*, granting Germany a total of 17 'rights of standing', against one for, say, France. From the point of view of national law, this is of course not true: in areas of exclusive competence of the federated entities, the federal government would not act. However, standing before the Court is not a matter for national constitutional law. It would be absurd to expect that the Court of Justice in each and every case verify which entity, federal or regional, was competent in a particular case, and which accordingly had standing under Article 230 EC. On the other hand, this is a difficult situation for federated entities, especially where they cannot force the federal government to bring the claim on their behalf. But this is, essentially, a matter for national constitutional law.[44]

Finally, can *parliaments*, as opposed to governments as representatives of the member States, bring an action under Article 230 EC? The text of Article 230 EC speaks of a 'Member State', without specifying which authority within the State may bring the action. The Statute of the Court of Justice, nor the Rules of Procedure are conclusive on the issue. Article 19 of the Statute merely states that *'the Member States (..) shall be represented before the Court by an agent appointed for each case (..)'*. Under Article 33 of the Rules of Procedure, these agents shall give proof of their status by producing an official document issued by the party for whom they act. In the *Walloon region* case the Court did say that the term 'Member State' referred only to 'government authorities of the Member States' as opposed to governments of regions or autonomous communities. The statement concerned the issue of central authorities as opposed to authorities of federated entities, rather than opposing governments against other authorities such as parliaments. It is, after all, common practice that 'the State', on the international plane and within the European Union, is represented by the government. Yet, does this exclude the possibility of parliament acting on behalf of the Member State, rather than the government? Presumably not, but the situation has not yet occurred.

The problem is primarily one of national constitutional law, as much or more so than one of European law. In many Member States parliament and/or the chambers of parliament do not have legal personality and do

---

[44] Piet Van Nuffel suggests that the Court should allow actions brought by a regional federated authority on behalf of the Member State: where a federated entity is authorized by the central government to act, the actions should be admissible under Article 230(1) EC, P Van Nuffel, *De rechtsbescherming van nationale overheden in het Europees recht*, (Deventer, Kluwer, 2000), at 552 *et seq*. While I am sympathetic to the situation of the federated entities, I consider the practical problems in the context of the current Article 230 EC too serious to be outweighed by these considerations.

not bring court cases. In federal systems it may be possible for cases to be brought before the federal constitutional court by or on behalf of a legislative body. In Belgium, for instance, the presidents of all legislative assemblies can bring an action before the *Cour d'arbitrage* at the request of two thirds of their members. In Germany one third of the Bundestag can request the *Bundesverfassungsgericht* to review the formal or material compatibility of federal or *Land* law with the Basic Law.[45] But in many Member States it is unthinkable for parliament or a chamber of parliament to conduct court proceedings. Until now, national parliaments have not, as such, been actors on the European field. Where the parliament's prerogatives were affected – in terms of competences – those of the Member States as such were presumably also affected. This is not however necessarily so: Consider the German situation, where Parliament consists of the *Bundestag* and *Bundesrat* representing the federal character of Germany, and where it may very well occur that the *Bundesrat* opposes European proposals which the Government and the *Bundestag* support. This brings us to the question what should be meant by 'Parliament'. Should it, in a bi-cameral system, be a joint position of both chambers, or would each have separate standing? These are difficult questions, and it is questionable whether they must be regulated at the European level.

If standing is left as it is and restricted to 'Member States', the question of whether the national government would be obliged to bring an action on request of the national parliament remains a matter for national constitutional law. It may be assumed that it is not difficult to make a provision at national level that where a majority in parliament requests the government to institute proceedings, the government is so obliged. This may be more complicated in federal States. Would it have to be provided that a claim of one regional parliament suffices to oblige the government to bring an action? Or would such obligation arise only where more than one, one third or more than half of the relevant parliaments 'raise the flag'? Would the federal government also be obliged to bring a action where the claim of one (or more) regional parliament(s) is obviously unfounded? Extremely sensitive situations can occur where the relevant piece of Union legislation divides the domestic national and regional parliaments. Which side is the government to chose? It could be argued that these are only national constitutional questions, which must be solved at the national level and should not carry consequences at the European level. Yet, even if it is regulated at the domestic level, it remains the case that the government is making a case on behalf of one of its – national or regional – organs, possibly not agreeing with it.

On the other hand, it is possible that the national and sub-national parliaments have been involved in the decision making procedure (under the

---

[45] Article 93(1), 2nd sentence of the Basic Law.

new *ex ante* provisions) as interested non-privileged actors and can therefore considered to have standing to bring an independent action for annulment under Article 230(4) EC.[46] However, if standing of regional and national parliaments must be located under Article 230(4) EC, it remains dependent on the position of the Court of Justice, which may alter. In addition, it would require the Court of Justice to investigate issues of an essentially national constitutional nature, for instance whether the relevant legislative chamber or organ actually had jurisdiction for this decision, as this will be decisive for the question whether or not the organ is directly and individually concerned. This clearly is a matter that the Court of Justice should not be concerned with.

24.2.3.2.6. *The Protocol on the Application of the Principles of Subsidiarity and Proportionality*

The Protocol provides in its Article 8 that '*The Court of Justice of the European Union shall have jurisdiction in actions on grounds of infringement of the principle of subsidiarity by a European legislative act, brought in accordance with the rules laid down in Article III-365 of the Constitution by Member States, or notified by them in accordance with their legal order on behalf of their national Parliament or a chamber of it*'. It would have been more elegant to also include this provision in the text of Article III-365. As for the procedure itself, the alternative would have been to award the national parliaments (and possibly even a chamber) *locus standi* in their own right on the basis of the Constitutional Treaty. They would then no longer be dependent on the national government to bring the action, while the detour via the Member States does not guarantee access to judicial review in all instances. It remains a half-way solution: it is intended to award national parliaments (and possibly their chambers) the right to bring actions for judicial review, but it does not actually give it to the parliaments themselves, and refers back to national law for the actual execution of that right. This is probably due to the disparities in national constitutional law depicted above, but this solution does not guarantee a right of access to all parliaments (or chambers) alike, in any situation. This is not satisfactory. As for the grounds for review, it must be assumed that the Court will only deal with subsidiarity issues: the reference to Article III-365 is probably not to the usual grounds for review, which would be much wider, and also include other competence issues, fundamental rights and the like.

24.3. CONCLUDING REMARKS

The judicial *Kompetenz Kompetenz* conflict between the Court of Justice and some of the national constitutional courts may still arise under the

---

[46] So apparently S Weatherill, 'Competence', in B De Witte (ed), *Ten Reflections on the Constitutional Treaty for Europe*, EUI, 2003, available on www.iue.it, 45, at 65.

Constitutional Treaty. The lists of competences lack clarity, and may possibly even give rise to more discussion than before. The introduction of the early warning system involving national parliaments may prove to be an important new asset, as it provides a (political) answer to the main concern of these courts, which is that the Union grabs competences which have not been transferred, leaving the Member States and their parliaments powerless. National parliaments will have a responsibility of their own not only at the time of assenting to Treaty amendments and new transfers of competences, but each time the Union intends to act under those competences. As this responsibility will thus return to a national organ (under unanimous decision-making, it can be argued, it resided in the national government representing the State in the Council), a role for the national *courts* as ultimate guardians will become much less critical. The role of the national parliaments in the early warning system remains restricted however to the principle of subsidiarity, and not to the remainer of competence issues. This may well prove to be too limited. The involvement of the national parliaments and the fact that they may via their government bring actions before the Court of Justice will lead to making a political issue justiciable, and to bring to the court room highly political questions. The Court of Justice will have to earn the confidence of the national courts and prove that it takes the issue of the delimitation of competences seriously. If it does take it seriously, the risk of the national courts exercising review over the exercise of competences will be reduced to extreme and almost hypothetical cases. In order to further restrict the risk of national courts claiming judicial *Kompetenz Kompetenz* or, worse yet, exercising it in a particular case, it would have been commendable to underline the exclusive jurisdiction of the Court of Justice as ultimate guardian in explicit Treaty provisions adopted to that effect, but neither *Foto-Frost*, nor a clear and unambiguous confirmation of the European Court's exclusive competence to guard the division of competences between the Member States and the Union have been included.

25

Conclusion

THE TREATY ESTABLISHING a Constitution for Europe, if ratified, will replace the current Treaties and become the basic document of a European Union, which will no longer have to be viewed as a Greek temple. However, this Constitution will remain only one element of the wider European Constitution, which continues to include the Constitutions of the Member States. Accordingly, the constitutional reality of a mixed constitutional system will continue to exist in co-existing documents.

It is difficult to predict at this stage the implications of the adoption of the Treaty for the national courts, but some remarks are in place. Firstly, Article I-29TCE probably contains the European mandate of national courts, but it is not well drafted and is old-fashioned in the sense that it is addressed only to the Member States without so much as mentioning the national courts. In addition, as the formulation is almost identical to terms copied from the *UPA* judgment of the Court of Justice, it may give the impression that it relates only to *UPA*-type situations, while it in fact could also be interpreted as the sanctioning in the Treaty of *effet utile*, and the ensuing mandate of the national courts to protect Union rights of individuals against the Member States.

Secondly, it is submitted that it was not necessary to incorporate the principle of primacy, due to its complexity and given the fact that it seems hardly possible to formulate it in an acceptable manner, and for reasons of legitimacy. Also, despite its appearance and the impression that it is only the confirmation of the current situation, the inclusion of the principle formulated as an absolute and unconditional principle applying to the entire Constitution and the law deriving from it does change the state of the law: it makes it a one-sided principle, and leaves out the national perspective.

With respect to fundamental rights protection, I consider accession to the ECHR far more important from the point of view of the national courts than the incorporation of the Charter. Accession is the only solution to conflicts of loyalty which may arise for a national court, and it would add considerable legitimacy to the Union and its Court of Justice. It is to be hoped that the Council will indeed take the necessary steps to actually accede. Whether incorporation of the Charter will alter the relationship between the national courts and the Court of Justice remains to be seen. Its value will probably lie elsewhere, increasing legitimacy to the Union and its institutions, making clear to the citizens of Europe that the Union does take fundamental rights seriously, and reminding the Union institutions and Member States acting in them that they are indeed bound to respect them.

As for the issue of judicial *Kompetenz Kompetenz*, it is regrettable that the Constitutional Treaty does not explicitly confirm the exclusive competence of the Court of Justice to decide conflicts over competence, and the obligation of all national courts to refer competence issues.

Bibliography

ABRAHAM, R., Droit international, droit communautaire et droit français, Paris, 1989

ACKERMAN, B., 'Constitutional Politics/Constitutional Law', 99 Yale LJ, 1989, 453

ACKERMAN, B., We the People: Foundations, Harvard, Harvard University Press, 1991

ACKERMAN, B., We the People: Transformations, Harvard, Harvard University Press, 1998

ADINOLFI, A., 'The Judicial Application of Community Law in Italy (1981–1997)', 35 CMLRev, 1998, 1313

ALBAEK JENSEN, J., 'Human Rights in Danish Law', 7 EPL, 2001, 1

AKEHURST, M., 'Parliamentary Sovereignty and the Supremacy of Community Law', BYIL, 1989, 351

ALBERTON, G., 'Le régime de la responsabilité du fait des lois confronté au droit communautaire: de la contradiction à la conciliation?', RFDA, 1997, 1017

ALBORS-LLORENS, A., 'Changes in the Jurisdiction of the European Court of Justice under the Treaty of Amsterdam', 35 CMLRev, 1998, 1273

ALKEMA, E.A., 'The Application of Internationally Guaranteed Human Rights in the Municipal Order', in Essays on the Development of the International Legal Order in Memory of Van Panhuys, F. Kalshoven (ed), Alphen Aan de Rijn, Sijthoff, 1980, 181

ALKEMA, E.A., Een meerkeuzetoets, Zwolle, W.E.J. Tjeenk Willink, 1985

ALLAN, T.R.S., 'Parliamentary Sovereignty: Lord Denning's Dexterous Revolution', 3 Oxford Journal of Legal Studies, 1983, 22

ALLAN, T.R.S., 'Parliamentary Sovereignty: Law, Politics and Revolution', LQR, 1997, 443

ALLAND, D., 'Consécration d'un paradoxe: primauté du droit interne sur le droit international', RFDA, 1998, 1094

ALLAND, D., 'Le droit international 'sous' la Constitution de la Ve République', RDP, 1998, 1649

ALSTON, Ph. (ed), The EU and Human Rights, Oxford, OUP, 1999

ALSTON, Ph. and Weiler, J.H.H., 'An "Ever Closer Union" in Need of a Human Rights Policy: The European Union and Human Rights', in The EU and Human Rights, Ph. Alston (ed), Oxford, OUP, 1999, 3

ALTER, K.J., and MEUNIER-AITSAHALIA, S., 'Judicial Politics in the European Community: European Integration and the Pathbreaking Cassis de Dijon Decision', Comparative Political Studies, 1994, 535

ALTER, K.J., 'The European Court's Political Power', West European Politics, 1996, 458

ALTER, K.J., 'Explaining National Court Acceptance of European Court Jurisprudence: A Critical Evaluation of Theories of Legal Integration', in The European Court and National Courts – Doctrine and Jurisprudence. Legal Change in Its Social Context, A.-M. Slaugther et al. (eds), Oxford, Hart Publishing, 1998, 227

Bibliography

ALTER, K., Establishing the Supremacy of European Law. The Making of an International Rule of Law in Europe, Oxford, OUP, 2001

AMOROSO, G., 'La giurisprudenza costituzionale nell'anno 1995 in tema di rapporto tra ordinamento comunitario e ordinamento nazionale: verso un 'quarta' fase?', Foro Italiano, 1996, V-4

ANAGNOSTARAS, G., 'State Liability v Retroactive Application of Belated Implementing Measures: Seeking the Optimum Means in Terms of Effectiveness of EC Law', 1 Web J, 2000, webjcli.ncl.ac.uk/200/issue1/anagnostaras1.html

ANAGNOSTARAS, G., 'The Principle of State Liability for Judicial Breaches: The Impact of European Community Law', EPL, 2001, 281

ANAGNOSTARAS, G., 'The allocation of responsibility in State liability actions for breach of Community law: a modern gordian knot?', 26 ELR, 2001, 139

ANAV, G., 'Parliamentary Sovereignty: An Anachronism?', 27 Columbia J Transnational L, 1989, 631

ANDENAS, M. and FAIRGRIEVE, D., 'Misfeasance in Public Office, Governmental Liability, and European Influences', 51 ICLQ, 2002, 757

ANDERSON, D., References to the European Court of Justice, London, Sweet & Maxwell, 1995

ARNULL, A., 'National courts and the validity of Community acts', ELR, 1988, 125

ARNULL, A., 'The Use and Abuse of Article 177', 52 MLR, 1989, 622

ARNULL, A., 'Liability for Legislative Acts under Article 215(2) EC', in The Action for Damages in Community Law, T. Heukels and A. McDonnell (eds), The Hague, Kluwer Law International, 1997, 129

ARNULL, A., European Union and its Court of Justice, Oxford, OUP, 1999

ARNULL, A., 'Judicial architecture or judicial folly? The challenge facing the European Union', 24 ELR, 1999, 516

ARNULL, A., 'Taming the Beast? The Treaty of Amsterdam and the Court of Justice', in Legal Issues of the Amsterdam Treaty, D. O'Keeffe and P. Twomey (eds), Oxford, Hart Publishing, 1999, 109

BALDASSARRE, A., Diritto comunitario europeo e diritto nazionale, Atti del seminario internazionale Roma 1995, Milano, Giuffrè, 1997

BARAV, A., 'Les effets du droit communautaire directement applicable', CDE, 1978, 265

BARAV, A., 'Cour constitutionnelle italienne et droit communautaire: le fantôme de Simmenthal', RTDEur, 1985, 313

BARAV, A., 'Damages in the Domestic Courts for Breach of Community Law by National Public Authorities', in Non-Contractual Liability of the European Communities, H.G. Schermers, T. Heukels and Ph. Mead (eds), Dordrecht, Kluwer Law International, 1988, 149

BARAV, A., 'Enforcement of Community Rights in the National Courts: the Case for Jurisdiction to Grant Interim Relief, 26 CMLRev, 1989, 369

BARAV, A., 'La plénitude de compétence du juge national en sa qualité de juge communautaire', in L'Europe et le droit, Mélanges en hommage à Jean Boulouis, Paris, 1991, 1

BARAV, A., 'Omnipotent Courts', in Institutional Dynamics of European Integration. Essays in Honour of H.G. Schermers, Vol 2, The Hague, Kluwer, 1994, 265

BARAV, A., 'State liability in damages for breach of Community law in the national courts', in The Action for Damages in Community Law, T. Heukels and A. McDonnell (eds), The Hague, Kluwer Law International, 1997, 363

BARENDT, E., An Introduction to Constitutional Law, Oxford, Clarendon Press, 1998

BARNARD, C. and SHARPSTON, E., 'The Changing Face of Article 177 References', 34 CMLRev, 1997, 1113

BEBR, G., 'How supreme is Community law in the national courts?', 11 CMLRev, 1974, 3

BEBR, G., 'Agreements concluded by the Community and their possible direct effect: From International Fruit Company to Kupferberg', 20 CMLRev, 1983, 35

BEBR, G., 'The Rambling Ghost of "Cohn-Bendit": Acte clair and the Court of Justice', 20 CMLRev, 1983, 439

BEBR, G., 'The Reinforcement of the Constitutional Review of Community Acts under Article 177 EEC Treaty', 25 CMLRev, 1988, 667

BELL, J., 'Sur le pouvoir du juge britannique d'addresser des injonction à la Couronne', RFDA, 1990, 920

BELL, J. and BRADLEY, A.W. (eds), Governmental Liability: A Comparative Study, Glasgow, UK Comparative Law Series, 1991

BELL, J., 'The Law of England and Wales', in Governmental Liability: A Comparative Study, J. Bell and A.W. Bradley (eds), Glasgow, UK Comparative Law Series, 1991

BELL, J., French Constitutional Law, Oxford, Clarendon Press, 1992

BELTRAMO, M., LONGO, G.E. and MERRYMAN, J.H., The Italian Civil Code and complementary legislation, Dobbs Ferry, NY, Oceana, 1996

BENGOETXEA, J., The Legal Reasoning of the Court of Justice: Towards a European Jurisprudence, Oxford, Clarendon Press, 1993

BENGOETXEA, J., MACCORMICK, N. and MORAL SORIANO, L., 'Integration and Integrity in the Legal Reasoning of the Court of Justice', in The European Court of Justice, G. de Búrca and J.H.H. Weiler (eds), Oxford, OUP, 2001, 43

BENNEKOM, TH.L. and others, Koopmans' Staatsrecht, 9th edn, Deventer, Kluwer, 2002

BENVENISTI, E., 'Judicial Misgivings Regarding the Application of International Law: An Analysis of Attitudes of National Courts', 4 EJIL, 1993, 159

BERNITZ, U., 'Sweden and the European Union: On Sweden's Implementation and Application of European Law', 38 CMLRev, 2001, 903

BERROD, F., 'La Cour de justice refuse l'invocabilité des accords OMC: essai de la régulation de la mondialisation', RTDeur, 2000, 419

BESSE, D., 'Die Bananenmarktordung im Lichte deutscher Grundrechte und das Kooperationsverhältnis zwischen BVerfG und EuGH, Juristische Schulung, 1996, 396

BESSELINK, L.F.M., Staatsrecht en buitenlands beleid, Nijmegen, Ars Aequi Cahiers, 1991

BESSELINK, L.F.M., 'Curing a "Childhood Sickness"? On Direct Effect, Internal Effect, Primacy and Derogation from Civil Rights. The Netherlands Council of State Judgment in the Metten Case', MJ, 1996, 165

BESSELINK, L.F.M., 'De zaak Metten: de Grondwet voorbij', NJB, 1996, 165

BESSELINK, L.F.M., 'An Open Constitution and European Integration: The Kingdom of The Netherlands', in Le droit constitutionnel national et l'intégration européenne, 17th FIDE Kongress, Berlin, 1996, 361

BESSELINK, L.F.M., et al., Europese Unie en nationale soevereiniteit, Staatsrechtconferentie 1997, Deventer, W.E.J. Tjeenk Willink, 1997

BESSELINK, L.F.M., 'Suiker en rijst uit de West – over Europees recht en de Koninkrijksverhoudingen', NJB, 1998, 1291

BESSELINK, L.F.M., 'Community Loyalty and Constitutional Loyalty', EPL, 2000, 169

BESSELINK, L.F.M., 'The Member States, the National Constitutions and the Scope of the Charter', 8 MJ, 2002, 68

BESSELINK, L.F.M., et al., De Nederlandse Grondwet en de Europese Unie, Groningen, Europa Law Publishing, 2002

BETLEM, G. and ROOD, E., 'Francovich-aansprakelijkheid. Schadevergoeding wegens schending van het gemeenschapsrecht', NJB, 1992, 250

BETLEM, G., 'Onrechtmatige Wetgeving: Overheidsaansprakelijkheid voor Schending van EG recht in het post-Francovich Tijdperk', RegelMaat, 1996, 128

BETLEM, G., 'The Doctrine of Constistent Interpretation – Managing Legal Uncertainty', 22 OJLS, 2002, 397

BIERING, P., 'The Application of EU Law in Denmark: 1986 to 2000', 37 CMLRev, 2000, 925

BIONDI, A., 'The European Court of Justice and Certain National Procedural Limitations: Not Such a Tough Relationship', 36 CMLRev, 1999, 1271

BLAIZOT-HAZARD, C., 'Les contradictions des articles 54 et 55 de la Constitution face à la hiérachie des normes', RDP, 1992, 1293

BLECKMANN, A., and PIEPER, S.U., 'Maastricht, die grundgesetzliche Ordnung und die "Superrevisionsinstanz"', RIW, 1993, 971

BLONDEAU, A., 'L'application du droit conventionnel par les juridictions françaises de l'ordre judiciaire', in L'application du droit international par le juge français, P.Reuter et al. (eds), Paris, Librairie Armand Colin, 1972, 43

BOCH, CHR.,'The Iroquois at the Kirchberg: Some Naïve Remarks on the Status and Relevance of Direct Effect', in The State of the European Union: Structure, Enlargement and Economic Union, J.A. Usher (ed), London, Longman, 2000, 21

BOK, A.J., 'Het Francovich-arrest en onrechtmatige wetgeving naar Nederlands recht', TPR, 1993, 27

BOLLEN, C., 'Verknoeit het Europees recht ook ons bestuursrecht? Terugvordering van in strijd met het Europese recht door de overheid verleende steun', in Uit de school geklapt? Opstellen uit Maastricht, M.A. Heldeweg et al. (eds), Den Haag, SdU, 1999, 39

BONICHOT, J.CL., 'Convergences et divergences entre le Conseil d'état et la Cour de justice des Communautés européennes', RFDA, 1989, 579

BONICHOT, J.-CL., 'Les pouvoirs d'injonction du juge national pour la protection des droits conférés par l'ordre juridique communautaire', RFDA, 1990, 912

BONTINCK, G., 'The TRIPs Agreement and the ECJ: A New Dawn? Some comments About Joined Cases C-300/98 and C-392/98 Parfums Dior and Assco Gerüste', Jean Monnet Working Paper 16/01

BOUJOUNG, K., 'Staatshaftung für legislatives und normatives Unrecht in der neueren Rechtsprechung des Bundesgerichtshofes', in Verantwortlichkeit und Freiheit. Festschrift für Willi Geiger zum 80. Geburtstag, H.J. Faller, P. Kirchhof and E. Träger (eds), 1989, 430

BOURGEOIS, J.H.J., 'The European Court of Justice and the WTO: Problems and Challenges', in The EU, the WTO and the NAFTA. Towards a Common Law of International Trade?, J.H.H. Weiler (ed), Oxford, OUP, 2000, 71

BOURGORGUE LARSEN, L., 'Espagne', in Les États membres de l'Union européenne. Adaptations, mutations, résistances, J. Rideau (ed), Paris, LGDJ, 1997, 135

BOYRON, S., 'The Conseil constitutionnel and the European Union', PL, 1993, 30

BRADLEY, A.W., 'The Sovereignty of Parliament – Form or Substance?', in The Changing Constitution, 4th edn, J. Jowell and D. Oliver (eds), Oxford, OUP, 2000, 23

BRADLEY, A.W., 'The Sovereignty of Parliament – In Perpetuity?', in The Changing Constitution, J. Jowell and D. Oliver (eds), 2nd edn, Oxford, OUP, 1989, 25

BRADLEY, A.W. and EWING, K.D., Wade & Bradley, Constitutional and Administrative Law, 11th edn, London, Longman, 1993

BRAIBANT, G., Le droit administratif français, 3rd edn, Paris, Dalloz, 1992

BRIBOSIA, H., 'Applicabilité directe et primauté des traités internationaux et du droit communautaire. Réflexions générales sur le point de vue de l'ordre juridique belge', RBDI, 1996, 33

BRIBOSIA, H., 'Report on Belgium', in The European Court and National Courts – Doctrine and Jurisprudence. Legal Change in Its Social Context, A.-M. Slaughter et al. (eds), Oxford, Hart Publishing, 1998, 3

BRICOUT, N.J., 'De l'ordre juridique européen', JT, 1974, 544

BRICOUT, N.J., 'Blijft de wet onschendbaar?', RW, 1974–1975, 2195

BRINKHORST, L.J., 'Le juge néerlandais et le droit communautaire' in Le juge national et le droit communautaire, A.M. Donner et al. (eds), Leyde, Sijthoff, 1966, 101

BROEKSTEEG J.W.L., et al., De Nederlandese Grondwet en de Europese Unie, Publikaties van de Staatsrechtkring, Deventer, Kluwer, 2003

BROUWER, J.G., 'Wijkt het Unie-Verdrag van Maastricht af van de Grondwet of van het Statuut?', NJB, 1992, 1045

BROUWER, J.G., 'Nederlandse gedachten over de Grondwet en het Verdrag', RW, 1992–1993, 1366

BUERGENTHAL, TH., 'Self-executing and Non-self-executing Treaties in National and International Law', Recueil des Cours, Collected Courses of the Hague Academy of International Law, Tome 235, 1992-IV, Dordrecht, Martinus Nijhoff, 1993

CALVET, H., 'Droit administratif de la responsabilité et droit communautaire', AJDA, 1996

CANDELA, J. and MONGIN, B., 'La loi européenne, désormais mieux protégée. Quelques réflexions sur la première décision de la Commission demandant à la Cour de justice de prononcer une sanction pécuniaire au sens de l'article 171 du Traité à l'encontre de certains États membres pour violation du droit communautaire', RMUE, 1997, 9

CANIVET, G., 'Le droit communautaire et l'office du juge national', Droit et Société, 1992, 133

CANOR, I., 'Primus inter pares. Who is the ultimate guardian of fundamental rights in Europe?', 25 ELR, 2000, 3.

CAPPELLETTI, M., The Judicial Process in Comparative Perspective, Oxford, OUP, 1989

CAPPELLETTI, M., Le pouvoir des juges, Paris, Economica/PUAM, 1990

CARANTA, R., 'Governmental Liability after Francovich', 52 CLJ, 1993, 272

Bibliography

CARTABIA, M., 'The Italian Constitutional Court and the Relationship between the Italian Legal System and the European Community', Michigan J Int L, 1990, 173

CASEY, J., Constitutional Law in Ireland, 3rd edn, Dublin, Sweet & Maxwell, 2000

CASSESE, A., 'Modern Constitutions and International Law', 192 Hague Recueil des cours, 1985-III, 331

CASSESE, A., International Law, Oxford, OUP, 2001

CHITI, M.P., 'The EC Notion of Public Administration: The Case of the Bodies Governed by Public Law', 8 EPL, 2002, 473

CLAES, M. and DE WITTE, B., 'Report on The Netherlands', in The European Court and National Courts – Doctrine and Jurisprudence. Legal Change in Its Social Context, A.-M. Slaughter, A. Stone Sweet and J.H.H. Weiler (eds), Oxford, Hart Publishing, 1998, 171

CLARICH, M., 'The Liability of Public Authorities in Italian Law', in Governmental Liability: A Comparative Study, J. Bell and A.W. Bradley (eds), Glasgow, UK Comparative Law Series, 1991, 225

CARTABIA, M., Principi inviolabili e integrazione europea, Milan, Giuffrè, 1995

CARTABIA, M., 'The Italian Constitutional Court and the Relationship Between the Italian Legal System and the European Union', in The European Court and National Courts – Doctrine and Jurisprudence. Legal Change in Its Social Context, Oxford, Hart Publishing, 1998, 133

CASSIA, P., 'Le juge administratif français et la validité des actes communautaires', RTDeur, 1999, 409

CATALANO, N., 'Portata dell'art. 11 della Costituzione in relazione ai trattati istitutive delle Comunità Europee', Foro Italiano, 1964, I, 465

CATALANO, N., 'La position du droit communautaire dans le droit des Etats membres', in Droit communautaire et droit national, Semaine de Bruges, Bruges, De Tempel, 1965, 55

CHALTIEL, F., 'Droit constitutionnel et droit communautaire', RTDeur, 1999, 395

CHALTIEL, F., 'La boîte de Pandore des relations entre la Constitution française et le droit comunautaire. À propos de l'arrêt SNIP du Conseil d'État du 3 décembre 2001', RMCUE, 2002, 595

CHEVALLIER, R.M., 'Le juge français et le droit communautaire', in Le juge national et le droit communautaire, A.M. Donner et al. (eds), Leiden, Sitnoff, 1966, 2

COHEN JONATHAN, G., 'Cour constitutionnelle allemande et règlements communautaires', CDE, 1975, 173

COLLINS, L., 'Foreign Relations and the Judiciary', 51 ICLQ, 2002, 85

CONSTANTINESCO, L.J., 'La spécificité du droit communautaire', RTDeur, 1966, 3.

CONSTANTINESCO, L.J., 'Effets et rang des traités et du droit communautaire en France', Riv.dir.civ., 1968, 259

CONSTANTINESCO, V., 'L'article 5 CEE, de la bonne foi à la loyauté communautaire', in Du droit international au droit de l'intégration. Liber Amicorum Pierre Pescatore, Baden-Baden, Nomos, 1987, 97

CONVERY, J., 'State Liability in the United Kingdom after Brasserie du Pêcheur', 34 CMLRev, 1997, 603

COPPEL, J. and O'NEILL, A., 'The European Court of Justice: Taking Rights Seriously?', CMLRev, 1992, 669

CORNELIS, I., Beginselen van het Belgische buitencontractuele aansprakelijkheid-srecht, Antwerpen, Maklu, 1989

COTTIER, TH. and NADAKAVUKAREN SCHEFER, K., 'The Relationship between World Trade Organization Law, National and Regional Law', JIEL, 1998, 83

CONFORTI, B., 'Notes on the Relationship between International and National Law', International Law FORUM du droit international, 2001, 18

CRAIG, P.P., 'Compensation in Public Law', LQR, 1980, 413

CRAIG, P.P., 'Sovereignty of the United Kingdom Parliament after Factortame', YEL, 1991, 221

CRAIG, P.P, 'Once upon a Time in the West: Direct Effect and the Federalization of EEC Law', OJLS, 1992, 453

CRAIG, P.P, 'The Domestic Liability of Public Authorities in Damages: Lessons from the European Community?', in New Directions in European Public Law, J. Beatson and T. Tridimas (eds), Oxford, Hart Publishing, 1998, 75

CRAIG, P.P, 'Report on the United Kingdom', in The European Court and National Courts – Doctrine and Jurisprudence. Legal Change in Its Social Context, A.-M. Slaughter et al. (eds), Oxford, Hart Publishing, 1998, 195

CRAIG, P.P., 'Britain in the European Union', in The Changing Constitution, J. Jowell and D. Oliver (eds), 4th ed, 2000, 61

CRAIG, P., 'Constitutions, Constitutionalism and the European Union', ELJ, 2001, 125

CRAIG, P. and DE BÚRCA, G., EU Law. Text, Cases and Materials, 3rd edn, Oxford, OUP, 2002

CRAUFURD SMITH, R., 'Remedies for Breaches of EU Law in National Courts: Legal Variation and Selection', in The Evolution of EU Law, Oxford, OUP, 1999, 286

CRIPPS, Y., 'European "rights", invalid actions and denial of damages', CLJ, 1986, 165

CURTIN, D., 'The Province of Government: Delimiting the Direct Effect of Directives in the Common Law Context', 15 ELR, 1990, 195

CURTIN, D., 'State Liability Under Community Law: A New Remedy for Private Parties', Industrial Law Journal, 1992, 74

CURTIN, D., 'The Constitutional Structure of the European Union: A Europe of Bits and Pieces', 30 CMLRev, 1993, 17

CURTIN, D. and MORTELMANS K., 'Application and Enforcement of Community Law by the Member States: Actors in Search of a Third Generation Script', in Institutional Dynamics of European Integration. Essays in Honour of H.G. Schermers, Vol. 2, D. Curtin and T. Heukels (eds), Dordrecht, Nijhoff, 1994, 423

CURTIN, D. and DEKKER, I., 'The EU as a "Layered" International Organization: Institutional Unity in Disguise', in The Evolution of EU Law, P. Craig and G. de Búrca (eds), Oxford, OUP, 1999, 83

CURTIN, D., 'The EU Human Rights Charter and the Union Legal Order: the "Banns" before the Marriage?', in Judicial Review in European Union Law. Liber Amicorum in Honour of Lord Slynn of Hadley, D. O'Keeffe and A. Bavasso (eds), The Hague, Kluwer Law International, 2000, 303

CURTIN, D. and DEKKER, I., 'The Constitutional Structure of the European Union: Some Reflections on Vertical Unity-in-Diversity', in Convergence and Divergence in European Public Law, P. Beaumont, C. Lyons and N. Walker (eds), Oxford, Hart Publishing, 2002, 59

Bibliography

DANIELE, L., 'Après l'arrêt Granital: Droit communautaire et droit national dans la jurisprudence récente de la Cour constitutionnelle italienne', CDE, 1992, 3

DANIELE, L., 'Italian Report', The Imposition of Sanctions for Breach of Community Law. XVth FIDE Congress, Lisbon, 1992, 259

DANIELE, L. and BARTOLE, S., in Le droit constitutionnel national et l'intégration européenne, 17th FIDE Congress, Berlin, 1996, 330

DANTONEL-COR, N., 'La mise en jeu de la respnsabilité de l'État français pour violation du droit communautaire', RTDeur, 1995, 471

DÄNZER-VANOTTI, W., 'Unzulässige Rechtsfortbildung des Europäischen Gerichtshofs', RIW, 1992, 733

DARRAS AND PIROTTE, 'La Cour constitutionnelle allemande a-t-elle mise en danger la primauté du droit communautaire?', RTDeur, 1976, 415

DASHWOOD, A. and JOHNSTON, A. (eds), The Future of the Judicial System of the European Union, Oxford, Hart Publishing, 2001

DAVIS, M.H., 'A Government of Judges: A Historical Re-view', AJCL, 1987, 559

DEARDS, E., '"Curiouser and Curiouser"? The Development of Member State Liability in the Court of Justice', 3 EPL, 1997, 117

DEARDS, E., 'Brasserie du Pêcheur: Snatching Defeat from the Jaws of Victory?', 22 ELR, 1997, 620

D. DE BÉCHILLON, 'De quelques incidences du contrôle de la conventionnalité internationale des lois par le juge ordinaire (Malaise dans la Constitution)', RFDA, 1998, 225

DE BERRANGER, Th. Constitutions nationales et construction communautaire, Paris, LGDJ, 1995

DE BERRANGER, Th., 'Danemark', in Les Etats membres de l'Union européenne. Adaptations – Mutations – Résistences, J. Rideau (ed), Paris, LGDJ, 1997, 97

DE BÚRCA, G. and SCOTT, J., The EU and the WTO. Legal and Constitutional Issues, Oxford, Hart Publishing, 2001

DE BÚRCA, G., 'The Drafting of the European Union Charter of Fundamental Rights', 26 ELR, 2001, 126

DE BÚRCA, G. and WEILER, J.H.H., (eds), The European Court of Justice, Oxford, OUP, 2001

DE CATERINI, P., 'La Cour constitutionnelle italienne et le droit communautaire', CDE, 1975, 122

DE GREVE, L. and MELCHIOR, M., Constitutionele bescherming en internationale bescherming van de mensenrechten: concurrentie of complementariteit, Report to the IXth Conference of European Constitutional Courts held in Paris, 1993

DEHAUSSY, J., 'La Constitution, les traités et les lois: à propos de la nouvelle jurisprudence du Conseil d'Etat sur les traités', JDI, 1999, 675

DEHOUSSE, R., The European Court of Justice, New York, St. Martin's Press, 1998

DEHOUSSE, R., La Cour de justice des Communautés européennes, Paris, Montchrestien, 1994

DE LOLME, J.L., The Rise and Process of the English Constitution, 1838

DELVOLVÉ, J.-L., 'Le pouvoir judiciaire et le Traité de Rome ou la diplomatie des juges', JCP, 1968, I, 2184

DE MOOR-VAN VUGT A., and VERMEULEN, E.M., Europees Bestuursrecht, Deventer, WEJ Tjeenk Willink, 1998

DENZA, E., 'Two legal orders: divergent or convergent?', 48 ICLQ, 1999, 257

DE SCHOUTHEETE, PH., 'Guest Editorial: the Intergovernmental Conference', 37 CMLRev, 2000, 845

DESMEDT, A., 'European Court of Justice on the Effect of WTO Agreements in the EC Legal Order', LIEI, 2000, 93

DETTERBECK, S., 'Staatshaftung für die Missachtung von EG-Recht', Verwaltungsarchiv, 1994, 159

DE WERD, M.F.J.M., 'Een Grafschrift op de Grondwet: de gebrekkige privaa-trechtelijke rechtspersoonlijkheid van de Nederlandse Staat', NJB, 1998, 213

DE WITTE, B., 'Retour à "Costa". La primauté du droit communautaire à la lumière du droit international', RTDeur, 1984, 425

DE WITTE, B., 'Sovereignty and European Integration: The Weight of Legal Tradition', 2 MJ, 1995, 145

DE WITTE, B., 'Interpreting the EC Treaty like a Constitution: The Role of the European Constitution in Comparative Perspective', in Judicial Control. Comparative Essays on Judicial Review, Antwerpen, Maklu, 1995, 133

DE WITTE, B., 'International Agreement or European Constitution?', in Reforming the Treaty on European Union: The Legal Debate, J. Winter, D. Curtin, A. Kellermann and B. De Witte (eds), The Hague, Kluwer Law International, 1996, 1

DE WITTE, B., 'The Pillar Structure and the Nature of the European Union: Greek Temple or French Gothis Cathedral?', in The European Union After Amsterdam, T. Heukels et al. (ed), The Hague, Kluwer Law International, 1998, 51

DE WITTE, B., 'Direct Effect, Supremacy and the Nature of the Legal Order', in The Evolution of EU Law, P. Craig and G. de Búrca (eds), Oxford, OUP, 1999, 177

DE WITTE, B., 'The Past and Future Role of the European Court of Justice in the Protection of Human Rights', in The EU and Human Rights, Ph. Alston (ed), Oxford, OUP, 1999, 859

DE WITTE, B., 'The Legal Status of the Charter: Vital Question or Non-issue?', 8 MJ, 2001, 81

DE WITTE, B., 'The Closest Thing to a Constitutional Conversation in Europe: The Semi-Permanent Treaty Revision Process', in Convergence and Divergence in European Public Law, P. Beaumont, C. Lyons and N. Walker (eds), Oxford, Hart Publishing, 2002, 39

DE WITTE, B., 'Do Not Mention The Word: Sovereignty in Two Europhile Countries, Belgium and The Netherlands', in Sovereignty in Transition, N. Walker (ed), Oxford, Hart Publishing, 2003, 359

DE WITTE, B., 'Clarifying the Delimitation of Powers. A Proposal with Comments', paper delivered at the Conference of the Jean Monnet Group on the Future of Europe, Europe 2004, Le Grand Débat, Setting the Agenda and Outlining the Options, available on www.ecsanet.org.

DE WITTE, B., 'The Primacy of Community Law: A Not-so-federal Principle?' unpublished paper, on file with the author

DE ZWAAN, J.W., 'Community Dimensions of the Second Pillar', in The European Union After Amsterdam, T. Heukels, N. Blokker and M. Brus (eds), The Hague, Kluwer Law International, 1998, 179

DICEY, A.V., The Law of the Constitution, E.C.S. Wade (ed), 10th edn, London, Macmillan, 1959

DOEHRING, K., Die allgemeinen Regeln des völkerrechtlichen Fremdenrechts und das deutsche Verfassungsrecht, Köln, 1963

Bibliography

DOHMOLD, H., 'Die Haftung des Staates für legislatives und normatives Unrecht in der neueren Rechtsprechung des Bundesgerichtshofes', DÖV, 1991, 152

LORD DONALDSON, 'Can the Judiciary control Acts of Parliament?', The Law Teacher, 1991, 4

DONNER, A.M. et al., Le juge national et le droit communautaire, Leyde, Sijthoff, 1966

DONNER, A.M., 'The Constitutional Powers of the Court of Justice of the European Communities', CMLRev, 1974, 127

DONNER, A.M., 'The Court of Justice as a Constitutional Court of the Communities', in Tussen het echte en het gemaakte, 1986, 343

DONNER, A.M., 'Uitlegging en toepassing', in Miscellanea Ganshof van der Meersch, Studia ab discipulis amicisque in honorem egregii professoris edita, Brussels, Bruylant, 1972, 103

DONY, M., 'Le droit français', in La responsabilité des Etats membres en cas de violation du droit communautaire. Etudes de droit communautaire et de droit national comparé, G. Vandersanden and M. Dony (eds), Bruxelles, Bruylant, 1997, 235

DORD, O., 'Le controle de constitutionnalité des actes communautaires dérivés: De la nécessité d'un dialogue entre les juridictions suprèmes de l'Union européenne', www.conseil-constitutionnel.fr/cahiers/ccc4/ccc4dord.htm

DUBOUIS, L., 'L'arrêt Nicolo et l'intégration de la règle internationale et communautaire dans l'ordre juridique français', RFDA, 1989, 1000

DUBOUIS, L., 'Le juge français et le conflit entre norme constitutionnelle et norme européenne', in L'Europe et le droit. Mélange en hommage à Jean Boulouis, Paris, Dalloz, 1991 205

DUBOUIS, L., 'Directive communautaire et loi française: primauté de la directive et respect de l'interprétation que la Cour de justice a donnée de ses dispositions', RFDA, 1992, 425

DUBOUIS, L., 'Le controle de la compatibilité des décisions de l'Union européenne avec la Constitution française', in Le droit des organsiations internationales. Recueil d'études à la mémoire de Jacques Schwob, J.-F. Flauss and P. Wachsmann (eds), Brussels, Bruylant, 1997, 330

DUBOUIS, L., 'Les trois logiques de la jurisprudence Sarran', RFDA, 1999, 57

DUBINSKY, P.R., 'The Essential Function of Federal Courts: The European Union and the United States Compared', Am J Comp L, 1994, 295

DUE, O. and GULMANN, C., 'Constitutional Implications of the Danish Accession to the European Communities', CMLRev, 1972, 256

DUE, O., 'A Constitutional Court for the European Communities', in Constitutional Adjudication in the European Community and National law, Essays for the Hon. Mr Justice T.F. O'Higgins, D. Curtin and D. O'Keeffe (eds), Dublin, Butterworth, 1992, 2

DUE, O., 'Artikel 5 van het EEG Verdrag. Een bepaling met een federaal karakter?', SEW, 1992, 355

DUE, O., 'Danish Preliminary References', in Judicial Review in European Union Law. Liber Amicorum in Honour of Lord Slynn of Hadley, Vol I, D. O'Keeffe and A. Bavasso (eds), The Hague, Kluwer Law International, 2000, 363

DUYNSTEE, J.F.M., Grondwetsherziening 1953. De nieuwe bepalingen omtrent de buitenlandse betrekkingen in de Grondwet, Deventer, Kluwer, 1953

EDWARD, D., 'Direct Effect, the Separation of Powers and the Judicial Enforcement of Obligations', in Scritti in onore di Giuseppe Federico Mancini, Vol II, Diritto dell'Unione Europea, Milano, Giuffrè, 1998, 423

EDWARD, D., Article 177 References to the European Court – Policy and Practice, London, Butterworths, 1994

EECKHOUT, P., 'The Domestic Legal Status of the WTO Agreement: Interconnecting Legal Systems', 34 CMLRev, 1997, 11

EECKHOUT, P., 'Liability of Member States in Damages and the Community System of Remedies', in New Directions in European Public Law, J. Beatson and T. Tridimas (eds), Oxford, Hart Publishing, 1998, 63

EECKHOUT, P., 'The European Court of Justice and the 'Area or Freedom, Security and Justice': Challenges and Problems', in Judicial Review in European Union Law. Liber Amicorum in Honour of Lord Slynn of Hadley, Vol. I, The Hague, Kluwer Law International, 2000, 153

EECKHOUT, P., 'The EU Charter of Fundamental Rights and the Federal Question', 39 CMLRev, 2002, 945

EDWARD, D., 'Reform of Article 234 Procedure: The Limits of the Possible', in Judicial Review in European Union Law, Liber Amicorum in Honour of Lord Slynn of Hadley, Vol I, D. O'Keeffe and A. Bavasso (eds), Kluwer Law International, 2000, 119

EEKELAAR, J., 'The Death of Parliamentary Sovereignty – A Comment', LQR, 1997, 185

EHLERMANN, C.D., 'Primauté du droit communautaire mise en danger par la Cour constitutionnelle fédérale allemande', RMC, 1975, 10

EHLERMANN, C.D., 'Zur Diskussion um einen "Solange III" – Beschluss: Rechtspolitische Pesrpektiven aus der Sicht des Gemeinschaftsrechts', EuR, 1991, 27

EISEMANN, P.M., Intégration du droit international et communautaire dans l'ordre juridique national. A Study of the Practice in Europe, The Hague, Kluwer, 1996

ELBERS, U. and URBAN, N., 'The Order of the German Federal Constitutional Court of 7 June 2000 and the Kompetenz Kompetenz in the European Judicial System', 7 EPL, 2001, 21

ELEFTERIADIS, P., 'The Direct Effect of Community Law: Conceptual Issues', YEL, 1996, 205

ERADES, L., 'Recht en rechter in Nederland en in de Europese Gemeenschappen', NTIR, 1960, 334

ERADES, L., 'Enkele vragen betreffende de artikelen 65 en 66 van de Grondwet', NJB, 1962, 357 and 385

ERADES, L., 'Poging tot ontwarring van de self-executing' knoop', NJB, 1963, 845

ERADES, L., 'International Law and the Netherlands Legal Order', in H.F. Van Panhuys et al. (eds), International Law in The Netherlands, Vol III, Alphen aan den Rijn, Sijthoff, 1980, 375

ERGEC, R., 'La consécration jurisprudentielle de la primauté du droit supranational de la Constitution', JT, 1997, 256

ESTELLA DE NORIEGA, A., 'A Dissident Voice: The Spanish Constitutional Court Case Law on European Integration', 5 EPL, 1999, 269

EVERLING, U., 'Brauchen wir "Solange III" – Zu den Forderungen nach Revision der Rechtsprechung des Bundesverfassungsgerichts', EuR, 1990, 195

Bibliography

EVERLING, U., 'The Maastricht Judgment of the German Federal Constitutional Court and its Significance for the Development of the European Union', YEL, 1994, 1

EVERLING, U., 'Will Europe Slip on Bananas? The Bananas Judgment of the Court of Justice and the National Courts', CMLRev, 1996, 401

EVERLING, U., 'Quis custodiet custodies ipsos? Zur Diskussion über die Kompetenzordnung der Europäischen Union und ein europäisches Kompetenzgericht', EuZW, 2002, 357

EVERSON, M., 'Beyond the Bundesverfassungsgericht: On the Necessary Cunning of Constitutional Reasoning', 4 ELJ, 1998, 389

EVRIGENIS, D., 'Legal and Constitutional Implications of Greek Accession to the European Communities', CMLRev, 1980, 157

FABERON, J.Y., 'Nouvelle Calédonie et Constitution: La révision constitutionnelle du 20 juillet 1998', RDP, 1999, 113

FAIRGREAVE, D., 'The Human Rights Act 1998, Damages and Tort Law', PL, 2001, 695

FAVOREU, L. (ed), Cours constitutionnelles européennes et droits fondamentaux, Paris, Economica, 1982

FAVOREU, L., 'Le Conseil constitutionnel et l'alternance', RFSP, 1984, 1002

FAVOREU, L. and JOLOWICZ, J.-A., Le contrôle juridictionnel des lois, Paris, Economica/PUAM, 1986

FAVOREU, L. and PHILIP, L. Les grandes décisions du conseil constitutionnel, Paris, Éd. Sirey, 6th edn, 1991

FAVOREU, L., Les cours constitutionnelles, Paris, PUF, 2nd edn, 1992

FAVOREU, L., 'Le contrôle de la constitutionnalité du Traité de Maastricht et le développement du "droit constitutionnel international"', 92 RGDIP, 1993, 39

FAVOREU, L., 'La légitimité du juge constitutionnel', RIDC, 1994, 557

FAVOREU, L., 'La notion de Cour constitutionnelle', in De la Constitution. Etudes en l'honneur de J.-F. Aubert, P. Zen-Ruffinen and A. Auer (eds), Basel, Helbing, 1996, 15

FAVOREU, L. and L. PHILIP, Les grandes décisions du Conseil constitutionnel, Paris, Dalloz, 11th edn, 2001

FENNELLY, N., 'Preserving the Legal Coherence within the New Treaty. The European Court of Justice after the Treaty of Amsterdam', 5 MJ, 1998, 185

FENNELLY, N., 'The Area of "Freedom, Security and Justice" and the European Court of Justice – A Personal View', 49 ICLQ, 2000, 1

FERIA TINTA, M., 'Due Process and the Right to Life in the Context of the Vienna Convention on Consular Relations: Arguing the LaGrand Case', 12 EJIL, 2001, 363

FERRERES COMELLA, V., 'Souveraineté nationale et intégration européenne dans le droit constitutionnel espagnol', www.conseil-constitutionnel.fr/cahiers/ccc9/comella.htm

FERSTENBERT, J., 'L'application du droit communautaire et la situation constitutionnelle du juge national', RTDeur, 1979, 32

FIGUEROA REGUEIRO, P.V., 'Invocability of Substitution and Invocability of Exclusion: Bringing Legal Realism to the Current Developments of the Case Law of "Horizontal" Direct Effects of Directives', Jean Monnet Working Paper, 7/02

FINER, S.E. et al., Comparing Constitutions, Oxford, Clarendon Press, 1995

FINES, F., 'Quelle obligation de réparer pour la violation du droit communautaire? Nouveaux développements jurisprudentiels sur la responsabilité de 'l'État normateur'', RTDeur, 1997, 69

FISCHER, P. and LENGAUER, A., 'The Adaptation of the Austrian Legal System Following EU Membership', 37 CMLRev, 2000, 763

FISCHER, J., 'From Confederacy to Federation. Thoughts on the Finality of European Integration', 12 May 2000, Humboldt Universität, Berlin

FITZMAURICE, M. and FLINTERMAN, C. (eds), L. Erades, Interactions Between International and Municipal Law: A Comparative Case Study, The Hague, TMC Asser Institute, 1993

FLINTERMAN, C., De Act of State doctrine, Antwerpen, 1981

FLINTERMAN, C., Heringa A.W. and Waddington, L. (eds), The Evolving Role of Parliaments in Europe, Antwerpen, Maklu, 1994

FORDER, C.J., 'Abortion: A Constitutional Problem in European Perspective', 1 MJ, 1994, 56

FOSTER, N.G., 'The German Constitution and EC Membership', PL, 1994, 392

FRANCESCAKIS, P., 'Remarques critiques sur le rôle de la Constitution dans le conflit entre le traité et la loi interne devant les tribunaux judiciaires', RCDIP, 1969, 425

FRIEND, M., 'Judicial Review, Private Rights and Community Law', PL, 1985, 21

FROMONT, M., 'Le droit constitutionnel national et l'intégration européenne', in Ergebnisse und Perspektiven, 17. FIDE Kongress, Berlin, 1996, 29

FROWEIN, J.A., 'Das Maastricht-Urteil und die Grenzen der Verfassungsgerichtsbarkeit', ZaöVR, 1994, 1

FROWEIN J.A. and OELLERS-FRAHM, K., 'Allemagne', in L'intégration du droit international et communautaire dans l'ordre juridique national. Étude à la pratique en Europe, P.M. Eisemann (ed), The Hague, Kluwer Law International, 1996, 69

GAÏA, P., 'Normes constitutionnelles et normes internationales', RFDA, 1996, 885

GAJA, G., 'New Developments in a Continuing Story: The Relationship between EEC Law and Italian Law', 27 CMLRev, 1990, 83

GAJA, G., 'The Growing Variety of Procedures concerning Preliminary Rulings', in Judicial Review in European Union Law. Liber Amicorum in Honour of Lord Slynn of Hadley, Vol. I, D. O'Keeffe and A. Bavasso (eds), The Hague, Kluwer Law International, 2000, 143

GALMOT, Y. and BONICHOT J.-CL., 'Le Cour de justice des Communauté européennes et la transposition des directives en droit national', RFDA, 1988, 1

GANSHOF VAN DER MEERSCH, W.J., 'Réflexions sur le droit international et la révision de la Constitution', mercuriale prononcée à l'audience solennelle de rentrée de la Cour de cassation le 2 septembre 1968, JT, 1968, 485

GANSHOF VAN DER MEERSCH, W.J., 'Le juge belge à l'heure du droit international et du droit communautaire', mercuriale 1969, JT, 1969, 537

GANSHOF VAN DER MEERSCH, W.J., 'Le droit communautaire et ses rapports avec le droit des États membres', in Les Novelles, Droit des Communautés européennes, W.J. Ganshof van der Meersch (ed), Bruxelles, Larcier, 1969, 41

GANSHOF VAN DER MEERSCH, W.J., 'Community Law and the Belgian Constitution', in In Memoriam J.D.B. Mitchell, St.John Bates et al. (ed), London, Sweet and Maxwell, 1983, 74

GAUDET, M., Conflits du Droit Communautaire avec les Droits Nationaux, Nancy, Centre européen universitaire, 1967

GENEVOIS, B., 'Responsabilité de la puissance publique', AJDA, 1984, 396

GENEVOIS, B., 'Entretien avec le Président de la Cour constitutionnelle italienne: Renato Granata', www.conseil-constitutionnel.fr/cahiers/ccc6/entretien.htm

GENEVOIS, B., 'Le Traité sur l'Union européenne et la Constitution', RFDA, 1992, 373

GERKRATH, J., 'L'arrêt du Bundesverfassungsgericht du 22 mars 1995 sur la directive 'télévision sans frontières'. Les difficultés de la répartition des compétences entre trois niveaux de législation', RTDeur, 1995, 539

GERKRATH, J., L'émergence d'un droit constitutionnel pour l'Europe, Brussels, Editions de l'Université de Bruxelles, 1997

GIMENO VERDEJO, C., 'L'Espagne', in La condition du droit communautaire dans le droit des Etats membres. Primauté et mise en oeuvre, cliché, CJCE, Division recherche et documentation, Luxembourg, 1994, 59

GOFFIN, L., 'A propos des principes régissant la responsabilité non contractuelle des États membres en cas de violation du droit communautaire', CDE, 1997, 531

GOHIN, O., 'La Constitution française et le droit d'origine externe', RFDA, 1999, 77

GOLDSWORTHY, J., The Sovereignty of Parliament. History and Philosophy, Oxford, Clarendon Press, 1999

GOLL, U. and KENNTNER, M., 'Brauchen wir ein Europäisches Kompetenzgericht? Vorschlage zur Sicherung der mitgliedstaatlichen Zuständigkeiten', EuZW, 2002, 101

GOLUB, J., 'The Politics of Judicial Discretion: Rethinking the Interaction between National Courts and the European Court of Justice', 19 West European Politics, 1996, 360

GRABITZ, E., 'Liability for Legislative Acts', in Non-contractual Liability of the European Communities, H.G. Schermers, T. Heukels and Ph. Mead (eds), Dordrecht, Martinus Nijhoff, 1988, 1

GRAVELLS, N.P., 'Disapplying an Act of Parliament pending a Preliminary Ruling: Constitutional Enormity or Community Law Right?', PL, 1989, 568

GRAVELLS, N.P., 'Part II of the Merchant Shipping Act 1988: A Sufficiently Serious Breach of European Community Law?', PL, 1998, 8

GREEN, N. and BARAV, A., 'Damages in National Courts for Breach of Community Law', YEL, 1986, 55

GRÉVISSE, F. and BONICHOT, J.-CL., 'Les incidences du droit communautaire sur l'organisation et l'exercice de la fonction juridictionnelle dans les États membres', in L'Europe et le droit, Mélanges Jean Boulouis, Paris, Dalloz, 1991, 297

GREWE, C. and RUIZ FABRI, H., Droits constitutionnels européens, Paris, PUF, 1995

GREWE, C., 'Le "traité de paix" avec la Cour de Luxembourg: l'arrêt de la Cour constitutionnelle allemande du 7 juin 2000 relatif au règlement du marché de la banane', 37 RTDeur, 2001, 1

GRILLER, S., 'Judicial Enforceability of WTO Law in the European Union. Annotation to Case C-146/96 Portugal v Council', JIEL, 2000, 441

GRIMM, D., 'Does Europe Need a Constitution?', 1 ELJ, 1995, 282

GRIMM, D., ' La Cour européenne de justice et les Juridictions nationales, vues sous l'angle du droit constitutionnel allemand. Situation après la 'Décision Maastricht' de la Cour Constitutionnelle fédérale d'Allemagne', drawn up for the 1997 Paris Conference of Constitutional Courts, www.conseil-constitutionnel. fr/cahiers/ccc4/ccc4grim.htm

GUASTINI, R., 'La primauté du droit communautaire: une révision tacite de la Constitution italienne', www.conseil-constitutionnel.fr/cahiers/ccc9/ guastini.htm

GUILLAUME, G., 'The Work of the Committee on International Law in International Courts of the International Law Association', International Law FORUM du droit international, 2001, 34

HABERMAS, J., 'Remarks on Dieter Grimm's 'Does Europe Need a Constitution'', 1 ELJ, 1995, 303

HAGUENAU, C., L'application effective du droit communautaire en droit interne, Bruxelles, Bruylant, 1995

HAILBRONNER, K., 'European Immigration and Asylum Law under the Amsterdam Treaty', 35 CMLRev, 1998, 1047

HANF, D., 'Le jugement de la Cour constitutionnelle fédérale allemande sur la constitutionnalité du Traité de Maastricht', RTDE, 1994, 391

HARCK, S., and PALMER OLSEN, H., 'Decision concerning the Maastricht Treaty', AJIL, 1999, 209

HARHOFF, F., 'Danemark', in L'intégration du droit international et communautaire dans l'ordre juridique national, P.M. Eisemann (ed), The Hague, Kluwer Law International, 1996

HARMSEN, R., 'National Responsibility for European Community Acts Under the Eruopean Convention on Human Rights: Recasting the Accession Debate', 7 EPL, 2001, 625

HARTKAMP, A.S., 'On European Freedoms and National Mandatory Rules: The Dutch Judiciary and the European Convention on Human Rights', 1 ERPL, 2000, 111

HARTLEY, T.C., 'The Community Legal Order: A British View', in Towards a New Constitution for the European Union? The Intergovernmental Conference 1996, J.-D. Mouton and Th. Stein (eds), Köln, 1997, 57

HARTLEY, T.C., Constitutional Problems of the European Union, Oxford, Hart Publishing, 1999

HASSELBACH, K., 'Der Voorrang des Gemeinschaftsrechts vor dem nationalen Verfassungsrecht nach dem Vertrag von Amsterdam', 52 JZ, 1997, 942

HAYOIT DE TERMICOURT, R., 'Conflict tussen het verdrag en de interne wet', mercuriale uitgesproken op de plechtige openingszitting van het Hof van Cassatie op 2 september 1963, RW, 1963, 73

HAYOIT DE TERMICOURT, R., 'Le conflit traité-loi interne', mercuriale 1963, JT, 1963, 481

HECQUARD-THERON, 'La notion d'État en droit communautaire', 26 RTDeur, 1990, 693

HEINTZEN, M., 'Die "Herrschaft" über die Europäische Gemeinschaftsverträge – Bundesverfassungsgericht und Europäischer Gerichtshof auf Konfliktkurs?', AÖR, 1994, 564

HENNEKENS, H.PH.J.A.M., Overheidsaansprakelijkheid op de weegschaal, Deventer, W.E.J. Tjeenk Willink, 2001

HERDEGEN, M., 'Maastricht and the German Constitutional Court: Constitutional Restraints for an "Ever Closer Union"', 31 CMLRev, 1994, 235

HERDEGEN, M., 'After the TV Judgment of the German Constitutional Court: Decision-making within the EU Council and the German Länder', 32 CMLRev, 1995, 1369

HERINGA, A.W., 'Terug naar af: waarom het begrip een ieder verbindende bepalingen van verdragen slechts tot verwarring leidt', Staatkundig Jaarboek, 1985

HERINGA, A.W., 'De verdragen van Maastricht in strijd met de Nederlandse Grondwet. Goedkeuring met twee derde meerderheid?', NJB, 1992, 749

HERVOUET, F., 'Politique jurisprudentielle de la Cour de Justice et des jurisdictions nationales. Réception du droit communautaire par le droit interne des États', RDP, 1992, 1257

HIGGINS, R., 'Dualism in the Face of a Changing Legal Culture', in Judicial review in International Perspective. Liber Amicorum in Honour of Lord Slynn of Hadley, Vol II, M. Andenas and D. Fairgrieve (eds), The Hague, Kluwer Law International, 2000, 9

HINS, A.W. and DE REEDE, J.L., 'Grondrechten, Europese integratie en nationale soevereiniteit', in Europese Unie en nationale soevereiniteit, L.F.M. Besselink et al. (eds), Staatsrechtconferentie 1997, Deventer, WEJ Tjeenk Willink, 1997, 1

HINSON, CHR. and DOWNES, T., 'Making Sense of Rights: Community Rights in EC Law', 24 ELR, 1999, 121

HINTON, E.F., 'Strengthening the Effectiveness of Community Law: Direct Effect, Article 5 EC and the European Court of Justice', 31 NYJILP, 1999, 307

HIRSCH, G., 'Europäischer Gerichtshof und Bundesverfassungsgericht – Kooperation oder Konfrontation', NJW, 1996, 2457

HØEGH, K.,' The Danish Maastricht Judgment', ELR, 1999, 80

HOFFMANN, L., 'The Convention on the Future of Europe – Thoughts on the Convention – Model', Jean Monnet Working Paper 11/02

HOFMANN, R., 'Der Oberste Gerichtshof Dänemarks und die europäische Integration', EuGRZ, 1999, 1

HOGAN, G. and WHELAN, A., Ireland and the European Union: constitutional and statutory texts and commentary, London, Sweet & Maxwell, 1995

HOGAN, G., 'The implementation of European Union Law in Ireland: The Meagher case and the democratic deficit', 1 Irish Journal of European Law, 1994, 190

HOGAN, G., 'The Meagher Case and the Executive Implementation of European Directives in Ireland', 2 MJ, 1995, 174

HOGAN, G. and WHYTE, G., Kelly's The Irish Constitution, 3rd edn, London, Butterworths, 1997

HOGAN, G., 'The Nice Treaty and the Irish Constitution', EPL, 2001, 565

HOOD PHILIPS, O., 'Has the "incoming tide" reached the Palace of Westminster?', 95 LQR, 1979, 167

Lord Hope of Craighead, 'The Human Rights Act 1998 – The Task of the Judges', in Judicial Review in International Perspective. Liber Amicorum in Honour of Lord Slynn of Hadley, Vol II, The Hague, Kluwer Law International, 2000, 415

HOPT, K., 'Report on Recent German Decisions'. 4 CMLRev, 1966, 93

HOSKINS, M., 'Tilting the Balance: Supremacy and National Procedural Rules' 21 ELR, 1996, 365

HOSKINS, M., 'Rebirth of the Innominate Tort?', in New Directions in European Public Law, J. Beatson and T. Tridimas (eds), Oxford, Hart Publishing, 1998, 91

ILIOPOULOS-STRANGAS, J., 'Le droit constitutionnel national et l'intégration européenne', in Le droit constitutionnel national et l'intégration européenne. 17. FIDE Kongress, Berlin, 1996, 120

ISAAC, G., Droit communautaire général, Paris, Masson, 1994

JACKSON, J.H., 'Status of Treaties in Domestic Legal Systems: A Policy Analysis', 86 AJIL, 1992, 310

JACOBS, F., 'Damages for breach of Article 86 EEC', ELR, 1983, 353

JACOBS, F.G., 'Enforcing Community Rights and Obligations in National Courts: Striking the Balance', in J. Lonbay and A. Biondi (eds), Remedies for Breach of EC Law, Chichester, Wiley, 1997, 25

JACOBS F.G. and ROBERTS, S. (eds), The Effect of Treaties in Domestic Law, London, Sweet & Maxwell, 1987

JACOBS, F., 'Is the Court of Justice of the European Communities a Constitutional Court?', in Constitutional Adjudication in the European Community and National law, Essays for the Hon. Mr Justice T.F. O'Higgins, D. Curtin and D. O'Keeffe (eds), Dublin, Butterworth (Ireland) Ltd, 1992, 25

F.G. JACOBS, 'The Community Legal Order – A Constitutional Order? A Perspective from the European Court of Justice', in Towards a New Constitution for the European Union? The Intergovernmental Conference 1996, J.-D. Mouton and Th. Stein (eds), Köln, 1997, 31

JACOBS, F., 'Enforcing Community Rights and Obligations in National Courts: Striking the Balance', in M. Lonbay and A. Biondi (eds), Remedies for Breach of EC Law, Chichester, Wiley, 1997, 25

JACOBS, F.G., 'Human Rights in the European Union: the Role of the Court of Justice', 26 ELR, 2001, 331

JACONELLI, J., 'Constitutional Review and Section 2(4) of the European Communities Act 1972', 28 ICLQ, 1979, 65

JACQUÉ, J.-P., 'Cours général de droit communautaire', Collected Courses of the Academy of European Law, Vol I, Book I, 1992, 49

JANS, J.H. et al., Inleiding tot het Europees bestuursrecht, 2de druk, Ars Aequi Libri, Utrecht, 2002

JARVIS, M., The Application of EC Law by National Courts: The Free Movement of Goods, Oxford, Clarendon Press, 1998

JENSEN, J.A., 'Human Rights in Danish Law', 7 EPL, 2001, 1

JONES, 'The Legal Nature of the European Community: A Jurisprudential Model Using H.L.A. Hart's Model of Law and Legal System', 17 Cornell International Law Journal, 1984, 1

JOWELL, J. and OLIVER, D., The Changing Constitution, Oxford, OUP, 4th edn, 2000

KELSEN, H., 'Les rapports de système entre droit interne et le droit international public', 14 Hague Recueil des cours, 1926-IV, 227

KILPATRICK, C., 'The Future of Remedies in Europe', in The Future of Remedies in Europe, Oxford, Hart Publishing, 2000

KILPATRICK, C., Novitz, T. and Skidmore, P. (eds), The Future of Remedies in Europe, Oxford, Hart Publishing, 2000

KILPATRICK, C., 'Turning Remedies Around: A Sectoral Analysis of the Court of Justice', in The European Court of Justice, G. de Búrca and J.H.H. Weiler (eds), Oxford, OUP, 2001, 143

KIRCHHOF, P., 'Deutsches Verfassungsrecht und Europäisches Gemeinschaftsrecht', EuR, 1991, 11

KIRCHHOF, P., in Handbuch des Staatsrecht der Bundesrepublik Deutschland, P. Kirchhof and J. Isensee (eds), 1993, 855

KIRCHHOF, P., 'Das Maastricht-Urteil des Bundesverfassungsgerichts', in Der Staatenverbund der Europäischen Union, P. Hommelhoff and P. Kirchhof (eds), Heidelberg, Müller, 1994

KIRCHHOF, P., 'The Balance of Powers Between National and European Institutions', 3 ELJ, 1999, 225

KNIPPENBERG, E.T.C., De Senaat. Rechtsvergelijkend onderzoek naar het House of Lords, de Sénat, de Eerste Kamer en de Bundesrat, De Haag, Sdu, 2002

KÖCK, H.F., 'EU Law and National Constitutions – the Austrian Case', report for the XXth FIDE Congress, London, 2002

KOEGLER, K.S., 'Ireland's Abortion Information Act of 1995', 29 Vanderbilt J of Transnational L, 1996, 1117

KOEKKOEK, A.K. (ed), Bijdragen aan een Europese Grondwet, Staatsrechtconferentie 2000, Deventer, WEJ Tjeenk Willink, 2000

KOKOTT, J., 'Deutschland im Rahmen der Europäischen Union. Zum Vertrag von Maastricht', AÖR, 1994, 207

KOKOTT, J., 'German Constitutional Jurisprudence and European Integration', EPL, 1996, 237, and 413

KOKOTT, J., 'Report on Germany', in The European Court and National Courts – Doctrine and Jurisprudence. Legal Change in Its Social Context, A.-M. Slaughter, A. Stone Sweet and J.H.H. Weiler (eds), Oxford, Hart Publishing, 1998, 77

KOKOTT, J., 'Federal States in Federal Europe: The German Länder and Problems of European Integration', in National Constitutions in the Era of Integration, A. Jyränki (ed), The Hague, Kluwer International Law, 1999, 175

KÖNING, D., 'Das Urteil des Bundesverfassungsgerichts zum Vertrag von Maastricht – Ein Stolperstein auf dem Weg in die europäische Integration?', ZaöVR, 1994, 17

KOOPMANS, T., 'Liability of Member States for legislative Omissions. The consequences of Francovich for national law', presentation at the Conference on The Liability of Member States for legislative Omissions – The Case Law of the Court of Justice following the Francovich Judgment, Trier, ERA, 1996, resumé on file with the author

KOOPMANS, T., 'The theory of interpretation and the Court of Justice', in Judicial Review in European Union Law. Liber Amicorum in Honour of Lord Slynn of Hadley, D. O'Keeffe and A. Bavasso (eds), The Hague, Kluwer Law International, 2000, 45

KOPELMANAS, L., 'La théorie du dédoublement fonctionnel et son utilisation pour la solution du problème dit des conflits des lois', in La technique et les principes du droit public, Etudes en l'honneur de Georges Scelle, Paris, 1950, 753

KORTMANN, C.A.J.M., 'European Union Law and National Constitutions: The Netherlands', XXth FIDE Congress, London, 2002

KORTMANN, S.C.J.J., 'Wie betaalt de rekening?', NJB, 1993, 921

KORTMANN, S.C.J.J., KORTMANN. J.S. and KORTMANN, L.P., 'Nogmaals de aansprake-lijkheid van de staat voor schade voortvloeiende uit rechterlijke uitspraken', in Grensverleggend Staatsrecht. Opstellen aangeboden aan C.A.J.M. Kortmann, Deventer, Kluwer, 2001, 207

KOVAR, R., 'La primauté du droit communautaire sur la loi française', RTDeur, 1975, 636

KOVAR, R., 'La contribution de la Cour de justice à l'édification de l'ordre juridique communautaire', Collected Courses of the Academy of European Law, 1993, Vol. IV Book 1, 15

KOVAR, R., 'Ordre juridique communautaire', in Juris-Classeur Europe, fasc. 431

KOVAR, R., 'The Relationship between Community law and national law', in Thirty Years of Community Law, 109

KOVAR, R., 'Le Conseil d'État et le droit communautaire: des progrès mais peut mieux faire', D. 1992, chron., 207

KULOVESI, K., 'International Relations in the New "Constitution of Finland"', 69 Nordic Journal of International Law, 2000, 513

KUMM, M., 'Who is the Final Arbiter of Constitutionality in Europe?: Three Conceptions of the Relationship Between the German Federal Constitutional Court and the European Court of Justice', 36 CMLRev, 1999, 351

KUTSCHER, H., 'Community Law and the National Judge', LQR, 1973, 487

KVJATKOVSKI, 'What is an 'Emanation of the State'? An Educated Guess', 3 EPL, 1997, 329

LACHAUME, J.-F., 'Une victoire de l'ordre juridique communautaire: l'arrêt Nicolo consacrant la supériorité des traités sur les lois postérieures', RMC, 1990, 384

LAFERRIÈRE, E., Traité de la juridiction administrative et des recours contentieux, Berger-Levrault, 1887

LAGRANGE, M., 'La primauté du droit communautaire sur le droit national', in Droit communautaire et droit national, Semaine de Bruges, Bruges, 1965, 22

LA PERGOLA, A. and DEL DUCA, P., 'Community law, International law and the Italian Constitution', AJIL, 1985, 598

LAVRANOS, N., 'Die Rechtswirkung von WTO panel reports im Europäischen Gemeinschaftsrecht sowie im deutschen Verfassungsrecht', EuR, 1999, 289

LAWSON, R., 'Confusion and Conflict? Divergent Interpretations of the European Convention on Human Rights in Strasbourg and Luxembourg', in The Dynamics of the Protection of Human Rights in Europe. Essays in Honour of H.G. Schermers, Vol III, R. Lawson and M. de Bloijs (eds), Dordrecht, Nijhoff, 1994, 219

LAWSON, R.A., Het EVRM en de Europese Gemeenschappen. Bouwstenen voor een aansprakelijkheidsregime voor het optreden van internationale organisaties, Deventer, Kluwer, 1999

LECOURT, R., 'Quel eût été le droit des Communautés sans les arrêts de 1963 et 1964?', in L'Europe et le droit, Mélanges en hommage de Jean Boulouis, Paris, Dalloz, 1991, 349

LECOURT, R., L'Europe des juges, Brussels, 1976

LECOURT, R., Le juge devant le Marché commun, Genève, Institut Universitaire de Hautes Études Internationales, 1970

LEE, I.B., 'In Search of a Theory of State Liability in the European Union', Harvard Jean Monnet Working Paper 9/99

LEHMANN, W., 'Attribution of Powers and Dispute Resolution in Selected Federal Systems', European Parliament Working Paper AFCO 103 EN

LEJEUNE, Y. and BROUWERS, PH., 'La Cour d'arbitrage face au controle de la constitutionnalité des traités', JT, 1992, 672

LEMMENS, P., 'The impact of Article 6, § 1, of the European Convention on Human Rights on the proceedings before the Belgian Council of State, available on the website of the Association of Councils of State, www.raadvst-consetat.be/colloquia/2000/Belgium.pdf

LEMMENS, P., 'The Relation between the Charter of Fundamental Rights of the European Union and the European Convention on Human Rights – Substantive Aspects', 8 MJ, 2001, 49

LENAERTS, K., 'Constitutionalism and the many Faces of Federalism', 38 AJCL, 1990, 205

LENAERTS, K. and ARTS, D., Europees Procesrecht, Antwerpen, Maklu, 1995

LENAERTS, K. and VAN NUFFEL, P., Europees recht in hoofdlijnen, Antwerpen, Maklu, 1995

LENAERTS, K. and DE SMIJTER, E., 'The European Union as an Actor under International Law', YEL, 1999, 95

LENAERTS, K., 'Fundamental Rights in the European Union', 25 ELR, 2000, 575

LENAERTS, K. and DE SMIJTER, E., 'A "Bill of Rights" for the European Union', 38 CMLRev, 2001, 273

LENAERTS, K. and DESOMER, M., 'New Models of Constitution-making in Europe: The Quest for Legitimacy', 39 CMLRev, 2002, 1217

LENZ, C.O. and GRILL, G., 'Zum Verhältnis zwischen dem Bundesfinanzhof und dem Gerichtshof der Europäischen Gemeinschaften', in Steuerrecht – Verfassungsrecht – Finanzpolitik – Festschrift für Franz Klein, P. Kirchhof et al. (eds), Köln, Otto Schmidt Verlag, 1994, 103

LEROY, M., 'La responsabilité de l'État législateur', JT, 1978, 321

LEROY, M., 'Responsabilité des pouvoirs public du chef de méconnaissance des normes supérieures de droit national par un pouvoir législatif', in La responsabilité des pouvoirs publics, Bruxelles, Bruylant, 1991, 299

LEVER, J., 'Aspects of Liability for the State and Public Bodies in English and Community Law', in European Community Law in the English Courts, M. Andenas and F. Jacobs (eds), Oxford, Clarendon Press, 1998, 67

LIISBERG, J.B., 'Does the EU Charter of Fundamental Rights Threaten the Supremacy of Community Law? Article 53 of the Charter: A Fountain of Law or just an Inkblot?', Harvard Jean Monnet Working Paper 04/01

LIISBERG, J.B., 'Does the EU Charter of Fundamental Rights Threaten the Supremacy of Community Law?', 38 CMLRev, 2001, 1171

LIMBACH, J., 'The Effects of the Jurisdiction of the German Federal Constitutional Court' EUI Distinguished Lectures of the Law Department, 99/5

LIMBACH, J., 'Das Bundesverfassungsgericht als politischer Machtsfaktor', Humboldt Forum Recht, 1996, Beitrag 12, www.rewi.hu-berlin.de/HFR/12-1996

LIMBACH, J., 'Die Kooperation der Gerichte in der zukünftigen europäischen Grundrechtsarchitektur', at www.rewi.hu-berlin.de

LIÑÁN NOGUERAS, D.J. and ROLDÁN BARBERO, J., 'The Judicial Application of Community Law in Spain', 30 CMLRev, 1993, 1135

LONBAY, J. and BIONDI, A., Remedies for Breach of EC Law, Chichester, Wiley, 1997

LÓPEZ CASTILLO, A. and POLAKIEWICZ, J., 'Verfassung und Gemeinschaftsrecht in Spanien. Zur Maastricht-Erklärung des Spanischen Verfassungsgerichts', EuGRZ, 1993, 277

Lord Lester of Hyrne Hill, 'Human Rights and the British Constitution', in The Changing Constitution, J. Jowell and D. Oliver (eds), Oxford, OUP, 2000, 89

Lord Lester of Herne Hill, 'Developing Constitutional Principles of Public Law', PL, 2001, 684

LOUIS, J.-V., 'La primauté, une valuer relative', CDE, 1995, 22

LOUIS, J.-V., 'La primauté du droit international et du droit communautaire après l'arrêt 'Le Ski'', in Mélanges F. Dehousse, Bruxelles, 1979, 237

LOUIS, J.-V., 'Le droit belge et l'ordre juridique international', JT, 1972, 437

LUCHAIRE, F., 'L'Union européenne et la Constitution', RDP, 1992, 589, 933, 956 and 1587

LUCHAIRE, F., 'Le Conseil constitutionnel et la souveraineté nationale', RDP, 1991, 1499

LUCIANI, M., 'La Constitution italienne et les obstacles à l'intégration européenne', RFDC, 1990, 663

LUCIANI, M., 'La Costituzione italiana e gli ostacoli all'integrazione europea', Politica del diritto, 1992, 557

MACCORMICK, N., Questioning Sovereignty. Law, State and Nation in the European Commonwealth, Oxford, OUP, 1999

MAESTRIPIERI, C., 'The Application of Community Law in Italy in 1973', CMLRev, 1975, 431

MAHER, I., 'Community law in the National Legal Order: A Systems Analysis', JCMS, 1998, 238

MALANCZUK, P., Akehurst's Modern Introduction to International Law, 7th revised edn, London, Routledge, 1997

MALFERRARI, L., 'State Liability for Violation of EC Law in Italy: The Reaction of the Corte di Cassazione to Francovich and Future Prospects in Lights of its Decision of July 22, 1999, No. 500', ZaORV, 1999, 809

MANCINI, G.F., 'The Making of a Constitution for Europe', CMLRev, 1989, 595

MANCINI, G.F. and KEELING, D.T., 'From CILFIT to ERT: the Constitutional Challenge facing the European Court', 11 YBEL, 1991, 1

MANCINI, G.F., Democracy and Constitutionalism in the European Union. Collected Essays, Oxford, Hart Publishing, 2000

MANGAS MARTÍN, A., 'Le droit constitutionnel espagnol et l'intégration européenne', in Le droit constitutionnel national et l'intégration européenne, 17. FIDE Kongress, Berlin, 1996, 206

MANIN, PH., 'The Nicolo case of the Conseil d'Etat: French constitutional law and the Supreme Administrative Court's Acceptance of the Primacy of Community Law over Subsequent National Statute Law', CMLRev, 1991, 499

MANIN, PH., 'L'invocabilité des directives: Quelques interrogations', RTDeur, 1990, 669

MANN, C.J., The Function of Judicial Decision in European Economic Integration, The Hague, Nijhoff, 1972

MARSHALL, G., 'The Maastricht Proceedings', PL, 1993, 402

MATHIEU, L., 'L'adhésion de la Communauté à la CDEH: un problème de compétence ou un problème de soumission?', RMUE, 1998, 31

MATHIEU, B. and VERPEAUX, M., 'Á propos de l'arrêt du Conseil d'Etat du 30 octobre 1998, Sarran et autres: le point de vue du constitutionnaliste', RFDA, 1999, 67

Bibliography

MATTHEWS, M.H., 'Injunctions, Interim Relief and Proceedings against Crown Servants', 8 Oxford Journal of Legal Studies, 1988, 154

MAUGÜÉ, CHR., 'L'arrêt Sarran, entre apparance et réalité', www.conseil-constitutionnel.fr/cahiers/ccc7/maugue.htm;

MAYER, F., 'Grundrechtsschutz gegen europäische Rechtsakte durch das BverfG: Zur Verfassungsmässigkeit der Bananenmarktordnung', EuZW, 2000, 685;

MAYER, F.C., 'Die drei Dimensionen der Europäischen Kompetenzdebatte', ZaöRV, 2001, 577

McCAFFREY, E., 'Equal Treatment, Unequal Retirement Ages and the Francovich Claim', 25 Industrial Law Journal, 1996, 144

McCRUDDEN, CHR., 'The Future of the EU Charter of Fundamental Rights', Jean Monnet Working Paper, 10/01

McMAHON and MURPHY, European Community Law in Ireland, Dublin, Round Hall, 1989

MEIER, G., 'Krieg der Richter – Was nun?', RIW, 1985, 748

MEIJ, A.W.H., 'Europese rechtspraak in de Nederlandse rechtspleging: impressies uit Den Haag en Luxemburg', Preadvies, in Internationale rechtspraak in de Nederlandse rechtsorde, Handelingen van de NJV, Deventer, Tjeenk Willink, 1999-I, 133

MEIJ, A.W.H., 'Guest Editorial: Architects or Judges? Some Comments in relation to the Current Debate', 37 CMLRev, 2000, 1039

MEINDL, T., 'Le controle de constitutionnalité des actes de droit communautaire dérivé en France. La possibilité d'une jurisprudence Solange II', RDP, 1997, 1665

MELCHIOR, M. and VANDERNOOT, P., 'Controle de constitutionnalité et droit communautaire dérivé', RBDC, 1998, 7

MENGOZZI, P. and DEL DUCA, P., European Community Law from Common Market to European Union, Dordrecht, Nijhoff, 1992

MEROLA, M. and BERETTA, M., 'Le droit italien', in La responsabilité des États membres en cas de violation du droit communautaire. Études de droit communautaire et de droit national comparé, G. Vandersanden and M. Dony (eds), Bruxelles, Bruylant, 1997, 289

MERTEN, D., (ed), Föderalismus und Europäische Gemeinschaften unter besondere Berücksichtigung von Umwelt und Gesundheit, Kultur und Bindung, Berlin, Duncker & Humblot, 1990

MERTENS DE WILMARS, J., 'De directe werking van het Europese recht', SEW, 1969, 66

MERTENS DE WILMARS, J., 'L'efficacité des différentes techniques nationales de protection juridique contre les violations du droit communautaire par les autorités nationales et les particuliers', CDE, 1981, 379

MISCHO, J., 'Un róle nouveau pour la Cour de justice?', RMC, 1990, 681

MITCHELL, J.D.B., 'The Sovereignty of Parliament andCommunity Law: The Stumbling Block that isn't There', International Affairs, 1979, 33

MITCHELL, J.D.B., Kuipers, S.A. and Gall, B., 'Constitutional Aspects of the Treaty and Legislation relating to British Membership', CMLRev, 1972, 134

MONAR, J., 'Justice and Home Affairs in the Treaty of Amsterdam: Reform at the Price of Fragmentation', ELR, 1998, 320

MONTIJN-SWINKELS, J.C.M. et. al., 'The imposition of sanctions for breaches of Community law. Report of the Netherlands Association for European Law for the FIDE Congress 1992', SEW, 1992, 256

MOREAU, J., 'L'influence du développement de la construction européenne sur le droit français de la responsabilité de la puissance publique', in L'Europe et le droit. Mélanges offertes à Jean Boulouis, Paris, Dalloz, 1991, 409

MOREAU, J., 'Internationalisation du droit administratif français et déclin de l'acte du gouvernement', in L'internationalisation du droit. Mélanges en honneur de Yvon Loussouarn, Paris, 1994, 293

MORGENSTERN, F., 'Judicial Practice and the Supremacy of International law', 27 BYBIL, 1950, 42

MORTELMANS, K., 'The relationship between the Treaty rules and Community measures for the Establishment and Functioning of the Internal Market. Towards a Concordance Rule', 39 CMLRev, 2002, 1303

MORTON, F.L., 'Judicial Review in France: A Comparative Analysis', AJCL, 1988, 89

MOSLER,H., Das Völkerrecht in der Praxis der deutsche Gerichte, Karlsruhe, 1957

MÜNCH, F., 'Compétence des juridictions nationales. Leur tâche dans l'application du droit communautaire', in Droit communautaire et droit national, Semaine de Bruges, N. Catalano et al. (eds), Bruges, De Tempel, 1965, 173

MURPHY, F., 'Maastricht: Implementation in Ireland', 19 ELR, 1994, 94

NAÔMÉ, C., 'Les relations entre le droit international et le droit interne belge après l'arrêt de la Cour d'arbitrage du 16 octobre 1991', RDIC, 1994, 24

NEIL, P., The European Court of Justice: A Case Study in Judicial Activism, London, European Policy Forum, 1995

NERI, S., 'Le juge italien et le droit communautaire', in Le juge national et le droit communautaire, A.M. Donner et al. (eds), Leyde, Sijthoff, 1966, 77

NERI, S., 'Le droit communautaire et l'ordre constitutionnel italien', CDE, 1966, 363

NETTESHEIM, M., 'Gemeinschaftsrechtliche Vorgaben für das deutsche Staatshaftungsrecht', DÖV, 1992, 999

NETTESHEIM, M., 'Art. 23 GG, nationale Grundrechte und EU-Recht', NJW, 1995, 2083

NEVILLE BROWN, L. and KENNEDY, T., The Court of Justice of the European Communities, London, Sweet & Maxwell, 5th edn, 2000

NICOLAYSEN, G., 'Tabakrauch, Gemeinschaftsrecht und Grundgesetz. Zum BVerfG-Beschluß vom 12.5.1989', EuR, 1989, 215

NOLLKAEMPER, A., 'The Direct Effect of Public International Law', in Direct Effect. Rethinking a Classic of EC Legal Doctrine, J.M. Prinssen and A. Schrauwen (eds), Groningen, Europa Law Publishing, 2002, 157

O'KEEFFE, D., 'Appeals Against an Order to Refer under Article 177 of the EEC Treaty', ELR, 1984, 87

O'KEEFFE, D., 'Can the Leopard Change its Spots? Visas, Immigration and Asylum – Following Amsterdam, in Legal Issues of the Amsterdam Treaty, D. O'Keeffe and P. Twomey (eds), Oxford, Hart Publishing, 1999, 271

O'KEEFFE, D. and BAVASSO, A. (eds), Judicial Review in European Union Law. Liber Amicorum in Honour of Lord Slynn of Hadley, The Hague, Kluwer Law International, 2000

OLIVER, P., 'Enforcing Community rights in the English Courts', MLR, 1987, 881

OLIVER, P., 'Interim Measures: Some Recent Developments', CMLRev, 1992, 7

OLIVER, P., 'The French Constitution and the Treaty of Maastricht', 43 ICLQ, 1994, 1

Bibliography

OLIVER, P., 'State Liability in Damages following Factortame III: A Remedy Seen in Context', in New Directions in European Public Law, J. Beatson and T. Tridimas (eds), Oxford, Hart Publishing, 1998, 49

O'NEILL, A., Decisions of the European Court of Justice and their Constitutional Implications, London Butterworths, 1994

O'NEILL, A., 'Fundamental Rights and the Constitutional Supremacy of Community law in the United Kingdom after Devolution and the Human Rights Act', PL, 2002, 724

ONIDA, V., 'L'état de la jurisprudence constitutionnelle sur les rapports entre le système juridique national et le système juridique communautaire: "harmonie dans la diversité" et questions ouvertes', paper on file with the author, also published in V. Onida, '"Ärmonia tra diversi" e problemi aperti. La giurisprudenza costituzionale sui rapporti tra ordinamento interno e ordinamento comunitario', Quaderni costituzionali, 2002, 549

OPPENHEIMER, A., The Relationship Between European Community Law and National Law: The Cases, Cambridge, CUP, 1994

OSSENBÜHL, F., 'Der gemeinschaftsrechtliche Staatshaftungsanspruch', DVBl, 1992, 993

OSSENBÜHL, F., 'Staatshaftung zwischen Europarecht und nationalem Recht', in Festschrift für Everling, O. Due, M. Lutter and J. Schwarze (eds), Baden Baden, Nomos, 1995, 1031

OSSENBÜHL, F., Staatshaftungsrecht, 5th edn München, Beck, 1998

PACHE, E., 'Das Ende der Bananenmarktordnung?', EuR, 1995, 95

PAPADIAS, L., 'Interim Protection under Community Law Before the National Courts: The Right to a Judge with Jurisdiction to Grant Interim Relief', LIEI, 1994, 153

PAPIER, H.-J., 'Staatshaftung', in Handbuch des Staatsrechts der Bundesrepublik Deutschlands, J. Isensee and P. Kirchhof (eds), Vol VI, 1989, 1353

PASSELECQ, O. et al., 'Les constitutions nationales face au droit européen. Conférence-débat, 12 juin 1996', RFDC, 1996, 675

PEDAIN, A., 'A hollow victory: The ECJ rules on direct effect of freedom of establishment provisions in Europe Agreements', CLJ, 2002, 284

PEDAIN, A., '"With or without me": The ECJ adopts a pose of studied neutrality towards EU enlargement', 51 ICLQ, 2002, 981

PEERS, S., 'Taking Supremacy Seriously', 23 ELR, 1998, 146

PEERS, S., 'Who's Judging the Watchmen? The Judicial System of the "Area of Freedom Security and Justice"', YEL, 1998, 337

PEERS, S., 'Human Rights and the Third Pillar', in The EU and Human Rights, Ph. Alston (ed), Oxford, OUP, 1999, 167

PEERS, S., 'Fundamental Right or Political Whim? WTO Law and the European Court of Justice', in The EU and the WTO. Legal and Constitutional Issues, G. de Búrca and J. Scott (eds), Oxford, Hart Publishing, 2001, 111

PELCKMANS, J., Sie Dhian Ho, M and Limonard, B. (eds), Nederland en de Europese grondwet, Amsterdam, Amsterdam University Press, 2003

PESCATORE, P., 'La Cour en tent que juridiction fédérale et constitutionnelle', in Zehh Jahre Rechtsprechuhg des EuGH, Kölner Schriften zum Europarecht, Band 1, 1965, 520

PESCATORE, P., 'L'application directe des traités européens par les juridictions nationales: la jurisprudence nationale', RTDeur, 1969, 697.

PESCATORE, P, 'International law and Community Law – A Comparative Analysis', 7 CMLRev, 1970, 167

PESCATORE, P., 'De werkzaamheden van de "juridische groep" bij de onderhandelingen over de verdragen van Rome', Studia Diplomatica, 1981, 167

PESCATORE, P., 'The Doctrine of "Direct Effect": An Infant Disease of Community Law', ELR, 1983, 155

PERNICE, I., 'Multilevel Constitutionalism and the Treaty of Amsterdam: European Constitution-making Revisited?', 36 CMLRev, 1999, 703

PERNICE, I., 'De la constitution composée de l'Europe', RTDEur, 2000, 623

PERNICE, I. and MAYER, F., 'De la Constitution composée de l'Europe', 36 RTDeur, 2000, 623

PERNICE, I., 'Zur Verfassungsdiskussion in der Europäischen Union', WHI Paper 2/01

PERNICE, I., 'Rethinking the Methods of Dividing and Controlling the Competencies of the Union', paper delivered at the Conference of the Jean Monnet Group on the Future of Europe, Europe 2004, Le Grand Débat, Setting the Agenda and Outlining the Options, available on www.ecsanet.org

PERREAU-SAUSSINE, A., 'A tale of two supremacies, four greengrocers, a fishmonger, and the seeds of a constitutional court', CLJ, 2002, 527

PETERS, A., 'The banans Decision (2000) of the German Federal Constitutional Court: Towards Reconciliation with the European Court of Justice as regards Fundamental Rights Protection In Europe', 43 German Yearbook of International Law, 2000, 276

PETRICCIONE, R.M., 'Supremacy of Community law over national law', ELR, 1986, 320

PHELAN, D.R., 'Right to Life of the Unborn v Promotion of Trade in Services: The European Court of Justice and the Normative Shaping of the European Union', 55 MLR, 1992, 670

PHELAN, D.R. and WHELAN, A., 'National Constitutional Law and European Integration', in Le droit constitutionnel national et l'intégration européenne, 17th FIDE Kongress, Berlin, 1996, 292

PHELAN, D.R., Revolt or Revolution. The Constitutional Boundaries of the European Community, Dublin, Sweet & Maxwell, Round Hall, 1997

PICARD, E., 'Petite exercice pratique de logique juridique. A propos de la décision du Conseil constitutionnel no. 98-399 DC du 5 mai 1998 'Séjour des étrangers et droit d'asile', RFDA, 1998, 620

PIRIS, J.-CL., ' L' Union européenne a't'elle une constitution? Lui en faut'il une?', RTDEur, 1999, 599

PIRIS, J.-CL., 'Does the European Union have a Constitution? Does It Need One?', Harvard Jean Monnet Working Paper, 5/00

PLAZA MARTIN, C., 'Furthering the Effectiveness of EC Directives and the Judicial Protection of Individual Rights Thereunder', 43 ICLQ, 1994, 26

PLÖTNER, J., 'Report on France', in The European Court and National Courts – Doctrine and Jurisprudence. Legal Change in Its Social Context, A.-M. Slaughter et al. (eds), Oxford, Hart Publishing, 1998, 41

PLOUVIER, L., 'L'arrêt de la cour constitutionnelle d'Italie du 22 octobre 1975 dans l'affaire I.C.I.C.', RTDEur, 1976, 271

POIARES MADURO, M., We, The Court. The European Court of Justice and the European Economic Constitution, Oxford, Hart Publishing, 1998

M. POIARES MADURO, 'Europe and the Constitution: What if this is as good as it gets?', ConWEB 5/2000

POIARES MADURO, M., 'EU Law and National Constitutions. Portuguese Report', report for the XXth FIDE Congress, London, 2002

POPELIER, P., 'Ongrondwettige verdragen: de rechtspraak van het Arbitragehof geplaatst in een monistisch tijdsperspectief', RW, 1994–1995, 1076

PRECHAL, S., 'Onrechtmatige (niet) wetgeving: nu procederen!', NJB, 1992, 1138

PRECHAL, S., Directives in European Community Law. A Study of Directives and Their Enforcement in National Courts, Oxford, Clarendon Press, 1995

PRECHAL, S., 'Community Law in National Courts: The Lessons from van Schijndel', 35 CMLRev, 1998, 681

PRECHAL, S., 'Does Direct Effect Still Matter', 37 CMLRev, 2000, 1047

PRECHAL, S., 'Direct Effect Reconsidered, Redefined and Rejected', in Direct Effect. Rethinking a Classic of EC Legal Doctrine, J.M. Prinssen and A. Schrauwen (eds), Groningen, Europa Law Publishing, 2002, 15

POHJOLAINEN, K., 'National Constitutional law and European Integration', in Le droit constitutionnel national et l'intégration européenne. 17 FIDE Kongress, Berlin, 1996, 399

QUESTIAUX, N., 'L'application du droit conventionnel par le Conseil d'état', in L'application du droit international par le juge français, P. Reuter et al. (eds), Paris, PUF, 1972, 63

RASMUSSEN, H., 'The European Court's Acte Clair Strategy in CILFIT', 9 ELR, 1984, 242

RASMUSSEN, H., On Law and Policy in the European Court of Justice: A Comparative Study in Judicial Policymaking, Dordrecht, Nijhoff, 1987

RASMUSSEN, H., 'Remedying the Crumbling Judicial System', 37 CMLRev, 2000, 1071

RASMUSSEN, H., 'Denmark's Maastricht Ratification Case: The Constitutional Dimension', in National Constitutions in the Era of Integration, A. Jyränki (ed), The Hague, Kluwer Law International, 1999, 87

RASMUSSEN, H., 'Confrontation or Peaceful Co-existence? On the Danish Supreme Court's Maastricht Ratification Judgment', in Judicial Review in European Union Law. Liber Amicorum in Honour of Lord Slynn of Hadley, Vol I, D. O'Keeffe and A. Bavasso (eds), The Hague, Kluwer Law International, 2000, 377

RAWLINGS, R., 'Legal Politics: The United Kingdom and Ratification of the Treaty on European Union', PL, 1994, 254 and 367

REESTMAN, J.H., Constitutionele toesting in Frankrijk. De Conseil constitutionnel en de grondwettigheid van wetten en verdragen, Utrecht Ars Aequi Libri, 1996

REICH, N., 'Judge-made "Europe à la carte": Some Remarks on Recent Conflicts between European and German Constitutional Law Provoked by the Banana litigation', 7 EJIL, 1996, 103

REICH, N., 'A European Constitution for Citizens: Reflections on the Rethinking of Union and Community Law', 3 ELJ, 1997, 131

REICH, N., 'Brauchen wir eine Diskussion um eine Europäische Kompetenzgericht?', EuZW, 2002, 257

RESS, G., 'Die Rundfunkfreiheit als Problem der europäischen Integration', ZfRV, 1992, 434

REUTER, P., 'Le droit international et la place du juge français dans l'ordre consti-tutionnel national', in L'application du droit international par le juge français, P. Reuter et al. (eds), Paris, Librairie Armand Colin, 1972, 17

RICHARDS, C., 'Sarran et Levacher: ranking legal norms in the French Republic', ELR, 2000, 192

RICHMOND, C., 'Preserving the Identity Crisis: Autonomy, System and Sovereignty in European law', in Constructing Legal Systems: "European Union" in Legal Theory, N. MacCormick (ed), Dordrecht, Kluwer Academic Publishers, 1997, 47

RIDEAU, J., Droit international et droit interne français, Paris, Librairie Armand Colin, 1971

RIDEAU, J., 'Constitution et droit international dans les Etats membres des Communautés européennes. Réflexions générales et situation française', RFDC, 1990, 259

RIDEAU, J., 'Aspects constitutionnels comparés de l'évolution vers l'Union européenne', in La Constitution et l'Europe, Paris, Montchrestien, 1992, 67

RIDEAU, J., La Constitution et l'Europe, Paris, Montchrestien, 1992

RIDEAU, J., Les États membres de l'Union européenne. Adaptations, mutations, résistances, Paris, LGDJ, 1997

RIDEAU, J. (ed), Le droit au juge dans l'Union européen, Paris, LGDJ, 1998

RIGAUX, A., and SIMON, D., '"Summum jus, summa injuria..." À propos de l'arrêt du Conseil d'État du 3 décembre 2001 SNIP', Europe, April 2002, 6

RINZE, J., 'The role of the European Court of Justice as a Federal Constitutional Court', PL, 1993, 426;

ROBERT, J., 'Constitutional and International Protection of Human Rights: Competing or Complementary Systems? General Report to the IXth Conference of European Constitutional Courts', HRLJ, 1994, 1

ROBERTSON, A., 'Effective Remedies in EEC Law before the House of Lords?', 109 LQR, 1993, 27

RODRIGUEZ IGLESIAS, G.C., 'Der Gerichtshof der Europäischen Gemeinschaften als Verfassungsgericht', EuR, 1992, 225

RODRIGUEZ IGLESIAS, G.C. and PUISSOCHET, J.-P., 'Rapport de la Cour de Justice des Communautés européénnes', report for the conference of constitutional courts on 'Droit communautaire dérivé et droit constitutionnel' organised by the Conseil constitutionnel in 1997, published on www.conseil-constitutionnel.fr/cahiers/ccc4/ccc4aver.htm

ROLIN, H., 'La force obligatoire des traités dans la jurisprudence belge', JT, 1953, 561

ROSS, M., 'Beyond Francovich', 56 MLR, 1993, 55

RUFFERT, M., 'Rights and Remedies in European Community Law; A Comparative View', 34 CMLRev, 1997, 307

RUFFERT, M., 'The Administration of Kosovo and East-Timor by the International Community', 50 ICLQ, 2001, 613

RÜFNER, W., 'Basic Elements of German Law on State Liability', in Governmental Liability: A Comparative Study, J. Bell and W. Bradley (eds), Glasgow, UK Comparative Law Series, 1991, 249

RUGGERI LADERCHI, F.P., 'Report on Italy', in The European Court and National Courts – Doctrine and Jurisprudence. Legal Change in Its Social Context, A.-M. Slaughter at el. (eds), Oxford, Hart Publishing, 1998, 147

RUPP, H., 'Die Ausschaltung des Bundesverfassungsgerichts durch den Amsterdamer Vertrag', 53 JZ, 1998, 213

RUPP-VON BRÜNNECK, W., 'Admonitory Functions of Constitutional Courts. Germany: The Federal Constitutional Court', 20 AJCL, 1972, 387

RYZIGER, P.-F., 'Le Conseil d'état et le droit communautaire: de la continuité au changement', RFDA, 1990, 850

SANTAOLALLA GADEA, F. and MATRINEZ LAGE, S., 'Spanish Accession to the European Communities: Legal and Constitutional Implications', 23 CMLRev, 1986, 11

SABOURIN, P., 'Le Conseil d'état face au droit communautaire. Méthodes et raisonnements', RDP, 1993, 397

SCELLE, G., Précis de Droit des gens, principes et systématique, Paris, Recueil Sirey, 1932–1934

SCELLE, G., 'Le phénomène juridique du dédoublement fonctionnel', in Rechtsfragen der internationalen Organisation, Festschrift für Hans Wehberg zu seinem 70. Geburtstag, W. Schätzel and H.-J. Schlochauer (eds), Frankfurt am Main, 1956, 324

SCHENKE, W.-R. and GUTTENBERG, U., 'Rechtsprobleme einer Haftung bei normativem Unrecht', DÖV, 1991, 945

SCHEPEL, H. and WESSELING, R. 'The Legal Community: Judges, Lawyers, Officials and Clerks in the Writing of Europe', ELJ, 1997, 165

SCHEPEL, H. and BLANKENBURG, E., 'Mobilizing the European Court of Justice', in The European Court of Justice, G. de Búrca and J.H.H. Weiler (eds), Oxford, OUP, 2001, 9

SCHERMERS, H.G., 'The Scales in Balance: National Constitutional Court v Court of Justice', 27 CMLRev, 1990, 97

SCHERMERS, H.G. and WAELBROECK, D.F. Judicial Protection in the European Union, The Hague, Kluwer Law International, 6th edn, 2001

SCHLEMMER-SCHULTE, S. and ÜKROW, J., 'Haftung des Staates gegenüber dem Marktbürger für gemeinschaftsrechtswidriges Verhalten', EuR, 1992, 82

SCHMID, C.U., 'From Pont d'Avignon to Ponte Vecchio: The Resolution of Constitutional Conflicts between the European Union and the Member States through the Principles of Public International Law', YEL, 1998, 415

SCHMID, C.U., 'All Bark and No Bite: Notes on the Federal Constitutional Court's 'Banana Decision'', 7 ELJ, 2001, 95

SCHOCKWEILER, F., WIVINES, G. and GODART, J.M., 'Le régime de la responsabilité extra-contractuelle du fait d'actes juridiques dans la Communauté européenne', RTDeur, 1990, 27

SCHOCKWEILER, F., 'La responsabilité de l'autorité nationale en cas de violation du droit communautaire', RTDeur, 1992, 27

SCHOKWEILER, F., 'Zur Kontrolle der Zuständigkeitsgrenzen der Gemeinschaft', EuR, 1996, 123

J.E. SCHOETTL, Rapport général drafted for the Conference of constitutional courts held in Paris, 1997, www.conseil-constitutionnel.fr/cahiers/ccc4/ccc4rage.htm

SCHOLZ, R., 'Wie lange bis "Solange III"', NJW, 1990, 941

SCHROEDER, W., 'Alles unter Karlsruher Kontrolle? Die Souveränitätsfrage im Maastricht-Urteil des BverfG', ZfRV, 1994, 143

SCHWARZE, J., 'Europapolitik unter deutschem Verfassungsrichtervorbehalt', NJ, 1994, 1

SCOTT, J., EC Environmental Law, London, Longman, 1998

SENELLE, R., 'De onschendbaarheid van de wet', RW, 1971, 641

SHAPIRO, M., 'Comparative law and Comparative Politics', 53 Southern California Law Review, 1980, 537

SHAPIRO, M., 'The European Court of Justice', in The Evolution of EU Law, P. Craig and G. de Búrca (eds), Oxford, OUP, 1999, 321

SHERLOCK, A., 'Self-executing Provisions in EC Law and under the Irish Constitution', 2 EPL, 1996, 103

SIMON, D. and BARAV, A., 'La responsabilité de l'administration nationale en cas de violation du droit communautaire', RMC, 1987, 165

SIMON, D. and BARAV, A., 'Le droit communautaire et la suspension provisoire des mesures nationales. Les enjeux de l'affaire Factortame', RMC, 1990, 591

SIMON, D., 'Les exigences de la primauté du droit communautaire: continuité ou métamorphoses?', in L'Europe et le droit. Mélanges en hommage à Jean Boulouis, Paris, Dalloz, 1991, 481

SIMON, D., 'Le Conseil d'État et les directives communautaires: du gallicisme à l'orthodoxie?', RTDeur, 1992, 265

SIMON, D., 'Droit communautaire et responsabilité de la puissance publique, glissements progressifs ou révolution tranquille?', AJDA, 1993, 235

SIMON, D., Le système juridique communautaire, Paris, PUF, 1997

SIMON, D., 'L'arrêt Sarran: dualisme incompressible ou monisme inversé?', Europe, no 3, 1999, 4

SIMON, D., 'The Sanction of Member States' Serious Violations of Community Law', in Judicial Review in European Union Law. Liber Amicorum in Honour of Lord Slynn of Hadley, D. O'Keeffe and A. Bavasso (eds), The Hague, Kluwer Law International, 2000, 275

SIMONART, H., 'La responsabilité du législateur en raison de la méconnaissance de normes supérieures de droit international', La responsabilité des pouvoirs publics, G. Vandersanden and M. Dony (eds) Bruxelles, Bruylant, 1991, 299

SLAUGTER, A.-M., STONE SWEET, A. and WEILER, J.H.H. (eds), The European Court and National Courts – Doctrine and Jurisprudence. Legal Change in Its Social Context, Oxford, Hart Publishing, 1998

SLOT, P.J., 'A Contribution to the Constitutional Debate in the EU in the Light of the Tobacco Judgment. What can be Learned from the USA?', European Business Law Review, 2002, 3

SLYNN OF HADLEY, G., 'What is a European Community law Judge?', CLJ, 1993, 234

SMITH, B.P.G., Constitution Building in the European Union. The Process of Treaty Reforms, The Hague, Kluwer Law International, 2002

SNYDER, F., 'Constitutional Law of the European Union', Collected Courses of the Academy of European Law 1995, Vol VI-1, Kluwer Law International, 1998, 41

SOARES, A.G., 'The Principle of Conferred Powers and the Division of Powers between the European Community and the Member States', 23 Liverpool Law Review, 2001, 57

Soulas de Russel, D. and Engles, U., 'L'intégration de l'Europe à l'heure de la décision de la Cour constitutionnelle fédérale du 24 mai 1974', RIDC, 1975, 377

Sørensen, M., 'Autonomous Legal Orders: Some Considerations relating to a Systems Analysis of International Organisations in the World Legal Order', 32 ICLQ, 1983, 559

Spielmann, D., 'Human Rights Case Law in the Strasbourg and Luxembourg Courts: Conflicts, Inconsistencies, and Complementarities', in The EU and Human Rights, Ph. Alston (ed), Oxford, OUP, 1999, 757

Spiermann, O., 'The Other Side of the Story: An Unpopular Essay on the Making a the European Community Legal Order', 10 EJIL, 1999, 763

Stahn, C., 'Constitution Without a State? Kosovo Under the United Nations Constitutional Framework for Self-Government', 14 LJIL, 2001, 531

Stein, E., 'Toward Supremacy of Treaty-Constitution by Judicial Fiat in the European Economic Community', Riv.dir.int., 1965, 3

Stein, E., 'Lawyers, Judges and the Making of a Transnational Constitution', 75 Am J of Int Law, 1981, 1

Stein, E., 'Conflicts between Treaties and subsequently enacted statutes in Belgium. Etat belge v Fromagerie franco-suisse Le Ski', Michigan Law Review, 1972, 118

Steiner, J., 'Drawing the line: Uses and Abuses of Article 30 EEC', 29 CMLRev, 1992, 749

Steiner, J., 'From direct effects to Francovich: Shifting means of enforcement of Community law', 18 ELR, 1993, 3

Stone Sweet, A., The Birth of Judicial Politics in France: The Constitutional Council in Comparative Perspective, Oxford, OUP, 1992

Stone Sweet, A. and Brunnell, T.L., 'The European Court of Justcie and the National Courts: A Statistical Analysis of Preliminary References, 1961–1995'

Storme, M., 'De rechterlijke macht', NJB, 1993, 917

Streinz, R., Bundesverfassungsrechtlicher Grundrechtsschutz und Europäisches Gemeinschaftsrecht, 1989

Streinz, R., 'Das Maastricht-Urteil des Bundesverfassungsgerichts', EuZW, 1994, 329

Svenningsen, J., 'The Danish Supreme Court Puts the Maastricht Treaty on Trial', 4 MJ, 1997, 101

Symmons, C., 'International Treaty Obligations and the Irish Constitution: The McGimpsey Case', 41 ICLQ, 1992, 311

Symmons, C.R., 'Ireland', in L'intégration du droit international et communautaire dans l'ordre juridique national, P.M. Eisemann (ed), The Hague, Kluwer Law International, 1996, 317

Szyszczak, E., 'Making Europe More Relevant to Its Citizens: Effective Judicial Process', 21 ELR, 1996, 351

Tammes, A.J.P., '"Een ieder verbindende" verdragsbepalingen', NJB, 1962, 69 and 89

Tash, Ph., 'Remedies for European Community Law Claims in Member State Courts: Toward a European Standard', 31 Columbia Journal of Transnational Law, 1993, 377

Tatham, A.F.T., 'Effect of European Community Directives in France: The Development of the Cohn-Bendit Jurisprudence', 40 ICLQ, 1991, 907

Temple Lang, J., 'European Community Law, Irish Law and the Irish Legal Profession', Frances E. Moran Memorial Lecture 1982

TEMPLE LANG, J., The duties of national courts under the constitutional law of the European Community, Dominik Lasok Lecture, Exeter, 1987

TEMPLE LANG, J., 'The Irish Court Case which Delayed the Single European Act: *Crotty v an Taoiseach and Others*', 24 CMLRev, 1989, 709

TEMPLE LANG, J., 'The Development of European Community Constitutional Law', The International Lawyer, 1991, 455

TEMPLE LANG, J., 'The Sphere in which Member States are obliged to Comply with the General Principles of Law and Community Fundamental Rights Principles', 2 LIEI, 1991

TEMPLE LANG, J., 'The Widening Scope of Community Law', in Constitutional Adjudication in European Community and National Law. Essays for the Hon. Mr. Justice T.F. O'Higgins, D. Curtin and D. O'Keeffe (eds), Dublin, Butterworth (Ireland) Ltd, 1992, 229

TEMPLE LANG, J., 'The Duties of National Courts under Community Constitutional Law', 22 ELR, 1997, 3

TEMPLE LANG, J., 'The Duties of National Authorities under Community Constitutional Law', 23 ELR, 1998, 109

TEMPLE LANG, J., 'The Duties of Co-operation of National Authorities and Courts under Article 10 EC: Two More Reflections', 26 ELR, 2001, 84

TEMPLE LANG, J., 'General Report: The Duties of Cooperation of the National Authorities and Courts and the Community Institutions under Article 10 EC Treaty, in XIX FIDE Congress, Helsinki, 2000, Vol I, 373

TEMPLE LANG, J., 'The Principle of Effective Judicial Protection of Community Law Rights', in Judicial Review in European Union Law. Liber Amicorum in Honour of Lord Slynn of Hadley, Vol I, The Hague, Kluwer Law International, 2000, 235

TESAURO, G., 'La sanction des infractions au droit communautaire', Rivista di diritto europeo, 1992, 477

TESAURO, G., ' Community Law and National Courts – An Italian Perspective', in Judicial Review in European Union Law. Liber Amicorum in Honour of Lord Slynn of Hadley, D. O'Keeffe and A. Bavasso (eds.), The Hague, Kluwer Law International, 2000, 391

TIMMERMANS, CHR., 'The Constitutionalisation of the European Union', YEL, 2002, 1

TOLIAS, 'Has the Problem concerning the Delimitation of the Community's Competence been Resolved since the Maastricht Judgment of the Bundesverfassungsgericht?', European Business Law Review, 2002, 267

TOMUSCHAT, CHR., 'Nein, und abermals Nein! Zum Urteil des BFH vom 25. April 1985', EuR, 1985, 346

TOMUSCHAT, CHR., 'Aller guten Dinge sind III?', EuR, 1990, 340

TOMUSCHAT, CHR., 'Die Europäische Union unter der Aufsicht des Bundesverfassungsgericht', EuGRZ, 1993, 489

TOMUSCHAT, CHR., 'Das Francovich-Urteil des EuGH – Ein Lehrstück zum Europarecht', in Festschrift für Ulrich Everling, O. Due, M. Lutter and J. Schwarze (eds), Baden-Baden, Nomos, 1995, 1585

TONER, H., 'Thinking the Unthinkable? State Liability for Judicial Acts after Factortame (III)', YEL, 1997, 165

TRAVERS, N., 'The implementation of directives into Irish law', 20 ELR, 1995, 103

TREVES, T. and FRIGESSI DI RATTALMA, M., 'Italie', in L'Intégration du droit international et communautaire dans l'ordre juridique national. Etude de la pratique en Europe, P.M. Eisemann (ed), The Hague, Kluwer Law International, 1996, 365

TRIDIMAS, T., 'Liability for Breach of Community Law: Growing up and Mellowing down?', 38 CMLRev, 2001, 301

TRIEPEL, C.H., 'Les rapports entre le droit interne et le droit international', 1 Hague Recueil des cours, 1923, 73

USHER, J., European Community Law and National Law. The Irreversible Transfer?, London, UACES, 1981

USHER, J.A., 'The imposition of sanctions for breaches of Community law', UK Report, FIDE 1992, Lisbon, 391

VAN BUUREN, P.J.J. and POLAK, J.E.M., De rechter en onrechtmatige wetgeving, Zwolle, WEJ Tjeenk Willink, 1987

VAN DEN BOSSCHE, P., 'The European Community and the Uruguay Round Agreements', in J. Jackson and A. Sykes (eds), Implementing the Uruguay Round, Oxford, Clarendon Press, 1997, 23

VAN DEN HEUVEL, H., Prejudiciële vragen en bevoegdheidsproblemen in het Europees recht, Deventer, Kluwer, 1962

VANDERSANDEN, G., 'Primauté du droit communautaire sur le droit national', RDIC, 1972, 847

VAN EMDE BOAS, M.J. and SUETENS, L.P., 'Gemeenschapsrecht en nationaal recht (Week van Brugge 1965)', SEW, 1965, 267

VAN EMDE BOAS, M.J., Jonkheer Haro Frederik van Panhuys (1916–1976), Bibliographical Essay, The Hague, TMC Asser Institute, 1987

VAN GERVEN, W., Hoe blauw is het bloed van de prins? De overheid in het verbintenissenrecht, Antwerpen, Kluwer, 1984

VAN GERVEN, W., 'De normatieve en rechterlijke aansprakelijkheid naar Europees en Belgisch recht', in Recht halen uit aansprakelijkheid, M. Storme (ed), Gent, Mys en Breesch, 1993, 396

VAN GERVEN, W., 'Toward a Coherent Constitutional System within the European Union', EPL, 1996, 81

VAN GERVEN, W., 'Taking Article 215(2) EC Seriously', in New Directions in European Public Law, J. Beatson and T. Tridimas (eds), Oxford, Hart Publishing, 1998, 35

VAN GERVEN, W., 'From Communitarisation of National Tort Rules to Europeanisation of Community Tort Law: The Invader Invaded', in Auslegung europäischen Privatrechts und angeglichenen Rechts, R. Scholz (ed), Baden-Baden, Nomos, 1999, 179

VAN GERVEN, W., 'Comparative Law in a Texture of Communitarization of National Laws and Europeanization of Community Law', in Judicial Review in European Union Law. Liber Amicorum in Honour of Lord Slynn of Hedley, Vol. I, D. O'Keeffe and A. Bavasso (eds), The Hague, Kluwer Law International, 2000, 433

VAN GERVEN, W., Cases, Materials and Text on National, Supranational and International Tort Law, Oxford, Hart Publishing, 2000

VAN GERVEN, W., 'Of Rights, Remedies and Procedures', 37 CMLRev, 2000, 501

VANHAMME, J., Volkenrechtelijke beginselen in het Europees recht, Groningen, Europa Law Publishing, 2001

VAN HOUTEN, M.L.P., Meer zicht op wetgeving, Rechterlijke toetsing van wetgeving aan de Grondwet en fundamentele rechtsbeginselen, Zwolle, 1997

VAN MAANEN, G.E. and DE LANGE, R., Onrechtmatige Overheidsdaad, Deventer, W.E.J. Tjeenk Willink, 2000

VAN MALE, R.M., Gevolgen van onrechtmatige regelgeving in Nederland, Zwolle, W.E.J. Tjeenk Willink, 1995

VAN NIEUWENHOVE, J., 'Over internationale verdragen, samenwerkingsakkoorden en "établissement". Enkele kanttekeningen bij de arresten 12/94, 17/94 en 33/94 van het Arbitragehof', RW, 1995–1995, 449

VAN NUFFEL, P., De rechtsbescherming van nationale overheden in het Europees recht, Deventer, Kluwer, 2000

VAN OEVELEN, A., 'De aansprakelijkheid van de Staat voor ambtsfouten van migistraten en de orgaantheorie na het Anca-arrest van het Hof van Cassatie van 19 december 1991', RW, 1992, 377

VAN OEVELEN, A., 'De materiële voorwaarden voor de aansprakelijkheid van de Staat voor de niet-uitvoering van zijn regelgevende bevoegdheid: een vergelijking tussen de rechtspraak van het Europese Hof van Justitie en die van het Hof van Cassatie', in Publiek recht, ruim bekeken, Opstellen aangeboden aan Prof. J. Gijssels, Antwerpen, Maklu, 1994, 427

VAN OMMESLAGHE, P., 'La responsabilité des pouvoirs publics et droit interne', in Recht halen uit aansprakelijkheid. Willy Delva Cyclus 1992–1993, M. Storme (ed), Gent, Mys & Breesch, 1993, 415

VAN PANHUYS, H.F, 'Relations and interaction between international and national scenes of law', Recueil des Cours de l'Académie de Droit international, 1964-II, 7

VAN PANHUYS, H.F., 'The Netherlands Constitution and International law', AJIL, 1964, 88, at 102, note 65

VAN PANHUYS, H.F., 'De verhouding tussen het volkenrecht, het Gemeenschapsrecht en het recht der lid-staten in het licht van het mandaat van rechters', in De rechtsorde der Europese Gemeenschappen tussen het internationale en nationale recht, H.F. Van Panhuys et al. (eds), Deventer, Kluwer

VAN ROOSMALEN, The King can do no wrong. Overheidsaansprakelijkheid naar Engels recht onder invloed van de jurisprudentie van het Hof van Justitie van de Europese Gemeenschappen, Leiden, 2000

VELU, J., 'Contrôle de constitutionnalité et contrôle de compatibilité avec les traités', mercuriale 1992, JT, 1992, 729 and 749

VELU, J., 'Toetsing van de grondwettigheid en toetsing van de verenigbaarheid met de verdragen', RW, 1992–1993, 481

VERHOEVEN, A., The European Union in Search of a Democratic and Constitutional Theory, The Hague, Kluwer Law International, 2002

VIRALLY, M., 'Sur un pont aux ânes: Les rapports entre le droit international et ldroit interne', in Mélanges offertes à Henri Rolin. Problèmes de droit des gens, Paris, Pédone, 1964, 488

VITORINO, A., 'The Convention as a Model for European Constitutionalisation', Vortrag am Walter Hallstein-Institut für Europäisches Verfassungsrecht der Humboldt Universität zu Berlin am 14 Juni 2001, FCE 6/01

VON BOGDANDY, A. and NETTESHEIM, M. 'Ex Pluribus Unum: Fusion of the European Communities into the European Union', 2 ELJ, 1996, 267

VON BOGDANDY, A., 'The Legal Case for Unity: The European Union as a Single Organization with a Single Legal System', 36 CMLRev, 1999, 887

VON BOGDANDY, A., 'A Bird's Eye View on the Science of European Law: Structures, Debates and Development Prospects of Basic Research on the Law of the European Union in a German Perspective', ELJ, 2000, 208

WACHSMANN, P., 'L'avis 2/94 de la Cour de justice relatif à l'adhésion de la Communauté européenne à la Convention de sauvegarde des droits de l'homme et des libertés fondamentales', RTDeur, 1996, 467

WADE, E.C.S. and BRADLEY, A.W., Constitutional and Administrative Law, 11th edn, 1993

WADE, H.W.R., 'The Basis of Legal Sovereignty', CLJ, 1955, 172

WADE, H.W.R., 'What has Happened to the Sovereignty of Parliament?', LQR, 1991

WADE, H.W.R., 'Sovereignty – Revolution or Evolution?', 112 LQR, 1996, 568

WAELBROECK, D.F., 'Treaty Violations and Liability of Member States: The Effect of the Francovich Case Law', in The Action for Damages in Community Law, The Hague, Kluwer Law International, 1997, 311

WAELBROECK, M., 'Le juge belge et le droit communautaire', in Le juge national et le droit communautaire, A.M. Donner et al. (eds), Leyde, Sijthoff, 1966, 29

WAELBROECK, M., Traités internationaux et juridictions internes dans les pays du Marché commun, Paris, Pedone, 1969

WAELBROECK, M., 'L'immédiateté communautaire, caractéristique de la suprana-tionalité: quelques conséquences pour la pratique', in Le droit international de demain, Neuchâtel, 1974, 85

WAKEFIELD, J., Judicial Protection through the Use of Article 288(2) EC, The Hague, Kluwer Law International, 2002

WALKER, N., 'Late Sovereignty in the European Union', in Sovereignty in Transition, N. Walker (ed), Oxford, Hart Publishing, 2003, 5

WALKER, N., 'The Idea of Constitutional Pluralism', 65 MLR, 2002, 317

WALKER, N., 'After the Constitutional Moment', in A Constitution for the European Union: First Comments on the 2003-Draft of the European Convention, I. Pernice and M. Poiares Maduro (eds), Baden Baden, Nomos, 2003

WALSH, B., 'Reflections of the Effects of Membership of the European Communities in Irish Law', in Du droit international au droit de l'intégration. Liber Amicorum P. Pescatore, F. Capotorti et al. (eds), Baden-Baden, Nomos, 1987, 805

WARD, A., 'The Limits of Uniform Application of Community Law and Effective Judicial Review: A Look Post-Amsterdam', in The Future of Remedies in Europe, C. Kilpatrick, T. Novitz and P. Skidmore (eds), Oxford, Hart Publishing, 2000, 213

WARD, I., A Critical Introduction to European Law, London, Butterworths, 1996

WASILKOWSKI, 'Monism and Dualism at present', in Theory of International law at the Threshold of the 21st Century. Essays in honour of Krzystof Skubiszewski, The Hague, Kluwer Law International, 1996, 323

WEATHERILL, S., Law and Integration in the European Union, Oxford, OUP, 1995

WEATHERILL, S., 'Is constitutional finality feasible or desirable? On the cases for European constitutionalism and a European Constitution', ConWEB 7/2002

WEATHERILL, S., 'Competence', in Ten Reflections on the Constitutional Treaty for Europe, B. De Witte (ed), EUI, 2003, 45

WEBER, A., 'Zur Kontrolle grundrechts – bzw. Kompetenzwidriger Rechtsakte der EG durch national Verfassungsgerichte, in Festschrift für Ulrich Everling, O. Due, M. Lutter and J. Schwarze (eds), Baden-Baden, Nomos, 1995, 1625

WEILER, J.H.H., 'The Transformation of Europe', 100 Yale Law Journal, 1991, 2403

WEILER, J.H.H.,'Journey to an Unknown Destination: A Retrospective and Prospective of the European Court of Justice in the Arena of Political Integration', 31 JCMS, 1993, 417

WEILER, J.H.H., 'Neither Unity nor Three Pillars. The Trinity Structure of the Treaty on European Union', in The Maastricht Treaty on European Union. Legal Complexity and Political Dynamic, J. Monar, et al. (eds), Brussels, EIP, 1993, 49

WEILER, J.H.H., 'Does Europe Need a Constitution? Demos, Telos and the German Maastricht Decision', 1 ELJ, 1995, 219

WEILER, J.H.H. and LOCKHART, N.J.S., '"Taking Rights Seriously" Seriously: The European Court and its Fundamental Rights Jurisprudence', 32 CMLRev, 1995, 51–94 and 579–627

WEILER, J.H.H. '"...We Will Do, and Hearken" (Ex. XXIV:7) Reflections on a Common Constitutional Law for the European Union', in The European Constitutional Area, R. Bieber and P. Widmer (eds), Zurich, Schulthess, 1995, 413

WEILER, J.H.H. and HALTERN, U., 'The Autonomy of the Community Legal Order: Through the Looking Glass', 37 Harvard International Law Journal, 1996, 411

WEILER, J., 'European Neo-Constitutionalism: In Search of Foundations for the European Constitutional Order', 44 Political Studies, 1996, 517

WEILER, J.H.H., 'The Reformation of European Constitutionalism', JCMS, 1997, 97

WEILER, J.H.H., 'The European Union Belongs to its Citizens: Three Immodest Proposals', 22 ELR, 1997, 150

WEILER, J.H.H., 'The European Court of Justice: Beyond "Beyond Doctrine" or the Legitimacy Crisis of European Constitutionalism', in The European Court and National Courts. Doctrine and Jurisprudence, A.-M. Slaughter, A. Stone Sweet and J.H.H. Weiler (eds), Oxford, Hart Publishing, 1998, 365

WEILER, J.H.H. and HALTERN, U., 'Constitutional or International? The Foundations of the Community Legal Order and the Question of Judicial Kompetenz Kompetenz', in The European Court and National Courts – Doctrine and Jurisprudence. Legal Change in Its Social Context, A.-M. Slaughter, A. Stone Sweet and J.H.H. Weiler (eds), Oxford, Hart Publishing, 1998, 331

WEILER, J.H.H., 'The Constitution of the Common Market Place: Text and Context in the Evolution of the Free Movement of Goods', in The Evolution of EU Law, P. Craig and G. de Búrca (eds), Oxford, OUP, 1999, 349

WEILER, J.H.H., The Constitution of Europe. 'Do the new clothes have an emperor?' and other essays on European integration, Cambridge, CUP, 1999

WEILER, J.H.H., 'Editorial: Does the European Union Truly Need a Charter of Rights?', 5 ELJ, 2000, 95

WEILER, J.H.H., 'Federalism and Constitutionalism: Europe's Sonderweg', Jean Monnet Working Paper 10/00

WEILER, J., 'Human Rights, Constitutionalism and Integration: Iconography and Fetishism', International Law FORUM du droit international, 2001, 227

WEILER, J.H.H., 'A Constitution for Europe? Some Hard Choices', 40 JCMS, 2002, 563

WEILER, J.H.H., 'Conclusions' of the Conference of the Jean Monnet Group on the Future of Europe, Europe 2004, Le Grand Débat, Setting the Agenda and Outlining the Options, available on www.ecsanet.org

WESSEL, R.A., 'The Inside Looking Out: Consistency and Delimitation in EU External Relations', 37 CMLRev, 2000, 1135

WHELAN, A., 'Article 29.4.3. and the Meaning of 'Necessity'', 2 Irish Student Law Review, 1992, 60

WHELAN, A., 'National Sovereignty in the European Union', in T. Murphy and P. Twomey (eds), Irelands evolving Constitution 1937–1997: Collected Essays, Oxford, Hart Publishing, 1998, 277

WHELAN, A., 'Constitutional Law – Meagher v Minister for Agriculture', 15 Dublin University Law Journal, 1993, 152

WHYTE, G., 'State responsibility in the context of European Community Law', in Contemporary Problems of International Law. Essays in Honour of G. Schwarzenberger, London, Stevens and Sons, 1988, 301

WIELAND, J., 'Germany in the European Union – The Maastricht Decision of the Bundesverfassungsgericht', 5 EJIL, 1994, 259

WINTER, J., 'Direct Applicability and Direct Effect: Two Distinct and Different Concepts in Community Law', 9 CMLR, 1972, 425

WISSINK, H.M., Richtlijnconforme interpretatie van burgerlijk recht, Deventer, Kluwer, 2001

WISSINK, M.H., 'De Nederlandse rechter en overheidsaansprakelijkheid krachtens Francovich en Brasserie du Pêcheur', SEW, 1997, 78

WIVINES, G., 'Le droit européen et les Constitutions nationales', FIDE, London, 2002

WIVINES, G., 'Rapport Luxembourgeois', for European Union Law and National Constitutions, XXth FIDE Congress, London, 2002, 22

WOUTERS, J., 'National Constitutions and the European Union', LIEI, 2000, 1

WYATT, D., 'New Legal Order, or Old?', ELR, 1982, 147

WYATT, D., 'Injunctions and Damages against the State for Breach of Community Law – A Legitimate Judicial Development', in European Community Law in the English Courts, M. Andenas and F. Jacobs (eds), Oxford, Clarendon Press, 1998, 87

YOUNG, A.L., 'Judicial Sovereignty and the Human Rights Acts 1998', 61 CLJ, 2002, 53

ZAHLE, H., 'National Constitutional Law and the European Integration', in National Constitutional Law vis-à-vis European Integration, 17 FIDE Kongress, Berlin, 1996, 60

ZAMPINI, E., 'Responsabilité de l'État pour violation du droit communautaire: l'exemple de l'Italie', RFDA, 1997, 1039

ZILLER, J., and LOTARSKI, J., 'Institutions et organes judiciaires', in Ten Reflections on the Constitutional Treaty for Europe, Florence, EUI, 2003, 67

ZONNEKEYN, G.A., 'The Status of WTO Law in the EC Legal Order. The Final Curtain?', 34 JWT, 2000, 111

Zonnekeyn, G.A., 'The status of WTO law in the Community legal order: some comments in the light of the Portuguese Textiles case', 25 ELR, 2000, 293

Zuleeg, M., 'Das Bundesverfassungsgericht als Hüter der Grundrechte gegenüber der Gemeinschaftsgewalt', DÖV, 1975, 44

Zuleeg, M., 'Die Verfassung der Europäischen Gemeinschaft in der Rechtsprechung des EuGH', Betriebs–Berater, 1994, 581

Zuleeg, M., 'Bundesfinanzhof und Gemeinschaftsrecht', in 75 Jahre Reichsfinanzhof – Bundesfinanzhof – Festschrift, Der Präsident des Bundesfinanzhofs (ed), Bonn, Stv, 1993, 115

Bibliography

Zonnekeyn, G.A., 'The status of WTO law in the Community legal order: some comments in the light of the Portuguese Textiles case', 25 ELR 2000, 293.

Zuleeg, M., Das Staatsvertragsrecht als Hüter der Grundrechte gegenüber der Gemeinschaftsgewalt, JÖR 1974, 1.

Zweig, M., Die Verfassung der Europäischen Gemeinschaft in der Rechtsprechung des BGH, Baden-Baden 1994/95.

Zuleeg, M., 'Unmittelbare und Gemeinschaftsrecht', in 75 Jahre Reichsfinanzhof Bundesfinanzhof – Text, hrsg. Dreßlett et al. Bundesfinanzhof (ed), Bonn, Stuttgart.

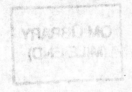